VOICES OF WISDOM

A Multicultural Philosophy Reader

EIGHTH EDITION

VOICES OF WISDOM

A Multicultural Philosophy Reader

GARY E. KESSLER

California State University, Bakersfield

WADSWORTH
CENGAGE Learning·

Australia • Brazil • Japan • Korea • Mexico • Singapore • Spain • United Kingdom • United States

WADSWORTH
CENGAGE Learning

Voices of Wisdom: A Multicultural Philosophy Reader, Eighth Edition

Gary E. Kessler

Publisher/Executive Editor: Clark Baxter

Senior Sponsoring Editor: Joann Kozyrev

Development Editor: Florence Kilgo

Assistant Editor: Joshua Duncan

Editorial Assistant: Mariko Straton

Associate Media Editor: Kimberly Apfelbaum

Marketing Program Manager: Sean Foy

Senior Art Director: Jennifer Wahi

Manufacturing Planner: Mary Beth Hennebury

Rights Acquisition Specialist: Shalice Shah-Caldwell

Production Management and Composition: PreMediaGlobal

Copy Editor: PreMediaGlobal

Cover Designer: Michelle DiMercurio

Cover Image: © Hemera Technologies/ Getty Images, © Kellis, © Hemera Technologies/Getty Images, © Don Bayley, Rapid Eye Media

> For product information and technology assistance, contact us at
> **Cengage Learning Customer & Sales Support, 1-800-354-9706**
>
> For permission to use material from this text or product, submit all requests online at **cengage.com/permissions.**
> Further permissions questions can be emailed to
> **permissionrequest@cengage.com**

Library of Congress Control Number: 2011941022

ISBN-13: 978-1-111-83467-8

ISBN-10: 1-111-83467-9

Wadsworth
20 Channel Center Street
Boston, MA 02210
USA

Cengage Learning is a leading provider of customized learning solutions with office locations around the globe, including Singapore, the United Kingdom, Australia, Mexico, Brazil and Japan. Locate your local office at international.cengage.com/region.

Cengage Learning products are represented in Canada by Nelson Education, Ltd.

For your course and learning solutions, visit **www.cengage.com.**

Purchase any of our products at your local college store or at our preferred online store **www.cengagebrain.com.**

Instructors: Please visit **login.cengage.com** and log in to access instructor-specific resources.

Printed in the United States of America
1 2 3 4 5 6 7 15 14 13 12 11

To all Who Struggle and Sacrifice for Liberty

CONTENTS

Since the publication of the first edition of *Voices of Wisdom,* I am gratified to note that more introductory textbooks now incorporate a multicultural perspective—a perspective that was unique to this introductory reader when it was first published in 1992. At that time the introductory readers that were available treated philosophy as if it were entirely an Anglo-European male phenomenon. Little or no attention was given to Hindu, Buddhist, Chinese, African, Native American, Latin American, and feminist philosophy. *Voices of Wisdom* helped to change that situation, offering to those who wished it the possibility of assigning significant readings that represent the global nature of philosophizing. This eighth edition continues to offer a multicultural perspective and has benefited from the teaching and learning experiences of the many instructors and students who used the previous editions. Readers have learned that ideas from other cultures are worth careful consideration and that these ideas make important contributions to human understanding.

PHILOSOPHY IN A MULTICULTURAL PERSPECTIVE

Although I wish to stress the universal nature of philosophizing, I am well aware of the dangers of anachronism. A text of this sort faces not only the problems associated with anachronism in the historical sense but also what we might term "cultural" anachronism. The writings of ancient philosophers mingle with modern texts, and thinkers from different cultures are brought together. The student may get the impression that Plato, Buddha, Nietzsche, Confucius, Descartes, and Aristotle are all contemporaries discussing the same issues with the same concepts in English! There are similarities. But there are also vast differences. Where appropriate, the important similarities and differences are stressed in my introductory remarks.

My selection of issues betrays my own Anglo-European perspective. Whereas many of the topics are fundamental and universal (How should one live? Is knowledge possible? What is really real?), their importance and centrality differ from tradition to tradition. The mind–body problem, the puzzle of freedom and determinism, the problem of moral skepticism—these problems are not necessarily the central ones that gripped the minds of Chinese or Indian philosophers. Just as Anglo-European philosophers have not had much to say about karma, Buddhist thinkers have not been overly concerned with proving the existence of God.

However, I do believe this Western way of organizing the material is justified in this instance. Even though the significance of the problems and the way they are formulated differ from culture to culture, many of the underlying issues are the same. One cannot reflect for long on karma and reincarnation without addressing issues relating to freedom and human identity. Furthermore, I think it best, for introductory and practical purposes, to organize the material around traditional Anglo-European philosophical themes. Many students already have some concern with these issues (for example, the existence of God). In addition, most introductory courses deal with these themes, and this book allows instructors to continue that practice, but some new and different voices are emphasized, thereby enriching philosophical thinking.

It should be noted that there exists no culturally neutral set of categories for organizing the material. If I had used the dominant concerns of, let us say, the Indian tradition (concerns such as release from suffering, duty and the stages of life, and the nature of bondage) to organize the selections, I would not thereby have escaped a cultural perspective. Perhaps, as a multicultural approach becomes more commonplace in introductory courses and as Western philosophy becomes more open and diverse, new categories will emerge. However, until that day, the sources need to be organized in some fashion. What is important is that we are aware of the limitations of our categories and that we continually remind ourselves of the diverse and subtle ways that long-held biases influence the way we select and organize materials.

Historical and cultural comparisons are inevitable, and I encourage them. However, I wish to stress that this reader is not meant to be primarily an exercise in comparative philosophy. It is meant to serve a course that introduces students to doing philosophy by drawing on multicultural resources. The students who read this text should be impressed with the rich diversity that comprises global philosophizing and should learn the art of philosophizing in a broader and more inclusive context than is usual.

I do wish to stress that it is global philosophizing with which I am concerned. Some associate the word "multicultural" almost exclusively with "multiethnic" and "minorities." Those who do so may expect more African American, Latin American, Native American, and feminist philosophers than I have included. These voices also need to be heard, and I have included many. However, my primary concern has been to provide sources that promote an international perspective. I believe it is important to educate students for the current century in which an understanding of the interconnectedness of all peoples will be increasingly important in determining the policies and practices of nations.

TOPICS

Voices of Wisdom includes much philosophical material that has come to be regarded as classic in the West. This material is included for two reasons. First, most students take an introductory philosophy course in conjunction with general education and, as part of that experience, it is important for them to read philosophical writings that are significant to the Western cultural tradition. Second, this writing is good philosophy (that is why it has become classic), and students should experience the ideas of profound philosophical minds. However, profound philosophical minds exist all over the world and, whereas other styles of thinking and other traditions may be very different, they are no less important.

Although the topics in this new edition remain largely unchanged, there are twenty-two new or revised selections. I have added a new chapter dealing with the basics of logic and arguments and with writing philosophy papers. The revisions not only reflect recent events such as terrorism but also add different perspectives and fresh material.

In addition, new to this edition, photographs pertaining to some of these topics also enhance the learning experience. Their content and caption help students connect in a fresh way with these topics.

CHANGES FOR THE EIGHTH EDITION

The following changes have been made for this new edition.

Your Book

- A new chapter on the basics of logic and arguments and on writing philosophy is added.
- Fourteen new readings complement the selection and offer fresh perspectives.
- Also new, images with captions highlight key ideas and connect to important themes and issues.

In addition,

- Six selections were revised and condensed.
- Learning Objectives were revised.
- More emphasis was given to contemporary continental philosophy.
- Reading and critical questions were revised.

Your Media

To access free study tools, search for this book on CengageBrain.com. The *Voices of Wisdom* **Premium Website,** new to this edition, also presents rich teaching and learning resources for students and instructors. Students will find videos with quizzing for every term in the text, as well as useful tools for review such as flashcards, a glossary, end-of-chapter quizzing, and Web links. Additionally, instructors have access to password-protected resources such as an Instructor's Manual, Test Bank, and Microsoft® PowerPoint® slides. Access may be packaged with the text for a nominal price. Instructors, contact your Cengage Learning representative for ordering details. Students may also purchase access to this resource through CengageBrain.com.

PEDAGOGICAL FEATURES

Learning Philosophy ... by Doing Philosophy I agree with John Dewey's notion that we learn by doing. In my experience, the more I can get my students to do for themselves, the more they learn. Thus, rather than providing summaries of the selections—a practice that can discourage careful reading by students—I provide the background information they need to understand the selections, and I supply questions that are designed to guide the students' reading prior to the selections as well as critical questions after the selections for discussion. This approach encourages students to read the selections for themselves and to formulate their own questions about the material. It also gives instructors an opportunity to require students to answer the questions in a philosophical journal before class meetings. The questions and the students' responses can then be used as the basis for class discussion. Students are thereby encouraged to become actively engaged in the process of figuring out what a text means. Instructors may wish to add their own questions, and I hope they will encourage students to create their own questions as well.

A Coherent and Flexible Structure   In most chapters the material is arranged chronologically. Sometimes, however, another sort of arrangement is more pedagogically useful, and so I have not restricted myself to the chronological pattern in all cases. I have written the chapters so that instructors may rearrange the material to meet their own interests and needs. I have also included more material than the average instructor will have time to cover in one course. I have done this so that instructors can select, from a wide range of options, the material that suits their purposes best.

Guidance with Technical and Foreign Terms   I have put technical terms in bold type on their first occurrence and provided brief definitions. A glossary (Appendix One) provides a convenient reference for those terms and their definitions.

Appendix Two provides a brief pronunciation guide to Chinese, Sanskrit, and Arabic words. Foreign words can be daunting to readers, and this pronunciation guide should alleviate some of the unease they may feel.

An Engaging Tone and a Clear Voice   I have written the introductory material in an informal, engaging, and, I trust, clear manner. I hope to engage students in the thinking process by connecting the selections to questions and issues students have already begun to encounter. The selections themselves have been classroom-tested and represent different degrees of difficulty. Most will challenge beginning students to think in more depth and in a more precise way.

Connection to Students' Lives   The images included in this edition help students further realize how the written word and old and new philosophical voices connect to today's world. They vividly show the relevance of the book's content to current events and to real life. They capture the attention of students and help them understand how the selections resonate beyond the printed page. The content of each image is tied to a specific section of the text. The relationship of the image to the text is clear and compelling. The image caption also guides students in reflecting more deeply on the concepts and issues raised in the text.

In addition, the online content offerings help enhance comprehension, and assist in studying the material and reviewing for tests. Taking advantage of the materials available on **CengageBrain** and, for users who purchased access to it, on the **Premium Web site,** will further enrich the students' experience.

ACKNOWLEDGMENTS

A book like this is written, edited, and revised by many people. The editors and staff at Wadsworth/Cengage have been most helpful. Joann Kozyrev, Holly Schaff, and

Florence Kilgo have been patient and understanding. Ms. Kilgo, in particular, has done a splendid job in selecting images and writing captions. Pushpa Munuswamy and the staff at PreMediaGlobal have handled production issues with patience and care. I have tried to keep students foremost in my mind as this new edition evolved. What will work in the classroom and what will stimulate students to engage philosophical issues is of fundamental importance. A special thanks goes to all those students who have shared their concerns, ideas, and suggestions. The reviewers of the last edition were particularly helpful. I wish it were possible to follow all of their valuable suggestions. I would like to thank the following reviewers for their ideas and comments: Louis Colombo, Bethune-Cookman University; Gregory Fahy, University of Maine at Augusta; Gael Grossman, Jamestown Community College; Chris Newcomb, Bethune-Cookman University; Lou Reich, Cal State University, San Bernardino; Robert Sweet, Clark State Community College; Donna Werner, Saint Louis Community College, Meramec; and Frank C. C. Young, Canada College.

A very special thanks goes to my wife Katy, whose ideas, insights, and loving support made this book possible. I also wish to thank all of you who used previous editions. Your responses have been gratifying and reinforce my hope that one day a global approach to the study, teaching, and doing of philosophy will be commonplace. I would appreciate hearing your responses to this new edition—about how it works and how it can be improved.

Gary E. Kessler
Bellingham, WA
e-mail: gkessler@csub.edu

CHAPTER ONE

What Is Philosophy?

... those who are eager to learn because they wonder at things are lovers of wisdom (philosophoi).

ALEXANDER OF APHRODISIAS

LEARNING OBJECTIVES

After studying this chapter students should be able to:
- explain as clearly as possible their understanding of what philosophy is,
- name and distinguish the major branches of philosophy,
- define foundationalism, constructivism, and state the differences,
- distinguish cognitive from moral relativism,
- distinguish ethnocentrism from ethnocentric imperialism,
- distinguish reading analytically from reading critically,
- identify Pythagoras, Sophists, Socrates, and Russell, and
- answer all the questions relating to the selections.

1.1 A DEFINITION OF PHILOSOPHY

Have you ever wondered about the purpose of life? Have you ever been curious about what you can reasonably believe? Have you ever marveled at the beauty of nature or been upset by suffering? Have you ever thought that life is unfair? Have you ever been puzzled about what you ought to do?

Perhaps you associate these kinds of questions with philosophy. If you do, why do you? What do you think is philosophical about these questions? When you hear the word *philosophy*, what do you think it means? Think about it awhile and write your answer.

The Greek philosopher Aristotle (384–322 BCE), who asserted that philosophy begins in wonder, was impressed by the ability of human beings to think. In fact, he defined humans as "rational animals." Aristotle maintained that philosophy arises from the human ability to reflect on experience, to wonder and be curious about what happens to us and to others.

Of course, wonder is not the sole cause of philosophizing. Sufficient leisure must be available to engage in reflection, and hence economic and cultural factors play an important role in promoting and influencing human curiosity. However, without the human capacity to wonder and be curious, it is doubtful that philosophical thinking would occur.

I hope this book will stimulate your natural ability to wonder, teach you something of the art of wondering, and help you learn how to live in wonder. Cultivating the art of wondering is important, Aristotle believed, because such an art leads us along the path toward wisdom.

The word *philosophy* comes from a combination of two Greek words—*philos*, meaning "loving," and *sophia*, meaning "wisdom." Etymologically, philosophy means the love of wisdom. To love something is to desire it. So, for many Greeks, the philosopher was the one who desired wisdom. The word *philos* also refers, for the Greeks, to the special kind of love found in close friendship. Hence the philosopher could also be characterized as the "friend of wisdom."

The historical origin of a word, however, often does not help us very much when we are searching for an adequate definition today. The meanings of words change. Also, meanings derived etymologically are sometimes unclear. If the philosopher is the lover or friend of wisdom, then what is wisdom? About that, philosophers—even Greek philosophers—disagree.

Philosophy in Western culture was born in the sixth century BCE among a group of thinkers called the Pre-Socratics. According to tradition, one of these thinkers, Pythagoras (about 570 BCE), coined the word *philosophy*. Along with other Pre-Socratics, he was intensely interested in nature, in knowing how the universe or cosmic order developed, and in figuring out what things were made of. These thinkers disagreed about the stuff out of which things are made (some said earth, some air, others fire, still others water or some combination of these elements), but many of them did think that wisdom consisted of knowledge about nature. To love wisdom, as far as they were concerned, was to search for knowledge about the universe.

A century later, another group of thinkers in Athens offered their services as teachers to those who could afford them. They claimed to teach virtue. The Greek word for virtue (*areté*) means "excellence or power." So to possess virtue is to possess power. Wisdom, they taught, is the possession of virtue. It is to have certain powers or abilities, especially in the social and political realm, to influence people and be successful. Since these teachers claimed to possess this wisdom, they came to be called "Sophists" or "The Wise Ones." For them, philosophy is not a search for knowledge about the universe, nor a *search* for wisdom. Rather, philosophy is the *possession* of wisdom and hence the possession of virtue or excellence, especially in the social and political dimensions of life.

Socrates (470–399 BCE) lived in Athens at the same time as the Sophists. He spent his days wandering around the marketplace, asking people questions about all kinds of things. He found himself perplexed by things other people claimed to know. For example, people claimed to know what knowledge, justice, virtue, and the right way to live are. The Sophists claimed to teach these things. However, under Socrates' relentless critical questioning, the definitions and grand theories that people held about these sorts of things collapsed.

The oracle at Delphi, a well-respected source of divine truth in the ancient world, said that Socrates was the wisest man in Athens. When word of this got to

Socrates, he was greatly puzzled. How could he, who knew next to nothing and spent his days asking others, be the wisest? What about the Sophists, the teachers of wisdom? Were not they the wisest? Socrates did believe he knew what virtue is; it is knowledge. But what is knowledge? He had to confess he did not know, so how could he be wise? And yet, he reasoned, the oracle of Delphi could not be lying. It was, after all, the voice of the god Apollo. But the oracle was tricky. You had to figure out what it meant.

Finally, Socrates understood. Wisdom, the oracle was telling him, is knowing that he did not know! Wisdom is the awareness of our ignorance, an awareness of the limitations of knowledge. Let the Sophists claim to be wise; the best Socrates could do was to claim he was a lover of wisdom. He lived his life in the pursuit of wisdom, as lovers live their lives in pursuit of the beloved. For him, philosophy was a critical examination of our pretensions to knowledge and the constant search for that final truth that always seems to be just beyond our grasp.

The Greeks were not the only ones to philosophize, for the pursuit of wisdom is common to all cultures. The Greeks were also not the only ones to disagree about the nature of wisdom. For example, in India some philosophers claimed that wisdom is coming to know one's true self as immortal. Yajnavalkya,[1] a wise man described in early Indian literature called the *Upanishads*, tells his wife Maitreyi that wealth will not gain one immortality; only the true self or *atman*, as he called it, is immortal. However, other Indian philosophers disagreed. Wisdom, they said, did not consist in the knowledge of a true immortal self or *atman*. Quite the opposite is the case. Genuine wisdom consists in knowing that there is no such thing as an eternal self or *atman*.

Clearly there are different understandings of what wisdom is and hence there are different understandings of what philosophy is about. No single definition can possibly capture all the nuances of the art of wondering in every place and time in which it appears. This does not mean, however, that we can define philosophy any way we wish, and it does not mean that some definitions are not better than others. Let me offer my definition, which, I think, states something important about philosophizing and helps us distinguish it from other types of thinking: *Philosophy is the rational attempt to formulate, understand, and answer fundamental questions.*

Many people think that philosophy is a body of doctrines and that philosophers are people who have answers to difficult questions about the meaning of life. My definition stresses that (1) philosophy is an activity rather than a body of set teachings and (2) philosophers are as concerned with formulating and understanding questions as they are with finding answers.

Formulating questions is very important. What we ask and how we ask it determine, in large part, where we look for answers and the kinds of answers we get. Progress in many fields consists, in part, of an ever-greater refinement of our questions and more precision and sophistication in our methods of interrogation. You will not get good answers if you do not ask the right questions.

For example, the title of this chapter is "What Is Philosophy?" and at the beginning of the chapter I asked you to think about the meaning of the word philosophy and to write your answer. Review your answer. Now think about the question,

[1]For a pronunciation guide for Sanskrit, Chinese, and Arabic words see Appendix II. To facilitate reading, I have left out diacritical marks that indicate sounds in other languages that are not normally part of English.

"What is it to philosophize?" If I had formulated the question about your understanding of philosophy as a question about what it is to philosophize and asked you to answer it, would your answer have been any different? If so, how would it have been different?

Understanding what we are after when we ask questions is as important as formulating questions. Words are often ambiguous and vague; we must be as clear as possible about what they mean. If I ask, "What is the meaning of life?" what do I mean? What am I looking for? Is this the best way to put it? What might count as a helpful answer? Where should I look for an answer? Am I asking about the purpose of life? Is life the sort of thing that has a purpose? Or am I interested in what makes life worthwhile? Is the purpose of life (if there is one) the same as what makes life valuable or worthwhile?

The purpose of formulating and understanding questions as precisely as we can is to find answers, but often our answers lead to further questions. Why assume some answer is final? Or why assume all questions we can ask have answers? Also, what counts as an answer? How do I know when I have a good one? Consider this conversation:

Yolanda: What is the meaning of life?
José: What do you mean by that question?
Yolanda: I mean, what is the purpose of life?
José: Oh, that's easy; its purpose is survival and reproduction. That's what my biology textbook says.

Is José's answer a good one? Is it the sort of answer Yolanda is after? Can this question be answered with factual information, or is it about values? When Yolanda asks, "What is the meaning of life?" is she asking, "What makes life ultimately valuable?" And if she is asking that, then the answer José gives may well miss the mark (unless, of course, Yolanda thinks survival and reproduction are more valuable than anything else).

I said in my definition that philosophers are concerned with *fundamental* questions. The word *fundamental* means "basic" and has to do with what is primary. Fundamental questions are *radical* questions in the sense of pertaining to roots. They are the most basic questions we can ask. Therefore, they are often *abstract* questions that have to do with a wide area of human experience.

However, even though the sorts of questions that concern philosophers are abstract, they are about concepts we employ every day. We are constantly making judgments about good and bad, right and wrong, true and false, reality and fiction, beautiful and ugly, just and unjust. But what is good? By what norms can we distinguish right behavior from wrong? What is truth? How can I distinguish appearance from reality? Is beauty only in the eye of the beholder? What is justice, and is it ever possible to achieve it?

Some of the main branches of Western philosophy are distinguished by the kinds of fundamental questions they ask. Many philosophers have regarded "What is truly real?" as a fundamental question. Note the word *truly*. I did not ask, "What is real?" but "What is *truly* real?" In other words, I am assuming that not everything that appears to be real is real. Or, to put that another way, by asking, "What is truly real?" I am asking how we might distinguish appearance from reality. The branch of philosophy called **metaphysics** deals with this and related issues. One of its purposes, some philosophers have claimed, is to develop a theory of reality or a theory of what is genuinely real. It is also concerned with what might be the most fundamental question we can think of: "Why is there something rather than nothing?"

What is knowledge and what is truth? These seem to be good candidates for fundamental questions because the concepts of knowledge and truth are basic to so much of our thinking, including all that we call science. The branch of Western philosophy known as **epistemology** concerns itself with the issues of knowledge and truth. Epistemologists search for a theory of what knowledge is and how it might be distinguished from opinion. They look for a definition of truth and wonder how we might correctly distinguish truth from error.

Axiology, the third main branch of Western philosophy, has to do with the study of value and the distinction between value and fact. Traditionally, it is divided into two main subdivisions: aesthetics and ethics. **Aesthetics** deals with such questions as the following: Is beauty a matter of taste, or is it something objective? What standards should be used to judge artistic work? Can we define art? **Ethics** attempts to decide what values and principles we should use to judge human action as morally right or wrong. What is the greatest good? How should one live? Applied ethics applies these values and principles to such social concerns as human rights, racial justice, globalization, environmental ethics, and animal rights in order to determine what would be the morally right thing to do.

Fundamental questions are not only basic and abstract; they are also *universal* questions. They are the sorts of questions any thinking person might ask anywhere and at any time. They arise out of our capacity to wonder about ourselves and the world in which we live. They arise naturally, as it were, as we search for wisdom.

Although fundamental questions are universal, or nearly so, it should be noted that the way I have described the organization of the field of philosophy (metaphysics, epistemology, axiology) is decidedly Western. Different societies organize knowledge in different ways. Also, what may seem fundamental in one society may seem far less important in another. For example, some Buddhist philosophers have been suspicious of intellectual speculation about metaphysical matters, especially questions like "Does God exist?" This question, so important to many people, excites little interest among these Buddhist thinkers.

It should also be noted that each of the three main branches of Western philosophy deals with important distinctions that all of us learn to make based on the standards our society teaches us. Hence, metaphysics is concerned with the distinction between *appearance and reality*, epistemology with the distinction between *knowledge and opinion*, and axiology with the distinction between *fact and value*. One important question is whether we can discover criteria that are universal and not merely relative to our own particular time in history and our own particular cultural view for making these distinctions. Fundamental and abstract questions about reality, knowledge, and value—and the distinctions these questions imply—may be universal in the sense that most cultures have developed intellectual traditions concerned with these issues. However, the concrete way the questions are asked, understood, and answered varies a great deal from one tradition to another.

For example, Plato (428–348 BCE) made the distinction between knowledge and opinion, at least in part, by claiming that *opinion* has to do with beliefs about the world, which are based on our sensations, but *knowledge* has to do with the reality we discover through our reason. For him, logic and mathematics constituted examples of knowledge, but information about physical objects based on sensation did not. Under the influence of physical science, many people today would be inclined to say almost the opposite of what Plato said. For instance, many of my students have maintained that knowledge is what empirical science provides, and opinion is a product of abstract speculation like philosophy.

As twenty-first century students living in a highly technological and pluralistic society, we live in a very different world from the ancient Greeks or Indians. Yet we, like them, wonder about life and ask basic questions about what is real, what is true, what is good, and what is beautiful. This is not to say that there are not vast differences among philosophies and ways of doing philosophy. There are. You are about to experience something of this variety firsthand as you read different philosophers from different cultures and different eras.

In sum, I think philosophy is the activity of rationally attempting to formulate, understand, and answer fundamental questions. I have discussed most of the parts of that definition except the word *rational*. Why must it be a rational attempt? And what is it to be rational, anyway? If we cannot agree on what rationality is, how can we know what constitutes a rational attempt to formulate and answer basic questions?

1.2 WHAT IS RATIONALITY?

This fundamental question is one of the most hotly debated issues in philosophy today. I cannot hope to settle the puzzles about rationality here, but I can give you some idea about what the issues are, describe some of the different views, and offer a few thoughts of my own.

William James (1842–1910), an important American philosopher, said that "philosophy is the unusually stubborn attempt to think clearly." Now *thinking* is a word with a much broader meaning than the word *rational*. To be rational is to think, but all thinking is not necessarily rational thinking. James does add the qualification "clearly." That narrows the field somewhat. But what is clear thinking, and how do we know it when we see it?

Consider this passage from a Chinese philosopher named Zhuangzi (Chuang Tzu)[2] who lived about 350 BCE.

> Suppose you and I have had an argument. If you have beaten me instead of my beating you, then are you necessarily right and am I necessarily wrong? If I have beaten you instead of your beating me, then am I necessarily right and are you necessarily wrong? Is one of us right and the other wrong? Are both of us right or are both of us wrong? If you and I don't know the answer, then other people are bound to be even more in the dark. Whom shall we get to decide what is right? Shall we get someone who agrees with you to decide? But if he already agrees with you, how can he decide fairly? Shall we get someone who agrees with me? But if he already agrees with me, how can he decide? Shall we get someone who disagrees with both of us? But if he already disagrees with both of us, how can he decide? Shall

[2]There are two methods in wide use today for romanticizing (translating into a Latin-based alphabetical system) Chinese words. One is called *Wade-Giles* and the other *Pinyin*. The first time a word or name is introduced, I have used the Pinyin spelling and provided the Wade-Giles spelling in parentheses. See the pronunciation guide for Chinese words in Appendix II. The quotation is from *Chuang Tzu: Basic Writings*, translated by Burton Watson (New York: Columbia University Press, 1996, p. 43).

we get someone who agrees with both of us? But if he already agrees with both of us, how shall he decide? Obviously, then, neither you nor I nor anyone else can know the answer. Shall we wait for still another person?

Zhuangzi wonders how we might decide who is right and who is wrong. You and I are not in a good position to make such a decision, at least not an objective one, because the fact that we are arguing shows that we disagree. According to Zhuangzi, bringing in a third party to settle the dispute does not help because he or she may not know what we are arguing about, may agree with both of us (which will not settle anything), or may disagree with you or with me or with both of us. What was a two-person argument will now become a three-person argument.

Zhuangzi is wondering how we might proceed to settle an argument. What procedures do we have that will eventuate in agreement? Should we appeal to authority? Perhaps some divine revelation? A long-standing tradition? Common sense? Force? Rationality? You might be tempted to say that we should settle it by applying rational standards. If we follow that course, then we can decide which argument is the most rational. Are there, however, objective and universal standards of rationality? Is rationality something entirely subjective or, at the very least, relative to particular historical periods and cultural communities?

Fundamental disagreements about the nature of rationality are very difficult to settle because in initially proceeding to approach the topic we have already made assumptions about what a rational way to proceed is. *Rationality* has to do with the way we proceed to investigate matters, settle disputes, evaluate evidence, and assess people's behaviors, practices, and beliefs. If we could get agreement about the standards of rationality, then the only thing left to argue about would be whether or not these standards were fairly and accurately applied. But how do we proceed if we cannot agree on the standards themselves?

Picture Zhaungzi's imaginary arguers debating the nature of rationality. Not only would they and some third party find an acceptable settlement of the dispute difficult to obtain, but they would not even know how to go about reaching a settlement. What would count as a rational solution to their disagreement if the very nature of rationality is itself the subject of the disagreement? With Zhaungzi we might ask, with more than a mere hint of futility, "Shall we wait for still another person?"

To avoid the futility of endless disagreements, some philosophers maintain that there must be objective and universal standards of rationality. This position on the question of rationality is called **foundationalism**. Generally (there are many different varieties of foundationalism), foundationalists hold that we can decide what is rational by appealing to principles that are undeniable to any rational person. For example, if I maintain that my belief about extraterrestrials visiting Peru is rational, I, according to this view, should be able to present good reasons in support of my belief. The reasons I present will be good ones insofar as they ultimately rest on a set of ideas that are *self-evidently true* for any person who can properly understand them.

What are these foundational principles? Many philosophers have maintained that they are the basic laws of logic and the rules and procedures deducible from those laws. Aristotle, for example, claims that the **law of noncontradiction** (a statement cannot be both true and false) stands at the foundation of all rational reasoning.

You cannot rationally assert *p* (where *p* stands for any statement) *and not-p*. If you claim *p* is true, you cannot also claim it is false and be rational. Furthermore, he argues, anyone who denies this law and who is prepared to defend that denial will be unable to advance her or his argument without relying on the very law supposedly rejected.

It would appear that people who argue that the law of noncontradiction is false are either perverse or irrational. Indeed, their own statement denying the law of noncontradiction could not be both true and false: it would have to be true but if could not be, because denying the law of noncontradiction means that it would have to be true and false at the same time. You would probably agree with me. However, you might quickly point out that being logical and correctly applying the laws of logic are, at best, necessary conditions of rationality. These are not sufficient. We can imagine someone applying logical procedures and arriving at the most absurd conclusions. If I were clever enough, I could justify my belief in extraterrestrials visiting Peru without violating any logical laws, but is that enough for you to conclude that my belief is rational?

So it would seem we need some fundamental principles, besides the laws of logic, in order to know both the necessary and sufficient conditions of rationality.[3] And here is where the fight really breaks out among foundationalists. Some (usually called *rationalists*) claim that these foundational principles of rationality amount to "clear and distinct ideas" that are innate in the human mind or can be discovered by a careful and critical analysis of our beliefs. Others (usually called *empiricists*) argue that immediate sense impressions form the foundations of rational beliefs. You will encounter something of this debate between rationalists and empiricists as you read this book, so I will not belabor the point here. I only wish you to understand that much philosophical energy has been expended in a search for the foundational principles of rational belief. If we can find such principles, then we will have agreed-upon procedures for sifting through the many different answers to metaphysical questions (What is real?), epistemological questions (What is knowledge?), and axiological questions (What is value?) and settling on those that prove the most rational.

I think you can see the attractiveness of the foundationalist position, especially if you have ever been in one of those arguments where someone keeps asking you, "How do you know that?" At first you are patient and display your reasons. But she or he persists. "How do you know those are good reasons?" You explain why. Again, "Well, how can you be so sure?" About now your blood pressure is rising because you are beginning to see an infinite, bottomless abyss opening up. This could go on forever! But have no fear. Foundationalism can ride to your rescue because foundationalism maintains that regress is not infinite, the pit is not bottomless, and there is a sure foundation of first principles that your questioner will recognize to be rational. There is a way, according to foundationalists, of settling Zhaungzi's imaginary dispute.

However, the foundation you reach on your descent may turn out to be a ledge that gives way under your weight. Why? Because all the philosophical energy that has been spent on the search for foundational principles has ended in disagreement.

---

[3]Something can be sufficient without being necessary and vice versa. A rock hitting a window is sufficient to break it, but not necessary because a baseball might do as well. Milk is necessary to make yogurt, but not sufficient.

Thus, many philosophers have declared the modern search for fundamental rational principles bankrupt. Welcome to the postmodern age of *anti-foundationalism*.

Just as there are many varieties of foundationalism, there are also many varieties of anti-foundationalism. In order to remove the negative connotations of the "anti," let us call the critics of foundationalism **constructivists** because many of them maintain that rationality is a social construction.

Some constructivists point to the failure of agreement among foundationalists as proof that the search for objective, universal, self-evident, rational principles is fruitless. Others argue that the so-called self-evident, objective, universal, ahistorical, transcultural foundations of rationality have been shown again and again to be little more than the elevation of the prejudices of an elite class, or of males, or of white culture, or of Western civilization to the honorific title of "self-evident rational principles." What is alleged to be "rational" turns out, after careful critical analysis, to be what Anglo-American European white males value! Foundationalism, this line of criticism maintains, is merely a variety of ethnocentric imperialism disguised with the mask of rationality.

Many constructivists argue that we are all so embedded in our cultures, our traditions, our religions, and our historical situations that we can never find some neutral point, some god's-eye view from which to pass judgment. Not one of our limited viewpoints is privileged. We are hopelessly culture-bound. There is no culturally neutral "third party," as Zhaungzi pointed out so clearly centuries ago, that can settle once and for all our important disputes. There are, of course, cultural procedures for settling disputes. However, it is a grave mistake to elevate such procedures to self-evident, universal marks of rationality.

Still other critics of foundationalism point out that foundationalism is fatally flawed because it is itself based on a contradiction. Foundationalism claims that a rational belief is one supported by good reasons. This means that before I accept your beliefs as rational, I should expect you to be able to display, if questioned, good reasons for such beliefs. If, after you have given me your good reasons, I persist and ask for more, sooner or later I shall have to be content with a belief whose truth is, you claim, "self-evident." So it turns out that good reasons rest on principles that we are asked to accept as self-evidently true and in need of no further support. Such principles would be irrational given the criterion initially assumed to be the hallmark of a rational belief—that is, a belief supported by good reasons.

Displaying the evidence and exploring the subtleties and shifts of argument between foundationalists and constructivists would take us too far afield. However, I should mention one major issue that this debate has engendered because it is particularly relevant to what this book is about. That is the issue of cognitive and ethical relativism. The foundationalists charge the constructivists with both **cognitive relativism** (the denial of universal truths) and **ethical relativism** (the denial of universally valid moral principles). They claim that if one denies the existence of transcultural, universal, objective standards of rationality, then what one is maintaining amounts to the view that there is no such thing as rationality; all there are, are *rationalities*. Eventually, this will lead the constructivist to assert moral relativism as well. One will be led down a slippery slope resulting in the conclusion that any culture's values, any religious tradition, any morality, indeed any set of beliefs, is as good or as rational as anyone else's. However, such relativism is self-defeating. If your view is no better or worse than my view, then all views are of equal merit.

Therefore, constructivists can have no justification to support their claim that foundationalism is wrong. Foundationalists' views of rationality as universal and ahistorical are no more rational or any less rational than constructivists' views of rationalities as local and historical (see Table 1.1).

This is a powerful response to the constructivist critique of foundationalism. Few of us would argue with others if we thought that all views of morality or all views of truth were of equal worth. Yet we do argue. Few of us would be willing to maintain that programs of "ethnic cleansing," which lamentably characterize so much of human political practice, are as rational or moral as programs that aim at getting human beings to live in peace with one another.

We seem to be caught on the horns of a dilemma. We do not wish to opt for either ethnocentric imperialism or a kind of relativism that advocates "anything goes." Is there any other choice? Is there a way out of this predicament? Much contemporary philosophy is presently concerned with finding a way out of this dilemma, a sort of middle ground that allows us to assert that some answers are better than others but stops short of imposing on others our own local views of what is rational and what is good.

One way to escape the horns of a dilemma is to make careful distinctions. There is a difference between ethnocentrism and ethnocentric *imperialism*. Perhaps it is impossible to totally escape an ethnocentric viewpoint, but we do not have to impose our views on others by presenting them as if they are the only true views.

Likewise some philosophers distinguish between different kinds of relativism. Not all relativism may be self-defeating, contrary to what some foundationalists believe. We must carefully distinguish between relativism in the *strong sense* (the claim there are no universally valid standards) and relativism in the *weak sense* (the claim that standards of rationality and morality are culturally diverse). It seems

TABLE 1.1

Foundationalism	Constructivism
Claim	*Claim*
One rationality that is universal and objective.	Many rationalities that are local and based on intersubjective agreement.
Argument	*Argument*
Beliefs are rational if supported by good reasons.	Rationality is conditioned by history and culture.
If an infinite regress of reasons is to be avoided, there must be a foundation of self-evident beliefs.*	Vast amounts of historical, cultural, anthropological, and linguistic evidence support the above claim.
Such foundational beliefs are the laws of logic or clear and distinct ideas or beliefs evident to the senses.	
Critique of Constructivism	*Critique of Foundationalism*
Constructivism amounts to a self-refuting relativism.	Foundationalism cannot agree on what counts as foundational beliefs; hence they are not self-evident. Its definition of rational beliefs is contradictory, and its claims amount to ethnocentric imperialism.

*Only *internalist* versions of foundationalism hold foundational beliefs are self-evident. *Externalist* versions reject this view and, according to one type of externalism, appeal to notions like reliability.

obvious that standards of rationality and morality are relative to historical and cultural conditions in the sense that they are related to such conditions (weak relativism). Standards of rationality do not float in some timeless, nonhuman space. However, concluding from this that all standards of rationality are of equal value or are equally true (the sort of self-defeating relativism the foundationalists charge the constructivists with) requires a big leap. It does not follow from the fact that there exist different understandings of rationality and morality that all understandings are of equal value, any more than it follows from the fact that there are different understandings of science that all of them are equally good or useful.

However, you might argue that if there are no objective standards of rationality or, at the very least, if we must admit we do not know what they might be, then all we are left with are rationalities bound to historical conditions and local cultural communities, and we have no way of determining which are better. Perhaps you are right. However, I think that we do have some options. We can remain convinced that our community has the last word on the subject and all others are wrong. Or, as we encounter other communities and other cultures, we can listen to them (and they to us) and try to discover ways of settling our disputes *together*. We can expand our conversations, listen to other voices, and together with them ask, What is real? What is knowledge? What is good? As we listen, as we enter into a dialogue, yes, and even as we argue, our standards of rationality will grow and, although we may still disagree in the end, at least we can say we have understood.

Hans-Georg Gadamer, a contemporary German philosopher, argues that truth is an understanding that occurs when there is a "fusion of horizons." Authentic conversation or dialogue occurs when we can recognize our own understanding as a horizon resulting from the perspective or bias we have acquired and when we are willing to risk our horizon in order to allow the horizon of the "other" to appear.

This book is an attempt to expand the philosophical dialogue. A wide variety of views will be heard—African American, Latino, Native American, feminist, and even Anglo-American European white males—and I hope these views will turn into meaningful voices of wisdom. We will not agree with all these voices, but we can learn from each, and we may discover wider areas of agreement than we thought possible.

My claim that agreement about what is rational can emerge out of dialogue and expanded cultural communication rests on the assumption that we can understand philosophical views held by people who live in times and places very different from our own and on the hope that learning about ourselves and others is a worthwhile enterprise. Some might argue that we can never understand what others who are very different from us are saying and that my hope is naive. I do not have the space to defend my assumption and my hope, but I do believe that good reasons can be given for them. In any case, we will never find out if we do not try.

Recall that I characterized philosophy as a rational activity of formulating, understanding, and answering fundamental questions. This activity, I wish to stress, relies heavily on the logical skills of analyzing, criticizing, and developing arguments. It is, however, more than this. If the goal of philosophy is to formulate, understand, and answer fundamental questions on both an intellectual and a practical level, then we can determine how rational this activity is only by assessing how successfully this goal is achieved by all those who participate in this sort of activity. I do not believe we can rule out any of the profound thinking about fundamental problems that the many peoples of the world have to offer by imposing some predetermined model of rationality. Hence, the very process of assessment is something we must learn as we go.

The Jains of India have a teaching called *syad-vada*, which might be translated as the "perhaps method." This teaching holds that 353 different viewpoints can be held on any question; hence, dogmatic closed-mindedness is inappropriate. To any perspective or any issue, the thoughtful will reply, "Perhaps." This "method" is based on the assumption that no single philosophical view or system can say all there is to be said about reality. It does not mean we should remain silent, nor does it mean that everything that is said (however partial) is of equal worth.

There are times, I think, when we can be a bit more definite than "perhaps," but the flexibility and openness this method recommends is a virtue we all need to practice when we have no privileged viewpoint from which we might settle a matter once and for all. Not all answers are rational. Some are better than others. However, the range of rational responses may be far broader than we realize.

1.3 READING PHILOSOPHY

Reading philosophy is both exciting and rewarding. Philosophy provides intellectual stimulation: the pleasure of discovering new ideas, the fascination of following the thread of a provocative argument, the challenge of rethinking inherited beliefs. For these reasons, reading philosophy can be enjoyable, but often it is not easy. As the image of Alice in Wonderland, in the color plates, reminds us, sometimes, when we read philosophy, we feel like Alice, who remarked, "Somehow it fills my head with ideas—only I don't know exactly what they are."

Philosophical texts come in a wide variety of types, ranging from technical essays to dramatic dialogues. They come from different cultures and different historical periods, and they are written in different languages. It is not easy to adjust to this variety. It takes practice to appreciate and understand ancient Greek dialogues, Buddhist fables, seventeenth-century French essays, and Chinese poetry.

Many of us are accustomed to reading secondary sources that explain the ideas of others. Textbooks digest what others say, explain what isn't clear, underline the important points, present summaries, and define technical words. Because much of our education has been centered on reading textbooks, not everyone is accustomed to wrestling with primary sources—the original texts and words—even in translation. If you are not used to digesting material on your own, explaining it to yourself, learning how to do your own summaries, and looking up words and references you do not understand, then at first you will find it difficult to read primary sources. Like anything else that is new, it will take some practice and some help from your instructor.

Voices of Wisdom is a combination of secondary material (my introductions to each chapter and to each selection in the chapters) and primary material (selections from the writings of philosophers past and present). Reading the primary texts may, in some cases, prove a rather difficult task. You need to learn how to read analytically and critically.

The purpose of analytical reading is to find out what the text says and to understand it as best you can. To do so requires analysis on your part. To analyze something is to break it into parts or smaller units. Thus you need to distinguish main ideas from supporting ideas and to determine what the author is trying to accomplish.

Critical reading involves evaluation. Your evaluation may be positive, negative, or some mixture of the two. Criticism requires you to make the effort to think about the ideas, analogies, arguments, evidence, and metaphors presented in the text, as well as their implications and assumptions.

Here are some suggestions that will help you understand philosophical texts and develop critical analysis skills.

1. Read the material at least twice.
2. Read actively and with a purpose.
3. Read analytically and sympathetically.

Here are some analytical questions that you can ask and answer as you read.

- What is the thesis (the central idea or main point)?
- What are the major points made in developing and supporting the thesis?
- How are key terms defined?
- What are the basic assumptions made by the author?
- What are the important implications of the author's position?

4. Read critically.

Here are some critical questions that will help you evaluate the strengths and weaknesses of the selections.

- Is what is said clear? If not, how is it unclear?
- Are adequate definitions given for important concepts? Can you think of counterexamples?
- Are the arguments adequate to support the claims; for example, are the premises true? the assumptions dubious?
- Do the implications of the text lead to absurd or false consequences?
- Are important aspects of the issue overlooked?
- How well did the author accomplish her or his goal?

5. After you have finished, review what you have read.
6. It is a good idea to keep a "philosophical notebook" in which you record your notes on the readings.

Before each selection are reading questions that will help you to analyze the reading. After each selection are critical questions designed to help you evaluate the reading. You can keep the answers to these questions in your philosophical notebook. For more on reading philosophy, as well as thinking logically and writing philosophy, see Chapter 2.

1.4 DOES PHILOSOPHY BAKE BREAD?

"Why should I study philosophy?" That is a question I often hear my students ask. It may be a question you are asking. Today many people approach their education pragmatically. They ask, "How will learning this prepare me for a job?" The implication of such a question is that if it does not help me get a job, it is not worth studying. If philosophy bakes no bread, why study it?

In the first two sections you have read about how we might define philosophy and about some debates over the nature of rationality. What have you learned that is of any importance? When you are interviewed for that first job upon graduation, do you think the interviewer might ask, "All right then, who do you think is right, the foundationalists or the constructivists?"

"Well," you might say, "I certainly don't think that the value of a field of study is completely exhausted by whether or not it leads to gainful employment. However, isn't it the case that philosophy, unlike science, never really settles anything? Philosophers just spin their wheels in endless debate."

It is true that uncertainty haunts the philosopher's study. Indeed, it is uncertainty that keeps the philosophical fires burning. If science could answer all our questions, if putting bread on the table were all there is to a happy life, if religion could provide all the answers we need, then I fear the philosopher in us would soon cease to exist. However, the philosophic wonder of which Aristotle spoke keeps our minds stirring largely because there are so many things about life that are uncertain.

There is an important sense, I think, in which we cannot help but philosophize. Life's circumstances and experiences compel us to think about things beyond our daily bread. If this line of reasoning is right, if we cannot help but philosophize, then should we not learn to do it well? One way of learning how to do it is to listen carefully to others who have philosophized from many different times and places. We can learn by example even when we disagree with the views of those from whom we learn.

If helping you get a job or answering with certainty the "big questions" is not the most important reason to study philosophy, it does not follow that philosophical study is totally without commercial value. I encourage you to visit the Web site of the American Philosophical Association (http://www.apaonline.org). There you will find all kinds of valuable information about philosophy and its study. Among other things you will find illustrations of both academic and nonacademic careers pursued by philosophy majors. These careers include educator, advertising executive, computer systems analyst, publisher, librarian, commodities broker, diplomat, attorney, TV producer, editor, minister, and so forth. The skills of critical thinking and clear expression that you can learn from the study of philosophy prove to be valuable in many different pursuits that do bake bread.

We continue with a Western example. Bertrand Russell (1872–1970) is the author of the following selection. He explicitly addressed the issue of the value of philosophy in a book called *The Problems of Philosophy* published in 1912. What he has to say may surprise you. Whatever you may think about his claims, it is clear that the questions about the usefulness of philosophy are neither new nor unimportant.

As you read what Russell has to say, see if you can answer the following reading questions and identify the passages that support your answers. Discuss in class the questions you had difficulty answering and the ones that stimulated your own thinking about the value of philosophy.

READING QUESTIONS

1. Where, according to Russell, is the value of philosophy to be found?
2. Why does Russell maintain that the "uncertainty of philosophy is more apparent than real"?
3. What does Russell mean when he asserts that the value of philosophy is to be sought in its "very uncertainty"?
4. According to Russell, what may be the chief value of philosophy?

On the Value of Philosophy

BERTRAND RUSSELL

Having now come to the end of our brief and very incomplete review of the problems of philosophy, it will be well to consider, in conclusion, what is the value of philosophy and why it ought to be studied. It is the more necessary to consider this question, in view of the fact that many men, under the influence of science or of practical affairs, are inclined to doubt whether philosophy is anything better than innocent but useless trifling, hairsplitting distinctions, and controversies on matters concerning which knowledge is impossible.

This view of philosophy appears to result, partly from a wrong conception of the ends of life, partly from a wrong conception of the kind of goods which philosophy strives to achieve. Physical science, through the medium of inventions, is useful to innumerable people who are wholly ignorant of it; thus the study of physical science is to be recommended, not only, or primarily, because of the effect on the student, but rather because of the effect on mankind in general. Thus utility does not belong to philosophy. If the study of philosophy has any value at all for others than students of philosophy, it must be only indirectly, through its effects upon the lives of those who study it. It is in these effects, therefore, if anywhere, that the value of philosophy must be primarily sought.

But further, if we are not to fail in our endeavour to determine the value of philosophy, we must first free our minds from the prejudices of what are wrongly called "practical" men. The "practical" man, as this word is often used, is one who recognizes only material needs, who realizes that men must have food for the body, but is oblivious of the necessity of providing food for the mind. If all men were well off, if poverty and disease had been reduced to their lowest possible point, there would still remain much to be done to produce a valuable society; and even in the existing world the goods of the mind are at least as important as the goods of the body. It is exclusively among the goods of the mind that the value of philosophy is to be found; and only those who are not indifferent to these goods can be persuaded that the study of philosophy is not a waste of time.

Philosophy, like all other studies, aims primarily at knowledge. The knowledge it aims at is the kind of knowledge which gives unity and system to the body of the sciences, and the kind which results from a critical examination of the grounds of our convictions, prejudices, and beliefs. But it cannot be maintained that philosophy has had any very great measure of success in its attempts to provide definite answers to its questions. If you ask a mathematician, a mineralogist, a historian, or any other man of learning, what definite body of truths has been ascertained by his science, his answer will last as long as you are willing to listen. But if you put the same question to a philosopher, he will, if he is candid, have to confess that his study has not achieved positive results such as have been achieved by other sciences. It is true that this is partly accounted for by the fact that, as soon as definite knowledge concerning any subject becomes possible, this subject ceases to be called philosophy, and becomes a separate science. The whole study of the heavens, which now belongs to astronomy, was once included in philosophy; Newton's great work was called "the mathematical principles of natural philosophy." Similarly, the study of the human mind, which was a part of philosophy, has now been separated from philosophy and has become the science of psychology. Thus, to a great extent, the uncertainty of philosophy is more apparent than real: those questions which are already capable of definite answers are placed in the sciences, while those only to which, at present, no definite answer can be given remain to form the residue which is called philosophy.

From Bertrand Russell, *The Problems of Philosophy* (London: Oxford University Press, 1912), pp. 153–161.

This is, however, only a part of the truth concerning the uncertainty of philosophy. There are many questions—and among them those that are of the profoundest interest to our spiritual life—which, so far as we can see, must remain insoluble to the human intellect unless its powers become of quite a different order from what they are now. Has the universe any unity of plan or purpose, or is it a fortuitous concourse of atoms? Is consciousness a permanent part of the universe, giving hope of indefinite growth in wisdom, or is it a transitory accident on a small planet on which life must ultimately become impossible? Are good and evil of importance to the universe or only to man? Such questions are asked by philosophy, and variously answered by various philosophers. But it would seem that, whether answers be otherwise discoverable or not, the answers suggested by philosophy are none of them demonstrably true. Yet, however slight may be the hope of discovering an answer, it is part of the business of philosophy to continue the consideration of such questions, to make us aware of their importance, to examine all the approaches to them, and to keep alive that speculative interest in the universe which is apt to be killed by confining ourselves to definitely ascertainable knowledge.

Many philosophers, it is true, have held that philosophy could establish the truth of certain answers to such fundamental questions. They have supposed that what is of most importance in religious beliefs could be proved by strict demonstration to be true. In order to judge of such attempts, it is necessary to take a survey of human knowledge, and to form an opinion as to its methods and its limitations. On such a subject it would be unwise to pronounce dogmatically; but if the investigations of our previous chapters have not led us astray, we shall be compelled to renounce the hope of finding philosophical proofs of religious beliefs. We cannot, therefore, include as part of the value of philosophy any definite set of answers to such questions. Hence, once more, the value of philosophy must not depend upon any supposed body of definitely ascertainable knowledge to be acquired by those who study it.

The value of philosophy is, in fact, to be sought largely in its very uncertainty. The man who has no tincture of philosophy goes through life imprisoned in the prejudices derived from common sense, from the habitual beliefs of his age or his nation, and from convictions which have grown up in his mind without the co-operation or consent of his deliberate reason. To such a man the world tends to become definite, finite, obvious; common objects rouse no questions, and unfamiliar possibilities are contemptuously rejected. As soon as we begin to philosophize, on the contrary, we find ... that even the most everyday things lead to problems to which only very incomplete answers can be given. Philosophy, though unable to tell us with certainty what is the true answer to the doubts which it raises, is able to suggest many possibilities which enlarge our thoughts and free them from the tyranny of custom. Thus, while diminishing our feeling of certainty as to what things are, it greatly increases our knowledge as to what they may be; it removes the somewhat arrogant dogmatism of those who have never travelled into the region of liberating doubt, and it keeps alive our sense of wonder by showing familiar things in an unfamiliar aspect.

Apart from its utility in showing unsuspected possibilities, philosophy has a value—perhaps its chief value—through the greatness of the objects which it contemplates, and the freedom from narrow and personal aims resulting from this contemplation. The life of the instinctive man is shut up within the circle of his private interests: family and friends may be included, but the outer world is not regarded except as it may help or hinder what comes within the circle of instinctive wishes. In such a life there is something feverish and confined, in comparison with which the philosophic life is calm and free. The private world of instinctive interests is a small one, set in the midst of a great and powerful world which must, sooner or later, lay our private world in ruins. Unless we can so enlarge our interests as to include the whole outer world, we remain like a garrison in a beleaguered fortress, knowing that the enemy prevents escape and that ultimate surrender is inevitable. In such a life there is no peace, but a constant strife between the insistence of desire and the powerlessness of will. In one way or another, if our life is to be great and free, we must escape this prison and this strife.

One way of escape is by philosophic contemplation. Philosophic contemplation does not, in its widest survey, divide the universe into two hostile camps—friends and foes, helpful and hostile, good and bad—it views the whole impartially. Philosophic contemplation, when it is unalloyed, does not aim at proving that the rest of the universe is akin to man. All acquisition of knowledge is an enlargement of the Self, but this enlargement is best attained when it is not directly sought. It is obtained when the desire for knowledge is alone operative, by a study which does not wish in advance that its objects should have this or that character, but adapts the Self to the characters which it finds in its objects. This enlargement of Self is not obtained when, taking the Self as it is, we try to show that the world is so similar to this Self that knowledge of it is possible without any admission of what seems alien. The desire to prove this is a form of self-assertion and, like all self-assertion, it is an obstacle to the growth of Self which it desires, and of which the Self knows that it is capable. Self-assertion, in philosophic speculation as elsewhere, views the world as a means to its own ends; thus it makes the world of less account than Self, and the Self sets bounds to the greatness of its goods. In contemplation, on the contrary, we start from the not-Self, and through its greatness the boundaries of Self are enlarged; through the infinity of the universe the mind which contemplates it achieves some share in infinity.

For this reason greatness of soul is not fostered by those philosophies which assimilate the universe to Man. Knowledge is a form of union of Self and not-Self; like all union, it is impaired by dominion, and therefore by any attempt to force the universe into conformity with what we find in ourselves. There is a widespread philosophical tendency towards the view which tells us that Man is the measure of all things, that truth is man-made, that space and time and the world of universals are properties of the mind, and that, if there be anything not created by the mind, it is unknowable and of no account for us. This view, if our previous discussions were correct, is untrue; but in addition to being untrue, it has the effect of robbing philosophic contemplation of all that gives it value, since it fetters contemplation to Self. What it calls knowledge is not a union with the not-Self, but a set of prejudices, habits, and desires, making an impenetrable veil between us and the world beyond. The man who finds pleasure in such a theory of knowledge is like the man who never leaves the domestic circle for fear his word might not be law.

The true philosophic contemplation, on the contrary, finds its satisfaction in every enlargement of the not-Self, in everything that magnifies the objects contemplated, and thereby the subject contemplating. Everything, in contemplation, that is personal or private, everything that depends upon habit, self-interest, or desire, distorts the object, and hence impairs the union which the intellect seeks. By thus making a barrier between subject and object, such personal and private things become a prison to the intellect. The free intellect will see as God might see, without a here and now, without hopes and fears, without the trammels of customary beliefs and traditional prejudices, calmly, dispassionately, in the sole and exclusive desire of knowledge—knowledge as impersonal, as purely contemplative, as it is possible for man to attain. Hence also the free intellect will value more the abstract and universal knowledge into which the accidents of private history do not enter, than the knowledge brought by the senses, and dependent, as such knowledge must be, upon an exclusive and personal point of view and a body whose sense organs distort as much as they reveal.

The mind which has become accustomed to the freedom and impartiality of philosophic contemplation will preserve something of the same freedom and impartiality in the world of action and emotion. It will view its purposes and desires as parts of the whole, with the absence of insistence that results from seeing them as infinitesimal fragments in a world of which all the rest is unaffected by any one man's deeds. The impartiality which, in contemplation, is the unalloyed desire for truth, is the very same quality of mind which, in action, is justice, and in emotion is that universal love which can be given to all, and not only to those who are judged useful or admirable. Thus contemplation enlarges not only the objects of our thoughts, but also the objects of our actions and our affections: it makes us citizens of the universe, not only of one walled city at war with all the rest. In this citizenship of the universe consists man's true freedom, and his liberation from the thraldom of narrow hopes and fears.

Thus, to sum up our discussion of the value of philosophy: Philosophy is to be studied, not for the sake of any definite answers to its questions, since no definite answers can, as a rule, be known to be true, but rather for the sake of the questions themselves; because these questions enlarge our conception of what is possible, enrich our intellectual imagination, and diminish the dogmatic assurance which closes the mind against speculation; but above all because, through the greatness of the universe which philosophy contemplates, the mind also is rendered great, and becomes capable of that union with the universe which constitutes its highest good.

◉ CRITICAL QUESTIONS

1. What do you think Russell means when he characterizes "true philosophic contemplation" as finding satisfaction in the "enlargement of the not-Self"? Is this clear?

2. How does Russell sum up the value of philosophical study? Do you agree with Russell? Why, or why not?

To access the *Voices of Wisdom*, 8th Edition, **Premium Website**, search for this book on CengageBrain.com.

CHAPTER TWO

Thinking and Writing Philosophically

Philosophy is the unusually stubborn attempt to think clearly.

WILLIAM JAMES

LEARNING OBJECTIVES

After studying this chapter students should be able to:
- understand what an argument is,
- analyze, criticize, and construct arguments,
- identify different kinds of arguments,
- identify different kinds of fallacies,
- write a philosophical essay, and
- successfully complete the exercises.

2.1 A LITTLE LOGIC

Philosophical thinking manifests great diversity of style, structure, method, and form. Metaphorical association, persuasive rhetoric, formal argument, analogical reasoning, word-plays, proverbial sayings, and much more can be found in philosophical writing. There is no simple or universal way to characterize philosophical thinking. It can be hypothetical, imaginative, deconstructive, constructive, and therapeutic. Many assert it is dialectical, although interpretations of what that means vary greatly. The word "dialectical" comes from a Greek word that means "to talk or think through." In a general sense, philosophical thinking involves thinking through an issue to a deeper level than is usual and trying to get clear about it.

Dialectical thinking usually involves some form of both analysis and criticism. In this sense it is closely related to the skills of analytical and critical reading of philosophical texts I discussed in the first chapter. Analysis, as we have already seen, is an activity of breaking up into smaller units or parts. Chemical analysis is a good example. A chemist analyzes a substance by breaking it up into its component parts. Thus water is found to consist of H_2O. Likewise, a philosopher analyzes an idea or issue

Adapted from Gary E. Kessler, *Reading, Thinking, and Writing Philosophically,* 2e. Belmont CA.: 2001. Reprinted by permission.

by uncovering the sub-ideas or issues that make it up. For example, a philosopher might analyze the concept of *free will* by first focusing on the various meanings of the term *free* and then trying to get clear about the notion of *will*.

Criticism comes from a Greek word that means "skilled in judging." To criticize is to judge whether an idea is true or false, or an argument strong or weak. Just as the chemist must evaluate the evidence resulting from her analysis of water, so the philosopher must evaluate her analysis of the idea of free will or some other notion.

If much philosophical thinking involves critical analysis, are there any rules to guide such thinking? Are there procedures and methods analogous to the procedures and methods of a chemist that can direct the process? Such rules do exist, but there is controversy over exactly what they are and whether they are appropriate to all cases. A subfield of philosophy called logic attempts to discover and articulate the rules that can help guide critical analysis.

Logic is the study of the norms or rules that ought to guide our reasoning if we wish to think clearly. It is important to note that many philosophers think of logic as a normative study, not a descriptive study. It does not describe how, in fact, we reason. Cognitive psychology does that. Rather, logic seeks to discover the norms or rules by which we ought to reason well.

I will consider three major aspects of logical reasoning. The first aspect deals with the analysis of arguments (breaking them into their parts), the second deals with the criticism or evaluation of arguments (distinguishing good ones from bad ones), and the third with the construction of arguments. The reason logic focuses on arguments is that we often express our reasoning by means of argumentation.

In the sections that follow, I am going to provide you with technical information about these three aspects in a condensed form, so you are going to have to read carefully and pay close attention. Be sure to answer the questions and do the exercises. Logical reasoning is a skill and, like all skills, is best learned by practice.

A. Analysis of Argument

To analyze arguments you need to familiarize yourself with the terms used to perform an analysis. You also need to follow four simple steps, as outlined below.

First step: recognize an argument

Statements (also called propositions) are sentences that assert something to be true or false. For example, "My name is Gary." Note that all statements are sentences, but not all sentences are statements. Thus the command, "Gary, get the ball!" is a sentence, but not a statement because it asserts nothing to be true (or false). Statements are the building blocks of arguments.

When you think of an argument, you probably think of a disagreement or a fight. In logic the word "argument" is used in a technical sense. It is an attempt to demonstrate that something is true by providing reasons in support of it. Hence an argument is a sequence of statements used to support, back up, prove, or give reasons for something.

Second step: distinguish the statements that are premises from the conclusion

Once you have identified an argument you need to distinguish premises from the conclusion. The supported statement is called the conclusion. The statement (there may be only one or there may be more than one) supporting the conclusion is called the premise.

> **Statements** are sentences that assert something to be true or false.
>
> An **argument** is a sequence of statements used to support, back up, prove, or give reasons for something.
>
> A **conclusion** is a statement in an argument that is supported or backed by other statements.
>
> A **premise** is a statement in an argument that supports, provides evidence, or gives the reasons for a conclusion.

Note that arguments are made up of statements. Note further that statements, when combined into an argument, are either premises or conclusions depending on the role they play in the argument. This indicates that arguments are not just a collection of any odd assortment or sequence of statements, but a collection in which the various statements are connected in a particular way.

Consider these examples:

EXAMPLE A		EXAMPLE B	
A1.	Is that water?	B1.	Either you are right or I am.
A2.	The book is open.	B2.	I am wrong.
A3.	Class is over	B3.	Therefore you are right.

Example B is an argument, but example A is not an argument. See if you can figure out why and state the differences in your own words.

When analyzing arguments, it is helpful to identify the conclusion first. Once that is done, the premises fall into place more easily. If you can find no conclusion, you may not be dealing with an argument. However, arguments can be incomplete. Sometimes the conclusion is not stated, but only implied. In such cases you must supply it. Arguments also can be complex. Each premise may be supported by one or more subarguments. In such cases, the premises of the main argument are themselves conclusions of the subarguments. Or there may be several major arguments; each linked so that the conclusion of one becomes a premise for the next one and so on. It is not always easy to reduce arguments to a simple premise and conclusion form. However, if you can explicitly identify the premises and conclusion, it helps in both understanding and evaluating arguments. Ask yourself, "What is the author trying to get me to believe, and why does he or she think I ought to believe it?"

Third step: determine whether arguments are inductive or deductive

Arguments come in two types: inductive and deductive. You have probably heard of inductive and deductive arguments. Many of you have been taught to think that inductive arguments move from specific cases to general cases and deductive arguments move from the general to the specific. This is certainly true of some kinds of deductive and inductive reasoning, but it is not true of all kinds. Hence, in logic, a more technical definition is used.

In logic, arguments are classified as inductive if their conclusions provide information in addition to the information contained in the premises. Hence, if the premises are true, the conclusion may or may not be true. Example: Suppose I conclude that all events have causes because every event observed so far has had a cause. What is the premise? What is the conclusion? If the premise is true, might the conclusion still be false? If so, this is an inductive argument.

Arguments are not always expressed with their premises stated first, their conclusion last, and each statement numbered. However, it is often helpful to rewrite them in this form so the connection between premises and conclusion can be seen more clearly. Thus the example above can be restated:

1. Every event observed so far has had a cause. (Premise)
2. Therefore, all events have causes. (Conclusion)

An argument is called deductive if the conclusion is inferred solely from the information contained in the premises. In other words, the conclusion provides no new information, but states explicitly what is already contained in the premises. For example, suppose I argue that I am bound to die because all humans die and I am a human. What is the conclusion? Which statements are the premises? Does the conclusion provide new information? Can you restate this argument in premise and conclusion form?

> An argument is **inductive** if its conclusion provides information in addition to the information contained in the premises.
> An argument is **deductive** if the conclusion is inferred solely from the information contained in the premises.

Fourth step: identify the kind of inductive or deductive argument with which you are dealing

There are several kinds of inductive arguments. One common type is called a generalization because the conclusion generalizes beyond the cases reported in the premises. For example, I might argue from the link between smoking and lung cancer in 10,000 cases to the likelihood of such a link in most cases. Another common type is analogy. Analogical arguments try to persuade us that something is true of one thing because of its similarity to another thing. For example, I might argue that the world is designed by some intelligent being because the world is like a machine and machines are designed by intelligent beings.

> An inductive argument is a **generalization** if the conclusion generalizes beyond the evidence cited in the premises.
> An inductive argument is an **analogy** if it asserts that something is true of one thing because of its similarity to another thing.

There are also several kinds of deductive arguments. Below I list five common kinds of deductive arguments in symbolic form.

1. *Modus ponens* (MP)

$$p \supset q$$
$$\underline{p}$$
$$\therefore q$$

p and q stand for any statement and $\supset$ stands for "If ... then"

∴ stands for "therefore" and the line marks the division between premises and conclusion.

This argument is read:

> "If p is true, then q is true."
> "p is true."
> "Therefore q is true."

If we substitute the statement "I am paying attention" for p and "I will learn logic" for q we get:

> "If I am paying attention, then I will learn logic."
> "I am paying attention."
> "Therefore, I will learn logic."

2. *Modus tollens* (MT)

$$p \supset q$$
$$\frac{\sim q}{}$$
$$\therefore \ \sim p$$

~ stands for "not."

Read: "If p is true, then q is true, q is *not* true. Therefore p is *not* true."

Using "I love logic" for p and "I love rock and roll" for q, you can write a *modus tollens* argument as follows:

> If I love logic, then I love rock and roll.
> I do not love rock and roll.
> Therefore, I do not love logic.

3. Hypothetical Syllogism (HS)

$$p \supset q$$
$$\frac{q \supset r}{}$$
$$\therefore p \supset r$$

Notice how the conclusion links the first statement (p) of the first premise with the last statement (r) of the second premise. This makes explicit the link that is established via statement q. You can extend the premises in this sort of argument indefinitely (at least theoretically) as long as you link the preceding premise with the subsequent premise via a common statement. The common statement will be the consequent (second statement) of one premise and the antecedent (first statement) of the next.

Example:

$$p \supset q$$
$$q \supset r$$
$$r \supset s$$
$$\frac{s \supset t}{}$$
$$\therefore p \supset t$$

4. Disjunctive Syllogism (DS). Two forms:

p v q   OR   p v q

~p   ~q

∴ q   ∴ p

v stands for "or."

The first form can be read "Either p is true or q is true. P is not true. Therefore q is true." The second form can be read "Either p is true or q is true, Q is not true. Therefore (fill in the blank) _____."

The v (or) is *exclusive* hence if we know that one of the statements is false (as the second premise tells us), then we can conclude that the other one is true.

5. Dilemma (D)

p v q   "Either p is true or q is true."

p ⊃ r   "If p is true, then r is true."

q ⊃ s   "If q is true, then s is true."

∴ r v s   "Therefore either r is true or s is true."

Notice that the two statements of the first premise constitute the antecedents of the second and third premises respectively. Also note that the disjunctive conclusion uses the consequent statements (r and s) of the second and third premises. The conclusion is often referred to as the "horns of the dilemma" if it presents a choice between two unpleasant options. If neither option is particularly attractive, and if there is no third option, then one faces a choice between being "impaled" by one of the horns or by the other one. Consider:

Either people do right (p) or people do wrong (q).
If people do right (p), then morality is unnecessary (r).
If people do wrong (q), then morality is ineffective (s).
Either _____ or _____.

Supply the conclusion to this dilemma and note its "horns."

FIVE TYPES OF DEDUCTIVE ARGUMENTS

Modus Ponens or MP
Modus Tollens or MT
Hypothetical Syllogism or HS
Disjunctive Syllogism or DS
Dilemma or D

Exercise I. Logic is a skill that needs to be practiced and applied. To see if you have understood this section on the analysis of arguments answer the following.

1. T or F. A premise is a statement supporting a conclusion.

2. T or F. "Are you happy?" is a statement.
3. Is the following an argument? If so, what is the conclusion? "It is right, too, that philosophy should be called the science of truth; for a theoretical science ends in truth, as a practical science ends in action." (Aristotle)
4. Consider this argument: Every time I have been to the dentist in the past, it has hurt. Therefore, I am afraid that when I go tomorrow it will hurt. This argument is _____.
   a. inductive
   b. deductive
   c. a *modus ponens*
   d. an analogy
   e. a dilemma
5. Consider: The brain is like a computer. Its structure is the hardware, and socialization is the software. Sensations are the input that it processes. Thus, just as the output of a computer is predictable once we know the hardware, software, and input, so the actions of the human being are predictable. This argument is _____.
   a. deductive
   b. a generalization
   c. an analogy
   d. inductive
   e. both c and d.
6. Consider: Either the soul is aware or it is not. If it is, then it changes. If it is not aware, then it does not exist. Hence, either the soul changes or it does not exist.
   a. The conclusion to this argument is the first sentence.
   b. The first sentence is the first premise.
   c. The conclusion is unstated.
   d. This is not an argument.
   e. This is a disjunctive syllogism.
7. T or F. If what is stated in question 6 is an argument, it is deductive.
8. Consider: "You have a choice of admitting that people are morally responsible for what they do or they are not morally responsible. After all, people are either free or they are not. If they are free, then they are morally responsible, but if they are not free, they are not morally responsible." This argument is _____.
   a. an analogy
   b. a generalization
   c. a *modus ponens*
   d. a dilemma
   e. a hypothetical syllogism
9. Confucius argued: "If words are not correctly used, then we will be deceived. If we are deceived, then dictators can rule. If words are not correctly used, then dictators can rule."
   a. The last sentence is the conclusion.
   b. This is a hypothetical syllogism.
   c. This is a *modus tollens*.
   d. This is a deductive argument.
   e. All except c.

10. Consider: If reforming the medical care system works, then the president has shown good judgment. Reforming the medical system has worked, therefore the president has shown good judgment. This argument is _____.
    a. inductive
    b. *modus tollens*
    c. *modus ponens*
    d. a dilemma
    e. a disjunctive syllogism.
11. Construct a disjunctive syllogism. Let p = Logic is fun, and q = Gumby exists.
12. Create a MT argument. Let p = I am unconscious. Use any statement you wish for q.
13. Construct an MP argument. Write it using anything you wish for p and q.

You can check your answers by looking up your textbook on CengageBrain. com.

B. Evaluating Arguments and Definitions

After analyzing an argument, we need to evaluate or criticize it in order to determine whether it is a good one or a bad one. If it is a good one, we may have some confidence that its conclusion can be accepted. If it is a bad one, we ought to be suspicious of the conclusion.

Step 1: Check to see if the terms are adequately defined

Arguments are made up of statements, but statements are made up of words. Some of these words are crucial to the argument and need to be adequately defined. Some philosophers maintain that definitions are not true or false; rather, they are more or less helpful. Their purpose is to draw boundaries and thereby distinguish one thing from another. If the boundaries are drawn in helpful ways, the definition is a good one. However, other philosophers have argued that good definitions express the essence of something. They tell us what something really is. If so, then definitions are more than just helpful in clarifying how we are using words. They truly express (or fail to express) the very essence of the thing being defined.

Here are some rules that you can use to evaluate definitions.

RULES FOR CRITICIZING DEFINITIONS
A good definition should:

1. be clear and precise;
2. be stated, if possible, in positive form rather than negative form (e.g., it should not include a negation such as "not");
3. be noncircular;
4. be broad enough to include all cases designated by actual usage;
5. be narrow enough to exclude cases beyond the range of actual usage; and
6. state, if analytic, essential characteristics.

Suppose we are discussing abortion, and we begin to wonder whether the fetus is a human being. I assert that it is not, and you ask me to define what I mean by "human being." I present Aristotle's famous definition: A human being is a rational animal.

Is this a good definition? Well, is it clear and precise? By clarity I mean is it free from ambiguity, and by precision I mean is it free from vagueness. Ambiguity refers to the fact that, because words mean different things, it is often not clear from the context which meaning is intended. For example, the word "animal" (according to Webster's dictionary) can mean: "1. a living organism capable of sensation and voluntary motion; 2. any creature other than man that is four-footed; 3. a brutish, debased or inhumane person." It is clear from the context of Aristotle's definition that he is using the word "animal" in the first sense. Hence, in this context its meaning is not ambiguous.

Vagueness refers to the range of applicability of a term. For example, the word "bald" is vague because it is unclear how much hair must be missing before one qualifies for that title. One might argue that the word "rational" in Aristotle's definition is vague. A wide range of actions might be termed rational. Where does one draw the line? Is a computer "rational" because it can calculate? Further clarification of the meaning of rational in this connection must be provided.

> **Ambiguity** refers to the fact that, because words mean different things, it is often not clear from the context which meaning is intended.
> **Vagueness** refers to the range of applicability of a term.

The definition we are considering ("humans are rational animals") is stated in a positive form and hence meets the second criterion. I think you can easily see the reason for this rule. If I defined humans as "not frogs" that would not be very helpful because it fails to sufficiently narrow the range of meaning. It should be noted, however, that in some cases negative definitions are the only kind possible. So God, some theologians have argued, can only be defined negatively, that is, God is not finite (infinite), not temporal (eternal), and so on.

The rule about circularity is obvious. It is not helpful to define a human being as "a being that is human." The definition ought to provide some useful information, not just repeat what is being defined (usually called the *definiendum*) in somewhat different terms. "Human beings are rational animals" does provide more information about what we consider human beings to be and hence is not circular.

When using rules 4 and 5 about broadness and narrowness, it is helpful to use a technique called counterexample. When checking definition, see if you can think of a clear-cut example of the *definiendum* that is not covered by the proposed definition or a clear-cut example of something that fits the definition, but is not an example of the *definiendum*. For instance, if I had defined human beings as "two-legged animals" you might have argued that this is far too broad because birds are two-legged animals, yet they are not humans. Or you might have argued that the definition I have given (rational animal) is too narrow because people in comas, people who are mentally disturbed, or very small infants who are not yet "rational" are still normally regarded as human.

> A *definiendum* is that which is being defined.
> A **counterexample** shares the alleged characteristics of the *definiendum* but is not an example of it or it is an example of the *definiendum* but does not have the characteristics stated in the definition.

In considering the last rule (#6) about essential characteristics we must note that there are different kinds of definition. One kind, called cluster definition, states that something will be an example of the *definiendum* if it has a number of a given set of characteristics. So, for instance, if I listed twenty-five characteristics of human beings (rational and animal being only two of the twenty-five) and said anything that had significant number of them I was willing to call "human" I would be offering a cluster definition. If this is the case, rule number 6 would not apply because I would not be claiming that any one of the twenty-five was essential. However, there is another kind of definition called analytic or essential, and in this case rule number 6 does apply.

Someone offering an analytic definition is attempting to express the essence of the *definiendum*. According to Aristotle, this sort of definition expresses the genus or class to which the *definiendum* belongs and the *differentiae* or characteristics that distinguish it from other members of its genus so, for example, "animal" is the genus or class and "rational" is the *differentia* or that trait distinguishing humans from other members of the genus "animal."

To express the essence of something is to state its necessary and sufficient characteristics. To claim that rationality and animality are the necessary characteristics of being human is to claim that anyone without these characteristics is not a human being. To claim that they are sufficient is to assert that anything that has these characteristics is human.

Please note that something can be sufficient without being necessary and vice versa. A rock hitting a window is sufficient to break it, but not necessary because a baseball might do as well. Milk is necessary to make yogurt, but not sufficient. However, essential characteristics must be both necessary and sufficient.

This rule is closely related to rules 4 and 5 and can be applied in a similar way by thinking about possible counterexamples. However, it is a bit different in that rules 4 and 5 have to do with the range of normal usage; this rule has to do with necessary and sufficient traits.

Let's consider a computer. It is not an animal and hence cannot be human according to Aristotle's definition, if being an animal is a necessary trait. It is clear that being an animal by itself is not a sufficient trait because there are lots of animals that are not human. However, computers can perform rational functions. They can calculate and solve problems that are too complex for the human mind. If they are rational in some sense, does that make them human? Only if being rational by itself is a sufficient condition for being human. If something must be both rational and animal to be a human being, then a computer, while qualifying on one count, fails to qualify on the other.

Often it is extremely difficult to express the essence of something (that is, to find a set of characteristics that are both sufficient and necessary) and, in some cases, there may be no set of traits that are both sufficient and necessary. Also, many philosophers question the idea of essence and deny that things have essential natures that can be expressed in definitions. Meaning is determined by use and context, they argue, not by fixed, unchanging essences.

A **cluster** definition states that something will be an example of the *definiendum* *if* it has most or all of a given set of characteristics.

An **analytic** or **essential** definition states the necessary and sufficient characteristics of *definiendum*.

A **necessary** trait or characteristic is a property or quality that must be present for something to be an example of the *definiendum*.

A **sufficient** trait is a quality that, should it occur, an example of the *definiendum* will occur.

A **genus** is a class containing related members or species.

A *differentia* is a trait that distinguishes members of a genus.

Step 2: Check to see if the statements are clear and precise

Just as words can be ambiguous and vague, so too can sentences. Check each of the premises and the conclusion to see whether the meaning is clear and precise. For example, if I asserted that this book contains 8,000 words, would you know whether it contains 8,000 different words or 8,000 words total? The statement "This book contains 8,000 words" is ambiguous. It may mean different things, and it is not clear exactly what is meant.

Step 3: Check to see if the premises are true

Since the conclusion of an argument depends on the premises, if one or more of the premises is false, the argument as a whole is thereby weakened. Of course, in many cases, we are not in a position to know whether the premises are true. In such cases we might ask ourselves whether the premises are plausible (could they be true?) or suspend judgment, provided we are in a position to do so. I add this qualification just in case you decide to remain in a building after someone has shouted, "Fire!" because you cannot smell any smoke. I would suggest you leave, just to be on the safe side, even if you are not certain there is strong evidence to support the conclusion that the building is on fire. Of course, if you are visiting a hospital for the mentally disabled and a patient tells you to leave because extraterrestrials have just invaded the grounds, you might consider staying.

Step 4: Check to see whether the assumptions upon which the argument rests are plausible and warranted

All arguments depend on theories and assumptions, which are sometimes unstated. If these theories and assumptions are implausible or unwarranted, the argument is thereby weakened. If I try to persuade you to buy a rug made out of fireproof material to place in front of your fireplace, you might be inclined to do so knowing that sparks from fireplaces can cause fires. However, if I tried to persuade you to wear red underwear to ward off the "evil eye," you might be inclined to dismiss my argument because the assumptions on which it was based seem to you implausible.

Step 5: Check to see whether the premises are relevant to the conclusion

We said above that one way of thinking about the connection between premises and conclusions is to think of premises as supporting conclusions. We might also express this relationship in terms of conclusions following from premises. Hence, we need to ask whether the conclusion follows from the information given in the premises. For example, does it follow from the fact that wars and famine reduce overpopulation that we ought to welcome them as blessings in disguise? Or does being a good president follow from the fact that someone is male? Does it follow that God exists because the Bible, Jesus, Muhammad, and the Qur'an have said so?

Step 6: Check to see if the argument is valid
An argument is valid if its form is valid. Validity refers to the form of an argument, not its content. If its form is such that the conclusion must be true if the premises are true, then it is valid. For example, all of the five types of deductive arguments (MP, MT, US, DS and D) described in section A are valid forms. Notice this rule of validity does not claim that premises have to be true. It just asserts that if they are true; then the conclusion must also be true. The premises of an argument may be false and the argument still valid. For example, the argument "If cows are purple, Gumby exists. Cows are purple. Therefore Gumby exists" is valid (MP), but all its premises are false.

A good way to check for validity is to see if the argument [fits] a standard valid form such as those we discussed in the last section. There are all kinds of valid forms and other ways of checking. You should consult any standard textbook on logic for additional information on how to check for validity.

There are also some argument forms that are known to be invalid. For example:
Fallacy of affirming the consequent

$$p \supset q$$
$$q$$
$$\therefore p$$

Fallacy of denying the antecedent

$$p \supset q$$
$$\sim p$$
$$\therefore \sim q$$

If the argument fits one of these forms, it is invalid Again, check a logic text for more information on invalid forms and on why they are invalid.

Since validity has to do with form, not content, also check to see if the premises are true after checking for validity. If the argument is valid and the premises are true, the argument is called sound. If the premises are not true, the argument is unsound even if its form is valid.

Validity and soundness apply to deductive arguments only. Inductive arguments are either strong or weak, but never valid or invalid. Further, we should not say that arguments are true or false because only statements are true or false. Rather, arguments, if deductive, are called valid or invalid, sound or unsound, and we designate inductive arguments as strong or weak.

An argument is **valid** if it is impossible for all of its premises to be true and, at the same time, its conclusion false.

An argument is **sound** if it is valid and all of its premises are true.

Step 7: Check to see whether the conclusion of an argument leads to an absurdity
There is a type of argument known as *reductio ad absurdum* (reduction to absurdity). It takes the form of *modus tollens.* Let p be the conclusion of some argument.

If p implies q, and if q is false or absurd, then p must also be absurd. This technique of evaluation will not tell you what is wrong with an argument, but it will tell you if something is fishy. For example, suppose I argue that thoughts are just electrical impulses in the brain because people without electrical activity in their brains are unconscious. You might try to show my reasoning wrong by arguing, "If thoughts are electrical impulses in the brain, then I should be able to read your thoughts by looking at the electrical activity of your brain. But it is absurd to claim I can read your mind by seeing the electrical impulses of your brain. Therefore, thoughts are not identical with electrical impulses."

Note that your *reductio* does not tell us what is wrong with my argument, it only tells us that we should be suspicious of it. What is wrong with it would be revealed by the application of step 5. The conclusion that thoughts and electrical brain activity are identical does not follow from the premise that the absence of such activity is correlated with the absence of thought. Perhaps this premise shows that thought and electrical activity in the brain are related in some way, perhaps even that thought is somehow dependent on electrical activity in the brain, but it does not show that thought and such activity are one and the same thing.

> A *reductio ad absurdum* argument shows some conclusion false by showing that it logically implies something that is false.

Step 8: Check to see if the argument is an example of one of the common fallacies
A fallacy is a bad argument and, by the application of the above steps, we have been checking for fallacies all along. There are formal fallacies (having to do with the structure of an argument) such as the two I discussed under step 6, and there are informal fallacies that involve the content of an argument or its wording. Any standard logic text includes a list of the most common fallacies and an explanation as to why they constitute faulty reasoning. I provide a very brief sample of some common informal fallacies here.

1. **Hasty generalization**. This fallacy occurs when someone uses an example that is not typical to make a general point covering all cases. Example: No one should drink alcohol in any amount, because my friend drank alcohol, became an alcoholic, and died.
2. **Begging the question**. This fallacy occurs when someone assumes what he or she is trying to prove. Example: God exists because the Bible says so and God wrote the Bible.
3. **Black and white**. This bit of faulty reasoning occurs when someone falsely limits alternatives. Example: "Either we attack that country or we appease it and history shows appeasement is futile. Therefore, let it be war!"
4. **Strawperson**. This names the situation (all too common) of misconstruing the argument of one's opponent and refuting the misconstrual rather than the actual argument. Example: Pete argues that he is pro-choice because he believes women, like men, have the right to decide matters relating to their own bodies. Jack responds by arguing that Pete is pro-choice because he is in favor of murder. Since murder is wrong, Pete's pro-choice position is wrong. In fact, Pete's reason for being pro-choice is quite different from Jack's charge.

5. **False analogy**. This is a common type of fallacy in which the alleged similarities either do not hold or are not relevant to the conclusion. Socrates, in a dialogue with his friend Crito, argues that he, Socrates, must obey the laws of the state because the state is like his parents. Because the state, like his parents, has nurtured him, he owes it respect and obedience. We might criticize this argument on the grounds that the analogy between the state and parents does not hold because states are not persons and do not nurture in the same sense parents do.

6. *Ad hominem* (argument against the person). This fallacy involves someone trying to undermine someone else's claim by calling attention to irrelevant personal characteristics. Of course, because personal characteristics sometimes do influence our views, it is often difficult to decide to what extent personal characteristics are irrelevant.

   So, for example, should the alleged dishonesty of some politicians or their religious convictions make their views on welfare or foreign policy wrong? Or should the fact that someone is a male (or female) make his (or her) views about justice wrong (or right)? Generally, one should consider the evidence people provide in support of their views on its own merits and not bring in personal factors unless it can be shown that such factors are distorting their views.

7. **Appeal to authority**. Appealing to expert authorities in your argument because of their expertise is quite appropriate, but appealing to authorities because of their positions of power and influence is quite another. Religious arguments often involve appeals to authority (the authority of the Bible, a prophet, a tradition, a creed), but such authorities only impress those who already believe them to be authorities. The issue is not who said "x" about something, but whether there are any good reasons for supposing that what is said is true. This fallacy is much like the *ad hominem* fallacy, but rather than attacking a claim because of who made it as in *ad hominem*, this fallacy tries to support a claim on the basis of who made it.

8. **Argument from ignorance**. It is usually not appropriate to argue for the truth of something based on the lack of evidence to the contrary. So, if I argue that there is life after death because no one has proved there is not, I would be arguing from the lack of proof or from ignorance about the matter, to a positive conclusion. At stake in this sort of argument is the issue of burden of proof. Thus, in a court of law where the burden of proof is on the prosecution to prove their case, their failure to do so is grounds for a not guilty verdict. However, if I believe in life after death and you don't, and I try to persuade you to change your views by pointing out you have no proof to the contrary, then I have shifted the burden of proof that rightly falls on my shoulders to your shoulders, and this is unfair.

A **fallacy** is a bad argument that appears to be a good one. There are formal fallacies having to do with the structure of an argument and informal fallacies having to do with the content or wording of an argument

Hasty generalization generalizing from unrepresentative or insufficient cases.

Begging the question assuming as true what needs to be proved.

Black and White assuming that alternatives are exhaustive when they are not.

Strawperson distorting someone's position and arguing against the distortion.

> **False analogy**   assuming similarities between two things hold when they do not or are relevant when they are not.
>
> *Ad hominem*   an attempt to discredit a position by discrediting the person holding it.
>
> **Appeal to authority**   assuming a claim is true from the fact that some alleged authority supports it.
>
> **Argument from ignorance**   assuming that the absence of evidence for or against something makes it true.

There is more to evaluating arguments than what I have covered here, but this is enough to get you started. A word of caution: Some people get so excited about their newfound critical tools that they go around picking arguments with people in order to refute them. Or they think that philosophy involves putting other people down and showing how stupid their reasoning is. The purpose of evaluating arguments is to improve our reasoning. Evaluation ought to be a constructive process. If you find an argument that is bad, find out why, see if you can remove the defect, and construct a better one. Our reasoning can always stand improvement.

Exercise II. In order to see if you have understood how to evaluate arguments, answer the following questions and check your answers by looking up your textbook on CengageBrain.com.

1. T or F. One would not be able to ask the question, "Are we having fun yet?" if the word "fun" were not vague.
2. T or F. In the definition "free will is voluntary choice," the genus is "choice."
3. T or F. In the definition "love is the feeling of intimacy and affection," the *differentiae* are intimacy and affection.
4. T or F. If being loved by God is a necessary condition of something being good, then nothing is good unless God loves it.
5. T or F. If being loved by God is a sufficient condition of goodness, then something that is not loved by God might still be good.
6. Consider: If Socrates should escape, then it is right to escape. It is not right to escape, therefore Socrates should not escape. This argument is _____.
   a. invalid
   b. a hasty generalization
   c. a fallacy of affirming the consequent
   d. valid
   e. both a and c.
7. John Calvin argues, "Since everything that God wills is fair and just for the very reason that He wills it, the terrible fate of the damned does not violate the principle of justice." This argument is an example of
   a. begging the question
   b. strawperson
   c. hasty generalization
   d. black and white
   e. the fallacy of denying the antecedent
8. Consider: Either Jesus is the Son of God or he is a liar. He is not a liar. Therefore, he must be the Son of God. This is an example of a _____.

   a. strawperson
   b. black and white
   c. hasty generalization
   d. argument from ignorance
   e. begging the question
 9. T or F. The following argument is a fallacy of appealing to authority: "Philosophy is just a matter of one's personal opinion. After all, there are no correct answers and no way to determine correct answers to philosophical questions. Anything goes. My opinion is as good as your opinion."
10. Consider this argument: There is no evidence that progress made in philosophical matters, therefore, no progress is made and philosophy is a waste of time. This argument is _____:
   a. based on a false analogy
   b. an argument from ignorance
   c. an appeal to authority
   d. a strawperson
   e. a formal fallacy
11. Use the rules of a good definition and discuss whether Hobbes's definition, "Jealousy is love with fear that the love is not returned," is a good one. Does Hobbes's definition presuppose that jealousy and envy are different?
12. Analyze and evaluate the following argument, then compare your analysis and criticism with another student's critical analysis and discuss how they differ. Remember, identify the conclusion first.

   Argument: If there is life after death, then life is meaningful. If life is meaningful, then there is a reason for my life. If there is life after death, then there is reason for my life.

C. Constructing Arguments

It is valuable to learn how to analyze and evaluate other people's arguments. People are always trying to persuade us of something. It helps to be able to follow their reasoning and evaluate it. However, ultimately we want to become independent thinkers. We want to reason for ourselves and construct our own arguments. Logic can help us do that too.

   Constructing your own arguments requires more creativity than analyzing and criticizing what someone else has said. I can give you some hints that will help you build your own arguments, but ultimately you are the one who has to do the thinking. And thinking can be hard work. It takes time, concentration, and leisure to think an issue or a problem through to some kind of solution.

1. Start with your conclusion

This seems like odd advice. A conclusion should come at the end of the thought process, not at the beginning. In a sense it does and my advice supposes that you have already thought about an issue and reached some kind of tentative conclusion about what you think. For example, most of you have already thought about abortion or the death penalty or God's existence and formulated some beliefs about those issues. Start there, with what you already believe about some problem, and work backwards. Suppose, for instance, you believe women should be treated as equal to men. State that as your conclusion and then look for your premises. (I need to thank Richard Purtill, *A Logical Introduction to Philosophy,* Prentice-Hall, 1989, for this example).

2. Examine your reasons

Why do you believe your conclusion? What has convinced you? List your reasons. These are your premises. State them as clearly and precisely as you can. For example, you think women ought to be treated as equal to men because there are no differences between men and women that justify unequal treatment. Further, it is unfair to treat people unequally unless such treatment is justified.

3. Use the appropriate argument type

Cast your argument in premise and conclusion form using one of the standard types as a guideline. For example, if your conclusion is a generalization from specific cases, or if your reasons involve an analogy, and if your conclusion adds new information not contained in the premises, then you should state it as an inductive type of argument. If it is possible to state your argument in a valid deductive form, then you may prefer that formulation because it presents a more compelling argument. (Remember, in a valid deductive argument, the conclusion must be true if the premises are true but in an inductive argument, the premises may all be true and the conclusion might still be false.) Be sure to select one of the known valid forms as your blueprint.

It is sometimes helpful to substitute letters for the statements of your argument. This will help you see which statements are equivalent, and it will aid you in arranging the statements into a valid format. For instance, let's see if we can get the argument about equality into a deductively valid form. Let q = "Women should be treated as equal to men." Let p = "There are no differences between women and men that justify unequal treatment." We can now use *modus ponens* to create the following valid argument:

1. If there are no differences between women and men that justify unequal treatment, then women should be treated as equal to men. (p ⊃ q)
2. There are no differences between women and men that justify unequal treatment, (p)
3. Therefore, women should be treated as equal to men. (q)

Note that I have left out one of the reasons given above, namely, that it is unfair to treat people unequally unless such treatment is justified. We could recast the argument in a more complex form to include this principle. Or as we develop our argument we might mention this as an assumption on which the argument is based. Presenting your argument in premise and conclusion form always involves some simplification. It is a shorthand way of stating things. However, stating it in this form has the advantage of clarity. You can always flesh things out and bring in the complications in the discussion of the argument.

Once you have your argument stated, evaluate it. Use the steps we discussed in the last section to examine your own argument. Play devil's advocate and try to expose its weaknesses. Then repair those weaknesses as you develop your argument.

4. Define your terms

You do not have to define every word you use, but you do need to define key words that might be unclear. In our example, I think words like "men" and "women" and "differences" are generally clear, but certain confusions ought to be mentioned so that people know more precisely what you are talking about. For example, people sometimes confuse sex and gender. Sex refers to a biological state often designated by the terms "male" and "female." Gender refers to certain psychological and behavioral traits usually designated by the terms "masculine" and "feminine" (although it can also be used to designate the biological state [sex], hence the confusions). Someone can be a female and have traits traditionally associated with masculinity in our culture and vice versa. People also sometimes confuse psychological differences with physical differences. This is analogous to the confusion over sex and gender. You will need to be precise about the sorts of differences you are talking about.

The term "equal treatment" is a key part of this argument and might well be vague or ambiguous. Your definition should try to remove any ambiguity or vagueness.

As we noted in the last section, there are different ways of defining words. Analytic definitions are particularly difficult to provide because of the need to state both the necessary and sufficient characteristics of the *definiendum*. It is easier to give a cluster type of definition in which you state what you take to be the most important (but not necessarily the essential) characteristics of the *definiendum*.

A helpful way to begin the task of definition is to start thinking about good examples of what the term means. Such examples can serve as models. General terms or concepts like "equal treatment" have two different types of meaning: denotative meaning and connotative meaning. A term's denotation, also called extension, is comprised of all objects to which the term refers, and its connotation, also called intension, is constituted by all the traits held in common by these objects. Your goal is to discover the connotative meaning of "equal treatment," but to get there it is helpful to start with the denotative meaning. List some clear-cut examples of actions you and most people would consider to be examples of equal treatment. For example, "equal pay for equal work," "equal employment opportunity for appropriately qualified people," and "equal access to higher education for qualified people." Now ask yourself, "What do all or most of the things on my list have in common?" Your answer will reveal the intensional meaning and provide you with a list of characteristics that might be useful for definitional purposes.

Suppose you think the main characteristics of the examples of equal treatment you have listed are impartial judgment, fair dealings, and balanced recompense (payback). If you do, then these would be your defining characteristics. Anything exemplifying one or more of these traits would be an example of equal treatment.

Be sure to use the criteria of a good definition to check your own definitions. For instance, are the words "impartial," "fair," and "balanced" any less vague than the word "equal"? If you find problems, try to improve the definition. It is best to try to think of concrete counterexamples and borderline cases (instances on the edge of the term's normal range of usage) and revise your definition with those in mind.

Denotative (extensive) meaning is constituted by all the objects referred to by a general term.

Connotative (intensive) meaning is constituted by all the properties held in common by the denoted objects.

Borderline cases are instances on the edge or boundary of the general range of the terms usage.

5. Support your premises and justify your assumptions

Are your premises true? Sometimes your premises and assumptions will be widely accepted principles or facts that do not require support or further justification. Other times they will be controversial. Support controversial premises and assumptions with evidence and additional argumentation.

For example, the first premise (if there are no differences between women and men that justify unequal treatment, then women should be treated as equal to men) of the argument about equality seems uncontroversial. Most people would agree that if unequal treatment is not justified, it ought not to be practiced. However, you may wish to make explicit the assumption on which this premise is based. The assumption is that it is unfair to treat people unequally unless such treatment is justified. In other words, you are assuming, all things being equal, that equal treatment is better than unequal treatment. This is a value judgment that, I believe, most people would accept. However, you need to make it explicit and, if someone should happen to challenge it, you would need to be prepared to support it by further argumentation.

Your second premise (there are no differences between women and men that justify unequal treatment) is controversial and therefore does require support. Most arguments that support inequality maintain that there are significant differences between men and women that do justify unequal treatment. How might you support the second premise? Well, you might make a list of all the differences that those who favor unequal treatment cite, such as: women are more emotional than men, men are stronger than women, men are better at math and science than women, and so on. The first thing you could do with such a list is sort the real differences from the apparent ones. For example, it is simply not true that women are more emotional than men. However, it is true that men are, on average, physically stronger than women, at least with respect to upper body strength. Once you have your list of real differences, the key question you need to ask is, "Do these real differences justify unequal treatment?" To be more concrete, "Is it right to pay women less than men if they have, on average, less upper body strength?" In seeking an answer to this question you will need to reintroduce the principle of fairness you have assumed.

Sometimes a good strategy is to assume the opposite of what you want to support and see where that leads (recall the *reductio* argument). Let's assume women should, in general, be paid less than men because they do, on average, have less upper body strength. Given the fairness principle, it follows that men who are physically weaker than other men and men who are weaker than women ought, in general, to be paid less. But this is absurd. Does a general pay scale, without respect to type of work, based on physical strength make any sense? This line of reasoning has uncovered a good general principle we can use to examine other differences. This general principle is: if a given difference is not used as a basis for unequal treatment of men, it is reasonable to conclude it should not be used as a basis for unequal treatment of women. You can now support the second premise by showing that all the alleged real differences between men and women also exist among men, and if they are not used to justify unequal treatment among men, they should not be used to justify unequal treatment among women.

When supporting your premises and developing your argument it is always best to state the strongest objections to your position. If you can refute the best objections, you thereby strengthen your argument. If you cannot refute them, you had better reconsider your reasoning.

> **Real** difference is a true difference or one that is the case.
> **Apparent** difference is a false difference or one that is not the case.

6. Use clear examples and illustrations

Confusion often arises on the abstract level. Bring your reasoning back down to earth with concrete illustrations. Often, just trying to think up good illustrations reveals a mistake in reasoning or opens up a new line of argument. Notice how, in developing the equality argument, we moved back and forth between concrete examples and more general principles.

7. Keep your audience in mind

We not only use logical reasoning to clarify our own thinking, to help us make decisions, and to arrive at solutions to problems, we also use it to persuade other people, defend ourselves, and refute other people's arguments. If you wish to convince someone else, persuasive and rhetorical considerations are important. Don't overstate your case. Don't claim more than you can demonstrate. Qualify your conclusions appropriately. Be courteous. Emphasize areas of agreement. Appeal to generally accepted principles and definitions. Be clear and use concrete examples. Make it clear that you are interested in arriving at the most reasonable conclusion and that you are not interested in just scoring points.

Keep in mind that there are many different uses of argument. Often we use arguments to persuade others, and I have assumed such a context in the example I have given. But we also use arguments to reconcile seemingly opposed ideas. For example, philosophers have been much concerned with reconciling the principle of causation with the view that humans are free. And we use arguments to dissolve problems. Philosophers in this century, for example, have spent much time and effort trying to show that some philosophical problems, such as the relationship between the mind and the body, are pseudo-problems. When evaluating and constructing arguments it is important to keep in mind their purpose. Convincing others is only one of the many uses of argument.

Exercise III. Answer the following questions. Check your answers to see what you have learned about constructing arguments by looking up your textbook on CengageBrain.com. If you get something wrong, see if you can determine your mistake.

1. If you are using the argument form called *modus ponens* and you knew the first premise is, "If the existence of God is a matter of faith, then it cannot be proved," what would be the second premise?
2. If you are using the argument form called *modus tollens* and you knew the conclusion is, "God does not exist" and the second premise is, "Not everything that happens is good," what would the first premise be?
3. Suppose you were using the hypothetical syllogism to construct an argument that concludes, "If I think, then I exist." What might your first and second premises be like?
4. Suppose you were using the disjunctive syllogism to show that "Mencius believes human nature is good." What might your first and second premises be like?
5. Give a definition of suffering.
6. Give a definition of happiness.

7. Give a definition of good.
8. Provide a concrete illustration of the principle, "We should not believe beyond the evidence."
9. Create an inductive argument using an analogy that concludes that God exists.
10. Create an argument in favor of the position that drugs ought to be legalized. Compare your argument with someone else's argument. Discuss which one is better and why.

2.2 HOW TO WRITE PHILOSOPHY

There are many different forms of philosophical writing, including drama, poetry, dialogue, fiction, and argumentative essay. Many different things are done in the course of philosophical writing, including interpretation, analysis, criticism, argumentation, definition, comparison, explanation, and summary. Here I will focus primarily on writing argumentative essays in which one develops and defends a thesis because this is the sort of writing many philosophy instructors expect their students to do. It is also the common form of writing one finds in philosophical journals. When writing an argumentative essay, one presents a thesis about some topic at the outset and then argues for it.

Even though a thesis is presented at the start of argumentative essay, it is a conclusion of a line of reasoning. (For more on conclusions and the nature of argumentation in general, see Section 2.1. The English word thesis comes from a Greek word that means stand or position. A thesis is a position or stand taken with respect to a particular topic or issue. It is usually a one sentence statement that answers some question about a topic or solves some problem.

A common mistake is to confuse a thesis with a topic. Suppose you are writing a paper on capital punishment. This is your topic, but your thesis is some position or stand that you take with respect to capital punishment. Below are several possible theses for which you might develop arguments.

Capital punishment is morally justified in certain instances.

Capital punishment is never morally justified.

Capital punishment can never be imposed fairly.

Capital punishment deters murder.

Capital punishment does not prevent others from murdering.

In what follows, I offer some guidelines designed to help you write good philosophical essays that develop and defend a thesis or position with respect to some topic. It is appropriate to begin with the process of thesis development because this is central to much philosophical writing.

Guidelines for Good Philosophical Writing

1. Pre-write
Before you write, get ready to write. Determine if you are genuinely interested in your subject. If it bores you, chances are what you write about will bore others. You should feel comfortable enough with your subject to write in detail about it. Familiarity will come as you research your topic and think about it. Relate it to your personal

experiences and think of questions relating to your subject. It helps to make a list of relevant questions and write down your preliminary answers. These answers will form the basis of your thesis.

Example: Suppose your topic is John Stewart Mill's version of utilitarianism.

Possible questions are:

1. What does Mill mean by utilitarianism?
2. Is utilitarianism an adequate moral theory?
3. How does Mill's utilitarian theory compare to Kant's moral theory?

Some possible answers that can form the basis of your thesis are:

1. By utilitarianism Mill means the principle of greatest happiness for the greatest number.
2. Mill's version of utilitarianism is not an adequate moral theory.
3. Mill's utilitarian theory is based on the assumption that the consequences of an action make it right, and Kant's moral theory is based on the assumption that motives make an action right.

A helpful format to use at this stage is:

My topic is _____
I intend to argue that _____ (thesis statement) _____.

Using number 2 of the above possible answers, your notes would read:

My topic is John Stewart Mill's version of utilitarianism.
I intend to argue that Mill's version of utilitarianism is not an adequate moral theory.

Ask yourself whether you have an interesting thesis that you can develop. The first thesis (listed above) on the meaning of Mill's utilitarianism is not particularly interesting because Mill's definition of utilitarian is straightforward and requires little thought to understand. The second thesis is more interesting because it involves an evaluation of Mill's ideas and hence requires some thought and argumentative development.

Elaborate on your thesis by making brief notes about important sub-themes and key terms you need to define. It is helpful, right after your note on the thesis, to add sentences beginning with because. As you jot down your thoughts about why you intend to argue your thesis, the reasons for your thesis will begin to develop and hence your argument will begin taking shape.

Example: I intend to argue that Mill's version of utilitarianism is not an adequate moral theory because _____.

Note the key words on which your thesis and reasons depend. These are the words you will need to define. In developing the above thesis about the adequacy of Mill's theory, for example, you would need to define utilitarianism and say something about what makes a moral theory adequate.

Determine your attitude toward your topic. This will be reflected in the tone you take in your writing, so give some thought to the language that you will use. Also, determine who your audience is and what its attitude toward your topic may be. If, for example, your audience consists of people who oppose your thesis, you will have to pay close attention to techniques of persuasion.

The following questions (adapted from Denise Lynch's article, "Easing the Process") will help you determine when you are ready to write. If you can answer yes to most of these questions, you are ready to start the creative process of writing your philosophical essay.

PRE-WRITING EVALUATION QUESTIONS

Am I interested in my subject?
Am I familiar enough with my subject to discuss it in detail?
Can I relate my subject to personal experiences?
Can I think of questions relating to my topic?
Do I have an interesting thesis?
Can I develop my thesis in some detail?
What is my attitude toward by topic?
Who is my audience?
What is my audience's attitude?
What sort of language is most appropriate?

---

2. Organize

Your presentation should be clearly and logically ordered. Outlining before you write is essential. Always keep your reader in mind and present ideas in an order that makes sense to your reader.

Most philosophy papers are organized into three parts. First, there is an introduction in which you catch the readers' interest, state your thesis, and tell your readers what you are going to do. Second, there is the body of your paper in which you develop your thesis by defining keywords and presenting arguments and evidence in support of your thesis. Third, there is a conclusion in which you briefly summarize what you have said and clearly state the conclusion (usually a restatement of your thesis) you wish your readers to accept.

3. Write simply

Do not use unnecessary words and do not use complex, technical words when ordinary words will do as well. Sometimes, of course, technical words are necessary because they are more precise. Part of learning any discipline, philosophy included, is learning a technical vocabulary. In the above examples, the word "utilitarianism" is a technical word I used because it is part of the philosophical vocabulary and there is no single ordinary word that will work as well. Whenever technical words are used, they should be explained as clearly possible.

4. Be Clear

This guideline is closely related to the second one above, but refers specifically to writing that is free from ambiguity and vagueness. I discussed ambiguity and vagueness previously and I refer you to that discussion for more information. Here I note that a word or sentence is ambiguous if its meaning is uncertain and it is vague if its range of application is uncertain.

For example, the sentence "Philosophy is an art" is ambiguous because the word "art" can mean so many different things. Rewriting the sentence as "Philosophy is the art of thinking" helps remove some of the ambiguity, but it is still vague because its range of application is unclear. Is all thinking philosophical?

How would you rewrite the following sentence in order to make it clearer?

Philosophy is the art of thinking.

5. Be human

Frequently students will be told to write impersonally because it sounds more objective. The word "one" is preferable, according to this advice, to the words "I," or "we." Likewise students are often admonished to avoid the word "you." One can, of course, overuse the words "I" and "we" and there are times when "you" is inappropriate in scholarly writing. However, I think it is important for you to let your humanity show through from time to time. An impersonal, technical, and abstract style is not always appropriate or effective.

Avoid, as much as possible, the use of the passive voice. Instead of "It has been argued that utilitarianism is an inadequate moral theory" write, "I have argued that ...

How would you rewrite the following example in order to make it more personal and less formal?

Example: One might say, if one wished, that philosophy is abstract thinking. While one can define it in this manner, one must define more precisely what abstract thinking means.

6. Use examples

It is particularly important, when dealing with abstract ideas, to provide concrete examples. Concrete examples not only help you test your own understanding, but aid your reader in understanding what you are talking about. For example, if you are writing about what philosophers call "synthetic statements," provide one or more examples of synthetic statements.

Example: A synthetic statement is any statement about matters of fact whose negation may be true. For example, "The lights are on in this room," is a synthetic statement whose negation ("The lights are not one in this room") may be true, depending on the facts of the case (that is, whether the lights are on or off).

7. Argue

Present arguments in support of your thesis. In the last section I discussed how to analyze, evaluate, and construct arguments. Review that discussion, especially the third part relating to the construction of arguments. At the heart of much philosophical writing is the presentation of arguments in support of some thesis. These arguments need to be persuasive and, the more controversial your thesis is, the more convincing you need to make your arguments. Your argument may be presented in a formal style, with premises and conclusions numbered and arranged logically, or it may be presented in an informal style without explicit identification of premises and conclusions. In either case, be sure to support your thesis with good arguments.

Example I Formal Argument:

Thesis: If determinism is true, then people are not responsible for what they do. Argument:

1. If determinism is true, then people cannot act in ways other than they do.

2. If people cannot act in ways other than they do, then people are not responsible for what they do.

3. Therefore, if determinism is true, then people are not responsible for what they do.

Example II Informal Argument:

I think people have never fully grasped the power of love. We have many examples of people doing things because they are forced to do them. We also have many examples of people doing things because of monetary compensation. The prevalence of both war and greed reinforce the impression that force and/or wealth make the world go round. However, we also have many examples of people acting out of love. We should not ignore these cases. Often the power of love will override both force and greed and motivate people to do heroic deeds that seem to defy common sense. For example, _____.

8. Consider objections and alternatives

Your arguments become more persuasive and thereby stronger if you state the most plausible objections to them and show that these objections either do not weaken your argument or can be incorporated into your argument.

Example: Some people might argue that no one is ever motivated by pure love because there is an element of selfishness in all that humans do. This may well be true, but it is irrelevant to my claim that people often underestimate the power of love. What we normally call love may well be a mixture of both altruistic and selfish elements, however, that does not make it any less powerful in situations where its motivating power overrides both physical force and greed.

9. Define key terms

Careful definition is important because it increases the reader's comprehension. In addition, definitions are important because they reduce the likelihood of getting into apparent disagreements in which arguments miss the mark because people are talking about different things in the mistaken belief they are talking about the same things. How many of you have gotten into arguments with people about some topic and argued long and hard only to discover that there was no real disagreement all along? Careful definition can help you avoid such situations.

I have discussed different kinds of definition and how one goes about defining key terms in section 2.1. You will want to review that material. Here I build on what I said by making a few remarks on different kinds of definition.

Much philosophical writing involves developing stipulative definitions that state the meaning of a new term introduced for special purposes, and precising definitions that reduce the vagueness and ambiguity of a term. One will also find some philosophers developing analytical definitions that attempt to adequately characterize the objects to which the word applies in terms of their essential features. Other philosophers, who may reject the idea of "essential features," offer cluster definitions that state some of the important resemblances between related objects.

These kinds of definition (stipulative, precising, analytical, cluster) should be distinguished from lexical definitions. Lexical definitions report a meaning or set of meanings a word has in some language. In other words, they specify the conventional meaning of a word. Lexical definitions are found in a good dictionary and every serious writer needs to consult one. The *Oxford English Dictionary* or OED is an invaluable source of information.

Lexical definitions, however, are often not adequate for philosophical writing. An adequate philosophical understanding of concepts cannot be gained by relying exclusively on what some dictionary says. The dictionary only reports the most common ways in which people use words in some language. Those common ways might be philosophically wrong or superficial. You may start with the lexical meaning of a philosophically interesting word like "justice" but you cannot stop there. For example, the first meaning I find in my *Webster's New Collegiate Dictionary* for *justice* is, "The maintenance or administration of that which is just, also, merited reward or punishment." The first part of the definition tells us very little about justice. It is a circular definition and thus philosophically inadequate. The second part about reward or punishment conflates at least two kinds of justice. Philosophers frequently distinguish between distributive justice, which has to do with the fair distribution of benefits such as wealth, rights, and honors among members of a society, and retributive justice, which has to do with a corrective distribution of burdens (such as punishment) to people who undeservedly enjoy benefits. There are other types of justice as well and the philosophical writer will carefully need to distinguish the different types.

Even though lexical definitions need to be made more precise to be philosophically useful, one should not ignore them. It is a good idea not to stray too far from common usage. If you do, then you disconnect from your readers. For example, if I define justice as creating a good personal balance between heartbeats and brainwaves, my definition would be so far removed from the ordinary lexical definition that my readers would be unable to relate to my thoughts. I advise starting with lexical definitions, and then making them more philosophically precise by expanding or narrowing their meaning.

10. Use the history of philosophy

It is helpful to show how your ideas are similar to or different from past philosophers. This will not only help the reader who knows something about philosophy understand you better, but also it will locate your own thinking within a historical context.

There are a variety of reference works available that will aid in the initial stage of connecting your ideas with the ideas of other philosophers. The *Cambridge Dictionary of Philosophy*, the *Routledge Encyclopedia of Philosophy*, and *The Encyclopedia of Philosophy* (MacMillan) are good places to begin. They contain hundreds of brief articles on philosophical concepts and philosophers. So, for example, if you were writing on the topic of justice, you could look up that word in the *Cambridge Dictionary of Philosophy* and find references to Aristotle, Kant, Marx and much more. Also, do not neglect Internet sources such as the Internet Encyclopedia of Philosophy and the Stanford Encyclopedia of Philosophy. Any sources you use must be used critically. Not every source is of equal value. Dictionaries, encyclopedias, and Internet resources can take you only so far, but they can get you going down the right path.

> Example: I have been arguing that our justified beliefs about the physical world ultimately rest on justified beliefs about our sensations. My position is supported by many logical positivists like A. J. Ayer who argue that sense-data have a privileged position in our claims to knowledge.

11. Revise, edit, and then revise some more

After you have completed a rough draft, go over it carefully looking for ways to improve it. Be tough on yourself. Very few of us write a first draft that can stand little or no improvement.

The fun part of writing is getting down on paper what you want to say. Revising and editing what you have written can be taxing. However, the rewards are worth the effort. You will be much happier with your creation after careful revision.

There are many things to keep track of as you reread what you have written. You need to check the content, style, and grammar to make sure you have written what you wanted to write in the way you wanted to write it. Rethink the organization. Can it be improved? Listen for the tone. Have you made good word choices? Check your examples. How can they be improved? Read each paragraph aloud. Is it coherent? Does it have a topic sentence? Does it develop one idea? Check to see if the thesis is clearly stated and the arguments are sufficiently developed. If you have written your essay on a word processor, run a spell and grammar check. Don't forget your audience. It often helps to have a friend read your draft and restate what he or she thinks you are saying in their own words. If what your friends have understood based on what you wrote is different from what you intended, you know you have to rewrite.

The following checklist, adapted from Denise Lynch's "Easing the Process," is useful when revising. If you answer any of the questions with a "no," you know where you need to revise in order to improve your philosophical writing.

REVISION CHECKLIST

Is the thesis of the essay clear?
Is the thesis adequately developed?
Are the examples helpful?
Does each paragraph build on the preceding one?
Does the introduction arouse interest?
Is my language appropriate?
What grammatical errors need to be corrected?
Is there a beginning, middle, and end?
Is there a clear summary and conclusion?
Have I accomplished what I set out to do?
Reread the writing assignment instructions if there are any and check to see if you have followed the instructions.

A Note about Philosophical Dialogues

In addition to the argumentative essay in which you formulate a thesis about some philosophical topic and argue for it, writing dialogues has been a time-honored way of writing philosophy. Some of the earliest philosophical writings that exist are dialogues. One of the most influential Western philosophers, Plato, developed the dialogue into a fine philosophical art.

Dialogues are good vehicles for presenting arguments, for incorporating objections, and for adding some drama to the process of thinking. Writing dialogues requires greater creativity than writing the standard philosophical essay because you must invent characters whose conversation sounds plausible and natural.

If you want to use the dialogue style, I would suggest that you get the approval of your instructor and then read some of the many fine philosophical dialogues available in order to develop a sense of how to proceed. Also go to or read plays and listen to the give and take of the characters in order to develop an ear for conversational style. Keep a notebook in which you record bits of interesting conversation you have heard. Tape record a conversation with a friend on some philosophical topic and note how it progresses.

Example: Suppose you want to write on the topic of God's existence and the problem of evil. One way to do it is to imagine a dialogue between an atheist (let's call her Veronica) who is convinced that the existence of evil disproves the existence of God, and a theist (let's call him Paul) who disagrees. Imagine what such people might say to one another. I offer a beginning below that you can finish in order to get a feel for how the dialogue style works.

Veronica: I just saw a report on AIDS in Africa. It was so awful, the suffering of thousands of people, even babies and children, that I began to cry. "How," I asked myself, "could God allow such a tragedy?"

Paul: There are no easy answers to that question Veronica, but I know God must have a purpose. Nothing happens in this world unless God allows it.

V: How do you know that? Surely the existence of such horrible evils as AIDS must show you that there is no merciful God in charge.

P: On the contrary, it shows me that God is concerned with the suffering of his children. I've seen those reports too, and I have great admiration for the doctors and missionaries that devote their lives to helping these people. God never promised us a rose garden, and the existence of goodness in the world counts just as much in favor of God's concern for the world as the existence of evil counts against it.

V: What? Are you saying that the existence of both goodness and evil have equal weight? If that is so, then _____.

EXERCISE

The only way to learn how to write philosophy is to write it. Guidelines can take you only so far. Like any skill—be it playing music or sports—you must do it. Write a practice argumentative essay on any one of the topics or questions listed below or select a topic of your own. If you pick a topic from my list, you will need to narrow it before you can write a manageable argumentative essay by asking appropriately focused questions. Exchange essays with a classmate and *constructively* critique each other's effort using the Revision Checklist.

Possible Topics:

1. Is knowledge possible?
2. Utopia.
3. The political views of John Locke and Thomas Hobbes.
4. Kant's theory of the categorical imperative.
5. Animal rights.
6. Plato's views on the good life.
7. Is a just society possible?

8. Are human actions free or determined?
9. Does God exist?
10. What is the nature of the self?
11. Can we survive death?

On the web, try www.apaonline.org for all kinds of interesting links. APA stands for the American Philosophical Association.

Take advantage of the materials available on **CengageBrain** and, for users who purchased access to it, on the **Premium Website,** to further enrich your learning experience.

CHAPTER THREE

How Should One Live?

The superior person is open-minded and not partisan.

CONFUCIUS

LEARNING OBJECTIVES

After studying this chapter students should be able to:
- explain how ambiguity differs from vagueness,
- state the difference between descriptive and normative,
- describe the Four Noble Truths and the Middle Way,
- define *ren, li, xiao,* and *yi,*
- explain why education is so important to living the good life for Confucius,
- describe the Socratic method and the divine command theory,
- define teleology and *eudaimonia,*
- describe how *dharma, karma, samsara,* and rebirth are interconnected in traditional Hindu thought,
- identify Siddhartha Gautama, Confucius, Plato, Socrates, Aristotle, *Bhagavad-Gita,* and Wolf, and
- answer all the questions relating to the selections.

3.1 INTRODUCTION

Have you ever wondered about how one should live? Should we live compassionately, pursuing a wisdom that liberates us from suffering? Should we live a virtuous and sincere life of balance, harmony, and family loyalty? Perhaps we should live a life of critical reflection, searching for truth and following an argument wherever it may lead. Should we live in pursuit of happiness? What exactly is happiness? How can we attain it? Perhaps we must unselfishly do what duty demands in devotion to God. Few of us would deny that we should live a meaningful life. A life without meaning and purpose is not desirable. However, what is a meaningful life, and how can it be pursued in a world that constantly threatens boredom if not meaninglessness?

The question of how one should live is fundamental to human existence. It is a question that has concerned ancient and modern peoples, Eastern and Western cultures. What do you understand by the question? If you had to write an essay on the topic, how would you begin? "One should live the good life," you might say. That seems a sensible way to start. The next question is, of course, what is the good life? Notice that the term "the good life" is both **ambiguous** (it can mean many different things and often it is not clear precisely to what it refers) and **vague** because the line between a good life and a bad life is not always clear. Is the good life one that is personally satisfying or one that possesses moral merit? Can it be both? Should it be both?

Let us assume that the good life is both, namely a personally satisfying life and a life of moral worth. Proceeding on this assumption you can continue your essay by exploring what is most important to you. What sorts of things do you value the most? Health? Wealth? Pleasure? However, just because you desire certain things, does that mean you *ought* to desire them? Desiring something is one thing, but claiming you ought to desire it is something else. The search for what is personally satisfying sooner or later runs into the issue of moral merit, and, if we assume the good life should be both personally satisfying and morally worthwhile, we must now explore the question in more depth.

What does *ought have* to do with this question about conducting one's life? "How *should* one live?" is not the same question as "How *ought* one to live?" You might say "I should go to the store," but that does not mean that you "ought" to in the sense that you are morally obligated to do so. Even so your sense of what you are morally obligated to do often grows out of your sense of what you should do.

Who is the "one" whom this question addresses? It is an impersonal one. "How *one* live?" is not the same question as "How should *I* live?" So does your answer hold good for you alone? What about others? Is there one way we all ought to live? Writing an essay about how you think you should live is one thing. Writing an essay about how you think everyone ought to live is another matter. For one thing, the latter essay is a lot more difficult to write.*

If you have ever wondered about how you or anyone else ought to live, you have been concerned with what philosophers call *ethics* or *moral philosophy.* Ethics comes from the Greek word *ethos,* which means "character." For the Greeks, ethics had to do with developing a virtuous character. They believed that if you develop such a character, you will not only know the right thing to do but also do it.

Today we use the word *ethics* in many different ways. Sometimes it refers to moral rules or a way of life based on a religiously inspired moral code. We speak of "Christian ethics" or "Buddhist ethics." However, sometimes it refers to the secular study of moral values and a search for the principles of right moral action. As a branch of philosophy, "ethics" is used in this latter sense to refer to reflection on or study of moral issues. It is concerned with such questions as: What is the morally right way to live? How can I know what is morally right? How can I decide morally difficult cases? What makes a society just?

---

*See Chapter 1, "Socrates' Question," in *Ethics and the Limits of Philosophy* by Bernard Williams (Cambridge, MA: Harvard University Press, 1985) for a discussion of the various ways the question "How should one live?" can be understood and for Williams's recommendation that we should not take it in the sense of a question about obligation. He argues that Western philosophy would do well to return to this question as the starting point of ethical reflection. Also see John Kekes, *The Morality of Pluralism* (Princeton, NJ: Princeton University Press, 1993) for an argument in support of moral pluralism (there are many good ways to live) and against moral monism (there is only one good way to live).

We can answer moral questions in different ways. One way is descriptive. We might *describe* the kinds of values people have and the sorts of principles they use in making moral judgments. Another way is **normative**. Normative reflection has to do with trying to discover *norms* or principles by which we *ought* to live. Many philosophers maintain that ethics is primarily a normative study. It is not only a description of what people find morally good and morally bad; it also seeks to discover norms that ought to guide our actions.

Although we can distinguish the kinds of questions moral philosophers ask, the answers often blend into one another. An answer to the question about how one should live will sooner or later have to address such issues as how we can know what is right, whether justice is possible, whether God exists, whether there is life after death, and many more. The readings in this chapter directly address the question of how one should live, in a broad sense, but this same question is addressed, in one way or another, by many of the other readings in *Voices of Wisdom*.

One useful way to approach the brief sampling of answers (which follow) to the question about how one should live is to see if you can find, explicitly or implicitly, answers to a set of what, how, and why questions. *What* is the good life? That is, what, according to the philosophers sampled here, is the goal of human life? Is the good life understood to be one that is primarily personally fulfilling or one of moral value? Is it understood to be both? *How* is the good life attained? That is, what are the means that the author recommends that would lead one (presumably) to the goal of living a good life? *Why* is the life as described a good one? That is, is the goal of human life the author envisions appropriate and right? Why is the means recommended appropriate? That is, what reasons (if any) does the author give for thinking that the means will in fact lead to the goal? The "why" question asks you to find out how the philosopher justifies his or her answer. At least two sorts of justification are called for: (1) a justification of the goal and (2) a justification of the means. You may wish to set up a grid like the one in Table 3.1 on which you can write brief answers to these questions based on your reading and then compare the answers that are given.

TABLE 3.1

	Buddha	Confucius	Socrates	Aristotle	Gita	Wolf
What						
How						
Why						

Analyzing the answers in this way not only allows you to discern differences and similarities among the answers but also provides an opportunity for you to evaluate the answers. Is the good life as described or presupposed truly good? Can you think of a better one? Are the justifications adequate? Why should we think that the way to live (the means) will result in a good life? Maybe there is something the authors have overlooked. What about luck? Maybe living a good life is not a matter of choice but dumb luck. Can we attain a good life if we live in a horrible society? Does social harmony or social disintegration have anything to do with it? What about illness or poverty? Are these significant factors?

As you read and think through these questions, your own understanding of the question and the issues should deepen, and your own answer should become clearer. What do you think the good life is, and how do you think it can be attained?

Socrates' question is abstract and complex. Thinking about it soon leads to thinking about all kinds of values—economic, political, social, moral—that influence what we do in many ways. One way to start thinking about your own views concerning how one should live is to focus on a concrete problem. Suppose there is a public good, such as clean air, which only can be attained by cooperative action. There will be a cost to each individual who joins the effort to clean the air but not every individual need pay that cost in order to obtain this public good. However, a significant number of individuals must assume the burden or the air will not get cleaned. Would you join in the effort and pay the cost or would you assume that enough other people would pay the cost, thereby allowing you to gain the benefit without paying the cost? You might think that this is such a desirable good enough people will pay the cost and thus you won't have to. Or you might think that not enough people will contribute to effort to clean the air because the cost is so high hence the probability is very low that your individual contribution will make any difference. You may end up paying the cost without getting the benefit. In either case the conclusion not to contribute seems the best course of action since it will save you the cost. If enough people reasoned like this, the benefit of clean air would not be realized.

As you think about this problem ask yourself how your reasoning reflects your values. If you decide not to contribute, it might be because you want to spend your money on yourself and hence do not want to pay the cost. Or it may be that you decide not to contribute because you value your independence and don't want others telling you how to live your life or restricting your lifestyle. Then again, you might decide to contribute because you want clean air and because you understand that even though there is a cost, the benefit is not likely to occur unless as many people as possible contribute to reaching that goal. You can't be sure what other people are going to do, but you can decide what you are going to do and hope that others will follow suit. Indeed you might even become an activist and urge others to join the effort.

Values effect our decisions about how we should live in many ways. If we desire self-respect more than social recognition, we will make decisions differently about what to do in countless situations. Desiring wealth more than health will also influence us one way or another. Valuing self-sacrifice more than self-interest will lead to ways of living that differ from putting self-interest before self-sacrifice. Our values are important not just to ourselves but also to others.

We cannot forget that neither our values nor we exist in a social vacuum. What makes the "clean air problem" I mentioned above difficult is its social context. It pits or seems to pit individual welfare (minimizing cost to oneself) against social welfare (the public good of clean air). But in this case the public welfare is also the individual welfare. Clean air is good for everyone and it cannot be achieved without cooperation. How you work through what you would do in situations like this and in countless other situations depends, in part, on how you answer the question how should one live.

3.2 THE BUDDHA AND THE MIDDLE WAY

The word *Buddha,* which means "the Enlightened One," is the title bestowed on Siddhartha Gautama, who was born into a royal family in Nepal around 563 BCE.

He lived a life of luxury and pleasure in the palace. On a trip outside the palace, he became aware of the suffering *(dukkha)* of humans. He witnessed people experiencing disease, old age, and death. At the age of twenty-nine, he left his life of comfort and became an ascetic in search of the solution to the problem of suffering.

Siddhartha studied with the sages of his day and practiced extreme austerities. Ironically, he nearly starved himself to death in his search for the answer to suffering. However, he found no satisfactory answer, either from his teachers or from his extreme ascetic practices. Eventually, he went his own way. One evening, he seated himself under a tree (later called the Bo-tree, or Tree of Enlightenment) and resolved not to stir from meditation until he discovered how to overcome suffering. He attained enlightenment and henceforth was called the Buddha.

After his enlightenment, he taught the wisdom he had realized and the practice for attaining that wisdom because he wished to help others gain **nirvana**, the release from suffering. He was convinced, based on his experience, that human beings should live free from suffering and that such a life was possible. He taught for forty-five years and founded an order of monks. He died at the age of eighty, in 483 BCE. From his teachings, a religion called Buddhism has grown and spread throughout Asia and much of the rest of the world. It is divided into three main groups: Theravada (Way of the Elders), Mahayana (Greater Vehicle), and Vajrayana (Diamond Vehicle). His teachings also inspired philosophical reflection, and various philosophical schools have also developed.

What follows is one selection from the "Long Discourses" (*Digha Nikaya*, Sutta 22:18-22), attributed to the Buddha himself, concerning the **Four Noble Truths**. These constitute the heart of his message and presumably express, in condensed form, what he learned under the Bo-tree. The second selection is a commentary, from a Theravadan viewpoint, on the Fourth Noble Truth (also called the **Middle Way** or the **Eightfold Path**) by a contemporary Sri Lankan Buddhist scholar, Dr. Walpola Rahula. A color plate inside this book shows a representation of the Eightfold Path. If you research the symbolism of this classic representation, you will discover the many intriguing facets of this ancient symbol.

◉ READING QUESTIONS

As you read the first selection, see if you can answer these questions:

1. What is suffering?
2. What is the relationship between craving and pleasure?
3. Why does the Buddha teach that the cessation of suffering (Third Noble Truth) is the extinction of craving?

As you read the commentary by Rahula, see if you can answer these questions:

4. Why is the Fourth Noble Truth called the Middle Path?
5. What is the relationship between compassion and wisdom?
6. What is the difference between knowing accordingly and penetration? Can you give an example of each from your own experience?

The Four Noble Truths

THE BUDDHA

17. "Again, monks, a monk abides contemplating mind-objects as mind-objects in respect of the Four Noble Truths. How does he do so? Here, a monk knows as it really is: 'This is suffering'; he knows as it really is: 'This is the origin of suffering'; he knows as it really is: 'This is the cessation of suffering'; he knows as it really is: 'This is the way of practice leading to the cessation of suffering'.

18. "And what, monks, is the Noble Truth of Suffering? Birth is suffering, aging is suffering, death is suffering, sorrow, lamentation, pain, sadness and distress are suffering. Being attached to the unloved is suffering, being separated from the loved is suffering, not getting what one wants is suffering. In short, the five aggregates of grasping are suffering....

"And how, monks, in short, are the five aggregates of grasping suffering? They are as follows: the aggregate of grasping that is form, the aggregate of grasping that is feeling, the aggregate of grasping that is perception, the aggregate of grasping that is the mental formations, the aggregate of grasping that is consciousness. These are, in short, the five aggregates of grasping that are suffering.[1] And that, monks, is called the Noble Truth of Suffering.

19. "And what, monks, is the Noble Truth of the Origin of Suffering? It is that craving which gives rise to rebirth, bound up with pleasure and lust, finding fresh delight now here, now there: that is to say sensual craving, craving for existence, and craving for non-existence.

"And where does this craving arise and establish itself? Wherever in the world there is anything agreeable and pleasurable, there this craving arises and establishes itself.

"And what is there in the world that is agreeable and pleasurable? The eye in the world is agreeable and pleasurable, the ear ... the nose ..., the tongue ..., the body ..., the mind in the world is agreeable and pleasurable, and there this craving arises and establishes itself. Sights, sounds, smells, tastes, tangibles, mind-objects in the world are agreeable and pleasurable, and there this craving arises and establishes itself.

"The craving for sights, sounds, smells, tastes, tangibles, mind-objects in the world is agreeable and pleasurable, and there this craving arises and establishes itself.[2]

"Thinking of sights, sounds, smells, tastes, tangibles, mind-objects in the world is agreeable and pleasurable, and there this craving arises and establishes itself.

"Pondering on sights, sounds, smells, tastes, tangibles and mind-objects in the world is agreeable and pleasurable, and there this craving arises and establishes itself. And that, monks, is called the Noble Truth of the Origin of Suffering.

20. "And what, monks, is the Noble Truth of the Cessation of Suffering? It is the complete fading-away and extinction of this craving, its forsaking and abandonment, liberation from it, detachment from it. And how does this craving come to be abandoned, how does its cessation come about? ...

21. "And what, monks, is the Noble Truth of the Way of Practice Leading to the Cessation of Suffering? It is just this Noble Eightfold Path, namely: Right View, Right Thought, Right Speech, Right Action, Right Livelihood; Right Effort, Right Mindfulness, Right Concentration.

---

[1][The five aggregates constitute the components of the individual human being. Form refers to the physical, feelings to the sensations that arise from the operation of the senses, perception to the cognition or awareness of sensation, mental formations to the emotions and dispositions to act based on sensations, and consciousness to the product or result of the interaction of the other four aggregates.—Ed.]

[2][In the West, we classify five senses as sight, sound, smell, taste, and touch. Buddhism adds a sixth, the mind.—Ed.]

"And what, monks, is Right View? It is, monks, the knowledge of suffering, the knowledge of the origin of suffering, the knowledge of the cessation of suffering, and the knowledge of the way of practice leading to the cessation of suffering. This is called Right View.

"And what, monks, is Right Thought? The thought of renunciation, the thought of non-ill-will, the thought of harmlessness. This, monks, is called Right Thought.

"And what, monks, is Right Speech? Refraining from lying, refraining from slander, refraining from harsh speech, refraining from frivolous speech. This is called Right Speech.

"And what, monks, is Right Action? Refraining from taking life, refraining from taking what is not given, refraining from sexual misconduct. This is called Right Action.

"And what, monks, is Right Livelihood? Here, monks, the Ariyan disciple, having given up wrong livelihood, keeps himself by right livelihood.

"And what, monks, is Right Effort? Here, monks, a monk rouses his will, makes an effort, stirs up energy, exerts his mind and strives to prevent the arising of unarisen evil unwholesome mental states. He rouses his will … and strives to overcome evil unwholesome mental states that have arisen. He rouses his will … and strives to produce unarisen wholesome mental states. He rouses his will, makes an effort, stirs up energy, exerts his mind and strives to maintain wholesome mental states that have arisen, not to let them fade away, to bring them to greater growth, to the full perfection of development. This is called Right Effort.

"And what, monks, is Right Mindfulness? Here, monks, a monk abides contemplating body as body, ardent, clearly aware and mindful, having put aside hankering and fretting for the world; he abides contemplating feelings as feelings …; he abides contemplating mind as mind …; he abides contemplating mind-objects as mind-objects, ardent, clearly aware and mindful, having put aside hankering and fretting for the world. This is called Right Mindfulness.

"And what, monks, is Right Concentration? Here, a monk, detached from sense-desires, detached from unwholesome mental states, enters and remains in the first *jhāna*,[3] which is with thinking and pondering, born of detachment, filled with delight and joy. And with the subsiding of thinking and pondering, by gaining inner tranquility and oneness of mind, he enters and remains in the second jhāna, which is without thinking and pondering, born of concentration, filled with delight and joy. And with the fading away of delight, remaining imperturbable, mindful and clearly aware, he experiences in himself the joy of which the Noble Ones say: 'Happy is he who dwells with equanimity and mindfulness,' he enters the third jhāna. And, having given up pleasure and pain, and with the disappearance of former gladness and sadness, he enters and remains in the fourth jhāna, which is beyond pleasure and pain, and purified by equanimity and mindfulness. This is called Right Concentration. And that, monks, is called the way of practice leading to the cessation of suffering."

---

[3][*Jhāna* (or *dhyana*) refers to altered states of consciousness that occur in meditation.—Ed.]

The Fourth Noble Truth

WALPOLA RAHULA

The fourth noble truth is that of the Way leading to the Cessation of Dukkha [suffering]. This is known as the "Middle Path," because it avoids two extremes: one extreme being the search for happiness through the pleasures of the senses, which is "low, common, unprofitable and the

---

way of the ordinary people;" the other being the search for happiness through self-mortification in different forms of asceticism, which is "painful, unworthy and unprofitable." Having himself first tried these two extremes, and having found them to be useless, the Buddha discovered through personal experience the Middle Path "which gives vision and knowledge, which leads to Calm, Insight, Enlightenment, Nirvāna." This Middle Path is generally referred to as the Noble Eightfold Path, because it is composed of eight categories or divisions: namely,

1. Right Understanding,
2. Right Thought,
3. Right Speech,
4. Right Action,
5. Right Livelihood,
6. Right Effort,
7. Right Mindfulness,
8. Right Concentration.

Practically the whole teaching of the Buddha, to which he devoted himself during 45 years, deals in some way or other with this Path. He explained it in different ways and in different words to different people, according to the stage of their development and their capacity to understand and follow him. But the essence of those many thousand discourses scattered in the Buddhist Scriptures is found in the Noble Eightfold Path.

It should not be thought that the eight categories or divisions of the Path should be followed and practised one after the other in the numerical order as given in the usual list above. But they are to be developed more or less simultaneously, as far as possible according to the capacity of each individual. They are all linked together and each helps the cultivation of the others.

These eight factors aim at promoting and perfecting the three essentials of Buddhist training and discipline: namely: (*a*) Ethical Conduct, (*b*) Mental Discipline, and (*c*) Wisdom. It will therefore be more helpful for a coherent and better understanding of the eight divisions of the Path, if we group them and explain them according to these three heads.

Ethical Conduct is built on the vast conception of universal love and compassion for all living beings, on which the Buddha's teaching is based.

It is regrettable that many scholars forget this great ideal of the Buddha's teaching, and indulge in only dry philosophical and metaphysical divagations when they talk and write about Buddhism. The Buddha gave his teaching "for the good of the many, for the happiness of the many, out of compassion for the world.

According to Buddhism, for a man to be perfect there are two qualities that he should develop equally: compassion on one side, and wisdom on the other. Here compassion represents love, charity, kindness, tolerance and such noble qualities on the emotional side, or qualities of the heart, while wisdom would stand for the intellectual side or the qualities of the mind. If one develops only the emotional neglecting the intellectual, one may become a good-hearted fool; while to develop only the intellectual side neglecting the emotional may turn one into a hard-hearted intellect without feeling for others. Therefore, to be perfect one has to develop both equally. That is the aim of the Buddhist way of life: in it wisdom and compassion are inseparably linked together, as we shall see later.

Now, in Ethical Conduct, based on love and compassion, are included three factors of the Noble Eightfold Path: namely, Right Speech, Right Action and Right Livelihood. (Nos. 3, 4 and 5 in the list.)

Right Speech means abstention (1) from telling lies, (2) from backbiting and slander and talk that may bring about hatred, enmity, disunity and disharmony among individuals or groups of people, (3) from harsh, rude, impolite, malicious and abusive language, and (4) from idle, useless and foolish babble and gossip. When one abstains from these forms of wrong and harmful speech one naturally has to speak the truth, has to use words that are friendly and benevolent, pleasant and gentle, meaningful and useful. One should not speak carelessly: speech should be at the right time and place. If one cannot say something useful, one should keep "noble silence."

Right Action aims at promoting moral, honourable and peaceful conduct. It admonishes us that we should abstain from destroying life, from stealing, from dishonest dealings, from illegitimate sexual intercourse, and that we should also help others to lead a peaceful and honourable life in the right way.

Right Livelihood means that one should abstain from making one's living through a profession that brings harm to others, such as trading in arms and lethal weapons, intoxicating drinks, poisons, killing animals, cheating, etc., and should live by a profession which is honourable, blameless and innocent of harm to others. One can clearly see here that Buddhism is strongly opposed to any kind of war, when it lays down that trade in arms and lethal weapons is an evil and unjust means of livelihood.

These three factors (Right Speech, Right Action and Right Livelihood) of the Eightfold Path constitute Ethical Conduct. It should be realized that the Buddhist ethical and moral conduct aims at promoting a happy and harmonious life both for the individual and for society. This moral conduct is considered as the indispensable foundation for all higher spiritual attainments. No spiritual development is possible without this moral basis.

Next comes Mental Discipline, in which are included three other factors of the Eightfold Path: namely, Right Effort, Right Mindfulness (or Attentiveness) and Right Concentration. (Nos. 6, 7 and 8 in the list).

Right Effort is the energetic will (1) to prevent evil and unwholesome states of mind from arising, and (2) to get rid of such evil and unwholesome states that have already arisen within a man, and also (3) to produce, to cause to arise, good and wholesome states of mind not yet arisen, and (4) to develop and bring to perfection the good and wholesome states of mind already present in a man.

Right Mindfulness (or Attentiveness) is to be diligently aware, mindful and attentive with regard to (1) the activities of the body, (2) sensations or feelings, (3) the activities of the mind, and (4) ideas, thoughts, conceptions and things.

The practice of concentration on breathing is one of the well-known exercises, connected with the body, for mental development. There are several other ways of developing attentiveness in relation to the body—as modes of meditation.

With regard to sensations and feelings, one should be clearly aware of all forms of feelings and sensations, pleasant, unpleasant and neutral, of how they appear and disappear within oneself.

Concerning the activities of mind, one should be aware whether one's mind is lustful or not, given to hatred or not, deluded or not, distracted or concentrated, etc. In this way one should be aware of all movements of mind, how they arise and disappear.

As regards ideas, thoughts, conceptions and things, one should know their nature, how they appear and disappear, how they are developed, how they are suppressed, and destroyed, and so on. These four forms of mental culture or meditation are treated in detail in the *Setting-up of Mindfulness*.

The third and last factor of Mental Discipline is Right Concentration leading to the four stages of *Dhyāna*, generally called trance or *recueillement*. In the first stage of *Dhyāna*, passionate desires and certain unwholesome thoughts like sensuous lust, ill-will, languor, worry, restlessness, and sceptical doubt are discarded, and feelings of joy and happiness are maintained, along with certain mental activities. In the second stage, all intellectual activities are suppressed, tranquillity and "one-pointedness" of mind developed, and the feelings of joy and happiness are still retained. In the third stage, the feeling of joy, which is an active sensation, also disappears, while the disposition of happiness still remains in addition to mindful equanimity. In the fourth stage of *Dhyāna*, all sensations, even of happiness and unhappiness, of joy and sorrow, disappear, only pure equanimity and awareness remaining.

Thus the mind is trained and disciplined and developed through Right Effort, Right Mindfulness, and Right Concentration. The remaining two factors, namely Right Thought and Right Understanding, go to constitute Wisdom.

Right Thought denotes the thoughts of selfless renunciation or detachment, thoughts of love and thoughts of non-violence, which are extended to all beings. It is very interesting and important to note here that thoughts of selfless detachment, love and non-violence are grouped on the side of wisdom. This clearly shows that true wisdom is endowed with these noble qualities, and that all thoughts of selfish desire, ill-will, hatred and violence are the result of a lack of wisdom—in all spheres of life whether individual, social, or political.

Right Understanding is the understanding of things as they are, and it is the Four Noble Truths that explain things as they really are. Right Understanding, therefore, is ultimately reduced to the understanding of the Four Noble Truths. This understanding is the highest wisdom which sees the Ultimate Reality. According to Buddhism there are two sorts of understanding: What we generally call understanding is knowledge, an accumulated memory, an intellectual grasping of a subject according to certain given data. This is called "knowing accordingly." It is not very deep. Real deep understanding is called "penetration," seeing a thing in its true nature, without name and label. This penetration is possible only when the mind is free from all impurities and is fully developed through meditation.

From this brief account of the Path, one may see that it is a way of life to be followed, practised and developed by each individual. It is self-discipline in body, word and mind, self-development and self-purification. It has nothing to do with belief, prayer, worship or ceremony. In that sense, it has nothing which may popularly be called "religious." It is a Path leading to the realization of Ultimate Reality, to complete freedom, happiness and peace through moral, spiritual and intellectual perfection.

In Buddhist countries there are simple and beautiful customs and ceremonies on religious occasions. They have little to do with the real Path. But they have their value in satisfying certain religious emotions and the needs of those who are less advanced, and helping them gradually along the Path.

With regard to the Four Noble Truths we have four functions to perform:

The First Noble Truth is *Dukkha,* the nature of life, its suffering, its sorrows and joys, its imperfection and unsatisfactoriness, its impermanence and insubstantiality. With regard to this, our function is to understand it as a fact, clearly and completely.

The Second Noble Truth is the Origin of *Dukkha,* which is desire, "thirst," accompanied by all other passions, defilements and impurities. A mere understanding of this fact is not sufficient. Here our function is to discard it, to eliminate, to destroy and eradicate it.

The Third Noble Truth is the Cessation of *Dukkha,* Nirvāna, the Absolute Truth, the Ultimate Reality. Here our function is to realize it.

The Fourth Noble Truth is the Path leading to the realization of Nirvāna. A mere knowledge of the Path, however complete, will not do. In this case, our function is to follow it and keep to it.

⊚ CRITICAL QUESTIONS

1. Present an argument showing that suffering can be good. What do you think might be wrong with your argument?

2. According to the Buddha, what is the good life, and how would he answer the question, "How should one live?" Do you agree? Why, or why not?

3.3 CONFUCIUS AND THE LIFE OF VIRTUE

Twelve years after the Buddha was born in India, Confucius (551–479 BCE) was born in the state of Lu in China. ("Confucius" is the latinization of Kong Fuzi (K'ung Fu Tzu),* which means "Master Kong.") He lived at a time when Chinese society had disintegrated into social and political chaos. Because of these circumstances, he became interested in the question of how the well-being of society could best be achieved and how this was related to the good life.

---

*There are two widely used methods for romanticizing (translating into a Latin-based alphabetical system) Chinese words. One is called Wade-Giles and the other Pinyin. The first time a word or name is introduced, I have used the Pinyin spelling and provided the Wade-Giles spelling in parentheses. See the pronunciation guide for Chinese words in Appendix II.

Biographical information is uncertain, but tradition tells us that Confucius was from the nobility. When he was three years old, his father died. At age nineteen he married and sought a government career. However, he was to make his name as an educator, not as a politician. He provided what we today would call a "humanistic" education to commoners and nobles alike, and he taught what might be termed a "humanistic social philosophy"—"social" because of his concern for achieving a good social order and "humanistic" because of his concern to cultivate humane qualities in the human spirit. His reputation in China became so immense that on the popular level he was deified, while among scholars he was venerated as a great sage.

Ren (jen) is one of the central ideas of his thought. It has been translated in a variety of ways: "goodness," "humanity," "benevolence," and "humanheartedness," to name only a few. The concept is so rich and used in such a variety of ways that no simple English translation captures its meaning. *Ren* is not something we are, but something we become by cultivating our aesthetic, moral, cognitive, and spiritual sensibilities. These qualities develop in social or community contexts involving ordered and ritualized relationships. *Ren* is closely related to the principle of reciprocity, which ought to govern relationships among humans. We should not, Confucius contended, do to others what we would not have them do to us. Long before Judaism and Christianity, Confucius had articulated a form of the "Golden Rule."

Li (pronounced "lee") is another central concept in Confucian philosophy. It can mean rules of proper behavior, ritual or rite, custom, etiquette, ceremony, worship, and propriety. Humans should behave appropriately. The models for appropriate behavior came, according to Confucius, from the traditional rites and customs handed down from a past Golden Age. He regarded himself as a traditionalist and spent much of his time teaching and interpreting the cultural classics (called the "Six Disciplines") from China's past. Tradition is important in his view because it provides an external check on what one may subjectively believe to be the right way to act and is a repository of the wisdom of the past with regard to proper conduct. However, tradition must be personally appropriated and made one's own. Otherwise rituals become dead ceremonies performed mechanically and without meaning.

One of the major traditional virtues in China associated with Confucianism is *xiao* (hsiao; pronounced "shee-ow"). *Xiao* is often translated as filial piety and involves the practice of kindness, honor, respect, and loyalty among family members. Confucius believed that a strong family is the basis of a strong society. In fact, the family is the microcosmic version of society. Society ought to be one large family, and ultimately *xiao* should be extended to the whole human community. Family harmony contributes to a wider social harmony and a social harmony supports family harmony.

Yi (pronounced "yee") is often translated as "rightness" and sometimes as "morals" or "morality." Many interpreters of Confucius, including the author of our next selection, D.C. Lau, think *yi,* or morality, becomes the primary concern of Confucius as he searches for the best way to live. While there is no denying that Confucius was concerned with what we today would call moral issues, the concept of *yi* is broader than morality. *Yi* refers to what is appropriate or fitting to do in a given situation. Hence it has aesthetic, political, social, and religious implications as well as moral ones.

Although it is usual to interpret Confucius as primarily concerned with moral, social, and political values, the aesthetic dimension of his thought needs to be emphasized as well. Ethics has to do with moral value; aesthetics has to do with artistic value or beauty. The Confucian concern with balance, harmony, and appropriateness reflects aesthetic values. Indeed, the very division between moral and aesthetic value is something Confucius probably did not recognize. For him to call an action right was not merely to pass a moral judgment, but an aesthetic judgment as well. Moral order is aesthetic order. The good and the beautiful are one.

Education plays a key role in the process of becoming a virtuous person because knowledge of the past is a clue to proper action in the present. Since becoming a virtuous person or developing good character is a process, it is something we must learn how to do. Hence, proper instruction and good education are keys to self-cultivation.

I have chosen to use a secondary source to introduce Confucius because it is rather difficult for a modern reader who has little or no background in Confucian philosophy to understand primary sources. Our guide to Confucius is D. C. Lau, respected translator and interpreter of Confucian thought. The following comes from the introduction to his widely used translation of Confucius's *Analects*.

◉ READING QUESTIONS

(Note: I have used the Wade-Giles spelling of Chinese terms in my questions because Lau uses Wade-Giles.)

1. What, according to Lau, is the most fundamental message of Confucius?
2. What is the difference between the *chün tzu* and the *hsiao jen?*
3. Can anyone become a *chün tzu?*
4. What is jen and how is it related to *chung* and *shu?*
5. Why are the obligations we owe others proportionate to the closeness of our relationship to them?
6. What is the relationship between *jen* and *li?*

Confucius and Moral Character

D. C. LAU

Before we proceed to look at what Confucius has to say about moral character, it is convenient, first of all, to dispose of two concepts which were already current in Confucius' time, viz., the Way *(tao)* and virtue *(te)*. The importance Confucius attached to the Way can be seen from his remark, "He has not lived in vain who dies the day he is told about the Way" (IV.8). Used in this sense, the Way seems to cover the sum total of truths about the universe and man, and not only the individual but also the state is said either to possess or not to possess the Way. As it is something which can be transmitted from teacher to disciple, it must be something that can be put into words. There is another slightly different sense in which the term is used. The way is said also to be

---

someone's way, for instance, "the ways of the Former Kings" (I.12), "the way of King Wen and King Wu" (XIX.22), or "the way of the Master" (IV. 15). When thus specified, the way naturally can only be taken to mean the way followed by the person in question. As for the Way, rival schools would each claim to have discovered it even though what each school claimed to have discovered turned out to be very different. The Way, then, is a highly emotive term and comes very close to the term "Truth" as found in philosophical and religious writings in the West.

There seems to be little doubt that the word *te*, virtue, is cognate with the word *te*, to get. Virtue is an endowment men get from Heaven. The word was used in this sense when Confucius, facing a threat to his life, said, "Heaven is author of the virtue that is in me" (VII.23), but this usage is rare in the *Analects*. By the time of Confucius, the term must have already become a moral term. It is something one cultivates, and it enables one to govern a state well. One of the things that caused him concern was, according to Confucius, his failure to cultivate his virtue (VII.3). He also said that if one guided the common people by virtue they would not only reform themselves but have a sense of shame (II.3).

Both the Way and virtue were concepts current before Confucius' time and, by then, they must have already acquired a certain aura. They both, in some way, stem from Heaven. It is, perhaps, for this reason that though he said little of a concrete and specific nature about either of these concepts, Confucius, nevertheless, gave them high precedence in his scheme of things. He said, "I set my heart on the Way, base myself on virtue, lean upon benevolence for support and take my recreation in the arts" (VII.6). Benevolence is something the achievement of which is totally dependent upon our own efforts, but virtue is partly a gift from Heaven.

Behind Confucius' pursuit of the ideal moral character lies the unspoken, and therefore, unquestioned, assumption that the only purpose a man can have and also the only worthwhile thing a man can do is to become as good a man as possible. This is something that has to be pursued for its own sake and with complete

indifference to success or failure. Unlike religious teachers, Confucius could hold out no hope of rewards either in this world or in the next. As far as survival after death is concerned, Confucius' attitude can, at best, be described as agnostic. When Tzu-lu asked how gods and spirits of the dead should be served, the Master answered that as he was not able even to serve man how could he serve the spirits, and when Tzu-lu further asked about death, the Master answered that as he did not understand even life how could he understand death (XI.12). This shows, at least, a reluctance on the part of Confucius to commit himself on the subject of survival after death. While giving men no assurance of an afterlife, Confucius, nevertheless, made great moral demands upon them. He said of the Gentleman[1] of purpose and the benevolent man that "while it is inconceivable that they should seek to stay alive at the expense of benevolence, it may happen that they have to accept death in order to have benevolence accomplished" (XV.9).

When such demands are made on men, little wonder that one of Confucius' disciples should have considered that a Gentleman's "burden is heavy and the road is long," for his burden was benevolence and the road came to an end only with death (VIII.7).

If a man cannot be assured of a reward after death, neither can he be guaranteed success in his moral endeavours in this life. The gatekeeper at the Stone Gate asked Tzu-lu, "Is that the K'ung who keeps working towards a goal the realization of which he knows to be hopeless?" (XIV.38). On another occasion, after an encounter with a recluse, Tzu-lu was moved to remark, "The gentleman takes office in order to do his duty. As for putting the Way into practice, he knows all along that it is hopeless" (XVIII.7). Since in being moral one can neither be assured of a reward nor guaranteed success, morality must be pursued for its own sake. This is, perhaps, the most fundamental message in Confucius' teachings, a message

---

[1]Throughout this book, "Gentleman" is used as an equivalent for *shih* while "gentleman" is used for *chün tzu*. *Shih* was the lowest rank of officials while *chün tzu* denoted either a man of moral excellence or a man in authority....

that marked his teachings from other schools of thought in ancient China.

For Confucius there is not one single ideal character but quite a variety. The highest is the sage (sheng jen). This ideal is so high that it is hardly ever realized. Confucius claimed neither to be a sage himself nor even to have seen such a man. He said, "How dare I claim to be a sage or a benevolent man?" (VII.34) and, on another occasion, "I have no hopes of meeting a sage" (VII.26). The only time he indicated the kind of man that would deserve the epithet was when Tzu-kung asked him, "If there were a man who gave extensively to the common people and brought help to the multitude, what would you think of him? Could he be called benevolent?" Confucius' answer was, "It is no longer a matter of benevolence with such a man. If you must describe him, 'sage' is, perhaps, the right word" (VI.30).

Lower down the scale there are the good man (shan jen) and the complete man (ch'eng jen). Even the good man Confucius said he had not seen, but the term "good man" seems to apply essentially to men in charge of government, as he said, for instance, "How true is the saying that after a state has been ruled for a hundred years by good men it is possible to get the better of cruelty and to do away with killing" (XIII.11), and "After a good man has trained the common people for seven years, they should be ready to take up arms" (XIII.29). On the one occasion when he was asked about the way of the good man, Confucius' answer was somewhat obscure (XI.20). As for the complete man, he is described in terms applied not exclusively to him. He "remembers what is right at the sight of profit," and "is ready to lay down his life in the face of danger" (XIV.12). Similar terms are used to describe the Gentleman (XIX.1).

There is no doubt, however, that the ideal moral character for Confucius is the chün tzu (gentleman), as he is discussed in more than eighty chapters in the Analects. Chün tzu and hsiao jen (small man) are correlative and contrasted terms. The former is used of men in authority while the latter of those who are ruled. In the Analects, however, chün tzu and hsiao jen

are essentially moral terms. The chün tzu is the man with a cultivated moral character, while the hsiao jen is the opposite. It is worth adding that the two usages indicating the social and moral status are not exclusive, and, in individual cases, it is difficult to be sure whether, besides their moral connotations, these terms may not also carry their usual social connotations as well.

As the gentleman is the ideal moral character, it is not to be expected that a man can become a gentleman without a great deal of hard work or cultivation, as the Chinese called it. There is a considerable number of virtues a gentleman is supposed to have and the essence of these virtues is often summed up in a precept. In order to have a full understanding of the complete moral character of the gentleman, we have to take a detailed look at the various virtues he is supposed to possess.

Benevolence (jen) is the most important moral quality a man can possess. Although the use of this term was not an innovation on the part of Confucius, it is almost certain that the complexity of its content and the pre-eminence it attained amongst moral qualities were due to Confucius. That it is *the* moral quality a gentleman must possess is clear from the following saying.

> If the gentleman forsakes benevolence, in what way can he make a name for himself? The gentleman never deserts benevolence, not even for as long as it takes to eat a meal. If he hurries and stumbles, one may be sure that it is in benevolence that he does so. (IV.5)

In some contexts "the gentleman" and "the benevolent man" are almost interchangeable terms. For instance, it is said in one place that "a gentleman is free from worries and fears" (XII.4), while elsewhere it is the benevolent man who is said not to have worries (IX.29, XIV.28). As benevolence is so central a concept, we naturally expect Confucius to have a great deal to say about it. In this we are not disappointed. There are no less than six occasions on which Confucius answered direct questions about benevolence, and as Confucius had the habit of framing his answers with the specific needs of the inquirer in mind, these answers, taken together, give us a reasonably complete picture.

The essential point about benevolence is to be found in Confucius' answer to Chung-kung:

> Do not impose on others what you yourself do not desire. (XII.2)

These words were repeated on another occasion.

> Tzu-kung asked, "Is there a single word which can be a guide to conduct throughout one's life?" The Master said, "It is perhaps the word 'shu'. Do not impose on others what you yourself do not desire." (XV.24)

By taking the two sayings together we can see that *shu* forms part of benevolence and, as such, is of great significance in the teachings of Confucius. This is confirmed by a saying of Tseng Tzu's. To the Master's remark that there was a single thread binding his way together, Tseng Tzu added the explanation, "The way of the Master consists in *chung* and *shu*. That is all" (IV.15). There is another saying which is, in fact, also about shu. In answer to a question from Tzu-kung, Confucius said,

> A benevolent man helps others to take their stand in so far as he himself wishes to take his stand, and gets others there in so far as he himself wishes to get there. The ability to take as analogy what is near at hand can be called the method of benevolence. (VI.30)

From this we can see that *shu* is the method of discovering what other people wish or do not wish done to them. The method consists in taking oneself—"what is near at hand"—as an analogy[2] and asking oneself what one would like or dislike were one in the position of the person at the receiving end. *Shu*, however, cannot be the whole of benevolence as it is only its method. Having found out what the other person wants or does not want, whether we go on to do to him what we believe he wants and refrain from doing to him what we believe he does not want must depend on something other than *shu*. As the

way of the Master consists of *chung* and *shu*, in *chung* we have the other component of benevolence. *Chung* is the doing of one's best and it is through *chung* that one puts into effect what one had found out by the method of *shu*. Tseng Tzu said on another occasion, "Every day I examine myself on three counts," and of these the first is "In what I have undertaken on another's behalf, have I failed to be *chung*?" (I.4). Again, when asked how a subject should serve his ruler, Confucius' answer was that he "should serve his ruler with *chung*" (III.19). Finally, it is also said that in dealing with others one should be *chung* (XIII.19). In all these cases there is no doubt at all that *chung* means "doing one's best."

Another answer Confucius gave to the question about benevolence was, "Love your fellow men" (XII.22). As he did not elaborate, his meaning is not very clear. But fortunately he used this phrase again on two other occasions. In I.5 he said, "In guiding a state of a thousand chariots … avoid excesses in expenditure and love your fellow men; employ the labour of the common people in the right seasons." Again, the Master, according to Tzu-yu, once said "that the gentleman instructed in the Way loves his fellow men and that the small man instructed in the Way is easy to command" (XVII.4). In the first case, the love for one's fellow men (*jen*) is contrasted with the employment of the common people (*min*) in the right seasons, while in the second the gentleman's loving his fellow men is contrasted with the small man's being easy to command. If we remember that the small man was probably different from the common people, we cannot rule out the possibility that when Confucius defined benevolence in terms of loving one's fellow men he did not have the common people in mind as well. Even if this is the case, it is perhaps not as strange as it may seem at first sight, and in order to see it in perspective, we should first take a look at the basis of Confucius' system of morals.

Confucius had a profound admiration for the Duke of Chou who, as regent in the early part of the reign of his young nephew, King Ch'eng, was the architect of the Chou feudal system some five hundred years before Confucius' time. It is beyond the scope of this introduction to discuss

---

[2]There is a more explicit definition of *shu* in one of the philosophers of the Warring States period. The *Shih tzu* says, "By 'shu' is meant using oneself as a measure." (*Ch'ün shu chih yao*, 36.19b)

in detail the influence of the Duke on Chinese society and the Chinese political system. It is sufficient simply to single out for mention his most important contribution, the clan inheritance system known as *tsung fa*. Under this system, succession passes to the eldest son by the principal wife. Younger sons or sons by concubines become founders of their own noble houses. Thus the feudal lord stands to the king in a double relationship. In terms of political relationship he is a vassal while in terms of blood ties he is the head of a cadet branch of the royal clan. Political allegiance has as its foundation family allegiance. This social system founded by the Duke of Chou proved its soundness by the durability of the Chou Dynasty.

Following the footsteps of the Duke of Chou, Confucius made the natural love and obligations obtaining between members of the family the basis of a general morality. The two most important relationships within the family are those between father and son and between elder and younger brother. The love one owes to one's parents is *hsiao* while the respect due one's elder brother is *t'i*. If a man is a good son and a good younger brother at home, he can be counted on to behave correctly in society. Tzu-yu said,

> It is rare for a man whose character is such that he is good as a son *(hsiao)* and obedient as a young man *(t'i)* to have the inclination to transgress against his superiors; it is unheard of for one who has no such inclination to be inclined to start a rebellion. (I.2)

He goes on to draw the logical conclusion that "being good as a son and obedient as a young man is, perhaps, the root of a man's character."

In later Confucianism an undue emphasis was put on being a good son, but we can see here that even in early Confucian teachings *hsiao* was one of the most basic virtues.

If being a good son makes a good subject, being a good father will also make a good ruler. Love for people outside one's family is looked upon as an extension of the love for members of one's own family. One consequence of this view is that the love, and so the obligation to love, decreases by degrees as it extends outwards.

Geographically, one loves members of one's own family more than one's neighbours, one's neighbours more than one's fellow villagers, and so on. Socially, one loves members of one's own social class more than those of another class. Thus it would not be surprising if benevolence was confined to one's fellow men *(jen)*, but what is much more important to remember is that this does not mean that one does not love the common people at all. One loves them, but to a lesser degree and, perhaps, in a different manner. In Confucius' terminology, one should be generous *(hui)* to the common people (V.16). This is in keeping with Confucius' general attitude towards obligations. Our obligation towards others should be in proportion to the benefit we have received from them. This seems to be the case even between parents and children. In commenting on Tsai Yü who wanted to cut short the three-year mourning period, Confucius said, "Was Yü not given three years' love by his parents?" (XVII.21). This may be taken to mean that the observance of the three-year mourning period is, in some sense, a repayment of the love received from one's parents in the first years of one's life. If this is so, it is not difficult to see why the obligations we owe to other people should also be in proportion to the closeness of our relationship to them. As to how a ruler should treat the common people, this is a topic to which we shall return.

Concerning the nature of benevolence, there is another answer given by Confucius which is of great importance because the question was put to him by his most talented disciple.

> Yen Yüan asked about benevolence. The Master said, "To return to the observance of the rites through overcoming the self constitutes benevolence. If for a single day a man could return to the observance of the rites through overcoming himself, then the whole Empire would consider benevolence to be his. However, the practice of benevolence depends on oneself alone, and not on others." (XII.1)

There are two points in this definition of benevolence which deserve attention. First, benevolence consists in overcoming the self. Second, to be benevolent one has to return to the observance of the rites.

Take the first point first. It is a central tenet in the teachings of Confucius that being moral has nothing to do with self-interest. To be more precise, to say that two things have nothing to do with each other is to say that there is no relationship whatsoever between them, either positive or negative. If being moral has nothing to do with pursuing one's own interest, neither has it anything to do with deliberately going against it. Why, then, it may be asked, is it so important to emphasize this lack of relationship between the two? The answer is this. Of all the things that are likely to distort a man's moral judgement and deflect him from his moral purpose, self-interest is the strongest, the most persistent and the most insidious. Confucius was well aware of this. That is why he said, more than once, that at the sight of profit one should think of what is right (XIV.12, XVI.10 and XIX.1). In another context he warned men in their old age against acquisitiveness (XVI.7). He also asked, "Is it really possible to work side by side with a mean fellow in the service of a lord? Before he gets what he wants, he worries lest he should not get it. After he has got it, he worries lest he should lose it, and when that happens he will not stop at anything" (XVII.15). Confucius came to the conclusion that he would not remain in undeserved wealth or position in spite of their being desirable objects (IV.5).

The point about returning to the observance of the rites is equally important. The rites (*li*) were a body of rules governing action in every aspect of life and they were the repository of past insights into morality. It is, therefore, important that one should, unless there are strong reasons to the contrary, observe them. Though there is no guarantee that observance of the rites necessarily leads, in every case, to behaviour that is right, the chances are it will, in fact, do so. To this point we shall return. For the moment, it is enough to say that Confucius had great respect for the body of rules which went under the name of *li*. That is why when Yen Yüan pressed for more specific details, he was told not to look or listen, speak or move, unless it was in accordance with the rites (XII.1). This, in Confucius' view, was no easy task, so much so that "if for a single day a man could

return to the observance of the rites through overcoming himself, then the whole Empire would consider benevolence to be his."

There are two occasions when answers are given which emphasize another aspect of benevolence. When Fan Ch'ih asked about benevolence, the Master said, "The benevolent man reaps the benefit only after overcoming difficulties" (VI.22). Similarly, when Ssu-ma Niu asked about benevolence, the Master said, "The mark of the benevolent man is that he is loath to speak," and then went on to explain, "When to act is difficult, is it any wonder that one is loath to speak?" (XII.3). That he considered benevolence difficult can be seen from his reluctance to grant that anyone was benevolent. He would not commit himself when asked whether Tzu-lu, Jan Ch'iu and Kung-hsi Ch'ih were benevolent (V.8). Nor would he grant that either Ling Yin Tzu-wen or Ch'en Wen Tzu was benevolent (V.19). He refused to claim benevolence for himself (VII.32). This is no more than one would expect from a man of modesty. However, he did say of Yen Yüan, "in his heart for three months at a time Hui does not lapse from benevolence," while "the others attain benevolence merely by fits and starts" (VI.7). This emphasis on the difficulty of practising benevolence is echoed, as we have seen, by Tseng Tzu who described benevolence as "a heavy burden" (VIII.7). But although Confucius emphasized the difficulty of practising benevolence, he also made it abundantly clear that whether we succeed or not depends solely on ourselves. As we have already seen, he said in answer to Yen Yüan's question that "the practice of benevolence depends on oneself alone, and not on others" (XII.1). He was quite clear that failure to practise benevolence was not due to lack of strength to carry it through. He said, "Is there a man who, for the space of a single day, is able to devote all his strength to benevolence? I have not come across such a man whose strength proves insufficient for the task" (IV.6). Thus when Jan Ch'iu excused himself by saying, "It is not that I am not pleased with your way, but rather that my strength gives out," Confucius' comment was, "A man whose strength gives out collapses along the course. In your case you set the limits beforehand" (VI.12). Confucius stated his conviction unambiguously when he said, "Is benevolence really far away? No sooner do I desire it than it is here" (VII.30). On the lines of the *Odes*

The flowers of the cherry tree,
How they wave about!

It's not that I do not think of you,
But your home is so far away,

Confucius commented, "He did not really think of her. If he did, there is no such thing as being far away" (IX.31). He must have made this comment with its possible application to benevolence in mind....

⊚ CRITICAL QUESTIONS

1. If benevolence requires the overcoming of self-interest, then why should our obligations to others be proportionate to the benefits we receive from them?

2. Do you agree with the Confucian vision of the good life? Why, or why not?

3.4 SOCRATES ON LIVING THE EXAMINED LIFE

Socrates (470–399 BCE), born in Athens nine years after Confucius died, lived during the golden era of Greek culture in a city that had become the intellectual and cultural center of the Mediterranean world. Many consider him the father of Western philosophy.

We have inherited contradictory pictures of Socrates. Plato, his most famous student and author of the dialogues in which Socrates stars, portrays him as the ideal philosopher. Aristophanes, in his play *The Clouds*, pictures him as a buffoon. Unlike the Pre-Socratics, Socrates showed little interest in natural philosophy. Like the Sophists, he was intensely interested in ethical and political problems. To many, he appeared to be just another Sophist, teaching the youth virtue. Plato contrasts him with the Sophists, however, claiming that he took no fee for his instruction and that his instruction was not a matter of *telling* others the truth but, like the activity of a midwife, of helping others give birth to and critically examine their own ideas.

His method (the **Socratic method**) consisted of asking people questions about matters they presumably knew something about. Socrates would usually begin by asking for a definition of a concept like justice. Once a definition was offered, he analyzed its meaning and critically examined it. If some defect was found, the definition was reformulated to avoid the defect. Then this new definition was critically examined until another defect appeared. The process went on as long as Socrates could keep the other parties talking.

As an example, let's consider the dialogue called *Euthyphro*. Socrates is at the courthouse in Athens because he has been charged with corrupting the youth and inventing new gods. The latter charge amounts to a charge of impiety, and so he is anxious to talk with Euthyphro, who has appeared at the courthouse on his way to prosecute his own father for the impious act of murder. He asks Euthyphro, who claims to be something of an expert in these matters, to define piety. Euthyphro responds by offering his own action of prosecuting his father for murder as an example of piety.

Socrates points out that this is an *example* of piety, but it is not the sort of definition he is seeking. He wants to know the *essential* characteristics of piety.

So Euthyphro tries again and defines piety as whatever is pleasing to the gods. This definition is soon found wanting when Socrates points out that the gods are often pleased by different things. What pleases Zeus does not always please his wife, Hera. So Euthyphro amends his definition. Piety is what is pleasing to *all* the gods. Socrates responds to this reformulation by asking, "Do the gods love piety because it is pious, or is it pious because the gods love it?" What is at issue is whether piety has some intrinsic characteristic that accounts for the fact that the gods love it, or whether the essential trait that determines piety is simply the fact that the gods love it. Euthyphro replies that the gods love piety because it is pious. Then Socrates shows him that he has not yet offered a good definition of piety itself, but only stated an effect of piety—namely that, whatever it is essentially, piety has the effect of pleasing all the gods. So Euthyphro, getting rather upset, offers another definition. This one, too, proves inadequate, but Euthyphro manages to make an excuse and leave before Socrates can drag yet another definition from him and demolish it. The dialogue ends, as so many do, with the issue of what piety is still up in the air. However, progress has been made. We now know more about what piety is not, but no positive, agreed-on definition has been formulated.

This dialogue not only illustrates the Socratic method but also probes the interesting and complex problem of the foundation of ethics. If we substitute the word *good* for the word *piety* and the word *will* for the word *love*, then, following Socrates' lead, we can ask, "Does God will the good because it is good, or is something good because God wills it?" In other words, is moral goodness an independent value, or is it something that depends on something else (like the will or command of God)? Some Jewish, Christian, and Islamic theologians have argued in favor of the divine command theory of ethics. According to this theory, God's command or will makes something morally right. Such a theory implies that the Ten Commandments, for example, are good only because God decreed them. Hence murder is not morally wrong in itself, but only if God should happen to forbid it. However, this sort of theory appears to make morality a matter of divine whim. If God decides to command just the opposite of the Ten Commandments, then this new set of commandments would become morally right. Surely we want to say that there is something intrinsically wrong about certain actions like murder, no matter what God might happen to command.

Socrates got into trouble with the people of Athens and was brought to trial in 399 BCE. Three Athenians—Meletus, Anytus, and Lycon—brought charges. There were 501 citizens on the jury. The image of a famous painting inspired by the eventual death of the philosopher is included in one of the book's color plates. It vividly shows Socrates' conviction as portrayed in the following excerpt. *The Apology*, which you are about to read, is Plato's account of the trial and Socrates' defense. It provides a dramatic statement of why Socrates believed that the pursuit of truth by the critical methods of rational inquiry is the way one should live. However, we should be cautious about interpreting Socrates' views in a purely intellectual way. He was concerned with the pursuit of wisdom and truth through the critical use of reason; there can be no doubt about that. However, this way of living is not unrelated to moral concerns. As he said at one point, his teaching had always been "not to take thought of yourself or your properties, but to care about the improvement of your soul." This "improvement of soul" is not acquired by money but by the practice of virtue. Indeed, he claimed that "from virtue come money and every other good of man, public as well as private."

⊛ READING QUESTIONS

1. What is the main point Socrates made by telling the story about the oracle of Delphi?
2. How did Socrates defend himself against the charge of corrupting the youth and the charge of atheism?
3. Why did Socrates think that fearing death is unwise?
4. At one point Socrates compared himself to a gadfly (horsefly) and the Athenians to a thoroughbred horse. What is the point of this comparison?
5. Why did Socrates not seek a public office?

The Apology

PLATO

Socrates. How you have felt, O men of Athens, hearing the speeches of my accusers, I cannot tell. I know their persuasive words almost made me forget who I was, such was their effect. Yet they hardly spoke a word of truth. But many as their falsehoods were, there was one of them which quite amazed me—I mean when they told you to be on your guard and not let yourselves be deceived by the force of my eloquence. They ought to have been ashamed of saying this, because they were sure to be detected as soon as I opened my lips and displayed my deficiency. They certainly did appear to be most shameless in saying this, unless by the force of eloquence they mean the force of truth; for then I do indeed admit that I am eloquent. But in how different a way from theirs!

Well, as I was saying, they have hardly uttered a word, or not more than a word, of truth. You shall hear from me the whole truth: not, however, delivered in their manner, in an oration ornamented with words and phrases. No, indeed! I shall use the words and arguments which occur to me at the moment. I am certain this is right, and at my time of life I should not appear before you, O men of Athens, in the character of a juvenile orator—let no one expect this of me. And I must beg you to grant me one favor, which is this—if you hear me using the same words in my defense which I have been in the habit of using, and which most of you may have heard in the agora, and at the tables of the money-changers, or anywhere else, I ask you not to be surprised at this, and not to interrupt me. I am more than 70 years of age and this is the first time I have ever appeared in a court of law, and I am a stranger to the ways of this place. Therefore I would have you regard me as if I was really a stranger whom you would excuse if he spoke in his native tongue and after the fashion of his country. That, I think, is not an unfair request. Never mind the way I speak, which may or may not be good, but think only of the justice of my cause, and give heed to that. Let the judge decide justly and the speaker speak truly.

First, I have to reply to the older charges and to my first accusers, and then I will go on to the later ones. I have had many accusers who accused me in the past and their false charges have continued during many years. I am more afraid of them than of Anytus and his associates, who are dangerous, too, in their own way. But far more dangerous are these, who began when you were children, and took possession of your minds with their falsehoods, telling of Socrates, a wise man, who speculated about the heavens above, and searched into the earth beneath, and made the worse argument defeat the better. These are the accusers whom I

The translation is based on Benjamin Jowett's nineteenth-century translation as updated and revised by Christopher Biffle, *A Guided Tour of Five Works by Plato* (Mountain View, CA: Mayfield, 1988), pp. 30–50. Reprinted by permission of Mayfield Publishing Company. Footnotes deleted.

fear because they are the circulators of this rumor and their listeners are too likely to believe that speculators of this sort do not believe in the gods. My accusers are many and their charges against me are of ancient date. They made them in days when you were impressionable—in childhood, or perhaps in youth—and the charges went by unanswered for there was none to answer. Hardest of all, their names I do not know and cannot tell, unless in the chance case of a comic poet. But the main body of these slanderers who from envy and malice have convinced you—and there are some of them who are convinced themselves, and impart their convictions to others—all these, I say, are most difficult to deal with. I cannot have them up here and examine them. Therefore, I must simply fight with shadows in my own defense and examine when there is no one who answers. I will ask you then to assume with me that my opponents are of two kinds: one more recent, the other from the past. I will answer the latter first, for these accusations you heard long before the others, and much more often.

Well, then, I will make my defense, and I will try in the short time allowed to do away with this evil opinion of me which you have held for such a long time. I hope I may succeed, if this be well for you and me, and that my words may find favor with you. But I know to accomplish this is not easy—I see the nature of the task. Let the event be as the gods will; in obedience to the law I make my defense.

I will begin at the beginning and ask what the accusation is which has given rise to this slander of me and which has encouraged Meletus to proceed against me. What do the slanderers say? They shall be my prosecutors and I will sum up their words in an affidavit. "Socrates is an evil-doer and a curious person, who searches into things under the earth and in the heavens. He makes the weaker argument defeat the stronger and he teaches these doctrines to others." That is the nature of the accusation, and that is what you have seen in the comedy of Aristophanes. He introduced a man whom he calls Socrates, going about and saying he can walk in the air, and talking a lot of nonsense concerning matters which I do not pretend to know anything about—however, I mean

to say nothing disparaging of anyone who is a student of such knowledge. should be very sorry if Meletus could add that to my charge. But the simple truth is, O Athenians, I have nothing to do with these studies. Very many of those here are witnesses to the truth of this and to them I appeal. Speak then, you who have heard me, and tell your neighbors whether any of you ever heard me hold forth in few words or in many upon matters of this sort.... You hear their answer. And from what they say you will be able to judge the truth of the rest.

There is the same foundation for the report I am a teacher, and take money; that is no more true than the other. Although, if a man is able to teach, I honor him for being paid. There is Gorgias of Leontium, Prodicus of Ceos, and Hippias of Elis, who go round the cities and are able to persuade young men to leave their own citizens, by whom they might be taught for nothing, and come to them, whom they not only pay but are thankful if they may be allowed to pay them.

There is actually a Parian philosopher residing in Athens who charges fees. I came to hear of him in this way: I met a man who spent a world of money on the sophists, Callias, the son of Hippo-nicus, and knowing he had sons, I asked him: "Callias," I said, "if your two sons were foals or calves, there would be no difficulty in finding someone to raise them. We would hire a trainer of horses, or a farmer probably, who would improve and perfect them in their own proper virtue and excellence. But, as they are human beings, whom are you thinking of placing over them? Is there anyone who understands human and political virtue? You must have thought about this because you have sons. Is there anyone?"

"There is," he said.

"Who is he?" said I. "And of what country? And what does he charge?"

"Evenus the Parian," he replied. "He is the man and his charge is five minae."

Happy is Evenus, I said to myself, if he really has this wisdom and teaches at such a modest charge. Had I the same, I would have been very proud and conceited; but the truth is I have no knowledge like this, O Athenians.

I am sure someone will ask the question, "Why is this, Socrates, and what is the origin of these accusations of you: for there must have been something strange which you have been doing? All this great fame and talk about you would never have come up if you had been like other men. Tell us then, why this is, as we should be sorry to judge you too quickly."

I regard this as a fair challenge, and I will try to explain to you the origin of this name of "wise," and of this evil fame. Please attend then and although some of you may think I am joking, I declare I will tell you the entire truth. Men of Athens, this reputation of mine has come from a certain kind of wisdom which I possess. If you ask me what kind of wisdom, I reply, such wisdom as is attainable by man, for to that extent I am inclined to believe I am wise. Whereas, the persons of whom I was speaking have a superhuman wisdom which I may fail to describe, because I do not have it. He who says I have, speaks false, and slanders me.

O men of Athens, I must beg you not to interrupt me, even if I seem to say something extravagant. For the word which I will speak is not mine. I will refer you to a wisdom which is worthy of credit, and will tell you about my wisdom—whether I have any, and of what sort—and that witness shall be the god of Delphi. You must have known Chaerephon. He was a friend of mine and also a friend of yours, for he shared in the exile of the people and returned with you. Well, Chaerephon, as you know, was very impetuous in all his doings, and he went to Delphi and boldly asked the oracle to tell him whether— as I said, I must beg you not to interrupt—he asked the oracle to tell him whether there was anyone wiser than I was. The Pythian prophetess answered, there was no man wiser. Chaerephon is dead, himself, but his brother, who is in court, will confirm the truth of this story.

Why do I mention this? Because I am going to explain to you why I have such an evil name. When I heard the answer, I said to myself, "What can the god mean and what is the interpretation of this riddle? I know I have no wisdom, great or small. What can he mean when he says I am the wisest of men? And yet he is a god, and cannot lie;

that would be against his nature." After long consideration, I at last thought of a method of answering the question.

I reflected if I could only find a man wiser than myself then I might go to the god with a refutation in my hand. I would say to him, "Here is a man who is wiser than I am, but you said I was the wisest." Accordingly I went to one who had the reputation of wisdom, and observed him—his name I need not mention; he was a politician whom I selected for examination. When I began to talk with him I could not help thinking he was not really wise, although he was thought wise by many, and wiser still by himself. I tried to explain to him that he thought himself wise, but was not really wise. The result was he hated me and his hatred was shared by several who were present who heard me. So I left him, saying to myself, as I went away: "Well, although I do not suppose either of us knows anything really beautiful and good, I am better off than he is—for he knows nothing and thinks that he knows. I neither know nor think that I know. In this latter, then, I seem to have an advantage over him." Then I went to another who had still higher philosophical pretensions and my conclusion was exactly the same. I made another enemy of him and of many others besides him.

After this I went to one man after another, being aware of the anger which I provoked and I lamented and feared this, but necessity was laid upon me. The word of the god, I thought, ought to be considered first. And I said to myself, "I must go to all who appear to know, and find out the meaning of the oracle." And I swear to you Athenians, by the dog, I swear!, the result of my mission was this: I found the men with the highest reputations were all nearly the most foolish and some inferior men were really wiser and better.

I will tell you the tale of my wanderings and of the Herculean labors, as I may call them, which I endured only to find at last the oracle was right. When I left the politicians, I went to the poets: tragic, dithyrambic, and all sorts. There, I said to myself, you will be detected. Now you will find out you are more ignorant than they are. Accordingly, I took them some of the most elaborate passages in their own writings, and asked what was the meaning of them—thinking the poets would teach me something. Will you believe me? I am almost ashamed to say this, but I must say there is hardly a person present who would not have talked better about their poetry than the poets did themselves. That quickly showed me poets do not write poetry by wisdom, but by a sort of inspiration. They are like soothsayers who also say many fine things, but do not understand the meaning of what they say. The poets appeared to me to be much the same and I further observed that upon the strength of their poetry they believed themselves to be the wisest of men in other things in which they were not wise. So I departed, conceiving myself to be superior to them for the same reason I was superior to the politicians.

At last I went to the artisans, because I was conscious I knew nothing at all and I was sure they knew many fine things. In this I was not mistaken, for they did know many things of which I was ignorant, and in this they certainly were wiser than I was. But I observed even the good artisans fell into the same error as the poets. Because they were good workmen, they thought they also knew all sorts of high matters and this defect in them overshadowed their wisdom. Therefore, I asked myself on behalf of the oracle whether I would like to be as I was, having neither their knowledge nor their ignorance, or like them in both. I answered myself and the oracle that I was better off as I was.

This investigation led to my having many enemies of the worst and most dangerous kind and has given rise also to many falsehoods. I am called wise because my listeners always imagine I possess the wisdom which I do not find in others. The truth is, O men of Athens, the gods only are wise and in this oracle they mean to say wisdom of men is little or nothing. They are not speaking of Socrates, only using my name as an illustration, as if they said, "He, O men, is the wisest who, like Socrates, knows his wisdom is in truth worth nothing." And so I go my way, obedient to the gods, and seek wisdom of anyone, whether citizen or stranger, who appears to be wise. If he is not wise, then in support of the oracle I show him he is not wise. This occupation quite absorbs me, and I have no time to give either to any public matter of interest or to any concern of my own, but I am in utter poverty by reason of my devotion to the gods.

There is another thing. Young men of the richer classes, who have little to do, gather around me of their own accord. They like to hear the pretenders examined. They often imitate me and examine others themselves. There are plenty of persons, as they soon enough discover, who think they know something, but really know little or nothing. Then those who are examined by the young men instead of being angry with themselves are angry with me. "This confounded Socrates," they say, "this villainous misleader of youth!" Then if somebody asks them, "Why, what evil does he practice or teach?," they do not know and cannot tell. But so they may not appear ignorant, they repeat the readymade charges which are used against all philosophers about teaching things up in the clouds and under the earth, and having no gods, and making the worse argument defeat the stronger. They do not like to confess their pretense to knowledge has been detected, which it has. They are numerous, ambitious, energetic and are all in battle array and have persuasive tongues. They have filled your ears with their loud and determined slanders. This is the reason why my three accusers, Meletus and Anytus and Lycon, have set upon me. Meletus has a quarrel with me on behalf of the poets, Anytus, on behalf of the craftsmen, Lycon, on behalf of the orators. As I said at the beginning, I cannot expect to get rid of this mass of slander all in a moment.

This, O men of Athens, is the truth and the whole truth. I have concealed nothing. And yet, I know this plainness of speech makes my accusers hate me and what is their hatred but a proof that I am speaking the truth? This is the reason for their slander of me, as you will find out either in this or in any future inquiry.

I have said enough in my defense against the first class of my accusers. I turn to the second class who are headed by Meletus, that good and patriotic man, as he calls himself. Now I will try to defend myself against them: These new accusers must also have their affidavit read. What do they say? Something of this sort: "Socrates is a doer of evil and corrupter of the youth, and he does not believe in the gods of the state. He has other new divinities of his own." That is their charge and now let us examine the particular counts. He says I am a doer of evil, who corrupts the youth but I say, O men of Athens, Meletus is a doer of evil and the evil is that he makes a joke of a serious matter. He is too ready to bring other men to trial from a pretended zeal and interest about matters in which he really never had the smallest interest. And the truth of this I will try to prove to you.

Come here, Meletus, and let me ask a question of you. You think a great deal about the improvement of youth?

Meletus: Yes I do.

Socrates: Tell the judges, then, who is their improver. You must know, as you have taken the pains to discover their corruptor and are accusing me before them. Speak then, and tell the judges who their improver is. Observe, Meletus, that you are silent and have nothing to say. But is this not rather disgraceful and a very great proof of what I was saying, that you have no interest in the matter? Speak up, friend, and tell us who their improver is.

Mel: The laws.

Soc: But that, my good sir, is not my meaning. I want to know who the person is, who, in the first place, knows the laws.

Mel: The jury, Socrates, who are present in court.

Soc: Do you mean to say, Meletus, they are able to instruct and improve youth?

Mel: Certainly they are.

Soc: All of them, or only some and not others?

Mel: All of them.

Soc: By the goddess Hera, that is good news! There are plenty of improvers, then. And what do you say of the audience—do they improve them?

Mel: Yes, they do.

Soc: And the senators?

Mel: Yes, the senators improve them.

Soc: But perhaps the members of the Assembly corrupt them? Or do they too improve them?

Mel: They improve them.

Soc: Then every Athenian improves and elevates them, all with the exception of myself. I alone am their corruptor? Is that what you say?

Mel: Most definitely.

Soc: I am very unfortunate if that is true. But suppose I ask you a question. Would you say that this also holds true in the case of horses? Does one man do them harm and everyone else good? Is not the exact opposite of this true? One man is able to do them good and not the many. The trainer of horses, that is to say, does them good, and others who deal with horses injure them? Is that not true, Meletus, of horses or any other animals? Yes, certainly. Whether you and Anytus say yes or no, that is no matter. Fortunate indeed would be the condition of youth if they had one corruptor only and all the rest of the world were their improvers. You, Meletus, have sufficiently shown you never had a thought about the young. Your carelessness is seen in your not caring about the matters spoken of in this very indictment.

And now, Meletus, I must ask you another question: Which is better, to live among bad citizens or among good ones? Answer, friend, I say, for that is a question which may be easily answered. Do not the good do their neighbors good and the bad do them evil?

Mel: Certainly.

Soc: And is there anyone who would rather be injured than benefited by those who associate with him? Answer, my good friend, the law requires you to answer—does anyone like to be injured?

Mel: Certainly not.

Soc: And when you accuse me of corrupting the youth, do you charge I corrupt them intentionally or unintentionally?

Mel: Intentionally, I say.

Soc: But you just admitted that the good do their neighbors good, and the evil do them evil. Now, is that a truth which your superior wisdom has recognized thus early in life, and am I, at my age, in such ignorance as not to know if a man with whom I associate is corrupted by me, I am very likely to be harmed by him? Yet you say I corrupt him, and intentionally too; of that you will never persuade me or any other human being. But either I do not corrupt them, or I corrupt them unintentionally, so that on either view of the case you lie. If my offense is unintentional, the law does not mention unintentional offenses. You ought to have taken me aside and warned me, because if I had been better advised, I should have stopped doing what I only did unintentionally—no doubt I should. Instead, you hated to talk with me or teach me and you indicted me in this court, which is a place not of instruction, but of punishment.

I have shown, Athenians, as I was saying, Meletus has no care at all, great or small, about the matter. But still I should like to know, Meletus, in what way do I corrupt the young. I suppose you mean, as I infer from your indictment, I teach them not to acknowledge the gods which the state acknowledges, but some other new divinities or spiritual agencies instead. These are the lessons which corrupt the youth, as you say.

Mel: Yes, I say that emphatically.

Soc: Then, by the gods, Meletus, of whom we are speaking, tell me and the court, in somewhat plainer terms, what you mean! I do not understand whether you charge I teach others to acknowledge some gods, and therefore do believe in gods, and am not an entire atheist—but only that they are not the same gods which the city recognizes, or, do you mean to say that I am atheist simply, and a teacher of atheism?

Mel: I mean the latter—that you are a complete atheist.

Soc: That is an extraordinary statement, Meletus. Why do you say that? Do you mean that I do not believe the sun or moon are gods, which is the common belief of all men?

Mel: I assure you, jurymen, he does not believe in them. He says the sun is stone and the moon, earth.

Soc: Friend Meletus, you think you are accusing Anaxagoras and you have a bad opinion of the jury, if you believe they do not know these doctrines are found in the books of Anaxagoras the Clazomenian. These are the doctrines which the youth are said to learn from

Socrates, when these doctrines can be bought in the marketplace. The youth might cheaply purchase them and laugh at Socrates if he pretends to father such eccentricities. And so, Meletus, you really think that I do not believe in any god?

Mel: I swear by Zeus that you absolutely believe in none at all.

Soc: You are a liar, Meletus, not believed even by yourself. I cannot help thinking, O men of Athens, Meletus is reckless and impudent and has written this indictment in a spirit of wantonness and youthful bravado. He has made a riddle, thinking to fool me. He said to himself: "I shall see whether this wise Socrates will discover my ingenious contradiction, or whether I shall be able to deceive him and the rest of them." For he certainly does appear to me to contradict himself in the indictment as much as if he said that Socrates is guilty of not believing in the gods, and yet of believing in them—but this surely is a piece of nonsense.

I should like you, O men of Athens, to join me in examining what I conceive to be his inconsistency and you, Meletus, answer. And I must remind you not to interrupt me if I speak in my accustomed manner.

Did any man, Meletus, ever believe in the existence of human things, and not human beings?... I wish, men of Athens, that he would answer and not be always trying to create an interruption. Did ever any man believe in horsemanship and not in horses? Or in flute playing and not in flute players? No, my friend, I will answer for you and to the court, as you refuse to answer for yourself. There is no man who ever did. But now, please answer the next question. Can a man believe in spiritual and divine activities and not in divine beings?

Mel: He cannot.

Soc: I am glad I have extracted that answer, by the assistance of the court. Nevertheless you swear in the indictment that I teach and believe in divine activities (new or old, no matter for that). At any rate, I believe in divine activities, as you swear in the affidavit, but if I believe in divine activities, I must believe in divine beings. Is that not true? Yes, that is true, for I may assume that your silence gives assent to that. Now what are divine beings?Are they not either gods or the sons of gods? Is that true?

Mel: Yes, that is true.

Soc: But this is just the ingenious riddle of which I was speaking. The divine beings are gods and you say first that I don't believe in gods, and then again that I do believe in gods; that is, if I believe in divine beings. For if the divine beings are the illegitimate sons of gods, whether by the nymphs or by any other mothers, as is thought, that, as all men will agree, necessarily implies the existence of their parents. You might as well affirm the existence of mules, and deny the existence of horses and donkeys. Such nonsense, Meletus, could only have been intended by you as a test of me. You have put this into the indictment because you have no real charge against me. But no one who has a particle of understanding will ever be convinced by you that the same men can believe in divine and superhuman activities, and yet not believe that there are gods and demigods.

I have said enough in answer to the charge of Meletus. Any elaborate defense is unnecessary but, as I was saying before, I certainly have many enemies and this will be my destruction if I am destroyed; of that I am certain—not Meletus, nor Anytus, but the envy and slander of the world, which has been the death of many good men and will probably be the death of many more. I will not be the last of them.

Someone will say: Are you not ashamed, Socrates, of a way of life which is likely to bring you to an untimely end? To him I answer: There you are mistaken, a man who is good for anything should not calculate the chance of living or dying. He should only consider whether in doing anything he is doing right or wrong and acting the part of a good man or of a bad. Whereas, according to your view, the heroes who fell at Troy were not good for much, and the son of Thetis above all, who altogether despised danger in comparison with disgrace. His goddess mother said to him, in

his eagerness to slay Hector, that if he avenged his companion Patroclus, and slew Hector, he would die himself.

"Fate," as she said, "waits upon you next after Hector."

He, hearing this, utterly despised danger and death, and instead of fearing them, feared rather to live in dishonor and not to avenge his friend.

"Let me die next," he replied, "and be avenged of my enemy, rather than stay here by the beaked ships to be mocked and a burden on the earth."

Had Achilles any thought of death and danger? For wherever a man's place is, whether the place which he has chosen or that in which he has been placed by a commander, there he should remain in the hour of danger. He should not consider death or anything else but only disgrace. And this, O men of Athens, is a true saying.

My conduct would be strange, O men of Athens, if I, who was ordered by the generals you chose to command me at Potidaea, Amphipolis, and Delium, remained where they placed me, like any other man facing death, should know when, as I believe, God orders me to fulfil the philosopher's mission of searching into myself and other men, desert my post through fear of death, or any other fear. That would indeed be strange, and I might be justly arraigned in court for denying the existence of the gods, if I disobeyed the oracle because I was afraid of death. Then I should be supposing I was wise when I was not wise.

This fear of death is indeed the imitation of wisdom, and not real wisdom, being the appearance of knowing the unknown. No one knows whether death, which they in their fear believe to be the greatest evil, may not be the greatest good. Is there not here the pretense of knowledge, which is a disgraceful sort of ignorance? This is the point that, as I think, I am superior to men in general and in which I might believe myself wiser than other men. Whereas I know little of the other world, I do not suppose that I know. But I do know that injustice and disobedience to a better, whether god or man, is evil and dishonorable, and I will never fear or avoid a possible good rather than a certain evil. Therefore if you let me go now, reject the advice of Anytus, who said if I were not put to death I should not have been prosecuted, and that if I escape now, your sons will all be utterly ruined by listening to my words. If you say to me, Socrates, this time we will not listen to Anytus and will let you off, but upon one condition, you are not to inquire and speculate in this way any more and if you are caught doing this again you shall die. If this was the condition on which you let me go, I would reply: Men of Athens, I honor and love you but I shall obey the god rather than you. While I have life and strength I shall never cease from practicing and teaching philosophy, exhorting anyone whom I meet in my usual way and convincing him, saying: O my friend, why do you, who are a citizen of the great and wise city of Athens, care so much about laying up the greatest amount of money, honor and reputation, and so little about wisdom, truth and the greatest improvement of the soul, which you never regard or heed at all? Are you not ashamed of this? If the person with whom I am arguing says: Yes, but I do care; I do not depart or let him go at once. I question, examine and cross-examine him, and if I think he has no virtue, but only says he has, I reproach him with undervaluing the greater, and overvaluing the lesser. This I would say to everyone I meet, young and old, citizen and alien, but especially to the citizens, inasmuch as they are my brethren. This is the command of the god, as I would have you know and I believe that to this day no greater good has ever happened in the state than my service to the god.

I do nothing but go about persuading you all, old and young alike, not to take thought of yourself or your properties, but to care about the improvement of your soul. I tell you virtue is not acquired with money, but that from virtue come money and every other good of man, public as well as private. This is my teaching, and if this is the doctrine which corrupts the young, my influence is certainly ruinous. If anyone says this is not my teaching, he is speaking a lie. Therefore, O men of Athens, I say to you, do as Anytus bids or not as Anytus bids, and either acquit me or not; but whatever you do, know that I shall never change my ways, not even if I have to die many times.

Men of Athens, do not interrupt, but hear me. There was an agreement between us that you should hear me out. I think what I am going to say will do you good: for I have something more to say, which you may be inclined to interrupt but I ask you not to do this.

I want you to know if you kill someone like me, you will injure yourselves more than you will injure me. Meletus and Anytus will not injure me. They cannot because it is not possible that a bad man should injure someone better than himself. I do not deny he may, perhaps, kill him, or drive him into exile, or deprive him of civil rights. He may imagine, and others may imagine, he is doing him a great injury but I do not agree with him. The evil of doing as Anytus is doing—of unjustly taking away another man's life is far greater.

Now, Athenians, I am not going to argue for my own sake, as you may think, but for yours, that you may not sin against the gods or lightly reject their favor by condemning me. If you kill me you will not easily find another like me, who, if I may use such a ludicrous figure of speech, am a sort of gadfly given to the State by the gods. The State is like a great and noble steed who is slow in his motions owing to his very size and needs to be stirred into life. I am that gadfly which the gods have given the State and all day long and in all places am always fastening upon you, arousing, persuading, and reproaching you. As you will not easily find another like me, I would advise you to spare me. I believe you may feel irritated at being suddenly awakened when you are caught napping. You may think if you were to strike me dead, as Anytus advises, which you easily might, then you would sleep on for the remainder of your lives, unless the god in his care of you gives you another gadfly. That I am given to you by the god is proved by this: if I had been like other men, I should not have neglected my own concerns all these years, and been occupied with yours, coming to you individually like a father or elder brother, exhorting you to think about virtue. This, I say, would not be like human nature. If I had gained anything, or if my exhortations had been paid, there would be some sense in that; but now, as you see not even my accusers dare to say I have ever sought pay from anyone. They have no witnesses for that. I have a witness of the truth of what I say; my poverty is my witness.

Someone may wonder why I go about in private giving advice and busying myself with the concerns of others, but do not come forward in public and advise the state. I will tell you the reason for this. You have often heard me speak of an oracle or sign which comes to me and is the divinity which Meletus ridicules in the indictment. This sign I have had ever since I was a child. The sign is a voice which comes to me and always forbids me to do something which I am going to do, but never commands me to do anything. This is what stands in the way of my being a politician. And correctly I think. For I am certain, O men of Athens, if I had engaged in politics, I would have perished long ago, and done no good either to you or to myself. Do not be offended at my telling you the truth. The truth is no man who goes to war with you or any other multitude, honestly struggling against acts of unrighteousness in the state, will save his life. He who will really fight for the right, if he would live even for a little while, must have a private station and not a public one.

I can give you proofs of this, not words only, but deeds, which you value more than words. Let me tell you a part of my own life which will prove to you I would never have yielded to injustice from any fear of death, and that if I had not yielded I should have died at once. I will tell you a story—tasteless perhaps and commonplace, but nevertheless true....

The only office of state which I ever held, O men of Athens, was when I served on the council. The clan Antiochis, which is my clan, had the presidency at the trial of the generals who had not taken up the bodies of the slain after the battle of Arginusae. You proposed to try them all together, which was illegal, as you all thought afterwards, but at the time I was the only one of the committee who was opposed to the illegality. I gave my vote against you. When the orators threatened to impeach and arrest me and have me taken away, and you called and shouted, I made up my mind I would run the risk, having law and justice with me, rather than take part in your injustice because I feared imprisonment and

death. This happened in the days of the democracy. But when the oligarchy of the Thirty was in power, they brought me and four others into the rotunda, and told us to bring in Leon from Salamis because they wanted to execute him. This was an example of the sort of commands which they were always giving in order to implicate as many as possible in their crimes. Then I showed, not in word only but in deed, if I may be allowed to use such an expression, I cared not a straw for death, and my only fear was the fear of doing an unrighteous or unholy thing. The strong arm of that oppressive power did not frighten me into doing wrong. When we came out of the rotunda the other four went to Salamis and fetched Leon, but I went quietly home. For this I might have lost my life, had not the power of the Thirty shortly afterwards come to an end. And to this many will witness.

Now do you really imagine I could have survived all these years if I had led a public life, supposing that like a good man I always supported the right and made justice, as I should, the first thing? No indeed, men of Athens, neither I nor any other. I have been always the same in all my actions, public as well as private, and never have yielded to any base agreement with those who are slanderously termed my disciples, or to any other. The truth is I have no regular disciples but if anyone likes to come and hear me while I am pursuing my mission, whether he be young or old, he may freely come. Nor do I converse with those who pay only, and not with those who do not pay; but anyone, whether he be rich or poor, may question and answer me and listen to my words. If he turns out to be a bad man or a good one, I am not responsible, as I never taught him anything. If anyone says he has ever learned or heard anything from me in private which all the world has not heard, I would like you to know that he is lying.

I will be asked, why do people delight in continually conversing with you? I have told you already, Athenians, the whole truth about this. They like to hear the cross-examination of the pretenders to wisdom; there is amusement in this. This is a duty which the gods have imposed upon me, as I am assured by oracles, visions, and in every sort of way which the will of divine power was ever made plain to anyone. This is true, O Athenians or, if not true, would be soon refuted. If I am really corrupting the youth and have corrupted some of them already, those who have grown up and are aware I gave them bad advice in the days of their youth should come forward as accusers and take their revenge. If they do not like to come themselves, some of their relatives, fathers, brothers, or other kinsmen, should say what evil their families suffered at my hands. Now is their time. I see many of them in the court.

There is Crito, who is of the same age and of the same township as myself, and there is Critobulus, his son, whom I also see. There is Lysanias of Sphettus, who is the father of Aeschines—he is present; and also there is Antiphon of Cephisus, who is the father of Epigenes; and there are the brothers of several who have associated with me. There is Nicostratus, the son of Theosdotides, and the brother of Theodotus (not Theodotus himself—he is dead, and therefore, he will not seek to stop him). There is Paralus, the son of Demodocus, who had a brother Theages; and Adeimantus, the son of Ariston, whose brother Plato is present; and Aeantodorus, who is the brother of Apollodorus, whom I also see. I might mention a great many others, any of whom Meletus could have produced as witnesses in the course of his speech. Let him still produce them, if he has forgotten—I will make way for him. Let him speak, if he has any testimony of this sort which he can produce. Nay, Athenians, the very opposite is the truth. For all these are ready to witness on behalf of the corruptor, of the destroyer of their kindred, as Meletus and Anytus call me; not the corrupted youth only—there might have been a motive for that—but their uncorrupted elder relatives. Why should they, too, support me with their testimony? Why indeed, except for the reason of truth and justice, and because they know I am speaking the truth and Meletus is lying.

Well, Athenians, this and similar to this is nearly all the defense I have to offer. Yet a word more. Perhaps there may be someone who is offended by me, when he calls to mind how he himself on a similar, or even a less serious occasion, had recourse to prayers and supplications with many tears, and how he produced his children in court, which was a moving spectacle, together with a group of his relations and friends. I, who am probably in danger of my life, will do none of these things. Perhaps this may come into his mind and he may be set against me, and vote in anger because he is displeased at this. Now if there is such a person among you I reply to him: My friend, I am a man, and like other men, a creature of flesh and blood and not of wood or stone, as Homer says. I have a family, yes, and sons, O Athenians, three in number, one of whom is growing up, and two others who are still young. Yet I will not bring any of them here in order to beg you for an acquittal. And why not? Not from any self-will or disregard of you. Whether I am, or am not, afraid of death is another question, of which I will not now speak. My reason is that I feel such conduct to be discreditable to myself, you and the whole state. One who has reached my years and who has a name for wisdom, whether deserved or not, should not lower himself. The world has decided that Socrates is in some way superior to other men. And if those among you who are said to be superior in wisdom, courage and any other virtue, lower themselves in this way, how shameful is their conduct!

I have seen men of reputation, when they have been condemned, behaving in the strangest manner. They seemed to believe they were going to suffer something dreadful if they died, and they could be immortal if you only allowed them to live. I think they were a dishonor to the state, and any stranger coming in would say the most eminent men of Athens, to whom the Athenians themselves give honor and command, are no better than women. I say these things ought not to be done by those of us who are of reputation; and if they are done, you ought not to permit them. You ought to show you are more inclined to condemn, not the man who is quiet, but the man who gets up a doleful scene and makes the city ridiculous.

Setting aside the question of dishonor, there seems to be something wrong in begging a judge and thus procuring an acquittal instead of informing and convincing him. For his duty is not to make a present of justice, but to give judgment. He has sworn he will judge according to the laws and not according to his own good pleasure. Neither he nor we should get into the habit of perjuring ourselves—there can be no piety in that. Do not require me to do what I consider dishonorable, impious and wrong, especially now, when I am being tried for impiety on the indictment of Meletus. For if, O men of Athens, by force of persuasion and entreaty, I could overpower your oaths, then I should be teaching you to believe there are no gods, and convict myself in my own defense of not believing in them. But that is not the case. I do believe there are gods and in a far higher sense than any of my accusers believe in them. To you and to the gods I commit my cause, to be determined by you as is best for you and me.

(The jury returns a guilty verdict and Meletus proposes death as a punishment.)

There are many reasons why I am not grieved, O men of Athens, at the vote of condemnation. I expected this and am only surprised the votes are so nearly equal. I thought the majority against me would have been far larger, but now, had thirty votes gone over to the other side, I would have been acquitted. And I may say I have escaped Meletus' charges. And I may say more; without the assistance of Anytus and Lycon, he would not have had a fifth part of the votes, as the law requires, in which case he would have incurred a fine of a thousand drachmae.

He proposes death as the penalty. What shall I propose on my part, O men of Athens? Clearly what is my due. What is that which I ought to pay or to receive? What shall be done to the man who has never been idle during his whole life, but has been careless of what the many care about— wealth, family interests, military offices and speaking in the Assembly, and courts, plots, and parties. Believing I was really too honest a man to follow in this way and live, I did not go where I could do no good to you or to myself. I went where I could do the greatest good privately to every one of you. I sought to persuade every man among you that he must look to himself and seek virtue and wisdom before he looks to his private interests, and look to the welfare of the State before he looks to the wealth of the State. This should be the order which he observes in all his actions. What shall be done to someone like me? Doubtless some good thing, O men of Athens, if he has his reward and the good should be suitable to him. What would be a reward suitable to a poor man who is your benefactor, who desires to instruct you? There can be no more fitting reward than maintenance in the Prytaneum, O men of Athens, a reward which he deserves far more than the citizen who wins the prize at Olympia in the horse or chariot race, whether the chariots were drawn by two horses or many. For I am in need and he has enough. He only gives you the appearance of happiness and I give you the reality. Thus, if I am to estimate the penalty justly, I say maintenance in the Prytaneum is just.

Perhaps you think I am mocking you in saying this, as in what I said before about the tears and prayers. But that is not the case. I speak because I am convinced I never intentionally wronged anyone, although I cannot convince you of that—for we have had a short conversation only. If there were a law at Athens, such as there is in other cities, that a case involving the death penalty should not be decided in one day, then I believe I would have convinced you. Now the time is too short. I cannot quickly refute great slanders and, as I am convinced that I never wronged another, I will assuredly not wrong myself. I will not say of myself that I deserve any evil, nor propose any penalty. Why should I? Because I am afraid of the penalty of death which Meletus proposes? When I do not know whether death is a good or an evil, why should I propose a penalty which would certainly be an evil? Shall I say imprisonment? And why should I live in prison, and be the slave of the judges of the year—of the Eleven? Or shall the penalty be a fine, and imprisonment until the fine is paid? There is the same objection. I should have to stay in prison for I have no money and cannot pay. And if I say exile, and this may be the penalty which you will affix, I must indeed be blinded by love of life, if I do not realize that you, who are my own citizens, cannot endure my words and have found them so hateful you want to silence them, others are likely to endure me. No indeed, men of Athens, that is not very likely. And what a life should I lead, at my age, wandering from city to city, living in ever-changing exile and always being driven out! For I am quite sure that whatever place I go, the young men will come to me. If I drive them away, their elders will drive me out. And, if I let them come, their fathers and friends will drive me out for their sakes.

Someone will say: Yes, Socrates, but can you not hold your tongue, and then go into a foreign city, and no one will interfere with you? Now I have great difficulty in making you understand my answer to this. If I tell you this would be a disobedience to a divine command, and therefore I cannot hold my tongue, you will not believe I am serious. If I say again that greatest good is daily to converse about virtue, and all that concerning which you hear me examining myself and others, and that the life which is unexamined is not worth living—that you are still less likely to believe. And yet what I say is true, although it is hard for me to persuade you. Moreover, I am not accustomed to thinking I deserve any punishment. Had I money I might have proposed to give you what I had and would have been none the worse. But you see I have none and can only ask you to proportion the fine to my means. However, I think I could afford a mina, and therefore I propose that penalty. Plato, Crito, Critobulus, and Apollodorus, my friends here, bid me say 30 minae and they will pay the fine. Well, then, say 30 minae, let that be the penalty for that they will be ample security to you.

(*The jury votes again to decide between Socrates' proposal of a fine and Meletus' proposal of the death penalty. The verdict is death.*)

Not much time will be gained, O Athenians, in return for the evil name you will get from the enemies of the city, who will say you killed Socrates, a wise man. They will call me wise even though I am not wise when they want to reproach you. If you waited a little while, your desire would have been fulfilled in the course of nature. I am far advanced in years, as you may perceive, and not far from death. I am speaking now only to those of you who have condemned me to death. And I have another thing to say to them: You think I was convicted through deficiency of words—I mean, if I had thought fit to leave nothing undone, nothing unsaid, I might have gained an acquittal. Not so, the deficiency which led to my conviction was not of words—certainly not. I did not have the boldness or impudence or inclination to address you as you would have liked me to address you, weeping, wailing, and lamenting, and saying and doing many things which you have been accustomed to hear from others, and which, as I say, are unworthy of me. I believed I should not do anything common or cowardly in the hour of danger. I do not now repent the manner of my defense. I would rather die having spoken after my manner than speak in your manner and live. Neither in war nor yet at law ought any man to use every way of escaping death. Often in battle there is no doubt if a man will throw away his arms and fall on his knees before his pursuers, he may escape death. In other dangers there are other ways of escaping death, if a man is willing to say and do anything.

The difficulty, my friends, is not in avoiding death, but in avoiding evil; for evil runs faster than death. I am old and move slowly, and the slower runner has overtaken me, and my accusers are keen and quick, and the faster runner, who is evil, has overtaken them. And now I depart hence condemned by you to suffer the penalty of death, and they, too, go their ways condemned by the truth to suffer the penalty of wickedness. I must abide by my award—let them abide by theirs. I suppose these things may be regarded as fated—and I think things are as they should be.

And now, O men who have condemned me, I would prophesy to you. I am about to die and that is the hour in which men are gifted with prophetic power. I prophesy to you who are my murderers that, immediately after my death, punishment far heavier than you have inflicted on me will await you. You have killed me because you wanted to escape the accuser, and not to give an account of your lives. That will not be as you suppose. I say there will be more accusers of you than there are now, accusers I have restrained: and as they are younger they will be more severe with you and you will be more offended at them. For if you

As the Chapter 1 introduction to *Reading Philosophy* suggests, we might identify with Alice in her voyage through Wonderland as we discover philosophy. Like Alice pursuing the rabbit, we follow the often strange path the great philosophers pioneered. Where do we want our own wonder to take us? What questions do we want answered? Or what questions do we even want to ask?

Craftsman making a Wheel of Dharma in Xining, China. This wheel has eight spokes, which represent the Eightfold Path described in the Chapter 3 excerpt, *The Fourth Noble Truth* by Walpola Rahula. Why do you think the Eightfold Path is represented as a wheel?

Tahrir Square recently was the central site of an eighteen-day protest to oust Egypt's President Mubarak. How do such recent and ongoing protests in some Islamic countries help (or not) the case that Khaled Abou El Fadl makes in Chapter 5's *Islam and Democracy*?

If you apply the argument that Khaled Abou El Fadl makes in Chapter 5's *Islam and Democracy*, what case can you make about what women's social position and rights ought to or might be in a democratic Islamic society?

think that by killing men you can avoid the accuser censuring your lives, you are mistaken; that is not a way of escape which is either possible or honorable. The easiest, noblest way is not to be crushing others but to be improving yourselves. This is the prophecy which I utter before my departure to the members of the jury who have condemned me.

Friends, who have acquitted me, I would like also to talk with you about this thing which has happened, while the judges are busy, and before I go to the place where I must die. Stay awhile, for we may as well talk with one another while there is time. You are my friends and I would like to show you the meaning of this event which has happened to me. O my judges—for you I may truly call judges—I should like to tell you of a wonderful occurrence. Before this, the familiar oracle within me has constantly been in the habit of opposing me even about trifles, if I was going to make a slip or error about anything. Now, as you see there has come upon me that which may be thought, and is generally believed to be, the last and worst evil. But the oracle made no sign of opposition, either as I was leaving my house and going out in the morning, or when I was going up into this court, or while I was speaking at anything I was going to say. I have often been stopped in the middle of a speech, but now in nothing I either said or did has the oracle opposed me. Why is this? I will tell you. I regard this as a proof that what has happened to me is a good, and that those of us who think that death is an evil are in error. This is a great proof to me of what I am saying, for the customary sign would surely have opposed me had I been going to evil and not to good.

Let us reflect in another way, and we shall see there is great reason to hope that death is a good. Either death is a state of nothingness and utter unconsciousness, or, as men say, there is a change and migration of the soul from this world to another. Now if you suppose there is no consciousness, but a sleep like the sleep of him who is undisturbed even by the sight of dreams, death will be an unspeakable gain. If a person were to select the night in which his sleep was undisturbed even by dreams and were to compare this with the other days and nights of his life, and then were to tell

us how many days and nights he passed in the course of his life better and more pleasantly than this one, I think any man, even a great king, will not find many such days or nights, when compared with the others. Now if death is like this, I say to die is to gain, for eternity is then only a single night. But if death is the journey to another place, and there, as men say, all the dead are, what good, O my friends and judges, can be greater than this? If indeed when the traveler arrives in the other world, he is delivered from the false judges in this world, and finds the true judges who are said to give judgment there, Minos, Rhadamanthus, Aeacus, and Triptolemus, and other sons of the gods who were righteous in their own life, that journey will be worth making. What would a man give if he might converse with Orpheus and Masaeus and Hesiod and Homer? Nay, if this is true, let me die again and again. I, too, shall have a wonderful interest in a place where I can converse with Palamedes, and Ajax, the son of Telamon, and other heroes of old who have suffered death through an unjust judgment. I think there will be pleasure, in comparing my own sufferings with theirs. Above all, I shall be able to continue my search into true and false knowledge. As in this world, so also in that; I shall find out who is wise, and who pretends to be wise but is not. What would a man give, O judges, to be able to examine the leader of the great Trojan expedition; or Odysseus or Sisyphus, or numberless others, men and women too! What infinite delight would there be in conversing with them and asking them questions! For in that world they do not put a man to death for such investigations, certainly not. For besides being happier in that world than in this, they will be immortal, if what is said is true.

Wherefore, O judges, be of good cheer about death, and know this truth—no evil can happen to a good man, either in life or after death. He and his are not neglected by the gods nor has my own approaching end happened by mere chance. I see clearly that to die and be released was better for me and therefore the oracle gave no sign. Because of this also, I am not angry with my accusers or my condemners. They have done me no harm, although neither of them meant to do me any good; and for this I gently blame them.

Still I have a favor to ask of them. When my sons are grown up, I would ask you, O my friends, to punish them. I would have you trouble them, as I troubled you, if they seem to care about riches, or anything, more than virtue. Or, if they pretend to be something when they are really nothing, then chastise them, as I chastised you, for not caring about what they ought to care, and thinking they are something when they are really nothing. And if you do this, I and my sons will have received justice at your hands. The hour of departure has arrived, and we go on our different ways—I to die, and you to live. Which is better only the god knows.

CRITICAL QUESTIONS

1. Socrates asserted that the unexamined life is not worth living. Imagine living your life using the Socratic method to examine your own beliefs and actions as well as the beliefs and actions of others. Would this be a good way to live? Why, or why not?

2. What are some basic assumptions made by Socrates in his response to the verdict of death?

3. What is one basic difference between Socrates' views of the good life and Buddha's? Support your answer with an argument.

3.5 ARISTOTLE ON HAPPINESS AND THE LIFE OF MODERATION

Aristotle (384–322 BCE) was a student of Plato and is recognized, along with Plato, as one of the greatest philosophic minds of the ancient Western world. He made significant contributions to all areas of philosophy, as well as to the natural sciences. He founded a school in Athens called the Lyceum. His students became known as the Peripatetics (which means "to walk around") because of his habit of strolling in the garden of the school while giving instruction.

Aristotle was from Macedonia and, while living there, tutored Alexander, the son of the king. Alexander the Great, as he was later called, established a vast empire. Legend has it that as he traveled toward India on his conquests, Alexander sent plant and animal specimens back to Aristotle. Alexander's death in 323 triggered anti-Macedonian sentiment in Athens. Realizing that his life might be in danger, Aristotle left in a hurry and, recalling what happened to Socrates, reputedly made the comment that he was leaving lest he provide an opportunity for the Athenians to "sin twice against philosophy."

Aristotle was a **teleologist**. He believed that all existing things have a purpose (in Greek the word for "end," "goal," or "purpose" is *telos*) and that their purpose constitutes their good. So, when seeking to answer the question "How should one live?" Aristotle naturally considered the issue of what is the good for humans. Notice he did not ask what is his good. He was not concerned with individual good but with the good for all humans. He called this good **eudaimonia**, which is here translated as "happiness." This translation is somewhat misleading because in English happiness refers to a feeling. For Aristotle happiness was more than a feeling; it was also a way of acting and living. Hence, some have translated it as human "flourishing." Since flourishing involves achieving excellence, any discussion of *eudaimonia* or human flourishing must pay attention to the notion of virtue.

The word *virtue* (*areté* in Greek) refers to an excellence. The excellence of a thing is the full development of the potentials of its essential nature. Because the human animal is essentially a "rational" animal according to Aristotle, the good for humans must involve the realization of their rational natures.

Reading Aristotle will test your reading skills. He is not easy to read, in part because you are reading the translation of lecture notes edited by someone else. However, he is also dealing with issues about how to live at a profound level, and one must get into his mind, so to speak, in order to follow his line of reasoning. The effort will, however, be repaid as you learn to think about the issue of how to conduct one's life at a deeper level.

Be sure to activate your "I-don't-understand" list and go over it with a classmate or in class for clarification.

◉ READING QUESTIONS

1. What, according to Aristotle, have others declared to be the good, and why? Why must the chief good be desired for its own sake?

2. Aristotle said that on a very abstract level, happiness can be considered as "living well and doing well." If so, the next question becomes, "Of what, specifically, does this consist?" Aristotle argued that what ever it is it must be something final, chosen for its own sake, self-sufficient, and an end of action. If this is so, why will not health or wealth or pleasure or honor (all of which are goods) count as the chief good or happiness?

3. How did Aristotle arrive at the conclusion that the human good (happiness) is an activity of soul in accordance with virtue? (*Hint:* His argument begins with the notion that human beings have a function.)

4. What are the two kinds of virtue, and do the moral virtues arise by nature (are we born with them?) or by learning and practice?

5. State in your own words what Aristotle meant when he claimed "Virtue, then, is a state of character concerned with choice, lying in a mean, i.e., the mean relative to us, this being determined by a rational principle, and by that principle by which the man of practical wisdom would determine it."

6. What are the excesses, deficiencies, and the means with respect to (a) feelings of fear and confidence, (b) giving and taking of money, (c) honor and dishonor, and (d) anger?

7. In Book II, Section 9, Aristotle gave some advice for those who wish to practice virtue (hit the mean). Summarize his advice.

Nicomachean Ethics

ARISTOTLE

BOOK I

1.

Every art and every inquiry, and similarly every action and pursuit, is thought to aim at some good; and for this reason the good has rightly been declared to be that at which all things aim. But a certain difference is found among ends; some are activities, others are products apart from the activities that produce them. Where there are ends apart from the actions, it is the nature of the products to be better than the activities. Now, as there are many actions, arts, and sciences, their ends also are many; the end of the medical art is health, that of shipbuilding a vessel, that of strategy victory, that of economics wealth. But where such arts fall under a single capacity—as bridlemaking and the other arts concerned with the equipment of horses fall under the art of riding, and this and every military action under strategy, in the same way other arts fall under yet others—in all of these the ends of the master

Reprinted from *Nicomachean Ethics*, translated by W. D. Ross (1925), Oxford University Press. Footnotes deleted.

arts are to be preferred to all the subordinate ends; for it is for the sake of the former that the latter are pursued. It makes no difference whether the activities themselves are the ends of the actions, or something else apart from the activities, as in the case of the sciences just mentioned.

2.

If, then, there is some end of the things we do, which we desire for its own sake (everything else being desired for the sake of this), and if we do not choose everything for the sake of something else (for at that rate the process would go on to infinity, so that our desire would be empty and vain), clearly this must be the good and the chief good. Will not the knowledge of it, then, have a great influence on life? Shall we not, like archers who have a mark to aim at, be more likely to hit upon what is right? If so, we must try, in outline at least to determine what it is, and of which of the sciences or capacities it is the object....

4.

Let us resume our inquiry and state, in view of the fact that all knowledge and every pursuit aims at some good, ... what is the highest of all goods achievable by action. Verbally there is very general agreement; for both the general run of men and people of superior refinement say that it is happiness, and identify living well and doing well with being happy; but with regard to what happiness is they differ, and the many do not give the same account as the wise. For the former think it is some plain and obvious thing, like pleasure, wealth, or honour; they differ, however, from one another—and often even the same man identifies it with different things, with health when he is ill, with wealth when he is poor; but, conscious of their ignorance, they admire those who proclaim some great ideal that is above their comprehension. Now some thought that apart from these many goods there is another which is self-subsistent and causes the goodness of all these as well. To examine all the opinions that have been held would no doubt be somewhat fruitless; it is enough to examine those that are most prevalent or that seem to have some reason in their favour....

5.

Let us, however, resume our discussion from the point at which we digressed. To judge from the lives that men lead, most men, and men of the most vulgar type, seem (not without some ground) to identify the good, or happiness, with pleasure; which is the reason why they love the life of enjoyment. For there are, we may say, three prominent types of life—that just mentioned, the political, and thirdly the contemplative life. Now the mass of mankind are evidently quite slavish in their tastes, preferring a life suitable to beasts, but they get some ground for their view from the fact that many of those in high places share the tastes of Sardanapallus. A consideration of the prominent types of life shows that people of superior refinement and of active disposition identify happiness with honour; for this is, roughly speaking, the end of the political life. But it seems too superficial to be what we are looking for, since it is thought to depend on those who bestow honour rather than on him who receives it, but the good we divine to be something proper to a man and not easily taken from him. Further, men seem to pursue honour in order that they may be assured of their goodness; at least it is by men of practical wisdom that they seek to be honoured, and among those who know them, and on the ground of their virtue; clearly, then, according to them, at any rate, virtue is better. And perhaps one might even suppose this to be, rather than honour, the end of the political life. But even this appears somewhat incomplete; for possession of virtue seems actually compatible with being asleep, or with life-long inactivity, and, further, with the greatest sufferings and misfortunes; but a man who was living so no one would call happy, unless he were maintaining a thesis at all costs. But enough of this; for the subject has been sufficiently treated even in the current discussions. Third comes the contemplative life, which we shall consider later. The life of money-making is one undertaken under compulsion, and wealth is evidently not the good we are seeking; for it is merely useful and for the sake of something else. And so one might rather take the aforenamed objects to be ends; for they are loved for themselves. But it is evident that not even these are ends; yet many arguments have been thrown away in support of them. Let us leave this subject, then....

7.

Let us again return to the good we are seeking, and ask what it can be. It seems different in different actions and arts; it is different in medicine, in strategy, and in the other arts likewise. What then is the good of each? Surely that for whose sake everything else is done. In medicine this is health, in strategy victory, in architecture a house, in any other sphere something else, and in every action and pursuit the end; for it is for the sake of this that all men do whatever else they do. Therefore, if there is an end for all that we do, this will be the good achievable by action, and if there are more than one, these will be the goods achievable by action.

So the argument has by a different course reached the same point; but we must try to state this even more clearly. Since there are evidently more than one end, and we choose some of these (e.g., wealth, flutes, and in general instruments) for the sake of something else, clearly not all ends are final ends; but the chief good is evidently something final. Therefore, if there is only one final end, this will be what we are seeking, and if there are more than one, the most final of these will be what we are seeking. Now we call that which is in itself worthy of pursuit more final than that which is worthy of pursuit for the sake of something else, and that which is never desirable for the sake of something else more final than the things that are desirable both in themselves and for the sake of that other thing, and therefore we call final without qualification that which is always desirable in itself and never for the sake of something else.

Now such a thing happiness, above all else, is held to be; for this we choose always for itself and never for the sake of something else, but honour, pleasure, reason, and every virtue we choose indeed for themselves (for if nothing resulted from them we should still choose each of them), but we choose them also for the sake of happiness, judging that by means of them we shall be happy.

Happiness, on the other hand, no one chooses for the sake of these, nor, in general, for anything other than itself....

[T]he self-sufficient we now define as that which when isolated makes life desirable and lacking in nothing; and such we think happiness to be; and further we think it most desirable of all things, without being counted as one good thing among others—if it were so counted it would clearly be made more desirable by the addition of even the least of goods; for that which is added becomes an excess of goods, and of goods the greater is always more desirable. Happiness, then, is something final and self-sufficient, and is the end of action.

Presumably, however, to say that happiness is the chief good seems a platitude, and a clearer account of what it is is still desired. This might perhaps be given, if we could first ascertain the function of man. For just as for a flute-player, a sculptor, or any artist, and, in general, for all things that have a function or activity, the good and the "well" is thought to reside in the function, so would it seem to be for man, if he has a function. Have the carpenter, then, and the tanner certain functions or activities, and has man none? Is he born without a function? Or as eye, hand, foot, and in general each of the parts evidently has a function, may one lay it down that man similarly has a function apart from all these? What then can this be? Life seems to be common even to plants, but we are seeking what is peculiar to man. Let us exclude, therefore, the life of nutrition and growth. Next there would be a life of perception, but it also seems to be common even to the horse, the ox, and every animal. There remains, then, an active life of the element that has a rational principle; of this, one part has such a principle in the sense of being obedient to one, the other in the sense of possessing one and exercising thought. And, as "life of the rational element" also has two meanings, we must state that life in the sense of activity is what we mean; for this seems to be the more proper sense of the term. Now if the function of man is an activity of soul which follows or implies a rational principle, and if we say "a so-and-so" and "a good so-and-so" have a function which is the same in kind, e.g., a lyre-player and a good lyre-player, and so without qualification in all cases, eminence in respect of goodness being added to the name of the function (for the function of a lyre-player is to play the lyre, and that of a good lyre-player is to do so well): if this is the case, [and we state the function of man to be a certain kind of life, and this to be an activity or actions of the soul implying a rational principle, and the function of a good man to be the good and noble performance of these, and if any action is well performed when it is performed in accordance with the appropriate excellence: if this is the case,] human good turns out to be activity of soul in accordance with virtue, and if there are more than one virtue, in accordance with the best and most complete.

But we must add "in a complete life." For one swallow does not make a summer, nor does one day; and so too one day, or a short time, does not make a man blessed and happy....

[*Editor's Note*: In Section 8, here omitted, Aristotle compares his view of happiness as living well and doing well with what most people say. He finds that many who have expressed their views on this topic agree in general with his own views. He takes this as confirmation that he is on the right track. Many regard happiness as consisting of three kinds of goods: worldly goods, bodily goods, and goods of the soul. While Aristotle wishes to stress in his account that happiness resides primarily in goods of the soul (the virtues), he acknowledges that we are not likely to call someone happy if they lack entirely worldly goods (wealth, friends, political influence) and bodily goods (noble family, handsome appearance, long life, and children). But both worldly goods and bodily goods often depend on circumstances beyond one's control. Can one be happy, even if misfortune diminishes some worldly and bodily goods? Some would say that happiness depends on good fortune. Others that it is a matter of acquiring virtue or excellence.]

13.

Since happiness is an activity of soul in accordance with perfect virtue, we must consider the nature of virtue; for perhaps we shall thus see better the nature of happiness....

BOOK II

1.

Virtue, then, being of two kinds, intellectual and moral, intellectual virtue in the main owes both its birth and its growth to teaching (for which reason it requires experience and time), while moral virtue comes about as a result of habit, whence also its name *ethiké* is one that is formed by a slight variation from the word *ethos* (habit). From this it is also plain that none of the moral virtues arises in us by nature; for nothing that exists by nature can form a habit contrary to its nature. For instance the stone which by nature moves downwards cannot be habituated to move upwards, not even if one tries to train it by throwing it up ten thousand times; nor can fire be habituated to move downwards, nor can anything else that by nature behaves in one way be trained to behave in another. Neither by nature, then, nor contrary to nature do the virtues arise in us; rather we are adapted by nature to receive them, and are made perfect by habit....

5.

Next we must consider what virtue is. Since things that are found in the soul are of three kinds—passions, faculties, states of character, virtue must be one of these. By passions I mean appetite, anger, fear, confidence, envy, joy, friendly feeling, hatred, longing, emulation, pity, and in general the feelings that are accompanied by pleasure or pain; by faculties the things in virtue of which we are said to be capable of feeling these, e.g., of becoming angry or being pained or feeling pity; by states of character the things in virtue of which we stand well or badly with reference to the passions, e.g., with reference to anger we stand badly if we feel it violently or too weakly, and well if we feel it moderately; and similarly with reference to the other passions.

Now neither the virtues nor the vices are *passions*, because we are not called good or bad on the ground of our passions, but are so called on the ground of our virtues and our vices, and because we are neither praised nor blamed for our passions (for the man who feels fear or anger is not praised, nor is the man who simply feels anger blamed, but the man who feels it in a certain way), but for our virtues and our vices we are praised or blamed.

Again, we feel anger and fear without choice, but the virtues are modes of choice or involve choice. Further, in respect of the passions we are said to be moved, but in respect of the virtues and the vices we are said not to be moved but to be disposed in a particular way.

For these reasons also they are not *faculties*; for we are neither called good nor bad, nor praised nor blamed, for the simple capacity of feeling the passions; again, we have the faculties by nature, but we are not made good or bad by nature; we have spoken of this before.

If, then, the virtues are neither passions nor faculties, all that remains is that they should be *states of character*.

Thus we have stated what virtue is in respect of its genus.

6.

We must, however, not only describe virtue as a state of character, but also say what sort of state it is. We may remark, then, that every virtue or excellence both brings into good condition the thing of which it is the excellence and makes the work of that thing be done well; e.g., the excellence of the eye makes both the eye and its work good; for it is by the excellence of the eye that we see well. Similarly the excellence of the horse makes a horse both good in itself and good at running and at carrying its rider and at awaiting the attack of the enemy. Therefore, if this is true in every case, the virtue of man also will be the state of character which makes a man good and which makes him do his own work well.

How this is to happen we have stated already, but it will be made plain also by the following consideration of the specific nature of virtue. In everything that is continuous and divisible it is possible to take more, less, or an equal amount, and that either in terms of the thing itself or relative to us; and the equal is an intermediate between excess and defect. By the intermediate in the object I mean that which is equidistant from each of the extremes, which is one and the same for all men; by the intermediate relative to us that which is neither too much nor too little—and this is not one, nor the same for all. For instance, if ten is many and two is few, six is the intermediate, taken in terms of the object; for it exceeds and is exceeded by an equal amount; this is intermediate according to arithmetical proportion. But the intermediate relative to us is not to be taken so; if ten pounds are too much for a particular person to eat and two too little, it does not follow that the trainer will order six pounds; for this also is perhaps too much for the person who is to take it, or too little—too little for Milo, too much for the beginner in athletic exercises. The same is true of running and wrestling. Thus a master of any art avoids excess and defect, but seeks the intermediate and chooses this—the intermediate not in the object but relative to us. If it is thus, then, that every art does its work well—by looking to the intermediate and judging its works by this standard (so that we often say of good works of art that it is not possible either to take away or to add anything, implying that excess and defect destroy the goodness of works of art, while the mean preserves it; and good artists, as we say, look to this in their work), and if, further, virtue is more exact and better than any art, as nature also is, then virtue must have the quality of aiming at the intermediate. I mean moral virtue; for it is this that is concerned with passions and actions, and in these there is excess, defect, and the intermediate. For instance, both fear and confidence and appetite and anger and pity and in general pleasure and pain may be felt both too much and too little, and in both cases not well; but to feel them at the right times, with reference to the right objects, towards the right people, with the right motive, and in the right way, is what is both intermediate and best, and this is characteristic of virtue. Similarly with regard to actions also there is excess, defect, and the intermediate. Now virtue is concerned with passions and actions, in which excess is a form of failure, and so is defect, while the intermediate is praised and is a form of success; and being praised and being successful are both characteristics of virtue. Therefore virtue is a kind of mean, since, as we have seen, it aims at what is intermediate.

Again, it is possible to fail in many ways (for evil belongs to the class of the unlimited, as the Pythagoreans conjectured, and good to that of the limited), while to succeed is possible only in one way (for which reason also one is easy and the other difficult—to miss the mark easy, to hit it difficult); for these reasons also, then, excess and defect are characteristic of vice, and the mean of virtue;

> For men are good in but one way, but bad in many.

Virtue, then, is a state of character concerned with choice, lying in a mean, i.e., the mean relative to us, this being determined by a rational principle, and by that principle by which the man of practical wisdom would determine it. Now it is a mean between two vices, that which depends on excess and that which depends on defect; and again it is a mean because the vices respectively fall short of or exceed what is right in both passions and actions, while virtue both finds and chooses that which is intermediate. Hence in respect of its substance and the definition which states its essence virtue is a mean, with regard to what is best and right an extreme.

But not every action nor every passion admits of a mean; for some have names that already imply badness, e.g., spite, shamelessness, envy, and in the case of actions adultery, theft, murder; for all of these and suchlike things imply by their names that they are themselves bad, and not the excesses or deficiencies of them. It is not possible, then, ever to be right with regard to them; one must always be wrong. Nor does goodness or badness with regard to such things depend on committing adultery with the right woman, at the right time, and in the right way, but simply to do any of them is to go wrong. It would be equally absurd, then, to expect that in unjust, cowardly, and voluptuous action there should be a mean, an excess, and a deficiency; for at that rate there would be a mean of excess and of deficiency, an excess of excess, and a deficiency of deficiency. But as there is no excess and deficiency of temperance and courage because what is intermediate is in a sense an extreme, so too of the actions we have mentioned there is no mean nor any excess and deficiency, but however they are done they are wrong; for in general there is neither a mean of excess and deficiency, nor excess and deficiency of a mean.

7.

We must, however, not only make this general statement, but also apply it to the individual facts. For among statements about conduct those which are general apply more widely, but those which are particular are more genuine, since conduct has to do with individual cases, and our statements must harmonize with the facts in these cases. We may take these cases from our table. With regard to feelings of fear and confidence courage is the mean; of the people who exceed, he who exceeds in fearlessness has no name (many of the states have no name), while the man who exceeds in confidence is rash, and he who exceeds in fear and falls short in confidence is a coward. With regard to pleasures and pains—not all of them, and not so much with regard to the pains—the mean is temperance, the excess self-indulgence. Persons deficient with regard to the pleasures are not often found; hence such persons also have received no name. But let us call them "insensible."

With regard to giving and taking of money, the mean is liberality, the excess and the defect prodigality and meanness. In these actions people exceed and fall short in contrary ways; the prodigal exceeds in spending and falls short in taking, while the mean man exceeds in taking and falls short in spending. (At present we are giving a mere outline or summary, and are satisfied with this; later these states will be more exactly determined.) With regard to money there are also other dispositions—a mean, magnificence (for the magnificent man differs from the liberal man; the former deals with large sums, the latter with small ones), and excess, tastelessness and vulgarity, and a deficiency, niggardliness; these differ from the states opposed to liberality, and the mode of their difference will be stated later.

With regard to honour and dishonour the mean is proper pride, the excess is known as a sort of "empty vanity," and the deficiency is undue humility; and as we said liberality was related to magnificence, differing from it by dealing with small sums, so there is a state similarly related to proper pride, being concerned with small honours while that is concerned with great. For it is possible to desire honour as one ought, and more than one ought, and less, and the man who exceeds in his desires is called ambitious, the man who falls short unambitious, while the intermediate person has no name. The dispositions also are nameless, except that that of the ambitious man is called ambition. Hence the people who are at the extremes lay claim to the middle place; and we ourselves sometimes call the intermediate person ambitious and sometimes unambitious, and sometimes praise the ambitious man and sometimes the unambitious. The reason of our doing this will be stated in what follows; but now let us speak of the remaining states according to the method which has been indicated.

With regard to anger also there is an excess, a deficiency, and a mean. Although they can scarcely be said to have names, yet since we call the intermediate person good-tempered let us call the mean good temper; of the persons at the extremes let the one who exceeds be called irascible, and his vice irascibility, and the man who falls short an inirascible sort of person, and the deficiency inirascibility....

9.

That moral virtue is a mean, then, and in what sense it is so, and that it is a mean between two vices, the one involving excess, the other deficiency, and that it is such because its character is to aim at what is intermediate in passions and in actions, has been sufficiently stated. Hence also it is no easy task to be good. For in everything it is no easy task to find the middle, e.g., to find the middle of a circle is not for everyone but for him who knows; so, too, any one can get angry—that is easy—or give or spend money; but to do this to the right person, to the right extent, at the right time, with the right motive, and in the right way, *that* is not for everyone, nor is it easy; wherefore goodness is both rare and laudable and noble. Hence he who aims at the intermediate must first depart from what is the more contrary to it, as Calypso advises—

Hold the ship out beyond that surf and spray.

For of the extremes one is more erroneous, one less so; therefore, since to hit the mean is hard in the extreme, we must as a second best, as people say, take the least of the evils; and this will be done best in the way we describe.

But we must consider the things towards which we ourselves also are easily carried away; for some of us tend to one thing, some to another; and this will be recognizable from the pleasure and the pain we feel. We must drag ourselves away to the contrary extreme; for we shall get into the intermediate state by drawing well away from error, as people do in straightening sticks that are bent....

CRITICAL QUESTIONS

1. Why did Aristotle conclude that virtue must be a state of character and do you agree or not? Why?
2. What are the similarities and differences between how a Confucian (see Section 3.3) would answer the question, "How should one live?" and how Aristotle would answer it? Does Aristotle's answer agree with Confucius's answer or not? Explain your reasoning.

3.6 THE SONG OF GOD

Have you ever faced a conflict of duties? For example, have you ever been torn between your duty to be loyal to a friend and your obligation to tell the truth? Have you ever confronted a situation in which, in order to do right, you had to do wrong? Have you ever been faced with options, neither of which were morally desirable? Have you ever felt sad because you live in a world where so often you must choose between doing the "lesser of two evils"?

In this same world, we are taught that we should strive for moral perfection. Reason demands that we should always do what is right and good, never what is wrong. Yes, we must face temptation and wrestle with evil, but in the end are we not expected to triumph over sin? Jesus reportedly said, "Be perfect, as your Father in heaven is perfect." But moral perfection, be it demanded by reason or by God, is impossible. Try as we might, we cannot make this a morally black-and-white world; too many choices are various shades of moral gray.

If you have ever faced moral conflicts or wondered how moral perfection is possible in a morally imperfect world, you ought to be able to identify with Arjuna, one of the main characters in the *Bhagavad-Gita* (*Song of God*). This Hindu poem forms part of India's greatest epic poem, *Mahabharata*. It was written sometime between the fourth and second centuries BCE. Much of the *Gita* is a conversation between Arjuna, who is a member of the warrior caste and a leader of the Pandava family, and Sri (Lord) Krishna, his cousin and the incarnation of the god Vishnu (Vishnu is the god responsible, according to traditional Hindu mythology, for sustaining the universe after it has been created by the god Brahman). This conversation is narrated by Sanjaya, a poet and charioteer. It takes place just before a horrendous battle, which is part of a civil war started by some of Arjuna's relatives. Krishna attempts to get Arjuna to do his duty, which, since he is a warrior and since he is on the side of right in this war, is to fight. However, Arjuna is reluctant because those whom he must fight and kill are his relatives and friends. We can formulate Arjuna's conflict as a dilemma:

1. Either Arjuna ought to fight or he ought not to fight.
2. If he fights, he will violate his duty to protect his relatives.
3. If he does not fight, he will violate his duty as a warrior and his obligation to fight in a just war.
4. Therefore, either he violates one set of duties or he violates another set of duties.

To appreciate the depth of this dilemma in the Indian context, we need some background information about Hinduism. The word for duty is **dharma**, which means, among other things, the order or law underlying the cosmos and embodied in social and ethical law codes. In this context, to violate one's duty is to violate dharma and thus to upset the natural, cosmic order. An immoral act has a negative impact on the whole universe. According to Hindu moral theory, there is a moral and natural law called the law of **karma**. Karma comes from the Sanskrit word *karman*, which means "action" or "the consequences of action." The law of karma states, "what you sow, so shall you reap." If you do good deeds, you will experience good things sometime in this or a future life; and if you act wrongly, you will suffer accordingly. The ultimate goal in life is to escape **samsara**, the cycle of rebirth, death, and suffering that characterizes human life. Our karma traps us in *samsara* because it determines our **reincarnation**, or rebirth into a new physical body. If the full consequences of our karma do not come in this life, we must live another life, and another, and another, and another, until there is no karma left and we get it right. In this context, the question of how one should live takes on added urgency because a wrong answer affects both the order of the universe and your future lives.

However, how can "getting it right" be possible? If, like Arjuna, we are faced with situations in which no matter what we do we will get bad karma, there seems no hope of breaking the cycle. Arjuna is doomed if he fights and doomed if he does not fight. We live in a morally imperfect world, and we can never hope to achieve moral perfection. However, even if we could, even if all our actions produced good karma, we would still be reborn. If we do evil, we are reborn to reap the bad consequences. If we do good, we are reborn to reap the good consequences.

We have now uncovered a more universal form of Arjuna's dilemma, what A. L. Herman calls the "dilemma of action." We can express it as follows:

1. Either you do good acts or you do bad acts.
2. If you do good acts, you are bound to be reborn to reap the good results.
3. If you do bad acts, you are bound to be reborn to reap the bad results.
4. Therefore, you reap good results or bad results, but, in either case, you are reborn.

We may not believe that transgressions of moral codes violate the natural order of things, and we may not believe in the law of karma or the idea of reincarnation. Nevertheless, each of us in his or her own way faces a form of Arjuna's dilemma—the conflict of duties, the necessity to do wrong in order to do right, the lack of moral perfection.

Is there a way out of these moral dilemmas? Read and find out.

◉ READING QUESTIONS

1. Why does Arjuna declare, "We don't know which weight is worse to bear—our conquering them or their conquering us"?
2. What reasons does Krishna present to Arjuna in support of his advice to fight?
3. What is the method of "spiritual discipline"?
4. According to Krishna, what are the characteristics of a person "deep in contemplation whose insight and thought are sure"?

Bhagavad-Gita

I. THE FIRST TEACHING: ARJUNA'S DEJECTION

Arjuna, his war flag a rampant monkey,
saw Dhritarashtra's sons assembled
as weapons were ready to clash,
and he lifted his bow.

He told his charioteer:
"Krishna,
halt my chariot
between the armies!

Far enough for me to see
these men who lust for war,
ready to fight with me
in the strain of battle.

I see men gathered here,
eager to fight,

bent on serving the folly
of Dhritarashtra's son."

When Arjuna had spoken,
Krishna halted
their splendid chariot
between the armies.

Facing Bhishma and Drona
and all the great kings,
he said, "Arjuna, see
the Kuru men assembled here!"

Arjuna saw them standing there:
fathers, grandfathers, teachers,
uncles, brothers, sons,
grandsons, and friends.

He surveyed his elders
and companions in both armies,
all his kinsmen
assembled together.

The greed that distorts their reason
blinds them to the sin they commit
in ruining the family, blinds them
to the crime of betraying friends.

How can we ignore the wisdom
of turning from this evil
when we see the sin
of family destruction, Krishna?

When the family is ruined,
the timeless laws of family duty
perish; and when duty is lost,
chaos overwhelms the family.

In overwhelming chaos, Krishna,
women of the family are corrupted;
and when women are corrupted,
disorder is born in society.

This discord drags the violators
and the family itself to hell;
for ancestors fall when rites
of offering rice and water lapse.

The sins of men who violate
the family create disorder in society
that undermines the constant laws
of caste and family duty.

Krishna, we have heard
that a place in hell
is reserved for men
who undermine family duties.

I lament the great sin
we commit when our greed
for kingship and pleasures
drives us to kill our kinsmen.

Dejected, filled with strange pity, he
said this:

"Krishna, I see my kinsmen
gathered here, wanting war.

My limbs sink,
my mouth is parched,

my body trembles,
the hair bristles on my flesh.

The magic bow slips
from my hand, my skin burns,
I cannot stand still, my mind reels.

I see omens of chaos,
Krishna; I see no good
in killing my kinsmen
in battle.

Krishna, I seek no victory,
or kingship or pleasures.
What use to us are kingship,
delights, or life itself?

We sought kingship, delights,
and pleasures for the sake of those
assembled to abandon their lives
and fortunes in battle.

They are teachers, fathers, sons,
and grandfathers, uncles, grandsons,
fathers and brothers of wives,
and other men of our family.

I do not want to kill them
even if I am killed, Krishna;
not for kingship of all three worlds,
much less for the earth!

What joy is there for us, Krishna,
in killing Dhritarashtra's sons?
Evil will haunt us if we kill them,
though their bows are drawn to kill.

Honor forbids us to kill
our cousins, Dhritarashtra's sons;
how can we know happiness
if we kill our own kinsmen?

If Dhritarashtra's armed sons
kill me in battle when I am unarmed
and offer no resistance,
it will be my reward."

Saying this in the time of war,
Arjuna slumped into the chariot
and laid down his bow and arrows,
his mind tormented by grief.

THE SECOND TEACHING: PHILOSOPHY AND SPIRITUAL DISCIPLINE

Sanjaya

Arjuna sat dejected,
filled with pity,
his sad eyes blurred by tears.
Krishna gave him counsel.

Lord Krishna

Why this cowardice
in time of crisis, Arjuna?
The coward is ignoble, shameful,
foreign to the ways of heaven.

Don't yield to impotence!
It is unnatural in you!
Banish this petty weakness from your heart.
Rise to the fight, Arjuna!

Arjuna

Krishna, how can I fight
against Bhishma and Drona
with arrows
when they deserve my worship?

It is better in this world
to beg for scraps of food
than to eat meals
smeared with the blood
of elders I killed
at the height of their power
while their goals
were still desires.

We don't know which weight
is worse to bear—
our conquering them
or their conquering us.
We will not want to live
if we kill the sons of Dhritarashtra
assembled before us.

The flaw of pity
blights my very being;
conflicting sacred duties
confound my reason.
I ask you to tell me

decisively—Which is better?
I am your pupil.
Teach me what I seek!

I see nothing
that could drive away
the grief
that withers my senses;
even if I won kingdoms
of unrivaled wealth
on earth
and sovereignty over gods.

Sanjaya

Arjuna told this
to Krishna—then saying,
"I shall not fight,"
he fell silent....

Lord Krishna

You grieve for those beyond grief;
and you speak words of insight;
but learned men do not grieve
for the dead or the living.

Never have I not existed,
nor you, nor these kings;
and never in the future
shall we cease to exist.

Just as the embodied self
enters childhood, youth, and old age,
so does it enter another body;
this does not confound a steadfast man.

Contacts with matter make us feel
heat and cold, pleasure and pain.
Arjuna, you must learn to endure
fleeting things—they come and go!

When these cannot torment a man,
when suffering and joy are equal
for him and he has courage,
he is fit for immortality.

Nothing of nonbeing comes to be,
nor does being cease to exist;
the boundary between these two
is seen by men who see reality.

Indestructible is the presence
that pervades all this;
no one can destroy
this unchanging reality.

Our bodies are known to end,
but the embodied self is enduring,
indestructible, and immeasurable;
therefore, Arjuna, fight the battle!

He who thinks this self a killer
and he who thinks it killed,
both fail to understand;
it does not kill, nor is it killed.

It is not born,
it does not die;
having been,
it will never not be;
unborn, enduring,
constant, and primordial,
it is not killed
when the body is killed.

Arjuna, when a man knows the self
to be indestructible, enduring, unborn,
unchanging, how does he kill
or cause anyone to kill?

As a man discards
worn-out clothes
to put on new
and different ones,
so the embodied self
discards
its worn-out bodies
to take on other new ones.

Weapons do not cut it,
fire does not burn it,
waters do not wet it,
wind does not wither it.

It cannot be cut or burned;
it cannot be wet or withered;
it is enduring, all-pervasive,
fixed, immovable, and timeless.

It is called unmanifest,
inconceivable, and immutable;

since you know that to be so,
you should not grieve!

If you think of its birth
and death as ever-recurring,
then too, Great Warrior,
you have no cause to grieve!

Death is certain for anyone born,
and birth is certain for the dead;
since the cycle is inevitable,
you have no cause to grieve!

Creatures are unmanifest in origin,
manifest in the midst of life,
and unmanifest again in the end.
Since this is so, why do you lament?

Rarely someone
sees it,
rarely another
speaks it,
rarely anyone
hears it—
even hearing it,
no one really knows it.

The self embodied in the body
of every being is indestructible;
you have no cause to grieve
for all these creatures, Arjuna!

Look to your own duty;
do not tremble before it;
nothing is better for a warrior
than a battle of sacred duty.

The doors of heaven open
for warriors who rejoice
to have a battle like this
thrust on them by chance.

If you fail to wage this war
of sacred duty,
you will abandon your own duty
and fame only to gain evil.

People will tell
of your undying shame,
and for a man of honor
shame is worse than death.

The great chariot warriors will think
you deserted in fear of battle;
you will be despised
by those who held you in esteem.

Your enemies will slander you,
scorning your skill
in so many unspeakable ways—
could any suffering be worse?

If you are killed, you win heaven;
if you triumph, you enjoy the earth;
therefore, Arjuna, stand up
and resolve to fight the battle!

Impartial to joy and suffering,
gain and loss, victory and defeat,
arm yourself for the battle,
lest you fall into evil.

Understanding is defined in terms of
    philosophy;
now hear it in spiritual discipline.
Armed with this understanding, Arjuna,
you will escape the bondage of action.

No effort in this world
is lost or wasted;
a fragment of sacred duty
saves you from great fear.

This understanding is unique
in its inner core of resolve;
diffuse and pointless are the ways
irresolute men understand.

Undiscerning men who delight
in the tenets of ritual lore
utter florid speech, proclaiming,
"There is nothing else!"

Driven by desire, they strive after heaven
and contrive to win powers and delights,
but their intricate ritual language
bears only the fruit of action in rebirth.

Obsessed with powers and delights,
their reason lost in words,
they do not find in contemplation
this understanding of inner resolve.

Arjuna, the realm of sacred lore
is nature—beyond its triad of qualities,
dualities, and mundane rewards,
be forever lucid, alive to your self.

For the discerning priest,
all of sacred lore
has no more value than a well
when water flows everywhere.

Be intent on action,
not on the fruits of action;
avoid attraction to the fruits
and attachment to inaction!

Perform actions, firm in discipline,
relinquishing attachment;
be impartial to failure and success—
this equanimity is called discipline.

Arjuna, action is far inferior
to the discipline of understanding;
so seek refuge in understanding—pitiful
are men drawn by fruits of action.

Disciplined by understanding,
one abandons both good and evil deeds;
so arm yourself for discipline—
discipline is skill in actions.

Wise men disciplined by understanding
relinquish the fruit born of action;
freed from these bonds of rebirth,
they reach a place beyond decay.

When your understanding passes beyond
the swamp of delusion,
you will be indifferent to all
that is heard in sacred lore.

When your understanding turns
from sacred lore to stand fixed,
immovable in contemplation,
then you will reach discipline.

Arjuna

Krishna, what defines a man
deep in contemplation whose insight
and thought are sure? How would he speak?
How would he sit? How would he move?

Lord Krishna

When he gives up desires in his mind,
is content with the self within himself,
then he is said to be a man
whose insight is sure, Arjuna.

When suffering does not disturb his mind,
when his craving for pleasures has vanished,
when attraction, fear, and anger are gone,
he is called a sage whose thought is sure.

When he shows no preference
in fortune or misfortune
and neither exults nor hates,
his insight is sure.

When, like a tortoise retracting
its limbs, he withdraws his senses
completely from sensuous objects,
his insight is sure.

Sensuous objects fade
when the embodied self abstains from food;
the taste lingers, but it too fades
in the vision of higher truth.

Even when a man of wisdom
tries to control them, Arjuna,
the bewildering senses
attack his mind with violence.

Controlling them all,
with discipline he should focus on me;
when his senses are under control,
his insight is sure.

Brooding about sensuous objects
makes attachment to them grow;
from attachment desire arises,
from desire anger is born.

From anger comes confusion;
from confusion memory lapses;
from broken memory understanding is lost;
from loss of understanding, he is ruined.

But a man of inner strength
whose senses experience objects
without attraction and hatred,
in self-control, finds serenity.

In serenity, all his sorrows
dissolve;
his reason becomes serene,
his understanding sure.

Without discipline,
he has no understanding or inner power;
without inner power, he has no peace; and
    without peace where is joy?

If his mind submits to the play
of the senses,
they drive away insight,
as wind drives a ship on water.

So, Great Warrior, when withdrawal
of the senses
from sense objects is complete,
discernment is firm....

When he renounces all desires
and acts without craving,
possessiveness,
or individuality, he finds peace.

This is the place of the infinite spirit;
achieving it, one is freed from delusion;
abiding in it even at the time of death,
one finds the pure calm of infinity.

◉ CRITICAL QUESTIONS

1. How would following Krishna's advice solve Arjuna's dilemma?
2. Do you think living the sort of life Krishna recommends (knowing the true nature of the self, doing one's moral duty, being unconcerned about the results of one's action, devotion to the divine) would be a good way to live? Why, or why not?
3. How do you think Socrates would respond to Krishna's advice? Support your answer with an argument.

3.7 WHAT IS THE MEANING OF LIFE?

Most of you have probably seen a cartoon of someone climbing a mountain and reaching a bearded guru in order to ask, "What is the meaning of life?" The answer is usually unexpected and slightly humorous.

Imagine a variation. Imagine the seeker reaching the guru and asking, "Why must life have a meaning?" Perhaps the guru is suddenly dumbfounded by this new version, so the seeker continues, "I mean, isn't it all right for life to be pointless?" This second version may seem odd because we all assume that life must have a meaning and that it is important that it does. The second version does not make that assumption. Instead it wonders about why we think it necessary or important that life have a meaning

Imagine a third version of the cartoon. The seeker reaches the guru and asks, "What does it mean to ask what is the meaning of life?" Perhaps this time the guru is not dumbfounded, but answers, "You have been studying too much philosophy." That may be true. You have already learned to question questions by asking how they might best be understood and formulated. So what are we to make of the question about the meaning of life? What does it mean?

If you think about it, it is a rather odd question. If what we do, think, and believe as we live our lives makes sense, why must life as a whole make sense? If there are good reasons for how I live my life in its details, why do I need a reason for my life taken as a whole? However, is the question even a question about my life? Is it not a question about every life? If we interpret the question this way, as a question about the whole of every human life (should we include animals and plants?), then the answer becomes both more difficult and more questionable. How could there be a good reason for every life that will ever be lived? Why should we think there is such a reason?

I have assumed that the question about the meaning of life is a question about finding a good reason for living. Shift your focus a bit and think about what might be a "good reason" for living. Is there only one? Could there be many? How is the search for a good reason for living connected to the search for the good life? Is finding your "passion" in life and pursuing it sufficient for living a meaningful life or is something else required? Does the answer to the question, "How should one live?" also provide an answer to the question, "What is the meaning of life?" If life has no meaning, no good reason, and no point, does it make any sense to worry about how we should conduct our lives?

Susan Wolf is the Edna J. Koury Professor of Philosophy at the University of North Carolina, Chapel Hill. The selection that follows is the first of two lectures delivered at Princeton University in 2007. The second lecture (on why this question matters) is not included here. Wolf is not here concerned with the "ultimate" meaning of life and she does not think that meaningfulness in life is necessarily related to morality or happiness. But she does think it is a value worth having. Read her lecture and see if you agree.

◉ READING QUESTIONS

1. What is the "false dichotomy" that Wolf describes and why does she think it is false?

2. What is the claim Wolf wants to defend?

3. What is Wolf's conception of "meaningfulness in life"?
4. What are the "fulfillment view" and the "larger-than-oneself view"? How does she think the two views should be combined in order to provide an adequate definition of a meaningful life?

Meaning in Life

SUSAN WOLF

A FALSE DICHOTOMY

Philosophical models of human psychology—or, more specifically, of human motivation—tend to fall into one of two categories. Perhaps the oldest and most popular model conceives of human beings as egoists, moved and guided exclusively by what they take to be in their own self-interest. However, there have long been defenders of a dualistic model of motivation as well, according to which people are capable of being moved not only by self-interest, but also by something "higher." Kant, for example, famously thought that in addition to being subject to inclinations, people are capable of being moved and directed by reason alone.

Closely linked to these two descriptive models of human motivation are prescriptive or normative models of practical reason. The descriptive thesis of psychological egoism, which holds that people exclusively seek their own good, is closely connected to (and frequently confused with) the normative thesis of rational egoism, which holds that people are only rational insofar as they seek to maximize their welfare. Corresponding to the dual conception of human motivation we find a dual conception of practical reason as well. This is perhaps most explicit in the writings of Henry Sidgwick, who held that two perspectives offer people equally valid reasons to act: the egoistic perspective, which issues recommendations of what is most in an agent's self-interest; and the impersonal perspective, which urges one to do what is best "from the point of view of the universe."

In ordinary discourse as well as philosophy we seem to have one of these two models in the backs of our minds when we offer justifications for our actions or our policies. Most often, when asked to explain or justify our choices, we offer reasons that seem to fall under the category of self-interest. When we are trying to persuade *someone else* to do something, we may appeal to self-interest—in this case, to the *other* person's self-interest—even more. Still, there are some occasions when invoking self-interest would simply be unconvincing, and others when such appeals would be unseemly, or at least beside the point. In these cases, we are likely to speak the language of duty: justice, compassion, or, simply, morality demands that we act in such and such a way, whether it contributes to our own good or not.

These models of motivation and practical reason, however, seem to me to leave out many of the motives and reasons that shape our lives. Moreover, the reasons left out are neither peripheral nor eccentric. Indeed, we might say that the reasons and motives omitted by these models are some of the most important and central ones in our lives. They are the reasons and motives that engage us in the activities that make our lives worth living; they give us a reason to go on; they make our worlds go round. They, and the activities they engender, give meaning to our lives.

My aim in this lecture is to bring out the distinctive character of these sorts of reasons and the special role they play in the quality of our lives. Specifically, I shall suggest that our susceptibility to these sorts of reasons is connected to the possibility that we live meaningful lives, understanding meaningfulness as an attribute lives can have that is not reducible to or subsumable under either happiness, as it is ordinarily understood, or morality. I shall be mainly concerned to explain the feature I call meaningfulness in life and to present it in such a way as to make it seem worth wanting, both for ourselves and for those about whom we care. As will be seen, however, what I have to say will be of little or no *practical* use. Though I shall offer a view of what it means for a life to be meaningful, I can offer only the most abstract advice about how to go about getting or living such a life.... As I shall argue, awareness that meaning is a third sort of value a life can possess should affect our understanding of the first two sorts: that is, adopting models of human motivation and reason that are attentive to meaningfulness should affect the way we think about happiness and morality—and about self-interest as well. Moreover, if the view I present in these lectures is right, we cannot so much as conceive of meaning without attributing a certain sort of objectivity to value judgments. It follows that if we want to continue to talk about, attend to, and encourage the acquisition of meaning in people's lives, we need to be willing to admit this sort of objectivity into our discussion of values.

Let me begin with some examples of the sorts of reasons and motives I have in mind—reasons and motives that are not best understood in terms of their contributions to either our happiness or our sense of what impersonal reason or morality demands. The most obvious examples of what I have in mind occur when we act out of love for individuals about whom we deeply and especially care. When I visit my brother in the hospital, or help my friend move, or stay up all night sewing my daughter a Halloween costume, I act neither for egoistic reasons nor for moral ones. I do not believe that it is *better for me* that I spend a depressing hour in a drab, cramped room, seeing my brother irritable and in pain, that I risk back injury trying to get my friend's sofa safely down two flights of stairs, or that I forego hours of much-wanted sleep to make sure that the wings will stand out at a good angle from the butterfly costume my

daughter wants to wear in the next day's parade. But neither do I believe myself duty-bound to perform these acts, or fool myself into thinking that by doing them I do what will be best for the world. I act neither out of self-interest nor out of duty or any other sort of impersonal or impartial reason. Rather, I act out of love.

As the egoistic and dualist models of practical reason leave out what we might call these "reasons of love,"[1] so they seem to me also to leave out many of the reasons that move us to pursue nonpersonal interests about which we are especially passionate. Writing philosophy, practicing the cello, keeping one's garden free of weeds, may demand more of one's time and attention than would be optimal from the point of view of one's own well-being. Yet in these cases, even more than in the cases involving beloved human beings, it is obvious that no impersonal perspective requires us to act. Just as, in the case of acting for a loved one, it is the good of that other person that provides us with a reason for our action, what draws us on in the nonpersonal pursuits I have in mind is a perceived or imagined value that lies outside of oneself. I agonize over the article I am trying to write because I want to get it right—that is, because I want the argument to be sound, the view to be correct, the writing to be clear and graceful. It is not for my sake—at least not only for my sake—that I struggle so with my work I do not know or care whether it is best for me—that is, whether it is best from the point of view of my self-interest—that I try to improve my work beyond a certain point, any more than I care whether it is best for me that I put so much energy into making my daughter happy. We might say that I struggle "for philosophy's sake" rather than for my own, but that would be misleading and obscure as well as pretentious. Still, it seems to me that it is the value of

[1]The phrase is used by Harry Frankfurt in much the same way as I use it and for purposes that largely overlap with mine in Harry Frankfurt, *The Reasons of Love* (Princeton: Princeton University Press, 2004). Like me, Frankfurt sees our susceptibility to reasons of love as essential to the possibility that we live meaningful lives. He forcefully rejects the conditions on which reasons for love can ground claims of meaning that I defend in what follows, however.

good philosophy that is driving and guiding my behavior in this instance, as it might be the beauty of the music or of the potential garden that moves the cellist or gardener to sacrifice ease and exercise discipline in pursuing her goal.

It does not seem unnatural or forced to speak of the subjects of these examples as *loving* philosophy or music or flowers, and their love for these things may not only explain but may also justify (or, more strictly, may contribute to the justification of) their choices and behavior more than their love for themselves or for morality or for some other impersonal and general good. Because of the similarities in the motivational and deliberative stance of these subjects to that of people who act out of love for individuals, I shall use the phrase "reasons of love" to cover both types of cases. My claim then is that reasons of love—whether of human individuals, other living creatures, or activities, ideals or objects of other sorts—have a distinctive and important role in our lives. They are not to be assimilated to reasons of self-interest or reasons of morality. Insofar as we fail to recognize and appreciate the legitimacy and value of these reasons, we misunderstand our values and ourselves and distort our concerns.

Not all actions that are motivated and guided by reasons of love are justified, however. Not all reasons of love are good reasons. For one thing, your love for something or someone is no guarantee that you know what is actually good for them. You may mean to help the object of your love, but your action may not benefit it. You might spoil your child, over-water your plants, cramp your philosophical style.

More interestingly, love can be misplaced or misguided; the energy or attention that you give to an object of love may be disproportionate to what that object merits.[2] A wonderful woman might give up her career, her home, her friendships to follow and serve a man the rest of us see does not "deserve her." An impressionable teenager might sign over his trust fund to a cult with which he has become enamored, thereby losing both his financial security and the opportunity to benefit worthier and needier groups.

What I wish to defend, then, is the justifiability and importance of a subset of those actions and decisions that are guided by reasons of love. Roughly, I want to defend the claim that acting in a way that positively engages with a *worthy* object of love can be perfectly justified even if it does not maximally promote either the agent's welfare or the good of the world, impartially assessed.

Actions and decisions based on the good of the beloved are part and parcel of love and its expression quite generally. When, in addition, the object of love is specified to be worthy of love, the justification of action on behalf of that object may be straightforward. Why shouldn't it be as justifiable for a person to act on behalf of a friend, for example, as it is for her to act on her own behalf? And why shouldn't it be as justifiable to act on behalf of one's friend as it is to do something of greater benefit to the world at large? Unless rational egoism or a particularly extreme form of consequentialism is presupposed, there is no reason to doubt the rational permissibility of acting on such reasons of love. Still, I want to say something stronger, something more favorable and more supportive of reasons of this sort. More precisely, I want to say something more favorable about a life that is prone to being moved and guided by such reasons. Proneness to being moved and guided by such reasons, I believe, is at the core of our ability to live meaningful lives. But it is far from clear what saying this amounts to.

A CONCEPTION OF MEANINGFULNESS IN LIFE

Academic philosophers do not talk much about meaningfulness in life. The term is more likely to be used by theologians or therapists, and by people who are in some way dissatisfied with their lives but are unable to pin down why. People sometimes complain that their lives lack meaning;

---

[2]The first way in which reasons of love may be mistaken parallels mistakes to which what we might call "reasons of self-interest" and "reasons of morality" are subject. I may think that something is in my self-interest when it is actually harmful; I may think morality requires or allows me to do what in fact is morally wrong. It is not obvious that the second way in which an apparent reason of love can be wrong has parallels in these other categories. There may be no such thing as caring too much about one's own good or about morality.

they yearn for meaning; they seek meaning. People sometimes judge others to be leading exceptionally meaningful lives, looking upon them with envy or admiration. Meaning is commonly associated with a kind of depth. Often the need for meaning is connected to the sense that one's life is empty or shallow. An interest in meaning is also frequently associated with thoughts one might have on one's deathbed, or in contemplation of one's eventual death. When the word "meaningful" is used in characterizing a life (or in characterizing what is missing from a life), it calls *something* to mind, but it is not clear what, nor is it clear that it calls or is meant to call the same thing to mind in all contexts.

In offering a conception of meaningfulness, I do not wish to insist that the term is always used in the same way, or that what I have to offer as an analysis of meaningfulness can be substituted for that term in every context. On the other hand, I do believe that much talk of meaning is aimed at capturing the same abstract idea, and that my proposal of what that idea is fits well with many of the uses to which the word is put. Whether or not my idea of meaningfulness captures what others mean when they use the term, it is an idea of philosophical interest, for it is an idea of a significant way in which a life can be good, a category or dimension of value, if you will, which we have a serious reason to want for ourselves and for those we care about, and which is neither subsumable under nor reducible to either happiness or morality.

According to the conception of meaningfulness I wish to propose, meaning arises from loving objects worthy of love and engaging with them in a positive way. The words "love" and "objects," however, are in some ways misleadingly specific, "engaging [with objects] in a positive way" regrettably vague, and the description of some objects but not others as being "*worthy* of love" may be thought to be contentious. Rather than try to clarify the view by taking up one word or phrase at a time, let me try to describe the view in other terms, bringing out what I take to be salient.

What is perhaps most distinctive about my conception of meaning, or about the category of value I have in mind, is that it involves subjective and objective elements, suitably and inextricably linked. "Love" is at least partly subjective, involving attitudes and feelings. In insisting that the requisite object must be "worthy of love," however, this conception of meaning invokes an objective standard. It is implicit in insisting that an object be worthy of love (in order to contribute meaning to the lover's life) that not any object will do. Nor is it guaranteed that the subject's own assessment of worthiness is privileged. One might paraphrase this by saying that, according to my conception, meaning arises when subjective attraction meets objective attractiveness.

Essentially, the idea is that a person's life can be meaningful only if she cares fairly deeply about some thing or things, only if she is gripped, excited, interested, engaged, or as I earlier put it, if she loves something—as opposed to being bored by or alienated from most or all that she does. Even a person who is so engaged, however, will not live a meaningful life if the objects or activities with which she is so occupied are worthless. A person who loves smoking pot all day long, or doing endless crossword puzzles, and has the luxury of being able to indulge in this without restraint does not thereby make her life meaningful. Finally, this conception of meaning specifies that the relationship between the subject and the object of her attraction must be an active one. The condition that says that meaning involves engaging with the (worthy) object of love in a positive way is meant to make clear that mere passive recognition and a positive attitude toward an object's or activity's value is not sufficient for a meaningful life. One must be able to be in some sort of relationship with the valuable object of one's attention—to create it, protect it, promote it, honor it, or more generally, to actively affirm it in some way or other.

Aristotle is well known for his use of the endoxic method in defending moral and conceptual claims. That is, he takes the *endoxa*,[3] "the things which are accepted by everyone, or by

---

[3] Aristotle, *Topics* 1.1 100b 21–3. For an excellent discussion of the endoxic method, see Richard Kraut, "How to Justify Ethical Propositions: Aristotle's Method," in *The Blackwell Guide to Aristotle's "Nicomachean Ethics"* (Oxford: Blackwell, 2006), pp. 76–95.

most people or by the wise" as a starting point in his inquiries. If a view can explain and support these common beliefs, or, even better, if it can bring them into harmony with each other, that counts as an argument in its favor. In that spirit, I suggest that my view might be seen as a combination, or a welding together, of two other, more popular views that one often hears offered, if not as analyses of meaning in life, then at least as ingredients—sometimes the *key* ingredients—in a life well lived.

The first view tells us that it doesn't matter what you do with your life as long as it is something you love. Do not get stuck, or settle into doing something just because it is expected of you, or because it is conventionally recognized as good, or because nothing better occurs to you. Find your passion. Figure out what turns you on, and go for it.[4]

The second view says that in order to live a truly satisfying life one needs to get involved in something "larger than oneself."[5] The reference to the size of the group or the object one wants to benefit or be involved with is perhaps misleading and unfortunate, but it is not unreasonable to understand such language metaphorically, as a way of gesturing toward the aim of participating in or contributing to something whose value *is independent* of oneself. Understood this way, the first view, ("find your passion") may be understood as a way of advocating something similar to the subjective element contained in my proposed analysis of meaningfulness, while the second view, ("be part of something larger than yourself") urges us to satisfy the objective condition.

Each of these more popular views is sometimes couched in the vocabulary of meaning, and in each case there is a basis for that choice in our ordinary uses of the term. When thinking about one's own life, for example, a person's worry or complaint that his life lacks meaning is apt to be an expression of dissatisfaction with the subjective quality of that life. Some subjective good is felt to be missing. One's life feels empty. One longs to find something to do that will fill this gap and make one feel, as it were, fulfilled.

On the other hand, when we consider the lives of others, our tendency to characterize some as especially meaningful and others as less so is apt to reflect differences in our assessments of the objective value of what these lives are about. When we look for paradigms of meaningful lives, who comes to mind? Gandhi, perhaps, or Mother Theresa, or Einstein, or Cézanne. Sisyphus, condemned to an endless cycle of rolling a huge stone up a hill, only to have it roll down again, is a standard exemplar of a meaningless existence. Our choice of these examples seems to be based on the value (or lack of value) we take these people's activities to have, rather than on the subjective quality of their inner lives.

Insofar as the conception of meaningfulness I propose welds these two popular views together, it may be seen as a partial affirmation of both. From my perspective, both these views have something right about them, but each also leaves out something crucial.

Why believe any of these views? The question is ambiguous. Understood as the question, "Why believe that any one of these views offers a correct analysis of meaningfulness in life?" the inquiry seems to focus on whether any of the views under consideration captures a property or feature or set of conditions that answers to most of the instances in which the term "meaningful" is used in ordinary discourse, in contexts in which the topic in question is meaningfulness in life (as opposed, say, to meaningfulness in language). In answering this question, we would want to look at how the term *is* used in ordinary discourse: In what sorts of situations do questions of meaning arise? What sorts of concerns is the presence of meaning in a person's life supposed to put to rest? What types of lives

---

[4]One of those silly books that were on sale at the cashiers' desks at Barnes & Noble a few years ago advanced that view. The book, by Bradley Trevor Greive (Kansas City: Andrews McMeel Publishing, 2002) was called *The Meaning of Life*. Richard Taylor offers a more serious and provocative defense of the view in Richard Taylor, *Good and Evil* (New York: Macmillan, 1970), Chapter 18.

[5]Not surprisingly, it is common to hear religious leaders speak in these terms, but many others do as well. For example, Peter Singer draws on this conception of the good life in his book, *How Are We To Live? Ethics in an Age of Self-interest* (Melbourne: The Text Publishing Company, 1993).

would be generally accepted as paradigms of meaning? What types would be accepted as paradigms of meaninglessness? I have already expressed some doubt about whether there is a single cleanly definable concept that is being invoked in all the contexts in which talk of meaningful (and meaningless) lives may naturally take place. More important than the question of how to use the term "meaning," in any event, is the question of what a good life should contain. Above all, when therapists, ministers, and motivational speakers tell you either to "find your passion" or to "contribute to something larger than yourself," they are offering advice about how to live. More important than asking which, if any, of these views offers a plausible conception of "meaningfulness," is asking which, if any of them, identifies key and distinctive ingredients of a fully flourishing, successful, good life....

THE FULFILLMENT VIEW

Let us turn our attention, then, to the first of the popular views I mentioned, the one that stresses the subjective element, urging each person to find his or her passion and pursue it. It is easy to see why someone would support this advice, and find plausible the claim that being able to pursue a passion adds something distinctive and deeply good to life. For the advice, at least as I understand it, rests on the plausible empirical supposition that doing what one loves doing, being involved with things one really cares about, gives one a kind of joy in life that one would otherwise be without. The reason one should find one's passion and go for it, then, is because doing so will give one's life a particular type of good feeling. Moreover, the distinctiveness of the type of good feeling in question makes it possible to see how the kind of life that engenders such feelings would be associated with meaningfulness, and how therefore one might be led to identify a meaningful life as a life lived pursuing one's passions.

Let us refer to the feelings one has when one is doing what one loves, or when one is engaging in activities by which one is gripped or excited, as feelings of fulfillment. Such feelings are the opposite of the very bad feelings of boredom and alienation. Although feelings of fulfillment are unquestionably good feelings, there are many other good feelings,

perhaps more comfortably classified as pleasures, that have nothing to do with fulfillment. Riding a roller coaster, meeting a movie star, eating a hot fudge sundae, finding a great dress on sale, can all give one pleasure, even intense pleasure. They are unlikely to contribute to a sense of fulfillment, however, and it would not be difficult to imagine a person who has an abundance of opportunities for such pleasures still finding something (subjectively) lacking in, her life.

Further, someone whose life is fulfilling has no guarantee of being happy in the conventional sense of that term. Many of the things that grip or engage us make us vulnerable to pain, disappointment, and stress. Consider, for example, writing a book, training for a triathlon, campaigning for a political candidate, caring for an ailing friend.

It may later be useful to bring to mind the fact that feelings of fulfillment are but one kind of positive feeling and potentially compete with other kinds: spending one's time, energy, money, and so on, on the projects that fulfill you necessarily reduces the resources you have for engaging in activities that are "merely" fun. Moreover, to the extent that one's sources of fulfillment are also sources of anxiety and suffering, the pleasure one gets from pursuing these things may be thought, at least from a hedonistic perspective, to be qualified or balanced by the negative feelings that accompany it. Still, the fact that most of us would willingly put up with a great deal of stress, anxiety, and vulnerability to pain in order to pursue our passions can be seen as providing support for the idea that fulfillment is indeed a great and distinctive good in life. Insofar as the view that urges us "to find our passion and go for it" expresses that idea, there is a lot to be said for it. From here on, I shall refer to that view as the "Fulfillment View."

Because feelings of fulfillment are different from and sometimes compete with other types of good feeling, types that are more paradigmatically associated with terms like "happiness" and "pleasure," it is plausible to interpret the Fulfillment View as a proposal for what gives meaning to life. To someone who finds himself puzzled by why, despite having a good job, a loving family, and a healthy body, he feels that something is missing from his life, it provides an answer. To someone trying to decide what career to pursue, or more generally, how to structure his life, it advises against focusing too narrowly on the superficial goals of ease, prestige, and material wealth. Nonetheless, the Fulfillment View, as I have interpreted it, is a form of hedonism, in that its prescription for the best possible life (in which is included the possession of meaning) rests exclusively on the question of how a life can attain the best qualitative character. Positive experience is, on this view, the only thing that matters.[6]

For this very reason, it seems to me, the view is inadequate as it stands. If, as the Fulfillment View suggests, the only thing that matters is the subjective quality of one's life, then it shouldn't matter, in our assessments of possible lives, which activities give rise to that quality. If the point of finding one's passion and pursuing it is simply to be fulfilled—that is, to get and keep the *feelings* of fulfillment, then it shouldn't matter what activities or objects one has a passion for. Considering a variety of lives, all equally fulfilling, but differing radically in the sorts of things that give rise to that fulfillment, however, may make us wonder whether we can really accept that view.

Imagine, in particular, a person whose life is dominated by activities that most of us would be tempted to call worthless, but which nonetheless give fulfillment to that person. I earlier gave the example of a person who simply loves smoking pot all day, and another (or maybe the same person) who is fulfilled doing crossword puzzles, or worse (as personal experience will attest), Sudokus. We might also consider more bizarre cases: a man who lives to make handwritten copies of the text of *War and Peace,* or a woman whose world revolves around her love for her pet goldfish. Do we think that, from the point of view of self-interest, these lives are as good as can be—provided, perhaps, that their affections and values are stable, and that the goldfish doesn't die?

Initially, perhaps, not everyone will answer these questions in the same way; some will not know what to think. In part, I believe this is because we are uncomfortable making negative judgments about other people's lives, even about imaginary other people who are conceived realistically enough to be stand-ins for real people. We are especially uncomfortable making negative judgments that diverge from the judgments the characters would make about their own lives. To avoid this problem, let me approach these questions by way of reflection on a more stylized philosophical example—namely, the case of Sisyphus Fulfilled.

Sisyphus, in the ancient myth, is condemned to an existence that is generally acknowledged to be awful. He is condemned eternally to a task that is boring, difficult, and futile. Because of this, Sisyphus's life, or more precisely, his afterlife, has been commonly treated as a paradigm of a meaningless existence.[7]

The philosopher Richard Taylor, however, in a discussion of life's absurdity, suggests a thought experiment according to which the gods take pity on Sisyphus and inject a substance in his veins that transforms him from someone for whom stone-rolling is nothing but a painful, arduous, and unwelcome chore to someone who loves stone-rolling more than anything else in the (after-) world.[8] There is nothing the transformed Sisyphus would rather do than roll that stone. Stone-rolling, in other words, fulfills him. Sisyphus has found his passion (or perhaps his passion has found him), and he is pursuing it to his life's content. The question is, what should *we* think of him? Has his life been transformed from horribly unfortunate to exceptionally good? Taylor thinks so, but some of us might disagree.

As I have already noted, the reason Sisyphus has traditionally been taken as a paradigm of a meaningless existence is that he is condemned to the perpetual performance of a task that is boring, difficult, and futile. In Taylor's variation, Sisyphus's task is no longer boring—no longer boring to Sisyphus, that is. But it remains futile. There is

---

[6]The Fulfillment View might be considered a plausible extension of J. S. Mill's view that an enlightened hedonist must take into account the differences in quality as well as quantity of pleasure in conceiving of the best possible life. See John Stuart Mill, *Utilitarianism* (1861), Chapter 2.

[7]See especially Albert Camus, *The Myth of Sisyphus and Other Essays* (New York: Alfred A. Knopf, 1955).
[8]See Taylor, *Good and Evil* (n. 4, above).

no value to his efforts; nothing ever comes of them. Even if due to divine intervention, Sisyphus comes to enjoy and even to feel fulfilled by his activity, the pointlessness of what he is doing doesn't change.

In light of this, many will feel that Sisyphus's situation remains far from enviable. Something desirable seems missing from his life despite his experience of fulfillment. Since what is missing is not a subjective matter—from the inside, we may assume that Sisyphus's life is as good as can be— we must look for an objective feature that characterizes what is lacking. The second popular view I brought up earlier names, or at least gestures toward, a feature that might fit the bill.

THE LARGER-THAN-ONESELF VIEW AND THE BIPARTITE VIEW

That second view tells us that the best sort of life is one that is involved in, or contributes to something "larger than oneself." Contemplation of the case of Sisyphus should, however, be enough to show that this "larger" must be understood metaphorically. We may, after all, imagine the rock Sisyphus is endlessly pushing uphill to be *very* large. We might rather understand the view as one that recommends involvement in something *more important* than ourselves—something, in other words, that is larger than ourselves not in size but in value. If the recommendation is to be taken as a criterion for a meaningful life, however, I would be inclined to argue against this interpretation, too. For one thing, if we assume that the value of one person's life is as great as the value of another's, it would seem to rule out the possibility that a life devoted to the care of a single other individual—a disabled partner, for example, or a frail, aging parent, or a child with special needs—could be a meaningful life, for the value of the one cared for is presumably just equal to and not larger than the value of the person who does the caring. When we try to assess projects and activities that are not principally aimed at the benefit of one or more human beings, the difficulties with such a view appear even more serious. Presumably, a dog is not more important than oneself—but what about two dogs, or six? And what about projects and activities that are not

directed toward promoting anyone's welfare at all? Is philosophy or poetry or basketball something "larger than oneself" in value? It is difficult to know exactly what the question is asking.

A more promising interpretation of the view that links meaningfulness to involvement with something larger than oneself takes the metaphor of size less seriously. According to this interpretation, the point is to recommend that one get involved not with something larger than oneself, but rather with something *other* than oneself— that is, with something the value of which is independent of and has its source *outside* of oneself. Presumably, Sisyphean stone-rolling has no such value—nor, it seems, does pot-smoking or Sudoku-solving. But devotion to a single, needy individual does satisfy this condition as much as devotion to a crowd. Philosophy and basketball appear to meet this criterion, too, since the value of these activities, whatever it is, does not depend on one's own contingent interest in them.

If we interpret the advice that one get involved with something "larger than oneself" in this way, it might be thought to represent a second and independent criterion for a fully successful and flourishing life. Combining this advice with the Fulfillment View, one might think, yields a better, bipartite conception of meaningfulness than either view taken on its own. The Fulfillment View directs our attention to a subjective component that a meaningful life must contain. But, as the case of Sisyphus Fulfilled led us to see, even a life that fully satisfies the subjective condition may be one we would be hesitant to describe as meaningful, if objectively that life were unconnected to anything or anyone whose value lay outside of the person whose life it was. By conjoining the Fulfillment View with the injunction to get involved with something "larger than oneself," we get a proposal that appears to remedy the problem. On this bipartite view, in order for a life to be meaningful both an objective and a subjective condition must be met: A meaningful life is a life that a.) the subject finds fulfilling, and b.) contributes to or connects positively with something the value of which has its source outside the subject.

If, however, meaningfulness is understood to refer to a coherent dimension of value, more specific than the general category of self-interest, or the even more general category of "all that is desirable in a life," it would be puzzling if it turned out to depend on the satisfaction of two unrelated conditions. The proposal I favor, which identifies meaning with a condition in which subjective and objective components are suitably linked, conceives of meaningfulness in a more unified way. My conception of meaningfulness sees subjective and objective elements fitting together to constitute a coherent feature a life might or might not possess. Besides, if we really consider the two conditions of meaningfulness proposed by the Bipartite View as criteria to be taken separately, it is not clear that they contribute to the goodness of a person's life at all.[9]

Consider again the suggestion that a life in which a person contributes to something larger than himself (suitably interpreted) is more meaningful than a life that serves only the needs and desires of the person whose life it is. I introduced this idea in answer to the question of what (desirable feature) might be missing from a life like that of Sisyphus Fulfilled (or the pot-smoker, or Sudoku-player), that prevents it from representing a life we would want for ourselves or for those we love. We could add stipulations to these examples that guaranteed that the protagonists' lives and activities did contribute to some independent value. If they had no interest in the external or objective or independent value with which their lives were involved, however, it is not clear that that involvement would make their lives any better or more desirable to them. Imagine, for example, that unbeknownst to Sisyphus, his stone-rolling scares away vultures who would otherwise attack a nearby community and spread terror and disease. Or imagine that the pot-smoker's secondary marijuana smoke is alleviating the pain of the AIDS victim next door. If Sisyphus and the pot-smoker do not care about the benefits their lives are producing, it is hard to see why the fact that their lives yield those benefits—that they contribute, in other words, to something larger or other than themselves—should make us any more

inclined to describe then-lives as meaningful (or to find their lives desirable) than we were before we learned of these consequences.

Even when we consider people whose involvement with something "larger" is less accidental, the contribution this makes to the quality of their own lives is limited at best if they are not emotionally engaged with the people or things or activities that make what they are doing valuable. People who do valuable work but who cannot identify or take pride in what they are doing—the alienated housewife, the conscripted soldier, the assembly line worker, for example—may know that what they are doing is valuable, yet reasonably feel that their lives lack something that might be referred to as meaning.

In any case, it seems to me that when the recommendation to get involved with something larger than oneself is offered, it is offered in the hope, if not the expectation, that if one does get so involved, it will make one feel good. The thought is that if one tries it, one will like it, and one will like it in part because of one's recognition that one is engaged with a person or an object or an activity that is independently valuable.[10] The suggestion, then, that one gets meaning in life through involvement with something larger than oneself may be most charitably interpreted as a suggestion that is not meant to be taken in isolation. It is not to be regarded as a criterion of meaningfulness separable from any assumptions about the attitudes the subject will have toward the project or activity in question. If one gets involved in something larger than oneself—or, as I have interpreted it, in something the value of which is (in part) independent of oneself—then, if one is lucky, one will find that involvement fulfilling, and if that happens, then one's life will both be and seem meaningful. If one's involvement brings no such reward, however, it is unclear that it contributes to meaning in one's life at all.

---

[9]I thank Cheshire Calhoun for pressing me to think about why the relation between the subjective and objective conditions of my conception of meaningfulness is important.

[10]This does not always work. It is a standard part of the requirements for a child who is training for a Bar or Bat Mitzvah, as it is for many middle and high school programs, that the child spend a specified number of hours engaged in community service. Not surprisingly, the degree to which this results in a gratifying experience, an enhanced social consciousness, or a lasting commitment varies widely.

Just as the objective condition sometimes associated with meaning—namely, that one's life be involved in something larger than oneself—is much more plausible when it is understood to function in conjunction with a positive subjective attitude to one's involvement, so it seems to me that the subjective condition—that one live in a way that one finds fulfilling—is more plausible when understood in conjunction with objective constraints. I suggested a moment ago that when someone recommends that you get involved in something larger than oneself, the hope, if not the expectation, that is lurking in the background is that you will find that involvement subjectively rewarding. Similarly, when someone recommends that you find your passion and go for it, there seems also to be a hope, if not an expectation, lurking in the background; namely, that the passion you find, the pursuit of which will be fulfilling, will be an intelligible one, within certain bounds. You will not be passionate—at least not for very long—about stone-rolling, or Sudokus, or caring for your goldfish, or making handwritten copies of *War and Peace*.

In my earlier discussion of Sisyphus Fulfilled, I expressed sympathy with those who, unlike Richard Taylor, found something desirable missing from Sisyphus's life, despite his being subjectively quite content. There is room for an even stronger disagreement with Taylor, however, that I want to consider now. Specifically, one might wonder whether the transformation that Sisyphus undergoes from being unhappy, bored, and frustrated to being blissfully fulfilled makes Sisyphus better off at all. One might think that it actually makes his situation worse.

From a hedonistic perspective, of course, Sisyphus's transformation *must* make his life better, for the only changes in Sisyphus are subjective. Negative feelings and attitudes are replaced by positive ones. From a nonhedonistic perspective, however, these changes come at a cost. When I try to understand the new Sisyphus's state of mind, when I try to imagine how someone might find stone-rolling fulfilling, I can only conceive of two possibilities: On the one hand, I can think of the substance in Sisyphus's veins as inducing delusions that make Sisyphus see something in stone-rolling that isn't really there. On the other hand, the drug in his veins may have lowered his intelligence and

reduced his imaginative capacity, thus eliminating his ability to perceive the dullness and futility of his labors or to compare them to other more challenging or worthwhile things that, had the gods not condemned him, he might have been doing instead. In either case, Sisyphus is in at least one respect worse off than he was before his transformation. He is either afflicted by mental illness or delusions or diminished in his intellectual powers.

Opinion may divide over whether, all things considered, the transformation makes Sisyphus worse or better off. Those in strongest sympathy with Mill's claim that it is better to be a human unsatisfied than a pig satisfied may think that however bad the fate of the classical Sisyphus, the fate of the transformed Sisyphus is worse. Others may conclude that since Sisyphus is condemned to roll stones in any case, it is better for him to be happy with, or more precisely, fulfilled by his lot than otherwise. Even those who hold the view that it is better to be Sisyphus happy than Sisyphus unhappy, however, may agree that it is better still not to be Sisyphus at all.

To me, the first scenario, in which the transformed Sisyphus is deluded, seems a more plausible way to understand what it would be for Sisyphus to be or to feel *fulfilled* by stone-rolling, for "fulfillment" seems to me to include a cognitive component that requires seeing the source or object of fulfillment as being, in some independent way, good or worthwhile. Even deep and intense pleasures, like lying on the beach on a beautiful day, or eating a perfectly ripe peach, would not naturally be described as fulfilling. To find something fulfilling is rather to find it such as to be characterizable in terms that would portray it as (objectively) good.[11]

---

[11]Though he does not use the language of "fulfillment" and "meaningfulness," Stephen Darwall discusses the profound contribution to welfare that comes from "the experience of connecting with something of worth in a way that enables the direct appreciation of the value of one's activity" in, *Welfare and Rational Care* (Princeton: Princeton University Press, 2002), p. 95. His discussion of such experiences, which I take to be more or less identical to what I am describing as experiences of fulfillment, offers an especially good characterization of the kind of appreciation of value at issue that avoids over-intellectualizing it. The account of human welfare he develops in Chapter Four has much in common with the description of meaningfulness I defend here.

Imagining Sisyphus in terms of either scenario, however, can explain why we might hesitate to describe the life of Sisyphus Fulfilled as meaningful—and similarly, I would argue, why we would withhold that label from the life of the fulfilled pot-smoker, goldfish-lover, or Tolstoy-copier. Imagining these characters on the model of either scenario would, in any case, help to explain why we might regard their lives as far from ideal. Earlier I suggested that we might judge these lives to be "missing something," a phrase that suggests a feature separable from fulfillment that these lives lack, rendering them less than optimally meaningful (if meaningful at all). In light of our discussion, we can now see that even the apparent condition of meaningfulness they do satisfy—that is, the condition of being fulfilled—is in a certain way defective and less desirable than fulfillment stemming from a more fitting or appropriate source....

◉ CRITICAL QUESTIONS

1. Construct an argument that supports the claim that *subjective* satisfaction with one's life is sufficient by itself for finding meaning in life.

2. Wolf's views on the meaning in life have been criticized as elitist. Do you think that is a fair criticism? Why or why not?

To access the *Voices of Wisdom*, 8th Edition, **Premium Website**, search for this book on CengageBrain.com.

CHAPTER FOUR

How Can I Know What Is Right?

Ethics is limitations on freedom of action in the struggle for existence.

ALDO LEOPOLD

LEARNING OBJECTIVES

After studying this chapter students should be able to:
- explain the differences among ethical skeptics, relativists, and absolutists,
- contrast teleogical ethical theories with deontological ethical theories,
- define utilitarianism and hedonism,
- explain some problems with the divine command theory,
- state the difference between ethical nihilism and emotivism,
- explain how, according to some psychological research, female moral reasoning differs from male moral reasoning,
- identify Kant, Bentham, Mill, Nietzsche, al-Ashari, Nielsen, Gilligan, Held, and Pojman, and
- answer all the questions relating to each selection.

4.1 INTRODUCTION

Have you ever wondered how you can know what is morally right? You have been told to do the right thing. But what is the *right* thing? Sometimes it is very hard to figure out. Sometimes our duties conflict. We know we should be loyal to our friends, but shouldn't we report them for cheating? Sometimes we must choose between alternatives, both of which seem wrong.

To know what is the right thing to do, we need to know what makes an action right. How can we know that? Do my motives make my actions right? If I intend to do my moral duty as best I understand it, isn't that enough? We call that acting out of a good will. However, maybe a good will is not enough. Maybe it is not my motives but the consequences of what I do that count. If my actions result in good things for most people, isn't that sufficient to justify my actions?

You might reply, "What about the act itself? It is surely either right or wrong in itself, no matter what my motives are or the consequences. Aren't some things just plain wrong? It is not right to steal even if my motives are good or the consequences will benefit some. Stealing is just plain wrong."

The philosopher wonders why it is "just plain wrong." What *makes* it wrong? How do I know that it is wrong?

We all know that people have different values and believe different things to be right. Are your moral beliefs any better than anyone else's? Some people are **ethical skeptics**. They doubt whether there is any such thing as moral truth. For them, there is no way we can know that stealing is wrong. It may be, but we cannot know that. To show that the ethical skeptic is mistaken, you would have to show how we can arrive at moral knowledge.

Some people are **ethical relativists**. They deny that there are any universally valid moral principles. Even stealing can be "right" if some culture recognizes it to be "right," even though others might think it "wrong." However, if we subscribe to ethical relativism, it appears that we must give up any basis for condemning someone like Hitler. Morally deplorable actions such as "ethnic cleansing" become "right" if some culture thinks them to be right. Surely there must be some moral absolutes.

While ethical skeptics doubt that we can know any moral absolutes, if there should happen to be any, and ethical relativists claim that there are, in fact, no such absolutes, **ethical absolutists** (also called universalists) claim there are. Moral values, they argue, are universal. They transcend time and place. What is right is right, regardless of what anyone may think. Stealing is wrong, even if it might be justified in some circumstances by some higher good and even if some culture might think it is "cool."

I should note that there are different varieties of ethical skeptics, relativists, and absolutists. My characterizations are intended to give an introductory first approximation. For example, as we shall see below, there are different kinds of ethical relativists.

Before we can know what might make an action right, we have to do a little bit of thinking about the parts of an action. It is evident that actions have consequences. Thus we might wonder whether the consequences or the results of an action make it right. People who advocate the view that consequences determine the rightness of an action support what philosophers call **teleological ethical theories**.

There is more to action, however, than its consequences. There is also the motive for the action, and it is worth asking whether motives, not consequences, make an action morally right. We know that people can do something that has good results, but do it for the wrong reasons. I may refrain from cheating on a test because I am afraid I will get caught. Not cheating has good consequences because it makes the test fair for all. However, is it right to praise me for being morally good simply because I was afraid to cheat? Should I not do the right thing because it is the right thing? Moral theories that advocate doing what is good because it is good, regardless of the consequences, are called **deontological ethical theories** (from the Greek *deon*, meaning "duty," and logos, meaning "science" or "study of").

4.2 KANT AND THE CATEGORICAL IMPERATIVE

Immanuel Kant (1724–1804) was born, spent his entire life, and died in Königsberg, Prussia. He studied natural science, mathematics, history, and philosophy at the University of Königsberg. After graduation he worked for a while as a tutor to the children of Prussian aristocrats, eventually landing a job as *Privatdozent* at the university. This meant that he was licensed by the university to offer lectures, but the university did not pay him. Rather, he was paid by the students who attended his lectures. For more than a dozen years, Kant lectured on a wide variety of subjects for up to 21 hours a week in order to make enough money to live.

Kant's monetary fortunes improved when he was finally appointed professor of logic and metaphysics in 1770 and was paid a decent wage by the university. In 1781 one of his many books appeared, *The Critique of Pure Reason*, which was destined to revolutionize Western philosophy. It earned Kant the reputation of being one of the greatest philosophical minds of the modern period.

The selection that follows is from *Groundwork of the Metaphysics of Morals*, which Kant published in 1785. He intended it to be a brief introduction to his theory, which he later elaborated in *The Critique of Practical Reason*. Even though this work is introductory, it is not easy to read. Take your time, think about what Kant is saying, and pay particular attention to what Kant means by the **categorical imperative**.

READING QUESTIONS

1. What is good without qualification?
2. Do the consequences or results of a good will make it good?
3. According to Kant, where does the moral value or worth of an action done from duty reside? In the results of the action? In the actual motive a person may in fact have *(the material principle)*? If not in these, where?
4. What do you think Kant meant when he said, "Duty is the necessity to act out of reverence for the law"?
5. What is the *categorical imperative*?

Groundwork of the Metaphysics of Morals

IMMANUEL KANT

THE GOOD WILL

It is impossible to conceive anything at all in the world, or even out of it, which can be taken as good without qualification, except a *good will*. Intelligence, wit, judgment, and any other *talents* of the mind we may care to name, or courage, resolution, and constancy of purpose, as qualities of *temperament*, are without doubt good and desirable in many respects; but they can also be extremely bad and hurtful when the will is not good which has to make use of these gifts of nature, and which for this reason has the term *"character"*

applied to its peculiar quality. It is exactly the same with *gifts of fortune*. Power, wealth, honour, even health and that complete well-being and contentment with one's state which goes by the name of *"happiness"* produce boldness, and as a consequence often over-boldness as well, unless a good will is present by which their influence on the mind—and so, too, the whole principle of action—may be corrected and adjusted to universal ends; not to mention that a rational and impartial spectator can never feel approval in contemplating the uninterrupted prosperity of a being graced by no touch of a pure and good will, and that consequently a

From I. Kant, *Groundwork of the Metaphysics of Morals*, translated by H. J. Paton (New York: Harper & Row, 1964), pp. 61–62, 64–71. Reprinted by permission of Unwin Hyman, Ltd. Translator's footnotes deleted.

good will seems to constitute the indispensable condition of our very worthiness to be happy.

Some qualities are even helpful to this good will itself and can make its task very much easier. They have none the less no inner unconditioned worth, but rather presuppose a good will which sets a limit to the esteem in which they are rightly held and does not permit us to regard them as absolutely good. Moderation in affections and passions, self-control, and sober reflexion are not only good in many respects: they may even seem to constitute part of the inner worth of a person. Yet they are far from being properly described as good without qualification (however unconditionally they have been commended by the ancients). For without the principles of a good will they may become exceedingly bad; and the very coolness of a scoundrel makes him, not merely more dangerous, but also immediately more abominable in our eyes than we should have taken him to be without it.

THE GOOD WILL AND ITS RESULTS

A good will is not good because of what it effects or accomplishes—because of its fitness for attaining some proposed end: it is good through its willing alone—that is, good in itself. Considered in itself it is to be esteemed beyond comparison as far higher than anything it could ever bring about merely in order to favour some inclination or, if you like, the sum total of inclinations. Even if, by some special disfavour of destiny or by the niggardly endowment of step-motherly nature, this will is entirely lacking in power to carry out its intentions; if by its utmost effort it still accomplishes nothing, and only good will is left (not, admittedly, as a mere wish, but as the straining of every means so far as they are in our control); even then it would still shine like a jewel for its own sake as something which has its full value in itself. Its usefulness or fruitlessness can neither add to, nor subtract from, this value. Its usefulness would be merely, as it were, the setting which enables us to handle it better in our ordinary dealings or to attract the attention of those not yet sufficiently expert, but not to commend it to experts or to determine its value....

THE GOOD WILL AND DUTY

We have now to elucidate the concept of a will estimable in itself and good apart from any further end. This concept, which is already present in a sound natural understanding and requires not so much to be taught as merely to be clarified, always holds the highest place in estimating the total worth of our actions and constitutes the condition of all the rest. We will therefore take up the concept of *duty*, which includes that of a good will, exposed, however, to certain subjective limitations and obstacles. These, so far from hiding a good will or disguising it, rather bring it out by contrast and make it shine forth more brightly.

THE MOTIVE OF DUTY

I will here pass over all actions already recognized as contrary to duty, however useful they may be with a view to this or that end; for about these the question does not even arise whether they could have been done *for the sake of duty* inasmuch as they are directly opposed to it. I will also set aside actions which in fact accord with duty, yet for which men have *no immediate inclination*, but perform them because impelled to do so by some other inclination. For there it is easy to decide whether the action which accords with duty has been done *from duty* or from some purpose of self-interest. This distinction is far more difficult to perceive when the action accords with duty and the subject has in addition an *immediate* inclination to the action. For example, it certainly accords with duty that a grocer should not overcharge his inexperienced customer; and where there is much competition a sensible shopkeeper refrains from so doing and keeps to a fixed and general price for everybody so that a child can buy from him just as well as anyone else. Thus people are served *honestly*; but this is not nearly enough to justify us in believing that the shopkeeper has acted in this way from duty or from principles of fair dealing; his interests required him to do so. We cannot assume him to have in addition an immediate inclination towards his customers, leading him, as it were out of love, to give no man preference over another in the matter of price. Thus the action was done neither from duty nor from immediate inclination, but solely from purposes of self-interest.

On the other hand, to preserve one's life is a duty, and besides this every one has also an immediate inclination to do so. But on account of this the often-anxious precautions taken by the greater part of mankind for this purpose have no inner worth, and the maxim of their action is without moral content. They do protect their lives *in conformity with duty*, but not *from the motive of duty*. When on the contrary, disappointments and hopeless misery have quite taken away the taste for life; when a wretched man, strong in soul and more angered at his fate than faint-hearted or cast down, longs for death and still preserves his life without loving it—not from inclination or fear but from duty; then indeed his maxim has a moral content.

To help others where one can is a duty, and besides this there are many spirits of so sympathetic a temper that, without any further motive of vanity or self-interest, they find an inner pleasure in spreading happiness around them and can take delight in the contentment of others as their own work. Yet I maintain that in such a case an action of this kind, however right and however amiable it may be, has still no genuinely moral worth. It stands on the same footing as other inclinations—for example, the inclination for honour, which if fortunate enough to hit on something beneficial and right and consequently honorable, deserves praise and encouragement, but not esteem; for its maxim lacks moral content, namely, the performance of such actions, not from inclination, but *from duty*. Suppose then that the mind of this friend of man were overclouded by sorrows of his own which extinguished all sympathy with the fate of others, but that he still had power to help those in distress, though no longer stirred by the need of others because sufficiently occupied with his own; and suppose that, when no longer moved by any inclination, he tears himself out of this deadly insensibility and does the action without any inclination for the sake of duty alone; then for the first time his action has its genuine moral worth. Still further: if nature had implanted little sympathy in this or that man's heart; if (being in other respects an honest fellow) he were cold in temperament and indifferent to the sufferings of others—perhaps because, being endowed with the special gift of patience and robust endurance in his own sufferings, he assumed the like in others or even demanded it; if such a man (who would in truth not be the worst product of nature) were not exactly fashioned by her to be a philanthropist, would he not still find in himself a source from which he might draw a worth far higher than any that a good-natured temperament can have? Assuredly he would. It is precisely in this that the worth of character begins to show— a moral worth and beyond all comparison the highest—namely, that he does good, not from inclination, but from duty.

To assure one's own happiness is a duty (at least indirectly); for discontent with one's state, in a press of cares and amidst unsatisfied wants, might easily become a great *temptation to the transgression of duty*. But here also, apart from regard to duty, all men have already of themselves the strongest and deepest inclination towards happiness, because precisely in this idea of happiness all inclinations are combined into a sum total. The prescription for happiness is, however, often so constituted as greatly to interfere with some inclinations, and yet men cannot form under the name of "happiness" any determinate and assured conception of the satisfaction of all inclinations as a sum. Hence it is not to be wondered at that a single inclination which is determinate as to what it promises and as to the time of its satisfaction may outweigh a wavering idea; and that a man, for example, a sufferer from gout, may choose to enjoy what he fancies and put up with what he can—on the ground that on balance he has here at least not killed the enjoyment of the present moment because of some possibly groundless expectations of the good fortune supposed to attach to soundness of health. But in this case also, when the universal inclination towards happiness has failed to determine his will, when good health, at least for him, has not entered into his calculations as so necessary, what remains over, here as in other cases, is a law—the law of furthering his happiness, not from inclination, but from duty; and in this for the first time his conduct has a real moral worth.

It is doubtless in this sense that we should understand too the passages from Scripture in which we are commanded to love our neighbour and even our enemy. For love out of inclination cannot be commanded; but kindness done from duty—although no inclination impels us, and even although natural and unconquerable disinclination stands in our way—is *practical*, and not *pathological*, love, residing in the will and not in the propensions [propensity] of feeling, in principles of action and not of melting compassion; and it is this practical love alone which can be an object of command.

THE FORMAL PRINCIPLE OF DUTY

Our second proposition is this: An action done from duty has its moral worth, not in the purpose to be attained by it, but in the maxim in accordance with which it is decided upon; it depends therefore, not on the realization of the object of the action, but solely on the principle of volition in accordance with which, irrespective of all objects of the faculty of desire, the action has been performed. That the purposes we may have in our actions, and also their effects considered as ends and motives of the will, can give to actions no unconditioned and moral worth is clear from what has gone before. Where then can this worth be found if we are not to find it in the will's relation to the effect hoped for from the action? It can be found nowhere but in the principle of the will, irrespective of the ends which can be brought about by such an action; for between its a priori principle, which is formal, and its a posteriori motive, which is material, the will stands, so to speak, at a parting of the ways; and since it must be determined by some principle, it will have to be determined by the formal principle of volition when an action is done from duty, where, as we have seen, every material principle is taken away from it.

REVERENCE FOR THE LAW

Our third proposition, as an inference from the two preceding, I would express thus: Duty is the

necessity to act out of reverence for the law. For an object as the effect of my proposed action I can have an inclination, but never reverence, precisely because it is merely the effect, and not the activity, of a will. Similarly for inclination as such, whether my own or that of another, I cannot have reverence: I can at most in the first case approve, and in the second case sometimes even love—that is, regard it as favourable to my own advantage. Only something which is conjoined with my will solely as a ground and never as an effect—something which does not serve my inclination, but outweighs it or at least leaves it entirely out of account in my choice—and therefore only bare law for its own sake, can be an object of reverence and therewith a command. Now an action done from duty has to set aside altogether the influence of inclination, and along with inclination every object of the will; so there is nothing left able to determine the will except objectively the law and subjectively pure reverence for this practical law, and therefore the maxim[1] of obeying this law even to the detriment of all my inclinations.

Thus the moral worth of an action does not depend on the result expected from it, and so too does not depend on any principle of action that needs to borrow its motive from this expected result. For all these results (agreeable states and even the promotion of happiness in others) could have been brought about by other causes as well, and consequently their production did not require the will of a rational being, in which, however, the highest and unconditioned good can alone be found. Therefore nothing but the idea of the law in itself, which admittedly is present only in a rational being—so far as it, and not an expected result, is the ground determining the will—can constitute that pre-eminent good which we call moral, a good which is already present in the person

---

[1]A maxim is the subjective principle of a volition: an objective principle (that is, one which would also serve subjectively as a practical principle for all rational beings if reason had full control over the faculty of desire) is a practical *law*.

acting on this idea and has not to be awaited merely from the result.[2]

THE CATEGORICAL IMPERATIVE

But what kind of law can this be the thought of which, even without regard to the results expected from it, has to determine the will if this is to be called good absolutely and without qualification? Since I have robbed the will of every inducement that might arise for it as a consequence of obeying any particular law, nothing is left but the conformity of actions to universal law as such, and this alone must serve the will as its principle. That is to say, I ought never to act except in such a way that I can also will that my maxim should become a universal law. Here bare conformity to universal law as such (without having as its base any law prescribing particular actions) is what serves the will as its principle, and must so serve it if duty is not to be everywhere an empty delusion and a chimerical concept. The ordinary reason of mankind also agrees with this completely in its

---

[2]It might be urged against me that I have merely tried, under cover of the word *"reverence"* to take refuge in an obscure feeling instead of giving a clearly articulated answer to the question by means of a concept of reason. Yet, although reverence is a feeling, it is not a feeling *received* through outside influence, but one *self-produced* by a rational concept, and therefore specifically distinct from feelings of the first kind, all of which can be reduced to inclination or fear. What I recognize immediately as law for me, I recognize with reverence, which means merely consciousness of the *subordination* of my will to a law without the mediation of external influences on my senses. Immediate determination of the will by the law and consciousness of this determination is called *"reverence"* so that reverence is regarded as the *effect* of the law on the subject and not as the *cause* of the law. Reverence is properly awareness of a value which demolishes my self-love. Hence, there is something which is regarded neither as an object of inclination nor as an object of fear, though it has at the same time some analogy with both. The *object* of reverence is the *law* alone—that law which we impose *on ourselves* but yet as necessary in itself. Considered as a law, we are subject to it without any consultation of self-love; considered as self-imposed it is a consequence of our will. In the first respect it is analogous to fear, in the second to inclination. All reverence for a person is properly only reverence for the law (of honesty and so on) of which that person gives us an example. Because we regard the development of our talents as a duty, we see too in a man of talent a sort of *example of the law* (the law of becoming like him by practice), and this is what constitutes our reverence for him. All moral *interest*, so-called, consists solely in *reverence* for the law.

practical judgments and always has the aforesaid principle before its eyes.

Take this question, for example. May I not, when I am hard pressed, make a promise with the intention of not keeping it? Here I readily distinguish the two senses which the question can have—Is it prudent, or is it right, to make a false promise? The first no doubt can often be the case. I do indeed see that it is not enough for me to extricate myself from present embarrassment by this subterfuge: I have to consider whether from this lie there may not subsequently accrue to me much greater inconvenience than that from which I now escape, and also—since, with all my supposed *astuteness*, to foresee the consequences is not so easy that I can be sure there is no chance, once confidence in me is lost, of this proving far more disadvantageous than all the ills I now think to avoid—whether it may not be a *more prudent* action to proceed here on a general maxim and make it my habit not to give a promise except with the intention of keeping it. Yet it becomes clear to me at once that such a maxim is always founded solely on fear of consequences. To tell the truth for the sake of duty is something entirely different from doing so out of concern for inconvenient results; for in the first case the concept of the action already contains in itself a law for me, while in the second case I have first of all to look around elsewhere in order to see what effects may be bound up with it for me. When I deviate from the principle of duty, this is quite certainly bad; but if I desert my prudential maxim, this can often be greatly to my advantage, though it is admittedly safer to stick to it. Suppose I seek, however, to learn in the quickest way and yet unerringly how to solve the problem "Does a lying promise accord with duty?" I have then to ask myself "Should I really be content that my maxim (the maxim of getting out of a difficulty by a false promise) should hold as a universal law (one valid both for myself and others)?" And could I really say to myself that everyone may make a false promise if he finds himself in a difficulty from which he can extricate himself in no other way? I then become aware at once that I can indeed will to lie, but I can by no means will a universal law of lying; for by such a law there could properly be no promises at all, since it would be futile to profess a will for future action to others who would not believe my profession or who, if they did so over-hastily, would pay me back in like coin; and consequently my maxim, as soon as it was made a universal law, would be bound to annul itself.

Thus I need no far-reaching ingenuity to find out what I have to do in order to possess a good will. Inexperienced in the course of world affairs and incapable of being prepared for all the chances that happen in it, I ask myself only "Can you also will that your maxim should become a universal law?" Where you cannot, it is to be rejected, and

that not because of a prospective loss to you or even to others, but because it cannot fit as a principle into a possible enactment of universal law. For such an enactment reason compels my immediate reverence, into whose grounds (which the philosopher may investigate) I have as yet no insight, although I do at least understand this much: reverence is the assessment of a worth which far outweighs all the worth of what is commended by inclination, and the necessity for me to act out of pure reverence for the practical law is what constitutes duty, to which every other motive must give way because it is the condition of a will good in itself, whose value is above all else.

⊚ CRITICAL QUESTIONS

1. According to Kant, a good will is manifested in acting for the sake of duty. He contends that "the worth of character begins to show" when a person "does good, not from inclination, but from duty." Why does Kant claim this and do you agree or not? Why?

2. Kant claimed we can will to lie, but we cannot will a universal law of lying. Do you think his argument is really, as Mill claimed, teleological rather than deontological? Why, or why not?

3. Kant said that if you want to know whether an action is morally right, determine the maxim or subjective principle on which it is based and then ask, "Can I also will that my maxim should become a universal law?" If the answer is no, it is

not the right thing to do. Apply Kant's advice to the following case: You are a bright individual who usually gets good grades. You want to go to law school, and you need good grades to get accepted by a good law school. You find yourself taking a philosophy test for which you are not well prepared, and you have an opportunity to cheat without being caught. By cheating, you will definitely improve your final grade for the course. Should you cheat? If you were a Kantian (a follower of Kant's theory), what would be your answer, and what would be your reasoning?

4. How did Kant answer the question, "How can I know what is right?" Do you agree with Kant's answer or not? Why, or why not?

4.3 UTILITARIANISM

Suppose you have to decide whether your lovable cat, who has been your companion for many years and is now very sick, should be "put to sleep," as we euphemistically say. How would you go about making the decision? Would you consider how much pain your cat (let's call her Jenny) is suffering? Would you consider Jenny's chances of recovery? Would and *should* you think about your own pain and loss if you put Jenny to sleep?

Now suppose that Jenny is your mother, not your cat. Suppose further that you lived in a state that allowed physician-assisted suicide. Suppose your mother is not able to tell a physician what she wants, and you must make a decision. How would you go about it? Would the same questions that occurred to you in the case of your cat also occur to you in this case? Would those questions be relevant? Should the decisionmaking process be essentially the same in both cases?

Now suppose that Jenny is the name you have selected for your newborn daughter who is so severely retarded and incapable of thought or action that she will be nothing but a burden to you and your family for as long as she may live. She will never know you, or have the capacity to love you. Suppose further that you live in a state that permits euthanasia. Should Jenny be "put to sleep"? How would you decide? Are the same sorts of considerations that you agonized about in the first two cases relevant to this case? Is there any way of thinking about these cases that might help us know what is right?

Jeremy Bentham (1748–1832), a British philosopher and social reformer, thought he could provide some help in deciding these difficult cases. He believed that a rational and scientific approach to social and moral issues is possible if we learn to apply what he called "the principle of utility."

Bentham's ethical theory is called **utilitarianism**. Classified as a teleological theory, it maintains that what makes an action right are its consequences. If the consequences are good, then the action is right. However, what are good consequences? Bentham answers that good consequences are those that result in the greatest amount of pleasure (happiness) for the "party whose interest is in question." The party may be the collection of individuals we call a community insofar as they share common interests or it may be a particular individual.

John Stuart Mill (1806–1873), a follower of Bentham, interpreted Bentham's discussion of the interests of the community to mean that Bentham was talking about the greatest happiness for the greatest number of people who are affected by the action in question. Whether this is what Bentham meant is a matter of scholarly dispute. However, it is clear that Bentham's principle of utility is intended to guide legislative (and individual) decision making by focusing attention on the amount of pleasure that might result from a particular law or course of action.

Because Mill believed that the good is pleasure, his utilitarian theory is also a variety of **hedonism**. According to hedonistic theories, the highest good is pleasure. Morality is thus grounded in feelings that are natural to the human animal. We, like all animals, act in order to avoid pain and maximize pleasure.

The following selection is from Chapters 2 through 4 of Mill's work, *Utilitarianism*, which was published in 1861. In the first chapter (not included here), Mill made general remarks about ethics and attacked Kant's theory. Kant believed that it is illogical and hence irrational to will universal immoral laws. Thus, although we can will to lie, we cannot will that everyone ought to lie. Mill said that Kant never proved that the adoption of immoral laws by all rational beings is illogical in the sense that it somehow involves a contradiction. All he ever showed is that the consequences of adopting immoral laws as universal would be so undesirable that no one would choose to do so. That is, we do not advocate that everyone should lie because it is irrational to do so; rather, we do not advocate it because we do not wish to live in societies where no one can be trusted. Thus Kant, in spite of his rejection of teleological ethical theories, ended up having to appeal to consequences but refusing to acknowledge he did, or so Mill contended.

In his last chapter (not included here), Mill turned to the issue of justice, acknowledging that providing an adequate theory of justice is one of the hardest problems for utilitarianism. Nevertheless, he argued that the fair treatment of all people in society can be justified on utilitarian grounds because it is in the best interests of all to promote a feeling of security. Fair treatment, extended to all, promotes such a feeling.

But I am getting too far ahead. Before we can compare Kant's deontological theory with Mill's teleological theory, we need to learn more about Mill's theory.

I think you will find Mill a lot easier to read than Kant, but answering the following questions will still prove helpful in understanding the main points of Mill's theory.

⊚ READING QUESTIONS

1. What is the "greatest happiness principle" (also called the "principle of utility")?
2. What does Mill mean by happiness?
3. What is the theory of life on which the utilitarian theory is based?

4. According to Mill, how can we determine whether one pleasure is more valuable than another?
5. How does Mill answer the question, "Why am I bound to promote the general happiness?"
6. How does Mill answer the question, "How can I know what is right?"

What Utilitarianism Is

JOHN STUART MILL

The creed which accepts as the foundation of morals "utility" or the "greatest happiness principle" holds that actions are right in proportion as they tend to promote happiness; wrong as they tend to produce the reverse of happiness. By "happiness" is intended pleasure and the absence of pain; by "unhappiness," pain and the privation of pleasure. To give a clear view of the moral standard set up by the theory, much more requires to be said; in particular, what things it includes in the ideas of pain and pleasure, and to what extent this is left an open question. But these supplementary explanations do not affect the theory of life on which this theory of morality is grounded—namely, that pleasure and freedom from pain are the only things desirable as ends; and that all desirable things (which are as numerous in the utilitarian as in any other scheme) are desirable either for pleasure inherent in themselves or as means to the promotion of pleasure and the prevention of pain.

Now such a theory of life excites in many minds, and among them in some of the most estimable in feeling and purpose, inveterate dislike. To suppose that life has (as they express it) no

higher end than pleasure—no better and nobler object of desire and pursuit—they designate as utterly mean and groveling, as a doctrine worthy only of swine, to whom the followers of Epicurus were, at a very early period, contemptuously likened; and modern holders of the doctrine are occasionally made the subject of equally polite comparisons by its German, French, and English assailants.

When thus attacked, the Epicureans have always answered that it is not they, but their accusers, who represent human nature in a degrading light; since the accusation supposes human beings to be capable of no pleasures except those of which swine are capable. If this supposition were true, the charge could not be gainsaid, but would then be no longer an imputation; for if the sources of pleasure were precisely the same to human beings and to swine, the rule of life which is good enough for the one would be good enough for the other. The comparison of the Epicurean life to that of beasts is felt as degrading, precisely because a beast's pleasures do not satisfy a human being's conceptions of happiness.

From "What Utilitarianism Is" by John Stuart Mill.

Human beings have faculties more elevated than the animal appetites and, when once made conscious of them, do not regard anything as happiness which does not include their gratification. I do not, indeed, consider the Epicureans to have been by any means faultless in drawing out their scheme of consequences from the utilitarian principle. To do this in any sufficient manner, many Stoic, as well as Christian elements require to be included. But there is no known Epicurean theory of life which does not assign to the pleasures of the intellect, of the feelings and imagination, and of the moral sentiments a much higher value as pleasures than to those of mere sensation. It must be admitted, however, that utilitarian writers in general have placed the superiority of mental over bodily pleasures chiefly in the greater permanency, safety, un-costliness, etc., of the former—that is, in their circumstantial advantages rather than in their intrinsic nature. And on all these points utilitarians have fully proved their case; but they might have taken the other and, as it may be called, higher ground with entire consistency. It is quite compatible with the principle of utility to recognize the fact that some kinds of pleasure are more desirable and more valuable than others. It would be absurd that, while in estimating all other things quality is considered as well as quantity, the estimation of pleasure should be supposed to depend on quantity alone.

If I am asked what I mean by difference of quality in pleasures, or what makes one pleasure more valuable than another, merely as a pleasure, except its being greater in amount, there is but one possible answer. Of two pleasures, if there be one to which all or almost all who have experience of both give a decided preference, irrespective of any feeling of moral obligation to prefer it, that is the more desirable pleasure. If one of the two is, by those who are competently acquainted with both, placed so far above the other that they prefer it, even though knowing it to be attended with a greater amount of discontent, and would not resign it for any quantity of the other pleasure which their nature is capable of, we are justified in ascribing to the preferred enjoyment a superiority in quality so far outweighing quantity as to render it, in comparison, of small account.

Now it is an unquestionable fact that those who are equally acquainted with and equally capable of appreciating and enjoying both do give a most marked preference to the manner of existence which employs their higher faculties. Few human creatures would consent to be changed into any of the lower animals for a promise of the fullest allowance of a beast's pleasures; no intelligent human being would consent to be a fool, no instructed person would be an ignoramus, no person of feeling and conscience would be selfish and base, even though they should be persuaded that the fool, the dunce, or the rascal is better satisfied with his lot than they are with theirs. They would not resign what they possess more than he for the most complete satisfaction of all the desires which they have in common with him. If they ever fancy they would, it is only in cases of unhappiness so extreme that to escape from it they would exchange their lot for almost any other, however undesirable in their own eyes. A being of higher faculties requires more to make him happy, is capable probably of more acute suffering, and certainly accessible to it at more points, than one of an inferior type; but in spite of these liabilities, he can never really wish to sink into what he feels to be a lower grade of existence. We may give what explanation we please of this unwillingness; we may attribute it to pride, a name which is given indiscriminately to some of the most and to some of the least estimable feelings of which mankind are capable; we may refer it to the love of liberty and personal independence, an appeal to which was with the Stoics one of the most effective means for the inculcation of it; to the love of power or to the love of excitement, both of which do really enter into and contribute to it; but its most appropriate appellation is a sense of dignity, which all human beings possess in one form or other, and in some, though by no means in exact, proportion to their higher faculties, and which is so essential a part of the happiness of those in whom it is strong that nothing which conflicts with it could be otherwise than momentarily an object of desire to them. Whoever supposes that this preference takes place at a sacrifice of happiness—that the superior being, in anything like equal circumstances, is not happier than the inferior—confounds the two very different ideas of happiness and content. It is indisputable that the being whose capacities of enjoyment are low has the greatest chance of having them fully satisfied; and a highly endowed being will always feel that any happiness which he can look for, as the world is constituted, is imperfect. But he can learn to bear its imperfections, if they are at all bearable; and they will not make him envy the being who is indeed unconscious of the imperfections, but only because he feels not at all the good which those imperfections qualify. It is better to be a human being dissatisfied than a pig satisfied; better to be Socrates dissatisfied than a fool satisfied. And if the fool or the pig are of a different opinion, it is because they only know their own side of the question. The other party to the comparison knows both sides.

It may be objected that many who are capable of the higher pleasures occasionally, under the influence of temptation, postpone them to the lower. But this is quite compatible with a full appreciation of the intrinsic superiority of the higher. Men often, from infirmity of character, make their election for the nearer good, though they know it to be the less valuable; and this no less when the choice is between two bodily pleasures than when it is between bodily and mental. They pursue sensual indulgences to the injury of health, though perfectly aware that health is the greater good. It may be further objected that many who begin with youthful enthusiasm for everything noble, as they advance in years, sink into indolence and selfishness. But I do not believe that those who undergo this very common change voluntarily choose the lower description of pleasures in preference to the higher. I believe that, before they devote themselves exclusively to the one, they have already become incapable of the other. Capacity for the nobler feelings is in most natures a very tender plant, easily killed, not only by hostile influences, but by mere want of sustenance; and in the majority of young persons it speedily dies away if the occupations to which their position in life has devoted them, and the society into which it has thrown them, are not favorable to keeping that higher capacity in exercise. Men lose their high aspirations as they lose their intellectual tastes, because they have not time or opportunity for indulging them; and

they addict themselves to inferior pleasures, not because they deliberately prefer them, but because they are either the only ones to which they have access or the only ones which they are any longer capable of enjoying. It may be questioned whether anyone who has remained equally susceptible to both classes of pleasures ever knowingly and calmly preferred the lower, though many, in all ages, have broken down in an ineffectual attempt to combine both.

From this verdict of the only competent judges, I apprehend there can be no appeal. On a question which is the best worth having of two pleasures, or which of two modes of existence is the most grateful to the feelings, apart from its moral attributes and from its consequences, the judgment of those who are qualified by knowledge of both, or, if they differ, that of the majority among them, must be admitted as final. And there needs be the less hesitation to accept this judgment respecting the quality of pleasures, since there is no other tribunal to be referred to even on the question of quantity. What means are there of determining which is the acutest of two pains, or the intensest of two pleasurable sensations, except the general suffrage of those who are familiar with both? Neither pains nor pleasures are homogeneous, and pain is always heterogeneous with pleasure. What is there to decide whether a particular pleasure is worth purchasing at the cost of a particular pain, except the feelings and judgment of the experienced? When, therefore, those feelings and judgment declare the pleasures derived from the higher faculties to be preferable *in kind*, apart from the question of intensity, to those of which the animal nature, disjoined from the higher faculties, is susceptible, they are entitled on this subject to the same regard....

OF THE ULTIMATE SANCTION OF THE PRINCIPLE OF UTILITY

The question is often asked, and properly so, in regard to any supposed moral standard—What is its sanction? What are the motives to obey? Or, more specifically, what is the source of its obligation? Whence does it derive its binding force? It is a necessary part of moral philosophy to provide the answer to this question, which, though frequently assuming the shape of an objection to the utilitarian morality, as if it had some special applicability to that above others, really arises in regard to all standards. It arises, in fact, whenever a person is called on to *adopt* a standard, or refer morality to any basis on which he has not been accustomed to rest it. For the customary morality, that which education and opinion have consecrated, is the only one which presents itself to the mind with the feeling of being *in itself* obligatory; and when a person is asked to believe that this morality *derives* its obligation from some general principle round which custom has not thrown the same halo, the assertion is to him a paradox; the supposed corollaries seem to have a more binding force than the original theorem; the superstructure seems to stand better without than with what is represented as its foundation. He says to himself, I feel that I am bound not to rob or murder, betray or deceive; but why am I bound to promote the general happiness? If my own happiness lies in something else, why may I not give that the preference?...

The ultimate sanction, therefore, of all morality (external motives apart) being a subjective feeling in our own minds, I see nothing embarrassing to those whose standard is utility in the question, What is the sanction of that particular standard? We may answer, the same as of all other moral standards—the conscientious feelings of mankind. Undoubtedly this sanction has no binding efficacy on those who do not possess the feelings it appeals to; but neither will these persons be more obedient to any other moral principle than to the utilitarian one. On them morality of any kind has no hold but through the external sanctions. Meanwhile the feelings exist, a fact in human nature, the reality of which, and the great power with which they are capable of acting on those in whom they have been duly cultivated, are proved by experience. No reason has ever been shown why they may not be cultivated to as great intensity in connection with the utilitarian as with any other rule of morals.

There is, I am aware, a disposition to believe that a person who sees in moral obligation a transcendental fact, an objective reality belonging to the province of "things in themselves," is likely to be more obedient to it than one who believes it to be entirely subjective, having its seat in human consciousness only. But whatever a person's opinion may be on this point of ontology, the force he is really urged by is his own subjective feeling, and is exactly measured by its strength. No one's belief that duty is an objective reality is stronger than the belief that God is so; yet the belief in God, apart from the expectation of actual reward and punishment, only operates on conduct through, and in proportion to, the subjective religious feeling. The sanction, so far as it is disinterested, is always in the mind itself; and the notion, therefore, of the transcendental moralists must be that this sanction will not exist in the mind unless it is believed to have its root out of the mind; and that if a person is able to say to himself, "That which is restraining me and which is called my conscience is only a feeling in my own mind," he may possibly draw the conclusion that when the feeling ceases the obligation ceases, and that if he find the feeling inconvenient, he may disregard it and endeavor to get rid of it. But is this danger confined to the utilitarian morality? Does the belief that moral obligation has its seat outside the mind make the feeling of it too strong to be got rid of? The fact is so far otherwise that all moralists admit and lament the ease with which, in the generality of minds, conscience can be silenced or stifled. The question, "Need I obey my conscience?" is quite as often put to themselves by persons who never heard of the principle of utility as by its adherents. Those whose conscientious feelings are so weak as to allow of their asking this question, if they answer it affirmatively, will not do so because they believe in the transcendental theory, but because of the external sanctions....

It is not necessary, for the present purpose, to decide whether the feeling of duty is innate or implanted. Assuming it to be innate, it is an open question to what objects it naturally attaches itself; for the philosophic supporters of that theory are now agreed that the intuitive perception is of principles of morality and not of the details. If there be anything innate in the matter, I see no reason why the feeling which is innate should not be that of regard to the pleasures and pains of others. If there is any principle of morals which is intuitively obligatory, I should say it must be that. If so, the intuitive ethics would coincide with the utilitarian, and there would be no further quarrel between them. Even as it is, the intuitive moralists, though they believe that there are other intuitive moral obligations, do already believe this to be one; for they unanimously hold that a large portion of morality turns upon the consideration due to the interests of our fellow creatures. Therefore, if the belief in the transcendental origin of moral obligation gives any additional efficacy to the internal sanction, it appears to me that the utilitarian principle has already the benefit of it.

On the other hand, if, as is my own belief, the moral feelings are not innate but acquired, they are not for that reason the less natural. It is natural to man to speak, to reason, to build cities, to cultivate the ground, though these are acquired faculties. The moral feelings are not indeed a part of our nature in the sense of being in any perceptible degree present in all of us; but this, unhappily, is a fact admitted by those who believe the most strenuously in their transcendental origin. Like the other acquired capacities above referred to, the moral faculty, if not a part of our nature, is a natural outgrowth from it; capable, like them, in a certain small degree, of springing up spontaneously; and susceptible of being brought by cultivation to a high degree of development. Unhappily it is also susceptible, by a sufficient use of the external sanctions and of the force of early impressions, of being cultivated in almost any direction, so that there is hardly anything so absurd or so mischievous that it may not, by means of these influences, be made to act on the human mind with all the authority of conscience. To doubt that the same potency might be given by the same means to the principle of utility, even if it had no foundation in human nature, would be flying in the face of all experience.

But moral associations which are wholly of artificial creation, when the intellectual culture goes on, yield by degrees to the dissolving force of analysis; and if the feeling of duty, when associated with utility, would appear equally arbitrary; if there were no leading department of our nature, no powerful class of sentiments, with which that association would harmonize, which would make us feel it congenial and incline us not only to foster it in others (for which we have abundant interested motives), but also to cherish it in ourselves—if there were not, in short, a natural basis of sentiment for utilitarian morality, it might well happen that this association also, even after it had been implanted by education, might be analyzed away.

But there *is* this basis of powerful natural sentiment; and this it is which, when once the general happiness is recognized as the ethical standard, will constitute the strength of the utilitarian morality. This firm foundation is that of the social feelings of mankind—the desire to be in unity with our fellow creatures, which is already a powerful principle in human nature, and happily one of those which tend to become stronger, even without express inculcation, from the influences of advancing civilization. The social state is at once so natural, so necessary, and so habitual to man, that, except in some unusual circumstances or by an effort of voluntary abstraction, he never conceives himself otherwise than as a member of a body; and this association is riveted more and more, as mankind are further removed from the state of savage independence. Any condition, therefore, which is essential to a state of society becomes more and more an inseparable part of every person's conception of the state of things which he is born into, and which is the destiny of a human being. Now society between human beings, except in the relation of master and slave, is manifestly impossible on any other footing than that the interests of all are to be consulted. Society between equals can only exist on the understanding that the interests of all are to be regarded equally. And since in all states of civilization, every person, except an absolute monarch, has equals, everyone is obliged to live on these terms with somebody; and in every age some advance is made toward a state in which it will be impossible to live permanently on other terms with anybody....

OF WHAT SORT OF PROOF THE PRINCIPLE OF UTILITY IS SUSCEPTIBLE

It has already been remarked that questions of ultimate ends do not admit of proof, in the ordinary acceptation of the term. To be incapable of proof by reasoning is common to all first principles, to the first premises of our knowledge, as well as to those of our conduct. But the former, being matters of fact, may be the subject of a direct appeal to the faculties which judge of fact—namely, our senses and our internal consciousness. Can an appeal be made to the same faculties on questions of practical ends? Or by what other faculty is cognizance taken of them?

Questions about ends are, in other words, questions about what things are desirable. The utilitarian doctrine is that happiness is desirable, and the only thing desirable, as an end; all other things being only desirable as means to that end. What ought to be required of this doctrine, what conditions is it requisite that the doctrine should fulfill—to make good its claim to be believed?

The only proof capable of being given that an object is visible is that people actually see it. The only proof that a sound is audible is that people hear it; and so of the other sources of our experience. In like manner, I apprehend, the sole evidence it is possible to produce that anything is desirable is that people do actually desire it. If the end which the utilitarian doctrine proposes to itself were not, in theory and in practice, acknowledged to be an end, nothing could ever convince any person that it was so. No reason can be given why the general happiness is desirable, except that each person, so far as he believes it to be attainable, desires his own happiness. This, however, being a fact, we have not only all the proof which the case admits of, but all which it is possible to require, that happiness is a good, that each person's happiness is a good to that person, and the general happiness, therefore, a good to the aggregate of all persons. Happiness has made out its title as *one* of the ends of conduct and, consequently, one of the criteria of morality.

But it has not, by this alone, proved itself to be the sole criterion. To do that, it would seem, by the same rule, necessary to show, not only that people desire happiness, but that they never desire anything else. Now it is palpable that they do desire things which, in common language, are decidedly distinguished from happiness. They desire, for example, virtue and the absence of vice no less really than pleasure and the absence of pain.

The desire of virtue is not as universal, but it is as authentic a fact as the desire of happiness. And hence the opponents of the utilitarian standard deem that they have a right to infer that there are other ends of human action besides happiness, and that happiness is not the standard of approbation and disapprobation.

But does the utilitarian doctrine deny that people desire virtue, or maintain that virtue is not a thing to be desired? The very reverse. It maintains not only that virtue is to be desired, but that it is to be desired disinterestedly, for itself. Whatever may be the opinion of utilitarian moralists as to the original conditions by which virtue is made virtue, however they may believe (as they do) that actions and dispositions are only virtuous because they promote another end than virtue, yet this being granted, and it having been decided, from considerations of this description, what is virtuous, they not only place virtue at the very head of the things which are good as means to the ultimate end, but they also recognize as a psychological fact the possibility of its being, to the individual, a good in itself, without looking to any end beyond it; and hold that the mind is not in a right state, not in a state conformable to utility, not in the state most conducive to the general happiness, unless it does love virtue in this manner—as a thing desirable in itself, even although, in the individual instance, it should not produce those other desirable consequences which it tends to produce, and on account of which it is held to be virtue. This opinion is not, in the smallest degree, a departure from the happiness principle. The ingredients of happiness are very various, and each of them is desirable in itself, and not merely when considered as swelling an aggregate. The principle of utility does not mean that any given pleasure, as music, for instance, or any given exemption from pain, as for example health, is to be looked upon as means to a collective something termed happiness, and to be desired on that account. They are desired and desirable in and for themselves; besides being means, they are a part of the end. Virtue, according to the utilitarian doctrine, is not naturally and originally part of the end, but it is capable of becoming so; and in those who live it disinterestedly it has become so, and is desired and cherished, not as a means to happiness, but as a part of their happiness....

It results from the preceding considerations that there is in reality nothing desired except happiness. Whatever is desired otherwise than as a means to some end beyond itself, and ultimately to happiness, is desired as itself a part of happiness, and is not desired for itself until it has become so. Those who desire virtue for its own sake desire it either because the consciousness of it is a pleasure, or because the consciousness of being without it is a pain, or for both reasons united; as in truth the pleasure and pain seldom exist separately, but almost always together—the same person feeling pleasure in the degree of virtue attained, and pain in not having attained more. If one of these gave him no pleasure, and the other no pain, he would not love or desire virtue, or would desire it only for the other benefits which it might produce to himself or to persons whom he cared for.

We have now, then, an answer to the question, of what sort of proof the principle of utility is susceptible. If the opinion which I have now stated is psychologically true—if human nature is so constituted as to desire nothing which is not either a part of happiness or a means of happiness—we can have

no other proof, and we require no other, that these are the only things desirable. If so, happiness is the sole end of human action, and the promotion of it the test by which to judge of all human conduct; from whence it necessarily follows that it must be the criterion of morality, since a part is included in the whole.

And now to decide whether this is really so, whether mankind does desire nothing for itself but that which is a pleasure to them, or of which the absence is a pain, we have evidently arrived at a question of fact and experience, dependent, like all similar questions, upon evidence. It can only be determined by practiced self-consciousness and self-observation, assisted by observation of others. I believe that these sources of evidence, impartially consulted, will declare that desiring a thing and finding it pleasant, aversion to it and thinking of it as painful, are phenomena entirely inseparable or, rather, two parts of the same phenomenon— in strictness of language, two different modes of naming the same psychological fact; that to think of an object as desirable (unless for the sake of its consequences) and to think of it as pleasant are one and the same thing; and that to desire anything except in proportion as the idea of it is pleasant is a physical and metaphysical impossibility....

⊚ CRITICAL QUESTIONS

1. How does Mill answer the objection that Epicureanism (a variety of hedonism) is a "doctrine only worthy of swine"? Do you think his answer is a good one? Why?
2. Mill claims it is "better to be Socrates dissatisfied than a fool satisfied." Do you agree or not? Why?
3. Summarize Mill's proof for the principle of utility. Some philosophers have argued that Mill's proof is faulty because it confuses the descriptive (what people actually desire) with the normative (what people ought to desire). Do you agree with this criticism or not? Why?

4. Refer back to the case of potential cheating recounted in Critical Question 3 in the section on Kant. If you were a utilitarian, how would you go about determining the right thing to do in this situation?
5. Some people object to utilitarianism on the grounds that it allows us to do things that are immoral. Can you think of an example of something that would be immoral that utilitarian theory would say is good? What is it?

4.4 REVALUATION OF VALUES

Consideration of the question "How can I know what is right?" leads to thinking about other questions, such as what makes an action right. The "what" in both these questions initiates a search for a "something" that not only makes for moral rightness but also is something we can know. Pondering what this "something" might be sends our minds along a path searching for what some have called the foundations of morality. Where does morality come from? What supports it? Why, in our struggle for existence, should we limit our behavior in any way, or at least in any way that might be called moral? Why be moral?

Many people have found a close association between religion and morality. Not only are the moral values we hold historically derived from certain religions like Judaism, Christianity, Islam, Hinduism, Confucianism, and others, but many have held that there must be some sort of divine source or foundation for morality. So some might say that the shortest answer to the question "How can I know what is right?" is "What does God say?"

This line of thought reflects a divine command theory of ethics (see Section 3.4). What is good is what God commands. However, this short answer is problematic. Which "god" are we talking about? How do we know what are the divine commands? Wars have been fought with both sides claiming they were acting according to God's will. And, as Socrates pointed out, if God's command or will determines what is good, then nothing is good in itself, but only if God should happen to will it. If the meaning of the concept "moral goodness" is equivalent to the meaning "God commands," then we have no independent standards for judging whether what God commands is good. It is good by definition. So, for example, if I believe God has commanded me to allow my diabetic child to go without medical treatment, then that is a good thing to do—by definition.

Another problem arises if we ask, "How do we know the divine will won't change?" One day murder may be wrong (forbidden by God) and the next day right (commanded by God). One can always counter that God is unchanging. The divine mind will never change with respect to morality. Of course, saying this is one thing; proving it is quite another. Thus this divine foundation of morality is beginning to appear very unstable, and moral goodness is beginning to look like little more than obedience to a superior power.

Some might say that if there is no God, then anything is morally permissible. There is no reason at all to limit our freedom to do what we want. Both Kant and Mill (see the two previous sections) were concerned with the issue of the foundation of morality and wanted to make a rational case for morality. If we cannot rely entirely on a religious answer to our question, perhaps human reason itself, without relying on alleged revelations of God's will, can supply an answer.

What if human reason should fail? What if Kant's categorical imperative and Mill's principle of utility turn out to be inadequate answers? Where might we turn next? Perhaps there is no answer (a view some have dubbed **ethical nihilism**) or, if there is, we cannot not know it (ethical skepticism).

Friedrich Nietzsche (1844–1900), a German philosopher, thought both the religious answer and the reliance on human reason failed. If all religious and rational accounts of morality fail, what are we left with? Some have argued that Nietzsche gave a negative answer. We are left with nothing (nihilism). Others have argued that Nietzsche tried to overcome ethical nihilism with a theory of his own. Exactly how to characterize this theory, however, is problematic. For some it amounts to a version of **ethical emotivism**, or the claim that moral judgments express the appraiser's attitudes of approval or disapproval. "A (where *A* is some action) is good" becomes, according to an emotivist theory, "I like *A*." It is a short step, some philosophers have argued, from this position to the view that people ought to do what is in their own self-interest. Much of the morality we have inherited stresses an altruistic viewpoint (the viewpoint that people ought, at least sometimes, to do what is in the interest of others), and Kant, as we have seen, finds selfishness at the root of immorality.

In order to understand Nietzsche, we must make a distinction between morality and ethics. The word morality can be used in both a wide and a narrow sense. In its wider sense it refers to any code of conduct or system of values. In this sense it is equivalent to the term *ethics*. In its narrow sense morality refers to a specific code or value system. Thus we speak about "honor among thieves" as a moral code, albeit one beyond morality as we normally think of it. In other words, morality in the narrow sense is only one of the possibilities for an ethical life (morality in the wider sense).

The selection that follows incorporates material from two of Nietzsche's most influential books, *Beyond Good and Evil*, first published in 1886, and *On the Genealogy of Morality*, first published in 1887. According to Nietzsche, the *Genealogy* was a "clarification and supplement to my last book, *Beyond Good and Evil*." In both books Nietzsche wanted to show how the life-affirming values of a noble and ruling class were revaluated into life-denying values of a slave class led by priests (Nietzsche singled out the role the Jews played early in this process, but his remarks should not be construed as anti-Semitic) and motivated by hatred directed at the ruling class.

◉ READING QUESTIONS

1. What are some of the basic differences between slave morality and master morality?
2. What is the "English psychologists'" theory of the origin of the concept "good" and why is it wrong?
3. According to Nietzsche, what is the real origin of the concepts good and bad?
4. Under what conditions does the opposition between unegoistic (altruistic) and egoistic (selfish) arise?
5. According to Nietzsche, what role does the priestly class play in the development of morality?
6. What role does *ressentiment* (grudge-bearing resentment) play in the creation of slave morality?

Beyond Good and Evil

FRIEDRICH NIETZSCHE

260.

In a tour of the many finer and coarser moralities which have ruled or still rule on earth I found certain traits regularly recurring together and bound up with one another: until at length two basic types were revealed and a basic distinction emerged. There is *master morality* and *slave morality*—I add at once that in all higher and mixed cultures attempts at mediation between the two are apparent and more frequently confusion and mutual misunderstanding between them, indeed sometimes their harsh juxtaposition—even within the same man, within *one* soul. The moral value-distinctions have arisen either among a ruling order which was pleasurably conscious of its distinction from the ruled—or among the ruled, the slaves and dependants of every degree. In the former case, when it is the rulers who determine the concept "good," it is the exalted, proud states of soul which are considered distinguishing and determine the order of rank. The noble human being separates from himself those natures in which the opposite of such exalted proud states find expression: he despises them. It should be noted at once that in this first type of morality the antithesis "good" and "bad" means the same thing as "noble" and "despicable"—the antithesis "good" and "evil" originates elsewhere. The cowardly, the timid, the petty, and those who think only of narrow utility are despised; as are the mistrustful with their constricted glance, those who abase themselves, the dog-like type of man who lets himself be mistreated, the fawning flatterer, above all the liar—it is a fundamental belief of all aristocrats that the common people are liars. "We who are truthful"—thus did the nobility of ancient Greece designate themselves. It is immediately obvious that designations of moral value were everywhere first applied to *human beings*, and only later and derivatively to *actions:* which is why it is a grave error when moral historians start from such questions as "why has the compassionate action been praised?" The noble type of man feels *himself to* be the determiner of values, he does not need to be approved of, he judges "what harms me is harmful in itself," he knows himself to be that which in general first accords honour to things, he *creates values.* Everything he knows to be part of himself, he honours: such a morality is self-glorification. In the foreground stands the feeling of plenitude, of power which seeks to overflow, the happiness of high tension, the consciousness of a wealth which would like to give away and bestow—the noble human being too aids the unfortunate but not, or almost not, from pity, but more from an urge begotten by superfluity of power. The noble human being honours in himself the man of power, also the man who has power over himself, who understands how to speak and how to keep silent, who enjoys practising severity and harshness upon himself and feels reverence for all that is severe and harsh. "A hard heart has Wotan set in my breast," it says in an old Scandinavian saga: a just expression coming from the soul of a proud Viking. A man of this type

is actually proud that he is *not* made for pity: which is why the hero of the saga adds as a warning: "he whose heart is not hard in youth will never have a hard heart." Brave and noble men who think that they are at the farthest remove from that morality which sees the mark of the moral precisely in pity or in acting for others or in *désintéressement;* belief in oneself, pride in oneself, a fundamental hostility and irony for "selflessness" belong just as definitely to noble morality as does a mild contempt for and caution against sympathy and the "warm heart."—It is the powerful who *understand* how to honour, that is their art, their realm of invention. Deep reverence for age and the traditional—all law rests on this twofold reverence—belief in and prejudice in favour of ancestors and against descendants, is typical of the morality of the powerful; and when, conversely, men of "modern ideas" believe almost instinctively in "progress" and "the future" and show an increasing lack of respect for age, this reveals clearly enough the ignoble origin of these "ideas." A morality of the rulers is, however, most alien and painful to contemporary taste in the severity of its principle that one has duties only towards one's equals; that towards beings of a lower rank, towards everything alien, one may act as one wishes or "as the heart dictates" and in any case "beyond good and evil"—: it is here that pity and the like can have a place. The capacity for and the duty of protracted gratitude and protracted revenge—both only among one's equals—subtlety in requittal, a refined conception of friendship, a certain need to have enemies (as conduit systems, as it were, for the emotions of envy, quarrelsomeness, arrogance—fundamentally so as to be able to be a *good friend*): all these are typical marks of noble morality which, as previously indicated, is not the morality of "modern ideas" and is therefore hard to enter into today, also hard to unearth and uncover—It is otherwise with the second type of morality, *slave morality.* Suppose the abused, oppressed, suffering, unfree, those uncertain of themselves and weary should moralize: what would their moral evaluations have in common? Probably a pessimistic mistrust of the entire situation of man will find expression, perhaps a condemnation of man together with his situation.

The slave is suspicious of the virtues of the powerful: he is sceptical and mistrustful, *keenly* mistrustful, of everything "good" that is honoured among them—he would like to convince himself that happiness itself is not genuine among them. On the other hand, those qualities which serve to make easier the existence of the suffering will be brought into prominence and flooded with light: here it is that pity, the kind and helping hand, the warm heart, patience, industriousness, humility, friendliness come into honour—for here these are the most useful qualities and virtually the only means of enduring the burden of existence. Slave morality is essentially the morality of utility. Here is the source of the famous antithesis "good" and "evil"—power and danger were felt to exist in evil, a certain dread-fulness, subtlety and strength which could not admit of contempt. Thus, according to slave morality the "evil" inspire fear; according to master morality it is precisely the "good" who inspire fear and want to inspire it, while the "bad" man is judged contemptible. The antithesis reaches its height when, consistently with slave morality, a breath of disdain finally also comes to be attached to the "good" of this morality—it may be a slight and benevolent disdain—because within the slaves' way of thinking the good man has in any event to be a *harmless* man: he is good-natured, easy to deceive, perhaps a bit stupid, *un bonhomme*. Wherever slave morality comes to predominate, language exhibits a tendency to bring the words "good" and "stupid" closer to each other.—A final fundamental distinction: the longing for *freedom*, the instinct for the happiness and the refinements of the feeling of freedom, belong just as necessarily to slave morality and morals as the art of reverence and devotion and the enthusiasm for them are the regular symptom of an aristocratic mode of thinking and valuating.—This makes it clear without further ado why love *as passion*—it is our European speciality—absolutely must be of aristocratic origin: it was, as is well known, invented by the poet-knights of Provence, those splendid, inventive men of the *"gai saber"* to whom Europe owes so much and, indeed, almost itself.—...

On the Genealogy of Morality

FRIEDRICH NIETZSCHE

FIRST TREATISE: "GOOD AND EVIL," "GOOD AND BAD"

1.

—These English psychologists whom we also have to thank for the only attempts so far to produce a history of the genesis of morality—they themselves are no small riddle for us; I confess, in fact, that precisely as riddles in the flesh they have something substantial over their books—they themselves are interesting! These English psychologists—what do they actually want? One finds them, whether voluntarily or involuntarily, always at the same task, namely of pushing the *partie honteuse*[1] of our inner world into the foreground and of seeking that which is actually effective, leading, decisive for our development, precisely where the intellectual pride of man would least of all *wish* to find it (for example in the *vis inertiae*[2] of habit or in forgetfulness or in

---

[1] *partie honteuse* shameful part (in the plural, this expression is the equivalent of the English "private parts").
[2] *vis inertiae* force of inactivity. In Newtonian physics, this term denotes the resistance offered by matter to any force tending to alter its state of rest or motion.

---

a blind and accidental interlacing and mechanism of ideas or in anything purely passive, automatic, reflexive, molecular, and fundamentally mindless)—what is it actually that always drives these psychologists in precisely *this* direction? Is it a secret, malicious, base instinct to belittle mankind, one that perhaps cannot be acknowledged even to itself? Or, say, a pessimistic suspicion, the mistrust of disappointed, gloomy idealists who have become poisonous and green? Or a little subterranean animosity and rancor against Christianity (and Plato) that has perhaps not yet made it past the threshold of consciousness? Or even a lascivious taste for the disconcerting, for the painful-paradoxical, for the questionable and nonsensical aspects of existence? Or finally—a little of everything, a little meanness, a little gloominess, a little anti-Christianity, a little tickle and need for pepper? ... But I am told that they are simply old, cold, boring frogs who creep and hop around on human beings, into human beings, as if they were really in their element there, namely in a *swamp*. I resist this, still more, I don't believe it; and if one is permitted to wish where one cannot know, then I wish from my heart that the reverse may be the case with them—that these explorers and microscopists of the soul are basically brave, magnanimous, and proud animals who know how to keep a rein on their hearts as well as their pain and have trained themselves to sacrifice all desirability to truth, to *every* truth, even plain, harsh, ugly, unpleasant, unchristian, immoral truth....For there are such truths.—

2.

Hats off then to whatever good spirits may be at work in these historians of morality! Unfortunately, however, it is certain that they lack the *historical spirit* itself, that they have been left in the lurch precisely by all the good spirits of history! As is simply the age-old practice among philosophers, they all think *essentially* ahistorically; of this there is no doubt. The ineptitude of their moral genealogy is exposed right at the beginning, where it is a matter of determining the origins of the concept and judgment "good." "Originally"—so they decree—"unegoistic actions were praised and called good from the perspective of

those to whom they were rendered, hence for whom they were *useful;* later one *forgot* this origin of the praise and, simply because unegoistic actions were as *a matter of habit* always praised as good, one also felt them to be good—as if they were something good in themselves." One sees immediately: this first derivation already contains all the characteristic traits of the idiosyncrasy of English psychologists—we have "usefulness," "forgetting," "habit," and in the end "error," all as basis for a valuation of which the higher human being has until now been proud as if it were some kind of distinctive prerogative of humankind. This pride *must* be humbled, this valuation devalued: has this been achieved? ... Now in the first place it is obvious to me that the actual genesis of the concept "good" is sought and fixed in the wrong place by this theory: the judgment "good" does *not* stem from those to whom "goodness" is rendered! Rather it was "the good" themselves, that is the noble, powerful, higher-ranking, and highminded who felt and ranked themselves and their doings as good, which is to say, as of the first rank, in contrast to everything base, low-minded, common, and vulgar. Out of this *pathos of distance* they first took for themselves the right to create values, to coin names for values: what did they care about usefulness! The viewpoint of utility is as foreign and inappropriate as possible, especially in relation to so hot an outpouring of highest rank-ordering, rank-distinguishing value judgments: for here feeling has arrived at an opposite of that low degree of warmth presupposed by every calculating prudence, every assessment of utility—and not just for once, for an hour of exception, but rather for the long run. As was stated, the pathos of nobility and distance, this lasting and dominant collective and basic feeling of a higher ruling nature in relation to a lower nature, to a "below"—*that is* the origin of the opposition "good" and "bad." (The right of lords to give names goes so far that we should allow ourselves to comprehend the origin of language itself as an expression of power on the part of those who rule: they say "this is such and such," they seal each thing and happening with a sound and thus, as it were, take possession of it.) It is because of this origin that from the outset the word "good" does *not* necessarily attach itself to "unegoistic" actions—as is the superstition of those genealogists of morality. On the contrary, only when aristocratic value judgments begin to *decline* does this entire opposition "egoistic" "unegoistic" impose itself more and more on the human conscience—to make use of my language, it is the *herd instinct* that finally finds a voice (also *words*) in this opposition. And even then it takes a long time until this instinct becomes dominant to such an extent that moral valuation in effect gets caught and stuck at that opposition (as is the case in present-day Europe: today the prejudice that takes "moral," "unegoistic," *"désintéressé"*[3] to be concepts of equal value already rules with the force of an *"idée fixe"*[4] and sickness in the head).

3.

In the second place, however: quite apart from the historical untenability of that hypothesis concerning the origins of the value judgment "good," it suffers from an inherent psychological absurdity. The usefulness of the unegoistic action is supposed to be the origin of its praise, and this origin is supposed to have been *forgotten:*—how is this forgetting even *possible*? Did the usefulness of such actions cease at some point? The opposite is the case: this usefulness has been the everyday experience in all ages, something therefore that was continually underscored anew; accordingly, instead of disappearing from consciousness, instead of becoming forgettable, it could not help but impress itself upon consciousness with ever greater clarity.

How much more reasonable is that opposing theory (it is not therefore truer—) advocated for example by Herbert Spencer—which ranks the concept "good" as essentially identical with the concept "useful," "purposive," so that in the judgments "good" and "bad" humanity has summed up and sanctioned its *unforgotten* and *unforgettable* experiences concerning what is useful-purposive, what is injurious-nonpurposive.

Good, according to this theory, is whatever has proved itself as useful from time immemorial: it may thus claim validity as "valuable in the highest degree," as "valuable in itself." This path of explanation is also false, as noted above, but at least the explanation is in itself reasonable and psychologically tenable.

4.

—The pointer to the *right* path was given to me by the question: what do the terms coined for "good" in the various languages actually mean from an etymological viewpoint? Here I found that they all lead back to the *same conceptual transformation*—that everywhere the basic concept is "noble," "aristocratic" in the sense related to the estates, out of which "good" in the sense of "noble of soul," "high-natured of soul," "privileged of soul" necessarily develops: a development that always runs parallel to that other one which makes "common," "vulgar," "base" pass over finally into the concept "bad." The most eloquent example of the latter is the German word *"schlecht"* [bad] itself: which is identical with *"schlicht"* [plain, simple]—compare *"schlechtweg,"* *"schlechterdings"* [simply or downright]—and originally designated the plain, the common man, as yet without a suspecting sideward glance, simply in opposition to the noble one. Around the time of the Thirty-Years' War, in other words late enough, this sense shifts into the one now commonly used.—With respect to morality's genealogy this appears to me to be an *essential* insight; that it is only now being discovered is due to the inhibiting influence that democratic prejudice exercises in the modern world with regard to all questions of origins. And this influence extends all the way into that seemingly most objective realm of natural science and physiology, as I shall merely hint at here. But the nonsense that this prejudice—once unleashed to the point of hate—is able to inflict, especially on morality and history, is shown by Buckle's notorious case; the *plebeianism* of the modern spirit, which is of English descent, sprang forth there once again on its native ground, vehemently like a muddy volcano and with that oversalted, overloud,

---

[3]*désintéressé* disinterested, unselfish, selfless.
[4]*idée fixe* obsession; literally: a fixed idea.

common eloquence with which until now all volcanoes have spoken.—…

7.

—One will already have guessed how easily the priestly manner of valuation can branch off from the knightly-aristocratic and then develop into its opposite; this process is especially given an impetus every time the priestly caste and the warrior caste confront each other jealously and are unable to agree on a price. The knightly-aristocratic value judgments have as their presupposition a powerful physicality, a blossoming, rich, even overflowing health, together with that which is required for its preservation: war, adventure, the hunt, dance, athletic contests, and in general everything which includes strong, free, cheerful-hearted activity. The priestly-noble manner of valuation—as we have seen—has other presuppositions: too bad for it when it comes to war! Priests are, as is well known, the *most evil enemies*—why is that? Because they are the most powerless. Out of their powerlessness their hate grows into something enormous and uncanny, into something most spiritual and most poisonous. The truly great haters in the history of the world have always been priests, also the most ingenious haters:—compared with the spirit of priestly revenge all the rest of spirit taken together hardly merits consideration. Human history would be much too stupid an affair without the spirit that has entered into it through the powerless:—let us turn right to the greatest example. Of all that has been done on earth against "the noble," "the mighty," "the lords," "the power-holders," nothing is worthy of mention in comparison with that which the *Jews* have done against them: the Jews, that priestly people who in the end were only able to obtain satisfaction from their enemies and conquerors through a radical revaluation of their values, that is, through an act of *spiritual revenge*. This was the only way that suited a priestly people, the people of the most suppressed priestly desire for revenge. It was the Jews who in opposition to the aristocratic value equation (good = noble = powerful = beautiful = happy = beloved of God) dared its inversion, with fear-inspiring consistency, and held it fast with teeth of the most unfathomable

hate (the hate of powerlessness), namely: "the miserable alone are the good; the poor, powerless, lowly alone are the good; the suffering, deprived, sick, ugly are also the only pious, the only blessed in God, for them alone is there blessedness,—whereas you, you noble and powerful ones, you are in all eternity the evil, the cruel, the lustful, the insatiable, the godless, you will eternally be the wretched, accursed, and damned!"… We know *who* inherited this Jewish revaluation.… In connection with the enormous and immeasurably doom-laden initiative provided by the Jews with this most fundamental of all declarations of war, I call attention to the proposition which I arrived at on another occasion ("Beyond Good and Evil" section 195)—namely, that with the Jews *the slave revolt in morality* begins: that revolt which has a two-thousand-year history behind it and which has only moved out of our sight today because it—has been victorious.…

10.

The slave revolt in morality begins when *ressentiment* itself becomes creative and gives birth to values: the *ressentiment* of beings denied the true reaction, that of the deed, who recover their losses only through an imaginary revenge. Whereas all noble morality grows out of a triumphant yes-saying to oneself, from the outset slave morality says "no" to an "outside," to a "different," to a "not-self": and *this* "no" is its creative deed. This reversal of the value-establishing glance—this *necessary* direction toward the outside instead of back onto oneself—belongs to the very nature of *ressentiment:* in order to come into being, slave-morality always needs an opposite and external world; it needs, psychologically speaking, external stimuli in order to be able to act at all,—its action is, from the ground up, reaction. The reverse is the case with the noble manner of valuation: it acts and grows spontaneously, it seeks out its opposite only in order to say "yes" to itself still more gratefully and more jubilantly—its negative concept "low" "common" "bad" is only an after-birth, a pale contrast-image in relation to its positive basic concept, saturated through and through with life and passion: "we noble ones, we good ones, we beautiful ones, we happy ones!" When the noble manner of valuation lays a hand on reality and sins against it, this occurs relative to the sphere with which it is not sufficiently acquainted, indeed against a real knowledge of which it rigidly defends itself: in some cases it forms a wrong idea of the sphere it holds in contempt, that of the common man, of the lower people; on the other hand, consider that the affect of contempt, of looking down on, of the superior glance—assuming that it does *falsify* the image of the one held in contempt—will in any case fall far short of the falsification with which the suppressed hate, the revenge of the powerless, lays a hand on its opponent—in effigy, of course. Indeed there is too much carelessness in contempt, too much taking-lightly, too much looking-away and impatience mixed in, even too much of a feeling of cheer in oneself; for it to be capable of transforming its object into a real caricature.... For the *ressentiment* of the noble human being, when it appears in him, runs its course and exhausts itself in an immediate reaction, therefore it does not *poison*—on the other hand it does not appear at all in countless cases where it is unavoidable in all the weak and powerless. To be unable for any length of time to take his enemies, his accidents, his *misdeeds* themselves seriously—that is the sign of strong, full natures in which there is an excess of formative, reconstructive, healing power that also makes one forget (a good example of this from the modern world is Mirabeau, who had no memory for insults and base deeds committed against him and who was only unable to forgive because he—forgot). Such a human is simply able to shake off with a single shrug a collection of worms that in others would dig itself in; here alone is also possible—assuming that it is at all possible on earth—the true *"love of one's enemies."* What great reverence for his enemies a noble human being has!—and such reverence is already a bridge to love.... After all, he demands his enemy for himself, as his distinction; he can stand no other enemy than one in whom there is nothing to hold in contempt and *a very* great *deal* to honor! On the other hand, imagine "the enemy" as the human being of *ressentiment* conceives of him—and precisely here is his deed, his creation: he has conceived of "the evil enemy," *"the evil one,"* and this indeed as the basic concept, starting from which he now also thinks up, as reaction and counterpart, a "good one"—himself! ...

11.

Precisely the reverse, therefore, of the case of the noble one, who conceives the basic concept "good" in advance and spontaneously, starting from himself that is, and from there first creates for himself an idea of "bad"! This "bad" of noble origin and that "evil" out of the brewing cauldron of unsatiated hate—the first, an after-creation, something on the side, a complementary color; the second, in contrast, the original, the beginning, the true *deed* in the conception of a slave morality—how differently the two words "bad" and "evil" stand there, seemingly set in opposition to the same concept "good"! But it is *not* the same concept "good": on the contrary, just ask yourself *who* is actually "evil" in the sense of the morality of *ressentiment*. To answer in all strictness: *precisely* the "good one" of the other morality, precisely the noble, the powerful, the ruling one, only recolored, only reinterpreted, only re-seen through the poisonous eye of *ressentiment*. There is one point we wish to deny least of all here: whoever encounters those "good ones" only as enemies encounters nothing but *evil enemies*, and the same humans who are kept so strictly within limits *inter pares*, by mores, worship, custom, gratitude, still more by mutual surveillance, by jealousy, and who on the other hand in their conduct towards each other prove themselves so inventive in consideration, self-control, tact, loyalty, pride, and friendship,—they are not much better than uncaged beasts of prey toward the outside world, where that which is foreign, the foreign world, begins. There they enjoy freedom from all social constraint; in the wilderness they recover the losses incurred through the tension that comes from a long enclosure and fencing-in within the peace of the community; they step *back* into the innocence of the beast-of-prey conscience, as jubilant monsters, who perhaps walk away from a hideous succession of murder, arson, rape, torture with such high spirits and equanimity that it seems as if they have only come the poets will again have something to

sing played a student prank, convinced that for years to and to praise....

◉ CRITICAL QUESTIONS

1. Do you think Nietzsche was right when he claimed that "slave morality is essentially a morality of utility"? Why, or why not?

2. Do you think that Nietzsche made a strong case for the claim that conventional morality is rooted in class conflict and resentment? Why, or why not?

4.5 THE DIVINE COMMAND THEORY

Although Friedrich Nietzsche (see Section 4.4) was clearly skeptical of the idea that morality was somehow grounded in religion, people have continued to find comfort in the idea that God and his commands are the true origin and hence foundation of what is morally right and wrong. We have had occasion to briefly discuss the divine command theory of ethics in Sections 3.4 and 4.4. Here we need to address the issue in more depth.

The two selections that follow focus on the idea that God and his will are the foundation of morality. The first is from a Muslim theologian of the tenth century named Abu al-Hasan al-Ashari. He was an Iraqi scholar who founded a school of thought named for him. He articulated a version of the divine command theory in its strongest form. His interpretation illustrates one possible inference from the belief that God (Allah) is an absolutely powerful sovereign who created all that exists, including morality. If that is true, as al-Ashari believed, then humans, who are the creatures of God, are in no position to pass judgment on anything that the divine wills. In this selection, a student asks al-Ashari questions, drawing out the startling implications and al-Ashari answers.

The second selection is from Kai Nielsen's controversial book, *Ethics Without God*. Nielsen is Professor Emeritus of Philosophy at the University of Calgary. He is the author of over twenty books and is not a friend of the divine command theory. In this selection he tells us why. In the course of his argument he makes use of a distinction between analytic and synthetic statements. This distinction is explained in Section 8.4.

◉ READING QUESTIONS

1. What is the underlying premise that al-Ashari uses to support his argument that whatever God wills is just and good?
2. What is the primary thrust of Nielsen's argument?
3. Why must we assume God is morally perfect in order for the divine command theory to be plausible?

4. Why must the concept of good be distinct from the concept of God?
5. Why does Nielsen conclude that religion must be based on morality rather than morality based on religion?

The Theology of Al-Ashari

AL-ASHARI

Question: Is God free to inflict pain on infants in the world to come?

Answer: God is free to do that, and in doing it would be just. In the same way, whenever He inflicts an infinite punishment for a finite sin, and subjects some living beings to others, and is gracious to some and not to others, and creates some knowing well that they will reject faith—all that is justice on His part. It would not be wrong on His part to create them in painful torments and make these everlasting. Nor would it be wrong on His part to punish the faithful and cause the rejecter to enter Paradise. We only say He will not do it because He has informed us that He will punish rejecters; and He cannot lie when He gives information. He is the Overwhelming Monarch, subject to no one. That being so, nothing can be wrong on God's part. For a thing is wrong on our part only when we go beyond the limit set for us and do what we have no right to do. But since the Creator is subject to no one, nothing can be wrong on His part.

Question: Then lying is wrong only because God has declared it to be wrong.

Answer: Quite so. And if He declared it good, it would be good; and if He commanded it, there could be no opposition to it.

From *Kitab al-Luma*, ed. by R. J. McCarthy, S.J., in *The Theology of Al-Ashari* (Beirut: Imprimerie Catholique, 1953), proposition 170, abridged in *The Word of Islam*, edited by John Alden Williams, Austin: University of Texas Press, 1994, p. 153. Copyright © 1994 by the University of Texas.

Ethics Without God

KAI NIELSEN

I

IT IS THE CLAIM of many influential Jewish and Christian theologians (Brunner, Buber, Barth, Niebuhr and Bultmann—to take outstanding examples) that the only genuine basis for morality is in religion. And any old religion is not good enough. The only truly adequate foundation for moral belief is a religion that acknowledges the absolute sovereignty of the Lord found in the prophetic religions.

These theologians will readily grant what is plainly true, namely, that as a matter of fact many non-religious people behave morally, but they contend that without a belief in God and his law there is no ground or reason for being moral. The sense of moral relativism, scepticism and nihilism rampant in our age is due in large measure to the general weakening of religious belief in an age of science. Without God there can be no objective foundation for our moral beliefs. As Brunner

From Kai Neilsen, *Ethics Without God* (Amherst, NY: Prometheus Books, 1990), pp. 51–69. Copyright 1990 by Kai Nielsen. All Rights Reserved. Used with permission of the publisher; www.prometheus-books.com

puts it,[1] 'The believer alone clearly perceives that the Good, as it is recognized in faith, is the sole Good, and all that is otherwise called good cannot lay claim to this title, at least in the ultimate sense of the word ... The Good consists in always doing what God wills at any particular moment.' Moreover, this moral Good can only be attained by our 'unconditional obedience' to God, the ground of our being. Without God life would have no point and morality would have no basis. Without religious belief, without the Living God, there could be no adequate answer to the persistently gnawing questions: What ought we to do? How ought I to live?

Is this frequently repeated claim justified? Are our moral beliefs and conceptions based on or grounded in a belief in the God of Judaism, Christianity and Islam? In trying to come to grips with question, we need to ask ourselves three fundamental questions.

1. Is being willed by God the, or even a, *fundamental* criterion for that which is so willed being morally good or for its being something that ought to be done?
2. Is being willed by God the *only* criterion for that which is so willed being morally good or for its being something that ought to be done?
3. Is being willed by God the only *adequate* criterion for that which is so willed being morally good or being something that ought to be done?

I shall argue that the fact that God wills something—if indeed that is a fact—cannot be a fundamental criterion for its being morally good or obligatory and thus it cannot be the only criterion or the only adequate criterion for moral goodness or obligation.

By way of preliminaries we should first get clear what is meant by a fundamental criterion. When we speak of the criterion for the goodness of an action or attitude we speak of some measure or test by virtue of which we may decide which actions or attitudes are good or desirable, or, at least, are the least undesirable of the alternate actions or attitudes open to us. A moral criterion is the measure we use for determining the value or worth of an action, principle, rule or attitude. We have such a measure or test when we have some generally relevant considerations by which we may decide whether something is whatever it is said to be. A fundamental moral criterion is *(a)* a test or measure used to judge the legitimacy of moral rules and/or acts or attitudes, and *(b)* a measure that one would give up last if one were reasoning morally. (In reality, there probably is no single fundamental criterion, although there are fundamental criteria.)

There is a further preliminary matter we need to consider. In asking about the basis or authority for our moral beliefs we are not asking about how we came to have them. If you ask someone where he got his moral beliefs, he, to be realistic, should answer that he got them from his parents, parent surrogates, teachers.[2] They are beliefs which he has been conditioned to accept. But the validity or soundness of a belief is independent of its origin. When one person naively asks another where he got his moral beliefs, most likely he is not asking how he came by them, but rather, (a) on what authority he holds these beliefs, or (b) what good reasons or justification he has for these moral beliefs. He should answer that he does not and cannot hold these beliefs on any authority. It is indeed true that many of us turn to people for moral advice and guidance in moral matters, but if we do what we do simply because it has been authorized, we cannot be reasoning and acting as moral agents; for to respond as a moral agent, one's moral principle must be something which is subscribed to by one's own deliberate commitment, and it must be something for which one is prepared to give reasons.

Keeping these preliminary clarifications in mind, we can return to my claim that the fact (if indeed it is a fact) that God has commanded, willed or ordained something cannot, in the very nature of the case, be a fundamental criterion for claiming that whatever is commanded, willed or ordained *ought* to be done.

II

Some perceptive remarks made by A. C. Ewing will carry us part of the way.[3] Theologians like Barth and Brunner claim that ethical principles gain their justification because they are God's decrees. But as Ewing points out, if 'being obligatory' means just 'willed by God', it becomes unintelligible to ask why God wills one thing rather than another. In fact, there can be no reason for his willing one thing rather than another, for his willing it *eo ipso* makes whatever it is he wills good, right or obligatory. 'God wills it because it ought to be done' becomes 'God wills it because God wills it'; but the first sentence, even as used by the most ardent believer, is not a tautology. 'If it were said in reply that God's commands determine what we ought to do but that these commands were only issued because it was good that they should be or because obedience to them did good, this would still make judgments about the good, at least, independent of the will of God, and we should not have given a definition of all fundamental ethical concepts in terms of God or made ethics dependent on God.'[4] Furthermore, it becomes senseless to say what the believer very much wants to say, namely, 'I ought always to do what God wills' if 'what I ought to do' and 'what God wills' have the same meaning. And to say I ought to do what God wills because I love God makes the independent assumption that I ought to love God and that I ought to do what God wills if I love him.

Suppose we say instead that we ought to do what God wills because God will punish us if we do not obey him. This may indeed be a cogent self-interested or prudential reason for doing what God commands, but it is hardly a morally good reason for doing what he commands since such considerations of self-interest cannot be an adequate basis for morality. A powerful being—an omnipotent and omniscient being—speaking out of the whirlwind cannot by his mere commands create an obligation. Ewing goes on to assert: 'Without a prior conception of God as good or his commands as right, God would have no more claim on our obedience than Hitler or Stalin except that he would have more power than even they had to make things uncomfortable for those who disobey him.'[5] Unless we assume that God is morally perfect, unless we assume the perfect goodness of God, there can be no necessary 'relation between being commanded or willed by God and being obligatory or good'.[6]

To this it is perfectly correct to reply that as believers we must believe that God is wholly and completely good, the most perfect of all conceivable beings.[7] It is not open for a Jew or a Christian to question the goodness of God. He must start with that assumption. Any man who seriously questions God's goodness or asks why he should obey God's commands shows by this very response that he is not a Jew or a Christian. Believers must claim that God is wholly and utterly good and that what he wills or commands is of necessity good, though this does not entail that the believer is claiming that the necessity here is a logical necessity. For a believer, God is all good; he is the perfect good. This being so, it would seem that the believer is justified in saying that he and we—if his claim concerning God is correct—ought to do what God wills and that our morality is after all grounded in a belief in God. But this claim of his is clearly dependent on his assumption that God is good. Yet I shall argue that even if God is good, indeed, even if God is the perfect good, it does not follow that morality can be based on religion and that we can know what we ought to do simply by knowing what God wishes us to do.

III

To come to understand the grounds for this last rather elliptical claim, we must consider the logical status of 'God is good.' Is it a non-analytic and in some way substantive claim, or is it analytic? (Can we say that it is neither?) No matter what we say, we get into difficulties.

Let us first try to claim that it is non-analytic, that it is in some way a substantive statement. So understood, God cannot then be by definition good. If the statement is synthetic and substantive, its denial cannot be self-contradictory; that is, it cannot be self-contradictory to assert that X is God but X is not good. It would always in fact be wrong to assert this, for God is the perfect good, but the denial of this claim is not self-contradictory, it is just false or in some way mistaken. The 'is' in 'God is the perfect good' is not 'is' of identity, perfect goodness is being predicated of on God in some logically contingent way. It is the religious experience of the believer and the events recorded in the Bible that lead the believer to the steadfast conviction that God has a purpose or vocation for him which he can fulfill only by completely submitting to God's will. God shall lead him and guide him in every thought, word and deed. Otherwise he will be like a man shipwrecked, lost in a vast and indifferent universe. Through careful attention to the Bible, he comes to understand that God is a wholly good being who has dealt faithfully with his chosen people. God is not by definition perfectly good or even good, but in reality, though not of logical necessity, he never falls short of perfection.

Assuming that 'God is good' is not a truth of language, how, then, do we know that God is good? Do we know or have good grounds for believing that the remarks made at the end of the above paragraph are so? The believer can indeed make such a claim, but how do we or how does he know that this is so? What grounds have we for believing that God is good? Naive people, recalling how God spoke to Job out of the whirlwind may say that God is good because he is omnipotent and omniscient. But this clearly will not do, for, as Hepburn points out, there is nothing logically improper about saying "X is omnipotent and omniscient and morally wicked."[8] Surely in the world as we know it there is no logical connection between being powerful and knowledgeable and being good. As far as I can see, all that God proved to Job when he spoke to him out of the whirlwind was that God was an immeasurably powerful being; but he did not prove his moral superiority to Job and he did nothing at all even to exhibit his moral goodness. (One might even argue that he exhibited moral wickedness.) We need not assume that omnipotence and omniscience bring with them goodness or even wisdom.

What other reason could we have for claiming that God is good? We might say that he is good because he tells us to do good in thought, word and deed and to love one another. In short, in his life and in his precepts God exhibits for us his goodness and love. Now one might argue that children's hospitals and concentration camps clearly show that such a claim is false. But let us assume that in some way God does exhibit his goodness to man. Let us assume that if we examine God's works we cannot but affirm that God is good.[9] We come to understand that he is not

cruel, callous or indifferent. But in order to make such judgments or to gain such an understanding, we must use our own logically independent moral criteria. In taking God's goodness as not being true by definition or as being some kind of conceptual truth, we have, in asserting 'God is good', of necessity made a moral judgment, a moral appraisal, using a criterion that cannot be based on a knowledge that God exists or that he issues commands. We call God good because we have experienced the goodness of his acts, but in order to do this, in order to know that he is good or to have any grounds for believing that he is good, we must have an independent moral criterion which we use in making this predication of God. So if 'God is good' is taken to be synthetic and substantive, then morality cannot simply be based on a belief in God. We must of logical necessity have some criterion of goodness that is not derived from any statement asserting that there is a deity.

IV

Let us alternatively, and more plausibly, take 'God is good' to be a truth of language. Now some truths of language (some analytic statements) are statements of identity, such as 'puppies are young dogs' or 'a father is a male parent.' Such statements are definitions and the 'is' indicates identity. But 'God is good' is clearly not such a statement of identity, for that 'God' does not have the same meaning as 'good' can easily be seen from the following case: Jane says to Betsy, after Betsy helps an old lady across the street, 'That was good of you.' 'That was good of you.' Most certainly does not mean 'that was God of you.' And when we say 'conscientiousness is good' we do not mean to say 'conscientiousness is God.' To say, as a believer does, that God is good is not to say that God is God. This clearly indicates that the word God does not have the same meaning as the word good. When we are talking about God we are not talking simply about morality.

'God is the perfect good' is somewhat closer to 'a father is a male parent,' but even here 'God' and 'the perfect good' are not identical in meaning. 'God is the perfect good' in some important respects is like 'a triangle is a trilateral.' Though something is a triangle if and only if it is a trilateral, it does not follow that 'triangle' and 'trilateral' have the same meaning. Similarly, something is God if and only if that something is the perfect good, but it does not follow that 'God' and 'the perfect good' have the same meaning. When we speak of God we wish to say other things about him as well, though indeed what is true of God will also be true of the perfect good. Yet what is true of the evening star will also be true of the morning star since they both refer to the same object, namely Venus, but, as Frege has shown, it does not follow that the two terms have the same meaning if they have the same referent.

Even if it could be made out that 'God is the perfect good' is in some way a statement of identity, (a) it would not make 'God is good' a statement of identity, and (b) we could know that X is the perfect good only if we already knew how to decide that X is good.[10] So even on the assumption that 'God is the perfect good' is a statement of identity, we need an independent way of deciding whether something is good; we must have an independent criterion for goodness.

Surely the alternative presently under consideration is more plausible than the alternative considered in section III. 'God is good' most certainly appears to be analytic in the way puppies are young', 'a bachelor is unmarried' or 'unjustified killing is wrong' are analytic. These statements are not statements of identity; they are not definitions, though they all follow from, definitions and to deny any of them is self-contradictory.

In short, it seems to me correct to maintain that 'God is good,', 'puppies are young' and 'triangles are three-sided' are all truths of language; the predicates partially define their subjects. That is to say—to adopt for a moment a Platonic sounding idiom—goodness is partially definitive of Godhood, as youngness is partially definitive of puppyhood and as three-sidedness is partially definitive of triangularity.

To accept this is not at all to claim that we can have no understanding of good without an

understanding of God; and the truth of the above claim, that God is good will not show that God is the, or even a, fundamental criterion for goodness. Let us establish first that and then how the fact of such truths of language does not show that we could have no understanding of good without having an understanding of God. We could not understand the full religious sense of what is meant by God without knowing that whatever is denoted by this term is said to be good; but, as 'young' or 'three-sided' are understood without reference to puppies or triangles though the converse cannot be the case, so 'good' is also understood quite independently of any reference to God. We can intelligibly say, 'I have a three-sided figure here that is most certainly not a triangle' and 'colts are young but they are not puppies.' Similarly, we can well say 'conscientiousness, under most circumstances at least, is good even in a world without God.' Such an utterance is clearly intelligible, to believer and non-believer alike. It is a well-formed English sentence with a use in the language. Here we can use the word good without either asserting or assuming the reality of God. Such linguistic evidence clearly shows that good is a concept which can be understood quite independently of any reference to the deity, that morality without religion, without theism, is quite possible. In fact, just the reverse is the case. Christianity, Judaism and theistic religions of that sort could not exist if people did not have a moral understanding that was, logically speaking, independent of such religions. We could have no understanding of the truth of 'God is good' or of the concept God unless we had an independent understanding of goodness.

That this is so can be seen from the following considerations. If we had no understanding of the word young, and if we did not know the criteria for deciding whether a dog was young, we could not know how correctly to apply the word puppy. Without such a prior understanding of what it is to be young, we could not understand the sentence 'puppies are young.' Similarly, if we had no understanding of the use of the word good, and if we did not know the criteria for deciding whether a being (or if you will, a power or a force) was good, we could not know how correctly to apply the word God. Without such a prior understanding of goodness, we could not understand the sentence 'God is good.' This clearly shows that our understanding of morality and knowledge of goodness are independent of any knowledge that we may or may not have of the divine. Indeed, without a prior and logically independent understanding of good and without some non-religious criterion for judging something to be good, the religious person could have no knowledge of God, for he could not know whether that powerful being who spoke out of the whirlwind and laid the foundations of the earth was in fact worthy of worship and perfectly good.

From my argument we should conclude that we cannot decide whether something is good or whether it ought to be done simply from finding out (assuming that we can find out) that God commanded it, willed it, enjoined it. Furthermore, whether 'God is good' is synthetic (substantive) or analytic (a truth of language), the concept of good must be understood as something distinct from the concept of God; that is to say, a man could know how to use 'good' properly and still not know how to use 'God.' Conversely, a man could not know how to use 'God' correctly unless he already understood how to use 'good.' An understanding of goodness is logically prior to, and is independent of, any understanding or acknowledgment of God.

V

In attempting to counter my argument for the necessary independence of morality—including a central facet of religious morality—from any beliefs about the existence or powers of the deity, the religious moralist might begin by conceding that *(a)* there are secular moralities that are logically independent of religion, and *(b)* that we must understand the meanings of moral terms independently of understanding what it means to speak of God. He might even go so far as to grant that only a man who understood what good and bad were could come to believe in God. 'Good,' he might grant, does not mean 'willed by God' or

anything like that; and 'there is no God, but human happiness is nonetheless good' is indeed perfectly intelligible as a moral utterance. But granting that, it is still the case that Jew and Christian do and must—on pain of ceasing to be Jew or Christian—take God's will as their final court of appeal in the making of moral appraisals or judgments. Any rule, act or attitude that conflicts with what the believer sincerely believes to be the will of God must be rejected by him. It is indeed true that in making moral judgments the Jew or Christian does not always use God's will as a criterion for what is good or what ought to be done. When he says 'fluoridation is a good thing' or 'the resumption of nuclear testing is a crime,' he need not be using God's will as a criterion for his moral judgment. But where any moral judgment or any other moral criterion conflicts with God's ordinances, or with what the person making the judgment honestly takes to be God's ordinances, he must accept those ordinances, or he is no longer a Jew or a Christian. This acceptance is a crucial test of his faith. In this way, God's will is his fundamental moral criterion.

That the orthodox Jew or Christian would reason in this way is perfectly true, but though he says that God's will is his fundamental criterion, it is still plain that he has a yet more fundamental criterion which he must use in order to employ God's will as a moral criterion. Such a religious moralist must believe and thus be prepared to make the moral claim that there exists a being whom he deems to be perfectly good or worthy of worship and whose will should always be obeyed. But to do this he must have a moral criterion (a standard for what is morally good) that is independent of God's will or what people believe to be God's will. In fact, the believer's moral criterion—'because it is willed by God'— is in logical dependence on some distinct criterion in virtue of which the believer judges that something is perfectly good, is worthy of worship. And in making this very crucial judgment he cannot appeal to God's will as a criterion, for, that there is a being worthy of the appellation 'God', depends in part on the above prior moral claim. Only if it is correct, can we justifiably say that there is a God.

It is crucial to keep in mind that 'a wholly good being exists who is worthy of worship' is not analytic, is not a truth of language, though 'God is wholly good' is. The former is rather a substantive moral statement (expressing a moral judgment) and a very fundamental one indeed, for the believer's whole faith rests on it. Drop this and everything goes.

It is tempting to reply to my above argument in this vein: 'but it is blasphemy to judge God; no account of the logical structure of the believer's argument can be correct if it says that the believer must judge that God is good.' Here we must beware of verbal magic and attend very carefully to precisely what it is we are saying. I did not—and could not on pain of contradiction—say that God must be judged worthy of worship, perfectly good; for God by definition is worthy of worship, perfectly good. I said something quite different, namely that the believer and non-believer alike must decide whether there exists or could conceivably exist a force, a being ('ground of being') that is worthy of worship or perfectly good; and I further said that in deciding this, one makes a moral judgment that can in no way be logically dependent on God's will. Rather, the moral standard, 'because it is willed by God,' is dependent for its validity on the acceptance of the claim that there is a being worthy of worship. And as our little word 'worthy' indicates, this is unequivocally a moral judgment for believer and non-believer alike.

There is a rather more baroque objection[11] to my argument that (a) nothing could count as the Judaeo-Christian God unless that reality is worthy of worship and (b) it is our own moral insight that must tell us if anything at all is or ever possibly could be worthy of worship or whether there is a being who possesses perfect goodness. My conclusion from (a) and (b) was that rather than morality being based on religion, it can be seen that religion in a very fundamental sense must be based on morality. The counter-argument claims that such a conclusion is premature because the judgment that something is worthy of worship is not a moral judgment; it is an evaluative judgment, a religious evaluation, but not a moral judgment. The grounds for this counter-claim are that if the judgment is a moral judgment, as I assumed, then demonolatry—the worship of evil spirits—would be self-contradictory. But although demonolatry is morally and religiously perverse, it is not self-contradictory. Hence my argument must be mistaken.

However, if we say 'Z is worthy of worship' or that, given Judaeo-Christian attitudes, 'if Z is what ought to be worshipped then Z must be good,' it does not follow that demonolatry is self-contradictory or incoherent. Not everyone uses language as Jews and Christians do and not everyone shares the conventions of those religious groups. To say that nothing can be God, the Judaeo-Christian God, unless it is thing as worthy of worship is a moral judgment, is not to deny that some people on some grounds could judge that what they believe to be evil spirits are worthy of worship. By definition, they could not be Jews or Christians—they show by their linguistic behaviour that they do not believe in the Judaeo-Christian God who, by definition, is perfectly good. Jews and Christians recognize that believers in demonolatry do not believe in God but in evil spirits whom such Joycean characters judge to be worthy of worship. The Christian and the demonolater make different moral judgments of a very fundamental sort reflecting different views of the World.

VI

The dialectic of our general argument about morality and divine commands should not end here. There are some further considerations that need to be brought to the forefront. Consider the theological claim that there is an infinite self-existent being upon whom all finite realities depend for their existence, but who in turn depends on nothing. Assuming the intelligibility of the key concepts in this claim and assuming also that we know this claim to be true, it still needs to be asked how we can know, except by the use of our own moral understanding, that this infinite, self-existent being is good or is a being whose commands we ought to obey. Since he—to talk about this being anthropomorphically by the use of the personal pronoun—is powerful enough, we might decide that it would be "the better part of valor" to obey him. But this decision would not at all entail that we ought to obey him. How do we know that this being is good, except by our own moral discernment? We could not discover that this being is good or just by discovering that he "laid the foundation of the world" or "created man in his image and likeness." No information about the behavior patterns of this being would of itself tell us that he was good, righteous, or just. We ourselves would have to decide that, or, to use the misleading idiom of the ethical intuitionist, we would have to intuit or somehow come to perceive or understand that the unique ethical properties of goodness, righteousness, and justness apply to this strange being or 'ground of all being' that we somehow discover to exist. Only if we independently knew what we would count as good, righteous, just, would we be in a position to know whether this being is good or whether his commands ought to be obeyed. That most Christians most of the time unquestionably assume that he is good only proves that this judgment is for them a fundamental moral judgment. But this should hardly be news.

At this point it is natural to reply: "Still, we would not even call this being God unless he was thought to be good. God, whatever else he may or may not be, is a fitting or proper object of worship." A person arguing thus might continue: "This is really a material mode statement about the use of the word 'God'; that is to say, we would not call Z God unless that Z were a fitting or proper object of worship or a being that ought to be worshipped. And if we say 'Z is a fitting object of worship' or 'Z ought to be worshipped' we must also be prepared to say 'Z is good.' Z could not be one without being the other; and if Z is a fitting object of worship, Z necessarily is a being we would call God. Thus, if Z is called God, then Z must also of necessity be called good since in Judeo-Christian contexts what ought to be worshipped must also be good. [This is a logical remark about the use of the phrase 'ought to be worshipped' in Judeo-Christian contexts.] God, by definition, is good. Though the word 'God' is not equivalent to the word 'good', we would

not call a being or power 'God' unless that being was thought to be good."

The above point is well taken, but it still remains the case that the believer has not derived a moral claim from a non-moral religious one. Rather, he has only indicated that the word 'God', like the words 'Saint', 'Santa Claus', 'Hunky', 'Nigger', 'Mick', or 'Kike', is not a purely descriptive term. 'God', like 'Saint', etc., has an evaluative force; it expresses a pro-attitude on the part of the believer and does not just designate or even describe a necessary being or transcendent power or immanent force. Such a believer—unlike Schopenhauer—means by 'God' something toward which he has an appropriate pro-attitude; employing this word with its usual evaluative force, he could not say, "God commands it but it is really evil to do it." If, on the other hand, we simply think of what is purportedly designated or described by the word 'God'—the descriptive force of the word—we can say, for example, without paradox, "An objective power commands it but it is evil to do it." By simply considering the reality allegedly denoted by the word 'God', we cannot discover whether this 'reality' is good. If we simply let Z stand for this reality, we can always ask, "Is it good?" This is never a self-answering question in the way it is if we ask, "Is murder evil?" Take away the evaluative force of the word 'God' and you have no ground for claiming that it must be the case that God is good; to make this claim, with our admittedly fallible moral understanding, we must decide if this Z is good.

"But"—it will be countered—"you have missed the significance of the very point you have just made. As you say yourself, 'God' is not just a descriptive word and God-sentences are not by any means used with a purely descriptive aim. 'God' normally has an evaluative use and God-sentences have a directive force. You cannot begin to understand them if you do not take this into consideration. You cannot just consider what Z designates or purports to designate."

My reply to this is that we can and must if we are going to attain clarity in these matters. Certain crucial and basic sentences like 'God created the Heavens and the earth' and 'God is in Christ', are by no means just moral or practical utterances and they would not have the evaluative force they do if it were not thought that in some strange way they described a mysterious objective power. The religious quest is a quest to find a Z such that Z is worthy of worship. This being the case, the evaluative force of the words and of the utterance is dependent on the descriptive force. How else but by our own moral judgment that Z is a being worthy to be worshipped are we enabled to call this Z "my Lord and God"? Christians say there is a Z such that Z should be worshipped. Nonbelievers deny this or remain skeptical. Findlay,[12] for example, points out that his atheism is in part moral because he does not believe that there can possibly be a Z such that Z is a worthy object of worship. Father Copleston,[13] on the other hand, says there is a Z such that Z ought to be worshipped. This Z, Father Copleston claims, is a 'necessary being' whose nonexistence is in some important sense inconceivable. But both Findlay and Copleston are using their own moral understanding in making their respective moral judgments. Neither is deriving or deducing his moral judgment from the statement 'there is a Z' or from noticing or adverting to the fact—if it is a fact—that Z is 'being-itself', 'a reality whose nonexistence is unthinkable', 'the ground of being', or the like.

Morality cannot be based on religion. If anything, the opposite is partly true, for nothing can be God unless he or it is an object worthy of worship, and it is our own moral insight that must tell us if anything at all could possibly be worthy of worship.

It is true that if some Z is God, then, by definition, Z is an object worthy of worship. But this does not entail there is such a Z; that there is such a Z would depend both on what is the case and on what we, as individuals, judge to be worthy of worship. 'God is worthy of worship' is—for most uses of 'God'—analytic. To understand this sentence requires no insight at all but only a knowledge of English; but that there is or can be a Z such that Z is worthy of worship depends, in part at least, on the moral insight—or lack thereof—of that fallible creature that begins and ends in dust.

In her puzzling article, "Modern Moral Philosophy,"[14] Miss Anscombe has made a different sort of objection to the type of approach taken here.

Moral uses of obligation statements, she argues, have no reasonable sense outside a divine-law conception of ethics. Without God, such conceptions are without sense. There was once a context, a religious way of life, in which these conceptions had a genuine application. 'Ought' was once equated, in the relevant context, with 'being obliged', 'bound', or 'required'. This came about because of the influence of the Torah. Because of the "dominance of Christianity for many centuries the concepts of being bound, permitted, or excused became deeply embedded in our language and thought."[15] But since this is no longer so unequivocally the case, these conceptions have become rootless. Shorn of this theistic Divine Law, shorn of the Hebrew-Christian tradition, these conceptions can only retain a "mere mesmeric force" and cannot be "inferred from anything whatever."[16] I think Miss Anscombe would say that I have shown nothing more than this in my above arguments. What I have said about the independence of morality from religion is quite correct for this "corrupt" age, where the basic principles of a divine-law conception of ethics appear merely as practical major premises on a par with the principle of utility and the like. In such contexts a moral 'ought' can only have a psychological force. Without God, it can have no "discernible content" for the conception of moral obligation "only operates in the context of law."[17] By such moves as I have made above, I have, in effect, indicated how moral obligation *now* has only a delusive appearance of content. And in claiming that without God there still can be genuine moral obligations I have manifested "a detestable desire to retain the atmosphere of the term 'morally obligatory' where the term itself no longer has a genuine use."[18] "Only if we believe in God as a law-giver can we come to believe that there is anything a man is categorically bound to do on pain of being a bad man."[19] The concept of obligation has, without God, become a Holmesless Watson. In our present context, Miss Anscombe argues, we should, if "psychologically possible," jettison the concepts of moral obligation, moral duty, and the like and approach ethics only after we have developed a philosophical psychology that will enable us to clarify what pleasure is, what a human action is, and what constitutes human virtue and a distinctively "human flourishing."[20]

I shall not be concerned here with the larger issues raised by Miss Anscombe's paradoxical, excessively obscure, yet strangely challenging remarks. I agree, of course, that philosophical psychology is important, but I am not convinced that we have not "done" ethics and cannot profitably "do" ethics without such a philosophical psychology. I shall, however, be concerned here only to point out that Miss Anscombe has not shown us that the notion of moral obligation is unintelligible or vacuous without God and his laws.

We have already seen that if so-and-so is called a divine command or an ordinance of God, then it is obviously something that the person who believes it to be a divine command or ordinance of God will believe he ought to obey, for he would not call anything a *divine* command or an ordinance of *God* unless he thought he ought to obey it. But we ourselves, by our own moral insight, must judge that such commands or promulgations are worthy of such an appellation. Yet no moral conceptions follow from a command or law as such. And this would be true at any time whatsoever. It is a logical and not a historical consideration.

Now it is true that if you believe in God in such a way as to accept God as your Lord and Master, and if you believe that something is an ordinance of God, then you ought to try to follow this ordinance. But if you behave like this, it is not because you base morals on religion or on a law concept of morality, but because he who can bring himself to say "my God" uses 'God' and cognate words evaluatively. To use such an expression is already to make a moral evaluation; the man expresses a decision that he is morally bound to do whatever God commands. 'I ought to do whatever this Z commands' is an expression of moral obligation. To believe in God, as we have already seen, involves the making of a certain value judgment; that is to say, the believer believes that there is a Z such that Z is worthy of worship. But his value judgment cannot be derived from just examining Z, or from hearing Z's commands or laws. Without a pro-attitude on the part of the believer toward Z, without a decision by the individual concerned that Z is worthy of worship, nothing of a moral kind follows. But no decision of this sort is entailed by discoveries about Z or by finding out what Z commands or wishes. It is finally up to the individual to decide that this Z is worthy of worship, that this Z ought to be worshipped, that this Z ought to be called his Lord and Master. We have here a moral use of 'ought' that is logically prior to any law conception of ethics. The command gains obligatory force because it is judged worthy of obedience. If someone says, "I do not pretend to appraise God's laws, I just simply accept them because God tells me to," similar considerations obtain. This person judges that there is a Z that is a proper object of obedience. This expresses his own moral judgment, his own sense of what he is obliged to do.

A religious belief depends for its viability on our sense of good and bad—our own sense of worth—and not vice versa. It is crucial to an understanding of morality that this truth about the uses of our language be understood. Morality cannot be based on religion and I (like Findlay) would even go so far as to deny in the name of morality that any Z whatsoever could be an object or being worthy of worship. But whether or not I am correct in this last judgment, it remains the case that each person with his own finite and fallible moral awareness must make decisions of this sort for himself. This would be so whether he was in a Hebrew-Christian tradition or in a "corrupt" and "shallow" consequentialist tradition or in any tradition whatsoever. A moral understanding must be logically prior to any religious assent.

NOTES

1. Brunner, Emil (1947), *The Divine Imperative*, translated by OliveWyon, Lutterworth PressLondon, chapter IX

2. Nowell-Smith, P. H. (1966), 'Morality: Religious and Secular' in Ramsey, Ian (ed), *Christian Ethics and Contemporary Philosophy*, London: SCM Press

3. Ewing, A. C. (1961), 'The Autonomy of Ethics' in Ramsey, Ian (ed), *Prospect for Metaphysics*, London: Allen and Unwin

4. ibid., p. 39

5. ibid., p. 40

6. ibid., p. 41

7. See Rees, D. A. (1961), 'Metaphysical Schemes and Moral Principles' in *Prospect for Metaphysics*, op. cit., p. 23

8. Hepburn, Ronald (1958), *Christianity and Paradox*, London: C. A. Watts, p. 132

9. This is surely to assume a lot

10. Finally we must be quite clear that X's being good is but a necessary condition for X's being the perfect good. But what would be a sufficient condition? Do we really know? I think we do not. We do not know how to identify the referent of 'the Perfect Good'. Thus in one clear sense we do not understand what such a phrase means.

11. This objection has been made in an unpublished paper by Professor T. P. Brown.

12. Findlay, J. N. (1955), "Can God's Existence be Disproved?" in Flew, Antony and MacIntyre, Alasdair (eds.), *New Essays in Philosophical Theology*, New York: Macmillan Company, pp. 47–56

13. Russell, Bertrand and Copleston, F. C. (1957), "The Existence of God: A Debate," in Russell, Bertrand, *Why I am not a Christian*, London: Allen and Unwin, pp. 145–47

14. Anscombe, Elizabeth (January 1958), "Modern Moral Philosophy," in *Philosophy 33*, no. 8.

15. Ibid., p. 5

16. Ibid., p. 8

17. Ibid., p. 18

18. Ibid.

19. Ibid., p. 6

20. Ibid., pp. 1, 15, 18

CRITICAL QUESTIONS

1. Whose argument do you find most persuasive, al-Ashari's or Kai Nielsen's? Why?

2. If there is no God, is there any reason to behave ethically? Why or why not?

4.6 THE ETHIC OF CARE

In 1982, Carol Gilligan, a developmental psychologist, published a book entitled *In a Different Voice*. She pointed out that empirical research into moral reasoning and moral development used samples consisting of mostly male subjects. Thus, most of the major psychological theories of moral reasoning took male reasoning and male development as the norm.

Gilligan began to listen to women and discovered that their approach to moral issues was different from the male approach. The male perspective toward relationships tends to emphasize reciprocity. Equality, justice, rights, impartiality, objectivity, generalization, fair rules, and logical reasoning emerge as central concerns of males when dealing with moral dilemmas. For example, an 11-year-old boy, Jake, is given the Heinz dilemma. A man named Heinz considers whether to steal a drug that he cannot afford to buy because the drug is essential for saving the life of his wife. Jake is confident that Heinz should steal the drug because this is a clear-cut case of a conflict between the values of property and life. Logically, he argues, since life is irreplaceable, it must be given greater priority than property.

The female approach to moral problems, according to Gilligan, tends to be responsive. Care, love, trust, dealing with specific persons who have specific needs, compassion, mercy, forgiveness, the importance of not hurting anyone, and the authority of feeling in solving problems emerge as central concerns of females when dealing with moral issues. For example, Amy, also 11 years old, when given the Heinz dilemma, says she is not sure whether Heinz should steal the drug since that would harm the druggist. Also, Heinz might harm himself if he is caught and has to go to jail. That would also harm his wife who needs him to take care of her. Of course, she shouldn't be allowed to die either. Some other way needs to be found (borrow the money, work out installment payments), and she suggests they all get together, talk about the problem, and find a solution acceptable to all concerned.

Lawrence Kohlberg, who originally designed the study and developed the theory to which Gilligan is responding, construed the Heinz dilemma as a conflict between life and property and thus would regard Jake's response as indicative of a higher level of moral reasoning than Amy's. Gilligan remarks that one is not "higher" than the other—they are just different.

The major and most influential theories in moral philosophy have been developed by men. They reflect what Gilligan sees as the male concern with logical consistency, impartiality, rights, and obligations. Gilligan's work in descriptive psychology inspired the development *of feminist ethical theories* by philosophers. These feminist theories often begin with a critique of the sexism hidden in traditional moral theories and then go on to develop theories that take seriously caring and nurturing.

However, some feminist philosophers have been critical of this development for several reasons. First, an ethic of care may itself be sexist by elevating to philosophic status gender stereotypes of women as more self-sacrificing and more nurturing than men. This can work against women by reinforcing the idea that women are best suited to raising children and working in the "caring" professions, thereby restricting their opportunities. Second, an ethic of care cannot be divorced from an ethic of justice or rights without severe consequences. Justice demands that we treat people fairly, and this is an ethical notion that has played an important role in the women's movement for liberation. For example, the "Seneca Falls Declaration" that resulted from the 1848 conference convened by Elizabeth Cady Stanton and Lucretia Mott in Seneca Falls, New York, to consider the "rights of women" states that "these truths [are] self-evident: that all men and *women* are created equal...." The implicit reference to the "Declaration of Independence" and the addition of the word *women* anchored the claim to equal rights in the values already widely accepted in the United States and thereby made it far more difficult for men to deny women fundamental rights (such as the right to vote).

Virginia Held is the Distinguished Professor of Philosophy at City University of New York, Graduate School. In the following selection she explores the contrast that is often drawn between theories of justice deriving from Kant, utilitarian theories, and an ethics of care (see the discussion of Gilligan above). Held is convinced that any comprehensive moral theory must mesh together in a consistent way a theory of care and of justice.

⦿ READING QUESTIONS

1. What is the most important change in moral theory that feminist thinking has brought about?
2. What are the major features of an ethics of care?

3. Why does Held reject the idea that an ethics of care is in conflict with an ethic of justice?
4. What is mistaken about allocating justice and care to the separate domains of public and private?

Justice, Utility, and Care

VIRGINIA HELD

A student studying ethics or a concerned citizen consulting a moral philosopher in the last third of the twentieth century would probably have encountered, among normative theories purporting to be able to address moral problems, one or both of the few theories dominant in that period. They would become acquainted with deontological, especially Kantian theories, and consequentialist, especially utilitarian theories. Both these kinds of theory are theories of right action. Both rely on universal norms and recommend simple, abstract principles assumed to be applicable to all cases in which decisions are to be made about what we morally ought to do. The moral epistemology of both Kantian and utilitarian theories is rationalist. To the Kantian we are to rely on reason to understand the implications of the categorical imperative and we are to act in accordance with the rational will, not our feelings. What matters morally is the motive with which we act, not the consequences that happen to result. To the utilitarian, we are to bring about the greatest happiness or utility or satisfaction of preferences for all concerned. The morality of the act depends entirely on its consequences, on whether it does or does not in fact alleviate human suffering or increase well-being. In deciding what morality requires us to do, we are to employ rational calculation and rely on reason to make rational choices.

Arguments have been pursued at length about which of these theories is superior or which has the least severe unacceptable implications. Arguments within both Kantian and utilitarian theories have been explored extensively. Within a Kantian approach, for instance, arguments about universalizability and formalism, about the connections between reasons and motives, about the responsibilities of agents, and

about ideal contracts have become ever more sophisticated—some would say scholastic. And within a utilitarian approach, arguments about interpersonal comparisons of utility, about rational choices and contracts in situations of uncertainty or conflict, about social choices and individual utilities and free riders, have also become ever more sophisticated—some would say removed from reality.

In the last quarter of the twentieth century, renewed interest in virtue theory arose. To some, virtue theory is an alternative to deontological and consequentialist theories and should replace them. If we cultivate good character in persons and achieve a society of virtuous persons, it is thought, we will not need additional theory: Virtuous persons will do what is best or what is morally required. Virtue theory recognizes the subtleties of human character and the complexities of moral situations.

Also in the last quarter of the century, feminist theory developed, and it led to feminist philosophy and feminist views in ethics. Feminist moral theory is increasingly recognized as a distinct and interesting alternative approach to moral issues. It is seen by many philosophers (not all of them women) as making an important contribution to normative ethics and to metaethics. There are by now a large number of books in the area of feminist morality, and a number of general texts now include segments on feminist ethics among their theories and topics covered.[1]

---

[1] See, for example, David Goldberg, ed., *Ethical Theory and Social Issues*, 2nd ed. (Fort Worth, Tex.: Harcourt Brace, 1995); and Steven M. Cahn and Peter Markie, eds., *Ethics: History, Theory, and Contemporary Issues*, 2nd ed. (New York: Oxford University Press, 2002).

FEMINIST MORAL INQUIRY

Before there was feminist philosophy, there was philosophical thinking about women. Much of it was appalling.

Aristotle held that women are defective men, human beings lacking in what is essential to the nature of man: the ability to reason. Though he thought women somewhat able to reason, he thought that whereas the nature or function of man is to reason in ways that are distinctively human, the nature and function of woman is to reproduce, like other animals.[2]

In the thirteenth century, Aquinas shared these conceptions of the natures of women and men. In the eighteenth century, Rousseau thought that society would crumble unless women were inculcated from childhood to be subservient to men. Kant, because he based morality entirely on reason and shared the view that women were deficient in reason, concluded that women are incapable of being full moral persons. In the twentieth century Freud extended comparable views into the domains studied by the new and growing fields concerned with human behavior, conceptualizing women as psychologically inferior through their anatomical deficiency: their lack of a penis.

In the long history of philosophy and in thought influenced by philosophy as almost all thought is, it had been thought that reason, to establish its honored place in human development and history, had to overcome and leave behind what were seen as the female and dark forces of unreason, passion, emotion, and bodily need. Although the conception of these dark forces changed at different times in history and in different places, the identification of them as female was almost constant. A long line of thinking about women had thus seen them as defective, deficient, and dangerous.[3]

Such ideas about women were both reflections within philosophy of dominant misconceptions of their times and in turn significant contributions to the continuation of male dominance. Philosophical ideas about women lent strong support to the failure to include women among those gaining political rights with the advent of democratic forms of government, the failure to extend to women the possibilities of economic advancement brought about by industrialization and the more widespread ownership of the property it produced, and the exclusion of women from most of the professions that burgeoned in the twentieth century.

Philosophical thought about women's inferiority was thus both an effect and a cause of women's subordination generally. Similarly, feminist philosophy in our time is both an effect and a cause of the growing equality of women in the wider society. It offers a very distinct and, for philosophy, almost entirely new contribution of women's voices concerning not only women but everything else in philosophy. And since philosophy concerns the most fundamental questions about all of our thinking about everything, feminist philosophy is rethinking life, society, and knowledge across the board. To challenge male dominance in our thinking is to challenge how we live and organize our worlds and pursue what we take to be knowledge and understanding and progress and value.

Instead of seeing the human as Man, with woman as the Other or the one lacking some essential capacity of Man, feminist thought sees human beings as women, men, and children. Feminist thought notes that although women *can* reason as well as men, it is doubtful that reason *should* leave behind all that belongs to emotion and the body. Feminist moral theorists, for instance, have emphasized the important and useful role of emotions such as caring and empathy in the moral life and moral understanding of human beings.

With respect to the body, instead of seeing women as, for instance, lacking a penis, feminist thought notices that women possess, among other abilities, a capacity men lack: the capacity to give birth to new human beings. When psychologists look for it, they can indeed find evidence of womb envy in little boys. One often fails to find what one is not looking for, and scientific research that has been looking for female weaknesses and passivities

---

[2]See Mary Mahowald, ed., *Philosophy of Woman: Classical to Current Concepts*, 3rd ed. (Indianapolis, Ind.: Hackett, 1994).
[3]See especially Genevieve Lloyd, *The Man of Reason: "Male" and "Female" in Western Philosophy* (Minneapolis: University of Minnesota Press, 1984).

has often failed to pay attention to women's strengths. Feminist thinking is changing what is looked for and what is found. It is making visible a vast amount of bias in what has been taken to be "knowledge," especially in the social sciences, psychology, history, and of course philosophy.[4] It is reconceptualizing such basic concepts as that of the "public," seen as the sphere of the human and the creative, and of the "private," seen as the locus of mere reproduction ... It is reshaping concepts of women, in all their diversity of race, sexual orientation, and economic, ethnic, and historical location, demanding that women's experiences be seen as of equal importance with those of privileged men's.[5] It leads us to reformulate our ideas of personhood, identity, self, and society. The most important change feminist thinking is bringing about in the area of moral theory is that it is making women's experience—including experience in the household and in bringing up children and in caring for the dependent—and the experience of children and of others who are not independent relevant to moral theory and moral inquiry in ways that had not been seen before. Dominant moral theories seem to have been modeled on the experience of men in the public life of state and market. Feminist perspectives illuminate the bias in such moralities.

Feminist moral theory of all varieties is united by certain core commitments: Men's domination of women should end; women are entitled to equal rights; the moral experience of women is as important as that of men. Of course the meanings and implications of all of these positions require much interpretation.

Feminist inquiry exploring the moral experience of women has led to a recognition of how this domain has been neglected by other moral theories and of how clumsy the dominant theories often are in dealing with the moral issues in it. Of course "women's experience" is potentially much more like men's experience than it has been, but historically women have had a vast amount of experience labeled "private" and "irrelevant." When it is recognized that it is anything but irrelevant, moral theory needs to be rethought accordingly.

As women care for children and others who need care, moral issues are ever present, yet this kind of experience has hardly entered into the thinking of moral theorists developing the dominant outlooks. Traditionally, women's caring activities have been assimilated to what is natural and instinctual, rather than to what has moral significance and involves moral choice. As recently as 1982, David Heyd, in a way that was entirely typical, dismissed a mother's sacrificing for her child as an example of the supererogatory because it belongs, as he put it, to "the sphere of natural relationships and instinctive feelings (which lie outside morality)."[6]

Among the clearest positions feminist moral theorists take is that such a dismissal of women's moral experience is unacceptable. In taking such experience seriously, much feminist moral inquiry has developed what has come to be best described as the ethics of care. Starting with Sara Ruddick's examination of the thinking involved in mothering, Carol Gilligan's empirical studies of the ways girls and women seem to interpret moral problems, and Nel Noddings's phenomenological inquiry into what caring involves and how we evaluate it, feminist moral inquiry has illuminated the importance of caring activities and relationships in human life, and has established the moral significance of care ... Caring well should be a moral goal, and basic caring relations are a moral necessity. The values involved in the practices of caring need to be understood and

---

[4]See, for example, Sandra Harding and Merrill Hintikka, eds., *Discovering Reality: Feminist Perspectives on Epistemology, Metaphysics, Methodology and Philosophy of Science* (Dordrecht: Reidel, 1983); and Linda Alcoff and Elizabeth Potter, eds., *Feminist Epistrmologies Epistemologies* (New York: Routledge, 1993).
[5]See, for example, Elizabeth V. Spelman, *Inessential Woman: Problems of Exclusion in Feminist Thought* (Boston: Beacon Press, 1988); Patricia Hill Collins, *Black Feminist Thought: Knowledge, Consciousness and the Politics of Empowerment* (Boston: Unwin Hyman, 1990); and Uma Narayan, *Dislocating Cultures: Identities, Traditions, and Third World Feminism* (New York: Routledge, 1997).

[6]David Heyd, *Supererogation: Its Status in Ethical Theory* (New York: Cambridge University Press, 1982), p. 134.

cultivated, and the failures of many practices to reflect these values also need to be understood. Caring as an actual practice should be continually evaluated and improved. To bring about such improvement, radical transformations may be needed in the social and political contexts in which caring takes place.

Many cautions have been raised about the ethics of care. To the extent that women have been confined to the work of caretaking, an ethic that reflects this may have the effect of prolonging inequality. It may mistake a merely historical fact—that women have done most of this labor—for a claim about women's outlooks on moral issues. To the extent that caring is for particular others with whom we have actual relationships, some critics fear it may draw attention away from the oppressive social structures in which such caring occurs. To elevate the activities of caring (which should be shared by men and not assigned automatically to women) into an ethic of care associated with women's experience, can thus be thought problematic.

How the ethics of care should be formulated continues to be a central subject of feminist moral inquiry, which includes far more than care ethics. I think the objections to it can be answered and result largely from an undue focus on a few early formulations only....

CARE VERSUS JUSTICE

As thinking about care developed, care and justice were often seen as alternative values. "Care" and "justice" were taken to name different approaches to moral problems and characteristically different recommendations concerning them. Care valued relationships between persons and empathetic understanding; justice valued rational action in accord with abstract principles. Carol Gilligan saw these as alternative interpretations that could be applied to given moral problems, yielding different ways of construing what the moral problem was and how it should be handled. For instance, should a contemplated abortion be interpreted as a way of avoiding or constituting a threat to the well-being of existing children and their relationships with their mother, or should it be interpreted as a

conflict of rights between a fetus and a pregnant woman? Gilligan saw both approaches as valid, but because interpretation from the perspective of care had been grossly neglected in the construction and study of dominant moral theories, it should now be seen as valid, and the deficiency corrected. Gilligan argued that if one sees a moral problem as an issue to be dealt with in terms of care, one cannot at the same time see is as an issue to be dealt with in terms of justice because the two perspectives organize the problem differently. A given person can recognize both interpretations and examine them one at a time. Morality, she argued, should include the concerns of both care and justice. But with respect to a given problem, this suggestion leaves us with alternative interpretations but no advice on choosing between them. *Why* should we see an issue as one of justice primarily or as one primarily of care?

If women are discriminated against in their chances for professional education, let's say, as they still are in many parts of the world, should we see this as an issue of justice or of care? If a parent hurts his child through his insensitivity, is this an issue of care or of justice? One can see how both points of view will illuminate different aspects of the problems. But which should we favor when their recommendations conflict? Seeing justice and care as alternative approaches did not help us decide.

Other theorists, Nel Noddings, for instance, thought care should replace justice as the central concept of morality. On this view, care could provide the guidance needed for whatever moral problems we face, and justice should be displaced to the sidelines. An ethic of care would be sufficient. But this view was open to many objections. How could care alone deal with the structural inequalities and discriminations of gender, race, class, and sexual orientation. How could sensitivity, responsiveness to the needs of the dependent, and cultivation of caring relations be adequate to preventing domestic violence, criminal coercion, and violent conflict between states? Moral decisions and outcomes seemed to require justice.

In these debates, the dominant ethic of justice was taken to include both Kantian and utilitarian approaches. John Rawls's *A Theory of Justice* was seen as emblematic of a Kantian approach.[7] Such theory requires abstract, universal principles to which all (taken as free, equal, and autonomous individual persons choosing impartially) could agree. It sees justice as the most important basis on which to judge the acceptability of political and social arrangements. It insists on respecting persons through recognition of their rights and provides moral constraints within which individuals may pursue their interests. It seeks fair distributions of positions of differential power and of the benefits of economic activity.

Utilitarianism is less obviously a morality of justice. It recommends maximizing the utility, or the preference satisfaction, of all, taken as individuals pursuing their own interests. It is better than Kantian and other deontological approaches in recognizing the importance of satisfying needs, because it can weigh them heavily in the calculus of preference satisfaction. But it still relies on an abstract universal principle appealing to rational individuals. In its requirement that the utility of each individual is to be seen as of equal importance to that of any other, it tries to build justice into its foundations. It justifies the political recognition of individual rights, the focus of justice, as highly conducive to general utility. Like Kantian moral theory's categorical imperative, utilitarianism has one very general universal principle, the principle of utility, on which it relies.

To those whose focus is on the differences between Kantian and utilitarian theories, it may seem unwarranted to classify them together as theories of justice, and defenders of both Kantian and utilitarian approaches have denied that they cannot well handle issues of care. Both have tried to assimilate care into their own favored frameworks.

Those developing the ethics of care, however, focus on persons responding with sensitivity to the needs of particular others with whom they share interests. From this perspective, the similarities between Kantian and utilitarian theories are of more significance than the differences: Both are rationalist in their moral epistemologies; both rely on simple, abstract, universal rules; both assume a concept of person that is individualistic and independent; both are theories of right action aimed at recommending rational choices; both can be interpreted as far more suitable for guiding the decisions of persons in "public" life than for dealing with moral issues of family life or of friendship or of group solidarity. Finally, both are concerned with issues such as justice—through rights and through public policy—though a Kantian foundation may be better and stronger for rights, and a utilitarian one for many issues of public policy.[8] In these ways the ethics of care contrasts with both. And to those focused on the values of care, it is apparent that if women, in their justifiable quest for equality, pursue justice at the expense of care, morality will suffer. For those previously engaged in care to become more and more like the free and equal, rational and unencumbered individuals of theories of justice will leave no one to nurture the relations of family and friendship, and to cultivate the ties of caring. To treat friends and family members as if relations between them were contractual bargains based on self-interest undermines mutuality and undercuts trust.[9]

For some time debates concerning an ethic of care became formulated as care versus justice. Participants were asked to consider which was more suitable for the concerns of feminists and their allies. Those concerned especially with oppressive social structures and unjust economic and political institutions were dubious about focusing on the family and personal relationships. They continued to see demands for equality as primary, although notions of liberal equality were often reconceptualized, and they saw such concerns as best handled through an ethic of justice. Some argued that justice required socialist institutions and economic

---

[7]John Rawls, *A Theory of Justice* (Cambridge, Mass.: Harvard University Press, 1971).

[8]For argument, see Virginia Held, *Rights and Goods: Justifying Social Action* (Chicago: University of Chicago Press, 1989).
[9]See Virginia Held, *Feminist Morality: Transforming Culture, Society, and Politics* (Chicago: University of Chicago Press, 1993); and Celeste M. Friend, "Trust and the Limits of Contract," Ph.D. dissertation, City University of New York, 1995.

democracy.[10] Many argued for the extension of justice to women in the household as well as in the workplace.[11] And others argued that an ethic of justice is superior to an ethic of care to protect women against violence and abuse.[12]

Others defended an ethic of care against charges that it is tied to women's traditional roles and complicit in them, making clear that the practices of care to be recommended were not those conducted under patriarchal oppression but those to be sought in postpatriarchal society. They showed how care could be extended beyond the contexts of family and friendship to call for deep restructurings of society; of economic, political, and legal institutions; of professional practices; and of international relations.[13] A caring society would reorder its social roles and transform its practices. Care could be seen as a public and not only a private value, if one uses those unsatisfactory concepts. As Monique Deveaux, introducing a symposium on care and justice wrote, "A care perspective relies centrally on a conception of human good and entails a deep commitment to a transformative politics." Not only have care thinkers asked "what difference contextual moral reasoning might make to politics, but more radically, they've asked what it would mean to fundamentally reorder our social and political priorities to reflect the central role of care in all of our lives."[14]

Instead of seeing law and government or the economy as the central and appropriate determinants of society, an ethic of care might see bringing up children and fostering trust between members of the society as the most important concerns of all. Other arrangements might then be evaluated in terms of how well or badly they contribute to the flourishing of children and the health of social relations. That would certainly require a radical restructuring of society! Just imagine reversing the salaries of business executives and those of child care workers.

Many questions become open in feminist theorizing rather than closed by what have become entrenched ways of thinking. Not only are arrangements *within* different spheres of society rethought from a feminist point of view—for instance, who does the housework and why, or why do laws against rape protect men from false accusations better than they protect minority women from forced sex? The relations *between* the spheres of society need also to be rethought from a feminist point of view. Practices to ensure bringing up children in the best possible ways should perhaps have the highest priority of all, along with education. What a change from recent years that might be, where in the United States most parents are left to scrounge as best they can for the few expensive places available for adequate child care, and many children grow up deeply deprived while social programs of all kinds are sacrificed in the race for global economic and military dominance.

Instead of leaving to the greed and vagaries of the market the creation and distribution of cultural images and influences, a feminist view of society would suggest that we take responsibility as a society for providing the best culture possible. The current media culture strongly shapes the aspirations and behavior of children, young people, and adults. To concede that the basis on which cultural arrangements will be structured is no more than that of commercial gain is morally irresponsible from many moral points of view, especially so from that of the ethics of care. This is not to say that commercial production should be forbidden or censored any more than private schools are. But modern states have made available for their members vast systems of public education, including higher education based on merit rather than wealth. They ought to support comparable public alternatives to commercial culture, protected by standards of artistic

---

[10]See, for example, Alison M. Jaggar, *Feminist Politics and Human Nature* (Totowa, N.J.: Rowman and Allanheld, 1983); and Carol C. Gould, *Rethinking Democracy: Freedom and Social Cooperation in Politics, Economy, and Society* (Cambridge: Cambridge University Press, 1988).

[11]See especially Susan Moller Okin, *Justice, Gender, and the Family* (New York: Basic Books, 1989).

[12]See, for example, Marilyn Friedman, *What Are Friends For? Feminist Perspectives on Personal Relationships and Moral Theory* (Ithaca, N.Y.: Cornell University Press, 1993).

[13]See, for example, Held, *Feminist Morality*, Joan C. Tronto, *Moral Boundaries: A Political Argument for an Ethic of Care* (New York: Routledge, 1993); and Rebecca Grant and Kathleen Newland, eds., *Gender and International Relations* (Bloomington: Indiana University Press, 1991).

[14]Monique Deveaux, "Shifting Paradigms: Theorizing Care and Justice in Political Theory," *Hypatia: A Journal of Feminist Philosophy* 10(2) (spring 1995): 117.

freedom matching those of academic freedom now recognized as at least an ideal for universities. Such alternatives would make it possible for the best artists and writers to offer the best cultural products, both popular and more selective, and thus to help societies improve morally and aesthetically through their culture. They would liberate culture from domination by commercial interests.

Of course a feminist concern for embodied persons will make the meeting of genuine economic needs a high priority. But an ethic of care would recommend that economic activity be organized to actually do so, rather than satisfy primarily the lust for wealth of the self-interested who manipulate society and its arrangements through culture, advertising, and influence on governments. The ethics of care would suggest that a great many activities should be outside the market rather than in it....

These are some examples of the kinds of social transformations that the ethics of care might demand. The charge that a feminist ethic of care is particularistic, limited to the contexts of family and friends, or merely descriptive of the kinds of restricted lives of caring for others to which women have traditionally been confined, is based, I believe, on a misunderstanding of this ethic. When one thinks about the restructurings that would be required by taking the ethics of care seriously, the idea that care ethics is a conservative ethic tied to women's traditional roles seems very implausible.

Feminism is a revolutionary program, since it is committed to overthrowing the deepest and most entrenched hierarchy of all—the hierarchy of gender. It does not seek to substitute women for men in the hierarchy of domination but to overcome domination itself. The care that is valued by the ethics of care can—and to be justifiable must—include caring for distant others in an interdependent world, and caring that the rights of all are respected and their needs met. It must include caring that the environment in which embodied human beings reside is well cared for. The ethics of care will strive to achieve these transformations in society and the world nonviolently and democratically but with persistence. A feminist ethic of care—and I have argued that no ethic

of care that is not feminist is entitled to call itself that—is an ethic for all who start out, as we all do, as human children.

At the same time, the concerns of justice must not be overlooked, though they may be more limited than had been thought. How to integrate the values of both justice and care have remained central concerns of feminist moral inquiry.

FEMINISM AND THE DISCOURSE OF RIGHTS

The ethics of care is not the same as feminist morality. As we have seen, some feminist moral theorists reject it. In my view, feminist moral theory will in time certainly include the ethics of care. Views that an ethic of justice alone, even revised in the light of feminist concerns, can be adequate are, I believe, coming to be seen as mistaken. But so is the view that an ethic of care alone is sufficient. Views that virtue ethics alone can substitute for justice or can incorporate care adequately are also unpersuasive.

Recent debates among feminist moral theorists have generally moved beyond the justice versus care formulations. The questions now being posed are often about how these core values should be thought to be related or combined. How should the framework that structures justice, equality, rights, and liberty, mesh with the network that delineates care, relatedness, and trust?

Feminist morality is surely concerned with the equality of women and with women's rights. If we look at the work of feminist legal theorists, we can see both criticisms of the justice approach, and a determination not to lose what it can provide. Catherine MacKinnon has argued, for example, that "in the liberal state, the rule of law—neutral, abstract, elevated, pervasive—both institutionalizes the power of men over women and institutionalizes power in its male form ... Male forms of power over women are affirmatively embodied as individual rights in law ... Abstract rights authorize the male experience of the world."[15] Many

---

[15]Catharine MacKinnon, *Toward a Feminist Theory of the State* (Cambridge, Mass.: Harvard University Press, 1989), pp. 238–48.

Critical Legal Studies and feminist legal scholars have been critical of focusing even legal argumentation (much less moral argument generally) on rights. They see rights claims as promoting individualistic, self versus other conflicts, and have argued that conceptualizations of issues in terms of rights claims "limit legal thinking and inhibit necessary social change."[16] Carol Smart shows how one can see a "congruence" between law and "masculine culture," and she examines the way law "disqualifies women's experience" and women's knowledge.[17] She urges feminists not to focus on law and rights in working to bring about the changes they seek. Feminist legal theorists have also shown, however, how rights cannot be replaced by what an ethic of care alone would provide. When rights are viewed in the context of social practices rather than in the abstract, they can effectively express the aspirations of a social movement and "articulate new values and political vision."[18] Patricia Williams, for instance, argues that "although rights may not be ends in themselves, rights rhetoric has been and continues to be an effective form of discourse for blacks," whereas describing needs has not been politically effective.[19] And Frances Olsen, well aware of the deficiencies in relying on law to reduce the subordination of women, nevertheless shows in detail how with respect to statutory rape, rights analyses can lead to reforms taking place and people's lives being changed in ways that empower women.[20]

The area of sexual harassment illustrates the potential of legal rights to bring about social change that decreases the subordination of women. Feminist jurisprudence turned the harms that women have long experienced in sexual harassment into a form of discrimination from which they could seek to be protected by the law. MacKinnon notes that the victims of sexual harassment "have been given a forum, legitimacy to speak, authority to make claims, and an avenue for possible relief.... The legal claim for sexual harassment made the events of sexual harassment illegitimate socially, as well as legally for the first time."[21] Women now have a name for the harm that occurs when sexual pressure is imposed on subordinates in the workplace or institution. This may well provide a strong argument for the potential of law to bring about social change for women.

The importance to women of reproductive rights has become ever clearer as such rights are threatened and constantly challenged and continue to be denied to vast numbers of women around the world. Reproductive freedom is thought by most feminists to be a precondition for other freedoms and for equality for women. Patricia Smith argues that "it is inconceivable that any issue that comparably affected the basic individual freedom of any man would not be under his control in a free society."[22] As women strive to overcome their subordination in other areas of society, their rights to control their own sexuality and reproduction and to avoid being commodified are especially crucial.[23]

Among feminist moral theorists (as distinct from legal theorists), there has also been much appreciation of the discourse of justice and rights along with the development of the ethics of care. Not all theorists have combined an interest in both, but there has been continued and mutually enlightening dialogue between those whose primary interests have been in one or the other approaches. I interpret many critiques of justice and rights as critiques of the dominance of this approach. That rights arguments serve well for some domains should not be taken to indicate

---

[16]Elizabeth M. Schneider, "The Dialectic of Rights and Politics: Perspectives from the Women's Movement," in *Feminist Legal Theory: Readings in Law and Gender*, eds. Katherine T. Bartlett and Rosanne Kennedy (Boulder, Colo.: Westview Press, 1989), p. 318.

[17]Carol Smart, *Feminism and the Power of Law* (London: Routledge, 1989).

[18]Schneider, "The Dialectic of Rights and Politics," p. 322.

[19]Patricia J. Williams, *The Alchemy of Race and Rights* (Cambridge, Mass.: Harvard University Press, 1991), p. 149.

[20]Frances Olsen, "Statutory Rape: A Feminist Critique of Rights Analysis," in *Feminist Legal Theory*, ed. Bartlett and Kennedy.

[21]Catherine MacKinnon, *Feminism Unmodified: Discourses on Life and Law* (Cambridge, Mass.: Harvard University Press, 1987), p. 104.

[22]Patricia Smith, ed., *Feminist Jurisprudence* (New York: Oxford University Press, 1993), p. 14.

[23]See ibid., part IV.

that they serve well for the entire spectrum of moral or political concerns, or that legal discourse should be the privileged or paradigmatic discourse of morality or social interpretation. The framework of justice and rights should be one among others rather than dominant.

Moralities of rights and justice can well be interpreted as generalizations to the whole of morality and social evaluation of ways of thinking developed in the contexts of law and public policy. Such expansions of legalistic approaches are and should be resisted by feminists. These ways of thinking are *unsuitable* for many contexts, and many of the contexts now thought best handled through justice and rights should be transformed so that a care approach could be employed and would be seen to be more suitable.

Even within the law, where justice and rights should generally have priority, various issues in family law can illustrate their limits, and how other moral considerations should play a larger role. Selma Sevenhuijsen has shown, for instance, how in decisions concerning the custody of children, an approach in terms of conflicting rights is a poor guide.[24] The ethics of care would do better at offering recommendations....

To argue that justice and rights should not dominate our moral thinking, however, does not mean that they are dispensable. Though the law does treat persons as conceptually self-contained individuals—a conception the ethics of care can recognize as an artificial and misleading abstraction—we can also assert that for some legal and political purposes, it may be a useful abstraction as long as it is not imagined to be the appropriate concept of the person for the whole of morality.

Feminist theorists are also well aware that women must have sufficient autonomy and individual subjectivity to resist and reformulate the ties of traditional communities and families. Rights may be needed to assure this. The feminist self is not absorbed into its social relationships.[25]

Feminist critiques of communitarianism make this clear.

THE MESHING OF CARE AND JUSTICE

Feminist understandings of justice and care have enabled us to see that these are different values, reflecting different ways of interpreting moral problems and expressing moral concern. Feminist discussion has also shown, I think, that neither justice nor care can be dispensed with: Both are extremely important for morality. Not all feminists agree, by any means, but this is how I see the debates of the last few decades on these issues.

What remains to be worked out is how justice and care and their related concerns fit together. How does the framework that structures justice, equality, rights, and liberty mesh with the network that delineates care, relatedness, and trust? Or are they incompatible views we must (at least at a given time and in a given context) choose between?

One clearly unsatisfactory possibility is to think that justice is a value appropriate to the public sphere of the political, whereas care belongs to the private domains of family and friends and charitable organizations. Feminist analyses have shown how faulty are traditional divisions between public and private, the political and the personal, but even if we use cleaned-up versions of these concepts, we can see how unsatisfactory it is to assign justice to public life and care to private, although in earlier work I may have failed to say enough along these lines.[26] I have argued that we need different moral approaches for different domains, and I have mapped out which are suitable for which domains. There is an initial plausibility, certainly, in thinking of justice as a primary value in the domain of law and care as a primary value in the domain of the family. But more needs to be said.

Justice is badly needed in the family as well as in the state: in a more equitable division of labor between women and men in the household, in the protection of vulnerable family members from domestic violence and abuse, in recognizing the

---

[24]Selma Sevenhuijsen, *Citizenship and the Ethics of Care* (London: Routledge, 1998), chap. 4.
[25]See, for example, Diana T. Meyers, *Subjection and Subjectivity: Psychoanalytic Feminism and Moral Philosophy* (New York: Routledge, 1994).

[26]Held, *Rights and Goods.*

rights of family members to respect for their individuality. In the practice of caring for children or the elderly, justice requires us to avoid paternalistic and maternalistic domination.

At the same time, we can see that care is badly needed in the public domain. Welfare programs are an intrinsic part of what contemporary states with the resources to do so provide, and no feminist should fail to acknowledge the social responsibilities they reflect, however poorly. The night watchman state is not a feminist goal. Almost all feminists recognize that there should be much more social and public concern for providing care than there now is in the United States, although it should be provided in appropriate and empowering ways very different from those in place. There should be greatly increased public concern for child care, education, and health care, infused with the values of care.

Care is needed by everyone when they are children, ill, or very old, and it is needed by some most of their lives. Assuring that care is available to those who need it should be a central political concern, not one imagined to be a solely private responsibility of families and charities. Providing care has always fallen disproportionately to women and minorities, who do the bulk of unpaid or badly paid actual work of caring for those needing it. But in addition to a fairer division of responsibilities for care, the care made available through the institutions of the welfare state needs to be strengthened as well as reformed. Care and justice, then, cannot be allocated to the separate spheres of the private and the public. But they are different, and they are not always compatible.

Consider the well-being of citizens that states seek to safeguard. One way of thinking about the issues surrounding it and recommending action would be from a perspective of justice, equality, and rights. We could then recognize basic well-being, or welfare, as something to which each person is entitled by right under conditions of need and ability of the society to provide. Welfare rights would be recognized as basic rights guaranteeing persons the resources needed to live.[27] Against the traditional liberal view that freedom is negative only, we would recognize the positive rights of persons to what they need to act freely. And persons in need would be seen as entitled to the means to live, not as undeserving supplicants for private or public charity. An interpretation of such rights within the framework of justice would then be likely to yield monetary payments, such as social security checks and unemployment insurance supplemented by other such payments for those in need. For many competent persons whose only major problem is a lack of money or a temporary lack of employment, such arrangements would seem recommended and would be preferable to an array of social workers who are expected to practice care but who, whether because of paternalistic tendencies or bureaucratic constraints, often threaten the autonomy of persons in need.

Many persons, however, are not competent, autonomous, and only temporarily unemployed. Often, due to deficiencies of care at earlier stages or in various areas of their lives, their needs are complex and persistent. Inadequately cared for as children at home, in school, and elsewhere or inadequately provided with work and earning experience, they have grown up with more serious problems than lack of money, or they suffer from illness or disability. In such cases, care itself is needed. It should be addressed to specific persons and their specific needs. Dealing with these needs requires other specific persons to provide actual care and caring labor, not a machine turning out equal payments, to all in a given category. The care should be sensitive and flexible, allowing for the interaction of care provider and care receiver in such a way that the receiver is gradually empowered to develop toward needing less care when such a decrease is part of a process of growth or training or recovery. When the care needed will be lasting, practices should evolve that preclude the provision of care from becoming dominating and the receiving of care from becoming humiliating. Much recent work on disability has illuminated the values in practices of care, not only of the disabled but also of others.[28]

---

[27]Ibid.

[28]See, for example, Kittay, *Love's Labor*, and Mary B. Mahowald, Anita Silvers, and David Wasserman, *Disability, Difference, Discrimination* (Lanham, Md.: Rowman and Littlefield, 1998).

Whether we employ the perspective of justice or care will affect how we interpret the moral problems involved and what we recommend as institutional policies or individual actions. We might try to combine care and justice into a recommendation concerning welfare that each person is entitled to the care needed for appropriate development, but such a recommendation will remain an abstract and empty formulation until we deal with just the kinds of very different policies and practices I have tried to outline.

If we try to see justice and care as alternative interpretations that we can apply to the same moral problem, as Carol Gilligan recommends, we can try to think of care and justice as different but equally valid. But we are still left with the question of which interpretation to apply when we act, or which to appeal to when we draw up our recommendations. If we are merely describing the problem and possible interpretations of it, as in alternative literary accounts, we could maintain both of these alternative moral frameworks and not have to reject either one. But if decisions must be made about the problem, we will sometimes have to choose between these interpretations. Moral theory should provide guidance for choice about actions and policies, as well as educate our sensibilities about possible attitudes. If a child must live with either one parent or the other because the parents are divorcing and live far apart, should the determination be made on grounds of the rights of the genetic parent or the parent with the higher income who can best "provide" for the child, or on grounds of who has been actually taking care of the child and with which parent does the child have the most trusting and solid relationship? The problems of choosing between the interpretive frameworks of justice and care often persist after we have clarified both frameworks and what they would suggest.

When the concerns of justice and care conflict, how should we try to reconcile these values? Does either have priority as a general rule? Many philosophers have supposed that justice is the primary value of political institutions to which other values could be assimilated, but the examples concerning welfare and child custody are from important functions of the modern state, and they do not yield the clear ability of justice to handle the moral problems even in the political or legal realm, and certainly not as deeper moral issues. To suppose that the "justice system" of courts and law enforcement is the only really important function of the contemporary state is surely unhelpful; to what extent it should or should not be would be among the very questions to be addressed by an adequately integrated ethic.

One possibility I have considered in the past is that justice deals with moral minimums, a floor of moral requirements beneath which we should not sink as we avoid the injustices of assault and disrespect. In contrast, care deals with what is above and beyond the floor of duty. Caring well for children, for instance, involves much more than honoring their rights to not be abused or deprived of adequate food; good care brings joy and laughter. But as a solution to our problem, I have come to think that this is not clear. Perhaps one can have ever more justice in the sense of more understanding of rights, equality, and respect. Certainly there are minimums of care, even of the kind that cannot be handled by a right to them, such as by rights to adequate nourishment or medical care, that must be provided for persons to develop normally, though excellent care will far exceed them.

Another possible metaphor is that justice and rights set more or less absolute bounds or moral constraints within which we pursue our various visions of the good life, which would for almost everyone include the development of caring relationships. But this metaphor collapses for many of the same reasons as does that of justice as a floor of moral minimums. For instance, if there is anything that sets near absolute constraints on our pursuit of anything, including justice, it is responding to the needs of our children for basic, including emotional, care.

I now think that caring relations should form the wider moral framework into which justice should be fitted. Care seems the most basic moral value. As a practice, we know that without care we cannot have anything else, since life requires it. All human beings require a great deal of care in their early years, and most of us need and want caring relationships throughout our lives. As a value, care indicates what many practices ought to involve. When, for instance, necessities are provided without the relational human caring children need, children do not develop well, if at all. When in society individuals treat each other with only the respect that justice requires but no further consideration, the social fabric of trust and concern can be missing or disappearing.

Though justice is surely among the most important moral values, much life has gone on without it, and much of that life has had moderately good aspects. There has, for instance, been little justice within the family in almost all societies but much care; so we know we can have care without justice. Without care, however, there would be no persons to respect and no families to improve. Without care, there would be no public system of rights—even if it could be just. But care is not simply causally primary, it is more inclusive as a value. Within a network of caring, we can and should demand justice, but justice should not then push care to the margins, imagining justice's political embodiment as the model of morality, which is what has been done.

From a perspective of care, persons are relational and interdependent, not the individualistic autonomous rational agents of the perspective of justice and rights. This relational view is the better view of human beings, of persons engaged in developing human morality. We can decide to treat such persons *as* individuals, to be the bearers of individual rights, for the sake of constructing just political and legal and other institutions. But we should not forget the reality and the morality this view obscures. Persons *are* relational and interdependent. We can and should value autonomy, but it must be developed and sustained within a framework of relations of trust.

At the levels of global society and our own communities, we should develop frameworks of caring about and for one another as human beings who are members of families and groups. We should care for one another as persons in need of a habitable environment with a sufficient absence of violence and with sufficient provision of care for human life to flourish. We need to

acknowledge the moral values of the practices and family ties underlying the caring labor on which human life has always depended, and we need to consider how the best of these values can be better realized. Within a recognized framework of care we should see persons as having rights and as deserving of justice, most assuredly. And we might even give priority to justice in certain limited domains. But we should embed this picture, I think, in the wider tapestry of human care.

FEMINIST MORALITY AND REDUCTIONISM

My own view, then, is that care and its related concerns should be seen as the wider network within which justice and utility and the virtues should be fit. This does not mean that the latter can all be essentially reduced to aspects of care, or that the ethics of care can substitute for ethics of justice. The model of reductionism seems to be the wrong model.

In her discussion of various influential conceptions of the self, Diana Meyers concludes that none is in itself satisfactory. She suggests that we should "drop the synthetic imperative" and think of the five conceptions as "five dimensions of subjective experience, five foci of value, five schemas for understanding oneself and others, and five foci of moral concern."[29] Admittedly, this may be confusing, but "parsimony and completeness may not be jointly attainable."[30] She finds promise in narrativity, since "in self-narratives, people effortlessly weave together the disparate themes that the unitary self, the social self, the divided self, the relational self, and the embodied self highlight."[31] She goes on to find deficiencies in narrativity also. But let's consider the metaphors with which we can try to conceptualize the relations between different theories. We can see them as different "dimensions" of the matter in question, different "foci" of what is important about

---

[29]Diana Tietjens Meyers, "Narrative and Moral Life," in *Setting the Moral Compass*, ed. Cheshire Calhoun (New York: Oxford University Press, 2004), p. 293.
[30]Ibid.
[31]Ibid.

them, and so on. We can resist the pressure to synthesize them and especially to reduce them to just one way of thinking about the issues.

Care seems to me to be the most basic of moral values. Without care as an empirically describable practice, we cannot have life at all since human beings cannot survive without it. Without some level of caring concern for other human beings, we cannot have any morality. These requirements are not just empirical givens. In every context of care, moral evaluations are needed. Then, without some level of caring moral concern for all other human beings, we cannot have a satisfactory moral theory.

Within a network of caring relations, we can demand ever better and more morally admirable care. We can demand justice, fairness, rights. Out of caring concern we can determine that it is sometimes best for the sake of justice to imagine persons as abstract individuals. But these ways of thinking, we need to remember, are suitable *only* for limited domains, such as those of public law, taxation policy, commercial transactions, assuring basic human rights and basic levels of equal treatment—including in the household. Although assuring basic rights is an enormously important task, it is not all that morality should concern itself with. Caring well for our children requires vastly more than simply treating them fairly and not violating their basic rights. And the discourse of justice and rights should not over-whelm other discourse, as has happened, as if the concerns of justice would suffice for morality in general.

We need new images for the relations between justice and care, rejecting the impulse toward reductionism. The idea that one kind of value can be reduced to another or one kind of moral recommendation to another, may be a leg-acy of imagining that deductive or scientific approaches are most suitable for moral under-standing. They are not. The aims of science are to describe or explain and predict what is the case in the natural world as seen from a third-person perspective. The aims of morality are fundamentally different: with it we seek to recom-mend how we ought to live and what we ought to do as seen from the first-person perspective of

the conscious moral agent choosing how to live and to act.[32]

Although we can acknowledge that our moral conceptions *could* be arranged along neat and clean lines if only the messy concerns of morality could be reduced to the categorical imperative or the principle of utility, actual experience with most moral problems and especially with those in the contexts of care—understood narrowly rather than as including all the rest—show that this is a mistaken goal. A generally Kantian approach does seem suitable for various legal contexts, but many other contexts such as those of friendship and family are not best handled with such approaches. Whereas utilitarian ways of thinking may be those that can often best guide the policy choices of governments, they are not well suited to uphold-ing rights and assuring fairness, and they are not suited for contexts such as those of family relations and friends, where it is the particularity of persons (not their universal features) that matters most.

If moral concerns about right action could be reduced to the cultivation of the virtues, it would simplify our efforts at moral education and at structuring society in justifiable ways. But I think they clearly cannot.[33] Although virtue theory is not (in my view) reducible to theories of right action—merely equating virtue with acting in accordance with principles of right action—neither are justice or utility reducible to whatever attitudes or dispositions virtuous persons will have. We need objective standards for the care of children, the safety and health of citizens, and so forth. Virtuous dispositions fail to tell us what they are, let alone ensure that we meet them.

The ethics of care, I have argued, cannot be reduced to an aspect of either kind of ethic of jus-tice or to virtue ethics. But if I argue for care as the wider moral network within which moral concerns are to be placed, is this not to argue for a reduction of justice, utility, and virtue to the ethics of care?

[32]For further discussion, see Virginia Held, "Moral Subjects: The Natural and the Normative," presidential address (APA Eastern Division). *Proceedings of the American Philosophical Association* (November 2002).
[33]For discussion, see Michael Slote, *From Morality to Virtue* (New York: Oxford University Press, 1992)....

The answer is no. We need new analogies, metaphors, and images to deal with these questions. We can appreciate the freedom with which some writers devise new metaphors with which to convey their ideas.[34] In the case of the ethics of care, instead of the metaphor of reduction through logical relation or conceptual analysis, perhaps we should think of a painting or a tapestry or a glass sculpture. There is an overall design within which are salient and less salient components. The overall moral design of feminist moral theory, I believe, will be one of caring relations. But within that overall design there will be a number of salient components organized around the values of justice and utility. And there will be many interesting and detailed elements concerning the virtues. The whole should be harmonious, but that does not mean that the components cannot differ significantly. I think less in terms of narrativity and more in terms of visual metaphors. But if we do think of narratives, the point might be that we should not try to reduce one genre to another or all genres to an underlying ur-genre [basic type].

Such a morality of care might lack the appeal of what various reductionist programs aim at but fail to achieve. It might, however, offer a design we could live with. To the objection that without clear and fairly simple principles we will not be able to teach morality to children, we should remember that children have never been taught the principle of utility or the categorical imperative. Children have been and should be taught aspects of the overall design of morality such as that we should care about the well-being of others, we should treat them fairly, and we should

not harm them. We should imagine or try to gain experience of how we would feel if treated as we treat others and be sensitive to how others actually feel in various situations. We should be the sorts of persons others can trust, and we should value the caring relations that connect us with those close to us and those far away with whom we share the global environment.

But how can a theory be like a work of art? A scientific theory is part of the practice of scientific inquiry, but a theory in philosophy of science is a theory about this practice. It may hold that biological theories are in some sense reducible to those in physics or that they are not.

The practice of morality, I think, should contain many recommendations that could be thought of as moral theories for particular areas of life: economic activity, medical practice, bringing up children, and so on. But the philosophy of morality should consider whether there is or is not some one underlying theory to which the others can be reduced. At this level the various theories embedded in various practices might more appropriately be thought to be features of an overall design for living good lives in caring relationships with others, rather than as abstract formulations logically reducible to simpler ones. Moral practice can certainly be thought of as an art. Perhaps it is possible to outline some general recommendations for the development of what we usually think of as art: seek to create what is beautiful and "true" independently of such pressures as those from tyrannical governments or commercial interests, strive for artistic integrity, and so on. But we do not imagine that the practice of painting can be reduced to that of needlework or glass-blowing. Perhaps morality in all its different forms is more like the practices of art than it is like the sciences.

---

[34]See, for example, the discussions of John Keane's *Global Civil Society?* and Anne-Marie Slaughter's *A New World Order....*

◉ CRITICAL QUESTIONS

1. Do you find Held's argument supporting the conclusion that the ethics of care cannot be reduced to either an ethic of justice or virtue ethics persuasive? Why or why not?

2. The concept of care is central to the ethics of care. How would you define care? What is the weakest part of your definition?

4.7 MORAL RELATIVISM

Does anything go? I mean, is any moral view with its associated actions acceptable? What about this: sacrificing humans by ripping their hearts out because some people believe that the Sun god requires it? What about this: killing Jews because some people believe Jews are somehow responsible for all the world's problems? What about this: beating and hanging Blacks because some believe Blacks are subhuman? What about this: sexually abusing boys and girls because some people sexually desire children and believe that having sex with them does no real harm?

Most of us (I would hope all of us) would condemn such actions and reject such beliefs as false. However, we often hear people say that we should not judge others or make them conform to our values. Many people support some version of moral relativism because they believe that the values of others are as valid as their own.

We must do some careful thinking when we wade into the waters of moral relativism. Precise distinctions are in order. It is true that moral values and codes differ with historical, cultural, and religious circumstances. Does it follow from this fact that it is wrong to render moral judgments about the rightness or wrongness of human action? (See the discussion of rationality in Chapter 1.) When conflicts in moral values and judgments arise, we rightly feel uncomfortable imposing our own values on others. However, we feel equally uncomfortable supporting an "anything goes" position. Are we forced to choose between a kind of moral relativism which holds that all human actions are of equal moral worth and a kind of moral universalism or absolutism which maintains that one and only one set of moral values is true?

Louis Paul Pojman (1935–2005) was Professor of Philosophy, Emeritus from the United States Military Academy at West Point where he received the Presidential award for Distinguished Service. He received his Ph.D. from Oxford University (1977) and Union Theological Seminary in New York (1972). He was the author of thirty-four books and numerous articles.

READING QUESTIONS

1. According to Pojman's analysis, what is the diversity thesis and the dependency thesis? What conclusions logically follow from these two theses?
2. What is the difference between the subjective or individualistic version of ethical relativism and conventionalism?
3. What is wrong with ethical relativism in both its subjective and conventional versions?
4. What is the difference between moral absolutism and moral objectivism?
5. Pojman describes two arguments for moral objectivism. What are these arguments *and* how do they differ?

A Critique of Ethical Relativism

LOUIS P. POJMAN

"WHO'S TO JUDGE WHAT'S RIGHT OR WRONG?"

Like many people, I have always been instinctively a moral relativist. As far back as I can remember … it has always seemed to be obvious that the dictates of morality arise from some sort of convention or understanding among people, that different people arrive at different understandings, and that there are no basic moral demands that apply to everyone. This seemed so obvious to me I assumed it was everyone's instinctive view, or at least everyone who gave the matter any thought in this day and age (Gilbert Harman, "Is There a Single True Morality," in *Morality Reason, and Truth*, ed. David Copp and David Zimmerman).

Ethical relativism is the doctrine that the moral rightness and wrongness of actions vary from society to society and that there are no absolute universal moral standards on all men at all times. Accordingly, it holds that whether or not it is right for an individual to act in a certain way depends on or is relative to the society to which he belongs (John Ladd, *Ethical Relativism*).

Gilbert Harman's intuitions about the self-evidence of relativism contrast strikingly with Plato's or Kant's equal certainly about a form of objectivism. On the basis of polls taken in my ethics and introduction to philosophy classes over the past several years, Harman's views may signal a shift in contemporary society's moral understanding. The polls showed a two-to-one ratio in favor of moral relativism over moral absolutism, with hardly 2 percent of the respondents recognizing that there might be a third position between these two polar opposites. Of course, I'm not suggesting that all of these students had a clear understanding of what relativism entails, for many who said that they were conventional relativists also contended in the same polls that abortion except to save the mother's life is always wrong, that capital punishment is always morally wrong, or that suicide is never morally permissible.

Among my university colleagues, a growing number seem to embrace moral relativism. Recently one of my nonphilosopher colleagues objected to a dissertation proposal because the student assumed an objectivist position in ethics. (Ironically, I found in this same colleague's works rhetorical treatment of individual liberty that raised it to the level of a non-negotiable absolute.) But irony and inconsistency aside, many relativists are aware of the tension between their own subjective positions and their metatheory that entails relativism. I confess that I too am tempted by the allurement of this view and that I find it, in some forms, plausible and worthy of serious examination. However, I am also deeply troubled by it.

In this essay I will examine the central notions of ethical relativism and look at the implications that seem to follow from it. Then I will present the outline of a very modest objectivism, one that takes into account many of the insights of relativism and yet stands as a viable option to it.

1. AN ANALYSIS OF RELATIVISM

Let us examine the theses contained in John Ladd's succinct statement on ethical (conventional) relativism that appears at the beginning of this essay. If we analyze it, we derive the following argument:

1. Moral rightness and wrongness of actions vary from society to society, so there are no universal moral standards held by all societies.

2. Whether or not it is right for individuals to act in a certain way depends on (or is relative to) the society to which they belong.

3. Therefore, there are no absolute or objective moral standards that apply to all people everywhere and at all times.

1. The first thesis, which may be called the *diversity thesis*, is simply a description that acknowledges the fact that moral rules differ from society to society. Eskimos allow their elderly to die by starvation, whereas we believe that this is morally wrong. The Spartans of ancient Greece and the Dobu of New Guinea believe that stealing is morally right, but we believe it is wrong. A tribe in East Africa throws deformed infants to the hippopotamuses, but we abhor infanticide. Ruth Benedict described a tribe in Melanesia that views cooperation and kindness as vices. Sexual practices vary over time and with climate. Some cultures permit, while others condemn, homosexual behavior. Some cultures practice polygamy, while others view it as immoral. Some cultures accept cannibalism, while we detest it. Cultural relativism is well documented, and custom seems king over all. There may or may not be moral principles held in common by every society, but if there are any, they seem to be few, at best. Certainly, it would be very difficult to derive any single "true" morality by observing various societies' moral standards.

2. The second thesis, the *dependency thesis*, asserts that individual acts are right or wrong depending on the nature of the society from which they emanate. Morality does not occur in a vacuum, and what is considered morally right or wrong must be seen in a context that depends on the goals, wants, beliefs, history, and environment of the society in question. We could, of course, distinguish between a weak and a strong thesis of dependency, for the nonrelativist can accept a certain degree of relativity in the way moral principles are *applied* in various cultures.

But the ethical relativist must maintain a stronger thesis, one that insists that the moral principles themselves are products of the culture and may vary from society to society. The ethical relativist contends that even beyond environmental factors and differences in beliefs, a fundamental disagreement exists among societies. The best way for the relativist to support this thesis is by appealing to an indeterminacy of translation thesis, which maintains that there is a conceptual relativity among language groups so that we cannot even translate into our language the worldviews of a culture with a radically different language.

In a sense, we all live in radically different worlds. But the relativist wants to go further and maintain that there is something conventional about *any* morality, so that every morality really depends on a level of social acceptance. Not only do various societies adhere to different moral systems, but the very same society could (and often does) change its moral views over place and time. For example, the majority of people in the southern United States now view slavery as immoral, whereas just over one hundred years ago, they did not. Our society's views on divorce and sexuality have changed somewhat as well.

3. The conclusion that there are no absolute or objective moral standards binding on all people follows from the first two propositions. Combining cultural relativism (the diversity thesis) with the dependency thesis yields ethical relativism in its classic form. If there are different moral principles from culture to culture and if all morality is rooted in culture, then it follows that there are no universal moral principles that are valid for all cultures and peoples at all times.

2. SUBJECTIVISM

Some people think that this conclusion is still too tame, and they maintain that morality is not dependent on the society but rather on the individual. As my students sometimes maintain, "Morality is in the eye of the beholder." This form of moral subjectivism has the sorry consequence that it makes morality a very useless concept, for, on its premises, little or no interpersonal criticism or judgment is logically possible. The only basis for judging John wrong would be if he failed to live up to his own principles, but, of course, one of his principles could be that hypocrisy is morally permissible (for him at least), so that it would be impossible for him to do wrong. For John hypocrisy and nonhyprocrisy are both morally permissible.

On the basis of subjectivism it could very easily turn out that Adolf Hitler was as moral as Gandhi, so long as each believed he was living by his chosen principles. Notions of moral good and bad, or right or wrong, cease to have interpersonal evaluative meaning. A student might not like it when her teacher gives her an F on a test paper, while he gives another student an A for a similar paper, but there is no way to criticize him for injustice, because justice is not one of his chosen principles.

Absurd consequences follow from subjectivism. If it is correct, then morality reduces to aesthetic tastes about which there can be neither argument nor interpersonal judgment. Although many students say that they espouse subjectivism, there is evidence that it conflicts with others of their moral views (for example, that Hitler truly was morally bad). A contradiction seems to exist between subjectivism and the very concept of morality, which it is supposed to characterize, for morality has to do with *proper* resolution of interpersonal conflict and the amelioration of the human predicament (both deontological and teleological systems do this, but in different ways …). Whatever else it does, it has a minimal aim of preventing a Hobbesian state of nature. But if so, subjectivism is no help at all in doing this, for it rests neither on social *agreement* of principle (as the conventionalist maintains) nor on an objectively independent set of norms that bind all people for the common good. If there were only one person on earth, there would be no occasion for morality because there wouldn't be any interpersonal conflicts to resolve or others whose suffering he or she would have a duty to ameliorate. Subjectivism implicitly assumes something of this atomism, a state of affairs in which only isolated individuals make up separate universes. In sum, subjectivism is solipsistic—philosophically unaware of human interaction and morality's social function.

3. CONVENTIONALISM

Conventional ethical relativism, the view that there are no objective moral principles but that all valid moral principles are justified by virtue of their cultural acceptance, recognizes the social nature of morality.[1] That is precisely its power and virtue. It does not seem subject to the same absurd consequences of subjectivism. Recognition of this contextual element has led many people to suppose that ethical relativism is the correct meta-ethical theory. Furthermore, they are drawn to it for its liberal philosophical stance. It seems to entail or strongly imply an attitude of tolerance toward other cultures. The most famous proponent of this position is the anthropologist Melville Herskovits, who argued that (1) since morality is relative to its culture and (2) we have no independent basis for criticizing any morality of any other culture, therefore (3) we ought to be tolerant of the moralities of other cultures.[2]

Tolerance is certainly a virtue, but is this a good argument for it? I think not. If morality simply is relative to each culture, then if the culture does not have a principle of tolerance, its members have no obligation to be tolerant. Herskovits seems to be treating the principle of tolerance as the one exception to his relativism. But from a relativistic point of view there is no more reason to be tolerant than to be intolerant, and neither stance is objectively morally better than the other.

Not only does the relativist fail to offer a basis for criticizing those who are intolerant, but he cannot also rationally criticize anyone who espouses what he might regard as a heinous principle. If criticism supposes an objective standard, he cannot morally criticize anyone outside his culture. Hitler's actions (so long as they are culturally tolerated) are as legitimate as Mother Teresa's. Genocide of unpopular minorities, oppression of the poor, slavery, and even advocacy of war for its own sake are as equally moral as their opposites. And if a subculture decided that starting a nuclear war was somehow morally acceptable, we could not morally criticize these people.

---

[1]Part of this section has been influenced by Fred Feldman's treatment of the same topic in *Introductory Ethics* (Prentice-Hall, 1978).

[2]Melville Herskovits, *Cultural Relativism* (Random House, 1972).

There are other disturbing consequences of ethical relativism. It seems to entail that reformers are always (morally) wrong because they go against the tide of cultural standards. William Wilberforce was wrong in the early nineteenth century to oppose slavery, and the British were immoral in opposing suttee in India (the burning of widows, which is now illegal there). Gandhi was wrong in trying to bring peace between Moslems and Hindus because the majority of each religious community felt hatred for the other. Jesus was immoral in advocating the beatitudes and principles of the Sermon on the Mount because it is clear that few in his time (or in ours) accepted them. Yet normally we feel just the opposite, that the reformer is the courageous innovator who is right, who has the truth, who is at odds with the mindless majority. We intuitively feel that Kierkegaard was right, that moral truth is often with the insightful individual and error with the crowd. Yet if relativism is correct, the opposite is necessarily the case: truth is with the crowd and error with the individual.

Similarly, moral relativism entails disturbing judgments about the law. Our normal view is that we have a *prima facie* duty to obey laws, because the law, in general, promotes the human good. According to most objective systems this obligation is not absolute, but rather is relative to the particular law's relationship to a higher moral order. Civil disobedience is warranted in some cases in which the law seems to be seriously in conflict with morality. However, if moral relativism is true, then neither law nor civil disobedience has a firm foundation. Civil disobedience will be morally wrong so long as the culture agrees with the law in question; but to those who belong to the subculture that doesn't recognize the law in question, disobedience will be morally permissible. Both a *prima facie* duty to obey the law and justification for breaking the law at certain times are dependent on a nonrelativist notion of morality.

A fundamental problem with the dependency thesis, the relativists' assumption that morality is dependent on culture or society, is that it is notoriously difficult to define a culture or society, especially in a pluralistic society like our own. One person may belong to several societies (subcultures) with different values and arrangements of principles. Persons may belong to the society-at-large and hold certain values of patriotism, honor, courage, and respect for the law (including some that are controversial but have majority acceptance, such as the law on abortion). But they may also belong to a church that opposes some secular laws, or they may be integral members of a socially mixed community in which different principles hold sway, or they may belong to clubs and families that adhere to still other rules.

Relativism would seem to contend that when people are members of societies with conflicting moralities they must be judged both wrong and not wrong (either right or permissible) whatever they do. For example, if Mary is a U.S. citizen and a member of the Roman Catholic [C]hurch, she is wrong (qua Catholic) if she chooses to have an abortion and not wrong (qua citizens of the United States) if she chooses to have an abortion. Likewise, if Sam and Alice are Jehovah's Witnesses, then they are morally wrong (qua Jehovah's Witnesses) in allowing their child, who might otherwise die, to have a blood transfusion, but they are not wrong (qua U.S. citizens) in allowing him to have a transfusion. And conversely, as U.S. citizens they are wrong in prohibiting the transfusion, but as Jehovah's Witnesses they are not wrong if they prohibit it.

Perhaps the relativist would adhere to a meta-principle that says that in such cases the individual may designate one group as primary. If Mary chooses to have an abortion, she is choosing to belong to the general society relative to that principle. The trouble with this feat is that it seems to lead back to counter-intuitive results. If Gangster Gus feels like killing bank president Ortcutt and wants to feel good about it, he identifies with the underworld society rather than the general public morality. Does this justify the killing? In fact, couldn't one justify anything simply by forming a small subculture that approved of it? Charles Manson would be morally pure in killing innocent people simply by forming a little coterie. How large must the group be in order to be a legitimate subculture or society? Does it need ten or fifteen people? How about just three? Come to think of it, why can't my burglary partner and I form our own society with a morality of its own? Of course, if my partner died, I could still claim that because I was acting from a set of norms that had an interpersonal origin, my act was morally correct. But why can't I dispense with the interpersonal agreements altogether and invent my own morality, since morality, in this view, is only an invention anyway? Conventionalist relativism seems to reduce to subjectivism. And subjectivism leads, as we have seen, to the demise of morality altogether.

If anyone objects that this argument is an instance of the slippery slope fallacy, let that person give an alternative analysis of what constitutes a viable social basis for generating valid moral principles. Perhaps we might agree (for the sake of argument, at least) that the very nature of morality entails two or more people making an agreement. This strategy saves the conventionalist from moral solipsism, but it still permits most any principle to count as moral, and what's more, those principles can be thrown out and their contraries substituted for them as the need arises. If two or three people decide that they will make cheating morally acceptable for them at their university (qua "Cheaters Anonymous"), then cheating is moral. Why not?

However, whereas we may fear the demise of morality as we have known it, this in itself may not be a good reason for rejecting relativism, that is, for judging it false. Alas, truth may not always be edifying. But the consequences of this position are sufficiently alarming to prompt us to look carefully for some weakness in the relativist's argument. So let us reexamine the premises and conclusion listed as the three theses of relativism at the beginning of this essay.

1. Moral rightness and wrongness of actions vary from society to society, so there are no universal moral standards held by all societies.

2. Whether or not it is right for individuals to act in a certain way depends on (or is relative to) the society to which they belong.

3. Therefore, there are no absolute or objective moral standards that apply to all people everywhere and at all times.

Does any one of these seem problematic? The first thesis, the diversity thesis, seems unexceptional. Cultural relativism is a fact, but it is a neutral fact. On the one hand, it does not establish the truth of ethical relativism, for it could be the case that some cultures simply lack correct moral principles. On the other hand, a denial of complete cultural relativism (that is, an admission of some universal principles) does not disprove ethical relativism. For even if we did find one or two universal principles, this would not prove that they had any objective status. We could still *imagine* a culture that was an exception to the rule and be unable to criticize it. So the first premise doesn't by itself imply ethical relativism, and its denial doesn't disprove ethical relativism.

Next we consider the crucial second thesis, the dependency thesis. Morality does not occur in a vacuum, but rather what is considered morally right or wrong must be seen in a context that depends on the goals, wants, beliefs, history, and environment of the society in question. Previously we mentioned weak and strong theses of dependency. The weak thesis says that the application of principles depends on the particular cultural predicament, whereas the strong thesis contends that the principles themselves depend on that predicament. The nonrelativist can accept a certain degree of relativity in the way moral principles are *applied* in various cultures.

For example, a raw environment with scarce natural resources may justify the Eskimos' practice of euthanasia to the objectivist, who would consistently reject that practice in another environment. A tribe in East Africa throws its deformed children into the river because of its belief that such infants *belong* to the hippopotamus, the god of the river. We believe that they have a false belief about this, but the point is that the same principles of respect for property and respect for human life are operative in these contrary practices. They differ from us only in belief, not in substantive moral principle. This example is an illustration of how nonmoral beliefs (for example, deformed children belong to the hippopotamus) cause moral principles (for example, give to each his due) to generate different actions. In our own culture the difference in the nonmoral belief about the status of a fetus generates opposite moral prescriptions.

So the fact that moral principles are weakly dependent doesn't show that ethical relativism is valid. In spite of this weak dependency on non-moral factors, a set of general moral norms that are applicable to all cultures (and even recognized in most) and that are disregarded at a culture's own expense could still exist.

What the relativist needs is a strong thesis of dependency that claims that somehow all principles are essentially cultural decisions. But why should we choose to view morality this way? Are there grounds to recommend the strong thesis of dependency over the weak one? One is the simple point that we don't have an obvious impartial standard from which to judge. Who's to say which culture is right and which is wrong? But we can reason and perform thought experiments in order to make a case for one system over another. We may not be able to know with certainty that we are right or relatively more right than the other culture, but we may be justified in believing that we are. If we can be closer to the truth regarding factual or scientific matters, why can't we be closer to the truth on moral matters? Why can't a culture simply be confused or wrong about its moral perceptions? Why can't we say that the society that sees nothing wrong with torturing children is less moral in that regard than the culture that cherishes children and grants them equal rights?

The only plausible argument that I know in favor of the strong dependency thesis is the indeterminacy of translation thesis, which holds that languages are often so fundamentally different from each other that we cannot accurately translate concepts or principles from one to another. But this thesis, while relatively true even within a language community, seems falsified by experience. We do learn foreign languages and learn to translate across linguistic frameworks. For example, people from a myriad of language groups come to the United States and learn to speak English and communicate perfectly well. Rather than a complete hiatus, the interplay between these other cultures eventually enriches the English language with new concepts (for example,

forte/foible, taboo, coup de grace), even as English has enriched (or "corrupted," as the purist might say) French and other languages as well. Even if it turns out that there is some indeterminacy of translation between language users, we should not infer from this that no translation is possible. It seems reasonable to believe that general moral principles are precisely those things that can be communicated transculturally. A sufficiently common human nature and human predicament seem to make it possible to speak cross-culturally of a common set of underlying moral principles.

If this is true, then the indeterminacy of translation thesis upon which relativism depends must itself be relativized to the point where it is no objection to objective morality.

4. THE CASE FOR OBJECTIVISM

If nonrelativists are to make their case, they will have to offer a better explanation of cultural diversity and give reasons for adhering to moral objectivism. One way of doing this is to appeal to a divine law and cite human sin that causes deviation from that law. Although I think that human greed, selfishness, pride, self-deception, and other maladies have a great deal to do with moral differences and that religion may lend great support to morality, I don't think that a religious justification is necessary for validation of moral principles. I shall not build a case for objectivism by an appeal to religion, but I shall instead outline a modest nonreligious objectivism by first appealing to our intuitions and then by giving a naturalist account of morality that transcends individual cultures.

First, I must make it clear that I am distinguishing moral absolutism from moral objectivism. The absolutist believes that there are moral principles that ought never be overridden or violated. Kant's system is a good example of this. One ought never break a promise, no matter what. Act utilitarianism also seems absolutist, for the principle—do that act that has the most promise of yielding the most utility—cannot be overridden. An objectivist need not posit any principles that cannot be overridden at least not in unqualified general forms. Moral principles are similar to

Ross's *prima facie* principles, which may or may not be arranged hierarchically, But even if they are, the principles may be overridden by another prima facie principle (for example whereas a principle of justice may generally outweigh a principle of benevolence, there are times when enormous good could be done by sacrificing a small amount of justice, so that an objectivist would be inclined to so act). An unqualified general principle would be of the form "Always do X" or "In general do X," but a qualified general principle would be of the form "In general do X except under condition C" or "Except under condition C, always do X." Suitably conditioned objective principles might turn out to be qualified absolutes.[3]

If we can establish or show that it is reasonable to believe that there is at least one objective moral principle that is binding on all people everywhere in some ideal sense, we shall have shown that relativism is probably false and that a limited objectivism is true. Actually, I believe that there are many qualified general ethical principles that are binding on all rational beings, but one will suffice to refute relativism. The principle I'll choose is the following:

A. It is morally wrong to torture people for the fun of it.

I claim that this principle is binding on all rational agents, so that if some agent, S, rejects A, we should not let that affect our intuition that A is a true principle, but rather try to explain S's behavior as perverse, ignorant, or irrational instead. For example, suppose Hitler didn't accept A. Should that affect our confidence in the truth of A? Is it not more reasonable to infer that Hitler was morally deficient, morally blind, ignorant, or irrational than to suppose that his noncompliance is evidence against the truth of A?

Suppose further that there is a tribe of people somewhere who enjoys torturing people. The whole culture accepts torturing others for the fun of it. Suppose that Mother Teresa or Gandhi tries unsuccessfully to convince them that they should stop torturing people altogether, and they respond by torturing them. Should this affect our confidence in A? Would it not be more reasonable to look for some explanation of the tribe's behavior? For example, we might hypothesize that this tribe lacked a developed sense of sympathetic imagination that is necessary for the moral life. Or we might theorize that this tribe was on a lower evolutionary level than most Homo sapiens. Or we might simply conclude that the tribe was closer to a Hobbesian state of nature than most societies, and as such probably would not survive. But we need not know why the tribe was in such bad shape in order to maintain our confidence in A as a moral principle. If A is a basic or core belief for us, then we will be more likely to doubt the tribe's sanity or ability to think morally than to doubt the validity of A.

Fortunately, it isn't as though A were an ad hoc belief, for we can give reasons for beliefs like A being central to any moral system that we deem adequate. Principles like the Golden Rule (suitably qualified), not killing innocent people, treating equals equally, truth-telling, promise-keeping, and the like are central to the fluid progression of social interaction and to the resolution of conflicts, which is what ethics is about (at least in the case of minimal morality, even though there may be more to morality than simply these kinds of concerns). For example, language itself depends on a general commitment to the principle of truth-telling. Every time we use words correctly we are telling the truth, and without this behavior, language wouldn't be possible. Likewise, without the recognition of a rule of promise-keeping, contracts are of no avail and cooperation is less likely to occur.

A morality would be adequate if it contained a requisite set of these objective principles (call them the stable core of morality), but there could be more than one adequate morality that contained different rankings of these and other principles that are consistent with the core. That is, there may be a certain relativity to secondary principles (whether to opt for monogamy rather than polygamy, whether to include a principle of high altruism in the set of moral duties, whether to allow for

---

[3]See Marcus Singer, "The Idea of a Rational Morality," *Proceedings of the American Philosophical Association* (September 1986: 28), in which he argues that such principles as "It is always wrong to lie for lying's sake" are absolutely wrong. "Given any moral rule to the effect that some kind of action is generally wrong, it follows that it is always wrong to do any act of that kind just for the sake of doing it."

limited euthanasia, and so forth), but in every morality a certain core will remain, though it may be applied somewhat differently because of differences in environment, belief, tradition, and the like.

Stated more positively, objectivists who base their moral systems on a common human nature with common needs and desires might construct the following argument for objectivism:

1. Human nature is relatively similar in essential respects, having a common set of needs and interests.

2. Moral principles are functions of human needs and interests and are instituted by reason in order to promote the most significant interests and needs of rational beings (and perhaps of others).

3. Some moral principles promote human interests and meet human needs better than others.

4. Those principles that meet essential needs and promote the most significant interests of humans in optimal ways can be said to be objectively valid moral principles.

5. Therefore, since there is a common human nature, there is an objectively valid set of moral principles that is applicable to all humanity.

If we leave out any reference to a common human nature, the argument would be even simpler:

1. Objectively valid moral principles are those adherence to which meets the needs and promotes the most significant interests of persons.

2. Some principles are such that adherence to them meets the needs and promotes the most significant interests of persons.

3. Therefore, some objectively valid moral principles exist.

Either argument would satisfy objectivism, but the former makes it clearer that is our common human nature that generates the common principles.[4]

---

[4]I owe the reformulation of the argument to Bruce Russell, who, along with Morton Winston, offered valuable criticisms of an earlier version of this article. An anonymous reader also aided in the revision of this article.

If either argument succeeds, there are ideal moralities (and not simply adequate ones). Of course, there could still be more than one ideal morality, which presumably an ideal observer would choose under optimal conditions. This ideal observer might conclude that out of an infinite set of moralities, three or more combinations would tie for first place. One would expect that these would be similar, but there is every reason to believe that all of these would contain the set of core principles.

Of course, we don't know what an ideal observer would choose, but we can imagine that the conditions which such an observer would choose would be conditions of maximal knowledge and impartiality, second-order qualities that ensure that agents have the best chance of making the best decisions. If this is so, then the more we learn to judge impartially and the more we know about possible forms of life, the better chance we have to approximate an ideal moral system. And if there is the possibility of approximating ideal moral systems with an objective core and other objective components, then ethical relativism is certainly false. We can confidently dismiss it as an aberration and get on with the job of working out better moral systems.

I have been arguing that morality has a point, so that not just anything can count as a valid moral principle. Let me illustrate: Imagine that you have been miraculously transported to the dark kingdom of hell, and there you get a glimpse of the sufferings of the damned. Their punishment is that they have eternal back itches that ebb and flow constantly. But they cannot scratch their backs, for their arms are paralyzed in a frontal position, so they writhe with itchiness through eternity. And just as you are beginning to feel the itch on your own back, you are suddenly transported to heaven. What do you see in the kingdom of the blessed? You see people who have eternal back itches and cannot scratch their own backs. But they are all smiling instead of writhing. Why? Because everyone has his or her arms stretched out to scratch someone else's back, and so, with their arrangement in one big circle, a hell of agony is turned into a heaven of ecstasy.

If we can imagine some states of affairs or cultures that are better than others in a way that depends on human action, we can ask what are those character traits that make them so. In our story, people in heaven, but not in hell, cooperate for the amelioration of suffering and the production of pleasure. These are very primitive goods, insufficient for a full-blown morality, but they give us a hint concerning the objectivity of morality. Moral goodness has something to do with the ameliorating of suffering, the resolution of conflict, and the promotion of human nourishing. If our heaven of scratching is really better than the eternal itchiness of hell, then whatever makes it so is constitutively related to moral rightness.

Why, then, is there such a strong inclination toward ethical relativism? I think that there are three reasons that haven't been emphasized. The first is the fact that options are usually presented as though absolutism and relativism were the only alternatives, so conventionalism wins out against an implausible competitor. We have seen that this dichotomy is unnecessary. One can have an objective morality without being absolutist.

The second reason is that our recent sensitivity to cultural relativism has made us conscious of the frailty of many aspects of our moral repertoire, so that there is a tendency to wonder who's to judge what's really right or wrong. However, the move from a reasonable cultural relativism, which rightly causes us to rethink our moral systems, to an ethical relativism, which causes us to give up the heart of morality altogether, is an instance of the fallacy of confusing factual or descriptive statements with normative ones. Cultural relativism doesn't entail ethical relativism.

We may well agree that cultures differ and that we ought to be cautious in condemning what we don't understand, but this in no way need imply that there are not better and worse ways of living. We can understand and excuse, to some degree at least, those who differ from our best notions of morality, and we can do this without abdicating the judgment that cultures that lack principles of justice or promise-keeping or protection of the innocent are morally poorer for these omissions.

The third reason, which is influential with philosophers who are overly impressed with meta-ethics, is that many philosophers believe that it is important to begin to do ethics with a morally neutral definition. As the *Webster's Ninth New Collegiate Dictionary* defines it, ethics is simply "the principles of conduct governing an individual or a group." No judgment is made from the outset about the content of those principles, and since the diversity thesis is plausible, one can be led to think that a certain relativism follows from this definition.

While this definition may be a fair one for sociology or anthropology, it is inadequate for philosophy. There is a narrower definition of the term that has to do with the Good, with human flourishing (and probably nonhuman sentient creatures' flourishing as well). And this flourishing involves the amelioration of suffering, the promotion of happiness, and the resolution of conflicts of interest. Given this content-laden conception of morality, we can explain why we are loathe to call Hitler's actions or torturing little children morally right regardless of whether a majority approves of them.

So, who's to judge what's right or wrong? We are. We are to do so on the basis of the best reasoning we can bring forth, and with sympathy and understanding.

◉ CRITICAL QUESTIONS

1. How might an ethical relativist counter Pojman's argument for moral objectivism?

2. Are you an ethical relativist, absolutist, or objectivist? Present an argument to support whichever position you take.

To access the *Voices of Wisdom*, 8th Edition, **Premium Website**, search for this book on CengageBrain.com.

CHAPTER FIVE

What Makes a Society Just?

The problem of setting up a state can be solved even by a nation of devils.

IMMANUEL KANT

LEARNING OBJECTIVES

After studying this chapter students should be able to:
- distinguish political from social philosophy,
- explain some of the philosophical issues that anarchism raises,
- describe the way Aristotle distinguishes between good and bad forms of government,
- provide examples of compensatory, retributive, and distributive justice,
- define egalitarianism,
- define theocracy and describe the Five Pillars of Islam,
- state the basic difference between Sunni and Shia Islam with respect to political ideas,
- distinguish the material from the formal principle of justice,
- state the differences among laissez-faire capitalism, socialism, communism, and totalitarianism,
- explain the social contract theory of governmental authority,
- identify Allah, Muslim, Islam, Mohammad, Averroës, el Fadl, Adam Smith, Locke, Marx, Engels, Rawls, Hobbes, Rousseau, King, Thoreau, Gandhi, and Deloria, and
- answer all the questions relating to the selections.

5.1 INTRODUCTION

Have you ever wondered, "What is justice?" Have you been curious about why we have governments? What is the best form of government? Who should rule? Where does the authority to rule come from? Have you ever thought, "Why should there be laws and why should we obey them? Are all people naturally wicked and do they need to be restrained from doing bad or forced to do good? Is it morally justifiable to break the law?" Have you noticed that we talk a lot about liberty, equality, and justice but have a hard time defining these concepts? Should liberty be sacrificed to promote equality? Or should liberty be protected at all costs, even if it means some people will not get an equal opportunity?

Have you wondered, "What should the government give the people—what they want or what is good for them? Who knows what is good for them? Should the state serve the interests of the individual, or should the interests of the individual be subordinate to the interests of the state?"

If you have thought about these sorts of questions, you have been concerned with the kinds of issues and problems that are normally studied by social and political philosophers. Political and social philosophies deal with issues of moral value at the level of the group. **Political philosophy** is primarily concerned with the justification of governmental authority to rule and with the nature of government or the state. **Social philosophy** is primarily concerned with who gets what and how.

Your pursuit of your own good occurs within a social context—that is, within a context in which others are also pursuing their own good. In such a social context, issues of fairness, social rights and responsibilities, the limits of political and economic power, and the welfare of your fellow human beings inevitably arise.

Like ethics, social–political philosophy is primarily *normative* rather than *descriptive*. For example, one goal of political philosophy is not just to describe the kinds of governments there are and how they function, but also to figure out which are the best forms of government and by what standards such a judgment can be made.

There are many issues and problems relating to social–political philosophy, and we can do no more than investigate a few of them in this chapter. However, two concepts are central to many of the debates in this field: authority and justice. A government is the exercise of power and coercive force by one person or group over the rest in a society. A fundamental political question has to do with what gives one group the authority to exercise such power. **Anarchism** is the position that governments are by nature immoral and should not be established. Those who argue in favor of anarchism maintain that each individual has the ultimate moral authority to live and act as he or she chooses. It is immoral for one group to rule another, and it is immoral of you, as an individual, to surrender your moral responsibility for the conduct of your own life to another. Of course, many people believe that anarchism would lead to social chaos, and so government of some kind seems necessary. But the question remains, by whose authority does one person or group rule another? And even if we grant that some kind of government is needed, the issues of what kind and the limits of its power must be answered.

Plato, in the *Republic* (see Section 10.3), describes an ideal society in which only the lovers of wisdom (philosophers) rule. Justice is achieved, according to Plato, when each of the classes of his ideal republic does well what they are best suited to do. Justice shall reign when the rulers rule wisely, the guardians protect courageously, and the producers produce and consume goods moderately. Plato's vision of a just society has been widely influential. However, his pupil Aristotle modified his teacher's political ideas.

Aristotle divided governments into three types: rule of one, rule of some, and rule of all. He divided these types again into those that were good because they had the common good in view and those that were bad because they had only self-interest or special interests in mind.

Type	Good	Bad
One	Monarchy	Tyranny
Some	Aristocracy	Oligarchy
All	Polity	Democracy

It might surprise you to find **democracy** (rule by the people) listed as the bad form of the rule of all, but Aristotle believed that democracies did not promote the common good. Rather, they promote the special interests of those who are able to exercise the most influence. For Aristotle, the moral entitlement to rule derives from whether those in power have their own interest in view or the interests of all segments of society. In other words, good governments promote the common good, and they do this by making human flourishing possible.

Some people have argued that one of the purposes of government is to ensure justice. Philosophers often distinguish among **compensatory justice**, **retributive justice**, and **distributive justice**. Affirmative action programs, which may provide for preferential treatment, constitute examples of compensatory (also called "corrective") justice because they involve providing benefits to persons who have suffered undeserved hardships or who have been denied benefits they deserve. The imposition of legal penalties (e.g., putting someone in prison) is an example of retributive justice because it involves placing burdens on people who have enjoyed benefits they did not deserve or who are guilty of failing to fulfill their responsibilities. Distributive justice is the fair distribution of both burdens and benefits to persons in situations of conflict of interest and relative scarcity. For example, not everyone can get into medical school, so how can we decide who should be accepted in a manner fair to all?

These three notions—compensation, retribution, and fair distribution—indicate that the concepts of fairness and desert are central to the concept of justice. What about the notion of equality? Isn't treating everyone equally the same as treating them justly? **Egalitarians** argue that all persons, simply because they are persons, should share equally in the distribution of all benefits and burdens. Yet treating everyone equally may not always be the just thing to do. Paying Harry $50,000 and paying Chong the same, even though Harry has worked only 5 years for the company and has a poor performance record whereas Chong is a 15-year veteran with an excellent record, does not seem just. Harry and Chong are both persons, but in the case of salary should this be the primary consideration? However, allowing some people, because of good luck or birth, to become extremely wealthy and others, because of misfortune or birth, to become extremely poor does not seem fair either. Is there a fair way to distribute wealth?

5.2 GOD AND JUSTICE

Aristotle did not list **theocracy** (the theory that only God has the right to rule) among his governmental types, but this has been a widespread and long-lasting theory of sovereignty. The Hebrew Bible (called by Christians the Old Testament) endorses a theocratic state in which a king rules with God's proxy. The monarchs of the ancient world ruled as divine stand-ins, and the emperors of China had the mandate of heaven as their charter. During the Middle Ages, the divine right of kings was a widely held political theory, which said, in effect, that the moral entitlement to exercise the power to rule is a divine right, and this right can be granted by God to those of his (her?) choice. The great monarchies of Europe were founded on this principle, and their power was maintained by the support of the Roman Catholic Church. Even today in the United States, one hears talk of the "restoration" of a theocratic state among fundamentalist Protestants, and the modern world is not without its theocracies.

The notion that God alone is sovereign is an idea that is found not only in ancient Judaism and Christianity but also in Islam. Muhammad (570–632) is considered by Muslims to be a prophet of **Allah** (God). A **Muslim** is one who submits to the will of Allah, and Islam is the name of a religious community that seeks to obey the commands of Allah. According to Islam, Allah revealed his will to the prophet Muhammad. Those revelations are recorded in the *Qur'an*, the holy book of Islam. Central to Islamic practice are the **five pillars of Islam**: witnessing that there is no God but Allah and that Muhammad is his Apostle; mandatory prayers, or *salat*; mandatory alms (*zakat*); fasting during the month of Ramadan; and *hajj*, or pilgrimage to Mecca.

Throughout Islamic history there has been and there continues to be considerable debate about the best type of government. The fundamental presupposition of this debate is that the right to rule belongs to God because only God is the perfectly just creator of all that exists. All parties agree on this theistic understanding of sovereignty. The disputes center on the political implications of divine sovereignty.

After the death of Muhammad, various schools of Islamic thought developed. Two of these schools—the **Sunni** and **Shi'i**—agreed that, since God does not rule human society directly, humans must devise governments that strive to realize as nearly as humans can the divine ideal of justice. According to the Sunni, a caliph (successor to the Prophet) should be selected or elected to provide political and military leadership. This caliphate would have, according to the Sunni, limited religious power although, ideally, the caliph himself would be a descendant from Muhammad's tribe if not from Muhammad himself. The Shi'i argued that leadership should be vested in an imam (leader) who is the direct descendant of the Prophet and his cousin and son-in-law Ali, who, according to the Shi'i, is the first true imam after the Prophet himself. The imam is a divinely inspired religious *and* political leader.

Islamic philosophers, while well aware of the debates within Islam over legitimate political succession, tended to take a different approach to the issue of what makes a society just. While acknowledging the sovereignty of Allah and the authority of revelation, philosophers such as Abu al-Walid Ibn Rushid (d. 595/1198), known in the West by his Latin name of Averroës, introduced ideas derived from both Aristotle and Plato into the debate. Criteria derived from reasonable reflection on the issues must also be considered. Proper genealogy is not enough. Just rulers are rational rulers, whatever may be their connection to the Prophet.

How should we understand Averroës's appeal to "rational criteria"? Today the debate within and outside the Muslim community of faith about issues of politics and justice often centers on whether democracy is compatible with the traditional values of Islam. As the view, on one of the color plates, of Tahrir Square in Cairo, Egypt, reminds us, this debate is particularly timely. Khaled Abou El Fadl (b. 1963 in Kuwait) is a professor of law at the UCLA School of Law. In the next selection he presents an argument for the compatibility of Islamic traditions and democracy.

The photo on another color plate shows another aspect of Islamic traditions that is a subject of debate in Western societies. See if you find in El Fadl's piece anything that offers these societies a possible response or persuasive argument regarding the role and position of women in Islamic countries.

◉ READING QUESTIONS

1. Why is democracy a formidable challenge for Islam?
2. What three values are socially and politically central to Muslim polity (a governmental or political organization)?
3. Put into your own words Fadl's "provisional case" for the compatibility of Islam and democracy.
4. Why, according to Fadl, does an "authoritarian view" denigrate God's sovereignty?
5. What is the paradox of Shari'ah and how does Fadl resolve this paradox?
6. What is the most "formidable challenge" to Fadl's argument, and how does he respond to it?

Islam and Democracy

KHALED ABOU EL FADL

A Muslim jurist writing a few centuries ago on the subject of Islam and government would have commenced his treatise by distinguishing three types of political systems. The first he would have described as a natural system—like a primitive state of nature, an uncivilized, anarchic world where the most powerful tyrannize the rest. Instead of law there would be custom; instead of government there would be tribal elders who would be obeyed only so long as they remained the strongest.

The jurist would then describe a second system, ruled by a prince or king whose word is the law. Because the law would be fixed by the arbitrary will of the ruler and the people would obey out of necessity or compulsion, this system, too, would be tyrannical and illegitimate.

The third and best system would be the caliphate, based on Shari'ah law—the body of Muslim religious law founded on the Qur'an and the conduct and statements of the Prophet. According to Muslim jurists, Shari'ah law fulfills the criteria of justice and legitimacy and binds the governed and governor alike. Because it is based on the rule of law and thus deprives human beings of arbitrary authority over each other, the caliphate system was considered superior to any other.[1]

In espousing the rule of law and limited government, classical Muslim scholars embraced core elements of modern democratic practice. Limited government and the rule of law, however, are only two elements in the system of government with the most compelling claim to legitimacy today. Democracy's moral power lies in the idea that the citizens of a nation are sovereign, and—in modern representative democracies—they express their sovereign will by electing representatives. In a democracy, the people are the source of the law, and the law in turn ensures the fundamental rights that protect the well-being and interests of the individual members of the sovereignty.

I am grateful to my wife, Grace, for her invaluable feedback and assistance. I thank Anver Emon and Mairaj Syed, my research assistants, for their diligent work on this chapter, and I also thank my assistant, Naheed Fakoor, for competently managing everything related to the timely production of my work. I am especially grateful to Joshua Cohen and Fred Appel, who believed in the importance of this project and who generously dedicated numerous hours of their time in order to ensure the successful completion of this book. My work is much richer because of their valuable insights. I am indebted to the staff at *Boston Review*, which was the first to suggest and promote this project, and I also thank the Boston NPR radio affiliate WBUR and its radio program, "On Point," *www.onpointradio.org*, which gave this project moral support and publicity.

[1] Abu al-Hasan al-Mawardi, *al-Ahkam al-Sultaniyya* (Beirut: Dar al-Kutub al-'Ilmiyya, 1985), 19–21; al-Qadi Abu Ya'la al-Farra', *al-Ahkam al-Sultaniyya* (Beirut: Dar al-Kutub al-'Ilmiyya, 1983), 28; Yusuf Ibish, *Nusus al-Fikr al-Siyasi al-Islami: al-Imama 'ind al-Sunna* (Beirut: Dar al-Tali'ah, 1966), 55; Nizam Barakat, *Muqaddima fi al-Fikr al-Siyasi al-Islami* (Riyadh: Jami'at al-Malik Su'ud, 1985), 119.

For Islam, democracy poses a formidable challenge. Muslim jurists have argued that law made by a sovereign monarch is illegitimate because it substitutes human authority for God's sovereignty. But law made by sovereign citizens faces the same problem of legitimacy. In Islam, God is the only sovereign and the ultimate source of legitimate law. How, then, can a democratic conception of the people's authority be reconciled with an Islamic understanding of God's authority?

Answering this question is extraordinarily important but also extraordinarily difficult, for both political and conceptual reasons. On the political side, democracy faces a number of practical hurdles in Islamic countries—authoritarian political traditions, a history of colonial and imperial rule, and state domination of the economy and society. But philosophical and doctrinal questions are important too, and I propose to focus on them here as the beginning of a discussion of the possibilities for democracy in the Islamic world.

A central conceptual problem is that modern democracy evolved over centuries within the distinctive context of a post-Reformation, market-oriented Christian Europe. Does it make sense to look for points of contact in a remarkably different context? My answer begins from the premise that democracy and Islam are defined in the first instance by their underlying moral values and the attitudinal commitments of their adherents—not by the ways that those values and commitments have been applied. If we focus on those fundamental moral values, we will see that the tradition of Islamic political thought contains both interpretive and practical possibilities that can be developed into a democratic system. To be sure, these doctrinal potentialities may remain unrealized: without willpower, an inspired vision, and a moral commitment there can be no democracy in Islam. But Muslims, for whom Islam is the authoritative frame of reference, can arrive at the conviction that democracy is an ethical good, and that the pursuit of this good does not require abandoning Islam.

DEMOCRACY AND DIVINE SOVEREIGNTY

Although Muslim jurists debated political systems, the Qur'an itself does not specify a particular form of government. But it does identify a set of social and political values that are central to a Muslim polity. Three values are of particular importance: pursuing justice through social cooperation and mutual assistance (49:13, 11:119); establishing a nonautocratic, consultative method of governance; and institutionalizing mercy and compassion in social interactions (6:12, 6:54, 21:107, 27:77, 29:51, 45:20). So, all else being equal, Muslims today ought to endorse the form of government that is most effective in helping them promote these values.

The Case for Democracy

Several considerations suggest that democracy—and especially a constitutional democracy that protects basic individual rights—is that form. My central argument (others will emerge later) is that democracy—by assigning equal rights of speech, association, and suffrage to all—offers the greatest potential for promoting justice and protecting human dignity, without making God responsible for injustice or the degradation of human beings. A fundamental Qur'anic idea is that God vested all of humanity with a kind of divinity by making every person the viceroy of God on this earth: "Remember, when your Lord said to the angels: 'I have to place a vicegerent on earth,' they said: 'Will you place one there who will create disorder and shed blood, while we intone Your litanies and sanctify Your name?' And God said: 'I know what you do not know'" (2:30). In particular, human beings, as God's vicegerents, are responsible for making the world more just. By assigning equal political rights to all adults, democracy expresses that special status of human beings in God's creation and enables them to discharge that responsibility.

Of course, God's vicegerent does not share God's perfection of judgment and will. A constitutional democracy, then, acknowledges the errors of judgment, temptations, and vices associated with human fallibility by enshrining some basic moral standards in a constitutional document—moral standards that express the dignity of individuals. To be sure, democracy does not ensure justice. But it does establish a basis for pursuing justice and thus for fulfilling a fundamental responsibility assigned by God to each one of us.

In a representative democracy some individuals have greater authority than others. But a democratic system makes those authorities accountable to all and thus resists the tendency of the powerful to render themselves immune from judgment. This requirement of accountability is consistent with the imperative of justice in Islam. If a political system has no institutional mechanisms to call the unjust to account, then the system itself is unjust, regardless of whether injustice has actually been committed. If criminal law does not assign punishment for rape, then it is unjust, quite apart from whether that crime was ever committed. It is a moral good in and of itself that a democracy, through the institutions of the vote, the separation and division of power, and the guarantee of pluralism at least offers the possibility of redress.

We have a provisional case for democracy, then, founded on a fundamental Islamic idea about the special status of human beings in God's creation. It is provisional because we have not yet considered the great challenge to that case: how can the higher law of Shari'ah, founded on God's sovereignty, be reconciled with the democratic idea that the people, as the sovereign, can be free to flout Shari'ah law?

God as the Sovereign

Early in Islamic history the issue of God's political dominion (*hakimiyyat Allah*) was raised by a group known as the Haruriyya (later known as the Khawarij) when they rebelled against the fourth Rightly Guided Caliph 'Ali Ibn Abi Talib. Initially the supporters of 'Ali, the Haruriyya turned against him when he agreed to arbitrate this political dispute with a competing political faction, which was led by a man named Mu'awiya.

'Ali himself had agreed to the arbitration on the condition that the arbitrators be bound by the Qur'an and give full consideration to the supremacy of the Shari'ah. But the Khawarij—pious, puritanical, and fanatical—believed that God's law clearly supported 'Ali. So they rejected arbitration as inherently unlawful and, in effect, a challenge to God's sovereignty. According to the Khawarij, 'Ali's behavior showed that he was willing to compromise God's supremacy by transferring decision making to human agency. They declared 'Ali a traitor to God, and after efforts to reach a peaceful resolution failed, they assassinated him. After 'Ali's death, Mu'awiya seized power and established himself as the first caliph of the Umayyad dynasty.

Anecdotal reports about the debates between 'Ali and the Khawarij reflect unmistakable tension about the meaning of legality and the implications of the rule of law. In one such report members of the Khawarij accused 'Ali of accepting the judgment and dominion (*hakimiyya*) of human beings instead of abiding by the dominion of God's law. Upon hearing of this accusation, 'Ali called on the people to gather around him and brought out a large copy of the Qur'an. 'Ali touched the Qur'an while instructing it to speak to the people and inform them about God's law. Surprised, the people who had gathered around 'Ali exclaimed, "What are you doing? The Qur'an cannot speak, for it is not a human being!" Upon hearing this, 'Ali exclaimed that this was exactly his point. The Qur'an, 'Ali explained, is but ink and paper, and it does not speak for itself. Instead, it is human beings who give effect to it according to their limited personal judgments and opinions.[2]

Such stories are subject to multiple interpretations, but this one points most importantly to the dogmatic superficiality of proclamations of God's sovereignty that sanctify human determinations. Notably, the Khawarij's rallying cry of "Dominion belongs to God" or "The Qur'an is the judge" (*la hukma illa li'llah* or *al-hukmu li'l-Qur'an*) is nearly identical to the slogans invoked by contemporary fundamentalist groups.[3] But considering the historical context, the Khawarij's sloganeering was initially a call for the symbolism of legality and the supremacy of law that later descended into an unequivocal radicalized demand for fixed lines of demarcation between what is lawful and unlawful.

---

[2]Muhammad b. 'Ali al-Shawkani, *Nayl al-Awtar Sharh Muntaqa al-Akhbar* (Cairo: Dar al-Hadith, n.d.), 7:166; Shihab al-Din Ibn Hajar al-'Asqalani, *Fath al-Bari bi Sharh Sahih al-Bukhari* (Beirut: Dar al-Fikr, 1993), 14:303.

[3]Ironically, Shi'i and Sunni fundamentalist groups detest the Khawarij and consider them heretics, but this is not because these modern groups disagree with the Khawarij's political slogans but because the Khawarij murdered 'Ali, the cousin of the Prophet. Epistemologically, however, the similarities between modern-day fundamentalist groups and the premodern Khawarij are numerous and undeniable.

To a believer, God is all-powerful and the ultimate owner of the heavens and earth. But when it comes to the laws in a political system, arguments claiming that God is the sole legislator endorse a fatal fiction that is indefensible from the point of view of Islamic theology. Such arguments pretend that some human agents have perfect access to God's will, and that human beings could become the perfect executors of the divine will without inserting their own human judgments and inclinations in the process.

Moreover, claims about God's sovereignty assume that the divine legislative will seeks to regulate all human interactions, that Shari'ah is a complete moral code that prescribes for every eventuality. But perhaps God does not seek to regulate all human affairs, and instead leaves human beings considerable latitude in regulating their own affairs as long as they observe certain minimal standards of moral conduct, including the preservation and promotion of human dignity and well-being. In the Qur'anic discourse, God commanded creation to honor human beings because of the miracle of the human intellect—an expression of the abilities of the divine. Arguably, the fact that God honored the miracle of the human intellect and the human being as a symbol of divinity is sufficient to justify a moral commitment to protecting and preserving the integrity and dignity of that symbol of divinity. But—and this is 'Ali's central point—God's sovereignty provides no escape from the burdens of human agency.[4]

When human beings search for ways to approximate God's beauty and justice, then, they do not deny God's sovereignty; they honor it. They also honor it in the attempt to safeguard the moral values that reflect the attributes of the divine. If we say that the only legitimate source of law is the divine text and that human experience and intellect are irrelevant to the pursuit of the divine will, then divine sovereignty will always stand as an instrument of authoritarianism and an obstacle to democracy.[5] But that authoritarian view denigrates God's sovereignty.

SHARI'AH AND THE DEMOCRATIC STATE

A case for democracy presented from within Islam must accept the idea of God's sovereignty; it cannot substitute popular sovereignty for divine sovereignty but must instead show how popular sovereignty—with its idea that citizens have rights and a correlative responsibility to pursue justice with mercy—expresses God's authority, properly understood. Similarly, it cannot reject the idea that God's law is given prior to human action but must show how democratic lawmaking respects that priority.

I have reserved the issue of Shari'ah and the state for the end of my essay because it was necessary to first lay the foundation for addressing it. As part of this foundation, it is important to appreciate the centrality of Shari'ah to Muslim life. Shari'ah is God's Way; it is represented by a set of normative principles, methodologies for the production of legal injunctions, and a set of positive legal rules. As is well known, Shari'ah encompasses a variety of schools of thought and approaches, all of which are equally valid and

---

[4]According to the Qur'an, God, at the moment of creation, as a symbol of the honor due to human beings, commanded the angels, who are incapable of sin, to prostrate themselves before Adam. The angels protested that God was commanding them to honor a being that is capable of sin and that is bound to commit evil and cause mischief. God affirmed that human beings are capable of causing much mischief but explained that the miracle of the intellect, in and of itself, deserves to be honored, and that furthermore, God had made human beings the vicegerents of divinity. Not having any choice but to obey, the angels prostrated themselves before Adam, but Satan, who was from the jinn and not an angel, defied God and refused to prostrate himself. Satan's attitude can be described as dismissive of the intellect, bigoted, and even ethnocentric. Satan argued that he was created of fire and Adam was created of clay, and according to Satan, everyone knows that fire is superior to clay. Therefore, it was inconceivable that he would have to prostrate himself before Adam. As a result of this anti-intellect position and as a consequence of his disobedience, Satan was damned through eternity. On this, see Fazlur Rahman, *Major Themes of the Qur'an* (Minneapolis: Bibliotheca Islamica, 1994), 17–36.

[5]One of the most important treatises, but also one of the most neglected, was written by Hasan Isma'il al-Hudaybi, a former chairman of the Muslim Brotherhood in Egypt, in which he effectively refuted the notion that divine hakimiyya means that God is the only legitimate legislator. Al-Hudaybi argued that political sovereignty, as opposed to moral sovereignty, belongs to the citizens of the state. Rather tellingly, the author's arguments, despite their liberal implications, would have been far more persuasive to medieval Muslim jurists than they are to contemporary fundamentalist activists. See Hasan Isma'il al-Hudaybi, *Du'ah la Qudah* (Cairo: Dar al-Nashr al-Islamiyya, 1977).

equally orthodox.[6] Nevertheless, Shari'ah as a whole, with all its schools and variant points of view, remains the Way and law of God.[7]

Shari'ah, for the most part, is not explicitly dictated by God. Rather, Shari'ah relies on the interpretive act of a human agent for its production and execution. Paradoxically, however, Shari'ah is the core value that society must serve. The paradox here is exemplified in the tension between the obligation to live by God's law and the fact that this law is manifested only through subjective interpretive determinations. Even if there is a unified realization that a particular positive command does express the divine law, there is still a vast array of possible subjective executions and applications. This dilemma was resolved to some extent in Islamic discourses by distinguishing between Shari'ah and *fiqh*. Shari'ah, it was argued, is the divine ideal, standing as if suspended in midair, unaffected and uncorrupted by life's vagaries. Fiqh is the human attempt to understand and apply that ideal. Therefore, Shari'ah is immutable, immaculate, and flawless; fiqh is not.[8]

As part of the doctrinal foundations for this discourse, Sunni jurists focused on the tradition attributed to the Prophet, stating, "Every mujtahid [jurist who strives to find the correct answer] is correct," or "Every *mujtahid* will be [justly] rewarded."[9] This implied that there could be more than a single correct answer to the same question. For Sunni jurists, this raised the issue of the purpose of or motivation behind the search for the divine will. What is the divine purpose of setting out indicators to the divine law and then requiring that human beings engage in a search? If the divine wants human beings to reach the correct understanding, then how could every interpreter or jurist be correct? Put differently, is there a correct legal response to all legal problems, and are Muslims charged with the legal obligation of finding that response?

The overwhelming majority of Sunni jurists agreed that good faith diligence in searching for the divine will is sufficient to protect a researcher from liability before God.[10] Beyond this, the jurists were divided into two main camps. The first school, known as the *mukhatti'ah*, argued that every legal problem ultimately has a correct answer; however, only God knows the correct response, and the truth will not be revealed until the Final

---

[6]The four surviving Sunni schools of law and legal thought are the Hanafi, Maliki, Shafi'i, and Hanbali. There are many schools of jurisprudence, such as the Jariri, Awza'i, Zahiri, and Thawri, that have become extinct in the sense that they no longer command a large number of adherents, but the texts of these schools remain extant in many cases.

[7]Even the puritanical Wahhabis, who considerably narrow the range and scope of subjects and issues on which Muslims may legitimately disagree, have not been able to deny the validity of this doctrine. The Wahhabis, and other Muslim extremists and literalists, could not deny the legitimacy of the various competing schools of thought in Islam. Rather, their tactic has been to claim the existence of agreement and consensus among the different schools of thought on certain points of law, when in fact agreement does not exist. The Wahhabis also claim that disagreement is acceptable only as to the branches (*furu'*) of religion, but not on the basics and fundamentals (*usul*). However, they proceed to widen the range and scope of the so-called fundamentals of religion to the point that disagreement becomes permissible only on the most marginal issues.

[8]I am simplifying this sophisticated doctrine to make a point. Muslim jurists engaged in lengthy attempts to differentiate between the two concepts of Shari'ah and fiqh. See Subhi Mahmasani, *Fasafat al-Tashri' fi al-Islam*, 3rd ed. (Beirut: Dar al-'Ilm li al-Malayin, 1961), 21–24, 199–200; Abu Zahra, *Usul al-Fiqh*, 291; Mustafa Zayd, *al-Maslaha fi Tashri' al-Islam wa Najm al-Din al-Tufi*, 2nd ed. (Cairo: Dar al-Fikr al-'Arabi, 1964), 22; Yusuf Hamid al-'Alim, *al-Maqasid al-Ammah li al-Shari'ah al-Islamiyya* (Herndon, VA: International Institute of Islamic Thought, 1991), 80; Muhammad b. Ali al-Shawkani, *Talab al-'Ilm wa Tabaqat al-Muta' allimin: Adab al-Talab wa Muntaha al-Arab* (n.p.: Dar al-Arqam, 1981), 145–151.

[9]In this context, Sunni jurists also debated a report attributed to the Prophet in which he says, "Whoever performs ijtihad and is correct will be rewarded twice, and whoever is wrong will be rewarded once." See Abu al-Husayn Muhammad al-Basri, *al-Mu'tamad fi Usul al-Fiqh* (Beirut: Dar al-Kutub al-'Ilmiyya, 1983), 2:370–372; al-Ghazali, *al-Mustasfa*, 2:363–367; Abu al-Ma'ali 'Abd al-Malik al-Juwayni, *Kitab al-Ijtihad min Kitab al-Talkhis* (Damascus: Dar al-Qalam, 1987), 26–32; al-Qarafi, *Sharh*, 438–441; al-Razi, *al-Mahsul*, 6:29–36; Jalal al-Din 'Abd al-Rahman al-Suyuti, *Ikthilaf al-Madhahib*, ed. 'Abd al-Qayyum Muhammad al-Bastawi (Cairo: Dar al-I'tisam, A.H. 1404), 38; Muhammad b. Idris al-Shafi'i, *al-Risalah*, ed. Ahmad Muhammad Shakir (n.p.: Dar al-Fikr, n.d.), 494; Abu Ishaq Yusuf al-Fayruzabadi al-Shirazi, *al-Tabsira fi Usul al-Fiqh* (Damascus: Dar al-Fikr, 1980), 499.

[10]This juristic position is to be distinguished from the early theological school of the Murji'a (Murji'ites) of the school of the suspension of judgment. The school of the Murji'a developed in reaction to the fanaticism of the Khawarij, who believed that the commission of a major sin renders a Muslim a nonbeliever. The Murji'a believed that major sins are offset by faith and argued that punishment in the Hereafter is not everlasting. They also refused to take a position on political disputes, arguing that judgment over any political dispute ought to be suspended until the Final Day. Most of the jurists I describe here did not adhere to Murji'i theology.

Day. Human beings for the most part cannot conclusively know whether they have found the correct response. In this sense, every mujtahid is correct in trying to find the answer; however, one reader might reach the truth while the rest might mistake it. God, on the Final Day, will inform all readers of who was right and who was wrong. Correctness here means that the mujtahid is to be commended for making the effort, but it does not mean that all responses are equally valid.[11]

The second school, known as the *musawwibah*, argued that there is no specific and correct answer (*hukm mu'ayyan*) that God wants human beings to discover; after all, if there were a correct answer, God would have made the evidence indicating a divine rule conclusive and clear.[12] God cannot charge human beings with the duty to find the correct answer when there is no objective means of discovering the correctness of a textual or legal problem. If there were an objective truth to everything, God would have made such a truth ascertainable in this life. Legal truth, or correctness, in most circumstances depends on belief and evidence, and the validity of a legal rule or act is often contingent on the rules of recognition that provide for its existence. Human beings are not charged with the obligation of finding some abstract or inaccessible, legally correct result. Rather, they are charged with the duty to diligently investigate a problem and

then follow the results of their own *ijtihad* (judgment or opinion). Al-Juwayni elaborates on this point by noting that "[t]he most a mujtahid would claim is a preponderance of belief [*ghalabat al-zann*] and the balancing of the evidence. However, certainty was never claimed by any of them [the early jurists].... If we were charged with finding [the truth,] we would not have been forgiven for failing to find it."[13] According to al-Juwayni, what God wants or intends is for human beings to search—to live a life fully and thoroughly engaged with the divine. Al-Juwayni explains: it is as if God has said to human beings, "My command to My servants is in accordance with the preponderance of their beliefs. So whoever preponderantly believes that they are obligated to do something, acting upon it becomes My command."[14] God's command to human beings is to diligently search, and God's law is suspended until a human being forms a preponderance of belief about the law. At the point that a preponderance of belief is formed, God's law comes in accordance with the preponderance of belief formed by that particular individual. In sum, if a person honestly and sincerely believes that such and such is the law of God, then for that person it is in fact God's law.[15]

The position of the second school in particular raises difficult questions about the application of the Shari'ah in society.[16] This position implies that God's law is to search for God's law; otherwise the legal charge (*taklif*) is entirely dependent on the subjectivity and sincerity of belief. Under

---

[11]Literalist schools of thought, including the modern-day Wahhabis, agree with this perspective, but they insist that when the Prophet declared that every mujtahid will be rewarded, the Prophet meant this to apply only to an exceedingly narrow range of issues, on which the text is vague or ambiguous. The literalists and extremist schools, in general, claim that the divine text is clear and unambiguous as to the vast majority of matters, and therefore, on most issues, there can be only one legitimate position or answer. Nonetheless, these literalists, and especially the Wahhabis, lack a methodology for systematically distinguishing between text that is clear, precise, and unambiguous and text that is not. In the final analysis, a text is considered unambiguous and clear because the Wahhabis say it is so.

[12]For discussions of the two schools, see 'Ala' al-Din b. Ahmai al-Bukhari, *Kashf al-Asrar 'an Usul Fakhr al-Islam*, ed. Muhammad al-Mu'tasin bi Allah (Beirut: Dar al-Kitab al-Arabi, 1997), 4:18; Abu Hamid Muhammad al-Ghazali, *al-Mankhul min Ta'liqat al-Usul* (Damascus: Dar al-Fikr, 1980), 455; idem. *al-Mustasfa*, 2:550–551; al-Razi, *al-Mahsul*, 2:500–508; al-Qarafi, *Sharh*, 438; al-Zuhayli, *al-Wasit*, 638–655; Hasab Allah, *Usul al-Tashri*, 82–83; Badran, *Usul al-Fiqh*, 474.

[13]Al-Juwayni, *Kitab al-Ijtihad*, 50–51.
[14]Ibid., 61.
[15]Sayf al-Din Abu al-Hasan 'Ali b. Abi 'Ali b.Muhammad al-Amidi, al-Ihkam fi Usul al-Ahkam, ed. 'Abd al-Razzaq 'Afifi, 2nd ed. (Beirut: al-Maktab al-Islami A.H. 1402), 4:183; Jamal al-Din Abi Muhammad 'Abd al-Rahim b. al-Hasan al-Asnawi, *al-Tamhidfi Takhrij al-Furu' 'ala al-Usul*, 3rd ed. (Beirut: Mu'assasat al-Risalah, 1984), 531–534; Muhammad b. al-Hasan al-Badakhshi, *Sharh al-Badakhshi Manahij al-'Uqul ma'a Sharh al-Asnawi Nihayat al-Sul* (Beirut: Dar al-Kutub al-'Ilmiyya, 1984), 3:275–281; Abu H amid al-Ghazali, *al-Mustasfa*, 2:375–378; al-Juwayni, *Kitab al-Ijtihad*, 41; Abu al-Thana' Mahmud b. Zayd al-Lamishi, *Kitab fi Usul al-Fiqh*, ed. 'Abd al-Majid Turki (Beirut: Dar al-Gharb al-Islami, 1995), 202–203; al-Qarafi, *Sharh*, 440; al-Din al-Razi, *al-Mahsul*, 6:34–35, 6:43–50.
[16]I deal much more extensively with these two schools of thought and their potential impact on modern Islam in my book *Speaking in God's Name*.

the first school of thought, whatever law the state applies is only potentially the law of God, and we will not find out until the Final Day. Under the second school of thought, any law applied by the state is not the law of God unless the person to which it applies believes it to be God's will and command. The first school suspends knowledge until we are done living, and the second school hinges knowledge to the validity of the process and ultimate sincerity of belief.

Building upon this intellectual heritage, I would suggest that Shari'ah ought to stand in an Islamic polity as a symbolic construct for the divine perfection that is unreachable by human effort. As Ibn Qayyim stated, this is the epitome of justice, goodness, and beauty as conceived and retained by God. Its perfection is preserved, so to speak, in the Mind of God, but anything that is channeled through human agency is necessarily marred by human imperfection. Put differently, Shari'ah as conceived by God is flawless, but as understood by human beings is imperfect and contingent. Jurists ought to continue to explore the ideal of Shari'ah and to expound their imperfect attempts at understanding God's perfection. As long as the argument constructed is normative, it is unfulfilled potential to reach the divine will. Significantly, any law applied is necessarily an unrealized potentiality. Shari'ah is not simply a collection of *ahkam* (a set of positive rules) but also a set of principles, a methodology, and a discursive process that searches for divine ideals. As such, Shari'ah is a work in progress that is never complete.

To put it more concretely: if a legal opinion is adopted and enforced by the state, it cannot be said to be God's law. By passing through the determinative and enforcement processes of the state, the legal opinion is no longer simply a potential—it has become an actual law, applied and enforced. But what has been applied and enforced is not God's law; it is the state's law. Effectively, a religious state law is a contradiction in terms. Either the law belongs to the state or it belongs to God, and as long as the law relies on the subjective agency of the state for its articulation and enforcement, any law enforced by the state is necessarily not God's law. Otherwise, we must be willing to admit that the failure of the law

of the state is in fact the failure of God's law and ultimately of God Himself. In Islamic theology, this possibility cannot be entertained.[17]

Of course, the most formidable challenge to this position is the argument that God and His Prophet have set out clear legal injunctions that cannot be ignored. Arguably, God provided unambiguous laws precisely because God wished to limit the role of human agency and foreclose the possibility of innovations. But—to return one last time to a point I have emphasized throughout—regardless of how clear and precise the statements of the Qur'an and Sunna are, the meaning derived from these sources is negotiated through human agency. For example, the Qur'an states, "As to the thief, male or female, cut off *[faqta'u]* their hands as a recompense for that which they committed, a punishment from God, and God is all-powerful and all-wise" (5:38). Although the legal import of the verse seems clear, it requires at a minimum that human agents struggle with the meaning of "thief," "cut off," "hands," and "recompense." The Qur'an uses the expression *iqta'u*, from the root word *qata'a*, which could mean to sever or cut off but could also mean to deal firmly, to bring to an end, to restrain, or to distance oneself.[18] Whatever the meaning derived

---

[17] I would go further and argue that the idea of state-implemented Shari'ah law could potentially establish and promote an idolatrous paradigm. Shari'ah is synonymous with divine perfection and immutability. The modern state, with all its human imperfections, cannot claim to represent or embody the divine perfection without falling into a paradigm that is idolatrous because, in effect, the state is claiming that it can partake in, share in, or even represent the divine perfection. This is theologically problematic, to say the least. In this regard, contemporary Islamic discourses suffer from a certain measure of hypocrisy. Often, Muslims confront a public relations crisis when the enforced, so-called state Shari'ah laws result in social hardship, suffering, or misery. In response to this crisis, Muslims often have claimed that there was a failure in the circumstances of implementation or that the divine law was not properly implemented. This indulgence in embarrassing apologetics could be avoided if Muslims would abandon the incoherent idea of Shari'ah state law.

[18] Al-'Allamah Ibn Manzur, *Lisan al-'Arab* (Riyadh: Dar al-Thabat, 1997), 11:220–228. Ahmed Ali argues in that the word used in the Qur'an does not mean to amputate a limb but rather, to "stop their hands from stealing by adopting deterrent means" (Ahmed Ali, *Al-Qur'an* [Princeton: Princeton University Press], 113). In classical jurisprudence, jurists placed conditions that were practically impossible to fulfill before a limb could be amputated.

from the text, can the human interpreter claim with certainty that the determination reached is identical to God's? And even when the issue of meaning is resolved, can the law be enforced in such a fashion that one can claim that the result belongs to God? Although God's knowledge and justice are perfect, it is impossible for human beings to determine or enforce the law in such a fashion that the possibility of a wrongful result is entirely excluded. This does not mean that the exploration of God's law is pointless; it means only that the interpretations of jurists are potential fulfillments of the divine will, but the laws as codified and implemented by the state cannot be considered the actual fulfillment of these potentialities.

Institutionally, it is consistent with the Islamic experience that the ulema [jurists] can and do act as the interpreters of the divine word, the custodians of the moral conscience of the community, and the curators who point the nation toward the ideal that is God.[19] But the law of the state, regardless of its origins or basis, belongs to the state. Under this conception, no religious laws

_____

[19]To regain their persuasive authority as curators of morality and interpreters and advocates of Shari'ah, and to play an effective mediating role in civil society, the ulema must first regain their institutional and moral independence from the state. As long as the ulema are controlled and directed by the state, their credibility and legitimacy as advocates and agents on behalf of God and Shari'ah will remain seriously suspect.

can or may be enforced by the state. All laws articulated and applied in a state are thoroughly human and should be treated as such. These laws are a part of Shari'ah law only to the extent that any set of human legal opinions can be said to be a part of Shari'ah. A code, even if inspired by Shari'ah, is not Shari'ah. Put differently, creation, with all its textual and nontextual richness, can and should produce foundational rights and organizational laws that honor and promote these rights. But these rights and laws do not mirror the perfection of divine creation.

According to this paradigm, democracy is an appropriate system for Islam because it both expresses the special worth of human beings—the status of vicegerency—and at the same time deprives the state of any pretense of divinity by locating ultimate authority in the hands of the people rather than the ulema. Moral educators have a serious role to play because they must be vigilant in urging society to approximate God. But not even the will of the majority—no matter how well educated morally—can embody the full majesty of God. And in the worst case—if the majority is not persuaded by the ulema, if the majority insists on turning away from God but still respects the fundamental rights of individuals, including the right to ponder creation and call to the way of God—those individuals who constituted the majority will still have to answer, in the Hereafter, to God.

⊚ CRITICAL QUESTIONS

1. Do you find Fadl's argument convincing? Why, or why not?

2. Is democracy compatible with Christianity? Why, or why not?

5.3 CAPITALISM AND EXPLOITATION

Should people be allowed to own property? That may be a startling question. We are so used to the notion of private property that it seems absurd to even ask such a question. Of course, we should be able to own property and, furthermore, do with it as we see fit. However, think a moment. Which society is better: one in which the wealthy are allowed to accumulate as much wealth as they can, or one in which the state regulates the distribution of wealth for the sake of the common good? Remember—we are not all born equal. Some of us are born into wealth and privilege. We can afford a good education, good medical care, excellent legal representation.

Others of us are born into poverty. We cannot afford education, medical care, or legal counsel. Is that fair?

Adam Smith (1723–1790), in his influential book *The Wealth of Nations*, published in 1776, argued for an economic philosophy called **laissez-faire capitalism**. He believed that, in the long run, a free competitive market would work for the common good. Smith thought that even though we are all selfish by nature, the laws that guided self-interested competitors would work like an "invisible hand" to the benefit of all.

Smith argued that the value of a commodity equals the amount of labor it commands (the labor theory of value). Those who acquire capital or "stock" can hire labor to produce a product. If a division of labor is efficiently established (in a famous example, Smith divided the process of making pins into eighteen different jobs, thereby increasing the number of pins per worker that could be produced), a surplus value over and above the expense of wages and materials will result. This profit is a repayment to the capitalists for their efforts and ingenuity.

Central to this theory is the concept of private property. John Locke (1632–1704), an English philosopher, articulated this concept long before Smith. He wrote in *Concerning Civil Government* that God gave "nature to humans to use for their benefit." The use of nature involves human labor. Once labor is mixed with the material God has given to humans, private property results. He wrote, "Whatsoever then, he [a human being] removes out of a state that nature hath provided and left it in, he hath mixed his labor with, and joined to it something that is his own, and thereby makes it his property." Since this property is private (owned by the individual), the individual should be free to use it as he or she sees fit. Thus, Locke argued for certain individual rights, among them the right to life, liberty, and the preservation of property. If those words sound at least partly familiar, it is because Thomas Jefferson (1743–1826) in the *Declaration of Independence* of the United States borrowed them from Locke but made one change, substituting the "pursuit of happiness" for "preservation of property."

The view that the freedom of the individual takes priority over the group is subject to some serious objections. For one thing, a community is more than an atomistic collection of individuals. It is an organic whole, and the good of each is not necessarily the good of all. In addition, the notion of "human rights" implies more than leaving people alone to compete with one another. Human rights include an equal opportunity to participate in and contribute to society. The right to work under safe conditions, to have access to education, to obtain adequate medical care, to enjoy a decent standard of living and a secure retirement—there is no provision for such rights in laissez-faire capitalism. And what about the intrinsic value of cooperation? Should not society promote cooperation? Laissez-faire capitalism promotes competition. Alienation, envy, corruption, greed—such can be the results when petty self-interest prevails.

Karl Marx (1818–1883) and Friedrich Engels (1820–1895) saw the results of Adam Smith's economic theory. They saw workers abused and degraded, children exploited, and society divided into two antagonistic classes: the proletariat (an urban population of wage-earning workers) and the bourgeoisie (the owners of production, along with bankers and financiers). All this was the result of the activity of capitalists whose primary interest was to maximize profits. One of the book's color plates shows a pyramid that represents the capitalist economic and social structure as Marx and Engels saw and described it.

Marx and Engels argued that the division of labor results in meaningless repetitive jobs that alienate workers from the product of their labors. The workers, even though they have "mixed" their labor with natural materials, do not own the result. The capitalist owns the product and can dispose of it as she or he wishes. They also argued that wage labor is necessarily exploitation because workers give more than they receive. If this were not the case, it would be crazy for a capitalist to hire a worker because the value produced by an hour's labor would not be worth more than the money paid for that hour's worth of work (plus materials and overhead). The so-called surplus value from which the capitalist makes a profit is, in fact, created by paying workers less than full value for their efforts.

Marx and Engels advocated **socialism** in place of capitalism. All citizens should own the means of production, and there should be rational planning of economic investment and growth. Production should exist for the sake of human need, not private profit. There should be a just distribution of goods and services. At first, a strong governmental role is needed to create such a system. Eventually, however, as full equality and universal prosperity are achieved, the classes will disappear and a society of naturally cooperative individuals will emerge. The need for a state will simply wither away. When this happens, **communism**, in its ideal form, will be achieved.

There are some serious objections to this position. For one thing, socialism, at least in centrally planned, one-party **totalitarian** states, does not seem to work well. The collapse of the Soviet Union is a case in point. People do not work very hard when they lack economic incentives. Voluntary cooperation is one thing, but forced cooperation is entirely different. The notion that eventually a classless society will be in place and government will disappear seems to be wishful thinking. If anything, government may get stronger and more absolute. Abuse of power may increase as control increases. The state may become more totalitarian and, while the human rights to education, employment, medical care, and shelter are ensured, the human rights of free assembly, free speech, and freedom of religion are often denied.

Both Marx and Engels believed that the revolution that could bring about economic justice needed to be led by the workers—those most exploited by capitalism. They wrote the *Manifesto of the Communist Party* in 1848, not only to explain their views and defend them, but also to call on the workers of the world to unite and throw off the chains of capitalistic exploitation. As you read parts of this manifesto, answer the questions and engage Marx and Engels in a critical dialogue about what makes a society just.

⊚ READING QUESTIONS

1. According to Marx and Engels, what form does the "history of class struggles" take in "our age"?
2. What effect has the bourgeoisie had on modern society?
3. What has happened to the worker or proletarian class because of the power of the capitalist class or bourgeoisie?
4. Outline the key points in the argument that Marx and Engels present.

Manifesto of the Communist Party

KARL MARX AND FRIEDRICH ENGELS

I. BOURGEOIS AND PROLETARIANS

The history of all hitherto existing society is the history of class struggles.

Freeman and slave, patrician and plebeian, lord and serf, guild master and journeyman, in a word, oppressor and oppressed, stood in constant opposition to one another, carried on an uninterrupted, now hidden, now open fight—a fight that each time ended either in a revolutionary reconstitution of society at large or in the common ruin of the contending classes.

In the earlier epochs of history, we find almost everywhere a complicated arrangement of society into various orders, a manifold gradation of social rank. In ancient Rome, we have patricians, knights, plebeians, slaves; in the Middle Ages, feudal lords, vassals, guild masters, journeymen, apprentices, serfs; in almost all of these classes, again, subordinate gradations.

The modern bourgeois society that has sprouted from the ruins of feudal society has not done away with class antagonisms. It has but established new classes, new conditions of oppression, new forms of struggle in place of the old ones.

Our epoch, the epoch of the bourgeoisie, possesses, however, this distinctive feature: it has simplified the class antagonisms. Society as a whole is more and more splitting up into two great hostile camps, into two great classes directly facing each other: bourgeoisie and proletariat.

From the serfs of the Middle Ages sprang the chartered burghers of the earliest towns. From these burgesses the first elements of the bourgeoisie were developed.

The discovery of America, the rounding of the Cape, opened up fresh ground for the rising bourgeoisie. The East Indian and Chinese markets, the colonisation of America, trade with the colonies, the increase in the means of exchange and in commodities generally, gave to commerce, to navigation, to industry, an impulse never before known, and thereby, to the revolutionary element in the tottering feudal society, a rapid development.

The feudal system of industry, under which industrial production was monopolised by closed guilds, now no longer sufficed for the growing wants of the new markets. The manufacturing system took its place. The guild masters were pushed on one side by the manufacturing middle class; division of labour between the different corporate guilds vanished in the face of division of labour in each single workshop.

Meantime the markets kept ever growing, the demand ever rising. Even manufacture no longer sufficed. Thereupon, steam and machinery revolutionised industrial production. The place of manufacture was taken by the giant, modern industry; the place of the industrial middle class, by industrial millionaires, the leaders of whole industrial armies, the modern bourgeois.

Modern industry has established the world market, for which the discovery of America paved the way. This market has given an immense development to commerce, to navigation, to communication by land. This development has, in its turn, reacted on the extension of industry; and in proportion as industry, commerce, navigation, railways extended, in the same proportion the bourgeoisie developed, increased its capital, and pushed into the background every class handed down from the Middle Ages.

We see, therefore, how the modern bourgeoisie is itself the product of a long course of development, of a series of revolutions in the modes of production and of exchange....

The bourgeoisie, historically, has played a most revolutionary part.

Selections from *Manifesto of the Communist Party*, first published in English by Friedrich Engels in 1888.

The bourgeoisie, wherever it has got the upper hand, has put an end to all feudal, patriarchal, idyllic relations. It has pitilessly torn asunder the motley feudal ties that bound man to his "natural superiors," and has left remaining no other nexus between man and man than naked self-interest, than callous "cash payment." It has drowned the most heavenly ecstasies of religious fervour, of chivalrous enthusiasm, of philistine sentimentalism, in the icy water of egotistical calculation. It has resolved personal worth into exchange value, and in place of the numberless indefeasible chartered freedoms, has set up that single, unconscionable freedom—free trade. In one word, for exploitation veiled by religious and political illusions, it has substituted naked, shameless, direct, brutal exploitation.

The bourgeoisie has stripped of its halo every occupation hitherto honoured and looked up to with reverent awe. It has converted the physician, the lawyer, the priest, the poet, the man of science, into its paid wage-labourers.

The bourgeoisie has torn away from the family its sentimental veil, and has reduced the family relation to a mere money relation....

The bourgeoisie cannot exist without constantly revolutionising the instruments of production, and thereby the relations of production, and with them the whole relations of society. Conservation of the old modes of production in unaltered form was, on the contrary, the first condition of existence for all earlier industrial classes. Constant revolutionising of production, uninterrupted disturbance of all social conditions, everlasting uncertainty and agitation distinguish the bourgeois epoch from all earlier ones. All fixed, fast-frozen relations, with their train of ancient and venerable prejudices and opinions, are swept away; all new-formed ones become antiquated before they can ossify. All that is solid melts into air, all that is holy is profaned, and man is at last compelled to face with sober senses his real conditions of life and his relations with his kind.

The need of a constantly expanding market for its products chases the bourgeoisie over the whole surface of the globe. It must nestle everywhere, settle everywhere, establish connexions everywhere.

The bourgeoisie has through its exploitation of the world market given a cosmopolitan character to production and consumption in every country. To the great chagrin of reactionists, it has drawn from under the feet of industry the national ground on which it stood. All old-established national industries have been destroyed or are daily being destroyed. They are dislodged by new industries, whose introduction becomes a life and death question for all civilised nations, by industries that no longer work up indigenous raw material, but raw material drawn from the remotest zones; industries whose products are consumed not only at home, but in every quarter of the globe. In place of the old wants, satisfied by the productions of the country, we find new wants, requiring for their satisfaction the products of distant lands and climes. In place of the old local and national seclusion and self-sufficiency, we have intercourse in every direction, universal interdependence of nations. And as in material, so also in intellectual production. The intellectual creations of individual nations become common property. National one-sidedness and narrow-mindedness become more and more impossible, and from the numerous national and local literatures there arises a world literature.

The bourgeoisie, by the rapid improvement of all instruments of production, by the immensely facilitated means of communication, draws all, even the most barbarian, nations into civilisation. The cheap prices of its commodities are the heavy artillery with which it batters down all Chinese walls, with which it forces the barbarians' intensely obstinate hatred of foreigners to capitulate. It compels all nations, on pain of extinction, to adopt the bourgeois mode of production; it compels them to introduce what it calls civilisation into their midst, that is, to become bourgeois themselves. In one word, it creates a world after its own image....

Modern bourgeois society with its relations of production, of exchange, and of property, a society that has conjured up such gigantic means of production and of exchange, is like the sorcerer who is no longer able to control the powers of the nether world whom he has called up by his spells. For many a decade past, the history of industry and commerce is but the history of the revolt of modern productive forces against modern conditions of production, against the property relations that are the conditions for the existence of the bourgeoisie and of its rule. It is enough to mention the commercial crises that by their periodical return put on its trial, each time more threateningly, the existence of the entire bourgeois society. In these crises a great part not only of the existing products, but also of the previously created productive forces, are periodically destroyed. In these crises there breaks out an epidemic that, in all earlier epochs, would have seemed an absurdity—the epidemic of overproduction. Society suddenly finds itself put back into a state of momentary barbarism; it appears as if a famine, a universal war of devastation, had cut off the supply of every means of subsistence; industry and commerce seem to be destroyed. And why? Because there is too much civilisation, too much means of subsistence, too much industry, too much commerce. The productive forces at the disposal of society no longer tend to further the development of the conditions of bourgeois property; on the contrary, they have become too powerful for these conditions by which they are fettered, and so soon as they overcome these fetters, they bring disorder into the whole of bourgeois society, endanger the existence of bourgeois property. The conditions of bourgeois society are too narrow to comprise the wealth created by them. And how does the bourgeoisie get over these crises? On the one hand, by enforced destruction of a mass of productive forces; on the other, by the conquest of new markets and by the more thorough exploitation of the old ones. That is to say, by paving the way for more extensive and more destructive crises, and by diminishing the means whereby crises are prevented.

The weapons with which the bourgeoisie felled feudalism to the ground are now turned against the bourgeoisie itself.

But not only has the bourgeoisie forged the weapons that bring death to itself; it has also called into existence the men who are to wield those weapons—the modern working class, the proletarians.

In proportion as the bourgeoisie, that is, capital, is developed, in the same proportion is the proletariat, the modern working class, developed—a class of labourers who live only so long as they find work and who find work only so long as their labour increases capital. These labourers, who must sell themselves piecemeal, are a commodity like every other article of commerce, and are consequently exposed to all the vicissitudes of competition, to all the fluctuations of the market.

Owing to the extensive use of machinery and to division of labour, the work of the proletarians has lost all individual character and, consequently, all charm for the workman. He becomes an appendage of the machine, and it is only the most simple, most monotonous, and most easily acquired knack that is required of him. Hence, the cost of production of a workman is restricted, almost entirely, to the means of subsistence that he requires for his maintenance and for the propagation of his race. But the price of a commodity, and therefore also of labour, is equal to its cost of production. In proportion, therefore, as the repulsiveness of the work increases, the wage decreases. Nay more, in proportion as the use of machinery and division of labour increases, in the same proportion the burden of toil also increases, whether by prolongation of the working hours, by increase of the work exacted in a given time, or by increased speed of the machinery, etc....

But with the development of industry the proletariat not only increases in number; it becomes concentrated in greater masses, its strength grows, and it feels that strength more. The various interests and conditions of life within the ranks of the proletariat are more and more equalised, in proportion as machinery obliterates all distinctions of labour, and nearly everywhere reduces wages to the same low level. The growing competition among the bourgeois, and the resulting commercial crises, make the wages of the workers ever more fluctuating. The unceasing improvement of machinery, ever more rapidly developing, makes their livelihood more and more precarious; the collisions between individual workmen and individual bourgeois take more and more the character of collisions between two classes. Thereupon the workers begin to form combinations (Trades Unions) against the bourgeois; they club together in order to keep up the rate of wages; they found permanent associations in order to make provision beforehand for these occasional revolts. Here and there the contest breaks out into riots....

In the conditions of the proletariat, those of old society at large are already virtually swamped. The proletarian is without property; his relation to his wife and children has no longer anything in common with the bourgeois family-relations; modern industrial labour, modern subjection to capital, the same in England as in France, in America as in Germany, has stripped him of every trace of national character. Law, morality, religion, are to him so many bourgeois prejudices, behind which lurk in ambush just as many bourgeois interests.

All the preceding classes that got the upper hand sought to fortify their already acquired status by subjecting society at large to their conditions of appropriation. The proletarians cannot become masters of the productive forces of society, except by abolishing their own previous mode of appropriation, and thereby also every other previous mode of appropriation. They have nothing of their own to secure and to fortify; their mission is to destroy all previous securities for, and insurances of, individual property.

All previous historical movements were movements of minorities, or in the interests of minorities. The proletarian movement is the self-conscious, independent movement of the immense majority, in the interests of the immense majority. The proletariat, the lowest stratum of our present society, cannot stir, cannot raise itself up, without the whole superincumbent strata of official society being sprung into the air.

Though not in substance, yet in form, the struggle of the proletariat with the bourgeoisie is at first a national struggle. The proletariat of each country must, of course, first of all settle matters with its own bourgeoisie.

In depicting the most general phases of the development of the proletariat, we traced the more or less veiled civil war, raging within existing society, up to the point where that war breaks out into open revolution, and where the violent overthrow of the bourgeoisie lays the foundation for the sway of the proletariat....

All property relations in the past have continually been subject to historical change consequent upon the change in historical conditions.

The French Revolution, for example, abolished feudal property in favour of bourgeois property.

The distinguishing feature of Communism is not the abolition of property generally, but the abolition of bourgeois property. But modern bourgeois private property is the final and most complete expression of the system of producing and appropriating products, that is based on class antagonisms, on the exploitation of the many by the few.

In this sense, the theory of the Communists may be summed up in the single sentence: Abolition of private property.

We Communists have been reproached with the desire of abolishing the right of personally acquiring property as the fruit of a man's own labour, which property is alleged to be the groundwork of all personal freedom, activity and independence.

Hard-won, self-acquired, self-earned property! Do you mean the property of the petty artisan and of the small peasant, a form of property that preceded the bourgeois form? There is no need to abolish that; the development of industry has to a great extent already destroyed it, and is still destroying it daily.

Or do you mean modern bourgeois private property?

But does wage-labour create any property for the labourer? Not a bit. It creates capital, i.e., that kind of property which exploits wage-labour, and which cannot increase except upon condition of begetting a new supply of wage-labour for fresh exploitation. Property, in its present form, is based on the antagonism of capital and wage-labour. Let us examine both sides of this antagonism.

To be a capitalist, is to have not only a purely personal, but a social *status* in production. Capital is a collective product, and only by the united action of many members, nay, in the last resort, only by the united action of all members of society, can it be set in motion.

Capital is, therefore, not a personal, it is a social power.

When, therefore, capital is converted into common property, into the property of all members of society, personal property is not thereby transformed into social property. It is only the social character of the property that is changed. It loses its class-character.

Let us now take wage-labour.

The average price of wage-labour is the minimum wage, *i.e.*, that quantum of the means of subsistence, which is absolutely requisite to keep the labourer in bare existence as a labourer. What, therefore, the wage-labourer appropriates by means of his labour merely suffices to prolong and reproduce a bare existence. We by no means intend to abolish this personal appropriation of the products of labour, an appropriation that is made for the maintenance and reproduction of human life, and that leaves no surplus wherewith to command the labour of others. All that we want to do away with is the miserable character of this appropriation, under which the labourer lives merely to increase capital, and is allowed to live only in so far as the interest of the ruling class requires it.

In bourgeois society, living labour is but a means to increase accumulated labour. In Communist society, accumulated labour is but a means to widen, to enrich, to promote the existence of the labourer.

In bourgeois society, therefore, the past dominates the present; in Communist society, the present dominates the past. In bourgeois society capital is independent and has individuality, while the living person is dependent and has no individuality.

And the abolition of this state of things is called by the bourgeois, abolition of individuality and freedom! And rightly so. The abolition of bourgeois individuality, bourgeois independence, and bourgeois freedom is undoubtedly aimed at.

By freedom is meant, under the present bourgeois conditions of production, free trade, free selling and buying.

But if selling and buying disappears, free selling and buying disappears also. This talk about free selling and buying, and all the other "brave words" of our bourgeoisie about freedom in general, have a meaning, if any, only in contrast with restricted selling and buying, with the fettered traders of the Middle Ages, but have no meaning when opposed to the Communistic abolition of buying and selling, of the bourgeois conditions of production, and of the bourgeoisie itself.

You are horrified at our intending to do away with private property. But in your existing society, private property is already done away with for nine-tenths of the population; its existence for the few is solely due to its non-existence in the hands of those nine-tenths. You reproach us, therefore, with intending to do away with a form of property, the necessary condition for whose existence is the non-existence of any property for the immense majority of society.

In one word, you reproach us with intending to do away with your property. Precisely so; that is just what we intend.

From the moment when labour can no longer be converted into capital, money, or rent, into a social power capable of being monopolised, i.e., from the moment when individual property can no longer be transformed into bourgeois property, into capital, from that moment, you say, individuality vanishes.

You must, therefore, confess that by "individual" you mean no other person than the bourgeois, than the middle-class owner of property. This person must, indeed, be swept out of the way, and made impossible.

Communism deprives no man of the power to appropriate the products of society; all that it does is to deprive him of the power to subjugate the labour of others by means of such appropriation.

It has been objected that upon the abolition of private property all work will cease, and universal laziness will overtake us.

According to this, bourgeois society ought long ago to have gone to the dogs through sheer idleness; for those of its members who work, acquire nothing, and those who acquire anything, do not work. The whole of this objection is but another expression of the tautology: that there can no longer be any wage-labour when there is no longer any capital.

All objections urged against the Communistic mode of producing and appropriating material products have, in the same way, been urged against the Communistic modes of producing and appropriating intellectual products. Just as, to the bourgeois, the disappearance of class property is the disappearance of production itself, so the disappearance of class culture is to him identical with the disappearance of all culture.

That culture, the loss of which he laments, is, for the enormous majority, a mere training to act as a machine.

But don't wrangle with us so long as you apply, to our intended abolition of bourgeois property, the standard of your bourgeois notions of freedom, culture, law, &c. Your very ideas are but the outgrowth of the conditions of your bourgeois production and bourgeois property, just as your jurisprudence is but the will of your class made into a law for all, a will, whose essential character and direction are determined by the economical conditions of existence of your class.

The selfish misconception that induces you to transform into eternal laws of nature and of reason, the social forms springing from your present mode of production and form of property—historical relations that rise and disappear in the progress of production—this misconception you share with every ruling class that has preceded you. What you see clearly in the case of ancient property, what you admit in the case of feudal property, you are of course forbidden to admit in the case of your own bourgeois form of property.

Abolition of the family! Even the most radical flare up at this infamous proposal of the Communists.

On what foundation is the present family, the bourgeois family, based? On capital, on private gain. In its completely developed form this family exists only among the bourgeoisie. But this state of things finds its complement in the practical absence of the family among the proletarians, and in public prostitution.

The bourgeois family will vanish as a matter of course when its complement vanishes, and both will vanish with the vanishing of capital.

Do you charge us with wanting to stop the exploitation of children by their parents? To this crime we plead guilty.

But, you will say, we destroy the most hallowed of relations, when we replace home education by social.

And your education! Is not that also social, and determined by the social conditions under which you educate, by the intervention, direct or indirect, of society, by means of schools, etc.? The Communists have not invented the intervention of society in education; they do but seek to alter the character of that intervention, and to rescue education from the influence of the ruling class. The bourgeois clap-trap about the family and education, about the hallowed co-relation of parent and child, becomes all the more disgusting, the more, by the action of Modern Industry, all family ties among the proletarians are torn asunder, and their children transformed into simple articles of commerce and instruments of labour.

But you Communists would introduce community of women, screams the whole bourgeoisie in chorus.

The bourgeois sees in his wife a mere instrument of production. He hears that the instruments of production are to be exploited in common, and, naturally, can come to no other conclusion than that the lot of being common to all will likewise fall to the women.

He has not even a suspicion that the real point aimed at is to do away with the status of women as mere instruments of production.

For the rest, nothing is more ridiculous than the virtuous indignation of our bourgeois at the community of women, which, they pretend, is to be openly and officially established by the Communists. The Communists have no need to introduce community of women; it has existed almost from time immemorial.

Our bourgeois, not content with having the wives and daughters of their proletarians at their disposal, not to speak of common prostitutes, take the greatest pleasure in seducing each other's wives.

Bourgeois marriage is in reality a system of wives in common and thus, at the most, what the Communists might possibly be reproached with is that they desire to introduce, in substitution for a hypocritically concealed, an openly legalised community of women. For the rest, it is self-evident that the abolition of the present system of production must bring with it the abolition of the community of women springing from that system, *i.e.*, of prostitution both public and private.

The Communists are further reproached with desiring to abolish countries and nationality.

The working men have no country. We cannot take from them what they have not got. Since the proletariat must first of all acquire political supremacy, must rise to be the leading class of the nation, must constitute itself *the* nation, it is, so far, itself national, though not in the bourgeois sense of the word.

National differences and antagonisms between peoples are daily more and more vanishing, owing to the development of the bourgeoisie, to freedom of commerce, to the world-market, to uniformity in the mode of production and in the conditions of life corresponding thereto.

The supremacy of the proletariat will cause them to vanish still faster. United action, of the leading civilised countries at least, is one of the first conditions for the emancipation of the proletariat.

In proportion as the exploitation of one individual by another is put an end to, the exploitation of one nation by another will also be put an end to. In proportion as the antagonism between classes within the nation vanishes, the hostility of one nation to another will come to an end.

The charges against Communism made from a religious, a philosophical, and, generally, from an ideological standpoint, are not deserving of serious examination.

Does it require deep intuition to comprehend that man's ideas, views and conceptions, in one word, man's consciousness, changes with every change in the conditions of his material existence, in his social relations and in his social life? What else does the history of ideas prove, than that intellectual production changes its character in proportion as material production is changed? The ruling ideas of each age have ever been the ideas of its ruling class.

When people speak of ideas that revolutionise society, they do but express the fact, that within

the old society, the elements of a new one have been created, and that the dissolution of the old ideas keeps even pace with the dissolution of the old conditions of existence.

When the ancient world was in its last throes, the ancient religions were overcome by Christianity. When Christian ideas succumbed in the 18th century to rationalist ideas, feudal society fought its death battle with the then revolutionary bourgeoisie. The ideas of religious liberty and freedom of conscience merely gave expression to the sway of free competition within the domain of knowledge.

"Undoubtedly," it will be said, "religious, moral, philosophical and juridical ideas have been modified in the course of historical development. But religion, morality, philosophy, political science, and law, constantly survived this change."

"There are, besides, eternal truths, such as Freedom, Justice, etc., that are common to all states of society. But Communism abolishes eternal truths, it abolishes all religion, and all morality, instead of constituting them on a new basis; it therefore acts in contradiction to all past historical experience."

What does this accusation reduce itself to? The history of all past society has consisted in the development of class antagonisms, antagonisms that assumed different forms at different epochs.

But whatever form they may have taken, one fact is common to all past ages, *viz.*, the exploitation of one part of society by the other. No wonder, then, that the social consciousness of past ages, despite all the multiplicity and variety it displays, moves within certain common forms, or general ideas, which cannot completely vanish except with the total disappearance of class antagonisms.

The Communist revolution is the most radical rupture with traditional property relations; no wonder that its development involves the most radical rupture with traditional ideas.

But let us have done with the bourgeois objections to Communism.

We have seen above, that the first step in the revolution by the working class, is to raise the proletariat to the position of ruling class, to win the battle of democracy.

The proletariat will use its political supremacy to wrest, by degrees, all capital from the bourgeoisie, to centralise all instruments of production in the hands of the State, *i.e.*, of the proletariat organised as the ruling class; and to increase the total of productive forces as rapidly as possible.

Of course, in the beginning, this cannot be effected except by means of despotic inroads on the rights of property, and on the conditions of bourgeois production; by means of measures, therefore, which appear economically insufficient and untenable, but which, in the course of the movement, outstrip themselves, necessitate further inroads upon the old social order, and are unavoidable as a means of entirely revolutionising the mode of production.

These measures will of course be different in different countries.

Nevertheless in the most advanced countries, the following will be pretty generally applicable.

1. Abolition of property in land and application of all rents of land to public purposes.
2. A heavy progressive or graduated income tax.
3. Abolition of all right of inheritance.
4. Confiscation of the property of all emigrants and rebels.
5. Centralisation of credit in the hands of the State, by means of a national bank with State capital and an exclusive monopoly.
6. Centralisation of the means of communication and transport in the hands of the State.
7. Extension of factories and instruments of production owned by the State; the bringing into cultivation of wastelands, and the improvement of the soil generally in accordance with a common plan.
8. Equal liability of all to labour. Establishment of industrial armies, especially for agriculture.
9. Combination of agriculture with manufacturing industries; gradual abolition of the distinction between town and country, by a more equable distribution of the population over the country.
10. Free education for all children in public schools. Abolition of children's factory labour in its present form. Combination of education with industrial production etc., etc.

When, in the course of development, class distinctions have disappeared, and all production has been concentrated in the hands of a vast association of the whole nation, the public power will lose its political character. Political power, properly so called, is merely the organised power of one class for oppressing another. If the proletariat during its contest with the bourgeoisie is compelled, by the force of circumstances, to organise itself as a class, if, by means of a revolution, it makes itself the ruling class, and, as such, sweeps away by force the old conditions of production, then it will, along with these conditions, have swept away the conditions for the existence of class antagonisms and of classes generally, and will thereby have abolished its own supremacy as a class.

In place of the old bourgeois society, with its classes and class antagonisms, we shall have an association, in which the free development of each is the condition for the free development of all.

IV. POSITION OF THE COMMUNISTS IN RELATION TO THE VARIOUS EXISTING OPPOSITION PARTIES

... The Communists everywhere support every revolutionary movement against the existing social and political order of things.

In all these movements they bring to the front, as the leading question in each, the property question, no matter what its degree of development at the time.

Finally, they labour everywhere for the union and agreement of the democratic parties of all countries.

The Communists disdain to conceal their views and aims. They openly declare that their ends can be attained only by the forcible overthrow of all existing social conditions. Let the ruling classes tremble at a Communistic revolution. The proletarians have nothing to lose but their chains. They have a world to win.

WORKING MEN OF ALL COUNTRIES, UNITE!

⊚ CRITICAL QUESTIONS

1. Do you think that the description of bourgeois society as essentially exploitive is accurate? Why or, why not?
2. What objections have been made to communism, and how do Marx and Engels answer those objections? Do you find their responses convincing? Why, or why not?
3. Marx and Engels list ten measures that they think will lead to a just society. Present an argument against or an argument for the justice of these measures.

5.4 THE ORIGINAL POSITION

What is the role of justice in a society? Is it very important or not so important? Is it more important than anything else? Should all the laws and all the major institutions of a society be changed or rejected if they are unjust?

You can imagine arguments on both sides of the issue. Someone might say that the promotion of law and order is of primary importance for any government. Justice must sometimes take a backseat to these more important goals. One could counter that law and order without justice is a sham. Peace and social stability at any price are just not worth it. There is no greater social good than justice.

If you read Kant, you might recognize a Kantian theme in the claim that justice is the highest social good. If you read Mill, you might recognize a utilitarian theme in the claim that justice must sometimes take a backseat to a greater good. So where do we go from here? How can we decide whether justice is the most important social good? Surely we must know what justice is before we can decide how important it is? What is justice?

Philosophers distinguish between the **material principle of justice** and the formal principle of justice. The material principle of justice is some particular trait that is used as a basis for distributing benefits and burdens. If someone claimed that race, ethnic background, sex, or sexual orientation is the basis on which he or she decided to deny (or give) someone a job, what would you say? Is this fair? If someone claimed that seniority, skill, or a record of good performance is the basis on which she or he decided to deny (or give) someone a job, what would you say? Is this fair? The **formal principle of justice** requires that benefits and burdens be distributed fairly according to *relevant* differences and similarities. So if I decide to award an A to all my students who wear something red on the first Tuesday of each month, is that fair?

"But," you might properly retort, "that is not relevant."

Why isn't it?

"Because," you say, "it has nothing to do with how well they perform on the exams."

That is a reasonable response. However, why is performance on exams relevant? How do we decide what is relevant and fair?

Imagine that you are faced with the task of creating a new society. You are in the dark about your status in that new society. You do not know if you will be rich or poor. You do not know if you will be healthy or sick. You do not know your race or gender or sexual orientation or religion. Not knowing any of these things, what sort of society would you create? What sort of government would it have? How would its laws be enacted? What would its public policies be like?

The philosopher John Rawls thinks he knows what kind of society you would create in such a situation. You would create a just society. In 1971 Rawls, professor of philosophy at Harvard University, published a now famous and influential book called *A Theory of Justice*. Below you will read some selections from that book in which Rawls answers some of the questions we have been thinking about here.

◎ READING QUESTIONS

1. What is the role of justice?
2. What is the subject of justice?
3. What is the main idea of Rawls's theory of justice?
4. What two principles of justice would persons in the original position be likely to choose? How are these principles related?

5. What is the "veil of ignorance," and why is it important in developing a contractarian theory of justice?

A Theory of Justice

JOHN RAWLS

1. THE ROLE OF JUSTICE

Justice is the first virtue of social institutions, as truth is of systems of thought. A theory however elegant and economical must be rejected or revised if it is untrue; likewise laws and institutions no matter how efficient and well-arranged must be reformed or abolished if they are unjust. Each person possesses an inviolability founded on justice that even the welfare of society as a whole cannot override. For this reason justice denies that the loss of freedom for some is made right by a greater good shared by others. It does not allow that the sacrifices imposed on a few are outweighed by the larger sum of advantages enjoyed by many. Therefore in a just society the liberties of equal citizenship are taken as settled; the rights secured by justice are not subject to political bargaining or to the calculus of social interests. The only thing that permits us to acquiesce in an erroneous theory is the lack of a better one; analogously, an injustice is tolerable only when it is necessary to avoid an even greater injustice. Being first virtues of human activities, truth and justice are uncompromising.

These propositions seem to express our intuitive conviction of the primacy of justice. No doubt they are expressed too strongly. In any event I wish to inquire whether these contentions or others similar to them are sound, and if so how they can be accounted for. To this end, it is necessary to work out a theory of justice in the light of which these assertions can be interpreted and assessed. I shall begin by considering the role of the principles of justice. Let us assume, to fix ideas, that a society is a more or less self-sufficient association of persons who in their relations to one another recognize certain rules of conduct as binding and who for the most part act in accordance with them. Suppose further that these rules specify a system of cooperation designed to advance the good of those taking part in it. Then, although a society is a cooperative venture for mutual advantage, it is typically marked by a conflict as well as by an identity of interests. There is an identity of interests since social cooperation makes possible a better life for all than any would have if each were to live solely by his own efforts. There is a conflict of interests since persons are not indifferent as to how the

---

From *A Theory of Justice* by John Rawls (Cambridge, MA: The Belknap Press of Harvard University Press), pp. 3–5, 7, 11–15, 60–62, 136–142. Copyright © 1971, 1999 by the President and Fellows Harvard College. Reprinted by permission of the publisher.

greater benefits produced by their collaboration are distributed, for in order to pursue their ends they each prefer a larger to a lesser share. A set of principles is required for choosing among the various social arrangements which determine this division of advantages and for underwriting an agreement on the proper distributive shares. These principles are the principles of social justice: they provide a way of assigning rights and duties in the basic institutions of society and they define the appropriate distribution of the benefits and burdens of social cooperation.

Now let us say that a society is well-ordered when it is not only designed to advance the good of its members but when it is also effectively regulated by a public conception of justice. That is, it is a society in which (1) everyone accepts and knows that the others accept the same principles of justice, and (2) the basic social institutions generally satisfy and are generally known to satisfy these principles. In this case while men may put forth excessive demands on one another, they nevertheless acknowledge a common point of view from which their claims may be adjudicated. If men's inclination to self-interest makes their vigilance against one another necessary, their public sense of justice makes their secure association together possible. Among individuals with disparate aims and purposes a shared conception of justice establishes the bonds of civic friendship; the general desire for justice limits the pursuit of other ends. One may think of a public conception of justice as constituting the fundamental charter of a well-ordered human association....

2. THE SUBJECT OF JUSTICE

Many different kinds of things are said to be just and unjust: not only laws, institutions, and social systems, but also particular actions of many kinds, including decisions, judgments, and imputations. We also call the attitudes and dispositions of persons, and persons themselves, just and unjust. Our topic, however, is that of social justice. For us the primary subject of justice is the basic structure of society, or more exactly, the way in which the major social institutions distribute fundamental rights and duties and determine the division of

advantages from social cooperation. By major institutions I understand the political constitution and the principal economic and social arrangements. Thus the legal protection of freedom of thought and liberty of conscience, competitive markets, private property in the means of production, and the monogamous family are examples of major social institutions. Taken together as one scheme, the major institutions define men's rights and duties and influence their life prospects, what they can expect to be and how well they can hope to do. The basic structure is the primary subject of justice because its effects are so profound and present from the start....

3. THE MAIN IDEA OF THE THEORY OF JUSTICE

My aim is to present a conception of justice which generalizes and carries to a higher level of abstraction the familiar theory of the social contract as found, say, in Locke, Rousseau, and Kant.[1] In order to do this we are not to think of the original contract as one to enter a particular society or to set up a particular form of government. Rather, the guiding idea is that the principles of justice for the basic structure of society are the object of the original agreement. They are the principles that free and rational persons concerned to further their own interests would accept in an initial position of equality as defining the fundamental terms of their association. These principles are to regulate all further agreements; they specify the kinds of social cooperation that can be entered into and the forms of government that can be established. This way of regarding the principles of justice I shall call justice as fairness.

---

[1]As the text suggests, I shall regard Locke's *Second Treatise of Government*, Rousseau's *The Social Contract*, and Kant's ethical works beginning with *The Foundations of the Metaphysics of Morals* as definitive of the contract tradition. For all of its greatness, Hobbes's *Leviathan* raises special problems. A general historical survey is provided by J. W. Gough, *The Social Contract*, 2nd ed. (Oxford: The Clarendon Press, 1957), and Otto Gierke, *Natural Law and the Theory of Society*, trans. with an introduction by Ernest Barker (Cambridge: The University Press, 1934). A presentation of the contract view as primarily an ethical theory is to be found in G. R. Grice, *The Grounds of Moral Judgment* (Cambridge: The University Press, 1967)....

Thus we are to imagine that those who engage in social cooperation choose together, in one joint act, the principles which are to assign basic rights and duties and to determine the division of social benefits. Men are to decide in advance how they are to regulate their claims against one another and what is to be the foundation charter of their society. Just as each person must decide by rational reflection what constitutes his good, that is, the system of ends which it is rational for him to pursue, so a group of persons must decide once and for all what is to count among them as just and unjust. The choice which rational men would make in this hypothetical situation of equal liberty, assuming for the present that this choice problem has a solution, determines the principles of justice.

In justice as fairness the original position of equality corresponds to the state of nature in the traditional theory of the social contract. This original position is not, of course, thought of as an actual historical state of affairs, much less as a primitive condition of culture. It is understood as a purely hypothetical situation characterized so as to lead to a certain conception of justice. Among the essential features of this situation is that no one knows his place in society, his class position or social status, nor does any one know his fortune in the distribution of natural assets and abilities, his intelligence, strength, and the like. I shall even assume that the parties do not know their conceptions of the good or their special psychological propensities. The principles of justice are chosen behind a veil of ignorance. This ensures that no one is advantaged or disadvantaged in the choice of principles by the outcome of natural chance or the contingency of social circumstances. Since all are similarly situated and no one is able to design principles to favor his particular condition, the principles of justice are the result of a fair agreement or bargain. For given the circumstances of the original position, the symmetry of everyone's relations to each other, this initial situation is fair between individuals as moral persons, that is, as rational beings with their own ends and capable, I shall assume, of a sense of justice. The original position is, one might say, the appropriate initial status quo, and thus the fundamental agreements reached in it are fair. This explains the propriety of the name "justice as fairness": it conveys the idea that the principles of justice are agreed to in an initial situation that is fair. The name does not mean that the concepts of justice and fairness are the same, any more than the phrase "poetry as metaphor" means that the concepts of poetry and metaphor are the same....

I shall maintain ... that the persons in the initial situation would choose two rather different principles: the first requires equality in the assignment of basic rights and duties, while the second holds that social and economic inequalities, for example inequalities of wealth and authority, are just only if they result in compensating benefits for everyone, and in particular for the least advantaged members of society. These principles rule out justifying institutions on the grounds that the hardships of some are offset by a greater good in the aggregate. It may be expedient but it is not just that some should have less in order that others may prosper. But there is no injustice in the greater benefits earned by a few provided that the situation of persons not so fortunate is thereby improved. The intuitive idea is that since everyone's well-being depends upon a scheme of cooperation without which no one could have a satisfactory life, the division of advantages should be such as to draw forth the willing cooperation of everyone taking part in it, including those less well situated. Yet this can be expected only if reasonable terms are proposed. The two principles mentioned seem to be a fair agreement on the basis of which those better endowed, or more fortunate in their social position, neither of which we can be said to deserve, could expect the willing cooperation of others when some workable scheme is a necessary condition of the welfare of all. Once we decide to look for a conception of justice that nullifies the accidents of natural endowment and the contingencies of social circumstance as counters in quest for political and economic advantage, we are led to these principles. They express the result of leaving aside those aspects of the social world that seem arbitrary from a moral point of view....

4. THE ORIGINAL POSITION AND JUSTIFICATION

I have said that the original position is the appropriate initial status quo which insures that the fundamental agreements reached in it are fair. This fact yields the name "justice as fairness." It is clear, then, that I want to say that one conception of justice is more reasonable than another, or justifiable with respect to it, if rational persons in the initial situation would choose its principles over those of the other for the role of justice. Conceptions of justice are to be ranked by their acceptability to persons so circumstanced. Understood in this way the question of justification is settled by working out a problem of deliberation: we have to ascertain which principles it would be rational to adopt given the contractual situation. This connects the theory of justice with the theory of rational choice....

11. TWO PRINCIPLES OF JUSTICE

I shall now state in a provisional form the two principles of justice that I believe would be chosen in the original position.... The first statement of the two principles reads as follows.

> First: each person is to have an equal right to the most extensive basic liberty compatible with a similar liberty for others.
>
> Second: social and economic inequalities are to be arranged so that they are both (a) reasonably expected to be to everyone's advantage, and (b) attached to positions and offices open to all.

There are two ambiguous phrases in the second principle, namely "everyone's advantage" and "open to all."...

By way of general comment, these principles primarily apply, as I have said, to the basic structure of society. They are to govern the assignment of rights and duties and to regulate the distribution of social and economic advantages. As their formulation suggests, these principles presuppose that the social structure can be divided into two more or less distinct parts, the first principle applying to the one, the second to the other. They distinguish between those aspects of the social system that define and secure the equal liberties of citizenship and those that specify and establish social and economic inequalities. The basic liberties of citizens are, roughly speaking, political liberty (the right to vote and to be eligible for public office) together with freedom of speech and assembly; liberty of conscience and freedom of thought; freedom of the person along with the right to hold (personal) property; and freedom from arbitrary arrest and seizure as defined by the concept of the rule of law. These liberties are all required to be equal by the first principle, since citizens of a just society are to have the same basic rights.

The second principle applies, in the first approximation, to the distribution of income and wealth and to the design of organizations that make use of differences in authority and responsibility, or chains of command. While the distribution of wealth and income need not be equal, it must be to everyone's advantage, and at the same time, positions of authority and offices of command must be accessible to all. One applies the second principle by holding positions open, and then, subject to this constraint, arranges social and economic inequalities so that everyone benefits.

These principles are to be arranged in a serial order with the first principle prior to the second. This ordering means that a departure from the institutions of equal liberty required by the first principle cannot be justified by, or compensated for, by greater social and economic advantages. The distribution of wealth and income, and the hierarchies of authority, must be consistent with both the liberties of equal citizenship and equality of opportunity.

It is clear that these principles are rather specific in their content, and their acceptance rests on certain assumptions that I must eventually try to explain and justify. A theory of justice depends upon a theory of society in ways that will become evident as we proceed. For the present, it should be observed that the two principles (and this holds for all formulations) are a special case of a more general conception of justice that can be expressed as follows.

> All social values—liberty and opportunity, income and wealth, and the bases of self-respect—are to be distributed equally unless an unequal distribution of any, or all, of these values is to everyone's advantage.

Injustice, then, is simply inequalities that are not to the benefit of all. Of course, this conception is extremely vague and requires interpretation.

As a first step, suppose that the basic structure of society distributes certain primary goods, that is, things that every rational man is presumed to want. These goods normally have a use whatever a person's rational plan of life. For simplicity, assume that the chief primary goods at the disposition of society are rights and liberties, powers and opportunities, income and wealth.... These are the social primary goods. Other primary goods such as health and vigor, intelligence and imagination are natural goods; although their possession is influenced by the basic structure, they are not so directly under its control. Imagine, then, a hypothetical initial arrangement in which all the social primary goods are equally distributed: everyone has similar rights and duties, and income and wealth are evenly shared. This state of affairs provides a benchmark for judging improvements. If certain inequalities of wealth and organizational powers would make everyone better off than in this hypothetical starting situation, then they accord with the general conception.

Now it is possible, at least theoretically, that by giving up some of their fundamental liberties men are sufficiently compensated by the resulting social and economic gains. The general conception of justice imposes no restrictions on what sort of inequalities are permissible; it only requires that everyone's position be improved. We need not suppose anything so drastic as consenting to a condition of slavery. Imagine instead that men forego certain political rights when the economic returns are significant and their capacity to influence the course of policy by the exercise of these rights would be marginal in any case. It is this kind of exchange which the two principles as stated rule out; being arranged in serial order they do not

permit exchanges between basic liberties and economic and social gains. The serial ordering of principles expresses an underlying preference among primary social goods. When this preference is rational so likewise is the choice of these principles in this order....

24. THE VEIL OF IGNORANCE

The idea of the original position is to set up a fair procedure so that any principles agreed to will be just. The aim is to use the notion of pure procedural justice as a basis of theory. Somehow we must nullify the effects of specific contingencies which put men at odds and tempt them to exploit social and natural circumstances to their own advantage. Now in order to do this I assume that the parties are situated behind a veil of ignorance. They do not know how the various alternatives will affect their own particular case and they are obliged to evaluate principles solely on the basis of general considerations.

It is assumed, then, that the parties do not know certain kinds of particular facts. First of all, no one knows his place in society, his class position or social status; nor does he know his fortune in the distribution of natural assets and abilities, his intelligence and strength, and the like. Nor, again, does anyone know his conception of the good, the particulars of his rational plan of life, or even the special features of his psychology such as his aversion to risk or liability to optimism or pessimism. More than this, I assume that the parties do not know the particular circumstances of their own society. That is, they do not know its economic or political situation, or the level of civilization and culture it has been able to achieve. The persons in the original position have no information as to which generation they belong. These broader restrictions on knowledge are appropriate in part because questions of social justice arise between generations as well as within them, for example, the question of the appropriate rate of capital saving and of the conservation of natural resources and the environment of nature. There is also, theoretically anyway, the question of a reasonable genetic policy. In these cases too, in order to carry through the idea of the original position, the parties must not know the contingencies that set them in opposition. They must choose principles the consequences of which they are prepared to live with whatever generation they turn out to belong to.

As far as possible, then, the only particular facts which the parties know [are] that their society is subject to the circumstances of justice and whatever this implies. It is taken for granted, however, that they know the general facts about human society. They understand political affairs and the principles of economic theory; they know the basis of social organization and the laws of human psychology. Indeed, the parties are presumed to know whatever general facts affect the choice of the principles of justice. There are no limitations on general information, that is, on general laws and theories, since conceptions of justice must be adjusted to the characteristics of the systems of social cooperation which they are to regulate, and there is no reason to rule out these facts. It is, for example, a consideration against a conception of justice that, in view of the laws of moral psychology, men would not acquire a desire to act upon it even when the institutions of their society satisfied it. For in this case there would be difficulty in securing the stability of social cooperation. It is an important feature of a conception of justice that it should generate its own support. That is, its principles should be such that when they are embodied in the basic structure of society men tend to acquire the corresponding sense of justice. Given the principles of moral learning, men develop a desire to act in accordance with its principles. In this case a conception of justice is stable. This kind of general information is admissible in the original position.

The notion of the veil of ignorance raises several difficulties. Some may object that the exclusion of nearly all particular information makes it difficult to grasp what is meant by the original position. Thus it may be helpful to observe that one or more persons can at any time enter this position, or perhaps, better, simulate the deliberations of this hypothetical situation, simply by reasoning in accordance with the appropriate restrictions. In arguing for a conception of justice we must be sure that it is among the permitted alternatives and satisfies the stipulated formal constraints. No considerations can be advanced in its favor unless they would be rational ones for us to urge were we to lack the kind of knowledge that is excluded. The evaluation of principles must proceed in terms of the general consequences of their public recognition and universal application, it being assumed that they will be complied with by everyone. To say that a certain conception of justice would be chosen in the original position is equivalent to saying that rational deliberation satisfying certain conditions and restrictions would reach a certain conclusion. If necessary, the argument to this result could be set out more formally. I shall, however, speak throughout in terms of the notion of the original position. It is more economical and suggestive, and brings out certain essential features that otherwise one might easily overlook.

These remarks show that the original position is not to be thought of as a general assembly which includes at one moment everyone who will live at some time; or, much less, as an assembly of everyone who could live at some time. It is not a gathering of all actual or possible persons. To conceive of the original position in either of these ways is to stretch fantasy too far; the conception would cease to be a natural guide to intuition. In any case, it is important that the original position be interpreted so that one can at any time adopt its perspective. It must make no difference when one takes up this viewpoint, or who does so: the restrictions must be such that the same principles are always chosen. The veil of ignorance is a key condition in meeting this requirement. It insures not only that the information available is relevant, but that it is at all times the same.

It may be protested that the condition of the veil of ignorance is irrational. Surely, some may object, principles should be chosen in the light of all the knowledge available. There are various replies to this contention. Here I shall sketch those which emphasize the simplifications that need to be made if one is to have any theory at all.... To begin with, it is clear that since the differences among the parties are unknown to them, and everyone is equally rational and similarly situated, each is convinced by the same arguments.

Therefore, we can view the choice in the original position from the standpoint of one person selected at random. If anyone after due reflection prefers a conception of justice to another, then they all do, and a unanimous agreement can be reached. We can, to make the circumstances more vivid, imagine that the parties are required to communicate with each other through a referee as intermediary, and that he is to announce which alternatives have been suggested and the reasons offered in their support. He forbids the attempt to form coalitions, and he informs the parties when they have come to an understanding. But such a referee is actually superfluous, assuming that the deliberations of the parties must be similar.

Thus there follows the very important consequence that the parties have no basis for bargaining in the usual sense. No one knows his situation in society nor his natural assets, and therefore no one is in a position to tailor principles to his advantage. We might imagine that one of the contractees threatens to hold out unless the others agree to principles favorable to him. But how does he know which principles are especially in his interests? The same holds for the formation of coalitions: if a group were to decide to band together to the disadvantage of the others, they would not know how to favor themselves in the choice of principles. Even if they could get everyone to agree to their proposal, they would have no assurance that it was to their advantage, since they cannot identify themselves either by name or description. The one case where this conclusion fails is that of saving. Since the persons in the original position know that they are contemporaries (taking the present time of entry interpretation), they can favor their generation by refusing to make any sacrifices at all for their successors; they simply acknowledge the principle that no one has a duty to save for posterity. Previous generations have saved or they have not; there is nothing the parties can now do to affect that. So in this instance the veil of ignorance fails to secure the desired result. Therefore I resolve the question of justice between generations in a different way by altering the motivation assumption. But with this adjustment no one is able to formulate principles especially designed to advance his own cause. Whatever his temporal position, each is forced to choose for everyone.

The restrictions on particular information in the original position are, then, of fundamental importance. Without them we would not be able to work out any definite theory of justice at all. We would have to be content with a vague formula stating that justice is what would be agreed to without being able to say much, if anything, about the substance of the agreement itself. The formal constraints of the concept of right, those applying to principles directly, are not sufficient for our purpose. The veil of ignorance makes possible a unanimous choice of a particular conception of justice. Without these limitations on knowledge the bargaining problem of the original position would be hopelessly complicated. Even if theoretically a solution were to exist, we would not, at present anyway, be able to determine it.

The notion of the veil of ignorance is implicit, I think, in Kant's ethics.... Nevertheless the problem of defining the knowledge of the parties and of characterizing the alternatives open to them has often been passed over, even by contract theories. Sometimes the situation definitive of moral deliberation is presented in such an indeterminate way that one cannot ascertain how it will turn out. Thus Perry's doctrine is essentially contractarian: he holds that social and personal integration must proceed by entirely different principles, the latter by rational prudence, the former by the concurrence of persons of good will. He would appear to reject utilitarianism on much the same grounds suggested earlier: namely, that it improperly extends the principle of choice for one person to choices facing society. The right course of action is characterized as that which best advances social aims as these would be formulated by reflective agreement given that the parties have full knowledge of the circumstances and are moved by a benevolent concern for one another's interests. No effort is made, however, to specify in any precise way the possible outcomes of this sort of agreement. Indeed, without a far more elaborate account, no conclusions can be drawn. I do not wish here to criticize others; rather, I want to explain the necessity for what may seem at times like so many irrelevant details.

Now the reasons for the veil of ignorance go beyond mere simplicity. We want to define the original position so that we get the desired solution. If a knowledge of particulars is allowed, then the outcome is biased by arbitrary contingencies. As already observed, to each according to his threat advantage is not a principle of justice. If the original position is to yield agreements that are just, the parties must be fairly situated and treated equally as moral persons. The arbitrariness of the world must be corrected for by adjusting the circumstances of the initial contractual situation. Moreover, if in choosing principles we required unanimity even when there is full information, only a few rather obvious cases could be decided. A conception of justice based on unanimity in these circumstances would indeed be weak and trivial. But once knowledge is excluded, the requirement of unanimity is not out of place and the fact that it can be satisfied is of great importance. It enables us to say of the preferred conception of justice that it represents a genuine reconciliation of interests.

A final comment. For the most part I shall suppose that the parties possess all general information. No general facts are closed to them. I do this mainly to avoid complications. Nevertheless a conception of justice is to be the public basis of the terms of social cooperation. Since common understanding necessitates certain bounds on the complexity of principles, there may likewise be limits on the use of theoretical knowledge in the original position. Now clearly it would be very difficult to classify and to grade for complexity the various sorts of general facts. I shall make no attempt to do this. We do however recognize an intricate theoretical construction when we meet one. Thus it seems reasonable to say that other things equal one conception of justice is to be preferred to another when it is founded upon markedly simpler general facts, and its choice does not depend upon elaborate calculations in the light of a vast array of theoretically defined possibilities. It is desirable that the grounds for a public conception of justice should be evident to everyone when circumstances permit. This consideration favors, I believe, the two principles of justice over the criterion of utility....

⊚ CRITICAL QUESTIONS

1. What do you think is wrong with Rawls's theory of justice? Why do you think it is wrong?
2. How would Rawls answer the question, "What makes a society just?" Compare his answer to the answer given by Marx and Engels. Clearly state the main differences and similarities.
3. Imagine yourself behind the Veil of Ignorance. Would you support gay marriage or not? Why?

5.5 OUR OBLIGATION TO THE STATE

In Chapter 3, we left Socrates condemned to death by the Athenian court. His execution was delayed because of a religious festival, and his friends made plans for his escape from prison. Crito went to Socrates in prison and tried to persuade him to escape. Socrates argued that the right thing for him to do was to obey the law. This argument was surprising because in the *Apology* he made it quite clear that his mission to search for the truth was of more value than conforming to the laws of Athens. Even if the Athenians should order him to stop his activities, he would continue because, as he so dramatically put it, "the unexamined life is not worth living."

So why did Socrates now argue that he should obey the laws of Athens and drink the hemlock? Should all laws be obeyed just because they are legally established? Where do governments get the authority to pass laws? Where do they get the authority to take a human life? If the laws are bad laws, isn't it right to break them? If someone is unjustly condemned, isn't it right to try to escape punishment? Or is it morally right to suffer the consequences of your actions, even if what you did was right?

At one point in his argument, Socrates made an allusion to an implied agreement that he had with the state. According to this agreement, the city-state of Athens had provided him and his family with certain benefits in return for his promise to keep the laws. By living in Athens, he had tacitly entered into a contract, and to break that contract now would be dishonest. Here we find the seeds for what has emerged as one of the dominant modern Western theories of political authority, the theory of the social contract (see Rawls's appeal to a contractarian position in the previous selection). The image of a famous painting depicting the philosopher as his punishment is being inflicted is included in one of the book's color plates. It shows him about to take the poison that will kill him, thereby, "fulfilling his contract" with the state.

Social contract theory states that the authority of government derives from a voluntary agreement among all the people to form a political community and to obey the laws passed by a government they collectively select. Thomas Hobbes (1588–1679), in his book *Leviathan*, imagined a state of nature that was pre-social. This condition he characterized as a "war of all against all" in which people pursued their own self-interest and the only right was the right to self-preservation. The desire for self-preservation eventually made it clear that peace was a desirable goal and that the only way to secure this was to give the "sword of sovereignty" to someone who could guarantee order.

Jean-Jacques Rousseau (1712–1778), in his book *Social Contract*, rejected Hobbes's view that humans are by nature selfish and warlike. Human nature is basically good, he argued; evil arises with society. Civilization corrupts us. However, even though we are born free and good, we are bound together in a social contract and obliged to obey the decisions of the group to which our agreement has bound us. Individually, we have unique desires and interests that express our individual will. But as voting citizens of a community, we manifest the "general will" of the group, and it is this general will that forms the foundation of political authority.

Social contract theory makes clear how closely political theories are tied to theories of human nature. If we think humans are by nature evil, governments will be seen as necessary goods that restrain evil and prevent chaos. Governments provide law and order. The stronger the government, the better. If we think humans are by nature good, governments will be seen as necessary evils that hamper free and spontaneous expression. Governments restrict our freedom, and the less government, the better.

◉ READING QUESTIONS

1. What are Crito's main arguments in favor of Socrates' escape?
2. Socrates first responds by stating certain principles with which he gets Crito to agree. What are these principles?

3. Socrates imagines that the laws of Athens are speaking to him. In this speech, what are the most important points in support of not escaping?
4. Based on your reading of the *Crito*, how do you think Socrates would answer the question, "What makes a society just?"

Crito

PLATO

Socrates: Why have you come at this hour, Crito? It must be quite early?

Crito: Yes, it certainly is.

Soc: What time is it?

Cr: The dawn is breaking.

Soc: I am surprised the keeper of the prison let you in.

Cr: He knows me because I come often, Socrates, and he owes me a favor.

Soc: Did you just get here?

Cr: No, I came some time ago.

Soc: Why did you sit and say nothing instead of waking me at once?

Cr: Why, indeed, Socrates, I myself would rather not have all this sleeplessness and sorrow. I have been wondering at your peaceful slumber and that was the reason why I did not (wake) you. I wanted you to be out of pain. I always thought you fortunate in your calm temperament but I never saw anything like the easy, cheerful way you bear this calamity.

Soc: Crito, when a man reaches my age he should not fear approaching death.

Cr: Other men of your age in similar situations fear death.

Soc: That may be. But you have not told me why you come at this early hour.

Cr: I bring you a sad and painful message; not sad, as I believe, for you, but to all of us who are your friends and saddest of all to me.

Soc: Has the ship come from Delos, on the arrival of which I am to die?

Cr: No, the ship has not actually arrived, but it will probably be here today because people who came from Sunium tell me they left it there. Therefore tomorrow, Socrates, will be the last day of your life.

Soc: Very well, Crito. If it is the will of the gods, I am willing but I believe there will be a delay of a day.

Cr: Why do you say that?

Soc: I will tell you. I am to die on the day after the arrival of the ship?

Cr: Yes, that is what the authorities say.

Soc: I do not think the ship will be here until tomorrow. I had a dream last night, or rather only just now, when you fortunately allowed me to sleep.

Cr: What was your dream?

Soc: I saw the image of a wondrously beautiful woman, clothed in white robes, who called to me and said: "O Socrates, the third day hence to fertile Phthia shalt thou go."

Cr: What a strange dream, Socrates!

Soc: I think there can be no doubt about the meaning, Crito.

Cr: Perhaps the meaning is clear to you. But, oh my beloved Socrates, let me beg you once more to take my advice and escape! If you die I shall not only lose a friend who can never be replaced, but there is another evil: People who do not know you and me will believe I might have saved you if I had been willing to spend money, but I did not care to do so. Now, can there be a worse disgrace than this—that I should be thought to value money more than the life of a friend? The many will not be persuaded I wanted you to escape and you refused.

Soc: But why, my dear Crito, should we care about the opinion of the many? Good men, and they are the only persons worth considering, will think of these things as they happened.

Cr: But do you see, Socrates, the opinion of the many must be regarded, as is clear in your

The original translation is by Benjamin Jowett and has been revised and updated by Chistopher Biffle, *A Guided Tour of Five Works of Plato* (Mountain View, CA: Mayfield, 1988), pp. 57–67. Reprinted by permission of Mayfield Publishing Company.

own case, because they can do the very greatest evil to anyone who has lost their good opinion.

Soc: I only wish, Crito, they could. Then they could also do the greatest good and that would be excellent. The truth is, they can do neither good nor evil. They cannot make a man wise or make him foolish and whatever they do is the result of chance.

Cr: Well, I will not argue about that. But please tell me, Socrates, if you are acting out of concern for me and your other friends. Are you afraid if you escape we may get into trouble with the informers for having stolen you away and lose either the whole or a great part of our property, or even a worse evil may happen to us? Now, if this is your fear, be at ease. In order to save you we should surely run this, or even a greater, risk. Be persuaded, then, and do as I say.

Soc: Yes, Crito, that is one fear which you mention, but by no means the only one.

Cr: Do not be afraid. There are persons who at no great cost are willing to save you and bring you out of prison. As for the informers, they are reasonable in their demands, a little money will satisfy them. My resources, which are ample, are at your service and if you are troubled about spending all mine, there are strangers who will give you theirs. One of them, Simmias the Theban, brought a sum of money for this very purpose. Cebes and many others are willing to spend their money, too. I say therefore, do not hesitate about making your escape and do not say, as you did in the court, you will have difficulty in knowing what to do with yourself if you escape. Men will love you in other places you may go and not only in Athens. There are friends of mine in Thessaly, if you wish to go to them, who will value and protect you and no Thessalian will give you any trouble. Nor can I think you are justified, Socrates, in betraying your own life when you might be saved. This is playing into the hands of your enemies and destroyers. Besides, I say you are betraying your children. You should bring them up and educate them; instead you go away and leave them, and they will have to grow up on their own. If they do not meet with the usual fate of orphans, there will be small thanks to you. No man should bring children into the world who is unwilling to continue their nurture and education. You are choosing the easier part, as I think, not the better and manlier, which you should as one who professes virtue in all his actions. Indeed, I am ashamed not only of you, but of us, your friends, when I think this entire business of yours will be attributed to our lack of courage. The trial need never have started or might have been brought to another conclusion. The end of it all, which is the crowning absurdity, will seem to have been permitted by us, through cowardice and baseness, who might have saved you. You might have saved yourself, if we had been good for anything, for there was no difficulty in escaping, and we did not see how disgraceful, Socrates, and also miserable all this will be to us as well as to you. Make up your mind then. Or rather, have your mind already made up, for the time of deliberation is over. There is only one thing to be done, which must be done if at all this very night, and which any delay will render all but impossible. I plead with you therefore, Socrates, to be persuaded by me, and do as I say.

Soc: Dear Crito, your zeal is invaluable if right. If wrong, the greater the zeal, the greater the evil. Therefore we must consider whether these things should be done or not. I am, and always have been, someone who must be guided by reason, whatever the reason may be which, upon reflection, appears to me to be the best. Now that this misfortune has come upon me, I cannot put away my old beliefs. The principles I honored and revered I still honor and unless we can find other and better principles, I will not agree with you. I would not even if the power of the multitude could inflict many more imprisonments, confiscations and deaths, frightening us like children with foolish terrors.

What will be the best way of considering the question? Shall I return to your old argument about the opinions of men, some of which should be considered, and others, as we were saying, are not to be considered. Now were we right in maintaining this before I was condemned? And has the argument which was once good, now proved to be talk for the sake of talking—in fact an amusement only and altogether foolish? That is what I want to consider with your help, Crito: whether, under my present circumstances, the argument appears to be in any way different or not and is to be followed by me or abandoned. That argument, I believe, is held by many who claim to be authorities, was to the effect, that the opinions of some men are to be considered and of other men not to be considered. Now you, Crito, are not going to die tomorrow—at least, there is no probability of this. You are therefore not likely to be deceived by the circumstances in which you are placed. Tell me, then, whether I am right in saying that some opinions are to be valued and other opinions are not to be valued. I ask you whether I was right in believing this?

Cr: Certainly.

Soc: The good opinions are to be believed and not the bad?

Cr: Yes.

Soc: And the opinions of the wise are good and the opinions of the foolish are evil?

Cr: Certainly.

Soc: And what was said about another matter? Is the gymnastics student supposed to attend to the praise and blame and opinion of every man, or of one man only—his physician or trainer, whoever that is?

Cr: Of one man only.

Soc: And he should fear the blame and welcome praise of that one only, and not of the many?

Cr: That is clear.

Soc: He should live and train, eat and drink in the way which seems good to his single teacher who has understanding, rather than according to the opinion of all other men put together?

Cr: True.

Soc: And if he disobeys and rejects the opinion and approval of the one, and accepts the opinion of the many who have no understanding, will he not suffer evil?

Cr: Certainly he will.

Soc: And how will the evil affect the disobedient student?

Cr: Clearly, it will affect his body; that is what is destroyed by the evil.

Soc: Very good. Is this not true, Crito, of other things which we need not separately consider? In the matter of the just and unjust, the fair and foul, the good and evil, which are the subjects of our present discussion, should we follow the opinion of the many and fear them, or the opinion of the one man who has understanding? Is he the one we ought to fear and honor more than all the rest of the world? If we leave him, shall we destroy and injure that principle in us which may be assumed to be improved by justice and deteriorated by injustice? Is there not such a principle?

Cr: Certainly there is, Socrates.

Soc: Take a similar case. If, acting under the advice of men who have no understanding, we ruined what is improved by health and destroyed by disease—when the body has been destroyed, I say, would life be worth having?

Cr: Yes.

Soc: Could we live having an evil and corrupted body?

Cr: Certainly not.

Soc: And will life be worth having, if the soul is crippled, which is improved by justice and harmed by injustice? Do we suppose the soul to be inferior to the body?

Cr: Certainly not.

Soc: More important, then?

Cr: Far more important.

Soc: Then, my friend, we must not consider what the many say of us, but what he, the one man who has understanding of the just and unjust will say, and what the truth will say. Therefore you begin in error when you suggest we should consider the opinion of the many about the just and unjust, the good and evil, the honorable and dishonorable, but what if someone says, "But the many can kill us."

Cr: Yes, Socrates, that will clearly be the answer.

Soc: Still I believe our old argument is unshaken. I would like to know whether I may say the same of another proposition—that not life, but a good life, is to be chiefly valued?

Cr: Yes, that is also true.

Soc: And a good life is equivalent to a just and honorable one—that is also true?

Cr: Yes, that is true.

Soc: From these beliefs I am ready to consider whether I should or should not try to escape without the consent of the Athenians. If I am clearly right in escaping, then I will make the attempt, but if not, I will remain here. The other considerations which you mention, of money and loss of reputation and the duty of educating children, are, I fear, only the beliefs of the many, who would be as ready to bring people to life, if they were able, as they are to put them to death. The only question remaining to be considered is whether we shall do right escaping or allowing others to aid our escape and paying them money and thanks or whether we shall not do right. If the latter, then death or any other calamity which may result from my remaining here must not be allowed to influence us.

Cr: I think you are right, Socrates. But, how shall we proceed?

Soc: Let us consider the matter together and either refute me if you can and I will be convinced; or else cease, my dear friend, from repeating to me that I ought to escape against the wishes of the Athenians. I am extremely eager to be persuaded by you, but not against my own better judgment. And now please consider my first position and do your best to answer me.

Cr: I will do my best.

Soc: Are we to say we are never intentionally to do wrong, or that in one way we should and in another way we should not do wrong? Or is doing wrong always evil and dishonorable, as I was just now saying? Are all our former admissions to be thrown away because of these last few days? Have we, at our age, been earnestly discoursing with one another all our life long only to discover we are no better than children? Or, are we convinced in spite of the opinion of the many and in spite of consequences of the truth of what we said, that injustice is always an evil and dishonor to him who acts unjustly? Shall we agree to that?

Cr: Yes.

Soc: Then we must do no wrong?

Cr: Certainly not.

Soc: Nor when injured should we injure in return, as the many imagine. We must injure no one at all?

Cr: Clearly not.

Soc: Again, Crito, can we do evil?

Cr: Surely not, Socrates.

Soc: And what of doing evil in return for evil, which is the morality of the many—is that just or not?

Cr: Not just.

Soc: For doing evil to another is the same as injuring him.

Cr: Very true.

Soc: Then we ought not to retaliate or render evil for evil to any one whatever evil we may have suffered from him. But I would have you consider, Crito, whether you really mean what you are saying. For this opinion has never been held, and never will be held, by many people. Those who are agreed and those who are not agreed upon this point have no common ground, and can only despise one another when they see how widely they differ. Tell me, then, whether you agree with my first principle, that neither injury nor retaliation nor returning evil for evil is ever right. Shall that be the premise of our argument? Or do you disagree? For this has been and still is my opinion; but, if you are of another opinion, let me hear what you have to say. If, however, you remain of the same mind as formerly, I will go to the next step.

Cr: You may proceed, for I have not changed my mind.

Soc: The next step may be put in the form of a question: Ought a man to do what he admits to be right, or ought he to betray the right?

Cr: He ought to do what he thinks right.

Soc: But if this is true, what is the application? In leaving the prison against the will of the Athenians, do I wrong anyone? Or do I wrong those whom I ought least to wrong? Do I abandon the principles which were acknowledged by us to be just. What do you say?

Cr: I cannot tell, Socrates, because I do not know.

Soc: Then consider the matter in this way— imagine I am about to escape, and the Laws and the State come and interrogate me: "Tell us, Socrates," they say, "what are you doing? Are you going to overturn us—the Laws and the State, as far as you are able? Do you imagine that a State can continue and not be overthrown, in which the decisions of Law have no power, but are set aside and overthrown by individuals?"

What will be our answer, Crito, to these and similar words? Anyone, and especially a clever orator, will have a good deal to say about the evil of setting aside the Law which requires a sentence to be carried out. We might reply, "Yes, but the State has injured us and given an unjust sentence." Suppose I say that?

Cr: Very good, Socrates.

Soc: "And was that our agreement with you?" the Law would say, "Or were you to abide by the sentence of the State?" And if I was surprised at their saying this, the Law would probably add: "Answer, Socrates, instead of opening your eyes: you are in the habit of asking and answering questions. Tell us what complaint you have against us which justifies you in attempting to destroy us and the State? In the first place did we not bring you into existence? Your father married your mother by our aid and conceived you. Say whether you have any objection against those of us who regulate marriage?" None, I should reply. "Or against those of us who regulate the system of care and education of children in which you were trained? Were not the Laws, who have the charge of this, right in commanding your father to train you in the arts and exercise?" Yes, I should reply.

"Well then, since you were brought into the world, nurtured and educated by us, can you deny in the first place that you are our child and slave, as your fathers were before you? And if this is true you are not on equal terms with us. Nor can you think you have a right to do to

us what we are doing to you. Would you have any right to strike or do any other evil to a father or to your master, if you had one, when you have been struck or received some other evil at his hands? And because we think it is right to destroy you, do you think that you have any right to destroy us in return, and your country so far as you are able? And will you, O expounder of virtue, say you are justified in this? Has a philosopher like you failed to discover your country is more to be valued and higher and holier by far than mother and father or any ancestor, and more regarded in the eyes of the gods and of men of understanding? It should be soothed and gently and reverently entreated when angry, even more than a father, and if not persuaded, it should be obeyed. And when we are punished by the State, whether with imprisonment or whipping, the punishment is to be endured in silence. If the State leads us to wounds or death in battle, we follow as is right; no one can yield or leave his rank, but whether in battle or in a court of law, or in any other place, he must do what his city and his country order him. Or, he must change their view of what is just. If he may do no violence to his father or mother, much less may he do violence to his country." What answer shall we make to this, Crito? Do the Laws speak truly, or do they not?

Cr: I think that they do.

Soc: Then the Laws will say: "Consider, Socrates, if this is true, that in your present attempt you are going to do us wrong. For, after having brought you into the world, nurtured and educated you, and given you and every other citizen a share in every good we had to give, we further give the right to every Athenian, if he does not like us when he has come of age and has seen the ways of the city, he may go wherever else he pleases and take his goods with him. None of us Laws will forbid or interfere with him. Any of you who does not like us and the city, and who wants to go to a colony or to any other city, may go where he likes, and take his possessions with him. But he who has experience of the way we order justice and administer the State, and still remains, has entered into an implied contract to do as we command him. He who disobeys us is, as we maintain, triply wrong; first, because in disobeying us he is disobeying his parents; second, because we are the authors of his education; third, because he has made an agreement with us that he will duly obey our commands. He neither obeys them nor convinces us our commands are wrong. We do not rudely impose our commands but give each person the alternative of obeying or convincing us. That is what we offer and he does neither. These are the sort of accusations to which, as we were saying, Socrates, you will be exposed if you do as you were intending; you, above all other Athenians."

Suppose I ask, why is this? They will justly answer that I above all other men have acknowledged the agreement.

"There is clear proof," they will say, "Socrates, that we and the city were not displeasing to you. Of all Athenians you have been the most constant resident in the city, which, as you never leave, you appear to love. You never went out of the city either to see the games, except once when you went to the Isthmus, or to any other place unless you were on military service; nor did you travel as other men do. Nor had you any curiosity to know other States or their Laws: Your affections did not go beyond us and our State; we were your special favorites and you agreed in our government of you. This is the State in which you conceived your children, which is a proof of your satisfaction. Moreover, you might, if you wished, have fixed the penalty at banishment in the course of the trial—the State which refuses to let you go now would have let you go then. You pretended you preferred death to exile and that you were not grieved at death. And now you have forgotten these fine sentiments and pay no respect to us, the Laws, who you destroy. You are doing what only a miserable slave would do, running away and turning your back upon the agreements which you made as a citizen. First of all, answer this very question: Are we right

in saying you agreed to be governed according to us in deed, and not in word only? Is that true or not?"

How shall we answer that, Crito? Must we not agree?

Cr: We must, Socrates.

Soc: Then will the Laws say: "You, Socrates, are breaking the agreements which you made with us at your leisure, not in any haste or under any compulsion or deception, but having had 70 years to think of them, during which time you were at liberty to leave the city, if we were not to your liking, or if our covenants appeared to you to be unfair. You might have gone either to Lacedaemon or Crete, which you often praise for their good government, or to some other Hellenic or foreign state. You, above all other Athenians, seemed to be so fond of the State and of us, her Laws, that you never left her. The lame, the blind, the maimed were not more stationary in the State than you were. Now you run away and forsake your agreements. Now, Socrates, if you will take our advice; do not make yourself ridiculous by escaping out of the city.

"Just consider, if you do evil in this way, what good will you do either yourself or your friends? That your friends will be driven into exile and lose their citizenship, or will lose their property, is reasonably certain. You yourself, if you fly to one of the neighboring cities, like Thebes or Megara, both of which are well-governed cities, will come to them as an enemy, Socrates. Their government will be against you and all patriotic citizens will cast suspicious eye upon you as a destroyer of the laws. You will confirm in the minds of the judges the justice of their own condemnation of you. For he who is a corruptor of the laws is more than likely to be corruptor of the young. Will you then flee from well-ordered cities and virtuous men? Is existence worth having on these terms? Or will you go to these cities without shame and talk to them, Socrates? And what will you say to them? Will you say what you say here about virtue, justice, institutions and laws being the best things among men? Would that be decent of you? Surely not.

"If you go away from well-governed states to Crito's friends in Thessaly, where there is a great disorder and immorality, they will be charmed to have the tale of your escape from prison, set off with ludicrous particulars of the manner in which you were wrapped in a goatskin or some other disguise and metamorphosed as the fashion of runaways is—that is very likely. But will there be no one to remind you in your old age you violated the most sacred laws from a miserable desire of a little more life. Perhaps not, if you keep them in a good temper. But if they are angry you will hear many degrading things; you will live, but how? As the flatterer of all men, and the servant of all men. And doing what? Eating and drinking in Thessaly, having gone abroad in order that you may get a dinner. Where will your fine sentiments about justice and virtue be then? Say that you wish to live for the sake of your children, that you may bring them up and educate them—will you take them into Thessaly and deprive them of Athenian citizenship? Is that the benefit which you would confer upon them? Or are you under the impression that they will be better cared for and educated here if you are still alive, although absent from them because your friends will take care of them? Do you think if you are an inhabitant of Thessaly they will take care of them, and if you are an inhabitant of the other world they will not take care of them? No, if they who call themselves friends are truly friends, they surely will.

"Listen, then, Socrates, to us who have brought you up. Think not of life and children first, and of justice afterwards, but of justice first, that you may be justified before the rulers of the other world. For neither will you nor your children be happier or holier in this life, or happier in another, if you do as Crito bids. Now you depart in innocence, a sufferer and not a doer of evil; a victim, not of the Laws, but of men. But if you escape, returning evil for evil and injury for injury, breaking the agreements which you have made with us, and wronging those whom you ought least to wrong, that is to say, yourself, your friends, your country, and us, we shall be angry with you while you live. Our brethren, the Laws in the other world, will receive you as an enemy because they will know you have done your best to destroy us. Listen, then, to us and not to Crito."

This is the voice which I seem to hear murmuring in my ears, like the sound of a divine flute in the ears of the mystic. That voice, I say, is humming in my ears and prevents me from hearing any other. I know anything more which you may say will be useless. Yet speak, if you have anything to say.

Cr: I have nothing to say, Socrates.

Soc: Then let me follow what seems to be the will of the gods.

CRITICAL QUESTIONS

1. Socrates asserts that "the really important thing is not to live, but to live well." Do you agree? Why, or why not?

2. Assume you are Crito. Offer Socrates your best argument for escaping that does not cause him to violate his principles.

3. Do you think the government is, as Socrates asserts, like your parents? Why?

4. Does living in a country amount to a tacit promise on your part to obey all its laws? Why, or why not?

5. What do you think Socrates should do and why?

5.6 CIVIL DISOBEDIENCE

Are there times when disobeying the law is morally justified? What are the responsibilities of a citizen? The dialogue *Crito* raised these issues, but in one way or another we have been asking these questions whenever the issue of governmental authority has arisen. The issue of civil disobedience also raises fundamental questions about the rule of law. Why do we need laws?

A case against the rule of law might go something like this: Laws limit human freedom and hinder spontaneity; they are sometimes unfair and repressive; common sense, social custom, and religion already provide enough guidance; and morality can never be legislated.

Many of course believe that the rule of law is both good and necessary. Laws protect people, create social stability, and provide opportunities to develop rights that people might not otherwise enjoy. The rights to life, liberty, and the pursuit of happiness need to be protected and defined by laws. In pluralistic societies, we cannot depend on customs and traditions to unite people. Nor can we depend on the virtue and goodwill of our leaders.

Only the rule of law can prevent abuse of power, but how can we tell the difference between good laws and bad laws? Are there minimal conditions for good laws? We might argue that good laws guarantee access to the resources necessary to live, provide for enforcement of contracts, and give security from violence. Such laws should be fairly enforced, adjudicated in courts free from prejudice, provide for due process, and be free from vagueness and ambiguity. Should we also add that the right of civil disobedience be granted, or would such a right undermine entirely the rule of law?

Civil disobedience has played and continues to play a major role in effecting political and legal change. In the nineteenth century, Henry David Thoreau went to jail for refusing to pay taxes to a government that supported slavery. He argued that conscience constitutes a higher law than the law of any land. We all have a moral duty to obey our consciences, but how many of us are willing to pay the legal penalty for disobeying the law?

Civil disobedience became a political strategy in many nations in the twentieth century. Gandhi used it to liberate India from British colonial rule. He carried a copy of Thoreau's *On Civil Disobedience* with him and used it as a blueprint for nonviolent resistance. Nelson Mandela used civil disobedience to change the apartheid system of South Africa. But when does civil disobedience become political revolution? When violence is used? Must one be willing to suffer the consequences of breaking the law in order to engage in a morally justifiable act of civil disobedience? Is *uncivil* disobedience morally justified? What makes disobedience civil rather than uncivil?

Martin Luther King, Jr. (1929–1968), a Baptist minister and winner of the Nobel Peace Prize, devoted his life to the struggle for racial justice in the United States. Like Thoreau and Gandhi, he argued for nonviolent methods. As a result, he found himself opposing those African Americans who would not renounce the use of violence.

A year before he won the Nobel Peace Prize and five years before his death from an assassin's bullet in Memphis, Tennessee, King served a sentence in the Birmingham, Alabama, jail for participating in a civil rights demonstration. Eight prominent Alabama clergy wrote an open letter critical of King's methods. In his famous "Letter from Birmingham Jail," King responded to their criticisms and, in the process, wrote a moving justification of civil disobedience.

◉ READING QUESTIONS

1. What does King mean when he says, "injustice anywhere is a threat to justice everywhere"?
2. What are the differences between unjust laws and just laws?
3. Under what conditions is it permissible to break the law?
4. According to King, what is the purpose of law and order?
5. What is the proper role of the Christian Church with respect to issues of social justice?

Letter from Birmingham Jail

MARTIN LUTHER KING, JR.

My dear fellow clergymen,

While confined here in the Birmingham city jail, I came across your recent statement calling our present activities "unwise and untimely." Seldom, if ever, do I pause to answer criticism of my work and ideas. If I sought to answer all of the criticisms that cross my desk, my secretaries would be engaged in little else in the course of the day, and I would have no time for constructive work. But since I feel that you are men of genuine good will and your criticisms are sincerely set forth, I would like to answer your statement in what I hope will be patient and reasonable terms.

I think I should give the reason for my being in Birmingham, since you have been influenced by the argument of "outsiders coming in." I have the honor of serving as president of the Southern Christian Leadership Conference, an organization operating in every southern state, with headquarters in Atlanta, Georgia. We have some 85 affiliate organizations all across the South—one being the Alabama Christian Movement for Human Rights. Whenever necessary and possible we share staff, educational and financial resources with our affiliates. Several months ago our local affiliate here in Birmingham invited us to be on call to engage in a nonviolent direct-action program if such were deemed necessary. We readily consented and when the hour came we lived up to our promises.

So I am here, along with several members of my staff, because we were invited here. I am here because I have basic organizational ties here.

Beyond this, I am in Birmingham because injustice is here. Just as the eighth century prophets left their little villages and carried their "thus saith the Lord" far beyond the boundaries of their hometowns; and just as the Apostle Paul left his little village of Tarsus and carried the gospel of Jesus Christ to practically every hamlet and city of the Graeco-Roman world, I too am compelled to carry the gospel of freedom beyond my particular hometown. Like Paul, I must constantly respond to the Macedonian call for aid.

Moreover, I am cognizant of the interrelatedness of all communities and states. I cannot sit idly by in Atlanta and not be concerned about what happens in Birmingham. Injustice anywhere is a threat to justice everywhere. We are caught in an inescapable network of mutuality, tied in a single garment of destiny. Whatever affects one directly affects all indirectly. Never again can we afford to live with the narrow, provincial "outside agitator" idea. Anyone who lives in the United States can never be considered an outsider anywhere in this country.

You deplore the demonstrations that are presently taking place in Birmingham. But I am sorry that your statement did not express a similar concern for the conditions that brought the demonstrations into being. I am sure that each of you would want to go beyond the superficial social analyst who looks merely at effects, and does not grapple with underlying causes. I would not hesitate to say that it is unfortunate that so-called demonstrations are taking place in Birmingham at this time, but I would say in more emphatic terms that it is even more unfortunate that the white power structure of this city left the Negro community with no other alternative.

In any nonviolent campaign there are four basic steps: (1) collection of the facts to determine whether injustices are alive, (2) negotiation, (3) self-purification, and (4) direct action. We have gone through all of these steps in Birmingham. There can be no gainsaying of the fact that racial injustice engulfs this community.

Birmingham is probably the most thoroughly segregated city in the United States. Its ugly record of police brutality is known in every section of this country. Its unjust treatment of Negroes in the courts is a notorious reality. There have been more unsolved bombings of Negro homes and churches in Birmingham than any city in this nation. These are the hard, brutal and unbelievable facts. On the basis of these conditions Negro leaders sought to negotiate with the city fathers. But the political leaders consistently refused to engage in good faith negotiation.

Then came the opportunity last September to talk with some of the leaders of the economic community. In these negotiating sessions certain promises were made by the merchants—such as the promise to remove the humiliating racial signs from the stores. On the basis of these promises Rev. Shuttlesworth and the leaders of the Alabama Christian Movement for Human Rights agreed to call a moratorium on any type of demonstrations. As the weeks and months unfolded we realized that we were the victims of a broken promise. The signs remained. Like so many experiences of the past we were confronted with blasted hopes, and the dark shadow of a deep disappointment settled upon us. So we had no alternative except that of preparing for direct action, whereby we would present our very bodies as a means of laying our case before the

conscience of the local and national community. We were not unmindful of the difficulties involved. So we decided to go through a process of self-purification. We started having workshops on nonviolence and repeatedly asked ourselves the questions, "Are you able to accept blows without retaliating?" "Are you able to endure the ordeals of jail?" We decided to set our direct-action program around the Easter season, realizing that with the exception of Christmas, this was the largest shopping period of the year. Knowing that a strong economic withdrawal program would be the by-product of direct action, we felt that this was the best time to bring pressure on the merchants for the needed changes. Then it occurred to us that the March election was ahead and so we speedily decided to postpone action until after election day. When we discovered that Mr. Connor was in the run-off, we decided again to postpone action so that the demonstrations could not be used to cloud the issues. At this time we agreed to begin our nonviolent witness the day after the run-off.

This reveals that we did not move irresponsibly into direct action. We, too, wanted to see Mr. Connor defeated; so we went through postponement after postponement to aid in this community need. After this we felt that direct action could be delayed no longer.

You may well ask, "Why direct action? Why sit-ins, marches, etc.? Isn't negotiation a better path?" You are exactly right in your call for negotiation. Indeed, this is the purpose of direct action. Nonviolent direct action seeks to create such a crisis and establish such creative tension that a community that has constantly refused to negotiate is forced to confront the issue. It seeks so to dramatize the issue that it can no longer be ignored. I just referred to the creation of tension as a part of the work of the nonviolent resister. This may sound rather shocking. But I must confess that I am not afraid of the word tension. I have earnestly worked and preached against violent tension, but there is a type of constructive nonviolent tension that is necessary for growth. Just as Socrates felt that it was necessary to create a tension in the mind so that individuals could rise from the bondage of myths and half-truths to the unfettered realm of creative analysis and objective appraisal, we must see the need of having nonviolent gadflies to create the kind of tension in society that will help men to rise from the dark depths of prejudice and racism to the majestic heights of understanding and brotherhood. So the purpose of the direct action is to create a situation so crisis-packed that it will inevitably open the door to negotiation. We, therefore, concur with you in your call for negotiation. Too long has our beloved Southland been bogged down in the tragic attempt to live in monologue rather than dialogue.

One of the basic points in your statement is that our acts are untimely. Some have asked, "Why didn't you give the new administration time to act?" The only answer that I can give to this inquiry is that the new administration must be prodded about as much as the outgoing one before it acts. We will be sadly mistaken if we feel that the election of Mr. Boutwell will bring the millennium to Birmingham. While Mr. Boutwell is much more articulate and gentle than Mr. Connor, they are both segregationists, dedicated to the task of maintaining the status quo. The hope I see in Mr. Boutwell is that he will be reasonable enough to see the futility of massive resistance to desegregation. But he will not see this without pressure from the devotees of civil rights. My friends, I must say to you that we have not made a single gain in civil rights without determined legal and nonviolent pressure. History is the long and tragic story of the fact that privileged groups seldom give up their privileges voluntarily. Individuals may see the moral light and voluntarily give up their unjust posture; but as Reinhold Niebuhr has reminded us, groups are more immoral than individuals.

We know through painful experience that freedom is never voluntarily given by the oppressor; it must be demanded by the oppressed. Frankly, I have never yet engaged in a direct action movement that was "well-timed," according to the timetable of those who have not suffered unduly from the disease of segregation. For years now I have heard the words "Wait!" It rings in the ear of every Negro with a piercing familiarity. This "Wait" has almost always meant "Never." It has been a tranquilizing thalidomide,

relieving the emotional stress for a moment, only to give birth to an ill-formed infant of frustration. We must come to see with the distinguished jurist of yesterday that "justice too long delayed is justice denied." We have waited for more than 340 years for our constitutional and God-given rights. The nations of Asia and Africa are moving with jetlike speed toward the goal of political independence, and we still creep at horse and buggy pace toward the gaining of a cup of coffee at a lunch counter. I guess it is easy for those who have never felt the stinging darts of segregation to say, "Wait." But when you have seen vicious mobs lynch your mothers and fathers at will and drown your sisters and brothers at whim; when you have seen hate-filled policemen curse, kick, brutalize and even kill your black brothers and sisters with impunity; when you see the vast majority of your twenty million Negro brothers smothering in an airtight cage of poverty in the midst of an affluent society; when you suddenly find your tongue twisted and your speech stammering as you seek to explain to your six-year-old daughter why she can't go to the public amusement park that has just been advertised on television, and see tears welling up in her little eyes when she is told that Funtown is closed to colored children, and see the depressing clouds of inferiority begin to form in her little mental sky, and see her begin to distort her little personality by unconsciously developing a bitterness toward white people; when you have to concoct an answer for a five-year-old son asking in agonizing pathos: "Daddy, why do white people treat colored people so mean?"; when you take a cross-country drive and find it necessary to sleep night after night in the uncomfortable corners of your automobile because no motel will accept you; when you are humiliated day in and day out by nagging signs reading "white" and "colored"; when your first name becomes "nigger" and your middle name becomes "boy" (however old you are) and your last name becomes "John," and when your wife and mother are never given the respected title "Mrs."; when you are harried by day and haunted by night by the fact that you are a Negro, living constantly at tiptoe stance never quite knowing what to expect next, and plagued with inner fears and outer resentments; when you are forever fighting a degenerating sense of "nobodiness"; then you will understand why we find it difficult to wait. There comes a time when the cup of endurance runs over, and men are no longer willing to be plunged into an abyss of injustice where they experience the blackness of corroding despair. I hope, sirs, you can understand our legitimate and unavoidable impatience.

You express a great deal of anxiety over our willingness to break laws. This is certainly a legitimate concern. Since we so diligently urge people to obey the Supreme Court's decision of 1954 outlawing segregation in the public schools, it is rather strange and paradoxical to find us consciously breaking laws. One may well ask, "How can you advocate breaking some laws and obeying others?" The answer is found in the fact that there are two types of laws: there are *just* and there are *unjust* laws. I would agree with Saint Augustine that "An unjust law is no law at all."

Now what is the difference between the two? How does one determine when a law is just or unjust? A just law is a man-made code that squares with the moral law or the law of God. An unjust law is a code that is out of harmony with the moral law. To put it in the terms of Saint Thomas Aquinas, an unjust law is a human law that is not rooted in eternal and natural law. Any law that uplifts human personality is just. Any law that degrades human personality is unjust. All segregation statutes are unjust because segregation distorts the soul and damages the personality. It gives the segregator a false sense of superiority, and the segregated a false sense of inferiority. To use the words of Martin Buber, the great Jewish philosopher, segregation substitutes an "I–it" relationship for the "I–thou" relationship, and ends up relegating persons to the status of things. So segregation is not only politically, economically and sociologically unsound, but it is morally wrong and sinful. Paul Tillich has said that sin is separation. Isn't segregation an existential expression of man's tragic separation, an expression of his awful estrangement, his terrible sinfulness? So I can urge men to disobey segregation ordinances because they are morally wrong.

Let us turn to a more concrete example of just and unjust laws. An unjust law is a code that a majority inflicts on a minority that is not binding on itself. This is difference made legal. On the other hand a just law is a code that a majority compels a minority to follow that it is willing to follow itself. This is sameness made legal.

Let me give another explanation. An unjust law is a code inflicted upon a minority which that minority had no part in enacting or creating because they did not have the unhampered right to vote. Who can say that the legislature of Alabama which set up the segregation laws was democratically elected? Throughout the state of Alabama all types of conniving methods are used to prevent Negroes from becoming registered voters and there are some counties without a single Negro registered to vote despite the fact that the Negro constitutes a majority of the population. Can any law set up in such a state be considered democratically structured?

These are just a few examples of unjust and just laws. There are some instances when a law is just on its face and unjust in its application. For instance, I was arrested Friday on a charge of parading without a permit. Now there is nothing wrong with an ordinance which requires a permit for a parade, but when the ordinance is used to preserve segregation and to deny citizens the First Amendment privilege of peaceful assembly and peaceful protest, then it becomes unjust.

I hope you can see the distinction I am trying to point out. In no sense do I advocate evading or defying the law as the rabid segregationist would do. This would lead to anarchy. One who breaks an unjust law must do it *openly, lovingly* (not hatefully as the white mothers did in New Orleans when they were seen on television screaming, "nigger, nigger, nigger"), and with a willingness to accept the penalty. I submit that an individual who breaks a law that conscience tells him is unjust, and willingly accepts the penalty by staying in jail to arouse the conscience of the community over its injustice, is in reality expressing the very highest respect for law.

Of course, there is nothing new about this kind of civil disobedience. It was seen sublimely in the refusal of Shadrach, Meshach and

Abednego to obey the laws of Nebuchadnezzar because a higher moral law was involved. It was practiced superbly by the early Christians who were willing to face hungry lions and the excruciating pain of chopping blocks, before submitting to certain unjust laws of the Roman Empire. To a degree academic freedom is a reality today because Socrates practiced civil disobedience.

We can never forget that everything Hitler did in Germany was "legal" and everything the Hungarian freedom fighters did in Hungary was "illegal." It was "illegal" to aid and comfort a Jew in Hitler's Germany. But I am sure that if I had lived in Germany during that time I would have aided and comforted my Jewish brothers even though it was illegal. If I lived in a Communist country today where certain principles dear to the Christian faith are suppressed, I believe I would openly advocate disobeying these antireligious laws. I must make two honest confessions to you, my Christian and Jewish brothers. First, I must confess that over the last few years I have been gravely disappointed with the white moderate. I have almost reached the regrettable conclusion that the Negro's great stumbling block in the stride toward freedom is not the White Citizen's Counciler or the Ku Klux Klanner, but the white moderate who is more devoted to "order" than to justice; who prefers a negative peace which is the absence of tension to a positive peace which is the presence of justice; who constantly says, "I agree with you in the goal you seek, but I can't agree with your methods of direct action"; who paternalistically feels that he can set the timetable for another man's freedom; who lives by the myth of time and who constantly advised the Negro to wait until a "more convenient season." Shallow understanding from people of good will is more frustrating than absolute misunderstanding from people of ill will. Lukewarm acceptance is much more bewildering than outright rejection.

I had hoped that the white moderate would understand that law and order exist for the purpose of establishing justice, and that when they fail to do this they become dangerously structured dams that block the flow of social progress. I had hoped that the white moderate would understand that the present tension of the South is merely a necessary phase of the transition from an obnoxious negative peace, where the Negro passively accepted his unjust plight, to a substance-filled positive peace, where all men will respect the dignity and worth of human personality. Actually, we who engage in nonviolent direct action are not the creators of tension. We merely bring to the surface the hidden tension that is already alive. We bring it out in the open where it can be seen and dealt with. Like a boil that can never be cured as long as it is covered up but must be opened with all its pus-flowing ugliness to the natural medicines of air and light, injustice must likewise be exposed, with all of the tension its exposing creates, to the light of human conscience and the air of national opinion before it can be cured.

In your statement you asserted that our actions, even though peaceful, must be condemned because they precipitate violence. But can this assertion be logically made? Isn't this like condemning the robbed man because his possession of money precipitated the evil act of robbery? Isn't this like condemning Socrates because his unswerving commitment to truth and his philosophical delvings precipitated the misguided popular mind to make him drink the hemlock? Isn't this like condemning Jesus because His unique God-consciousness and never-ceasing devotion to His will precipitated the evil act of crucifixion? We must come to see, as federal courts have consistently affirmed, that it is immoral to urge an individual to withdraw his efforts to gain his basic constitutional rights because the quest precipitates violence. Society must protect the robbed and punish the robber.

I had also hoped that the white moderate would reject the myth of time. I received a letter this morning from a white brother in Texas which said: "All Christians know that the colored people will receive equal rights eventually, but it is possible that you are in too great of a religious hurry. It has taken Christianity almost two thousand years to accomplish what it has. The teachings of Christ take time to come to earth." All that is said here grows out of a tragic misconception of time. It is the strangely irrational notion that there is something in the very flow of time that will inevitably cure all ills. Actually time is neutral. It can be used either destructively or constructively. I am coming to feel that the people of ill will have used time much more effectively than the people of good will. We will have to repent in this generation not merely for the vitriolic words and actions of the bad people, but for the appalling silence of the good people. We must come to see that human progress never rolls in on wheels of inevitability. It comes through the tireless efforts and persistent work of men willing to be co-workers with God, and without this hard work time itself becomes an ally of the forces of social stagnation. We must use time creatively, and forever realize that the time is always ripe to do right. Now is the time to make real the promise of democracy, and transform our pending national elegy into a creative psalm of brotherhood. Now is the time to lift our national policy from the quicksand of racial injustice to the solid rock of human dignity.

You spoke of our activity in Birmingham as extreme. At first I was rather disappointed that fellow clergymen would see my nonviolent efforts as those of the extremist. I started thinking about the fact that I stand in the middle of two opposing forces in the Negro community. One is a force of complacency made up of Negroes who, as a result of long years of oppression, have been so completely drained of self-respect and a sense of "somebodiness" that they have adjusted to segregation, and, of a few Negroes in the middle class who, because of a degree of academic and economic security, and because at points they profit by segregation, have unconsciously become insensitive to the problems of the masses. The other force is one of bitterness and hatred, and comes perilously close to advocating violence. It is expressed in the various black nationalist groups that are springing up over the nation, the largest and best known being Elijah Muhammad's Muslim movement. This movement is nourished by the contemporary frustration over the continued existence of racial discrimination. It is made up of people who have lost faith in America, who have absolutely repudiated Christianity, and who have concluded that the white man is an incurable "devil." I have tried to stand between these two forces, saying that we need not follow the

"do-nothingism" of the complacent or the hatred and despair of the black nationalist. There is the more excellent way of love and nonviolent protest. I'm grateful to God that, through the Negro church, the dimension of nonviolence entered our struggle. If this philosophy had not emerged, I am convinced that by now many streets of the South would be flowing with floods of blood. And I am further convinced that if our white brothers dismiss us as "rabble-rousers" and "outside agitators" those of us who are working through the channels of nonviolent direct action and refuse to support our non-violent efforts, millions of Negroes, out of frustration and despair, will seek solace and security in black nationalist ideologies, a development that will lead inevitably to a frightening racial nightmare.

Oppressed people cannot remain oppressed forever. The urge for freedom will eventually come. This is what happened to the American Negro. Something within has reminded him of his birthright of freedom; something without has reminded him that he can gain it. Consciously and unconsciously, he has been swept in by what the Germans call the *Zeitgeist*, and with his black brothers of Africa, and his brown and yellow brothers of Asia, South America and the Caribbean, he is moving with a sense of cosmic urgency toward the promised land of racial justice. Recognizing this vital urge that has engulfed the Negro community, one should readily understand public demonstrations. The Negro has many pent-up resentments and latent frustrations. He has to get them out. So let him march sometime; let him have his prayer pilgrimages to the city hall; understand why he must have sit-ins and freedom rides. If his repressed emotions do not come out in these nonviolent ways, they will come out in ominous expressions of violence. This is not a threat; it is a fact of history. So I have not said to my people "get rid of your discontent." But I have tried to say that this normal and healthy discontent can be channelized through the creative outlet of nonviolent direct action. Now this approach is being dismissed as extremist. I must admit that I was initially disappointed in being so categorized.

But as I continued to think about the matter, I gradually gained a bit of satisfaction from being considered an extremist. Was not Jesus an extremist in love—"Love your enemies, bless them that curse you, pray for them that despitefully use you." Was not Amos an extremist for justice—"Let justice roll down like waters and righteousness like a mighty stream." Was not Paul an extremist for the gospel of Jesus Christ—"I bear in my body the marks of the Lord Jesus." Was not Martin Luther an extremist—"Here I stand; I can do none other so help me God." Was not John Bunyan an extremist—"I will stay in jail to the end of my days before I make a butchery of my conscience." Was not Abraham Lincoln an extremist—"This nation cannot survive half slave and half free." Was not Thomas Jefferson an extremist—"We hold these truths to be self-evident, that all men are created equal." So the question is not whether we will be extremist but what kind of extremist will we be. Will we be extremists for hate or will we be extremists for love? Will we be extremists for the preservation of injustice—or will we be extremists for the cause of justice? In that dramatic scene on Calvary's hill, three men were crucified. We must not forget that all three were crucified for the same crime—the crime of extremism. Two were extremists for immorality, and thusly fell below their environment. The other, Jesus Christ, was an extremist for love, truth and goodness, and thereby rose above his environment. So, after all, maybe the South, the nation and the world are in dire need of creative extremists.

I had hoped that the white moderate would see this. Maybe I was too optimistic. Maybe I expected too much. I guess I should have realized that few members of a race that has oppressed another race can understand or appreciate the deep groans and passionate yearnings of those that have been oppressed and still fewer have the vision to see that injustice must be rooted out by strong, persistent and determined action. I am thankful, however, that some of our white brothers have grasped the meaning of this social revolution and committed themselves to it. They are still all too small in quantity, but they are big in quality. Some like Ralph McGill, Lillian Smith, Harry Golden and James Dabbs have written about our struggle in eloquent, prophetic and understanding terms. Others have marched with us down nameless streets of the South. They have languished in filthy roach-infested jails, suffering the abuse and brutality of angry policemen who see them as "dirty nigger-lovers." They, unlike so many of their moderate brothers and sisters, have recognized the urgency of the moment and sensed the need for powerful "action" antidotes to combat the disease of segregation.

Let me rush on to mention my other disappointment. I have been so greatly disappointed with the white church and its leadership. Of course, there are some notable exceptions. I am not unmindful of the fact that each of you has taken some significant stands on this issue. I commend you, Rev. Stallings, for your Christian stance on this past Sunday, in welcoming Negroes to your worship service on a non-segregated basis. I commend the Catholic leaders of this state for integrating Springhill College several years ago.

But despite these notable exceptions I must honestly reiterate that I have been disappointed with the church. I do not say that as one of the negative critics who can always find something wrong with the church. I say it as a minister of the gospel, who loves the church; who was nurtured in its bosom; who has been sustained by its spiritual blessings and who will remain true to it as long as the cord of life shall lengthen.

I had the strange feeling when I was suddenly catapulted into the leadership of the bus protest in Montgomery several years ago that we would have the support of the white church. I felt that the white ministers, priests and rabbis of the South would be some of our strongest allies. Instead, some have been outright opponents, refusing to understand the freedom movement and misrepresenting its leaders; all too many others have been more cautious than courageous and have remained silent behind the anesthetizing security of the stained-glass windows.

In spite of my shattered dreams of the past, I came to Birmingham with the hope that the white religious leadership of this community would see the justice of our cause, and with deep moral concern, serve as the channel through which our just grievances would get to the power structure. I had hoped that each of you would understand. But again I have been disappointed. I have heard numerous religious leaders of the South call upon their worshippers to comply with a desegregation decision because it is the *law*, but I have longed to hear white ministers say, "Follow this decree because integration is morally *right* and the Negro is your brother." In the midst of blatant injustices inflicted upon the Negro, I have watched white churches stand on the sideline and merely mouth pious irrelevancies and sanctimonious trivialities. In the midst of a mighty struggle to rid our nation of racial and economic injustice, I have heard so many ministers say, "Those are social issues with which the gospel has no real concern," and I have watched so many churches commit themselves to a completely otherworldly religion which made a strange distinction between body and soul, the sacred and the secular.

So here we are moving toward the exit of the twentieth century with a religious community largely adjusted to the status quo, standing as a tail-light behind other community agencies rather than a headlight leading men to higher levels of justice.

I have traveled the length and breadth of Alabama, Mississippi and all the other southern states. On sweltering summer days and crisp autumn mornings I have looked at her beautiful churches with their lofty spires pointing heavenward. I have beheld the impressive outlay of her massive religious education buildings. Over and over again I have found myself asking: "What kind of people worship here? Who is their God? Where were their voices when the lips of Governor Barnett dripped with words of interposition and nullification? Where were they when Governor Wallace gave the clarion call for defiance and hatred? Where were their voices of support when tired, bruised and weary Negro men and women decided to rise from the dark dungeons of complacency to the bright hills of creative protest?"

Yes, these questions are still in my mind. In deep disappointment, I have wept over the laxity of the church. But be assured that my tears have been tears of love. There can be no deep disappointment where there is not deep love. Yes, I love the church; I love her sacred walls. How could I do otherwise? I am in the rather unique position of being the son, the grandson and the great-grandson of preachers. Yes, I see the church as the body of Christ. But, oh! How we have blemished and scarred that body through social neglect and fear of being nonconformists.

There was a time when the church was very powerful. It was during that period when the early Christians rejoiced when they were deemed worthy to suffer for what they believed. In those days the church was not merely a thermometer that recorded the ideas and principles of popular opinion; it was a thermostat that transformed the mores of society. Wherever the early Christians entered a town the power structure got disturbed and immediately sought to convict them for being "disturbers of the peace" and "outside agitators." But they went on with the conviction that they were "a colony of heaven," and had to obey God rather than man. They were small in number but big in commitment. They were too God-intoxicated to be "astronomically intimidated." They brought an end to such ancient evils as infanticide and gladiatorial contest.

Things are different now. The contemporary church is often a weak, ineffectual voice with an uncertain sound. It is so often the arch-supporter of the status quo. Far from being disturbed by the presence of the church, the power structure of the average community is consoled by the church's silent and often vocal sanction of things as they are.

But the judgment of God is upon the church as never before. If the church of today does not recapture the sacrificial spirit of the early church, it will lose its authentic ring, forfeit the loyalty of millions, and be dismissed as an irrelevant social club with no meaning for the twentieth century. I am meeting young people every day whose disappointment with the church has risen to outright disgust.

Maybe again, I have been too optimistic. Is organized religion too inextricably bound to the status quo to save our nation and the world? Maybe I must turn my faith to the inner spiritual church, the church within the church, as the true *ecclesia* and the hope of the world. But again I am thankful to God that some noble souls from the ranks of organized religion have broken loose from the paralyzing chains of conformity and joined us as active partners in the struggle for freedom. They have left their secure congregations and walked the streets of Albany, Georgia, with us. They have gone through the highways of the South on tortuous rides for freedom. Yes, they have gone to jail with us. Some have been kicked out of their churches, and lost support of their bishops and fellow ministers. But they have gone with the faith that right defeated is stronger than evil triumphant. These men have been the leaven in the lump of the race. Their witness has been the spiritual salt that has preserved the true meaning of the gospel in these troubled times. They have carved a tunnel of hope through the dark mountain of disappointment.

I hope the church as a whole will meet the challenge of this decisive hour. But even if the church does not come to the aid of justice, I have no despair about the future. I have no fear about the outcome of our struggle in Birmingham, even if our motives are presently misunderstood. We will reach the goal of freedom in Birmingham and all over the nation, because the goal of America is freedom. Abused and scorned though we may be, our destiny is tied up with the destiny of America. Before the Pilgrims landed at Plymouth, we were here. Before the pen of Jefferson etched across the pages of history the majestic words of the Declaration of Independence, we were here. For more than two centuries our fore-parents labored in this country without wages; they made cotton king; and they built the homes of their masters in the midst of brutal injustice and shameful humiliation—and yet out of a bottomless vitality they continued to thrive and develop. If the inexpressible cruelties of slavery could not stop us, the opposition we now face will surely fail. We will win our freedom because the sacred heritage of our nation and the eternal will of God are embodied in our echoing demands.

I must close now. But before closing I am impelled to mention one other point in your statement that troubled me profoundly. You warmly commended the Birmingham police force for keeping "order" and "preventing violence." I don't believe you would have so warmly commended the police force if you had seen its angry violent dogs literally biting six unarmed, nonviolent Negroes. I don't believe you would so quickly commend the policemen if you would observe their ugly and inhuman treatment of Negroes here in the city jail; if you would watch them push and curse old Negro women and young Negro girls; if you would see them slap and kick old Negro men and young boys; if you will observe them, as they did on two occasions, refuse to give us food because we wanted to sing our grace together. I'm sorry that I can't join you in your praise for the police department.

It is true that they have been rather disciplined in their public handling of the demonstrators. In this sense they have been rather publicly "nonviolent." But for what purpose? To preserve the evil system of segregation. Over the last few years I have consistently preached that nonviolence demands that the means we use must be as pure as the ends we seek. So I have tried to make it clear that it is wrong to use immoral means to attain moral ends. But now I must affirm that it is just as wrong, or even more so, to use moral means to preserve immoral ends. Maybe Mr. Connor and his policemen have been rather publicly nonviolent, as Chief Pritchett was in Albany, Georgia, but they have used the moral means of nonviolence to maintain the immoral end of flagrant racial injustice. T. S. Eliot has said that there is no greater treason than to do the right deed for the wrong reason.

I wish you had commended the Negro sit-inners and demonstrators of Birmingham for their sublime courage, their willingness to suffer and their amazing discipline in the midst of the most inhuman provocation. One day the South will recognize its real heroes. They will be the James Merediths, courageously and with a majestic sense of purpose facing jeering and hostile mobs and the agonizing loneliness that characterizes the life of the pioneer. They will be old, oppressed, battered Negro women, symbolized in a seventy-two-year-old woman of Montgomery, Alabama, who rose up with a sense of dignity and with her people decided not to ride the segregated buses, and responded to one who inquired about her tiredness with ungrammatical profundity: "My feet is tired, but my soul is rested." They will be the young high school and college students, young ministers of the gospel and a host of their elders courageously and nonviolently sitting-in at lunch counters and willingly going to jail for conscience's sake. One day the South will know that when these disinherited children of God sat down at lunch counters they were in reality standing up for the best in the American dream and the most sacred values in our Judeo-Christian heritage, and thusly, carrying our whole nation back to those great wells of democracy which were dug deep by the Founding Fathers in the formulation of the Constitution and the Declaration of Independence.

Never before have I written a letter this long (or should I say a book?). I'm afraid that it is much too long to take your precious time. I can assure you that it would have been much shorter if I had been writing from a comfortable desk, but what else is there to do when you are alone for days in the dull monotony of a narrow jail cell other than write long letters, think strange thoughts, and pray long prayers?

If I have said anything in this letter that is an overstatement of the truth and is indicative of an unreasonable impatience, I beg you to forgive me. If I have said anything in this letter that is an understatement of the truth and is indicative of my having a patience that makes me patient with anything less than brotherhood, I beg God to forgive me.

I hope this letter finds you strong in the faith. I also hope that circumstances will soon make it possible for me to meet each of you, not as an integrationist or a civil rights leader, but as a fellow clergyman and a Christian brother. Let us all hope that the dark clouds of racial prejudice will soon pass away and the deep fog of misunderstanding will be lifted from our fear-drenched communities and in some not too distant tomorrow the radiant stars of love and brotherhood will shine over our great nation with all of their scintillating beauty.

Yours for the cause of Peace and Brotherhood,

Martin Luther King, Jr.

⊚ CRITICAL QUESTIONS

1. Write a brief letter in response to King from the point of view of the clergy who originally criticized him.

2. How do you think King would answer the question, "What makes a society just?" Compare his answer to Marx and Engels' views of justice. Clearly state the differences and similarities.

5.7 GOD IS RED

Have you ever wondered why oppression exists? Have you wondered how oppression might be eliminated? Surely one of the features of societies that make them unjust is the existence of oppression. Oppression can take many forms: economic, racial, sexual. The rich dominate the poor and get richer at their expense. In the United States and elsewhere, whites discriminate against blacks. Men limit the opportunities for women. Gays and lesbians are denied the rights and opportunities others enjoy. Native Americans have suffered near extinction and cultural destruction at the hands of the European invaders and their descendants. Mexican Americans have been brutally exploited as farm laborers, and prevented, until recently, from gaining any significant political power. Unfortunately, I could go on and on recounting example after example.

Oppressors need to justify their position, and so they convince themselves that those whom they oppress are inferior, immoral, heathen, lazy, stupid, dirty, or somehow deserving of their lot in life. In effect, they dehumanize the oppressed while keeping for themselves the image of full humanity. For example, during the westward expansion in the United States, it was often said that "The only good Indian is a dead Indian."

Oppressors also need to justify their positions by legal means. If what one does is immoral, that fact can be disguised by making it appear legal. An obvious example is the many treaties the United States entered into with the native population only to later break them or fail to enforce them on the pretense of some legal technicality. A less obvious example is the way in which courts interpret the meaning and application of laws to the detriment of Native Americans.

In the selection that follows, Vine Deloria (1933–2005) a prominent and influential Native American philosopher (Yankton Sioux), shows how the First Amendment guaranteeing freedom of religion to all Americans has been applied to some Native American cases based on ignorance of what counts as "religion" for Indians and on prejudices. The result has been injustice, which continues to the present day.

It is difficult to see how a society can be just if it cannot adequately ensure religious freedom for its citizens. The First Amendment was designed to prevent the government from imposing one particular sectarian religious viewpoint on all Americans. However, Christianity has come to shape and pervade American society. This has led to a tendency to understand and judge all forms of spiritual expression by comparison, implicit or explicit, to Christianity.

⊚ READING QUESTIONS

1. What does Deloria find most troubling about the Supreme Court's decision in *Lyng v. Northwest Indian Cemetery Association*?
2. What is the "great gulf" between Western thinking about religion and the Indian perspective on religion?
3. What are the first two types of sacred places, and what is the main difference between them?
4. Why does Deloria think that non-Indians cannot understand the sense of relatedness to the land and animals that Indians have?
5. How does Deloria counter the argument of those who deliberately violate holy places and then claim that the lack of ill effects proves such places are not really sacred?
6. Summarize the main thrust of Deloria's argument in your own words.

Sacred Places and Moral Responsibility

VINE DELORIA, JR.

When the tribes were forced from their aboriginal homelands and confined to small reservations, many of the tribal religious rituals were prohibited by the BIA in the 1870s and 1880s because of an inordinately large number of Christian zealots as Indian agents. We read … how traditional people had to adopt various subterfuges so that their religious life could be continued. Some tribes shifted their ceremonial year to coincide with the whites' holidays and conducted their most important rituals on national holidays and Christian feast days, explaining to curious whites that they were simply honoring George Washington and celebrating Christmas and Easter. Many shrines and holy places were located far away from the new reservation homelands, but because they were not being exploited economically or used by settlers, it was not difficult for small parties of people

From Vine Deloria, Jr., *God is Red: A Native American View of Religions* (Golden, CO: Fulcrum Publishing, 1994), pp. 159–161, 267–282. Copyright © 1994 Vine Deloria. Jr.

to go into the mountains or to remote lakes and buttes and conduct ceremonies without interference from non-Indians.

Since World War II, this situation has changed dramatically. We have seen a greatly expanding national population, the introduction of corporate farming practices that have placed formerly submarginal lands under cultivation, more extensive mining and timber industry activities, and a greatly expanded recreation industry—all of which have severely impacted the use of public lands in the United States. Few rural areas now enjoy the isolation of half a century ago, and as multiple use of lands increased, many of the sacred sites that were on public lands were threatened by visitors and subjected to new uses. Tribal religious leaders were often able to work out informal arrangements with federal and state agencies to allow them access to these places for religious purposes. But as the personnel changed in state and federal agencies, a new generation of bureaucrats, catering to developers, recreation interest, and the well-established economic groups who have always used public lands for a pittance, began to restrict Indian access to sacred sites by establishing increasingly narrow rules and regulations for managing public lands.

In 1978, in a symbolic effort to clarify the status of traditional religious practices and practitioners, Congress passed a Joint Resolution entitled the American Indian Religious Freedom Act. This act declared that it was the policy of Congress to protect and preserve the inherent right of American Indians to believe, express, and practice their traditional religions. The resolution identified the problem as one of a "lack of knowledge or the insensitive and inflexible enforcement of Federal policies and regulations." Section 2 of the resolution directed the president to require the various federal departments to evaluate their policies and procedures, report back to Congress on the results of their survey, and make recommendations for legislative actions.[1]

Many people assumed that this resolution clarified the federal attitude toward traditional religions, and it began to be cited in litigation involving the construction of dams, roads, and the management of federal lands. Almost unanimously, however, the federal courts have since ruled that the resolution did not protect or preserve the right of Indians to practice their religion and conduct ceremonies at sacred sites on public lands.[2] Some courts even hinted darkly that any formal recognition of the existence of tribal practices would be tantamount to establishing a state religion,[3] an interpretation that, upon analysis, is a dreadful misreading of American history and the Constitution and may have been an effort to inflame anti-Indian feelings.

A good example for making this claim was the 1988 Supreme Court decision in the *Lyng v. Northwest Indian Cemetery Protective Association* case that involved protecting the visitation rights of the traditional religious leaders of three tribes to sacred sites in the Chemistry Rock area of the Six Rivers National Forest in Northern California. The Forest Service proposed to build a 6-mile paved road that would have opened part of the area to commercial logging. This area, known by three Indian tribes as the "High Country," was the center of their religious and ceremonial life. The lower federal courts prohibited the construction of the road on the grounds that it would have made religious ceremonial use of the area impossible. Before the Supreme Court could hear the appeal, Congress passed the California Wilderness Act that made the question of constructing the road moot for all practical purposes.

---

[1] 92 Stat 469, 42 U.S.C. §1996.

[2] See *Wilson v. Block*, 708 F 2d. 735 (D.C. Cir 1983). Hopi and Navajo sacred sites and shrines on San Francisco peak were destroyed by the U.S. Forest Service to make room for a new ski lift. In *Fools Crow v. Gullet*, 706 F. 2d 856 (8th Cir 1983) the court upheld intrusions by the U.S. Park Service on Sioux vision quest use of Bear Butte. In *Badoni v. Higginson*, 638 F. 2d. 172 (10th Cir 1980) the court allowed the destruction of a Navajo sacred site at Rainbow Bridge in the Grand Canyon area.

[3] The majority decision in *Lyng* even suggested that to recognize traditional Indian religious freedom would make it seem as if the Indians owned the federal lands.

No disrespect for these practices is implied when one notes that such beliefs could easily require de facto beneficial ownership of some rather spacious tracts of public property. Even without anticipating future cases, the diminution of the government's property rights, and the concomitant subsidy of the Indian religion, would in this case be far from trivial.... 108 S. Ct 1319, 1327 (1988).

But the Supreme Court insisted on hearing the appeal of the Forest Service and deciding the religious issues. It turned the tribes down flat, ruling that the Free Exercise clause did not prevent the government from using its property in any way it saw fit and in effect rolling back the religious use of the area completely.

Most troubling about the Supreme Court's decision was the insistence on analyzing tribal religions within the same conceptual frame work as western organized religions. Justice O'Connor observed, "A broad range of government activities—from social welfare programs to foreign aid to conservation projects—will always be considered essential to the spiritual well-being of some citizens, often on the basis of sincerely held religious beliefs. Others will find the very same activity deeply offensive, and perhaps incompatible with their own search for spiritual fulfillment and with the tenets of their religion."[4]

Thus, ceremonies and rituals that had been performed for thousands of years were treated as if they were popular fads or simply matters of personal preference based upon the erroneous assumption that religion was only a matter of individual aesthetic choice.

Justice Brennan's dissent vigorously attacked this spurious line of reasoning, outlining with some precision the communal aspect of the tribal religions and their relationship to the mountains. But his argument failed to gather support within the Court. Most observers of the Supreme Court were simply confounded at the majority's conclusion that suggested that destroying a religion "did not unduly burden it" and that no constitutional protections were available to the Indians.[5]

When informed of the meaning of this decision, most people have shown great sympathy for the traditional religious people. At the same time, they have had great difficulty understanding why it is so important that these ceremonies be held, that they be conducted only at certain locations, and that they be held in secrecy and privacy. This lack of understanding highlights the great gulf that exists between traditional Western thinking about religion and the Indian perspective. It is the difference between individual conscience and commitment (Western) and communal tradition (Indian), these views can only be reconciled by examining them in a much broader historical and geographical context.

Justice Brennan attempted to make this difference clear when he observed, "Although few tribal members actually made medicine at the most powerful sites, the entire tribe's welfare hinges on the success of individual practitioner."[6] More than that, however, the "world renewal" ceremonies conducted by the tribes were done on behalf of the earth and all forms of life. To describe these ceremonies as if they were comparable to Oral Roberts seeking funds or Jimmy Swaggart begging forgiveness for his continuing sexual misconduct or Justice O'Connor's matters of community aesthetic preference is to miss the point entirely. In effect, the Court declared that Indians cannot pray for the planet or for other people and other forms of life in the manner required by their religion.

Two contradictory responses seem to characterize the non-Indian attitudes toward traditional tribal religions. Some people want the traditional healers to share their religious beliefs in the same manner that priests, rabbis, and ministers expound publicly the tenets of their denominations. Other people feel that Indian ceremonials are simply remnants of primitive life and should be abandoned. Neither perspective understands that Indian tribes are communities in ways that are fundamentally different than other American communities and organizations. Tribal communities are wholly defined by the family relationships; the non-Indian communities are defined primarily

---

[4]At 1327.
[5]Justice Brennan's dissent makes this point specifically. The Court today, however, ignores *Roy's* emphasis on the internal nature of the government practice at issue there, and instead construes that case as further support for the proposition that governmental action that does not coerce conduct inconsistent with religious faith simply does not implicate the concerns of the Free Exercise Clause. That such a reading is wholly untenable, however, is demonstrated by the cruelly surreal result it produces here: *governmental action that will virtually destroy a religion is nevertheless deemed not to "burden" that region* (at 1337). (Emphasis added.)

---

[6]At 1332.

by residence, by an arbitrary establishment of political jurisdiction, or by agreement with generally applicable sets of intellectual beliefs.

Ceremonial and ritual knowledge is possessed by everyone in the Indian community, although only a few people may actually be chosen to perform these acts. Authorization to perform ceremonies comes from higher spiritual powers and not by certification through an institution or any formal organization.

A belief in the sacredness of lands in the non-Indian context may become the preferred belief of an individual or group of people based on their experiences or on an intensive study of preselected evidence. But this belief becomes the subject of intense criticism and does not, except under unusual circumstances, become an operative principle in the life and behavior of the non-Indian group. The same belief, when seen in the Indian context, is an integral part of the experiences of the people—past, present, and future. The idea does not become a bone of contention among the people for even if someone does not have the experience or belief in the sacredness of lands, he or she accords tradition the respect that it deserves. Indians who have never visited certain sacred sites nevertheless know of these places from the community knowledge, and they intuit this knowing to be an essential part of their being.

Justice Brennan, in countering the arguments raised by Justice O'Connor that any recognition of the sacredness of certain sites would allow traditional Indian religions to define the use of all public lands, suggested that the burden of proof be placed on the traditional people to demonstrate why some sites are central to their practice and other sites, while invoking a sense of reverence, are not as important. This requirement is not unreasonable, but it requires a willingness on the part of non-Indians and the courts to entertain different ideas about the nature of religion—ideas which until the present have not been a part of their experience or understanding.

If we were to subject the topic of the sacredness of lands to a Western rational analysis, fully recognizing the [sic.] such an analysis is merely for our convenience in discussion and does not represent the nature of reality, we would probably find four major categories of description. Some of these categories are overlapping because some groups might not agree with the description of certain sites in the categories in which other Indians would place them. Nevertheless, it is the principle of respect for the sacred that is important.

The first and most familiar kind of sacred lands are places to which we attribute sanctity because the location is a site where, within our own history, something of great importance has taken place. Unfortunately, many of these places are related to instances of human violence. Gettysburg National Cemetery is a good example of this kind of sacred land. Abraham Lincoln properly noted that we cannot hallow the Gettysburg battlefield because others, the men who fought there, had already consecrated it by giving "that last full measure of devotion." We generally hold these places sacred because people did there what we might one day be required to do—give our lives in a cause we hold dear. Wounded Knee, South Dakota, has become such a place for many Indians where a band of Sioux Indians were massacred. On the whole, however, the idea of regarding a battlefield as sacred was entirely foreign to most tribes because they did not see war as a holy enterprise. The Lincoln Memorial in Washington, D.C., might be an example of a nonmartial location, and, although Justice O'Connor felt that recognizing the sacredness of land and location might inspire an individual to have a special fondness for this memorial, it is important to recognize that we should have some sense of reverence in these places.

Every society needs these kinds of sacred places because they help to instill a sense of social cohesion in the people and remind them of the passage of generations that have brought them to the present. A society that cannot remember and honor its past is in peril of losing its soul. Indians, because of our considerably longer tenure on this continent, have many more sacred places than do non-Indians. Many different ceremonies can be and have been held at these locations; there is both an exclusivity and an inclusiveness, depending upon the occasion and the ceremony.

In this classification the site is all important, but it is sanctified each time ceremonies are held and prayers offered.

A second category of sacred lands has a deeper, more profound sense of the sacred. It can be illustrated in Old Testament stories that have become the foundation of three world religions. After the death of Moses, Joshua led the Hebrews across the River Jordan into the Holy Land. On approaching the river with the Ark of the Covenant, the waters of the Jordan "rose up" or parted and the people, led by the Ark, crossed over on "dry ground," which is to say they crossed without difficulty. After crossing, Joshua selected one man from each of the Twelve Tribes and told him to find a large stone. The twelve stones were then placed together in a monument to mark the spot where the people had camped after having crossed the river successfully. When asked about this strange behavior, Joshua then replied, "That this may be a sign among you, that when your children ask their fathers in time to come, saying 'What mean ye by these stones?' Then you shall answer them: That the waters of Jordan were cut off before the Ark of the Covenant of the Lord, when it passed over Jordan."[7]

In comparing this site with Gettysburg, we must understand a fundamental difference. Gettysburg is made sacred by the actions of men. It can be described as exquisitely dear to us, but it is not a location where we have perceived that something specifically other than ourselves is present, something mysteriously religious in the proper meaning of those words has happened or been made manifest. In the crossing of the River Jordan, the sacred or higher powers have appeared in the lives of human beings. Indians would say something holy has appeared in an otherwise secular situation. No matter how we might attempt to explain this event in later historical, political, or economic terms, the essence of the event is that the sacred has become a part of our experience.

Some of the sites that traditional religious leaders visit are of this nature. Buffalo Gap at the southeastern edge of the Black Hills of South Dakota marks the location where the buffalo emerged each spring to begin the ceremonial year of the Plains Indians, and it has this aspect of sacred/secular status. It may indeed be the starting point of the Great Race that determined the primacy between two-legged and four-legged creatures at the beginning of the world. Several mountains in New Mexico and Arizona mark places where the Pueblo, Hopi, and Navajo peoples completed their migrations, were told to settle, or where they first established their spiritual relationships with bear, deer, eagle, and other peoples who participate in the ceremonials.

Every identifiable region has sacred places peculiar to its geography and as we extend the circle geographically from any point in North America, we begin to include an ever-increasing number of sacred sites. Beginning in the American Southwest we must include the Apache, Ute, Comanche, Kiowa, and other tribes as we move away from the Pueblo and Navajo lands. These lands would be sacred to some tribes but secular to the Pueblo, Hopi, and Navajo. The difference would be in the manner of revelation and what the people experienced. There is immense particularity in the sacred and it is not a blanket category to be applied indiscriminately. Even east of the Mississippi, though many places have been nearly obliterated, people retain knowledge of these sacred sites. Their sacredness does not depend on human occupancy but on the stories that describe the revelation that enabled human beings to experience the holiness there.

In the religious world of most tribes, birds, animals, and plants compose the "other peoples" of creation. Depending on the ceremony, various of these "peoples" participate in human activities. If Jews and Christians see the action of a deity at sacred places in the Holy Land and in churches and synagogues, traditional Indian people experience spiritual activity as the whole of creation becomes active participants in ceremonial life. Because the relationship with the "other peoples" is so fundamental to the human community, most traditional practitioners are reluctant to articulate the specific elements of either the ceremony or the locations. Because some rituals involve the continued prosperity of the "other peoples" discussing

---

[7]Joshua 4:6–7.

the nature of the ceremony would violate the integrity of these relationships. Thus, traditional people explain that these ceremonies are being held for "all our relatives" but are reluctant to offer any further explanations. It is these ceremonies in particular that are now to be denied protection under the Supreme Court rulings.

It is not likely that non-Indians have had many of these kinds of religious experiences, particularly because most churches and synagogues have special rituals that are designed to cleanse the buildings so that their services can be held there untainted by the natural world. Non-Indians have simply not been on this continent very long; their families have rarely settled in one place for any period of time so that no profound relationship with the environment has been possible. Additionally, non-Indians have engaged in the senseless killing of wildlife and utter destruction of plant life. It is unlikely that they would have understood efforts by other forms of life to communicate with humans. Although, some non-Indian families who have lived continuously in isolated rural areas tell stories about birds and animals similar to the traditions of many tribes indicating that lands and the "other peoples" do seek intimacy with our species.

The third kind of sacred lands are places of overwhelming holiness where the Higher Powers, on their own initiative, have revealed themselves to human beings. Again, we can illustrate this in the Old Testament narrative. Prior to his journey to Egypt, Moses spent his time herding his father-in-law's sheep on or near Mount Horeb. One day he took the flock to the far side of the mountain and to his amazement saw a bush burning with fire but not being consumed by it. Approaching this spot with the usual curiosity of a person accustomed to the outdoor life, Moses was startled when the Lord spoke to him from the bush, warning, "Draw not hither; put off thy shoes from thy feet, for the place where on thou standest is holy ground."[8]

This tradition tells us that there are places of unquestionable, inherent sacredness on this earth, sites that are holy in and of themselves. Human societies come and go on this earth and any prolonged occupation of a geographical region will produce shrines and sacred sites discerned by the occupying people, but there will always be a few sites at which the highest spirits dwell. The stories that explain the sacred nature of these locations will frequently provide startling parallels to the account about the burning bush. One need only look at the shrines of present-day Europe. Long before Catholic or Protestant churches were built in certain places, other religions had established shrines and temples of that spot. These holy places are locations where people have always gone to communicate and commune with higher spiritual powers.

This phenomenon is worldwide and all religions find that these places regenerate people and fill them with spiritual powers. In the Western Hemisphere these places, with few exceptions, are known only by American Indians. Bear Butte, Blue Lake, and the High Places in the *Lyng* case are all well-known locations that are sacred in and of themselves. People have been commanded to perform ceremonies at these holy places so that the earth and all its forms of life might survive and prosper. Evidence of this moral responsibility that sacred places command has come through the testimony of traditional people when they have tried to explain to non-Indians at various times in this century—in court, in conferences, and in conversations—that they must perform certain ceremonies at specific times and places in order that the sun may continue to shine, the earth prosper, and the stars remain in the heavens. Tragically, this attitude is interpreted by non-Indians as indicative of the traditional leader's personal code or philosophy and is not seen as a simple admission of a moral duty.

Skeptical non-Indians, and representatives of other religions seeking to discredit tribal religions, have sometimes deliberately violated some of these holy places with no ill effects. They have then come to believe that they have demonstrated the false nature of Indian beliefs. These violations reveal a strange non-Indian belief in a form of mechanical magic that is touchingly adolescent, a belief that an impious

[8]Exodus 3:5.

act would, or could trigger an immediate response from the higher spiritual powers. Surely these impious acts suggest a deity who jealously guards his or her prerogatives and wreaks immediate vengeance for minor transgressions—much as some Protestant sects have envisioned God and much as an ancient astronaut wanting to control lesser beings might act.

It would be impossible for the thoughtless or impious acts of one species to have an immediate drastic effort on the earth. The cumulative effect of continuous secularity, however, poses a different kind of danger. Long-standing prophecies tell us of the impious people who would come here, defy the creator, and cause the massive destruction of the planet. Many traditional people believe that we are now quite near that time. The cumulative evidence of global warming, acid rain, the disappearance of amphibians, overpopulation, and other products of civilized life certainly testify to the possibility of these prophecies being correct.

Of all the traditional ceremonies extant and actively practiced at the time of contact with non-Indians, ceremonies derived from or related to these holy places have the highest retention rate because of their extraordinary planetary importance. Ironically, traditional people have been forced to hold these ceremonies under various forms of subterfuge and have been abused and imprisoned for doing them. Yet the ceremonies have very little to do with individual or tribal prosperity. Their underlying theme is one of gratitude expressed by human beings on behalf of all forms of life. They act to complete and renew the entire and complete cycle of life, ultimately including the whole cosmos present in its specific realizations, so that in the last analysis one might describe ceremonials as the cosmos becoming thankfully aware of itself.

Having used Old Testament examples to show the objective presence of the holy places, we can draw additional conclusions about the nature of these holy places from the story of the Exodus. Moses did not demand that the particular location of the burning bush become a place of worship for his people, although there was every reason to suppose that he could have done so. Lacking information, we must conclude that the

holiness of this place precluded its use as a shrine. If Moses had been told to perform annual ceremonies at that location during specific days or times of the year, world history would have been entirely different.

Each holy site contains its own revelation. This knowledge is not the ultimate in the sense that Near Eastern religions like to claim the universality of their ideas. Traditional religious leaders tell us that in many of the ceremonies new messages are communicated to them. The ceremonies enable humans to have continuing relationships with higher spiritual powers so that each bit of information is specific to the time, place, and circumstances of the people. No revelation can be regarded as universal because times and conditions change.

The second and third kinds of sacred lands result from two distinctly different forms of sacred revelations where the sacred is actively involved in secular human activities and where the sacred takes the initiative to chart out a new historical course for humans. Because there are higher spiritual powers who can communicate with people, there has to be a fourth category of sacred lands. People must always be ready to experience new revelations at new locations. If this possibility did not exist, all deities and spirits would be dead. Consequently, we always look forward to the revelation of new sacred places and ceremonies. Unfortunately, some federal courts irrationally and arbitrarily circumscribe this universal aspect of religion by insisting that traditional religious practitioners restrict their identification of sacred locations to places that were historically visited by Indians, implying that at least for the federal courts, God is dead.

In denying the possibility of the continuing revelation of the sacred in our lives, federal courts, scholars, and state and federal agencies refuse to accord credibility to the testimony of religious leaders. They demand evidence that a ceremony or location has *always* been central to the beliefs and practices of an Indian tribe and impose exceedingly rigorous standards of proof on Indians who appear before them. This practice allows the Supreme Court to command what should not to [sic.] be done, it lets secular institutions rule on the substance of religious belief and practice. Thus, courts will protect a religion that shows every symptom of being dead but will create formidable barriers if it appears to be alive. Justice Scalia made this posture perfectly clear when he announced in *Smith*, that it would be unconstitutional to ban the casting of "statues that are used for worship purposes" or to prohibit bowing down before a golden calf.

We live in time and space and receive most of our signals about proper behavior from each other and the environment around us. Under these circumstances, the individual and the group *must* both have some kind of sanctity if we are to have a social order at all. By recognizing the various aspects of the sacredness of lands as we have described, we place ourselves in a realistic context in which the individual and the group can cultivate and enhance the sacred experience. Recognizing the sacredness of lands on which previous generations have lived and died is the foundation of all other sentiment. Instead of denying this dimension of our emotional lives, we should be setting aside additional places that have transcendent meaning. Sacred sites that higher spiritual powers have chosen for manifestation enable us to focus our concerns on the specific form of our lives. These places remind us of our unique relationship with the spiritual forces that govern the universe and call us to fulfill our religious vocations. These kinds of religious experiences have shown us something of the nature of the universe by an affirmative manifestation of themselves and this knowledge illuminates everything else that we know.

The nature of tribal religion brings contemporary America a new kind of legal problem. Religious freedom has existed as a matter of course in America *only* when religion has been conceived as a set of objective beliefs. This condition is actually not freedom at all because it would be exceedingly difficult to read minds and determine what ideas were being entertained at the time. So far in American history religious freedom has not involved the consecration and setting aside of lands for religious purposes or allowing sincere but highly divergent behavior by individuals and groups. The issue of sacred lands, as we have seen,

was successfully raised in the case of the Taos Pueblo people. Nevertheless, a great deal more remains to be done to guarantee Indian people the right to practice their own religion.

A number of other tribes have sacred sanctuaries in lands that have been taken by the government for purposes other than religion. These lands must be returned to the respective Indian tribes for their ceremonial purposes. The greatest number of Indian shrines are located in New Mexico and here the tribal religions have remained comparatively strong. Cochiti Pueblo needs some 24,000 acres of land for access to and use of religious shrines in what is now Bandelier National Monument. The people also have shrines in the Tetilla Peak area. San Juan Pueblo has also been trying to get lands returned for religious purposes. Santa Clara Pueblo requested the Indian Claims Commission to set aside 30,000 acres of the lands that have religious and ceremonial importance to its people but are presently in the hands of the National Forest Service and Atomic Energy Commission.

In Arizona the Hopi people have a number of shrines that are of vital importance to their religion. Traditionals regard the Black Mesa area as sacred, but it is being leased to Peabody Coal by the more assimilative tribal council. The San Francisco Peaks within the Coconino National Forest are sacred because they are believed to be the homes of the Kachinas who play a major part in the Hopi ceremonial system. The Navajo have a number of sacred mountains now under federal ownership. Mount Taylor in the Cibola National Forest, Blanca Peak in southern Colorado, Hesperus Peak in the San Juan National Forest, Huerfano Mountain on public domain lands, and Oak Creek canyon in the Coconino National Forest are all sites integral to the Navajo tradition. Part of the Navajo religion involves the "mountain chant" that describes the seven sacred mountains and a sacred lake located within these mountains. The Navajo believe their ancestors arose from this region at the creation. Last, but certainly not least, is the valiant struggle now being waged by the Apache people to prevent the University of Arizona from building several telescopes on Mount Graham in southern Arizona.

In other states several sacred sites are under threat of exploitation. The Forest Service is proposing to construct a major parking lot and observation platform at the Medicine Wheel site near Powell, Wyoming, that is sacred to many tribes from Montana, the Dakotas, and Wyoming. Because the only value of this location is its relationship to traditional Indian religions that need isolation and privacy, it seems ludicrous to pretend that making it accessible to more tourists and subject to increasing environmental degradation is enhancing it. The Badger Two Medicine area of Montana, where oil drilling has been proposed, is a sacred area for traditional Blackfeet who live in the vicinity. The Pipestone Quarry in southwestern Minnesota was confiscated from the Yankton Sioux in the closing decades of the last century when some missionaries pressured the federal government to eliminate Indian access to this important spot.

Finally, there is the continuing struggle over the Black Hills of South Dakota. Many Americans are now aware of this state thanks to the success of the movie *Dances with Wolves* that not only depicted the culture of the Sioux Indians but also filled the screen with the magnificent landscape of the northern Great Plains. Nineteen ninety-one was a year of great schizophrenia and strange anomalies in South Dakota. Local whites shamelessly capitalized on the success of the movie at the same time they were frothing at the mouth over the continuing efforts of the Sioux people to get the federal lands in the Black Hills returned to them. Governor George Mickelson announced a "Year of Reconciliation" that simply became twelve months of symbolic maneuvering for publicity and renewal of political images. When some of the Sioux elders suggested that the return of Bear Butte near Sturgis would be a concrete step toward reconciliation, non-Indians were furious that reconciliation might require them to make good-faith effort to heal the wounds from a century of conflict.

The question that must be addressed in the issue of sacred lands is the extent to which the tribal religions can be maintained if sacred lands are restored. Would restoration of the sacred Pipestone Quarry result in more people seeking to follow the traditional religious life or would it result in continued use of the stone for tourism and commercial purposes? A small group of Sioux people have made a living during this century from making ashtrays and decorative carvings from this sacred rock; they refuse to stop their exploitation. A major shift in focus is needed by traditional Sioux people to prepare to reconsecrate the quarry and return to the old ways of reverence.

A very difficult task lies ahead for the people who continue to believe in the old tribal religions. In the past, these traditions have been ridiculed by disbelievers, primarily missionaries and social scientists. Today injuries nearly as grievous are visited on traditional religions by the multitude of non-Indians who seek entrance and participation in ceremonies and rituals. Many of these non-Indians blatantly steal symbols, prayers and teaching by laying claim to alleged offices in tribal religions. Most non-Indians see in tribal religions the experiences and reverence that are missing in their own heritage. No matter how hard they try, they always reduce the teachings and ceremonies to a complicated word game and ineffectual gestures. Lacking communities and extended families, they are unable to put the religion into practice.

Some major efforts must be made by the Indians of this generation to demonstrate the view of the world that their tradition teaches has an integrity of its own and represents a sensible and respectable perspective of the world and a valid means of interpreting experiences. There are many new studies that seem to confirm certain tribal practices as reasonable and sometimes even as sophisticated techniques for handling certain kinds of problems. It might be sufficient to show that these patterns of behavior are indicative of a consistent attitude toward the world and include the knowledge that everything is alive and related.

Sacred places are the foundation of all other beliefs and practices because they represent the presence of the sacred in our lives. They properly inform us that we are not larger than nature and that we have responsibilities to the rest of the natural world that transcend our own personal desires and wishes. This lesson must be learned by each generation; unfortunately the technology of industrial society always leads us in the other direction. Yet it is certain that as we permanently foul our planetary nest, we shall have to learn a most bitter lesson. There probably is not sufficient time for the non-Indian population to understand the meaning of sacred lands and incorporate the idea into their lives and practices. We can but hope that some protection can be afforded these sacred places before the world becomes wholly secular and is destroyed.

⊚ CRITICAL QUESTIONS

1. Deloria claims that "A society that cannot remember and honor its past is in peril of losing its soul." While Deloria offers no argument to support this claim, how might it be supported?

2. Deloria maintains that the Supreme Court, contrary to its own standards, allowed "secular institutions [to] rule on the substance of religious belief and practices" in the case of American Indian spirituality. Do you agree? Why, or why not?

To access the *Voices of Wisdom*, 8th Edition, **Premium Website**, search for this book on CengageBrain.com.

CHAPTER SIX

Is Justice for All Possible?

The test of our progress is not whether we add more to the abundance of those who have too much: it is whether we provide enough for those who have too little.

PRESIDENT FRANKLIN D. ROOSEVELT, INAUGURAL ADDRESS, 1937

LEARNING OBJECTIVES

After studying this chapter students should be able to:
- distinguish between individual and institutional sexism, racism, and homophobia,
- define sexism, racism, and homophobia,
- explain why sexism, racism, and homophobia are unjust,
- explain globalization and cosmopolitanism,
- state the difference between the "just war" approach to terrorism and the ethic of care approach,
- explain why it is so difficult to define terrorism,
- describe critical theory, subjective and objective violence,
- explain what the "tragedy of the commons" is,
- describe Regan's argument for animal rights,
- identify hooks, West, Pharr, Williams, Singer, Bat-Ami Bar On, Borradori, Habermas, Hardin, and Regan, and
- answer all the questions about each selection.

6.1 INTRODUCTION

When I ask students to write a brief essay on whether they think a just society is possible, the responses I get are overwhelmingly negative. They do not think a just society is possible because, as one student put it, "Someone will always be unhappy with the way things are."

The United States, as well as other countries, faces a number of complex issues requiring some sort of legislation. Yet every time a law is passed or a judicial decision is made, someone is going to feel cheated. Even so, decisions must be made, and we can only hope that the decisions make good moral sense even if someone may be "unhappy."

Racism, sexism, and homophobia have plagued many countries. Can they be eliminated? Is a society that tolerates racism, sexism, and homophobia a just society? Can there ever be justice for those who have been victims of racism, sexism, and homophobia? Are affirmative action programs justified? One often hears such programs justified on the grounds of compensatory justice. However, many argue that the correction of a past injustice leads to a present injustice.

Terrorism, which has an ancient history, has recently emerged with a renewed fury in a frantic attempt to achieve justice by any means possible. If globalization is shrinking the world and spreading exploitation of the poor by the rich, terrorism is balkanizing the world, creating "us-versus-them" mentalities. Any serious consideration of the problems of achieving justice for all today must contend with both of these forces.

Environmental issues appear in the news almost daily. Many predict that in the twenty-first century a good portion of our time and resources will be spent cleaning up the mess left by the last century's insensitivity to the environment. As international businesses expand and globalization becomes more and more entrenched, the temptations to exploit humans, other-than-human animals, and our environment in the name of "progress" (read "profit") will multiply.

Social philosophy discusses these sorts of issues (and many more). Philosophers try to illuminate the issues, sort out the reasonable positions, and argue for policies that make moral sense. We will become a part of some of these discussions in this chapter, and, I trust, our thinking about them will deepen. We may, in some cases, still be uncertain about what is the best thing to do, and we still may realize that some people will be unhappy no matter what is done, but at least our vision of social justice in some areas may become clearer.

6.2 SEXISM, RACISM, AND HOMOPHOBIA

Suppose I ask you to list five types of the most common social injustices. I would wager that both racism and sexism are somewhere on that list. Both these social wrongs appear to be so widespread and difficult to eliminate because race and sex are such fundamental features of human existence. However, it clearly is not possible to achieve justice for all as long as racial prejudice and sexual discrimination exist.

Would you include homophobia on your list of social injustices? Homophobia has led to widespread discrimination against homosexuals. Recently some governments have even tried to write laws forbidding certain civil rights to gays, such as marriage, thereby denying an important right that heterosexuals enjoy. One of the book's color plates shows a poster of the movie *The Kids Are All Right*. The story told in that film suggests perhaps that, at least in popular culture in the United States, lesbianism is alive and well—though popular culture may not be an accurate reflection of current and accepted realities.

It is important to distinguish individual sexism, racism, and homophobia from its institutional forms. Individuals have and do hold negative attitudes and prejudicial beliefs about people of another race, or sex, or sexual orientation that often result in negative actions such as sexual harassment, racial slurs, and homophobic epithets. Institutional forms of sexism, racism, and homophobia involve official agencies and various kinds of organizations treating people unfairly based solely on their race, sex, or sexual orientation. For example, women did not have the right to vote in the United States until 1920. As the photo in one of the color plates shows, some still commemorate the hard-won suffrage for women, acquired in some states before it was for the nation as a whole. For many years, also, blacks and women could not serve in police forces. Even today women are not supposed to serve in combat roles.

It has proven very difficult to eliminate the injustices of racism, sexism, and homophobia. Just when we think progress is being made, new forms emerge. In part, this is due to our tendencies to see the world from an egocentric viewpoint. In part it is due to the power, prestige, and benefits that result from being in the advantaged group.

The author of our first selection is bell hooks, a professor of English at City College of New York. She was born Gloria Watkins but writes under the name of her great-grandmother in order to pay homage to the unheard voices of black women, past and present. She writes her name all in lowercase, thereby symbolizing her skepticism about the importance of fame even though her book, *Ain't I a Woman*, from which the following selection is taken, brought her fame as an author, activist, and important social critic.

Cornel West, University Professor of Religion at Princeton University, is the author of numerous books and articles. He has taught at Harvard as well as Princeton. The second selection comes from his highly acclaimed book, *Race Matters*.

Our third selection in this section comes from Suzanne Pharr's *Homophobia as a Weapon of Sexism*. She is an author, educator, activist, and a founding member of the Women's Project of Little Rock, Arkansas.

◉ READING QUESTIONS

1. What does hooks mean when she claims that the feminist movement in America perpetuated "the myth that the social status of all women in America is the same"?
2. What is Sojourner Truth's argument against the innate physical inferiority of women?
3. According to West, what is the fundamental crisis of black America?
4. Why, according to West, has affirmative action not been a "major solution to poverty nor a sufficient means to equality"?
5. According to Pharr, what is the relationship among economics, violence, and homophobia?
6. How is calling someone lesbian or gay a threat to all women and men?

Ain't I a Woman

bell hooks

RACISM AND FEMINISM: THE ISSUE OF ACCOUNTABILITY

American women of all races are socialized to think of racism solely in the context of race hatred. Specifically in the case of black and white people, the term racism is usually seen as synonymous with discrimination or prejudice against black people by white people. For most women, the first knowledge of racism as institutionalized oppression is engendered either by direct personal experience or through information gleaned from conversations, books, television, or movies. Consequently, the American woman's understanding of racism as a political tool of colonialism and imperialism is severely limited. To experience the pain of race hatred or to witness that pain is not to understand its origin, evolution, or impact on world history. The inability of American women to understand racism in the context of American politics is not due to any inherent

From bell hooks, *Ain't I a Woman: Black Women and Feminism* (Boston: South End Press, 1981), pp. 159–161, 194–196. Copyright © 1981 by Gloria Watkins. Reprinted by permission of South End Press.

deficiency in woman's psyche. It merely reflects the extent of our victimization.

No history books used in public schools informed us about racial imperialism. Instead we were given romantic notions of the "new world," the "American dream," America as the great melting pot where all races come together as one. We were taught that Columbus *discovered* America; that "Indians" were scalphunters, killers of innocent women and children; that black people were enslaved because of the biblical curse of Ham, that God "himself had decreed they would be hewers of wood, tillers of the field, and bringers of water. No one talked of Africa as the cradle of civilization, of the African and Asian people who came to America before Columbus. No one mentioned mass murders of Native Americans as genocide, or the rape of Native American and African women as terrorism. No one discussed slavery as a foundation for the growth of capitalism. No one described the forced breeding of white wives to increase the white population as sexist oppression.

I am a black woman. I attended all-black public schools. I grew up in the south where all around me was the fact of racial discrimination, hatred, and forced segregation. Yet my education as to the politics of race in American society was not that different from that of white female students I met in integrated high schools, in college, or in various women's groups. The majority of us understood racism as a social evil perpetuated by prejudiced white people that could be overcome through bonding between blacks and liberal whites, through militant protest, changing of laws or racial integration. Higher educational institutions did nothing to increase our limited understanding of racism as a political ideology. Instead professors systematically denied us truth, teaching us to accept racial polarity in the form of white supremacy and sexual polarity in the form of male dominance.

American women have been socialized, even brainwashed, to accept a version of American history that was created to uphold and maintain racial imperialism in the form of white supremacy and sexual imperialism in the form of patriarchy. One measure of the success of such indoctrination is that we perpetuate both consciously and unconsciously the very evils that oppress us. I am certain that the black female sixth grade teacher who taught us history, who taught us to identify with the American government, who loved those students who could best recite the pledge of allegiance to the American flag was not aware of the contradiction; that we should love this government that segregated us, that failed to send schools with all black students supplies that went to schools with only white pupils. Unknowingly she implanted in our psyches a seed of the racial imperialism that would keep us forever in bondage. For how does one overthrow, change, or even challenge a system that you have been taught to admire, to love, to believe in? Her innocence does not change the reality that she was teaching black children to embrace the very system that oppressed us, that she encouraged us to support it, to stand in awe of it, to die for it.

That American women, irrespective of their education, economic status, or racial identification, have undergone years of sexist and racist socialization that has taught us to blindly trust our knowledge of history and its effect on present reality, even though that knowledge has been formed and shaped by an oppressive system, is nowhere more evident than in the recent feminist movement. The group of college-educated white middle and upper class women who came together to organize a women's movement brought a new energy to the concept of women's rights in America. They were not merely advocating social equality with men. They demanded a transformation of society, a revolution, a change in the American social structure. Yet as they attempted to take feminism beyond the realm of radical rhetoric and into the realm of American life, they revealed that they had not changed, had not undone the sexist and racist brainwashing that had taught them to regard women unlike themselves as Others. Consequently, the Sisterhood they talked about has not become a reality, and the women's movement they envisioned would have a transformative effect on American culture has not emerged. Instead, the hierarchical pattern of race and sex relationships already established in American society merely took a different form under "feminism": the form of women being classed as an oppressed group under affirmative action programs further perpetuating the myth that the social status of all women in America is the same; the form of women's studies programs being established with all-white faculty teaching literature almost exclusively by white women about white women and frequently from racist perspectives; the form of white women writing books that purport to be about the experience of American women when in fact they concentrate solely on the experience of white women; and finally the form of endless argument and debate as to whether or not racism was a feminist issue.

If the white women who organized the contemporary movement toward feminism were at all remotely aware of racial politics in American history, they would have known that overcoming barriers that separate women from one another would entail confronting the reality of racism, and not just racism as a general evil in society but the race hatred they might harbor in their own psyches. Despite the predominance of patriarchal rule in American society, America was colonized on a racially imperialistic base and not on a sexually imperialistic base. No degree of patriarchal bonding between white male colonizers and Native American men overshadowed white racial imperialism. Racism took precedence over sexual alliances in both the white world's interaction with Native Americans and African Americans, just as racism overshadowed any bonding between black women and white women on the basis of sex. Tunisian writer Albert Memmi emphasizes in *The Colonizer and the Colonized* the impact of racism as a tool of imperialism:

> Racism appears ... not as an incidental detail, but as a consubstantial part of colonialism. It is the highest expression of the colonial system and one of the most significant features of the colonialist. Not only does it establish a fundamental discrimination between colonizer and colonized, a sine qua non of colonial life, but it also lays the foundation for the immutability of this life.

While those feminists who argue that sexual imperialism is more endemic to all societies than racial imperialism are probably correct, American society is one in which racial imperialism supersedes sexual imperialism.

In America, the social status of black and white women has never been the same. In 19th and early 20th century America, few if any similarities could be found between the life experiences of the two female groups. Although they were both subject to sexist victimization, as victims of racism black women were subjected to oppressions no white woman was forced to endure. In fact, white racial imperialism granted all white women, however victimized by sexist oppression they might be, the right to assume the role of oppressor in relationship to black women and black men. From the onset of the contemporary move toward feminist revolution, white female organizers attempted to minimize their position in the racial caste hierarchy of American society. In their efforts to disassociate themselves from white men (to deny connections based on shared racial caste), white women involved in the move toward feminism have charged that racism is endemic to white male patriarchy and have argued that they cannot be held responsible for racist oppression. Commenting on the issue of white female accountability in her essay "'Disloyal to Civilization': Feminism, Racism, and Gynephobia," radical feminist Adrienne Rich contends:

> If Black and White feminists are going to speak of female accountability, I believe the word racism must be seized, grasped in our bare hands, ripped out of the sterile or defensive consciousness in which it so often grows, and transplanted so that it can yield new insights for our lives and our movement. An analysis that places the guilt for active domination, physical and institutional violence, and the justifications embedded in myth and language, on white women not only compounds false consciousness; it allows us all to deny or neglect the charged connection among black and white women from the historical conditions of slavery on, and it impedes any real discussion of women's instrumentality in a system which oppresses all women and in which hatred of women is also embedded in myth, folklore, and language.

No reader of Rich's essay could doubt that she is concerned that women who are committed to feminism work to overcome barriers that separate black and white women. However, she fails to understand that from a black female perspective, if white women are denying the existence of black women, writing "feminist" scholarship as if black women are not a part of the collective group American women, or discriminating against black women, then it matters less that North America was colonized by white patriarchal *men* who institutionalized a racially imperialistic social order than that white women who purport to be feminists support and actively perpetuate anti-black racism.

To black women the issue is not whether white women are more or less racist than white men, but that they are racist. If women committed to feminist revolution, be they black or white, are to achieve any understanding of the "charged connections" between white women and black women, we must first be willing to examine woman's relationship to society, to race, and to American culture as it is and not as we would ideally have it be. That means confronting the reality of white female racism. Sexist discrimination has prevented white women from assuming the dominant role in the perpetuation of white racial imperialism, but it has not prevented white women from absorbing, supporting, and advocating racist ideology or acting individually as racist oppressors in various spheres of American life....

BLACK WOMEN AND FEMINISM

More than a hundred years have passed since the day Sojourner Truth stood before an assembled body of white women and men at an anti-slavery rally in Indiana and bared her breasts to prove that she was indeed a woman. To Sojourner, who had traveled the long road from slavery to freedom, the baring of her breasts was a small matter. She faced her audience without fear, without shame, proud of having been born black and female. Yet the white man who yelled at Sojourner, "I don't believe you really are a woman," unwittingly voiced America's contempt and disrespect for black womanhood. In the eyes of the 19th century white public, the black female was a creature unworthy of the title woman; she was mere chattel, a thing, an animal. When Sojourner Truth stood before the second annual convention of the women's rights movement in Akron, Ohio, in 1852, white women who deemed it unfitting that a black woman should speak on a public platform in their presence screamed: "Don't let her speak! Don't let her speak! Don't let her speak!" Sojourner endured their protests and became one of the first feminists to call their attention to the lot of the black slave woman who, compelled by circumstance to labor alongside black men, was a living embodiment of the truth that women could be the work-equals of men.

It was no mere coincidence that Sojourner Truth was allowed on stage after a white male spoke against the idea of equal rights for women, basing his argument on the notion that woman was too weak to perform her share of manual labor—that she was innately the physical inferior to man. Sojourner quickly responded to his argument, telling her audience:

> ... Well, children, whar dar is so much racket dar must be something out o' kilter. I tink dat 'twixt de niggers of de Souf and de women at de Norf all a talkin 'bout rights, de white men will be in a fix pretty soon. But what's all dis here talkin' 'bout? Dat man ober dar say dat women needs to be helped into carriages, and lifted ober ditches, and to have de best places ... and ain't I a woman? Look at me! Look at my arm! ... I have plowed, and planted, and gathered into barns, and no man could head me—and ain't I a woman? I could work as much as any man (when I could get it), and bear de lash as well—and ain't I a woman? I have borne five children and I seen 'em mos all sold off into slavery, and when I cried out with a mother's grief, none but Jesus hear—and ain't I a woman?

Unlike most white women's rights advocates, Sojourner Truth could refer to her own personal life experience as evidence of woman's ability to function as a parent; to be the work equal of man; to undergo persecution, physical abuse, rape, torture; and to not only survive but emerge triumphant....

It is a contradiction that white females have structured a women's liberation movement that is racist and excludes many non-white women. However, the existence of that contradiction should not lead any woman to ignore feminist issues. Oftentimes I am asked by black women to explain why I would call myself a feminist and by using that term ally myself with a movement that is racist. I say, "The question we must ask again and again is how can racist women call themselves feminists." It is obvious that many women have appropriated feminism to serve their own ends, especially those white women who have been at the forefront of the movement; but rather than resigning myself to this appropriation I choose to re-appropriate the term "feminism," to focus on the fact that to be "feminist" in any authentic sense of the term is to want for all people, female and male, liberation from sexist role patterns, domination, and oppression.

Today masses of black women in the U.S. refuse to acknowledge that they have much to gain by feminist struggle. They fear feminism. They have stood in place so long that they are afraid to move. They fear change. They fear losing what little they have. They are afraid to openly confront white feminists with their racism or black males with their sexism, not to mention confronting white men with their racism and sexism. I have sat in many a kitchen and heard black women express a belief in feminism and eloquently critique the women's movement explaining their refusal to participate. I have witnessed their refusal to express these same views in a public setting. I know their fear exists because they have seen us trampled upon, raped, abused, slaughtered, ridiculed and mocked. Only a few black women have rekindled the spirit of feminist struggle that stirred the hearts and minds of our 19th century sisters. We, black women who advocate feminist ideology, are pioneers. We are clearing a path for ourselves and our sisters. We hope that as they see us reach our goal—no longer victimized, no longer unrecognized, no longer afraid—they will take courage and follow.

Race Matters

CORNEL WEST

Institutionalized rejection of *difference* is an absolute necessity in a profit economy which needs outsiders as surplus people.

As members of such an economy, we have all been programmed to respond to the human differences between us with fear and loathing and to handle that difference in one of three ways: ignore it, and if that is not possible, copy it if we think it is dominant, or destroy it if we think it is subordinate.

But we have no patterns for relating across our human differences as equals. As a result, those differences have been misnamed and misused in the service of separation and confusion.

—AUDRE LORDE, *Sister Outsider* (1984)

The fundamental crisis in black America is twofold: too much poverty and too little self-love. The urgent problem of black poverty is primarily due to the distribution of wealth, power, and income—a distribution influenced by the racial caste system that denied opportunities to most "qualified" black people until two decades ago.

The historic role of American progressives is to promote redistributive measures that enhance the standard of living and quality of life for the have-nots and have-too-littles. Affirmative action was one such redistributive measure that surfaced in the heat of battle in the 1960s among those fighting for racial equality. Like earlier *de facto* affirmative action measures in the American past—contracts, jobs, and loans to select immigrants granted by political machines; subsidies to certain farmers; FHA mortgage loans to specific home buyers; or GI Bill benefits to particular courageous Americans—recent efforts to broaden access to America's prosperity have been based upon preferential policies. Unfortunately, these policies always benefit middle-class Americans disproportionately. The political power of big business in big government circumscribes redistributive measures and thereby tilts these measures away from the have-nots and have-too-littles.

Every redistributive measure is a compromise with and concession from the caretakers of American prosperity—that is, big business and big government. Affirmative action was one such compromise and concession achieved after the protracted struggle of American progressives and liberals in the courts and in the streets. Visionary progressives always push for substantive redistributive measures that make opportunities available to the have-nots and have-too-littles, such as more federal support to small farmers, or more FHA mortgage loans to urban dwellers as well as suburban home buyers. Yet in the American political system, where the powers that be turn a skeptical eye toward any program aimed at economic redistribution, progressives must secure whatever redistributive measures they can, ensure their enforcement, then extend their benefits if possible.

If I had been old enough to join the fight for racial equality in the courts, the legislatures, and the boardrooms in the 1960s (I *was* old enough to be in the streets), I would have favored—as I do now—a class-based affirmative action in principle. Yet in the heat of battle in American politics, a redistributive measure in principle with no power and pressure behind it means no redistributive measure at all. The prevailing discriminatory practices during the sixties, whose targets were working people, women, and people of color, were atrocious. Thus, an *enforceable* race-based—and later gender-based—affirmative action policy was the best possible compromise and concession.

Progressives should view affirmative action as neither a major solution to poverty nor a sufficient means to equality. We should see it as primarily playing a negative role—namely, to ensure that discriminatory practices against women and people of color are abated. Given the history of this country, it is a virtual certainty that without affirmative action, racial and sexual discrimination would return with a vengeance. Even if affirmative action fails significantly to reduce black poverty or contributes to the persistence of racist perceptions in the workplace, without affirmative action, black access to America's prosperity would be even more difficult to obtain and racism in the workplace would persist anyway.

This claim is not based on any cynicism toward my white fellow citizens; rather, it rests upon America's historically weak will toward racial justice and substantive redistributive measures. This is why an attack on affirmative action is an attack on redistributive efforts by progressives unless there is a real possibility of enacting and enforcing a more wide-reaching class-based affirmative action policy.

In American politics, progressives must not only cling to redistributive ideals, but must also fight for those policies that—out of compromise and concession—imperfectly conform to those ideals. Liberals who give only lip service to these ideals, trash the policies in the name of *realpolitik*, or reject the policies as they perceive a shift in the racial bellwether give up precious ground too easily. And they do so even as the sand is disappearing under our feet on such issues as regressive taxation, layoffs or takebacks from workers, and cutbacks in health and child care.

Affirmative action is not the most important issue for black progress in America, but it is part of a redistributive chain that must be strengthened if we are to confront and eliminate black poverty. If there were social democratic redistributive measures that wiped out black poverty, and if racial and sexual discrimination could be abated through the good will and meritorious judgments of those in power, affirmative action would be unnecessary. Although many of my liberal and progressive citizens view affirmative action as a redistributive measure whose time is over or whose life is no longer worth preserving, I question their view because of the persistence of discriminatory practices that increase black social misery, and the warranted suspicion that good will and fair judgment among the powerful does not loom as large toward women and people of color.

If the elimination of black poverty is a necessary condition of substantive black progress, then the affirmation of black humanity, especially among black people themselves, is a sufficient condition of such programs. Such affirmation speaks to the existential issues of what it means to be a degraded African (man, woman, gay, lesbian, child) in a racist society. How does one affirm oneself without re-enacting negative black stereotypes or overreacting to white supremacist ideals?

The difficult and delicate quest for black identity is integral to any talk about racial equality. Yet it is not solely a political or economic matter. The quest for black identity involves self-respect and self-regard, realms inseparable from, yet not identical to, political power and economic status. The flagrant self-loathing among black middle-class professionals bears witness to this painful process. Unfortunately, black conservatives focus on the issue of self-respect as if it were the one key that would open all doors to black progress. They illustrate the fallacy of trying to open all doors with one key: they wind up closing their eyes to all doors except the one the key fits.

Progressives, for our part, must take seriously the quest for self-respect, even as we train our eye on the institutional causes for black social misery. The issues of black identity—both black self-love and self-contempt—sit alongside black poverty as realities to confront and transform. The uncritical acceptance of self-degrading ideals that call into question black intelligence, possibility, and beauty not only compounds black social misery but also paralyzes black middle-class efforts to defend broad redistributive measures.

This paralysis takes two forms: black bourgeois preoccupation with white peer approval and black nationalist obsession with white racism.

The first form of paralysis tends to yield a navel-gazing posture that conflates the identity crisis of the black middle class with the state of siege raging in black working-poor and very poor communities. That unidimensional view obscures the need for redistributive measures that significantly affect the majority of blacks, who are working people on the edge of poverty.

The second form of paralysis precludes any meaningful coalition with white progressives because of an undeniable white racist legacy of the modern Western world. The anger this truth engenders impedes any effective way of responding to the crisis in black America. Broad redistributive measures require principled coalitions, including multiracial alliances. Without such measures, black America's sufferings deepen. White racism indeed contributes to this suffering. Yet an obsession with white racism often comes at the expense of more broadly based alliances to effect social change and borders on a tribal mentality. The more xenophobic versions of this viewpoint simply mirror the white supremacist ideals we are opposing and preclude any movement toward redistributive goals.

How one defines oneself influences what analytical weight one gives to black poverty. Any progressive discussion about the future of racial equality must speak to black poverty and black identity. My views on the necessity and limits of affirmative action in the present moment are informed by how substantive redistributive measures and human affirmative efforts can be best defended and expanded....

We are living in one of the most frightening moments in the history of this country. Democracies are quite rare and usually short-lived in the human adventure. The precious notion of ordinary people living lives of decency and dignity—owing to their participation in the basic decision making in those fundamental institutions that affect their life chances—is difficult to sustain over space and time. And every historic effort to forge a democratic project has been undermined by two fundamental realities: *poverty* and *paranoia*. The persistence of poverty generates levels of *despair* that deepen social conflict; the escalation of paranoia produces levels of *distrust that* reinforce cultural division. Race is the most explosive issue in American life precisely because it forces us to confront the tragic facts of poverty and paranoia, despair and distrust. In short, a candid examination of *race* matters takes us to the core of the crisis of American democracy. And the degree to which race *matters* in the plight and predicament of fellow citizens is a crucial measure of whether we can keep alive the best of this democratic experiment we call America.

Needless to say, this fragile experiment began by taking for granted the ugly conquest of Amerindians and Mexicans, the exclusion of women, the subordination of European working-class men and the closeting of homosexuals. These realities made many of the words of the revolutionary Declaration of Independence ring a bit hollow. Yet the enslavement of Africans—over 20 percent of the population—served as the linchpin of American democracy; that is, the much-heralded stability and continuity of American democracy was predicated upon black oppression and degradation. Without the presence of black people in America, European-Americans would not be "white"—they would be only Irish, Italians, Poles, Welsh, and others engaged in class, ethnic, and gender struggles over resources and identity. What made America distinctly American for them was not simply the presence of unprecedented opportunities, but the struggle for seizing these opportunities in a new land in which black slavery and racial caste served as the floor upon which white class, ethnic, and gender struggles could be diffused and diverted. In other words, white poverty could be ignored and whites' paranoia of each other could be overlooked primarily owing to the distinctive American feature: the basic racial divide of black and white peoples. From 1776 to 1964—188 years of our 218-year history—this racial divide would serve as a basic presupposition for the expansive functioning of American democracy, even as the concentration of wealth and power remained in the hands of a few well-to-do white men.

The era of the sixties was a watershed period in American history because for the first time we decided as a people to overcome the racial divide *and* declare war on poverty. Within two years, *legal* barriers against black access to civil and voting rights were erased. Within eight years, half of America's poor people were lifted out of poverty. And within a decade, the number of poor old people was more than cut in half. Contrary to the popular myths about the sixties, this was a brief moment in which we bravely confronted our most explosive issues as a people: *racial hierarchy and the maldistribution of wealth and power*. But it did not last long. As the economy slumped, black rage escalated and white backlash set in. And, for nearly two decades, we witnessed a decline in the real wages of most Americans, a new racial divide in the minds and streets of fellow citizens, a massive transfer of wealth from working people to the well-to-do, and an increase in drugs and guns (along with fear and violence) in American life. Many conservative Republicans played the old racial card to remain in office and most liberal Democrats lacked the courage to tell the truth about the new levels of decline and decay engulfing us. Instead, we as a

people tolerated levels of suffering and misery among the disadvantaged (especially among poor children of all colors, caught in a vicious natural lottery!), lost faith in our money-driven political system, and lived lives of hedonistic evasion and narcissistic avoidance as the racial divide expanded and the gaps between rich, poor, and working people increased. We now find ourselves hungry for quick solutions and thirsty for overnight cures for deep economic, cultural, and political problems that were allowed to fester for decades. And, most sadly, we seem to lack the patience, courage, and hope necessary to reconstruct our public life— the very life blood of any democracy.

My aim in this book is to revitalize our public conversation about race, in light of our paralyzing pessimism and stultifying cynicism as a people. As a radical democrat, I believe it is late—but maybe not too late—to confront and overcome the poverty and paranoia, the despair and distrust that haunt us. Since democracy is, as the great Reinhold Niebuhr noted, a proximate solution to insoluble problems, I envision neither a social utopia nor a political paradise. My goal is to be as bold and defiant in my criticism of any form of xenophobia, as honest and candid about the need for civil responsibility and social accountability of each one of us, and as charitable and compassionate toward any political perspective from which we can gain insight and wisdom to empower us.

In these downbeat times, we need as much hope and courage as we do vision and analysis; we must accent the best of each other even as we point out the vicious effects of our racial divide and the pernicious consequences of our maldistribution of wealth and power. We simply cannot enter the twenty-first century at each other's throats, even as we acknowledge the weighty forces of racism, patriarchy, economic inequality, homophobia, and ecological abuse on our necks. We are at a crucial crossroad in the history of this nation—and we either hang together by combating these forces that divide and degrade us or we hang separately. Do we have the intelligence, humor, imagination, courage, tolerance, love, respect, and will to meet the challenge? Time will tell. None of us alone can save the nation or world. But each of us can make a positive difference if we commit ourselves to do so.

Homophobia as a Weapon of Sexism

SUZANNE PHARR

Patriarchy—an enforced belief in male dominance and control—is the ideology and sexism is the system that holds it in place. The catechism goes like this: Who do gender roles serve? Men and the women who seek power from them. Who suffers from gender roles? Women most completely and men in part. How are gender roles maintained? By the weapons of sexism: economics, violence, homophobia.

Why then don't we ardently pursue ways to eliminate gender roles and therefore sexism? It is my profound belief that all people have a spark in them that yearns for freedom, and the history of the world's atrocities—from the Nazi concentration camps to white dominance in South Africa to the battering of women—is the story of attempts to snuff out that spark. When that spark doesn't move forward to full flame, it is because the weapons designed to control and destroy have wrought such intense damage over time that the spark has been all but extinguished.

Sexism, that system by which women are kept subordinate to men, is kept in place by three powerful weapons designed to cause or threaten women with pain and loss. As stated before, the three are economics, violence, and homophobia....

What would happen if women gained the earning opportunities and power that men have? What would happen if these opportunities were distributed equitably, no matter what sex one was, no matter what race one was born into, and no matter where one lived? What if educational and training opportunities were equal? Would women spend most of our youth preparing for marriage? Would marriage be based on economic survival for women? What would happen to issues of power and control? Would women stay with our batterers? If a woman had economic independence in a society where women had equal opportunities, would she still be thought of as owned by her father or husband?

Economics is the great controller in both sexism and racism. If a person can't acquire food, shelter, and clothing and provide them for children, then that person can be forced to do many things in order to survive. The major tactic, worldwide, is to provide unrecompensed or inadequately recompensed labor for the benefit of those who control wealth. Hence, we see women performing unpaid labor in the home or filling low-paid jobs, and we see people of color in the lowest-paid jobs available.

The method is complex: limit educational and training opportunities for women and for people of color and then withhold adequate paying jobs with the excuse that people of color and women are incapable of filling them. Blame the economic victim and keep the victim's self-esteem low through invisibility and distortion within the media and education. Allow a few people of color and women to succeed among the profit-makers so that blaming those who don't "make it" can be intensified. Encourage those few who succeed in gaining power now to turn against those who remain behind rather than to use their resources to make change for all. Maintain the myth of scarcity—that there are not enough jobs, resources, etc., to go around—among the middleclass so that they will not unite with laborers, immigrants, and the unemployed. The method keeps in place a system of control and profit by a few and a constant source of cheap labor to maintain it.

If anyone steps out of line, take her/his job away. Let homelessness and hunger do their work. The economic weapon works. And we end up saying, "I would do this or that—be openly who I am, speak out against injustice, work for civil rights, join a labor union, go to a political march, etc.—if I didn't have this job. I can't afford to lose it." We stay in an abusive situation because we see no other way to survive....

Violence is the second means of keeping women in line, in a narrowly defined place and role. First, there is the physical violence of battering, rape, and incest. Often when battered women come to shelters and talk about their lives, they tell stories of being not only physically beaten but also raped and their children subjected to incest. Work in the women's anti-violence movement during almost two decades has provided significant evidence that each of these acts, including rape and incest, is an attempt to seek power over and control of another person. In each case, the victim is viewed as an object and is used to meet the abuser's needs. The violence is used to wreak punishment and to demand compliance or obedience.

Violence against women is directly related to the condition of women in a society that refuses us equal pay, equal access to resources, and equal status with males. From this condition comes men's confirmation of their sense of ownership of women, power over women, and assumed right to control women for their own means. Men physically and emotionally abuse women because they *can,* because they live in a world that gives them permission. Male violence is fed by their sense of their *right* to dominate and control, and their sense of superiority over a group of people who, because of gender, they consider inferior to them.

It is not just the violence but the threat of violence that controls our lives. Because the burden of responsibility has been placed so often on the potential victim, as women we have curtailed our freedom in order to protect ourselves from violence. Because of the threat of rapists, we stay on alert, being careful not to walk in isolated places, being careful where we park our cars, adding incredible security measures to our homes—massive locks, lights, alarms, if we can afford them—and we avoid places where we will appear vulnerable or unprotected while the abuser walks with freedom. Fear, often now so commonplace that it is unacknowledged, shapes our lives, reducing our freedom....

The threat of violence against women who step out of line or who are disloyal is made all the more powerful by the fact that women do not have to do anything—they may be paragons of virtue and subservience—to receive violence against our lives: the violence still comes. It comes because of the woman-hating that exists throughout society. Chance plays a larger part than virtue in keeping women safe. Hence, with violence always a threat to us, women can never feel completely secure and confident. Our sense of safety is always fragile and tenuous.

Many women say that verbal violence causes more harm than physical violence because it damages self-esteem so deeply. Women have not wanted to hear battered women say that the verbal abuse was as hurtful as the physical abuse: to acknowledge that truth would be tantamount to acknowledging that *virtually every woman is a battered woman.* It is difficult to keep strong against accusations of being a bitch, stupid, inferior, etc., etc. It is especially difficult when these individual assaults are backed up by a society that shows women in textbooks, advertising, TV programs, movies, etc., as debased, silly, inferior, and sexually objectified, and a society that gives tacit approval to pornography. When we internalize these messages, we call the result "low self-esteem," a therapeutic individualized term. It seems to me we should use the more political expression: when we internalize these messages, we experience *internalized sexism,* and we experience it in common with all women living in a sexist world. The violence against us is supported by a society in which woman-hating is deeply imbedded....

Homophobia works effectively as a weapon of sexism because it is joined with a powerful arm, heterosexism. Heterosexism creates the climate for homophobia with its assumption that the world is and must be heterosexual and its display of power and privilege as the norm. Heterosexism is the systemic display of homophobia in the institutions of society. Heterosexism and homophobia work together to enforce compulsory heterosexuality and that bastion of patriarchal power, the nuclear family. The central focus of the rightwing attack against women's liberation is that women's equality, women's self-determination, women's control of our own bodies and lives will damage what they see as the crucial societal institution, the nuclear family. The attack has been led by fundamentalist ministers across the country. The two areas they have focused on most consistently are abortion and homosexuality, and their passion has led them to bomb women's clinics and to recommend deprogramming for homosexuals and establishing camps to quarantine people with AIDS. To resist marriage and/or heterosexuality is to risk severe punishment and loss....

There was a time when the two most condemning accusations against a woman meant to ostracize and disempower her were "whore" and "lesbian." The sexual revolution and changing attitudes about heterosexual behavior may have led to some lessening of the power of the word *whore,* though it still has strength as a threat to sexual property and prostitutes are stigmatized and abused. However, the word *lesbian* is still fully charged and carries with it the full threat of loss of power and privilege, the threat of being cut asunder, abandoned, and left outside society's protection.

To be a lesbian is to be *perceived* as someone who has stepped out of line, who has moved out of sexual/economic dependence on a male, who is woman-identified. A lesbian is perceived as someone who can live without a man, and who is therefore (however illogically) against men. A lesbian is perceived as being outside the acceptable, routinized order of things. She is seen as someone who has no societal institutions to protect her and who is not privileged to the protection of individual males. Many heterosexual women see her as someone who stands in contradiction to the sacrifices they have made to conform to compulsory heterosexuality. A lesbian is perceived as a threat to the nuclear family, to male dominance and control, to the very heart of sexism.

Gay men are perceived also as a threat to male dominance and control, and the homophobia expressed against them has the same roots in sexism as does homophobia against lesbians. Visible gay men are the objects of extreme hatred and fear by heterosexual men because their breaking ranks with male heterosexual solidarity is seen as a damaging rent in the very fabric of sexism. They are seen as betrayers, as traitors who must be punished and eliminated. In the beating and killing of gay men we see clear evidence of this hatred. When we see the fierce homophobia expressed toward gay men, we can begin to understand the ways sexism also affects males through imposing rigid, dehumanizing gender roles on them. The two

circumstances in which it is legitimate for men to be openly physically affectionate with one another are in competitive sports and in the crisis of war. For many men, these two experiences are the highlights of their lives, and they think of them again and again with nostalgia. War and sports offer a cover of all-male safety and dominance to keep away the notion of affectionate openness being identified with homosexuality. When gay men break ranks with male roles through bonding and affection outside the arenas of war and sports, they are perceived as not being "real men," that is, as being identified with women, the weaker sex that must be dominated and that over the centuries has been the object of male hatred and abuse. Misogyny gets transferred to gay men with a vengeance and is increased by the fear that their sexual identity and behavior will bring down the entire system of male dominance and compulsory heterosexuality.

If lesbians are established as threats to the status quo, as outcasts who must be punished, homophobia can wield its power over all women through lesbian baiting. Lesbian baiting is an attempt to control women by labeling us as lesbians because our behavior is not acceptable, that is, when we are being independent, going our own way, living whole lives, fighting for our rights, demanding equal pay, saying no to violence, being self-assertive, bonding with and loving the company of women, assuming the right to our bodies, insisting upon our own authority, making changes that include us in society's decision-making; lesbian baiting occurs when women are called lesbians because we resist male dominance and control. And it has little or nothing to do with one's sexual identity.

To be named as lesbian threatens all women, not just lesbians, with great loss. And any woman who steps out of role risks being called a lesbian. To understand how this is a threat to all women, one must understand that any woman can be called a lesbian and there is no real way she can defend herself: there is no way to credential one's sexuality. ("The Children's Hour," a Lillian Hellman play, makes this point when a student asserts two teachers are lesbians and they have no way to disprove it.) She may be married or divorced, have children, dress in the most feminine manner, have sex with men, be celibate—but there are lesbians who do all those things. *Lesbians look like all women and all women look like lesbians.* There is no guaranteed method of identification, and as we all know, sexual identity can be kept hidden. (The same is true for men. There is no way to prove their sexual identity, though many go to extremes to prove heterosexuality.) Also, women are not necessarily born lesbian. Some seem to be, but others become lesbians later in life after having lived heterosexual lives. Lesbian baiting of heterosexual women would not work if there were a definitive way to identify lesbians (or heterosexuals)....

If, then, any woman can be named a lesbian and be threatened with terrible losses, what is it she fears? Are these fears real? Being vulnerable to a homophobic world can lead to these losses:

- *Employment.* The loss of job leads us right back to the economic connection to sexism. This fear of job loss exists for almost every lesbian except perhaps those who are self-employed or in a business that does not require societal approval. Consider how many businesses or organizations you know that will hire and protect people who are openly gay or lesbian.
- *Family.* Their approval, acceptance, love.
- *Children.* Many lesbians and gay men have children, but very, very few gain custody in court challenges, even if the other parent is a known abuser. Other children may be kept away from us as though gays and lesbians are abusers. There are written and unwritten laws prohibiting lesbians and gays from being foster parents or from adopting children. There is an irrational fear that children in contact with lesbians and gays will become homosexual through influence or that they will be sexually abused. Despite our knowing that 95 percent of those who sexually abuse children are heterosexual men, there are no policies keeping heterosexual men from teaching or working with children, yet in almost every school system in America, visible gay men and lesbians are not hired through either written or unwritten law.
- *Heterosexual privilege and protection.* No institutions, other than those created by lesbians and gays—such as the Metropolitan Community Church, some counseling centers, political

organizations such as the National Gay and Lesbian Task Force, the National Coalition of Black Lesbians and Gays, the Lambda Legal Defense and Education Fund, etc.—affirm homosexuality and offer protection. Affirmation and protection cannot be gained from the criminal justice system, mainline churches, educational institutions, the government.

- *Safety.* There is nowhere to turn for safety from physical and verbal attacks because the norm presently in this country is that it is acceptable to be overtly homophobic. Gay men are beaten on the streets; lesbians are kidnapped and "deprogrammed." The National Gay and Lesbian Task Force, in an extended study, has documented violence against lesbians and gay men and noted the inadequate response of the criminal justice system. One of the major differences between homophobia/heterosexism and racism and sexism is that because of the Civil Rights Movement and the women's movement racism and sexism are expressed more covertly (though with great harm); because there has not been a major, visible lesbian and gay movement, it is permissible to be overtly homophobic in any institution or public forum. Churches spew forth homophobia in the same way they did racism prior to the Civil Rights Movement. Few laws are in place to protect lesbians and gay men, and the criminal justice system is wracked with homophobia.
- *Mental health.* An overtly homophobic world in which there is full permission to treat lesbians and gay men with cruelty makes it difficult for lesbians and gay men to maintain a strong sense of well-being and self-esteem. Many lesbians and gay men are beaten, raped, killed, subjected to aversion therapy, or put in mental institutions. The impact of such hatred and negativity can lead one to depression and, in some cases, to suicide. The toll on the gay and lesbian community is devastating.
- *Community.* There is rejection by those who live in homophobic fear, those who are afraid of association with lesbians and gay men. For many in the gay and lesbian community, there is a loss of public acceptance, a loss of allies, a loss of place and belonging.

- *Credibility.* This fear is large for many people: the fear that they will no longer be respected, listened to, honored, believed. They fear they will be social outcasts.

The list goes on and on. But any one of these essential components of a full life is large enough to make one deeply fear its loss. A black woman once said to me in a workshop, "When I fought for Civil Rights, I always had my family and community to fall back on even when they didn't fully understand or accept what I was doing. I don't know if I could have borne losing them. And you people don't have either with you. It takes my breath away."

What does a woman have to do to get called a lesbian? Almost anything, sometimes nothing at all, but certainly anything that threatens the status quo, anything that steps out of role, anything that asserts the rights of women, anything that doesn't indicate submission and subordination. Assertiveness, standing up for oneself, asking for more pay, better working conditions, training for and accepting a non-traditional (you mean a man's?) job, enjoying the company of women, being financially independent, being in control of one's life, depending first and foremost upon oneself, thinking that one can do whatever needs to be done, but above all, working for the rights and equality of women.

In the backlash to the gains of the women's liberation movement, there has been an increased effort to keep definitions man-centered. Therefore, to work on behalf of women must mean to work against men. To love women must mean that one hates men. A very effective attack has been made against the word *feminist* to make it a derogatory word. In current backlash usage, *feminist* equals *man-hater* which equals *lesbian.* This formula is created in the hope that women will be frightened away from their work on behalf of women. Consequently, we now have women who believe in the rights of women and work for those rights while from fear deny that they are feminists, or refuse to use the word because it is so "abrasive."…

Women in many of these organizations, out of fear of all the losses we are threatened with, begin to modify our work to make it more acceptable and less threatening to the male-dominated society which we originally set out to change. The work can no longer be radical (going to the root cause of the problem) but instead must be reforming, working only on the symptoms and not the cause. Real change for women becomes thwarted and stopped. The word *lesbian* is instilled with the power to halt our work and control our lives. And we give it its power with our fear.

In my view, homophobia has been one of the major causes of the failure of the women's liberation movement to make deep and lasting change. (The other major block has been racism.) We were fierce when we set out but when threatened with the loss of heterosexual privilege, we began putting on brakes. Our best-known nationally distributed women's magazine was reluctant to print articles about lesbians, began putting a man on the cover several times a year, and writing articles about women who succeeded in a man's world. We worried about our image, our being all right, our being "real women" despite our work. Instead of talking about the elimination of sexual gender roles, we stepped back and talked about "sex role stereotyping" as the issue. Change around the edges for middleclass white women began to be talked about as successes. We accepted tokenism and integration, forgetting that equality for all women, for all people—and not just equality of white middleclass women with white men—was the goal that we could never put behind us.

But despite backlash and retreats, change is growing from within. The women's liberation movement is beginning to gain strength again because there are women who are talking about liberation for all women. We are examining sexism, racism, homophobia, classism, anti-Semitism, ageism, ableism, and imperialism, and we see everything as connected. This change in point of view represents the third wave of the women's liberation movement, a new direction that does not get mass media coverage and recognition. It has been initiated by women of color and lesbians who were marginalized or rendered invisible by the white heterosexual leaders of earlier efforts. The first wave was the 19th and early 20th century campaign for the vote; the second, beginning in the 1960s, focused on the Equal Rights Amendment and abortion rights. Consisting of predominantly white middleclass women, both failed in recognizing issues of equality and empowerment for all women. The third wave of the movement, multi-racial and multi-issued, seeks the transformation of the world for us all. We know that we won't get there until everyone gets there; that we must move forward in a great strong line, hand in hand, not just a few at a time.

We know that the arguments about homophobia originating from mental health and Biblical/religious attitudes can be settled when we look at the sexism that permeates religious and psychiatric history. The women of the third wave of the women's liberation movement know that *without the existence of sexism, there would be no homophobia.*

Finally, we know that as long as the word lesbian can strike fear in any woman's heart, then work on behalf of women can be stopped; the only successful work against sexism must include work against homophobia.

CRITICAL QUESTIONS

1. Has your own education been similar to the socialization process hooks describes? If not, how has it been different? If it has been similar, whose interest does this sort of socialization serve?

2. Do you think West is right when he claims that the "tragic facts of poverty and paranoia, despair and distrust" create a crisis for American democracy? Why, or why not?

3. Do you think, as Pharr does, that homophobia and sexism are linked? Why, or why not?

4. Apply the formal and material principles of justice discussed in the introduction of Chapter 5, Section 4 to the issue of whether gays should be given the right to legally marry. Also apply the idea of the "veil of ignorance" to this same issue. Indicate your reasoning and the conclusion(s) you draw.

6.3 ILLEGAL IMMIGRATION

What to do about illegal immigration is dividing America. Many conservatives want to "get tough," and close the borders, round up and deport millions (by some estimates nearly twelve million) of undocumented aliens, most of whom are Hispanic. Arizona has led the way by passing SB 1070, which is to date the most stringent anti-illegal immigration measure in the United States. If it becomes law, it would require police to, among other things, stop people they suspect might be illegal and require them to show proof of legal residency. If they cannot, they would be arrested and eventually deported.

Moderates and liberals want what they consider to be a more humane and practical approach to the problem by developing Federal legislation that provides a path to permanent residency for undocumented aliens as long as certain requirements are met, such as length of residency in the United States. So far the divisions and heated rhetoric that have characterized the divisions in the states is mirrored on the Federal level and no comprehensive immigration reform legislation has been passed. Can philosophy shed any more reasoned light on the problem? What is fair for all concerned? How do we determine fairness when dealing with this social issue? What is the morally right thing to do?

Reginald Williams, chair of the Department of Philosophy at Bakersfield College, sees the issue of illegal immigration as a problem that social and political philosophy can illuminate. Careful analysis and reasoned thought can point us, he believes, in the right direction. In the following selection he presents a clear and careful argument for a solution that he thinks satisfies the demands of justice.

READING QUESTIONS

1. What is Williams's main point?

2. Summarize the "five underappreciated facts" that Williams cites in your own words and explain how

they support his claim that illegal migrant laborers have earned the right to permanent residency.

3. What is Kershnar's argument, and how does Williams counter it?

4. Select three of what you consider to be the strongest objections to Williams' argument, summarize the objections, and describe how Williams counters them.

A Case for Residency

REGINALD WILLIAMS

1. INTRODUCTION

This paper argues that illegal migrant laborers who are currently in the U.S. should be granted permanent residency if they have contributed to its economy for a certain period of time which I will not attempt to specify and if they have not committed any serious crimes in the country (i.e., if the only criminal statute of the U.S. which they have violated is that against illegal entry into the country). My argument is theoretical and tentative. For some of my points would benefit from empirical support, but there are no definitive statistics on the relevant issues. The aim, accordingly, is to create a framework, and I hope a demand, for empirical investigations of illegal immigration that could lend factual support to my claims.[i]

2. THE ARGUMENT

There are five underappreciated facts that, when combined with certain normative considerations identified below, provide strong support for granting illegal migrant laborers permanent residency in the U.S.:

1. Some American companies have recruiting stations in Mexico which solicit the labor of illegal immigrants and even transport them to the U.S.;

2. The illegal migrant laborers whom some American companies recruit are financially desperate, and it is primarily because of this that they are inclined to immigrate to the U.S.;

3. American companies tend to pay illegal migrant laborers less than America's minimum legal wage to work in the U.S.;

4. America's economy could not have expanded to the extent that it has, as quickly as it has, without the inexpensive labor of illegal immigrants; and

5. The vast majority of Americans, including a vast majority of those calling for the deportation of illegal immigrants, have created a demand for, and benefited from, the labor of these immigrants by consuming the goods and services which they have supplied in the U.S.

My basic contention will be that it is unfair for America to deport its illegal migrant laborers when some of its own companies have invited and transported some of these laborers to the U.S. and when the vast majority of Americans have consumed, and thus benefited from, the inexpensive goods and services which these laborers have contributed to America's economy. To establish this claim, however, each of my argument's five premises must be defended.

2.1: On the Recruitment of Illegal Immigrants

It would strengthen my argument if I could specify how many recruiting stations exist in Mexico or the number of illegal immigrants that American companies recruit each year. Predictably, though, neither American employers nor the government keeps such records; they simply do not exist. What

From "Illegal Immigration: A Case for Residency," *Public Affairs Quarterly*, 23.4 (October, 2009), 309–324. Reprinted by permission.

can be said in defense of my first premise—beyond my first-hand knowledge, living in an agricultural hub of California's Central Valley—is that American companies have recruited enough illegal migrant laborers to have prompted Congress's Committee on Education and Labor to hear testimony on the matter in 2007.[ii]

This is interesting because in America we see government officials and residents of our agricultural communities—people who know about these recruiting practices—debating 'what should be done about' illegal immigrants in the U.S. But do we ever see these people debating how to hold American companies accountable for facilitating illegal immigration? Do people protest these companies' products as they protest the fur industry?

News agencies tend to frame the illegal immigration debate as a debate over whether the U.S. should tolerate people's literally *running* across its border with Mexico. Even Michael Taylor, who defends granting illegal immigrants citizenship, does so by appealing to the risks and harms that they face when breaching the U.S./Mexico border:

> To get work, immigrants must cross the border illegally, and in doing so they subject themselves to significant risks and sometimes to injury or even death. They may be caught by the Border Patrol or armed militia groups such as the "Minutemen." The occasional irate landowner may take a pot shot at them. There are formidable obstacles that must be negotiated if the crossing is made, as it increasingly is, in remote areas, which heighten the risk of dehydration, hunger, exposure, and accident. Finally, there is lethal risk if they happen to be abandoned in a locked truck or railway car....[iii]

Taylor's argument is problematic, though, because we do not usually grant one rights for incurring risks or hardships while breaking the law. Given that a law is just, that those who wrote and passed it are not inducing people to break it, and so forth, we hold violators responsible for breaking the law. We would not take a trespasser, for instance, to deserve anything for taking risks and incurring hardships while breaking into someone's house.

More attention should be paid to the fact some American companies encourage illegal immigrants to enter the U.S. and assist them in doing so. If illegal immigration is a problem, then companies which encourage, recruit, and transport illegal immigrants to the U.S. are part of the problem. Indeed, these companies are exacerbating any social problem that is associated with illegal immigration: crime, rising healthcare costs, etc. Many illegal immigrants would not enter the U.S. were it not for the financial incentives and transportation provided by American companies. Furthermore, any company which recruits and transports illegal immigrants to America is as guilty of violating America's immigration laws as illegal immigrants are for being in the country.

The question here is who should bear the burden of solving whatever problems illegal immigration has created in the U.S. Who should have to pay the costs of illegal immigration: illegal immigrants, who as a class have provided the U.S. with an abundance of cheap arduous labor, or American companies and citizens who have benefited from this labor?

Given that many illegal migrant laborers were encouraged to enter the U.S. in the first place, and given that American companies benefited from illegal migrant labor (if they had not, they would not have recruited or employed it), it seems unfair for illegal migrant laborers to bear the burden of correcting the problems associated with their presence in the U.S. It seems unfair for these laborers to bear the additional burden of being deported: a substantial burden considering that many of them have resided in the U.S. for years at this point. It seems particularly unfair to deport a class of hardworking laborers to a region whose poverty rendered it vulnerable to the recruiting practices described above. It seems only fair that those who have most benefited from illegal migrant labor bear the burden of correcting the problems associated with it: American companies and ultimately, I will argue, American consumers.

2.2 On the Financial Desperation of Illegal Migrant Laborers

One need only visit illegal migrant laborers, in America or in their homeland, to see that they live in poverty. Were they not poor in the first place, they would not leave their homes and families to undertake arduous, precarious work in a foreign country. The immigration debate needs to better appreciate that poverty motivates illegal migrant laborers to enter the U.S. For, to build on my first premise, American companies which recruit illegal migrant laborers in Mexico are not recruiting just anyone to work in the U.S.; they are knowingly recruiting the desperately poor. This raises an important question: Are such companies exploiting the financial desperation of these people?

This issue is contentious because illegal migrant laborers earn more for their service in the U.S. than in their homeland; they would not immigrate otherwise. Given this, one could deny that a company which offers to pay these laborers more than they are used to earning is exploiting their financial desperation. Indeed, one could argue that such a company is doing these laborers a favor.

The problem with this view is that one can presumably benefit another and still exploit his or her financial desperation. As Alan Wertheimer notes, 'In many cases of alleged exploitation, A takes advantage of B's circumstances to get B to agree to a mutually advantageous transaction to which B would not have agreed under better or perhaps more just background conditions, where A has no special obligation to repair those conditions, and where B is fully informed as to the consequences of various choices'.[iv] The 'adult' film industry presumably exploits the hardship of any performer who enters the industry to avoid living on the streets, even if the performer benefits by having a paycheck and a residence. And a company likewise exploits the hardship of potential laborers when it enters their poor neighborhoods outside the U.S., recruiting them to work in the U.S. for the kinds of wages they garner here.

These wages *are* higher than those which illegal migrant laborers make back home, but they are not merely *low* by U.S. standards; they are *illegally low*. Moreover, there is a good reason that America's minimum legal wage should apply to all laborers in the U.S.—be they legal or illegal, accustomed or unaccustomed to earning more. The reason is that anyone who resides in the U.S. must live in accord with its cost of living.

2.3 On the Compensation of Illegal Migrant Laborers

It is difficult to find reliable statistics on the wages that illegal migrant laborers earn in the U.S., and the best professional studies on the topic appear to have been done in the 1990s.[v] 'Undocumented laborers' are just that: undocumented. There is ample evidence that these laborers are paid less than Americans for doing the same work. A common criticism of illegal immigration, after all, is that it drives down American wages.[vi] But for this to obtain, illegal migrant laborers must earn less than Americans for the same work. Furthermore, one recent study leaves little doubt that at least one large pool of illegal migrant laborers earns less than America's minimum legal wage—i.e., those living in Los Angeles.

In 2006, the Economic Roundtable, a nonprofit, public research organization, published the results of an extensive study, conducted in 2004, of the 'informal economy' of Los Angeles: the city's 'underground', or off-the-record, employment and taxation trends.[vii] The study concluded that, in 2004, approximately 679,000 illegal laborers were employed in Los Angeles: a staggering 15% of the city's entire labor force. In addition, the average annual income of these laborers was just above $12,000. And this is telling because in 2004, California's minimum legal wage was $6.75/hour. So at $6.75/hour, one who worked 40 hours/week for 50 weeks in 2004 would have made $13,500, not $12,000. Conversely, to earn $12,000 in 2004, one who worked 40 hours/week for 50 weeks would have been earning $6.00/hour, not $6.75/hour.

One could object that if these laborers worked in agriculture, these figures are consistent with their having earned California's minimum legal wage in 2004 (even more). For jobs in agriculture are seasonal; field work does not span 50 weeks/year. While field work is seasonal, and while this paper will focus on illegal migrant labor in agriculture, most of the illegal migrant laborers in Los Angeles, which is not an agricultural area, are employed in factories, warehouses, restaurants, office buildings, nursing homes, and private residences.[viii] These jobs tend to span not only 50 weeks/year but also to involve more than 40 hours/week. So an illegal laborer in Los Angeles who earned just above $12,000 in 2004 likely earned even less than $6.00/hour.

Taking the illegal migrant labor market of Los Angeles as indicative of broader American trends, then, there is strong evidence that illegal migrant laborers often work in the U.S. for less than its minimum legal wage. And this again means that they must find a way to live on their wages and yet in accord with America's cost of living.

2.4 On the Economic Contributions of Illegal Migrant Laborers

More than half of the immigrants working in America's agriculture sector are undocumented.[ix] As noted, moreover, Congress considered America's illegal migrant labor force to be sufficiently important in 2007 to hold hearings on it. Peter Schuck has also recently observed:

> The interest groups that pressed in the late 1980s both for more legal immigrants and for amnesties or others bars to removal of illegals continue to do so. Perhaps the most important of these is growers, whose demand for agricultural labor seems inexhaustible and whose prosperity is vital to the economies and political establishments in many of our states, including the most populous ones (e.g., California, Texas, Florida, and New York).[x]

Finally, there is a powerful, straightforward case for thinking that at least some vital sectors of America's economy have expanded on a scale and at a rate which would have been impossible without illegal laborers:

A) Some important American companies (e.g., in agriculture) have managed to pay illegal migrant laborers less than they could have paid *legal* laborers for the same work since the U.S. has a minimum *legal* wage.

B) Paying illegal migrant laborers less for doing this work has enabled some important American companies to supply more goods and services per cost than they could have supplied without employing illegal migrant laborers.

C) Supplying more goods and services per cost has enabled some important American

companies to charge American consumers less for their products than they could have realistically charged without employing illegal migrant laborers.

D) Therefore, since American consumers have been charged less than they otherwise realistically could have been charged for the goods and services which illegal migrant laborers have supplied, most notably for their food but again for manufactured goods and for a variety of services as well, Americans have been able to save more money, thus generating investment income, and to spend more money on other goods and services: from furniture and cars to education, medicine, and technology.

Assuming that illegal migrant laborers have not imposed costs on the economy which outweigh their contributions—an issue that I will discuss at the end of this paper—I see no way to avoid the conclusion that illegal migrant laborers have helped America's economy expand on a scale and at a rate that would have been impossible without their contributions. One could object that, given sufficient demand, American companies would supply the same levels of goods and services with or without illegal migrant laborers; these companies would just generate less profit without these laborers. This objection, however, contradicts three of the most basic principles of American business (if not of capitalism). First, companies pass on their costs to consumers. Second, the more a good or service costs, the less consumers demand it. Third, companies normally refuse to supply goods and services for less than 'normal profit' (unless the government mandates that they do so).

Given these principles, illegal migrant laborers have contributed to America's economy, and the vast majority of Americans have benefited from their contributions. One could object that Americans have not only benefited from the labor which illegal immigrants have provided American companies; Americans have benefited from *these companies' employing* such laborers as well. In addition, the immigrants themselves have benefited from obtaining this employment; otherwise, as noted, they would not have left their homes to obtain it. Indeed, one could add, if America's illegal migrant laborers were deported tomorrow, they would still be better off having worked here temporarily than not at all; many of these laborers manage to send some of their earnings to family at home.

So what, exactly, is the problem here? If Americans, American companies, and illegal migrant laborers have all benefited from America's immigration policy, why grant illegal migrant laborers residency? Everyone seems to benefit from the way things are.

The problem which I will develop in Section 2.5 below is that America's current and long-standing immigration policy has fostered in illegal migrant laborers a rational expectation that they will not be deported from the U.S., which over time can be taken to undermine the legitimacy of deporting those who have been in the country contributing to it. Furthermore, as illegal migrant laborers would not enter the U.S. if they did not stand to benefit from doing so, they would presumably be anxious to get back home when their work in the U.S. is done if they did not believe that they stood to benefit more by staying in the country. So even if illegal migrant laborers are better off having lived and worked temporarily in the U.S. than not at all, the question remains open whether it is acceptable for these laborers to be deported, given the facts highlighted in this paper, and given that these laborers prefer not to be deported.

2.5 On the Benefits of Illegal Migrant Labor

Much of the immigration debate in America ignores the ways in which Americans have benefited from illegal immigration. The debate often does not even juxtapose the benefits of such immigration and the problems with it. Stephen Kershnar, for instance, has recently used the following thought experiment to argue that immigration can harm a country's current citizens by 'changing the character of the institutions to which [they] have consented':

> Imagine that one hundred of us are members of a private club and that we agree upon certain arrangements that allow our club to be quite enjoyable to all or nearly all members. Then one big-hearted member decides he would like to add another 120 members, where these members will likely bring about great changes to our club, of which we might not approve. For example, if the new members are Hasidic Jews, they might not approve of some of the scantily clad social events that the club traditionally sponsors. The big-hearted member would be changing the nature of our club, probably in significant ways, without the permission of its members. This would seem to infringe upon their rights, especially their contractual rights. Hence, it would seem that there is no right to join the club, and that allowing a flood of new members without the consent of the current membership would be unjust.[xi]

This scenario emphasizes some important aspects of immigration in the U.S. For example, the fact that the new members of Kershnar's club bring with them a radically different culture represents the fact that many Americans feel that illegal immigration detrimentally affects their nation's culture or ethos. In addition, and relevant here, the fact that one member of Kershnar's club invites the new members without the consent of the other original members parallels the fact that even if Americans create demand for illegal migrant laborers, as I contend, most of those who create this demand did not invite illegal migrant laborers to the U.S. or consent to their being in the country. American companies invited some of these laborers, and the rest of them entered the U.S. without invitation.

There are, however, at least two respects in which Kershnar's thought experiment does not parallel illegal immigration in the U.S. The first problem concerns Kershnar's choice of numbers. A club with 100 members would be over-run and difficult to sustain if 120 new members joined; the original members would be literally outnumbered. But these numbers hardly represent the U.S., whose official population exceeds 300 million and whose illegal migrant population is an estimated 12 million.[xii] Second, Kershnar's thought experiment seems to assume that the effects of 'new members' on an institution will be wholly negative. Like so much of the immigration debate in America, Kershnar's thought experiment does not consider that new members could be both a partial burden and a partial boon to the original members of an institution.[xiii]

Granted, the original members of an institution may prefer to forgo the benefits which new members could provide in order to maintain the character of their institution. In this event, though, the original members should *actually forgo* these benefits as much as possible. Few Americans forgo the benefits of having an illegal migrant labor force; the vast majority reaps these benefits daily. Every dollar that one saves on food which illegal migrant laborers produce or harvest in the U.S. is a dollar that one can spend on one's education, on a home, on a mutual fund, etc. The benefits which accrue from such savings endure long after one has digested one's food, and it is unfair for America to deport a class of immigrants from whose labor its citizens have thus benefited, especially when one considers these benefits in conjunction with the following claims that I have sought to defend:

- American companies have often recruited illegal migrant laborers in their homeland and helped them enter the U.S., violating its immigration laws in the process.
- These companies exploit the severe poverty of a region, luring particularly desperate people away from their homes and families.
- The people then work in the U.S. for less than its minimum legal wage, struggling to live in accord with its cost of living.
- They have helped its economy to expand to an extent, and at a rate, that would have been impossible without their inexpensive labor, labor for which the vast majority of Americans have created a demand.

One could object that despite being encouraged to enter the U.S., illegal migrant laborers had to realize that their being in the country was against the law, and that they faced deportation if discovered. The question, then, becomes why think it unfair to deport these laborers. Why not see deportation as a risk which they knowingly and willingly took in order to earn an income that was unavailable to them back home, and one whose consequences they must face if discovered in the U.S. To deport an illegal migrant laborer, after all, is but to enforce an immigration law that is on the books in the U.S. Illegal migrant laborers do realize that their being in America is against the law, and that they

could be deported if discovered in the country. They also realize, however, that for decades the U.S. has not deported them: despite the ease with which it could have done so. To deport illegal migrant laborers in large numbers, the government need only visit America's farmlands during harvest season.

By not deporting illegal immigrants whom it could easily deport, the U.S. has fostered in these persons a rational expectation that they will not be deported. And even if it is not *unjust* for the U.S. to violate this expectation and to deport these laborers—granting that America's failure to enforce its immigration laws does not render it forever unjust to enforce them—America's failure to enforce its immigration laws does weaken the normative force of these laws. In particular, given its long-standing tendency not to deport illegal migrant laborers, it seems unfair for America now, without an official and widely publicized change of policy, to begin deporting those who have been allowed to live in the U.S. for years with the rational expectation that they will not be deported.

The U.S. should grant residency to illegal migrant laborers who are presently in the country and have contributed to it for a period of time which I will, again, not specify. Moreover, if Americans wish to end illegal immigration, the government should announce that it will begin immediately to police its borders and as of some specific date will begin to deport illegal immigrants unless they can provide evidence of having been productively employed for a certain period. Such a policy would be more fair than deporting a hardworking class of laborers in which America has fostered a rational expectation of living in the country. There remain, however, eight objections to my argument that merit replies.

3. OBJECTIONS AND REPLIES

First, one could object that even if the vast majority of Americans have consumed goods and services which illegal immigrants supply, many Americans are either unaware that they have done so or could not realistically avoid doing so. The issue, however, is whether the benefits which Americans have accrued by consuming these goods and services establish a debt to those who have supplied them. One need not voluntarily or knowingly benefit from something to owe another a debt for providing it. I, for instance, would presumably owe part of my tax dollars to police agencies even if I did not voluntarily entrust them with securing my society and even if I did not realize that they did so. Similarly, I would argue that my society owes a debt to illegal migrant laborers who have provided it with the benefits highlighted in this paper, even if those who have benefited have not voluntarily or knowingly done so.

Second, one could object that the reasons which I have offered for granting illegal migrant laborers U.S. residency better support deporting them with added compensation for their contributions to the country. The companies which employed these laborers, for example, might be required to pay them a stipend when they are deported: one that compensates them for working in America for less than its minimum legal wage. While this is an interesting proposal, it is an unviable as a matter of public policy. For approximately 12 million people, again, currently reside illegally in the U.S., and companies which employ them tend not to keep records on them. Specifically, these companies tend not to record the names of their illegal migrant laborers, the duration of their employment, or their earnings with the company. So even if we could identify the companies which have recruited illegal migrant laborers and paid them less than America's minimum legal wage, the prospects of determining what these companies should pay such laborers at the time of their deportation are very low.

Third, one could object that if I am right and illegal migrant laborers should be granted U.S. residency, why not take their contributions to warrant making illegal migrant laborers full-blown citizens of the U.S.? Is there any principled reason to grant them only residency? The question of citizenship is different from that of residency, and it must be answered on different criteria. Residents of the U.S. should be allowed to apply for citizenship at some point, but deciding whether they should be made citizens would require considerations that go beyond the scope of this paper: beyond their economic contributions to the country. One does not have a claim to become the citizen of a country by merely contributing to its economy.

Fourth, one could object that temporary but legal migrant laborers contribute to America's economy (even to its agriculture sector). But we do not see them as entitled to stay in the U.S. permanently. So why should the U.S. treat illegal migrant laborers differently? Temporary migrant laborers do not work for years in the U.S. for less than its minimum legal wage, and thus the labor of temporary migrants has not helped keep American production costs and prices down to the extent that illegal migrant laborers have. In addition, temporary migrant laborers work with a contract which specifies how long they will be employed and allowed to live in the U.S. These laborers do not therefore form a rational expectation to live in America indefinitely as many illegal migrant laborers do. My argument, then, provides a basis for granting illegal migrant laborers residency in the U.S. which does not extend to temporary migrant laborers.

Fifth, one could object that if my argument establishes that illegal migrant laborers who contribute sufficiently to America's economy should be granted residency, what about current residents of other countries who would be happy to enter the U.S. illegally and contribute to its economy if doing so earned them residency? Does not my argument sanction such immigration? The answer is no. For my argument concerns how illegal migrant laborers who are *now in the U.S.* ought to be treated, not the terms under which migrant laborers should be allowed to *enter* the country. It might have been wrong for these immigrants to enter the U.S. in the first place; my argument is consistent with this claim, and with my suggestion that illegal immigration should stop at some determinate and publicized date in the future. The fact is that many illegal migrant laborers are now in the U.S. and have contributed to its economy for some time, which provide grounds for granting them residency.

Sixth, one could object that illegal migrant laborers are not the only persons who work for American companies for less than America's minimum legal wage, thus helping America's economy to expand in a way that would be impossible without their labor. Countless foreign laborers do the same thing every day in sweatshops which American companies operate abroad. One could thus ask: If this paper is correct and illegal migrant laborers should be made residents of the U.S., ought these foreign laborers to be offered residency as well?

There may or may not be good independent reasons to oppose an American company's paying foreign laborers less than America's minimum legal wage; this matter cannot be resolved here. In either event, my argument does not entail that such laborers should be offered U.S. residency. For one thing, even if foreign laborers contribute to America's economy as much as illegal migrant laborers do, only the latter must manage to live in accord with America's cost of living on a lower wage than its law sanctions. One at least hopes that while American companies pay foreign laborers less than America's minimum legal wage, the countries which house American sweatshops have lower costs of living which allow people to live on less money than one needs to live in the U.S.

One could reply: If America's standard of living is higher than are the standards of living in countries which house American sweatshops, and if illegal migrant laborers in the U.S. enjoy even some of the advantages that America's standard of living offers, why take illegal migrant laborers in the U.S. to deserve residency more than do foreign laborers who provide similar services without receiving the benefits of living and working temporarily in the U.S.?

There are advantages to living and working even temporarily in the U.S., but there is another important difference between illegal migrant laborers in the U.S. and foreign laborers who work for American companies. The former laborers, again, leave their homes, their families, essentially the *lives* to which they are accustomed, to work for American companies. They sacrifice the opportunity to stroll familiar streets, to eat at familiar tables, to see their loved ones and friends: even to communicate with locals if they do not speak English. Foreign laborers who work for American sweatshops do not face these hardships. And thus while such laborers earn less than America's minimum legal wage, and while they help America's economy expand as do illegal migrant laborers, my argument provides grounds for not extending residency rights to them.

Seventh, one could object that for residency rights to mean anything to illegal migrant laborers, the U.S. would have to offer their spouses and children residency, particularly as my argument emphasizes that these laborers are often recruited away from their families. And even if one is convinced that the treatment and contributions of illegal migrant laborers warrant making them U.S. residents at some point, one could deny that the U.S. can or should accommodate the families of these laborers, who have not been so treated or contributed anything to the country. Indeed, extending residency rights to these laborers' families could be economically disastrous. For, again, there are approximately 12 million illegal immigrants in America today; so if even twenty percent of them had just a spouse back home (a conservative estimate), then extending residency rights to these families would increase America's population by more than two million, and this at a time when America's economy is already strained.

This is a difficult objection. Perhaps the best way to implement the immigration policy that I am defending would be to offer residency to the family of an illegal migrant laborer only if the laborer has moved beyond entry level work (e.g., in agriculture fields) and secured employment (e.g., a management position) which can be proven stable and sufficient to support the laborer and his or her family without government assistance. We might require that illegal migrant laborers earn twice the income they need to support themselves in order for a spouse or domestic partner to become a resident and an additional percentage of their income for each child to become a resident, as many apartments require that prospective tenets earn three times the rent to secure a lease. While no doubt imperfect, such a policy would have advantages. It would allow illegal migrant laborers a realistic hope that their families could eventually join them in the U.S., making the right of residency that I would extend to them meaningful. It would provide an incentive for illegal migrant laborers to move up in their employment. And it would prevent a deluge of new immigrants from entering the U.S. because many of the illegal migrant laborers who are in the U.S. do not currently earn enough to secure residency for their families.

Eighth, and finally, I have presupposed that the debate over illegal immigration in America should be framed in terms of the economic contributions that illegal migrant laborers have made to the country. I take this focus to be important because those who debate immigration in America often ignore or trivialize these contributions. It is more common to see this debate framed in terms of the burden that illegal immigrants pose to America's healthcare system or the crimes which some of them commit. But, of course, illegal immigrants do require healthcare; and some of them commit serious crimes as well.[xiv] Moreover, while the number of working illegal immigrants is substantial, sufficiently substantial again to motivate Congressional Hearings and interest groups in Washington, many other illegal immigrants in America are *not* working. In fact, a recent report to Congress indicates that the 'typical crop worker' only performs farm labor 66% of the

year. And 16% of these workers are unemployed the rest of the year.[xv]

These facts are important. For if the costs of illegal immigration are high, they might override my argument by showing illegal immigration to impose a net loss on America's economy. My argument, however, is consistent with America's denying residency to illegal migrant laborers who have consumed too much of its healthcare or committed serious crimes. The U.S. should implement the immigration policy that I have defended on a case-by-case basis, performing background checks on each prospective resident and verifying that he or she has in fact made a net contribution to America's economy. The problem is that, as of now, such verification is impossible because there are not adequate records of, or studies on, the economic contributions of illegal migrant laborers. The hope again is that my argument will motivate research in the area.[xvi]

NOTES

i. Not only have economists failed to pursue the issues that concern me in this paper; historically, very little philosophical attention has been paid to these matters as well. Thus, in a recent survey article, Michael Blake writes: 'Immigration has not received a great deal of philosophical attention. While the issues surrounding immigration have become subjects of vigorous public discussion, a like discussion has not been forthcoming in the philosophical community. Indeed, there may be no other area of political life in which so many heated issues have met with so little sustained normative theorizing'. See 'Immigration.' *A Companion to Applied Ethics* (Eds.) R. G. Frey and Christopher Heath Wellman. (Malden, MA: Blackwell, 2003), pp. 224. x

ii. For Baldemar Velasquez's testimony on American companies' recruitment of illegal immigrant laborers, go to www.floc.com/documents/BV%20Testimony%20HR1763.pdf.

iii. See 'Illegal Immigration and Moral Obligation'. *Public Affairs Quarterly* 22.1 (2008), p. 32.

iv. See *Exploitation* (Princeton: Princeton University Press, 1996), p. 27. See also Joel Feinberg, *Harmless Wrongdoing* (New York: Oxford University Press, 1998), p. 179.

v. I have in mind Francisco L. Rivera-Batiz, 'Underground Workers in the Labor Market: An Analysis of the Earnings of Legal and Illegal Mexican Immigrants in the U.S.' *Journal of Population Economics* 12.1 (1999), pp. 91–116.

vi. See, for example, Peter Brimelow, 'Economics of Immigration and the Course of the Debate since 1994'. *Debating Immigration*. Ed. Carol M. Swain (New York: Cambridge University Press, 2007), pp. 163–4.

vii. See Richard D. Vogel, 'Harder Times: Undocumented Workers and the U.S. Informal Economy'. *Monthly Review* 58.3 (July–August 2006), available at www.monthlyreview.org/0706vogel.htm.

viii. Ibid.

ix. A recent report to Congress indicates that since 1997, 'unauthorized aliens' comprise more than 50% of the 'estimated 1.8 million workers' on America's farmlands. See Linda Levine. 'Congressional Research Service Report for Congress: Farm Labor Shortages and Immigration Policy' (September 5, 2007), p. 2.

x. See 'The Disconnect between Public Attitudes and Policy Outcomes in Immigration' in Carol Swain (ed.), *Debating Immigration*, p. 22.

xi. See 'There is No Moral Right to Immigrate to the United States'. *Public Affairs Quarterly* 14 (2000), pp. 141–158.

xii. See Adam Davidson, 'Q & A: Illegal Immigrants and the U.S. Economy', NPR (September 30, 2008), available at www.npr.org/templates/story/story.php?storyId=5312900.

xiii. In fairness to Kershnar, one could read his thought experiment as a purely theoretical argument against the 'cosmopolitan' view that liberal political theory entails an open borders policy on immigration. That is, it could be read as having nothing to do with immigration as it actually exists in the U.S., for instance. This, however, would seem a bit of a stretch, interpretively, given the title of Kershnar's paper: 'There is no Moral Right to Immigrate to the United States.' Furthermore, in either event, the present investigation will proceed to discuss immigration in a way that is hopefully of practical significance. In this way, then, the present investigation will be in the spirit of Shelley Wilcox's recent concern with 'cosmopolitanism': 'The "open borders" position on immigration is an attractive cosmopolitan ideal, and the freedom of movement argument may be plausible at the level of ideal theory. However, I will suggest that this argument fails to provide adequate normative guidance concerning immigration in the world as it is today'. See 'Immigrant Admissions and Global Relations of Harm'. *Journal of Social Philosophy* 38.2 (2007), pp. 274–291.

xiv. It is surprisingly difficult to get official numbers or percentages of U.S. crimes that are committed by illegal immigrants. U.S. jails and prison systems tend not to record whether crimes were committed by citizens or illegal immigrants. In addition, the INS and Department of Homeland Security tend not to classify illegal immigrant offenders in terms of their specific offenses. So [long] as being in the U.S. illegally is a criminal offense, one is hard pressed to get reliable numbers on how many of these persons have committed violent or even property crimes in America. What one does find is much speculation on these matters. On the one hand, there is no question that illegal immigrants commit some serious crimes. A 2006 *Time Magazine* article, for instance, reported that from October 1st of 2003 to July 20th of 2004, 9,051 people with criminal records were apprehended by Tuscon border patrol agents, 378 of them with active warrants, two of these warrants in a one-week period being for homicide. See Donald L. Barlett and James B. Steele, 'Who Left the Door Open?' (Thursday, March 30), p. 14, available at www.time.com/time/magazine/article/0,9171,995145-14,00.html. On the other hand, a careful, well-researched 2005 paper by the Federal Reserve Bank of Dallas concluded that while increased patrolling of the U.S./Mexico border between 1991 and 2000 was correlated with a reduction in violent crime along the border, this reduction was lower than that observed on the national level in America during the same period. See Robert Coronado and Pia M. Orrenius, 'The Effect of Undocumented Immigration and Border Enforcement on Crime Rates along the U.S.-Mexico Border', p. 19, available at www.dallasfed.org/research/papers/2003/wp0303.pdf.

xv. See Linda Levine, 'Congressional Research', p. 12.

xvi. I would like to thank Jeff McMahan for providing extensive comments on several drafts of this paper. I would also like to thank René Trujillo and Jeremy Oxford for research assistance, and Joseph Carens, Stephen Kershnar, and Shelley Wilcox for helpful correspondences.

◉ CRITICAL QUESTIONS

1. Do you find Williams's argument persuasive? Why or why not?

2. Do you think that framing the debate over illegal immigration in economic terms undermines Williams's moral argument that it is only fair not to deport illegal immigrants given the benefits that the United States has derived from their labor? Why or why not?

6.4 GLOBALIZATION AND JUSTICE

Anyone who follows the news must be dismayed by the power of the two opposing forces now shaping global events. On the one hand, the world appears to be disintegrating into smaller and smaller units intent on pursuing their own agendas for self-determination. On the other hand, the forces of telecommunications and globalization render the world more interconnected and interdependent than it has ever been. Muslim women wear lipstick and nail polish under their black burkas while sipping Pepsi through straws in the openings of their veils.

How can both disintegration and integration be happening all at once? How can people around the world become both closer and further apart at the same time? What are the political and ethical implications of globalization? Is the idea of nationalism passé? Is the notion of sovereign nations pursuing their own self-interests viable any more?

Philosophers have long considered the ideal of cosmopolitanism. Greek and Roman Stoic philosophers proclaimed themselves citizens of the world (although their idea of the world was certainly very different from and smaller than our own). However, the forces of nationalism are strong. The attempts to build a League of Nations after the First World War failed, and the formation of the United Nations almost crashed on the shores of nationalism. Is it time, given the age in which we live, to take up seriously once more the ancient idea of world citizenship? Is a global ethic of justice possible?

Peter Singer, the Ira W. De Camp Professor of Bioethics at Princeton University, gave the prestigious Terry Lectures at Yale University in 2000. Those lectures constitute the core of one of his many books, *One World: The Ethics of Globalization*, from which I take the following selection.

◉ READING QUESTIONS

1. What is the "fundamental ethical issue" Singer wishes to consider?
2. What is the argument in favor of the position that "the abstract ethical idea that all humans are entitled to equal consideration cannot govern the duties of a political leader"?
3. What is the difference between an international order and a global order? How does this distinction relate to Singer's critique of Rawls's theory of justice?
4. How does Singer use Marx's claims about technology and Friedman's idea of "a Golden Straitjacket" to advance his argument?

One World: The Ethics of Globalization

PETER SINGER

Consider two aspects of globalization: first, planes exploding as they slam into the World Trade Center, and second, the emission of carbon dioxide from the exhausts of gas-guzzling sport utility vehicles. One brought instant death and left unforgettable images that were watched on television screens all over the world; the other makes a contribution to climate change that can be detected only by scientific instruments. Yet both are indications of the way in which we are now one world, and the more subtle changes to which sport utility vehicle owners unintentionally contribute will almost certainly kill far more people than the highly visible one. When people in rich nations switch to vehicles that use more fuel than the cars they used to drive, they contribute to changes in the climate of Mozambique or Bangladesh—changes that may cause crops to fail, sea levels to rise, and tropical diseases to spread. As scientists pile up the evidence that continuing greenhouse gas emissions will imperil millions of lives, the leader of the nation that emits the largest share of these gases has said: "We will not do anything that harms our economy, because first things first are the people who live in America."[1] Consistently with this approach, as sales of sport utility vehicles increase, the average gas mileage of cars sold in the United States falls, and each year the U.S. Congress rejects measures to raise fuel efficiency standards for cars and trucks. The last time federal standards were raised was in 1985.[2]

President George W. Bush's remarks were not an aberration, but an expression of an ethical view that he has held for some time. In the second presidential debate against Vice-President Gore, then-Governor Bush was asked what use he would make of America's power and influence in the world. He said that he would use it for the benefit of all Americans. He may have learned this ethic from his father. The first President George Bush had said much the same thing at the 1992 Earth Summit in Rio de Janeiro. When representatives of developing nations asked Bush senior to put on the agenda the over-consumption of resources by the developed countries, especially the United States, he said "the American lifestyle is not up for negotiation." It was not negotiable, apparently, even if maintaining this lifestyle will lead to the deaths of millions of people subject to increasingly

unpredictable weather and the loss of land used by tens of millions more people because of rising ocean levels and local flooding.[3]

But it is not only the two Bush administrations that have put the interests of Americans first. When it came to the crunch in the Balkans, the Clinton-Gore administration made it very clear that it was not prepared to risk the life of a single American in order to reduce the number of civilian casualties. In the context of the debate over whether to intervene in Bosnia to stop Serb "ethnic cleansing" operations directed against Bosnian Moslems, Colin Powell, then chairman of the Joint Chiefs of Staff, quoted with approval the remark of the nineteenth-century German statesman Otto von Bismarck, that all the Balkans were not worth the bones of a single one of his soldiers.[4] Bismarck, however, was not thinking of intervening in the Balkans to stop crimes against humanity. As Chancellor of Imperial Germany, he assumed that his country followed its national interest. To use his remark today as an argument against humanitarian intervention is to return to nineteenth-century power politics, ignoring both the bloody wars that style of politics brought about in the first half of the twentieth century, and the efforts of the second half of the twentieth century to find a better foundation for peace and the prevention of crimes against humanity.

In Kosovo, though the policy of giving absolute priority to American lives did not prevent intervention to defend the Kosovars, it led to the restriction of intervention to aerial bombardment. This strategy was a total success: NATO forces suffered not a single casualty in combat. Approximately 300 Kosovar, 209 Serb, and 3 Chinese civilians were killed. Observing the American policy, Timothy Garton Ash wrote: "It is a perverted moral code that will allow a million innocent civilians of another race to be made destitute because you are not prepared to risk the life of a single professional soldier of your own." This blunt condemnation of the approach to the duties of a national leader taken by—at least—the last three American presidents forces us to consider a fundamental ethical issue. To what extent

[1] *New York Times*, 30 March 2001, p. A11.
[2] David Rosenbaum, "Senate Deletes Higher Mileage Standard in Energy Bill," *New York Times*, 14 March 2002, p. A28.
[3] Philip Elmer-Dewitt, "Summit to Save the Earth: Rich vs. Poor," *Time*, 139:2, June 1992, pp. 42–48, www.cddc.vt.edu/tim/tims/Tim599.htm.

[4] Bill Keller, "The World According to Colin Powell," *New York Times Sunday Magazine*, 25 November 2001, p. 67.

should political leaders see their role narrowly, in terms of promoting the interests of their citizens, and to what extent should they be concerned with the welfare of people everywhere?

Romano Prodi, at the time President of the Commission of the European Union, and a former Prime Minister of Italy, responded to President George W. Bush's "first things first" statement by saying that "if one wants to be a world leader, one must know how to look after the entire earth and not only American industry." But the question is not only one for those who aspire to be world leaders. The leaders of smaller nations must also consider, in contexts like global warming, trade pacts, foreign aid, and the treatment of refugees, to what extent they are prepared to consider the interests of "outsiders."

As Ash suggests, there is a strong ethical case for saying that it is wrong for leaders to give absolute priority to the interests of their own citizens. The value of the life of an innocent human being does not vary according to nationality. But, it might be said, the abstract ethical idea that all humans are entitled to equal consideration cannot govern the duties of a political leader. Just as parents are expected to provide for the interests of their own children, rather than for the interests of strangers, so too in accepting the office of president of the United States, George W. Bush has taken on a specific role that makes it his duty to protect and further the interests of Americans. Other countries have their leaders, with similar roles in respect of the interests of their fellow citizens. There is no world political community, and as long as that situation prevails, we must have nation-states, and the leaders of those nation-states must give preference to the interests of their citizens. Otherwise, unless electors were suddenly to turn into altruists of a kind never before seen on a large scale, democracy could not function. American voters would not elect a president who gave no more weight to their interests than he or she gave to the interests of Bosnians or Afghans. Our leaders feel that they must give some degree of priority to the interests of their own citizens, and they are, so this argument runs, right to do so. But what does "some degree of priority" amount to, in practice?

Related to this question about the duties of national leaders is another one: Is the division of the world's people into sovereign nations a dominant and unalterable fact of life? Here our thinking has been affected by the horrors of Bosnia, Rwanda, and Kosovo. In Rwanda, a United Nations inquiry took the view that 2,500 military personnel, given the proper training and mandate, might have saved 800,000 lives.[5] Secretary-General Kofi Annan, who, as Under-Secretary-General for Peace-Keeping Operations at the time, must bear some responsibility for what the inquiry has termed a "terrible and humiliating" paralysis, has learned from this situation. Now he urges, "the world cannot stand aside when gross and systematic violations of human rights are taking place." What we need, he has said, are "legitimate and universal principles" on which we can base intervention.[6] This means a redefinition of state sovereignty, or more accurately, an abandonment of the absolute idea of state sovereignty that has prevailed in Europe since the Treaty of Westphalia in 1648.

The aftermath of the attacks on September 11, 2001 underlined in a very different way the extent to which our thinking about state sovereignty has changed over the past century. In the summer of 1914 another act of terrorism shocked the world: the assassination of the Austrian Crown Prince Franz Ferdinand and his wife in Sarajevo, by a Bosnian Serb nationalist. In the wake of that outrage Austria-Hungary presented an ultimatum to Serbia in which it laid out the evidence that the assassins were trained and armed by the Black Hand, a shadowy Serbian organization headed by the chief of Serbian military intelligence. The Black Hand was tolerated or supported by other Serbian government officials, and Serbian officials arranged safe passage across the border into Bosnia for the seven conspirators in the assassination plot.[7] Accordingly, Austria-Hungary's ultimatum demanded that the Serbs bring those responsible to justice and allow

---

[5] *Report of the Independent Inquiry into the Actions of the United Nations During the 1994 Genocide in Rwanda*, United Nations, Office of the Spokesman for the Secretary-General, New York, 15 December 1999, www.un.org/News/ossg/rwanda_report.htm.
[6] Kofi Annan, "Two Concepts of Sovereignty," *The Economist*, 18 September 1999, www.un.org/Overview/SG/kaecon.htm.
[7] John Langdon, *July 1914: The Long Debate*, 1918–1990, Berg, New York, 1991, p. 175.

Austro-Hungarian officials to inspect the files to ensure that this had been done properly.

Despite the clear evidence of the involvement of Serbian officials in the crime—evidence that, historians agree, was substantially accurate—the ultimatum Austria-Hungary presented was widely condemned in Russia, France, Britain, and the United States. "The most formidable document I have ever seen addressed by one State to another that was independent," the British Foreign Minister, Sir Edward Grey, called it.[8] The American Legion's official history of the Great War used less diplomatic language, referring to the ultimatum as a "vicious document of unproven accusation and tyrannical demand."[9] Many historians studying the origins of the First World War have condemned the Austro-Hungarian ultimatum as demanding more than one sovereign nation may properly ask of another. They have added that the Austro-Hungarian refusal to negotiate after the Serbian government accepted many, but not all, of its demands, is further evidence that Austria-Hungary, together with its backer Germany, wanted an excuse to declare war on Serbia. Hence they must bear the guilt for the outbreak of the war and the nine million deaths that followed.

Now consider the American response to the terrorist attacks of September 11. The demands made of the Taliban by the Bush administration in 2001 were scarcely less stringent than those made by Austria-Hungary of Serbia in 1914. (The main difference is that the Austro-Hungarians insisted on the suppression of hostile nationalist propaganda. Freedom of speech was not so widely regarded, then, as a human right.) Moreover the American demand that the Taliban hand over Osama bin Laden was made without presenting to the Taliban any evidence at all linking him to the attacks of September 11. Yet the U.S. demands, far from being condemned as a mere pretext for aggressive war, were endorsed as reasonable and justifiable by a wide-ranging coalition of nations. When President Bush said, in speeches and press conferences after September 11, that he would not draw a distinction between terrorists and regimes that harbor terrorists, no ambassadors, foreign ministers, or United Nations representatives denounced this as a "vicious" doctrine or a "tyrannical" demand on other sovereign nations. The Security Council broadly endorsed it, in its resolution of September 28, 2001.[10] It seems that world leaders now accept that every nation has an obligation to every other nation of the world to suppress activities within its borders that might lead to terrorist attacks carried out in other countries, and that it is reasonable to go to war with a nation that does not do so. If Kaisers Franz Joseph I and Wilhelm II could see this, they might well feel that, since 1914, the world has come round to their view.

Shortly before the September 11 attacks, a United Nations panel issued a report pointing out that even if there were no altruistic concern among the rich nations to help the world's poor, their own self-interest should lead them to do so:

> In the global village, someone else's poverty very soon becomes one's own problem: of lack of markets for one's products, illegal immigration, pollution, contagious disease, insecurity, fanaticism, terrorism.[11]

Terrorism has made our world an integrated community in a new and frightening way. Not merely the activities of our neighbors, but those of the inhabitants of the most remote mountain valleys of the farthest-flung countries of our planet, have become our business. We need to extend the reach of the criminal law there and to have the means to bring terrorists to justice without declaring war on an entire country in order to do it. For this we need a sound global system of criminal justice, so justice does not become the victim of national differences of opinion. We also need, though it will be far more difficult to achieve, a sense that we really are one community, that we are people who recognize not

[8]G. P. Gooch and H. Temperley, eds., *British Documents on the Origins of the War*, 1898–1914, London, 1926–1938, vol. XI, no. 91; cited in Zara Steiner, *Britain and the Origins of the First World War*, St. Martin's Press, New York, 1977, pp. 221–222.
[9]Charles Horne, ed., *Source Records of the Great War*, vol. I, The American Legion, Indianapolis, 1931, p. 285.

[10]Security Council Resolution 1373 (2001), www.un.org/Docs/scres/2001/res1373e.pdf.
[11]Report of the High-Level Panel on Financing for Development appointed by the United Nations Secretary-General, United Nations General Assembly, Fifty-fifth Session, Agenda item 101, 26 June 2001, A/55/1000, p. 3, www.un.org/esa/ffd/a55–1000.pdf.

only the force of prohibitions against killing each other but also the pull of obligations to assist one another. This may not stop religious fanatics from carrying out suicide missions, but it will help to isolate them and reduce their support. It was not a coincidence that just two weeks after September 11, conservative members of the U.S. Congress abandoned their opposition to the payment of $582 million in back dues that the United States owed to the United Nations.[12] Now that America was calling for the world to come to its aid to stamp out terrorism, it was apparent that America could no longer flout the rules of the global community to the extent that it had been doing before September 11.

We have lived with the idea of sovereign states for so long that they have come to be part of the background not only of diplomacy and public policy but also of ethics. Implicit in the term "globalization" rather than the older "internationalization" is the idea that we are moving beyond the era of growing ties between nations and are beginning to contemplate something beyond the existing conception of the nation-state. But this change needs to be reflected in all levels of our thought, and especially in our thinking about ethics.

To see how much our thinking about ethics needs to change, consider the work that, better than any other, represents late-twentieth-century thinking on justice in the liberal American establishment: John Rawls's *A Theory of Justice*. When I first read this book, shortly after its publication in 1971, I was astonished that a book with that title, nearly 600 pages long, could utterly fail to discuss the injustice of the extremes of wealth and poverty that exist between different societies. Rawls's method (this is like mother's milk to every philosophy or politics student now) is to seek the nature of justice by asking what principles people would choose if they were choosing in conditions that prevented them from knowing what position they themselves would occupy. That is, they must choose without knowing whether they themselves would be rich or poor, a member of the dominant ethnic majority or of an ethnic minority, a religious believer or an atheist,

highly skilled or unskilled, and so on. If we were to apply this method globally rather than for a given society, it would immediately be obvious that one fact about which those making the choice should be ignorant is whether they are citizens of a rich nation such as the United States or of a poor nation such as Haiti. In setting up his original choice, however, Rawls simply assumes that the people making the choice all belong to the same society and are choosing principles to achieve justice *within* their society. Hence when he argues that people choosing under the conditions he prescribes would choose a principle that, subject to constraints intended to protect equal liberty and fair equality of opportunity, seeks to improve the position of the worst-off, he limits the conception of "worst-off" to those within one's own society. If he accepted that to choose justly, people must also be ignorant of their citizenship, his theory would become a forceful argument for improving the prospects of the worst-off people in the world. But in the most influential work on justice written in twentieth-century America, this question *never even arises*.[13] Rawls does address it in his most recent book, *The Law of Peoples*, and I shall say something later about what he says there. His approach, however, remains firmly based on the idea that the unit for deciding what is just remains something like today's nation-state. Rawls's model is that of an international order, not a global order. This assumption needs reconsidering.

For most of the eons of human existence, people living only short distances apart might as well, for all the difference they made to each other's lives, have been living in separate worlds. A river, a mountain range, a stretch of forest or desert, a sea—these

---

[12]Juliet Eilperin, "House Approves U.N. Payment Legislation Would Provide $582 Million for Back Dues," *Washington Post*, 25 September 2001, p. A01.

[13]See John Rawls, *A Theory of Justice*, Oxford University Press, Oxford, 1971. The objection to Rawls that I have put here was made by Brian Barry in *The Liberal Theory of Justice*, Oxford University Press, Oxford, 1973, pp. 129–130. See also the same author's *Theories of Justice*, University of California Press, Berkeley, 1989. Other arguments to the same end have been pressed by Charles Beitz, *Political Theory and International Relations*, Princeton University Press, Princeton, 1979, and "Social and Cosmopolitan Liberalism," *International Affairs*, 75:3, 1999, pp. 515–529; by Thomas Pogge, *Realizing Rawls*, Cornell University Press, Ithaca, N.Y., 1990, and "An Egalitarian Law of Peoples," *Philosophy and Public Affairs*, 23:3, 1994; and by Andrew Kuper, "Rawlsian Global Justice: Beyond *The Law of Peoples* to a Cosmopolitan Law of Persons," *Political Theory* 28:5, 2000, pp. 640–674.

were enough to cut people off from each other. Over the past few centuries the isolation has dwindled, slowly at first, then with increasing rapidity. Now people living on opposite sides of the world are linked in ways previously unimaginable.

One hundred and fifty years ago, Karl Marx gave a one-sentence summary of his theory of history:

> The handmill gives you society with the feudal lord; the steam mill, society with the industrial capitalist.[14]

Today he could have added:

> The jet plane, the telephone, and the Internet give you a global society with the transnational corporation and the World Economic Forum.

Technology changes everything—that was Marx's claim, and if it was a dangerous half-truth, it was still an illuminating one. As technology has overcome distance, economic globalization has followed. In London supermarkets, fresh vegetables flown in from Kenya are offered for sale alongside those from nearby Kent. Planes bring illegal immigrants seeking to better their own lives in a country they have long admired. In the wrong hands the same planes become lethal weapons that bring down tall buildings. Instant digital communication spreads the nature of international trade from actual goods to skilled services. At the end of a day's trading, a bank based in New York may have its accounts balanced by clerks living in India. The increasing degree to which there is a single world economy is reflected in the development of new forms of global governance, the most controversial of which has been the World Trade Organization, but the WTO is not itself the creator of the global economy.

Global market forces provide incentives for every nation to put on what Thomas Friedman has called "a Golden Straitjacket," a set of policies that involve freeing up the private sector of the economy, shrinking the bureaucracy, keeping inflation low, and removing restrictions on foreign investment. If a country refuses to wear the Golden Straitjacket, or

tries to take it off, then the electronic herd—the currency traders, stock and bond traders, and those who make investment decisions for multinational corporations—could gallop off in a different direction, taking with it the investment capital that countries want to keep their economy growing. When capital is internationally mobile, to raise your tax rates is to risk triggering a flight of capital to other countries with comparable investment prospects and lower taxation. The upshot is that as the economy grows and average incomes rise, the scope of politics may shrink—at least as long as no political party is prepared to challenge the assumption that global capitalism is the best economic system. When neither the government nor the opposition is prepared to take the risk of removing the Golden Straitjacket, the differences between the major political parties shrink to differences over minor ways in which the Straitjacket might be adjusted.[15] Thus even without the WTO, the growth of the global economy itself marks a decline in the power of the nation-state.

Marx argued that in the long run we never reject advances in the means by which we satisfy our material needs. Hence history is driven by the growth of productive forces. He would have been contemptuous of the suggestion that globalization is something foisted on the world by a conspiracy of corporate executives meeting in Switzerland, and he might have agreed with Thomas Friedman's remark that the most basic truth about globalization is "*No one is in charge.*"[16] For Marx this is a statement that epitomizes humanity in a state of alienation, living in a world in which, instead of ruling ourselves, we are ruled by our own creation, the global economy. For Friedman, on the other hand, all that needs to be said about Marx's alternative—state control of the economy—is that *it doesn't work.*[17] (Whether there are alternatives to both capitalism and centrally controlled socialism that could work is another question, but not one for this book.)

Marx also believed that a society's ethic is a reflection of the economic structure to which its

---

[14]"The Poverty of Philosophy," in David McLellan, ed., Karl Marx: Selected Writings, Oxford University Press, Oxford, 1977, p. 202.

[15]Thomas Friedman, *The Lexus and the Olive Tree*, Anchor Books, New York, 2000, pp. 104–106.
[16]Friedman, *Lexus and the Olive Tree*, p. 112.
[17]Friedman, *Lexus and the Olive Tree*, p. 140.

technology has given rise. Thus a feudal economy in which serfs are tied to their lord's land gives you the ethic of feudal chivalry based on the loyalty of knights and vassals to their lord, and the obligations of the lord to protect them in time of war. A capitalist economy requires a mobile labor force able to meet the needs of the market, so it breaks the tie between lord and vassal, substituting an ethic in which the right to buy and sell labor is paramount. Our newly interdependent global society, with its remarkable possibilities for linking people around the planet, gives us the material basis for a new ethic. Marx would have thought that such an ethic would serve the interests of the ruling class, that is, the rich nations and the transnational corporations they have spawned. But perhaps our ethics is related to our technology in a looser, less deterministic, way than Marx thought. Ethics appears to have developed from the behavior and feelings of social mammals. It became distinct from anything we can observe in our closest nonhuman relatives when we started using our reasoning abilities to justify our behavior to other members of our group. If the group to which we must justify ourselves is the tribe, or the nation, then our morality is likely to be tribal, or nationalistic. If, however, the revolution in communications has created a global audience, then we might feel a need to justify our behavior

to the whole world. This change creates the material basis for a new ethic that will serve the interests of all those who live on this planet in a way that, despite much rhetoric, no previous ethic has ever done.[18]

If this appeal to our need for ethical justification appears to be based on too generous a view of human nature, there is another consideration of a very different kind that leads in the same direction. The great empires of the past, whether Persian, Roman, Chinese, or British, were, as long as their power lasted, able to keep their major cities safe from threatening barbarians on the frontiers of their far-flung realms. In the twenty-first century the greatest superpower in history was unable to keep the self-appointed warriors of a different world-view from attacking both its greatest city and its capital. The thesis of this book is that how well we come through the era of globalization (perhaps whether we come through it at all) will depend how we respond ethically to the idea that we live in one world. For the rich nations not to take a global ethical viewpoint has long been seriously morally wrong. Now it is also, in the long term, a danger to their security.

---

[18]On the evolution of ethics, see Peter Singer, *The Expanding Circle* Farrar, Straus and Giroux, New York, 1981. On globalization as the basis for a new ethic, see Clive Kessler, "Globalization: Another False Universalism?," *Third World Quarterly*, 21, 2000, pp. 931–942.

⊚ CRITICAL QUESTIONS

1. How has terrorism "made our world an integrated community," and what does that require of us? Do you think Singer is right about this? Why, or why not?

2. Do you agree with Singer's thesis? Why, or why not?

6.5 TERRORISM AND MORALITY

One day when we were having a lively discussion of terrorism in one of my classes, a student suddenly asked, "So what is really wrong with terrorism?" The room fell silent and after the initial shock wore off, someone said, "What a stupid question!"

Is it not the case that terrorism is self-evidently wrong? We don't have to figure out what is wrong about it; everyone knows it is morally reprehensible. If that is the case, then one wonders why so many people have been and are willing to engage in terrorist acts. The picture gets complicated when we realize that terrorists usually feel morally justified. They see themselves as doing the right thing, not the wrong thing. Of course we can always say that they are deluded, or insane, or gravely (no pun intended) misled. Somehow these responses seem inadequate when we confront the sincerity of terrorists' beliefs and the integrity, even to the point of suicide (or martyr-dom depending on one's perspective), of their actions.

One reason terrorists, especially those who are politically or religiously motivated, feel morally justified in terrorizing others is because they approach terrorism from the "just war" tradition. According to that tradition, one of the conditions (among others) that justifies violence is that the use of force is in a "just cause." If the critics of terrorism also approach the issue of the morality of terrorism from the "just war" tradition, they share the same general moral framework as the terrorists. The major difference is that those who condemn terrorism do not see the cause of the terrorist as just, or at least just enough to warrant violence against innocent people.

Bat-Ami Bar On, a professor of philosophy at the State University of New York at Binghamton, argues in the next selection that philosophers and others who think about terrorism from the viewpoint of an ethic of justice or rights miss one of the most important features of terrorism, one that makes it immoral. If we morally assess terrorism from the ethic of care perspective (see Section 4.6), then it is cruelty, not unjust causes, that emerge as the central moral problem with terrorism. Bat-Ami Bar On wrote this essay before 9/11. However much the events of that dreaded day may have changed the world, her ideas about terrorism and violence are still relevant. Read it and see if you agree.

◉ READING QUESTIONS

1. How does the author define terrorism, and why does she reject any sharp conceptual difference between a terrorist and a freedom fighter?
2. What do terrorism, "seasoning," and torture have in common as a "formative process"?

3. Why is cruelty immoral?
4. What is the "just war" tradition, and why, according to Bat-Ami Bar On, is it inadequate for understanding what is morally problematic about terrorism?

Why Terrorism Is Morally Problematic

BAT-AMI BAR ON

In my life and in the lives of members of my family, terrorism has been a formative force. In this essay I will examine how terrorism forms the terrorized. I will argue that what is morally problematic about terrorism is that it produces people who are psychologically and morally diminished and it is, therefore, cruel. This brute fact is not addressed by the standard moral arguments offered by contemporary philosophers about terrorism. Those arguments appeal to the "just war" tradition and thus to abstract principles. Looking at the way in which terrorism forms the terrorized reveals that such appeals are insufficient to condemn and especially to condone terrorism.

That terrorism operates psychologically in certain ways became clearest for me just after the

Versions of this chapter were read at the SUNY College at Oswego and at Le Moyne College. I would like to thank the Central New York Feminist Philosophers Study Group, Sandra Bartky, and Claudia Card for their insightful comments.

intifada[1] started. I was in Israel and talking with one of my cousins about the situation. I argued that the formation of an independent Palestinian state was the only realistic compromise solution to the Jewish-Israeli[2]–Palestinian conflict. I was told in response that the formation of an independent Palestinian state would endanger the state of Israel with a war. When I claimed that the *intifada* together with the militarily enforced official Israeli repression constitute a war, I was told that at least this war is not happening within Israel's borders and thus does not endanger the majority of the Jewish-Israeli population.

I realized as the discussion developed that my cousin genuinely believed that for the Palestinians an independent state would be first and foremost a means to assert a destructive power against her and her family and against the Jewish-Israeli population. Motivating this belief was a deep-seated fear that also motivated a clinging to the Israeli military as the only shield against the expected destruction and a commitment to the deployment and use, including inhumane use, of the military against the Palestinians.

Since Jewish-Israeli life within the 1948 disengagement lines, which delineate what is popularly believed to form the pre-1967 Israeli borders, seemed undisturbed by the *intifada,* my cousin's fear can make sense only given the history of the Jewish-Israeli-Palestinian relationship. Looked at from the Jewish-Israeli perspective, this relationship has been colored by Palestinian terrorism ever since the beginning of Jewish settlement in the area at the end of the nineteenth century. My cousin's fear, a fear I recognize in myself, is a product of growing up under and living with the constant threat of terrorism. Although this threat was magnified by the Israeli government's official pronouncements and the official history of Israel,[3] it was nonetheless real.

For the purpose of this essay the only salient fact about terrorism is that it is a practice of terrorization in which terror is a means to an end other than itself.[4] The means used to terrorize, the possible distinctions among the ends, and the practitioners of terrorism are all insignificant insofar as this essay is concerned. Knowing the means, ends, and practitioners may help one to list the different kinds of terrorism, to chart it historically and culturally, to understand the relation between it and technology, or to see its place in local or global social, political, or economic structures or power relations.[5] But knowledge of the means, ends, and practitioners of terrorism does not shed light on terrorism as a formative process.

Letting terrorism be understood as a practice of terrorization in which terror is a means to an end other than itself does not permit one to categorize as terroristic a random attack on a school by a psychotic person, no matter how violent and terrifying, since it is not a means to a further end. On the

---

[1]The *intifada* is the Palestinian uprising in the areas that were occupied by the state of Israel in the 1967 Six Days War. Following the Israeli War of Independence in 1948, these areas were held by Jordan (the West Bank, or Judaea and Samaria) and Egypt (the Gaza Strip), respectively. The *intifada* began in December 1988. Its declared end is the formation of an independent Palestinian state.

[2]I am using the term "Jewish-Israeli" in order both to emphasize the multinational character of the Israeli population in which the Jews form the majority, and to locate the conflict more accurately.

[3]Recent revisionist historical work is very suggestive. See, for example, Bernard Avishai, *The Tragedy of Zionism: Revolution and Democracy in the Land of Israel* (New York: Farrar, Straus, Giroux, 1985); Simha Flapan, *The Birth of Israel: Myths and Realities* (New York: Pantheon, 1987); Yosef Gorny, *The Arab Question and the Jewish Problem* (Tel-Aviv: Am Oved, 1985); and Michael Janson, *Dissonance in Zion* (London: Zed, 1987).

[4]There are many discussions of the definition of terrorism and a consensus on the use of terrorization as a means to an end in terrorism. The following are a few examples of analyses of the concept of terrorism: Eugene Victor Walter, "Violence and the Process of Terror," *American Sociological Review* 29, no. 2 (April 1964): 248–257; Grant Wardlaw, "The Problem of Defining Terrorism," in Wardlaw, *Political Terrorism: Theory, Tactics, and Counter-Measures* (Cambridge: Cambridge University Press, 1982), 3–17; and Carl Wellman, "On Terrorism Itself," *Journal of Value Inquiry* 13 (1979): 250–258.

[5]For attempts to list, chart, and understand the history, culture, and social, economic, and political place of terrorism, see H. Edward Price, Jr., "The Strategy and Tactics of Revolutionary Terrorism," *Comparative Studies in Society and History* 19 (1977): 52–66; Luigi Bonanate, "Some Unanticipated Consequences of Terrorism," *Journal of Peace Research* 16 (1979): 192–212; William Gutteridge (editor for the Institute for the Study of Conflict), *Contemporary Terrorism* (New York: Facts on File, 1986); Alberto Melucci, "New Movements, Terrorism, and the Political System: Reflections on the Italian Case," *Socialist Review* 11, no. 2 (March-April 1981): 97–136; Christopher Dobson and Ronald Payne, *The Terrorists: Their Weapons, Leaders, and Tactics* (New York: Facts on File, 1982); and Noel O'Sullivan, ed., *Terrorism, Ideology, and Revolution: The Origins of Modern Political Violence* (Brighton, England: Wheatsheaf Books, 1986).

other hand, such a conception of terrorism does permit one to categorize as terroristic certain practices of nation-states—for example, the repressive actions of the Argentinian junta during the "dirty war," the nuclear strategies of the United States and the USSR, the actions of criminal organizations such as the Colombian drug cartel, and the U.S. government's tactics of intimidation against organized crime—since they do have ends other than terrorization.

The inclusive conception of terrorism that I have adopted here would trouble anyone committed to a distinction between terrorism and freedom fighting, be the source of the commitment politically on the left or on the right—hence, a commitment to the work of groups such as the El Salvadoran Farabundo Marti National Liberation Front (FMLN), or the Afghan Mujahadin, respectively. Conor Cruise O'Brien, who believes that a distinction between freedom fighters and terrorists is viable, says:

> We reserve the use [of the words "terrorism" and "terrorist"] in practice for politically motivated violence *of which we disapprove*. The words imply a judgement about the political context in which those whom we decide to call terrorists operate, and above all about the nature of the regime under which and against which they operate. We imply that the regime itself is *legitimate*. If we call them "freedom fighters" we imply that the regime is illegitimate.

O'Brien's claims, which focus on what he calls "politically motivated violence," first suggest that in ordinary usage "terrorism" and "freedom fighting" are terms used not merely to describe but also to morally condemn and commend. His analysis then points out that the basis for the moral condemnation or commendation is the end of the "politically motivated violence" and that it is the ends with the moral meanings attached to them that are used to distinguish between terrorism and freedom fighting.

Although O'Brien's analysis of the ordinary usage of terrorism and freedom fighting is not wrong, the ordinary-language distinction between the two terms is not strong enough to be able to claim that the two are conceptually distinct. They are not. The ordinary-usage distinction between

terrorism and freedom fighting presupposes that the ends of a practice are the necessary and sufficient criteria to distinguish among practices, and this is just not so. Furthermore, according to the ordinary usage, the terms "terrorism" and "freedom fighting" have certain normative connotations that are important for the distinction between them. Yet these connotations are simply the products of Western politics.

"Terrorism" as a negative term was coined in 1795 by the French Directory to refer specifically to the repressive measures practiced by Robespierre's government. It later was used to describe the activities of nineteenth-century clandestine oppositional groups in Russia. Not surprisingly, because these groups were considered revolutionary, "terrorism" retained its negative connotations in the dictionaries of the time even though these groups were different from the French revolutionaries, and their ends differed also. Furthermore, these groups did not necessarily consider themselves terroristic, and if they did, they viewed terrorism positively. As they saw it, they were freedom fighters.

I think this brief discussion shows that terrorism and freedom fighting are not conceptually distinct and thus that terrorists can be freedom fighters and freedom fighters can be terrorists. One could similarly show that other distinctions people attempt to make to save some action from being classified as terroristic will not work. If terrorism is a practice, then, as uncomfortable as it may be to think so, the Allies' strategic use of air raids against the German civilian population during the Second World War was as terroristic as the Germans' bombardment of London with V rockets. The Irish Republican Army relies on terrorism in its war of liberation, as did the Palestine Liberation Organization. And the South African and Salvadoran death squads, even if only covertly supported by their governments, are also terroristic.

Suppose, then, that terrorism is a practice of terrorization in which terror is a means to an end other than itself. What can be said about it as a process through which the terrorized are formed?

In *The Demon Lover: On the Sexuality of Terrorism*, Robin Morgan claims that terrorism democratizes violence and brings men to experience the world in relation to each other similarly, though not identically, to how women experience the world in relation to men. She begins with the description of the woman.

> Look closely at her. She crosses a city street, juggling her briefcase and her sack of groceries. Or she walks down the dirt road, balancing a basket on her head. Or she hurries toward her locked car, pulling a small child along with her. Or she trudges home from the fields, the baby strapped to her back. Suddenly there are footsteps behind her. Heavy, rapid. A man's footsteps. She knows this immediately, just as she knows that she must not look around. She quickens her pace in time to the quickening of her pulse. She is afraid. He could be a rapist. He could be a soldier, a harasser, a robber, a killer. He could be none of these. He could be a man in a hurry. He could be a man merely walking at his normal pace. But she fears him. She fears him because he is a man. She has reason to fear. She does not feel the same way—on a city street or dirt road, in parking lot or field—if she hears a woman's footsteps behind her.

Morgan later adds the comparable description of the man:

> Now look closely at him. He hurries through the airport to catch his plane. Or he pedals his bicycle, basket laden with books to the university. Or he mounts the steps to his embassy on official business. Or he snaps a fresh roll of film into his camera and starts out on an assignment. Suddenly, there are footsteps behind him. Heavy, rapid. A man's footsteps. In the split second before he turns around, he knows he's afraid. He tells himself he has no reason to fear. But he fears. *He does not feel the same way if he hears a woman's footsteps behind him.*

Morgan's descriptions make it vividly clear that as a formative process, terrorism produces people who are afraid. Terrorized people's fear is deep and easily triggered by the slightest indication of possible danger. Yet the fear is triggered by things and movements that are not extraordinary within an ordinary day-to-day context. And the day-to-day ordinariness of the terrorized circumstances does not dissipate the fear.

Morgan does not talk about the consequences of living a life in which fear is triggered

so easily under what should be ordinary circumstances. Some of the consequences are described by Leo Lowenthal in his "Terror's Atomization of Man," an essay written in 1946 about fascist state terrorism. According to Lowenthal, terrorism interrupts the causal relation between what people do and what happens to them. As a result, the terrorized's sense of a continuous experience and memory weakens and even breaks down. This in turn leads to a shrinking or breakdown of personality.

How this happens can be clarified somewhat by a comparison of terrorism with seasoning, the process used by pimps to form prostitutes. Kathleen Barry discusses the process in *Female Sexual Slavery*, and Marilyn Frye elaborates on it in *The Politics of Reality*. Frye writes:

> While he holds her in captivity and isolation he brutalizes the victim in as many ways as there are to brutalize.... The abductor's brutality functions in several ways. By placing the victim in a life-threatening and absolutely aversive situation, he maximizes the urgency of the victim's taking action in her own behalf while making it utterly impossible for her to do so. This puts maximum force into the process of alienating her from herself through total helplessness. The result is radical loss of self-esteem, self-respect and any sense of capacity or agency.... After having been in a situation where her presence as agent has been reduced to nothing, she now has the opportunity to try to act in support of her physical survival. She can try to discover what pleases and what displeases the man, and try to please him and avoid displeasing him.

Like seasoning, terrorism places its victims in a life-threatening situation in which one feels both a need to do something to save oneself and a helplessness. The terrorized too will experience an alienation from self and a loss of the sense of oneself as an agent capable of acting on her or his own behalf and deserving of respect. The sense of alienation from self together with the lack of a sense of agency and dignity constitute a dissolution of the individual self. What is left is a will to survive, as evidenced in the case of the victim of seasoning, who attempts to live through satisfying the pimp.

Another way to understand terrorism as a formative process is by comparing it with torture, which, like seasoning, is also a practice in which brutalization is used as a means to break a person down. In *The Body in Pain*, Elaine Scarry analyzes several aspects of torture. Like Morgan, Scarry begins with the transformation of the ordinary. Like Lowenthal, she emphasizes the consequences of torture, which also constitute the dissolution of the ordinary world. Scarry describes the transformation of a room:

> In torture the world is reduced to a single room or set of rooms. Called "guest rooms" in Greece and "safe houses" in the Philippines, the torture rooms are often given names that acknowledge and call attention to the generous, civilizing impulse normally present in the human shelter. They call attention to the impulse only as a prelude to announcing its annihilation. The torture room is not just the setting in which the torture occurs.... It is itself literally converted into another weapon, into an agent of pain. All aspects of the basic structure—walls, ceiling, window, doors—undergo this conversion.

Scarry proceeds from here to focus on the interrogation and its end—the confession—and calls attention to elements that Frye focuses on in her discussion of seasoning. Scarry writes: "Torture systematically prevents the prisoner from being the agent of anything and simultaneously pretends that he is the agent of some things. Despite the fact that in reality he has been deprived of all control over, and therefore all responsibility for, his world, his words, his body, he is to understand his confession as it will be understood by others, as an act of self-betrayal."

It is not only confession that will be experienced as self-betrayal. The torturer controls the tortured body and voice and can make the tortured act or stop acting, speak, sing, or scream or stop speaking, singing, or screaming. The torturer's control is a function of the ability to cause pain, and it is through the experience of pain that the tortured is formed into a self-betrayer because this experience dissolves the distinction between outside and inside the body, conflates the private and the public, destroys language, and obliterates the contents of consciousness.

Like the tortured, the terrorized may come to experience themselves as self-betrayers, and the possibility of self-betrayal is one of the things they fear most, because the terrorized, like the tortured, realize very quickly once their terrorization begins that what is at issue for their tormentors is the length of time it may take for them to break down and betray themselves by accepting the terrorists' demands. Indeed, from the point of view of the terrorist, as from the point of view of the torturer, terrorization consists of a series of tests of strength that are designed to reveal the weakness of their victims to the terrorist and to the victims.

When the victims feel tested, they know that what is being tested is the strength of their will. As they become aware of their weakness, they also become aware of the erosion of their will. This is accompanied by a diminishing sense of self, since under these conditions the self becomes the will. Everything else is stripped away. When the will erodes totally or when it feels as if it has been broken, nothing is left of the self.

One may want to claim that although a comparison of terrorism with seasoning or torture may provide some insight, terrorism actually differs significantly from both because it does not occur in circumstances that allow for the kind of intensity that takes place in seasoning or torture. After all, in the case of terrorism, the terrorized are not totally at the mercy of the terrorists. In fact, only some terrorized are not at the mercy of the terrorists, usually those living under the threat of some form of political terrorism, especially when it is an oppositional practice. When, for example, a state is in the business of terrorizing its citizenry and has in place the organizations necessary for carrying out the terrorizing—such as the Nicaraguan national guard during Somoza's rule—the people are very much at the mercy of their state. Under these conditions, people can usually find refuge from their government only by becoming exiles. Resistance is a viable alternative to exile only when the resistance movement has succeeded in occupying and maintaining a territory in which its members are relatively safe, as the Sandinistas did in Nicaragua.

Still, most torture happens within Goffmanian total institutions such as jails, prisons, concentration camps, and special torture camps. Seasoning has in common with torture the confinement and isolation of its victims. Being and feeling at the mercy of torturers and pimps is the function of the confinement and isolation. Terrorists, on the other hand, do not confine and isolate the terrorized.

Again, too much is claimed about terrorism in general. But even in the case of those terrorized by oppositional political terrorism—the kind of terrorism that at the outset seems just not to take place in circumstances resembling the confinement and isolation of the tortured—the situation is much more complicated. This fact is testified to by the practices states institute to control terrorism (such as careful inspection of people and luggage in airports) and the general fear that terrorism endangers the liberal democratic state.

This general fear, noted by many contemporary experts on international oppositional political terrorism, causes liberal democratic states to risk violating civil liberties because of the practices they have to institute to prevent terrorism within their borders. To be effective they have to work like a screen that does not permit infiltration by terrorists into the state. They must also facilitate tracing an infiltration if and when it occurs.

Thus in Israel, for example, roads at certain intervals have checkpoints staffed by military personnel, who stop and inspect all cars. For buses, the armed soldiers get in and inspect the luggage racks, making sure that every item has an owner among the people on the bus. To maximize security on its campus, the University of Tel-Aviv is surrounded by a fence, and at the gates, security personnel check every bag that is brought in. Security personnel check every bag brought into every public building in Israel, including movie theaters. Helicopters patrol the seashores on the hour, and a civilian militia patrols them on foot. It also patrols the streets of every town twenty-four hours a day. Children at summer camps and at schools are always accompanied by armed guards on their field trips. Everyone in Israel is expected to carry officially issued identity papers and produce them upon the demand of the police, militia, or army. Everywhere in Israel there are posters that remind the public of terrorism and of the people's obligation to be alert and vigilant, to always survey their environment for suspicious items, movement, or individuals.

These various practices instituted by states to combat terrorism confine and isolate the citizenry and put it under constant surveillance. Surveillance makes one feel simultaneously safer and more vulnerable. One feels safer because one feels protected by it. But at the same time, one feels more exposed and not only to one's own government, especially if terrorists have been successful in their attempts, because this means that they are even better at surveillance than the government. The consequences of this state of affairs are best captured by Foucault's explanation of the workings of Bentham's panopticon in *Discipline and Punish*. According to him the panoptic mechanism arranges things so that it is possible to see everyone constantly and recognize everyone immediately, and anyone can use it at anytime. The effect is to induce in those who are observed a state of conscious and permanent visibility that assures the automatic functioning of power.

Thus even in the case of terrorists who do not confine and isolate their victims, circumstances are altered in response to their terrorism. The new situation has within it the elements needed to create for the terrorized an intense experience of feeling totally at the mercy of the terrorists. This suffices to start the process of the formation of the self as the self of a terrorized person, a fearful self that contracts and is organized more and more around its experience as a certain level of strength of will.

My description of terrorism can tempt one to argue that what is morally problematic with terrorism is that it is a coercive practice, a practice whose structure Marilyn Frye describes as follows: "The structure of coercion, then, is this: to coerce someone into doing something, one has to manipulate the situation so that the world as perceived by the victim presents the victim with a range of options the least unattractive of which (or the most attractive of which) in the judgement of the victim is the act one wants the victim to do." But to argue this, though formally correct, requires the conceptual classification of terrorism with practices that do not involve the intentional erosion of selves and the intentional breaking of wills, such as a state's paternalistic imposition of seatbelts, helmets, or a 55-mile-per-hour speed limit. Conceiving terrorism as a practice of terrorization through which a self is intentionally eroded and a will is intentionally broken implies, I believe, that *what morally problematizes terrorism is that it is cruel.*

That cruelty is the crux of what is morally problematic with terrorism becomes clearer when one thinks about the things terrorists do when they terrorize: bombing a city, shooting indiscriminately in an airport, abducting and killing people. Such events provide the occasion for a variety of possible attitudes and moral dispositions toward those who suffer as a result of these terroristic acts. Some people are motivated to help the victims of terrorism. Others are motivated to increase their suffering. The latter disposition is cruelty. One expects people who intentionally induce and increase suffering either to take pleasure in other people's pain or to be indifferent to it. Tom Regan notes these two kinds of cruelty in "Cruelty, Kindness, and Unnecessary Suffering."

> The central case of cruelty appears to be the case where, in Locke's apt phase, one takes "a seeming kind of pleasure" in causing another to suffer.... Not all cruel people are cruel in this sense. Some cruel people do not take pleasure in making others suffer. Indeed, they seem not to feel anything. Their cruelty is manifested by a lack of what is judged as appropriate feeling ... for the plight of the individual whose suffering they cause.... [T]hey are ... insensitive to the suffering they inflict, unmoved by it, as if they were unaware of it or failed to appreciate it as suffering.

Terrorists intentionally intensify the suffering of people whom they intentionally victimize. And although they may not take pleasure in this, in some important sense they have to be indifferent to the pain they cause. Sergey Nechaev and Mikhail Bakunin express this clearly in their *Revolutionary Catechism*, written in 1869 for clandestine Russian oppositional groups. In this booklet, they say:

> 1. The revolutionary is a lost man; he has no interests of his own, no cause of his own, no feelings, no habits, no belongings, he does not even have a name....
>
> 2. In the very depths of his being, not just in words but in deed, he has broken every tie with the

civil order, with the educated world and all laws, conventions, and generally accepted conditions and with the ethics of this world....

> ...
>
> 6. Hard with himself, he must be hard toward others. All the tender feelings of family life, of friendship, love, gratitude, and even honour must be stifled in him by a single cold passion for the revolutionary cause....
>
> ...
>
> 13. ...He is not a revolutionary if he feels pity for anything in this world. If he is able to, he must face the annihilation of a situation, of a relationship, or of any person who is part of this world—everything and everyone must be equally odious to him.

Terrorists are cruel, therefore, not only because they create and worsen in an obvious way the suffering that comes through the body but also because they create the anguish that the terrorized experience as they feel their selves erode and fear they will break.

So, if cruelty morally problematizes terrorism, what, then, is morally wrong with cruelty? It is not easy to capture what is morally wrong with cruelty. But cruelty horrifies, and Steven G. Smith suggests that the repugnance felt is a "protesting recoil from a violation" of normative, value-laden "shoulds" and "should nots." Given Smith's analysis, in the case of a terrorist's cruelty, the violated "should not" seems to be the Kantian categorical imperative prohibiting the use of people as means only. Yet there are also "shoulds" that seem to be violated by cruelty: the "shoulds" of compassion, kindness, and hospitality.

Lawrence Blum believes compassion is directed at "a person in a negative condition, suffering from harm, difficulty, or danger (past, present or future)." He points out that it characteristically involves "imaginative dwelling on the condition of another person, an active regard for his good, a view of him as a fellow human being, and emotional responses of a certain degree of intensity." Tom Regan contrasts cruelty with kindness: "A kind person is one who is inclined (disposed) to act with the intention of forwarding the interest of others, not for reasons of self-gain, but out of love, affection or compassion for the individuals whose interests are forwarded."

Philip Hallie contrasts cruelty with hospitality. In "From Cruelty to Goodness," he says that he learned that the two were opposites after reading about the Huguenot French village of Le Chambon de Ligon, which saved about six thousand people, many of them Jewish children, from the Nazis. The village, whose population was poor, had about thirty-five hundred people. Beginning in 1940, the villagers sheltered the refugees, taking many of them across the mountains to neutral Geneva. What was so special about the villagers of Le Chambon was that they sincerely welcomed the refugees, shared everything they had with them and were surprised when asked why they did it. According to them, even though this endangered them as individuals and as a community, this is what they should have done if they were to manifest their belief in a love for humanity.

Neither cruelty nor compassion, kindness nor hospitality, enters the standard moral discussions of terrorism with their limited focus on political and especially oppositional terrorism. These discussions are usually framed by the Western "just war" tradition. According to this tradition, one has to distinguish between the general question of whether some resort to force is morally justified and the particular question of whether this or that specific form of force is morally justified. The answers to these two questions, which are presumed to be independent of each other, can be found by following certain guidelines. These guidelines define the "just war" tradition.

To assess whether some resort to force is morally justified one needs to decide (1) whether there is a just cause for the use of force, that is, some wrong to be redressed through it; (2) whether there is a legitimate authority seeking to use it, popular support for it, and ways of controlling it; (3) whether force is being used as the last resort; and (4) whether the overall damage that will result from the use of force is at least balanced by the good that will be attained by it. On the other hand, to assess whether a specific form of the use of force is morally justified, one needs to decide (1) what is the balance of proximate good and bad that would result from using a specific form of force, and (2) whether this specific form of force discriminates between combatants and noncombatants.

Michael Walzer frames his discussion of political oppositional terrorism very strictly within the "just war" tradition. He argues that it is morally unjustifiable because it fails to discriminate between combatants and noncombatants. R. M. Hare argues that political oppositional terrorism, which he distinguishes from revolutionary violence, is morally unjustifiable because it leads to more destruction than good. Among the latest variations on both arguments is that of C. A. J. Coady. He argues that no form of political terrorism could be morally justified because it fails to discriminate between combatants and noncombatants and because it is ineffective.

Those who morally object to terrorism are not the only ones who rely on the "just war" tradition. Robert Young appeals to this tradition by arguing that revolutionary terrorism is morally justifiable because of its just cause, because it is a tactic of last resort, and because it is more economical than a war, achieving the same results with less destruction. According to Young, even if revolutionary terrorism involves harming non-combatants, it is not ultimately morally unjustifiable. It just requires a more complex justification.

Though the "just war" tradition has provided a framework for the standard discussions of terrorism, most of the arguments either for or against terrorism do not use all of the criteria or guidelines for assessment that the tradition provides. In addition, they do not clearly distinguish between the assessment of use of force in general and the assessment of a specific use of force. Thus, for example, both Hare and Young, while treating terrorism as a specific use of force, discuss it primarily in terms designed for assessing the use of force in general. And no one seems to bother to assess whether terrorism has a legitimate authority behind it.

For me, this problem of legitimate authority is not as important as the fact that from the beginning of its construction by Augustine, the "just war" tradition was designed to legitimate certain wars. A war's just cause was given priority to make this possible. Limitations on the legitimate use of force were put in place to mitigate its destructiveness. In using the "just war" framework to discuss terrorism, the issue becomes the possibility of its legitimation. Just cause is made the most important criterion of assessment. Destructiveness is a concern only in relation to the possible need to limit it.

I do not know why just cause was given priority over other criteria. I think that concern only about the physical destructiveness of certain forms of force—about the extent of injury, death, and rubble—is much too limited a moral worry, at least in the case of terrorism. The most important issue is not the balance between advantages gained and material destruction. The most important issue is the formation of persons through terrorization and the fact that terrorism requires terrorists to be cruel rather than compassionate, kind, and hospitable.

It could be said that my issue is addressed by concerns about destruction typical of the "just war" tradition because what I worry about is psychic injury, a worry that need not be restricted to the terrorized but can be extended to the terrorist. In the process of terrorization, terrorists also form themselves as psychically injured persons.

Further, if my concerns are seen as belonging to an "ethics of care," which gives precedence to empathy, their conflict with the standard moral discussions of terrorism, insofar as they are framed by the "just war" tradition, can be viewed as a conflict with justice. An "ethics of justice" gives precedence to abstract moral principles concerned with justice, and the "just war" tradition seems to be motivated by concerns situated within this kind of ethics.

However, my concern with how individuals are formed through terrorization, be it the terrorized or the terrorists, is not merely a concern with the physical damage inflicted, and I am not unconcerned with justice. Like others who have tried to argue that an ethics of care and an ethics of justice, though different, are not really in conflict, I am interested in challenging the prioritization of justice and not in its substitution by empathy. Both empathy and justice have to be accorded a serious place in moral thinking.

I am not certain how to accord both empathy and justice a serious place in moral thinking. Yet when I reflect on terrorism, I find that responses to the terrorism of organized crime or perhaps to covert right-wing state terrorism (for example, that practiced in Guatemala) are helpful in clarifying the relation between empathy and justice in the moral assessment of terrorism. As I see it, the difference between the responses to these two forms of terrorism is that though both horrify because both are cruel, the horror in the case of organized crime is not accompanied by surprise at or disillusionment with the cruelty of the criminals, whereas the horror in state terrorism is accompanied by surprise at and disillusionment with the cruelty of politicians. Unlike the terrorism of organized crime, the terrorism of a state against its citizens leaves the victims with a deep sense of betrayal.

I believe this difference in response can be accounted for by expectations from the relation between the ends and the means used to achieve them. The ends of organized crime—the accumulation of wealth and power—do not limit the means that can be used to obtain them. On the other hand, unless one is already disillusioned and corrupted by cynicism, one cannot view the means to the ends that politicians ought to have—the service and maintenance of communities for the good of their members—as independent of these ends. Organized crime can achieve its ends by all means necessary. Criminals need not be just or decent. However, politicians must be just and decent and so cannot use all means necessary to achieve their ends.

Moreover, there are means that would not fit organized crime's ends but would undermine them just as there are means that would not fit the ends that politicians ought to have but would undermine them. Terrorism is not a means that would undermine the ends of organized crime. Yet even if one could show, as the Guatemalan right-wing politicians try to, that terrorism may serve a greater communal good in the future (for example, increase the wealth available for distribution to all the members of the community, thereby making the community better and more just), it is very hard to see how this should count for more than what happens to the people who are terrorized and who terrorize. Terrorism produces fearful people with diminished selves organized around the experience of the fear of the loss of their strength of will. It also produces cruel people, people who feel no compassion or kindness and are inhospitable. Could such people enjoy the promised future goods?

If there is a promised future good whose value seems overwhelming, it is freedom from conditions in which people are formed as they are by terrorism. Contrary to Fanon and Sartre, I doubt very much that such a future can be brought about by terrorism. Fanon's patients are much more resilient than I think people really are, especially given the growing evidence on post-traumatic stress disorder. Post-traumatic stress shapes the lives not only of individuals whose experiences resulted in the stress but the young people who grow up with them as well.

The children of Holocaust survivors have Holocaust nightmares.

So in the case of terrorism, it seems that one cannot fail to give precedence to empathy, to concern about what happens to people who are terrorized and to people who terrorize. Yet this concern has its foundation not merely in care for people as individuals and the possibility that they may be harmed but also in care for them as members of communities. As producers and distributors of wealth and power, communities can continue for a long time independently of the kind of people who populate them. But good communities—communities that are fairly just, that get along not only contractually but generously, that take each other concretely into consideration, and whose members are free of daily fears for their survival and physical well-being—these communities need people who care. Neither the terrorized nor the terrorists can care well enough—for themselves or for others.

CRITICAL QUESTION

1. Do you agree with the author that the essential fact about terrorism that makes it immoral is cruelty? Why, or why not?

6.6 PHILOSOPHY IN A TIME OF TERROR

Noam Chomsky retells a story that the Christian theologian St. Augustine (354–430) told about Alexander the Great (356–323 BCE). Alexander captured a pirate and asked him how he had the audacity to molest the sea. The pirate answered, "How dare you molest the whole world?" He added, "Because I do it with a little ship only, I am called a thief: you doing it with a great navy are called an Emperor." Augustine, as the story goes, found the pirate's answer "excellent."[1]

The word *terrorism* was coined to name the violent repression by governments against their own citizens. Eventually its meaning was extended to include violent acts by individuals or groups against the state. While it is important to discuss the morality of terrorism as we did in the last selection, it is also important to address issues of definition and use. Exactly what do we mean by terrorism and how do we use (or overuse) that term? How does the terrorist differ from the guerilla, or how do terrorist groups differ from national liberation movements? Wars are fought between or among nations, but can a war, properly speaking, be

[1]Noam Chomsky, *Pirates and Emperors Old and New: International Terrorism in the Real World* (Cambridge, MA: South End Press, 2002), p. vii.

fought against a terrorist movement and its ideology? Does such language make terrorists soldiers? If they are soldiers, how must they be treated when captured? Does the Geneva Convention apply?

Terrorism is a slippery concept that can be exploited to make some people appear in a favorable light and others in a decidedly unfavorable light. There is state terrorism and retaliatory terrorism of those who believe they have been terrorized by the state. How do terrorists differ from freedom fighters? At one time the Taliban and Osama bin Laden were hailed by the United States as freedom fighters in their war with the Soviets. Now they are condemned as criminals and vicious terrorists. Do historical circumstances make a group "freedom fighters" and the same group "terrorists" at different times?

The tragedy of 9/11 spawned the invasion of two countries and so far has resulted in thousands of mostly civilian deaths and injuries. It changed international relations, ignited religious bigotry, and so far cost billions of dollars. People now speak of a "war on terror" and some claim we live in an "age of terror." The tragic events of September 11 also provoked philosophers to think about how those events affect the doing of philosophy at the beginning of a new century.

Giovanna Borradori is a professor of philosophy at Vassar College who, shortly after the attacks on 9/11, interviewed one of the most influential contemporary European philosophers, Jürgen Habermas. Selections from her interview appear below.

Habermas is a German philosopher and sociologist who has been influenced by both **critical theory** and American pragmatism (see Sections 7.2 and 8.5). Critical theory developed from the Marxist philosophical tradition. It differs from "traditional theory" in explicitly seeking ways to develop and apply ideas that liberate humans from limiting and repressive social and economic conditions. It is, at the same time, practical, theoretically explanatory, and normative. Habermas is best known for developing the ideas of communicative action and the public sphere. Ideally communication should involve open and free public dialogue in which people treat each other as equals and seek a common consensus on norms for guiding action in society. From his perspective, terrorism is the result of a "communicative pathology" created by globalization and unfettered capitalism. These forces led to a rigid social stratification dividing the rich and the poor. The dialogue and understanding required and fostered by communicative action in the public sphere collapses under these pressures.

◉ READING QUESTIONS

1. According to Habermas, what is the "new quality" of terrorism after September 11, 2001, and how might this lead to the nation under threat to overreact?

2. How does global terrorism differ from other types?

3. Why does Habermas think that Bush's call for a "war against terrorism" was a mistake?

Fundamentalism and Terror

JÜRGEN HABERMAS

A Dialogue with Jürgen Habermas

Borradori: Do you consider what we now tend to call "September 11" an unprecedented event, one that radically alters the way we see ourselves?

Habermas: Allow me to say in advance that I shall be answering your questions at a distance of three months.[1] Therefore, it might be useful to mention my personal experience in relation to the event. At the start of October I was beginning a two-month stay in Manhattan. I must confess I somehow felt more of a stranger this time than I did on previous visits to the "capital of the twentieth century," a city that has fascinated me for more than three decades. It was not only the flag-waving and rather defiant "United We Stand" patriotism that had changed the climate, nor was it the peculiar demand for solidarity and the accompanying susceptibility to any presumed "anti-Americanism." The impressive American liberality toward foreigners, the charm of the eager, sometimes also self-consciously accepting embrace—this noble openhearted mentality seemed to have given way to a slight mistrust. Would we, the ones who had not been present, now also stand by them unconditionally? Even those who hold an unquestionable *record*, as I do among my American friends, needed to be cautious with regard to criticism. Since the intervention in Afghanistan, we suddenly began to notice when, in political discussions, we found ourselves only among Europeans (or among Israelis).

On the other hand, only there did I first feel the full magnitude of the event. The terror of this disaster, which literally came bursting out of the blue, the horrible convictions behind this treacherous assault, as well as the stifling depression that set over the city, were a completely different experience there than at home. Every friend and colleague could remember exactly what they were doing that day shortly after 9:00 A.M. In short, only there did I begin to better comprehend the foreboding atmosphere that already echoes in your question. Also among the left there is a widespread awareness of living at a turning point in history. I do not know whether the U.S. government itself was slightly paranoid or merely shunning responsibility. At any rate, the repeated and utterly nonspecific announcements of possible new terror attacks and the senseless calls to "be alert" further stirred a vague feeling of angst along with an uncertain readiness—precisely the intention of the terrorists. In New York people seemed ready for the worst. As a matter of course, the anthrax scares (even the plane crash in Queens)[2] were attributed to Osama bin Laden's diabolical machinations.

Given this background, you can understand a certain tendency toward skepticism. But is what we contemporaries think at the moment that important for a long-term diagnosis? If the September 11 terror attack is supposed to

---

[1]This dialogue took place in December 2001, three months after the attacks of 9/11.

[2]On November 12, 2001, only two months and one day after the 9/11 attacks, a commercial plane crashed in the Queens section of New York City, killing 260 people aboard and 5 on the ground. The city was completely shut down in fear that the crash was the result of another terrorist attack. Habermas, who was then visiting New York, lived that moment firsthand.

From Giovanna Borradori, *Philosophy in a Time of Terror: Dialogues with Jürgen Habermas and Jacques Derrida* (Chicago: The University of Chicago Press, 2003), pp. 25–30, 33–36, 85–90, 100–109, 179, 186, 189–190. Copyright © 2003 by the University of Chicago Press. Reprinted by permission. Translated from the German by Luis Guzman. Revised by Jürgen Habermas in English.

constitute a caesura in world history, as many think, then it must be able to stand comparison to other events of world historical impact. For that matter, the comparison is not to be drawn with Pearl Harbor but rather with the aftermath of August 1914. The outbreak of World War I signaled the end of a peaceful and, in retrospect, somewhat unsuspecting era, unleashing an age of warfare, totalitarian oppression, mechanistic barbarism and bureaucratic mass murder. At the time, there was something like a widespread foreboding. Only in retrospect will we be able to understand if the symbolically suffused collapse of the capitalistic citadels in lower Manhattan implies a break of that type or if this catastrophe merely confirms, in an inhuman and dramatic way, a long-known vulnerability of our complex civilization. If an event is not as unambiguously important as the French Revolution once was— not long after that event Kant had spoken about a "historical sign" that pointed toward a "moral tendency of humankind"—only "effective history" can adjudicate its magnitude in retrospect.

Perhaps at a later point important developments will be traced back to September 11. But for now we do not know which of the many scenarios depicted today will actually hold in the future. The clever, albeit fragile, coalition against terrorism brought together by the U.S. government might, in the most favorable case, be able to advance the transition from classical international law to a cosmopolitan order. At all events, a hopeful signal was the Afghanistan conference in Bonn, which, under the auspices of the UN, set the agenda in the right direction.[3] However, after September 11 the European governments have completely failed. They are obviously incapable of seeing beyond their own national scope of interests and lending at least their support to the U.S. Secretary of State Colin Powell against the hard-liners. The Bush administration seems to be continuing, more or less undisturbed, the self-centered course of a callous superpower. It is fighting now as it has in the past against the appointment of an international criminal court, relying instead on military tribunals of its own. These constitute, from the viewpoint of international law, a dubious innovation. It refuses to sign the Biological Weapons Convention. It one-sidedly terminated the ABM Treaty and absurdly sees its plan to deploy a missile defense system validated by the events of September 11. The world has grown too complex for this barely concealed unilateralism. Even if Europe does not rouse itself to play the civilizing role, as it should, the emerging power of China and the waning power of Russia do not fit into the *pax Americana* model so simply. Instead of the kind of international police action that we had hoped for during the war in Kosovo, there are wars again— conducted with state-of-the-art technology but still in the old style.

The misery in war-torn Afghanistan is reminiscent of images from the Thirty Years' War. Naturally there were good reasons, even normative ones, to forcibly remove the Taliban regime, which brutally oppressed not only women but the entire population. They also refused the legitimate demand to hand over bin Laden. However, the asymmetry between the concentrated destructive power of the electronically controlled clusters of elegant and versatile missiles in the air and the archaic ferocity of the swarms of bearded warriors outfitted with Kalashnikovs on the ground remains a morally obscene sight. This feeling is more properly understood when one recalls the bloodthirsty colonial history that Afghanistan suffered, its arbitrary geographic dismemberment, and its continued instrumentalization at the hands of the European power play. In any case, the Taliban regime already belongs to history.

Borradori: True, but our topic is terrorism, which seems to have taken up new meaning and definition after September 11.

Habermas: The monstrous act itself was new. And I do not just mean the action of the suicide

---

[3]Here, Habermas refers to the peace talks that took place in late November 2001 near Bonn, Germany. These brought together the political leaders of the Northern Alliance, made up mostly of ethnic Tajiks, Uzbeks, and Hazaras, and three ethnic Pashtun-dominated factions of exiles known as the Rome, Cyprus, and Peshawar groups. The Rome group represented allies of the former king, whose return as even a figurehead leader was rejected by the Northern Alliance.

hijackers who transformed the fully fueled airplanes together with their hostages into living weapons, or even the unbearable number of victims and the dramatic extent of the devastation. What was new was the symbolic force of the targets struck. The attackers did not just physically cause the highest buildings in Manhattan to collapse; they also destroyed an icon in the household imagery of the American nation. Only in the surge of patriotism that followed did one begin to recognize the central importance the towers held in the popular imagination, with their irreplaceable imprint on the Manhattan skyline and their powerful embodiment of economic strength and projection toward the future. The presence of cameras and of the media was also new, transforming the local event simultaneously into a global one and the whole world population into a benumbed witness. Perhaps September 11 could be called the first historic world event in the strictest sense: the impact, the explosion, the slow collapse—everything that was not Hollywood anymore but, rather, a gruesome reality, literally took place in front of the "universal eyewitness" of a global public. God only knows what my friend and colleague *experienced,* watching the second airplane explode into the top floors of the World Trade Center only a few blocks away from the roof of his house on Duane Street. No doubt it was something completely different from what I *experienced* in Germany in front of the television, though we *saw* the same thing.

Certainly, no observation of a unique event can provide an explanation per se for why terrorism itself should have assumed a new characteristic. In this respect, one factor above all seems to me to be relevant: one never really knows who one's enemy is. Osama bin Laden, the person, more likely serves the function of a stand-in. Compare the new terrorists with partisans or conventional terrorists, for example, in Israel. These people often fight in a decentralized manner in small, autonomous units, too. Also, in these cases there is no concentration of forces or central organization, a feature that makes them difficult targets. But

partisans fight on familiar territory with professed political objectives in order to conquer power. This is what distinguishes them from terrorists who are scattered around the globe and networked in the fashion of secret services. They allow their religious motives of a fundamentalist kind to be known, though they do not pursue a program that goes beyond the engineering of destruction and insecurity. The terrorism we associate for the time being with the name "al-Qaeda" makes the identification of the opponent and any realistic assessment of the danger impossible. This intangibility is what lends terrorism a new quality.

Surely the uncertainty of the danger belongs to the essence of terrorism. But the scenarios of biological or chemical warfare painted in detail by the American media during the months after September 11, the speculations over the various kinds of nuclear terrorism, only betray the inability of the government to at least determine the magnitude of the danger. One never knows if there's anything to it. In Israel, people at least know *what* can happen to them if they take a bus, go into a department store, discotheque, or any open area—and *how frequently* it happens. In the U.S.A. or Europe, one cannot circumscribe the risk; there is no realistic way to estimate the type, magnitude, or probability of the risk, nor any way to narrow down the potentially affected regions.

This brings a threatened nation, which can react to such uncertain dangers solely through administrative channels, to the truly embarrassing situation of perhaps overreacting and, yet, because of the inadequate level of secret intelligence, remaining unable to know whether or not it is in fact overreacting. Because of this, the state is in danger of falling into disrepute due to the evidence of its inadequate resources; both domestically, through a militarizing of the security measures, which endanger the constitutional state, and internationally, through the mobilization of a simultaneously disproportionate and ineffective military and technological superiority. With transparent motives, U.S. Defense Secretary Donald Rumsfeld warned again of *unspecified* terror threats at the NATO conference in Brussels in mid-December [2001]: "When we look at the destruction they caused in the U.S.A., imagine what they could do in New York, or London, or Paris, or Berlin with nuclear, chemical or biological weapons."[4] Of a wholly different kind were the measures—necessary and prudent, but only effective in the long term—the U.S. government took after the attack: the creation of a worldwide coalition of countries against terrorism, the effective control over suspicious financial flows and international bank associations, the networking of relevant information flows among national intelligence agencies, as well as the worldwide coordination of corresponding police investigations.

Borradori: Philosophically speaking, do you consider terrorism to be a wholly political act?

Habermas: Not in the subjective sense in which Mohammed Atta, the Egyptian citizen who came from Hamburg and piloted the first of the two catastrophic airplanes, would offer you a political answer. No doubt today's Islamic fundamentalism is also a cover for political motifs. Indeed, we should not overlook the political motifs we encounter in forms of religious fanaticism. This explains the fact that some of those drawn into the "holy war" had been secular nationalists only a few years before. If one looks at the biographies of these people, remarkable continuities are revealed. Disappointment over nationalistic authoritarian regimes may have contributed to the fact that today religion offers a new and subjectively more convincing language for old political orientations.

Borradori: How would you actually define terrorism? Can a meaningful distinction be drawn between national and international or even global terrorism?

Habermas: In one respect, Palestinian terrorism still possesses a certain outmoded characteristic in that it revolves around murder, around the indiscriminate annihilation of enemies, women, and children—life against life. This is what distinguishes it from the terror that appears in the

paramilitary form of guerilla warfare. This form of warfare has characterized many national liberation movements in the second half of the twentieth century—and has left its mark today on the Chechnyan struggle for independence, for example. In contrast to this, the global terror that culminated in the September 11 attack bears the anarchistic traits of an impotent revolt directed against an enemy that cannot be defeated in any pragmatic sense. The only possible effect it can have is to shock and alarm the government and population. Technically speaking, since our complex societies are highly susceptible to interferences and accidents, they certainly offer ideal opportunities for a prompt disruption of normal activities. These disruptions can, with minimum expense, have considerably destructive consequences. Global terrorism is extreme both in its lack of realistic goals and in its cynical exploitation of the vulnerability of complex systems.

Borradori: Should terrorism be distinguished from ordinary crime and other types of violence?

Habermas: Yes and no. From a moral point of view, there is no excuse for terrorist acts, regardless of the motive or the situation under which they are carried out. Nothing justifies our "making allowance for" the murder or suffering of others for one's own purposes. Each murder is one too many. Historically, however, terrorism falls in a category different from crimes that concern a criminal court judge. It differs from a private incident in that it deserves public interest and requires a different kind of analysis than murder out of jealousy, for example. Otherwise, we would not be having this interview. The difference between political terror and ordinary crime becomes clear during the change of regimes, in which former terrorists come to power and become well-regarded representatives of their country. Certainly, such a political transition can be hoped for only by terrorists who pursue political goals in a realistic manner; who are able to draw, at least retrospectively, a certain legitimation for their criminal actions, undertaken to overcome a manifestly unjust situation. However, today I cannot imagine a context that would some

---

[4]See *Süddeutsche Zeitung*, December 19, 2001.

day, in some manner, make the monstrous crime of September 11 an understandable or comprehensible political act.

Borradori: Do you think it was good to interpret 9/11 as a declaration of war?

Habermas: Even if the term "war" is less misleading and, morally, less controvertible than "crusade," I consider Bush's decision to call for a "war against terrorism" a serious mistake, both normatively and pragmatically. Normatively, he is elevating these criminals to the status of war enemies; and pragmatically, one cannot lead a war against a "network" if the term "war" is to retain any definite meaning.

Borradori: If the West needs to develop greater sensitivity and adopt more self-criticism in its dealings with other cultures, how should it go about doing that? Philosophically, you have articulated the interrelation between "translation" and the "search for a common language." Can this be the key to a new political course?

Habermas: Since September 11 I have often been asked whether or not, in light of this violent phenomenon, the whole conception of "communicative action" I developed in my theory has been brought into disrepute. We in the West do live in peaceful and well-to-do societies, and yet they contain a *structural* violence that, to a certain degree, we have gotten used to, that is, unconscionable social inequality, degrading discrimination, pauperization, and marginalization. Precisely because our social relations are permeated by violence, strategic action and manipulation, there are two other facts we should not overlook. On the one hand, the praxis of our daily living together rests on a solid base of common background convictions, self-evident cultural truths and reciprocal expectations. Here the coordination of action runs through the ordinary language games, through mutually raised and at least implicitly recognized validity claims *in the public space of more or less good reasons*. On the other hand, due to this, conflicts arise from *distortion in communication*, from misunderstanding and incomprehension, from insincerity and

deception. When the consequences of these conflicts become painful enough, they land in court or at the therapist's office. The spiral of violence begins as a spiral of distorted communication that leads through the spiral of uncontrolled reciprocal mistrust, to the breakdown of communication. If violence thus begins with a distortion in communication, after it has erupted it is possible to know what has gone wrong and what needs to be repaired.

This trivial insight can be applied to the conflicts you speak of. The matter is more complicated here because cultures, ways of life, and nations are at a greater distance from and, thus, are more foreign to one another. They do not encounter each other like members of a society who might *become alienated* from each other only through systematically distorted communication. Furthermore, in *international relations*, the curbing power of the law plays a comparatively weak role. And in *intercultural* relations, the legal system achieves at best an institutional framework for formal meetings, such as the World Conference on Human Rights held in Vienna by the United Nations. As important as the multi-leveled intercultural discourse on the controversial interpretations of human rights may be, such formal encounters cannot by themselves interrupt the spiral of stereotyping. The desired transformation of a mentality happens, rather, through the improvement of living conditions, through a sensible relief from oppression and fear. Trust must be able to develop in communicative everyday practices. Only then can a broadly effective enlightenment extend into media, schools, and homes. And it must do so by affecting the premises of its own political culture.

In this context, the type of normative self-representation vis-à-vis other cultures becomes important for ourselves, too. In the process of such revision of its self-image, the West could learn, for example, how it would need to change its politics if it wants to be perceived as a shaping power with a civilizing impact. Without the political taming of an unbounded capitalism, the devastating stratification of world society will remain intractable. The disparities in the dynamic of world economic development would have to at least be balanced out regarding their most destructive consequences—the deprivation and misery of complete regions and continents comes to mind. This does not merely concern the discrimination toward, the humiliation of, or the offense to other cultures. The so-called "clash of civilizations" [Kampf der Kul-turen] is often the veil masking the vital material interests of the West (accessible oilfields and a secured energy supply, for example).[5]

---

[5]Habermas refers to the debate opened by Samuel P. Huntington's article, "The Clash of Civilizations?" published in *Foreign Affairs* in 1993. Huntington's argument is that world politics is being reconfigured along cultural lines so that future conflicts will not be fought for economic or political motives but for the sake of different cultural values. The Islamic, Western, and Asian "cultures" are the ones that Huntington seems to be most worried about. See Samuel P. Huntington et al., "The Clash of Civilizations? The Debate" (*Foreign Affairs*, 1993); *Many Globalizations. Cultural Diversity in the Contemporary World*, ed. Peter L. Berger and Samuel P. Huntington (Oxford University Press, 2002).

CRITICAL QUESTION

1. Create a counter-argument to Habermas's claim that conflicts arise from a "distortion in communication."

6.7 THE PROBLEM OF TOO MANY PEOPLE

Connect to www.nineplanets.org/earth.html for a glimpse of our home from outer space. This planet earth that we call our home looks beautiful from afar, but looks can be deceiving because runaway pollution already threatens our lives and livelihoods. And what does the future hold? "Imagine a future of relentless storms and floods; islands and heavily inhabited coastal regions inundated by rising sea levels; fertile soils rendered barren by drought and the desert's advance; mass emigrations of environmental refugees; and armed conflicts over water and other precious natural resources."

The preceding quotation paints a far from rosy picture of the future. It comes from page A18 of *Time*'s special report on the environment (August 26, 2002). The following facts also come from that special report, which was prepared in anticipation of the World Summit 2002 on Sustainable Development, held in South Africa.

- By 2050 the earth's population will increase from its present 6.1 billion to 9.3 billion.
- The average temperature of the earth will climb eight degrees Fahrenheit by 2100.
- The United States produces more greenhouse gases per person than any other country.
- More than 15 percent of the Amazon rainforests have been destroyed in only 30 years.
- As much as 86 percent of Indonesia's coral reefs are severely damaged by pollution and overfishing.
- As many as half of all species presently alive could vanish in this century.
- In 25 years, two-thirds of the human population may live in countries that are running dangerously short of fresh water.
- Presently one-third of the world goes hungry.

World population was 1 billion in 1800. Today it is 7 billion and counting. The more people there are on the planet the more resources they consume. The more resources they consume the more the climate is affected negatively given present technology. By 2050, as I indicated above, the projected world population will be 9.3 billion. Can the planet earth comfortably sustain so many people? If we assume there is a limit to resources, then at some point we will face severe problems, some of which, global warming for example, are appearing already. Garrett Hardin (1915–2003), an American ecologist, is the author of the next selection and is famous for his 1968 paper, "The Tragedy of the Commons." He is also known for his "First Law of Ecology," which is, "You cannot do only one thing."

The tragedy he describes has important moral implications. One is that neither utilitarianism nor Kantian ethical systems appear adequate to the task of guiding us through such a tragedy (see Sections 4.2 and 4.3). If Hardin is right and our present ethical thinking is no longer adequate to deal with the problems that will arise as humans swarm over the face of Mother Earth, what will guide us in making the hard decisions we face today and will face in the future with increasing urgency?

READING QUESTIONS

1. How does Hardin define a "technical solution"?
2. Why can't the population problem be solved by technology?
3. Why can't the utilitarian goal of "the greatest happiness for the greatest number" be achieved?
4. What is the "tragedy of the commons"?
5. Why is the freedom to breed intolerable?
6. Create your own reading question relating to this essay *and* answer it.

The Tragedy of the Commons

GARRETT HARDIN

At the end of a thoughtful article on the future of nuclear war, Wiesner and York concluded that:

> Both sides in the arms race are ... confronted by the dilemma of steadily increasing military power and steadily decreasing national security. It *is our considered professional judgment that this dilemma has no technical solution.* If the great powers continue to look for solutions in the area of science and technology only, the result will be to worsen the situation.[1]

I would like to focus your attention not on the subject of the article (national security in a nuclear world) but on the kind of conclusion they reached, namely that there is no technical solution to the problem. An implicit and almost universal assumption of discussions published in professional and semipopular scientific journals is that the problem under discussion has a technical solution. A technical solution may be defined as one that requires a change only in the techniques of the natural sciences, demanding little or nothing in the way of change in human values or ideas of morality.

In our day (though not in earlier times) technical solutions are always welcome. Because of previous failures in prophecy, it takes courage to assert that a desired technical solution is not possible. Wiesner and York exhibited this courage; publishing in a science journal, they insisted that the solution to the problem was not to be found in the natural sciences. They cautiously qualified their statement with the phrase, "It is our considered professional judgment." Whether they were right or not is not the concern of the present article. Rather, the concern here is with the important concept of a class of human problems which can be called "no technical solution problems," and, more specifically, with the identification and discussion of one of these.

It is easy to show that the class is not a null class. Recall the game of tick-tack-toe. Consider the problem "How can I win the game of tick-tack-toe?" It is well known that I cannot, if I assume (in keeping with the conventions of game theory) that my opponent understands the game perfectly. Put another way, there is no "technical solution" to the problem. I can win only by giving a radical meaning to the word "win." I can hit my opponent over the head; or I can drug him; or I can falsify the records. Every way in which I "win" involves, in some sense, an abandonment of the game, as we intuitively understand it. (I can also, of course, openly abandon the game—refuse to play it. This is what most adults do.)

The class of "no technical solution problems" has members. My thesis is that the "population problem," as conventionally conceived, is a member of this class. How it is conventionally conceived needs some comment. It is fair to say that most people who anguish over the population problem are trying to find a way to avoid the evils of overpopulation without relinquishing any of the privileges they now enjoy. They think that farming the seas or developing new strains of wheat will solve the problem—technologically. I try to show here that the solution they seek cannot be found. The population problem cannot be solved in a technical way, any more than can the problem of winning the game of tick-tack-toe.

WHAT SHALL WE MAXIMIZE?

Population, as Malthus said, naturally tends to grow "geometrically," or, as we would now say,

exponentially. In a finite world this means that the per capita share of the world's goods must steadily decrease. Is ours a finite world?

A fair defense can be put forward for the view that the world is infinite; or that we do not know that it is not. But, in terms of the practical problems that we must face in the next few generations with the foreseeable technology, it is clear that we will greatly increase human misery if we do not, during the immediate future, assume that the world available to the terrestrial human population is finite. "Space" is no escape.[2]

A finite world can support only a finite population; therefore, population growth must eventually equal zero. (The case of perpetual wide fluctuations above and below zero is a trivial variant that need not be discussed.) When this condition is met, what will be the situation of mankind? Specifically, can Bentham's goal of "the greatest good for the greatest number" be realized?

No—for two reasons, each sufficient by itself. The first is a theoretical one. It is not mathematically possible to maximize for two (or more) variables at the same time. This was clearly stated by von Neumann and Morgenstern,[3] but the principle is implicit in the theory of partial differential equations, dating back at least to D'Alembert (1717–1783).

The second reason springs directly from biological facts. To live, any organism must have a source of energy (for example, food). This energy is utilized for two purposes: mere maintenance and work. For man, maintenance of life requires about 1,600 kilocalories a day ("maintenance calories"). Anything that he does over and above merely staying alive will be defined as work, and is supported by "work calories" which he takes in. Work calories are used not only for what we call work in common speech; they are also required for all forms of enjoyment, from swimming and automobile racing to playing music and writing poetry. If our goal is to maximize population it is obvious what we must do: We must make the work calories per person approach as close to zero as possible. No gourmet meals, no vacations, no sports, no music, no literature, no art.... I think that everyone will grant, without argument or proof, that maximizing population does not maximize goods. Bentham's goal is impossible.

In reaching this conclusion I have made the usual assumption that it is the acquisition of energy that is the problem. The appearance of atomic energy has led some to question this assumption. However, given an infinite source of energy, population growth still produces an inescapable problem. The problem of the acquisition of energy is replaced by the problem of its dissipation, as J. H. Fremlin has so wittily shown.[4] The arithmetic signs in the analysis are, as it were, reversed; but Bentham's goal is still unobtainable.

The optimum population is, then, less than the maximum. The difficulty of defining the optimum is enormous; so far as I know, no one has seriously tackled this problem. Reaching an acceptable and stable solution will surely require more than one generation of hard analytical work—and much persuasion.

We want the maximum good per person; but what is good? To one person it is wilderness, to another it is ski lodges for thousands. To one it is estuaries to nourish ducks for hunters to shoot; to another it is factory land. Comparing one good with another is, we usually say, impossible because goods are incommensurable. Incommensurables cannot be compared.

Theoretically this may be true; but in real life incommensurables *are* commensurable. Only a criterion of judgment and a system of weighting are needed. In nature the criterion is survival. Is it better for a species to be small and hidable, or large and powerful? Natural selection commensurates the incommensurables. The compromise achieved depends on a natural weighting of the values of the variables.

Man must imitate this process. There is no doubt that in fact he already does, but unconsciously. It is when the hidden decisions are made explicit that the arguments begin. The problem for the years ahead is to work out an acceptable theory of weighting. Synergistic effects, nonlinear variation, and difficulties in discounting the future make the intellectual problem difficult, but not (in principle) insoluble.

Has any cultural group solved this practical problem at the present time, even on an intuitive level? One simple fact proves that none has: there is no prosperous population in the world today

that has, and has had for some time, a growth rate of zero. Any people that has intuitively identified its optimum point will soon reach it, after which its growth rate becomes and remains zero.

Of course, a positive growth rate might be taken as evidence that a population is below its optimum. However, by any reasonable standards, the most rapidly growing populations on earth today are (in general) the most miserable. This association (which need not be invariable) casts doubt on the optimistic assumption that the positive growth rate of a population is evidence that it has yet to reach its optimum.

We can make little progress in working toward optimum population size until we explicitly exorcize the spirit of Adam Smith in the field of practical demography. In economic affairs, *The Wealth of Nations* (1776) popularized the "invisible hand," the idea that an individual who "intends only his own gain," is, as it were, "led by an invisible hand to promote ... the public interest."[5] Adam Smith did not assert that this was invariably true, and perhaps neither did any of his followers. But he contributed to a dominant tendency of thought that has ever since interfered with positive action based on rational analysis, namely, the tendency to assume that decisions reached individually will, in fact, be the best decisions for an entire society. If this assumption is correct it justifies the continuance of our present policy of laissez-faire in reproduction. If it is correct we can assume that men will control their individual fecundity so as to produce the optimum population. If the assumption is not correct, we need to reexamine our individual freedoms to see which ones are defensible.

TRAGEDY OF FREEDOM IN A COMMONS

The rebuttal to the invisible hand in population control is to be found in a scenario first sketched in a little-known pamphlet in 1833 by a mathematical amateur named William Forster Lloyd (1794–1852).[6] We may well call it "the tragedy of the commons," using the word "tragedy" as the philosopher Whitehead used it: "The essence of dramatic tragedy is not unhappiness. It resides in the solemnity of the remorseless working of things." He then goes on to say, "This inevitableness of destiny can only be illustrated in terms of human life by incidents which in fact involve unhappiness. For it is only by them that the futility of escape can be made evident in the drama."[7]

The tragedy of the commons develops in this way. Picture a pasture open to all. It is to be expected that each herdsman will try to keep as many cattle as possible on the commons. Such an arrangement may work reasonably satisfactorily for centuries because tribal wars, poaching, and disease keep the numbers of both man and beast well below the carrying capacity of the land. Finally, however, comes the day of reckoning, that is, the day when the long-desired goal of social stability becomes a reality. At this point, the inherent logic of the commons remorselessly generates tragedy.

As a rational being, each herdsman seeks to maximize his gain. Explicitly or implicitly, more or less consciously, he asks, "What is the utility to me of adding one more animal to my herd?" This utility has one negative and one positive component.

1. The positive component is a function of the increment of one animal. Since the herdsman receives all the proceeds from the sale of the additional animal, the positive utility is nearly +1.

2. The negative component is a function of the additional overgrazing created by one more animal. Since, however, the effects of overgrazing are shared by all the herdsmen, the negative utility for any particular decision-making herdsman is only a fraction of −1.

Adding together the component partial utilities, the rational herdsman concludes that the only sensible course for him to pursue is to add another animal to his herd. And another; and another... But this is the conclusion reached by each and every rational herdsman sharing a commons. Therein is the tragedy. Each man is locked into a system that compels him to increase his herd without limit—in a world that is limited. Ruin is the destination toward which all men rush, each pursuing his own best interest in a society that believes in the freedom of the commons. Freedom in a commons brings ruin to all.

Some would say that this is a platitude. Would that it were! In a sense, it was learned thousands of years ago, but natural selection favors the forces of psychological denial.[8] The individual benefits as an individual from his ability to deny the truth even though society as a whole, of which he is a part, suffers.

Education can counteract the natural tendency to do the wrong thing, but the inexorable succession of generations requires that the basis for this knowledge be constantly refreshed.

A simple incident that occurred a few years ago in Leominster, Massachusetts, shows how perishable the knowledge is. During the Christmas shopping season the parking meters downtown were covered with plastic bags that bore tags reading: "Do not open until after Christmas. Free parking courtesy of the mayor and city council." In other words, facing the prospect of an increased demand for already scarce space, the city fathers reinstituted the system of the commons. (Cynically, we suspect that they gained more votes than they lost by this retrogressive act.)

In an approximate way, the logic of the commons has been understood for a long time, perhaps since the discovery of agriculture or the invention of private property in real estate. But it is understood mostly only in special cases which are not sufficiently generalized. Even at this late date, cattlemen leasing national land on the western ranges demonstrate no more than an ambivalent understanding, in constantly pressuring federal authorities to increase the head count to the point where overgrazing produces erosion and weed dominance. Likewise, the oceans of the world continue to suffer from the survival of the philosophy of the commons. Maritime nations still respond automatically to the shibboleth of the "freedom of the seas." Professing to believe in the "inexhaustible resources of the oceans," they bring species after species of fish and whales closer to extinction.[9]

The National Parks present another instance of the working out of the tragedy of the commons. At present, they are open to all, without limit. The parks themselves are limited in extent—there is only one Yosemite Valley—whereas population seems to grow without limit. The values that visitors seek in the parks are steadily eroded. Plainly, we must soon cease to treat the parks as commons or they will be of no value to anyone.

What shall we do? We have several options. We might sell them off as private property. We might keep them as public property, but allocate the right to enter them. The allocation might be on the basis of wealth, by the use of an auction system. It might be on the basis of merit, as defined by some agreed-upon standards. It might be by lottery. Or it might be on a first-come, first-served basis, administered to long queues. These, I think, are all the reasonable possibilities. They are all objectionable. But we must choose—or acquiesce in the destruction of the commons that we call our National Parks.

POLLUTION

In a reverse way, the tragedy of the commons reappears in problems of pollution. Here it is not a question of taking something out of the commons, but of putting something in—sewage, or chemical, radioactive, and heat wastes into water; noxious and dangerous fumes into the air; and distracting and unpleasant advertising signs into the line of sight. The calculations of utility are much the same as before. The rational man finds that his share of the cost of the wastes he discharges into the commons is less than the cost of purifying his wastes before releasing them. Since this is true for everyone, we are locked into a system of "fouling our own nest," so long as we behave only as independent, rational, free-enterprisers.

The tragedy of the commons as a food basket is averted by private property, or something formally like it. But the air and waters surrounding us cannot readily be fenced, and so the tragedy of the commons as a cesspool must be prevented by different means, by coercive laws or taxing devices that make it cheaper for the polluter to treat his pollutants than to discharge them untreated. We have not progressed as far with the solution of this problem as we have with the first. Indeed, our

particular concept of private property, which deters us from exhausting the positive resources of the earth, favors pollution. The owner of a factory on the bank of a stream—whose property extends to the middle of the stream, often has difficulty seeing why it is not his natural right to muddy the waters flowing past his door. The law, always behind the times, requires elaborate stitching and fitting to adapt it to this newly perceived aspect of the commons.

The pollution problem is a consequence of population. It did not much matter how a lonely American frontiersman disposed of his waste. "Flowing water purifies itself every ten miles," my grandfather used to say, and the myth was near enough to the truth when he was a boy, for there were not too many people. But as population became denser, the natural chemical and biological recycling processes became overloaded, calling for a redefinition of property rights.

HOW TO LEGISLATE TEMPERANCE?

Analysis of the pollution problem as a function of population density uncovers a not generally recognized principle of morality, namely: *the morality of an act is a function of the state of the system at the time it is performed.*[10] Using the commons as a cesspool does not harm the general public under frontier conditions, because there is no public; the same behavior in a metropolis is unbearable. A hundred and fifty years ago a plainsman could kill an American bison, cut out only the tongue for his dinner, and discard the rest of the animal. He was not in any important sense being wasteful. Today, with only a few thousand bison left, we would be appalled at such behavior.

In passing, it is worth noting that the morality of an act cannot be determined from a photograph. One does not know whether a man killing an elephant or setting fire to the grassland is harming others until one knows the total system in which his act appears. "One picture is worth a thousand words," said an ancient Chinese; but it may take 10,000 words to validate it. It is as tempting to ecologists as it is to reformers in general to try to persuade others by way of the photographic shortcut. But the essence of an argument cannot be photographed: it must be presented rationally—in words.

That morality is system-sensitive escaped the attention of most codifiers of ethics in the past. "Thou shalt not ..." is the form of traditional ethical directives which make no allowance for particular circumstances. The laws of our society follow the pattern of ancient ethics, and therefore are poorly suited to governing a complex, crowded, changeable world. Our epicyclic solution is to augment statutory law with administrative law. Since it is practically impossible to spell out all the conditions under which it is safe to burn trash in the back yard or to run an automobile without smog-control, by law we delegate the details to bureaus. The result is administrative law, which is rightly feared for an ancient reason—*Quis custodiet ipsos custodes?*—"Who shall watch the watchers themselves?" John Adams said that we must have "a government of laws and not men." Bureau administrators, trying to evaluate the morality of acts in the total system, are singularly liable to corruption, producing a government by men, not laws.

Prohibition is easy to legislate (though not necessarily to enforce); but how do we legislate temperance? Experience indicates that it can be accomplished best through the mediation of administrative law. We limit possibilities unnecessarily if we suppose that the sentiment of *Quis custodiet* denies us the use of administrative law. We should rather retain the phrase as a perpetual reminder of fearful dangers we cannot avoid. The great challenge facing us now is to invent the corrective feedbacks that are needed to keep custodians honest. We must find ways to legitimate the needed authority of both the custodians and the corrective feedbacks.

FREEDOM TO BREED IS INTOLERABLE

The tragedy of the commons is involved in population problems in another way. In a world governed solely by the principle of "dog eat dog"—if indeed there ever was such a world—how many children a family had would not be a matter of public concern. Parents who bred too exuberantly

would leave fewer descendants, not more, because they would be unable to care adequately for their children. David Lack and others have found that such a negative feedback demonstrably controls the fecundity of birds.[11] But men are not birds, and have not acted like them for millenniums, at least.

If each human family were dependent only on its own resources; *if* the children of improvident parents starved to death; *if*, thus, overbreeding brought its own "punishment" to the germ line— *then* there would be no public interest in controlling the breeding of families. But our society is deeply committed to the welfare state,[12] and hence is confronted with another aspect of the tragedy of the commons.

In a welfare state, how shall we deal with the family, the religion, the race, or the class (or indeed any distinguishable and cohesive group) that adopts overbreeding as a policy to secure its own aggrandizement?[13] To couple the concept of freedom to breed with the belief that everyone born has an equal right to the commons is to lock the world into a tragic course of action.

Unfortunately this is just the course of action that is being pursued by the United Nations. In late 1967, some thirty nations agreed to the following:

> The Universal Declaration of Human Rights describes the family as the natural and fundamental unit of society. It follows that any choice and decision with regard to the size of the family must irrevocably rest with the family itself, and cannot be made by someone else.[14]

It is painful to have to deny categorically the validity of this right; denying it, one feels as uncomfortable as a resident of Salem, Massachusetts, who denied the reality of witches in the seventeenth century. At the present time, in liberal quarters, something like a taboo acts to inhibit criticism of the United Nations. There is a feeling that the United Nations is "our last and best hope," that we shouldn't find fault with it; we shouldn't play into the hands of the archconservatives. However, let us not forget what Robert Louis Stevenson said: "The truth that is suppressed by friends is the readiest weapon of the enemy." If we love the truth we must openly deny the validity of the Universal Declaration of Human Rights, even though it is promoted by the United Nations. We should also join with Kingsley Davis[15] in attempting to get Planned Parenthood-World Population to see the error of its ways in embracing the same tragic ideal.

CONSCIENCE IS SELF-ELIMINATING

It is a mistake to think that we can control the breeding of mankind in the long run by an appeal to conscience. Charles Galton Darwin made this point when he spoke on the centennial of the publication of his grandfather's great book. The argument is straightforward and Darwinian.

People vary. Confronted with appeals to limit breeding, some people will undoubtedly respond to the plea more than others. Those who have more children will produce a larger fraction of the next generation than those with more susceptible consciences. The difference will be accentuated, generation by generation.

In C. G. Darwin's words: "It may well be that it would take hundreds of generations for the progenitive instinct to develop in this way, but if it should do so, nature would have taken her revenge, and the variety *Homo contracipiens* would become extinct and would be replaced by the variety *Homo progenitivus*"[16].

The argument assumes that conscience or the desire for children (no matter which) is hereditary—but hereditary only in the most general formal sense. The result will be the same whether the attitude is transmitted through germ cells, or exosomatically, to use A. J. Lotka's term. (If one denies the latter possibility as well as the former, then what's the point of education?) The argument has here been stated in the context of the population problem, but it applies equally well to any instance in which society appeals to an individual exploiting a commons to restrain himself for the general good—by means of his conscience. To make such an appeal is to set up a selective system that works toward the elimination of conscience from the race.

PATHOGENIC EFFECTS OF CONSCIENCE

The long-term disadvantage of an appeal to conscience should be enough to condemn it; but it has serious short-term disadvantages as well. If we ask a man who is exploiting a commons to desist "in the name of conscience," what are we saying to him? What does he hear?—not only at the moment but also in the wee small hours of the night when, half asleep, he remembers not merely the words we used but also the nonverbal communication cues we gave him unawares? Sooner or later, consciously or subconsciously, he senses that he has received two communications, and that they are contradictory: (1, intended communication) "If you don't do as we ask, we will openly condemn you for not acting like a responsible citizen"; (2, the unintended communication) "If you *do* behave as we ask, we will secretly condemn you for a simpleton who can be shamed into standing aside while the rest of us exploit the commons."

Everyman then is caught in what Bateson has called a "double bind." Bateson and his co-workers have made a plausible case for viewing the double bind as an important causative factor in the genesis of schizophrenia.[17] The double bind may not always be so damaging, but it always endangers the mental health of anyone to whom it is applied. "A bad conscience," said Nietzsche, "is a kind of illness."

To conjure up a conscience in others is tempting to anyone who wishes to extend his control beyond the legal limits. Leaders at the highest level succumb to this temptation. Has any President during the past generation failed to call on labor unions to moderate voluntarily their demands for higher wages, or to steel companies to honor voluntary guidelines on prices? I can recall none. The rhetoric used on such occasions is designed to produce feelings of guilt in noncooperators.

For centuries it was assumed without proof that guilt was a valuable, perhaps even an indispensable, ingredient of the civilized life. Now, in this post-Freudian world, we doubt it. Paul Goodman speaks from the modern point of view when he says: "No good has ever come from feeling guilty, neither intelligence, policy, nor compassion. The guilty do not pay attention to the object but only to themselves, and not even to their own interests, which might make sense, but to their anxieties".[18]

One does not have to be a professional psychiatrist to see the consequences of anxiety. We in the Western world are just emerging from a dreadful two-centuries-long Dark Ages of Eros that was sustained partly by prohibition laws, but perhaps more effectively by the anxiety-generating mechanisms of education. Alex Comfort has told the story well in *The Anxiety Makers*;[19] it is not a pretty one.

Since proof is difficult, we may even concede that the results of anxiety may sometimes, from certain points of view, be desirable. The larger question we should ask is whether, as a matter of policy, we should ever encourage the use of a technique the tendency (if not the intention) of which is psychologically pathogenic. We hear much talk these days of responsible parenthood; the coupled words are incorporated into the titles of some organizations devoted to birth control. Some people have proposed massive propaganda campaigns to instill responsibility into the nation's (or the world's) breeders. But what is the meaning of the word responsibility in this context? Is it not merely a synonym for the word conscience? When we use the word responsibility in the absence of substantial sanctions are we not trying to browbeat a free man in a commons into acting against his own interest? Responsibility is a verbal counterfeit for a substantial *quid pro quo*. It is an attempt to get something for nothing.

If the word responsibility is to be used at all, I suggest that it be in the sense Charles Frankel uses it.[20] "Responsibility," says this philosopher, "is the product of definite social arrangements." Notice that Frankel calls for social arrangements— not propaganda.

MUTUAL COERCION MUTUALLY AGREED UPON

The social arrangements that produce responsibility are arrangements that create coercion, of some sort. Consider bank robbing. The man who takes money from a bank acts as if the bank were a commons. How do we prevent such action? Certainly not by trying to control his behavior solely by a verbal appeal to his sense of responsibility. Rather than rely on propaganda we follow Frankel's lead and insist that a bank is not a commons; we seek the definite social arrangements that will keep it from becoming a commons. That we thereby infringe on the freedom of would-be robbers we neither deny nor regret.

The morality of bank robbing is particularly easy to understand because we accept complete prohibition of this activity. We are willing to say "Thou shalt not rob banks," without providing for exceptions. But temperance also can be created by coercion. Taxing is a good coercive device. To keep downtown shoppers temperate in their use of parking space we introduce parking meters for short periods, and traffic fines for longer ones. We need not actually forbid a citizen to park as long as he wants to; we need merely make it increasingly expensive for him to do so. Not prohibition, but carefully biased options are what we offer him. A Madison Avenue man might call this persuasion; I prefer the greater candor of the word coercion.

Coercion is a dirty word to most liberals now, but it need not forever be so. As with the four-letter words, its dirtiness can be cleansed away by exposure to the light, by saying it over and over without apology or embarrassment. To many, the word coercion implies arbitrary decisions of distant and irresponsible bureaucrats; but this is not a necessary part of its meaning. The only kind of coercion I recommend is mutual coercion, mutually agreed upon by the majority of the people affected.

To say that we mutually agree to coercion is not to say that we are required to enjoy it, or even to pretend we enjoy it. Who enjoys taxes? We all grumble about them. But we accept compulsory taxes because we recognize that voluntary taxes would favor the conscienceless. We institute and (grumblingly) support taxes and other coercive devices to escape the horror of the commons.

An alternative to the commons need not be perfectly just to be preferable. With real estate and other material goods, the alternative we have chosen is the institution of private property coupled with legal inheritance. Is this system perfectly just? As a genetically trained biologist I deny that it is. It seems to me that, if there are to be differences in individual inheritance, legal possession should be perfectly correlated with biological inheritance—that those who are biologically more fit to be the custodians of property and power should legally inherit more. But genetic recombination continually makes a mockery of the doctrine of "like father, like son" implicit in our laws of legal inheritance. An idiot can inherit millions, and a trust fund can keep his estate intact. We must admit that our legal system of private property plus inheritance is unjust—but we put up with it because we are not convinced, at the moment, that anyone has invented a better system. The alternative of the commons is too horrifying to contemplate. Injustice is preferable to total ruin.

It is one of the peculiarities of the warfare between reform and the status quo that it is thoughtlessly governed by a double standard. Whenever a reform measure is proposed it is often defeated when its opponents triumphantly discover a flaw in it. As Kingsley Davis has pointed out, worshippers of the status quo sometimes imply that no reform is possible without unanimous agreement, an implication contrary to historical fact.[21] As nearly as I can make out, automatic rejection of proposed reforms is based on one of two unconscious assumptions: (1) that the status quo is perfect; or (2) that the choice we face is between reform and no action; if the proposed reform is imperfect, we presumably should take no action at all, while we wait for a perfect proposal.

But we can never do nothing. That which we have done for thousands of years is also action. It also produces evils. Once we are aware that the status quo is action, we can then compare its discoverable advantages and disadvantages with the predicted advantages and disadvantages of the proposed reform, discounting as best we can for our lack of experience. On the basis of such a comparison, we can make a rational decision which will not involve the unworkable assumption that only perfect systems are tolerable.

RECOGNITION OF NECESSITY

Perhaps the simplest summary of this analysis of man's population problems is this: the commons, if justifiable at all, is justifiable only under conditions of low population density. As the human population has increased, the commons has had to be abandoned in one aspect after another.

First we abandoned the commons in food gathering, enclosing farm land and restricting pastures and hunting and fishing areas. These restrictions are still not complete throughout the world.

Somewhat later we saw that the commons as a place for waste disposal would also have to be abandoned. Restrictions on the disposal of domestic sewage are widely accepted in the Western world; we are still struggling to close the commons to pollution by automobiles, factories, insecticide sprayers, fertilizing operations, and atomic energy installations.

In a still more embryonic state is our recognition of the evils of the commons in matters of pleasure. There is almost no restriction on the propagation of sound waves in the public medium. The shopping public is assaulted with mindless music, without its consent. Our government is paying out billions of dollars to create supersonic transport which will disturb 50,000 people for every one person who is whisked from coast to coast three hours faster. Advertisers muddy the airwaves of radio and television and pollute the view of travelers. We are a long way from outlawing the commons in matters of pleasure. Is this because our Puritan inheritance makes us view pleasure as something of a sin, and pain (that is, the pollution of advertising) as the sign of virtue?

Every new enclosure of the commons involves the infringement of somebody's personal liberty. Infringements made in the distant past are accepted because no contemporary complains of a loss. It is the newly proposed infringements that we vigorously oppose; cries of "rights" and "freedom" fill the air. But what does "freedom" mean? When men mutually agreed to pass laws against robbing, mankind became more free, not less so. Individuals locked into the logic of the commons are free only to bring on universal ruin; once they see the necessity of mutual coercion, they become free to pursue other goals. I believe it was Hegel who said, "Freedom is the recognition of necessity."

The most important aspect of necessity that we must now recognize is the necessity of abandoning the commons in breeding. No technical solution can rescue us from the misery of overpopulation. Freedom to breed will bring ruin to all. At the moment, to avoid hard decisions many of us are tempted to propagandize for conscience and responsible parenthood. The temptation must be resisted, because an appeal to independently acting consciences selects for the disappearance of all conscience in the long run, and an increase in anxiety in the short.

The only way we can preserve and nurture other and more precious freedoms is by relinquishing the freedom to breed, and that very soon. "Freedom is the recognition of necessity"—and it is the role of education to reveal to all the necessity of abandoning the freedom to breed. Only so can we put an end to this aspect of the tragedy of the commons.

NOTES

1. J. B. Wiesner and H. F. York, *Scientific American*, 211: 4(1964), 27. Offprint 319.
2. G. Hardin, *Journal of Heredity*, 50 (1959), 68; S. von Hoernor, *Science*, 137 (1962), 18.
3. J. von Neumann and O. Morgenstern, *Theory of Games and Economic Behavior* (Princeton: Princeton University Press, 1947), 11.
4. J. H. Fremlin, *New Science*, 415 (1964), 285.
5. A. Smith, *The Wealth of Nations* (New York: Modern Library, 1937), 423.
6. W. F. Lloyd, *Two Lectures on the Checks to Population* (Oxford: Oxford University Press, 1833), reprinted (in part) in G. Hardin (ed.), *Population, Evolution, and Birth Control,* 2nd edn. (San Francisco: W. H. Freeman and Company, 1969), 28.
7. A. N. Whitehead, *Science and the Modern World* (New York: Mentor, 1948), p. 17.
8. Hardin, *Population, Evolution, and Birth Control,* 46.
9. S. McVay, *Scientific American*, 216: 8(1966), 13. Offprint 1046.
10. J. Fletcher, *Situation Ethics* (Philadelphia: Westminster, 1966).
11. D. Lack, *The Natural Regulation of Animal Numbers* (Oxford: Clarendon Press, 1954).
12. H. Girvetz, *From Wealth to Welfare* (Stanford, Calif.: Stanford University Press, 1950).
13. G. Hardin, *Perspectives in Biology and Medicine*, 6 (1963), 366.
14. U. Thant, *International Planned Parenthood News*, 168 (February 1968), 3.
15. K. Davis, *Science*, 158 (1967), 730.
16. S. Tax (ed.), *Evolution after Darwin* (Chicago: University of Chicago Press, 1960), ii. 469.
17. G. Bateson, D. D. Jackson, J. Haley, J. Weakland, *Behavioral Science*, 1 (1956), 251.
18. P. Goodman, *New York Review of Books*, 10: 8 (23 May 1968), 22.
19. A. Comfort, *The Anxiety Makers* (London: Nelson, 1967).
20. C. Frankel, *The Case for Modern Man* (New York: Harper, 1955), 203.
21. J. D. Roslansky, *Genetics and the Future of Man* (New York: Appleton-Century-Crofts, 1966), 177.

◉ CRITICAL QUESTIONS

1. Do you agree that we cannot delay action on the problem Hardin describes? Why or why not?

2. Do you agree that "the role of education [is] to reveal to all the necessity of abandoning the freedom to breed"? Why or why not?

6.8 ANIMAL RIGHTS

Do other-than-human animals have moral rights? That is, do we as humans have a moral obligation or duty to animals that are not human?

At first you might be inclined to answer, "Yes." After all, if someone has a pet cat or dog and they neglect or mistreat that animal, we hold them both morally and legally responsible for their actions. What if my neighbor kicks or injures my dog Arthur? Isn't that wrong, and can I not call on the police to prosecute my neighbor for animal abuse?

Why do we hold people responsible for pet abuse? "Well," you might say, "because to harm a pet harms the owner of the pet or at least harms the interests that humans have in that pet and its safety." Does it not, however, harm the animal too? If we only argue that it is wrong to harm animals because it is in the interests of human animals not to do so, we would be assuming that animals have no intrinsic or inherent rights, and we have only indirect duties to them.

Do we not have direct obligations? Isn't it wrong to harm pets, not only because it harms human interests in having healthy and happy other-than-human companions, but also because it inflicts suffering on our pets directly, and they have a right to be free from suffering?

Some of you might view pets as a special case. While it is true many societies punish and forbid pet abuse, many societies also permit painful medical, cosmetic, and chemical research to be done on dogs, cats, rabbits, monkeys, and other animals (although we forbid such research on human animals). We allow farmers to raise calves in confined quarters in order to produce better quality veal, and we allow slaughterhouses to kill and butcher animals so people can eat them, not to mention permitting hunters to hunt them, trappers to trap them, and furriers to skin them. Society clearly allows quite a bit of animal suffering to occur legally, so maybe we do not have any moral obligations to animals in general—only to our pets and the pets of others. But why single out one group? If we have direct moral obligations to some animals, why not to all animals—human and other-than-human alike? Can the case be made that all or most animals have rights? How might we go about developing that sort of argument?

In the selection that follows, Tom Regan, professor of philosophy at North Carolina State University, explores how we might develop a strong moral argument for animal rights.

⬤ READING QUESTIONS

1. How do the concepts of direct duties and indirect duties relate to the debate about animal rights?

2. What is wrong with the contractarian and utilitarian moral theories?

3. How does the rights view of morality support the case for animal rights?

The Case for Animal Rights

TOM REGAN

I regard myself as an advocate of animal rights—as a part of the animal rights movement. That movement, as I conceive it, is committed to a number of goals, including:

- the total abolition of the use of animals in science;
- the total dissolution of commercial animal agriculture;
- the total elimination of commercial and sport hunting and trapping.

There are, I know, people who profess to believe in animal rights but do not avow these goals. Factory farming, they say, is wrong—it violates animals' rights—but traditional animal agriculture is all right. Toxicity tests of cosmetics on animals violates their rights, but important medical research—cancer research, for example—does not. The clubbing of baby seals is abhorrent, but not the harvesting of adult seals. I used to think I understood this reasoning. Not any more. You don't change unjust institutions by tidying them up.

What's wrong—fundamentally wrong—with the way animals are treated isn't the details that vary from case to case. It's the whole system. The forlornness of the veal calf is pathetic, heart wrenching; the pulsing pain of the chimp with electrodes planted deep in her brain is repulsive; the slow, torturous death of the raccoon caught in the leg-hold trap is agonizing. But what is wrong isn't the pain, isn't the suffering, isn't the deprivation. These compound what's wrong. Sometimes—often—they make it much, much worse. But they are not the fundamental wrong.

The fundamental wrong is the system that allows us to view animals as *our resources,* here for *us*—to be eaten, or surgically manipulated, or exploited for sport or money. Once we accept this view of animals—as our resources—the rest is

as predictable as it is regrettable. Why worry about their loneliness, their pain, their death? Since animals exist for us, to benefit us in one way or another, what harms them really doesn't matter—or matters only if it starts to bother us, makes us feel a trifle uneasy....

In the case of animals in science, whether and how we abolish their use ... are to a large extent political questions. People must change their beliefs before they change their habits. Enough people, especially those elected to public office, must believe in change—must want it—before we will have laws that protect the rights of animals. This process of change is very complicated, very demanding, very exhausting, calling for the efforts of many hands in education, publicity, political organization and activity, down to the licking of envelopes and stamps. As a trained and practicing philosopher, the sort of contribution I can make is limited but, I like to think, important. The currency of philosophy is ideas—their meaning and rational foundation—not the nuts and bolts of the legislative process, say, or the mechanics of community organization. That's what I have been exploring over the past ten years or so in my essays and talks and, most recently, in my book, *The Case for Animal Rights.* I believe the major conclusions I reach in the book are true because they are supported by the weight of the best arguments. I believe the idea of animal rights has reason, not just emotion, on its side.

In the space I have at my disposal here I can only sketch, in the barest outline, some of the main features of the book. Its main themes—and we should not be surprised by this—involve asking and answering deep, foundational moral questions about what morality is, how it should be understood and what is the best moral theory, all considered. I hope I can convey something of the

From *In Defense of Animals,* edited by Peter Singer (Oxford: Basil Blackwell, 1985), pp. 13–26. Reprinted by permission of the author and the publisher.

shape I think this theory takes. The attempt to do this will be (to use a word a friendly critic once used to describe my work) cerebral, perhaps too cerebral. But this is misleading. My feelings about how animals are sometimes treated run just as deep and just as strong as those of my more volatile compatriots. Philosophers do—to use the jargon of the day—have a right side to their brains. If it's the left side we contribute (or mainly should), that's because what talents we have reside there.

How to proceed? We begin by asking how the moral status of animals has been understood by thinkers who deny that animals have rights. Then we test the mettle of their ideas by seeing how well they stand up under the heat of fair criticism. If we start our thinking in this way, we soon find that some people believe that we have no duties directly to animals, that we owe nothing to them, that we can do nothing that wrongs them. Rather, we can do wrong acts that involve animals, and so we have duties regarding them, though none to them. Such views may be called indirect duty views. By way of illustration: suppose your neighbor kicks your dog. Then your neighbor has done something wrong. But not to your dog. The wrong that has been done is a wrong to you. After all, it is wrong to upset people, and your neighbor's kicking your dog upsets you. So you are the one who is wronged, not your dog. Or again: by kicking your dog your neighbor damages your property. And since it is wrong to damage another person's property, your neighbor has done something wrong—to you, of course, not to your dog. Your neighbor no more wrongs your dog than your car would be wronged if the windshield were smashed. Your neighbor's duties involving your dog are indirect duties to you. More generally, all of our duties regarding animals are indirect duties to one another—to humanity.

How could someone try to justify such a view? Someone might say that your dog doesn't feel anything and so isn't hurt by your neighbor's kick, doesn't care about the pain since none is felt, is as unaware of anything as is your windshield. Someone might say this, but no rational person will, since, among other considerations, such a view will commit anyone who holds it to the position that no human being feels pain either—that

human beings also don't care about what happens to them. A second possibility is that though both humans and your dog are hurt when kicked, it is only human pain that matters. But, again, no rational person can believe this. Pain is pain wherever it occurs. If your neighbor's causing you pain is wrong because of the pain that is caused, we cannot rationally ignore or dismiss the moral relevance of the pain that your dog feels.

Philosophers who hold indirect duty views—and many still do—have come to understand that they must avoid the two defects just noted: that is, both the view that animals don't feel anything as well as the idea that only human pain can be morally relevant. Among such thinkers the sort of view now favored is one or other form of what is called *contractarianism*.

Here, very crudely, is the root idea: morality consists of a set of rules that individuals voluntarily agree to abide by, as we do when we sign a contract (hence the name contractarianism). Those who understand and accept the terms of the contract are covered directly; they have rights created and recognized by, and protected in, the contract. And these contractors can also have protection spelled out for others who, though they lack the ability to understand morality and so cannot sign the contract themselves, are loved or cherished by those who can. Thus young children, for example, are unable to sign contracts and lack rights. But they are protected by the contract nonetheless because of the sentimental interests of others, most notably their parents. So we have, then, duties involving these children, duties regarding them, but no duties to them. Our duties in their case are indirect duties to other human beings, usually their parents.

As for animals, since they cannot understand contracts, they obviously cannot sign; and since they cannot sign, they have no rights. Like children, however, some animals are the objects of the sentimental interest of others. You, for example, love your dog or cat. So those animals that enough people care about (companion animals, whales, baby seals, the American bald eagle), though they lack rights themselves, will be protected because of the sentimental interests of people. I have, then, according to contractarianism, no duty directly to your dog or any other animal, not even the duty not to cause them pain or suffering; my duty not to hurt them is a duty I have to those people who care about what happens to them. As for other animals, where no or little sentimental interest is present—in the case of farm animals, for example, or laboratory rats—what duties we have grow weaker and weaker, perhaps to vanishing point. The pain and death they endure, though real, are not wrong if no one cares about them.

When it comes to the moral status of animals, contractarianism could be a hard view to refute if it were an adequate theoretical approach to the moral status of human beings. It is not adequate in this latter respect, however, which makes the question of its adequacy in the former case, regarding animals, utterly moot. For consider: morality, according to the (crude) contractarian position before us, consists of rules that people agree to abide by. What people? Well, enough to make a difference—enough, that is, *collectively* to have the power to enforce the rules that are drawn up in the contract. That is very well and good for the signatories but not so good for anyone who is not asked to sign. And there is nothing in contractarianism of the sort we are discussing that guarantees or requires that everyone will have a chance to participate equally in framing the rules of morality. The result is that this approach to ethics could sanction the most blatant forms of social, economic, moral and political injustice, ranging from a repressive caste system to systematic racial or sexual discrimination. Might, according to this theory, does make right. Let those who are the victims of injustice suffer as they will. It matters not so long as no one else—no contractor, or too few of them—cares about it. Such a theory takes one's moral breath away ... as if, for example, there would be nothing wrong with apartheid in South Africa if few white South Africans were upset by it. A theory with so little to recommend it at the level of the ethics of our treatment of our fellow humans cannot have anything more to recommend it when it comes to the ethics of how we treat our fellow animals.

The version of contractarianism just examined is, as I have noted, a crude variety, and in fairness to those of a contractarian persuasion it must be noted that much more refined, subtle and ingenious varieties are possible. For example, John Rawls, in his *A Theory of Justice,* sets forth a version of contractarianism that forces contractors to ignore the accidental features of being a human being—for example, whether one is white or black, male or female, a genius or of modest intellect. Only by ignoring such features, Rawls believes, can we ensure that the principles of justice that contractors would agree upon are not based on bias or prejudice. Despite the improvement a view such as Rawls's represents over the cruder forms of contractarianism, it remains deficient: it systematically denies that we have direct duties to those human beings who do not have a sense of justice—young children, for instance, and many mentally retarded humans. And yet it seems reasonably certain that, were we to torture a young child or a retarded elder, we would be doing something that wronged him or her, not something that would be wrong if (and only if) other humans with a sense of justice were upset. And since this is true in the case of these humans, we cannot rationally deny the same in the case of animals.

Indirect duty views, then, including the best among them, fail to command our rational assent. Whatever ethical theory we should accept rationally, therefore, it must at least recognize that we have some duties directly to animals, just as we have some duties directly to each other....

Some people think that the theory we are looking for is utilitarianism. A utilitarian accepts two moral principles. The first is that of equality: everyone's interests count, and similar interests must be counted as having similar weight or importance. White or black, American or Iranian, human or animal—everyone's pain or frustration matter[s], and matter[s] as much as the equivalent pain or frustration of anyone else. The second principle a utilitarian accepts is that of utility: do the act that will bring about the best balance between satisfaction and frustration for everyone affected by the outcome.

As a utilitarian, then, here is how I am to approach the task of deciding what I morally ought to do: I must ask who will be affected if I choose to do one thing rather than another, how much each individual will be affected, and where the best results are most likely to lie—which option, in other words, is most likely to bring about the best results, the best balance between satisfaction and frustration. That option, whatever it may be, is the one I ought to choose. That is where my moral duty lies.

The great appeal of utilitarianism rests with its uncompromising *egalitarianism*: everyone's interests count and count as much as the like interests of everyone else. The kind of odious discrimination that some forms of contractarianism can justify—discrimination based on race or sex, for example—seems disallowed in principle by utilitarianism, as is speciesism, systematic discrimination based on species membership.

The equality we find in utilitarianism, however, is not the sort an advocate of animal or human rights should have in mind. Utilitarianism has no room for the equal moral rights of different individuals because it has no room for their equal inherent value or worth. What has value for the utilitarian is the satisfaction of an individual's interests, not the individual whose interests they are. A universe in which you satisfy your desire for water, food and warmth is, other things being equal, better than a universe in which these desires are frustrated. And the same is true in the case of an animal with similar desires. But neither you nor the animal have any value in your own right. Only your feelings do.

Here is an analogy to help make the philosophical point clearer. A cup contains different liquids, sometimes sweet, sometimes bitter, sometimes a mix of the two. What has value are the liquids: the sweeter the better, the bitterer the worse. The cup, the container, has no value. It is what goes into it, not what they go into, that has value. For the utilitarian you and I are like the cup; we have no value as individuals and thus no equal value. What has value is what goes into us, what we serve as receptacles for; our feelings of satisfaction have positive value, our feelings of frustration negative value.

Serious problems arise for utilitarianism when we remind ourselves that it enjoins us to bring about the best consequences. What does this mean? It doesn't mean the best consequences for me alone, or for my family or friends, or any other person taken individually. No, what we must do is, roughly, as follows: we must add up (somehow!) the separate satisfactions and frustrations of everyone likely to be affected by our choice, the satisfactions in one column, the frustrations in the other. We must total each column for each of the options before us. That is what it means to say the theory is aggregative. And then we must choose that option which is most likely to bring about the best balance of totaled satisfactions over totaled frustrations. Whatever act would lead to this outcome is the one we ought morally to perform—it is where our moral duty lies. And that act quite clearly might not be the same one that would bring about the best results for me personally, or for my family or friends, or for a lab animal. The best aggregated consequences for everyone concerned are not necessarily the best for each individual.

That utilitarianism is an aggregative theory—different individuals' satisfactions or frustrations are added, or summed, or totaled—is the key objection to this theory. My Aunt Bea is old, inactive, a cranky, sour person, though not physically ill. She prefers to go on living. She is also rather rich. I could make a fortune if I could get my hands on her money, money she intends to give me in any event, after she dies, but which she refuses to give me now. In order to avoid a huge tax bite, I plan to donate a handsome sum of my profits to a local children's hospital. Many, many children will benefit from my generosity, and much joy will be brought to their parents, relatives and friends. If I don't get the money rather soon, all these ambitions will come to naught. The once-in-a-lifetime opportunity to make a real killing will be gone. Why, then, not kill my Aunt Bea? Oh, of course I *might* get caught. But I'm no fool and, besides, her doctor can be counted on to cooperate (he has an eye for the same investment and I happen to know a good deal about his shady past). The deed can be done … professionally, shall we say. There is very little chance of getting caught. And as for my conscience being guilt-ridden, I am a resourceful sort of fellow and will take more than sufficient comfort—as I lie on the beach at Acapulco—in contemplating the joy and health I have brought to so many others.

Suppose Aunt Bea is killed and the rest of the story comes out as told. Would I have done anything wrong? Anything immoral? One would have thought that I had. Not according to utilitarianism. Since what I have done has brought about the best balance between totaled satisfaction and frustration for all those affected by the outcome, my action is not wrong. Indeed, in killing Aunt Bea the physician and I did what duty required.

This same kind of argument can be repeated in all sorts of cases, illustrating, time after time, how the utilitarian's position leads to results that impartial people find morally callous. It is wrong to kill my Aunt Bea in the name of bringing about the best results for other. A good end does not justify an evil means. Any adequate moral theory will have to explain why this is so. Utilitarianism fails in this respect and so cannot be the theory we seek.

What to do? Where to begin anew? The place to begin, I think, is with the utilitarian's view of the value of the individual—or, rather, lack of value. In its place, suppose we consider that you and I, for example, do have value as individuals—what we'll call *inherent value.* To say we have such value is to say that we are something more than, something different from, mere receptacles. Moreover, to ensure that we do not pave the way for such injustices as slavery or sexual discrimination, we must believe that all who have inherent value have it equally, regardless of their sex, race, religion, birthplace and so on. Similarly to be discarded as irrelevant are one's talents or skills, intelligence and wealth, personality or pathology, whether one is loved and admired or despised and loathed. The genius and the retarded child, the prince and the pauper, the brain surgeon and the fruit vendor, Mother Teresa and the most unscrupulous used-car salesman—all have inherent value, all possess it equally, and all have an equal right to be treated with respect, to be treated in ways that do not reduce them to the status of things, as if they existed as resources for others. My value as an individual is independent of my usefulness to you. Yours is not dependent on your usefulness to me. For either of us to treat the other in ways that fail to show respect for the other's independent value is to act immorally, to violate the individual's rights.

Some of the rational virtues of this view—what I call the rights view—should be evident. Unlike (crude) contractarianism, for example, the rights view *in principle* denies the moral tolerability of any and all forms of racial, sexual or social discrimination; and unlike utilitarianism, this view *in principal* denies that we can justify good results by using evil means that violate an individual's rights—denies, for example, that it could be moral to kill my Aunt Bea to harvest beneficial consequences for others. That would be to sanction the disrespectful treatment of the individual in the name of the social good, something the rights view will not—categorically will not—ever allow.

The rights view, I believe, is rationally the most satisfactory moral theory. It surpasses all other theories in the degree to which it illuminates and explains the foundation of our duties to one another—the domain of human morality. On this score it has the best reasons, the best arguments, on its side. Of course, if it were possible to show that only human beings are included within its scope, then a person like myself, who believes in animal rights, would be obliged to look elsewhere.

But attempts to limit its scope to humans only can be shown to be rationally defective. Animals, it is true, lack many of the abilities humans possess. They can't read, do higher mathematics, build a bookcase or make *baba ghanoush.* Neither can many human beings, however, and yet we don't (and shouldn't) say that they (these humans) therefore have less inherent value, less of a right to be treated with respect, than do others. It is the *similarities* between those human beings who most clearly, most noncontroversially have such value (the people reading this, for example), not our differences, that matter most. And the really crucial, the basic similarity is simply this: we are each of us the experiencing subject of a life, a conscious creature having an individual welfare that has importance to us whatever our usefulness to others. We want and prefer things, believe and feel things, recall and expect things. And all these dimensions of our life, including our pleasure and pain, our enjoyment and suffering, our satisfaction and frustration, our continued existence or our untimely death—all make a difference to the quality of our life as lived, as experienced, by us as individuals. As the same is true of those animals that concern us, ... they too must be viewed as the experiencing subjects of a life, with inherent value of their own.

Some there are who resist the idea that animals have inherent value. "Only humans have such value," they profess. How might this narrow view be defended? Shall we say that only humans have the requisite intelligence, or autonomy, or reason? But there are many, many humans who fail to meet these standards and yet are reasonably viewed as having value above and beyond their usefulness to others. Shall we claim that only humans belong to the right species, the species *Homo sapiens*? But this is blatant speciesism. Will it be said, then, that all—and only—humans have immortal souls? Then our opponents have their work cut out for them. I am myself not ill-disposed to the proposition that there are immortal souls. Personally, I profoundly hope I have one. But I would not want to rest my position on a controversial ethical issue on the even more controversial question about who or what has an immortal soul. That is to dig one's hole deeper, not to climb out. Rationally, it is better to resolve moral issues without making more controversial assumptions than are needed. The question of who has inherent value is such a question, one that is resolved more rationally without the introduction of the idea of immortal souls than by its use.

Well, perhaps some will say that animals have some inherent value, only less than we have. Once again, however, attempts to defend this view can be shown to lack rational justification. What could be the basis of our having more inherent value than animals? Their lack of reason, or autonomy, or intellect? Only if we are willing to make the same judgment in the case of humans who are similarly deficient. But it is not true that such humans—the retarded child, for example, or the mentally deranged—have less inherent value than you or I. Neither, then, can we rationally sustain the view that animals, like them in being the experiencing subjects of a life, have less inherent value. *All* who have inherent value have it *equally*, whether they be human animals or not.

Inherent value, then, belongs equally to those who are the experiencing subjects of a life. Whether it belongs to others—to rocks and rivers, trees and glaciers, for example—we do not know and may never know. But neither do we need to know, if we are to make the case for animal rights. We do not need to know, for example, how many people are eligible to vote in the next presidential election before we can know whether I am. Similarly, we do not need to know how many individuals have inherent value before we can know that some do. When it comes to the case for animal rights, then, what we need to know is whether the animals that, in our culture, are routinely eaten, hunted and used in our laboratories, for example, are like us in being subjects of a life. And we do know this. We do know that many—literally, billions and billions—of these animals are the subjects of a life in the sense explained and so have inherent value if we do. And since, in order to arrive at the best theory of our duties to one another, we must recognize our equal inherent value as individuals, reason—not sentiment, not emotion—reason compels us to recognize the equal inherent value of these animals and, with this, their equal right to be treated with respect.

That, *very* roughly, is the shape and feel of the case for animal rights. Most of the details of the supporting argument are missing. They are to be found in the book to which I alluded earlier. Here, the details go begging, and I must, in closing, limit myself to four final points.

The first is how the theory that underlies the case for animal rights shows that the animal rights movement is a part of, not antagonistic to, the human rights movement. The theory that rationally grounds the rights of animals also grounds the rights of humans. Thus those involved in the animal rights movement are partners in the struggle to secure respect for human rights—the rights of women, for example, or minorities, or workers. The animal rights movement is cut from the same moral cloth as these.

Second, having set out the broad outlines of the rights view, I can now say why its implications for … science, among other fields, are both clear and uncompromising. In the case of the use of animals in science, the rights view is categorically abolitionist. Lab animals are not our tasters; we are not their kings. Because these animals are treated routinely, systematically as if their value were reducible to their usefulness to others, they are routinely, systematically treated with a lack of respect, and thus are their rights routinely, systematically violated. This is just as true when they are used in trivial, duplicative, unnecessary or unwise research as it is when they are used in studies that hold out real promise of human benefits. We can't justify harming or killing a human being (my Aunt Bea, for example) just for these sorts of reason. Neither can we do so even in the case of so lowly a creature as a laboratory rat. It is not just refinement or reduction that is called for, not just larger, cleaner cages, not just more generous use of anesthetic or the elimination of multiple surgery, not just tidying up the system. It is complete replacement. The best we can do when it comes to using animals in science is—not to use them. That is where our duty lies, according to the rights view....

My last two points are about philosophy, my profession. It is, most obviously, no substitute for political action. The words I have written here and in other places by themselves don't change a thing. It is what we do with the thoughts that the words express—our acts, our deeds—that changes things. All that philosophy can do, and all I have attempted, is to offer a vision of what our deeds should aim at. And the why. But not the how.

Finally, I am reminded of my thoughtful critic, the one I mentioned earlier, who chastised me for being too cerebral. Well, cerebral I have been: indirect duty views, utilitarianism, contractarianism—hardly the stuff deep passions are made of. I am also reminded, however, of the image another friend once set before me— the image of the ballerina as expressive of disciplined passion. Long hours of sweat and toil, of loneliness and practice, of doubt and fatigue: those are the discipline of her craft. But the passion is there too, the fierce drive to excel, to speak through her body, to do it right, to pierce our minds. That is the image of philosophy I would leave with you, not "too cerebral" but *disciplined passion*. Of the discipline enough has been seen. As for the passion: there are times, and these not infrequent, when tears come to my eyes when I see, or read, or hear of the wretched plight of animals in the hands of humans. Their pain, their suffering, their loneliness, their innocence, their death. Anger. Rage. Pity. Sorrow. Disgust. The whole creation groans under the weight of the evil we humans visit upon these mute, powerless creatures. It is our hearts, not just our heads, that call for an end to it all, that demand of us that we overcome, for them, the habits and forces behind their systematic oppression. All great movements, it is written, go through three stages: ridicule, discussion, adoption. It is the realization of this third stage, adoption, that requires both our passion and our discipline, our hearts and our heads. The fate of animals is in our hands. God grant we are equal to the task.

⊚ CRITICAL QUESTION

1. Present the best argument you can against the idea that animals have rights.

To access the *Voices of Wisdom*, 8th Edition, **Premium Website**, search for this book on CengageBrain.com.

CHAPTER SEVEN

What Is Aesthetic Value?

If the world were clear, art would not exist.

ALBERT CAMUS, *THE MYTH OF SISYPHUS*

LEARNING OBJECTIVES

After studying this chapter students should be able to:
- distinguish philosophy of art and aesthetics,
- give examples of the kinds of questions with which philosophy of art and aesthetics deal,
- describe the concerns that prompted Dewey's philosophy of art,
- characterize pragmatism,
- explain the "myth of the great artist,"
- identify Zen Buddhism,
- explain *wabi* and *sabi,*
- distinguish fine arts from crafts,
- explain the difficulties involved in defining art,
- define postmodernism,
- define ideology,
- identify Dewey, Hume, Nochlin, D. T. Suzuki, Danto, Hicks, and Caso, and
- answer all the questions related to the selections.

7.1 INTRODUCTION

All artistic objects are aesthetic objects, but not all aesthetic objects are artistic. If you grasp why this claim is true, you have understood the difference between aesthetics and **philosophy of art**.

Imagine walking through a wooded area of a university campus. You know that art students often make sculptures that they place in natural settings. You notice a shape in the distance in the woods. You find it interesting, even beautiful, and think, "what a lovely sculpture." Then you realize as you get closer that it is not a sculpture at all. It is a branch with an unusually pleasing shape that has fallen from a tree. What you thought was artwork created by some talented student now becomes for you not artwork at all but a natural object. Although it is no longer an artistic object for you, it has not ceased to be an aesthetic object.

The word *aesthetics* comes from Greek and means "perception." Typically it is used to name what is valuable about perceptions that we find pleasing. The answer to what makes them pleasing is often designated by the word *beauty*. Thus, in a rough and general way, we can say that aesthetic experiences are enjoyable experiences produced by the perception of beautiful objects. It is not surprising, given this general approximation, that many philosophers have claimed that beauty is the chief aesthetic value just as good is the chief moral value and truth the primary intellectual value.

Aesthetic objects can be of many sorts such as natural events (sunsets) and objects (beautifully shaped tree branches). Art objects constitute a subset of the category aesthetic objects. Unlike sunsets and tree branches, art is created by humans for aesthetic purposes.

Aesthetics (a branch of philosophy that emerged in the eighteenth century) and philosophy of art, while closely related and overlapping in many ways, are nevertheless distinguishable.

Aesthetics is concerned with questions like, what is an aesthetic experience? What is an aesthetic attitude? Are there aesthetic properties that objects and events possess? What is beauty? Is beauty only in the eye of the beholder? How does aesthetic value relate to moral value and to truth?

Although all of the above questions (and more) are relevant to the philosophy of art, that field of study is more narrowly focused on questions like, what is the nature of art? Are there criteria on which we can all agree for judging art? Can art be ugly, revolting, distasteful, weird, strange, and so on and still be an aesthetic object? Is the value of a work of art merely a matter of taste? Can standards of taste be objective? How does art relate to culture, and if different cultures have different standards of taste, how could there ever be a universal standard of beauty?

We cannot deal with all of these questions in this short introduction to aesthetics. However, we can look at some of them and sample what some philosophers have said and the sorts of arguments they have advanced to support their positions.

7.2 ART AS EXPERIENCE

Most of our experiences are rather humdrum. Everyday experiences are not memorable and do not stand out from the routine of life. There is not much exciting about brushing your teeth, nor is there much to "write home about" when you feel hungry for a beef taco.

Some of our experiences are not humdrum. They are interesting, intense, and exciting. Such experiences seem alive, even transforming. They are memorable. They break out of the routine and mechanical experiences that characterize so much of our lives. On the surface these more intense experiences may not be different in content from our more ordinary experiences, but there is a vitality and unity about them that sets them apart. There is eating a beef taco and there is *really* eating a beef taco. In the latter eating, we are more intensely aware of what is going on—we savor the spicy sauce, feel the coolness of the lettuce in contrast to the heat of the meat, delight in the crispness of the tortilla, and the complexity of aromas. We remember it. We say things like, "wow, that was really a fantastic taco" or "best taco I ever had."

We have all had ordinary everyday experiences that are unremarkable and experiences that stand out in our memory as impressive and exciting. If I asked you which of these kinds of experiences is like aesthetic appreciation of a work of art, what would you say? And if I asked you which of these experiences characterize your own experience of the art created by others, what would you say?

John Dewey (1859–1952), the author of the next selection, was disturbed by the fact that too often people's experiences of art were drab and ordinary. Sometimes art seemed like something imported into life from some place not very familiar and the "aesthetic" (Dewey used the alternative spelling "esthetic") for many meant something artificial, contrived, and reserved for museums or concert halls. Yet Dewey was convinced that art and aesthetic experience were rooted in common experiences, and to truly understand and appreciate art we had to recover its connection to experience.

Dewey was an important and influential American philosopher best known for his philosophy of education and theory of knowledge. His contributions to the philosophical movement known as **pragmatism** (see Section 8.5 for more on pragmatism) spread his influence in the United States and abroad. Pragmatism (Dewey preferred the term *instrumentalism*) was, in part, a reaction to an idealistic philosophy that abstracted concepts from the rich context of actual lived experience. This idea, when applied to art, meant for Dewey that we had to recover the connection between art and experience in order to understand and appreciate aesthetic value.

While many think philosophy's job is to create theories of art, Dewey argued that theories get in the way of genuine art appreciation. The ways in which art enriches our lives and illuminates otherwise unseen areas of experience become lost when theory separates aesthetic value from experience thereby obscuring something of importance to human happiness. Too often theories of art reduce our aesthetic experiences to passing "pleasurable excitations." Dewey thought that philosophy of art needed to make clear the connection of art to lived experience and thereby mend the gap created by abstract theories of art appreciation.

READING QUESTIONS

1. How does Dewey distinguish between experience and having "*an* experience"?
2. Explain what Dewey means by the "consummating phase of every developing integral experience."
3. How does Dewey contrast non-aesthetic and aesthetic experience?
4. Why is it regrettable that there is no word in English that connects the two words *artistic* and *aesthetic*?
5. What is the difference between recognition and perception?

Having an Experience

JOHN DEWEY

Experience occurs continuously, because the interaction of live creature and environing conditions is involved in the very process of living. Under conditions of resistance and conflict, aspects and elements of the self and the world that are implicated in this interaction qualify experience with emotions and ideas so that conscious intent emerges. Oftentimes, however, the experience had is inchoate. Things are experienced but not in such a way that they are composed into *an* experience. There is distraction and dispersion; what we observe and what we think, what we desire and what we get, are at odds with each other. We put our hands to the plow and turn back; we start and then we stop, not because the experience has reached the end for the sake of which it was initiated but because of extraneous interruptions or of inner lethargy.

In contrast with such experience, we have an experience when the material experienced runs its course to fulfillment. Then and then only is it integrated within and demarcated in the general stream of experience from other experiences. A piece of work is finished in a way that is satisfactory; a problem receives its solution; a game is played through; a situation, whether that of eating a meal, playing a game of chess, carrying on a conversation, writing a book, or taking part in a political campaign, is so rounded out that its close is a consummation and not a cessation. Such an experience is a whole and carries with it its own individualizing quality and self-sufficiency. It is *an* experience.

Philosophers, even empirical philosophers, have spoken for the most part of experience at large. Idiomatic speech, however, refers to experiences each of which is singular, having its own beginning and end. For life is no uniform uninterrupted march or flow. It is a thing of histories, each with its own plot, its own inception and movement toward its close, each having its own particular rhythmic movement; each with its own unrepeated quality pervading it throughout. A flight of stairs, mechanical as it is, proceeds by individualized steps, not by undifferentiated progression, and an inclined plane is at least marked off from other things by abrupt discreteness.

Experience in this vital sense is defined by those situations and episodes that we spontaneously refer to as being "real experiences"; those things of which we say in recalling them, "that *was* an experience." It may have been something of tremendous importance—a quarrel with one who was once an intimate, a catastrophe finally averted by a hair's breadth. Or it may have been something that in comparison was slight—and which perhaps because of its very slightness illustrates all the better what is to be an experience. There is that meal in a Paris restaurant of which one says "that *was* an experience." It stands out as an enduring memorial of what food may be. Then there is that storm one went through in crossing the Atlantic—the storm that seemed in its fury, as it was experienced, to sum up in itself all that a storm can be, complete in itself, standing out because marked out from what went before and what came after.

In such experiences, every successive part flows freely, without seam and without unfilled blanks, into what ensues. At the same time there is no sacrifice of the self-identity of the parts. A river, as distinct from a pond, flows. But its flow gives a definiteness and interest to its successive portions greater than exist in the homogenous portions of a pond. In an experience, flow is from something to something. As one part leads into another and as one part carries on what went before, each gains distinctness in itself. The

From John Dewey, *Art As Experience* (New York: Capricorn Books, 1958), pp. 35–49. Copyright © 1934 by John Dewey.

enduring whole is diversified by successive phases that are emphases of its varied colors.

Because of continuous merging, there are no holes, mechanical junctions, and dead centers when we have *an* experience. There are pauses, places of rest, but they punctuate and define the quality of movement. They sum up what has been undergone and prevent its dissipation and idle evaporation. Continued acceleration is breathless and prevents parts from gaining distinction. In a work of art, different acts, episodes, occurrences melt and fuse into unity, and yet do not disappear and lose their own character as they do so—just as in a genial conversation there is a continuous interchange and blending, and yet each speaker not only retains his own character but manifests it more clearly than is his wont.

An experience has a unity that gives it its name, *that* meal, that storm, that rupture of friendship. The existence of this unity is constituted by a single *quality* that pervades the entire experience in spite of the variation of its constituent parts. This unity is neither emotional, practical, nor intellectual, for these terms name distinctions that reflection can make within it. In discourse *about* an experience, we must make use of these adjectives of interpretation. In going over an experience in mind *after* its occurrence, we may find that one property rather than another was sufficiently dominant so that it characterizes the experience as a whole. There are absorbing inquiries and speculations which a scientific man and philosopher will recall as "experiences" in the emphatic sense. In final import they are intellectual. But in their actual occurrence they were emotional as well; they were purposive and volitional. Yet the experience was not a sum of these different characters; they were lost in it as distinctive traits. No thinker can ply his occupation save as he is lured and rewarded by total integral experiences that are intrinsically worthwhile. Without them he would never know what it is really to think and would be completely at a loss in distinguishing real thought from the spurious article. Thinking goes on in trains of ideas, but the ideas form a train only because they are much more than what an analytic psychology calls ideas. They are phases, emotionally

and practically distinguished, of a developing underlying quality; they are its moving variations, not separate and independent like Locke's and Hume's so-called ideas and impressions, but are subtle shadings of a pervading and developing hue.

We say of an experience of thinking that we reach or draw a conclusion. Theoretical formulation of the process is often made in such terms as to conceal effectually the similarity of "conclusion" to the consummating phase of every developing integral experience. These formulations apparently take their cue from the separate propositions that are premises and the proposition that is the conclusion as they appear on the printed page. The impression is derived that there are first two independent and ready-made entities that are then manipulated so as to give rise to a third. In fact, in an experience of thinking, premises emerge only as a conclusion becomes manifest. The experience, like that of watching a storm reach its height and gradually subside, is one of continuous movement of subject matters. Like the ocean in the storm, there are a series of waves; suggestions reaching out and being broken in a clash, or being carried onwards by a coöperative wave. If a conclusion is reached, it is that of a movement of anticipation and cumulation, one that finally comes to completion. A "conclusion" is no separate and independent thing; it is the consummation of a movement.

Hence *an* experience of thinking has its own esthetic quality. It differs from those experiences that are acknowledged to be esthetic, but only in its materials. The material of the fine arts consists of qualities; that of experience having intellectual conclusion are signs or symbols having no intrinsic quality of their own, but standing for things that may in another experience be qualitatively experienced. The difference is enormous. It is one reason why the strictly intellectual art will never be popular as music is popular. Nevertheless, the experience itself has a satisfying emotional quality because it possesses internal integration and fulfillment reached through ordered and organized movement. This artistic structure may be immediately felt. In so far, it is esthetic. What is even more important is that not only is this quality a significant motive in undertaking intellectual inquiry and in keeping it honest, but that no intellectual activity is an integral event (is *an* experience), unless it is rounded out with this quality. Without it, thinking is inconclusive. In short, esthetic cannot be sharply marked off from intellectual experience since the latter must bear an esthetic stamp to be itself complete.

The same statement holds good of a course of action that is dominantly practical, that is, one that consists of overt doings. It is possible to be efficient in action and yet not have a conscious experience. The activity is too automatic to permit of a sense of what it is about and where it is going. It comes to an end but not to a close or consummation in consciousness. Obstacles are overcome by shrewd skill, but they do not feed experience. There are also those who are wavering in action, uncertain, and inconclusive like the shades in classic literature. Between the poles of aimlessness and mechanical efficiency, there lie those courses of action in which through successive deeds there runs a sense of growing meaning conserved and accumulating toward an end that is felt as accomplishment of a process. Successful politicians and generals who turn statesmen like Caesar and Napoleon have something of the showman about them. This of itself is not art, but it is, I think, a sign that interest is not exclusively, perhaps not mainly, held by the result taken by itself (as it is in the case of mere efficiency), but by it as the outcome of a process. There is interest in completing an experience. The experience may be one that is harmful to the world and its consummation undesirable. But it has esthetic quality.

The Greek identification of good conduct with conduct having proportion, grace, and harmony, the *kalon-agathon,* is a more obvious example of distinctive esthetic quality in moral action. One great defect in what passes as morality is its anesthetic quality. Instead of exemplifying wholehearted action, it takes the form of grudging piecemeal concessions to the demands of duty. But illustrations may only obscure the fact that any practical activity will, provided that it is integrated and moves by its own urge to fulfillment, have esthetic quality.

A generalized illustration may be had if we imagine a stone, which is rolling down hill, to have an experience. The activity is surely sufficiently "practical." The stone starts from somewhere, and moves, as consistently as conditions permit, toward a place and state where it will be at rest—toward an end. Let us add, by imagination, to these external facts, the ideas that it looks forward with desire to the final outcome; that it is interested in the things it meets on its way, conditions that accelerate and retard its movement with respect to their bearing on the end; that it acts and feels toward them according to the hindering or helping function it attributes to them; and that the final coming to rest is related to all that went before as the culmination of a continuous movement. Then the stone would have an experience, and one with esthetic quality.

If we turn from this imaginary case to our own experience, we shall find much of it is nearer to what happens to the actual stone than it is to anything that fulfills the conditions fancy just laid down. For in much of our experience we are not concerned with the connection of one incident with what went before and what comes after. There is no interest that controls attentive rejection or selection of what shall be organized into the developing experience. Things happen, but they are neither definitely included nor decisively excluded; we drift. We yield according to external pressure, or evade and compromise. There are beginnings and cessations, but no genuine initiations and concludings. One thing replaces another, but does not absorb it and carry it on. There is experience, but so slack and discursive that it is not *an* experience. Needless to say, such experiences are anesthetic.

Thus the non-esthetic lies within two limits. At one pole is the loose succession that does not begin at any particular place and that ends—in the sense of ceasing—at no particular place. At the other pole is arrest, constriction, proceeding from parts having only a mechanical connection with one another. There exists so much of one and the other of these two kinds of experience that unconsciously they come to be taken as norms of all experience. Then, when the esthetic appears, it so sharply contrasts with the picture that has been formed of experience, that it is impossible to combine its special qualities with the features of the picture and the esthetic is given an outside place and status. The account that has been given of experience dominantly intellectual and practical is intended to show that there is no such contrast involved in having an experience; that, on the contrary, no experience of whatever sort is a unity unless it has esthetic quality.

The enemies of the esthetic are neither the practical nor the intellectual. They are the humdrum; slackness of loose ends; submission to convention in practice and intellectual procedure. Rigid abstinence, coerced submission, tightness on one side and dissipation, incoherence and aimless indulgence on the other are deviations in opposite directions from the unity of an experience. Some such considerations perhaps induced Aristotle to invoke the "mean proportional" as the proper designation of what is distinctive of both virtue and the esthetic. He was formally correct. "Mean" and "proportion" are, however, not self-explanatory, nor to be taken over in a prior mathematical sense, but are properties belonging to an experience that has a developing movement toward its own consummation.

I have emphasized the fact that every integral experience moves toward a close, an ending, since it ceases only when the energies active in it have done their proper work. This closure of a circuit of energy is the opposite of arrest, of *stasis*. Maturation and fixation are polar opposites. Struggle and conflict may be themselves enjoyed, although they are painful, when they are experienced as means of developing an experience; members in that they carry it forward, not just because they are there. There is, as will appear later, an element of undergoing, of suffering in its large sense, in every experience. Otherwise there would be no taking in of what preceded. For "taking in" in any vital experience is something more than placing something on the top of consciousness over what was previously known. It involves reconstruction which may be painful. Whether the necessary undergoing phase is by itself pleasurable or painful is a matter of particular conditions. It is indifferent to the total esthetic quality, save that there are

few intense esthetic experiences that are wholly gleeful. They are certainly not to be characterized as amusing, and as they bear down upon us they involve a suffering that is none the less consistent with, indeed a part of, the complete perception that is enjoyed.

I have spoken of the esthetic quality that rounds out an experience into completeness and unity as emotional. The reference may cause difficulty. We are given to thinking of emotions as things as simple and compact as are the words by which we name them. Joy, sorrow, hope, fear, anger, curiosity, are treated as if each in itself were a sort of entity that enters full-made upon the scene, an entity that may last a long time or a short time, but whose duration, whose growth and career, is irrelevant to its nature. In fact emotions are qualities, when they are significant, of a complex experience that moves and changes. I say, when they are *significant,* for otherwise they are but the outbreaks and eruptions of a disturbed infant. All emotions are qualifications of a drama and they change as the drama develops. Persons are sometimes said to fall in love at first sight. But what they fall into is not a thing of that instant. What would love be were it compressed into a moment in which there is no room for cherishing and for solicitude? The intimate nature of emotion is manifested in the experience of one watching a play on the stage or reading a novel. It attends the development of a plot; and a plot requires a stage, a space, wherein to develop, and time in which to unfold. Experience is emotional but there are no separate things called emotions in it.

By the same token, emotions are attached to events and objects in their movement. They are not, save in pathological instances, private. And even an "objectless" emotion demands something beyond itself to which to attach itself, and thus it soon generates a delusion in lack of something real. Emotion belongs of a certainty to the self. But it belongs to the self that is concerned in the movement of events toward an issue that is desired or disliked. We jump instantaneously when we are scared, as we blush on the instant when we are ashamed. But fright and shamed modesty are not in this case emotional states. Of themselves they are but automatic reflexes.

This image depicts the capitalist system as described by Marx and Engels in the *Manifesto of the Communist Party,* in Chapter 5. On what layer of this pyramid does the bourgeoisie reside?

The Death of Socrates by Jacques-Louis David (1787) is one of several representations of the philosopher's demise. In Chapter 5, the excerpt, *Crito*, by Plato, relates a conversation between Socrates and his friend, Crito, in which the philosopher explains why he will not accept help escaping from prison, but will, instead, face his death. Does the argument made by Socrates resonate with you? Why or why not?

According to bell hooks, in Chapter 6's *Ain't I a Woman*, "American society is one in which racial imperialism supersedes sexual imperialism." How does this notion square up with the fact that the Fifteenth Amendment to the Constitution, ratified in 1870, gave black men the right to vote but excluded women from that right, which was granted to them by the Nineteenth Amendment to the Constitution signed into law in 1920?

ANNETTE **BENING**   JULIANNE **MOORE**   MARK **RUFFALO**

THE KIDS ARE ALL RIGHT

TWO TEENS   TWO MOMS   ONE SPERM DONOR
THE PERFECT FAMILY

KidsAreAllRightMovie.com

In the movie *The Kids Are All Right*, two women in a long-term committed relationship have two teen-age children from a sperm donor. How does this sort of popular entertainment inform, belie, or support Suzanne Pharr's claim that homophobia and sexism are linked, as she posits in Chapter 6's *Homophobia as a Weapon of Sexism*?

In order to become emotional they must become parts of an inclusive and enduring situation that involves concern for objects and their issues. The jump of fright becomes emotional fear when there is found or thought to exist a threatening object that must be dealt with or escaped from. The blush becomes the emotion of shame when a person connects, in thought, an action he has performed with an unfavorable reaction to himself of some other person.

Physical things from far ends of the earth are physically transported and physically caused to act and react upon one another in the construction of a new object. The miracle of mind is that something similar takes place in experience without physical transport and assembling. Emotion is the moving and cementing force. It selects what is congruous and dyes what is selected with its color, thereby giving qualitative unity to materials externally disparate and dissimilar. It thus provides unity in and through the varied parts of an experience. When the unity is of the sort already described, the experience has esthetic character even though it is not, dominantly, an esthetic experience.

Two men meet; one is the applicant for a position, while the other has the disposition of the matter in his hands. The interview may be mechanical, consisting of set questions, the replies to which perfunctorily settle the matter. There is no experience in which the two men meet, nothing that is not a repetition, by way of acceptance or dismissal, of something which has happened a score of times. The situation is disposed of as if it were an exercise in bookkeeping. But an interplay may take place in which a new experience develops. Where should we look for an account of such an experience? Not to ledger entries nor yet to a treatise on economics or sociology or personnel psychology, but to drama or fiction. Its nature and import can be expressed only by art, because there is a unity of experience that can be expressed only as an experience. The *experience* is of material fraught with suspense and moving toward its own consummation through a connected series of varied incidents. The primary emotions on the part of the applicant may be at the beginning hope or despair, and elation or disappointment at the close. These emotions qualify the experience as a unity. But as the interview proceeds, secondary emotions are evolved as variations of the primary underlying one. It is even possible for each attitude and gesture, each sentence, almost every word, to produce more than a fluctuation in the intensity of the basic emotion; to produce, that is, a change of shade and tint in its quality. The employer sees by means of his own emotional reactions the character of the one applying. He projects him imaginatively into the work to be done and judges his fitness by the way in which the elements of the scene assemble and either clash or fit together. The presence and behavior of the applicant either harmonize with his own attitudes and desires or they conflict and jar. Such factors as these, inherently esthetic in quality, are the forces that carry the varied elements of the interview to a decisive issue. They enter into the settlement of every situation, whatever its dominant nature, in which there are uncertainty and suspense.

There are, therefore, common patterns in various experiences, no matter how unlike they are to one another in the details of their subject matter. There are conditions to be met without which an experience cannot come to be. The outline of the common pattern is set by the fact that every experience is the result of interaction between a live creature and some aspect of the world in which he lives. A man does something; he lifts, let us say, a stone. In consequence he undergoes, suffers, something: the weight, strain, texture of the surface of the thing lifted. The properties thus undergone determine further doing. The stone is too heavy or too angular, not solid enough; or else the properties undergone show it is fit for the use for which it is intended. The process continues until a mutual adaptation of the self and the object emerges and that particular experience comes to a close. What is true of this simple instance is true, as to form, of every experience. The creature operating may be a thinker in his study and the environment with which he interacts may consist of ideas instead of a stone. But interaction of the two constitutes the total experience that is had, and the close which completes it is the institution of a felt harmony.

An experience has pattern and structure, because it is not just doing and undergoing in alternation, but consists of them in relationship. To put one's hand in the fire that consumes it is not necessarily to have an experience. The action and its consequence must be joined in perception. This relationship is what gives meaning; to grasp it is the objective of all intelligence. The scope and content of the relations measure the significant content of an experience. A child's experience may be intense, but, because of lack of background from past experience, relations between undergoing and doing are slightly grasped, and the experience does not have great depth or breadth. No one ever arrives at such maturity that he perceives all the connections that are involved. There was once written (by Mr. Hinton) a romance called "The Unlearner." It portrayed the whole endless duration of life after death as a living over of the incidents that happened in a short life on earth, in continued discovery of the relationships involved among them.

Experience is limited by all the causes which interfere with perception of the relations between undergoing and doing. There may be interference because of excess on the side of doing or of excess on the side of receptivity, of undergoing. Unbalance on either side blurs the perception of relations and leaves the experience partial and distorted, with scant or false meaning. Zeal for doing, lust for action, leaves many a person, especially in this hurried and impatient human environment in which we live, with experience of an almost incredible paucity, all on the surface. No one experience has a chance to complete itself because something else is entered upon so speedily. What is called experience becomes so dispersed and miscellaneous as hardly to deserve the name. Resistance is treated as an obstruction to be beaten down, not as an invitation to reflection. An individual comes to seek, unconsciously even more than by deliberate choice, situations in which he can do the most things in the shortest time.

Experiences are also cut short from maturing by excess of receptivity. What is prized is then the mere undergoing of this and that, irrespective of perception of any meaning. The crowding together of as many impressions as possible is thought to be "life," even though no one of them is more than a flitting and a sipping. The sentimentalist and the day-dreamer may have more fancies and impressions pass through their consciousness than has the man who is animated by lust for action. But his experience is equally distorted, because nothing takes root in mind when there is no balance between doing and receiving. Some decisive action is needed in order to establish contact with the realities of the world and in order that impressions may be so related to facts that their value is tested and organized.

Because perception of relationship between what is done and what is undergone constitutes the work of intelligence, and because the artist is controlled in the process of his work by his grasp of the connection between what he has already done and what he is to do next, the idea that the artist does not think as intently and penetratingly as a scientific inquirer is absurd. A painter must consciously undergo the effect of his every brush stroke or he will not be aware of what he is doing and where his work is going. Moreover, he has to see each particular connection of doing and undergoing in relation to the whole that he desires to produce. To apprehend such relations is to think, and is one of the most exacting modes of thought. The difference between the pictures of different painters is due quite as much to differences of capacity to carry on this thought as it is to differences of sensitivity to bare color and to differences in dexterity of execution. As respects the basic quality of pictures, difference depends, indeed, more upon the quality of intelligence brought to bear upon perception of relations than upon anything else—though of course intelligence cannot be separated from direct sensitivity and is connected, though in a more external manner, with skill.

Any idea that ignores the necessary role of intelligence in production of works of art is based upon identification of thinking with use of one special kind of material, verbal signs and words. To think effectively in terms of relations of qualities is as severe a demand upon thought as to think in terms of symbols, verbal and mathematical. Indeed, since words are easily manipulated in mechanical ways, the production of a work of genuine art probably demands more intelligence than does most of the so-called thinking that goes on among those who pride themselves on being "intellectuals."

I have tried to show in these chapters that the esthetic is no intruder in experience from without, whether by way of idle luxury or transcendent ideality, but that it is the clarified and intensified development of traits that belong to every normally complete experience. This fact I take to be the only secure basis upon which esthetic theory can build. It remains to suggest some of the implications of the underlying fact.

We have no word in the English language that unambiguously includes what is signified by the two words "artistic" and "esthetic." Since "artistic" refers primarily to the act of production and "esthetic" to that of perception and enjoyment, the absence of a term designating the two processes taken together is unfortunate. Sometimes, the effect is to separate the two from each other, to regard art as something superimposed upon esthetic material, or, upon the other side, to an assumption that, since art is a process of creation, perception and enjoyment of it have nothing in common with the creative act. In any case, there is a certain verbal awkwardness in that we are compelled sometimes to use the term "esthetic" to cover the entire field and sometimes to limit it to the receiving perceptual aspect of the whole operation. I refer to these obvious facts as preliminary to an attempt to show how the conception of conscious experience as a perceived relation between doing and undergoing enables us to understand the connection that art as production and perception and appreciation as enjoyment sustain to each other.

Art denotes a process of doing or making. This is as true of fine as of technological art. Art involves molding of clay, chipping of marble, casting of bronze, laying on of pigments, construction of buildings, singing of songs, playing of instruments, enacting rôles on the stage, going through rhythmic movements in the dance. Every art does something with some physical material, the body or something outside the body, with or without the use of intervening tools, and with a view to production of something visible, audible, or tangible. So marked is the active or "doing" phase of art that the dictionaries usually define it in terms of skilled action, ability in execution. The Oxford Dictionary illustrates by a quotation from John Stuart Mill: "Art is an endeavor after perfection in execution" while Matthew Arnold calls it "pure and flawless workmanship."

The word "esthetic" refers, as we have already noted, to experience as appreciative, perceiving, and enjoying. It denotes the consumer's rather than the producer's standpoint. It is Gusto, taste; and, as with cooking, overt skillful action is on the side of the cook who prepares, while taste is on the side of the consumer, as in gardening there is a distinction between the gardener who plants and tills and the householder who enjoys the finished product.

These very illustrations, however, as well as the relation that exists in having an experience between doing and undergoing, indicate that the distinction between esthetic and artistic cannot be pressed so far as to become a separation. Perfection in execution cannot be measured or defined in terms of execution; it implies those who perceive and enjoy the product that is executed. The cook prepares food for the consumer and the measure of the value of what is prepared is found in consumption. Mere perfection in execution, judged in its own terms in isolation, can probably be attained better by a machine than by human art. By itself, it is at most technique, and there are great artists who are not in the first ranks as technicians (witness Cézanne), just as there are great performers on the piano who are not great esthetically, and as Sargent is not a great painter.

Craftsmanship to be artistic in the final sense must be "loving"; it must care deeply for the subject matter upon which skill is exercised. A sculptor comes to mind whose busts are marvelously exact. It might be difficult to tell in the presence of a photograph of one of them and of a photograph of the original which was of the person himself. For virtuosity they are remarkable. But one doubts whether the maker of the busts had an experience of his own that he was concerned to have those share who look at his products. To be truly artistic, a work must also be esthetic—that is, framed for enjoyed receptive perception. Constant observation is, of course, necessary for the maker while he is producing. But if his perception is not also esthetic in nature, it is a colorless and cold recognition of what has been done, used as a stimulus to the next step in a process that is essentially mechanical.

In short, art, in its form, unites the very same relation of doing and undergoing, outgoing and incoming energy, that makes an experience to be an experience. Because of elimination of all that does not contribute to mutual organization of the factors of both action and reception into one another, and because of selection of just the aspects and traits that contribute to their interpenetration of each other, the product is a work of esthetic art. Man whittles, carves, sings, dances, gestures, molds, draws and paints. The doing or making is artistic when the perceived result is of such a nature that *its* qualities *as perceived* have controlled the question of production. The act of producing that is directed by intent to produce something that is enjoyed in the immediate experience of perceiving has qualities that a spontaneous or uncontrolled activity does not have. The artist embodies in himself the attitude of the perceiver while he works.

Suppose, for the sake of illustration, that a finely wrought object, one whose texture and proportions are highly pleasing in perception, has been believed to be a product of some primitive people. Then there is discovered evidence that proves it to be an accidental natural product. As an external thing, it is now precisely what it was

before. Yet at once it ceases to be a work of art and becomes a natural "curiosity." It now belongs in a museum of natural history, not in a museum of art. And the extraordinary thing is that the difference that is thus made is not one of just intellectual classification. A difference is made in appreciative perception and in a direct way. The esthetic experience—in its limited sense—is thus seen to be inherently connected with the experience of making.

The sensory satisfaction of eye and ear, when esthetic, is so because it does not stand by itself but is linked to the activity of which it is the consequence. Even the pleasures of the palate are different in quality to an epicure than in one who merely "likes" his food as he eats it. The difference is not of mere intensity. The epicure is conscious of much more than the taste of the food. Rather, there enter into the taste, as directly experienced, qualities that depend upon reference to its source and its manner of production in connection with criteria of excellence. As production must absorb into itself qualities of the product as perceived and be regulated by them, so, on the other side, seeing, hearing, tasting become esthetic when relation to a distinct manner of activity qualifies what is perceived.

There is an element of passion in all esthetic perception. Yet when we are overwhelmed by passion, as in extreme rage, fear, jealousy, the experience is definitely non-esthetic. There is no relationship felt to the qualities of the activity that has generated the passion. Consequently, the material of the experience lacks elements of balance and proportion. For these can be present only when, as in the conduct that has grace or dignity, the act is controlled by an exquisite sense of the relations which the act sustains—its fitness to the occasion and to the situation....

⊛ CRITICAL QUESTIONS

1. Is Dewey's claim that experience "is emotional but there are no separate things called emotions in it" clear? Why, or why not?

2. Create your own critical question about what Dewey says and answer it.

7.3 WOMEN AND ART

Imagine yourself at a party with several art students present, both male and female. Someone, after the third glass of wine, decides to liven things up a bit by loudly asking, why are there no great women artists? After the groans subside, someone, a male, says that the answer is obvious. Women are just not as good at art as men are. After the cries of sexism fade, someone else, a female, says, "Oh, but there are," and proceeds to name several. As the people shift their focus to debating the merits of this or that female artist that had been mentioned, someone, again a female, claims that women's art exhibits a different kind of greatest than men's art. The debate now shifts again to focus on the difference in characteristics between women's art and men's art.

We can imagine further shifts in the discussion as someone else begins to outline the social and cultural conditions of oppression that have prevented women from living up to their full artistic potential in the world of art. The fact that this deceptively simple question about why there are no great women artists has opened up so many different avenues of discussion and debate reveals that such questions carry freight. They come with unanalyzed assumptions concerning what art is, what "great" art is, how we judge art, and how the cultural and institutional context of art production influences what we eventually call good if not great art.

Linda Nochlin, the author of the next selection, graduated from Vassar College with a B.A. in philosophy and took her doctorate in art history at the Institute of Fine Arts at New York University. She is Distinguished Professor of Art History at the Graduate Center of the City University of New York and Lila Acheson Wallace Professor of Modern Art at the Institute of Fine Arts, New York University. This selection, originally published in *Art News* (January 1971, Vol. 69) during the early days of the feminist movement, has become a classic in the field of feminist art history.

⊚ READING QUESTIONS

1. What must be corrected in order to gain a more accurate view of the history of art?
2. What is the "naïve idea" of art?
3. What does making art involve?
4. What is the "myth of the Great Artist," and how does it influence our understanding of the question, "Why have there been no great women artists"?
5. What is the significance of the fact that until recently most female art students were denied access to both male and female nude models?

Why Have There Been No Great Women Artists?

LINDA NOCHLIN

While the recent upsurge of feminist activity in this country has indeed been a liberating one, its force has been chiefly emotional—personal, psychological, and subjective—centered, like the other radical movements to which it is related, on the present and its immediate needs, rather than on historical analysis of the basic intellectual issues which the feminist attack on the status quo automatically raises.[1] Like any revolution, however, the feminist one ultimately must come to grips with the intellectual and ideological basis of the various intellectual or scholarly disciplines—history, philosophy, sociology, psychology, etc.—in the same way that it questions the ideologies of present social institutions. If, as John Stuart Mill suggested, we tend to accept whatever *is* as natural, this is just as true in the realm of academic investigation as it is in our social arrangements. In the former, too, "natural" assumptions must be questioned and the mythic basis of much so-called fact brought to light. And it is here that the very position of woman as an acknowledged outsider, the maverick "she" instead of the presumably neutral "one"—in reality the white-male-position-accepted-as-natural, or the hidden "he" as the subject of all scholarly predicates—is a decided advantage, rather than merely a hindrance or a subjective distortion.

In the field of art history, the white Western male viewpoint, unconsciously accepted as *the* viewpoint of the art historian, may—and does—prove to be inadequate not merely on moral and ethical grounds, or because it is elitist, but on purely intellectual ones. In revealing the failure of much academic art history, and a great deal of history in general, to take account of the unacknowledged value system, the very *presence* of an intruding subject in historical investigation, the feminist critique at the same time lays bare its conceptual smugness, its meta-historical naïveté. At a moment when all disciplines are becoming more self-conscious, more aware of the nature of their presuppositions as exhibited in the very languages and structures of the various fields of scholarship, such uncritical acceptance of "what is" as "natural" may be intellectually fatal. Just as Mill saw male domination as one of a long series of social injustices that had to be overcome if a truly just social order were to be created, so we may see the unstated domination of white male subjectivity as one in a series of intellectual distortions which must be corrected in order to achieve a more adequate and accurate view of historical situations.

It is the engaged feminist intellect (like John Stuart Mill's) that can pierce through the cultural-ideological limitations of the time and its specific "professionalism" to reveal biases and inadequacies not merely in dealing with the question of women, but in the very way of formulating the crucial questions of the discipline as a whole. Thus, the so-called woman question, far from being a minor, peripheral, and laughably provincial sub-issue grafted on to a serious, established discipline, can become a catalyst, an intellectual instrument, probing basic and "natural" assumptions, providing a paradigm for other kinds of internal questioning, and in turn providing links with paradigms established by radical approaches in other fields. Even a simple question like "Why have there been no great women artists?" can, if answered adequately, create a sort of chain reaction, expanding not merely to encompass the accepted assumptions of the single field, but outward to embrace history and the social sciences, or even psychology and literature, and thereby, from the outset, can challenge the assumption that the traditional divisions of intellectual inquiry are still adequate to deal with the meaningful questions of our time, rather than the merely convenient or self-generated ones.

Let us, for example, examine the implications of that perennial question (one can, of course, substitute almost any field of human endeavor, with appropriate changes in phrasing): "Well, if women really *are* equal to men, why have there never been any great women artists (or composers, or mathematicians, or philosophers, or so few of the same)?"

"Why have there been no great women artists?" The question tolls reproachfully in the background of most discussions of the so-called woman problem. But like so many other so-called questions involved in the feminist "controversy," it falsifies the nature of the issue at the same time that it insidiously supplies its own answer: "There are no great women artists because women are incapable of greatness."

The assumptions behind such a question are varied in range and sophistication, running anywhere from "scientifically proven" demonstrations of the inability of human beings with wombs rather than penises to create anything significant, to relatively open-minded wonderment that women, despite so many years of near-equality—and after all, a lot of men have had their disadvantages too—have still not achieved anything of exceptional significance in the visual arts.

The feminist's first reaction is to swallow the bait, hook, line and sinker, and to attempt to answer the question as it is put: that is, to dig up examples of worthy or insufficiently appreciated women artists throughout history; to rehabilitate rather modest, if interesting and productive careers; to "rediscover" forgotten flower painters or David followers and make out a case for them; to demonstrate that Berthe Morisot was really less dependent upon Manet than one had been led to think—in other words, to engage in the normal activity of the specialist scholar who makes a case for the importance of his very own neglected or minor master. Such attempts, whether undertaken from a feminist point of view, like the ambitious article on women artists which appeared in the 1858 *Westminster Review,*[2] or more recent scholarly studies on such artists as Angelica Kauffmann and Artemisia Gentileschi,[3] are certainly worth the effort, both in adding to our knowledge of women's achievement and of art history generally. But they do nothing to question the assumptions lying behind the question "Why have there been no great women artists?" On the contrary, by attempting to answer it, they tacitly reinforce its negative implications.

Another attempt to answer the question involves shifting the ground slightly and asserting, as some contemporary feminists do, that there is a different kind of "greatness" for women's art than for men's, thereby postulating the existence of a distinctive and recognizable feminine style, different both in its formal and its expressive qualities and based on the special character of women's situation and experience.

This, on the surface of it, seems reasonable enough: in general, women's experience and situation in society, and hence as artists, is different from men's, and certainly the art produced by a group of consciously united and purposefully articulate women intent on bodying forth a group consciousness of feminine experience might indeed be

stylistically identifiable as feminist, if not feminine, art. Unfortunately, though this remains within the realm of possibility it has so far not occurred. While the members of the Danube School, the followers of Caravaggio, the painters gathered around Gauguin at Pont-Aven, the Blue Rider, or the Cubists may be recognized by certain clearly defined stylistic or expressive qualities, no such common qualities of "femininity" would seem to link the styles of women artists generally, any more than such qualities can be said to link women writers, a case brilliantly argued, against the most devastating, and mutually contradictory, masculine critical clichés, by Mary Ellmann in her *Thinking about Women.*[4] No subtle essence of femininity would seem to link the work of Artemesia Gentileschi, Mme Vigée-Lebrun, Angelica Kauffmann, Rosa Bonheur, Berthe Morisot, Suzanne Valadon, Käthe Kollwitz, Barbara Hepworth, Georgia O'Keeffe, Sophie Taeuber-Arp, Helen Frankenthaler, Bridget Riley, Lee Bontecou, or Louise Nevelson, any more than that of Sappho, Marie de France, Jane Austen, Emily Brontë, George Sand, George Eliot, Virginia Woolf, Gertrude Stein, Anaïs Nin, Emily Dickinson, Sylvia Plath, and Susan Sontag. In every instance, women artists and writers would seem to be closer to other artists and writers of their own period and outlook than they are to each other.

Women artists are more inward-looking, more delicate and nuanced in their treatment of their medium, it may be asserted. But which of the women artists cited above is more inward-turning than Redon, more subtle and nuanced in the handling of pigment than Corot? Is Fragonard more or less feminine than Mme Vigée-Lebrun? Or is it not more a question of the whole Rococo style of eighteenth-century France being "feminine," if judged in terms of a binary scale of "masculinity" versus "femininity"? Certainly, if daintiness, delicacy, and preciousness are to be counted as earmarks of a feminine style, there is nothing fragile about Rosa Bonheur's *Horse Fair,* nor dainty and introverted about Helen Frankenthaler's giant canvases. If women have turned to scenes of domestic life, or of children, so did Jan Steen, Chardin, and the Impressionists—Renoir and Monet as well as Morisot and Cassatt. In any case, the mere choice of a certain realm of subject matter, or the restriction to certain subjects, is not to be equated with a style, much less with some sort of quintessentially feminine style.

The problem lies not so much with some feminists' concept of what femininity is, but rather with their misconception—shared with the public at large—of what art is: with the naïve idea that art is the direct, personal expression of individual emotional experience, a translation of personal life into visual terms. Art is almost never that, great art never is. The making of art involves a self-consistent language of form, more or less dependent upon, or free from, given temporally defined conventions, schemata, or systems of notation, which have to be learned or worked out, either through teaching, apprenticeship, or a long period of individual experimentation. The language of art is, more materially, embodied in paint and line on canvas or paper, in stone or clay or plastic or metal—it is neither a sob story nor a confidential whisper.

The fact of the matter is that there have been no supremely great women artists, as far as we know, although there have been many interesting and very good ones who remain insufficiently investigated or appreciated; nor have there been any great Lithuanian jazz pianists, nor Eskimo tennis players, no matter how much we might wish there had been. That this should be the case is regrettable, but no amount of manipulating the historical or critical evidence will alter the situation; nor will accusations of male-chauvinist distortion of history. There *are* no women equivalents for Michelangelo or Rembrandt, Delacroix or Cézanne, Picasso or Matisse, or even, in very recent times, for de Kooning or Warhol, any more than there are black American equivalents for the same. If there actually were large numbers of "hidden" great women artists, or if there really should be different standards for women's art as opposed to men's—and one can't have it both ways—then what are feminists fighting for? If women have in fact achieved the same status as men in the arts, then the status quo is fine as it is.

But in actuality, as we all know, things as they are and as they have been, in the arts as in a

hundred other areas, are stultifying, oppressive, and discouraging to all those, women among them, who did not have the good fortune to be born white, preferably middle class and, above all, male. The fault lies not in our stars, our hormones, our menstrual cycles, or our empty internal spaces, but in our institutions and our education—education understood to include everything that happens to us from the moment we enter this world of meaningful symbols, signs, and signals. The miracle is, in fact, that given the overwhelming odds against women, or blacks, that so many of both have managed to achieve so much sheer excellence, in those bailiwicks of white masculine prerogative like science, politics, or the arts.

It is when one really starts thinking about the implications of "Why have there been no great women artists?" that one begins to realize to what extent our consciousness of how things are in the world has been conditioned—and often falsified—by the way the most important questions are posed. We tend to take it for granted that there really is an East Asian Problem, a Poverty Problem, a Black Problem—and a Woman Problem. But first we must ask ourselves who is formulating these "questions," and then, what purposes such formulations may serve. (We may, of course, refresh our memories with the connotations of the Nazis' "Jewish Problem.") Indeed, in our time of instant communication, "problems" are rapidly formulated to rationalize the bad conscience of those with power: thus the problem posed by Americans in Vietnam and Cambodia is referred to by Americans as the "East Asian Problem," whereas East Asians may view it, more realistically, as the "American Problem"; the so-called Poverty Problem might more directly be viewed as the "Wealth Problem" by denizens of urban ghettos or rural wastelands; the same irony twists the White Problem into its opposite, a Black Problem; and the same inverse logic turns up in the formulation of our own present state of affairs as the "Woman Problem."

Now the "Woman Problem," like all human problems, so-called (and the very idea of calling anything to do with human beings a "problem" is, of course, a fairly recent one) is not amenable to "solution" at all, since what human problems involve is reinterpretation of the nature of the situation, or a radical alteration of stance or program *on the part of the "problems" themselves.* Thus women and their situation in the arts, as in other realms of endeavor, are not a "problem" to be viewed through the eyes of the dominant male power elite. Instead, *women* must conceive of themselves as potentially, if not actually, equal subjects, and must be willing to look the facts of their situation full in the face, without self-pity, or cop-outs; at the same time they must view their situation with that high degree of emotional and intellectual commitment necessary to create a world in which equal achievement will be not only made possible but actively encouraged by social institutions.

It is certainly not realistic to hope that a majority of men, in the arts or in any other field, will soon see the light and find that it is in their own self-interest to grant complete equality to women, as some feminists optimistically assert, or to maintain that men themselves will soon realize that they are diminished by denying themselves access to traditionally "feminine" realms and emotional reactions. After all, there are few areas that are really "denied" to men, if the level of operations demanded be transcendent, responsible, or rewarding enough: men who have a need for "feminine" involvement with babies or children gain status as pediatricians or child psychologists, with a nurse (female) to do the more routine work; those who feel the urge for kitchen creativity may gain fame as master chefs; and, of course, men who yearn to fulfill themselves through what are often termed "feminine" artistic interests can find themselves as painters or sculptors, rather than as volunteer museum aides or part-time ceramists, as their female counterparts so often end up doing; as far as scholarship is concerned, how many men would be willing to change their jobs as teachers and researchers for those of unpaid, part-time research assistants and typists as well as full-time nannies and domestic workers?

Those who have privileges inevitably hold on to them, and hold tight, no matter how marginal the advantage involved, until compelled to bow to superior power of one sort or another.

Thus the question of women's equality—in art as in any other realm—devolves not upon the relative benevolence or ill-will of individual men, nor the self-confidence or abjectness of individual women, but rather on the very nature of our institutional structures themselves and the view of reality which they impose on the human beings who are part of them. As John Stuart Mill pointed out more than a century ago, "Everything which is usual appears natural. The subjection of women to men being a universal custom, any departure from it quite naturally appears unnatural."[5] Most men, despite lip service to equality, are reluctant to give up this "natural" order of things in which their advantages are so great; for women, the case is further complicated by the fact that, as Mill astutely pointed out, unlike other oppressed groups or castes, men demand of them not only submission but unqualified affection as well; thus women are often weakened by the internalized demands of the male-dominated society itself, as well as by a plethora of material goods and comforts: the middle-class woman has a great deal more to lose than her chains.

The question "Why have there been no great women artists?" is simply the top tenth of an iceberg of misinterpretation and misconception; beneath lies a vast dark bulk of shaky *idées reçues* [customary ideas] about the nature of art and its situational concomitants, about the nature of human abilities in general and of human excellence in particular, and the role that the social order plays in all of this. While the "woman problem" as such may be a pseudo-issue, the misconceptions involved in the question "Why have there been no great women artists?" points to major areas of intellectual obfuscation beyond the specific political and ideological issues involved in the subjection of women. Basic to the question are many naïve, distorted, uncritical assumptions about the making of art in general, as well as the making of great art. These assumptions, conscious or unconscious, link together such unlikely superstars as Michelangelo and van Gogh, Raphael and Jackson Pollock under the rubric of "Great"—an honorific attested to by the number of scholarly monographs devoted to the artist in question—and the Great Artist is, of course, conceived of as one who has "Genius"; Genius, in turn, is thought of as an atemporal and mysterious power somehow embedded in the person of the Great Artist.[6] Such ideas are related to unquestioned, often unconscious, meta-historical premises that make Hippolyte Taine's race-milieu-moment formulation of the dimensions of historical thought seem a model of sophistication. But these assumptions are intrinsic to a great deal of art-historical writing. It is no accident that the crucial question of the conditions *generally* productive of great art has so rarely been investigated, or that attempts to investigate such general problems have, until fairly recently, been dismissed as unscholarly, too broad, or the province of some other discipline, like sociology. To encourage a dispassionate, impersonal, sociological, and institutionally oriented approach would reveal the entire romantic, elitist, individual-glorifying, and monograph-producing substructure upon which the profession of art history is based, and which has only recently been called into question by a group of younger dissidents.

Underlying the question about woman as artist, then, we find the myth of the Great Artist—subject of a hundred monographs, unique, godlike—bearing within his person since birth a mysterious essence, rather like the golden nugget in Mrs. Grass's chicken soup, called Genius or Talent, which, like murder, must always out, no matter how unlikely or unpromising the circumstances.

The magical aura surrounding the representational arts and their creators has, of course, given birth to myths since the earliest times. Interestingly enough, the same magical abilities attributed by Pliny to the Greek sculptor Lysippos in antiquity—the mysterious inner call in early youth, the lack of any teacher but Nature herself—is repeated as late as the nineteenth century by Max Buchon in his biography of Courbet. The supernatural powers of the artist as imitator, his control of strong, possibly dangerous powers, have functioned historically to set him off from others as a godlike creator, one who creates Being out of nothing. The fairy tale of the discovery by an older artist or discerning patron of the Boy Wonder, usually in the guise of a lowly shepherd boy, has been a stock-in-trade

of artistic mythology ever since Vasari immortalized the young Giotto, discovered by the great Cimabue while the lad was guarding his flocks, drawing sheep on a stone; Cimabue, overcome with admiration for the realism of the drawing, immediately invited the humble youth to be his pupil.[7] Through some mysterious coincidence, later artists including Beccafumi, Andrea Sansovino, Andrea del Castagno, Mantegna, Zurbarán, and Goya were all discovered in similar pastoral circumstances. Even when the young Great Artist was not fortunate enough to come equipped with a flock of sheep, his talent always seems to have manifested itself very early, and independent of any external encouragement: Filippo Lippi and Poussin, Courbet and Monet are all reported to have drawn caricatures in the margins of their schoolbooks instead of studying the required subjects—we never, of course, hear about the youths who neglected their studies and scribbled in the margins of their notebooks without ever becoming anything more elevated than department-store clerks or shoe salesmen. The great Michelangelo himself, according to his biographer and pupil, Vasari, did more drawing than studying as a child. So pronounced was his talent, reports Vasari, that when his master, Ghirlandaio, absented himself momentarily from his work in Santa Maria Novella, and the young art student took the opportunity to draw "the scaffolding, trestles, pots of paint, brushes and the apprentices at their tasks" in this brief absence, he did it so skillfully that upon his return the master exclaimed: "This boy knows more than I do."

As is so often the case, such stories, which probably have some truth in them, tend both to reflect and perpetuate the attitudes they subsume. Even when based on fact, these myths about the early manifestations of genius are misleading. It is no doubt true, for example, that the young Picasso passed all the examinations for entrance to the Barcelona, and later to the Madrid, Academy of Art at the age of fifteen in but a single day, a feat of such difficulty that most candidates required a month of preparation. But one would like to find out more about similar precocious qualifiers for art academies who then went on to achieve nothing but mediocrity or failure—in whom, of course, art historians are uninterested—or to study in greater detail the role played by Picasso's art-professor father in the pictorial precocity of his son. What if Picasso had been born a girl? Would Señor Ruiz have paid as much attention or stimulated as much ambition for achievement in a little Pablita?

What is stressed in all these stories is the apparently miraculous, nondetermined, and asocial nature of artistic achievement; this semi-religious conception of the artist's role is elevated to hagiography in the nineteenth century, when art historians, critics, and, not least, some of the artists themselves tended to elevate the making of art into a substitute religion, the last bulwark of higher values in a materialistic world. The artist, in the nineteenth-century Saints' Legend, struggles against the most determined parental and social opposition, suffering the slings and arrows of social opprobrium like any Christian martyr, and ultimately succeeds against all odds—generally, alas, after his death—because from deep within himself radiates that mysterious, holy effulgence: Genius. Here we have the mad van Gogh, spinning out sunflowers despite epileptic seizures and near-starvation; Cézanne, braving paternal rejection and public scorn in order to revolutionize painting; Gauguin throwing away respectability and financial security with a single existential gesture to pursue his calling in the tropics; or Toulouse-Lautrec, dwarfed, crippled, and alcoholic, sacrificing his aristocratic birthright in favor of the squalid surroundings that provided him with inspiration.

Now no serious contemporary art historian takes such obvious fairy tales at their face value. Yet it is this sort of mythology about artistic achievement and its concomitants which forms the unconscious or unquestioned assumptions of scholars, no matter how many crumbs are thrown to social influences, ideas of the times, economic crises, and so on. Behind the most sophisticated investigations of great artists—more specifically, the art-historical monograph, which accepts the notion of the great artist as primary, and the social and institutional structures within which he lived and worked as mere secondary "influences" or "background"—lurks the golden-nugget theory of genius and the free-enterprise conception of individual achievement. On this basis, women's lack of major achievement in art may be formulated as a syllogism: If women had the golden nugget of artistic genius then it would reveal itself. But it has never revealed itself. Q.E.D. Women do not have the golden nugget of artistic genius. If Giotto, the obscure shepherd boy, and van Gogh with his fits could make it, why not women?

Yet as soon as one leaves behind the world of fairy tale and self-fulfilling prophecy and, instead, casts a dispassionate eye on the actual situations in which important art production has existed, in the total range of its social and institutional structures throughout history, one finds that the very questions which are fruitful or relevant for the historian to ask shape up rather differently. One would like to ask, for instance, from what social classes artists were most likely to come at different periods of art history, from what castes and subgroup. What proportion of painters and sculptors, or more specifically, of major painters and sculptors, came from families in which their fathers or other close relatives were painters and sculptors or engaged in related professions? As Nikolaus Pevsner points out in his discussion of the French Academy in the seventeenth and eighteenth centuries, the transmission of the artistic profession from father to son was considered a matter of course (as it was with the Coypels, the Coustous, the Van Loos, etc.); indeed, sons of academicians were exempted from the customary fees for lessons.[8] Despite the noteworthy and dramatically satisfying cases of the great father-rejecting *révoltés* of the nineteenth century, one might be forced to admit that a large proportion of artists, great and not-so-great, in the days when it was normal for sons to follow in their fathers' footsteps, had artist fathers. In the rank of major artists, the names of Holbein and Dürer, Raphael and Bernini, immediately spring to mind; even in our own times, one can cite the names of Picasso, Calder, Giacometti, and Wyeth as members of artist-families.

As far as the relationship of artistic occupation and social class is concerned, an interesting paradigm for the question "Why have there been no great women artists?" might well be provided by trying to answer the question "Why have there been no great artists from the aristocracy?" One can scarcely think, before the antitraditional nineteenth century at least, of any artist who sprang from the ranks of any more elevated class than the upper bourgeoisie; even in the nineteenth century, Degas came from the lower nobility—more like the haute bourgeoisie, in fact—and only Toulouse-Lautrec, metamorphosed into the ranks of the marginal by accidental deformity, could be said to have come from the loftier reaches of the upper classes. While the aristocracy has always provided the lion's share of the patronage and the audience for art—as, indeed, the aristocracy of wealth does even in our more democratic days— it has contributed little beyond amateurish efforts to the creation of art itself, despite the fact that aristocrats (like many women) have had more than their share of educational advantages, plenty of leisure and, indeed, like women, were often encouraged to dabble in the arts and even develop into respectable amateurs, like Napoleon III's cousin, the Princess Mathilde, who exhibited at the official Salons, or Queen Victoria, who, with Prince Albert, studied art with no less a figure than Landseer himself. Could it be that the little golden nugget—genius—is missing from the aristocratic makeup in the same way that it is from the feminine psyche? Or rather, is it not that the kinds of demands and expectations placed before both aristocrats and women—the amount of time necessarily devoted to social functions, the very kinds of activities demanded—simply made total devotion to professional art production out of the question, indeed unthinkable, both for upper-class males and for women generally, rather than its being a question of genius and talent?

When the right questions are asked about the conditions for producing art, of which the production of great art is a subtopic, there will no doubt have to be some discussion of the situational concomitants of intelligence and talent generally, not merely of artistic genius. Piaget and others have stressed in their genetic epistemology that in the development of reason and in the unfolding of imagination in young children, intelligence—or, by implication, what we choose to call genius—is a dynamic activity rather than a static essence, and an activity of a subject *in a*

situation. As further investigations in the field of child development imply, these abilities, or this intelligence, are built up minutely, step by step, from infancy onward, and the patterns of adaptation-accommodation may be established so early within the subject-in-an-environment that they may indeed *appear* to be innate to the unsophisticated observer. Such investigations imply that, even aside from meta-historical reasons, scholars will have to abandon the notion, consciously articulated or not, of individual genius as innate, and as primary to the creation of art.[9]

The question "Why have there been no great women artists?" has led us to the conclusion, so far, that art is not a free, autonomous activity of a super-endowed individual, "influenced" by previous artists, and, more vaguely and superficially, by "social forces," but rather, that the total situation of art making, both in terms of the development of the art maker and in the nature and quality of the work of art itself, occur in a social situation, are integral elements of this social structure, and are mediated and determined by specific and definable social institutions, be they art academies, systems of patronage, mythologies of the divine creator, artist as he-man or social outcast.

THE QUESTION OF THE NUDE

We can now approach our question from a more reasonable standpoint, since it seems probable that the answer to why there have been no great women artists lies not in the nature of individual genius or the lack of it, but in the nature of given social institutions and what they forbid or encourage in various classes or groups of individuals. Let us first examine such a simple, but critical, issue as availability of the nude model to aspiring women artists, in the period extending from the Renaissance until near the end of the nineteenth century, a period in which careful and prolonged study of the nude model was essential to the training of every young artist, to the production of any work with pretensions to grandeur, and to the very essence of History Painting, generally accepted as the highest category of art. Indeed, it was argued by defenders of traditional painting in the nineteenth century that there could be no great painting *with* clothed figures, since costume inevitably destroyed both the temporal universality and the classical idealization required by great art. Needless to say, central to the training programs of the academies since their inception late in the sixteenth and early in the seventeenth centuries was life drawing from the nude, generally male, model. In addition, groups of artists and their pupils often met privately for life-drawing sessions from the nude model in their studios. While individual artists and private academies employed the female model extensively, the female nude was forbidden in almost all public art schools as late as 1850 and after—a state of affairs which Pevsner rightly designates as "hardly believable."[10] Far more believable, unfortunately, was the complete unavailability to the aspiring woman artist of *any* nude models at all, male or female. As late as 1893, "lady" students were not admitted to life drawing at the Royal Academy in London, and even when they were, after that date, the model had to be "partially draped."[11]

A brief survey of representations of life-drawing sessions reveals an all-male clientele drawing from the female nude in Rembrandt's studio; men working from male nudes in eighteenth-century representations of academic instruction in The Hague and Vienna; men working from the seated male nude in Boilly's charming painting of the interior of Houdon's studio at the beginning of the nineteenth century. Léon-Mathieu Cochereau's scrupulously veristic *Interior of David's Studio* [I], exhibited in the Salon of 1814, reveals a group of young men diligently drawing or painting from a male nude model, whose discarded shoes may be seen before the models' stand.

The very plethora of surviving "Academies"—detailed, painstaking studies from the nude studio model—in the youthful oeuvre of artists down through the time of Seurat and well into the twentieth century attests to the central importance of this branch of study in the pedagogy and development of the talented beginner. The formal academic program itself normally proceeded, as a matter of course, from copying from drawings and engravings, to drawing from casts of famous works of sculpture, to drawing from the living model. To be deprived of this ultimate stage of training meant, in effect, to be deprived of the possibility of creating major art works, unless one were a very ingenious lady indeed, or simply, as most of the women aspiring to be painters ultimately did, restricting oneself to the "minor" fields of portraiture, genre, landscape, or still life. It is rather as though a medical student were denied the opportunity to dissect or even examine the naked human body.

There exist, to my knowledge, no historical representations of artists drawing from the nude model which include women in any role but that of the nude model itself, an interesting commentary on rules of propriety: that is, it is all right for a ("low," of course) woman to reveal herself naked-as-an-object for a group of men, but forbidden to a woman to participate in the active study and recording of naked-man-as-an-object, or even of a fellow woman. An amusing example of this taboo on confronting a dressed lady with a naked man is embodied in a group portrait of the members of the Royal Academy in London in 1772, represented by Zoffany as gathered in the life room before two nude male models: all the distinguished members are present with but one noteworthy exception—the single female member, the renowned Angelica Kauffmann, who, for propriety's sake, is merely present in effigy, in the form of a portrait hanging on the wall. A slightly earlier drawing, *Ladies in the Studio* by the Polish artist Daniel Chodowiecki, shows the ladies portraying a modestly dressed member of their sex. In a lithograph dating from the relatively liberated epoch following the French Revolution, the lithographer Marlet has represented some women sketchers in a group of students working from the male model, but the model himself has been chastely provided with what appears to be a pair of bathing trunks, a garment hardly conducive to a sense of classical elevation; no doubt such license was considered daring in its day, and the young ladies in question suspected of doubtful morals, but even this liberated state of affairs seems to have lasted only a short while. In an English stereoscopic color view of the interior of a studio of about 1865, the standing, bearded male model is so heavily draped that not an iota of his anatomy escapes from the discreet toga, save for a single bare shoulder and arm: even so, he obviously had the grace to avert his eyes in the presence of the crinoline-clad young sketchers.

The women in the Women's Modeling Class at the Pennsylvania Academy were evidently not allowed even this modest privilege. A photograph by Thomas Eakins of about 1885 reveals these students modeling from a cow (bull? ox? the nether regions are obscure in the photograph), a naked cow to be sure, perhaps a daring liberty when one considers that even piano legs might be concealed beneath pantalettes during this era. (The idea of introducing a bovine model into the artist's studio stems from Courbet, who brought a bull into his short-lived studio academy in the 1860s.) Only at the very end of the nineteenth century, in the relatively liberated and open atmosphere of Repin's studio and circle in Russia, do we find representations of women art students working uninhibitedly from the nude—the female model, to be sure—in the company of men. Even in this case, it must be noted that certain photographs represent a private sketch group meeting in one of the women artists' homes; in another, the model is draped; and the large group portrait, a cooperative effort by two men and two women students of Repin's, is an imaginary gathering together of all of the Russian realist's pupils, past and present, rather than a realistic studio view.

I have gone into the question of the availability of the nude model, a single aspect of the automatic, institutionally maintained discrimination against women, in such detail simply to demonstrate both the universality of this discrimination and its consequences, as well as the institutional rather than individual nature of but one facet of the necessary preparation for achieving mere proficiency, much less greatness, in the realm of art during a long period. One could equally well examine other dimensions of the situation, such as the apprenticeship system, the academic educational pattern which, in France especially, was almost the only key to success and which had a regular progression and set competitions, crowned by the Prix de Rome which enabled the young winner to work in the French Academy in that

city—unthinkable for women, of course—and for which women were unable to compete until the end of the nineteenth century, by which time, in fact, the whole academic system had lost its importance anyway. It seems clear, to take France in the nineteenth century as an example (a country which probably had a larger proportion of women artists than any other—that is to say, in terms of their percentage in the total number of artists exhibiting in the Salon), that "women were not accepted as professional painters."[12] In the middle of the century, there were only a third as many women as men artists, but even this mildly encouraging statistic is deceptive when we discover that out of this relatively meager number, *none* had attended that major stepping stone to artistic success, the École des Beaux-Arts, only 7 percent had received any official commission or had held any official office—and these might include the most menial sort of work—only 7 percent had ever received any Salon medal, and *none* had ever received the Legion of Honor. Deprived of encouragements, educational facilities and rewards, it is almost incredible that a certain percentage of women did persevere and seek a profession in the arts.

It also becomes apparent why women were able to compete on far more equal terms with men—and even become innovators—in literature. While art making traditionally has demanded the learning of specific techniques and skills, in a certain sequence, in an institutional setting outside the home, as well as becoming familiar with a specific vocabulary of iconography and motifs, the same is by no means true for the poet or novelist. Anyone, even a woman, has to learn the language, can learn to read and write, and can commit personal experiences to paper in the privacy of one's room. Naturally this oversimplifies the real difficulties and complexities involved in creating good or great literature, whether by man or woman, but it still gives a clue as to the possibility of the existence of an Emily Brontë or an Emily Dickinson and the lack of their counterparts, at least until quite recently, in the visual arts.

Of course we have not gone into the "fringe" requirements for major artists, which would have been, for the most part, both psychically and socially closed to women, even if hypothetically they could have achieved the requisite grandeur in the performance of their craft: in the Renaissance and after, the great artist, aside from participating in the affairs of an academy, might well be intimate with members of humanist circles with whom he could exchange ideas, establish suitable relationships with patrons, travel widely and freely, perhaps politic and intrigue; nor have we mentioned the sheer organizational acumen and ability involved in running a major studio-factory, like that of Rubens. An enormous amount of self-confidence and worldly knowledgeability, as well as a natural sense of well-earned dominance and power, was needed by the great *chef d'école,* both in the running of the production end of painting, and in the control and instruction of the numerous students and assistants....

CONCLUSION

I have tried to deal with one of the perennial questions used to challenge women's demand for true, rather than token, equality, by examining the whole erroneous intellectual substructure upon which the question "Why have there been no great women artists?" is based; by questioning the validity of the formulation of so-called problems in general and the "problem" of women specifically; and then, by probing some of the limitations of the discipline of art history itself. By stressing the *institutional*—that is, the public—rather than the *individual,* or private, preconditions for achievement or the lack of it in the arts, I have tried to provide a paradigm

for the investigation of other areas in the field. By examining in some detail a single instance of deprivation or disadvantage—the unavailability of nude models to women art students—I have suggested that it was indeed *institutionally* made impossible for women to achieve artistic excellence, or success, on the same footing as men, *no matter what* the potency of their so-called talent, or genius. The existence of a tiny band of successful, if not great, women artists throughout history does nothing to gainsay this fact, any more than does the existence of a few superstars or token achievers among the members of any minority groups. And while great achievement is rare and difficult at best, it is still rarer and more difficult if, while you work, you must at the same time wrestle with inner demons of self-doubt and guilt and outer monsters of ridicule or patronizing encouragement, neither of which have any specific connection with the quality of the art work as such.

What is important is that women face up to the reality of their history and of their present situation, without making excuses or puffing mediocrity. Disadvantage may indeed be an excuse; it is not, however, an intellectual position. Rather, using as a vantage point their situation as underdogs in the realm of grandeur, and outsiders in that of ideology, women can reveal institutional and intellectual weaknesses in general, and, at the same time that they destroy false consciousness, take part in the creation of institutions in which clear thought—and true greatness—are challenges open to anyone, man or woman, courageous enough to take the necessary risk, the leap into the unknown.

NOTES

1. Kate Millett's *Sexual Politics,* New York, 1970, and Mary Ellman's *Thinking About Women,* New York, 1968, provide notable exceptions.
2. "Women Artists." Review of *Die Frauen in die Kunstgeschichte* by Ernst Guhl in *The Westminster Review* (American Edition), LXX, July 1858, pp. 91–104. I am grateful to Elaine Showalter for having brought this review to my attention.
3. See, for example, Peter S. Walch's excellent studies of Angelica Kauffmann or his unpublished doctoral dissertation, "Angelica Kauffmann,"

Princeton University, 1968, on the subject; for Artemisia Gentileschi, see R. Ward Bissell, "Artemisia Gentileschi—A New Documented Chronology," *Art Bulletin,* L (June 1968): 153–68.
4. New York, 1968.
5. John Stuart Mill, *The Subjection of Women* (1869) in *Three Essays by John Stuart Mill,* World's Classics Series, London, 1966, p. 441.
6. For the relatively recent genesis of the emphasis on the artist as the nexus of esthetic experience, see M. H. Abrams, *The Mirror and the Lamp:*

Romantic Theory and the Critical Tradition, New York, 1953, and Maurice Z. Shroder, *Icarus: The Image of the Artist in French Romanticism*, Cambridge, Massachusetts, 1961.

7. A comparison with the parallel myth for women, the Cinderella story, is revealing: Cinderella gains higher status on the basis of a passive, "sex-object" attribute—small feet—whereas the Boy Wonder always proves himself through active accomplishment. For a thorough study of myths about artists, see Ernst Kris and Otto Kurz. *Die Legende vom Künstler: Ein Geschichtlicher Versuch,* Vienna, 1934.

8. Nikolaus Pevsner, *Academies of Art, Past and Present.* Cambridge, 1940, p. 96f.

9. Contemporary directions—earthworks, conceptual art, art as information, etc.—certainly point *away* from emphasis on the individual genius and his salable products; in an history, Harrison C. and

Cynthia A. White's *Canvases and Careers: Institutional Change in the French Painting World*, New York, 1965, opens up a fruitful new direction of investigation, as did Nikolaus Pevsner's pioneering *Academies of Art*, Ernst Gombrich and Pierre Francastel, in their very different ways, always have tended to view art and the artist as part of a total situation rather than in lofty isolation.

10. Female models were introduced in the life class in Berlin in 1875, in Stockholm in 1839, in Naples in 1870, at the Royal College of Art in London after 1875. Pevsner, op. cit., p. 231. Female models at the Pennsylvania Academy of the Fine Arts wore masks to hide their identity as late as about 1866—as attested to in a charcoal drawing by Thomas Eakins—if not later.

11. Pevsner, op. cit., p. 231.

12. H. C. and C. A. White, op. cit., p. 51.

⊙ CRITICAL QUESTIONS

1. Has Nochlin adequately supported her claim that "it was indeed *institutionally* made impossible for women to achieve artistic excellence or success, on the same footing as men, *no matter what* the potency of their so-called talent, or genius"? Provide reasons to support your answer.

2. How would you answer the question, "Why have there been no great women artists?" Justify your answer with an argument.

7.4 ZEN CULTURE

Have you ever thought of drinking tea as an art? One can imagine it being an aesthetic experience of pleasure just as one can imagine that eating a taco can be an aesthetic experience. But can you imagine it being a form of art?

If aesthetic taste reflects experiences rooted in human nature, then why do cultural tastes vary so much? Some cultures prefer what is complex and others what is simple. Some cultures elevate certain activities to the level of art, even fine art, and others find aesthetic value in the mundane and everyday simplicity of life. Think of the differences between Japanese art and American art. Are these differences purely a matter of culture and history?

One reason to think about art and aesthetic value is because both reflect and express a culture. To understand a culture we must understand its art. The reverse is also true. To point out the close connection between art and culture is not to say that aesthetics is not a valuable study in its own right. However, we need to keep in mind the complex and significant links between art and the cultural values that provide its context.

Religions and philosophies also reflect culture. Often they are intertwined with art in subtle ways. Buddhism is both a religion and a philosophy in a broad sense of recommending a good way to live (see Section 3.2). Like many such movements, it gave birth to various schools. One of these schools emphasized the importance of meditation and was called Chan in Chinese and Zen in Japanese. Both words mean meditation and both schools gave rise to distinctive aesthetic values. The legendary and traditional founder of Chan Buddhism is Bodhidarma (470–543) who taught that meditation is the heart of Buddhist practice.

D. T. Suzuki (1870–1966) was born Suzuki Teitaro. One of his Zen teachers gave him the name Daisetsu, which means "great simplicity." He came to the United States in 1897 and through his writings, teaching, and public lectures became one of the primary Japanese scholars who introduced Zen Buddhism to Americans and Europeans. He brought Zen from the East to the West and gathered a devoted following. The relationship between art and culture was one of his many interests and in the selection that follows he discusses artistic ideas and aesthetic values that he regards as characteristic of Japanese culture, art, and Zen.

◉ READING QUESTIONS

1. What is the "one-corner" style and how does the Japanese "thrifty brush" tradition illustrate it?
2. What does *wabi* mean?

3. What is *sabi*?
4. How can the "imperfection" of asymmetry be beautiful?

Japanese Culture and Art

D. T. SUZUKI

Before proceeding further, we may make a few general remarks about one of the peculiar features of Japanese art, which is closely related to and finally deducible from the world conception of Zen.

Among things which strongly characterize Japanese artistic talents we may mention the so-called "one-corner" style, which originated with Bayen (Ma Yüan, fl. 1175–1225), one of the greatest Southern Sung artists. The "one-corner" style is psychologically associated with the Japanese painters' "thrifty brush" tradition of retaining the least possible number of lines or strokes which go to represent forms on silk or paper. Both are very much in accord with the spirit of Zen. A simple fishing boat in the midst of the rippling waters is enough to awaken in the mind of the beholder a sense of the vastness of the sea and at the same time of peace and contentment—the Zen sense of the Alone. Apparently the boat floats helplessly. It is a primitive structure with no mechanical device

for stability and for audacious steering over the turbulent waves, with no scientific apparatus for braving all kinds of weather—quite a contrast to the modern ocean liner. But this very helplessness is the virtue of the fishing canoe, in contrast with which we feel the incomprehensibility of the Absolute encompassing the boat and all the world. Again, a solitary bird on a dead branch, in which not a line, not a shade, is wasted, is enough to show us the loneliness of autumn, when days become shorter and nature begins to roll up once more its gorgeous display of luxurious summer vegetation.[1] It makes one feel somewhat pensive, but it gives one opportunity to withdraw the attention towards the inner life, which, given attention enough, spreads out its rich treasures ungrudgingly before the eyes.

---

[1] For a picture of a similar nature, see my *Zen Essays*, III, facing p. 310. (See bibliography for full references.) Here the fishing boat as one of the most representative specimens is reproduced.

From *Zen and Japanese Culture* by D. T. Suzuki (Princeton University Press, 1959), 22–28.

Here we have an appreciation of transcendental aloofness in the midst of multiplicities–which is known as *wabi* in the dictionary of Japanese cultural terms. *Wabi* really means "poverty," or, negatively, "not to be in the fashionable society of the time." To be poor, that is, not to be dependent on things worldly—wealth, power, and reputation—and yet to feel inwardly the presence of something of the highest value, above time and social position: this is what essentially constitutes *wabi*. Stated in terms of practical everyday life, *wabi* is to be satisfied with a little hut, a room of two or three *tatami* (mats), like the log cabin of Thoreau, and with a dish of vegetables picked in the neighboring fields, and perhaps to be listening to the pattering of a gentle spring rainfall. While later I will say something more about *wabi*, let me state here that the cult of *wabi* has entered deeply into the cultural life of the Japanese people. It is in truth the worshiping of poverty—probably a most appropriate cult in a poor country like ours. Despite the modern Western luxuries and comforts of life which have invaded us, there is still an ineradicable longing in us for the cult of *wabi*. Even in the intellectual life, not richness of ideas, not brilliancy or solemnity in marshaling thoughts and building up a philosophical system, is sought; but just to stay quietly content with the mystical contemplation of Nature and to feel at home with the world is more inspiring to us, at least to some of us.

However "civilized," however much brought up in an artificially contrived environment, we all seem to have an innate longing for primitive simplicity, close to the natural state of living. Hence the city people's pleasure in summer camping in the woods or traveling in the desert or opening up an unbeaten track. We wish to go back once in a while to the bosom of Nature and feel her pulsation directly. Zen's habit of mind, to break through all forms of human artificiality and take firm hold of what lies behind them, has helped the Japanese not to forget the soil but to be always friendly with Nature and appreciate her unaffected simplicity. Zen has no taste for complexities that lie on the surface of life. Life itself is simple enough, but when it is surveyed

by the analyzing intellect it presents unparalleled intricacies. With all the apparatus of science we have not yet fathomed the mysteries of life. But, once in its current, we seem to be able to understand it, with its apparently endless pluralities and entanglements. Very likely, the most characteristic thing in the temperament of the Eastern people is the ability to grasp life from within and not from without. And Zen has just struck it.

In painting especially, disregard of form results when too much attention or emphasis is given to the all-importance of the spirit. The "one-corner" style and the economy of brush strokes also help to effect aloofness from conventional rules. Where you would ordinarily expect a line or a mass or a balancing element, you miss it, and yet this very thing awakens in you an unexpected feeling of pleasure. In spite of shortcomings or deficiencies that no doubt are apparent, you do not feel them so; indeed, this imperfection itself becomes a form of perfection. Evidently, beauty does not necessarily spell perfection of form. This has been one of the favorite tricks of Japanese artists—to embody beauty in a form of imperfection or even of ugliness.

When this beauty of imperfection is accompanied by antiquity or primitive uncouthness, we have a glimpse of *sabi*, so prized by Japanese connoisseurs. Antiquity and primitiveness may not be an actuality. If an object of art suggests even superficially the feeling of a historical period, there is *sabi* in it. *Sabi* consists in rustic unpretentiousness or archaic imperfection, apparent simplicity or effortlessness in execution, and richness in historical associations (which, however, may not always be present); and, lastly, it contains inexplicable elements that raise the object in question to the rank of an artistic production. These elements are generally regarded as derived from the appreciation of Zen. The utensils used in the tearoom are mostly of this nature.

The artistic element that goes into the constitution of *sabi*, which literally means "loneliness" or "solitude," is poetically defined by a teamaster thus:

As I come out
To this fishing village,
Late in the autumn day,
No flowers in bloom I see,
Nor any tinted maple leaves.[2]

Aloneness indeed appeals to contemplation and does not lend itself to spectacular demonstration. It may look most miserable, insignificant, and pitiable, especially when it is put up against the Western or modern setting. To be left alone, with no streamers flying, no fireworks crackling, and this amidst a gorgeous display of infinitely varied forms and endlessly changing colors, is indeed no sight at all. Take one of those *sumiye* sketches, perhaps portraying Kanzan and Jittoku (Han-shan and Shihtê),[3] hang it in a European or an American art gallery, and see what effect it will produce in the minds of the visitors. The idea of aloneness belongs to the East and is at home in the environment of its birth.

It is not only to the fishing village on the autumnal eve that aloneness gives form but also to a patch of green in the early spring—which is in all likelihood even more expressive of the idea of *sabi* or *wabi*. For in the green patch, as we read in the following thirty-one-syllable verse, there is an indication of life impulse amidst the wintry desolation:

To those who only pray for the cherries to bloom,
How I wish to show the spring
That gleams from a patch of green
In the midst of the snow-covered mountain-
*   village!*[4]

This is given by one of the old teamasters as thoroughly expressive of *sabi*, which is one of the four principles governing the cult of tea, *cha-no-yu*. Here is just a feeble inception of life power as asserted in the form of a little green patch, but in it he who has an eye can readily discern the spring shooting out from underneath the forbidding snow. It may be said to be a mere suggestion that stirs his mind, but just the same it is life itself and not its feeble indication. To the artist, life is as much here as when the whole field is overlaid with verdure and flowers. One may call this the mystic sense of the artist.

Asymmetry is another feature that distinguishes Japanese art. The idea is doubtlessly derived from the "one-corner" style of Bayen. The plainest and boldest example is the plan of Buddhist architecture. The principal structures, such as the Tower Gate, the Dharma Hall, the Buddha Hall, and others, may be laid along one straight line; but structures of secondary or supplementary importance, sometimes even those of major importance, are not arranged symmetrically as wings along either side of the main line. They may be found irregularly scattered over the grounds in accordance with the topographical peculiarities. You will readily be convinced of this fact if you visit some of the Buddhist temples in the mountains, for example, the Iyeyasu shrine at Nikko. We can say that asymmetry is quite characteristic of Japanese architecture of this class.

This can be demonstrated *par excellence* in the construction of the tearoom and in the tools used in connection with it. Look at the ceiling, which may be constructed in at least three different styles, and at some of the utensils for serving tea, and again at the grouping and laying of the steppingstones or flagstones in the garden. We find so many illustrations of asymmetry, or, in a way, of imperfection, or of the "one-corner" style.

Some Japanese moralists try to explain this liking of the Japanese artists for things asymmetrically formed and counter to the conventional, or rather geometrical, rules of art by the theory that the people have been morally trained not to be obtrusive but always to efface themselves, and that this mental habit of self-annihilation manifests itself accordingly in art—for example, when the artist leaves the important central space unoccupied. But, to my mind, this theory is not quite

---

[2]Fujiwara Sadaiye (1162–1241).
[3]Zen poet-recluses of the T'ang dynasty. A collection of their poems known as the *Kanzan Shi* (*Han-shan Shih*) or *Sanrai Shi* (*San-lai Shih*) or *Sanin Shi* (*San-yin shih*) is still in existence. The pair together, Kanzan and Jittoku, has been a favorite subject for Far Eastern painters. There is something in their transcendental air of freedom which attracts us even in these modern days. We give two sets of representative pictures of the T'ang poet-recluses.
[4]Fujiwara Iyetaka (1158–1237).

correct. Would it not be a more plausible explanation to say that the artistic genius of the Japanese people has been inspired by the Zen way of looking at individual things as perfect in themselves and at the same time as embodying the nature of totality which belongs to the One?

The doctrine of ascetic aestheticism is not so fundamental as that of Zen aestheticism. Art impulses are more primitive or more innate than those of morality. The appeal of art goes more directly into human nature. Morality is regulative, art is creative. One is an imposition from without, the other is an irrepressible expression from within. Zen finds its inevitable association with art but not with morality. Zen may remain unmoral but not without art. When the Japanese artists create objects imperfect from the point of view of form, they may even be willing to ascribe their art motive to the current notion of moral asceticism; but we need not give too much significance to their own interpretation or to that of the critics. Our consciousness is not, after all, a very reliable standard of judgment.

However this may be, asymmetry is certainly characteristic of Japanese art, which is one of the reasons informality or approachability also marks to a certain degree Japanese objects of art. Symmetry inspires a notion of grace, solemnity, and impressiveness, which is again the case with logical formalism or the piling up of abstract ideas. The Japanese are often thought not to be intellectual and philosophical, because their general culture is not thoroughly impregnated with intellectuality. This criticism, I think, results somewhat from the Japanese love of asymmetry. The intellectual primarily aspires to balance, while the Japanese are apt to ignore it and incline strongly towards imbalance.

Imbalance, asymmetry, the "one-corner," poverty, *sabi* or *wabi*, simplification, aloneness, and cognate ideas make up the most conspicuous and characteristic features of Japanese art and culture. All these emanate from one central perception of the truth of Zen, which is "the One in the Many and the Many in the One," or better, "the One remaining as one in the Many individually and collectively."

◉ CRITICAL QUESTIONS

1. Do you think it is true that we all seem to long for a "primitive simplicity" close to nature as Suzuki claims? Present an argument in support of your answer.

2. Do you agree that artistic impulses are more innate than moral impulses? Justify your answer with an example.

7.5 THE END OF ART AND THE CITIZEN ARTIST

What is art? It may be relatively easy to define specific arts such as music or drawing, but what is art itself? Sometimes art is used in an honorific sense such as the "fine arts" as opposed to the "crafts." The fine arts are, presumably, human-made objects whose primary value is aesthetic while the crafts are often thought of as the "useful arts" because, unlike fine art, their primary value resides in their use. For example, a painting of a table is usually classified as a fine art while building a table is often called a craft. If one asks what a painting of a table is good for, the obvious answer is that it is good for looking at and perhaps enjoying if it is an attractive painting. If one asks what building a table is good for, the obvious answer is to produce a useful object for supporting things. What counts as a fine art or as a craft often depends on cultural and historical taste. And of course some creative activities, such as architecture, blur the distinction. A building is useful and its construction involves a number of crafts. But an important function of buildings is to look good, that is, be pleasing to the eye. Here the useful and aesthetic overlap.

However, before we can decide what kinds of arts there are and what human productions belong to which, we must know what counts as art. When we ask this question things become difficult because it seems that just about anything can be art from paintings of nudes to splashes of dots on paper.

There are many definitions of art that reflect various theories of art. Art as imitation, as representation, as the expression of feelings, as form, and so on have all been proposed at one time or another. All have been found defective in one way or another. Even those who argue that a necessary condition of all art is that it be made by humans face accounting for the "paintings" produced by elephants and apes. Can other than human animals do art? The problem with most definitions is that they are either too inclusive or too exclusive. As soon as somebody defines art as imitation of nature someone will ask "so how does music imitate nature"? If one defines art as an expression of feeling, someone will create a poem by randomly picking words out of a hat and putting them together. The outcome cannot be known ahead of time, so how could the resulting poem express a feeling of the poet who did it?

The art world is always changing. It flows like water and not always in a predictable direction. It is very difficult to define an everchanging creative field. How could a single definition capture all the many different things and events people from different cultures call art, and how could it cover all historical periods along with all future periods? The task seems impossible and, indeed, some philosophers have declared it as such.

Other philosophers claim that art has entered a postmodern age and reflects what some call **postmodernism**. This term is used in a wide variety of ways but frequently it is used to refer to a style of art that self-consciously goes beyond the modernist movement in art. Postmodern art reveals in subtle and not so subtle ways that conventional assumptions about beauty reflect class, gender, religious, political, and historically specific ideologies that claim universal and absolute value for what is in fact relative and culturally specific. An **ideology** is a group of interrelated attitudes, beliefs, and concepts about what is real, valuable, and important. It functions to justify and support actions, practices, institutions, and ideas that express and embody the attitudes, beliefs, and concepts that make up an ideology. The term can be used both positively and negatively. As a positive term it refers to different cultural, political, and religious ideas and symbols. Negatively it can refer to a system of ideas that distorts reality by hiding the human, class, and cultural origin of a particular ideology by making it appear that certain values, attitudes, and beliefs are a part of nature or ordained by God and hence are part of the eternal and natural order of things.

The notion that art and even aesthetic value is ideological raises a number of issues. One such issue is whether art should or can serve political purposes and remain art. If art does serve ideological functions, then the aesthetic ideal of art for art's sake appears abandoned.

Arthur C. Danto, author of our first selection below, is both an art critic and a philosopher. He has, in spite of the problems, ventured a definition of art. Art, Danto maintains, has three features. The first two can be stated at the present time because they have already emerged in the history art, but the third is yet to be articulated. Artworks are (1) about something and (2) embody their meaning in the sense that the mode of presentation *says something* of what it is about. In other words, works of art offer interpretations of what they are about. He famously argues the startling thesis that in the present day, art has ended. To find out what he means by this you will have to read the selection below.

Emily Hicks is the author of our second selection. She is both an artist and a philosopher of Chicana/o Studies at San Diego State University. Traditionally the views of Mexican philosophers about art and aesthetics have been quite conservative. Antonio Caso (1883–1946), for example, argued that art has no other purpose than to delight. When we respond to art we, if our attitude is appropriately aesthetic, should seek nothing more than to enjoy a work of art for its own sake.[1] As Hicks makes clear below, a lot has changed in the art world of Mexican artists. The enjoyment of art has taken a backseat to political and social uses.

---

[1]See John H. Haddox, *Antonio Caso: Philosopher of Mexico* (Austin, TX: University of Texas Press, 1971), p. 43.

READING QUESTIONS

1. Why did something like Warhol's Brillo Box mean that in order to understand what art is one had to "turn to philosophy"?
2. Why did "pressing against boundaries" make possible a "general philosophy of art"?
3. According to Danto, what are the marks of contemporary art?
4. What does Danto mean by the "appropriated image" and what marks the "philosophical coming of age of art"?
5. According to Hicks, what are the features of performance art that link it to **postmodernism**?
6. According to Hicks, what is the problem of high culture vs. mass culture?
7. How does "recontextualizing" images relate to **postmodernism**?
8. How is the art Hicks describes different from postmodern art?

After the End of Art

ARTHUR C. DANTO

The sixties was a paroxysm of styles, in the course of whose contention, it seems to me—and this was the basis of my speaking of the "end of art" in the first place—it gradually became clear, first through the *nouveaux réalistes* and pop, that there was no special way works of art had to look in contrast to what I have designated "mere real things." To use my favorite example, nothing need mark the difference, outwardly, between Andy Warhol's Brillo Box and the Brillo boxes in the supermarket. And conceptual art demonstrated that there need not even be a palpable visual object for something to be a work of visual art. That meant that you could no longer teach the meaning of art by example. It meant that as far as appearances were concerned, anything could be a work of art, and it meant that if you were going to find out what art was, you had to turn

---

from sense experience to thought. You had, in brief, to turn to philosophy.

In an interview in 1969, conceptual artist Joseph Kosuth claimed that the only role for an artist at the time "was to investigate the nature of art itself." This sounds strikingly like the line in Hegel that gave support to my own views about the end of art: "Art invites us to intellectual consideration, and that not for the purpose of creating art again, but for knowing philosophically what art is." Joseph Kosuth is a philosophically literate artist to an exceptional degree, and he was one of the few artists working in the sixties and seventies who had the resources to undertake a philosophical analysis of the general nature of art. As it happened, relatively few philosophers of the time were ready to do this, just because so few of them could have imagined the possibility of art like that being produced in such dizzying disjunctiveness. The philosophical question of the nature of art, rather, was something that arose within art when artists pressed against boundary after boundary, and found that the boundaries all gave way. All typical sixties artists had that vivid sense of boundaries, each drawn by some tacit philosophical definition of art, and their erasure has left us the situation we find ourselves in today. Such a world is not, by the way, the easiest kind of world to live in, which explains why the political reality of the present seems to consist in drawing and defining boundaries wherever possible. Nevertheless, it was only in the 1960s that a serious philosophy of art became a possibility, one which did not base itself on purely local facts—for example, that art was essentially painting and sculpture. Only when it became clear that anything could be a work of art could one think, philosophically, about art. Only then did the possibility arise of a true general philosophy of art. But what of art itself? What of "Art after Philosophy"—to use the title of Kosuth's essay—which, to make the point, may indeed itself be a work of art? What of art after the end of art, where, by "after the end of art," I mean "after the ascent to philosophical self-reflection?" Where an artwork can consist of any object whatsoever that is enfranchised as art, raising the question "Why am I a work of art?"

With that question the history of modernism was over. It was over because modernism was too local and too materialist, concerned as it was with shape, surface, pigment, and the like as defining painting in its purity. Modernist painting, as Greenberg defined it, could only ask the question "What is it that I have and that no other kind of art can have?" And sculpture asked itself the same kind of question. But what this gives us is no general picture of what art is, only what some of the arts, perhaps historically the most important arts, essentially were. What question does Warhol's Brillo Box ask, or one of Beuys's multiples of a square of chocolate stuck to a piece of paper? What Greenberg had done was to identify a certain local style of abstraction with the philosophical truth of art, when the philosophical truth, once found, would have to be consistent with art appearing every possible way.

What I know is that the paroxysms subsided in the seventies, as if it had been the internal intention of the history of art to arrive at a philosophical conception of itself, and that the last stages of that history were somehow the hardest to work through, as art sought to break through the toughest outer membranes, and so itself became, in the process, paroxysmal. But now that the integument was broken, now that at least the glimpse of self-consciousness had been attained, that history was finished. It had delivered itself of a burden it could now hand over to the philosophers to carry. And artists, liberated from the burden of history, were free to make art in whatever way they wished, for any purposes they wished, or for no purposes at all. That is the mark of contemporary art, and small wonder, in contrast with modernism, there is no such thing as a contemporary style.

I think the ending of modernism did not happen a moment too soon. For the art world of the seventies was filled with artists bent on agendas having nothing much to do with pressing the limits of art or extending the history of art, but with putting art at the service of this or that personal or political goal. And artists had the whole inheritance of art history to work with, including the history of the avant-garde, which placed at the disposition of the artist all those marvelous possibilities the avant-garde had worked out and which modernism did its utmost to repress. In my own view, the major artistic contribution of the decade was the emergence of the appropriated image—the taking over of images with established meaning and identity and giving them a fresh meaning and identity. Since any image could be appropriated, it immediately follows that there could be no perceptual stylistic uniformity among appropriated images. One of my favorite examples is Kevin Roche's 1992 addition to the Jewish Museum in New York. The old Jewish Museum was just the Warburg mansion on Fifth Avenue, with its baronial associations and connotations of the Gilded Age. Kevin Roche brilliantly decided to duplicate the old Jewish Museum, and the eye is unable to tell a single difference. But the building belongs to the postmodern age perfectly: a postmodern architect can design a building which looks like a Mannerist chateau. It was an architectural solution that had to have pleased the most conservative and nostalgic trustee, as well as the most avant-garde and contemporary one, but of course for quite different reasons.

These artistic possibilities are but realizations and applications of the immense philosophical contribution of the 1960s to art's self-understanding: that artworks can be imagined, or in fact produced, which look exactly like mere real things which have no claim to the status of art at all, for the latter entails that you can't define artworks in terms of some particular visual properties they may have. There is no a priori constraint on how works of art must look—they can look like anything at all. This alone finished the modernist agenda, but it had to wreak havoc with the central institution of the art world, namely the museum of fine arts. The first generation of great American museums took it for granted that its contents would be treasures of great visual beauty and that visitors would enter the tresorium to be in the presence of spiritual truth of which the visually beautiful was the metaphor. The second generation, of which the Museum of Modern Art is the great exemplar, assumed that the work of art is to be defined in formalist terms and appreciated under the perspective of a narrative not remarkably different

from the one Greenberg advanced: a linear progressive history the visitor would work through, learning to appreciate the work of art together with learning the historical sequences. Nothing was to distract from the formal visual interest of the works themselves. Even picture frames were eliminated as distractions, or perhaps as concessions to an illusionistic agenda modernism had outgrown: paintings were no longer windows onto imagined scenes, but objects in their own right, even if they had been conceived as windows. It is, incidentally, easy to understand why surrealism has to be repressed in the light of such an experience: it would be too distracting, not to mention irrelevantly illusionistic. Works had plenty of space to themselves in galleries emptied of everything but those works.

In any case, with the philosophical coming of age of art, visuality drops away, as little relevant to the essence of art as beauty proved to have been. For art to exist there does not even have to be an object to look at, and if there are objects in a gallery, they can look like anything at all. Three attacks on established museums are worth noting in this respect. When Kirk Varnedoe and Adam Gopnick admitted pop into the galleries of the Museum of Modern Art in the "High and Low" show of 1990, there was a critical conflagration. When Thomas Krens deaccessioned a Kandinsky and a Chagall to acquire part of the Panza collection, a good bit of it conceptual and much of which did not exist as objects, there was a critical conflagration. And when, in 1993, the Whitney compiled a Biennial consisting of works that really typified the way the art world had gone after the end of art, the outpouring of critical hostility—in which I am afraid I shared—was by an inestimable factor unprecedented in the history of Biennial polemics. Whatever art is, it is no longer something primarily to be looked at. Stared at, perhaps, but not primarily looked at. What, in view of this, is a post-historical museum to do, or to be?

It must be plain that there are three models at least, depending upon the kind of art we are dealing with, and depending upon whether it is beauty, form, or what I shall term engagement that defines our relationship to it. Contemporary art is too pluralistic in intention and realization to allow itself to be captured along a single dimension, and indeed an argument can be made that enough of it is incompatible with the constraints of the museum that an entirely different breed of curator is required, one who bypasses museum structures altogether in the interests of engaging the art directly with the lives of persons who have seen no reason to use the museum either as tresorium of beauty or sanctum of spiritual form. For a museum to engage this kind of art, it has to surrender much of the structure and theory that define the museum in its other two modes.

But the museum itself is only part of the infrastructure of art that will sooner or later have to deal with the end of art and with art after the end of art. The artist, the gallery, the practices of art history, and the discipline of philosophical aesthetics must all, in one or another way, give way and become different, and perhaps vastly different, from what they have so far been. I can only hope to tell part of the philosophical story in the chapters that follow. The institutional story must wait upon history itself.

The Artist as Citizen

EMILY HICKS

A flamenco surfer surrounded by waves of blood/ a tourist donkey cart strategically placed and later perceived as a threat to public safety/a rock concert in the midst of the coffins and debris after an earthquake/a portrait of the man who discovered blood plasma and later died of lack of blood in a Southern hospital.

These images appear in the work of Guillermo Gómez-Peña, Felipe Ehrenberg, David Avalos and Judy Baca. Some artists in Mexico City, Los Angeles and the U.S.-Mexico border region are producing work that is profoundly political and linked to "performance" in its largest sense. Their work may offer a narrow conceptual passageway between the Scylla and Charybdis of performance [art] and mass culture. To negotiate this passageway is to broaden the definition of the artist.

The notion of art as cultural intervention—or what Mexican muralist Arnold Belkin, in his attempt to define Mexican interdisciplinary artist

Felipe Ehrenberg, calls "the artist as citizen"— stretches the definition of art beyond even the flexible boundaries of postmodernism.[1]

As the critic Fredric Jameson has pointed out, postmodernism has many variants, some that are progressive and others that are not.[2] And yet, it is within the debates of postmodernist criticism in North American and European art journals that performance artists like these are again redefining themselves. Among the features that link their work to a postmodernist critique are 1) the medium changes according to the requirements of the cultural intervention—it can be community organizing, mural art, journalism, radio, criticism, multimedia performance, etc.; 2) works may be collaborative, even anonymously so; 3) works may be changed or compounded by other artists; 4) the meaning depends on the active participation of a politicized audience.

Most importantly, many North American performance artists have experienced the isolation of

---

[1]When this article originally appeared, I failed to thank Philip Brookman for his help with information about the work of Felipe Ehrenberg.

[2]Fredric Jameson, "The Politics of Theory: Ideological Positions in the Postmodernism Debate," *Critical Inquiry*, January 1985, pp. 53–65.

From Emily Hicks, *The Artist as Citizen: Guillermo Gómez-Pena Felipe Ehrenberg David Avalos and Judy Baca*. Copyright © 2002 Community Arts Network. http://www.communityarts.net/readingroom/ archivefiles/2002/09/artist_as_citiz.php. Retrieved January 10, 2008.

small, specialized audiences and the pressure to do more accessible work. Postmodernist critics have christened this dilemma as the problem of high culture vs. mass culture. Artists experience it as a problem of performance vs. entertainment.[3] But consider instead the alternative response of an artist like Felipe Ehrenberg and his project of the reconstruction of Mexico City after the 1985 earthquake. For him, the goal is not to be a pop star, but a responsible citizen/activist. At the moment, his community is Tepito, the devastated neighborhood in the city of his birth, Mexico D.F.

For muralist Judy Baca, who grew up in Pacoima, California, the definition of community includes the relationships of ethnic groups, the interrelationships of social problems, and the question of who occupies a public space. The community for her mural projects began in East Los Angeles, but then expanded to include blacks in South Central Los Angeles, Filipinos in Echo Park and Japanese in Little Tokyo.

For David Avalos, who grew up in National City, California, 20 miles from the U.S.-Mexican border, the creative context is the Chicano community, which he calls "a community outside the law." Using site-specific works and media-art strategies, he explores the notions of "citizenship" and "identity" in relation to the labor provided by the undocumented worker, a "citizen" whose civic rights are systematically denied.

For Gómez-Peña, a performance artist and writer from Mexico City, the community is the border region of Tijuana-San Diego, where he has lived since 1983, and which, for him, represents a microcosm of U.S.-Latin American relations. Through collaborative, interdisciplinary art projects, involving people from both countries, he attempts to create a binational dialogue that supersedes mass-media-produced misconceptions and transcultural fears.

These citizen-artists, involved in cultural projects that often include performance, get excellent media coverage and reach very large audiences without striving to be pop stars. The recent

activities of Felipe Ehrenberg in Mexico City have received wide coverage in the international press. A performance by Gómez-Peña appeared in a Louis Malle film on new immigrants to the U.S. that aired nationally on HBO. Baca's *Great Wall* is perhaps one of the most widely viewed and discussed Chicano murals, and Avalos' donkey cart sparked a national media scandal involving a federal judge. What do these artists have in common?

In a recent site-work, after being authorized by city officials, Avalos brought his own version of a Tijuana donkey cart to the Federal Building in San Diego, where the Immigration and Naturalization Service (INS) office is located. Traditional Tijuana donkey carts are decorated with hats, serapes and images of Aztec warriors and buxom Indian princesses. Tourists, including middle-class North American families and U.S. military personnel, pose for photographs on the carts. Avalos' cart, instead, is painted with the image of an undocumented worker being frisked by a border-patrol agent. While the traditional carts give the tourist a romanticized taste of Mexico, Avalos' version gives the viewer the opportunity to identify with a daily experience of an undocumented worker. Declared "dangerous" and "anti-American" by a federal judge, the cart was ordered removed immediately. When Avalos refused to remove the artwork, it was confiscated and detained in a storage area of the Federal Building. This resulted both in television interviews and national feature articles in which Avalos was paradoxically allowed to address the social contradictions embodied in the artwork and often avoided by the media, and to expose the authoritarian censorship of the judge. At this point, we can say the piece was completed.

Gómez-Peña creates border stereotypes in order to deconstruct their underlying oppositions: a *cholo/punk*, a wrestler/shaman, a Latin American general/movie star, a *"bruja"/maid*. His works involve a continuous recycling of images and texts. A recent text that began as a radio art show on the U.S.-Mexico and the U.S.-Canadian borders entitled *Border-X-Frontera,* later inspired a performance by Poyesis GenÉtica around Avalos' donkey cart in front of Sushi Gallery (San Diego). Another version then appeared on a

[3]Jacki Apple, "Commerce on the Edge," *High Performance*, no. 34, vol. IX, no. 2, 1986, pp. 34–38.

local cable station. This sparked *Cabaret Babylon Aztlán,* a multimedia work performed at the Centro Cultural de la Raza. Malle filmed a segment of this version, with the donkey cart as the set, and juxtaposed Gómez-Peña's performance describing thousands of "Waspbacks" illegally crossing the border into Mexico, with anti-undocumented worker statements by Harold Ezell, Western Regional Commissioner of the INS. The same text appeared on the cover of the bilingual art journal *La Línea Quebrada,* in *Uno-más-uno,* the most important newspaper in Mexico, and in two art exhibits accompanying an upside-down map of the continent. This strategy of recontextualizing image and texts has much in common with postmodernism. It undermines the sanctity of the single creator, the finished piece, and the work of art as a commodity.

Baca's work, in its mixture of the mural tradition and community organizing, also undermines the sanctity of the single creator. In 1976, Judy Baca began the *Great Wall Mural Project,* the largest of its kind in the world, in the Tujunga Wash Channel of the San Fernando Valley. Baca envisioned the channel, which had been built by the Army Corps and was being developed into a park, as a wall that could bring the diverse mural groups she had been organizing together at one site. It began with 80 teenagers and nine artists. The mural depicts the history of California, from pre-Colombian times to the present. Images include Tomás Alva Edison;[4] Jeanette Rankin, who opposed WW II; Charles Drew, who discovered blood plasma; David Gonzales, recipient of a Congressional Medal of Honor; Pulitzer Prize-winner Gwendolyn Brooks; zoot suiters, athletes and many other recognized and previously unrecognized historical figures. The opportunity to paint murals was not the only benefit for participants in the *Great Wall Project.* They also received counseling on the draft, sexuality, drugs, incest and other social problems. For Baca, art is merely a catalyst for the regeneration of the community.

In the case of Ehrenberg, cultural intervention took the form of entering the disaster area of Tepito

in Mexico City immediately after the earthquake. Ehrenberg took some artists, friends, and his own family into Tepito in order to organize brigades to comfort survivors, who had been left without homes, electricity and social services, and to distribute food and clothing. Volunteers who made up the brigades included psychologists, musicians, teachers, actors, university students and painters.

While the Mexican government prevented supplies from reaching Mexico City by insisting that they go through government channels, Ehrenberg and the Tepitenos began to raise money and opened bank account #228333 at the Banco de Crédito Mexicano. To administer the account, he organized the Committee for the Reconstruction of Tepito, which included community representatives, well-known cultural activists, scientists and specialists in fields from urbanism to finance. Between September 25 and October 1, his group managed to give food, medical attention and drinkable water to nearly 5,000 people a day. On October 6, Ehrenberg organized a "Festival of Life," which included music by rock groups, to celebrate, in Ehrenberg's words, "that we are alive, that Tepito didn't fold, and to be aware that we have to help ourselves." In addition, children's theater, concerts and a library were organized. Citizens of Tepito have recently appeared in the press carrying banners saying *"No nos moverán de aquí"* ("They won't move us from here"), referring to their desire to reconstruct Tepito rather than be relocated by the government. In a sense, these activities can be considered an epic performance installation, in which an entire city functions as a gallery space.

While the above artists' work shares several of the previously mentioned features of postmodernist critiques, what they do not share with some of those critiques is their ultimate goal: the transformation of social conditions. Socially committed artists commonly have very broad backgrounds, and they point to the other influences on their work as more important than their experiences in art schools.

Ehrenberg was a painter who had worked with Margaret Randall on the legendary bilingual journal *The Plumed Horn.* After the massacre of students in October, 1968, Ehrenberg and his

---

[4]Better known in the United States as Thomas Edison.

wife left the country. He lived in England for several years, directing the famous Beau Geste Press. He later returned to Mexico where, during the 1970s, he nurtured both a widespread movement of alternative small-press publications called *Neográfica,* and the creation of a network of art collectives that opposed the gallery system. In 1982, he ran for office on the United Socialist Party of Mexico ticket (PSUM). Ehrenberg's decision to participate in *la reconstrucción* was inspired by the work of his brother, who went to Nicaragua during the revolution as a cameraman and joined the southern guerrilla front.

David Avalos is a product of the tradition of political activism in the border region. Jose Montoya, one of the godfathers of the Chicano movement, sees Avalos as a Chicano artist who "hasn't succumbed to the false, hedonistic tendency of so many Hispanics who consider being Chicano to be one of the unpleasant realities of these times, and who have eagerly embraced Reagan's redefinition of our national character ... the I'm OK, you're poor, poverty sucks bunch."[5] Avalos, who studied communications at UC San Diego and Stanford, is a self-taught artist and has been, since 1976, a member of the Committee on Chicano Rights, which monitors the activities of the INS in the border region. In 1982, he and a group of artists including Gómez-Peña formed BAW/TAF (Border Arts Workshop/*Taller de Arte Fronterizo*). This group includes Chicano, Mexican and Anglo artists, and offers a successful example of multicultural, multidisciplinary artmaking.

Gómez-Peña came to the United States from Mexico City, where he studied linguistics and was a student activist at the Autonomous National University of Mexico (UNAM). He entered CalArts in 1979, and two years later cofounded with Sara Jo Berman the *Poyesis Genética* troupe in order to explore artistic and political contradictions between the United States and Mexico. The troupe toured Europe in 1982 and relocated to the Mexican–American border in 1983. Gómez-Peña's art projects include bicultural journalism for radio and newspapers and binational interdisciplinary art projects involving people from both countries. Both activities proceed from the same set of concerns, but utilize different formats in order to reach different audiences.

Judy Baca attended Cal State Northridge and received a master's degree in art education. Her decision to define herself as an artist came halfway through her career, because she "couldn't align art with her sense of political commitment." Her community organizing as a director of mural projects has resolved this conflict; she has been personally involved with more than 150 murals. Furthermore, her cultural activities in Los Angeles have created a bridge between feminism and the Chicano movement.

In the Mexican and Chicano art worlds, the relationship between art and politics is a much more widely shared reference code. This is particularly true in the case of Ehrenberg, Baca, Avalos and Gómez-Peña, who are bicultural, have identified with the upheavals of the 1960s, and have been involved in social activism outside the art world. In the context of the economic crisis and the earthquake in Mexico, politics and art are clearly connected for many artists in a way that they are not in the art scenes of New York and Los Angeles. When one is of Latino descent living in the border region, confronting everyday violations of human rights, media distortions and the ethnic insensitivity of the general population, one has no choice but to engage in some kind of social/political discourse.

It is unfortunate, but probably true, that the best reaction many North American mainstream artists may hope for is that a painting will sell or a performance piece will be reviewed. This is a less satisfactory response than the attainment of the more ambitious goal of the activist: a profound cultural impact outside of the art world. The question of why many artists settle for less than being understood, and for merely a career, may have something to do with their inability to conceive of themselves in historical terms and therefore to understand the world as a political structure.

The vast majority of North American artists have not experienced the political repression in

[5]This interview originally appeared in *High Performance* magazine, Fall 1986.

El Salvador and Guatemala, the fear of invasion by Reagan in Nicaragua, the war against "subversives" in Argentina and the U.S.-Mexico border region, police brutality in Chile or in the Chicano barrios, or the ecological deterioration of Mexico City. Instead, their primary experiences are likely to be art school, art openings, "relationships" and mass culture. Their sense of belonging in the world is mediated by mass-media images. And their problems are "personal," not social. Few have engaged in cultural activism. Those who have most likely have experienced other cultures and other political regimes.

For artists not currently involved in socially committed activities, there may be something to learn from cultural activists. Will art schools encourage students to form multicultural groups and begin to produce a new generation of artist/citizens? There are isolated examples like Rutgers University and UC San Diego, but a mass movement is very unlikely. However, at least we can recognize non-New York, non-master-discourse-packaged art forms in whatever contexts they occur. Mexico City, the border region and the Chicano barrios of California are three such contexts. A multicultural redefinition of the "art world" and a willingness to become fluent in many art languages could facilitate an interchange among artists from a variety of contexts, including those mentioned above and the Anglo art world.

⊚ CRITICAL QUESTIONS

1. How do you think Danto, based on what you have read here, would react to the claim that if anything can be art, then nothing is art?
2. How is it possible for art to exist after the end of art history if a necessary condition for something being artwork is to be located within art history?
3. What is the definition of art presupposed by the following argument? If something claims to be art and serves political and social purposes, it is not art but ideology.
4. Is the definition of art that Hicks presupposes like Danto's definition? Explain your answer.

To access the *Voices of Wisdom*, 8th Edition, **Premium Website**, search for this book on CengageBrain.com.

CHAPTER EIGHT

Is Knowledge Possible?

A heap see, but a few know.

CAROLYN CHASE'S AUNT

LEARNING OBJECTIVES

After studying this chapter students should be able to:
- explain the difference between empiricism and rationalism,
- distinguish the different kinds of skepticism,
- define Sufism,
- contrast direct with indirect realism,
- explain the significance of *cogito, ergo sum*,
- explain the difference between necessity and constant conjunction,
- explain the difference between analytic and synthetic statements,
- define evidentialism,
- distinguish the pragmatic, correspondence, and coherence theories of truth,
- explain the four kinds of *pramanas*,
- describe standpoint epistemology,
- identify Pyrrho, al-Ghazali, Averröes, Descartes, Galileo, Hume, Clifford, James, Koller, and Tanesini, and
- answer all the questions relating to the selections.

8.1 INTRODUCTION

Have you ever thought that people didn't really know what they were talking about? Have you ever wondered whether we can trust our intuition? Have you ever thought about the limits of human reason? Are there things that we cannot know? But how could we know that? Have you thought about how we can know what happened before we were born? Does everything we know come from experience? Have you been puzzled by the question, "What is truth"? Have you wondered whether we can be certain about any of our beliefs? Do we need evidence, and if so, what kind, to support our beliefs?

If you have wondered about these kinds of questions, you have been thinking about what philosophers call epistemology (the study of knowledge). The epistemologist wants to know how we can distinguish between opinion and knowledge.

We've all had the experience of listening to someone tell us something she thinks she knows. Perhaps we have dismissed what was said with the comment, "Oh, that's just your opinion." How do we know it is only her opinion? However we know it, the very fact that we call it opinion indicates that we assume that it is possible to distinguish between opinion and knowledge.

Let's start with a game. How do you know, if you know, the following?

You exist.	This book exists.
It will snow tomorrow.	All fat cats are fat.
It rained yesterday.	Two plus two equals four.
God exists.	Every event has a cause.

I imagine that you said you knew some of the things on this list because of sense experiences you've had. For example, you might have said that you know this book exists because you can see it and touch it. One important epistemological theory is called **empiricism**. According to this theory, we know things because we experience them with our senses. We see, touch, taste, smell, and hear things. That is how we gain knowledge about them. If someone tells me something is true, but what he says is neither based on experience nor verifiable by reference to experience, I would say, if I were an empiricist, "Oh, that's just a matter of opinion."

However, there are some things on the preceding list that you might say you knew because of reason. For example, you might have said that you know two plus two equals four because that's the way it works out when you add. Addition is a rational activity, one that requires you to reason, and you reason, in this case, by applying the rules of addition. If you apply the rules correctly, the answer has to be four.

If some of you identified reason as the source of knowledge, you would be reflecting the ideas of another important epistemological theory called **rationalism**. According to this theory, we know things by the use of reason. Reason tells us what is true. If someone says he knows there are some fat cats that are not fat because he has seen one, you might want to suggest that this is not merely a matter of opinion. Fat cats, by definition, are fat. Whatever he saw, he is mistaken.

Let us contrast these two basic theories of knowledge a bit more to be sure we grasp how they are different. Empiricism usually claims that the human mind, prior to sense experience, is like a blank slate (*tabula rasa*) or empty tablet. Sensations make impressions on this slate via our senses. It is from these impressions that we learn what is true and false and thereby, over the years, slowly build up a fund of knowledge. Hence, our knowledge is **a posteriori** (after experience). We cannot know anything until after we have had experiences, and if we wish to test or verify what we believe, we do so by checking it against further experiences. Knowledge, according to the empiricist, is also largely inductive because we induce some future events from past or present experiences. Of course our inductions may be wrong. The conclusions we draw are only probable, but probability is the best we can hope for if we want to know something about the world in which we live.

Rationalists reject the idea that the human mind is blank. We have, they usually claim, innate ideas, or ideas already built into our minds at birth, like the wiring built into a computer that allows it to compute. We use these innate ideas to make sense of our sensations. How do we know such **innate ideas** are true? By direct intellectual intuition (reason). Sensation does not tell us that every event has a cause since we cannot experience every event. Reason tells us that. We know it intuitively. Hence, knowledge is **a priori** (prior to or independent from experience). We do know things not learned from sensation, and we can prove things true without reference to sensation. Our proofs are deductive, and we can deduce that a fat cat is fat from the definition of *fat cat*. It follows necessarily. It is certain.

Ponder the contrast between the following:

Empiricism	*Rationalism*
tabula rasa	innate ideas
sensation	reason
a posteriori	a priori
inductive	deductive

"But wait," some of you might be saying, "what about those of us who are not sure that anything on that first list can be known at all? After all, you said, 'How do you know if you know?' Well, I don't think some of these things can be known. For example, God. I think we just believe or we don't, but we can't know."

This response raises the issue of **skepticism**. The word *skepticism* comes from a Greek word that means "to reflect on," "consider," or "examine." We often associate the word with doubt or the suspension of judgment. The skeptic is a doubter.

There are various kinds of skepticism. One kind, what we might call **common-sense skepticism**, refers to the activity of doubting or suspending judgment about some things at one time or another. In this sense, we are all skeptics because we have all doubted. This sort of skepticism is healthy. It prevents an overly credulous attitude and is a good antidote to intellectual arrogance. If you are too gullible, you can be manipulated by others who claim to have knowledge when they do not.

Another kind of skepticism is **methodical skepticism**. This is the sort of skepticism that is used by some philosophers and scientists in their search for truth. If, for example, I want to be as certain as I can be that water freezes at 32 degrees Fahrenheit, I might doubt that hypothesis and conduct several experiments under differing circumstances to see if evidence supports it. Such doubt can be enormously constructive because it stimulates our intellectual curiosity and energizes our search for truth.

There is yet a third kind of skepticism, **absolute skepticism**, which, somewhat ironically, some philosophers have presented as a theory of knowledge. Unlike both rationalism and empiricism, this theory doubts the very possibility of knowledge. Pyrrho of Elis (about 300 BCE) founded a school of philosophers who advocated absolute skepticism. He claimed to be following Socrates and just asking questions. However, he also claimed that every argument cancels out its opposite. In other words, arguments on opposite sides of an issue balance out, thereby canceling any definitive conclusion. Try as we might, we cannot know what is true.

"Well," you might say, "that is ridiculous. If we cannot know what is true, then how can Pyrrho or any other skeptic know that we cannot know?" That is a good question. You are suggesting that absolute skepticism is self-refuting. If it is true that we cannot know anything, then how do we know that it is true that we cannot know anything? If absolute skepticism is true, then it must be false!

Pyrrho himself anticipated a similar criticism. He retorted that he was not certain that he was not certain of anything. Of course, one wonders whether he was not certain that he was not certain that.... This conversation could go on forever! Yet self-refuting propositions are puzzling and provocative things. Consider:

The sentence in this box is false.

Think about that. If "the sentence in the box is false" is false, then it must be true. And if it is true, it must be false. However, one claim central to two-valued logics is that sentences must be either true or false. They presumably cannot be both. Here we have, however, a sentence that seems to be both. What are we to make of this? Is the claim of the absolute skeptic another example of a proposition of this sort? Perhaps certainty is simply not possible for humans, and, if we mean by "knowledge" certainty (knowing without the possibility of doubt), then we may have to be more humble when we claim to know something.

8.2 SUFI MYSTICISM

Abu Hamid Muhammad al-Ghazali was born at Tus, Persia, in 450 AH (1058). He was appointed a professor of Islamic theology at the university in Baghdad at the early age of thirty-three. Four years later, he had an emotional and spiritual crisis and came to believe that his way of life was too worldly. He left his academic post and became an ascetic, studying both the teachings and the practices of Islamic mystics. He later returned to teaching; he died in 505 AH. *Deliverance from Error*, from which the following selection is taken, constitutes al-Ghazali's spiritual and intellectual autobiography.

Al-Ghazali embarked on a quest for certainty. He studied theology but was disappointed with its intellectual achievements. His quest prompted him to study philosophy, but once again he was disappointed, especially with its unfounded metaphysical claims and with the fact that philosophers held beliefs contrary to Islamic revelation. He turned to the Batiniyah, who taught that truth is attained not by reason, but by accepting the pronouncements of the infallible imam (religious leader). At the time, this teaching had important political implications because it was the official ideology of the Fatimid caliphate with its center in Cairo. However, al-Ghazali found the teachings of the imams to be trivial. He characterized their knowledge as "feeble" and "emaciated." Finally he investigated **Sufism**, an Islamic mystical movement, which taught that direct and immediate experience of Allah is possible. It was among the Sufis that his restless soul found peace.

Al-Ghazali was not satisfied with empiricism, rationalism, or skepticism. Hence, he sought to discover a source or means to knowledge that escapes the skeptic's doubts and provides a firmer foundation than either empiricism or rationalism. He believed he found such a source in mystical experience—that is, an experience of intimate union or contact with the Divine.

Of course, al-Ghazali's motivation was not entirely philosophical or scientific. He did not merely want to know about the world that sense experience could show him, nor about the abstract world of mathematics and metaphysics that reason could reveal. Nor was he content to be a doubter. His motivation was also spiritual; he wanted to know about the Divine. His quest may reveal to us something about the limited nature of epistemological theories. Each theory may be appropriate in a limited domain. If you want to know about the world, empiricism is attractive. If you want to know about mathematics or abstract realities, rationalism commends itself. However, what if you want to know about God? Is either empiricism or rationalism adequate?

Al-Ghazali's views are controversial because many would be skeptical about the claim that adequate knowledge can be grounded in some sort of mystical experience. How do we know that mystical experience is not an illusion, just like some sense experiences? Within Islamic philosophy, al-Ghazali was not without his critics. Another Islamic philosopher, Averroës (Ibn Rushid, 1126–1198), wrote a book called *The Incoherence of the Incoherence*, referring to a book al-Ghazali wrote entitled, *The Incoherence of the Philosophers*. Averroës attacked al-Ghazali's views, arguing that the philosophic reliance on reason and sense experience is, in fact, an adequate method for knowing.

◉ READING QUESTIONS

1. How does al-Ghazali define knowledge?
2. What leads him to doubt beliefs based on sense perception and on intellect?
3. What is distinctive about mysticism?
4. What credal principles were firmly rooted in al-Ghazali after his study of theology and philosophy?
5. What is the mystic way, and what did al-Ghazali learn from following it?
6. How does the author distinguish among *knowledge*, *immediate experience*, and *faith*?
7. What method does he suggest we use to arrive at the knowledge that someone is a prophet? Why is this method better than relying on miracles as proof?

Deliverance from Error

AL-GHAZALI

To thirst after a comprehension of things as they really are was my habit and custom from a very early age. It was instinctive with me, a part of my God-given nature, a matter of temperament and not of my choice or contriving. Consequently as I drew near the age of adolescence the bonds of mere authority (*taqlid*) ceased to hold me and inherited beliefs lost their grip upon me, for I saw that Christian youths always grew up to be Christians, Jewish youths to be Jews and Muslim youths to be Muslims. I heard, too, the Tradition related of the Prophet of God according to which he said:

"Everyone who is born is born with a sound nature; it is his parents who make him a Jew or a Christian or a Magian." My inmost being was moved to discover what this original nature really was and what the beliefs derived from the authority of parents and teachers really were. The attempt to distinguish between these authority-based opinions and their principles developed the mind, for in distinguishing the true in them from the false differences appeared.

I therefore said within myself: "To begin with, what I am looking for is knowledge of

"Deliverance from Error," from *The Faith and Practice of Al-Ghazali*, trans. by W. Montgomery Watt, pp. 21–26, 54–57, 59, 60–68. Copyright © 1953 by George Allen and Unwin. Reproduced by permission of HarperCollins Publishers. Footnotes deleted.

what things really are, so I must undoubtedly try to find what knowledge really is." It was plain to me that sure and certain knowledge is that knowledge in which the object is disclosed in such a fashion that no doubt remains along with it, that no possibility of error or illusion accompanies it, and that the mind cannot even entertain such a supposition. Certain knowledge must also be infallible; and this infallibility or security from error is such that no attempt to show the falsity of the knowledge can occasion doubt or denial, even though the attempt is made by someone who turns stones into gold or a rod into a serpent. Thus, I know that ten is more than three. Let us suppose that someone says to me: "No, three is more than ten, and in proof of that I shall change this rod into a serpent"; and let us suppose that he actually changes the rod into a serpent and that I witness him doing so. No doubts about what I know are raised in me because of this. The only result is that I wonder precisely how he is able to produce this change. Of doubt about my knowledge there is no trace.

After these reflections I knew that whatever I do not know in this fashion and with this mode of certainty is not reliable and infallible knowledge; and knowledge that is not infallible is not certain knowledge.

PRELIMINARIES: SCEPTICISM AND THE DENIAL OF ALL KNOWLEDGE

Thereupon I investigated the various kinds of knowledge I had, and found myself destitute of all knowledge with this characteristic of infallibility except in the case of sense-perception and necessary truths. So I said: "Now that despair has come over me, there is no point in studying any problems except on the basis of what is self-evident, namely, necessary truths and the affirmations of the senses. I must first bring these to be judged in order that I may be certain on this matter. Is my reliance on sense-perception and my trust in the soundness of necessary truths of the same kind as my previous trust in the beliefs I had merely taken over from others and as the trust most men have in the results

of thinking? Or is it a justified trust that is in no danger of being betrayed or destroyed?"

I proceeded therefore with extreme earnestness to reflect on sense-perception and on necessary truths, to see whether I could make myself doubt them. The outcome of this protracted effort to induce doubt was that I could no longer trust sense-perception either. Doubt began to spread here and say: "From where does this reliance on sense-perception come? The most powerful sense is that of sight. Yet when it looks at the shadow (sc. of a stick or the gnomon of a sundial), it sees it standing still, and judges that there is no motion. Then by experiment and observation after an hour it knows that the shadow is moving and, moreover, that it is moving not by fits and starts but gradually and steadily by infinitely small distances in such a way that it is never in a state of rest. Again, it looks at the heavenly body (sc. the sun) and sees it small, the size of a shilling; yet geometrical computations show that it is greater than the earth in size."

In this and similar cases of sense-perception the sense as judge forms his judgements, but another judge, the intellect, shows him repeatedly to be wrong; and the charge of falsity cannot be rebutted.

To this I said: "My reliance on sense-perception also has been destroyed. Perhaps only those intellectual truths which are first principles (or derived from first principles) are to be relied upon, such as the assertion that ten are more than three, that the same thing cannot be both affirmed and denied at one time, that one thing is not both generated in time and eternal, nor both existent and nonexistent, nor both necessary and impossible."

Sense-perception replied: "Do you not expect that your reliance on intellectual truths will fare like your reliance on sense-perception? You used to trust in me; then along came the intellect-judge and proved me wrong; if it were not for the intellect-judge you would have continued to regard me as true. Perhaps behind intellectual apprehension there is another judge who, if he manifests himself, will show the falsity of intellect in its judging, just as, when intellect manifested itself, it showed the falsity of sense in its judging. The fact that such a supra-intellectual apprehension has not manifested itself is no proof that it is impossible."

My ego hesitated a little about the reply to that, and sense-perception heightened the difficulty by referring to dreams. "Do you not see," it said, "how, when you are asleep, you believe things and imagine circumstances, holding them to be stable and enduring, and, so long as you are in that dream-condition, have no doubts about them? And is it not the case that when you awake you know that all you have imagined and believed is unfounded and ineffectual? Why then are you confident that all your waking beliefs, whether from sense or intellect, are genuine? They are true in respect of your present state; but it is possible that a state will come upon you whose relation to your waking consciousness is analogous to the relation of the latter to dreaming. In comparison with this state your waking consciousness would be like dreaming! When you have entered into this state, you will be certain that all the suppositions of your intellect are empty imaginings. It may be that that state is what the Sufis claim as their special 'state' (*sc.* mystic union or ecstasy), for they consider that in their 'states' (or ecstasies), which occur when they have withdrawn into themselves and are absent from their senses, they witness states (or circumstances) which do not tally with these principles of the intellect. Perhaps that 'state' is death; for the Messenger of God (God bless and preserve him) says: 'The people are dreaming; when they die, they become awake.' So perhaps life in this world is a dream by comparison with the world to come; and when a man dies, things come to appear differently to him from what he now beholds, and at the same time the words are addressed to him: 'We have taken off thee thy covering, and thy sight today is sharp'" (Q. 50, 21).

When these thoughts had occurred to me and penetrated my being, I tried to find some way of treating my unhealthy condition; but it was not easy. Such ideas can only be repelled by demonstration; but a demonstration requires a knowledge of first principles; since this is not admitted, however, it is impossible to make the demonstration. The disease was baffling, and lasted almost two months, during which I was a sceptic in fact though not in theory nor in outward expression. At length God cured me of the malady; my being was restored to health and an even balance; the necessary truths of the intellect became once more accepted, as I regained confidence in their certain and trustworthy character.

This did not come about by systematic demonstration or marshalled argument, but by a light which God most high cast into my breast. That light is the key to the greater part of knowledge. Whoever thinks that the understanding of things Divine rests upon strict proofs has in his thought narrowed down the wideness of God's mercy. When the Messenger of God (peace be upon him) was asked about "enlarging" and its meaning in the verse, "Whenever God wills to guide a man, He enlarges his breast for *islām* (i.e. surrender to God)" (Q. 6, 125), he said, "It is a light which God most high casts into the heart." When asked, "What is the sign of it?," he said, "Withdrawal from the mansion of deception and return to the mansion of eternity." It was about this light that Muhammad (peace be upon him) said, "God created the creatures in darkness, and then sprinkled upon them some of His light." From that light must be sought an intuitive understanding of things Divine. That light at certain times gushes from the spring of Divine generosity, and for it one must watch and wait—as Muhammad (peace be upon him) said: "In the days of your age your Lord has gusts of favour; then place yourselves in the way of them."

The point of these accounts is that the task is perfectly fulfilled when the quest is prosecuted up to the stage of seeking what is not sought (but stops short of that). For first principles are not sought, since they are present and to hand; and if what is present is sought for, it becomes hidden and lost. When, however, a man seeks what is sought (and that only), he is not accused of falling short in the seeking of what is sought....

THE WAYS OF MYSTICISM

I knew that the complete mystic "way" includes both intellectual belief and practical activity; the latter consists in getting rid of the obstacles in the self and in stripping off its base characteristics and vicious morals, so that the heart may attain to freedom from what is not God and to constant recollection of Him.

The intellectual belief was easier to me than the practical activity. I began to acquaint myself with their belief by reading their books.... I thus comprehended their fundamental teachings on the intellectual side, and progressed, as far as is possible by study and oral instruction, in the knowledge of mysticism. It became clear to me, however, that what is most distinctive of mysticism is something which cannot be apprehended by study, but only by immediate experience (*dhawq*—literally "tasting"), by ecstasy and by a moral change. What a difference there is between *knowing* the definition of health and satiety, together with their causes and presuppositions, and *being* healthy and satisfied! What a difference between being acquainted with the definition of drunkenness—namely, that it designates a state arising from the domination of the seat of the intellect by vapours arising from the stomach—and being drunk! Indeed, the drunken man while in that condition does not know the definition of drunkenness nor the scientific account of it; he has not the very least scientific knowledge of it. The sober man, on the other hand, knows the definition of drunkenness and its basis, yet he is not drunk in the very least. Again the doctor, when he is himself ill, knows the definition and causes of health and the remedies which restore it, and yet is lacking in health. Similarly there is a difference between knowing the true nature and causes and conditions of the ascetic life and actually leading such a life and forsaking the world.

I apprehended clearly that the mystics were men who had real experiences, not men of words, and that I had already progressed as far as was possible by way of intellectual apprehension. What remained for me was not to be attained by oral instruction and study but only by immediate experience and by walking in the mystic way.

Now from the sciences I had laboured at and the paths I had traversed in my investigation of the revelational and rational sciences (that is, presumably, theology and philosophy), there had come to me a sure faith in God most high, in prophethood (or revelation), and in the Last Day. These three credal principles were firmly rooted in my being, not through any carefully argued proofs, but by reason of various causes, coincidences and experiences which are not capable of being stated in detail.

It had already become clear to me that I had no hope of the bliss of the world to come save through a God-fearing life and the withdrawal of myself from vain desire. It was clear to me too that the key to all this was to sever the attachment of the heart to worldly things by leaving the mansion of deception and returning to that of eternity, and to advance towards God most high with all earnestness. It was also clear that this was only to be achieved by turning away from wealth and position and fleeing from all time-consuming entanglements.

Next I considered the circumstances of my life, and realized that I was caught in a veritable thicket of attachments. I also considered my activities, of which the best was my teaching and lecturing, and realized that in them I was dealing with sciences that were unimportant and contributed nothing to the attainment of eternal life.

After that I examined my motive in my work of teaching, and realized that it was not a pure desire for the things of God, but that the impulse moving me was the desire for an influential position and public recognition. I saw for certain that I was on the brink of a crumbling bank of sand and in imminent danger of hell-fire unless I set about to mend my ways.

I reflected on this continuously for a time, while the choice still remained open to me. One day I would form the resolution to quit Baghdad and get rid of these adverse circumstances; the next day I would abandon my resolution. I put one foot forward and drew the other back. If in the morning I had a genuine longing to seek eternal life, by the evening the attack of a whole host of desires had reduced it to impotence. Worldly desires were striving to keep me by their chains just where I was, while the voice of faith was calling, "To the road! to the road! What is left of life is but little and the journey before you is long. All that keeps you busy, both intellectually and practically, is but hypocrisy and delusion. If you do not prepare *now* for eternal life, when will you prepare? If you do not now sever these attachments, when will you sever them?" On hearing that, the impulse would be stirred and the resolution made to take to flight....

I left Baghdad, then. I distributed what wealth I had, retaining only as much as would suffice myself and provide sustenance for my children. This I could easily manage, as the wealth of Iraq was available for good works, since it constitutes a trust fund for the benefit of the Muslims. Nowhere in the world have I seen better financial arrangements to assist a scholar to provide for his children....

In general, then, how is a mystic "way" (*tariqah*) described? The purity which is the first condition of it (*sc.* as bodily purity is the prior condition of formal Worship for Muslims) is the purification of the heart completely from what is other than God most high; the key to it, which corresponds to the opening act of adoration in prayer, is the sinking of the heart completely in the recollection of God; and the end of it is complete absorption (*fanā'*) in God. At least this is its end relatively to those first steps which almost come within the sphere of choice and personal responsibility; but in reality in the actual mystic "way" it is the first step, what comes before it being, as it were, the ante-chamber for those who are journeying towards it.

With this first stage of the "way" there begin the revelations and visions. The mystics in their waking state now behold angels and the spirits of the prophets; they hear these speaking to them and are instructed by them. Later, a higher state is reached; instead of beholding forms and figures, they come to stages in the "way" which it is hard to describe in language; if a man attempts to express these, his words inevitably contain what is clearly erroneous.

In general what they manage to achieve is nearness to God; some, however, would conceive of this as "inherence," some as "union," and some as "connection." All that is erroneous. In my book, *The Noblest Aim*, I have explained the nature of the error here. Yet he who has attained the mystic "state" need do no more than say:

> Of the things I do not remember, what was, was;
> Think it good; do not ask an account of it.
> (Ibn al-Mu'tazz)

In general the man to whom He has granted no immediate experience at all, apprehends no more of what prophetic revelation really is than the name. The miraculous graces given to the saints are in truth the beginnings of the prophets; and that was the first "state" of the Messenger of God (peace be upon him) when he went out to Mount Hirā', and was given up entirely to his Lord, and worshipped, so that the bedouin said, "Muhammad loves his Lord passionately."

Now this is a mystical "state" which is realized in immediate experience by those who walk in the way leading to it. Those to whom it is not granted to have immediate experience can become assured of it by trial (*sc.* contact with mystics or observation of them) and by hearsay, if they have sufficiently numerous opportunities of associating with mystics to understand that (*sc.* ecstasy) with certainty by means of what accompanies the "states." Whoever sits in their company derives from them this faith; and none who sits in their company is pained.

Those to whom it is not even granted to have contacts with mystics may know with certainty the possibility of ecstasy by the evidence of demonstration, as I have remarked in the section entitled *The Wonders of the Heart* of my *Revival of the Religious Sciences*.

Certainty reached by demonstration is *knowledge ('ilm)*; actual acquaintance with that "state" is *immediate experience (dhawq)*; the acceptance of it as probable from hearsay and trial (or observation) is *faith (imān)*. These are three degrees. "God will raise those of you who have faith and those who have been given knowledge in degrees (*sc.* of honour)" (Q. 58, 12).

Behind the mystics, however, there is a crowd of ignorant people. They deny this fundamentally, they are astonished at this line of thought, they listen and mock. "Amazing," they say. "What nonsense they talk!" About such people God most high has said: "Some of them listen to you, until, upon going out from you, they say to those to whom knowledge has been given, 'What did he say just now?' These are the people on whose hearts God sets a seal and they follow their passions" (Q. 47, 18). He makes them deaf, and blinds their sight.

Among the things that necessarily became clear to me from my practice of the mystic "way" was the true nature and special characteristics of prophetic revelation. The basis of that must undoubtedly be indicated in view of the urgent need for it.

THE TRUE NATURE OF PROPHECY AND THE COMPELLING NEED OF ALL CREATION FOR IT

You must know that the substance of man in his original condition was created in bareness and simplicity without any information about the worlds of God most high. These worlds are many, not to be reckoned save by God most high Himself. As He said, "None knows the hosts of thy Lord save He" (Q. 74, 34). Man's information about the world is by means of perception; and every perception of perceptibles is created so that thereby man may have some acquaintance with a world (or sphere) from among existents. By "worlds (or spheres)" we simply mean "classes of existents."

The first thing created in man was the sense of *touch*, and by it he perceives certain classes of existents, such as heat and cold, moisture and dryness, smoothness and roughness. Touch is completely unable to apprehend colours and noises. These might be non-existent so far as concerns touch.

Next there is created in him the sense of *sight*, and by it he apprehends colours and shapes. This is the most extensive of the worlds of sensibles. Next hearing is implanted in him, so that he hears sounds of various kinds. After that taste is created in him; and so on until he has completed the world of sensibles.

Next, when he is about seven years old, there is created in him discernment (or the power of distinguishing). This is a fresh stage in his development. He now apprehends more than the world of sensibles; and none of these additional factors (*sc.* relations, etc.) exists in the world of sense.

From this he ascends to another stage, and *intellect* (or reason) is created in him. He apprehends things necessary, possible, impossible, things which do not occur in the previous stages.

Beyond intellect there is yet another stage. In this another eye is opened, by which he beholds the unseen, what is to be in the future, and other things which are beyond the ken of intellect in the same way as the objects of intellect are beyond the ken of the faculty of discernment and the objects of discernment are beyond the ken of sense. Moreover, just as the man at the stage of discernment would reject and disregard the objects of intellect were these to be presented to him, so some intellectuals reject and disregard the objects of prophetic revelation. That is sheer ignorance. They have no ground for their view except that this is a stage which they have not reached and which for them does not exist; yet they suppose that it is non-existent in itself. When a man blind from birth, who has not learnt about colours and shapes by listening to people's talk, is told about these things for the first time, he does not understand them nor admit their existence.

God most high, however, has favoured His creatures by giving them something analogous to the special faculty of prophecy, namely dreams. In the dream-state a man apprehends what is to be in the future, which is something of the unseen; he does so either explicitly or else clothed in a symbolic form whose interpretation is disclosed.

Suppose a man has not experienced this himself, and suppose that he is told how some people fall into a dead faint, in which hearing, sight and the other senses no longer function, and in this condition perceive the unseen. He would deny that this is so and demonstrate its impossibility. "The sensible powers," he would say, "are the causes of perception (or apprehension); if a man does not perceive things (*sc.* the unseen) when these powers are actively present, much less will he do so when the senses are not functioning." This is a form of analogy which is shown to be false by what actually occurs and is observed. Just as intellect is one of the stages of human development in which there is an "eye" which sees the various types of intelligible objects, which are beyond the ken of the senses, so prophecy also is the description of a stage in which there is an eye endowed with light such that in that light the unseen and other supra-intellectual objects become visible.

Doubt about prophetic revelation is either (a) doubt of its possibility in general, or (b) doubt of its actual occurrence, or (c) doubt of the attainment of it by a specific individual.

The proof of the possibility of there being prophecy and the proof that there has been prophecy is that there is knowledge in the world the attainment of which by reason is inconceivable; for example, in medical science and astronomy. Whoever researches in such matters knows of necessity that this knowledge is attained only by Divine inspiration and by assistance from God most high. It cannot be reached by observation. For instance there are some astronomical laws based on phenomena which occur only once in a thousand years; how can these be arrived at by personal observation? It is the same with the properties of drugs.

This argument shows that it is possible for there to be a way of apprehending these matters which are not apprehended by the intellect. This is the meaning of prophetic revelation. That is not to say that prophecy is merely an expression for such knowledge. Rather, the apprehending of this class of extra-intellectual objects is *one* of the properties of prophecy; but it has many other properties as well. The said property is but a drop in the ocean of prophecy. It has been singled out for mention because you have something analogous to it in what you apprehend in dreaming, and because you have medical and astronomical knowledge belonging to the same class, namely, the miracles of the prophets, for the intellectuals cannot arrive at these at all by any intellectual efforts.

The other properties of prophetic revelation are apprehended only by immediate experience from the practice of the mystic way, but this property of prophecy you can understand by an analogy granted you, namely, the dream-state. If it were not for the latter you would not believe in that. If the prophet possessed a faculty to which you had nothing analogous and which you did not understand, how could you believe in it? Believing presupposes understanding. Now that analogous experience comes to a man in the early stages of the mystic way. Thereby he attains to a kind of immediate experience, extending as far as that to which he has attained, and by analogy to a kind of belief (or assent) in respect of that to which he has not attained. Thus this single property is a sufficient basis for one's faith in the principle of prophecy.

If you come to doubt whether a specific person is a prophet or not, certainty can only be reached by acquaintance with his conduct, either by personal observation, or by hearsay as a matter of common knowledge. For example, if you are familiar with medicine and law, you can recognise lawyers and doctors by observing what they are, or, where observation is impossible, by hearing what they have to say. Thus you are not unable to recognise that al-Shāfi'i (God have mercy upon him) is a lawyer and Galen a doctor; and your recognition is based on the facts and not on the judgment of someone else. Indeed, just because you have some knowledge of law and medicine, and examine their books and writings, you arrive at a necessary knowledge of what these men are.

Similarly, if you understand what it is to be a prophet, and have devoted much time to the study of the Qur'an and the Traditions, you will arrive at a necessary knowledge of the fact that Muhammad (God bless and preserve him) is in the highest grades of the prophetic calling. Convince yourself of that by trying out what he said about the influence of devotional practices on the purification of the heart—how truly he asserted that "whoever lives out what he knows will receive from God what he does not know"; how truly he asserted that "if anyone aids an evildoer, God will give that man power over him"; how truly he asserted that "if a man rises up in the morning with but a single care (*sc.* to please God), God most high will preserve him from all cares in this world and the next." When you have made trial of these in a thousand or several thousand instances, you will arrive at a necessary knowledge beyond all doubt.

By this method, then, seek certainty about the prophetic office, and not from the transformation of a rod into a serpent or the cleaving of the moon. For if you consider such an event by itself, without taking account of the numerous circumstances accompanying it—circumstances readily eluding the grasp of the intellect—then you might perhaps suppose that it was magic and deception and that it came from God to lead men astray; for "He leads astray whom He will, and guides whom He will." Thus the topic of miracles will be thrown back upon you; for if your faith is based on a reasoned argument involving the probative force of the miracle, then your faith is destroyed by an ordered argument showing the difficulty and ambiguity of the miracle.

Admit, then, that wonders of this sort are one of the proofs and accompanying circumstances out of the totality of your thought on the matter; and that you attain necessary knowledge and yet are unable to say specifically on what it is based.

The case is similar to that of a man who receives from a multitude of people a piece of information which is a matter of common belief.... He is unable to say that the certainty is derived from the remark of a single specific person; rather, its source is unknown to him; it is neither from outside the whole, nor is it from specific individuals. This is strong, intellectual faith. Immediate experience, on the other hand, is like actually witnessing a thing and taking it in one's hand. It is only found in the way of mysticism.

This is a sufficient discussion of the nature of prophetic revelation for my present purpose.

◉ CRITICAL QUESTIONS

1. What is the proof of prophecy, and do you find the proof convincing? Why, or why not?

2. How does al-Ghazali answer the question, "Is knowledge possible?" What do you think is wrong with his answer, if anything?

8.3 IS CERTAINTY POSSIBLE?

Have you ever been plagued by doubt? Would you like to be certain about something? Have you ever longed for an absolute truth that would never let you down? Have you ever gotten tired of questions, questions, questions?

You might be inclined to answer, "Yes, especially when studying philosophy." Uncertainty is not a pleasant state for anyone, even philosophers. It leaves us up in the air, juggling things that might fall and break at any moment. Uncertainty is unsettling. However, if we really want to know what is true, if we really want absolutely certain knowledge, must we not question and doubt until we find it?

René Descartes (sounds like "day kart") was born in France in 1596 and died in Sweden in 1650. He was a brilliant philosopher and mathematician, who has been called the father of modern philosophy. Like many of you, and like al-Ghazali (see the previous selection), he sought something about which he could be absolutely certain. He was willing to undergo the turmoil of doubt to find it because he believed that we should accept as true only that which is supported by sound arguments.

Descartes was a methodical skeptic because he employed the method of doubt in his quest for certainty. This method deals with *logical possibility*. He was not concerned with beliefs that people actually doubt or with beliefs that are in fact false. Rather, he was concerned with those beliefs that are logically possible to doubt. If it is possible for a belief to be false, then it is possible to doubt it, whether or not, as a matter of fact, anyone has ever doubted it and whether or not, as a matter of fact, it is false.

However, Descartes could not be content with skepticism. Ultimately he sought knowledge firmly grounded in reason. Like Plato he was a rationalist, holding that beliefs based on sensations are little more than opinions, but beliefs based on reason constitute genuine knowledge. He refined Plato's distinction between opinion and knowledge. By *certainty* he meant that about which logical doubt is impossible. A belief is certain (or "clear and distinct" as Descartes liked to put it) if it is *not* logically possible to doubt its truth. Only such beliefs constitute knowledge. Because it is logically possible to doubt the truth of beliefs based on sensations, such beliefs must constitute opinion, not knowledge.

To grasp Descartes's philosophical project, we must take a brief look at the historical context. Descartes lived at the time when modern science was replacing medieval science, which had been based on the philosophies of Aristotle and Plato. Medieval science assumed as true a theory (ultimately derived from Aristotle) called **direct realism**. According to this theory, there is a reality that exists apart from human sensations, and our senses put us *directly* in touch with this reality.

This theory of direct realism had proved increasingly problematic because it seemed to lead to all sorts of contradictions. I see a house as small from a distance and as large when close up. Is the house both small and large? "Hardly," you say. If, however, our senses put us *directly* in touch with the real house, then what else can we conclude? Likewise, in the photo on one of the book's color plates, are the items seen in the foreground actually larger than the ones in the background or do they appear to be so?

Galileo Galilei (1564–1642), who had reintroduced the atomistic theory of matter into physical science, also rejected direct realism because it was rather obvious that we do not directly sense atoms. If what is really out there are atoms and if we don't sense them, then we cannot be directly in touch with physical reality via our senses.

So what role do our senses play? Galileo proposed a theory called **indirect** or **representational realism**. According to this theory, our sensations represent physical reality. We are not directly in touch with physical reality; we are only directly in touch with our sensations *of* physical reality.

How did Galileo know that? How did he know, or how does anyone know, that our sensations represent an external reality? We cannot get outside of sensations to see. We cannot compare our image of a fat cat with the real fat cat as we can compare a picture of a fat cat with our sensations of a fat cat. Here we have a problem that seems to undermine the epistemic certainty the new science promises.

Descartes believed that science ought to provide us with certainty. Its great promise was to give us knowledge. Knowledge is certainty as far as Descartes was concerned, but how can science provide us with knowledge if the theory on which it is built, the theory of indirect or representational realism, cannot be proved true? Without a proof of representational realism, science is without a firm foundation, or so Descartes thought.

Descartes wrote his famous *Meditations on First Philosophy* in order to arrive at certainty and to prove representational realism correct. Here you will read only the first two *Meditations* because they deal directly with his epistemological theory.

In the first *Meditation*, Descartes employed the method of doubt to show that all our beliefs based on sensations can be doubted and that we cannot even be sure we have not made a mistake in calculation when we do mathematics. In the second *Meditation*, he showed that one thing cannot be doubted: "I exist as a thinking thing when I think." This is the famous *"cogito, ergo sum"* ("I think, therefore I am") argument (although Descartes did not use that exact language here), and Descartes maintained this is an absolutely certain truth that cannot be doubted. In later

Meditations, Descartes attempted to rationally deduce the existence of God from his own existence as a thinking thing and to show that God is perfectly good and hence no deceiver.

"So what?" you say. Well, if we can be certain that we exist and if we can be certain that God exists and if we can be certain that God is no deceiver, we can also be certain that our sensations must truly represent an external reality. If they did not, we would live in constant error and ignorance, like Plato's prisoners in the cave, and this, surely, a good and gracious God would not allow.

◉ READING QUESTIONS

1. What was Descartes's goal, and what method did he employ to get there?
2. Many of our beliefs are based on sensation. Descartes offered two arguments, the arguments from deception and dreaming, to show that beliefs based on sensations are not trustworthy. State these arguments in your own words.
3. Some of our beliefs—for example, that two plus three equals five—are based on reasoning, not sensation. Descartes argued that even arithmetic calculations can be doubted. What is his argument?
4. Descartes ended the first *Meditation* with the famous evil demon argument. What is the point of this argument?

5. Descartes concluded that the statement "I am, I exist" must be true whenever he thought it. Why? What reasons support this conclusion?
6. The next step in Descartes's argument is to reach the conclusion that he is a thinking thing. How did he reach that conclusion? Why did he not conclude instead that he was a physical thing?
7. In the final paragraph of *Meditation II*, Descartes listed several things he had learned from his consideration of a piece of wax. What are they, and how did he arrive at these conclusions?
8. If you studied the previous selection, what similarities and differences do you notice between al-Ghazali's quest for knowledge and Descartes's quest?

Meditations I and II

RENÉ DESCARTES

MEDITATION I

On What Can Be Called into Doubt

For several years now, I've been aware that I accepted many falsehoods as true in my youth, that what I built on the foundations of those falsehoods was dubious, and accordingly that once in my life I would need to tear down everything and begin anew from the foundations if I wanted to establish any stable and lasting knowledge. But the task seemed enormous, and I waited until I was so old that no better time for undertaking it would be likely to follow. I have thus delayed so

long that it would be wrong for me to waste in indecision the time left for action. Today, then, having rid myself of worries and having arranged for some peace and quiet, I withdraw alone, free at last earnestly and wholeheartedly to overthrow all my beliefs.

To do this, I don't need to show each of them to be false: I may never be able to do that. But, since reason now convinces me that I ought to withhold my assent just as carefully from what isn't obviously certain and indubitable as from what's obviously false, I can justify the rejection

---

From René Descartes's *Meditations on First Philosophy*, translated by Ronald Rubin (Claremont, CA: Areté Press, 1986), pp. 1–13. Reprinted by permission of Areté Press.

has been deceived by senses

of all my beliefs if in each I can find some ground for doubt. And, to do this, I need not run through my beliefs one by one, which would be an endless task. Since a building collapses when its foundation is cut out from under it, I will go straight to the principles on which all my former beliefs rested.

Of course, whatever I have so far accepted as supremely true I have learned either from the senses or through the senses. But I have occasionally caught the senses deceiving me, and it's prudent never completely to trust those who have cheated us even once.

But, while my senses may deceive me about what is small or far away, there may still be other things which I take in by the senses but which I cannot possibly doubt—like that I am here, sitting before the fire, wearing a dressing gown, touching this paper. And on what grounds might I deny that my hands and the other parts of my body exist?—unless perhaps I liken myself to madmen whose brains are so rattled by the persistent vapors of melancholy that they are sure that they're kings when in fact they are paupers, or that they wear purple robes when in fact they're naked, or that their heads are clay, or that they are gourds, or made of glass. But these people are insane, and I would seem just as crazy if I were to apply what I say about them to myself.

This would be perfectly obvious—if I weren't a man accustomed to sleeping at night whose experiences while asleep are at least as far-fetched as those that madmen have while awake. How often, at night, I've been convinced that I was here, sitting before the fire, wearing my dressing gown, when in fact I was undressed and between the covers of my bed! But now I am looking at this piece of paper with my eyes wide open; the head that I am shaking has not been lulled to sleep; I put my hand out consciously and deliberately and feel. None of this would be as distinct if I were asleep. As if I can't remember having been tricked by similar thoughts while asleep! When I think very carefully about this, I see so plainly that there are no reliable signs by which I can distinguish sleeping from waking that I am stupefied—and my stupor itself suggests that I am asleep!

Suppose, then, that I am dreaming. Suppose, in particular, that my eyes are not open, that my head is not moving, and that I have not put out my hand. Suppose that I do not have hands, or even a body. I must still admit that the things I see in sleep are like painted images which must have been patterned after real things and, hence, that things like eyes, heads, hands, and bodies are real rather than imaginary. For, even when painters try to give bizarre shapes to sirens and satyrs, they are unable to give them completely new natures; they only jumble together the parts of various animals. And, even if they were to come up with something so novel that no one had ever seen anything like it before, something entirely fictitious and unreal, at least there must be real colors from which they composed it. Similarly, while things like eyes, heads, and hands may be imaginary, it must be granted that some simpler and more universal things are real—the "real colors" from which the true and false images in our thoughts are formed.

Things of this sort seem to include general bodily nature and its extension, the shape of extended things, their quantity (that is, their size and number), the place in which they exist, the time through which they endure, and so on.

Perhaps we can correctly infer that, while physics, astronomy, medicine, and other disciplines that require the study of composites are dubious, disciplines like arithmetic and geometry, which deal only with completely simple and universal things without regard to whether they exist in the world, are somehow certain and indubitable. For, whether we are awake or asleep, two plus three is always five, and the square never has more than four sides. It seems impossible even to suspect such obvious truths of falsity.

Nevertheless, the traditional view is fixed in my mind that there is a God who can do anything and by whom I have been made to be as I am. How do I know that He hasn't brought it about that, while there is in fact no earth, no sky, no extended thing, no shape, no magnitude, and no place, all of these things seem to me to exist, just as they do now? I think that other people sometimes err in what they believe themselves to know perfectly well. Mightn't I be deceived when I add two and three, or count the sides of a square, or do even simpler things, if we can even suppose that there is anything simpler? Maybe it will be denied that God deceives me, since He is said to be supremely good. But, if God's being good is incompatible with His having created me so that I am deceived always, it seems just as out of line with His being good that He permits me to be deceived sometimes—as he undeniably does.

Maybe some would rather deny that there is an omnipotent God than believe that everything else is uncertain. Rather than arguing with them, I will grant everything I have said about God to be fiction. But, however these people think I came to be as I now am—whether they say it is by fate, or by accident, or by a continuous series of events, or in some other way—it seems that he who errs and is deceived is somehow imperfect. Hence, the less power that is attributed to my original creator, the more likely it is that I am always deceived. To these arguments, I have no reply. I'm forced to admit that nothing that I used to believe is beyond legitimate doubt—not because I have been careless or playful, but because I have valid and well-considered grounds for doubt. Hence, I must withhold my assent from my former beliefs as carefully as from obvious falsehoods if I want to arrive at something certain.

But it's not enough to have noticed this: I must also take care to bear it in mind. For my habitual views constantly return to my mind and take control of what I believe as if our longstanding, intimate relationship has given them the right to do so, even against my will. I'll never break the habit of trusting and giving in to these views while I see them for what they are—things somewhat dubious (as I have just shown) but nonetheless probable, things that I have much more reason to believe than to deny. That's why I think it will be good deliberately to turn my will around, to allow myself to be deceived, and to suppose that all my previous beliefs are false and illusory. Eventually, when I have counterbalanced the weight of my prejudices, my bad habits will no longer distort my grasp of things. I know that there is no danger of error here and that I won't overindulge in skepticism, since I'm now concerned, not with action, but only with gaining knowledge.

I will suppose, then, not that there is a supremely good God who is the source of all truth, but that there is an evil demon, supremely powerful and cunning, who works as hard as he can to deceive me. I will say that sky, air, earth, color, shape, sound, and other external things are just dreamed illusions which the demon uses to ensnare my judgment. I will regard myself as not having hands, eyes, flesh, blood, and senses—but as having the false belief that I have all these things. I will obstinately concentrate on this meditation and will thus ensure by mental resolution that, if I do not really have the ability to know the truth, I will at least withhold assent from what is false and from what a deceiver may try to put over on me, however powerful and cunning he may be. But this plan requires effort, and laziness brings me back to my ordinary life. I am like a prisoner who happens to enjoy the illusion of freedom in his dreams, begins to suspect that he is asleep, fears being awakened, and deliberately lets the enticing illusions slip by unchallenged. Thus, I slide back into my old views, afraid to awaken and to find that after my peaceful rest I must toil, not in the light, but in the confusing darkness of the problems just raised.

MEDITATION II

On the Nature of the Human Mind, Which Is Better Known Than the Body

Yesterday's meditation has hurled me into doubts so great that I can neither ignore them nor think my way out of them. I am in turmoil, as if I have accidentally fallen into a whirlpool and can neither touch bottom nor swim to the safety of the surface. I will struggle, however, and try to follow the path that I started on yesterday. I will reject whatever is open to the slightest doubt just as though I have found it to be entirely false, and I will continue until I find something certain—or at least until I know for certain that nothing is certain. Archimedes required only one fixed and immovable point to move the whole earth from its place, and I too can hope for great things if I can find even one small thing that is certain and unshakable.

I will suppose, then, that everything I see is unreal. I will believe that my memory is unreliable and that none of what it presents to me ever happened. I have no senses. Body, shape, extension, motion, and place are fantasies. What then is true? Perhaps just that nothing is certain.

But how do I know that there isn't something different from the things just listed which I do not have the slightest reason to doubt? Isn't there a God, or something like one, who puts my thoughts into me? But why should I say so when I may be the author of those thoughts? Well, isn't it at least the case that I am something? But I now am denying that I have senses and a body. But I stop here. For what follows from these denials? Am I so bound to my body and to my senses that I cannot exist without them? I have convinced myself that there is nothing in the world—no sky, no earth, no minds, no bodies. Doesn't it follow that I don't exist? No, surely I must exist if it's me who is convinced of something. But there is a deceiver, supremely powerful and cunning, whose aim is to see that I am always deceived. But surely I exist, if I am deceived. Let him deceive me all he can, he will never make it the case that I am nothing while I think that I am something. Thus having fully weighed every consideration, I must finally conclude that the statement "I am, I exist" must be true whenever I state it or mentally consider it.

But I do not yet fully understand what this "I" is that must exist. I must guard against inadvertently taking myself to be something other than I am, thereby going wrong even in the knowledge that I put forward as supremely certain and evident. Hence, I will think once again about what I believed myself to be before beginning these meditations. From this conception, I will subtract everything challenged by the reasons for doubt which I produced earlier, until nothing remains except what is certain and indubitable.

What, then, did I formerly take myself to be? A man, of course. But what is a man? Should I say a rational animal? No, because then I would need to ask what an animal is and what it is to be rational. Thus, starting from a single question, I would sink into many which are more difficult, and I do not have the time to waste on such subtleties. Instead, I will look here at the thought which occurred to me spontaneously and naturally when I reflected on what I was. The first thought

to occur to me was that I have a face, hands, arms, and all the other equipment (also found in corpses) which I call a body. The next thought to occur to me was that I take nourishment, move myself around, sense, and think—that I do things which I trace back to my soul. Either I didn't stop to think about what this soul was, or I imagined it to be a rarified air, or fire, or ether permeating the denser parts of my body. But, about physical objects, I didn't have any doubts whatever: I thought that I distinctly knew their nature. If I had tried to describe my conception of this nature, I might have said this: "When I call something a physical object, I mean that it is capable of being bounded by a shape and limited to a place; that it can fill a space so as to exclude other objects from it; that it can be perceived by touch, sight, hearing, taste, and smell; that it can be moved in various ways, not by itself, but by something else in contact with it." I judged that the powers of self-movement, of sensing, and of thinking did not belong to the nature of physical objects, and, in fact, I marveled that there were some physical objects in which these powers could be found.

But what should I think now, while supposing that a supremely powerful and "evil" deceiver completely devotes himself to deceiving me? Can I say that I have any of the things that I have attributed to the nature of physical objects? I concentrate, think, reconsider—but nothing comes to me; I grow tired of the pointless repetition. But what about the things that I have assigned to soul? Nutrition and self-movement? Since I have no body, these are merely illusions. Sensing? But I cannot sense without a body, and in sleep I've seemed to sense many things that I later realized I had not really sensed. Thinking? It comes down to this: Thought and thought alone cannot be taken away from me. I am, I exist. That much is certain. But for how long? As long as I think—for it may be that, if I completely stopped thinking, I would completely cease to exist. I am not now admitting anything unless it must be true, and I am therefore not admitting that I am anything at all other than a thinking thing—that is, a mind, soul, understanding, or reason (terms whose meaning I did not previously know). I know that I am a real, existing thing, but what kind of thing? As I have said, a thing that thinks.

What else? I will draw up mental images. I'm not the collection of organs called a human body. Nor am I some rarified gas permeating these organs, or air, or fire, or vapor, or breath—for I have supposed that none of these things exist. Still, I am something. But couldn't it be that these things, which I do not yet know about and which I am therefore supposing to be nonexistent, really aren't distinct from the "I" that I know to exist? I don't know, and I'm not going to argue about it now. I can only form judgments on what I do know. I know that I exist, and I ask what the "I" is that I know to exist. It's obvious that this conception of myself doesn't depend on anything that I do not yet know to exist and, therefore, that it does not depend on anything of which I can draw up a mental image. And the words "draw up" point to my mistake. I would truly be creative if I were to have a mental image of what I am, since to have a mental image is just to contemplate the shape or image of a physical object. I now know with certainty that I exist and at the same time that all images—and, more generally, all things associated with the nature of physical objects—may just be dreams. When I keep this in mind, it seems just as absurd to say "I use mental images to help me understand what I am" as it would to say "Now, while awake, I see something true—but, since I don't yet see it clearly enough, I'll go to sleep and let my dreams present it to me more clearly and truly." Thus I know that none of the things that I can comprehend with the aid of mental images bear on my knowledge of myself. And I must carefully draw my mind away from such things if it is to see its own nature distinctly.

But what then am I? A thinking thing. And what is that? Something that doubts, understands, affirms, denies, wills, refuses, and also senses and has mental images.

That's quite a lot, if I really do all of these things. But don't I? Isn't it me who now doubts nearly everything, understands one thing, affirms this thing, refuses to affirm other things, wants to know much more, refuses to be deceived, has mental images (sometimes involuntarily), and is

aware of many things "through his senses?" Even if I am always dreaming, and even if my creator does what he can to deceive me, isn't it just as true that I do all these things as that I exist? Are any of these things distinct from my thought? Can any be said to be separate from me? That it's me who doubts, understands, and wills is so obvious that I don't see how it could be more evident. And it's also me who has mental images. While it may be, as I am supposing, that absolutely nothing of which I have a mental image really exists, the ability to have mental images really does exist and is a part of my thought. Finally, it's me who senses—or who seems to gain awareness of physical objects through the senses. For example, I am now seeing light, hearing a noise, and feeling heat. These things are unreal, since I am dreaming. But it is still certain that I seem to see, to hear, and to feel. This seeming cannot be unreal, and it is what is properly called sensing. Strictly speaking, sensing is just thinking.

From this, I begin to learn a little about what I am. But I still can't stop thinking that I apprehend physical objects, which I picture in mental images and examine with my senses, much more distinctly than I know this unfamiliar "I," of which I cannot form a mental image. I think this, even though it would be astounding if I comprehended things which I've found to be doubtful, unknown, and alien to me more distinctly than the one which I know to be real: my self. But I see what's happening. My mind enjoys wandering, and it won't confine itself to the truth. I will therefore loosen the reins on my mind for now so that later, when the time is right, I will be able to control it more easily.

Let's consider the things commonly taken to be the most distinctly comprehended: physical objects that we see and touch. Let's not consider physical objects in general, since general conceptions are very often confused. Rather, let's consider one, particular object. Take, for example, this piece of wax. It has just been taken from the honeycomb; it hasn't yet completely lost the taste of honey; it still smells of the flowers from which it was gathered; its color, shape, and size are obvious; it is hard, cold, and easy to touch; it makes a sound when rapped. In short, everything seems to be present in the wax that is required for me to know it as distinctly as possible. But, as I speak, I move the wax towards the fire; it loses what was left of its taste; it gives up its smell; it changes color; it loses its shape; it gets bigger; it melts; it heats up; it becomes difficult to touch; it no longer makes a sound when struck. Is it still the same piece of wax? We must say that it is: no one denies it or thinks otherwise. Then what was there in the wax that I comprehended so distinctly? Certainly nothing that I reached with my senses—for, while everything having to do with taste, smell, sight, touch, and hearing has changed, the same piece of wax remains.

Perhaps what I distinctly knew was neither the sweetness of honey, not the fragrance of flowers, nor a sound, but a physical object which once appeared to me one way and now appears differently. But what exactly is it of which I now have a mental image? Let's pay careful attention, remove everything that doesn't belong to the wax, and see what's left. Nothing is left except an extended, flexible, and changeable thing. But what is it for this thing to be flexible and changeable? Is it just that the wax can go from round to square and then to triangular, as I have mentally pictured? Of course not. Since I understand that the wax's shape can change in innumerable ways, and since I can't run through all the changes in my imagination, my comprehension of the wax's flexibility and changeability cannot have been produced by my ability to have mental images. And what about the thing that is extended? Are we also ignorant of its extension? Since the extension of the wax increases when the wax melts, increases again when the wax boils, and increases still more when the wax gets hotter, I will be mistaken about what the wax is unless I believe that it can undergo more changes in extension than I can ever encompass with mental images. I must therefore admit that I do not have an image of what the wax is—that I grasp what it is with only my mind. (While I am saying this about a particular piece of wax, it is even more clearly true about wax in general.) What then is this piece of wax that I grasp only with my mind? It is something that I see, feel, and mentally picture—exactly what

I believed it to be at the outset. But it must be noted that, despite the appearances, my grasp of the wax is not visual, tactile, or pictorial. Rather, my grasp of the wax is the result of a purely mental inspection, which can be imperfect and confused, as it was once, or clear and distinct, as it is now, depending on how much attention I pay to the things of which the wax consists.

I'm surprised by how prone my mind is to error. Even when I think to myself non-verbally, language stands in my way, and common usage comes close to deceiving me. For, when the wax is present, we say that we see the wax itself, not that we infer its presence from its color and shape. I'm inclined to leap from this fact about language to the conclusion that I learn about the wax by eyesight rather than by purely mental inspection. But, if I happen to look out my window and see men walking in the street, I naturally say that I see the men just as I say that I see the wax. What do I really see, however, but hats and coats that could be covering robots? I *judge* that there are men. Thus I comprehend with my judgment, which is in my mind, objects that I once believed myself to see with my eyes.

One who aspires to wisdom above that of the common man disgraces himself by deriving doubt from common ways of speaking. Let's go on, then, to ask when I most clearly and perfectly grasped what the wax is. Was it when I first looked at the wax and believed my knowledge of it to come from the external senses—or at any rate from the so-called "common sense," the power of having mental images? Or is it now, after I have carefully studied what the wax is and how I come to know it? Doubt would be silly here. For what was distinct in my original conception of the wax? How did that conception differ from that had by animals? When I distinguish the wax from its external forms—when I "undress" it and view it "naked"—there may still be errors in my judgments about it, but I couldn't possibly grasp the wax in this way without a human mind.

What should I say about this mind—or, in other words, about myself? (I am not now admitting that there is anything to me but a mind.) What is this "I" that seems to grasp the wax so distinctly? Don't I know myself much more truly and certainly, and also much more distinctly and plainly, than I know the wax? For, if I base my judgment that the wax exists on the fact that I see it, my seeing it much more obviously implies that I exist. It's possible that what I see is not really wax, and it's even possible that I don't have eyes with which to see—but it clearly is not possible that, when I see (or, what now amounts to the same thing, when I think I see), the "I" which thinks is not a real thing. Similarly, if I base my judgment that the wax exists on the fact that I feel it, the same fact makes it obvious that I exist. If I base my judgment that the wax exists on the fact that I have a mental image of it or on some other fact of this sort, the same thing can obviously be said. And what I've said about the wax applies to everything else that is outside me. Moreover, if I seem to grasp the wax more distinctly when I detect it with several senses than when I detect it with just sight or touch, I must

know myself even more distinctly—for every consideration that contributes to my grasp of the piece of wax or to my grasp of any other physical object serves better to reveal the nature of my mind. Besides, the mind has so much in it by which it can make its conception of itself distinct that what comes to it from physical objects hardly seems to matter.

And now I have brought myself back to where I wanted to be. I now know that physical objects are grasped, not by the senses or the power of having mental images, but by understanding alone. And, since I grasp physical objects in virtue of their being understandable rather than in virtue of their being tangible or visible, I know that I can't grasp anything more easily or plainly than my mind. But, since it takes time to break old habits of thought, I should pause here to allow the length of my contemplation to impress the new thoughts more deeply into my memory.

CRITICAL QUESTIONS

1. List some examples of occasions when you have been deceived by your senses. Do these examples support Descartes's view? Why, or why not?
2. Have you ever had a dream that you were totally convinced was true? How do you know you are not now dreaming?
3. Play Descartes's game for a moment and imagine there is an all-powerful force that has nothing better to do than to deceive you. Give this force a name and imagine it, like some mad puppeteer

pulling the strings behind the scenes, constantly arranging things so that your beliefs are false even though you think they are true. Now ask yourself, "Is there anything about which this wicked force could not deceive me?" If there is anything you can think of, what is it?
4. How did Descartes answer the question, "Is knowledge possible?" What is one major problem with his answer, and why is it a major problem?

8.4 EMPIRICISM AND LIMITED SKEPTICISM

David Hume (1711–1776) was a Scottish philosopher regarded by some as the greatest philosopher to write in the English language. There is little doubt about his brilliance. He graduated from the University of Edinburgh at the ripe old age of fifteen and headed for law school. Deciding he did not like law, he began writing a philosophical work called *A Treatise on Human Nature* (1739–1740), which he hoped would bring him fame and fortune. It did not. Very few people understood what he was talking about. Disappointed, he wrote a more popular version called *An Enquiry Concerning Human Understanding* (1748) from which the following selection is taken. You can judge for yourself how popular this version might have been.

Hume presented an empiricist theory of knowledge: Everything we can know about the world is ultimately derived from our senses. He developed empiricism into a critical tool for checking ideas. If you want to know what an idea or concept means, said Hume, trace it back to the impressions from which it came. For example, in a famous section (VII, not included here) Hume sought to find out what the concept of cause means. This is a basic idea because so much of science and, for that matter, common sense presupposes the law of cause and effect.

Usually people mean three things by cause—namely, that event *A* is the cause of event *B* if *A* occurs before *B, A* is contiguous to *B* in some way, and *A* is necessarily connected with *B*. It is this last idea that puzzled Hume. What is a necessary connection? From what impression does it arise? The only impression Hume could find was the impression of *constant conjunction*. We say *A* is the cause of *B* because in our experience *A* and *B* are constantly conjoined. Yet the concept of a necessary connection goes far beyond constant conjunction. If *A* and *B* are necessarily connected, then whenever *A* occurs, *B* will necessarily occur. However, from the fact that *A* and *B* have been constantly conjoined in the past, can we conclude that they will be so connected in the future? It is likely that they will be connected, even highly probable, but high probability is not the same as necessity.

This conclusion shocked the intellectual community of Hume's day because, if Hume was right, a fundamental law of thought and of science was without foundation in experience. This issue of the foundation of knowledge was of central importance to Hume. The rationalists claimed there was a foundation found in reason; the empiricists claimed there was a foundation found in experience. Hume, while sympathetic to empiricism, questioned whether there are in fact any firm foundations on which knowledge rests other than customary and habitual associations of ideas.

Hume brought the assumption that knowledge had a foundation into question by discovering the **problem of induction**. Although Hume did not call it by this name, the problem of induction, simply stated, is the problem of discovering rational foundations for all the conclusions we draw based on experience.

Later philosophers, inspired by Hume, drew a distinction between **analytic statements** such as "All bachelors are unmarried men" and **synthetic statements** such as "My cat is fat." Hume used the terms *relations of ideas* and *matters of fact* for these two kinds of statements because analytic statements are about how ideas are related and synthetic statements are about facts. You can test to see if any given statement is analytic by applying this rule: "If it is not logically possible for the negation of the statement to be true, the statement is analytic." For example, the claim that "some bachelors are married" cannot be true because the word *bachelor* means "unmarried man." You can test to see if a statement is synthetic by applying this rule: "If it is logically possible for the negation of the statement to be true, the statement is synthetic." For example, it is quite possible that, in fact, my cat is not fat.

See if you understand these rules by determining which of these statements are analytic and which synthetic.

1. The sun is round.
2. The lights are on.
3. $2 + 2 = 4$
4. Philosophy is fun.
5. Blind bats cannot see.

Note that statements about the relation of ideas (analytic) are *necessarily true*. That is, they are true by virtue of the meaning of the terms. Statements about matters of fact (synthetic) are *contingently true* because their truth depends on a certain state of affairs actually obtaining. Some philosophers have also maintained that the truth of analytic statements is justified a priori by deductive reasoning, whereas the truth of synthetic statements is justified a posteriori by inductive reasoning.

Let us return to the problem of induction. Conclusions based on experience presuppose, according to Hume, that the future will resemble the past. Now how is this presupposition justified? Read Hume and see.

READING QUESTIONS

1. Into what two categories can the "perceptions of the mind" be divided, and how are they distinguished from one another? Give an example of each.
2. According to Hume, all reasoning concerning matters of fact is founded on the relation of cause and effect. This relation, Hume argued, is not discoverable by reason, only by experience.
Summarize the argument Hume used to support this claim.
3. Why can we not prove the principle "the future will resemble the past" deductively (Hume's term was "by demonstrative reasoning")?
4. Why can we not prove this principle inductively ("by moral reasoning")?

An Enquiry Concerning Human Understanding

DAVID HUME

SECTION II

Of the Origin of Ideas

Every one will readily allow, that there is a considerable difference between the perceptions of the mind, when a man feels the pain of excessive heat, or the pleasure of moderate warmth, and when he afterwards recalls to his memory this sensation, or anticipates it by his imagination. These faculties may mimic or copy the perceptions of the senses; but they never can entirely reach the force and vivacity of the original sentiment. The utmost we say of them, even when they operate with greatest vigour, is, that they represent their object in so lively a manner, that we could *almost* say we feel or see it: But, except the mind be disordered by disease or madness, they never can arrive at such a pitch of vivacity, as to render these perceptions altogether indistinguishable. All the colours of poetry, however splendid, can never paint natural objects in such a manner as to make the description be taken for a real landscape. The most lively thought is still inferior to the dullest sensation.

We may observe a like distinction to run through all the other perceptions of the mind. A man in a fit of anger, is actuated in a very different manner from one who only thinks of that emotion. If you tell me, that any person is in love, I easily understand your meaning, and form a just conception of his situation; but never can mistake that conception for the real disorders and agitations of the passion. When we reflect on our past sentiments and affections, our thought is a faithful mirror, and copies its objects truly; but the colours which it employs are faint and dull, in comparison of those in which our original perceptions were clothed. It requires no nice discernment or metaphysical head to mark the distinction between them.

Here therefore we may divide all the perceptions of the mind into two classes or species, which are distinguished by their different degrees of force and vivacity. The less forcible and lively are commonly denominated *Thoughts* or *Ideas*. The other species want a name in our language, and in most others; I suppose, because it was not

---

Excerpts from Sections II and IV of David Hume's *An Enquiry Concerning Human Understanding* (Oxford: Clarendon Press, 1748).

requisite for any, but philosophical purposes, to rank them under a general term or appellation. Let us, therefore, use a little freedom, and call them *Impressions;* employing that word in a sense somewhat different from the usual. By the term *impression,* then, I mean all our more lively perceptions, when we hear, or see, or feel, or love, or hate, or desire, or will. And impressions are distinguished from ideas, which are the less lively perceptions, of which we are conscious, when we reflect on any of those sensations or movements above mentioned.

Nothing, at first view, may seem more unbounded than the thought of man, which not only escapes all human power and authority, but is not even restrained within the limits of nature and reality. To form monsters, and join incongruous shapes and appearances, costs the imagination no more trouble than to conceive the most natural and familiar objects. And while the body is confined to one planet, along which it creeps with pain and difficulty; the thought can in an instant transport us into the most distant regions of the universe; or even beyond the universe, into the unbounded chaos, where nature is supposed to lie in total confusion. What never was seen, or heard of, may yet be conceived; nor is any thing beyond the power of thought, except what implies an absolute contradiction.

But though our thought seems to possess this unbounded liberty, we shall find, upon a nearer examination, that it is really confined within very narrow limits, and that all this creative power of the mind amounts to no more than the faculty of compounding, transposing, augmenting, or diminishing the materials afforded us by the senses and experience. When we think of a golden mountain, we only join two consistent ideas, *gold*, and *mountain*, with which we were formerly acquainted. A virtuous horse we can conceive; because, from our own feeling, we can conceive virtue; and this we may unite to the figure and shape of a horse, which is an animal familiar to us. In short, all the materials of thinking are derived either from our outward or inward sentiment: the mixture and composition of these belongs alone to the mind and will. Or, to express myself in philosophical language, all our ideas or

more feeble perceptions are copies of our impressions or more lively ones.

To prove this, the two following arguments will, I hope, be sufficient. First, when we analyze our thoughts or ideas, however compounded or sublime, we always find that they resolve themselves into such simple ideas as were copied from a precedent feeling or sentiment. Even those ideas, which, at first view, seem the most wide of this origin, are found, upon a nearer scrutiny, to be derived from it. The idea of God, as meaning an infinitely intelligent, wise, and good Being, arises from reflecting on the operations of our own mind, and augmenting, without limit, those qualities of goodness and wisdom. We may prosecute this enquiry to what length we please; where we shall always find, that every idea which we examine is copied from a similar impression. Those who would assert that this position is not universally true nor without exception, have only one, and that an easy method of refuting it; by producing that idea, which, in their opinion, is not derived from this source. It will then be incumbent on us, if we would maintain our doctrine, to produce the impression, or lively perception, which corresponds to it.

Secondly. If it happen, from a defect of the organ, that a man is not susceptible of any species of sensation, we always find that he is as little susceptible of the correspondent ideas. A blind man can form no notion of colours; a deaf man of sounds. Restore either of them that sense in which he is deficient; by opening this new inlet for his sensations, you also open an inlet for the ideas; and he finds no difficulty in conceiving these objects. The case is the same, if the object, proper for exciting any sensation, has never been applied to the organ. A Laplander or Negro has no notion of the relish of wine. And though there are few or no instances of a like deficiency in the mind, where a person has never felt or is wholly incapable of a sentiment or passion that belongs to his species; yet we find the same observation to take place in a less degree. A man of mild manners can form no idea of inveterate revenge or cruelty; nor can a selfish heart easily conceive the heights of friendship and generosity. It is readily allowed, that other beings may possess many senses of which we can have no conception; because the ideas of them have never been introduced to us in the only manner by which an idea can have access to the mind, to wit, by the actual feeling and sensation....

SECTION IV

Sceptical Doubts Concerning the Operations of the Understanding
Part 1

All the objects of human reason or enquiry may naturally be divided into two kinds, to wit, *Relations of Ideas*, and *Matters of Fact*. Of the first kind are the sciences of Geometry, Algebra, and Arithmetic; and in short, every affirmation which is either intuitively or demonstratively certain. *That the square of the hypothenuse is equal to the square of the two sides*, is a proposition which expresses a relation between these figures. *That three times five is equal to the half of thirty*, expresses a relation between these numbers. Propositions of this kind are discoverable by the mere operation of thought, without dependence on what is anywhere existent in the universe. Though there never were a circle or triangle in nature, the truths demonstrated by Euclid would for ever retain their certainty and evidence.

Matters of fact, which are the second objects of human reason, are not ascertained in the same manner; nor is our evidence of their truth, however great, of a like nature with the foregoing. The contrary of every matter of fact is still possible; because it can never imply a contradiction, and is conceived by the mind with the same facility and distinctness, as if ever so conformable to reality. *That the sun will not rise to-morrow* is no less intelligible a proposition, and implies no more contradiction than the affirmation, *that it will rise*. We should in vain, therefore, attempt to demonstrate its falsehood. Were it demonstratively false, it would imply a contradiction, and could never be distinctly conceived by the mind.

It may, therefore, be a subject worthy of curiosity, to enquire what is the nature of that evidence which assures us of any real existence and matter of fact, beyond the present testimony of our senses, or the records of our memory. This part of philosophy, it is observable, has been little cultivated, either by the ancients or moderns; and therefore our doubts and errors, in the prosecution of so important an enquiry, may be the more excusable; while we march through such difficult paths without any guide or direction. They may even prove useful, by exciting curiosity, and destroying that implicit faith and security, which is the bane of all reasoning and free enquiry. The discovery of defects in the common philosophy, if any such there be, will not, I presume, be a discouragement, but rather an incitement, as is usual, to attempt something more full and satisfactory than has yet been proposed to the public.

All reasonings concerning matter of fact seem to be founded on the relation of *Cause and Effect*. By means of that relation alone we can go beyond the evidence of our memory and senses. If you were to ask a man, why he believes any matter of fact, which is absent; for instance, that his friend is in the country, or in France; he would give you a reason; and this reason would be some other fact; as a letter received from him, or the knowledge of his former resolutions and promises. A man finding a watch or any other machine in a desert island, would conclude that there had once been men in that island. All our reasonings concerning fact are of the same nature. And here it is constantly supposed that there is a connexion between the present fact and that which is inferred from it. Were there nothing to bind them together, the inference would be entirely precarious. The hearing of an articulate voice and rational discourse in the dark assures us of the presence of some person: Why? because these are the effects of the human make and fabric, and closely connected with it. If we anatomize all the other reasonings of this nature, we shall find that they are founded on the relation of cause and effect, and that this relation is either near or remote, direct or collateral. Heat and light are collateral effects of fire, and the one effect may justly be inferred from the other.

If we would satisfy ourselves, therefore, concerning the nature of that evidence, which assures us of matters of fact, we must enquire how we arrive at the knowledge of cause and effect.

I shall venture to affirm, as a general proposition, which admits of no exception, that the knowledge of this relation is not, in any instance, attained by reasonings *a priori*; but arises entirely from experience, when we find that any particular objects are constantly conjoined with each other. Let an object be presented to a man of ever so strong natural reason and abilities; if that object be entirely new to him, he will not be able, by the most accurate examination of its sensible qualities, to discover any of its causes or effects. Adam, though his rational faculties be supposed, at the very first, entirely perfect, could not have inferred from the fluidity and transparency of water that it would suffocate him, or from the light and warmth of fire that it would consume him. No object ever discovers, by the qualities which appear to the senses, either the causes which produced it, or the effects which will arise from it; nor can our reason, unassisted by experience, ever draw any inference concerning real existence and matter of fact....

We fancy, that were we brought on a sudden into this world, we could at first have inferred that one Billiard-ball would communicate motion to another upon impulse; and that we needed not to have waited for the event, in order to pronounce with certainty concerning it. Such is the influence of custom, that, where it is strongest, it not only covers our natural ignorance, but even conceals itself, and seems not to take place, merely because it is found in the highest degree.

But to convince us that all the laws of nature, and all the operations of bodies without exception, are known only by experience, the following reflections may, perhaps, suffice. Were any object presented to us, and were we required to pronounce concerning the effect, which will result from it, without consulting past observation; after what manner, I beseech you, must the mind proceed in this operation? It must invent or imagine some event, which it ascribes to the object as its effect; and it is plain that this invention must be entirely arbitrary. The mind can

never possibly find the effect in the supposed cause, by the most accurate scrutiny and examination. For the effect is totally different from the cause, and consequently can never be discovered in it. Motion in the second Billiard-ball is a quite distinct event from motion in the first; nor is there anything in the one to suggest the smallest hint of the other. A stone or piece of metal raised into the air, and left without any support, immediately falls: but to consider the matter *a priori*, is there anything we discover in this situation which can beget the idea of a downward, rather than an upward, or any other motion, in the stone or metal?

And as the first imagination or invention of a particular effect, in all natural operations, is arbitrary, where we consult not experience; so must we also esteem the supposed tie or connexion between the cause and effect, which binds them together, and renders it impossible that any other effect could result from the operation of that cause. When I see, for instance, a Billiard-ball moving in a straight line towards another; even suppose motion in the second ball should by accident be suggested to me, as the result of their contact or impulse; may I not conceive, that a hundred different events might as well follow from that cause? May not both these balls remain at absolute rest? May not the first ball return in a straight line, or leap off from the second in any line or direction? All these suppositions are consistent and conceivable. Why then should we give the preference to one, which is no more consistent or conceivable than the rest? All our reasonings *a priori* will never be able to show us any foundation for this preference....

Part II

But we have not yet attained any tolerable satisfaction with regard to the question first proposed. Each solution still gives rise to a new question as difficult as the foregoing, and leads us on to farther enquiries. When it is asked, *What is the nature of all our reasonings concerning matter of fact?* the proper answer seems to be, that they are founded on the relation of cause and effect. When again it is asked, *What is the foundation of all our reasonings and conclusions concerning that relation?* it may be replied in one word, Experience. But if we still carry on our sifting humour, and ask, *What is the foundation of all conclusions from experience?* this implies a new question, which may be of more difficult solution and explication. Philosophers, that give themselves airs of superior wisdom and sufficiency, have a hard task when they encounter persons of inquisitive dispositions, who push them from every corner to which they retreat, and who are sure at last to bring them to some dangerous dilemma. The best expedient to prevent this confusion, is to be modest in our pretensions; and even to discover the difficulty ourselves before it is objected to us. By this means, we may make a kind of merit of our very ignorance.

I shall content myself, in this section, with an easy task, and shall pretend only to give a negative answer to the question here proposed. I say then, that, even after we have experience of the operations of cause and effect, our conclusions from that experience are *not* founded on reasoning, or any process of the understanding. This answer we must endeavour both to explain and to defend.

It must certainly be allowed, that nature has kept us at a great distance from all her secrets, and has afforded us only the knowledge of a few superficial qualities of objects; while she conceals from us those powers and principles on which the influence of those objects entirely depends. Our senses inform us of the colour, weight, and consistence of bread; but neither sense nor reason can ever inform us of those qualities which fit it for the nourishment and support of a human body. Sight or feeling conveys an idea of the actual motion of bodies; but as to that wonderful force or power, which would carry on a moving body for ever in a continued change of place, and which bodies never lose but by communicating it to others; of this we cannot form the most distant conception. But notwithstanding this ignorance of natural powers and principles, we always presume, when we see like sensible qualities, that they have like secret powers, and expect that effects, similar to those which we have experienced, will follow from them. If a body of like colour and consistence with that bread, which we have formerly [eaten], be presented to us, we make no scruple of repeating the experiment, and foresee, with certainty, like nourishment and support. Now this is a process of the mind or thought, of which I would willingly know the foundation. It is allowed on all hands that there is no known connexion between the sensible qualities and the secret powers; and consequently, that the mind is not led to form such a conclusion concerning their constant and regular conjunction, by anything which it knows of their nature. As to past *Experience*, it can be allowed to give *direct* and *certain* information of those precise objects only, and that precise period of time, which fell under its cognizance: but why this experience should be extended to future times, and to other objects, which for aught we know, may be only in appearance similar; this is the main question on which I would insist. The bread, which I formerly [ate], nourished me; that is, a body of such sensible qualities was, at that time, endued with such secret powers: but does it follow, that other bread must also nourish me at another time, and that like sensible qualities must always be attended with like secret powers? The consequence seems nowise necessary. At least, it must be acknowledged that there is here a consequence drawn by the mind; that there is a certain step taken; a process of thought, and an inference, which wants to be explained. These two propositions are far from being the same, *I have found that such an object has always been attended with such an effect*, and *I foresee, that other objects, which are, in appearance, similar, will be attended with similar effects*. I shall allow, if you please, that the one proposition may justly be inferred from the other: I know, in fact, that it always is inferred. But if you insist that the inference is made by a chain of reasoning, I desire you to produce that reasoning. The connexion between these propositions is not intuitive. There is required a medium, which may enable the mind to draw such an inference, if indeed it be drawn by reasoning and argument. What that medium is, I must confess, passes my comprehension; and it is incumbent on those to produce it, who assert that it really exists; and is the origin of all our conclusions concerning matter of fact.

This negative argument must certainly, in process of time, become altogether convincing, if many penetrating and able philosophers shall turn their enquiries this way and no one be ever able to discover any connecting proposition or intermediate step, which supports the understanding in this conclusion. But as the question is yet new, every reader may not trust so far to his own penetration, as to conclude, because an argument escapes his enquiry, that therefore it does not really exist. For this reason it may be requisite to venture upon a more difficult task; and enumerating all the branches of human knowledge, endeavour to show that none of them can afford such an argument.

All reasonings may be divided into two kinds, namely, demonstrative reasoning, or that concerning relations of ideas, and moral reasoning, or that concerning matter of fact and existence. That there are no demonstrative arguments in the case seems evident; since it implies no contradiction that the course of nature may change, and that an object, seemingly like those which we have experienced, may be attended with different or contrary effects. May I not clearly and distinctly conceive that a body, falling from the clouds, and which, in all other respects, resembles snow, has yet the taste of salt or feeling of fire? Is there any more intelligible proposition than to affirm, that all the trees will flourish in December and January, and decay in May and June? Now whatever is intelligible, and can be distinctly conceived, implies no contradiction, and can never be proved false by any demonstrative argument or abstract reasoning *a priori*.

If we be, therefore, engaged by arguments to put trust in past experience, and make it the standard of our future judgment, these arguments must be probable only, or such as regard matter of fact and real existence, according to the division above mentioned. But that there is no argument of this kind, must appear, if our explication of that

species of reasoning be admitted as solid and satisfactory. We have said that all arguments concerning existence are founded on the relation of cause and effect; that our knowledge of that relation is derived entirely from experience; and that all our experimental conclusions proceed upon the supposition that the future will be conformable to the past. To endeavour, therefore, the proof of this last supposition by probable arguments, or arguments regarding existence, must be evidently going in a circle, and taking that for granted, which is the very point in question.

In reality, all arguments from experience are founded on the similarity which we discover among natural objects, and by which we are induced to expect effects similar to those which we have found to follow from such objects. And though none but a fool or madman will ever pretend to dispute the authority of experience, or to reject that great guide of human life, it may surely be allowed a philosopher to have so much curiosity at least as to examine the principle of human nature, which gives this mighty authority to experience, and makes us draw advantage from that similarity which nature has placed among different objects. From causes which appear similar we expect similar effects. This is the sum of all our experimental conclusions. Now it seems evident that, if this conclusion were formed by reason, it would be as perfect at first, and upon one instance, as after ever so long a course of experience. But the case is far otherwise. Nothing so like as eggs; yet no one, on account of this appearing similarity, expects the same taste and relish in all of them. It is only after a long course of uniform experiments in any kind, that we attain a firm reliance and security with regard to a particular event. Now where is that process of reasoning which, from one instance, draws a conclusion, so different from that which it infers from a hundred instances that are nowise different from that single one? This question I propose as much for the sake of information, as with an intention of raising difficulties. I cannot find, I cannot imagine any such reasoning. But I keep my mind still open to instruction, if any one will vouchsafe to bestow it on me.

CRITICAL QUESTIONS

1. Hume presented two arguments to prove "all our ideas ... are copies of our impressions." State these arguments in your own words. Are these arguments convincing? Why, or why not?

2. In answer to the question "What is the foundation of all conclusions from experience?" Hume challenged the reader to supply the foundation for the inference from the fact that I have found objects (like bread) to produce certain effects (like nourishment) in the past to the conclusion that the same will occur in the future. Can you supply the basis for the connection or inference between these two statements? If so, what is it?

3. How do you think Hume would have answered the question, "Is knowledge possible?" How would his answer differ from the answers given by al-Ghazali and Descartes? Which of these answers do think is better and why?

8.5 SHOULD WE BELIEVE BEYOND THE EVIDENCE?

Should you believe something to be true even though you have insufficient evidence that it is true? Do you have a moral obligation to refrain from believing something true or false if the available evidence is not sufficient? Suppose you loan your old car to a friend. You have not checked the brakes in some time, but you dismiss all doubts about the brakes from your mind, confident that they will work because they have in the past. Suppose your friend crashes and dies due to faulty brakes. Are you to blame? Suppose your friend does not crash and die. Are you to blame for putting her life in danger? According to William K. Clifford (1845–1879), if you do not have sufficient evidence that the brakes are in working order, then you are to blame no matter what happens.

Clifford, a British mathematician interested in philosophical and religious topics, wrote an essay entitled "The Ethics of Belief." Clifford's argument reflects an epistemological position called evidentialism. **Evidentialism** holds that we should not accept any statement as true unless we have good evidence to support its truth. Our beliefs about the truth of things—be they moral, religious, or scientific beliefs—must meet appropriate epistemic standards. *Practical* standards, such as aiding me in accomplishing certain goals or possibly resulting in my eternal happiness, will not do. William James (1842–1910), an American philosopher, wrote a famous essay in reply to Clifford, called "The Will to Believe." James advocated a philosophy called **pragmatism** (see Sections 7.2 and 9.2).

James characterized pragmatism (from the Greek word *pragma*, meaning "action") as a method for settling philosophical disputes. This method was based on a distinctive theory of truth, called the pragmatic theory of truth. According to this theory, some proposition p is true if and only if the belief that "p is true" works.

"And what does *works* mean?" you ask. James used words like *useful, adaptive, serviceable, satisfying, verifiable,* and *agreeing with reality* to try to explain what it means. He also asserted that for any proposition to "work" and hence to be taken as true, it must be consistent with what we already take to be true, and it must be in agreement with our sense experience. Thus, my belief that "my fat, blind cat is on the rug by the fire" works as long as it is consistent with my other beliefs (he is not outside, he is not in the kitchen eating my dinner, he is not in the pool practicing his backstroke, etc.), and when I look at the rug I get "fat-blind-cat"-type sensations.

We can grasp James's theory better by contrasting it with two other theories of truth, both of which derive from Plato. They have been the two dominant theories of truth in Western thought. The first is called the **correspondence theory of truth**. According to this theory, p is true if and only if p corresponds to the facts. My believing p to be true or false has nothing to do with the matter of its truth, or so this theory would maintain. "My cat is on the rug" is true if, indeed, that is where the cat is and is false if the cat is not there. Even if I don't look and no matter how I feel or what I believe, it is true or false independent of my actions or beliefs.

The second theory of truth is called the **coherence theory of truth**. According to this view, p is true if and only if p is logically implied by q, where q is a true statement, and q in turn is logically implied by r, and so on. Truth, on this account, is the coherence of a whole system of statements in which each statement is entailed by all the others. We have only fragments of this whole, but when and if we ever discover the entire system, we will have arrived at absolute truth. Thus, "My fat, blind cat is on the rug" is true if a whole host of other propositions are true such as "My cat is blind," "The rug exists," "Cats exist," and so on.

James ascribed both the correspondence and coherence theories to philosophers he called "intellectualists and rationalists." He objected to these theories on the grounds that they present truth as a static property existing prior to and independent of human experience and investigation. James saw truth as something dynamic, something that happens to ideas when they lead humans into ever more satisfactory experiences. The rationalists accused James, in turn, of denying objectivity, reducing truth to a matter of what we want to believe, and making it relative to the context in which we verify propositions.

From James's point of view, Clifford's argument rests in part on a reliance on a static theory of truth, which too narrowly confines our thinking. His insistence on purely epistemic standards, and his refusal to admit practical standards, not only denies the facts involved in how humans come to hold many of their beliefs, but also restricts us to a very narrow range of beliefs and forbids us to have beliefs about some of the most important matters that make human life worth living.

What follows are selections from both Clifford's essay and James's. Read their arguments and decide for yourself whether we have a right to believe beyond the evidence.

⊚ READING QUESTIONS

1. What do the examples of the shipowner and the commission show?
2. Summarize Clifford's argument in your own words.
3. What, according to James, is a genuine option? Give an example.
4. What is James's thesis?
5. How, according to James, does Clifford's attitude differ from James's with respect to "our first and great commandments as would-be knowers"?

The Ethics of Belief

WILLIAM K. CLIFFORD

A shipowner was about to send to sea an emigrant-ship. He knew that she was old, and not over-well built at the first; that she had seen many seas and climes, and often had needed repairs. Doubts had been suggested to him that possibly she was not seaworthy. These doubts preyed upon his mind, and made him unhappy; he thought that perhaps he ought to have her thoroughly

From *Lectures and Essays*, Vol. 2 (London: Macmillan, 1897), pp. 177–188. Footnotes deleted.

overhauled and refitted, even though this should put him to great expense. Before the ship sailed, however, he succeeded in overcoming these melancholy reflections. He said to himself that she had gone safely through so many voyages and weathered so many storms that it was idle to suppose she would not come safely home from this trip also. He would put his trust in providence, which could hardly fail to protect all these unhappy families that were leaving their fatherland to seek for better times elsewhere. He would dismiss from his mind all ungenerous suspicions about the honesty of builders and contractors. In such ways he acquired a sincere and comfortable conviction that his vessel was thoroughly safe and seaworthy; he watched her departure with a light heart, and benevolent wishes for the success of the exiles in their strange new home that was to be; and he got his insurance-money when she went down in mid-ocean and told no tales.

What shall we say of him? Surely this, that he was verily guilty of the death of those men. It is admitted that he did sincerely believe in the soundness of his ship; but the sincerity of his conviction can in no wise help him, because *he had no right to believe on such evidence as was before him*. He had acquired his belief not by honestly earning it in patient investigation, but by stifling his doubts. And although in the end he may have felt so sure about it that he could not think otherwise, yet inasmuch as he had knowingly and willingly worked himself into that frame of mind, he must be held responsible for it.

Let us alter the case a little, and suppose that the ship was not unsound after all; that she made her voyage safely, and many others after it. Will that diminish the guilt of her owner? Not one jot. When an action is once done, it is right or wrong for ever; no accidental failure of its good or evil fruits can possibly alter that. The man would not have been innocent, he would only have been not found out. The question of right or wrong has to do with the origin of his belief, not the matter of it; not what it was, but how he got it; not whether it turned out to be true or false, but whether he had a right to believe on such evidence as was before him.

There was once an island in which some of the inhabitants professed a religion teaching neither the doctrine of original sin nor that of eternal punishment. A suspicion got abroad that the professors of this religion had made use of unfair means to get their doctrines taught to children. They were accused of wresting the laws of their country in such a way as to remove children from the care of their natural and legal guardians; and even of stealing them away and keeping them concealed from their friends and relations. A certain number of men formed themselves into a society for the purpose of agitating the public about this matter. They published grave accusations against individual citizens of the highest position and character, and did all in their power to injure these citizens in the exercise of their professions. So great was the noise they made, that a Commission was appointed to investigate the facts; but after the Commission had carefully inquired into all the evidence that could be got, it appeared that the accused were innocent. Not only had they been accused on insufficient evidence, but the evidence of their innocence was such as the agitators might easily have obtained, if they had attempted a fair inquiry. After these disclosures the inhabitants of that country looked upon the members of the agitating society, not only as persons whose judgment was to be distrusted, but also as no longer to be counted honourable men. For although they had sincerely and conscientiously believed in the charges they had made, yet *they had no right to believe on such evidence as was before them*. Their sincere convictions, instead of being honestly earned by patient inquiring, were stolen by listening to the voice of prejudice and passion.

Let us vary this case also, and suppose, other things remaining as before, that a still more accurate investigation proved the accused to have been really guilty. Would this make any difference in the guilt of the accusers? Clearly not; the question is not whether their belief was true or false, but whether they entertained it on wrong grounds....

In the two supposed cases which have been considered, it has been judged wrong to believe on insufficient evidence, or to nourish belief by suppressing doubts and avoiding investigation. The reason of this judgment is not far to seek: it is that in both these cases the belief held by one man was of great importance to other men. But forasmuch as no belief held by one man, however seemingly trivial the belief, and however obscure the believer, is ever actually insignificant or without its effect on the fate of mankind, we have no choice but to extend our judgment to all cases of belief whatever....

It is not only the leader of men, statesman, philosopher, or poet, that owes this bounden duty to mankind. Every rustic who delivers in the village alehouse his slow, infrequent sentences, may help to kill or keep alive the fatal superstitions which clog his race. Every hard-worked wife of an artisan may transmit to her children beliefs which shall knit society together, or rend it in pieces. No simplicity of mind, no obscurity of station, can escape the universal duty of questioning all that we believe....

The harm which is done by credulity in a man is not confined to the fostering of a credulous character in others, and consequent support of false beliefs. Habitual want of care about what I believe leads to habitual want of care in others

about the truth of what is told to me. Men speak the truth to one another when each reveres the truth in his own mind and in the other's mind; but how shall my friend revere the truth in my mind when I myself am careless about it, when I believe things because I want to believe them, and because they are comforting and pleasant? Will he not learn to cry, "Peace," to me, when there is no peace? By such a course I shall surround myself with a thick atmosphere of falsehood and fraud, and in that I must live. It may matter little to me, in my cloud-castle of sweet illusions and darling lies; but it matters much to Man that I have made my neighbours ready to deceive. The credulous man is father to the liar and the cheat; he lives in the bosom of this his family, and it is no marvel if he should become even as they are. So closely are our duties knit together, that whoso shall keep the whole law, and yet offend in one point, he is guilty of all.

To sum up: it is wrong always, everywhere, and for anyone, to believe anything upon insufficient evidence....

The Will to Believe

WILLIAM JAMES

Let us give the name of *hypothesis* to anything that may be proposed to our belief; and just as the electricians speak of *live* and *dead* wires, let us speak of any hypothesis as either live or dead. A live hypothesis is one which appeals as a real possibility to him to whom it is proposed. If I ask you to believe in the Mahdi, the notion makes no electric connection with your nature—it refuses to scintillate with any credibility at all. As an hypothesis it is completely dead. To an Arab, however (even if he be not one of the Mahdi's followers), the hypothesis is among the mind's possibilities: it is alive. This shows that deadness and liveness in an hypothesis are

not intrinsic properties, but relations to the individual thinker. They are measured by his willingness to act. The maximum of liveness in an hypothesis means willingness to act irrevocably. Practically, that means belief; but there is some believing tendency wherever there is willingness to act at all.

Next, let us call the decision between two hypotheses an *option.* Options may be of several kinds. They may be—1, *living or dead;* 2, *forced or avoidable;* 3, *momentous or trivial;* and for our purposes we may call an option a *genuine* option when it is of the forced, living and momentous kind.

From William James, *The Will to Believe and Other Essays in Popular Philosophy* (New York: Henry Holt, 1912), pp. 1–31.

1. A living option is one in which both hypotheses are live ones. If I say to you: "Be a theosophist or be a mahomedan," it is probably a dead option, because for you neither hypothesis is likely to be alive. But if I say "Be an agnostic or be a Christian," it is otherwise: trained as you are, each hypothesis makes some appeal, however small, to your belief.
2. Next, if I say to you: "Choose between going out with your umbrella or without it," I do not offer you a genuine option, for it is not forced. You can easily avoid it by not going out at all. Similarly, if I say "Either love me or hate me," "Either call my theory true or call it false," your option is avoidable. You may remain indifferent to me, neither loving nor hating, and you may decline to offer any judgment as to my theory. But if I say "Either accept this truth or go without it," I put on you a forced option, for there is no standing place outside of the alternative. Every dilemma based on a complete logical disjunction, with no possibility of not choosing, is an option of this forced kind.
3. Finally, if I were Dr. Nansen[1] and proposed to you to join my North Pole expedition, your option would be momentous; for this would probably be your only similar opportunity, and your choice now would either exclude you from the North Pole sort of immortality altogether or put at least the chance of it into your hands. He who refuses to embrace a unique opportunity loses the prize as surely as if he tried and failed. *Per contra*, the option is trivial when the opportunity is not unique, when the stake is insignificant, or when the decision is reversible if it later prove[s] unwise. Such trivial options abound in the scientific life. A chemist finds an hypothesis live enough to spend a year in its verification: he believes in it to that extent. But if his

experiments prove inconclusive either way, he is quit for his loss of time, no vital harm being done....

The thesis I defend is, briefly stated, this: *Our passional nature not only lawfully may, but must, decide an option between propositions, whenever it is a genuine option that cannot by its nature be decided on intellectual grounds; for to say, under such circumstances, "Do not decide, but leave the question open," is itself a passional decision—just like deciding yes or no—and is attended with the same risk of losing the truth....*

There are two ways of looking at our duty in the matter of opinion—ways entirely different, and yet ways about whose difference the theory of knowledge seems hitherto to have shown very little concern. *We must know the truth; and we must avoid error*—these are our first and great commandments as would-be knowers; but they are not two ways of stating an identical commandment, they are two separable laws. Although it may indeed happen that when we believe the truth A, we escape as an incidental consequence from believing the falsehood B, it hardly ever happens that by merely disbelieving B we necessarily believe A. We may in escaping B fall into believing other falsehoods, C or D, just as bad as B; or we may escape B by not believing anything at all, not even A.

Believe truth! Shun error!—these, we see, are two materially different laws; and by choosing between them we may end by colouring differently our whole intellectual life. We may regard the chase for truth as paramount, and the avoidance of error as secondary; or we may, on the other hand, treat the avoidance of error as more imperative, and let truth take its chance. Clifford ... exhorts us to the latter course. Believe nothing, he tells us, keep your mind in suspense forever, rather than by closing it on insufficient evidence incur the awful risk of believing lies. You, on the other hand, may think that the risk of being in error is a very small matter when compared with the blessings of real knowledge, and be ready to be duped many times in your investigation rather than postpone indefinitely the chance of guessing true. I myself find it impossible to go with Clifford. We must remember that these feelings of our duty about either truth or error are

---

[1]Dr. Fridtjof Nansen (1861–1930) was a Norwegian explorer, scientist, and Nobel Laureate who led a famous North Pole expedition in 1893–96. [Ed.]

in any case only expressions of our passional life. Biologically considered, our minds are as ready to grind out falsehood as veracity, and he who says "Better go without belief forever than believe a lie!" merely shows his own preponderant private horror of becoming a dupe. He may be critical of many of his desires and fears, but this fear he slavishly obeys. He cannot imagine anyone questioning its binding force. For my own part, I have also a horror of being duped; but I can believe that worse things than being duped may happen to a man in this world: so Clifford's exhortation has to my ears a thoroughly fantastic sound. It is like a general informing his soldiers that it is better to keep out of battle forever than to risk a single wound. Not so are victories either over enemies or over nature gained. Our errors are surely not such awfully solemn things. In a world where we are so certain to incur them in spite of all our caution, a certain lightness of heart seems healthier than this excessive nervousness on their behalf....

Wherever the option between losing truth and gaining it is not momentous, we can throw the chance of *gaining truth* away, and at any rate save ourselves from any chance of *believing falsehood*, by not making up our minds at all till objective evidence has come. In scientific questions, this is almost always the case; and even in human affairs in general, the need of acting is seldom so urgent that a false belief to act on is better than no belief at all. Law courts, indeed, have to decide on the best evidence attainable for the moment, because a judge's duty is to make law as well as to ascertain it, and (as a learned judge once said to me) few cases are worth spending much time over: the great thing is to have them decided on *any* acceptable principle, and got out of the way. But in our dealings with objective nature we obviously are recorders, not makers, of the truth; and decisions for the mere sake of deciding promptly and getting on to the next business would be wholly out of place. Throughout the breadth of physical nature facts are what they are quite independently of us, and seldom is there any such hurry about them that the risks of being duped by believing a premature theory need be faced. The questions here are always trivial options, the hypotheses are hardly living (at any rate not living for us

spectators), the choice between believing truth or falsehood is seldom forced. The attitude of sceptical balance is therefore the absolutely wise one if we would escape mistakes....

[But] are there not somewhere forced options in our speculative questions, and can we (as men who may be interested at least as much in positively gaining truth as in merely escaping dupery) always wait with impunity till the coercive evidence shall have arrived?...

Moral questions immediately present themselves as questions whose solution cannot wait for sensible proof. A moral question is a question not of what sensibly exists, but of what is good, or would be good if it did exist. Science can tell us what exists; but to compare the *worths*, both of what exists and of what does not exist, we must consult not science, but what Pascal calls our heart. Science herself consults her heart when she lays it down that the infinite ascertainment of fact and correction of false belief are the supreme goods for man. Challenge the statement and science can only repeat it oracularly, or else prove it by showing that such ascertainment and correction bring man all sorts of other goods which man's heart in turn declares. The question of having moral beliefs at all or not having them is decided by our will. Are our moral preferences true or false, or are they only odd biological phenomena, making things good or bad for *us*, but in themselves indifferent? How can your pure intellect decide? If your heart does not *want* a world of moral reality, your head will assuredly never make you believe in one....

Turn now from these wide questions of good to a certain class of questions of fact, questions concerning personal relations, states of mind between one man and another. *Do you like me or not?*—for example. Whether you do or not depends, in countless instances, on whether I meet you half-way, am willing to assume that you must like me, and show you trust and expectation. The previous faith on my part in your liking's existence is in such cases what makes your liking come. But if I stand aloof, and refuse to budge an inch until I have objective evidence, ... ten to one your liking never comes. How many women's hearts are vanquished by the mere sanguine insistence of some man that they *must* love him! [H]e will not consent to the hypothesis that they cannot. The desire for a certain kind of truth here brings about that special truth's existence; and so it is in innumerable cases of other sorts. Who gains promotions, boons, appointments, but the man in whose life they are seen to play the part of live hypotheses, who discounts them, sacrifices other things for their sake before they have come, and takes risks for them in advance? His faith acts on the powers above him as a claim, and creates its own verification.

A social organism of any sort whatever, large or small, is what it is because each member proceeds to his own duty with a trust that the other members will simultaneously do theirs. Wherever a desired result is achieved by the co-operation of many independent persons, its existence as a fact is a pure consequence of the precursive faith in one another of those immediately concerned. A government, an army, a commercial system, a ship, a college, an athletic team, all exist on this condition, without which not only is nothing achieved, but nothing is even attempted. A whole train of passengers (individually brave enough) will be looted by a few highwaymen, simply because the latter can count on one another, while each passenger fears that if he makes a movement of resistance, he will be shot before anyone else backs him up. If we believed that the whole car-full would rise at once with us, we should each severally rise, and train-robbing would never even be attempted. There are, then, cases where a fact cannot come at all unless a preliminary faith exists in its coming. *And where faith in a fact can help create the fact*, that would be an insane logic which should say that faith running ahead of scientific evidence is the "lowest kind of immorality" into which a thinking being can fall. Yet such is the logic by which our scientific absolutists pretend to regulate our lives!

In truths dependent on our personal action, then, faith based on desire is certainly a lawful and possibly an indispensable thing.

But now, it will be said, these are all childish human cases, and have nothing to do with great cosmical matters, like the question of religious faith. Let us then pass on to that. Religions differ so much in their accidents that in discussing the religious question we must make it very generic and broad. What then do we now mean by the religious hypothesis? Science says things are; morality says some things are better than other things; and religion says essentially two things.

First, she says that the best things are the most eternal things, the overlapping things, the things in the universe that throw the last stone, so to speak, and say the final word. "Perfection is eternal"—this phrase of Charles Secrétan seems a good way of putting this first affirmation of religion, an affirmation which obviously cannot yet be verified scientifically at all.

The second affirmation of religion is that we are better off even now if we believe her first affirmation to be true.

Now let us consider what the logical elements of this situation *are in case the religious hypothesis in both its branches be really true.* (Of course, we must admit that possibility at the outset. If we are to discuss the question at all, it must involve a living option. If for any of you religion be a hypothesis that cannot, by any living possibility be true, then you need go no farther. I speak to the "saving remnant" alone.) So proceeding, we see, first, that religion offers itself as a *momentous* option. We are supposed to gain, even now, by our belief, and to lose by our non-belief, a certain vital good. Secondly, religion is a *forced* option, so far as that good goes. We cannot escape the issue by remaining sceptical and waiting for more light, because, although we do avoid error in that way *if religion be untrue*, we lose the good, *if it be true*, just as certainly as if we positively chose to disbelieve. It is as if a man should hesitate indefinitely to ask a certain woman to marry him because he was not perfectly sure that she would prove an angel after he brought her home. Would he not cut himself off from that particular angel-possibility as decisively as if he went and married someone else? Scepticism, then, is not avoidance of option; it is option of a certain particular kind of risk. *Better risk loss of truth than chance of error*— that is your faith-vetoer's exact position. He is actively playing his stake as much as the believer is; he is backing the field against the religious hypothesis, just as the believer is backing the religious hypothesis against the field. To preach scepticism to us as a duty until "sufficient evidence" for religion be found, is tantamount therefore to telling us, when in presence of the religious hypothesis, that to yield to our fear of its being error is wiser and better than to yield to our hope that it may be true. It is not intellect against all passions, then; it is only intellect with one passion laying down its law. And by what, forsooth, is the supreme wisdom of this passion warranted? Dupery for dupery, what proof is there that dupery through hope is so much worse than dupery through fear? I, for one, can see no proof; and I simply refuse obedience to the scientist's command to imitate his kind of option, in a case where my own stake is important enough to give me the right to choose my own form of risk. If religion be true and the evidence for it be still insufficient, I do not wish, by putting your extinguisher upon my nature (which feels to me as if it had after all some business in this matter), to forfeit my sole chance in life of getting upon the winning side—that chance depending, of course, on my willingness to run the risk of acting as if my passional need of taking the world religiously might be prophetic and right.

All this is on the supposition that it really may be prophetic and right, and that, even to us who are discussing the matter, religion is a live hypothesis which may be true. Now to most of us religion comes in a still farther way that makes a veto on our active faith even more illogical. The more perfect and more eternal aspect of the universe is represented in our religions as having personal form. The universe is no longer a mere *It* to us, but a *Thou*, if we are religious; and any relation that may be possible from person to person might be possible here. For instance, although in one sense we are passive portions of the universe, in another we show a curious autonomy, as if we were small active centres on our own account. We feel, too, as if the appeal of religion to us were made to our own active good-will, as if evidence might be forever withheld from us unless we met the hypothesis half-way. To take a trivial illustration: just as a man who in a company of gentlemen made no advances, asked a warrant for every concession, and believed no one's word without proof, would cut himself off by such churlishness from all the social rewards that a more trusting spirit would

earn—so here, one who should shut himself up in snarling logicality and try to make the gods extort his recognition willy-nilly, or not get it at all, might cut himself off forever from his only opportunity of making the gods' acquaintance. This feeling, forced on us we know not whence, that by obstinately believing that there are gods (although not to do so would be so easy both for our logic and our life) we are doing the universe the deepest service we can, seems part of the living essence of the religious hypothesis. If the hypothesis were true in all its parts, including this one, then pure intellectualism, with its veto on our making willing advances, would be an absurdity; and some participation of our sympathetic nature would be logically required. I, therefore, for one, cannot see my way to accepting the agnostic rules for truth-seeking, or wilfully agree to keep my willing nature out of the game. I cannot do so for this plain reason, that *a rule of thinking which would absolutely prevent me from acknowledging certain kinds of truth if those kinds of truth were really there, would be an irrational rule.* That for me is the long and short of the formal logic of the situation, no matter what the kinds of truth might materially be.

I confess I do not see how this logic can be escaped. But sad experience makes me fear that some of you may still shrink from radically saying with me, *in abstracto*, that we have the right to believe at our own risk any hypothesis that is live enough to tempt our will. I suspect, however, that if this is so, it is because you have got away from the abstract logical point of view altogether, and are thinking (perhaps without realizing it) of some particular religious hypothesis which for you is dead. The freedom to "believe what we will" you apply to the case of some patent superstition; and the faith you think of is the faith defined by the schoolboy when he said, "Faith is when you believe something that you know ain't true." I can only repeat that this is misapprehension. *In concreto*, the freedom to believe can only cover living options which the intellect of the individual cannot by itself resolve; and living options never seem absurdities to him who has them to consider. When I look at the religious question as it really puts itself to concrete men, and when I think of all the possibilities which both practically and theoretically it involves, then this command that we shall put a stopper on our heart, instincts and courage, and *wait*—acting of course meanwhile more or less as if religion were *not* true—till doomsday, or till such time as our intellect and senses working together may have raked in evidence enough—this command, I say, seems to me the queerest idol ever manufactured in the philosophic cave. Were we scholastic absolutists, there might be more excuse. If we had an infallible intellect with its objective certitudes, we might feel ourselves disloyal to such a perfect organ of knowledge in not trusting to it exclusively, in not waiting for its releasing word. But if we are empiricists, if we believe that no bell in us tolls to let us know for certain when truth is in our grasp, then it seems a piece of idle fantasticality to preach so solemnly our duty of waiting for the bell. Indeed we *may* wait if we will—I hope you do not think that I am denying that—but if we do so, we do so at our peril as much as if we believed. In either case we *act*, taking our life in our hands. No one of us ought to issue vetoes to the other, nor should we bandy words of abuse. We ought, on the contrary, delicately and profoundly to respect one another's mental freedom—then only shall we bring about the intellectual republic; then only shall we have that spirit of inner tolerance without which all our outer tolerance is soulless, and which is empiricism's glory; then only shall we live and let live, in speculative as well as in practical things....

CRITICAL QUESTIONS

1. Do you agree with Clifford's contention that all of us have a duty to question our beliefs? Why, or why not?
2. Do you think that Clifford's claim that it is "wrong always, everywhere, and for anyone, to believe anything upon insufficient evidence" is true? Why, or why not?
3. What do you think Clifford meant by "sufficient evidence"? How much evidence is sufficient?
4. How did James support his own attitude? What examples did he use? Do his examples support his thesis? Why, or why not?
5. Who do you think is right, Clifford or James? Why?

8.6 CLASSICAL INDIAN EPISTEMOLOGY

Some people think of Indian philosophy as "spiritual" and unconcerned with technical issues relating to truth and knowledge. Popular culture associates India with mysticism, meditation, and religion. Students often study about India in religious studies courses but seldom in philosophy classes.

This picture of Indian thought as spiritual is misleading. Among the various schools of Indian philosophy, careful attention is given to logical and epistemological issues. For example, Udayana, an Indian philosopher who lived about 1000, combined two previous schools of philosophy, the Vaisesika and the **Nyaya** ("nyah-yah") schools, into what is usually called **Naiyayika**. This philosophic school advanced an epistemological theory (first developed in Nyaya philosophy) that influenced much of Indian philosophy. According to this theory, the correct causes of knowledge (called *pramanas*) can be analyzed into four kinds: perception, inference, comparison (analogy), and reliable testimony.

According to Nyaya, the concept of knowledge can be analyzed into four different parts. The selection that follows concentrates primarily on the fourth component, "the means whereby the object comes to be known." The author, John M. Koller, professor of Asian and Comparative Philosophy at the Rensselaer Polytechnic Institute, guides us through the complexities of the Nyaya theory. If you have ever wondered about the sources of knowledge, this selection should stimulate further thought. There are some surprises.

1. What is the principle for distinguishing among the various means of knowledge?
2. How can genuine perceptions be distinguished from perceptual mistakes?
3. What is the sixth kind of perceptual knowledge, and why do you think it is more important than the other five kinds?
4. What is inference, and how does it work?

Knowledge and Reality

JOHN M. KOLLER

As we have seen, the Upanishads emphasize the ultimate nature of reality as the identity of *Atman* and *Brahman*, while Samkhya emphasizes the dualistic nature of reality in order to explain both our experience of the ordinary world and the experience of the ultimate Self, the *purusha*. The Nyaya tradition, however, focuses on the nature of knowledge, asking, What is knowledge? and What are the valid means of knowledge? Vaisheshika is a tradition closely linked to Nyaya. It borrows the Nyaya theory of knowledge and goes on to ask, What exists? In answering this question, it develops an atomistic view of existence, a view of existence adopted also by Nyaya.

THE PROBLEM OF KNOWLEDGE

The basic problem of knowledge is that of ascertaining whether or not what is claimed as knowledge is actually knowledge, rather than just mistaken opinion. Mistakes are easily made in matters of perception and inference. For instance, in dim light, a discarded rope appears to be a snake; it could cause someone to claim knowledge of a snake on the path. But if there were only a rope on the path, obviously no one could have *knowledge* of a snake on the path. As examples such as this are considered, it becomes possible to speculate that perhaps what appears to us is always different from what is really there. It might be that the eyes always present things as

red, yellow, and blue, whereas all things are really orange, black, and green. It might be that the ear presents sounds differently from what they really are, and that the other senses equally distort the reality with which they come in contact. Skeptical considerations of this sort push philosophers in the direction of trying to analyze what knowledge is and when it can be claimed to be valid.

In Nyaya, the analysis of knowledge is taken up in terms of the knowing subject, the object to be known, the known object, and the means of coming to know the object. Analysis of claims to knowledge reveals that these four factors are involved in all knowledge, for there is no knowledge except when someone knows something. The one who knows is the subject; the something known is the object. The object is either the object to be known or the object that is known. The whole point of coming to know things is to pass from ignorance, in which case the subject is separated from the object, to knowledge, in which case the subject, by various means, comes to be related to the object in certain ways. These relations constitute knowledge of the object. Consequently, anyone wishing to come to an understanding of what knowledge is must inquire into these four topics: (1) the knowing subject, (2) the object to be known, (3) the object as known, and (4) the means of knowledge whereby the object comes to be known.

From *Asian Philosophies*, 4th Edition by John M. Koller (Upper Saddle River, NJ: Pearson Education, Inc.), pp. 67–73. © 2002 Pearson Education, Inc.

THE MEANS OF KNOWLEDGE

According to Nyaya, the main characteristic of knowledge is that it illumines and reveals what exists. If we had no eyes to illumine and reveal the green grass, we would not know that it exists or that it is green. The means of knowledge are distinguished according to the different causes responsible for the revelation of the object in knowledge. This principle of distinction yields perception, inference, analogy, and testimony as the four basic means, or sources, of knowledge. The reason for distinguishing between these sources is that a person is doing four basically different things in coming to know something in each of the different ways. We begin our discussion of the Nyaya theory of knowledge with an analysis of these four valid means of knowledge, showing how they constitute different ways of knowing.

Perceptual Knowledge

Perceptual knowledge is defined as the true and determinate knowledge arising from the contact of the senses with their proper objects. It is known, by means of perception, that these words appear on a piece of paper because of the contact of the eyes with the words. If one were a considerable distance from the paper and perceived only dark spots on the paper, it would not be a genuine case of perception, for the object perceived would not be determinate. If one were to mistake these words for logic symbols, this would not be a case of genuine perception either, for it would not be true knowledge, since there were no symbols there to be perceived.

Even in the case of mistaken perception, an external object is actually perceived, though it is wrongly identified as something other than what it really is. If the words on this page are mistaken for symbols, the ink marks that constitute the words are actually perceived, though they are mistaken for symbols. Unless the senses made contact with an external object, there would be nothing revealed. To assume that perception can occur without perceiving an external object is to assume that the perceptive act creates the object, rather than revealing it. If the senses created their objects, rather than revealing them, asks Nyaya,

how could mistaken perceptions be detected or corrected? There would be no external object to which the perceptions could be compared.

But how can genuine perceptions be distinguished from perceptual mistakes? The Nyaya explanation of this point rests on a distinction between two kinds of perception. Determinate perception—perception of words on this paper—is preceded by the indeterminate perception of sense contact with the marks on the paper prior to the recognition and classification of them as words. To talk about a perceptual mistake in reference to the indeterminate perception does not make any sense, for nothing is taken to be anything, and therefore it cannot be taken for something other than what it is. Indeterminate perception is simply the contact of the sense with its object. It is the most elementary sensory experience, limited to precisely what is given by sense contact. Since it is not determinate, mere sensory contact is not classified as perceptual knowledge.

Perceptual knowledge requires determinate perception in which the basic sensory experience of the indeterminate perception is determined to be some kind of thing with various qualities and relations. Determinate perception is, in principle, nameable. Thus, a distinction is made between an immediate sensory experience and perception, though the latter always includes the former. Consequently, there is also a distinction between ignorance and error.

Ignorance may be due either to a lack of the immediate sensory experience or to a lack of determinate perception. Error, on the other hand, results from mistaking what is given in immediate sensory experience for something other than what it is. In terms of the example of erroneously perceiving a snake instead of a rope, the immediate sensory experience reveals a dark-colored, elongated, and twisted shape. But in perception, this content of sensory experience is seen as a snake when it is, in fact, a rope. The result is the erroneous claim that a snake has been seen. From this it is evident that true perceptual knowledge is the perception of what is perceived as it really is, and error is the perception of something as other than what it really is.

But now the question may be raised as to how a particular perceptual judgment can be known to be true. Obviously, it is impossible to directly test the correspondence between the perception and the reality being perceived, for this would mean knowing what is true knowledge by going outside of knowledge itself. But to know something outside of knowing is impossible. If, however, the correspondence is tested within the framework of knowledge, all we get is another knowledge claim about the claimed correspondence. And this can go on indefinitely without ever revealing anything about the actual correspondence between the knowledge claim and reality.

This is why Nyaya suggests that mistaken knowledge claims are detected, ultimately, in terms of the successfulness of practice. If one's perception of the finely granulated white stuff in the bowl on the table as sugar is erroneous because the bowl in reality contains salt, it will not help to take another look at it. Rather, it is necessary to take some action based on the perception and see how the action turns out. If the perception is nonerroneous, a spoonful of the contents of the bowl will make the coffee a pleasant drink. If the perception is erroneous because the bowl contains salt, a spoonful in the coffee will make the contents of the cup undrinkable. Expanding this pragmatic principle of verification of perceptual claims, the position is reached that whatever works—in the sense that it provides for successful activity, and eventually, human happiness and liberation—is true because it is seen to correspond to reality as attested to by the successful activity. In this way, the Nyaya philosophers define true perception in terms of correspondence to reality. But they advocate practice as the means of testing this correspondence.

Different kinds of perceptual knowledge can be distinguished according to the ways in which contact is established between the senses and their objects. Ordinary perception occurs when the eye sees colors, the ear hears sounds, the nose smells odors, the tongue tastes flavors, the body feels resistance, or the mind comes into contact with physical states and processes. The first five kinds of perceptual knowledge yield indeterminate perception, or merely the basic sensory experience

itself. The sixth kind of perceptual knowledge, which is internal, is a matter of becoming aware of the sensory experiences and perceiving them to be something or the other. It corresponds to ordinary determinate perception.

In addition, Nyaya admits extra-ordinary perception. Not only are there basic sensory experiences and perceptions of individual things, but there are also perceptions of the natures of things. Visual experience of certain color shapes is not simply perceived to be an individual thing called Rama, but is perceived to be that man, Rama. Since the perception of the nature of the individual, that by virtue of which the individual can be recognized as a member of a class (e.g., the class "man"), is not given in ordinary perception, it is regarded as one of the three kinds of extra-ordinary perception.

The second kind of extra-ordinary perception accounts for how what is proper to one sense organ can become the object of another sense. For example, it is often said that ice looks cold, or that flowers look soft. But coldness and softness are not the proper objects of sight. Consequently, these kinds of perceptual experiences are regarded as extra-ordinary.

The third kind of extra-ordinary perception recognized by Nyaya refers to the perception of things in the past or future, or hidden, or infinitely small in size by one who possesses unusual powers generated by disciplined mediation, or *yoga*.

Inference

Although perception is the basic kind of knowledge, three other means of knowledge are recognized by Nyaya. *Inference*, the second means of valid knowledge, is regarded as an independent means of valid knowledge that is defined in the *Nyaya Sutra* as producing "a knowledge that comes after other knowledge" (I.5). For example, from perceptual knowledge, it is possible to infer something about reality that has never actually been perceived. We know that dinosaurs existed because of certain fossil remains that have been seen.

Inference proceeds from what has been perceived to something that has not been perceived by means of a third "something" called a *reason*, which functions as a middle term in syllogistic reasoning. For example, in the syllogistic inference, "there is fire on the hill because there is smoke on the hill, and wherever there is smoke there is fire," the universal connection between smoke and fire is the reason (the third "something") for affirming fire on the hill, even though the fire was not actually perceived.

The full syllogistic form of this commonly used example of inference is, according to Nyaya, as follows:

1. Yonder hill has fire.
2. Because it has smoke.
3. Whatever has smoke has fire, for example, a stove.
4. Yonder hill has smoke such as is always accompanied by fire.
5. Therefore yonder hill has fire.

The essential part of the inference in this example is the coming to know that there is fire on the hill on the basis of (1) the perceived smoke and (2) the reason constituted by the invariable connection between smoke and fire. The first proposition represents the new knowledge claim. The second proposition gives the perceptual grounds for the new claim. The third proposition asserts the reason for moving from a claim about smoke to one about fire. The fourth proposition asserts that the reason applies in this case. The fifth proposition repeats the claim, now not as a matter for testing, but as a valid knowledge claim, as established by the reasons provided.

Clearly, the most crucial part of the inferential process is establishing the invariable connection between two objects or events. Nyaya philosophers regard the enumeration of individual objects or events as an important part of the establishment of universal connections between events or objects. If ten black crows and no nonblack crows are seen, some probability exists that there is a universal connection between being a crow and being black. But if thousands of crows have been observed, all of them black, the probability is increased. Even if a million crows, all black, have been observed, however, and the next crow observed is white, the probability that there is a universal connection between being a crow and being black is zero, even though we might want

to say that the probability is very high that the millionth-and-second crow will be black.

But if this is the case, it would seem that no number of confirming instances would ever establish a necessary connection between events or objects, for it would always be possible that the very next observed case would refute the necessity of the connection. In light of this possibility, even though Nyaya places much emphasis upon presence of confirming experience and absence of disconfirming experience, the matter is not left here. After all, they argue, there is a difference between claims such as, Wherever there is smoke there is fire, on the one hand, and All crows are black, on the other. The difference is that nothing in the nature of a crow requires blackness. But something about the nature of smoke invariably connects it with fire.

Nevertheless, even if there really is a difference between these cases, the question still arises as to how it is possible to determine that in some cases the connection is universal and necessary because it is causal, while in others the connection is mere coincidence, without any causal basis. Since inference proceeds from perceptual knowledge, if knowledge of a universal and necessary connection between events or objects is possible, it must be that this necessity is perceived, and not inferred. Accordingly, Nyaya includes in perceptual knowledge the perception of the class-nature of the individual. This is a kind of extra-ordinary perception whereby the individual is perceived not merely to be this particular thing or event, but as both this particular thing and a thing of a certain *kind*, or class, of things.

Inferences involving universal connection are of two kinds. Either (1) the unperceived effect can be inferred from the perceived cause, or (2) the unperceived cause can be inferred from the perceived effect. All other inferences depend upon a noncausal and nonnecessary uniformity and cannot be shown to be necessarily true.

Inferential Fallacies

To aid in avoiding certain common mistakes in drawing inferences, the Nyaya philosophers have listed a number of fallacies to be avoided. A *fallacy* is defined as that which appears to be a valid reason for inference, but which is really not a valid reason. In the inference, "There is fire on the hill because there is smoke on the hill and where there is smoke there is fire," the inferred knowledge is that there is fire on the hill. The assertion "There is fire" is being made about the hill. Technically, the term "fire" is called *sadhya*. The term "hill" is called *paksha*. The reason for the assertion, namely, "there is smoke," is called *hetu*. Unless what is taken to be a reason for connecting the *sadhya* with the *paksha* is really a reason, the inference will be invalid. To ensure that the given reason will really be a reason, several rules must be observed: (1) the reason must be present in the *paksha* and in all other objects having the *sadhya* in it; (2) the reason must be absent from objects not possessing the *sadhya*; (3) the inferred claim should not be contradicted by valid perception; and (4) the reason should not make possible a conclusion contradicting the inferred claim.

Comparison

The third means of valid knowledge recognized by Nyaya philosophers is knowledge by comparison based on similarity. For example, if you knew what a cow was, and were told that a deer was like a cow in certain respects, you might come to know that the animal you met in the woods was a deer. This is different from being told what name to apply to a certain object. If, for example, one were to see a deer for the first time and be told "that is a deer," the knowledge would be due to testimony, not to comparison. Knowledge by

means of comparison is attained when the association of the name of an unknown object is made by the knower on the basis of experiencing the similarity of the unknown object with a known object. The crucial aspect of this means of knowledge is the observation of the similarity. Nyaya thinkers hold that similarities are objective and perceivable. Accordingly, knowledge of the nature of a new object on the strength of its similarity to a known object constitutes a separate means of knowledge. While comparative knowledge involves both perception and inference, it cannot be reduced to either of them, and therefore is to be counted as a third means of knowledge.

Testimony

The fourth means of valid knowledge recognized in Nyaya is technically called shabda. Literally, it means "word," and it refers to the knowledge achieved as a result of being told something by a reliable person. Opinion is not the same thing as knowledge, for opinion might be erroneous, but knowledge cannot be. Consequently, simply hearing the opinion of another person is not a means of knowledge. But when the knowledge claims of another person are heard and understood, then genuine knowledge is attained.

The three criteria of knowledge based on the testimony of another person are (1) the person speaking must be absolutely honest and reliable; (2) the person speaking must actually know that which is communicated; and (3) the hearer must understand exactly what is being heard.

⊚ CRITICAL QUESTIONS

1. What are the three "extra-ordinary" perceptions? Would you classify these as "perceptions"? Why, or why not?
2. How does the Nyaya claim that necessary connections can be perceived solve Hume's problem of induction (see Section 8.4)? Have you ever perceived a necessary connection? If so, explain.

3. What three criteria of knowledge must testimony satisfy in order to constitute a valid source of knowledge? Can you imagine a counterexample that would satisfy these three criteria and not be an example of knowledge? If so, what is it?

8.7 FEMINIST EPISTEMOLOGY

Is knowledge universal? If we know what it means to know something in one culture, do we know what it means in all cultures? Who is the subject of knowledge? Who is the knower? Is knowing the knower at all relevant to knowing what knowledge is or whether it is possible? How does the social position of the knower make an impact on the production and transmission of knowledge? Is all knowledge expressible in the form of propositions? Is knowledge the result of the exercise of social power?

These questions are not easy to answer, and even to raise them is somewhat unsettling because they introduce political and social questions into philosophic reflection on the nature and possibility of knowledge. Feminist epistemology, however, has not shied away from asking such questions or from interjecting moral and political considerations into the epistemological project.

Feminist epistemology began as a critique of existing theories of knowledge. This critique revealed and continues to reveal how large a role gender has played in supposedly universal and objective theories of knowledge. Genevieve Lloyd (1984) documents how rationality has been associated with males and with masculine qualities in the development of Western philosophy. Men, supposedly, are rational whereas women are emotional. Thus, not only are women excluded from the sacred halls of knowers, but also an unwarranted division is created between knowledge and emotion.

Janice Moulton (1983) argues that philosophy has relied heavily on the adversary *paradigm*. This model pictures rational activity aimed at producing knowledge as one of an opponent defending a belief against an attacker. According to this model, the best way to arrive at the truth is to subject our beliefs to the strongest possible objections.

Undoubtedly, there are advantages to this method, especially in courts of law, but it has severe limitations if it is transposed into a universal model of knowledge-production. Not only is it tainted with sexism insofar as it assumes that aggressive (male-type) thinking is the best thinking, but also the adversary paradigm leads to bad reasoning. By restricting reasoning to an adversarial situation, we ignore the sorts of reasoning that might be appropriate in different situations, such as figuring something out for oneself, exploring a topic among like-minded people, or trying to show how two apparently opposed positions might be in harmony.

It is not enough, however, to unmask the ways traditional theories of knowledge have been tainted by male bias. We must go on, feminist philosophers maintain, to find new frameworks for thinking about problems relating to knowledge. So some feminists argue that a **"standpoint" epistemology** that frankly acknowledges that all knowing substantially involves the social and historical context of the knowers is a better place to begin our philosophical reflection on the possibility of knowledge. Others point out how the community—as the place where knowledge is generated, stored, and communicated—has been neglected in favor of the traditional views that the "isolated individual" is the epistemic agent. Still others call for a recognition of the significant role that emotions play in the production of knowledge.

Alessandra Tanesini teaches philosophy at the University of Wales, Cardiff. She is the author of several books and numerous articles on epistemological issues. In the following selection she critically examines different versions of standpoint epistemology and concludes that they share the conviction that objectivity, a crucial feature of successful claims to knowledge, can be achieved from "partial perspectives."

1. What are the "two constitutive elements" of standpoint epistemology?
2. How do feminist philosophers employ the tools of Marxist analysis in developing their own versions of standpoint epistemology?
3. What is distinctive about "women's cognitive style" according to Rose and Hartsock, and how does this alleged distinctiveness support the claim to epistemic privilege?
4. What objections have been raised against some versions of standpoint epistemology, and what does Tanesini conclude from her analysis of these objections?
5. Explain Harding's alternative notion of standpoint epistemology in your own words.

The Importance of Standpoint in Feminism

ALESSANDRA TANESINI

When people look at things from different perspectives, what they see is likely to be different. This platitude is the starting point of one of the most popular feminist approaches to knowledge, namely standpoint epistemology, according to which there is a distinctive perspective on reality which pertains to feminists or to women. They have a distinctive outlook because their experiences are different from those of people who occupy other positions in society. This feminist or womanly perspective, furthermore, is not merely different from, say, a masculinist perspective, it is also a privileged perspective. It is a perspective that makes it possible to understand reality better, perhaps to understand it as it really is.

What I have given is only a rough sketch of standpoint epistemology from which more sophisticated versions diverge on several accounts. Nevertheless, it is already evident that standpoint epistemology employs notions such as 'experience' and 'privileged perspective' which require a closer scrutiny. In this chapter I first discuss formulations of standpoint based on the notion of women's experience, and then several problems which later formulations of standpoint attempt to resolve.

WHAT IS A STANDPOINT?: BEGINNING FROM WOMEN'S EXPERIENCE

There are at least two constitutive aspects of the several versions of standpoint epistemology: first, the notion of a standpoint or perspective; second, the notion that some perspectives are epistemically privileged. Thus, this sort of epistemology needs to establish that there is a distinctive perspective which pertains to women or to feminists, and that this perspective is privileged.

Feminist standpoint epistemology finds its ancestor in the Marxian notion of a standpoint of the proletariat. According to Marx the positions occupied in society by different classes give them distinct perspectives on social reality. These positions constitute different standpoints which provide dissimilar understandings of social relations. These standpoints are not only different in content, they also differ in accuracy. The understanding of society available from the standpoint of the working class is less distorted than those offered by other perspectives or standpoints.

For Marx, knowledge emerges through active engagement with social and natural reality. Thus, knowledge does not pertain to a theoretical sphere which is independent of practical activities.

From *An Introduction to Feminist Epistemologies*, (Malden, Mass.: Blackwell Publishers, 1999), pp. 138–159. Copyright © Alessandra Tanesini 1999. Footnotes edited.

Rather, understanding of the social and natural world results from individuals' labor; that is, from their involvement in the process of production. What, for Marx, characterizes the capitalist political system is the class division of labor. In this system intellectual and manual labor are kept strictly separate, so that some economically privileged individuals perform only intellectual work. It is these individuals alone who are recognized as producers of knowledge, whereas the knowledge possessed by manual laborers goes unacknowledged. Marx, however, does not merely claim that the working classes possess knowledge which is not usually recognized. He also claims that the working class has a distinctive understanding of social reality under the capitalist system, an understanding which is more accurate than the understanding available to members of the other economic classes.

The perspective of the working class is distinctive because it emerges from their practical activities. The class division of labor ensures that some manual productive work is done only by members of the proletariat; thus, working-class people's lives are systematically different from those of the members of other classes. This difference grounds or gives rise to a distinct perspective on social reality. This unique perspective of the proletariat in a capitalist system is privileged from an epistemic viewpoint because the working class plays a crucial economic function in preserving the system while it has no vested interest in its continuation. In other words, for Marx, it is possible to gain a more accurate understanding of the social reality of capitalism from the perspective of that class which is socially marginal but economically central. The social marginality of this class ensures that its members have no vested interest in preserving the system and are, therefore, not likely to be blind to its shortcomings. Its economic centrality guarantees that the members of this class have first-hand acquaintance with the workings of the capitalist system.[1] Thus understood, Marxian epistemology claims that to acquire accurate knowledge of a phenomenon one must be in a position to experience it and its effects, and one also must have no vested interests, no biases, which would lead to a distorted understanding.[2]

Some standpoint feminist epistemologists, notably Nancy Hartsock (1983), Hilary Rose (1983), and Dorothy Smith (1988), have explicitly modeled their theories on this Marxist account. In particular, they have developed explanations of the division of labor which ground the claim for a distinctive perspective pertaining to women or to feminists, and have supplemented these with analyses of social reality which show women to be both central and marginal in relevant ways.

Feminist critics of Marxist political theory have notoriously exposed the gender blindness of its crucial notions. In particular, they have noted that the Marxist focus on systems of production excludes and naturalizes those systems of reproduction which are central to many women's lives. Similarly, the exclusive focus on capitalism as an economic system ignores the system of patriarchy, a distinct set of social relations, which contributes to the continuation of women's oppression.[3] These concepts of 'reproductive labor' and 'patriarchy' can provide the tools to formulate an account of standpoint epistemology within a feminist context. Women's reproductive labor provides them with a distinctive perspective on reality; their socially marginal role under patriarchy, when combined with their essential function in its preservation, guarantees the epistemic privilege of their perspective.

These tools have been employed by Hartsock (1983) in her formulation of a feminist standpoint. Starting from the Marxian tenet that the material conditions of a person's everyday life inform the understanding of society developed by that person, Hartsock finds in the specificity of women's experiences the basis for a distinctive perspective.

For her a feminist standpoint emerges from what she calls 'the sexual division of labor' (1983: 284). She chooses the term 'sexual' instead of 'gendered' to remind us that 'there is some biological, bodily component to human existence' (1983: 289). This bodily component is deeply linked to one of the aspects of life which distinguishes women's work from men's: namely, their production of other human beings, their reproductive capacities. Childbearing and childrearing are complex social activities which give rise to distinct experiences (1983: 294).[4] Even in the sphere of the production of goods for subsistence, women's activities differ structurally from men's. Women spend more time than men in the production of goods in the house, goods which are not sold as commodities (1983: 292). In both cases, women's labor is distinct from men's and involves an unification of mind and body. Hence, as Hartsock remarks, 'women's lives differ structurally from those of men' (1983: 284).

Hartsock is not alone in believing that the distinctiveness of women's work grounds a notion of women's experience which differs structurally from men's. This experience is the basis of women's distinctive understanding of the social and natural worlds. Similar claims have also been supported by Rose (1983), who adds that women's work concerning reproduction is distinctive especially because it is a 'labor of love' (1983: 83–4; 1986: 164–6). Women's caring work, for her, does not just unify hand and brain, as Hartsock claims, but also the heart (1983: 83). A crucial aspect of feminist standpoint epistemology is for Rose an acknowledgment of the central role of emotional involvement in the process of knowledge acquisition: this is an aspect of feminist epistemology that opposes the abstract and depersonalized character of traditional science (1983: 84).

Both Rose and Hartsock find in the division of labor by sex–gender[5] the origin for the character of women's experience; an experience that differs structurally from that of men. Women's experience is, as Rose remarks, a 'subjective shared experience of oppression' (1983: 88).

This focus on experience as the basis of a feminist standpoint is also present in the sociological theory of Smith. For her, to acquire knowledge in the way recommended by standpoint epistemology is 'to begin our work from our experience as women' (1988: 78). Division of labor accounts for the difference between men's and women's experience since women do the work which makes it possible for men to engage in intellectual work (1988: 83). In other words, women's work releases men from any concern with care of bodies and their needs.

What characterizes women's experience is, for Smith, 'a point of rupture,' 'a line of fault' (1988: 49). This line of fault is the perceived 'disjuncture between experience and the forms in which experience is socially expressed (becoming thereby intelligible …)' (1988: 50). It is, that is, a perceived mismatch between what one actually experiences and the conceptual framework socially available to put one's experiences into words.[6] The cause of this experiential rupture is found in men's oppression of women, or, more precisely, in patriarchy as a set of oppressive social relations (1988: 51).

For Smith what makes women's experience valuable from an epistemic viewpoint is their dual marginal and central position in the current set of social relations. Women's position is central because they do the work which sustains the current patriarchal system and also produce the invisibility of such work as work (1988: 81). They are marginal because they do not occupy a position of power within the system. As a consequence, 'for women (as also for others in the society similarly excluded), the organization of daily experience, the work routines, and the structuring of our lives through time has been and to a large extent still is determined and ordered by processes external to, and beyond, our everyday world' (1988: 65). Thus, women occupy the position of insiders/outside: insiders because they are crucial to the continuation of the current system, but also outsiders since they have no power within it.

It is because they occupy this dual social role that women's experiences reflect more accurately than men's the reality of current relations. From their position, relations which are invisible from dominant positions become visible. Since women have a direct experience of what is invisible to men, they come to perceive a rupture between what the world is like for them and what dominant views say about it. It is this line of fault which alerts women that something is amiss. Starting from their experiences it is possible for them to expose those aspects of social reality that are invisible from other positions.

Thus, Smith does not only argue for the distinctiveness of women's standpoint but also for its epistemic privilege. Before addressing the problematic nature of Smith's appeals to women's experience, I would like to return to Hartsock's argument for the epistemic privilege of that distinctive feminist standpoint which, she has explained, is based on women's experiences.

Hartsock draws an explicit parallel between the feminist standpoint and that of the proletariat. She holds that

> just as Marx's understanding of the world from the standpoint of the proletariat enabled him to go beneath bourgeois ideology, so a feminist standpoint can allow us to understand patriarchal institutions and ideologies as perverse inversions of more humane social relations. (1983: 284)

Hence Hartsock also exploits the Marxian argument that those who occupy a position which is central to the preservation of a social system, but are oppressed by it, have a better understanding of the real nature of the system in question. Even if we accept this argument, however, the scope of its application is limited to knowledge of society and cannot be automatically extended to other domains.

Hartsock's argument could only establish that the reality of the patriarchal system is better understood from the feminist standpoint; the same argument could not justify a claim for the superiority of the feminist standpoint in knowing other aspects of the world.[7] This is reflected in Smith's use of her formulation of standpoint as the methodological basis of a sociology of everyday life. The perspective of women's experience is granted an epistemic advantage only concerning matters that have to do with social relations shaped by the system of patriarchy.

Rose and Hartsock, on the other hand, aspire to provide greater applicability to the notion of a feminist standpoint. To do so, they need to argue both for the distinctiveness of women's perspective in other fields of inquiry, and for the epistemic privilege of that perspective in these fields. It is, I believe, possible to find arguments for a broader distinctive feminist perspective in both Rose and Hartsock, although they do not explicitly take these arguments to fulfill such a purpose.[8] Crucially, for standpoint theorists, women's experiences, grounded in the sex–gender division of labor, give women access to knowledge which is denied to members of other groups. That is, under patriarchy women have experiences of social relations whose content is different from those of men's; furthermore the content of women's experience reflects more adequately this social reality. For example, men might experience women's childrearing as involving nothing more than the deployment of instinctual attitudes, but women's own experience of childrearing reflects the fact that socially acquired skills are involved in this activity. Considerations of this sort indicate that women's experiences about some social relations under patriarchy are more reliable than men's. However, these considerations cannot, as I said, be automatically extended to other fields of inquiry. It is at this point that both Rose and Hartsock modify the nature of their claims: instead of holding that women have experiences whose content differs from the experiences of members of other groups, they hold that women have a different way of experiencing, or more precisely a different cognitive style from that employed by men. Thus, for Rose, women's caring labor endows them with an affective way of knowing; Hartsock employs psychoanalytic object relations theory to a similar effect. She holds that there is a distinctive female subjectivity with a specific way of being in the world. Girls develop a 'female sense of self as connected to the world' (1983: 295) which informs all their experiences. Object relations theory therefore explains how the sexual division of labor gives rise to a distinctively female way of experiencing.

It thus becomes possible for Rose and Hartsock to hold that the distinctiveness of women's perspective has general application, since what makes it distinct is women's cognitive style rather than just the specific contents of their experiences.[9] Of course, to say this is not to unearth a contradiction in Rose and Hartsock, rather it becomes now possible for them to claim that women's different cognitive style is the cause of the difference in content of their experiences. Nevertheless, an invocation of a distinctive cognitive style that belongs to women makes it rather difficult to explain why this style would be epistemically privileged for the whole range of its application. The Marxist claim that oppressed groups, central to the system of their oppression, have a better understanding of that system cannot in this case provide an adequate explanation. Instead, one perhaps could argue for the superiority of this female cognitive style over traditional ones by showing how it embodies certain epistemic virtues which are absent from the traditional masculinist approach. There is, however, little evidence for this claim which does not seem to possess much initial credibility. Further, even if one could provide a convincing argument in its favor, this claim would constitute a move away from the Marxist origins of standpoint epistemology.

Be that as it may, there are serious feminist objections to talk of a distinctively female cognitive style. Genevieve Lloyd has pointed out that the view that women have a distinctive way of reasoning is an unintended consequence of Descartes's mind--body dualism. While men were seen to possess Reason, conceived as 'a highly abstract mode of thought,' women were associated with a different sort of intellectual character, one that involved emotional and practical thinking (1984: 49). Although a reevaluation of these latter cognitive functions is overdue.[10] Lloyd doubts that an endorsement of the division by sex–gender of ways of thinking is either empirically correct or politically useful.[11]

This is only one of several objections that have been raised against the version of standpoint epistemology developed by Hartsock (1983), Rose (1983), and Smith (1988). Other objections include: (i) the charge that this theory of knowledge rests on the assumption that there is a female nature or essence; (ii) arguments against the assumption that there are enough experiences all women share which could constitute the basis of a standpoint, (iii) arguments against grounding knowledge on the notion of experience. These three objections are interrelated and I shall discuss them together in what follows. Another set of objections focuses on the understanding of marginality implicit in the versions of standpoint epistemology discussed so far; these criticisms, voiced by Bat-Ami Bar On (1993), assert that: (i) marginality should be understood as a locus of

resistance rather than primarily as a matter of being victims of oppression, and (ii) people at the margins are not free from the dominant ideology. I shall also consider these objections, and argue that they derive in part from a misunderstanding of standpoint. Nevertheless, they point toward the need for more reflection on the notion of marginal position.

Several critics, including Sandra Harding (1986 and 1991) and Bar On (1993), have remarked that standpoint epistemology appears to entail false essentialisms and universalizations. To claim that there is a unique cognitive style or set of experiences which pertains to women seems to presuppose that women have essential features and to ignore the many important differences among women.[12]

It is true that, as Harding remarks, standpoint theorists 'tend to center a difference between the genders ... at the expense of clearly focusing on differences between women or between men in different races, classes, and cultures' (1991: 178). That is, standpoint thinkers, like Smith, talk about the position of 'women in general' (1988: 86), or about 'women's oppression,' and ignore the differences between the positions occupied, and the oppressions experienced by, women of different races, classes, and sexual orientations. However, unless we support what Susan Bordo has aptly termed 'a new skepticism about the use of gender as an analytic category' (1990: 135), this observation alone is not sufficient to reject standpoint theory. A recognition of differences among women should not automatically lead to the assumption that there is nothing useful to be said about women in general. A recognition of the importance of, say, race and sexual orientation in the lives of some women, does not mean that every feminist analysis of some aspect of social reality should focus on all these dimensions (1990: 139). This is exactly the position held by Hartsock who, with regard to her Marxist strategy, says

> I adopt this strategy with some reluctance, since it contains the danger of making invisible the experience of lesbians or women of color. At the same time, I recognize that the effort to uncover a feminist standpoint assumes that there are some things common to all women's lives in Western class societies. (1983: 290)

Hartsock is aware of the risks involved in focusing on commonalties at the expense of differences among women, nevertheless she believes in the theoretical fruitfulness of using gender as a category in this context. To believe in this fruitfulness is to believe in the separability, at least in thought, of gender from other dimensions such as class and race. Unless this is, at least sometimes, possible, gender cannot be a useful analytic category. It has been argued by Elizabeth Spelman that this view entails what 'we might call tootsie roll metaphysics: each part of my identity is separable from every other part, and the significance of each part is unaffected by the other parts' (1990: 136). Spelman claims that it is not possible to abstract from the racial identities of white and black women in order to focus on a certain 'womanness' they have in common (1990: 135). Spelman, who is white, supports her claim by asking us to consider the following counterfactual (contrary to fact) situation:

> we should have no trouble imagining that had I been Black I could have had just the same understanding of myself as a woman as I in fact do, and that no matter how differently people would have treated me had I been Black, nevertheless what it would have meant to them that I was a woman would have been just the same. (1990: 135)

Although Spelman is correct to point out that we cannot assume that what it means to be a woman is the same for white and black women, this does not necessarily mean that we cannot ever abstract from race to consider issues of gender. Such an abstraction does not commit one to the view that there is an essence all women share. Similarly, we are not embracing essentialism when we abstract from all other features to claim of a group of people that they are all students in British universities. This claim does not even commit one to the view that being a student means the same to each one of them. Nevertheless, it is still possible to say a few politically important things about all these students, such as that they are likely to have financial worries since their grants have been cut, and therefore are likely to have a part-time job.

Similarly, to recognize that gender, race, class, and sexual orientation are not neatly separable

does not entail that nothing can be said about gender without mentioning all other aspects.[13] It means, however, that this is possible only in limited and carefully chosen contexts. In particular, it means that it is not easy to make generalizations about women's experiences because this is a context where the other dimensions of one's identity seem to make an important difference. Women belonging to different social classes, races, and sexual orientations face very different problems, and encounter different forms of oppression. While it is reasonable to claim that we all are 'victims' of racism, insofar as racism affects in negative ways everybody's life, the experience that non-white people have of racism is, of course, very different from what is experienced by whites. Furthermore, the institution of racism has consequences on the division of labor: non- white people usually do less well paid menial work, they face discrimination in the workplace, and tend to be excluded from professional occupations. More importantly, given Hartsock's claims, black women's experience of childbearing and childrearing are likely to be different from that of white women. If we do not conceive reproduction as a purely biological set of activities, we quickly come to realize that it is deeply affected by social factors such as wealth, family structure, and cultural assumptions, to name but a few. Raising a black child in a racist society is very different from raising a white child. One could also notice that it is often black women who take care of bodies so as to free white women from these chores. Therefore, neither Smith's nor Hartsock's assumption that it is possible to talk about women in general in the context of these aspects of social life are empirically correct. Instead, we are drawn toward the opposite conclusion that the life of a black woman is likely to be structurally different from the life of a white one. There are enough relevant differences in the conditions of women's lives to make it impossible to talk meaningfully about the experiences of women in general as the basis of standpoint.

Hartsock has managed to overlook these facts partly because she implicitly assumes that all women share some experiences in virtue of having a female body. It is this biological fact of embodiment, a fact she highlights in her preference of the term 'sex' over the less biological category of 'gender,' which I believe guides Hartsock's thinking in these matters. However, even if it is necessarily true that we are embodied, and biologically true that bodies are sexed, it does not follow that people with the same kind of body must have the same experiences of embodiment. This would only follow if one assumed that experiences are not mediated by social factors. Furthermore, even if having a female body were a source of identical experiences for all women, we still could not derive from this a standpoint unless we assumed that these experiences, which would have a purely biological source, were crucial to being a woman. Unless, that is, we assume that there is a female nature which is somehow grounded in facts about embodiment. Since Hartsock subscribes to Marx's opposition to a fixed human nature, she could not hold this position; nevertheless it is only by giving a crucial role to a female nature that one could support her claim that women have the same experience of reproductive labor.

To summarize, the version of standpoint theory based on shared experiences seriously underestimates the importance of differences between women. It thus runs the risk of essentialism; furthermore, since it employs unwarranted generalizations it is also in danger of making invisible the experiences of women who are poor or black or lesbians. Standpoint theorists like Hartsock took these dangers to be avoidable, but they were mistaken in doing so.

We must, however, also be careful to avoid the opposite error of putting too much emphasis on differences among women. Firstly, because this attitude tends to construe people with identities other than ours as complete and mysterious 'Others' with whom we have nothing in common. When we do this it becomes easy to fall prey to all sorts of generalizations which merely reflect our prejudices: e.g., that all black people must be poor. Secondly, an emphasis on difference may lead one to claim that people can only talk on behalf of their own group. Thus, although it may appear to be a step in the right direction to

state that, say, only lesbians can talk for the lesbian community, the result is that claims such as this one are often taken to entail their converse. Thus, lesbians would be entitled only to talk about themselves. This is what Gayatri Chakravorty Spivak has called 'clinging to marginality' which, by teaching a person to speak for oneself works 'precisely to contain the ones whom this person is supposed to represent' (1994: 162). In other words, if persons belonging to groups which are taken to be marginal in society can only speak for themselves, what they have to say is taken to be relevant only to their groups and can, therefore, be safely ignored by everybody else.

What I have said so far suggests that shared experience might not be the correct starting point for a feminist epistemology. And, indeed, there are versions of standpoint epistemology which do not rely on this notion: an example is the theory developed by Harding which is the topic of the next section. The notion of 'experience' itself has been the focus of intense criticisms, especially by feminists who are sympathetic to post-structuralist views. What feminists like Joan Scott find objectionable is not 'experience' in its colloquial sense; rather, they argue against the philosophical conception according to which experience is the basis of all human knowledge. Although Scott is explicitly concerned with historical knowledge, her critique of experience is couched in general terms and is easily applicable to knowledge in many other fields. Scott criticizes the use of 'experience' as a 'foundational ground' of knowledge (1992: 26). In this sense experience would function as the ultimate and 'uncontestable evidence' for a claim to knowledge (1992: 24). Scott rightly argues that experience is fallible, and therefore contestable. Further, she claims that experience cannot be taken as a ground for all other knowledge, because this would amount to ignoring 'the constructed nature of experience' (1992: 25). Usually post-structuralist claims about the construction of a given entity carry several ontological commitments, but in this context it is possible to read Scott simply as endorsing anti-foundationalism. Thus, it is not possible merely to have an experience, one must also somehow conceptualize what is happening, and hence what one experiences will depend on the concepts available to that person.[14] This is a position which is widely accepted also in analytic philosophy, and which I discussed in chapter 4. As that discussion has I hope made clear, anti-foundationalism does not require abandoning the notion of experience altogether, but it involves both accepting that experience is fallible and that it is not independent of theory.[15]

Most standpoint theorists do not adopt a conception of experience as untheoretical or immediately given. Hartsock, for example, is quite explicit in her claim that the 'vision of the oppressed group must be struggled for and represents an achievement which requires both science … and education' (1983: 285). The experience of oppression as oppression is not something which is immediately available to the oppressed; instead, it represents an achievement obtained by thinking and producing theories about one's situation.[16] On the other hand, Smith appears to appeal to a notion of immediate experience when she distinguishes between experience and the categories for its expression. Thus, she believes that there is a world which is immediately and directly experienced (1988: 55). Experience is employed here to give some authority to the views held by people occupying marginal positions, but, as Scott has argued, foundationalist accounts of experience are ultimately incorrect.

Besides being criticized for its universalism and for its use of experience, standpoint epistemology has been accused of misconceiving the notion of marginality. Bar On suggests that we understand it not in terms of oppression but, as has been done by bell hooks, as a matter of resistance (Bar On, 1993: 87). Bar On also points out that even practices of resistance are tainted by the dominant ideology from which it is impossible to escape completely (1993: 94). Bar On is correct on both counts. These points, however, help to articulate further the notion of standpoint—they do not oppose it. I discuss these issues in the next section. For now, it suffices to say that both points had already been acknowledged by Hartsock when she claims that a struggle is necessary to achieve a standpoint and that the 'vision of the ruling class (or gender) structures the material

relations in which all parties are forced to participate' (1983: 285).

In conclusion, the versions of standpoint which start from women's experiences discussed so far have enormous problems because they assume that there are experiences shared by all women. What is needed, it would seem, is a standpoint which is based on something other than experience.

STARTING FROM MARGINAL LIVES

A fruitful attempt to provide such an alternative notion of standpoint epistemology has been developed by Harding. She claims that there are several reasons why it is not possible to use experience as the basis of standpoint. First, she makes the same point raised by Scott (1992) which I discussed above: women's experience cannot provide the foundations of knowledge because 'experience itself is shaped by social relations' (1991: 123). Second, women's experiences are not homogeneous. It is, she adds, possible to understand different sorts of feminism as based on the experiences of different historical groups of women. Hence, she concludes that 'both "women's experiences" and "what women say" … would not seem to be reliable grounds for deciding just which claims to knowledge are preferable' (1991: 123).

Harding does not deny the importance of experience, but she holds that:

> For a position to count as a standpoint, rather than as a claim—equally valuable but for different reasons—for the importance of listening to women tell us about their lives and experiences, we must insist on an objective location—women's lives—as the place from which feminist research should begin. (1991: 123)

Experience is a useful pointer toward the correct starting point for feminist research, but the grounds of feminist knowledge are theories and observations that 'start out from, that look at the world from the perspective of, women's lives' (1991: 124). In this way Harding attempts to avoid basing feminist knowledge on a notion of experience conceived as immediate and infallible. Instead, she stresses that even experiences are shaped by social reality. For example, one experiences a remark about one's body from a work colleague as either a normal form of interaction between men and women in the workplace, or as an instance of sexual harassment. Thus, what we experience is influenced by our understanding of social relations. Similarly, in the case of natural science what I experience as mere lines on a surface, a physicist may experience as the traces of the path of an elementary particle. In both cases, experiences are not something that we just have; instead, there is a lot that needs to be learned before we are capable of having them.

Harding shares with those standpoint theorists whose views I discussed in the previous section a belief that the lives of women and of people belonging to marginal groups differ structurally from those of men in dominant groups. She also believes that these differences are a source of new understandings of social reality. She holds, however, that research should start from the objective facts of these lives rather than from the experiences of those who conduct such lives. She makes this move because she wants to avoid the problems encountered by early versions of standpoint theory. As I said above, for Harding these problems are centered on the problematic notion of immediate experience and on the risk of erasing differences among women. Starting from women's lives rather than experiences contributes to a solution of both problems. First, it recognizes that experience is not immediately given but presupposes some theory and understanding. Second, it acknowledges that women belonging to different groups lead different lives.

Harding provides an indication of some resources available when one starts research in this fashion. Looking at social reality from the perspective of women's lives permits a recognition of the partiality of dominant understandings (1991: 121). Due to the nature of many women's activities, their lives are the ideal ground for understanding both the processes which have created our social reality (1991: 128) and the cultural character of phenomena which current ideology takes to be natural (1991: 131). That is, women's work in childrearing and in the general care of bodies makes it possible for others to dedicate themselves to socially recognized activities; but, since such work is invisible from the dominant perspective, social theories fail to recognize the indispensability of women's labor for our current social arrangements. The invisibility of women's work as work makes possible current ideological conceptions of it as a natural and instinctual activity.

Furthermore, starting research from the lives of oppressed groups makes possible an understanding of the mechanisms of oppression (1991: 126); it also increases the objectivity of the results of research in many areas of inquiry because it is only through social struggles to change the current social reality that we come to understand previously hidden aspects of social relations (1991: 127). Finally, the position of marginal lives as outsiders within the social order is a valuable source of understanding because it brings to 'research just the combination of nearness and remoteness, concern and indifference, that are central to maximizing objectivity' (1991: 124).

A concern with a stronger notion of objectivity is prominent in Harding's later work, and it is the contribution of standpoint to achieving such objectivity that she finds most valuable. She holds that scientific method as traditionally conceived is incapable of identifying and screening out the ideological values of dominant groups in society and scientific communities What is instead needed is an approach which, like standpoint, scientifically studies those assumptions that appear unremarkable from dominant perspectives (1991: 150).

Harding's account of standpoint builds upon the work of other feminist thinkers, in particular she adopts Patricia Hill Collins's notion of the position of 'outsider-within.' This is the position occupied by people who are within a community or society but inhabit its margins. Within academia, for example, 'black women remain outsiders within, individuals whose marginality provides a distinctive angle of vision on the theories put forth by ... intellectual communities' (1991: 12).

The perspective of marginal people, such as black women, is a standpoint. It provides a preferred stance to understand oppression because it is less likely than dominant perspectives to deny the links between its claims and political ideological interests (1991: 234). Each marginal group has its own perspective, and each of these is partial (1991: 234). As Collins says: 'No group has a clear angle of vision' (1991: 234). Thus, no group can legitimately claim to possess that unique standpoint which permits a completely adequate account of social reality.

While Hartsock and Smith seem to take a standpoint to be capable, at least in principle, of offering a complete account of social oppressive relations, Collins denies the possibility of such completeness. She criticizes these earlier Marxist accounts of standpoint for sharing 'the positivist belief in one "true" interpretation of reality' (1991: 235). There is, however, more than one way of interpreting claims about the partiality of any standpoint. One may follow Harding's talk of perspectives which are less false than others, claiming that not even 'our "best" representations of the world are transparent to the world' (1991: 185). That is, our best claims are themselves situated. None of our claims can represent the world as it is in itself independently of human interests. Nevertheless, some perspectives furnish less distorted understandings of the world of human concerns. A perspective is, thus, partial because it is not a transparent representation. One could, however, provide a different account of partial perspectives according to which what counts as 'true' is simply a matter of negotiation and agreement between those involved in discussion. This might amount to some sort of relativism, and it is rightly rejected by Collins (1991: 235).

For Collins, although every perspective is partial, not all claims to knowledge are equal. Instead, the standpoints of 'outsiders-within' are to be preferred to that of dominant groups.[17] Collins hold that each marginal group has its own partial perspective. Her approach envisages a coalition among marginal groups.

> Each group speaks from its own standpoint and shares itown partial, situated knowledge. But because each group perceives its own truth as partial, its knowledge is unfinished. Each group

> becomes better able to consider other groups' standpoints without relinquishing the uniqueness of its own standpoint or suppressing other groups' partial perspectives. (1991: 236)

Acknowledgment of the partiality of one's own angle on reality encourages a politics of solidarity in the awareness that one does not have a complete knowledge of social reality: one may thus be disposed to learn what other marginal standpoints have to offer. This approach does not only have political advantages, it also facilitates more accurate knowledge of social relations. Its epistemic superiority originates from awareness that systems of oppression are deeply related. It is only through the combination of the insights of different standpoints that it is possible to study how these systems interconnect, so that each needs the others in order to function (1991: 222).

The account of standpoint epistemology provided by Collins, thus, avoids some of the problems encountered by its earlier versions. First, since she recognizes that each group has its own perspective, she does not erase differences among women. There is, for instance, a black lesbian's perspective, one that pertains to poor latinas, and so on. Second, she avoids additive analyses of oppression. The search for a unique privileged standpoint may lead one to assume that it must belong to the most oppressed group of all.[18] Such an assumption would betray a mistaken understanding of oppression as composed of separate layers rather than deeply related phenomena (1991: 207). As Collins points out, oppression is a matrix with no pure victims and no pure oppressors. All groups have some different amount of privilege and underprivilege depending on the context. There is no group which is the most oppressed of all, because oppression is not quantifiable in this manner. Instead, we are all partly victims and partly oppressors to a varying degree depending on the situation. Furthermore, each system of oppression—along the axes of gender, race, class, and sexual orientation—is interlocked with all others without which it could not function in the way it does. Thus, Collins's approach has the double advantage of making explicit that it is not possible to understand one kind of oppression independently of all others, and that the members of no group can be seen as pure victims of oppression. On the other hand, earlier standpoint epistemologies encouraged both the view that the oppression of women can be understood in isolation, and the belief that women do not themselves oppress anyone.

Further, Collins's understanding of oppression as a matrix is combined with a conception of marginal positions as sites of resistance. Marginal positions thus become sites of, using bell hooks's apt phrase, 'counter-hegemonic discourse' (1984: 15). They are both locations of oppression and resistance (hooks, 1990: 151). If margins, all margins, are sites of resistance, we do not need Marx's account of standpoint as pertaining uniquely to that group which is both oppressed by a system and central to its continuation. What for Marx was the result of occupying a double central and marginal position is for hooks and Collins proper to all marginal positions. For them the very condition of marginality provides the materials for understanding oppression. And since there are different marginalized groups, there will be different standpoints.

Marginality can by itself be a source of knowledge because it is not seen just as the position occupied by victims; it is instead the space where oppressed people organize their resistance. Hooks and Collins rightly insist that the experiences of oppressed people are not just experiences of oppression and powerlessness, they are also experiences of struggle to preserve one viewpoint, to resist oppression (hooks, 1990: 150). Thus, they avoid what has been perceived as early standpoint theory's tendency to view women as victims rather than agents of resistance.[19] This non-Marxist conception of marginality finds support in Foucault's conception of power. Power stops being seen as the unique property of institutions to limit the liberty of individuals, and it becomes also a positive force or ability to make new freedoms possible. Power does not just work top-down, but is a force permeating every level which enables new possibilities while impeding others.

Collins's standpoint theory, thus, avoids those problems encountered by earlier standpoint theory. Nevertheless, she employs the notion of lived experience as a crucial source of knowledge. At times her position may seem similar to Harding's, for example when she suggests that we look at African-American women's family lives to denaturalize the notion of the nuclear family (1991: 223). In this case the starting point of her research appears to be the lives of marginal people rather than their experiences of those lives. More frequently, however, Collins explicitly claims that the primary source of knowledge is provided by the experiences of marginal people. These experiences give rise to a concrete wisdom developed in the struggle for survival and which is opposed to the knowledge of dominant groups (1991: 208). Collins does not, however, understand experience as something which is infallible, immediately given and untheoretical. If it is correct to say that Collins's account avoids those problems encountered by early versions of standpoint even though she relies on the notion of experience, the source of trouble for standpoint is not its use of 'experience' but rather the assumptions made by early theorists. They assumed that women have the same experiences, and Smith also assumed that these are infallible, immediate and independent of theory. Once these assumptions are rejected, it becomes possible to put the notion of experience to fruitful employment. Thus, more recently some feminists have tried to rethink experience in new ways.

Morwenna Griffiths, for example, has recently argued that feminist epistemology cannot dispense with experience because of its concern with subjectivity. What characterized traditional epistemology was its willingness to hide the role played by the subject in the process of achieving knowledge. The contribution of the subjectivity of usually white male knowers was thus left unchecked. On the contrary, what characterizes many feminist theories of knowledge is a recognition of the role played by subjectivity in the process of knowledge acquisition (1995: 59). Hence, experience is necessarily a starting point for acquiring knowledge—one must start from a perspective. Experience is, of course, only a starting point since it must always be subjected to a process of critical revision (1995: 6). While Griffiths argues for the indispensability of experience Oshadi Mangena provides an account of how true universality, the mark of adequate knowledge, can emerge from a recognition of concrete experiences in all their very specific differences.

For Mangena there is no common experience as a consequence of gender to which race and class can simply be added on (1994: 281). These dimensions of identity are inextricably linked and, as Collins also points out, can be better understood by foregrounding their relations. Furthermore, gender itself is thoroughly relational. Hence, 'we cannot examine the experience of woman in society without taking into account the fact of their interconnectedness with men' (Mangena, 1994: 280). This is especially true in African societies where both men and women are oppressed, and where these oppressions, although systematically different, are inextricably linked. Similarly, the condition of women in the South of the planet must be linked to the global condition of women. The concrete experiences of individuals belonging to different groups not only differ in very specific ways, they are also interrelated. The causal processes underlying those experiences can be therefore adequately represented only if we understand them as processes of interaction (1994: 280). We can understand social reality only if we look at it in a global manner taking into account all the relations that constitute this reality.

Mangena's emphasis on experience is based on her acknowledgment that subjectivity always colors scientific knowledge (1994: 227). Experience cannot, therefore, be excised from knowledge. What characterizes traditional science is that the, usually male, investigator considers only his experience of reality. This very specific form of experience is then invested with the title of knowledge. Because the investigator has the exclusive right to the process of objectification that transforms experience into knowledge, what is usually termed 'knowledge' is a collection of falsifying universalisms. What results is abstract universality,

a false universality achieved by giving universal character to only one form of experience.

Instead, for Mangena, feminist epistemology should indicate how to achieve true or concrete universality (1994: 278). Such universality can be obtained when we assume 'a holistic approach to knowledge in the sense that both subjects and objects of experience are together involved in the process of formulating human knowledge from their distinct but interrelated situational experiences' (1994: 278). Knowledge is a process by means of which experiences are represented and objectified, and human experiences are always situational insofar as they emerge our of our relations with others. Thus, adequate knowledge requires a sort of participatory democracy. Everybody must be invited to participate to the process of objectification of experience so that all experiences are taken into account. In this manner, we can produce theories which represent the whole situation since they reflect the interrelated character of the experiences themselves (1994: 280). This participatory process gives rise to a concrete universality because it is possible to bring together all these different perspectives as a coherent whole (1994: 281). The resulting claims would have true universal applicability 'in the sense that they would refer to a multiplicity of concrete experience, although in general terms' (1994: 281).

To summarize, in recent years some feminists have claimed that experience can be a useful tool for epistemology as long as it is not understood as giving us an immediate and infallible access to the object of knowledge. Starting from experience is a sound starting point of inquiry if it is understood as a matter as starting from a perspective which is inevitably partial and subject to revision. The problem encountered by earlier versions of standpoint epistemology can be avoided if we acknowledge differences among women. We can, thus, admit the existence of multiple standpoints, which can perhaps be unified as Mangena suggests. Even if this unification is impossible, the multiplicity of viewpoints need not lead to relativism. We can admit the legitimacy of more than one perspective without claiming the all perspectives are as good as any other.

What is characteristic of all the very different versions of standpoint epistemology which I have discussed is the belief that objectivity can be achieved from partial perspectives. This claim requires that the very notion of 'objectivity' is given new meanings....

NOTES

1. For a good discussion of social marginality and economic centrality in the context of Marxist theory see Bar On (1993: 85–6).
2. Marxist theory of knowledge is, therefore, closer to traditional conceptions than one might expect, since it claims that lack of bias is a necessary condition for knowledge. This is an aspect of the theory which has been modified in some of its feminist reappropriations.
3. The debate over the need to supplement Marxism with accounts of patriarchy and of the sexual division of reproductive labor has been central to socialist feminist theories in the 1980s. Some feminists, for example Heidi Hartmann (1981), have argued for a dual theory of women's oppression in terms both of the structure of relations in society which constitutes capitalism, and of that which constitutes patriarchy. Others, such as Alison Jaggar (1983), have attempted to provide a unified theory which nevertheless takes into account the specificity of women's reproductive labor. For an overview of this debate, see chapter 6 of Rosemarie Tong (1992); for a discussion of these issues in a specifically epistemological context, see Rose (1986).
4. For a theoretically sophisticated account of gender-specific experiences, see Vrinda Dalmiya and Linda Alcoff (1993).
5. Hartstock (1983: 284) talks of division of labor by sex; but, as Rose (1986: 176) notices, this sort of talk 'pulls her arguments too strongly back to nature' and extenuates the socially sanctioned character of this division of labor.
6. For this interpretation see Harding (1986: 157). Although it seems quite clear that this is how Smith intends to characterize the experiential line of fault, her claim is too strong. If there truly were no way in our current society to give a name to one's experiences they could not constitute the basis for knowledge. We can, however, interpret Smith as claiming that it is not easy to give a name to one's actual experiences because they do not correspond to what, according to socially sanctioned norms, one ought to experience.

7. The issue here is made more complex by the Marxian rejection of a sharp dichotomy between natural and social worlds. Nevertheless, no feminist would argue that patriarchy is sufficient to explain every aspect of reality, therefore even complete knowledge about patriarchy will not be sufficient to have knowledge about other aspects of the world.
8. Thus, Rose (1994: 74) provides a very different explanation from the one I provide below of the role of object relations theory in standpoint epistemology.
9. The notion of a distinctive cognitive style of women has been explicitly endorsed, for example, by Shulamit Reinharz (1983: 183). For a critical discussion of this issue see Harding (1991: 121–2).
10. One must not assume that, were such a reevaluation to take place, women's perceived intellectual status would be improved. When the romantic movement glorified emotions and passions, women were seen to be deficient because they did not have them as much as men (Battersby, 1989: 113).
11. As Judith Grant (1987) notices this division seems to reinscribe rather than challenge patriarchal assumptions.
12. Marnia Lazreg (1994) raises these objections and finds their origin in an underexamined acceptance of the empiricist conception of experience.
13. In this context, for ease of exposition, I have chosen to leave unquestioned the received view about identity claims. According to this view, identity attributions describe features that individuals possess in virtue of their psychology, or of the social role they occupy.
14. Strictly speaking even a foundationalist can accept this point and argue that experience functions as evidence independent of theory, although one needs the theory to conceptualize experience.
15. Although Lazreg (1994) is right to claim that the notion of immediate experience is an outgrowth of classical empiricism, it is incorrect to deduce, as she does, from this that the projects of a

feminist standpoint or of a feminist empiricism must be abandoned. This unacceptable conception of experience is not essential to either.

16. Hartsock's view is similar to Wilfrid Sellars's anti-foundationalism, which I explained in chapter 1. Although experiential knowledge is not inferential, it counts as knowledge only against the background of other knowledge.

17. I follow Collins here in using 'standpoint' as synonymous with 'perspective.'

18. This would, of course, go against Marxian accounts of epistemic privilege of a standpoint.

19. As I said above this criticism of early standpoint theories is not entirely accurate.

⊚ CRITICAL QUESTION

1. Assuming that claims to knowledge reflect some particular standpoint, what would convince you that one standpoint is more privileged than another? Support your answer with an argument.

To access the *Voices of Wisdom*, 8th Edition, **Premium Website**, search for this book on CengageBrain.com.

CHAPTER NINE

Does Science Tell Us the Whole Truth and Nothing but the Truth?

Science is far from a perfect instrument of knowledge.
It is just the best we have.

CARL SAGAN, *"THE DEMON-HAUNTED WORLD"*

LEARNING OBJECTIVES

After studying this chapter students should be able to:
- explain the issues with which the philosophy of science deals,
- define scientism,
- define abduction and semiotics,
- describe the deductive-nomological model (covering law model),
- describe the hypothetico-deductive method,
- contrast normal with revolutionary science,
- explain why anomalies are important,
- define a paradigm in Kuhn's sense of the word,
- explain incommensurable and its relationship to paradigms,
- define theodicy,
- explain discursive formations and how they are related to the archeology and genealogy of knowledge,
- identify Peirce, Popper, Kuhn, Appiah, and Longino, and
- answer all the questions relating to the selections.

9.1 INTRODUCTION

As is our philosophical custom, a custom I trust you have all become accustomed to, let us begin by asking some questions about science. What makes a theory scientific? What is the difference between superstition and science? Does science progress at a steady pace, carefully building on previous discoveries? Is science objective? Is it value-free? What is the place of science in human life? Should it be subordinated to ethical and religious concerns? What is the relationship between scientific thinking and traditional modes of problem solving? Are scientific explanations and religious explanations logically similar?

These questions raise some of the issues we will explore in this chapter and some of the issues associated with an area of philosophical research known as the

philosophy of science. This branch of philosophy centers on a critical analysis of the various sciences, such as the physical, life, and behavioral sciences. To the extent that all of these sciences (physics, biology, psychology, and so on) share certain assumptions about the production of knowledge, the philosophy of science often focuses on methodological issues generally associated with all the sciences. Philosophers of science concern themselves with such topics as theory formation, the nature of hypotheses, the role of observation and experiment in the processes of verification and falsification, and the nature of explanation.

Clearly the philosophy of science is closely related to epistemology because of its concern with the role science plays in generating true statements that constitute knowledge about ourselves and the world in which we live. Questions about the nature of truth and the nature of knowledge inevitably arise as philosophical reflection on science proceeds. One cannot long ponder what is meant by such talk as "verifying a hypothesis" without wondering about truth and its possibility.

We live in a time and a place that puts a great deal of trust in science to tell us the truth and nothing but the truth. Many of our decisions, both public and private, are based on scientific information. We are wowed and amazed at the technological spin-offs scientific research engenders. Today we can do what only yesterday seemed like magic. We can travel in outer space and communicate within seconds with people on the other side of the earth.

Many people also mistrust science. They are uncertain about how reliable scientific theory is, what the limits of science are, and whether the technological marvels are ultimately conducive to living a better life. In the photo on one of the book's color plates, also, for example, some might see a timely reminder that the technological fruits of science can be dangerous and are not always safe under all conditions. Some scholars warn of **scientism**, a kind of blind faith in the power of science to determine all truth. Still others worry about the religious and moral implications of the trust many have in science.

I do not know how much interest you have in science or in the philosophy of science. It is, I think, very interesting from a theoretical point of view. Questions about the nature of scientific truth (if there is any) and questions about the differences between superstition and science can be fascinating in their own right. But the pursuit of answers to such questions may seem remote from the business of everyday life.

Studying the philosophy of science may seem irrelevant to our daily concerns, but it is not. We face a host of public policy debates, from global warming to genetic engineering, in which scientific evidence often plays a crucial role. The more we understand about the nature of scientific theories and the procedures of science, the better informed we will be when we make the difficult judgments we must make as we create public policy that will have a significant impact on our own future, as well as on the future of our children.

Is it a mark of scientific objectivity to present, as the media supposedly does, "all sides of the issue"? Or is it more objective to follow scientific consensus even when some scientists disagree with that consensus? How important is scientific consensus when it comes to matters of truth? Would good science counsel us to adopt a precautionary principle when it comes to new technologies? We require drug companies to prove scientifically that a new drug is safe before it is introduced to the public. However, we do not apply the same principle to environmental concerns. We allow the release of all kinds of chemicals into the atmosphere without any requirements that such actions be proved scientifically safe ahead of time. Why? Why do we trust science sometimes and reject it at other times? Why do we treat the controversies between creationists and evolutionists differently from conflicting claims between the Flat Earth Society and contemporary astronomers?

9.2 HOW DO WE COME TO BELIEVE?

Suppose you want to wax your car. How would you decide what wax to use? Well, you might use what I call the method of pondering. It is a method I very much favor when it is time to mow the lawn. You think about it. Roll it around in your mind. Examine the idea of auto wax from every angle and break it down into its various parts. You then reassemble them in different ways and, if you do this long enough in a comfortable deck chair on a warm sunny afternoon, you will soon fall asleep but will probably not wake up with a fixed belief about what wax is best, unless, of course, you have had a dream that reveals the truth about auto wax.

Waking up too late to wax the car, you decide on another method: the method of authority. You turn on the television and see what auto wax is advertised. After watching eight hours of ads for everything from tires and soap to dieting methods that will cause you to lose 50 pounds in less than 15 days without changing what you eat or getting off the couch in front of the TV, you decide this is taking far too long. But you have, you must admit, avoided waxing the car for two days now. Unfortunately you have no fixed belief about what wax to use, and the car remains wax free. At least you have flexibility.

Charles Sanders Peirce (1839–1914) would probably like this example of methods for fixing belief (as he would put it) about the best wax. Peirce was amazed at all the different methods for arriving at fixed beliefs that humans use, many of which don't work very well.

Peirce is the author of the next selection. He was a maverick but brilliant philosopher, mathematician, logician, and scientist who held no permanent academic post during his lifetime. Yet his ideas lay at the foundation of the distinctive American philosophy called pragmatism (Section 8.5). In addition to the two standard forms of logical reasoning called induction and deduction, Peirce added a third, which he called *abduction*. Abduction is a method for discovering (as opposed to justifying) the best scientific hypotheses out of a nearly infinite number available to our minds when we confront problems that need solutions. He also made significant contributions to a general theory of signs called *semiotics*. He developed the pragmatist principle for clarifying concepts, although he disagreed with the interpretation of this principle by his friend William James. In response to James's interpretation of pragmatism as a theory of truth centering on the notion of what, in the long run, "works," he renamed his version *pragmaticism*.

In the opening section (not included here) of the following essay, Peirce provides a brief history of inquiry and a very general look at logical reasoning. We pick up the story at the point he begins to consider the difference between belief and doubt.

The Fixation of Belief

CHARLES SANDERS PEIRCE

We generally know when we wish to ask a question and when we wish to pronounce a judgment, for there is a dissimilarity between the sensation of doubting and that of believing.

But this is not all which distinguishes doubt from belief. There is a practical difference. Our beliefs guide our desires and shape our actions. The Assassins, or followers of the Old Man of the Mountain, used to rush into death at his least command, because they believed that obedience to him would insure everlasting felicity. Had they doubted this, they would not have acted as they did. So it is with every belief, according to its degree. The feeling of believing is a more or less sure indication of there being established in our nature some habit which will determine our actions. Doubt never has such an effect.

Nor must we overlook a third point of difference. Doubt is an uneasy and dissatisfied state from which we struggle to free ourselves and pass into the state of belief; while the latter is a calm and satisfactory state which we do not wish to avoid, or to change to a belief in anything else.[1]

On the contrary, we cling tenaciously, not merely to believing, but to believing just what we do believe.

Thus, both doubt and belief have positive effects upon us, though very different ones. Belief does not make us act at once, but puts us into such a condition that we shall behave in a certain way, when the occasion arises. Doubt has not the least effect of this sort, but stimulates us to action until it is destroyed. This reminds us of the irritation of a nerve and the reflex action produced thereby; while for the analogue of belief, in the nervous system, we must look to what are called nervous associations—for example, to that habit of the nerves in consequence of which the smell of a peach will make the mouth water.

The irritation of doubt causes a struggle to attain a state of belief. I shall term this struggle *inquiry*, though it must be admitted that this is sometimes not a very apt designation.

The irritation of doubt is the only immediate motive for the struggle to attain belief. It is certainly best for us that our beliefs should be such as may truly guide our actions so as to satisfy our desires; and this reflection will make us reject any belief which does not seem to have been so formed as to insure this result. But it will only do so by creating a doubt in the place of that belief.

---

[1] I am not speaking of secondary effects occasionally produced by the interference of other impulses.

From "The Fixation of Belief," by Charles Sanders Peirce, from *Popular Science Monthly*, Vol. 12 (November, 1977), pp. 3–15. Footnotes renumbered.

With the doubt, therefore, the struggle begins, and with the cessation of doubt it ends. Hence, the sole object of inquiry is the settlement of opinion. We may fancy that this is not enough for us, and that we seek, not merely an opinion, but a true opinion. But put this fancy to the test, and it proves groundless; for as soon as a firm belief is reached we are entirely satisfied, whether the belief be true or false. And it is clear that nothing out of the sphere of our knowledge can be our object, for nothing which does not affect the mind can be the motive for a mental effort. The most that can be maintained is, that we seek for a belief that we shall *think* to be true. But we think each one of our beliefs to be true, and, indeed, it is mere tautology to say so.

That the settlement of opinion is the sole end of inquiry is a very important proposition. It sweeps away, at once, various vague and erroneous conceptions of proof. A few of these may be noticed here.

1. Some philosophers have imagined that to start an inquiry it was only necessary to utter a question or set it down upon paper, and have even recommended us to begin our studies with questioning everything! But the mere putting of a proposition into the interrogative form does not stimulate the mind to any struggle after belief. There must be a real and living doubt, and without this all discussion is idle.
2. It is a very common idea that a demonstration must rest on some ultimate and absolutely indubitable propositions. These, according to one school, are first principles of a general nature; according to another, are first sensations. But, in point of fact, an inquiry, to have that completely satisfactory result called demonstration, has only to start with propositions perfectly free from all actual doubt. If the premises are not in fact doubted at all, they cannot be more satisfactory than they are.
3. Some people seem to love to argue a point after all the world is fully convinced of it. But no further advance can be made. When doubt ceases, mental action on the subject comes to an end; and, if it did go on, it would be without a purpose.

If the settlement of opinion is the sole object of inquiry, and if belief is of the nature of a habit, why should we not attain the desired end, by taking any answer to a question which we may fancy, and constantly reiterating it to ourselves, dwelling on all which may conduce to that belief, and learning to turn with contempt and hatred from anything which might disturb it? This simple and direct method is really pursued by many men. I remember once being entreated not to read a certain newspaper lest it might change my opinion upon free-trade. "Lest I might be entrapped by its fallacies and misstatements," was the form of expression. "You are not," my friend said, "a special student of political economy. You might, therefore, easily be deceived by fallacious arguments upon the subject. You might, then, if you read this paper, be led to believe in protection. But you admit that free-trade is the true doctrine; and you do not wish to believe what is not true." I have often known this system to be deliberately adopted. Still oftener, the instinctive dislike of an undecided state of mind, exaggerated into a vague dread of doubt, makes men cling spasmodically to the views they already take. The man feels that, if he only holds to his belief without wavering, it will be entirely satisfactory. Nor can it be denied that a steady and immovable faith yields great peace of mind. It may, indeed, give rise to inconveniences, as if a man should resolutely continue to believe that fire would not burn him, or that he would be eternally damned if he received his *ingesta* otherwise than through a stomach-pump. But then the man who adopts this method will not allow that its inconveniences are greater than its advantages. He will say, "I hold steadfastly to the truth, and the truth is always wholesome." And in many cases it may very well be that the pleasure he derives from his calm faith overbalances any inconveniences resulting from its deceptive character. Thus, if it be true that death is annihilation, then the man who believes that he will certainly go straight to heaven when he dies, provided he has fulfilled certain simple observances in this life, has a cheap pleasure which will not be followed by the least disappointment. A similar consideration seems to have weight with many persons in religious topics, for we frequently hear it said, "Oh, I could not believe so-and-so, because I should be wretched if I did." When an ostrich buries its head in the sand as danger approaches, it very likely takes the happiest course. It hides the danger, and then calmly says there is no danger; and, if it feels perfectly sure there is none, why should it raise its head to see? A man may go through life, systematically keeping out of view all that might cause a change in his opinions, and if he only succeeds—basing his method, as he does, on two fundamental psychological laws—I do not see what can be said against his doing so. It would be an egotistical impertinence to object that his procedure is irrational, for that only amounts to saying that his method of settling belief is not ours. He does not propose to himself to be rational, and, indeed, will often talk with scorn of man's weak and illusive reason. So let him think as he pleases.

But this method of fixing belief, which may be called the method of tenacity, will be unable to hold its ground in practice. The social impulse is against it. The man who adopts it will find that other men think differently from him, and it will be apt to occur to him, in some saner moment, that their opinions are quite as good as his own, and this will shake his confidence in his belief. This conception, that another man's thought or sentiment may be equivalent to one's own, is a distinctly new step, and a highly important one. It arises from an impulse too strong in man to be suppressed, without danger of destroying the human species. Unless we make ourselves hermits, we shall necessarily influence each other's opinions; so that the problem becomes how to fix belief, not in the individual merely, but in the community.

Let the will of the state act, then, instead of that of the individual. Let an institution be created which shall have for its object to keep correct doctrines before the attention of the people, to reiterate them perpetually, and to teach them to the young; having at the same time power to prevent contrary doctrines from being taught, advocated, or expressed. Let all possible causes of a change of mind be removed from men's apprehensions. Let them be kept ignorant, lest they should learn of some reason to think otherwise than they do. Let their passions be enlisted, so that they may regard private and unusual opinions with hatred and horror. Then, let all men who reject the established belief be terrified into silence. Let the people turn out and tar-and-feather such men, or let inquisitions be made into the manner of thinking of suspected persons, and, when they are found guilty of forbidden beliefs, let them be subjected to some signal punishment. When complete agreement could not otherwise be reached, a general massacre of all who have not thought in a certain way has proved a very effective means of settling opinion in a country. If the power to do this be wanting, let a list of opinions be drawn up, to which no man of the least independence of thought can assent, and let the faithful be required to accept all these propositions, in order to segregate them as radically as possible from the influence of the rest of the world.

This method has, from the earliest times, been one of the chief means of upholding correct theological and political doctrines, and of preserving their universal or catholic character. In Rome, especially, it has been practised from the days of Numa Pompilius to those of Pius Nonus. This is the most perfect example in history; but wherever there is a priesthood—and no religion has been without one—this method has been more or less made use of. Wherever there is an aristocracy, or a guild, or any association of a class of men whose interests depend or are supposed to depend on certain propositions, there will be inevitably found some traces of this natural product of social feeling. Cruelties always accompany this system; and when it is consistently carried out, they become atrocities of the most horrible kind in the eyes of any rational man. Nor should this occasion surprise, for the officer of a society does not feel justified in surrendering the interests of that society for the sake of mercy, as he might his own private interests. It is natural, therefore, that sympathy and fellowship should thus produce a most ruthless power.

In judging this method of fixing belief, which may be called the method of authority, we must, in the first place, allow its immeasurable mental and moral superiority to the method of tenacity. Its success is proportionately greater; and, in fact, it has over and over again worked the most majestic results. The mere structures of stone which it has caused to be put together—in Siam, for example, in Egypt, and in Europe—have many of them a sublimity hardly more than rivaled by the greatest works of Nature. And, except the geological epochs, there are no periods of time so vast as those which are measured by some of these organized faiths. If we scrutinize the matter closely, we shall find that there has not been one of their creeds which has remained always the same; yet the change is so slow as to be imperceptible during one person's life, so that individual belief remains sensibly fixed. For the mass of mankind, then, there is perhaps no better method than this. If it is their highest impulse to be intellectual slaves, then slaves they ought to remain.

But no institution can undertake to regulate opinions upon every subject. Only the most important ones can be attended to, and on the rest men's minds must be left to the action of natural causes. This imperfection will be no source of weakness so long as men are in such a state of culture that one opinion does not influence another—that is, so long as they cannot put two and two together. But in the most priestridden states some individuals will be found who are raised above that condition. These men possess a wider sort of social feeling; they see that men in other countries and in other ages have held to very different doctrines from those which they themselves have been brought up to believe; and they cannot help seeing that it is the mere accident of their having been taught as they have, and of their having been surrounded with the manners and associations they have, that has caused them to believe as they do and not far differently. And their candor cannot resist the reflection that there is no reason to rate their own views at a higher value than those of other nations and other centuries; and this gives rise to doubts in their minds.

They will further perceive that such doubts as these must exist in their minds with reference to

every belief which seems to be determined by the caprice either of themselves or of those who originated the popular opinions. The willful adherence to a belief, and the arbitrary forcing of it upon others, must, therefore, both be given up, and a new method of settling opinions must be adopted, which shall not only produce an impulse to believe, but shall also decide what proposition it is which is to be believed. Let the action of natural preferences be unimpeded, then, and under their influence let men, conversing together and regarding matters in different lights, gradually develop beliefs in harmony with natural causes. This method resembles that by which conceptions of art have been brought to maturity. The most perfect example of it is to be found in the history of metaphysical philosophy. Systems of this sort have not usually rested upon any observed facts, at least not in any great degree. They have been chiefly adopted because their fundamental propositions seemed "agreeable to reason." This is an apt expression; it does not mean that which agrees with experience, but that which we find ourselves inclined to believe. Plato, for example, finds it agreeable to reason that the distances of the celestial spheres from one another should be proportional to the different lengths of strings which produce harmonious chords. Many philosophers have been led to their main conclusions by considerations like this; but this is the lowest and least developed form which the method takes, for it is clear that another man might find Kepler's theory, that the celestial spheres are proportional to the inscribed and circumscribed spheres of the different regular solids, more agreeable to *his* reason. But the shock of opinions will soon lead men to rest on preferences of a far more universal nature. Take, for example, the doctrine that man only acts selfishly—that is, from the consideration that acting in one way will afford him more pleasure than acting in another. This rests on no fact in the world, but it has had a wide acceptance as being the only reasonable theory.

This method is far more intellectual and respectable from the point of view of reason than either of the others which we have noticed. But its failure has been the most manifest. It makes of inquiry something similar to the development of taste; but taste, unfortunately, is always more or less a matter of fashion, and accordingly metaphysicians have never come to any fixed agreement, but the pendulum has swung backward and forward between a more material and a more spiritual philosophy, from the earliest times to the latest. And so from this, which has been called the *a priori* method, we are driven, in Lord Bacon's phrase, to a true induction. We have examined into this *a priori* method as something which promised to deliver our opinions from their accidental and capricious element. But development, while it is a process which eliminates the effect of some casual circumstances, only magnifies that of others. This method, therefore, does not differ in a very essential way from that of authority. The government may not have lifted its finger to influence my convictions; I may have been left outwardly quite free to choose, we will say, between monogamy and polygamy, and, appealing to my conscience only, I may have concluded that the latter practice is in itself licentious. But when I come to see that the chief obstacle to the spread of Christianity among a people of as high culture as the Hindoos has been a conviction of the immorality of our way of treating women, I cannot help seeing that, though governments do not interfere, sentiments in their development will be very greatly determined by accidental causes. Now, there are some people, among whom I must suppose that my reader is to be found, who, when they see that any belief of theirs is determined by any circumstance extraneous to the facts, will from that moment not merely admit in words that that belief is doubtful, but will experience a real doubt of it, so that it ceases to be a belief.

To satisfy our doubts, therefore, it is necessary that a method should be found by which our beliefs may be caused by nothing human, but by some external permanency—by something upon which our thinking has no effect. Some mystics imagine that they have such a method in a private inspiration from on high. But that is only a form of the method of tenacity, in which the conception of truth as something public is not yet developed. Our external permanency would not be external, in our sense, if it was restricted in its influence to one individual. It must be something which affects, or might affect, every man. And, though these affections are necessarily as various as are individual conditions, yet the method must be such that the ultimate conclusion of every man shall be the same. Such is the method of science. Its fundamental hypothesis, restated in more familiar language, is this: There are real things, whose characters are entirely independent of our opinions about them; those realities affect our senses according to regular laws, and though our sensations are as different as our relations to the objects, yet, by taking advantage of the laws of perception, we can ascertain by reasoning how things really are, and any man, if he have sufficient experience and reason enough about it, will be led to the one true conclusion. The new conception here involved is that of reality. It may be asked how I know that there are any realities. If this hypothesis is the sole support of my method of inquiry, my method of inquiry must not be used to support my hypothesis. The reply is this: 1. If investigation cannot be regarded as proving that there are real things, it at least does not lead to a contrary conclusion; but the method and the conception on which it is based remain ever in harmony. No doubts of the method, therefore, necessarily arise from its practice, as is the case with all the others. 2. The feeling which gives rise to any method of fixing belief is a dissatisfaction at two repugnant propositions. But here already is a vague concession that there is some one thing to which a proposition should conform. Nobody, therefore, can really doubt that there are realities, or, if he did, doubt would not be a source of dissatisfaction. The hypothesis, therefore, is one which every mind admits. So that the social impulse does not cause me to doubt it. 3. Everybody uses the scientific method about a great many things, and only ceases to use it when he does not know how to apply it. 4. Experience of the method has not led me to doubt it, but, on the contrary, scientific investigation has had the most wonderful triumphs in the way of settling opinion. These afford the explanation of my not doubting the method or the hypothesis which it supposes; and not having any doubt, nor believing that anybody else whom I could influence has, it would be the merest babble for me to say more about it. If there be anybody with a living doubt upon the subject, let him consider it.

To describe the method of scientific investigation is the object of this series of papers. At present I have only room to notice some points of contrast between it and other methods of fixing belief. This is the only one of the four methods which presents any distinction of a right and a wrong way. If I adopt the method of tenacity and shut myself out from all influences, whatever I think necessary to doing this is necessary according to that method. So with the method of authority: the state may try to put down heresy by means which, from a scientific point of view, seem very ill-calculated to accomplish its purposes; but the only test *on that method* is what the state thinks, so that it cannot pursue the method wrongly. So with the *a priori* method. The very essence of it is to think as one is inclined to think. All metaphysicians will be sure to do that, however they may be inclined to judge each other to be perversely wrong. The Hegelian system recognizes every natural tendency of thought as logical, although it be certain to be abolished by counter-tendencies. Hegel thinks there is a regular system in the succession of these tendencies, in consequence of which, after drifting one way and the other for a long time, opinion will at last go right. And it is true that metaphysicians get the right ideas at last; Hegel's system of Nature represents tolerably the science of that day; and one may be sure that whatever scientific investigation has put out of doubt will presently receive *a priori* demonstration on the part of the metaphysicians. But with the scientific method the case is different. I may start with known and observed facts to proceed to the unknown; and yet the rules which I follow in doing so may not be such as investigation would approve. The test of whether I am truly following the method is not an immediate appeal to my feelings and purposes, but, on the contrary, itself involves the application of the method. Hence it is that bad reasoning as well as

good reasoning is possible; and this fact is the foundation of the practical side of logic.

It is not to be supposed that the first three methods of settling opinion present no advantage whatever over the scientific method. On the contrary, each has some peculiar convenience of its own. The *a priori* method is distinguished for its comfortable conclusions. It is the nature of the process to adopt whatever belief we are inclined to, and there are certain flatteries to the vanity of man which we all believe by nature, until we are awakened from our pleasing dream by some rough facts. The method of authority will always govern the mass of mankind; and those who wield the various forms of organized force in the state will never be convinced that dangerous reasoning ought not to be suppressed in some way. If liberty of speech is to be untrammeled from the grosser forms of constraint, then uniformity of opinion will be secured by a moral terrorism to which the respectability of society will give its thorough approval. Following the method of authority is the path of peace. Certain non-conformities are permitted; certain others (considered unsafe) are forbidden. These are different in different countries and in different ages; but, wherever you are, let it be known that you seriously hold a tabooed belief, and you may be perfectly sure of being treated with a cruelty less brutal but more refined than hunting you like a wolf. Thus, the greatest intellectual benefactors of mankind have never dared, and dare not now, to utter the whole of their thought; and thus a shade of *prima facie* doubt is cast upon every proposition which is considered essential to the security of society. Singularly enough, the persecution does not all come from without; but a man torments himself and is oftentimes most distressed at finding himself believing propositions which he has been brought up to regard with aversion. The peaceful and sympathetic man will, therefore, find it hard to resist the temptation to submit his opinions to authority. But most of all I admire the method of tenacity for its strength, simplicity, and directness. Men who pursue it are distinguished for their decision of character, which becomes very easy with such a mental rule. They do not waste time in trying to make up their minds what they want, but, fastening like lightning upon whatever alternative comes first, they hold to it to the end, whatever happens, without an instant's irresolution. This is one of the splendid qualities which generally accompany brilliant, unlasting success. It is impossible not to envy the man who can dismiss reason, although we know how it must turn out at last.

Such are the advantages which the other methods of settling opinion have over scientific investigation. A man should consider well of them; and then he should consider that, after all, he wishes his opinions to coincide with the fact, and that there is no reason why the results of these three methods should do so. To bring about this effect is the prerogative of the method of science. Upon such considerations he has to make his choice—a choice which is far more than the adoption of any intellectual opinion, which is one of the ruling decisions of his life, to which, when once made, he is bound to adhere. The force of habit will sometimes cause a man to hold on to old beliefs, after he is in a condition to see that they have no sound basis. But reflection upon the state of the case will overcome these habits, and he ought to allow reflection its full weight. People sometimes shrink from doing this, having an idea that beliefs are wholesome which they cannot help feeling rest on nothing. But let such persons suppose an analogous though different case from their own. Let them ask themselves what they would say to a reformed Mussulman who should hesitate to give up his old notions in regard to the relations of the sexes; or to a reformed Catholic who should still shrink from reading the Bible. Would they not say that these persons ought to consider the matter fully, and clearly understand the new doctrine, and then ought to embrace it, in its entirety? But, above all, let it be considered that what is more wholesome than any particular belief is integrity of belief, and that to avoid looking into the support of any belief from a fear that it may turn out rotten is quite as immoral as it is disadvantageous. The person who confesses that there is such a thing as truth, which is distinguished from falsehood simply by this, that if acted on it will carry us to the point we aim at and not astray, and then, though convinced of this, dares not know the truth and seeks to avoid it, is in a sorry state of mind indeed.

Yes, the other methods do have their merits: a clear logical conscience does cost something—just as any virtue, just as all that we cherish, costs us dear. But we should not desire it to be otherwise. The genius of a man's logical method should be loved and reverenced as his bride, whom he has chosen from all the world. He need not condemn the others; on the contrary, he may honor them deeply, and in doing so he only honors her the more. But she is the one that he has chosen, and he knows that he was right in making that choice. And having made it, he will work and fight for her, and will not complain that there are blows to take, hoping that there may be as many and as hard to give, and will strive to be the worthy knight and champion of her from the blaze of whose splendors he draws his inspiration and his courage.

⊚ CRITICAL QUESTIONS

1. How does Peirce answer the question about how one can know that there are any "realities"? Do you find his answer satisfactory? Why, or why not?

2. Do you think that the method of science is a better way for gaining truth than other methods? Why, or why not?

9.3 THE GROWTH OF SCIENTIFIC KNOWLEDGE

What exactly is science? What do we mean when we call an idea or a theory scientific? How does a scientific idea differ from the ideas of common sense? Certainly one can make a case that science is nothing but just plain, good common sense. Do not both science and common sense share the same goals?

In thinking about these questions I am sure the concept of explanation came to your mind. Science explains things. It answers the "why" and the "how" questions about natural events. It explains what causes what. In good philosophical fashion, however, we must press further and ask what an explanation is.

Many (but not all) philosophers of science subscribe to the **deductive-nomological model** (also called the **covering law model**) of explanation. According to this model, an explanation of an event consists in "covering" or "subsuming" the event under some law. In other words, explaining something requires that a description of it is deducible from the relevant laws of nature. One might explain, for example, the expansion of some metal by appealing to some law such as "metal expands when heated." (Note: this is a highly simplified and nontechnical version of the physical laws involved. One can still ask why heat causes expansion.)

So science is concerned with laws, the laws of nature as some would say. Here science seems to go beyond common sense. Scientists discover and formulate natural laws, and science allows us to accomplish much more than common sense allows. The concept of law is important in science because it makes predictions possible, and predictions make control possible. If I can predict exactly how much a metal will expand when heated to such and such a degree, I have much greater control over the behavior of, let us say, a combustion engine, than I would otherwise. So philosophers of science need to ponder the nature of natural laws and how they are discovered. They must explore how scientists construct scientific concepts.

In addition to problems about the nature of explanation and the construction of scientific concepts like natural law, the philosopher of science must give some account of how scientific conclusions are validated. How do we know when we have arrived at a scientific truth? Is it significantly different from how we know when we have arrived at a common sense truth?

Karl Popper (1902–1994) was an Austrian-born British philosopher who took issue with the notion that scientific progress consists in extending the laws of nature to explain more and more hitherto unexplained events. Although Popper did not totally reject the deductive-nomological model, he did try to refocus the attention of philosophers of science on issues surrounding the testability of what he liked to call *conjectures*. Science grows not so much by deducing hypotheses from some known laws as it does by making interesting guesses and then subjecting those guesses to rigorous criticism. It is more fruitful, Popper maintained, to try to disprove or falsify a conjecture than to verify or confirm it.

◉ READING QUESTIONS

1. What is Popper's first thesis, and what does it imply?
2. What is the difference between the verificationists and the falsificationists?
3. According to Popper, what makes scientific theorizing rational?
4. What did Popper mean when he asserted "truth is not the only aim of science"?
5. What are the three requirements of a good scientific theory?
6. How does the third requirement differ from the first two?

Conjectures and Refutations

KARL POPPER

I

My aim in this lecture is to stress the significance of one particular aspect of science—its need to grow, or, if you like, its need to progress. I do not have in mind here the practical or social significance of this need. What I wish to discuss is rather its intellectual significance. I assert that continued growth is essential to the rational and empirical character of scientific knowledge; that if science ceases to grow it must lose that character. It is the way of its growth which makes science rational and empirical; the way, that is, in which scientists discriminate between available theories and choose the better one or (in the absence of a satisfactory theory) the way they give reasons for rejecting all the available theories, thereby suggesting some of the conditions with which a satisfactory theory should comply.

You will have noticed from this formulation that it is not the accumulation of observations which I have in mind when I speak of the growth of scientific knowledge, but the repeated overthrow of scientific theories and their replacement by better or more satisfactory ones. This, incidentally, is a procedure which might be found worthy of attention even by those who see the most important aspect of the growth of scientific knowledge in new experiments and in new observations. For our critical examination of our theories leads us to attempts to test and to overthrow them; and these lead us further to experiments and observations of a kind which nobody would ever have dreamt of without the stimulus and guidance both of our theories and of our criticism of them. For indeed, the most interesting experiments and observations were carefully designed by us in order to test our theories, especially our new theories.

In this paper, then, I wish to stress the significance of this aspect of science and to solve some of the problems, old as well as new, which are connected with the notions of scientific progress and of discrimination among competing theories. The new problems I wish to discuss are mainly those connected with the notions of objective truth, and of getting nearer to the truth—notions which seem to me of great help in analysing the growth of knowledge.

Although I shall confine my discussion to the growth of knowledge in science, my remarks are applicable without much change, I believe, to the growth of pre-scientific knowledge also—that is to say, to the general way in which men, and even animals, acquire new factual knowledge about the world. The method of learning by trial and error—of learning from our mistakes—seems to be fundamentally the same whether it is practised by lower or by higher animals, by chimpanzees or by men of science. My interest is not merely in the theory of scientific knowledge, but rather in the theory of knowledge in general. Yet the study of the growth of scientific knowledge is, I believe, the most fruitful way of studying the growth of knowledge in general. For the growth of scientific knowledge may be said to be the growth of ordinary human knowledge *writ large* (as I have pointed out in the 1958 Preface to my *Logic of Scientific Discovery*).

But is there any danger that our need to progress will go unsatisfied, and that the growth of scientific knowledge will come to an end? In particular, is there any danger that the advance of science will come to an end because science has completed its task? I hardly think so, thanks to the infinity of our ignorance. Among the real dangers to the progress of science is not the likelihood of

From Karl R. Popper, *Conjectures and Refutations: The Growth of Scientific Knowledge* (London: Routledge, 1963), pp. 215–217, 228–231, 240–244. Footnotes deleted. Copyright © Karl R. Popper 1963. Copyright © since 1994 The Estate of Sir Karl Popper.

its being completed, but such things as lack of imagination (sometimes a consequence of lack of real interest); or a misplaced faith in formalization and precision …; or authoritarianism in one or another of its many forms.

Since I have used the word "progress" several times, I had better make quite sure, at this point, that I am not mistaken for a believer in a historical law of progress. Indeed I have before now struck various blows against the belief in a law of progress, and I hold that even science is not subject to the operation of anything resembling such a law. The history of science, like the history of all human ideas, is a history of irresponsible dreams, of obstinacy, and of error. But science is one of the very few human activities—perhaps the only one—in which errors are systematically criticized and fairly often, in time, corrected. This is why we can say that, in science, we often learn from our mistakes, and why we can speak clearly and sensibly about making progress there. In most other fields of human endeavour there is change, but rarely progress (unless we adopt a very narrow view of our possible aims in life); for almost every gain is balanced, or more than balanced, by some loss. And in most fields we do not even know how to evaluate change.

Within the field of science we have, however, a *criterion of progress:* even before a theory has ever undergone an empirical test we may be able to say whether, provided it passes certain specified tests, it would be an improvement on other theories with which we are acquainted. This is my first thesis.

To put it a little differently, I assert that we *know* what a good scientific theory should be like, and—even before it has been tested—what kind of theory would be better still, provided it passes certain crucial tests. And it is this (meta-scientific) knowledge which makes it possible to speak of progress in science, and of a rational choice between theories.

II

Thus it is my first thesis that we can know of a theory, even before it has been tested, that if it passes certain tests it will be better than some other theory.

My first thesis implies that we have a criterion of relative *potential* satisfactoriness, or of *potential* progressiveness, which can be applied to a theory even before we know whether or not it will turn out, by the passing of some crucial tests, to be satisfactory *in fact*.

This criterion of relative potential satisfactoriness (which I formulated some time ago, and which, incidentally, allows us to grade theories according to their degree of relative potential satisfactoriness) is extremely simple and intuitive. It characterizes as preferable the theory which tells us more; that is to say, the theory which contains the greater amount of empirical information or *content*; which is logically stronger; which has the greater explanatory and predictive power; and which can therefore be *more severely tested* by comparing predicted facts with observations. In short, we prefer an interesting, daring, and highly informative theory to a trivial one.

All these properties which, it thus appears, we desire in a theory can be shown to amount to one and the same thing: to a higher degree of empirical *content* or of testability….

IX

Like many other philosophers I am at times inclined to classify philosophers as belonging to two main groups—those with whom I disagree, and those who agree with me. I also call them the verificationists or the justificationist philosophers of knowledge (or of belief), and the falsificationists or fallibilists or critical philosophers of knowledge (or of conjectures). I may mention in passing a third group with whom I also disagree. They may be called the disappointed justificationists—the irrationalists and sceptics.

The members of the first group—the verificationists or justificationists—hold, roughly speaking, that whatever cannot be supported by positive reasons is unworthy of being believed, or even of being taken into serious consideration.

On the other hand, the members of the second group—the falsificationists or fallibilists—say, roughly speaking, that what cannot (at present) in principle be overthrown by criticism is (at present) unworthy of being seriously considered; while what can in principle be so overthrown and yet resists all our critical efforts to do so may quite possibly be false, but is at any rate not unworthy of being seriously considered and perhaps even of being believed—though only tentatively.

Verificationists, I admit, are eager to uphold that most important tradition of rationalism—the fight of reason against superstition and arbitrary authority. For they demand that we should accept a belief *only if it can be justified by positive evidence*; that is to say, *shown* to be true, or, at least, to be highly probable. In other words, they demand that we should accept a belief only if it can be *verified,* or probabilistically *confirmed.*

Falsificationists (the group of fallibilists to which I belong) believe—as most irrationalists also believe—that they have discovered logical arguments which show that the programme of the first group cannot be carried out: that we can never give positive reasons which justify the belief that a theory is true. But, unlike irrationalists, we falsificationists believe that we have also discovered a way to realize the old ideal of distinguishing rational science from various forms of superstition, in spite of the breakdown of the original inductivist or justificationist programme. We hold that this ideal can be realized, very simply, by recognizing that the rationality of science lies not in its habit of appealing to empirical evidence in support of its dogmas—astrologers do so too—but solely in the *critical approach*—in an attitude which, of course, involves the critical use, among other arguments, of empirical evidence (especially in refutations). For us, therefore, science has nothing to do with the quest for certainty or probability or reliability. We are not interested in establishing scientific theories as secure, or certain, or probable. Conscious of our fallibility we are only interested in criticizing them and testing them, in the hope of finding out where we are mistaken; of learning from our mistakes; and, if we are lucky, of proceeding to better theories.

Considering their views about the positive or negative function of argument in science, the first group—the justificationists—may be also nicknamed the "positivists" and the second—the group to which I belong—the critics or the "negativists." These are, of course, mere nicknames.

Yet they may perhaps suggest some of the reasons why some people believe that only the positivists or verificationists are seriously interested in truth and in the search for truth, while we, the critics or negativists, are flippant about the search for truth, and addicted to barren and destructive criticism and to the propounding of views which are clearly paradoxical.

This mistaken picture of our views seems to result largely from the adoption of a justificationist programme, and of the mistaken subjectivist approach to truth which I have described.

For the fact is that we too see science as the search for truth, and that, at least since Tarski, we are no longer afraid to say so. Indeed, it is only with respect to this aim, the discovery of truth, that we can say that though we are fallible, we hope to learn from our mistakes. It is only the idea of truth which allows us to speak sensibly of mistakes and of rational criticism, and which makes rational discussion possible—that is to say, critical discussion in search of mistakes with the serious purpose of eliminating as many of these mistakes as we can, in order to get nearer to the truth. Thus the very idea of error—and of fallibility—involves the idea of an objective truth as the standard of which we may fall short. (It is in this sense that the idea of truth is a *regulative* idea.)

Thus we accept the idea that the task of science is the search for truth, that is, for true theories (even though as Xenophanes pointed out we may never get them, or know them *as true* if we get them). Yet we also stress that *truth is not the only aim of science.* We want more than mere truth: what we look for is *interesting truth*—truth which is hard to come by. And in the natural sciences (as distinct from mathematics) what we look for is truth which has a high degree of explanatory power, which implies that it is logically improbable.

For it is clear, first of all, that we do not merely want truth—we want more truth, and new truth. We are not content with "twice two equals four," even though it is true: we do not resort to reciting the multiplication table if we are faced with a difficult problem in topology or in physics. Mere truth is not enough; what we look for are *answers to our problems.* The point has been well put by the German humorist and poet Busch, of Max-and-Moritz fame, in a little nursery rhyme—I mean a rhyme for the epistemological nursery:

> *Twice two equals four: 'tis true,*
> *But too empty, and too trite.*
> *What I look for is a clue*
> *To some matters not so light.*

Only if it is an answer to a problem—a difficult, a fertile problem, a problem of some depth—does a truth, or a conjecture about the truth, become relevant to science. This is so in pure mathematics, and it is so in the natural sciences. And in the latter, we have something like a logical measure of the depth or significance of the problem in the increase of logical improbability or explanatory power of the proposed new answer, as compared with the best theory or conjecture previously proposed in the field. This logical measure is essentially the same thing which I have described above as the logical criterion of potential satisfactoriness and of progress.

My description of this situation might tempt some people to say that truth does not, after all, play a very big role with us negativists even as a regulative principle. There can be no doubt, they will say, that negativists (like myself) much prefer an attempt to solve an interesting problem by a bold conjecture, *even if it soon turns out to be false,* to any recital of a sequence of true but uninteresting assertions. Thus it does not seem, after all, as if we negativists had much use for the idea of truth. Our ideas of scientific progress and of attempted problem-solving do not seem very closely related to it.

This, I believe, would give quite a mistaken impression of the attitude of our group. Call us negativists, or what you like: but you should realize that we are as much interested in truth as anybody—for example, as the members of a court of justice. When the judge tells a witness that he should speak "The truth, the *whole truth,* and nothing but the truth," then what he looks for is as much of the *relevant truth* as the witness may be able to offer. A witness who likes to

wander off into irrelevancies is unsatisfactory as a witness, even though these irrelevancies may be truisms, and thus part of "the whole truth." It is quite obvious that what the judge—or anybody else—wants when he asks for "the whole truth" is as much *interesting and relevant* true information as can be got; and many perfectly candid witnesses have failed to disclose some important information simply because they were unaware of its relevance to the case.

Thus when we stress, with Busch, that we are not interested in mere truth but in interesting and relevant truth, then, I contend, we only emphasize a point which everybody accepts. And if we are interested in bold conjectures, even if these should soon turn out to be false, then this interest is due to our methodological conviction that only with the help of such bold conjectures can we hope to discover interesting and relevant truth.

There is a point here which, I suggest, it is the particular task of the logician to analyse. "Interests," or "relevance," in the sense here intended, can be *objectively* analysed; it is relative to our problems; and it depends on the explanatory power, and thus on the content or improbability, of the information. The measures alluded to earlier … are precisely such measures as take account of some *relative content* of the information—its content relative to a hypothesis or to a problem.

I can therefore gladly admit that falsificationists like myself much prefer an attempt to solve an interesting problem by a bold conjecture, *even (and especially) if it soon turns out to be false,* to any recital of a sequence of irrelevant truisms. We prefer this because we believe that this is the way in which we can learn from our mistakes; and that in finding that our conjecture was false, we shall have learnt much about the truth, and shall have got nearer to the truth.

I therefore hold that both ideas—the idea of truth, in the sense of correspondence with the facts and the idea of content (which may be measured by the same measure as testability)—play about equally important roles in our considerations, and that both can shed much light on the idea of progress in science....

XVIII

… What is the general problem situation in which the scientist finds himself? He has before him a scientific problem: he wants to find a new theory capable of explaining certain experimental facts; facts which the earlier theories successfully explained; others which they could not explain; and some by which they were actually falsified. The new theory should also resolve, if possible, some theoretical difficulties (such as how to dispense with certain *ad hoc* hypotheses, or how to unify two theories). Now if he manages to produce a theory which is a solution to all these problems, his achievement will be very great.

Yet it is not enough. I have been asked, "What more do you want?" My answer is that there are many more things which I want; or rather, which I think are required by the logic of the general problem situation in which the scientist finds himself; by the task of getting nearer to the truth. I shall confine myself here to the discussion of three such requirements.

The first requirement is this. The new theory should proceed from some *simple, new*, and *powerful, unifying idea* about some connection or relation (such as gravitational attraction) between hitherto unconnected things (such as planets and apples) or facts (such as inertial and gravitational mass) or new "theoretical entities" (such as field and particles). This *requirement of simplicity* is a bit vague, and it seems difficult to formulate it very clearly. It seems to be intimately connected with the idea that our theories should describe the structural properties of the world—an idea which it is hard to think out fully without getting involved in an infinite regress. (This is so because any idea of a particular structure of the world— unless, indeed, we think of a purely *mathematical* structure—already presupposes a universal theory; for example, explaining the laws of chemistry by interpreting molecules as structures of atoms, or of subatomic particles, presupposes the idea of universal laws that regulate the properties and the behaviour of the atoms, or of the particles.) Yet one important ingredient in the idea of simplicity can be logically analysed. It is the idea of

testability. This leads us immediately to our second requirement.

For, secondly, we require that the new theory should be *independently testable*. That is to say, apart from explaining all the *explicanda* which the new theory was designed to explain, it must have new and testable consequences (preferably consequences of a *new kind*); it must lead to the prediction of phenomena which have not so far been observed.

This requirement seems to me indispensable since without it our new theory might be *ad hoc*; for it is always possible to produce a theory to fit any given set of explicanda. Thus our two first requirements are needed in order to restrict the range of our choice among the possible solutions (many of them uninteresting) of the problem in hand.

If our second requirement is satisfied then our new theory will represent a potential step forward, whatever the outcome of the new tests may be. For it will be better testable than the previous theory: the fact that it explains all the explicanda of the previous theory, and that, in addition, it gives rise to new tests, suffices to ensure this.

Moreover, the second requirement also ensures that our new theory will, to some extent, be fruitful as an instrument of exploration. That is to say, it will suggest to us new experiments, and even if these should at once lead to the refutation of the theory, our factual knowledge will have grown through the unexpected results of the new experiments. Moreover, they will confront us with new problems to be solved by new explanatory theories.

Yet I believe that there must be a third requirement for a good theory. It is this. We require that the theory should pass some new, and severe, tests.

XIX

Clearly, this requirement is totally different in character from the previous two. These could be seen to be fulfilled, or not fulfilled, largely by analysing the old and the new theories logically. (They are "formal requirements.") The third requirement, on the other hand, can be found to be fulfilled, or not fulfilled, only by testing the new theory empirically. (It is a "material requirement," a requirement of *empirical success.*)

Moreover, the third requirement clearly cannot be indispensable in the same sense as are the two previous ones. For these two are indispensable for deciding whether the theory in question should be at all accepted as a serious candidate for examination by empirical tests; or in other words, whether it is an interesting and promising theory. Yet on the other hand, some of the most interesting and most admirable theories ever conceived were refuted at the very first test. And why not? The most promising theory may fail if it makes predictions of a new kind....

Refutations have often been regarded as establishing the failure of a scientist, or at least of his theory. It should be stressed that this is an inductivist error. Every refutation should be regarded as a great success; not merely a success of the scientist who refuted the theory, but also of the scientist who created the refuted theory and who thus in the first instance suggested, if only indirectly, the refuting experiment.

Even if a new theory (such as the theory of Bohr, Kramers, and Slater) should meet an early death, it should not be forgotten; rather its beauty should be remembered, and history should record our gratitude to it—for bequeathing to us new and perhaps still unexplained experimental facts and, with them, new problems; and for the services it has thus rendered to the progress of science during its successful but short life.

All this indicates clearly that our third requirement is not indispensable: even a theory which fails to meet it can make an important contribution to science. Yet in a different sense, I hold, it is indispensable none the less. (Bohr, Kramers and Slater rightly aimed at more than making an important contribution to science.)

In the first place, I contend that further progress in science would become impossible if we did not reasonably often manage to meet the third requirement; thus if the progress of science is to continue, and its rationality not to decline, we need not only successful refutations, but also positive successes. We must, that is, manage reasonably often to produce theories that entail new predictions, especially predictions of new effects, new testable consequences, suggested by the new theory and never thought of before. Such a new prediction was that planets would under certain circumstances deviate from Kepler's laws; or that light, in spite of its zero mass, would prove to be subject to gravitational attraction (that is, Einstein's eclipse-effect). Another example is Dirac's prediction that there will be an anti-particle for every elementary particle. New predictions of these kinds must not only be produced, but they must also be reasonably often corroborated by experimental evidence, I contend, if scientific progress is to continue....

CRITICAL QUESTIONS

1. Why did Popper think that "every refutation should be regarded as a great success"? Do you think he is right about this? Why, or why not?

2. If we adopt Popper's view of science, how can we distinguish science from superstition?

9.4 SCIENTIFIC REVOLUTIONS

If I asked you to tell me something about scientific procedure, you might start talking about the scientific method of observation, which leads to theories from which predictive hypotheses are deduced and then tested by making further observations. This is called the **hypothetico-deductive method** because it involves deducing consequences (predictions) that should hold if the hypothesis is correct and then designing experiments to see if they do indeed hold true.

Your version of the scientific method might also include a belief that science is incremental in the sense that truth slowly accumulates over time. Scientists build on past discoveries and theories. Many people working very carefully, but slowly and surely, add to an ever-growing understanding of the way the world operates. Present theories absorb past theories, and each generation makes progress toward the ideal of understanding everything scientifically.

This picture of science is what philosophers often call **normal science** or standard science. It can be contrasted with a picture of science that might be new to you, a picture called **revolutionary science**. According to this picture, scientists sometimes reject traditional, time-honored, and well-established theories of how the world runs in favor of new and incompatible theories. Old problems and puzzles that people worked on so carefully now seem irrelevant, and a host of new problems emerges, clamoring for attention. **Anomalies** or new events that do not fit with prevailing beliefs generate new and deep questions about accepted scientific views. Theories once thought true now appear inadequate, and new theories must be invented.

According to Thomas Kuhn (1922–1996), one of the most influential and controversial philosophers of science in the last century, one of the main differences between normal science and revolutionary science has to do with what he calls paradigms. A **paradigm** is a scientific achievement so deep and impressive that it defines the daily practice for a particular community of scientists. It settles fundamental issues, provides a general set of assumptions, and offers a kind of basic model, thereby generating research puzzles with definite solutions. Normal science works within a paradigm, solving slowly but surely the puzzles and problems the paradigm generates. Within the boundaries of the paradigm, we may speak of scientific progress. Then anomalies occur. Unexpected experimental results that are incompatible with prevailing theory generate a crisis that leads to a paradigm shift. This shift in paradigms is the work of revolutionary science, which tears down established frameworks and creates something new. Once revolutionary science has done its work, a new paradigm reigns and a new round of normal science begins, now operating within the bounds of the new paradigm.

I think you can see that if Kuhn is right, science does not always make gradual and smooth progress. Crises generated by anomalies create shifts in vision. What people see and how they see it changes very much like gestalt shifts in vision that occur when one suddenly sees a figure that first appeared to be a rabbit, now appears to be a duck (or vice versa). These shifts are not built on the old paradigm. In fact the old and new paradigms are **incommensurable**, not only in the sense of being incompatible, but also in the sense that given any two paradigms, we would not be able to say which one is better or more accurate because we lack paradigm-transcending criteria for making such extra-paradigmatic judgments. From the point of view of revolutionary science, science does not progress in a traditional sense. It changes direction.

The following selection comes from Kuhn's most influential book, *The Structure of Scientific Revolutions*. To present the key ideas, I have edited many of the examples that Kuhn uses to support his views (examples that give a thickness to his ideas) so the resulting version may seem overly thin, abstract, and unconnected to familiar scientific theories. Even so, what Kuhn has to say will get you to think about science and its ability to generate knowledge in a way you have not thought about before.

◉ READING QUESTIONS

1. How does Kuhn describe normal science?
2. What, according to Kuhn, are two essential characteristics of a paradigm?
3. What is the nature of normal science in relationship to a paradigm?

4. Why are anomalies important in science?
5. What influences the decision to reject a paradigm?
6. What are scientific revolutions, and what is their function in scientific development?

The Structure of Scientific Revolutions

THOMAS S. KUHN

II. THE ROUTE TO NORMAL SCIENCE

In this essay, "normal science" means research firmly based upon one or more past scientific achievements, achievements that some particular scientific community acknowledges for a time as supplying the foundation for its further practice. Today such achievements are recounted, though seldom in their original form, by science textbooks, elementary and advanced. These textbooks expound the body of accepted theory, illustrate many or all of its successful applications, and compare these applications with exemplary observations and experiments. Before such books became popular early in the nineteenth century (and until even more recently in the newly matured sciences), many of the famous classics of science fulfilled a similar function. Aristotle's *Physica,* Ptolemy's *Almagest,* Newton's *Principia and Opticks,* Franklin's *Electricity,* Lavoisier's *Chemistry,* and Lyell's *Geology*—these and many other works served for a time implicitly to define the legitimate problems and methods of a research field for succeeding generations of practitioners. They were able to do so because they shared two essential characteristics. Their achievement was sufficiently unprecedented to attract an enduring group of adherents away from competing modes of scientific activity. Simultaneously, it was sufficiently open-ended to leave all sorts of

problems for the redefined group of practitioners to resolve.

Achievements that share these two characteristics I shall henceforth refer to as "paradigms," a term that relates closely to "normal science." By choosing it, I mean to suggest that some accepted examples of actual scientific practice—examples which include law, theory, application, and instrumentation together—provide models from which spring particular coherent traditions of scientific research. These are the traditions which the historian describes under such rubrics as "Ptolemaic astronomy" (or "Copernican"), "Aristotelian dynamics" (or "Newtonian"), "corpuscular optics" (or "wave optics"), and so on. The study of paradigms, including many that are far more specialized than those named illustratively above, is what mainly prepares the student for membership in the particular scientific community with which he will later practice. Because he there joins men who learned the bases of their field from the same concrete models, his subsequent practice will seldom evoke overt disagreement over fundamentals. Men whose research is based on shared paradigms are committed to the same rules and standards for scientific practice. That commitment and the apparent consensus it produces are prerequisites for normal science, i.e., for the genesis and continuation of a particular research tradition....

From Thomas S. Kuhn, *The Structure of Scientific Revolutions,* 2nd Edition, enlarged (Chicago: The University of Chicago Press, 1970), pp. 10–11, 23–24, 52–53, 64–65, 77–78, 92–96, 109, 111–112, 160, 162–173. Footnotes omitted. Copyright © 1962, 1970 by the University of Chicago Press. Reprinted by permission.

III. THE NATURE OF NORMAL SCIENCE

What then is the nature of the more professional and esoteric research that a group's reception of a single paradigm permits? If the paradigm represents work that has been done once and for all, what further problems does it leave the united group to resolve? Those questions will seem even more urgent if we now note one respect in which the terms used so far may be misleading. In its established usage, a paradigm is an accepted model or pattern, and that aspect of its meaning has enabled me, lacking a better word, to appropriate "paradigm" here. But it will shortly be clear that the sense of "model" and "pattern" that permits the appropriation is not quite the one usual in defining "paradigm." In grammar, for example, "*amo, amas, amat*" is a paradigm because it displays the pattern to be used in conjugating a large number of other Latin verbs, e.g., in producing "*audo, laudas, laudat.*" In this standard application, the paradigm functions by permitting the replication of examples any one of which could in principle serve to replace it. In a science, on the other hand, a paradigm is rarely an object for replication. Instead, like an accepted judicial decision in the common law, it is an object for further articulation and specification under new or more stringent conditions.

To see how this can be so, we must recognize how very limited in both scope and precision a paradigm can be at the time of its first appearance. Paradigms gain their status because they are more successful than their competitors in solving a few problems that the group of practitioners has come to recognize as acute. To be more successful is not, however, to be either completely successful with a single problem or notably successful with any large number. The success of a paradigm—whether Aristotle's analysis of motion, Ptolemy's computations of planetary position, Lavoisier's application of the balance, or Maxwell's mathematization of the electromagnetic field—is at the start largely a promise of success discoverable in selected and still incomplete examples. Normal science consists in the actualization of that promise, an actualization achieved by extending the knowledge of those facts that the paradigm

displays as particularly revealing, by increasing the extent of the match between those facts and the paradigm's predictions, and by further articulation of the paradigm itself.

Few people who are not actually practitioners of a mature science realize how much mop-up work of this sort a paradigm leaves to be done or quite how fascinating such work can prove in the execution. And these points need to be understood. Mopping-up operations are what engage most scientists throughout their careers. They constitute what I am here calling normal science. Closely examined, whether historically or in the contemporary laboratory, that enterprise seems an attempt to force nature into the preformed and relatively inflexible box that the paradigm supplies. No part of the aim of normal science is to call forth new sorts of phenomena; indeed those that will not fit the box are often not seen at all. Nor do scientists normally aim to invent new theories, and they are often intolerant of those invented by others. Instead, normal-scientific research is directed to the articulation of those phenomena and theories that the paradigm already supplies....

VI. ANOMALY AND THE EMERGENCE OF SCIENTIFIC DISCOVERIES

Normal science, the puzzle-solving activity we have just examined, is a highly cumulative enterprise, eminently successful in its aim, the steady extension of the scope and precision of scientific knowledge. In all these respects it fits with great precision the most usual image of scientific work. Yet one standard product of the scientific enterprise is missing. Normal science does not aim at novelties of fact or theory and, when successful, finds none. New and unsuspected phenomena are, however, repeatedly uncovered by scientific research, and radical new theories have again and again been invented by scientists. History even suggests that the scientific enterprise has developed a uniquely powerful technique for producing surprises of this sort. If this characteristic of science is to be reconciled with what has already been said, then research under a paradigm must be a particularly effective way of inducing paradigm change. That is what fundamental novelties of fact and theory do. Produced inadvertently by a game played under one set of rules, their assimilation requires the elaboration of another set. After they have become parts of science, the enterprise, at least of those specialists in whose particular field the novelties lie, is never quite the same again.

We must now ask how changes of this sort can come about, considering first discoveries, or novelties of fact, and then inventions, or novelties of theory. That distinction between discovery and invention or between fact and theory will, however, immediately prove to be exceedingly artificial. Its artificiality is an important clue to several of this essay's main theses. Examining selected discoveries in the rest of this section, we shall quickly find that they are not isolated events but extended episodes with a regularly recurrent structure. Discovery commences with the awareness of anomaly, i.e., with the recognition that nature has somehow violated the paradigm-induced expectations that govern normal science. It then continues with a more or less extended exploration of the area of anomaly. And it closes only when the paradigm theory has been adjusted so that the anomalous has become the expected. Assimilating a new sort of fact demands a more than additive adjustment of theory, and until that adjustment is completed—until the scientist has learned to see nature in a different way—the new fact is not quite a scientific fact at all....

In the development of any science, the first received paradigm is usually felt to account quite successfully for most of the observations and experiments easily accessible to that science's practitioners. Further development, therefore, ordinarily calls for the construction of elaborate equipment, the development of an esoteric vocabulary and skills, and a refinement of concepts that increasingly lessens their resemblance to their usual common-sense prototypes. That professionalization leads, on the one hand, to an immense restriction of the scientist's vision and to a considerable resistance to paradigm change. The science has become increasingly rigid. On the other hand, within those areas to which the paradigm directs the attention of the group, normal science leads to

a detail of information and to a precision of the observation-theory match that could be achieved in no other way. Furthermore, that detail and precision of match have a value that transcends their not always very high intrinsic interest. Without the special apparatus that is constructed mainly for anticipated functions, the results that lead ultimately to novelty could not occur. And even when the apparatus exists, novelty ordinarily emerges only for the man who, knowing *with precision* what he should expect, is able to recognize that something has gone wrong. Anomaly appears only against the background provided by the paradigm. The more precise and far-reaching that paradigm is, the more sensitive an indicator it provides of anomaly and hence of an occasion for paradigm change. In the normal mode of discovery, even resistance to change has a use that will be explored more fully in the next section. By ensuring that the paradigm will not be too easily surrendered, resistance guarantees that scientists will not be lightly distracted and that the anomalies that lead to paradigm change will penetrate existing knowledge to the core. The very fact that a significant scientific novelty so often emerges simultaneously from several laboratories is an index both to the strongly traditional nature of normal science and to the completeness with which that traditional pursuit prepares the way for its own change....

VIII. THE RESPONSE TO CRISIS

Let us then assume that crises are a necessary precondition for the emergence of novel theories and ask next how scientists respond to their existence. Part of the answer, as obvious as it is important, can be discovered by noting first what scientists never do when confronted by even severe and prolonged anomalies. Though they may begin to lose faith and then to consider alternatives, they do not renounce the paradigm that has led them into crisis. They do not, that is, treat anomalies as counterinstances, though in the vocabulary of philosophy of science that is what they are. In part this generalization is simply a statement from historic fact, based upon examples like those given above and, more extensively, below. These hint what our later examination of paradigm rejection will disclose more fully: once it has achieved the status of paradigm, a scientific theory is declared invalid only if an alternate candidate is available to take its place. No process yet disclosed by the historical study of scientific development at all resembles the methodological stereotype of falsification by direct comparison with nature. That remark does not mean that scientists do not reject scientific theories, or that experience and experiment are not essential to the process in which they do so. But it does mean—what will ultimately be a central point—that the act of judgment that leads scientists to reject a previously accepted theory is always based upon more than a comparison of that theory with the world. The decision to reject one paradigm is always simultaneously the decision to accept another, and the judgment leading to that decision involves the comparison of both paradigms with nature *and* with each other.

There is, in addition, a second reason for doubting that scientists reject paradigms because confronted with anomalies or counterinstances. In developing it my argument will itself foreshadow another of this essay's main theses. The reasons for doubt sketched above were purely factual; they were, that is, themselves counterinstances to a prevalent epistemological theory. As such, if my present point is correct, they can at best help to create a crisis or, more accurately, to reinforce one that is already very much in existence. By themselves they cannot and will not falsify that philosophical theory, for its defenders will do what we have already seen scientists doing when confronted by anomaly. They will devise numerous articulations and *ad hoc* modifications of their theory in order to eliminate any apparent conflict. Many of the relevant modifications and qualifications are, in fact, already in the literature. If, therefore, these epistemological counterinstances are to constitute more than a minor irritant, that will be because they help to permit the emergence of a new and different analysis of science within which they are no longer a source of trouble. Furthermore, if a typical pattern, which we shall later observe in scientific revolutions, is applicable here, these anomalies will then no longer seem to be

simply facts. From within a new theory of scientific knowledge, they may instead seem very much like tautologies, statements of situations that could not conceivably have been otherwise....

IX. THE NATURE AND NECESSITY OF SCIENTIFIC REVOLUTIONS

These remarks permit us at last to consider the problems that provide this essay with its title. What are scientific revolutions, and what is their function in scientific development? Much of the answer to these questions has been anticipated in earlier sections. In particular, the preceding discussion has indicated that scientific revolutions are here taken to be those non-cumulative developmental episodes in which an older paradigm is replaced in whole or in part by an incompatible new one. There is more to be said, however, and an essential part of it can be introduced by asking one further question. Why should a change of paradigm be called a revolution? In the face of the vast and essential differences between political and scientific development, what parallelism can justify the metaphor that finds revolutions in both?

One aspect of the parallelism must already be apparent. Political revolutions are inaugurated by a growing sense, often restricted to a segment of the political community, that existing institutions have ceased adequately to meet the problems posed by an environment that they have in part created. In much the same way, scientific revolutions are inaugurated by a growing sense, again often restricted to a narrow subdivision of the scientific community, that an existing paradigm has ceased to function adequately in the exploration of an aspect of nature to which that paradigm itself had previously led the way. In both political and scientific development the sense of malfunction that can lead to crisis is prerequisite to revolution. Furthermore, though it admittedly strains the metaphor, that parallelism holds not only for the major paradigm changes, like those attributable to Copernicus and Lavoisier, but also for the far smaller ones associated with the assimilation of a new sort of phenomenon, like oxygen or X-rays. Scientific revolutions ... seem revolutionary only to those whose paradigms are affected by them. To outsiders they may, like the Balkan revolutions of the early twentieth century, seem normal parts of the developmental process. Astronomers, for example, could accept X-rays as a mere addition to knowledge, for their paradigms were unaffected by the existence of the new radiation. But for men like Kelvin, Crookes, and Roentgen, whose research dealt with radiation theory or with cathode ray tubes, the emergence of X-rays necessarily violated one paradigm as it created another. That is why these rays could be discovered only through something's first going wrong with normal research.

This genetic aspect of the parallel between political and scientific development should no longer be open to doubt. The parallel has, however, a second and more profound aspect upon which the significance of the first depends. Political revolutions aim to change political institutions in ways that those institutions themselves prohibit. Their success therefore necessitates the partial relinquishment of one set of institutions in favor of another, and in the interim, society is not fully governed by institutions at all. Initially it is crisis alone that attenuates the role of political institutions as we have already seen it attenuate the role of paradigms. In increasing numbers individuals become increasingly estranged from political life and behave more and more eccentrically within it. Then, as the crisis deepens, many of these individuals commit themselves to some concrete proposal for the reconstruction of society in a new institutional framework. At that point the society is divided into competing camps or parties, one seeking to defend the old institutional constellation, the others seeking to institute some new one. And, once that polarization has occurred, *political recourse fails*. Because they differ about the institutional matrix within which political change is to be achieved and evaluated, because they acknowledge no suprainstitutional framework for the adjudication of revolutionary difference, the parties to a revolutionary conflict must finally resort to the techniques of mass persuasion, often including force. Though revolutions have had a vital role in the evolution of political institutions, that role depends upon their being partially extrapolitical or extrainstitutional events.

The remainder of this essay aims to demonstrate that the historical study of paradigm change reveals very similar characteristics in the evolution of the sciences. Like the choice between competing political institutions, that between competing paradigms proves to be a choice between incompatible modes of community life. Because it has that character, the choice is not and cannot be determined merely by the evaluative procedures characteristic of normal science, for these depend in part upon a particular paradigm, and that paradigm is at issue. When paradigms enter, as they must, into a debate about paradigm choice, their role is necessarily circular. Each group uses its own paradigm to argue in that paradigm's defense.

The resulting circularity does not, of course, make the arguments wrong or even ineffectual. The man who premises a paradigm when arguing in its defense can nonetheless provide a clear exhibit of what scientific practice will be like for those who adopt the new view of nature. That exhibit can be immensely persuasive, often compellingly so. Yet, whatever its force, the status of the circular argument is only that of persuasion. It cannot be made logically or even probabilistically compelling for those who refuse to step into the circle. The premises and values shared by the two parties to a debate over paradigms are not sufficiently extensive for that. As in political revolutions, so in paradigm choice—there is no standard higher than the assent of the relevant community. To discover how scientific revolutions are effected, we shall therefore have to examine not only the impact of nature and of logic, but also the techniques of persuasive argumentation effective within the quite special groups that constitute the community of scientists.

To discover why this issue of paradigm choice can never be unequivocally settled by logic and experiment alone, we must shortly examine the nature of the differences that separate the proponents of a traditional paradigm from their revolutionary successors. That examination is the principal object of this section and the next. We have, however, already noted numerous examples of such differences, and no one will doubt that history can supply many others. What is more likely to be doubted than their existence—and what must therefore be considered first—is that such examples provide essential information about the nature of science. Granting that paradigm rejection has been a historic fact, does it illuminate more than human credulity and confusion? Are there intrinsic reasons why the assimilation of either a new sort of phenomenon or a new scientific theory must demand the rejection of an older paradigm?

First notice that if there are such reasons, they do not derive from the logical structure of scientific knowledge. In principle, a new phenomenon might emerge without reflecting destructively upon any part of past scientific practice. Though discovering life on the moon would today be destructive of existing paradigms (these tell us things about the moon that seem incompatible with life's existence there), discovering life in some less well-known part of the galaxy would not. By the same token, a new theory does not have to conflict with any of its predecessors. It might deal exclusively with phenomena not previously known, as the quantum theory deals (but, significantly, not exclusively) with subatomic phenomena unknown before the twentieth century. Or again, the new theory might be simply a higher level theory than those known before, one that linked together a whole group of lower level theories without substantially changing any. Today, the theory of energy conservation provides just such links between dynamics, chemistry, electricity, optics, thermal theory, and so on. Still other compatible relationships between old and new theories can be conceived. Any and all of them might be exemplified by the historical process through which science has developed. If they were, scientific development would be genuinely cumulative. New sorts of phenomena would simply disclose order in an aspect of nature where none had been seen before. In the evolution of science new knowledge would replace ignorance rather than replace knowledge of another and incompatible sort.

Of course, science (or some other enterprise, perhaps less effective) might have developed in that fully cumulative manner. Many people have believed that it did so, and most still seem to suppose that cumulation is at least the ideal that historical development would display if only it had not so often been distorted by human idiosyncrasy. There are important reasons for that belief. In Section X we shall discover how closely the view of science-as-cumulation is entangled with a dominant epistemology that takes knowledge to be a construction placed directly upon raw sense data by the mind.... Nevertheless, despite the immense plausibility of that ideal image, there is increasing reason to wonder whether it can possibly be an image of *science*. After the pre-paradigm period the assimilation of all new theories and of almost all new sorts of phenomena has in fact demanded the destruction of a prior paradigm and a consequent conflict between competing schools of scientific thought. Cumulative acquisition of unanticipated novelties proves to be an almost non-existent exception to the rule of scientific development. The man who takes historic fact seriously must suspect that science does not tend toward the ideal that our image of its cumulativeness has suggested. Perhaps it is another sort of enterprise....

By shifting emphasis from the cognitive to the normative functions of paradigms, the preceding examples enlarge our understanding of the ways in which paradigms give form to the scientific life. Previously, we had principally examined the paradigm's role as a vehicle for scientific theory. In that role it functions by telling the scientist about the entities that nature does and does not contain and about the ways in which those entities behave. That information provides a map whose details are elucidated by mature scientific research. And since nature is too complex and varied to be explored at random, that map is as essential as observation and experiment to science's continuing development. Through the theories they embody, paradigms prove to be constitutive of the research activity. They are also, however, constitutive of science in other respects, and that is now the point. In particular, our most recent examples show that paradigms provide scientists not only with a map but also with some of the directions essential for map-making. In learning a paradigm the scientist acquires theory, methods, and standards together, usually in an inextricable mixture. Therefore, when paradigms change, there are usually significant shifts in the criteria determining the legitimacy both of problems and of proposed solutions….

X. REVOLUTIONS AS CHANGES OF WORLD VIEW

Examining the record of past research from the vantage of contemporary historiography, the historian of science may be tempted to exclaim that when paradigms change, the world itself changes with them. Led by a new paradigm, scientists adopt new instruments and look in new places. Even more important, during revolutions scientists see new and different things when looking with familiar instruments in places they have looked before. It is rather as if the professional community had been suddenly transported to another planet where familiar objects are seen in a different light and are joined by unfamiliar ones as well. Of course, nothing of quite that sort does occur: there is no geographical transplantation; outside the laboratory everyday affairs usually continue as before. Nevertheless, paradigm changes do cause scientists to see the world of their research-engagement differently. In so far as their only recourse to that world is through what they see and do, we may want to say that after a revolution scientists are responding to a different world.

It is as elementary prototypes for these transformations of the scientist's world that the familiar demonstrations of a switch in visual gestalt prove so suggestive. What were ducks in the scientist's world before the revolution are rabbits afterwards. The man who first saw the exterior of the box from above later sees its interior from below. Transformations like these, though usually more gradual and almost always irreversible, are common concomitants of scientific training. Looking at a contour map, the student sees lines on paper, the cartographer a picture of a terrain. Looking at a bubble-chamber photograph, the student sees confused and broken lines, the physicist a record of familiar subnuclear events. Only after a number of such transformations of vision does the student become an inhabitant of the scientist's world, seeing what the scientist sees and responding as the scientist does. The world that the student then enters is not, however, fixed once and for all by the nature of the environment, on the one hand, and of science, on the other. Rather, it is determined jointly by the environment and the particular normal-scientific tradition that the student has been trained to pursue. Therefore, at times of revolution, when the normal-scientific tradition changes, the scientist's perception of his environment must be reeducated—in some familiar situations he must learn to see a new gestalt. After he has done so the world of his research will seem, here and there, incommensurable with the one he had inhabited before. That is another reason why schools guided by different paradigms are always slightly at cross-purposes.

In their most usual form, of course, gestalt experiments illustrate only the nature of perceptual transformations. They tell us nothing about the role of paradigms or of previously assimilated experience in the process of perception. But on that point there is a rich body of psychological literature, much of it stemming from the pioneering work of the Hanover Institute. An experimental subject who puts on goggles fitted with inverting lenses initially sees the entire world upside down. At the start his perceptual apparatus functions as it had been trained to function in the absence of the goggles, and the result is extreme disorientation, an acute personal crisis. But after the subject has begun to learn to deal with his new world, his entire visual field flips over, usually after an intervening period in which vision is simply confused. Thereafter, objects are again seen as they had been before the goggles were put on. The assimilation of a previously anomalous visual field has reacted upon and changed the field itself. Literally as well as metaphorically, the man accustomed to inverting lenses has undergone a revolutionary transformation of vision….

XIII. PROGRESS THROUGH REVOLUTIONS

The preceding pages have carried my schematic description of scientific development as far as it can go in this essay. Nevertheless, they cannot quite provide a conclusion. If this description has at all caught the essential structure of a science's continuing evolution, it will simultaneously have posed a special problem: Why should the enterprise sketched above move steadily ahead in ways that, say, art, political theory, or philosophy does not? Why is progress a perquisite reserved almost exclusively for the activities we call science? The most usual answers to that question have been denied in the body of this essay. We must conclude it by asking whether substitutes can be found....

It can, however, only clarify, not solve, our present difficulty to recognize that we tend to see as science any field in which progress is marked. There remains the problem of understanding why progress should be so noteworthy a characteristic of an enterprise conducted with the techniques and goals this essay has described. That question proves to be several in one, and we shall have to consider each of them separately. In all cases but the last, however, their resolution will depend in part upon an inversion of our normal view of the relation between scientific activity and the community that practices it. We must learn to recognize as causes what have ordinarily been taken to be effects. If we can do that, the phrases "scientific progress" and even "scientific objectivity" may come to seem in part redundant. In fact, one aspect of the redundancy has just been illustrated. Does a field make progress because it is a science, or is it a science because it makes progress?

Ask now why an enterprise like normal science should progress, and begin by recalling a few of its most salient characteristics. Normally, the members of a mature scientific community work from a single paradigm or from a closely related set. Very rarely do different scientific communities investigate the same problems. In those exceptional cases the groups hold several major paradigms in common. Viewed from within any single community, however, whether of scientists or of non-scientists, the result of successful creative work is progress. How could it possibly be anything else? We have, for example, just noted that while artists aimed at representation as their goal, both critics and historians chronicled the progress of the apparently united

group. Other creative fields display progress of the same sort. The theologian who articulates dogma or the philosopher who refines the Kantian imperatives contributes to progress, if only to that of the group that shares his premises. No creative school recognizes a category of work that is, on the one hand, a creative success, but is not, on the other, an addition to the collective achievement of the group. If we doubt, as many do, that non-scientific fields make progress, that cannot be because individual schools make none. Rather, it must be because there are always competing schools, each of which constantly questions the very foundations of the others. The man who argues that philosophy, for example, has made no progress emphasizes that there are still Aristotelians, not that Aristotelianism has failed to progress....

With respect to normal science, then, part of the answer to the problem of progress lies simply in the eye of the beholder. Scientific progress is not different in kind from progress in other fields, but the absence at most times of competing schools that question each other's aims and standards makes the progress of a normal-scientific community far easier to see. That, however, is only part of the answer and by no means the most important part. We have, for example, already noted that once the reception of a common paradigm has freed the scientific community from the need constantly to re-examine its first principles, the members of that community can concentrate exclusively upon with precision and detail. In the process the community will sustain losses. Often some old problems must be banished. Frequently, in addition, revolution narrows the scope of the community's professional concerns, increases the extent of its specialization, and attenuates its communication with other groups, both scientific and lay. Though science surely grows in depth, it may not grow in breadth as well. If it does so, that breadth is manifest mainly in the proliferation of scientific specialties, not in the scope of any single specialty alone. Yet despite these and other losses to the individual communities, the nature of such communities provides a virtual guarantee that both the list of problems solved by science and the precision of individual problem-solutions will grow and grow. At least, the nature of the community provides such a guarantee if there is any way at all in which it can be provided. What better criterion than the decision of the scientific group could there be?

These last paragraphs point the directions in which I believe a more refined solution of the problem of progress in the sciences must be sought. Perhaps they indicate that scientific progress is not quite what we had taken it to be. But they simultaneously show that a sort of progress will inevitably characterize the scientific enterprise so long as such an enterprise survives. In the sciences there need not be progress of another sort. We may, to be more precise, have to relinquish the notion, explicit or implicit, that changes of paradigm carry scientists and those who learn from them closer and closer to the truth.

It is now time to notice that until the last very few pages the term "truth" had entered this essay only in a quotation from Francis Bacon. And even in those pages it entered only as a source for the scientist's conviction that incompatible rules for doing science cannot coexist except during revolutions when the profession's main task is to eliminate all sets but one. The developmental process described in this essay has been a process of evolution *from* primitive beginnings—a process whose successive stages are characterized by an increasingly detailed and refined understanding of nature. But nothing that has been or will be said makes it a process of evolution *toward* anything. Inevitably that lacuna will have disturbed many readers. We are all deeply accustomed to seeing science as the one enterprise that draws constantly nearer to some goal set by nature in advance.

But need there be any such goal? Can we not account for both science's existence and its success in terms of evolution from the community's state of knowledge at any given time? Does it really help to imagine that there is some one full, objective, true account of nature and that the proper measure of scientific achievement is the extent to which it brings us closer to that ultimate goal? If we can learn to substitute evolution-from-what-we-do-know for evolution-toward-what-we-wish-to-know, a number of vexing problems may vanish in the process. Somewhere in this maze, for example, must lie the problem of induction.

I cannot yet specify in any detail the consequences of this alternate view of scientific advance. But it helps to recognize that the conceptual transposition here recommended is very close to one that the West undertook just a century ago. It is particularly helpful because in both cases the main obstacle to transposition is the same. When Darwin first published his theory of evolution by natural selection in 1859, what most bothered many professionals was neither the notion of species change nor the possible descent of man from apes. The evidence pointing to evolution, including the evolution of man, had been accumulating for decades, and the idea of evolution had been suggested and widely disseminated before. Though evolution, as such, did encounter resistance, particularly from some religious groups, it was by no means the greatest of the difficulties the Darwinians faced. That difficulty stemmed from an idea that was more nearly Darwin's own. All the well-known pre-Darwinian evolutionary theories—those of Lamarck, Chambers, Spencer, and the German *Naturphilosophen*—had taken evolution to be a goal-directed process. The "idea" of man and of the contemporary flora and fauna was thought to have been present from the first creation of life, perhaps in the mind of God. That idea or plan had provided the direction and the guiding force to the entire evolutionary process. Each new stage of evolutionary development was a more perfect realization of a plan that had been present from the start.

For many men the abolition of that teleological kind of evolution was the most significant and least palatable of Darwin's suggestions. The *Origin of Species* recognized no goal set either by God or nature. Instead, natural selection, operating in the given environment and with the actual organisms presently at hand, was responsible for the gradual but steady emergence of more elaborate, further articulated, and vastly more specialized organisms. Even such marvelously adapted organs as the eye and hand of man—organs whose design had previously provided powerful arguments for the existence of a supreme artificer and an advance plan—were products of a process that moved steadily *from* primitive beginnings but *toward* no goal. The belief that natural selection, resulting from mere competition between organisms for survival, could have produced man together with the higher animals and plants was the most difficult and disturbing aspect of Darwin's theory. What could "evolution," "development," and "progress" mean in the absence of a specified goal? To many people, such terms suddenly seemed self-contradictory.

The analogy that relates the evolution of organisms to the evolution of scientific ideas can easily be pushed too far. But with respect to the issues of this closing section it is very nearly perfect. The process described in Section XII [not included here] as the resolution of revolutions is the selection by conflict within the scientific community of the fittest way to practice future science. The net result of a sequence of such revolutionary selections, separated by periods of normal research, is the wonderfully adapted set of instruments we call modern scientific knowledge. Successive stages in that developmental process are marked by an increase in articulation and specialization. And the entire process may have occurred, as we now suppose biological evolution did, without benefit of a set goal, a permanent fixed scientific truth, of which each stage in the development of scientific knowledge is a better exemplar.

Anyone who has followed the argument this far will nevertheless feel the need to ask why the evolutionary process should work. What must nature, including man, be like in order that science be possible at all? Why should scientific communities be able to reach a firm consensus unattainable in other fields? Why should consensus endure across one paradigm change after another? And why should paradigm change invariably produce an instrument more perfect in any sense than those known before? From one point of view those questions, excepting the first, have already been answered. But from another they are as open as they were when this essay began. It is not only the scientific community that must be special. The world of which that community is a part must also possess quite special characteristics, and we are no closer than we were at the start to knowing what these must be. That problem—What must the world be like in order that man may know it?—was not, however, created by this essay. On the contrary, it is as old as science itself, and it remains unanswered. But it need not be answered in this place. Any conception of nature compatible with the growth of science by proof is compatible with the evolutionary view of science developed here. Since this view is also compatible with close observation of scientific life, there are strong arguments for employing it in attempts to solve the host of problems that still remain.

◉ CRITICAL QUESTIONS

1. In Section X, do you think Kuhn is claiming that both the way the scientist sees the world and the world itself change when a paradigm shift occurs? Why, or why not?
2. How does Kuhn explain scientific progress? Do you think his answer is better than the traditional picture of science as progressing by drawing closer to the truth about the way things are? Why, or why not?
3. Do you think Kuhn's ideas about science imply that knowledge is relative? Why, or why not?

9.5 SCIENCE AND TRADITIONAL THOUGHT

Do you believe in spirits? Do you think that if you got ill, you could go to a shrine, have a priest sacrifice a chicken, and get well? If you think this would work, why? If you do not think going to spirit-shrines and sacrificing chickens would cure illness, why not?

Do you think false beliefs can survive for long periods of time? If you think there are no spirits who cure people in response to sacrificed chickens, why do you think some people believe there are? Let us suppose that the people who believe there are indeed such spirits have held this view for centuries, and that in fact there are no such spirits. What sustains false beliefs in healing spirits over centuries? Why do they persist if they are false?

I am going to call something a traditional religious belief if it is based on positing spirit-agents as causes of events. You go to the priest, she sacrifices a chicken, and you get well. The priest, who holds traditional religious beliefs, would say that the spirit of the shrine healed you. Is this traditional religious belief scientific? Why, or why not?

Suppose you go to a medical doctor and, instead of the doctor sacrificing a chicken, she gives you a shot and you get well. The medical doctor, who holds scientific beliefs, tells you that you have a bacterial infection and that the antibiotic she has just given you will destroy the bacteria. How is this scientific belief different from a traditional religious belief? Is there a significant difference between the two explanations of why you got well?

Some African people build granaries on poles to store their harvests above the ground so mice will not get into the grain. When it is hot, people sometimes sit under these granaries to get shade and sometimes, because termites weaken the supports, these granaries fall and kill or injure some of the people. If you ask why the granaries fell and people were injured, you would be told it was because of witchcraft. Witches did it! Everyone knows about the termites, and they know what termites have done to the supports, yet they still explain this unfortunate event by appealing to witchcraft. Witchcraft is their **theodicy** or answer to the problem of evil. It explains why bad things happen. Is it a scientific explanation? Why, or why not?

Suppose a friend, a religious and good person, is suddenly killed in an auto accident caused by a drunk driver. At the funeral the minister asks why bad things happen to good people and answers, "I believe this tragic event is part of God's plan." Everyone knows the accident was caused by a drunk driver, yet the minister says it is part of God's plan. Is this a scientific explanation of the tragic accident? Is it an explanation at all? If it is, what kind of explanation is it?

Kwame Anthony Appiah, professor of philosophy at Princeton University and author of the following selection, is a person of "two worlds." Before earning his PhD from Cambridge University, he was trained in Africa to be a leader of the Asante. His father, a British barrister, was from the royal house of the Asante, the most powerful kinship group in Ghana, and his mother, a published author, a member of the British establishment. One of his worlds is the world of traditional African belief and thought. The other world is the world of modern European scientific belief and thought. Here he offers some intriguing philosophical reflections on the relationship between these worlds.

⊚ READING QUESTIONS

1. What is Durkheim's argument for treating religion as symbolic?
2. Why, according to Appiah, is Durkheim wrong?
3. Why are the concepts of "underdetermination" and "theory-laden" important in this context?
4. What is the analogy between traditional religion and natural science?
5. How, according to Horton, do traditional religious beliefs differ from natural science, and why?
6. Which sort of explanation is missing in Horton's account, and why?
7. What is the difference between an "adversarial style" and an "accommodative style," and why is this difference important?

Old Gods, New Worlds

KWAME ANTHONY APPIAH

In coming to terms with what it means to be modern, Western and African intellectuals have interests they should share.... [A]s I shall suggest, neither of us will understand what modernity is until we understand each other....

[O]ne of the marks of traditional life is the extent to which beliefs, activities, habits of mind, and behavior in general are shot through with what Europeans and Americans would call "religion." ... Most intellectuals outside ... [traditional societies] think they know, after all, that there are no such spirits [as can be summoned by sacrificing, for example, gold or sheep and chickens at a shrine]. That, for all the requests in the priest's prayer, no unseen agent will come to inhabit the shrine; no one will answer the questions "What made this person ill?" or "Would we win if we went to war?" or "How should we cure the king's elder?" Yet here is a culture [Asante] where, for at least several hundred years, people have been setting up just such shrines and asking them just such questions and asking the spirits they believe are in them to perform just such tasks. Surely by now they should know, if they are rational, that it won't work? ... And if we press the question how these beliefs can be sustained in the face of a falsity that is obvious, at least to us, we shall return, in the end, to the question whether we have really understood what is going on....

[W]e need, I think, to bear in mind at least these three separate types of understanding: first, understanding the ritual and the beliefs that underlie it; second, understanding the historical sources of both ritual and belief; and, third, understanding what sustains them.

[T]o understand these ritual acts what is necessary is what is necessary in the understanding of any acts: namely to understand what beliefs and intentions underlie them, so that we know what the actors think they are doing, what they are trying to do. Indeed if we cannot do this we cannot even say what the ritual is. To say that what is going on here is that these people are inviting a spirit to take up its place in a shrine is already to say something about their beliefs and their intentions. It is to say, for example, that they believe that there is a spirit, Ta Kwesi, and believe too that asking the spirit to do something is a way of getting that spirit to do it; it is to say that they want the spirit to inhabit the shrine....

But if we are to face the question of the rationality of traditional belief we must turn, finally, to my third set of questions: those about what keeps these beliefs, which outsiders judge so obviously false, alive.

It is in asking these questions that some have been led by another route to treating religion symbolically. The British anthropologist John Beattie, for example, has developed a "symbolist" view of Africa's traditional religions, whose "central tenet," as Robin Horton (a philosopher-anthropologist, who is a British subject and a longtime Nigerian resident) puts it, "is that traditional religious thought is basically different from and incommensurable with Western scientific thought"; so that the symbolists avoid "comparisons with science and turn instead to comparisons with symbolism and art...."[1] Simply put, the symbolists are able to treat traditional believers as reassuringly rational only because they deny that traditional people mean what they say. Now Robin Horton has objected—correctly—that ... [i]t is

---

[1] Robin Horton, "Spiritual Beings and Elementary Particles—A Reply to Mr. Pratt," *Second Order* 1, No. 1 (1972), p. 30.

From Gary Varner, *In Nature's Interests?: Interests, Animal Rights, And Environmental Ethics* (Oxford University Press, 1998), pp. 107–136.

peculiarly unsatisfactory to treat a system of propositions as symbolic when those whose propositions they are appear to treat them literally and display, in other contexts, a clear grasp of the notion of symbolic representation.

I have mentioned Durkheim ... and it is in his work that we can find the clearest statement of the connection between the urge to treat religion as symbolic and the question why such patently false beliefs survive. For Durkheim cannot allow that religious beliefs are false, because he thinks that false beliefs could not survive. Since if they are false they would not have survived, it follows that they must be true: and since they are not literally true, they must be symbolically true.[2] This argument is based on a misunderstanding of the relationship between the rationality of beliefs, their utility and their truth; it is important to say why.

Rationality is best conceived of as an ideal, both in the sense that it is something worth aiming for and in the sense that it is something we are incapable of realizing. It is an ideal that bears an important internal relation to that other great cognitive ideal, Truth. And, I suggest, we might say that rationality in belief consists in being disposed so to react to evidence and reflection that you change your beliefs in ways that make it more likely that they are true....[3]

With such an account of reasonableness, we can see why the apparently obvious falsehood of the beliefs of the Asante priest might be regarded as evidence of his unreasonableness. For how could

he have acquired and maintained such beliefs if he was following the prescription always to try to change his beliefs in ways that made it more likely that they were true? The answer is simple. The priest acquired his beliefs in the way we all acquire the bulk of our beliefs: by being told things as he grew up. As Evans-Pritchard says of the Zande people, they are "born into a culture with ready-made patterns of belief which have the weight of tradition behind them."[4] And of course, so are we. On the whole, little has happened in his life to suggest they are not true. So too, in our lives.

Now it may seem strange to suggest that accepting beliefs from one's culture and holding onto them in the absence of countervailing evidence can be reasonable, if it can lead to having beliefs that are, from the point of view of Western intellectuals, so wildly false. And this is especially so if you view reasonableness as a matter of trying to develop habits of belief acquisition that make it likely that you will react to evidence and reflection in ways that have a tendency to produce truth....

We may also fail to see how reasonable the priest's views should seem, because, in assessing the religious beliefs of other cultures, we start, as is natural enough, from our own. But it is precisely the absence of this, our alien, alternative point of view in traditional culture, that makes it reasonable to adopt the "traditional" worldview. The evidence that spirits exist is obvious: priests go into trance, people get better after the application of spiritual remedies, people die regularly from the action of inimical spirits. The reinterpretation of this evidence, in terms of medical-scientific theories or of psychology, requires that there be such alternative theories and that people have some reason to believe in them; but again and again, and especially in the area of mental and social life, the traditional view is likely to be confirmed. We have theories explaining some of this, the theory of suggestion and suggestibility, for example, and if we were to persuade traditional thinkers of these theories, they might become skeptical of the theories held in their own culture.

---

[2]John Skorupski has persuaded me that Durkheim does indeed offer this apparently crude argument; see Skorupski's *Symbol and Theory* (Cambridge: Cambridge University Press, 1976), chap. 2, for an excellent discussion.

[3]... This conception of rationality belongs to a family of recent proposals that treat a concept as being defined by the *de re* relations of agents to the world.... As Gettler [1963] showed, a belief can be justified and true, but not a piece of knowledge, because the justification fails to be appropriately related *de re* to the facts.... Similarly, I want to say a belief can be reasonable (subjectively), but irrational (objectively). Since questions of rationality, therefore, raise questions about how other people stand in relation to reality; and since these questions cannot be answered while leaving open, as I wish to do, questions about who is right, I shall talk from now on about reasonableness rather than rationality. Someone is reasonable, on my view, if they are trying to be rational: if they are trying to act so as to maximize the chance of their beliefs being true.

---

[4]Evans-Pritchard, *Witchcraft, Oracles and Magic among the Azande* (Oxford: Oxford University Press, 1976), p. 202.

But we cannot begin by asking them to assume their beliefs are false, for they can always make numerous moves in reasonable defense of their beliefs. [Blaming some extant auxiliary hypothesis or adding some excusing auxiliary, for example.] It is this fact that entitles us to oppose the thesis that traditional beliefs are simply unreasonable....

Philosophers of science have names for this: they say that theory is "underdetermined" by observation, and that observation is "theory-laden." And they mean by underdetermination the fact that French philosopher-physicist Pierre Duhem noticed in the early part of this century: that the application of theory to particular cases relies on a whole host of other beliefs, not all of which can be checked at once. By the theory-ladenness of observation, relatedly, they mean that our theories both contribute to forming our experience and give meaning to the language we use for reporting it. Sir Karl Popper's claim that science should proceed by attempts at falsification, as we all know after reading Thomas Kuhn, is incorrect. If we gave up every time an experiment failed, scientific theory would get nowhere. The underdetermination of our theories by our experience means that we are left even by the most unsuccessful experiment with room for maneuver. The trick is not to give up too soon or go on too long. In science, as everywhere else, there are babies and there is bathwater....

[T]raditional religious theory is in certain respects more like modern natural science ... which we may summarize in the slogan "explanation, prediction, and control." It is his systematic development of the analogy between natural science and traditional religion that has made the work of Robin Horton so important in the philosophy of African traditional religions, and it will be useful begin with him.[5]

Horton's basic point is just the one I made earlier: the fundamental character of these religious systems is that the practices arise from the

belief, literal and not symbolic, in the powers of invisible agents. Horton argues persuasively, and I believe correctly, that spirits and such function in explanation, prediction, and control much as do other theoretical entities: they differ from those of natural science in being persons and not material forces and powers, but the logic of their function in explanation and prediction is the same.

Horton's view, then, is that religious beliefs of traditional peoples constitute explanatory theories and that traditional religious actions are reasonable attempts to pursue goals in the light of these beliefs—attempts, in other words, at prediction and control of the world. In these respects, Horton argues, traditional religious belief and action are like theory in the natural sciences and the actions based on it.... Horton's thesis is not that traditional religion is a kind of science but that theories in the two domains are similar in these crucial respects. The major difference in the contents of the theories, he argues, is that traditional religious theory is couched in terms of personal forces, while natural scientific theory is couched in terms of impersonal forces. The basic claim strikes me as immensely plausible....

Horton himself is, of course, aware that traditional religious beliefs are certainly unlike those of natural science in at least two important respects. First of all, as I have already insisted, he points out that the theoretical entities invoked are agents and not material forces.... And he offers us an account of why this might be. He suggests that this difference arises out of the fundamental nature of explanation as the reduction of the unfamiliar to the familiar. In traditional cultures nature, the wild, is untamed, alien, and a source of puzzlement and fear. Social relations and persons are, on the contrary, familiar and well understood. Explaining the behavior of nature in terms of agency is thus reducing the unfamiliar forces of the wild to the familiar explanatory categories of personal relations.

In the industrial world, on the other hand, industrialization and urbanization have made social relations puzzling and problematic. We move between social environments—the rural and the urban, the workplace and the home—in which different conventions operate; in the new,

[5]Horton's most famous paper is his "African Traditional Religion and Western Science."... All my thought on these questions has been stimulated and enlivened by reading and talking with him, and so many of the ideas I shall be offering are his that I make now a general acknowledgement.

urban, factory, market environment we deal with people whom we know only through our common productive projects. As a result the social is relatively unfamiliar. On the other hand, our relations with objects in the city are relations that remain relatively stable across all these differing social relations. Indeed, if factory workers move between factories, the skills they take with them are precisely those that depend on a familiarity not with other people but with the workings of material things. It is no longer natural to try to understand nature through social relations; rather, we understand it through machines, through matter whose workings we find comfortably familiar. It is well known that the understanding of gases in the nineteenth-century was modeled on the behavior of miniature billiard balls—for nineteenth-century scientists in Europe know the billiard table better than they knew, for example, their servants. Alienation is widely held to be the characteristic state of modern man: the point can be overstated, but it cannot be denied…. [Horton's] story works so well that it is hard not to feel that there is something right about it; it would indeed explain the preference for agency over matter, the first of the major differences Horton acknowledges between traditional religion and science.

And yet this *cannot* be quite right. All cultures—in modest mood, I might say, all the cultures I have knowledge of—have the conceptual resources for at least two fundamental sorts of explanation. On the one hand, all have some sort of notion of what Aristotle called "efficient" causation: the causality of push and pull through which we understand the everyday interactions of material objects and forces. On the other, each has a notion of explanation that applies paradigmatically to human action, the notion that the American philosopher Daniel Dennett has characterized as involving the "intentional stance."[6] This sort of explanation relates actions to beliefs, desires, intentions, fears, and so on—the so-called propositional attitudes—and is fundamental … to folk psychology. We might say, analogously, that efficient

_____
[6]See Daniel Dennett's *The Intentional Stance* (Cambridge, Mass.: Bradford Books, 1987).

causality is central to what cognitive psychologists now call "naive" or "folk physics."

These kinds of explanations are, of course, interconnected: when I explain the death of the elephant by talking of your need for food, your hunt, your firing the gun, there are elements of folk physics and of folk psychology involved in each stage on this narrative. To say that mechanical explanation is unfamiliar to preindustrial peoples is, of course, to say something true. Mechanical explanation is explanation in terms of machines, which are, of course, exactly what preindustrial cultures do not have. But mechanical explanation is by no means the only kind of nonintentional explanation: there is more to folk physics than a view of machines. And the fact is that the stability of the causal relations of objects in the preindustrial world is surely quite substantial: not only do people make tools and utensils, using the concepts of efficient causation, but their regular physical interactions with the world—in digging, hunting, walking, dancing—are as stable and as well understood as their familial relations. More than this, preindustrial Homo is already Homo Faber, and the making of pots and of jewelry, for example, involves intimate knowledge of physical things and an expectation of regularity in their behavior….

What we need to bring back into view here is a kind of explanation that is missing from Horton's story: namely, functional explanation, which we find centrally (but by no means uniquely) in what we might call "folk biology." Functional explanation is the sort of explanation that we give when we say that the flower is there to attract the bee that pollinates it; that the liver is there to purify the blood; that the rain falls to water the crops.

This sort of explanation is missing from Horton's story for a very good reason—namely, that the positivist philosophy of science on which Horton relies sought either to eradicate functional explanation or to reduce it to other sorts of explanation, in large part because it reeked of teleology—of the sort of Aristotelian "final" causation that positivism took to have been shown to be hopeless by the failure of vitalism in nineteenth-century biology. And, surely, what is most striking about the "unscientific" explanations that most precolonial African cultures offer is not just that they appeal to agency but that they are addressed to the question "Why?" understood as asking what the event in question was for. Evans-Pritchard in his account of Zande belief insists that the Azande do not think that "unfortunate events" ever happen by chance:[7] their frequent appeal to witchcraft—in the absence of other acceptable explanations of misfortunate—demonstrates their unwillingness to accept the existence of contingency. But to reject the possibility of the contingent is exactly to insist that everything that happens serves some purpose: a view familiar in Christian tradition in such formulas as "And we know that all things work together for good to them that love God" (Rom. 8:28), or in the deep need people feel—in Europe and America as in Africa—for answers to the question "Why do bad things happen to good people?" Zande witchcraft beliefs depend on an assumption that the universe is in a certain sort of evaluative balance; in short, on the sort of assumption that leads monotheistic theologians to develop theodicies.

What Zande people will not accept, as Evans-Pritchard's account makes clear, is not that "unfortunate events" have no explanation—the granary falls because the termites have eaten through the stilts that support it—but that they are meaningless; that there is no deeper reason why the person sitting in the shade of the granary was injured. And in that sense they share an attitude that we find in Christian theodicy from Irenaeus to Augustine to Karl Barth: that the cosmos works to a plan. Precolonial African cultures, pre- and nonscientific thinkers everywhere, are inclined to suppose that events in the world have meaning; they worry not about the possibility of the unexplained (what has no efficient cause nor agent explanation) but of the meaningless (what has no function, no point). And this marks those who accept the scientific worldview—a minority, of course, even in the industrialized world—from almost all other humans throughout history. For it

is a distinctive feature of that scientific worldview that it accepts that not everything that happens has a human meaning. To explain this difference between scientific and nonscientific visions we need, I think, to begin with the fact that the world, as the sciences conceive of it, extends so hugely far beyond the human horizon, in time as in space. As Alexandre Korye indicated in the title of his well-known study of the birth of modern celestial physics, the Newtonian revolution took the intellectual path *From the Closed World to the Infinite Universe,* and the Victorian dispute between science and religion had at its center a debate about the age of the earth, with geology insisting that the biblical time scale of thousands of years since the creation radically underestimated the age of our planet. Copernicus turned European scientists away from a geocentric to a heliocentric view of the universe and began a process, which Darwin continued, that inevitably displaced humankind from the center of the natural sciences. A recognition that the universe does not seem to have been made simply for us is the basis of the radically nonanthropocentric character of scientific theories of the world. This nonanthropocentrism is part of the change in view that develops with the growth of capitalism, of science, and of the modern state. The change to which, for example, Weber's account of modernization was addressed, and it contributes profoundly to the sense of the universe as disenchanted that Weberians have taken to be so central a feature of modernity (a claim that makes more sense as a claim about the life of professional intellectuals than as one about the culture as a whole)....

But Horton in his original work made, as I said, a second important claim for difference: he summarized it by calling the cognitive world of traditional cultures "closed" and that of modern cultures "open." "What I take to be the key difference is a very simple one," he writes. "It is that in traditional cultures there is no developed awareness of alternatives to the established body of theoretical tenets; whereas in scientifically oriented cultures, such an awareness is highly developed."... And it is here, when we turn from questions about the content and logic of traditional and scientific explanation to the social contexts in which those theories

---

[7]See Evans-Pritchard, *Witchcraft, Oracles and Magic among the Azande,* chap. 2.

are constructed and mobilized, that Horton's account begins to seem less adequate....

Remember the answer the priest gave to the question about the gold dust ... "We do it because the ancestors did it." In the open society this will no longer do as a reason. The early modern natural scientists, the natural philosophers of the Renaissance, stressed often the unreasonableness of appeals to authority. And if modern scholarship suggests that they overstressed the extent to which their predecessors were bound by a hidebound traditionalism, it is still true that there is a difference—if only in degree—in the extent to which modernity celebrates distance from our predecessors, while the traditional world celebrates cognitive continuity.

Now Horton's account of the sense in which the traditional worldview is closed has—rightly—been challenged. The complexities of war and trade, dominance and clientage, migration and diplomacy, in much of precolonial Africa are simply not consistent with the image of peoples unaware that there is a world elsewhere....

It is also possible to find first-rate speculative thinkers in traditional societies whose individual openness is not to be denied. I think here of Ogotemmêli, whose cosmology Griaule has captured ... and Barry Hallen has provided evidence from Nigerian sources of the existence, within African traditional modes of thought, of styles of reasoning that are open neither to Wiredu's stern strictures nor to Horton's milder ones....[8] Horton's original stress on the "closed" nature of traditional modes of thought does look less adequate in the face of Africa's complex history of cultural exchanges and of Hallen's babalawo, or in the presence of the extraordinary metaphysical synthesis of the Dogon elder, Ogotemmêli.... In a recent book—written with the Nigerian philosopher J. O. Sodipo—Hallen insists on the presence among Yoruba doctors of theories of witchcraft rather different from those of their fellow

country-men.[9] Here, then, among doctors, speculation inconsistent with ordinary folk belief occurs....

Horton has recently come—in response, in part, to Hallen's critique—to speak not of the closedness of traditional belief systems but, borrowing a term from Wole Soyinka, of their being "accommodative." He discusses work by students of Evans-Pritchard that not only addresses the kind of static body of belief that is captured in Evans-Pritchard's picture of the Azande thought world but also stresses the dynamic and—as Horton admits—"open" way in which they "devise explanations for novel elements in ... experience," and "their capacity to borrow, re-work and integrate alien ideas in the course of elaborating such explanations." "Indeed," he continues, "it is this 'open-ness' that has given the traditional cosmologies such tremendous durability in the face of immense changes that the 20th century has brought to the African scene." Horton then contrasts this accommodative style with the "adversary" style of scientific theory, which is characterized by the way in which the main stimulus to change of belief is not "novel experience but rival theory."[10]

And it seems to me that this change from the Popperian terminology of "open" and "closed" allows Horton to capture something important about the difference between traditional religion and science; something to do not with individual cognitive strategies but with social ones. If we want to understand the significance of social organization in differentiating traditional religion and natural science, we can do no better than to begin with those of Evans-Pritchard's answers to the question why the Azande do not see the falsity of their magic beliefs that mention social facts about the organization of those beliefs.

Evans-Pritchard wrote:

> Scepticism, far from being smothered, is recognized, even inculcated. But it is only about certain

[8]Barry Hallen, "Robin Horton on Critical Philosophy and Traditional Thought." ... Wiredu, of course, does not deny the existence of skeptics in traditional cultures. See pp. 20–21, 37, 143 of *Philosophy and an African Culture* (London: Cambridge University Press, 1980).

[9]Barry Hallen and J. Sodipo, *Knowledge, Belief and Witchcraft: Analytic Experiments in African Philosophy* (London: Ethnographica, 1986)—summarized here in Chapter 9.
[10]This work is in the paper, "Traditional Thought and the Emerging African Philosophy Department: A Reply to Dr. Hallen," unpublished manuscript.

medicines and certain magicians. By contrast it tends to support other, medicines and other magicians.... Each man and each kinship group acts without cognizance of the actions of others. People do not pool their ritual experiences....They are not experimentally inclined.... Not being experimentally inclined, they do not test the efficacy of their medicines.[11]

And, he added, "Zande beliefs are generally vaguely formulated. A belief, to be easily contradicted by experience ... must be clearly shared and intellectually developed."[12]

Whatever the practices of imperfect scientists are actually like, none of these things is supposed to be true of natural science. In our official picture of the sciences, skepticism is encouraged even about foundational questions—indeed, that is where the best students are supposed to be directed.... The scientific community is experimentally inclined, and, of course, scientific theory is formulated as precisely as possible in order that those experiments can be carried out in a controlled fashion.... [S]cience is, crucially, adversarial, and the norms of publication and reproducibility of results, even though only imperfectly adhered to, are explicitly intended to lay theories and experimental claims open to attack by one's peers, and thus make competition from the adventurous "young Turk" possible.

More important than the hugely oversimplified contrast between an experimental, skeptical, science and an unexperimental, "dogmatic" traditional mode of thought is the difference in images of knowledge that are represented in the differences in the social organization of inquiry in modern as opposed to "traditional" societies. Scientists, like the rest of us, hold onto theories longer than they may be entitled to; suppress, unconsciously or half consciously, evidence they do not know how to handle; lie a little. In precolonial societies there were, we can be sure, individual doubters who kept their own counsel, resisters against the local dogma. But what is interesting about modern modes of theorizing is that they are organized around an image of constant change: we expect new theories, we reward and encourage the search for them, we believe that today's best theories will be revised beyond recognition if the enterprise of science survives. My ancestors in Asante never organized a specialized activity that was based around this thought. They knew that some people know more than others, and that there are things to be found out. But they do not seem to have thought it necessary to invest social effort in working out new theories of how the world works, not for some practical end (this they did constantly) but, as we say, for its own sake.

The differences between traditional religious theory and the theories of the sciences reside in the social organization of inquiry, as a systematic business, and it is differences in social organization that account, I think, both for the difference we feel in the character of natural scientific and traditional religious theory—they are products of different kinds of social process—and for the spectacular expansion of the domain of successful prediction and control, an expansion that characterizes natural science but is notably absent in traditional society. Experimentation, the publication and reproduction of results, the systematic development of alternative theories in precise terms, all these ideals, however imperfectly they are realized in scientific practice, are intelligible only in an organized social enterprise of knowledge.

But what can have prompted this radically different approach to knowledge? Why have the practitioners of traditional religion, even the priests, who are the professionals, never developed the organized "adversarial" methods of the sciences? There are, no doubt, many historical sources. A few, familiar suggestions strike one immediately.

[11]This is not to say that they do not have the concepts necessary to understand the idea of an experiment, merely to say that they are not interested in disinterested experimentation simply to find out how things work. For the Azande are very aware, for example, that an oracle needs to be run carefully if it is to be reliable. They therefore test its reliability on every occasion of its use. There are usually two tests: *bambata sima* and *gingo*; the first and second tests. Generally, in the first test, the question is asked so the death of a chicken means yes and in the second so that death means no; but it may be the other way round. Inconsistent results invalidate the procedure. The Azande also have a way of confirming that an oracle is not working; namely to ask it a question to which they already know the answer. Such failures can be explained by one of the many obstacles to an oracle's functioning properly: breach of taboo; witchcraft; the fact that the benge poison used in the oracle has been "spoiled" (as the Azande believe) because it has been near a menstruating woman.
[12]Evans-Pritchard, Witchcraft, *Oracles and Magic among the Azande*, 202–4.

Social mobility leads to political individualism, of a kind that is rare in the traditional polity; political individualism allows cognitive authority to shift, also, from priest to king to commoner; and social mobility is a feature of industrial societies.

Or, in traditional societies, accommodating conflicting theoretical views is part of the general process of accommodation necessary for those who are bound to each other as neighbors for life.... In Ghana, but not in America, it is impolite to disagree, to argue, to confute. And this accommodating approach to conversation is part of the same range of attitudes that leads to theoretical accommodations....

[I]t seems to me that there is one other fundamental difference between traditional West African culture and the culture of the industrial world, and that it plays a fundamental role in explaining why the adversarial style never established itself in West Africa. And it is that these cultures were largely nonliterate.

Now literacy has, as Jack Goody has pointed out in his influential book *The Domestication of the Savage Mind,* important consequences; among them is the fact that it permits a kind of consistency that oral culture cannot and does not demand. Write down a sentence and it is there, in principle, forever; that means that if you write down another sentence inconsistent with it, you can be caught out. It is this fact that is at the root of the possibility of the adversarial style. How often have we seen Perry Mason—on television in Ghana or the United States or England (for television, at least, there is only one world)—ask the stenographer to read back from the record? In the traditional culture the answer can only be: "What record?" In the absence of written records, it is not possible to compare the ancestors' theories in their actual words with ours; nor, given the limitations of quantity imposed by oral transmission, do we have a detailed knowledge of what those theories were. We know more about the thought of Isaac Newton on one or two subjects than we know about the entire population of his Asante contemporaries.

The accommodative style is possible because orality makes it hard to discover discrepancies. And so it is possible to have an image of knowledge as unchanging lore, handed down from the ancestors. It is no wonder, with this image of knowledge, that there is no systematic research: nobody need ever notice that the way that traditional theory is used requires inconsistent interpretations. It is literacy that makes possible the precise formulation of questions that we have just noticed as one of the characteristics of scientific theory, and it is precise formulation that points up inconsistency. This explanation, which we owe to Horton, is surely very plausible....

CRITICAL QUESTIONS

1. Explain what Appiah means when he says that the "differences between traditional religious theory and the theories of the sciences reside in the social organization of inquiry." Do you think he is right about this? Why, or why not?

2. According to Appiah, what accounts for modern scientific cultures being adversarial and traditional religious cultures being accommodative? Explain why you think he may be right or wrong in making this claim.

9.6 FEMINISM AND SCIENCE

Is there such a thing as a feminist science? If there were, would it not seriously compromise the political and ethical neutrality that "good science" is supposed to practice? Would not a science that reflected feminist values amount to "bad science"?

A powerful philosophical influence on our conception of science stems from a movement called **logical positivism**. According to positivism, good science should be objective and value-free. It needs to maintain a sharp distinction between facts and values. If science does not maintain that distinction, then junk science is the result, because bias and prejudices can distort the data and thereby taint the conclusions drawn from that data. This can have devastating and dangerous consequences in the fields of biology and physics that effect practices and technologies from medicine to space exploration.

Could it be, however, that not allowing values such as feminist values to influence the practice of science actually produces bad science? Could it be that the exclusion of values from the production of scientific knowledge distorts the truth that is the goal of such knowledge? But if we allow values into the practice of science are we not opening the door to subjectivity? Is it wise to sacrifice scientific objectivity or is there a legitimate place for values in the practice of science that does not compromise objectivity?

There is, in the philosophy of science, something called the **underdetermination thesis**. According to this thesis, some scientific theory is always undetermined, to a greater or lesser degree, by the evidence that is cited in its support. One consequence is that quite often different and even incompatible theories are supported by the same body of evidence. Debates over everything from global warming to vaccination of infants are often fueled by debates over precisely what theory best explains the evidence. If (and that is a big IF) the evidence can support two different theories, then politics often steps in to try to shape public policy according to different value–commitments.

Could some version of the underdetermination thesis open enough space for values to actually influence, hopefully constructively, the inferences scientists draw from the facts? If so, would science still remain objective even if it were no longer value-neutral?

Professor Helen E. Longino, a philosopher of science, a feminist, and chair of the Department of Philosophy at Stanford University, thinks that the underdetermination thesis does open a space that allows for a "feminist scientific inquiry" that does not compromise scientific objectivity. Read the following selection and see how she argues her case.

◉ READING QUESTIONS

1. What problem does Longino wish to address?
2. What are the problems with thinking that feminist science expresses a "distinctive female cognitive temperament"?
3. On what does Longino wish to focus?
4. Give examples of the two kinds of values relevant to science that Longino distinguishes.
5. Why is the underdetermination thesis important for Longino's account of "feminist scientific inquiry"?
6. According to Longino, what is the argument that demonstrates all of science is not value-free?
7. How does Longino's example of the research she did with Doell on the influence of sex hormones on human behavior illustrate her argument that contextual values do enter into the practice of science?

Can There Be a Feminist Science?

HELEN E. LONGINO

This paper explores a number of recent proposals regarding "feminist science" and rejects a content-based approach in favor of a process-based approach to characterizing feminist science. Philosophy of science can yield models of scientific reasoning that illuminate the interaction between cultural values and ideology and scientific inquiry. While we can use these models to expose masculine and other forms of bias, we can also use them to defend the introduction of assumptions grounded in feminist political values.

I

The question of this title conceals multiple ambiguities. Not only do the sciences consist of many distinct fields, but the term "science" can be used to refer to a method of inquiry, a historically changing collection of practices, a body of knowledge, a set of claims, a profession, a set of social groups, etc. And as the sciences are many, so are the scholarly disciplines that seek to understand them: philosophy, history, sociology, anthropology, psychology. Any answer from the perspective of some one of these disciplines will, then, of necessity, be partial. In this essay, I shall be asking about the possibility of theoretical natural science that is feminist and I shall ask from the perspective of a philosopher. Before beginning to develop my answer, however, I want to review some of the questions that could be meant, in order to arrive at the formulation I wish to address.

The question could be interpreted as factual, one to be answered by pointing to what feminists in the sciences are doing and saying: "Yes, and this is what it is." Such a response can be perceived as question-begging, however. Even such a friend of feminism as Stephen Gould dismisses the idea of a distinctively feminist or even female contribution to the sciences. In a generally positive review of Ruth Bleier's book, *Science and Gender*, Gould

(1984) brushes aside her connection between women's attitudes and values and the interactional science she calls for. Scientists (male, of course) are already proceeding with wholist and interactionist research programs. Why, he implied, should women or feminists have any particular, distinctive, contributions to make? There is not masculinist and feminist science, just good and bad science. The question of a feminist science cannot be settled by pointing, but involves a deeper, subtler investigation.

The deeper question can itself have several meanings. One set of meanings is sociological, the other conceptual. The sociological meaning proceeds as follows. We know what sorts of social conditions make misogynist science possible. The work of Margaret Rossiter (1982) on the history of women scientists in the United States and the work of Kathryn Addelson (1983) on the social structure of professional science detail the relations between a particular social structure for science and the kinds of science produced. What sorts of social conditions would make feminist science possible? This is an important question, one I am not equipped directly to investigate, although what I can investigate is, I believe, relevant to it. This is the second, conceptual, interpretation of the question: what sort of sense does it make to talk about a feminist science? Why is the question itself not an oxymoron, linking, as it does, values and ideological commitment with the idea of impersonal, objective, value-free, inquiry? This is the problem I wish to address in this essay.

The hope for a feminist theoretical natural science has concealed an ambiguity between content and practice. In the content sense the idea of a feminist science involves a number of assumptions and calls a number of visions to mind. Some theorists have written as though a feminist science is one of the theories which encode a particular world

From *Hypatia*, Vol. 2, no. 3 (Fall 1987), pp. 51–64. © by Helen E. Longino.

view, characterized by complexity, interaction and wholism. Such a science is said to be feminist because it is the expression and valorization of a female sensibility or cognitive temperament. Alternatively, it is claimed that women have certain traits (dispositions to attend to particulars, interactive rather than individualist and controlling social attitudes and behaviors) that enable them to understand the true character of natural processes (which are complex and interactive).[1] While proponents of this interactionist view see it as an improvement over most contemporary science, it has also been branded as soft— misdescribed as non-mathematical. Women in the sciences who feel they are being asked to do not better science, but inferior science, have responded angrily to this characterization of feminist science, thinking that it is simply new clothing for the old idea that women can't do science. I think that the interactional view can be defended against this response, although that requires rescuing it from some of its proponents as well. However, I also think that the characterization of feminist science as the expression of a distinctive female cognitive temperament has other drawbacks. It first conflates feminine with feminist. While it is important to reject the traditional derogation of the virtues assigned to women, it is also important to remember that women are *constructed* to occupy positions of social subordinates. We should not uncritically embrace the feminine.

This characterization of feminist science is also a version of recently propounded notions of a 'women's standpoint' or a 'feminist standpoint' and suffers from the same suspect universalization that these ideas suffer from. If there is one such standpoint, there are many as Maria Lugones and Elizabeth Spelman spell out in their tellingly entitled article, "Have We Got a Theory for You: Feminist Theory, Cultural Imperialism, and the Demand for 'The Woman's Voice,'" women are too diverse in our experiences to generate a single cognitive framework (Lugones and Spelman 1983). In addition, the sciences are themselves too diverse for me to think that they might be equally transformed by such a framework. To reject this concept of a feminist science, however, is not to disengage science from

feminism. I want to suggest that we focus on science as practice rather than content, as process rather than product, hence, not on feminist science, but on doing science as a feminist.

The doing of science involves many practices: how one structures a laboratory (hierarchically or collectively), how one relates to other scientists (competitively or cooperatively), how and whether one engages in political struggles over affirmative action. It extends also to intellectual practices, to the activities of scientific inquiry, such as observation and reasoning. Can there be a feminist scientific inquiry? This possibility is seen to be problematic against the background of certain standard presuppositions about science. The claim that there could be a feminist science in the sense of an intellectual practice is either nonsense because oxymoronic as suggested above, or the claim is interpreted to mean that established science (science as done and dominated by men) is wrong about the world. Feminist science in this latter interpretation is presented as correcting the errors of masculine, standard science and as revealing the truth that is hidden by masculine 'bad' science, as taking the sex out of science.

Both of these interpretations involve the rejection of one approach as incorrect and the embracing of the other as the way to a truer understanding of the natural world. Both trade one absolutism for another. Each is a side of the same coin, and that coin, I think, is the idea of a value-free science. This is the idea that scientific methodology guarantees the independence of scientific inquiry from values of value-related considerations. A science or a scientific research program informed by values is *ipso facto* "bad science." "Good science" is inquiry protected by methodology from values and ideology. This same idea underlies Gould's response to Bleier, so it bears closer scrutiny. In the pages that follow, I shall examine the idea of value-free science and then apply the results of that examination to the idea of feminist scientific inquiry.

II

I distinguish two kinds of values relevant to the sciences. Constitutive values, internal to the sciences, are the source of the rules determining what constitutes acceptable scientific practice or scientific method. The personal, social and cultural values, those group or individual preferences about what ought to be I call contextual values, to indicate that they belong to the social and cultural context in which science is done (Longino 1983c). The traditional interpretation of the value-freedom of modern natural science amounts to a claim that its constitutive and contextual features are clearly distinct from and independent of one another, that contextual values play no role in the inner workings of scientific inquiry, in reasoning and observation. I shall argue that this construal of the distinction cannot be maintained.

There are several ways to develop such in argument. One scholar is fond of inviting her audience to visit any science library and peruse the titles on the shelves. Observe how subservient to social and cultural interests are the inquiries represented by the book titles alone! Her listeners would soon abandon their ideas about the value-neutrality of the sciences, she suggests. This exercise may indeed show the influence of external, contextual considerations on what research gets done/supported (i.e., on problem selection). It does not show that such considerations affect reasoning or hypothesis acceptance. The latter would require detailed investigation of particular cases or a general conceptual argument. The conceptual arguments involve developing some version of what is known in philosophy of science as the underdetermination thesis, i.e., the thesis that a theory is always underdetermined by the evidence adduced in its support, with the consequence that different or incompatible theories are supported by or at least compatible with the same body of evidence. I shall sketch a version of the argument that appeals to features of scientific inference.

One of the rocks on which the logical positivist program foundered was the distinction between theoretical and observational language. Theoretical statements contain, as fundamental descriptive terms, terms that do not occur in the description of data. Thus, hypotheses in particle physics contain terms like "electron," "pion," "muon," "electron spin," etc. The evidence for a hypothesis such as "A pion decays sequentially into a muon, then a positron" is obviously not direct observations of pions, muons and positrons, but consists largely in photographs taken in large and complex experimental apparati accelerators, cloud chambers, bubble chambers. The photographs show all sorts of squiggly lines and spirals. Evidence for the hypotheses of particle physics is presented as statements that describe these photographs. Eventually, of course, particle physicists point to a spot on a photograph and say things like "Here a neutrino hits a neutron." Such an assertion, however, is an interpretive achievement which involves collapsing theoretical and observational moments. A skeptic would have to be supplied a complicated argument linking the elements of the photograph to traces left by particles and these to particles themselves. What counts as theory and what as data in a pragmatic sense change over time, as some ideas and experimental procedures come to be securely embedded in a particular framework and others take their place on the horizons. As the history of physics shows, however, secure embeddedness is no guarantee against overthrow.

Logical positivists and their successors hoped to model scientific inference formally. Evidence for hypotheses, data, were to be represented as logical consequences of hypotheses. When we try to map this logical structure onto the sciences, however, we find that hypotheses are, for the most part, not just generalizations of data statements. The links between data and theory, therefore, cannot be adequately represented as formal or syntactic, but are established by means of assumptions that make or imply substantive claims about the field over which one theorizes. Theories are confirmed via the confirmation of their constituent hypotheses, so the confirmation of hypotheses and theories is relative to the assumptions relied upon in asserting the evidential connection. Conformation of such assumptions, which are often unarticulated, is itself subject to similar relativization. And it is these assumptions that can be the vehicle for the involvement of considerations motivated primarily by contextual values (Longino 1979, 1983a).

The point of this extremely telescoped argument is that one can't give an a priori specification of confirmation that effectively eliminates the role of value-laden assumptions in legitimate scientific inquiry without eliminating auxiliary hypotheses (assumptions) altogether. This is not to say that all scientific reasoning involves value-related assumptions. Sometimes auxiliary assumptions will be supported by mundane inductive reasoning. But sometimes they will not be. In any given case, they may be metaphysical in character, they may be untestable with present investigative techniques, they may be rooted in contextual, value-related considerations. If, however, there is no a priori way to eliminate such assumptions from evidential reasoning generally, and, hence, no way to rule out value-laden assumptions, then there is no formal basis for arguing that an inference mediated by contextual values is thereby bad science. A comparable point is made by some historians investigating the origins of modern science. James Jacob (1977) and Margaret Jacob (1976) have, in a series of articles and books, argued that the adoption of conceptions of matter by 17th century scientists like Robert Boyle was inextricably intertwined with political considerations. Conceptions of matter provided the foundation on which physical theories were developed and Boyle's science, regardless of his reasons for it, has been fruitful in ways that far exceed his imaginings. If the presence of contextual influences were grounds for disallowing a line of inquiry, then early modern science would not have gotten off the ground.

The conclusion of this line of argument is that constitutive values conceived as epistemological (i.e., truth-seeking) are not adequate to screen out the influence of contextual values in the very structuring of scientific knowledge. Now the ways in which contextual values do, if they do, influence this structuring and interact, if they do, with constitutive values has to be determined separately for different theories and fields of science. But this argument, if it's sound, tells us that this sort of inquiry is perfectly respectable and involves no shady assumptions or unargued intuitively based rejections of positivism. It also opens the possibility that one can make explicit value commitments and still do "good" science. The conceptual argument doesn't show that all science is value-laden (as opposed to metaphysics-laden)—that must be established on a case-by-case basis, using the tools not just of logic and philosophy but of history and sociology as well. It does show that not all science is value-free and, more importantly, that it is not necessarily in the nature of science to be value-free. If we reject that idea we're in a better position to talk about the possibilities of feminist science.

III

In earlier articles (Longino 1981, 1983b, Longino and Doell 1983), I've used similar considerations to argue that scientific objectivity has to be reconceived as a function of the communal structure of scientific inquiry rather than as a property of individual scientists. I've then used these notions about scientific methodology to show that science displaying masculine bias is not *ipso facto* improper or 'bad' science, that the fabric of science can neither rule out the expression of bias nor legitimate it. So I've argued that both the expression of masculine bias in the sciences and feminist criticism of research exhibiting that bias are—shall we say—business as usual, that scientific inquiry should be expected to display the deep metaphysical and normative commitments of the culture in which it flourishes, and finally that criticism of the deep assumptions that guide scientific reasoning about data is a proper part of science. The argument I've just offered about the idea of a value-free science is similar in spirit to those earlier arguments. I think it makes it possible to see these questions from a slightly different angle.

There is a tradition of viewing scientific inquiry as somehow inexorable. This involves supposing that the phenomena of the natural world are fixed in determinate relations with each other, that these relations can be known and formulated in a consistent and unified way. This is not the old "unified science" idea of the logical positivists, with its privileging of physics. In its "unexplicated" or "pre-analytic" state, it is simply the idea that there is one consistent, integrated or coherent, true theoretical treatment of all natural phenomena. (The indeterminacy principle of quantum physics is restricted to our understanding of the behavior of certain particles which themselves ·underlie the fixities of the natural world. Stochastic theories reveal fixities, but fixities among ensembles rather than fixed relations among individual objects or events.) The scientific inquirer's job is to discover those fixed relations. Just as the task of Plato's philosophers was to discover the fixed relations among forms and the task of Galileo's scientists was to discover the laws written in the language of the grand book of nature, geometry, so the scientist's task in this tradition remains the discovery of fixed relations however conceived. These ideas are part of the realist tradition in the philosophy of science.

It's no longer possible, in a century that has seen the splintering of the scientific disciplines, to give such a unified description of the objects of inquiry. But the belief that the job is to discover fixed relations of some sort, and that the application of observation, experiment and reason leads ineluctably to unifiable, if not unified, knowledge of an independent reality, is still with us. It is evidenced most clearly in two features of scientific rhetoric the use of the passive voice as in "it is concluded that" or "it has been discovered that" and the attribution of agency to the data, as in "the data suggest." Such language has been criticized for the abdication of responsibility it indicates. Even more, the scientific inquirer, and we with her, become passive observers, victims of the truth. The idea of a value-free science is integral to this view of scientific inquiry. And if we reject that idea we can also reject our roles as passive onlookers, helpless to affect the course of knowledge.

Let me develop this point somewhat more concretely and autobiographically. Biologist Ruth Doell and I have been examining studies in three areas of research on the influence of sex hormones on human behavior and cognitive performance research on the influence of pre-natal, *in utero,* exposure to higher or lower than normal levels of androgens and estrogens on so-called 'gender-role' behavior in children, influence of androgens (pre- and post-natal) on homosexuality in women, and influence of lower than normal (for men) levels of androgen at puberty on spatial abilities (Doell and Longino, forthcoming). The studies we looked at are vulnerable to criticism of their data and their observation methodologies. They

also show clear evidence of androcentric bias—in the assumption that there are just two sexes and two genders (us and them), in the designation of appropriate and inappropriate behaviors for male and female children, in the caricature of lesbianism, in the assumption of male mathematical superiority. We did not find, however, that these assumptions mediated the inferences from data to theory that we found objectionable. These sexist assumptions did affect the way the data were described. What mediated the inferences from the alleged data (i.e., what functioned as auxiliary hypotheses or what provided auxiliary hypotheses) was what we called the linear model—the assumption that there is a direct one-way causal relationship between pre- or post-natal hormone levels and later behavior or cognitive performance. To put it crudely, fetal gonadal hormones organize the brain at critical periods of development. The organism is thereby disposed to respond in a range of ways to a range of environmental stimuli. The assumption of unidirectional programming is supposedly supported by the finding of such a relationship in other mammals, in particular, by experiments demonstrating the dependence of sexual behaviors—mounting and lordosis—on pen-natal hormone exposure and the finding of effects of sex hormones on the development of rodent brains. To bring it to bear on humans is to ignore, among other things, some important differences between human brains and those of other species. It also implies a willingness to regard humans in a particular way—to see us as produced by factors over which we have no control. Not only are we, as scientists, victims of the truth, but we are the prisoners of our physiology.[2] In the name of extending an explanatory model, human capacities for self-knowledge, self-reflection, self-determination are eliminated from any role in human action (at least in the behaviors studied).

Doell and I have therefore argued for the replacement of that linear model of the role of the brain in behavior by one of much greater complexity that includes physiological, environmental, historical and psychological elements. Such a model allows not only for the interaction of physiological and environmental factors but also for the interaction of these with a continuously self-modifying, self-representational (and self-organizing) central processing system. In contemporary neurobiology, the closest model is that being developed in the group selectionist approach to higher brain function of Gerald Edelman and other researchers (Edelman and Mountcastle 1978). We argue that a model of at least that degree of complexity is necessary to account for the human behaviors studies in the sex hormones and behavior research and that if gonadal hormones function at all at these levels, they will probably be found at most to facilitate or inhibit neural processing in general. The strategy we take in our argument is to show that the degree of intentionality involved in the behaviors in question is greater than is presupposed by the hormonal influence researchers and to argue that this degree of intentionality implicates the higher brain processes.

To this point Ruth Doell and I agree. I want to go further and describe what we've done from the perspective of the above philosophical discussion of scientific methodology.

Abandoning my polemical mood for a more reflective one, I want to say that, in the end, commitment to one or another model is strongly influenced by values or other contextual features. The models themselves determine the relevance and interpretation of data. The linear or complex models are not in turn independently or conclusively supported by data. I doubt for instance that value-free inquiry will reveal the efficacy or inefficacy of intentional states or of physiological factors like hormone exposure in human action. I think instead that a research program in neuroscience that assumes the linear model and sex-gender dualism will show the influence of hormone exposure on gender-role behavior. And I think that a research program in neuroscience and psychology proceeding on the assumption that humans do possess the capacities for self-consciousness, self-reflection, and self-determination, and which then asks how the structure of the human brain and nervous system enables the expression of these capacities, will reveal the efficacy of intentional states (understood as very complex sorts of brain states).

While this latter assumption does not itself contain normative terms, I think that the decision to adopt it is motivated by value-laden considerations—by the desire to understand ourselves and others as self-determining (at least some of the time), that is, as capable of acting on the basis of concepts or representations of ourselves and the world in which we act. (Such representations are not necessarily correct, they are surely mediated by our cultures, all we wish to claim is that they are efficacious.) I think further that this desire on Ruth Doell's and my part is, in several ways, an aspect of our feminism. Our preference for a neurobiological model that allows for agency, for the efficacy of intentionality is partly a validation of our (and everyone's) subjective experience of thought, deliberation, and choice. One of the tenets of feminist research is the valorization of subjective experience, and so our preference in this regard conforms to feminist research patterns. There is, however, a more direct way in which our feminism is expressed in this preference. Feminism is many things to many people, but it is at its core in part about the expansion of human potentiality. When feminists talk of breaking out and do break out of socially prescribed sex-roles, when feminists criticize the institutions of domination, we are thereby insisting on the capacity of humans—male and female—to act on perceptions of self and society and to act to bring about changes in self and society on the basis of those perceptions. (Not overnight and not by a mere act of will. The point is that we act.) And so our criticism of theories of the hormonal influence or determination of so-called gender-role behavior is not just a rejection of the sexist bias in the description of the phenomena—the behavior of the children studied, the sexual lives of lesbians, etc.—but of the limitations on human capacity imposed by the analytic model underlying such research.[3]

While the argument strategy we adopt against the linear model rests on a certain understanding of intention, the values motivating our adoption of that understanding remain hidden in that polemical context. Our political commitments, however, presuppose a certain understanding of human action, so that when faced with a conflict between these commitments and a particular model of brain-behavior relationships we allow the political commitments to guide the choice.

The relevance of my argument about value-free science should be becoming clear. Feminists—in and out of science—often condemn masculine bias in the sciences from the vantage point of commitment to a value-free science. Androcentric bias, once identified, can then be seen as a violation of the rules, as "bad" science. Feminist science, by contrast, can eliminate that bias and produce better, good, more true or gender free science. From that perspective the process I've just described is anathema. But if scientific methods generated by constitutive values cannot guarantee independent from contextual values, then that approach to sexist science won't work. We cannot restrict ourselves simply to the elimination of bias, but must expand our scope to include the detection of limiting and interpretive frameworks and the finding or construction of more appropriate frameworks. We need not, indeed should not, wait for such a framework to emerge from the data. In waiting, if my argument is correct, we run the danger of working unconsciously with assumptions still laden with values from the context we seek to change. Instead of remaining passive with respect to the data and what the data suggest, we can acknowledge our ability to affect the course of knowledge and fashion or favor research programs that are consistent with the values and commitments we express in the rest of our lives. From this perspective, the idea of a value-free science is not just empty, but pernicious. Accepting the relevance to our practice as scientists of our political commitments does not imply simple and crude impositions of those ideas onto the corner of the natural world under study. If we recognize, however, that knowledge is shaped by the assumptions, values and interests of a culture and that, within limits, one can choose one's culture, then it's clear that as scientists/theorists we have a choice. We can continue to do establishment science, comfortably wrapped in the myths of scientific rhetoric or we can alter our intellectual allegiances. While remaining committed to an abstract goal of understanding, we can choose to whom, socially and politically, we are accountable in our pursuit of that goal. In

particular we can choose between being accountable to the traditional establishment or to our political comrades.

Such accountability does not demand a radical break with the science one has learned and practiced. The development of a "new" science involves a more dialectical evolution and more continuity with established science than the familiar language of scientific revolutions implies.

In focusing on accountability and choice, this conception of feminist science differs from those that proceed from the assumption of a congruence between certain models of natural processes and women's inherent modes of understanding.[4] I am arguing instead for the deliberate and active choice of an interpretive model and for the legitimacy of basing that choice on political considerations in this case. Obviously model choice is also constrained by (what we know of) reality, that is, by the data. But reality (what we know of it) is, I have already argued, inadequate to uniquely determine model choice. The feminist theorists mentioned above have focused on the relation between the content of a theory and female values or experiences, in particular on the perceived congruence between interactionist, wholist visions of nature and a form of understanding and set of values widely attributed to women. In contrast, I am suggesting that a feminist scientific practice admits political considerations as relevant constraints on reasoning, which, through their influence on reasoning and interpretation, shape content. In this specific case, those considerations in combination with the phenomena support an explanatory model that is highly interactionist, highly complex. This argument is so far, however, neutral on the issue of whether an interactionist and complex account of natural processes will always be the preferred one. If it is preferred, however, this will be because of explicitly political considerations and not because interactionism is the expression of "women's nature."

The integration of a political commitment with scientific work will be expressed differently in different fields. In some, such as the complex of research programs having a bearing on the understanding of human behavior, certain moves, such as the one described above, seem quite obvious. In others it may not be clear how to express an alternate set of values in inquiry, or what values would be appropriate. The first step, however, is to abandon the idea that scrutiny of the data yields a seamless web of knowledge. The second is to think through a particular field and try to understand just what its unstated and fundamental assumptions are and how they influence the course of inquiry. Knowing something of the history of a field is necessary to this process, as is continued conversation with other feminists.

The feminist interventions I imagine will be local (i.e., specific to a particular area of research), they may not be exclusive (i.e., different feminist perspectives may be represented in theorizing), and they will be in some way continuous with existing scientific work. The accretion of such interventions, of science done by feminists as feminists, and by members of other disenfranchised groups, has the potential, nevertheless, ultimately to transform the character of scientific discourse. Doing science differently requires more than just the will to do so and it would be disingenuous to pretend that our philosophies of science are the only barrier. Scientific inquiry takes place in a social, political and economic context which imposes a variety of institutional obstacles to innovation, let alone to the intellectual working out of oppositional and political commitments. The nature of university career ladders means that one's work must be recognized as meeting certain standards of quality in order that one be able to continue it. If those standards are

intimately bound up with values and assumptions one rejects, incomprehension rather than conversion is likely. Success requires that we present our work in a way that satisfies those standards and it is easier to do work that looks just like work known to satisfy them than to strike out in a new direction. Another push to conformity comes from the structure of support for science. Many of the scientific ideas argued to be consistent with a feminist politics have a distinctively non-production orientation.[5] In the example discussed above, thinking of the brain as hormonally programmed makes intervention and control more likely than does thinking of it as a self-organizing complexly interactive system. The doing of science, however, requires financial support and those who provide that support are increasingly industry and the military. As might be expected they support research projects likely to meet their needs, projects which promise even greater possibilities for intervention in and manipulation of natural processes. Our sciences are being harnessed to the making of money and the waging of war. The possibility of alternate understandings of the natural world is irrelevant to a culture driven by those interests. To do feminist science we must change the social and political context in which science is done. So can there be a feminist science? If this means is it in principle possible to do science as a feminist, the answer must be yes. If this means can we in practice do science as feminists, the answer must be, not until we change present conditions.

NOTES

I am grateful to the Wellesley Center for Research on Women for the Mellon Scholarship during which I worked on the ideas in this essay. I am also grateful to audiences at UC Berkeley, Northeastern University, Brandeis University and Rice University for their comments and to the anonymous reviewers for *Hypatia* for their suggestions. An earlier version appeared as Wellesley Center for Research on Women Working Paper iC63.

1. This seems to be suggested in Bleier (1984), Rose (1983), and in Sandra Harding's (1980) early work.
2. For a striking expression of this point of view see Witelson (1985).
3. Ideological commitments other than feminist ones may lead to the same assumptions and the variety of feminisms means that feminist commitments can lead to different and incompatible assumptions.
4. Cf note 1, above.

5. This is not to say that interactional ideas may not be applied in productive contexts, but that, unlike linear causal models, they are several steps away from the manipulation of natural processes immediately suggested by the latter. See Keller (1985), especially Chapter 10.

◉ REFERENCES

Addelson, Kathryn Pine. 1983. The man of professional wisdom. In *Discovering reality*, ed. Sandra Harding and Merrill Hintikka. Dordrecht: Reidel.

Bleier, Ruth. 1984. *Science and gender*. Elmsford, NY: Pergamon.

Doell, Ruth, and Helen E. Longino. N.d. *Journal of Homosexuality*. Forthcoming.

Edelman, Gerald and Vernon Mountcastle. 1978. *The mindful brain*. Cambridge, MA: MIT Press.

Gould, Stephen J. 1984. Review of Ruth Bleier, *Science and gender*. *New York Times Book Review*, VVI, 7 (August 12): 1.

Harding, Sandra. 1980. The norms of inquiry and masculine experience. In *PSA 1980*, Vol. 2, ed. Peter Asquith and Ronald Giere. East Lansmg, MI: Philosophy of Science Association.

Jacob, James R. 1977. *Robert Boyle and the English Revolution, A study in social and intellectual change*. New York: Franklin.

Jacob, Margaret C. 1976. *The Newtonians and the English Revolution, 1689–1720*. Ithaca, NY: Cornell University Press.

Keller, Evelyn Fox. 1985. *Reflections on gender and science*. New Haven, CT: Yale University Press.

Longino, Helen. 1979. Evidence and hypothesis. *Philosophy of Science* 46 (1): 35–56.

——— 1981. Scientific objectivity and feminist theorizing. *Liberal Education* 67 (3): 33–41.

——— 1983a. The idea of a value free science. Paper presented to the Pacific Division of the American Philosophical Association, March 25, Berkeley, CA.

——— 1983b. Scientific objectivity and logics of science. *Inquiry* 26 (1): 85–106.

——— 1983c. Beyond "bad science." *Science, Technology and Human Values* 8 (1): 7–17.

Longino, Helen and Ruth Doell. 1983. Body, bias and behavior. *Signs* 9 (2): 206–227.

Lugones, Maria and Elizabeth Spelman. 1983. Have we got a theory for you! Feminist theory, cultural imperialism and the demand for "the woman's voice." *Hypatia I*, published as a special issue of *Women's Studies International Forum 6* (6): 573–581.

Rose, Hilary. 1983. Hand, brain, and heart: A feminist epistemology for the natural sciences. *Signs* 9 (1): 73–90.

Rossiter, Margaret. 1982. *Women scientists in America: Struggles and strategies to 1940*. Baltimore, MD: Johns Hopkins University Press.

Witelson, Sandra. 1985. An exchange on gender. *New York Review of Books* (October 24).

◉ CRITICAL QUESTIONS

1. Do you think Longino and Doell are correct in allowing their commitments to feminist values to influence their choice of models (linear vs. complex) to explain hormonal influences on gender-role behavior? Why or why not?

2. Can Longino have it both ways, that is, preserve the objectivity of scientific research and allow contextual values to influence the choices researchers must make? Why or why not?

To access the *Voices of Wisdom*, 8th Edition, **Premium Website**, search for this book on CengageBrain.com.

CHAPTER TEN

What Is Really Real?

If the doors of perception were cleansed everything would appear to man as it is, infinite.

WILLIAM BLAKE

LEARNING OBJECTIVES

After studying this chapter students should be able to:
- define ontology,
- distinguish the material from the immaterial,
- contrast materialism and idealism,
- distinguish dualism, monism, and pluralism,
- describe the three main concerns of metaphysics,
- explain the problem of the one and the many,
- compare process and substance ontologies,
- describe the relationship between *Dao* and *De*,
- explain *Wuwei*,
- characterize the relationship between *yin* and *yang*,
- explain Plato's theory of Forms,
- provide a brief outline of the *Republic*,
- describe how *Atman* and *Brahman* are related according to *Shankara*,
- explain sublation,
- state the difference between objective and subjective idealism,
- differentiate direct and indirect realism,
- distinguish primary from secondary qualities,
- explain "*esse* is *percipi*,"
- identify Laozi, Dao De Jing, The Republic, Plato, Shankara, Advaita Vedanta, Berkeley, Locke, *The Principles of Human Knowledge*, Valedez, and Heidegger, and
- answer all of the questions relating to the selections.

10.1 INTRODUCTION

Have you ever wondered if what you *think* is real is *actually* real? Someone has undoubtedly asked you, with a smile, "If a tree falls in a forest and no one is there, does it make a sound?" What do you think? Have you ever thought about the question, "Why is there something rather than nothing?" Have you ever thought, "Is the world we experience real or an illusion?" Have you ever been puzzled by the question, "What are time and space?" Do you think something can come from nothing? What are ideas made of? Is nature all there is, or is there some sort of supernatural reality?

If you have wondered about these sorts of questions, you have been concerned with what philosophers call *metaphysics*. Metaphysics has to do with the construction and criticism of theories about what is truly real. Metaphysics deals with abstract issues, but its concerns arise out of everyday experiences. For example, you may have been traveling down a road and seen, ahead on the highway, what looked like an animal; but when you got closer, you discovered that it was really a bush. It appeared to be one thing and turned out to be another. The question about what is *genuinely* or *really* real presupposes a distinction between appearance and reality. Metaphysics generalizes that distinction and asks, "If some things in the world appear to be real but turn out not to be, what about the world itself? Is the universe appearance or reality?"

Some philosophers maintain that the chief part of metaphysics is what they call **ontology** (literally, "the study of being"). One ontological concern has to do with the *kinds* of things that exist. For example, try to categorize the items in the following list into two general groups, material and immaterial:

chairs	trees	cats	ideas
seeing	anger	stones	atoms
God	space	time	you

Did you have a hard time sorting these? One problem is that some things seem to be a mixture of the material and the immaterial. For example, you have a body, which is material, but you also have a mind, which some would claim to be immaterial. Another problem has to do with definitions. What do we mean by *material* and *immaterial*? How can we classify things until we know how to distinguish between them?

This last question leads us directly into a second concern of ontology, namely the *definition* of different kinds of being. For example, some philosophers have argued that material beings can be distinguished from immaterial beings according to the following characteristics:

Material	*Immaterial*
spatial	nonspatial
public	private
mechanical	teleological

According to this list, material things like chairs take up space (hence are spatial), but immaterial things like ideas do not take up space (hence are nonspatial). It makes good sense to ask how wide a chair is, but does it make any sense to ask how wide my *idea* of a chair is? Material things are also public in the sense that they can be viewed by different people. I can see a chair or a tree, and so can you.

However, I cannot see your *idea* of a chair or a tree. Your idea is private; it is not open to public inspection. Finally, material objects are causally determined in a purely **mechanistic** way. They are nonintentional—that is, they behave not according to purposes but according to the laws of physics. That chair is in the corner of the room not because it *wants* to be there, but because it was *placed* there by external forces. But what about you? Is your behavior purely mechanistic (machinelike)? Or is your behavior teleological, that is, governed by goals and purposes? Are you in the corner of the room because of external forces, or are you there because you want to leave and the door is located there?

A third concern of ontology has to do with what is *ultimately* real. Once we have discovered all the kinds of beings that seem to exist and have adequately defined each of the kinds, which if any of these kinds are really real? Is matter the really real? If you answer yes, you would be an advocate of materialism. **Materialism** is the metaphysical theory that matter is truly real and immaterial things are not. Note that we should not confuse materialism with physical science. Physical science is clearly concerned with matter and the study of physical things. The claim, however, that only physical things are real is not a scientific claim, it is a metaphysical claim. It is a claim about the *whole* of reality.

Some of you might be inclined to argue that being, or reality, is fundamentally immaterial. One widespread philosophical version of this theory is called idealism. The metaphysical theory of **idealism** asserts that ideas (in the broad sense of thoughts, concepts, minds) are ultimately real. Do not confuse idealism as a metaphysical doctrine with idealism as a moral theory about ideals. Idealism, as I am using that term here, has to do with ideas, not ideals.

One major problem with idealism, as you might expect, is to explain our experience of things that seem both material and real. The chair I am sitting on seems physical, solid, and real to me, and I certainly hope it is. Could it be that this chair is nothing more than a bundle of sensations or ideas? If materialism needs to explain the mental in terms of the physical, idealism must explain the physical in terms of the mental.

Maybe you want to suggest that both these sorts of things (the material and the immaterial) are genuinely real. This dualistic approach seems reasonable. It certainly escapes the problems of explaining away chairs, bodies, minds, and ideas. **Dualism** is the theory that reality is both material and immaterial. My body is real, and the material chair it is sitting on is real (what a relief), but my mind and its ideas are also real (that's good to know, too). However, if reality is both material and immaterial, how are the two related? How, for example, are our minds related to our brains? The major problem of dualism is to relate the material and the immaterial.

Those who argue that being, or reality, is fundamentally of one nature avoid this problem. They are called monists, and their theory (in contrast to dualism) is called monism. **Monism** holds that there is a single reality. Notice that a monist can be either a materialist or an idealist. The contrast here is between monism and dualism, not between materialism and idealism.

Discussions of dualism versus monism soon lead to the **problem of the one and the many**. Is there one reality, or are there many different real things that cannot be reduced to a single thing? **Pluralism** is the position that there are many different real things. This question of one or many, along with the question about what is really real, constitute two fundamental metaphysical problems.

Metaphysics may seem abstract and totally unrelated to real-world problems. What difference does it make whether reality is one undivided whole or is made up of many parts? Although it may not seem like it, metaphysical assumptions (largely unexamined and often unconscious) influence our lives on a daily basis. They also play a vital role in moral debates. For example, arguments about stem cell research and abortion depend on a variety of metaphysical ideas about the existence or non-existence of souls and the nature of human beings. Debates about environmental policies rely on metaphysical assumptions about individuals, communities, ecosystems, and so forth. How we treat others with whom we share this planet depends, in part, on metaphysical assumptions about how all things are related (or not related). Although some philosophers have argued that metaphysical speculation is a meaningless activity because we cannot discover any solid, verifiable answers to metaphysical questions about the nature of reality, most philosophers realize that we cannot escape thinking about what is really real.

10.2 THE DAO

The name "Daoism" (Wade-Giles spelling is Taoism) was first coined by Han scholars to refer to the philosophy developed by Laozi. As the name implies, central to this philosophical view is the notion of *Dao,* often translated as the "way of nature." Laozi is the alleged author of a book popularly known as the *Dao DeJing* (Wade-Giles *Tao Te Ching*).

We have legends about Laozi and when he lived, but we have very little firm historical information. According to tradition he was a contemporary of Confucius (551–479 BCE), but most scholars have placed his book later, during the Warring States Period (403–221 BCE).

The *Dao De Jing* is a classic of world literature. Each time you come back to it, you will find something new and profound. However, the first time you read it you are likely to find it obscure. This is why I have included the translator's comments along with the translation.

You may find it obscure for a variety of reasons. First, it is written in a poetic and cryptic style. Poetry employs symbols and metaphors, uses paradoxes and unexpected contrasts in order to stimulate thought. It thrives on ambiguity. Second, this is a translation from ancient Chinese, and our English words often do not convey the richness of the Chinese concepts. Third, although 80 percent of the book deals with ethics (how one should live) and politics (what is the best way to govern), the rest deals with difficult metaphysical issues about the basic principles of reality, and it is these metaphysical portions of the text that are included here.

According to Aristotelian logic, a good definition should be positive and not negative. You should state what something is, not what it is not. Telling you that a pencil is "not a cat" does not help much if you do not know what a pencil is. However, what if there are realities that transcend the definitional abilities of human language? In such cases (and the *Dao* is such a case), the best we might hope for are negative indications, analogies, metaphors, and symbols.

Daoism has been characterized as a process ontology in contrast to a substance ontology. **Process ontologies** emphasize change and becoming as fundamentally real. In addition, they often emphasize the interrelatedness of an everflowing reality in which nothing is totally independent. **Substance ontologies** emphasize permanence and unchanging being as fundamentally real. Reality, a substantialist asserts, is made up of one or more substances that can exist independently.

Before you plunge into this bewildering, fascinating, and thought-provoking book about the *Dao,* it may be helpful to say something about some of the key concepts of Daoism. Let us begin with the word *Dao* itself.

The word *Dao* means "road" or "way" in Chinese. Before Laozi, the word had been used by the Confucians to refer to the way of humans, that is, the proper way that human beings ought to live. Laozi extends the term and gives it a cosmic and metaphysical meaning (at least according to some interpreters). It now becomes the way of the universe and the source of all reality. Reality consists of all the sorts of things we think exist (which we can classify as being) as well as what we take to be nonexistent (which we can classify as nonbeing). Already we encounter something odd from a traditional Western perspective. How can the nonexistent be real? Where we tend to identify the real with what exists (being) and the unreal with what does not (nonbeing), the Daoist distinguishes between reality and existence so that both the existent and nonexistent can be classified as real.

The *Dao,* because it is the source of all reality, is not a thing (a being or a substance). It is beyond distinctions and hence beyond the definitional powers of language. To define is to distinguish. However, how do you define that which is the source of all distinctions? So the *Dao* is called "the nameless," that is, the indefinable.

This negative designation suggests that the *Dao* is closer to nonbeing than to being, and indeed, Daoists say that the *Dao* is nonbeing. It is, however, not nonbeing in the Western sense of total nothingness. It is nonbeing in the sense of "no-thingness." It is real, but not a thing. Laozi compares it to a *positive emptiness,* that is, an emptiness (like the hollow of a bowl) that makes being (the usefulness of the bowl) possible. This notion of nonbeing as positive and creative is a unique insight of the *Dao De Jing.* For the Greeks, and much of the Western tradition since the Greeks, something cannot come from nothing. Nothing is absolute nothingness. It is a totally negative void. Laozi sees things differently. Something can come from nothing; indeed, this whole marvelous universe did come from the *no-thing* that is the way of all things.

De can be translated as "virtue," "power," or "excellence," so the title of Laozi's mind-expanding poem has been translated as "The Book of the Way and Its Power." It is a book *(jing)* about the excellence or power of the *Dao. De* is sometimes thought of as the *Dao* itself viewed from the perspective of individual things. The excellence (perfection, power) of each thing is called its *de,* and this is the *Dao* manifesting itself on the individual level. To actualize the potential of one's nature in an excellent way is to exhibit *de.* For humans (as for all natural things), this actualization occurs by living in accord with the *Dao.*

Wuwei literally means "no action" and refers to the manner in which the *Dao* acts. The way that is no-thing acts by not acting. Now there is a bit of philosophy on which to chew! Let me repeat it. The way that is no-thing acts by not acting. This rather mysterious claim can be elucidated somewhat by looking at the various levels of meaning of *wuwei.* Laozi provides advice to rulers in his book. He tells them to govern according to *wuwei.* In this political context, *wuwei* means that rulers should not interfere unnecessarily in the lives of the people. In other words, the less government, the better. On a moral level, *wuwei* means acting unselfishly and spontaneously, free of all selfish attachment to the consequences of our actions. And on the cosmic level, wuwei refers to the way nature acts—spontaneously, freely, and naturally. There is nothing artificial in natural events. Nature does not calculate how to act, it just acts.

Finally, we need to speak of the Daoist use of the *yin/yang* concept. The Daoists adopted this concept to characterize the universe that stems from the *Dao*. *Yin* and *yang* stand for complementary opposites: *yin* for all things that manifest a passive or receptive force; *yang* for all things that manifest an active or aggressive force. The passive and the active are complementary opposites; you cannot have one without the other.

There is a little bit of *yang* in *yin* and a little bit of *yin* in *yang*. In time, opposites will change into each other. Hence, the universe is essentially a vast, harmonious process. This can be illustrated by the seasonal cycle. Winter is the most *yin* season because it is cold and dark, and life processes are slow. However, winter contains an element of *yang*, which expands over time until we reach spring with its warmth, light, and flourishing life. *Yang* continues to expand and reaches its zenith in summer. Yet summer contains an element of *yin*, which expands into fall and eventually winter again. Such is the operation of *Dao* by means of *yin* and *yang*.

So the *Dao*, which is not a thing, acts naturally, freely, spontaneously, unselfishly, without force, thereby producing and sustaining a universe of harmonious processes in such a way that it is possible for each individual thing to manifest its own excellence. This is the way of nature, the way of genuine reality. I hope this profound vision of reality whets your appetite for more. Read on, and as you do, see if you can answer the following questions.

◉ READING QUESTIONS

1. What does it mean to say that the *Dao* (*Tao*) is nameless, and why do you think it is "named" that?
2. What is the main idea that Chapter 2 of the *Dao De Jing* conveys about the nature of opposites?
3. How is it possible for the sage (wise person) to act without acting and teach without speaking?
4. What do you think the comparison between the *Dao* and a bowl implies about the relationship between the substance of a thing and its function?
5. Analogies are drawn between the *Dao* and a valley, a female, the water, the hub of a wheel, a utensil, and a room. What do these analogies tell us about the *Dao*?
6. How does the *Dao* "run" the universe?
7. What does it mean to say that "reversion is the action of *Dao*"?

Dao De Jing

LAOZI

1

The Tao that can be told of is not the eternal Tao;
The name that can be named is not the eternal name.
The Nameless is the origin of Heaven and Earth;
The Named is the mother of all things.

Therefore let there always be non-being, so we may see their subtlety,
And let there always be being, so we may see their outcome.
The two are the same,
But after they are produced, they have different names.

They both may be called deep and profound.
Deeper and more profound,
The door of all subtleties!

COMMENT

This is the most important of all chapters, for in one stroke the basic characteristics of Tao as the eternal, the nameless, the source, and the substance of all things are explicitly or implicitly affirmed. It is no wonder the opening sentences are among the most often quoted or even chanted sayings in Chinese.

The key Taoist concepts of the named and the nameless are also introduced here. The concept of name is common to all ancient Chinese philosophical schools, but Taoism is unique in this respect. Most schools insist on the correspondence of names and actualities and accept names as necessary and good; Taoism, on the contrary, rejects names in favor of the nameless. This, among other things, shows its radical and unique character. To Lao Tzu, Tao is nameless and is the simplicity without names; when names arise, that is, when the simple oneness of Tao is split up into individual things with names, it is time to stop.

The cardinal ideas of being and non-being are also important here, for in Taoism the nameless (*wu-ming*) is equivalent to non-being and the named (*yu-ming*) is equivalent to being. For this reason, when he comments on the saying about the named and the nameless, Wang Pi says, "All being originated in non-being." As students of Chinese thought well know, the ideas of being and non-being have been dominant throughout the history of Chinese philosophy. They are central concepts in Neo-Taoism, Chinese Buddhism, and also Neo-Confucianism. It was the importance of these concepts, no doubt, that led the Neo-Confucianist Wang An-shih to deviate from tradition and punctuate the phrases "always be no desires" and "always be desires" to read "Let there always be non-being, so we may ...," and "Let there always be being, so we may ..."

Wang's punctuation not only underlines the importance of these ideas; it also shows the new metaphysical interest in Neo-Confucianism. Confucianism had been fundamentally ethical in tradition, but under the impact of Buddhist and Taoist metaphysics, the Neo-Confucianists developed

Confucianism along metaphysical lines. In this case, in substituting the ideas of being and non-being for the ideas of having desires and having no desires, Wang shows a greater recognition of the philosophical content of the *Lao Tzu*, as it deserves.

2

When the people of the world all know beauty as
*   beauty,*
There arises the recognition of ugliness.
When they all know the good as good,
There arises the recognition of evil.
Therefore:
*   Being and non-being produce each other;*
*   Difficult and easy complete each other;*
*   Long and short contrast each other;*
*   High and low distinguish each other;*
*   Sound and voice harmonize each other;*
*   Front and behind accompany each other.*

Therefore the sage manages affairs without
*   action*
And spreads doctrines without words.
All things arise, and he does not turn away
*   from them.*
He produces them but does not take possession
*   of them.*
He acts but does not rely on his own ability.
He accomplishes his task but does not claim
*   credit for it.*
It is precisely because he does not claim credit
*   that his*
accomplishment remains with him.

COMMENT

That everything has its opposite, and that these opposites are the mutual causations of each other, form a basic part of Chuang Tzu's philosophy and later Chinese philosophy. It is important to note that opposites are here presented not as irreconcilable conflicts but as complements. The traditional Chinese ideal that opposites are to be synthesized and harmonized can be said to have originated with Lao Tzu.

The idea of teaching without words anticipated the Buddhist tradition of silent transmission of the mystic doctrine, especially in the Zen (Ch'an) school. This is diametrically opposed to the Confucian ideal, according to which a superior man acts and thus "becomes the model of the world," and speaks and thus "becomes the pattern for the world." It is true that Confucianists say that a superior man "is truthful without any words," but they would never regard silence itself as a virtue....

4

> Tao is empty (like a bowl).
>> It may be used but its capacity is never exhausted.
> It is bottomless, perhaps the ancestor of all things.
> It blunts its sharpness, It unties its tangles.
> It softens its light.
> It becomes one with the dusty world.
> Deep and still, it appears to exist forever.
> I do not know whose son it is.
> It seems to have existed before the Lord.

COMMENT

This chapter, on the substance and function of Tao, shows clearly that in Taoism function is no less important than substance. Substance is further described in chapters 14 and 21, but here, as in chapters 11 and 45, function (*yung*, also meaning "use") is regarded with equal respect. There is no deprecation of phenomena, as is the case with certain Buddhist schools. To describe the world as dusty may suggest a lack of enthusiasm for it; indeed both Buddhism and later Taoism employ the word "dust" to symbolize the dirty world from which we should escape. It is significant to note, however, that Taoism in its true sense calls for identification with, not escape from, such a world....

6

> The spirit of the valley never dies.
>> It is called the subtle and profound female.
> The gate of the subtle and profound female
>> Is the root of Heaven and Earth.
> It is continuous, and seems to be always existing.
> Use it and you will never wear it out.

COMMENT

The valley and the female, like the infant and water, are Lao Tzu's favorite symbols for Tao. The symbol of the valley is employed again and again. There is nothing mysterious about it or its spirit; it simply stands for vacuity, vastness, openness, all-inclusiveness, and lowliness or humility, all of which are outstanding characteristics of Tao. This is the interpretation of Wang Pi, and commentators, with only a few exceptions, have followed him. To understand the "continuous" operation as breathing, or the valley as the belly or the Void, and then to interpret the whole passage as one on the yoga technique of breathing, or to single out the characteristic of stillness of the valley and then to present it as an evidence of Taoist quietism, is to fail to interpret the passages in the context of the whole. These interpretations are not supported by the symbolic meaning of the valley elsewhere in the book.

The spirit of the chapter is far from quietism. Instead, it involves the idea of natural transformation and continuous creation. As Chu Hsi has said, "The valley is vacuous. As sound reaches it, it echoes. This is the spontaneity of spiritual transformation. To be subtle and profound means to be wonderful. The female is one who receives something and produces things. This is a most wonderful principle and it has the meaning of production and reproduction."...

8

> The best (man)[1] is like water.
>> Water is good; it benefits all things and does not compete with them.
> It dwells in (lowly) places that all disdain.
> This is why it is so near to Tao

---

[1]Most commentators and translators have understood the Chinese phrase literally as the highest good, but some commentators and translators, including Lin Yutang, Cheng Lin, and Bynner, have followed Wang Pi and taken the phrase to mean the best man. Both interpretations are possible. The former interpretation has a parallel in chapter 38, which talks about the highest virtue, while the latter has a parallel in chapter 17, where both Wang Pi and Ho-shang Kung interpret "the best" to mean the best ruler. I have followed Wang Pi, not only because his commentary on the text is the oldest and most reliable, but also because the *Lao Tzu* deals with man's way of life more than abstract ideas.

(The best man) in his dwelling loves the earth.
In his heart, he loves what is profound.
In his associations, he loves humanity.
In his words, he loves faithfulness.
In government, he loves order.
In handling affairs, he loves competence.
In his activities, he loves timeliness.
It is because he does not compete that he is
*   without reproach.*

COMMENT

Water is perhaps the most outstanding among Lao Tzu's symbols for Tao. The emphasis of the symbolism is ethical rather than metaphysical or religious. It is interesting to note that, while early Indian philosophers associated water with creation and the Greek philosophers looked upon it as a natural phenomenon, ancient Chinese philosophers, whether Lao Tzu or Confucius, preferred to learn moral lessons from it. Broadly speaking, Western thought, derived chiefly from the Greeks, has been largely interested in metaphysical and scientific problems, Indian thought largely interested in religious problems, and Chinese thought largely interested in moral problems. It is not too much to say that these different approaches to water characterize the Western, the Indian, and the Chinese systems of thought....

11

Thirty spokes are united around the hub to
*   make a wheel,*
*   But it is on its non-being that the utility of*
*   the carriage depends.*
Clay is molded to form a utensil,
*   But it is on its non-being that the utility of*
*   the utensil depends.*
Doors and windows are cut out to make a room,
*   But it is on its non-being that the utility of*
*   the room depends.*
Therefore turn being into advantage, and turn
non-being into utility.

COMMENT

Nowhere else in Chinese philosophy is the concept of non-being more strongly emphasized. This chapter alone should dispel any idea that Taoism

is negativistic, for non-being—the hole in the hub, the hollowness of a utensil, the empty space in the room—is here conceived not as nothingness but as something useful and advantageous.

The Taoist interest in non-being has counteracted the positivistic tendency in certain Chinese philosophical schools, especially the Legalist and Confucian, which often overlook what seems to be nonexistent. It has prepared the Chinese mind for the acceptance of the Buddhist doctrine of Emptiness, although neither the Taoist concept of non-being nor that of vacuity is identical with that of the Buddhist Void. In addition, it was because of the Taoist insistence on the positive value of non-being that empty space has been utilized as a constructive factor in Chinese landscape painting. In this greatest art of China, space is used to combine the various elements into an organic whole and to provide a setting in which the onlooker's imagination may work. By the same token, much is left unsaid in Chinese poetry, for the reader must play a creative role to bring the poetic idea into full realization. The Zen Buddhists have developed to the fullest the themes that real existence is found in the nonexistent and that true words are spoken in silence, but the origin of these themes must be traced to early Taoism....

14

We look at it and do not see it;
*   Its name is The Invisible.*
We listen to it and do not hear it;
*   Its name is The Inaudible.*
We touch it and do not find it;
*   Its name is The Subtle (formless).*

These three cannot be further inquired into,
And hence merge into one.
Going up high, it is not bright, and coming
*   down low, it is not dark.*
Infinite and boundless, it cannot be given any
*   name;*
It reverts to nothingness.
This is called shape without shape
Form without objects.
It is The Vague and Elusive.
Meet it and you will not see its head.
Follow it and you will not see its back.

Hold on to the Tao of old in order to master the things of the present.
From this one may know the primeval beginning (of the universe).
This is called the bond[2] of Tao.

COMMENT

Subtlety is an important characteristic of Tao and is more important than its manifestations. The Confucianists, on the other hand, emphasize manifestation. There is nothing more manifest than the hidden (subtle), they say, and "a man who knows that the subtle will be manifested can enter into virtue." The Buddhists and Neo-Confucianists eventually achieved a synthesis, saying that "there is no distinction between the manifest and the hidden."

To describe reality in terms of the invisible, the inaudible, and the subtle is an attempt to describe it in terms of non-being. Because the three Chinese words are pronounced *i, hsi,* and *wei,* respectively, they have been likened to *Jod, Heh, Vav,* indicating the name Jehovah, and to the Hindu god Ishvara, but any similarity is purely accidental. The threefold description does not suggest any idea of trinity either. Basically, Taoist philosophy is naturalistic, if not atheistic, and any idea of a god is alien to it....

16

Attain complete vacuity.
Maintain steadfast quietude.

All things come into being,
And I see thereby their return.
All things flourish,
But each one returns to its root.
This return to its root means tranquillity.
It is called returning to its destiny.
To return to destiny is called the eternal (Tao).
To know the eternal is called enlightenment.
Not to know the eternal is to act blindly to result in disaster.

He who knows the eternal is all-embracing.
Being all-embracing, he is impartial.
Being impartial, he is kingly (universal).
Being kingly, he is one with Nature.
Being one with Nature, he is in accord with Tao.
Being in accord with Tao, he is everlasting
And is free from danger throughout his lifetime.

COMMENT

The central idea here is returning to the root, which is to be achieved through tranquillity. Generally speaking, in Taoist philosophy Tao is revealed most fully through tranquillity rather than activity. Under its influence, Wang Pi has commented on the hexagram *fu* (to return) in the *Book of Changes* in the same light. He says, "Although Heaven and Earth are vast, possessing the myriad things in abundance, where thunder moves and winds circulate, and while there is an infinite variety of changes and transformations, yet its original [substance] is absolutely quiet and perfect non-being. Therefore only with the cessation of activities within Earth can the mind of Heaven and Earth be revealed."

This Taoistic position is directly opposed by the Neo-Confucianists, who insist that the mind of Heaven and Earth is to be seen in a state of activity. As Ch'eng I says, "Former scholars all said that only in a state of tranquillity can the mind of Heaven and Earth be seen. They did not realize that the mind of Heaven and Earth is found in the beginning of activity."...

22

To yield is to be preserved whole.
To be bent is to become straight.
To be empty is to be full.
To be worn out is to be renewed.
To have little is to possess.
To have plenty is to be perplexed.
Therefore the sage embraces the One
And becomes the model of the world.
He does not show himself; therefore he is luminous.
He does not justify himself; therefore he becomes prominent.
He does not boast of himself; therefore he is given credit.

---

[2]Chi, literally, "a thread," denotes tradition, discipline, principle, order, essence, etc. Generally, it means the system, principle, or continuity that binds things together.

*He does not brag; therefore he can endure for
long.*

*It is precisely because he does not compete that
the world cannot compete with him.*
*Is the ancient saying, "To yield is to be preserved
whole," empty words?*
*Truly he will be preserved and (prominence
and credit) will come to him.*

COMMENT

Taoism seems to be advocating a negative morality. In this respect, it is not much different from
the Christian doctrine taught in the Sermon on
the Mount, which extols meekness, poverty, and
so forth. Whatever negativism there may seem to
be, it pertains to method only; the objective is
entirely positive....

25

*There was something undifferentiated and yet
complete,*
Which existed before heaven and earth.
*Soundless and formless, it depends on nothing
and does not change.*
It operates everywhere and is free from danger.
It may be considered the mother of the universe.
I do not know its name; I call it Tao.
If forced to give it a name, I shall call it Great.
Now being great means functioning everywhere.
Functioning everywhere means far-reaching.
*Being far-reaching means returning to the
original point.*

Therefore Tao is great. Heaven is great.
Earth is great.
And the king[3] is also great.
*There are four great things in the universe, and
the king is one of them.*
Man models himself after Earth.

Earth models itself after Heaven.
Heaven models itself after Tao.
And Tao models itself after Nature.

COMMENT

Taoist cosmology is outlined here simply but
clearly. In the beginning there is something undifferentiated, which is forever operating; it produces
heaven and earth and then all things. In essence this
cosmology is strikingly similar to that of the *Book of
Changes.* In the system of Change, the Great Ultimate produces the Two Modes (yin and yang),
which in turn produce all things. We don't know
to what extent Taoist thought has influenced the
Book of Changes, which the Confucianists have
attributed to their ancient sages, chiefly Confucius.
At any rate, this naturalistic philosophy has always
been prominent in Chinese thought, and later contributed substantially to the naturalistic pattern of
Neo-Confucian cosmology, especially through
Chou Tun-i. As will be noted, he has added the
concept of the Non-ultimate to the philosophy of
the *Book of Changes* in order better to explain the
originally undifferentiated. It is to be noted that the
term "Non-ultimate" comes from the *Lao Tzu....*

34

The Great Tao flows everywhere.
It may go left or right.
*All things depend on it for life, and it does not
turn away from them.*
*It accomplishes its task, but does not claim
credit for it.*
*It clothes and feeds all things but does not claim
to be master over them.*
*Always without desires, it may be called The
Small.*
*All things come to it and it does not master
them; it may be called The Great.*
*Therefore (the sage) never strives himself for the
great, and thereby the great is achieved.*

COMMENT

In commenting on this chapter, Yen Fu says that
the left and the right, the small and the great,
are relative terms, and that Tao in its original
substance transcends all these relative qualities.

---

[3]The Fu I and Fan Ying-yüan texts have "man" in place of
"king." This substitution has been accepted by Hsi T'ung, Ma
Hsü-lun, Ch'en Chu, Jen Chi-yü, and Ch'u Ta-kao. They
have been influenced, undoubtedly, by the concept of the trinity of Heaven, Earth, and man, without realizing that the king
is considered here as representative of men. Moreover, in
chapters 16 and 39, Heaven, Earth, and the king are spoken of
together.

Of greater significance, however, is the paradoxical character of Tao. This character is affirmed more than once in the *Lao Tzu*. In Neo-Confucianism, principle is both immanent and transcendent, as is the Christian God. Ultimate being or reality is by nature paradoxical....

37

> *Tao invariably takes no action, and yet there is nothing left undone.*
> *If kings and barons can keep it, all things will transform spontaneously.*
> *If, after transformation, they should desire to be active,*
> *I would restrain them with simplicity, which has no name.*
> *Simplicity, which has no name, is free of desires.*
> *Being free of desires, it is tranquil.*
> *And the world will be at peace of its own accord.*

COMMENT

"Transform spontaneously" seems to be a passing remark here, but the idea became a key concept in the *Chuang Tzu* and later formed a key tenet in the Neo-Taoism of Kuo Hsiang. In the *Lao Tzu*, things transform themselves because Tao takes no action or leaves things alone. Chuang Tzu goes a step further, saying that everything is in incessant change and that is self-transformation. In his commentary on the *Chuang Tzu*, Kuo Hsiang goes even further, stressing that things transform themselves spontaneously because they are self-sufficient, and there is no Nature behind or outside of them. Nature, he says, is but a general name for things....

40

> *Reversion is the action of Tao.*
> *Weakness is the function of Tao.*
> *All things in the world come from being.*
> *And being comes from non-being.*[4]

---

[4]Cf. chapter 1. This seems to contradict the saying, "Being and non-being produce each other," in chapter 3, but to produce means not to originate but to bring about.

COMMENT

The doctrine of returning to the original is a prominent one in the *Lao Tzu*.[5] It has contributed in no small degree to the common Chinese cyclical concept, according to which the Chinese believe that both history and reality operate in cycles....

42

> *Tao produced the One.*
> *The One produced the two.*
> *The two produced the three.*
> *And the three produced the ten thousand things.*
> *The ten thousand things carry the yin and embrace the yang, and through the blending of the material force they achieve harmony.*
> *People hate to be children without parents, lonely people without spouses, or men without food to eat,*
> *And yet kings and lords call themselves by these names.*
> *Therefore it is often the case that things gain by losing and lose by gaining.*
> *What others have taught, I teach also:*
> *"Violent and fierce people do not die a natural death"*
> *I shall make this the father of my teaching.*

COMMENT

It is often understood that the One is the original material force of the Great Ultimate, the two are yin and yang, the three are their blending with the

---

[5]The doctrine is also encountered in one sense or another in chapters 14, 16, 25, 28, 30, and 52. To D. C. Lau, returning to the root is not a cyclical process. According to him, the main doctrine of the *Lao Tzu* is the preservation of life, which is to be achieved through "abiding by softness." Softness is real strength, because when strength is allowed to reach its limit, it falls, whereas softness preserves itself. Thus opposites are neither relative nor paradoxical, and their process is not circular but a gradual development to the limit and then an inevitable and sudden decline. This idea may be implied in the *Lao Tzu*, but there is no explicit passage to support Lau's theory. See his "The Treatment of Opposites in Lao Tzu," *Bulletin of the School of Oriental and African Studies*, XXI (1958), 349–50, 352–7.

original material force, and the ten thousand things are things carrying yin and embracing yang. The similarity of this process to that of the *Book of Changes,* in which the Great Ultimate produces the Two Forces (yin and yang) and then the myriad things, is amazing. The important point, however, is not the specific similarities, but the evolution from the simple to the complex. This theory is common to nearly all Chinese philosophical schools.

It should be noted that the evolution here, as in the *Book of Changes,* is natural. Production (*sheng*) is not personal creation or purposeful origination, but natural causation.

◉ CRITICAL QUESTIONS

1. If the *Dao* is invisible, inaudible, and formless, how can it be known? Do you think this makes sense? Why, or why not?
2. Is Daoist metaphysics a materialism, idealism, dualism, monism, or something that these categories fail to express adequately? Provide evidence to support your answer.

10.3 PLATONIC DUALISM

We have encountered Plato and Socrates before (see Chapter 3). Plato (428–347 BCE) was Socrates' star pupil and one of the most creative and influential minds in the whole history of Western philosophy. He lived in Athens, founded the first "university" (called the Academy) in the West, and wrote a number of dialogues in which Socrates frequently appeared.

Alfred North Whitehead, a twentieth-century British-American philosopher, remarked that "all Western philosophy is but a footnote to Plato." This might be overstating the case for Plato's importance, but there can be little doubt that his ideas have influenced and still influence the thoughts and values of people who do not even know his name.

Do you believe in the immortality of the soul? Do you think that there is a material reality and an immaterial or spiritual reality and that the latter is more important than the former? Do you think logical and mathematical methods of reasoning are ideal models for arriving at truth? Do you believe that things have an essential nature? Do you believe you ought to control your passions by the use of reason? Do you think politicians ought to have the good of the people in mind? Do you think virtue is its own reward? If you answered some of these questions in the affirmative, you are reflecting ideas that Plato articulated almost twenty-four centuries ago.

Plato wrote on almost every aspect of philosophy. Here we are concerned primarily with his metaphysical ideas. Plato's metaphysics has been classified as dualistic because he argued that reality could be divided into two radically different parts. There is the reality of matter characterized by change (becoming) and the reality of what he called the **Forms**, or Ideas characterized by permanence (being). Being is immaterial and of greater value than the material.

Along with this general ontological dualism between being and becoming, Plato taught a soul–body dualism. Human beings are composed of bodies and souls. One power that our souls have is the power of thought (the mind), and this is by far our most valuable thing. Our minds and souls are immaterial in contrast to our material bodies.

Plato's metaphysics is also classified as an idealism because it centers on the **theory of Forms** (Ideas) and because, although the reality of matter is not denied, matter is regarded as less real than the immaterial Forms. What is the theory of Forms? The English word *form* is often used to translate the Greek word for idea or concept. So, in the first instance, a form is the mental concept or idea we have of something. For example, how do you recognize a table as a table when you see one? After all, each table is different. How are you able to classify a whole group of different-looking objects into the class "table"? Well, you can do this, we might say, because you have the concept or idea of a table. If someone asked you what a table is, you could give a definition. This definition would constitute the expression of your concept.

Your definition (if it were the "correct" definition in Socrates's sense) would also express the essential nature of table. That is, it would not tell us what this or that particular table is, but it would tell us what *all* tables are insofar as they are tables. So, in the second place, a form is an essence.

Now most of us think that the concepts of things exist only in human minds and the essences of things (if there are such) either exist in our minds or somehow exist in the things themselves. If we might use the word *tableness* to designate the Form of tables, then most of us would be inclined to say that if there were no tables, there would be no tableness. Not so Plato. Or at least, not so Plato as interpreted by his star pupil, Aristotle. For Plato, according to Aristotle, essences (Forms) exist objectively apart from the minds that think them and the objects that instantiate them. They constitute ideals, perfect models if you will, that are even more real than the material things that reflect them.

Think of a square. Any particular material square you can draw will be imperfect. Its angles and lines will not be exact. But the square as such (squareness or the pure abstract geometric shape that we can define with mathematical precision) is another matter. It is perfect, and its definition will never change. Is not that which is perfect and permanent more real than that which is imperfect and ever-changing? Plato answers yes.

The selection that follows is from Plato's most famous dialogue, *The Republic*. This is one of the masterpieces of Western literature, and someday you should read all of it. It is filled with stories, myths, striking analogies, and political ideas that are still debated. For now, we will have to be content with just a little bit. However, to appreciate this little bit, some idea of what the whole is about will help.

Socrates, along with others, has been invited to the home of Cephalus. The question "What is justice?" arises and after examining and finding fault with several definitions, Thrasymachus (pronounced Thra-*sim*-a-kus) argued that justice is whatever is in the interest of the stronger party. Socrates disagreed and argued that power and knowledge must be combined because the art of government, like other arts, requires skill and knowledge. In particular, it requires knowledge of what is good for people because government ought to serve the needs of those who are governed, not merely the interests of the strongest.

In Book 2, Glaucon and Adeimantus pressed Socrates to prove that the just life is worth living. Socrates argued that virtue is its own reward and began an analysis of political justice. The ideal state needs philosopher-kings (wisdom-loving rulers), guardians (soldiers and police), and producers (artisans, tradesmen, farmers). When each class does its proper business without interfering with the others, political justice is achieved. By analogy with the state, Socrates argued that the just person is one in whom the three basic elements of human nature—the rational, the spirited, and the appetitive—are properly ordered. Proper order consists of the rule of rationality or reason over the spirited and appetitive parts of the soul.

Books 3–5 describe in some detail Socrates's vision of the ideal state. In the ideal republic, the classes are carefully controlled by breeding, education, and selection. Just as reason should rule in the individual if personal justice is to be realized, so the "lovers of wisdom" (philosophers) should rule the state. This means that the rulers (philosopher-kings) need to know what is good and so must be properly educated. These ideas lead to a discussion of what the good is and what the proper education of the guardians should be. This discussion takes place in Books 6 and 7, from which the following selection comes.

Socrates admitted that the good itself is the proper object of the philosopher's quest, but he could not say directly what the good is. He offered three analogies. The first compares the good to the Sun. The second, called the simile of the divided line, compares *opinion* (which derives from sensations of material objects) with *knowledge* (which derives from knowing the Forms via reason and understanding). The third, called the allegory of the cave, compares the philosopher to a prisoner who has escaped from a cave and seen the light of the real world.

The last three books of *The Republic* deal with political change, the decline of the state, and various forms of government. *The Republic* closes with an argument for the immortality of the soul. By loving justice (i.e., by harmonizing reason, spirit, and appetite under the rule of rationality), we can keep our souls healthy and thereby prosper forever.

You should read what follows slowly and carefully, pausing to think about what Socrates is saying. Socrates is the main speaker. In this translation, the words of the speaker who responds to Socrates are sometimes indicated only by a dash (—). The following questions should help you catch the main ideas.

⊚ READING QUESTIONS

1. What is the difference between the *many things* and the *Forms?*
2. In what ways are the Sun and the Good alike?
3. Give examples of what Socrates means by *images* and by *objects of sense.*
4. What is the difference between *reasoning* and *understanding?*
5. What do you think the allegory of the cave means?
6. What is the relationship between the image of the divided line and the story about the cave?
7. What conclusion about education does Socrates draw from the allegory of the cave?

The Republic

PLATO

...But you also, Socrates, must tell us whether you consider the good to be knowledge, or pleasure, or something else.

What a man! I said. It has been clear for some time that the opinion of others on this subject would not satisfy you.

From *Plato's Republic,* translated by G. M. A. Grube, Hackett Publishing Co., Inc. Copyright © 1974, pp. 161–172. Reprinted with permission of Hackett Publishing Company, Inc. All rights reserved. Translator's footnotes have been retained but renumbered.

Well, Socrates, he said, it does not seem right to me to be able to tell the opinions of others and not one's own, especially for a man who has spent so much time as you have occupying himself with this subject.

Why? said I. Do you think it right to talk about things one does not know as if one knew them? Not as if one knew them, he said, but for a man who has an opinion to say what that opinion is.

And have you not noticed that opinions not based on knowledge are ugly things? The best of them are blind; or do you think that those who express a true opinion without knowledge are any different from blind people who yet follow the right road?—They are no different.

Do you want to contemplate ugly, blind, and crooked things when you can hear bright and beautiful things from others?

By Zeus, Socrates, said Glaucon, do not stand off as if you had come to the end. We shall be satisfied if you discuss the Good in the same fashion as you did justice, moderation, and the other things.

That, my friend, I said, would also quite satisfy me, but I fear I shall not be able to do so, and that in my eagerness I shall disgrace myself and make myself ridiculous. But, my excellent friends, let us for the moment abandon the quest for the nature of the Good itself, for that I think is a larger question than what we started on, which was to ascertain my present opinion about it. I am willing to tell you what appears to be the offspring of the Good and most like it, if that is agreeable to you. If not, we must let the question drop.

Well, he said, tell us. The story of the parent remains a debt which you will pay us some other time.

I wish, I said, that I could pay it in full now, and you could exact it in full and not, as now, only receive the interest.[1] However, accept then this offspring and child of the Good. Only be careful that I do not somehow deceive you unwillingly by giving

a counterfeit account of this offspring.—We shall be as careful as we can. Only tell us.

I will, I said, after coming to an agreement with you and reminding you of the things we said before, and also many times elsewhere.—What are these things?

We speak of many beautiful things and many good things, and we say that they are so and so define them in speech.—We do.

And Beauty itself and Goodness itself, and so with all the things which we then classed as many; we now class them again according to one Form of each, which is one and which we in each case call that which is.—That is so.

And we say that the many things are the objects of sight but not of thought, while the Forms are the objects of thought but not of sight.—Altogether true.

With what part of ourselves do we see the objects that are seen?—With our sight.

And so things heard are heard by our hearing, and all that is perceived is perceived by our other senses?—Quite so.

Have you considered how very lavishly the maker of our senses made the faculty of seeing and being seen?—I cannot say I have.

Look at it this way: do hearing and sound need another kind of thing for the former to hear and the latter to be heard, and in the absence of this third element the one will not hear and the other not be heard.—No, they need nothing else.

Neither do many other senses, if indeed any, need any such other thing, or can you mention one?—Not I.

But do you not realize that the sense of sight and that which is seen do have such a need?—How so?

Sight may be in the eyes, and the man who has it may try to use it, and colours may be present in the objects, but unless a third kind of thing is present, which is by nature designed for this very purpose, you know that sight will see nothing and the colours remain unseen.—What is this third kind of thing?

What you call light, I said.—Right.

So to no small extent the sense of sight and the power of being seen are yoked together by a

---

[1] Plato is punning on the Greek word tokos, which means a child, and in the plural was used also of the interest on capital, a pleasant and common metaphor.

more honourable yoke than other things which are yoked together, unless light is held in no honour.—That is far from being the case.

Which of the gods in the heavens can you hold responsible for this, whose light causes our sight to see as beautifully as possible, and the objects of sight to be seen?—The same as you would, he said, and as others would; obviously the answer to your question is the sun.

And is not sight naturally related to the sun in this way?—Which way?

Sight is not the sun, neither itself nor that in which it occurs which we call the eye.—No indeed.

But I think it is the most sun-like of the organs of sense.—Very much so.

And it receives from the sun the capacity to see as a kind of outflow.—Quite so.

The sun is not sight, but is it not the cause of it, and is also seen by it?—Yes.

Say then, I said, that it is the sun which I called the offspring of the Good, which the Good begot as analogous to itself. What the Good itself is in the world of thought in relation to the intelligence and things known, the sun is in the visible world, in relation to sight and things seen.—How? Explain further.

You know, I said, that when one turns one's eyes to those objects of which the colours are no longer in the light of day but in the dimness of the night, the eyes are dimmed and seem nearly blind, as if clear vision was no longer in them.— Quite so.

Yet whenever one's eyes are turned upon objects brightened by sunshine, they see clearly, and clear vision appears in those very same eyes?—Yes indeed.

So too understand the eye of the soul: whenever it is fixed upon that upon which truth and reality shine, it understands and knows and seems to have intelligence, but whenever it is fixed upon what is mixed with darkness—that which is subject to birth and destruction—it opines and is dimmed, changes its opinions this way and that, and seems to have no intelligence.—That is so.

Say that what gives truth to the objects of knowledge, and to the knowing mind the power to know, is the Form of Good. As it is the cause of knowledge and truth, think of it also as being the object of knowledge. Both knowledge and truth are beautiful, but you will be right to think of the Good as other and more beautiful than they. As in the visible world light and sight are rightly considered sun-like, but it is wrong to think of them as the sun, so here it is right to think of knowledge and truth as Good-like, but wrong to think of either as the Good, for the Good must be honoured even more than they.

This is an extraordinary beauty you mention, he said, if it provides knowledge and truth and is itself superior to them in beauty. You surely do not mean this to be pleasure!

Hush! said I, rather examine the image of it in this way.—How?

You will say, I think, that the sun not only gives to the objects of sight the capacity to be seen, but also that it provides for their generation, increase, and nurture, though it is not itself the process of generation.—How could it be?

And say that as for the objects of knowledge, not only is their being known due to the Good, but also their reality being, though the Good is not being but superior to and beyond being in dignity and power.

Glaucon was quite amused and said: By Apollo, a miraculous superiority!

It is your own fault, I said, you forced me to say what I thought about it.

Don't you stop, he said, except for a moment, but continue to explain the similarity to the sun in case you are leaving something out.

I am certainly leaving out a good deal, I said.—Don't omit the smallest point.

Much is omitted, I said. However, as far as the explanation can go at present, I will not omit anything.—Don't you!

Understand then, I said, that, as we say, there are those two, one reigning over the intelligible kind and realm, the other over the visible (not to say heaven, that I may not appear to play the sophist about the name[2]). So you have two kinds, the visible and the intelligible.—Right.

---

[2]He means play on the similarity of sound between *ouranos*, the sky, and *horaton*, visible.

It is like a line divided[3] into two unequal parts, and then divide each section in the same ratio, that is, the section of the visible and that of the intelligible. You will then have sections related to each other in proportion to their clarity and obscurity. The first section of the visible consists of images—and by images I mean shadows in the first instance, then the reflections in water and all those on close-packed, smooth, and bright materials, and all that sort of thing, if you understand me.—I understand.

In the other section of the visible, place the models of the images, the living creatures around us, all plants, and the whole class of manufactured things.—I so place them.

Would you be willing to say that, as regards truth and untruth, the division is made in this proportion: as the opinable is to the knowable so the image is to the model it is made like?—Certainly.

Consider now how the section of the intelligible is to be divided.—How?

In such a way that in one section the soul, using as images what before were models, is compelled to investigate from hypotheses, proceeding from these not to a first principle but to a conclusion. In the second section which leads to a first

principle that is not hypothetical, the soul proceeds from a hypothesis without using the images of the first section, by means of the Forms themselves and proceeding through these.—I do not, he said, quite understand what you mean.

Let us try again, I said, for you will understand more easily because of what has been said. I think you know that students of geometry, calculation, and the like assume the existence of the odd and the even, of figures, of three kinds of angles, and of kindred things in each of their studies, as if they were known to them. These they make their hypotheses and do not deem it necessary to give any account of them either to themselves or to others as if they were clear to all; these are their starting points, and going through the remaining steps they reach an agreed conclusion on what they started out to investigate.—Quite so, I understand that.

You know also that they use visible figures and talk about them, but they are not thinking about them but about the models of which these are likenesses; they are making their points about the square itself, the diameter itself, not about the diameter which they draw, and similarly with the others. These figures which they fashion and draw, of which shadows and reflections in the water are images, they now in turn use as images, in seeking to understand those others in themselves, which one cannot see except in thought.—That is true.

This is what I called the intelligible class, and said that the soul is forced to use hypotheses in its search for it, not travelling up to a first principle, since it cannot reach beyond its hypotheses, but it uses as images those very things which at a lower level were models and which, in comparison with their images, were thought to be clear and honoured as such.—I understand, he said, that you mean what happens in geometry and kindred sciences.

Understand also that by the other section of the intelligible I mean that which reason itself grasps by the power of dialectic. It does not consider its hypotheses as first principles, but as hypotheses in the true sense of stepping stones and starting points, in order to reach that which is beyond hypothesis, the first principle of all that

---

[3]It is clear that Plato visualizes a vertical line ... with B as the highest point in the scale of reality and A as the lowest form of existence. The main division is at C. AC is the visible, CB being the intelligible world, AD is the world of images (and perhaps, though Plato does not say so, works of art), mathematical realities are contained in CE, the Platonic Forms in EB, with the Good presumably at B.

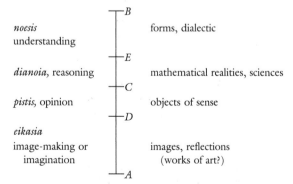

noesis understanding	—B	forms, dialectic
dianoia, reasoning	—E	mathematical realities, sciences
pistis, opinion	—C	objects of sense
eikasia image-making or imagination	—D	images, reflections (works of art?)
	—A	

The names of the four mental processes—*noesis, dianoia, pistis,* and *eikasia*—are more or less arbitrary, and Plato does not use them regularly in these precise senses in the rest of the *Republic*.

exists. Having reached this and keeping hold of what follows from it, it does come down to a conclusion without making use of anything visible at all, but proceeding by means of Forms and through Forms to its conclusions which are Forms.

I understand, he said, but not completely, for you seem to be speaking of a mighty task—that you wish to distinguish the intelligible reality contemplated by the science of dialectic as clearer than that viewed by the so-called sciences, for which their hypotheses are first principles. The students of these so-called sciences are, it is true, compelled to study them by thought and not by sense perception, yet because they do not go back to a first principle but proceed from hypotheses, you do not think that they have any clear understanding of their subjects, although these can be so understood if approached from a first principle. You seem to me to call the attitude of mind of geometers and such reasoning but not understanding, reasoning being midway between opinion and understanding.

You have grasped this very satisfactorily, I said. There are four such processes in the soul, corresponding to the four sections of our line: understanding for the highest, reasoning for the second; give the name of opinion to the third, and imagination to the last. Place these in the due terms of a proportion and consider that each has as much clarity as the content of its particular section shares in truth.—I understand, and I agree and arrange them as you say.

BOOK VII

Next, I said, compare the effect of education and the lack of it upon our human nature to a situation like this: imagine men to be living in an underground cave-like dwelling place, which has a way up to the light along its whole width, but the entrance is a long way up. The men have been there from childhood, with their neck and legs in fetters, so that they remain in the same place and can only see ahead of them, as their bonds prevent them turning their heads. Light is provided by a fire burning some way behind and above them. Between the fire and the prisoners, some way behind them and on a higher ground, there is a

path across the cave and along this a low wall has been built, like the screen at a puppet show in front of the performers who show their puppets above it.—I see it.

See then also men carrying along that wall, so that they overtop it, all kinds of artifacts, statues of men, reproductions of other animals in stone or wood fashioned in all sorts of ways, and, as is likely, some of the carriers are talking while others are silent.—This is a strange picture, and strange prisoners.

They are like us, I said. Do you think, in the first place, that such men could see anything of themselves and each other[4] except the shadows which the fire casts upon the wall of the cave in front of them?—How could they, if they have to keep their heads still throughout life?

And is not the same true of the objects carried along the wall?—Quite.

If they could converse with one another, do you not think that they would consider these shadows to be the real things?—Necessarily.

What if their prison had an echo which reached them from in front of them? Whenever one of the carriers passing behind the wall spoke, would they not think that it was the shadow passing in front of them which was talking? Do you agree?—By Zeus I do.

Altogether then, I said, such men would believe the truth to be nothing else than the shadows of the artifacts?—They must believe that.

Consider then what deliverance from their bonds and the curing of their ignorance would be if something like this naturally happened to them. Whenever one of them was freed, had to stand up suddenly, turn his head, walk, and look up toward the light, doing all that would give him pain, the flash of the fire would make it impossible for him to see the objects of which he had earlier seen the shadows. What do you think he would say if he was told that what he saw then was foolishness,

---

[4]These shadows of themselves and each other are never mentioned again. A Platonic myth or parable, like a Homeric simile, is often elaborated in considerable detail. These contribute to the vividness of the picture but often have no other function, and it is a mistake to look for any symbolic meaning in them. It is the general picture that matters.

that he was now somewhat closer to reality and turned to things that existed more fully, that he saw more correctly? If one then pointed to each of the objects passing by, asked him what each was, and forced him to answer, do you not think he would be at a loss and believe that the things which he saw earlier were truer than the things now pointed out to him?—Much truer.

If one then compelled him to look at the fire itself, his eyes would hurt, he would turn round and flee toward those things which he could see, and think that they were in fact clearer than those now shown to him.—Quite so.

And if one were to drag him thence by force up the rough and steep path and did not let him go before he was dragged into the sunlight, would he not be in physical pain and angry as he was dragged along? When he came into the light, with the sunlight filling his eyes, he would not be able to see a single one of the things which are now said to be true.—Not at once, certainly.

I think he would need time to get adjusted before he could see things in the world above; at first he would see shadows most easily, then reflections of men and other things in water, then the things themselves. After this he would see objects in the sky and the sky itself more easily at night, the light of the stars and the moon more easily than the sun and the light of the sun during the day.—Of course.

Then, at last, he would be able to see the sun, not images of it in water or in some alien place, but the sun itself in its own place, and be able to contemplate it.—That must be so.

After this he would reflect that it is the sun which provides the seasons and the years, which governs everything in the visible world, and is also in some way the cause of those other things which he used to see.—Clearly that would be the next stage.

What then? As he reminds himself of his first dwelling place, of the wisdom there and of his fellow prisoners, would he not reckon himself happy for the change, and pity them?—Surely.

And if the men below had praise and honours from each other, and prizes for the man who saw most clearly the shadows that passed before them, and who could best remember which usually came earlier and which later, and which came together and thus could most ably prophesy the future, do you think our man would desire those rewards and envy those who were honoured and held power among the prisoners, or would he feel, as Homer put it, that he certainly wished to be "serf to another man without possessions upon the earth"[5] and go through any suffering, rather than share their opinions and live as they do?— Quite so, he said, I think he would rather suffer anything.

Reflect on this too, I said. If this man went down into the cave again and sat down in the same seat, would his eyes not be filled with darkness, coming suddenly out of the sunlight?—They certainly would.

And if he had to contend again with those who had remained prisoners in recognizing those shadows while his sight was affected and his eyes had not settled down—and the time for this adjustment would not be short—would he not be ridiculed? Would it not be said that he had returned from his upward journey with his eyesight spoiled, and that it was not worthwhile even to attempt to travel upward? As for the man who tried to free them and lead them upward, if they could somehow lay their hands on him and kill him, they would do so.—They certainly would.

This whole image, my dear Glaucon, I said, must be related to what we said before. The realm of the visible should be compared to the prison dwelling, and the fire inside it to the power of the sun. If you interpret the upward journey and the contemplation of things above as the upward journey of the soul to the intelligible realm, you will grasp what I surmise since you were keen to hear it. Whether it is true or not only the god knows, but this is how I see it, namely that in the intelligible world the Form of the Good is the last to be seen, and with difficulty; when seen it must be reckoned to be for all the cause of all that is right and beautiful, to have produced in the visible world both light and the fount of

---

[5] *Odyssey* 11, 489–90, where Achilles says to Odysseus, on the latter's visit to the underworld, that he would rather be a servant to a poor man on earth than king among the dead.

light, while in the intelligible world it is itself that which produces and controls truth and intelligence, and he who is to act intelligently in public or in private must see it.—I share your thought as far as I am able.

Come then, share with me this thought also: do not be surprised that those who have reached this point are unwilling to occupy themselves with human affairs, and that their souls are always pressing upward to spend their time there, for this is natural if things are as our parable indicates.— That is very likely.

Further, I said, do you think it at all surprising that anyone coming to the evils of human life from the contemplation of the divine behaves awkwardly and appears very ridiculous while his eyes are still dazzled and before he is sufficiently adjusted to the darkness around him, if he is compelled to contend in court or some other place about the shadows of justice or the objects of which they are shadows, and to carry through the contest about these in the way these things are understood by those who have never seen Justice itself?—That is not surprising at all.

Anyone with intelligence, I said, would remember that the eyes may be confused in two ways and from two causes, coming from light into darkness as well as from darkness into light. Realizing that the same applies to the soul, whenever he sees a soul disturbed and unable to see something, he will not laugh mindlessly but will consider whether it has come from a brighter life and is dimmed because unadjusted, or has come from greater ignorance into greater light and is filled with a brighter dazzlement. The former he would declare happy in its life and experience, the latter he would pity, and if he should wish to laugh at it, his laughter would be less ridiculous than if he laughed at a soul that has come from the light above.—What you say is very reasonable.

We must then, I said, if these things are true, think something like this about them, namely that education is not what some declare it to be; they say that knowledge is not present in the soul and that they put it in, like putting sight into blind eyes.—They surely say that.

Our present argument shows, I said, that the capacity to learn and the organ with which to do so are present in every person's soul. It is as if it were not possible to turn the eye from darkness to light without turning the whole body; so one must turn one's whole soul from the world of becoming until it can endure to contemplate reality, and the brightest of realities, which we say is the Good.—Yes.

Education then is the art of doing this very thing, this turning around, the knowledge of how the soul can most easily and most effectively be turned around; it is not the art of putting the capacity of sight into the soul; the soul possesses that already but it is not turned the right way or looking where it should. This is what education has to deal with.—That seems likely.

Now the other so-called virtues of the soul seem to be very close to those of the body—they really do not exist before and are added later by habit and practice—but the virtue of intelligence belongs above all to something more divine, it seems, which never loses its capacity but, according to which way it is turned, becomes useful and beneficial or useless and harmful. Have you never noticed in men who are said to be wicked but clever, how sharply their little soul looks into things to which it turns its attention? Its capacity for sight is not inferior, but it is compelled to serve evil ends, so that the more sharply it looks the more evils it works.—Quite so.

Yet if a soul of this kind had been hammered at from childhood and those excrescences had been knocked off it which belong to the world of becoming and have been fastened upon it by feasting, gluttony, and similar pleasures, and which like leaden weights draw the soul to look downward—if, being rid of these, it turned to look at things that are true, then the same soul of the same man would see these just as sharply as it now sees the things towards which it is directed.—That seems likely.

Further, is it not likely, I said, indeed it follows inevitably from what was said before, that the uneducated who have no experience of truth would never govern a city satisfactorily, nor would those who are allowed to spend their whole life in the process of educating themselves; the former would fail because they do not have a single goal at which all their actions, public and private, must aim; the latter because they would refuse to act, thinking that they have settled, while still alive, in the faraway islands of the blessed.—True.

It is then our task as founders, I said, to compel the best natures to reach the study which we have previously said to be the most important, to see the Good and to follow that upward journey.

When they have accomplished their journey and seen it sufficiently, we must not allow them to do what they are allowed to do today.—What is that?

To stay there, I said, and to refuse to go down again to the prisoners in the cave, there to share both their labours and their honours, whether these be of little or of greater worth.

CRITICAL QUESTIONS

1. Are you inclined to agree with Plato about the existence of some higher, immaterial, intelligible reality beyond this material world? Why, or why not?

2. How would Plato answer the question, "What is really real?" Do you think he is right? Why, or why not?

10.4 NONDUALISM

Shankara (ca. 788–820) is one of the most important figures in Indian philosophy. In his short life, he traveled extensively, founded four monasteries, and made major contributions to the development of philosophical and religious ideas. He wrote extensive commentaries interpreting important Hindu scriptures and became the leading advocate for a school of philosophy known as **Advaita** (nondual) **Vedanta** (end of the *Vedas*). Shankara preferred to be thought of as a *nondualist* rather than a monist because he taught that ultimate reality is an undifferentiated unity beyond all positive predication. Hence, it can be defined only by saying what it is not.

Brahman was the word used by Shankara for ultimate reality. The word **Atman** had been used for the true Self (the real identity behind our individual egos). Shankara thought of the Atman as pure consciousness (consciousness per se) and identified it with the Brahman. Hence, Atman is the word used for the Brahman "within," and Brahman is the word used for the Atman "without." But, of course, since they are identical and since there is no other absolute reality, ultimately there is no division between within and without. Philosophically, Shankara struggled to articulate more precisely what these ideas mean and to understand how they are related. Religiously, he sought to discover the way to experience the identity of Atman and Brahman.

Like Plato, Shankara believed that the more permanent something is, the more real it is. That which is absolutely permanent is absolutely real. Everything else is but an appearance of this eternal reality. The supposed "reality" of the impermanent is nothing but an illusion. We must learn how to discriminate between the permanent and the impermanent if we want to know what is really real.

To distinguish things, we need a principle of discrimination, which we can term *sublation*. **Sublation** is the act of correcting a previous judgment in light of a subsequent one. For example, when I think the shiny surface up ahead on the road is water but decide, as I get closer, that it is only the sun reflecting off the asphalt, I am engaging in an act of sublation and thereby discriminating appearance from reality. Sublatability is the quality a thing has that allows us to correct our judgment about it. If something is sublatable, it must be impermanent. If the "water" I saw up ahead were permanent, when I got closer I would still see water. It would not be a temporary mirage.

Shankara defines *reality* as that which cannot be sublated, *appearance* as that which can be sublated, and *unreality* as neither sublatable nor unsublatable because it does not exist. Armed with these distinctions and the principle of sublation, our task is to examine all the sorts of things we think are real to see if they really are real or just the appearance of what is real.

In the selection from *The Crest-Jewel of Discrimination* that follows, Shankara, speaking as the master, leads a disciple through an examination of various "coverings" in search of the true Self (Atman). The master then claims that the Atman, which is unsublatable, is the same as the Brahman, the really real.

Some scholars do not believe Shankara is the author of this text. Nevertheless, tradition has attributed it to him, and it undoubtedly expresses ideas associated with his philosophy, even if he did not write it.

Read the text slowly and carefully, keeping in mind that to qualify as really real, something must be permanent and unsublatable. I have added footnotes at key points to explain technical terms. Be sure to read them; they will help.

⊚ READING QUESTIONS

1. What does discrimination mean?
2. Why do you think renunciation, tranquillity, self-control, faith, self-surrender, the longing for liberation, and devotion are necessary to gain knowledge of the Atman?
3. What is ignorance, and how is it overcome?
4. Why is your body (physical covering) not your true Self?

5. What are the differences among the fool, the intelligent person, and the wise person?
6. Why are the vital covering, the mental covering, and the covering of the intellect not the Atman?
7. How is the universe related to Brahman?

The Crest-Jewel of Discrimination

SHANKARA

A man should be intelligent and learned, with great powers of comprehension, and able to overcome doubts by the exercise of his reason. One who has these qualifications is fitted for knowledge of the Atman.

He alone may be considered qualified to seek Brahman who has discrimination, whose mind is turned away from all enjoyments, who possesses tranquillity and the kindred virtues, and who feels a longing for liberation.

In this connection, the sages have spoken of four qualifications for attainment. When these are present, devotion to the Reality will become complete. When they are absent, it will fail.

First is mentioned discrimination between the eternal and the non-eternal. Next comes renunciation of the enjoyment of the fruits of action, here and hereafter. Then come the six treasures of virtue, beginning with tranquillity. And last, certainly, is the longing for liberation.

From Shankara's *Crest-Jewel of Discrimination with a Garland of Questions and Answers*, translated by Swami Prabhavananda and Christopher Isherwood (New York: New American Library, 1970), pp. 37–39, 52–61, 65–69. Reprinted by permission of Vedanta Press, 1946 Vedanta Pl., Hollywood, CA 90068.

Brahman is real; the universe is unreal. A firm conviction that this is so is called *discrimination* between the eternal and the non-eternal.

Renunciation is the giving-up of all the pleasures of the eyes, the ears, and the other senses, the giving-up of the desire for a physical body as well as for the highest kind of spirit-body of a god.

To detach the mind from all objective things by continually seeing their imperfection, and to direct it steadfastly toward Brahman, its goal—this is called *tranquillity.*

To detach both kinds of sense-organs—those of perception and those of action—from objective things, and to withdraw them to rest in their respective centers—this is called *self-control.* True *mental poise* consists in not letting the mind react to external stimuli.

To endure all kinds of afflictions without rebellion, complaint or lament—this is called *forbearance.*

A firm conviction, based upon intellectual understanding that the teachings of the scriptures and of one's master are true—this is called by the sages the *faith* which leads to realization of the Reality.

To concentrate the intellect repeatedly upon the pure Brahman and to keep it fixed there always—this is called *self-surrender.* This does not mean soothing the mind, like a baby, with idle thoughts.

Longing for liberation is the will to be free from the fetters forged by ignorance—beginning with the ego-sense and so on, down to the physical body itself—through the realization of one's true nature.

Even though this longing for liberation may be present in a slight or moderate degree, it will grow intense through the grace of the teacher, and through the practice of renunciation and of virtues such as tranquillity, etc.: And it will bear fruit.

When renunciation and the longing for liberation are present to an intense degree within a man, then the practice of tranquillity and the other virtues will bear fruit and lead to the goal.

Where renunciation and longing for liberation are weak, tranquillity and the other virtues are a mere appearance, like the mirage in the desert.

Among all means of liberation, devotion is supreme. To seek earnestly to know one's real nature—this is said to be devotion.

In other words, devotion can be defined as the search for the reality of one's own Atman. The seeker after the reality of the Atman, who possesses the above-mentioned qualifications, should approach an illumined teacher from whom he can learn the way to liberation from all bondage....

Now I shall tell you the nature of the Atman. If you realize it, you will be freed from the bonds of ignorance, and attain liberation.

There is a self-existent Reality, which is the basis of our consciousness of ego. That Reality is the witness of the three states of our consciousness, and is distinct from the five bodily coverings.[1]

That Reality is the knower in all states of consciousness—waking, dreaming and dreamless sleep. It is aware of the presence or absence of the mind and its functions. It is the Atman.

That Reality sees everything by its own light. No one sees it. It gives intelligence to the mind and the intellect, but no one gives it light.

That Reality pervades the universe, but no one penetrates it. It alone shines. The universe shines with its reflected light.

Because of its presence, the body, senses, mind and intellect apply themselves to their respective functions, as though obeying its command.

Its nature is eternal consciousness. It knows all things, from the sense of ego to the body itself. It is the knower of pleasure and pain and of the sense-objects. It knows everything objectively—just as a man knows the objective existence of a jar.

This is the Atman, the Supreme being, the ancient. It never ceases to experience infinite joy. It is always the same. It is consciousness itself.

---

[1][The five bodily coverings will be discussed later. They are the physical, the vital, the mental, the intellectual, and the covering of bliss. These are called "coverings" because Shankara pictures them as progressively thinner bodies or sheaves (like those dolls within dolls) that cover the Atman. This is based on the idea that matter extends from a gross level (the physical body as we think of it) to subtler or finer levels. Notice that things like mind and intellect, which in the West have usually been thought of as immaterial, are here thought of as material (but matter of a finer sort).—Ed.]

The organs and vital energies function under its command.

Here, within this body, in the pure mind, in the secret chamber of intelligence, in the infinite universe within the heart, the Atman shines in its captivating splendour, like a noonday sun. By its light, the universe is revealed.

It is the knower of the activities of the mind and of the individual man. It is the witness of all the actions of the body, the sense-organs and the vital energy. It seems to be identified with all these, just as fire appears identified with an iron ball. But it neither acts nor is subject to the slightest change.

The Atman is birthless and deathless. It neither grows nor decays. It is unchangeable, eternal. It does not dissolve when the body dissolves. Does the ether cease to exist when the jar that enclosed it is broken?

The Atman is distinct from Maya,[2] the primal cause, and from her effect, the universe. The nature of the Atman is pure consciousness. The Atman reveals this entire universe of mind and matter. It cannot be defined. In and through the various states of consciousness—the waking, the dreaming and the sleeping—it maintains our unbroken awareness of identity. It manifests itself as the witness of the intelligence.

THE MIND

With a controlled mind and an intellect which is made pure and tranquil, you must realize the Atman directly, within yourself. Know the Atman as the real I. Thus you cross the shoreless ocean of worldliness, whose waves are birth and death. Live always in the knowledge of identity with Brahman, and be blessed.

Man is in bondage because he mistakes what is non-Atman for his real Self. This is caused by ignorance. Hence follows the misery of birth and death. Through ignorance, man identifies the Atman with the body, taking the perishable for the real. Therefore he nourishes this body, and anoints it, and guards it carefully. He becomes enmeshed in the things of the senses like a caterpillar in the threads of its cocoon.

Deluded by his ignorance, a man mistakes one thing for another. Lack of discernment will cause a man to think that a snake is a piece of rope. When he grasps it in this belief he runs a great risk. The acceptance of the unreal as real constitutes the state of bondage. Pay heed to this, my friend.

The Atman is indivisible, eternal, one without a second. It is eternally made manifest by the power of its own knowledge. Its glories are infinite. The veil of tamas[3] hides the true nature of the Atman, just as an eclipse hides the rays of the sun.

When the pure rays of the Atman are thus concealed, the deluded man identifies himself with his body, which is non-Atman. Then rajas, which has the power of projecting illusory forms, afflicts him sorely. It binds him with chains of lust, anger and the other passions.

His mind becomes perverted. His consciousness of the Atman is swallowed up by the shark of total ignorance. Yielding to the power of rajas, he identifies himself with the many motions and changes of the mind. Therefore he is swept hither and thither, now rising, now sinking, in the boundless ocean of birth and death, whose waters are full of the poison of sense-objects. This is indeed a miserable fate.

The sun's rays bring forth layers of cloud. By them, the sun is concealed; and so it appears that the clouds alone exist. In the same way, the ego, which is brought forth by the Atman, hides the true nature of the Atman; and so it appears that the ego alone exists.

On a stormy day the sun is swallowed up by thick clouds; and these clouds are attacked by

[2][*Maya* is sometimes translated as "illusion" and sometimes as "appearance." It refers to the illusions done by magicians, and Shankara uses this analogy to indicate the nature of the pluralistic universe we usually experience. In general, *Maya* is the impermanent that appears to be real but is not. It stands in contrast to the permanence of Atman-Brahman, which is what is truly real.—Ed.]

[3][Tamas are one of the three gunas that make up all material things. Gunas are qualities. In ancient Hindu cosmology, it was thought that everything material is made up of some combination or mixture of the gunas. Tamas is the quality of stupor, laziness, stupidity, heaviness, and inaction in general. Rajas, another guna, is the active principle and hence the opposite of tamas. Sattva, the third guna, is associated with the pure, the fine, and the calm.—Ed.]

sharp, chill blasts of wind. So, when the Atman is enveloped in the thick darkness of tamas, the terrible power of rajas attacks the deluded man with all kinds of sorrows.

Man's bondage is caused by the power of these two—tamas and rajas. Deluded by these, he mistakes the body for the Atman and strays on to the path that leads to death and rebirth.

Man's life in this relative world may be compared to a tree. Tamas is the seed. Identification of the Atman with the body is its sprouting forth. The cravings are its leaves. Work is its sap. The body is its trunk. The vital forces are its branches. The sense-organs are its twigs. The sense-objects are its flowers. Its fruits are the sufferings caused by various actions. The individual man is the bird who eats the fruit of the tree of life.

The Atman's bondage to the non-Atman springs from ignorance. It has no external cause. It is said to be beginningless. It will continue indefinitely until a man becomes enlightened. As long as a man remains in this bondage it subjects him to a long train of miseries—birth, death, sickness, decrepitude, and so forth.

This bondage cannot be broken by weapons, or by wind, or by fire, or by millions of acts. Nothing but the sharp sword of knowledge can cut through this bondage. It is forged by discrimination and made keen by purity of heart, through divine grace.

A man must faithfully and devotedly fulfill the duties of life as the scriptures prescribe. This purifies his heart. A man whose heart is pure realizes the supreme Atman. Thereby he destroys his bondage to the world, root and all.

Wrapped in its five coverings, beginning with the physical, which are the products of its own Maya, the Atman remains hidden, as the water of a pond is hidden by a veil of scum.

When the scum is removed, the pure water is clearly seen. It takes away a man's thirst, cools him immediately and makes him happy.

When all the five coverings are removed, the pure Atman is revealed. It is revealed as God dwelling within; as unending, unalloyed bliss; as the supreme and self-luminous Being.

The wise man who seeks liberation from bondage must discriminate between Atman and non-Atman. In this way, he can realize the Atman, which is Infinite Being, Infinite Wisdom and Infinite Love. Thus he finds happiness.

The Atman dwells within, free from attachment and beyond all action. A man must separate this Atman from every object of experience, as a stalk of grass is separated from its enveloping sheath. Then he must dissolve into the Atman all those appearances which make up the world of name and form. He is indeed a free soul who can remain thus absorbed in the Atman alone.

THE BODY

This body is the "physical covering." Food made its birth possible; on food it lives; without food it must die. It consists of cuticle, skin, flesh, blood, bone and water. It cannot be the Atman, the ever-pure, the self-existent.

It did not exist before birth, it will not exist after death. It exists for a short while only, in the interim between them. Its very nature is transient, and subject to change. It is a compound, not an element. Its vitality is only a reflection. It is a sense-object, which can be perceived, like a jar. How can it be the Atman—the experiencer of all experiences?

The body consists of arms, legs and other limbs. It is not the Atman—for when some of these limbs have been cut off, a man may continue to live and function through his remaining organs. The body is controlled by another. It cannot be the Atman, the controller.

The Atman watches the body, with its various characteristics, actions and states of growth. That this Atman, which is the abiding reality, is of another nature than the body, must be self-evident.

The body is a bundle of bones held together by flesh. It is very dirty and full of filth. The body can never be the same as the self-existent Atman, the knower. The nature of the Atman is quite different from that of the body.

It is the ignorant man who identifies himself with the body, which is compounded of skin, flesh, fat, bone and filth. The man of spiritual discrimination knows the Atman, his true being, the one supreme reality, as distinct from the body.

The fool thinks, "I am the body." The intelligent man thinks, "I am an individual soul united with the body." But the wise man, in the greatness of his knowledge and spiritual discrimination, sees the Atman as reality and thinks, "I am Brahman."

O fool, stop identifying yourself with this lump of skin, flesh, fat, bones and filth. Identify yourself with Brahman, the Absolute, the Atman in all beings. That is how you can attain the supreme peace.

The intelligent man may be learned in Vedanta and the moral laws. But there is not the least hope of his liberation until he stops mistakenly identifying himself with the body and the sense-organs. This identification is caused by delusion.

You never identify yourself with the shadow cast by your body, or with its reflection, or with the body you see in a dream or in your imagination. Therefore you should not identify yourself with this living body, either.

Those who live in ignorance identify the body with the Atman. This ignorance is the root-cause of birth, death and rebirth. Therefore you must strive earnestly to destroy it. When your heart is free from this ignorance, there will no longer be any possibility of your rebirth. You will reach immortality.

That covering of the Atman which is called "the vital covering" is made up of the vital force and the five organs of action. The body is called "the physical covering." It comes to life when it is enveloped by the vital covering. It is thus that the body engages in action.

This vital covering is not the Atman—for it is merely composed of the vital airs. Air-like, it enters and leaves the body. It does not know what is good or bad for itself, or for others. It is always dependent upon the Atman.

PURIFICATION

The mind, together with the organs of perception, forms the "mental covering." It causes the sense of "I" and "mine." It also causes us to discern objects. It is endowed with the power and faculty of differentiating objects by giving them various names. It is manifest, enveloping the "vital covering."

The mental covering may be compared to the sacrificial fire. It is fed by the fuel of many desires. The five organs of perception serve as priests. Objects of desire are poured upon it like a continuous stream of oblations. Thus it is that this phenomenal universe is brought forth.

Ignorance is nowhere, except in the mind. The mind is filled with ignorance, and this causes the bondage of birth and death. When, in the enlightenment of the Atman, a man transcends the mind, the phenomenal universe disappears from him. When a man lives in the domain of mental ignorance, the phenomenal universe exists for him.

In dream, the mind is emptied of the objective universe, but it creates by its own power a complete universe of subject and object. The waking state is only a prolonged dream. The phenomenal universe exists in the mind.

In dreamless sleep, when the mind does not function, nothing exists. This is our universal experience. Man seems to be in bondage to birth and death. This is a fictitious creation of the mind, not a reality.

The wind collects the clouds, and the wind drives them away again. Mind creates bondage, and mind also removes bondage.

The mind creates attachment to the body and the things of this world. Thus it binds a man, as a beast is tied by a rope. But it is also the mind which creates in a man an utter distaste for sense-objects, as if for poison. Thus it frees him from his bondage.

The mind, therefore, is the cause of man's bondage and also of his liberation. It causes bondage when it is darkened by rajas. It causes liberation when it is freed from rajas and tamas, and made pure.

If discrimination and dispassion are practiced, to the exclusion of everything else, the mind will become pure and move toward liberation. Therefore the wise man who seeks liberation must develop both these qualities within himself.

That terrible tiger called an impure mind prowls in the forest of the sense-objects. The wise man who seeks liberation must not go there.

The mind of the experiencer creates all the objects which he experiences, while in the waking or the dreaming state. Ceaselessly, it creates the differences in men's bodies, color, social condition and race. It creates the variations of the gunas. It creates desires, actions and the fruits of actions.

Man is pure spirit, free from attachment. The mind deludes him. It binds him with the bonds of the body, the sense-organs and the life-breath. It creates in him the sense of "I" and "mine." It makes him wander endlessly among the fruits of the actions it has caused.

The error of identifying Atman with non-Atman is the cause of man's birth, death and rebirth. This false identification is created by the mind. Therefore, it is the mind that causes the misery of birth, death and rebirth for the man who has no discrimination and is tainted by rajas and tamas.

Therefore the wise, who know Reality, have declared that the mind is full of ignorance. Because of this ignorance, all the creatures of the universe are swept helplessly hither and thither, like masses of cloud before the wind.

Therefore, the seeker after liberation must work carefully to purify the mind. When the mind has been made pure, liberation is as easy to grasp as the fruit which lies in the palm of your hand.

Seek earnestly for liberation, and your lust for sense-objects will be rooted out. Practice detachment toward all actions. Have faith in the Reality. Devote yourself to the practice of spiritual disciplines, such as hearing the word of Brahman, reasoning and meditating upon it. Thus the mind will be freed from the evil of rajas.

The "mental covering," therefore, cannot be the Atman. It has a beginning and an end, and is subject to change. It is the abode of pain. It is an object of experience. The seer cannot be the thing which is seen.

THE COVERING OF INTELLECT

The discriminating faculty with its powers of intelligence, together with the organs of perception, is known as the "covering of intellect." To be the doer is its distinguishing characteristic. It is the cause of man's birth, death and rebirth.

The power of intelligence that is in the "covering of intellect" is a reflection of the Atman, the pure consciousness. The "covering of intellect" is an effect of Maya. It possesses the faculty of

knowing and acting. It always identifies itself entirely with the body, sense-organs, etc.

It has no beginning. It is characterized by its sense of ego. It constitutes the individual man. It is the initiator of all actions and undertakings. Impelled by the tendencies and impressions formed in previous births, it performs virtuous or sinful actions and experiences their results.

It gathers experiences by wandering through many wombs of higher or lower degree. The states of waking and dreaming belong to this "covering of intellect." It experiences joy and sorrow.

Because of its sense of "I" and "mine," it constantly identifies itself with the body, and the physical states, and with the duties pertaining to the different stages and orders of life. This "covering of intellect" shines with a bright light because of its proximity to the shining Atman. It is a garment of the Atman, but man identifies himself with it and wanders around the circle of birth, death and rebirth because of his delusion.

The Atman, which is pure consciousness, is the light that shines in the shrine of the heart, the center of all vital force. It is immutable, but it becomes the "doer" and "experiencer" when it is mistakenly identified with the "covering of intellect."

The Atman assumes the limitations of the "covering of intellect" because it is mistakenly identified with that covering, which is totally different from itself. This man, who is the Atman, regards himself as being separate from it, and from Brahman, who is the one Atman in all creatures. An ignorant man, likewise, may regard a jar as being different from the clay of which it was made.

By its nature, the Atman is forever unchanging and perfect. But it assumes the character and nature of its coverings because it is mistakenly identified with them. Although fire is formless, it will assume the form of red-hot iron....

ATMAN IS BRAHMAN

The Disciple: Master, if we reject these five coverings as unreal, it seems to me that nothing remains but the void. How, then, can there be an existence which the wise man may realize as one with his Atman?

The Master: That is a good question, O prudent one. Your argument is clever. Nevertheless, there must be an existence, a reality, which perceives the ego-sense and the coverings and is also aware of the void which is their absence. This reality by itself remains unperceived. Sharpen your discrimination that you may know this Atman, which is the knower.

He who experiences is conscious of himself. Without an experiencer, there can be no self-consciousness.

The Atman is its own witness, since it is conscious of itself. The Atman is no other than Brahman.

The Atman is pure consciousness, clearly manifest as underlying the states of waking, dreaming and dreamless sleep. It is inwardly experienced as unbroken consciousness, the consciousness that I am I. It is the unchanging witness that experiences the ego, the intellect and the rest, with their various forms and changes. It is realized within one's own heart as existence, knowledge and bliss absolute. Realize this Atman within the shrine of your own heart.

The fool sees the reflection of the sun in the water of a jar, and thinks it is the sun. Man in the ignorance of his delusion sees the reflection of Pure Consciousness upon the coverings, and mistakes it for the real I.

In order to look at the sun, you must turn away from the jar, the water, and the sun's reflection in the water. The wise know that these three are only revealed by the reflection of the self-luminous sun. They are not the sun itself.

The body, the covering of intellect, the reflection of consciousness upon it—none of these is the Atman. The Atman is the witness, infinite consciousness, revealer of all things but distinct from all, no matter whether they be gross or subtle. It is the eternal reality, omnipresent, all-pervading, the subtlest of all subtleties. It has neither inside nor outside. It is the real I, hidden in the shrine of the heart. Realize fully the truth of the Atman. Be free from evil and impurity, and you shall pass beyond death.

Know the Atman, transcend all sorrows, and reach the fountain of joy. Be illumined by this knowledge, and you have nothing to fear. If you wish to find liberation, there is no other way of breaking the bonds of rebirth.

What can break the bondage and misery of this world? The knowledge that the Atman is Brahman. Then it is that you realize Him who is one without a second, and who is the absolute bliss.

Realize Brahman, and there will be no more returning to this world—the home of all sorrows. You must realize absolutely that the Atman is Brahman.

Then you will win Brahman for ever. He is the truth. He is existence and knowledge. He is absolute. He is pure and self-existent. He is eternal, unending joy. He is none other than the Atman.

The Atman is one with Brahman: this is the highest truth. Brahman alone is real. There is none but He. When He is known as the supreme reality there is no other existence but Brahman.

THE UNIVERSE

Brahman is the reality—the one existence, absolutely independent of human thought or idea. Because of the ignorance of our human minds, the universe seems to be composed of diverse forms. It is Brahman alone.

A jar made of clay is not other than clay. It is clay essentially. The form of the jar has no independent existence. What, then, is the jar? Merely an invented name!

The form of the jar can never be perceived apart from the clay. What, then, is the jar? An appearance! The reality is the clay itself.

This universe is an effect of Brahman. It can never be anything else but Brahman. Apart from Brahman, it does not exist. There is nothing beside Him. He who says that this universe has an independent existence is still suffering from delusion. He is like a man talking in his sleep.

"The universe is Brahman"—so says the great seer of the Atharva Veda. The universe, therefore, is nothing but Brahman. It is superimposed upon Him. It has no separate existence, apart from its ground.

If the universe, as we perceive it, were real, knowledge of the Atman would not put an end to our delusion. The scriptures would be untrue. The revelations of the Divine Incarnations would make no sense. These alternatives cannot be considered either desirable or beneficial by any thinking person.

Sri Krishna, the Incarnate Lord, who knows the secret of all truths, says in the Gita: "Although I am not within any creature, all creatures exist within me. I do not mean that they exist within me physically. That is my divine mystery. My Being sustains all creatures and brings them to birth, but has no physical contact with them."

If this universe were real, we should continue to perceive it in deep sleep. But we perceive nothing then. Therefore it is unreal, like our dreams.

The universe does not exist apart from the Atman. Our perception of it as having an independent existence is false, like our perception of blueness in the sky. How can a superimposed attribute have any existence, apart from its substratum? It is only our delusion which causes this misconception of the underlying reality.

No matter what a deluded man may think he is perceiving, he is really seeing Brahman and nothing else but Brahman. He sees mother-of-pearl and imagines that it is silver. He sees Brahman and imagines that it is the universe. But this universe, which is superimposed upon Brahman, is nothing but a name.

I AM BRAHMAN

Brahman is supreme. He is the reality—the one without a second. He is pure consciousness, free from any taint. He is tranquillity itself. He has neither beginning nor end. He does not change. He is joy for ever.

He transcends the appearance of the manifold, created by Maya. He is eternal, forever beyond reach of pain, not to be divided, not to be measured, without form, without name, undifferentiated, immutable. He shines with His own light. He is everything that can be experienced in this universe.

The illumined seers know Him as the uttermost reality, infinite, absolute, without parts—the pure consciousness. In Him they find that knower, knowledge and known have become one.

They know Him as the reality which can neither be cast aside (since He is ever-present within the human soul) nor grasped (since He is beyond the power of mind and speech). They know Him immeasurable, beginningless, endless, supreme in glory. They realize the truth: "I am Brahman."

CRITICAL QUESTIONS

1. Shankara says all kinds of things about the Atman and yet claims that it cannot be defined. Is this a contradiction? Present an argument in support of your answer.

2. Do you agree that the "mind of the experiencer creates all the objects which he experiences" while in the waking and the dreaming state? Why, or why not?

3. How does the master answer the disciple's question, "How, then, can there be an existence which the wise man may realize as one with his Atman?" Do you find the answer convincing? Provide an argument in support of your answer.

4. If you were in a debate with Shankara, what would be the major objection you would make to his ideas? How do you think he would defend himself?

10.5 SUBJECTIVE IDEALISM

George Berkeley was born in 1685 in Kilkenny, Ireland. At age fifteen he went to Trinity College, Dublin, where he studied classics, mathematics, and the then-new and controversial physics of Newton. In 1704, after graduation, he became a Fellow of his college and was ordained to the ministry. By the age of twenty-five, he had worked out the basic ideas of his philosophy in reaction to the philosophy of

John Locke (1632–1704). He saw himself as a defender of common sense in a skeptical age and a defender of religion against a science that pictured the universe as a vast machine operating according to blind natural laws. Berkeley lived in the American colonies for a while, married in 1728, and was appointed Bishop of Cloyne in south Ireland in 1734 after his attempt to start a college in Bermuda to educate colonists, Native Americans, and Africans failed due to lack of funding. He died at Oxford in 1753.

Berkeley's metaphysics is called **subjective idealism**. His views constitute a variety of idealism because he argued that reality consists of finite or created minds, an infinite mind (God), and the ideas (thoughts, feelings, and sensations) these minds have. All of these things are immaterial. This idealism is termed *subjective* because physical objects do not exist apart from some subject (mind) who perceives them. This kind of idealism stands in contrast to **objective idealism**, which holds that although reality is mental, it does exist independently of the human knower because it is a manifestation of an absolute mind. Objective idealism is usually monistic (or at least nondualistic), maintaining that there is one absolute mind and the universe is a manifestation of it. Berkeley's subjective idealism, though nondualistic in the sense of asserting that all reality is mental or immaterial, is pluralistic in the sense that there are many finite minds independent of God's mind.

The denial of the objective or independent existence of physical objects seems so utterly fantastic that one wonders how Berkeley could view himself as a champion of common sense. Indeed, when he published his views in 1710, many thought him insane. However, Berkeley's rejection of matter seems more plausible if we understand the historical circumstances that led him to that conclusion.

We must return, for a moment, to Plato. Plato was a dualist, arguing that reality is twofold: material and immaterial. This dualism was revived and given a modern formulation by the French philosopher René Descartes in the early seventeenth century. Descartes argued for a position known as indirect or representational realism. His position is called **realism** because he believed objects can exist apart from any knower or mind. It is called *indirect* or *representational* because he also argued that sensations indirectly represent objects that exist outside the mind. This sort of realism stands in contrast to direct or naive realism, which holds that we are directly in touch with real objects via our senses.

John Locke, an English philosopher, combined Descartes's realism with empiricism. Empiricism is the view that knowledge derives from sense experience and that knowledge claims are tested by reference to sense experience. If empiricism is true, then all we can know *directly* or immediately are the ideas or sensations that occur in our minds. Although these ideas are themselves mental, they resemble and are caused by nonmental or physical objects existing outside the mind, or so the indirect realist claims. Hence, according to Locke, there are two substances: *immaterial substances* or minds, that have ideas *caused* by *material substances*.

This distinction between ideas and the physical objects they represent was accompanied by a distinction between primary and secondary qualities. **Primary qualities** are characteristics that constitute the properties of physical objects. Locke believed them to be extension, figure, motion, rest, solidity, and number. **Secondary qualities** are characteristics of our *sensation* of physical objects: color, flavor, odor, texture, sound, hot, cold, and the like. The theory of indirect realism combined with the distinction between secondary and primary qualities allowed Locke to explain, for example, how it is that an object looks a different color in different light or feels cold to one person but hot to another. Direct realism was unable to explain such common experiences, because if we are *directly* in touch with real physical objects via our senses, an object would have to be both blue and green or hot and cold if it were so experienced. However, if we are *indirectly* in touch with objects, and if color and heat are secondary qualities, then we can say that the object *appears* both blue and green or feels both hot and cold, but *in fact* it is simply in a certain state of motion.

Berkeley pondered Locke's ideas as an undergraduate and found them nonsensical. He felt that since all we can really know are immaterial ideas, there is no way of knowing that they represent anything at all outside the mind. To know that this picture is a likeness of my friend, I can look at my friend and compare that image to the picture image. However, I cannot do that with sensations because I can never get outside of sensations to compare them with the physical objects that supposedly caused them.

Locke, Berkeley thought, had created a duplex world. We have a world of physical objects duplicated by a world of mental images. It also turns out that there are problems involved in trying to explain how physical objects can cause nonphysical sensations. Why not just simplify things by getting rid of physical objects? Isn't it true that we only know for sure that ideas or sensations exist, but we have no way of knowing for sure that physical objects do? What we *do* know is that what we call a physical object is for us a bundle of sensations (colors, odors, flavors, etc.). Because sensations cannot exist without being sensed, why not say the obvious, that nothing can exist without being experienced. Hence, Berkeley concluded that "*esse* is *percipi*"—that is, *to be is to be perceived.* We don't really need the materialistic hypothesis—or so Berkeley argued.

Notice how Berkeley's argument is heavily dependent on an empirical epistemological theory. This may surprise you, because many people associate empiricism with materialism. Berkeley argued that this association is wrong. If empiricism is right in claiming that the only thing we can know are things that appear to our minds such as sensations, feelings, and ideas, then why assume we can know matter or some physical reality apart from what appears to our minds. Notice further how epistemological arguments and metaphysical assertions come together. The philosophical concern with knowledge will, sooner or later, lead us into metaphysical territory and theories of reality.

READING QUESTIONS

1. Give an example of each of the three kinds of ideas that constitute, according to Berkeley, the objects of human knowledge.
2. What is the difference between *ideas* and the *mind*?
3. Why did Berkeley assert that the existence (*esse*) of the objects of knowledge consists in their being perceived (*percipi*)?
4. How would Berkeley answer that old question, "If a tree fell in the forest and no one was there to hear it, would it make a sound?"
5. Why did Berkeley reject the distinction between primary and secondary qualities, and why did he claim that the very notion of matter is contradictory?
6. In Sections 16–20, Berkeley advanced a series of arguments against the idea that material objects exist outside our minds. Briefly summarize the main ideas of these arguments.

The Principles of Human Knowledge

GEORGE BERKELEY

PART I

1. It is evident to anyone who takes a survey of the objects of human knowledge, that they are either ideas actually imprinted on the senses; or else such as are perceived by attending to the passions and operations of the mind; or lastly, ideas formed by help of memory and imagination—either compounding, dividing, or barely representing those originally perceived in the aforesaid ways.—By sight I have the ideas of light and colours, with their several degrees and variations. By touch I perceive hard and soft, heat and cold, motion and resistance, and of all these more and less either as to quantity or degree. Smelling furnishes me with odours; the palate with tastes; and hearing conveys sounds to the mind in all their variety of tone and composition.—And as several of these are observed to accompany each other, they come to be marked by one name, and so to be reputed as one thing. Thus, for example, a certain colour, taste, smell, figure and consistence having been observed to go together, are accounted one distinct thing, signified by the name apple; other collections of ideas constitute a stone, a tree, a book, and the like sensible things—which as they are pleasing or disagreeable excite the passions of love, hatred, joy, grief, and so forth.

2. But, besides all that endless variety of ideas or objects of knowledge, there is likewise something which knows or perceives them; and exercises divers operations, as willing, imagining, remembering, about them. This perceiving, active being is what I call mind, spirit, soul, or myself. By which words I do not denote any one of my ideas, but a thing entirely distinct from them, wherein they exist, or, which is the same thing, whereby they are perceived—for the existence of an idea consists in being perceived.

3. That neither our thoughts, nor passions, nor ideas formed by the imagination, exist without the mind, is what everybody will allow.—And to me it is no less evident that the various sensations, or ideas imprinted on the sense, however blended or combined together (that is, whatever objects they compose), cannot exist otherwise than in a mind perceiving them—I think an intuitive knowledge may be obtained of this by anyone that shall attend to what is meant by the term exist when applied to sensible things. The table I write on I say exists, that is, I see and feel it; and if I were out of my study I should say it existed—meaning thereby that if I was in my study I might perceive it, or that some other spirit actually does perceive it. There was an odour, that is, it was smelt; there was a sound, that is, it was heard; a colour or figure, and it was perceived by sight or touch. This is all that I can understand by these and the like expressions.—For as to what is said of the absolute existence of unthinking things without any relation to their being perceived, that is to me perfectly unintelligible. Their esse is percipi, nor is it possible they should have any existence out of the minds or thinking things which perceive them.

4. It is indeed an opinion strangely prevailing amongst men, that houses, mountains, rivers, and in a word all sensible objects, have an existence, natural or real, distinct from their being perceived by the understanding. But, with how great an assurance and acquiescence soever this principle may be entertained in the world, yet whoever shall find in his heart to call it in question may, if I mistake not, perceive it to involve a manifest contradiction. For, what are the forementioned objects but the things we perceive by sense? and what do we perceive besides our own ideas or sensations? and is it not plainly repugnant that

From George Berkeley, *A Treatise Concerning the Principles of Human Knowledge* (1710), Sections 1–10, 14–20.

any one of these, or any combination of them, should exist unperceived?

5. If we thoroughly examine this tenet it will, perhaps, be found at bottom to depend on the doctrine of abstract ideas. For can there be a nicer strain of abstraction than to distinguish the existence of sensible objects from their being perceived, so as to conceive them existing unperceived? Light and colours, heat and cold, extension and figures—in a word the things we see and feel—what are they but so many sensations, notions, ideas, or impressions on the sense? and is it possible to separate, even in thought, any of these from perception? For my part, I might as easily divide a thing from itself. I may, indeed, divide in my thoughts, or conceive apart from each other, those things which, perhaps, I never perceived by sense so divided. Thus, I imagine the trunk of a human body without the limbs, or conceive the smell of a rose without thinking on the rose itself. So far, I will not deny, I can abstract—if that may properly be called abstraction which extends only to the conceiving separately such objects as it is possible may really exist or be actually perceived asunder. But my conceiving or imagining power does not extend beyond the possibility of real existence or perception. Hence, as it is impossible for me to see or feel anything without an actual sensation of that thing, so is it impossible for me to conceive in my thoughts any sensible thing or object distinct from the sensation or perception of it.

6. Some truths there are so near and obvious to the mind that a man need only open his eyes to see them. Such I take this important one to be, viz. that all the choir of heaven and furniture of the earth, in a word all those bodies which compose the mighty frame of the world, have not any subsistence without a mind—that their being is to be perceived or known; that consequently so long as they are not actually perceived by me, or do not exist in my mind or that of any other created spirit, they must either have no existence at all, or else subsist in the mind of some Eternal Spirit—it being perfectly unintelligible, and involving all the absurdity of abstraction, to attribute to any single part of them an existence independent of a spirit. To be convinced of which, the reader need only reflect, and try to separate in his own thoughts the being of a sensible thing from its being perceived.

7. From what has been said it is evident there is not any other Substance than spirit, or that which perceives. But, for the fuller demonstration of this point, let it be considered the sensible qualities are colour, figure, motion, smell, taste, &c., i.e., the ideas perceived by sense. Now, for an idea to exist in an unperceiving thing is a manifest contradiction; for to have an idea is all one as to perceive; that therefore wherein colour, figure, &c. exist must perceive them; hence it is clear there can be no unthinking substance or substratum of those ideas.

8. But, say you, though the ideas themselves do not exist without the mind, yet there may be things like them, whereof they are copies or resemblances, which things exist without the mind in an unthinking substance. I answer, an idea can be like nothing but an idea; a colour or figure can be like nothing but another colour or figure. If we look but never so little into our own thoughts, we shall find it impossible for us to conceive a likeness except only between our ideas. Again, I ask whether those supposed originals or external things, of which our ideas are the pictures or representations, be themselves perceivable or no? If they are, then they are ideas and we have gained our point; but if you say they are not, I appeal to anyone whether it be sense to assert a colour is like something which is invisible; hard or soft, like something which is intangible; and so of the rest.

Some there are who make a distinction betwixt primary and secondary qualities. By the former they mean extension, figure, motion, rest, solidity or impenetrability, and number; by the latter they denote all other sensible qualities, as colours, sounds, tastes, and so forth. The ideas we have of these they acknowledge not to be the resemblances of anything existing without the mind, or unperceived, but they will have our ideas of the primary qualities to be patterns or images of things which exist without the mind, in an unthinking substance which they call matter. By matter, therefore, we are to understand an inert, senseless substance, in which extension, figure, and motion do actually subsist. But it is evident, from what we have already shewn, that extension, figure, and motion are only ideas existing in the mind, and that an idea can be like nothing but another idea, and that consequently neither they nor their archetypes can exist in an unperceiving substance. Hence, it is plain that the very notion of what is called matter or corporeal substance, involves a contradiction in it.

They who assert that figure, motion, and the rest of the primary or original qualities do exist without the mind in unthinking substances, do at the same time acknowledge that colours, sounds, heat, cold, and such like secondary qualities, do not—which they tell us are sensations existing in the mind alone, that depend on and are occasioned by the different size, texture, and motion of the minute particles of matter. This they take for an undoubted truth, which they can demonstrate beyond all exception. Now, if it be certain that those original qualities are inseparably united with the other sensible qualities, and not, even in thought, capable of being abstracted from them, it plainly follows that they exist only in the mind. But I desire any one to reflect and try whether he can, by any abstraction of thought, conceive the extension and motion of a body without all other sensible qualities. For my own part, I see evidently that it is not in my power to frame an idea of a body extended and moving, but I must withal give it some colour or other sensible quality which is acknowledged to exist only in the mind. In short, extension, figure, and motion, abstracted from all other qualities, are inconceivable. Where therefore the other sensible qualities are, there must these be also, to wit, in the mind and nowhere else....

14. I shall farther add, that, after the same manner as modern philosophers prove certain sensible qualities to have no existence in matter, or without the mind, the same thing may be likewise proved of all other sensible qualities whatsoever. Thus, for instance, it is said that heat and cold are affections only of the mind, and not at all patterns of real beings, existing in the corporeal substances which excite them, for [the reason] that the same body which appears cold to one hand seems warm to another. Now, why may we not as well argue that figure and extension are not patterns or resemblances of qualities existing in matter,

because to the same eye at different stations, or eyes of a different texture at the same station, they appear various, and cannot therefore be the images of anything settled and determinate without the mind? Again, it is proved that sweetness is not really in the sapid [tasty] thing, because the thing remaining unaltered the sweetness is changed into bitter, as in case of a fever or otherwise vitiated palate. Is it not as reasonable to say that motion is not without the mind, since if the succession of ideas in the mind become swifter, the motion, it is acknowledged, shall appear slower without any alteration in any external object?

15. In short, let any one consider those arguments which are thought manifestly to prove that colours and tastes exist only in the mind, and he shall find they may with equal force be brought to prove the same thing of extension, figure, and motion. Though it must be confessed this method of arguing does not so much prove that there is no extension or colour in an outward object, as that we do not know by sense which is the true extension or colour of the object. But the arguments foregoing plainly shew it to be impossible that any colour or extension at all, or other sensible quality whatsoever, should exist in an unthinking subject without the mind, or in truth, that there should be any such thing as an outward object.

16. But let us examine a little the received opinion.—It is said extension is a mode or accident of Matter, and that Matter is the substratum that supports it. Now I desire that you would explain to me what is meant by Matter's supporting extension. Say you, I have no idea of Matter and therefore cannot explain it. I answer, though you have no positive, yet, if you have any meaning at all, you must at least have a relative idea of Matter; though you know not what it is, yet you must be supposed to know what relation it bears to accidents, and what is meant by its supporting them. It is evident "support" cannot here be taken in its usual or literal sense—as when we say that pillars support a building; in what sense therefore must it be taken?

17. If we inquire into what the most accurate philosophers declare themselves to mean by material substance, we shall find them acknowledge they have no other meaning annexed to those

sounds but the idea of being in general, together with the relative notion of its supporting accidents. The general idea of Being appeareth to me the most abstract and incomprehensible of all other; and as for its supporting accidents, this, as we have just now observed, cannot be understood in the common sense of those words; it must therefore be taken in some other sense, but what that is they do not explain. So that when I consider the two parts or branches which make the signification of the words material substance, I am convinced there is no distinct meaning annexed to them. But why should we trouble ourselves any farther, in discussing this material substratum or "support" of figure, and motion, and other sensible qualities? Does it not suppose they have an existence without the mind? And is not this a direct repugnancy, and altogether inconceivable?

18. But, though it were possible that solid, figured, moveable substances may exist without the mind, corresponding to the ideas we have of bodies, yet how is it possible for us to know this? Either we must know it by Sense or by Reason.—As for our senses, by them we have the knowledge only of our sensations, ideas, or those things that are immediately perceived by sense, call them what you will: but they do not inform us that things exist without the mind, or unperceived, like to those which are perceived. This the Materialists themselves acknowledge.—It remains therefore that if we have any knowledge at all of external things, it must be by Reason inferring their existence from what is immediately perceived by sense. But what reason can induce us to believe the existence of bodies without the mind, from what we perceive, since the very patrons of Matter themselves do not pretend there is any necessary connexion betwixt them and our ideas? I say it is granted on all hands—and what happens in dreams, frenzies, and the like, puts it beyond dispute—that it is possible we might be affected with all the ideas we have now, though there were no bodies existing without resembling them. Hence, it is evident the supposition of external bodies is not necessary for producing our ideas; since it is granted they are

produced sometimes, and might possibly be produced always in the same order we see them in at present, without their concurrence.

19. But, though we might possibly have all our sensations without them, yet perhaps it may be thought easier to conceive and explain the manner of their production, by supposing external bodies in their likeness rather than otherwise; and so it might be at least probable there are such things as bodies that excite their ideas in our minds. But neither can this be said; for, though we give the materialists their external bodies, they by their own confession are never the nearer knowing how our ideas are produced; since they own themselves unable to comprehend in what manner body can act upon spirit, or how it is possible it should imprint any idea in the mind. Hence it is evident the production of ideas or sensations in our minds can be no reason why we should suppose Matter or corporeal substances, since that is acknowledged to remain equally inexplicable with or without this supposition. If therefore it were possible for bodies to exist without the mind, yet to hold they do so must needs be a very precarious opinion; since it is to suppose, without any reason at all, that God has created innumerable beings that are entirely useless, and serve to no manner of purpose.

20. In short, if there were external bodies, it is impossible we should ever come to know it; and if there were not, we might have the very same reasons to think there were that we have now. Suppose—what no one can deny possible—an intelligence without the help of external bodies, to be affected with the same train of sensations or ideas that you are, imprinted in the same order and with like vividness in his mind. I ask whether that intelligence hath not all the reason to believe the existence of corporeal substances, represented by his ideas, and exciting them in his mind, that you can possibly have for believing the same thing? Of this there can be no question—which one consideration were enough to make any reasonable person suspect the strength of whatever arguments he may think himself to have, for the existence of bodies without the mind.

1. How did Berkeley respond to the claim that things exist apart from minds (unthinking or material substances), which our ideas copy or resemble? Do you find his response convincing? Why, or why not?

2. Do you find any of the arguments in Sections 16–20 of *The Principles of Human Knowledge* convincing? Provide an argument in support of your answer.

3. If you got into a debate with Berkeley, what sort of objections would you raise against his claim that matter does not exist? How do you think he would respond to your objections?

4. Formulate and answer a question comparing Berkeley's views with any of the other metaphysical views you have studied in this chapter. How are they the same, and how are they different?

10.6 PRE-COLUMBIAN COSMOLOGIES

Cultural critiques have often lamented the fragmentation of modern life. Many think this fragmentation stems from modern scientific developments that have slowly chipped away at a more integrated view of the cosmos. Others lay the blame at the doorstep of modern metaphysical views, which deny the interconnectedness of fact and values, mind and matter, faith and science.

Comparisons can be illuminating. In fact, comparing one thing to another is one of the primary ways we add depth to our understanding. However helpful comparisons can be, they can also be misleading. Sometimes we view the "other" in the comparison as inferior to ourselves or to some viewpoint we prefer. Sometimes we view the "other" as superior, romanticizing a past no longer existent, but one for which we long. Comparisons are particularly difficult when comparing the views of a culture that has conquered another culture or when comparing existing cultural viewpoints with those that no longer exist. In such situations we must imagine the "other," and imagination—as we all know—can be both helpful and misleading.

Jorge Valadez, author of the next selection, teaches philosophy at Marquette University. His research focuses on ontology, social and political philosophy, and pre-Columbian philosophy. The selection that follows is part of a larger essay that includes a discussion of the Maya, Aztec, and Inca worldviews along with the changes that took place in the colonial and post-colonial period in Latin America.

Valadez is convinced that the metaphysical views of ancient Mesoamerican cultures have not been fully appreciated because of the Eurocentrism brought by the conquering Spanish. When we think of these cultures we think of wild-eyed priests in feathered headdresses brutally sacrificing humans to their sun god. However dreadful the practice of human sacrifice may be, it was embedded in a metaphysical view that we need to understand. We must not lose sight of the more positive elements that may be found in this ancient metaphysic, especially when compared with modern views.

1. How did the metaphysical views of the Spanish influence their treatment of the Aztecs?

2. What four different kinds of integration characterized Mesoamerican metaphysics?

3. Why, according to Valadez, did the conflict between science and religion that characterizes modern Western thought not occur among the Mesoamericans?

4. How is the "Legend of the Four Suns" related to human sacrifice and the need for a warrior class?

Pre-Columbian Philosophical Perspectives

JORGE VALADEZ

Nothing in the experience of the much-traveled soldiers of Hernán Cortés's invading army could have prepared them for what they saw when they marched into Tenochtitlán, the ancient site of present-day Mexico City, in 1519. They encountered great buildings and ceremonial centers, vast and beautiful floating gardens, splendid murals, impressive sculptures and other works of art, and large and well-organized markets. The Spaniards were witnessing the splendors of one of the greatest civilizations in history. Their amazement was magnified by the fact that this civilization was so utterly foreign and unexpected. The Spaniards were denizens of the Old World, where diverse cultures had interacted and influenced one another for thousands of years. But here was a civilization that had evolved in isolation from the rest of the world and yet was highly advanced in astronomy and agriculture, had created architectural wonders, practiced sophisticated types of surgery, and developed complex and unique systems of religious belief and social organization.

This unprecedented and extraordinary encounter of two diverse cultures was destined to have catastrophic consequences for the people of the Americas. In less than two centuries diseases like smallpox and diphtheria, which the inhabitants of the New World had no defenses against because of their genetic isolation, decimated approximately two-thirds of the population of the Americas. In Mesoamerica (a region covering the southern two-thirds of Mexico and Guatemala, El Salvador, Belize, and certain areas of Nicaragua, Honduras, and Costa Rica), tens of millions of native people died either in battles with the technologically superior invading army or, more commonly, as the result of infection with these new diseases. The Spaniards

eventually conquered the Aztec capital, Tenochtitlán, plundered it for its gold and silver (melting many pieces of jewelry and religious figurines into gold bullion), and enslaved many of its inhabitants.

But there was another kind of destruction that the Spaniards were to wreak on the Aztecs and other people of Mesoamerica—the almost wholesale destruction of their culture. The social, religious, and political organization of early Mesoamerican society—including the structure of its large urban centers, forms of religious ritual, cultural customs, artistic styles, philosophy of education, and architectural forms—were all based on a religious and cosmological perspective that was completely foreign and incomprehensible to the Europeans.

The worldview of the Spaniards was determined by their Christian beliefs, and hence they were at once amazed and repulsed by what they saw: human sacrifices, rituals involving bloodletting, adoration of pagan gods, cannibalism, sculptures of what they considered monstrous creatures, and so on. According to their Christian metaphysical perspective there was a clear and straightforward way to categorize these practices; they were to be considered evil and the work of the Devil. One of the most famous chroniclers of the native culture, the Spanish Franciscan priest Bernardino de Sahagun, firmly believed that the existence of Aztec religious beliefs and customs was an ingenious and elaborate manifestation of the power of Satan's influence. Thus, the religious practices of the Aztecs not only had no claim to cultural legitimacy, they had to be stopped at whatever cost. Bolstered by such ethical and cultural chauvinism, the Spaniards undertook what is perhaps the most extensive and systematic (and certainly the most large-scale) destruction of a civilization in the

From Jorge Valadez, "Pre-Columbian and Modern Philosophical Perspectives in Latin America," in *From Africa to Zen: An Invitation to World Philosophy*, edited by Robert C. Solomon and Kathleen M. Higgins (Lanham, MD: Rowman and Littlefield, 1993), pp. 81–89. Copyright © 1993 by Rowman and Littlefield Publishers, Inc. Reprinted by permission.

world's history. In that the civilizations of Meso-america were essentially grounded in a radically different religious and cosmological vision, this conquest was nothing less than an attempt at meta-physical annihilation, that is, an attempt to destroy the worldviews of the native people. Nevertheless, despite the efforts of the Spaniards to eradicate the cosmological roots of these cultures, we shall see that some important features of the ancient world-views can still be found in some contemporary Mesoamerican cultures.

Given their imperialistic orientations and the closed nature of their religious perspective, it was perhaps inevitable that the Spaniards would fail so completely to understand the Aztec culture and the other cultures of ancient Mesoamerica. In fact, it is only in the latter half of the twentieth century that it has been possible, through a variety of archaeological sources and different kinds of interpretive techniques, to understand the reli-gious and metaphysical worldview of early Meso-american cultures.

This essay will present a systematic exposition of some of the central concepts and principles of the early Mesoamerican cosmological perspec-tives, ... I will draw contrasts and comparisons between the Mesoamerican metaphysical perspec-tives and some perspectives that have been of predominant importance in the Western philo-sophical tradition. These comparisons will help us to appreciate more fully the uniqueness and depth of the ancient Mesoamerican worldviews and will further our understanding of some of the Western European philosophical perspectives by placing them within a wider global cultural context.

PRECOLONIAL LATIN AMERICAN COSMOLOGIES

Cultures throughout history have developed a variety of answers to certain fundamental and perennial questions: What place do human beings have in the universe? What is the structure of the cosmos? How can we explain or account for the origin of the world? The cultures of Mesoamerica developed complex and fascinating answers to such questions. In order to provide a general

understanding of how they approached these questions, we will look first at some central meta-physical principles common to the Mayan and Aztec cosmologies, and then examine the struc-ture of each of these worldviews in more detail.

One of the most striking features of the Mesoamerican metaphysical perspective was the remarkable degree to which it interconnected or integrated different aspects or components of real-ity. Four different kinds of integration character-ized its cosmology: (1) the internal structural interconnection of the different components of the universe, (2) the integration of fundamental dualities that were perceived as complementary instead of oppositional, (3) the holistic integration of astronomical science and religious beliefs, and, most important, (4) the integration of everyday life with the cycles and rhythms of the cosmos through the practice of rituals that were perceived as necessary for sustaining the very existence of the universe. To arrive at a unified view of the Meso-american metaphysical perspective, we must under-stand each of these four aspects of Mesoamerican cosmology....

The Interactive Universe

The people of Mesoamerica believed that the uni-verse consisted of three different planes or levels: a celestial plane, a terrestrial plane, and an under-world plane. There were further divisions within the celestial and underworld levels. (The Aztecs, for example, believed that there were thirteen celestial levels and nine underworld levels.) There was also a constant interaction of supernat-ural forces or powers among these levels, which was made possible by the existence of spiral-shaped channels called mallinalis. These supernat-ural forces were thought to enter the terrestrial level through caves, sunlight, fire, and animals. Some of the rituals of the Mesoamerican cultures were designed to tap and redirect or harness these supernatural cosmic forces. Thus their universe was not a static universe, but rather an interactive one, with three dynamic levels of reality.

Time itself also existed at different planes or levels: human or terrestrial time; the time of myth; and the transcendent time in which the gods dwelled. Terrestrial time originated in the interaction of cosmic forces from the celestial and under-world levels converging at the terrestrial level. In other words, human time originated in the interaction of forces from two distinct spatial planes.

Myth time existed prior to terrestrial time, and in it the actions of the gods, as they were depicted in their myths, took place. For example, in one of the Mayan myths about death, two heroic twin brothers descend to the underworld to challenge the Lords of Death. After a long series of trials and ordeals, the brothers defeat the Lords of the Underworld and emerge victorious. This myth is an expression of the Mayan belief that death repre-sents a challenge which, through courage and for-titude, can be overcome. It was also during this myth time, which still progresses and has not ceased to be, that many supernatural beings who exert cyclical influences on humans at the terrestrial level were born or created.

In transcendent time lived the most powerful gods at the apex of the divine hierarchy who cre-ated and grounded the universe. (Apparently these powerful creator gods existed in two tempo-ral dimensions, namely, mythic and transcendent time.) The gods and supernatural beings that inhabited transcendent time, like those that lived in mythic time, had periodic or cyclical influences on the events and beings that existed in terrestrial time. The early Mesoamerican calendars marked the occasions during the year when these periodic influences occurred.

Thus, in the Mesoamerican worldview, space and time were not understood as existing inde-pendently of one another; instead, they formed a complex, unified whole…. For the ancient Mesoa-mericans, the world was replete with cosmic forces resulting from the intersection of the various spatial and temporal levels that comprised the universe.

In addition, their universe did not consist of isolated, discrete entities; rather, it consisted of entities, events, and forces that were in constant interaction with one another and that existed in different spaciotemporal planes. Absolute space, conceived as an empty vacuum in which entities exist and events take place, and absolute time, understood as an infinite linear progression of moments, had no reality in the Mesoamerican cos-mological perspective. For the people of early Mesoamerica, space and time constituted the very fabric of existence; that is, they affected, shaped, and determined everything that exists. This is why Mesoamerican cultures were so preoc-cupied with developing accurate calendars and astronomical techniques for measuring time, determining the spatial location of celestial bodies, and anticipating the occurrence of astronomical events. The capacity to measure and predict the solar, lunar, planetary, and astral cycles enabled them to understand the various complex cosmic forces that they believed affected human events at the terrestrial level. By knowing the particular times at which certain cosmic forces affected events at the human level, they tried to mediate and channel these forces through rituals. From such observations we can appreciate the great extent to which the different components of the Mesoamerican universe were interrelated and interconnected with one another.

Complementary Dualities

The second kind of integration in Mesoamerican cosmology concerns the complementary nature of fundamental dualities. Dualities such as life/death, celestial world/underworld, male/female, night/day, and so forth were of central impor-tance in the Mesoamerican worldview. These dualities were not conceived as being oppositional in nature; instead, they were understood as being different and necessary aspects of reality. One of the clearest examples of this type of nonopposi-tional duality was the supreme dual god of the Aztecs, Ometeotl. This supreme deity, who was the ultimate originator of all that exists, had a dual male and female nature. Ometeotl was some-times called Tonacatecuhtli-Tonacacihuatl, which means "lord and lady of our maintenance," and often he/she was referred to as "our mother, our father." The dual nature of Ometeotl enabled him/her to beget other beings and the universe from his/her own essence. It is clear that the Aztecs wanted to incorporate both the male and the female principle within a single supreme entity and that they saw no contradiction in a deity who was simultaneously male and female.

It is interesting and instructive to compare the conception of a male/female dual god with the monotheistic God of the Judeo-Christian tradition. Traditionally, the Christian god has been characterized primarily as having male qualities and has been referred to in explicitly male terms. For example, the first two substantive terms in the expression "the father, the son, and the holy ghost" refer to God in terms that are unequivocally male, while the third substantive term, "the holy ghost," has traditionally never been spoken of in female terms. And historically, rarely if ever have we heard the Christian God referred to by the female pronoun "she" or by the phrase "holy mother." He is usually characterized by predominantly male qualities that emphasized his power and authority instead of, say, his nurturance and unconditional acceptance. Some contemporary theologians have argued that these gender-specific characterizations of the Christian God deny women full spiritual participation in the Christian religious tradition. In any case, we can see that the Aztec conceptualization of the supreme deity Ometeotl incorporates the two aspects of the male/female duality into a single divine entity.

We find another case of the Mesoamerican tendency to think in terms of nonoppositional dualities in the Mayan understanding of the life/death duality. From the Mayan perspective, death, whether of humans or of plants, was an integral part of a never-ending life cycle of birth, death, and regeneration. Death was not seen as the discontinuity of life, but rather as a necessary phase in the regeneration of life. Upon death, humans went to the underworld of Xibalba, where they experienced various ordeals and struggles with the supernatural entities of the underworld. Then they would be reborn and ascend to the celestial or terrestrial level, where they might become a part of a heavenly body, an ancestral spiritual entity, or a maize plant. Through this transformation and process of rebirth, individuals would be integrated into one of the eternal life cycles of the universe. In similar fashion, the death of plant life in the seasonal and agricultural cycles was merely one phase in the recurring pattern of sowing, sprouting, dying, and regenerating. One of the central ideas in the Mayan cosmology was that the earth was a living entity that was continually in the process of regeneration, and that the death of plant life was an integral part of this process.

In short, death was not seen as the negation, or as the polar opposite, of life. Rather, death was a process that either (1) made possible the continuation of the life process or (2) allowed for the integration of the life of the individual into the eternal cosmic cycles. In the plant world, the death of plants enabled new vegetation to sprout and develop; that is, death was an integral part of the process of regeneration. In the human realm, death was, as we have seen, a process in which the individual would eventually become a part of the astral or earthly cycles of the universe. In contrast to some Western views on death, in which the soul of the individual continues to exist in an otherworldly spiritual realm, in the early Mesoamerican cosmology the spirits of the dead return to become a part of the world we can see, touch, and feel. That is, they became part of the world of everyday experience.

A Scientific-Religious Worldview

The third kind of structural integration that characterizes the Mesoamerican cosmology concerns the intimate linkage between Mesoamerican scientific and religious perspectives. Astronomy was by far the most fully developed science of the cultures of Mesoamerica. The accuracy of their calendars equaled or surpassed those of other cultures in the world at that time, and their astronomical observations were as extensive and accurate as those of any other civilization. Insofar as they possessed a scientific, empirically validated form of knowledge, it was their astronomy. This was the knowledge that allowed them to correctly predict celestial events, carry out extensive and accurate calendrical computations (some of which involved dates many millions of years into the future), and measure agricultural cycles. But their astronomical science was also closely interconnected with their religious ideas and beliefs, especially the fundamentally important concept of the renewal or regeneration of agricultural and human life cycles. They believed that the influences of the supernatural forces and beings that permeated the earth and supported these life cycles could be tracked and predicted by their calendars. In addition, they maintained that through religious rituals they could harness and successfully mediate these cosmic forces.

Thus, the intense interest of the people of ancient Mesoamerica in astronomical observation and the measurement of time was not motivated merely by the desire to acquire knowledge for its own sake; the continuation of the life cycles of the universe depended on the performance of the appropriate religious rituals at specific points in time. Their scientifically validated observations were united with their fundamental religious ideas and with the rituals they believed were crucial for the continued existence of the cosmos. This unification of their two most basic kinds of knowledge gave rise to a holistic conceptual unity in their thinking that is difficult for us to understand and appreciate. The reason this conceptual integration is so foreign to us is that there is a fundamental fragmentation in modern thought between scientific knowledge and religious belief.

Science tells us that reality consists of physical entities and forces that exist independently of human consciousness and that are utterly indifferent to the human search for meaning and cosmic significance. According to the contemporary scientific worldview, everything that occurs in the universe is explainable in terms of universal physical laws, not in terms of the acts of a divine will. Because according to this worldview it is physics, and not the will of God, that explains why events occur, modern scientific knowledge conflicts with the age-old reliance on a supernatural, spiritual being to explain what happens in the universe. And if, as the modern scientific perspective tells us, reality consists exclusively of impersonal physical forces and entities governed by universal laws, where in such a universe can we find a basis for human spiritual meaning and significance? This scientific perspective has also deeply influenced nonreligious, philosophical attempts to find a basis for the meaning of human existence. For the past several centuries (a period coinciding with the emergence of modern science and the decline of the religious worldview), Western philosophers have wrestled with questions concerning the meaning of life. Here again the problem has been to find a basis for grounding existential significance and human

values in an indifferent, impersonal universe consisting solely of objective physical forces and entities. In short, a basic dilemma has arisen in modern Western thought as a result of the scientific view of the universe as an objectively existing physical realm in which there is no room for the principles of human subjective experience as expressed in religious and philosophic thought. By contrast, in the Mesoamerican cosmological view there was no conflict between science and religion; on the contrary, Mesoamerican scientific and religious world-views complemented and reinforced one another.

Cosmic Responsibility

We have already alluded to the fourth kind of integration characteristic of the Mesoamerican metaphysical perspective. It concerns the belief that religious rituals were of central importance for maintaining the existence of the cosmos. Perhaps the clearest expression of this belief can be found in the Aztec Legend of the Four Suns. According to this legend, there have been four ages that have been dominated by four different suns. Each of these ages—which correspond to each of the four directions, east, south, west, and north—had ended in a catastrophic manner with the destruction of the human race and the world. The Aztecs believed that they lived in the age of the Fifth Sun, which was created at Tenochtitlán, the ancient site of Mexico City, as the result of the self-sacrifice of the gods Nanahuatzin and Tecuciztecatl. After the destruction of the Fourth Sun, all was darkness except for the divine hearth (the teotexcalli), where the gods gathered to create the new sun that would usher in the new age. The gods ordered Tecuciztecatl to leap into the great fire, but he was unable to do so out of fear. After Tecuciztecatl attempted and failed four times to leap into the fire, the gods ordered Nanahuatzin to sacrifice himself in the giant blaze. Nanahuatzin braced himself, closed his eyes, and threw himself in. Upon seeing this, Tecuciztecatl finally gained enough courage to jump into the fire. As the result of his courage and sacrifice, Nanahuatzin reemerges from the east as the new, blazing red sun.

The Legend of the Suns expresses some central ideas of the Aztec cosmology. One of these is the centrality of cataclysmic change in the evolution of the universe. Each of the previous four ages had been destroyed by sudden, catastrophic disasters and the present age was also susceptible to an abrupt, massive destruction. The Aztec universe was thus highly unstable and vulnerable to extinction. Another prominent theme in this myth is that of sacrifice. The Aztecs believed that the present age began with a sacrifice by the gods, and that in order to prevent this age from ending they had continually to provide the sun with life-sustaining blood and with the energy concentrated in certain parts of the body of sacrificial victims. This is the primary explanation for the religious rituals involving human sacrifice.

The need for sacrificial victims demanded the continued capture of enemy warriors and the creation of a warrior class to satisfy this need. This sense of cosmic responsibility reinforced certain authoritarian orientations in Aztec culture. Theirs was a society that did not tolerate a great deal of individual freedom or challenges to the established social order.

Human actions had great significance in the cosmology of the Aztecs, because the very existence of the universe depended on the proper performance of religious rituals, including human sacrifice. Without a doubt, most of us would find the practice of human sacrifice, and the extent to which it was practiced by the Aztecs, to be morally objectionable and repugnant in the extreme. Nevertheless, this practice was based on a religious doctrine that was of central importance in the Aztec cosmological perspective. Within their worldview, human sacrifice was not only justified, it was absolutely essential. Indeed, the profound sense of cosmic responsibility that was so central to the Aztec worldview was a double-edged sword. It provided them with an unquestioned faith in their relevance and importance as a people, but it also burdened them with the heavy obligation of maintaining the existence of the cosmos. It can truly be said that the Aztecs elaborated a highly imaginative, though severe, answer to the question concerning the role and relevance of human existence in the universe....

◉ CRITICAL QUESTIONS

1. How do the Mesoamerican views of space and time, the divine, and death differ from your own? Do you see any reason to modify your views based on the differences? If so, how would you change your views and why? If you see no reason to change, state your reasons.
2. Can you think of a modern practice as morally objectionable as human sacrifice? If you can, how is it linked to our metaphysical views?

10.7 WHY IS THERE SOMETHING RATHER THAN NOTHING?

Philosophers from around the world have wondered about whether there is some Archimedian point, some firm and solid foundation, some privileged perspective from which we can distinguish with confidence dreaming from waking, good from bad, reality from appearance. Some have claimed to have found such a foundation; others have claimed it does not exist. Is there some sort of "God's-eye view" that humans can adopt that will allow them to see things as they really are? What do you think?

"Not that question again," I hear some of you say. Wondering can be frustrating business, and being constantly challenged to think for ourselves can be intimidating. Yet thinking is what philosophy is about. Of course, from time to time we all wonder what we have accomplished by all this thought. Sometimes it seems we just go in circles, but the circles get bigger and after a while begin to form a spiral. New ideas arise. Fresh distinctions emerge. Questions are refined and plateaus of clarity reached. You may not be in a position to say with absolute certainty exactly what is really real, but think about all you have learned in thinking about metaphysical issues in conversation with others from around the world.

I do hope that this experience encourages you to continue to wonder because wondering has given birth to some of the greatest of human accomplishments. One metaphysical question that I mentioned in passing at the beginning of this chapter has left people who consider it wondering. It does not focus on ontology, but on how we might explain why anything at all exists. It would appear there is just as good a reason for nothing to exist (if we can talk this way about nothing and make sense),as for something to exist. Martin Heidegger (1889–1976) called this question about why something exists rather than nothing the most fundamental question humans can ask. Heidegger was one of the most brilliant, obscure, and controversial philosophers of the last century. He is usually categorized as an existentialist because of his influential book *Being and Time* (1953). The selection that follows is from the published text of a lecture he delivered at the University of Freiberg in 1935. It does not answer the question, why is there something rather than nothing, but it probes the significance of that question for human existence. It is a question that, as someone remarked, keeps the metaphysical clock ticking endlessly, fascinating those who think about it. It is the ultimate "why" question.

◉ READING QUESTIONS

1. What does the word *essents* mean?
2. Why is the question, "Why are there essents" the widest, deepest, and most fundamental question we can ask?
3. In what way does the question "recoil" on itself?

Introduction to Metaphysics

MARTIN HEIDEGGER

Why are there essents* rather than nothing? That is the question. Clearly it is no ordinary question. "Why are there essents, why is there anything at all, rather than nothing?"—obviously this is the first of all questions, though not in a chronological sense. Individuals and peoples ask a good many questions in the course of their historical passage through time. They examine, explore, and test a good many things before they run into the question "Why are there essents rather than nothing?"

Many men never encounter this question, if by encounter we mean not merely to hear and read about it as an interrogative formulation but to ask the question, that is, to bring it about, to raise it, to feel its inevitability.

And yet each of us is grazed at least once, perhaps more than once, by the hidden power of this question, even if he is not aware of what is happening to him. The question looms in moments of great despair, when things tend to lose all their weight and all meaning becomes obscured. Perhaps it will strike but once like a muffled bell that rings into our life and gradually

---

*"Essents"="existents," things that are.

From *An Introduction to Metaphysics*, trans. Ralph Manheim, (New Haven, CT.: Yale University Press, 1959), pp. 1–6. © 1959 by Yale University Press, Inc.

dies away. It is present in moments of rejoicing, when all the things around us are transfigured and seem to be there for the first time, as if it might be easier to think they are not than to understand that they are and are as they are. The question is upon us in boredom, when we are equally removed from despair and joy, and everything about us seems so hopelessly commonplace that we no longer care whether anything is or is not—and with this the question "Why are there essents rather than nothing?" is evoked in a particular form.

But this question may be asked expressly, or, unrecognized as a question, it may merely pass through our lives like a brief gust of wind; it may press hard upon us, or, under one pretext or another, we may thrust it away from us and silence it. In any case it is never the question that we ask first in point of time.

But it is the first question in another sense—in regard to rank. This may be clarified in three ways. The question "Why are there essents rather than nothing?" is first in rank for us first because it is the most far reaching, second because it is the deepest, and finally because it is the most fundamental of all questions.

It is the widest of all questions. It confines itself to no particular essent of whatever kind. The question takes in everything, and this means not only everything that is present in the broadest sense but also everything that ever was or will be. The range of this question finds its limit only in nothing, in that which simply is not and never was. Everything that is not nothing is covered by this question, and ultimately even nothing itself; not because it is *something*, since after all we speak of it, but because it *is* nothing. Our question reaches out so far that we can never go further. We do not inquire into this and that, or into each essent in turn, but from the very outset into the essent as a whole, or, as we say for reasons to be discussed below: into the essent as such in its entirety.

This broadest of questions is also the deepest: Why are there essents…? Why, that is to say, on what ground? from what source does the essent derive? on what ground does it stand? The question is not concerned with particulars, with what essents are and of what nature at any time, here

and there, with how they can be changed, what they can be used for, and so on. The question aims at the ground of what is insofar as it is. To seek the ground is to try to get to the bottom; what is put in question is thus related to the ground….

Finally, this broadest and deepest question is also the most fundamental. What do we mean by this? If we take the question in its full scope, namely the essent as such in its entirety, it readily follows that in asking this question we keep our distance from every particular and individual essent, from every this and that. For we mean the essent as a whole, without any special preference. Still, it is noteworthy that in this questioning *one* kind of essent persists in coming to the fore, namely the men who ask the question. But the question should not concern itself with any particular essent. In the spirit of its unrestricted scope, all essents are of equal value. An elephant in an Indian jungle "is" just as much as some chemical combustion process at work on the planet Mars, and so on.

Accordingly, if our question "Why are there essents rather than nothing?" is taken in its fullest sense, we must avoid singling out any special, particular essent, including man. For what indeed is man? Consider the earth within the endless darkness of space in the universe. By way of comparison it is a tiny grain of sand; between it and the next grain of its own size there extends a mile or more of emptiness; on the surface of this grain of sand there lives a crawling, bewildered swarm of supposedly intelligent animals, who for a moment have discovered knowledge. And what is the temporal extension of a human life amid all the millions of years? Scarcely a move of the second hand, a breath. Within the essent as a whole there is no legitimate ground for singling out this essent which is called mankind and to which we ourselves happen to belong….

…This question and all the questions immediately rooted in it, the questions in which this one question unfolds—this question "why" is incommensurable with any other. It encounters the search for its own why. At first sight the question "Why the why?" looks like a frivolous repetition ad infinitum of the same interrogative formulation, like an empty and unwarranted brooding over words. Yes, beyond a doubt, that is how it looks. The question is only whether we wish to be taken in by this superficial look and so regard the whole matter as settled, or whether we are capable of finding a significant event in this recoil of the question "why" upon itself.

But if we decline to be taken in by surface appearances we shall see that this question "why," this question as to the essent as such in its entirety, goes beyond any mere playing with words, provided we possess sufficient intellectual energy to make the question actually recoil into its "why"—for it will not do so of its own accord. In so doing we find out that this privileged question "why" has its ground in a leap through which man thrusts away all the previous security, whether real or imagined, of his life. The question is asked only in this leap; it *is* the leap; without it there is no asking....Our questioning is not yet the leap; for this it must undergo a transformation; it still stands perplexed in the face of the essent. Here it may suffice to say that the leap in this questioning opens up its own source—with this leap the question arrives at its own ground. We call such a leap, which opens up its own source, the original source or origin <Ursprung>, the finding of one's own ground. It is because the question "Why are there essents rather than nothing?" breaks open the ground for all authentic questions and is thus at the origin <Ursprung> of them all that we must recognize it as the most fundamental of all questions.

CRITICAL QUESTIONS

1. What do you think Heidegger means when he says that this widest, deepest, most fundamental of all questions "opens up its own source"? Support your answer with an argument.

2. Some critics have claimed that Heidegger's writing is vague and ambiguous nonsense disguised as profundity. Would you agree? Why or why not?

To access the *Voices of Wisdom*, 8th Edition, **Premium Website**, search for this book on CengageBrain.com.

CHAPTER ELEVEN

Are We Free or Determined?

All theory is against freedom of the will; all experience is for it.

SAMUEL JOHNSON, *BOSWELL'S LIFE OF JOHNSON*

LEARNING OBJECTIVES

After studying this chapter students should be able to:
- distinguish simple determinism, fatalism, and predestination,
- explain the problem of freedom and determinism,
- distinguish hard and soft determinism (incompatibilism/compatibilism),
- explain libertarianism,
- characterize existentialism,
- explain the law of karma,
- describe agent causation,
- identify Taylor, Blatchford, Sartre, Radhakrishnan, and Holmstrom, and
- answer all the questions relating to the selections.

11.1 INTRODUCTION

Determinism (sometimes called simple determinism in order to distinguish it from other types) refers to the idea that all events are caused. For every event there is a set of conditions such that if the conditions were repeated, the event would recur. Simple determinism implies that the universe and what happens in it is lawful, that is, that the law of causality (or law of cause and effect) governs events. Hence, we can assume that any given event is determined (caused) by some set of antecedent events even if we are not fully aware of what those antecedent events are.

Some philosophers maintain that simple determinism should not be confused with fatalism or with predestination. **Fatalism** is the belief that events are **predetermined** by some impersonal cosmic force or power; **predestination** is the belief that events are predetermined by some personal power. Although fatalism and predestination differ about what predetermines events, they share the idea that if an event or action is fated or predestined, it will happen *no matter what.*

Simple determinism does not claim that events or actions are predetermined by personal or impersonal cosmic powers, nor does it claim that events will happen no matter what. Rather, it holds that events happen *only* if particular causes of those events occur. If the causes of a possible event do not occur, that event will not occur. While simple determinism is clearly different from predestination, one might argue that it is very close to fatalism. If we think about a chain of cause and effect going all the way back to the very beginning of the universe, it is difficult to deny that the way things are now may well have been set in motion a very long time ago and long before humans entered the scene.

Although there are important differences among simple determinism, fatalism, and predestination, all three positions clearly raise questions about human freedom. If all events are caused (whether their cause be fate, a god, or some set of antecedent events), how can any human actions (assuming human actions are events), like your act of reading these words, be free? This is one way of formulating what philosophers call the **problem of freedom and determinism** (sometimes called the *problem of free will*).

This problem is important for a number of reasons. One of the most important has to do with moral responsibility. If the choices we make and the actions we perform are not free, it seems to make no sense to praise or blame people for what they do. Indeed, why bother to search for how one should live, or how to make correct moral choices, or how to create a just society if, in fact, all our choices are determined by antecedent factors over which we have no control?

The issue of moral responsibility allows us to probe more deeply the problem of freedom and determinism by formulating that problem as a dilemma.

1. Human choice is either free, or it is not free.
2. If it is free, then the law of causality is false.
3. If it is not free, then people are not responsible for their actions.
4. Therefore, either the law of causality is false, or people are not responsible for their actions.

Neither of the choices given in conclusion (4) is very attractive. On the one hand, we want to believe in the law of causality. All of science and technology depend on it. Surely, if there are uncaused events, then there are events that can never be explained, or predicted. So why search for a cure for cancer, or why try to eliminate crime, or why try to invent a pollution-free form of rapid transportation? There may be no causes for these things and hence no means of prediction or control. If the law of causality is false, the universe appears chaotic, disordered, unreliable, and events seem unexplainable.

On the other hand, we want to hold people morally responsible for what they do. What sense would praise or blame make if we aren't responsible? If you are not free and hence not responsible for what you do, then what sense does it make to say you *earned* a good grade in philosophy, or you *merited* a promotion, or you *ought* to be punished for behaving badly? Indeed, what sense would morality make if people cannot freely choose what they do? In addition, our legal systems are vital for establishing law and order in society. However, these systems do this by trying to ascertain guilt and innocence and assign appropriate punishments to the guilty as well as award benefits to wronged parties. If people are not actually responsible for what they do, legal systems could collapse as people lost confidence in the very idea of justice.

In this chapter, we explore some of the solutions people have proposed to the problem of freedom and determinism. As we explore these solutions, our understanding of the problem will grow, and alternatives that may not have occurred to us will present themselves.

11.2 DO WE HAVE REAL CHOICES?

Deliberation is an experience common to all of us. You might right now be thinking about whether you should continue reading or play a new computer game with friends. You might be trying to decide how important all of this stuff is. Should you skim it, hoping to pick up enough to pass a test? Or should you read it carefully and in detail?

Imagine for a moment that you have already taken an exam on this chapter. Would you still deliberate about how carefully you should read? What would be the point? Either you are happy that you decided to read it carefully and did well on the exam or you regret skimming it too rapidly and doing poorly on the exam. The time for deliberation has passed. We cannot deliberate about the past, only about the future. Are there other restrictions on what we can deliberate about?

One other restriction may be the absence of feeling that it is up to us whether to read carefully or not. If you have no other choice, if for some reason you *must* read this chapter carefully, then deliberation seems pointless. We must feel that it is up to us to do or not to do something in order for deliberation to make sense.

Our experiences of deliberation and our feelings that some decisions are up to us are important supports for the argument that we are free and not determined. If we had no such experiences, if every choice seemed forced by powers beyond our control, if nothing ever felt like it was up to us, chances are we would all be determinists. The question of freedom would not even arise.

Richard Taylor (1919–2003) explores these issues and more in the following selection. For many years he was professor of philosophy at the University of Rochester and is best known for his work in metaphysics and virtue ethics.

◉ READING QUESTIONS

1. What does Taylor mean by "deliberation" and "it is up to me," and how do they relate to the discussion of freedom and determinism?
2. What is soft determinism, and what is wrong with it?
3. Describe simple indeterminism and the problems both it and determinism face.
4. Create a reading question of your own and answer it.

Freedom and Determinism

RICHARD TAYLOR

We want to learn, if we can, whether determinism is true, and this is a question of metaphysics. It can, like all good questions of philosophy, be answered only on the basis of certain data; that is, by seeing whether or not it squares with certain things which every man knows, or believes himself to know, or things of which every man is at least more sure than the answer to the question at issue.

Now I could, of course, simply affirm that I am a morally responsible being, in the sense in

From Richard Taylor, *Metaphysics*, Second edition (Englewood Cliffs, NJ: Prentice-Hall, 1974), pp. 40–57. Copyright © 1974, 1963 by Prentice-Hall, Inc.

which my responsibility for my behavior implies that I could have avoided that behavior. But this would take us into the nebulous realm of ethics, and it is, in fact, far from obvious that I am responsible in that sense. Many have doubted that they are responsible in that sense, and it is in any case not difficult to doubt it, however strongly one might feel about it.

There are, however, two things about myself of which I feel quite certain and which have no necessary connection with morals. The first is that I sometimes deliberate, with the view to making a decision; a decision, namely, to do this thing or that. And the second is that whether or not I deliberate about what to do it is sometimes up to me what I do. This might all be an illusion, of course; but so also any philosophical theory, such as the theory of determinism, might be false. The point remains that it is far more difficult for me to doubt that I sometimes deliberate, and that it is sometimes up to me what to do, than to doubt any philosophical theory whatever, including the theory of determinism. We must, accordingly, if we ever hope to be wiser, adjust our theories to our data and not try to adjust our data to our theories.

Let us, then, get these two data quite clearly before us so we can see what they are, what they presuppose, and what they do and do not entail.

DELIBERATION

Deliberation is an activity, or at least a kind of experience, that cannot be defined, or even described without metaphors. We speak of weighing this and that in our minds, of trying to anticipate consequences of various possible courses of action, and so on, but such descriptions do not convey to us what deliberation is unless we already know.

Whenever I deliberate, however, I find that I make certain presuppositions, whether I actually think of them or not. That is, I assume that certain things are true, certain things which are such that, if I thought they were not true, it would be impossible for me to deliberate at all. Some of these can be listed as follows.

First, I find that I can deliberate only about my own behavior and never about the behavior of

another. I can try to guess, speculate, or figure out what another person is going to do; I can read certain signs and sometimes infer what he will do; but I cannot deliberate about it. When I deliberate I try to decide something, to make up my mind, and this is as remote as anything could be from speculating, trying to guess, or to infer from signs. Sometimes one *does* speculate on what he is going to do, by trying to draw conclusions from certain signs or omens—he might infer that he is going to sneeze, for instance, or speculate that he is going to become a grandfather—but he is not then deliberating whether to do these things or not. One does, to be sure, sometimes deliberate about whether another person will do a certain act, when that other person is subject to his command or otherwise under his control; but then he is not really deliberating about another person's acts at all, but about his own—namely, whether or not to have that other person carry out the order.

Second, I find that I can deliberate only about future things, never things past or present. I may not know what I did at a certain time in the past, in case I have forgotten, but I can no longer deliberate whether to do it then or not. I can, again, only speculate, guess, try to infer, or perhaps try to remember. Similarly, I cannot deliberate whether or not to be doing something now; I can only ascertain whether or not I am in fact doing it. If I am sitting I cannot deliberate about whether or not to be sitting. I can only deliberate about whether to remain sitting—and this has to do with the future.

Third, I cannot deliberate about what I shall do, in case I already know what I am going to do. If I were to say, for example, "I know that I am going to be married tomorrow and in the meantime I am going to deliberate about whether to get married," I would contradict myself. There are only two ways that I could know now what I am going to do tomorrow; namely, either by inferring this from certain signs and omens or by having already decided what I am going to do. But if I have inferred from signs and omens what I am going to do, I cannot deliberate about it—there is just nothing for me to decide; and similarly, if I have already decided. If, on the other hand, I can still deliberate about what I am going to do, to that extent I must regard the signs and omens as unreliable, and the inference uncertain, and I therefore do not know what I am going to do after all.

And finally, I cannot deliberate about what to do, even though I may not know what I am going to do, unless I believe that it is up to me what I am going to do. If I am within the power of another person, or at the mercy of circumstances over which I have no control, then, although I may have no idea what I am going to do, I cannot deliberate about it. I can only wait and see. If, for instance, I am a conscript, and regulations regarding uniforms are posted each day by my commanding officer and are strictly enforced by him, then I shall not know what uniforms I shall be wearing from time to time, but I cannot deliberate about it. I can only wait and see what regulations are posted; it is not up to me. Similarly, a woman who is about to give birth to a child cannot deliberate whether to have a boy or a girl, even though she may not know. She can only wait and see; it is not up to her. Such examples can be generalized to cover any case wherein one does not know what he is going to do, but believes that it is not up to him, and hence no matter for his decision and hence none for his deliberation.

"IT IS UP TO ME"

I sometimes feel certain that it is, at least to some extent, up to me what I am going to do; indeed, I must believe this if I am to deliberate about what to do. But what does this mean? It is, again, hard to say, but the idea can be illustrated, and we can fairly easily see what it does *not* mean.

Let us consider the simplest possible sort of situation in which this belief might be involved. At this moment, for instance, it seems quite certain to me that, holding my finger before me, I can move it either to the left or to the right, that each of these motions is possible for me. This does not mean merely that my finger can move either way, although it entails that, for this would be true in case nothing obstructed it, even if I had no control over it at all. I can say of a distant, fluttering leaf that it can move either way, but not that I can move it, since I have no control

over it. How it moves is not up to me. Nor does it mean merely that my finger can be moved either way, although it entails this too. If the motions of my finger are under the control of some other person or of some machine, then it might be true that the finger can be moved either way, by that person or machine, though false that I can move it at all.

If I say, then, that it is up to me how I move my finger, I mean that I can move it in this way and I can move it in that way, and not merely that it can move or be moved in this way and that. I mean that the motion of my finger is within my direct control. If someone were to ask me to move it to the right, I could do that, and if he were to ask me to move it to the left, I could do that too. Further, I could do these simple acts without being asked at all, and, having been asked, I could move it in a manner the exact opposite of what was requested, since I can ignore the request. There are, to be sure, some motions of my finger that I cannot make, so it is not *entirely* up to me how it moves. I cannot bend it backward, for instance, or bend it into a knot, for these motions are obstructed by the very anatomical construction of the finger itself; and to say that I can move my finger at all means at least that nothing obstructs such a motion, though it does not mean merely this. There is, however, at this moment, no obstruction, anatomical or otherwise, to my moving it to the right, and none to my moving it to the left.

This datum, it should be noted, is properly expressed as a conjunction and not as a disjunction. That is, my belief is that I can move my finger in one way, *and* that I can also move it another way; and it does not do justice to this belief to say that I can move it one way *or* the other. It is fairly easy to see the truth of this, for the latter claim, that I can move it one way *or* the other, would be satisfied in case there were only one way I could move it, and *that* is not what I believe. Suppose, for instance, my hand were strapped to a device in such a fashion that I could move my finger to the right but not to the left. Then it would still be entirely true that I could move it either to the left *or* to the right— since it would be true that I could move it to the right. But that is not what I now believe. My finger is not strapped to anything, and nothing obstructs its motion in either direction. And what I believe, in this situation, is that I can move it to the right *and* I can move it to the left.

We must note further that the belief expressed in our datum is not a belief in what is logically impossible. It is the belief that I now *can* move my finger in different ways but not that I can move it in different ways at once. What I believe is that I am now able to move my finger one way and that I am now equally able to move it another way, but I do not claim to be able now or any other time to move it both ways simultaneously. The situation here is analogous to one in which I might, for instance, be offered a choice of either of two apples but forbidden to take both. Each apple is such that I may select it, but neither is such that I may select it together with the other.

Now are these two data—the belief that I do sometimes deliberate, and the belief that it is sometimes up to me what I do—consistent with the metaphysical theory of determinism? We do not know yet. We intend to find out. It is fairly clear, however, that they are going to present difficulties to that theory. But let us not, in any case, try to avoid those difficulties by just denying the data themselves. If we eventually deny the data, we shall do so for better reasons than this. Virtually all men are convinced that beliefs such as are expressed in our data are sometimes true. They cannot be simply dismissed as false just because they might appear to conflict with a metaphysical theory that hardly any men have ever really thought much about at all. Almost any man, unless his fingers are paralyzed, bound, or otherwise incapable of movement, believes sometimes that the motions of his fingers are within his control, in exactly the sense expressed by our data. If consequences of considerable importance to him depend on how he moves his fingers, he sometimes deliberates before moving them, or at least, he is convinced that he does, or that he can. Philosophers might have different notions of just what things are implied by such data, but there is in any case no more, and in fact considerably less, reason for denying the data than for denying some philosophical theory....

FREEDOM

To say that it is, in a given instance, up to me what I do, is to say that I am in that instance *free* with respect to what I then do. Thus, I am sometimes free to move my finger this way and that, but not, certainly, to bend it backward or into a knot. But what does this mean?

It means, first, that there is no *obstacle* or *impediment* to my activity. Thus, there is sometimes no obstacle to my moving my finger this way and that, though there are obvious obstacles to my moving it far backward or into a knot. Those things, accordingly, that pose obstacles to my motions limit my freedom. If my hand were strapped in such a way as to permit only a leftward motion of my finger, I would not then be free to move it to the right. If it were encased in a tight cast that permitted no motion, I would not be free to move it at all. Freedom of motion, then, is limited by obstacles.

Further, to say that it is, in a given instance, up to me what I do, means that nothing *constrains or forces* me to do one thing rather than another. Constraints are like obstacles, except that while the latter prevent, the former enforce. Thus, if my finger is being forcibly bent to the left—by a machine, for instance, or by another person, or by any force that I cannot overcome—then I am not free to move it this way and that. I cannot, in fact, move it at all; I can only watch to see how it is moved, and perhaps vainly resist: its motions are not up to me, or within my control, but in the control of some other thing or person.

Obstacles and constraints, then, both obviously limit my freedom. To say I am free to perform some action thus means at least that there is no obstacle to my doing it, and that nothing constrains me to do otherwise.

Now if we rest content with this observation, as many have, and construe free activity simply as activity that is unimpeded and unconstrained, there is evidently no inconsistency between affirming both the thesis of determinism and the claim that I am sometimes free. For to say that some action of mine is neither impeded nor constrained does not by itself imply that it is not causally determined. The absence of obstacles and constraints are mere negative conditions, and do not by themselves rule out the presence of positive causes. It might seem, then, that we can say of some of my actions that there are conditions antecedent to their performance so that no other actions were possible, and also that these actions were unobstructed and unconstrained. And to say that would logically entail that such actions were both causally determined, and free.

SOFT DETERMINISM

It is this kind of consideration that has led many philosophers to embrace what is sometimes called "soft determinism." All versions of this theory have in common three claims, by means of which, it is naïvely supposed, a reconciliation is achieved between determinism and freedom. Freedom being, furthermore, a condition of moral responsibility and the only condition that metaphysics seriously questions, it is supposed by the partisans of this view that determinism is perfectly compatible with such responsibility. This, no doubt, accounts for its great appeal and wide acceptance, even by some men of considerable learning.

The three claims of soft determinism are (1) that the thesis of determinism is true, and that accordingly all human behavior, voluntary or other, like the behavior of all other things, arises from antecedent conditions, given which no other behavior is possible—in short, that all human behavior is caused and determined; (2) that voluntary behavior is nonetheless free to the extent that it is not externally constrained or impeded; and (3) that, in the absence of such obstacles and constraints, the causes of voluntary behavior are certain states, events, or conditions within the agent himself; namely, his own acts of will or volitions, choices, decisions, desires, and so on.

Thus, on this view, I am free, and therefore sometimes responsible for what I do, provided nothing prevents me from acting according to my own choice, desire, or volition, or constrains me to act otherwise. There may, to be sure, be other conditions for my responsibility—such as, for example, an understanding of the probable consequences of my behavior, and that sort of thing—but absence of constraint or impediment

is, at least, one such condition. And, it is claimed, it is a condition that is compatible with the supposition that my behavior is caused—for it is, by hypothesis, caused by my own inner choices, desires, and volitions.

THE REFUTATION OF THIS

The theory of soft determinism looks good at first—so good that it has for generations been solemnly taught from numberless philosophical chairs and implanted in the minds of students as sound philosophy—but no great acumen is needed to discover that far from solving any problem, it only camouflages it.

My free actions are those unimpeded and unconstrained motions that arise from my own inner desires, choices, and volitions; let us grant this provisionally. But now, whence arise those inner states that determine what my body shall do? Are they within my control or not? Having made my choice or decision and acted upon it, could I have chosen otherwise or not? Here the determinist, hoping to surrender nothing and yet to avoid the problem implied in that question, bids us not to ask it; the question itself, he announces, is without meaning. For to say that I could have done otherwise, he says, means only that I *would* have done otherwise *if* those inner states that determined my action had been different; if, that is, I had decided or chosen differently. To ask, accordingly, whether I could have chosen or decided differently is only to ask whether, had I decided to decide differently or chosen to choose differently, or willed to will differently, I would have decided or chosen or willed differently. And this, of course, *is* unintelligible nonsense.

But it is not nonsense to ask whether the causes of my actions—my own inner choices, decisions, and desires—are themselves caused. And of course they are, if determinism is true, for on that thesis everything is caused and determined. And if they are, then we cannot avoid concluding that, given the causal conditions of those inner states, I could not have decided, willed, chosen, or desired otherwise than I in fact did, for this is a logical consequence of the very definition of determinism. Of course we can still say that, *if* the causes of those inner states, whatever they were, had been different, then their effects, those inner states themselves, would have been different, and that in this hypothetical sense I could have decided, chosen, willed, or desired differently—but that only pushes our problem back still another step. For we will then want to know whether the causes of those inner states were within my control; and so on, *ad infinitum*. We are, at each step, permitted to say "could have been otherwise" only in a provisional sense—provided, that is, something else had been different—but must then retract it and replace it with "could not have been otherwise" as soon as we discover, as we must at each step, that whatever would have to have been different could not have been different.

EXAMPLES

Such is the dialectic of the problem. The easiest way to see the shadowy quality of soft determinism, however, is by means of examples.

Let us suppose that my body is moving in various ways, that these motions are not externally constrained or impeded, and that they are all exactly in accordance with my own desires, choices, or acts of will and what not. When I will that my arm should move in a certain way, I find it moving in that way, unobstructed and unconstrained. When I will to speak, my lips and tongue move, unobstructed and unconstrained, in a manner suitable to the formation of the words I choose to utter. Now given that this is a correct description of my behavior, namely, that it consists of the unconstrained and unimpeded motions of my body in response to my own volitions, then it follows that my behavior is free, on the soft determinist's definition of "free." It follows further that I am responsible for that behavior; or at least, that if I am not, it is not from any lack of freedom on my part.

But if the fulfillment of these conditions renders my behavior free—that is to say, if my behavior satisfies the conditions of free action set forth in the theory of soft determinism—then my behavior will be no less free if we assume further conditions that are perfectly consistent with those already satisfied.

We suppose further, accordingly, that while my behavior is entirely in accordance with my own volitions, and thus "free" in terms of the conception of freedom we are examining, my volitions themselves are caused. To make this graphic, we can suppose that an ingenious physiologist can induce in me any volition he pleases, simply by pushing various buttons on an instrument to which, let us suppose, I am attached by numerous wires. All the volitions I have in that situation are, accordingly, precisely the ones he gives me. By pushing one button, he evokes in me the volition to raise my hand; and my hand, being unimpeded, rises in response to that volition. By pushing another, he induces the volition in me to kick, and my foot, being unimpeded, kicks in response to that volition. We can even suppose that the physiologist puts a rifle in my hands, aims it at some passer-by, and then, by pushing the proper button, evokes in me the volition to squeeze my finger against the trigger, whereupon the passerby falls dead of a bullet wound.

This is the description of a man who is acting in accordance with his inner volitions, a man whose body is unimpeded and unconstrained in its motions, these motions being the effects of those inner states. It is hardly the description of a free and responsible agent. It is the perfect description of a puppet. To render a man your puppet, it is not necessary forcibly to constrain the motions of his limbs, after the fashion that real puppets are moved. A subtler but no less effective means of making a man your puppet would be to gain complete control of his inner states, and ensuring, as the theory of soft determinism does ensure, that his body will move in accordance with them.

The example is somewhat unusual, but it is no worse for that. It is perfectly intelligible, and it does appear to refute the soft determinist's conception of freedom. One might think that, in such a case, the agent should not have allowed himself to be so rigged in the first place, but this is irrelevant; we can suppose that he was not aware that he was, and was hence unaware of the source of those inner states that prompted his bodily motions. The example can, moreover, be modified in perfectly realistic ways, so as to coincide with actual and familiar cases. One can, for instance, be given a compulsive desire for certain drugs, simply by having them administered to him over a course of time. Suppose, then, that I do, with neither my knowledge nor consent, thus become a victim of such a desire and act upon it.

Do I act freely, merely by virtue of the fact that I am unimpeded in my quest for drugs? In a sense I do, surely, but I am hardly free with respect to whether or not I shall use drugs. I never chose to have the desire for them inflicted upon me.

Nor does it, of course, matter whether the inner states which allegedly prompt all my "free" activity are evoked in me by another agent or by perfectly impersonal forces. Whether a desire which causes my body to behave in a certain way is inflicted upon me by another person, for instance, or derived from hereditary factors, or indeed from anything at all matters not the least. In any case, if it is in fact the cause of my bodily behavior, I cannot but act in accordance with it. Wherever it came from whether from personal or impersonal origins, it was entirely caused or determined, and not within my control. Indeed, if determinism is true as the theory of soft determinism holds it to be, all those inner states which cause my body to behave in whatever ways it behaves must arise from circumstances that existed before I was born; for the chain of causes and effects is infinite, and none could have been the least different, given those that preceded.

SIMPLE INDETERMINISM

We might at first now seem warranted in simply denying determinism, and saying that, insofar as they are free, my actions are not caused; or that, if they are caused by my own inner states—my own desires, impulses, choices, volitions, and whatnot—then these, in any case, are not caused. This is a perfectly clear sense in which a man's action, assuming that it was free, could have been otherwise. If it was uncaused, then, even given the conditions under which it occurred and all that preceded, some other act was nonetheless possible, and he did not have to do what he did. Or if

his action was the inevitable consequence of his own inner states, and could not have been otherwise given these, we can nevertheless say that these inner states, being uncaused, could have been otherwise, and could thereby have produced different actions.

Only the slightest consideration will show, however, that this simple denial of determinism has not the slightest plausibility. For let us suppose it is true, and that some of my bodily motions—namely, those that I regard as my free acts—are not caused at all or, if caused by my own inner states, that these are not caused. We shall thereby avoid picturing a puppet, to be sure—but only by substituting something even less like a man; for the conception that now emerges is not that of a free man, but of an erratic and jerking phantom, without any rhyme or reason at all.

Suppose that my right arm is free, according to this conception; that is, that its motions are uncaused. It moves this way and that from time to time, but nothing causes these motions. Sometimes it moves forth vigorously, sometimes up, sometimes down, sometimes it just drifts vaguely about—these motions all being wholly free and uncaused. Manifestly I have nothing to do with them at all; they just happen, and neither I nor anyone can ever tell what this arm will be doing next. It might seize a club and lay it on the head of the nearest bystander, no less to my astonishment than his. There will never be any point in asking why these motions occur, or in seeking any explanation of them, for under the conditions assumed there is no explanation. They just happen, from no causes at all.

This is no description of free, voluntary, or responsible behavior. Indeed, so far as the motions of my body or its parts are entirely uncaused, such motions cannot even be ascribed to me as my behavior in the first place, since I have nothing to do with them. The behavior of my arm is just the random motion of a foreign object. Behavior that is mine must be behavior that is within my control, but motions that occur from no causes are without the control of anyone. I can have no more to do with, and no more control over, the uncaused motions of my limbs than a gambler has over the motions of an honest roulette wheel. I can only, like him, idly wait to see what happens.

Nor does it improve things to suppose that my bodily motions are caused by my own inner states, so long as we suppose these to be wholly uncaused. The result will be the same as before. My arm, for example, will move this way and that, sometimes up and sometimes down, sometimes vigorously and sometimes just drifting about, always in response to certain inner states, to be sure. But since these are supposed to be wholly uncaused, it follows that I have no control over them and hence none over their effects. If my hand lays a club forcefully on the nearest bystander, we can indeed say that this motion resulted from an inner club-wielding desire of mine; but we must add that I had nothing to do with that desire, and that it arose, to be followed by its inevitable effect, no less to my astonishment than to his. Things like this do, alas, sometimes happen. We are all sometimes seized by compulsive impulses that arise we know not whence and we do sometimes act upon these. But because they are far from being examples of free, voluntary, and responsible behavior, we need only to learn that behavior was of this sort to conclude that it was not free, voluntary, or responsible. It was erratic, impulsive, and irresponsible.

DETERMINISM AND SIMPLE INDETERMINISM AS THEORIES

Both determinism and simple indeterminism are loaded with difficulties, and no one who has thought much on them can affirm either of them without some embarrassment. Simple indeterminism has nothing whatever to be said for it, except that it appears to remove the grossest difficulties of determinism, only, however, to imply perfect absurdities of its own. Determinism, on the other hand, is at least initially plausible. Men seem to have a natural inclination to believe in it; it is, indeed, almost required for the very exercise of practical intelligence. And beyond this, our experience appears always to confirm it, so long as we are dealing with everyday facts of common experience, as distinguished from the esoteric

researches of theoretical physics. But determinism, as applied to human behavior, has implications which few men can casually accept, and they appear to be implications which no modification of the theory can efface.

Both theories, moreover, appear logically irreconcilable to the two items of data that we set forth at the outset; namely, (1) that my behavior is sometimes the outcome of my deliberation, and (2) that in these and other cases it is sometimes up to me what I do. Because these were our data, it is important to see, as must already be quite clear, that these theories cannot be reconciled to them.

I can deliberate only about my own future actions, and then only if I do not already know what I am going to do. If a certain nasal tickle warns me that I am about to sneeze, for instance, then I cannot deliberate whether to sneeze or not; I can only prepare for the impending convulsion. But if determinism is true, then there are always conditions existing antecedently to everything I do, sufficient for my doing just that, and such as to render it inevitable. If I can know what those conditions are and what behavior they are sufficient to produce, then I can in every such case know what I am going to do and cannot then deliberate about it.

By itself this only shows, of course, that I can deliberate only in ignorance of the causal conditions of my behavior; it does not show that such conditions cannot exist. It is odd, however, to suppose that deliberation should be a mere substitute for clear knowledge. Ignorance is a condition of speculation, inference, and guesswork, which have nothing whatever to do with deliberation. A prisoner awaiting execution may not know when he is going to die, and he may even entertain the hope of reprieve, but he cannot deliberate about this. He can only speculate, guess—and wait.

Worse yet, however, it now becomes clear that I cannot deliberate about what I am going to do, if it is even possible for me to find out in advance, whether I do in fact find out in advance or not. I can deliberate only with the view to deciding what to do, to making up my mind;

and this is impossible if I believe that it could be inferred what I am going to do, from conditions already existing, even though I have not made that inference myself. If I believe that what I am going to do has been rendered inevitable by conditions already existing, and could be inferred by anyone having the requisite sagacity, then I cannot try to decide whether to do it or not, for there is simply nothing left to decide. I can at best only guess or try to figure it out myself or, all prognostics failing, I can wait and see; but I cannot deliberate. I deliberate in order to *decide* what *to do*, not to *discover* what it is that I *am going* to do. But if determinism is true, then there are always antecedent conditions sufficient for everything that I do, and this can always be inferred by anyone having the requisite sagacity; that is, by anyone having a knowledge of what those conditions are and what behavior they are sufficient to produce.

This suggests what in fact seems quite clear, that determinism cannot be reconciled with our second datum either, to the effect that it is sometimes up to me what I am going to do. For if it is ever really up to me whether to do this thing or that, then, as we have seen, each alternative course of action must be such that I can do it; not that I can do it in some abstruse or hypothetical sense of "can"; not that I could do it if only something were true that is not true; but in the sense that it is then and there within my power to do it. But this is never so, if determinism is true, for on the very formulation of that theory whatever happens at any time is the only thing that can then happen, given all that precedes it. It is simply a logical consequence of this that whatever I do at any time is the only thing I can then do, given the conditions that precede my doing it. Nor does it help in the least to interpose, among the causal antecedents of my behavior, my own inner states, such as my desires, choices, acts of will, and so on. For even supposing these to be always involved in voluntary behavior—which is highly doubtful in itself—it is a consequence of determinism that these, whatever they are at any time, can never be other than what they then are. Every chain of causes and effects, if

determinism is true, is infinite. This is why it is not now up to me whether I shall a moment hence be male or female. The conditions determining my sex have existed through my whole life, and even prior to my life. But if determinism is true, the same holds of anything that I ever am, ever become, or ever do. It matters not whether we are speaking of the most patent facts of my being, such as my sex; or the most subtle, such as my feelings, thoughts, desires, or choices. Nothing could be other than it is, given what was; and while we may indeed say, quite idly, that something—some inner state of mine, for instance—*could* have been different, had only something *else* been different, any consolation of this thought evaporates as soon as we add that whatever would have to have been different could not have been different.

It is even more obvious that our data cannot be reconciled to the theory of simple indeterminism. I can deliberate only about my own actions; this is obvious. But the random, uncaused motion of any body whatever, whether it be a part of my body or not, is no action of mine and nothing that is within my power. I might try to guess what these motions will be, just as I might try to guess how a roulette wheel will behave, but I cannot deliberate about them or try to decide what they shall be, simply because these things are not up to me. Whatever is not caused by anything is not caused by me, and nothing could be more plainly inconsistent with saying that it is nevertheless up to me what it shall be.

THE THEORY OF AGENCY

The only conception of action that accords with our data is one according to which men—and perhaps some other things too—are sometimes, but of course not always, self-determining beings; that is, beings which are sometimes the causes of their own behavior. In the case of an action that is free, it must be such that it is caused by the agent who performs it, but such that no antecedent conditions were sufficient for his performing just that action. In the case of an action that is both free and rational, it must be such that the agent who performed it did so for some reason, but this reason cannot have been the cause of it.

Now this conception fits what men take themselves to be; namely, beings who act, or who are agents, rather than things that are merely acted upon, and whose behavior is simply the causal consequence of conditions which they have not wrought. When I believe that I have done something, I do believe that it was I who caused it to be done, I who made something happen, and not merely something within me, such as one of my own subjective states, which is not identical with myself. If I believe that something not identical with myself was the cause of my behavior—some event wholly external to myself, for instance, or even one internal to myself, such as a nerve impulse, volition, or whatnot—then I cannot regard that behavior as being an act of mine, unless I further believe that I was the cause of that external or internal event. My pulse, for example, is caused and regulated by certain conditions existing within me, and not by myself. I do not, accordingly, regard this activity of my body as my action, and would be no more tempted to do so if I became suddenly conscious within myself of those conditions or impulses that produce it. This is behavior with which I have nothing to do, behavior that is not within my immediate control, behavior that is not only not free activity, but not even the activity of an agent to begin with; it is nothing but a mechanical reflex. Had I never learned that my very life depends on this pulse beat, I would regard it with complete indifference, as something foreign to me, like the oscillations of a clock pendulum that I idly contemplate.

Now this conception of activity, and of an agent who is the cause of it, involves two rather strange metaphysical notions that are never applied elsewhere in nature. The first is that of a *self* or *person*—for example, a man—who is not merely a collection of things or events, but a substance and a self-moving being. For on this view it is a man himself, and not merely some part of him or something within him, that is the cause of his own activity. Now we certainly do not know that a man is anything more than an assemblage of physical things and processes, which act in accordance with those laws that describe the behavior of all other physical things and processes. Even though a man is a living being, of enormous complexity, there is nothing, apart from the requirements of this theory, to suggest that his behavior is so radically different in its origin from that of other physical objects, or that an understanding of it must be sought in some metaphysical realm wholly different from that appropriate to the understanding of non-living things.

Second, this conception of activity involves an extraordinary conception of causation, according to which an agent, which is a substance and not an event, can nevertheless be the cause of an event. Indeed, if he is a free agent then he can, on this conception, cause an event to occur—namely, some act of his own—without anything else causing him to do so. This means that an agent is sometimes a cause, without being an antecedent sufficient condition; for if I affirm that I am the cause of some act of mine, then I am plainly not saying that my very existence is sufficient for its occurrence, which would be absurd. If I say that my hand causes my pencil to move, then I am saying that the motion of my hand is, under the other conditions then prevailing, sufficient for the motion of the pencil. But if I then say that I cause my hand to move, I am not saying anything remotely like this, and surely not that the motion of my self is sufficient for the motion of my arm and hand, since these are the only things about me that are moving.

This conception of the causation of events by beings or substances that are not events is, in fact, so different from the usual philosophical conception of a cause that it should not even bear the same name, for "being a cause" ordinarily just means "being an antecedent sufficient condition or set of conditions." Instead, then, of speaking of agents as *causing* their own acts, it would perhaps be better to use another word entirely, and say, for instance, that they *originate* them, *initiate* them, or simply that they *perform* them.

Now this is on the face of it a dubious conception of what a man is. Yet it is consistent with our data, reflecting the presuppositions of deliberation, and appears to be the only conception that is consistent with them, as determinism and simple indeterminism are not. The theory of agency avoids the absurdities of simple indeterminism by conceding that human behavior is caused, while at the same time avoiding the difficulties of determinism by denying that every chain of causes and effects is infinite. Some such causal chains, on this view, have beginnings, and they begin with agents themselves. Moreover, if we are to suppose that it is sometimes up to me what I do, and understand this in a sense which is not consistent with determinism, we must suppose that I am an agent or a being who initiates his own actions, sometimes under conditions which do not determine what action he shall perform. Deliberation becomes, on this view, something that is not only possible but quite rational, for it does make sense to deliberate about activity that is truly my own and that depends in its outcome upon me as its author, and not merely upon something more or less esoteric that is supposed to be intimately associated with me, such as my thoughts, volitions, choices, or whatnot.

One can hardly affirm such a theory of agency with complete comfort, however, and wholly without embarrassment, for the conception of men and their powers which is involved in it is strange indeed, if not positively mysterious. In fact, one can hardly be blamed here for simply denying our data outright, rather than embracing this theory to which they do most certainly point. Our data—to the effect that men do sometimes deliberate before acting, and that when they do, they presuppose among other things that it is up to them what they are going to do—rest upon nothing more than fairly common consent. These data might simply be illusions. It might in fact be that no man ever deliberates, but only imagines that he does, that from pure conceit he supposes himself to be the master of his behavior and the author of his acts. Spinoza has suggested that if a stone, having been thrown into the air, were suddenly to become conscious, it would suppose itself to be the source of its own motion, being then conscious of what it was doing but not aware of the real cause of its behavior. Certainly men are *sometimes* mistaken in believing that they are behaving as a result of choice deliberately arrived at. A man might, for example, easily imagine that his embarking upon matrimony is the result of the most careful and rational deliberation, when in fact the causes, perfectly sufficient for that behavior, might be of an entirely physiological, unconscious origin. If it is sometimes false that we deliberate and then act as the result of a decision deliberately arrived at, even when we suppose it to be true, it might always be false. No one seems able, as we have noted, to describe deliberation without metaphors, and the conception of a thing's being "within one's power" or "up to him" seems to defy analysis or definition altogether, if taken in a sense which the theory of agency appears to require.

These are, then, dubitable conceptions, despite their being so well implanted in the common sense of mankind. Indeed, when we turn to the theory of fatalism, we shall find formidable metaphysical considerations which appear to rule them out altogether. Perhaps here, as elsewhere in metaphysics, we should be content with discovering difficulties, with seeing what is and what is not consistent with such convictions as we happen to have, and then drawing such satisfaction as we can from the realization that, no matter where we begin, the world is mysterious and the men who try to understand it are even more so. This realization can, with some justification, make one feel wise, even in the full realization of his ignorance.

⊚ CRITICAL QUESTION

1. Create an argument in support of the theory of agency. Be sure your argument meets the objection that such a theory is so strange that it is better, in the name of intellectual honesty, to regard both deliberation and the feeling that decisions are "up to me" as illusions and affirm, however reluctantly, that determinism is the best alternative.

11.3 WE ARE DETERMINED

One proposed solution to the problem of freedom and determinism is called hard **determinism**. Hard determinism holds that every event has a cause and that this fact is *incompatible* with free will. Nothing happens for which there is no sufficient reason; hence, free will is an illusion. People should not be held morally responsible for their actions since a given act is unavoidable if the appropriate antecedent conditions obtain. If we want to change people's behavior, we need to develop a science of behavior that will show us how to manipulate the causes of human behavior.

Notice that hard determinism is a form of simple determinism insofar as it holds that every event has a cause. However, unlike simple determinism, hard determinism claims, in addition, that determinism and free will are incompatible, that free will is an illusion, and that humans are not in fact responsible for what they do in the sense that they could have made choices other than they did.

Supporters of this position usually appeal to the physical sciences and concepts like "natural law" to back up their views. Science seeks to give a description of objective facts. It also seeks to discover uniformity in nature. That is, it seeks to explain facts by discovering the networks of cause and effect according to which events are ordered.

Two opposing tendencies drive our thoughts. On the one hand, we want to believe that some inner agent called the "I" controls what we do no matter what our genetic inheritance or life experiences. On the other hand, we want to know what makes us and others tick. We want science to tell us what accounts for addiction, intelligence, sexual preference, crime, and a host of other behaviors. Can we have it both ways? Can we believe both that some free agent called the self is responsible for people's actions and that there are factors beyond people's control that cause them to do what they do?

The hard determinist says we cannot have it both ways. Free will and determinism are incompatible. The idea of a free agent who is in control of what we do so that we could have done otherwise at many choice points in our lives is an illusion. It is a convenient fiction we maintain out of our desire to punish and blame others for wrongdoing and to congratulate ourselves for doing the right thing.

Robert Blatchford (1851–1943) believed in hard determinism and crusaded in England for that position. He argued that heredity and environment determine human behavior. Hence rewards and punishments should not be linked to the notion of responsibility. His arguments are aimed against a particular conception of free will, namely, that humans are free to do other than what their heredity and environment cause them to do. He did not deny that humans make choices and that they even make choices in accord with their wishes, desires, likes, and dislikes. Nor did he deny that many of the choices humans make are voluntary in the sense that no other person forced them to make a particular choice. All he denied is that humans are free to somehow rise above heredity and environment.

◉ READING QUESTIONS

1. According to Blatchford, what is the "point" that the free will discussion turns on?
2. What is Blatchford's main point?
3. What arguments did Blatchford present to support his main point?
4. Why, according to Blatchford, should we not blame someone for his or her conduct?

According to direct realism, as defined in Chapter 8's section, **Is Certainty Possible?**, we are directly in touch with the reality that exists apart from human sensations through our senses. In this image, the cherries are all about the same size but appear to be of different sizes: the closest to us appear to be larger. Such observations led to doubts about the validity of this theory.

Chapter 9's introduction invites us to examine how science might also illuminate our understanding of the world. This picture, taken in South Korea, shows a TV news report on the Fukushima-Daiichi Nuclear Power Plant, where an explosion took place and a meltdown was feared following the earthquake and Tsunami that hit Japan on Friday March 11th, 2011. What does scientific evidence say about the safety of nuclear power?

In Chapter 11, we are asked to ponder what the mind, the body, the brain are and what the relationship between them is. Are our brains nothing more than complex machines, that is, basically, computers, just like Watson who defeated two Jeopardy champions?

Buckingham Browne and Nichols School, Cambridge, MA

Chapter 13 introduces Deirdre McCloskey in her own words, in the excerpt *Crossing*. This photo shows Deirdre, who was born Donald McCloskey and cross-dressed for 41 years before proceeding to change gender. What do you think are areas of a person's life, beyond the physical and material realms, that gender identity affects?

Not Guilty

ROBERT BLATCHFORD

The free will delusion has been a stumbling block in the way of human thought for thousands of years. Let us try whether common sense and common knowledge cannot remove it. Free will is a subject of great importance to us in this case; and it is one we must come to with our eyes wide open and our wits wide awake; not because it is very difficult, but because it has been tied and twisted into a tangle of Gordian knots by twenty centuries full of wordy but unsuccessful philosophers.

The free will party claim that man is responsible for his acts, because his will is free to choose between right and wrong.

We reply that the will is not free, and that if it were free man could not know right from wrong until he was taught.

As to the knowledge of good and evil the free will party will claim that conscience is an unerring guide. But I have already proved that conscience does not and cannot tell us what is right and what is wrong: it only reminds us of the lessons we have learnt as to right and wrong.

The "still small voice" is not the voice of God: it is the voice of heredity and environment.

And now to the freedom of the will.

When a man says his will is free, he means that it is free of all control or interference: that it can overrule heredity and environment.

We reply that the will is ruled by heredity and environment.

The cause of all the confusion on this subject may be shown in a few words.

When the free will party say that man has a free will, they mean that he is free to act as he chooses to act.

There is no need to deny that. *But what causes him to choose?*

That is the pivot upon which the whole discussion turns.

The free will party seem to think of the will as something independent of the man, as something outside him. They seem to think that the will decides without the control of the man's reason.

If that were so, it would not prove the man responsible. "The will" would be responsible, and not the man. It would be as foolish to blame a man for the act of a "free" will, as to blame a horse for the action of its rider.

But I am going to prove to my readers, by appeals to their common sense and common knowledge, that the will is not free; and that it is ruled by heredity and environment.

To begin with, the average man will be against me. He knows that he chooses between two courses every hour, and often every minute, and he thinks his choice is free. But that is a delusion: his choice is not free. He can choose, and does choose. But he can only choose as his heredity and his environment cause him to choose. He never did choose and never will choose except as his heredity and his environment—his temperament and his training—cause him to choose. And his heredity and his environment have fixed his choice before he makes it.

The average man says "I know that I can act as I wish to act." But what causes him to wish? The free will party say, "We know that a man can and does choose between two acts." But what settles the choice?

There is a cause for every wish, a cause for every choice; and every cause of every wish and choice arises from heredity, or from environment.

For a man acts always from temperament, which is heredity, or from training, which is environment.

And in cases where a man hesitates in his choice between two acts, the hesitation is due to

From *Not Guilty* by Robert Blatchford (New York: Albert and Charles Boni, Inc., 1913), pp. 108–120, 130–131.

a conflict between his temperament and his train-ing, or as some would express it, "between his desire and his conscience."

A man is practising at a target with a gun, when a rabbit crosses his line of fire. The man has his eye and his sights on the rabbit, and his finger on the trigger. The man's will is free. If he presses the trigger the rabbit will be killed.

Now, how does the man decide whether or not he shall fire? He decides by feeling, and by reason.

He would like to fire, just to make sure that he could hit the mark. He would like to fire, because he would like to have the rabbit for sup-per. He would like to fire, because there is in him the old, old hunting instinct, to kill.

But the rabbit does not belong to him. He is not sure that he will not get into trouble if he kills it. Perhaps—if he is a very uncommon kind of man—he feels that it would be cruel and cowardly to shoot a helpless rabbit.

Well. The man's will is free. He can fire if he likes: he can let the rabbit go if he likes. How will he decide? On what does his decision depend?

His decision depends upon the relative strength of his desire to kill the rabbit, and of his scruples about cruelty, and the law.

Not only that, but, if we knew the man fairly well, we could guess how his free will would act before it acted. The average sporting Briton would kill the rabbit. But we know that there are men who on no account shoot any harmless wild creature.

Broadly put, we may say that the sportsman would will to fire, and that the humanitarian would not will to fire.

Now, as both their wills are free, it must be something outside the wills that makes the difference.

Well. The sportsman will kill, because he is a sportsman: the humanitarian will not kill, because he is a humanitarian.

And what makes one man a sportsman and another a humanitarian? Heredity and environ-ment: temperament and training.

One man is merciful, another cruel, by nature; or one is thoughtful and the other thoughtless, by nature. That is a difference of heredity.

One may have been taught all his life that to kill wild things is "sport"; the other may have been taught that it is inhuman and wrong: that is a difference of environment.

Now, the man by nature cruel or thoughtless, who has been trained to think of killing animals as sport, becomes what we call a sportsman, because heredity and environment have made him a sportsman.

The other man's heredity and environment have made him a humanitarian.

The sportsman kills the rabbit, because he is a sportsman, and he is a sportsman because heredity and environment have made him one.

That is to say the "free will" is really con-trolled by heredity and environment.

Allow me to give a case in point. A man who had never done any fishing was taken out by a fisherman. He liked the sport, and for some months followed it eagerly. But one day an acci-dent brought home to his mind the cruelty of catching fish with a hook, and he instantly laid down his rod, and never fished again.

Before the change he was always eager to go fishing if invited: after the change he could not be persuaded to touch a line. His will was free all the while. How was it that his will to fish changed to his will not to fish? It was the result of environ-ment. He had learnt that fishing was cruel. This knowledge controlled his will.

But, it may be asked, how do you account for a man doing the thing he does not wish to do? No man ever did a thing he did not wish to do. When there are two wishes the stronger rules.

Let us suppose a case. A young woman gets two letters by the same post; one is an invitation to go with her lover to a concert, the other is a request that she will visit a sick child in the slums. The girl is very fond of music, and is rather afraid of the slums. She wishes to go to the concert, and to be with her lover; she dreads the foul street and the dirty home, and shrinks from the risk of mea-sles or fever. But she goes to the sick child, and she foregoes the concert. Why?

Because her sense of duty is stronger than her self-love.

Now, her sense of duty is partly due to her nature—that is, to her heredity—but it is chiefly due to environment. Like all of us, this girl was born without any kind of knowledge, and with only the rudiments of a conscience. But she has been well taught, and the teaching is part of her environment.

We may say that the girl is free to act as she chooses, but she *does* act as she has been *taught* that she *ought* to act. This teaching, which is part of her environment, controls her will.

We may say that a man is free to act as he chooses. He is free to act as *he* chooses, but *he* will choose as heredity and environment cause *him* to choose. For heredity and environment have made him that which he is....

As we want to get this subject as clear as we can, let us take one or two familiar examples of the action of the will.

Jones and Robinson meet and have a glass of whisky. Jones asks Robinson to have another. Robinson says, "no thank you, one is enough." Jones says, "all right: have another cigarette." Robinson takes the cigarette. Now, here we have a case where a man refuses a second drink, but takes a second smoke. Is it because he would like another cigarette, but would not like another glass of whisky? No. It is because he knows that it is *safer* not to take another glass of whisky.

How does he know that whisky is dangerous? He has learnt it—from his environment.

"But he *could* have taken another glass if he wished."

But he could not wish to take another, because there was something he wished more strongly—to be safe.

And why did he want to be safe? Because he had learnt—from his environment—that it was unhealthy, unprofitable, and shameful to get drunk. Because he had learnt—from his environment—that it is easier to avoid forming a bad habit than to break a bad habit when formed. Because he valued the good opinion of his neighbors, and also his position and prospects.

These feelings and this knowledge ruled his will, and caused him to refuse the second glass. But there was no sense of danger, no well-learnt lesson of risk to check his will to smoke another cigarette. Heredity and environment did not warn

him against that. So, to please his friend, and himself, he accepted.

Now suppose Smith asks Williams to have another glass. Williams takes it, takes several, finally goes home—as he often goes home. Why?

Largely because drinking is a habit with him. And not only does the mind instinctively repeat an action, but, in the case of drink, a physical craving is set up, and the brain is weakened. It is easier to refuse the first glass than the second; easier to refuse the second than the third; and it is very much harder for a man to keep sober who has frequently got drunk.

So, when poor Williams has to make his choice, he has habit against him, he has a physical craving against him, and he has a weakened brain to think with.

"But Williams could have refused the first glass."

No. Because in this case the desire to drink, or to please a friend, was stronger than his fear of the danger. Or he may not have been so conscious of the danger as Robinson was. He may not have been so well taught, or he may not have been so sensible, or he may not have been so cautious. So that his heredity and environment, his temperament and training, led him to take the drink, as surely as Robinson's heredity and environment led him to refuse it.

And now, it is my turn to ask a question. If the will is "free," if conscience is a sure guide, how is it that the free will and the conscience of Robinson caused him to keep sober, while the free will and the conscience of Williams caused him to get drunk?

Robinson's will was curbed by certain feelings which failed to curb the will of Williams. Because in the case of Williams the feelings were stronger on the other side.

It was the nature and the training of Robinson which made him refuse the second glass, and it was the nature of the training of Williams which made him drink the second glass.

What had free will to do with it?

We are told that *every* man has a free will, and a conscience.

Now, if Williams had been Robinson, that is to say if his heredity and his environment had been exactly like Robinson's, he would have done exactly as Robinson did.

It was because his heredity and environment were not the same that his act was not the same. Both men had free wills. What made one do what the other refused to do?

Heredity and environment. To reverse their conduct we should have to reverse their heredity and environment....

And, again, as to that matter of belief. Some moralists hold that it is wicked not to believe certain things, and that men who do not believe those things will be punished.

But a man cannot believe a thing he is told to believe: he can only believe a thing which he *can* believe; and he can only believe that which his own reason tells him is true.

It would be no use asking Sir Roger Ball to believe that the earth is flat. He *could not* believe it.

It is no use asking an agnostic to believe the story of Jonah and the whale. He *could not* believe it. He might pretend to believe it. He might try to believe it. But his reason would not allow him to believe it.

Therefore it is a mistake to say that a man "knows better," when the fact is that he has been told "better" and cannot believe what he has been told.

That is a simple matter, and looks quite trivial; but how much ill-will, how much intolerance, how much violence, persecution, and murder have been caused by the strange idea that a man is wicked because *his* reason *cannot* believe that which to another man's reason seems quite true.

Free will has no power over a man's belief. A man cannot believe by will, but only by conviction. A man cannot be forced to believe. You may threaten him, wound him, beat him, burn him; and he may be frightened, or angered, or pained; but he cannot *believe,* nor can he be made to believe. Until he is convinced.

Now, truism as it may seem, I think it necessary to say here that a man cannot be convinced by abuse, nor by punishment. He can only be convinced by *reason.*

Yes. If we wish a man to believe a thing, we shall find a few words of reason more powerful than a million curses, or a million bayonets. To burn a man alive for failing to believe that the sun goes round the world is not to convince him. The fire is searching, but it does not seem to him to be relevant to the issue. He never doubted that fire would burn; but perchance his dying eyes may see the sun sinking down into the west, as the world rolls on its axis. He dies in his belief. And knows no "better."...

We are to ask whether it is true that everything a man does is the only thing he could do, at the instant of his doing it.

This is a very important question, because if the answer is yes, all praise and all blame are undeserved.

All praise and *all* blame.

Let us take some revolting action as a test.

A tramp has murdered a child on the highway, has robbed her of a few coppers, and has thrown her body into a ditch.

"Do you mean to say that tramp could not help doing that? Do you mean to say he is not to blame? Do you mean to say he is not to be punished?"

Yes. I say all those things; and if all those things are not true this book is not worth the paper it is printed on.

Prove it? I have proved it. But I have only instanced venial acts, and now we are confronted with murder. And the horror of murder drives men almost to frenzy, so that they cease to think: they can only feel.

Murder. Yes, a brutal murder. It comes upon us with a sickening shock. But I said in my first chapter that I proposed to defend those whom God and man condemn, and to demand justice for those whom God and man have wronged. I have to plead for the *bottom* dog: the lowest, the most detested, the worst.

The tramp has committed a murder. Man would loathe him, revile him, hang him: God would cast him into outer darkness.

"Not," cries the pious Christian, "if he repents."

I make a note of the repentance and pass on. The tramp has committed a murder.

It was a cowardly and cruel murder, and the motive was robbery.

But I have proved that all motives and all powers; all knowledge and capacity, all acts and all words, are caused by heredity and environment. I have proved that a man can only be good or bad as heredity and environment cause him to be good or bad; and I have proved these things because I have to claim that all punishments and rewards, all praise and blame, are undeserved.... Punishment has never been just, has never been effectual. Punishment has always failed of its purpose: the greater its severity, the more abject its failure.

Men cannot be made good and gentle by means of violence and wrong. The real tamers and purifiers of human hearts are love and charity and reason....

◉ CRITICAL QUESTIONS

1. Present the best counterargument you can to Blatchford's position.
2. If what you believe about the existence of free will is determined (as Blatchford claimed) by heredity and environment, why would Blatchford even try to convince you that hard determinism is true?

11.4 WE ARE FREE

Some of you may find hard determinism unconvincing. Some of you might still be wondering whether we are free in the sense that our choices are not always caused or determined by heredity or environment.

Libertarianism is the position that some human choices, in particular moral choices for which we are responsible, are not determined by antecedent events. (Note: This kind of libertarianism should not be confused with the political movement and theory of the same name.) One version of this theory holds that the self (sometimes called "soul") is an agent with a power to choose that transcends heredity and environment in the sense that the self can choose contrary to these factors. Another version holds that humans are radically free in the sense that they are free to create their own selves. The self is not a fixed essence determined by heredity, environment, or any other factor except our capacity for choice. We create who we are (ourselves) by the choices we make. It follows that humans, when freely deciding to act in a particular way, not only can be but also ought to be held responsible for what they do.

Jean-Paul Sartre (1905-1980) was a French novelist, playwright, and philosopher. In 1939 he was called up by the French army to fight the German invasion. He was captured by the Germans in 1940 but returned to France after the armistice and became active in the resistance movement. After the war, he emerged as a leading French intellectual, a major figure in the philosophical movement called **existentialism**, and he became involved in a number of radical causes. His major philosophical work is *Being and Nothingness* (1943).

In 1945 Sartre gave a lecture that was published the following year as *L'Existentialisme est un Humanisme*. The selection that follows is from that lecture. Sartre was not only concerned with defining existentialism and defending it against its critics, but he was also concerned with free choice. Sartre realized that, if human nature is not something determined beforehand but is something we create as we make the decisions that come to constitute our lives, we are radically free. This is central to the existentialist view of human beings and, as Sartre also clearly realized, has important implications for ethics. If you are free to do whatever you wish, if for you everything is permissible, then what will you do?

◉ READING QUESTIONS

1. What does *existence precedes essence* mean?
2. What is the first principle of existentialism?
3. Why did Sartre claim that "in choosing myself, I choose man"?
4. What is meant by *anguish*?
5. What does *forlornness* mean?
6. Why did Sartre say we are condemned to be free?
7. What does Sartre mean by *despair*?

Existentialism

JEAN-PAUL SARTRE

What is meant by the term existentialism? Most people who use the word would be rather embarrassed if they had to explain it, since, now that the word is all the rage, even the work of a musician or painter is being called existentialist. A gossip columnist in *Clartés* signs himself *The Existentialist*, so that by this time the word has been so stretched and has taken on so broad a meaning that it no longer means anything at all. It seems that for want of an advance-guard doctrine analogous to surrealism, the kind of people who are eager for scandal and flurry turn to this philosophy which in other respects does not at all serve their purposes in this sphere.

Actually, it is the least scandalous, the most austere of doctrines. It is intended strictly for specialists and philosophers. Yet it can be defined easily. What complicates matters is that there are two kinds of existentialist; first, those who are Christian, among whom I would include Jaspers and Gabriel Marcel, both Catholic; and on the other hand the atheistic existentialists, among whom I class Heidegger, and then the French existentialists and myself. What they have in common is that they think that existence precedes essence, or, if you prefer, that subjectivity must be the starting point.

Just what does that mean? Let us consider some object that is manufactured, for example, a book or a paper-cutter: here is an object which has been made by an artisan whose inspiration came from a concept. He referred to the concept of what a paper-cutter is and likewise to a known method of production, which is part of the concept, something which is, by and large, a routine. Thus, the paper-cutter is at once an object produced in a certain way and, on the other hand, one having a specific use; and one can not postulate a man who produces a paper-cutter but does not know what it is used for. Therefore, let us say that, for the paper-cutter, essence—that is, the ensemble of both the production routines and the properties which enable it to be both produced and defined—precedes existence. Thus, the presence of the paper-cutter or book in front of me is determined. Therefore, we have here a technical view of the world whereby it can be said that production precedes existence.

When we conceive God as the Creator, He is generally thought of as a superior sort of artisan. Whatever doctrine we may be considering, whether one like that of Descartes or that of Leibniz, we always grant that will more or less follows understanding or, at the very least, accompanies it, and that when God creates He knows exactly what He is creating. Thus, the concept of man in the mind of God is comparable to the concept of paper-cutter in the mind of the manufacturer, and, following certain techniques and a conception, God produces man, just as the artisan, following a definition and a technique, makes a paper-cutter. Thus, the individual man is the realization of a certain concept in the divine intelligence.

Jean-Paul Sartre, *Existentialism*, translated by Bernard Frechtman (New York: The Philosophical Library, 1947), pp. 14–42. Reprinted by permission of The Philosophical Library, Inc.

In the eighteenth century, the atheism of the *philosophes* discarded the idea of God, but not so much for the notion that essence precedes existence. To a certain extent, this idea is found everywhere; we find it in Diderot, in Voltaire, and even in Kant. Man has a human nature; this human nature, which is the concept of the human, is found in all men, which means that each man is a particular example of a universal concept, man. In Kant, the result of this universality is that the wild-man, the natural man, as well as the bourgeois, are circumscribed by the same definition and have the same basic qualities. Thus, here too the essence of man precedes the historical existence that we find in nature.

Atheistic existentialism, which I represent, is more coherent. It states that if God does not exist, there is at least one being in whom existence precedes essence, a being who exists before he can be defined by any concept, and that this being is man, or, as Heidegger says, human reality. What is meant here by saying that existence precedes essence? It means that, first of all, man exists, turns up, appears on the scene, and, only afterwards, defines himself. If man, as the existentialist conceives him, is indefinable, it is because at first he is nothing. Only afterward will he be something, and he himself will have made what he will be. Thus, there is no human nature, since there is no God to conceive it. Not only is man what he conceives himself to be, but he is also only what he wills himself to be after this thrust toward existence.

Man is nothing else but what he makes of himself. Such is the first principle of existentialism. It is also what is called subjectivity, the name we are labeled with when charges are brought against us. But what do we mean by this, if not that man has a greater dignity than a stone or table? For we mean that man first exists, that is, that man first of all is the being who hurls himself toward a future and who is conscious of imagining himself as being in the future. Man is at the start a plan which is aware of itself, rather than a patch of moss, a piece of garbage, or a cauliflower; nothing exists prior to this plan; there is nothing in heaven; man will be what he will have planned to be. Not what he will want to be. Because by the word

"will" we generally mean a conscious decision, which is subsequent to what we have already made of ourselves. I may want to belong to a political party, write a book, get married; but all that is only a manifestation of an earlier, more spontaneous choice that is called "will." But if existence really does precede essence, man is responsible for what he is. Thus, existentialism's first move is to make every man aware of what he is and to make the full responsibility of his existence rest on him. And when we say that a man is responsible for himself, we do not only mean that he is responsible for his own individuality, but that he is responsible for all men.

The word subjectivism has two meanings, and our opponents play on the two. Subjectivism means, on the one hand, that an individual chooses and makes himself; and, on the other, that it is impossible for man to transcend human subjectivity. The second of these is the essential meaning of existentialism. When we say that man chooses his own self, we mean that every one of us does likewise; but we also mean by that that in making this choice he also chooses all men. In fact, in creating the man that we want to be, there is not a single one of our acts which does not at the same time create an image of man as we think he ought to be. To choose to be this or that is to affirm at the same time the value of what we choose, because we can never choose evil. We always choose the good, and nothing can be good for us without being good for all. If, on the other hand, existence precedes essence, and if we grant that we exist and fashion our image at one and the same time, the image is valid for everybody and for our whole age. Thus, our responsibility is much greater than we might have supposed, because it involves all mankind. If I am a working man and choose to join a Christian trade-union rather than be a communist, and if by being a member I want to show that the best thing for man is resignation, that the kingdom of man is not of this world, I am not only involving my own case—I want to be resigned for everyone. As a result, my action has involved all humanity. To take a more individual matter, if I want to marry, to have children; even if this marriage depends solely on my own circumstances or passion or wish, I am involving all humanity in monogamy and not merely myself. Therefore, I am responsible for myself and for everyone else. I am creating a certain image of man of my own choosing. In choosing myself, I choose man.

This helps us understand what the actual content is of such rather grandiloquent words as anguish, forlornness, despair. As you will see, it's all quite simple.

First, what is meant by anguish? The existentialists say at once that man is anguish. What that means is this: the man who involves himself and who realizes that he is not only the person he chooses to be, but also a law-maker who is, at the same time, choosing all mankind as well as himself, can not help escape the feeling of his total and deep responsibility. Of course, there are many people who are not anxious; but we claim that they are hiding their anxiety, that they are fleeing from it. Certainly, many people believe that when they do something, they themselves are the only ones involved, and when someone says to them, "What if everyone acted that way?" they shrug their shoulders and answer, "Everyone doesn't act that way." But really, one should always ask himself, "What would happen if everybody looked at things that way?" There is no escaping this disturbing thought except by a kind of double-dealing. A man who lies and makes excuses for himself by saying "not everybody does that," is someone with an uneasy conscience, because the act of lying implies that a universal value is conferred upon the lie.

Anguish is evident even when it conceals itself. This is the anguish that Kierkegaard called the anguish of Abraham. You know the story: an angel has ordered Abraham to sacrifice his son; if it really were an angel who has come and said, "You are Abraham, you shall sacrifice your son," everything would be all right. But everyone might first wonder, "Is it really an angel, and am I really Abraham? What proof do I have?"

There was a madwoman who had hallucinations; someone used to speak to her on the telephone and give her orders. Her doctor asked her, "Who is it who talks to you?" She answered, "He says it's God." What proof did she really have that it was God? If an angel comes to me, what proof is

there that it's an angel? And if I hear voices, what proof is there that they come from heaven and not from hell, or from the subconscious, or a pathological condition? What proves that they are addressed to me? What proof is there that I have been appointed to impose my choice and my conception of man on humanity? I'll never find any proof or sign to convince me of that. If a voice addresses me, it is always for me to decide that this is the angel's voice; if I consider that such an act is a good one, it is I who will choose to say that it is good rather than bad. Now, I'm not being singled out as an Abraham, and yet at every moment I'm obliged to perform exemplary acts. For every man, everything happens as if all mankind had its eyes fixed on him and were guiding itself by what he does. And every man ought to say to himself, "Am I really the kind of man who has the right to act in such a way that humanity might guide itself by my actions?" And if he does not say that to himself, he is masking his anguish.

There is no question here of the kind of anguish which would lead to quietism, to inaction. It is a matter of a simple sort of anguish that anybody who has had responsibilities is familiar with. For example, when a military officer takes the responsibility for an attack and sends a certain number of men to death, he chooses to do so, and in the main he alone makes the choice. Doubtless, orders come from above, but they are too broad; he interprets them, and on this interpretation depend the lives of ten or fourteen or twenty men. In making a decision he can not help having a certain anguish. All leaders know this anguish. That doesn't keep them from acting; on the contrary, it is the very condition of their action. For it implies that they envisage a number of possibilities, and when they choose one, they realize that it has value only because it is chosen. We shall see that this kind of anguish, which is the kind that existentialism describes, is explained, in addition, by a direct responsibility to the other men whom it involves. It is not a curtain separating us from action, but is part of action itself.

When we speak of forlornness, a term Heidegger was fond of, we mean only that God does not exist and that we have to face all the consequences of this. The existentialist is strongly opposed to a certain kind of secular ethics which would like to abolish God with the least possible expense. About 1880, some French teachers tried to set up a secular ethics which went something like this: God is a useless and costly hypothesis; we are discarding it; but, meanwhile, in order for there to be an ethics, a society, a civilization, it is essential that certain values be taken seriously and that they be considered as having an *a priori* existence. It must be obligatory, *a priori,* to be honest, not to lie, not to beat your wife, to have children, etc. So we're going to try a little device which will make it possible to show that values exist all the same, inscribed in a heaven of ideas, though otherwise God does not exist. In other words—and this, I believe, is the tendency of everything called reformism in France—nothing will be changed if God does not exist. We shall find ourselves with the same norms of honesty, progress, and humanism, and we shall have made of God an outdated hypothesis which will peacefully die off by itself.

The existentialist, on the contrary, thinks it very distressing that God does not exist, because all possibility of finding values in a heaven of ideas disappears along with Him; there can no longer be an *a priori* Good, since there is no infinite and perfect consciousness to think it. Nowhere is it written that the Good exists, that we must be honest, that we must not lie; because the fact is we are on a plane where there are only men. Dostoievsky said, "If God didn't exist, everything would be possible." That is the very starting point of existentialism. Indeed, everything is permissible if God does not exist, and as a result man is forlorn, because neither within him or without does he find anything to cling to. He can't start making excuses for himself.

If existence really does precede essence, there is no explaining things away by reference to a fixed and given human nature. In other words, there is no determinism, man is free, man is freedom. On the other hand, if God does not exist, we find no values or commands to turn to which legitimize our conduct. So, in the bright realm of values, we have no excuse behind us, nor justification before us. We are alone, with no excuses.

That is the idea I shall try to convey when I say that man is condemned to be free. Condemned, because he did not create himself, yet, in other respects is free; because, once thrown into the world, he is responsible for everything he does. The existentialist does not believe in the power of passion. He will never agree that a sweeping passion is a ravaging torrent which fatally leads a man to certain acts and is therefore an excuse. He thinks that man is responsible for his passion.

The existentialist does not think that man is going to help himself by finding in the world some omen by which to orient himself. Because he thinks that man will interpret the omen to suit himself. Therefore, he thinks that man, with no support and no aid, is condemned every moment to invent man. Ponge, in a very fine article, has said, "Man is the future of man." That's exactly it. But if it is taken to mean that this future is recorded in heaven, that God sees it, then it is false, because it would really no longer be a future. If it is taken to mean that, whatever a man may be, there is a future to be forged, a virgin future before him, then this remark is sound. But then we are forlorn.

To give you an example which will enable you to understand forlornness better, I shall cite the case of one of my students who came to see me under the following circumstances: His father was on bad terms with his mother, and, moreover, was inclined to be a collaborationist; his older brother had been killed in the German offensive of 1940, and the young man, with somewhat immature but generous feelings, wanted to avenge him. His mother lived alone with him, very much upset by the half-treason of her husband and the death of her older son; the boy was her only consolation.

The boy was faced with the choice of leaving for England and joining the Free French Forces—that is, leaving his mother behind—or remaining with his mother and helping her to carry on. He was fully aware that the woman lived only for him and that his going-off—and perhaps his death—would plunge her into despair. He was also aware that every act that he did for his mother's sake was a sure thing, in the sense that it was helping her to carry on, whereas every effort he made toward going off and fighting was an uncertain move which might run aground and prove completely useless; for example, on his way to England he might, while passing through Spain, be detained indefinitely in a Spanish camp; he might reach England or Algiers and be stuck in an office at a desk job. As a result, he was faced with two very different kinds of action: one, concrete, immediate, but concerning only one individual; the other concerned an incomparably vaster group, a national collectivity, but for that very reason was dubious, and might be interrupted en route. And, at the same time, he was wavering between two kinds of ethics. On the one hand, an ethics of sympathy, of personal devotion; on the other, a broader ethics, but one whose efficacy was more dubious. He had to choose between the two.

Who could help him choose? Christian doctrine? No. Christian doctrine says, "Be charitable, love your neighbor, take the more rugged path, etc." But which is the more rugged path? Whom should he love as a brother? The fighting man or his mother? Which does the greater good, the vague act of fighting in a group, or the concrete one of helping a particular human being to go on living? Who can decide *a priori*? Nobody. No book of ethics can tell him. The Kantian ethics says, "Never treat any person as a means, but as an end." Very well, if I stay with my mother, I'll treat her as an end and not as a means; but by virtue of this very fact, I'm running the risk of treating the people around me who are fighting, as means; and, conversely, if I go to join those who are fighting, I'll be treating them as an end, and, by doing that, I run the risk of treating my mother as a means.

If values are vague, and if they are always too broad for the concrete and specific case that we are considering, the only thing left for us is to trust our instincts. That's what this young man tried to do; and when I saw him, he said, "In the end, feeling is what counts. I ought to choose whichever pushes me in one direction. If I feel that I love my mother enough to sacrifice everything else for her—my desire for vengeance, for action, for adventure—then I'll stay with her. If, on the contrary, I feel that my love for my mother isn't enough, I'll leave."

But how is the value of a feeling determined? What gives his feeling for his mother value? Precisely the fact that he remained with her. I may say that I like so-and-so well enough to sacrifice a certain amount of money for him, but I may say so only if I've done it. I may say "I love my mother well enough to remain with her" if I have remained with her. The only way to determine the value of this affection is, precisely, to perform an act which confirms and defines it. But, since I require this affection to justify my act, I find myself caught in a vicious circle.

On the other hand, Gide has well said that a mock feeling and a true feeling are almost indistinguishable; to decide that I love my mother and will remain with her, or to remain with her by putting on an act, amount somewhat to the same thing. In other words, the feeling is formed by the acts one performs; so, I can not refer to it in order to act upon it. Which means that I can neither seek within myself the true condition which will impel me to act, nor apply to a system of ethics for concepts which will permit me to act. You will say, "At least, he did go to a teacher for advice." But if you seek advice from a priest, for example, you have chosen this priest; you already knew, more or less, just about what advice he was going to give you. In other words, choosing your adviser is involving yourself. The proof of this is that if you are a Christian, you will say, "Consult a priest." But some priests are collaborating, some are just marking time, some are resisting. Which to choose? If the young man chooses a priest who is resisting or collaborating, he has already decided on the kind of advice he's going to get. Therefore, in coming to see me he knew the answer I was going to give him, and I had only one answer to give: "You're free; choose, that is, invent." No general ethics can show you what is to be done; there are no omens in the world. The Catholics will reply, "But there are." Granted—but, in any case, I myself choose the meaning they have.

When I was a prisoner, I knew a rather remarkable young man who was a Jesuit. He had entered the Jesuit order in the following way: he had had a number of very bad breaks; in childhood, his father died, leaving him in poverty, and he was a scholarship student at a religious institution where he was constantly made to feel that he was being kept out of charity; then, he failed to get any of the honors and distinctions that children like; later on, at about eighteen, he bungled a love affair; finally, at twenty-two, he failed in military training, a childish enough matter, but it was the last straw.

This young fellow might well have felt that he had botched everything. It was a sign of something, but of what? He might have taken refuge in bitterness or despair. But he very wisely looked upon all this as a sign that he was not made for secular triumphs, and that only the triumphs of religion, holiness, and faith were open to him. He saw the hand of God in all this, and so he entered the order. Who can help seeing that he alone decided what the sign meant?

Some other interpretation might have been drawn from this series of setbacks; for example, that he might have done better to turn carpenter or revolutionist. Therefore, he is fully responsible for the interpretation. Forlornness implies that we ourselves choose our being. Forlornness and anguish go together.

As for despair, the term has a very simple meaning. It means that we shall confine ourselves to reckoning only with what depends upon our will, or on the ensemble of probabilities which make our action possible. When we want something, we always have to reckon with probabilities. I may be counting on the arrival of a friend. The friend is coming by rail or street-car; this supposes that the train will arrive on schedule, or that the street-car will not jump the track. I am left in the realm of possibility; but possibilities are to be reckoned with only to the point where my action comports with the ensemble of these possibilities, and no further. The moment the possibilities I am considering are not rigorously involved by my action, I ought to disengage myself from them, because no God, no scheme, can adapt the world and its possibilities to my will. When Descartes said, "Conquer yourself rather than the world," he meant essentially the same thing.

The Marxists to whom I have spoken reply, "You can rely on the support of others in your action, which obviously has certain limits because you're not going to live forever. That means: rely on both what others are doing elsewhere to help you, in China, in Russia, and what they will do later on, after your death, to carry on the action and lead it to its fulfillment, which will be the revolution. You even *have* to rely upon that, otherwise you're immoral." I reply at once that I will always rely on fellow-fighters insofar as these comrades are involved with me in a common struggle, in the unity of a party or a group in which I can more or less make my weight felt; that is, one whose ranks I am in as a fighter and whose movements I am aware of at every moment. In such a situation, relying on the unity and will of the party is exactly like counting on the fact that the train will arrive on time or that the car won't jump the track. But, given that man is free and that there is no human nature for me to depend on, I can not count on men whom I do not know by relying on human goodness or man's concern for the good of society. I don't know what will become of the Russian revolution; I may make an example of it to the extent that at the present time it is apparent that the proletariat plays a part in Russia that it plays in no other nation. But I can't swear that this will inevitably lead to a triumph of the proletariat. I've got to limit myself to what I see.

Given that men are free and that tomorrow they will freely decide what man will be, I can not be sure that, after my death, fellow-fighters will carry on my work to bring it to its maximum perfection. Tomorrow, after my death, some men may decide to set up Fascism, and the others may be cowardly and muddled enough to let them do it. Fascism will then be the human reality, so much the worse for us.

Actually, things will be as man will have decided they are to be. Does that mean that I should abandon myself to quietism? No. First, I should involve myself; then, act on the old saw, "Nothing ventured, nothing gained." Nor does it mean that I shouldn't belong to a party, but rather that I shall have no illusions and shall do what I can. For example, suppose I ask myself, "Will socialization, as such, ever come about?" I know nothing about it. All I know is that I'm going to do everything in my power to bring it about. Beyond that, I can't count on anything. Quietism is the attitude of people who say, "Let others do what I can't do." The doctrine I am presenting is the very opposite of quietism, since it declares, "There is no reality except in action." Moreover, it goes further, since it adds, "Man is nothing else than his plan; he exists only to the extent that he fulfills himself; he is therefore nothing else than the ensemble of his acts, nothing else than his life."

According to this, we can understand why our doctrine horrifies certain people. Because often the only way they can bear their wretchedness is to think, "Circumstances have been against me. What I've been and done doesn't show my true worth. To be sure, I've had no great love, no great friendship, but that's because I haven't met a man or woman who was worthy. The books I've written haven't been very good because I haven't had the proper leisure. I haven't had children to devote myself to because I didn't find a man with whom I could have spent my life. So there remains within me, unused and quite viable, a host of propensities, inclinations, possibilities, that one wouldn't guess from, the mere series of things I've done."

Now, for the existentialist there is really no love other than one which manifests itself in a person's being in love. There is no genius other than one which is expressed in works of art; the genius of Proust is the sum of Proust's works; the genius of Racine is his series of tragedies. Outside of that, there is nothing. Why say that Racine could have written another tragedy, when he didn't write it? A man is involved in life, leaves his impress on it, and outside of that there is nothing. To be sure, this may seem a harsh thought to someone whose life hasn't been a success. But, on the other hand, it prompts people to understand that reality alone is what counts, that dreams, expectations, and hopes warrant no more than to define a man as a disappointed dream, as miscarried hopes, as vain expectations. In other words, to define him negatively and not positively. However, when we say, "You are nothing else than your life," that does not imply that the artist will be judged solely on the basis of his works of art; a thousand other things will contribute toward summing him up. What we mean is that a man is nothing else than a

series of undertakings, that he is the sum, the organization, the ensemble of the relationships which make up these undertakings.

When all is said and done, what we are accused of, at bottom, is not our pessimism, but an optimistic toughness. If people throw up to us our works of fiction in which we write about people who are soft, weak, cowardly, and sometimes even downright bad, it's not because these people are soft, weak, cowardly, or bad; because if we were to say, as Zola did, that they are that way because of heredity, the workings of environment, society, because of biological or psychological determinism, people would be reassured. They would say, "Well, that's what we're like, no one can do anything about it." But when the existentialist writes about a coward, he says that this coward is responsible for his cowardice. He's not like that because he has a cowardly heart or lung or brain; he's not like that on account of his physiological makeup; but he's like that because he has made himself a coward by his acts. There's no such thing as a cowardly constitution; there are nervous constitutions; there is poor blood, as the common people say, or strong constitutions. But the man whose blood is poor is not a coward on that account, for what makes cowardice is the act of renouncing or yielding. A constitution is not an act; the coward is defined on the basis of the acts he performs. People feel, in a vague sort of way, that this coward we're talking about is guilty of being a coward, and the thought frightens them. What people would like is that a coward or a hero be born that way.

One of the complaints most frequently made about *The Ways of Freedom*[1] can be summed up as follows: "After all, these people are so spineless, how are you going to make heroes out of them?" This objection almost makes me laugh, for it assumes that people are born heroes. That's what people really want to think. If you're born cowardly, you may set your mind perfectly at rest; there's nothing you can do about it; you'll be cowardly all your life, whatever you may

---

[1] *Les Chemins de la Liberté*. M. Sartre's projected trilogy of novels, two of which, *L'Age de Raison (The Age of Reason)* and *Le Sursis (The Reprieve)* have already appeared.—Translator's note.

do. If you're born a hero, you may set your mind just as much at rest; you'll be a hero all your life; you'll drink like a hero and eat like a hero. What the existentialist says is that the coward makes himself cowardly, that the hero makes himself heroic. There's always a possibility for the coward not to be cowardly any more and for the hero to stop being heroic. What counts is total involvement; some one particular action or set of circumstances is not total involvement.

Thus, I think we have answered a number of the charges concerning existentialism. You see

that it can not be taken for a philosophy of quietism, since it defines man in terms of action; nor for a pessimistic description of man—there is no doctrine more optimistic, since man's destiny is within himself; nor for an attempt to discourage man from acting, since it tells him that the only hope is in his acting and that action is the only thing that enables a man to live. Consequently, we are dealing here with an ethics of action and involvement....

CRITICAL QUESTIONS

1. Do you agree with the assertion that "everything is permissible if God does not exist"? Why, or why not?
2. If we create moral value and there is no guarantee that our values are correct or will produce good

results, why bother to become socially and politically involved at all? How did Sartre answer this question? Do you agree with his answer? Support your answer with the best argument you can.

11.5 KARMA AND FREEDOM

The contemporary Western discussion of the problem of freedom and determinism usually takes place in the context of the natural and social sciences. Many philosophers believe that some type of determinism is one of the basic assumptions of science. If it is, then the scene is set for a conflict between a scientific view and the moral or religious view of human freedom and responsibility. The law of causality, as understood by science, is an amoral law. That is, it operates regardless of moral considerations. The social or behavioral sciences (psychology, sociology, anthropology, economics, and history) have extended this view to human behavior. They assume that human action, like physical action, is understandable only when the causal factors determining such action are described and explained by reference to some kind of "natural" law.

In the Asian (primarily Indian) context, the discussion of the problem of freedom and determinism often takes place in a moral and religious context. The law of causality that concerns much Indian and Buddhist philosophy is moral, not amoral. Very early in Indian philosophy (500 BCE?), the idea of the *law of karma* developed. This law states that as each of us sows, so shall we reap. If this law is valid, then your past and present actions determine your future spiritual, moral, and physical conditions. If there is a life beyond this one, then your actions also determine it.

The teaching of karma posits the existence of a perfect law of moral justice that operates automatically within the universe. Habitual liars in this life, for example, will pay for lying in the future. Perhaps they will be falsely accused at some future date or, when reborn, will have relatives who lie, cheat, and deceive them. In contrast, an honest person will be treated honestly by others.

The law of karma provides a good deal of comfort. It assures us that the universe is a just place. It tells us that evil people and good people will eventually get their just deserts. However, the notion of karma also raises questions about human freedom. If what is happening to me now is the effect of my own actions in the past, how can I be free? Are not my life and the circumstances of my life determined? It seems to be the case, according to the law of karma, that, for example, if you are poor, this condition is due to what you did in the past, and hence, it would seem, you are no more in control of your poverty than you are in control of the orbit of Earth.

Some Indian philosophers have drawn fatalistic conclusions from the doctrine of karma and have denied human freedom. The majority of Indian philosophers, however, have affirmed human freedom and argued that freedom and karma are compatible ideas. One such philosopher was Sarvepalli Radhakrishnan (1888–1975), a scholar and statesman who held chairs of philosophy at several Indian universities and was president of India from 1962 until 1967. He was a leading exponent of neo-Hinduism, maintaining that all religions are but different expressions of one truth and that spiritual reality is more fundamental than material reality. The following selection comes from his book *An Idealist View of Life*, which contains his Hibbert lectures given in 1929 and 1930.

Radhakrishnan supports a type of libertarianism. Though he believes that human action is determined to a large extent (and hence would not subscribe to Sartre's radical libertarianism), he also believes in self-determination. If a choice is caused by the whole self, rather than part of the self (such as character or environment), such choice is free. In other words, he subscribes to what is often called *agent causation*. When your self (not a part of your self but your whole self) is the agent that causes you to choose and act, then you are free. A crucial question now becomes, what is the self?

◉ READING QUESTIONS

1. According to Radhakrishnan, what is the law of karma?
2. What are the two aspects of karma?
3. How did Radhakrishnan define *freedom of the will*?
4. According to Radhakrishnan, what is *self-determination*?
5. How did he respond to the argument that self-determination is not really freedom?
6. According to Radhakrishnan, what is *choice*?

Karma and Freedom

SARVEPALLI RADHAKRISHNAN

The two pervasive features of all nature, connection with the past and creation of the future, are present in the human level. The connection with the past at the human stage is denoted by the word "Karma" in the Hindu systems. The human individual is a self-conscious, efficient portion of universal nature with his own uniqueness. His history stretching back to an indefinite period of time binds him with the physical and vital conditions of the world. Human life is an organic whole where

From *An Idealist View of Life* by S. Radhakrishnan (London: George Allen & Unwin, 1932), pp. 274–281. Reprinted by kind permission of The Hibbert Trust.

each successive phase grows out of what has gone before. We are what we are on account of our affinity with the past. Human growth is an ordered one and its orderedness is indicated by saying that it is governed by the law of Karma.

Karma literally means action, deed. All acts produce their effects which are recorded both in the organism and the environment. Their physical effects may be short-lived but their moral effects (samskāra) are worked into the character of the self. Every single thought, word and deed enters into the living chain of causes which makes us what we are. Our life is not at the mercy of blind chance or capricious fate. The conception is not peculiar to the Oriental creeds. The Christian Scriptures refer to it. "Be not deceived; God is not mocked: for whatsoever a man soweth, that shall he also reap." Jesus is reported to have said on the Mount, "Judge not that ye be not judged, for with what judgment ye judge, ye shall be judged, and with what measure ye mete, it shall be measured to you again."

Karma is not so much a principle of retribution as one of continuity. Good produces good, evil, evil. Love increases our power of love, hatred our power of hatred. It emphasizes the great importance of right action. Man is continuously shaping his own self. The law of Karma is not to be confused with either a hedonistic or a juridical theory of rewards and punishments. The reward for virtue is not a life of pleasure nor is the punishment for sin pain. Pleasure and pain may govern the animal nature of man but not his human. Love which is a joy in itself suffers; hatred too often means a perverse kind of satisfaction. Good and evil are not to be confused with material well-being and physical suffering.

All things in the world are at once causes and effects. They embody the energy of the past and exert energy on the future. Karma or connection with the past is not inconsistent with creative freedom. On the other hand it is implied by it. The law that links us with the past also asserts that it can be subjugated by our free action. Though the past may present obstacles, they must all yield to the creative power in man in proportion to its sincerity and insistence. The law of Karma says that each individual will get the return according to the energy he puts forth. The universe will respond to and implement the demands of the self. Nature will reply to the insistent call of spirit. "As is his desire, such is his purpose; as is his purpose, such is the action he performs; what action he performs, that he procures for himself." "Verily I say unto you that whoever shall say to this mountain, 'Be lifted up and cast into the sea,' and shall not doubt in his heart but believe fully that what he says shall be, it shall be done for him." When Jesus said, "Destroy this temple and I will raise it again in three days" he is asserting the truth that the spirit within us is mightier than the world of things. There is nothing we cannot achieve if we want it enough. Subjection to spirit is the law of universal nature. The principle of Karma has thus two aspects, a retrospective and a prospective, continuity with the past and creative freedom of the self.

The urge in nature which seeks not only to maintain itself at a particular level but advance to a higher becomes conscious in man who deliberately seeks after rules of life and principles of progress. "My father worketh hitherto, and I work." Human beings are the first among nature's children who can say "I" and consciously collaborate with the "father," the power that controls and directs nature, in the fashioning of the world. They can substitute rational direction for the slow, dark, blundering growth of the subhuman world. We cannot deny the free action of human beings however much their origin may be veiled in darkness. The self has conative tendencies, impulses to change by its efforts the given conditions, inner and outer, and shape them to its own purpose.

The problem of human freedom is confused somewhat by the distinction between the self and the will. The will is only the self in its active side and freedom of the will really means the freedom of the self. It is determination by the self.

It is argued that self-determination is not really freedom. It makes little difference whether the self is moved from without or from within. A spinning top moved from within by a spring is as mechanical as one whipped into motion from without. The self may well be an animated automaton. A drunkard who takes to his glass habitually does so in obedience to an element in his nature.

The habit has become a part of his self. If we ana-lyze the contents of the self, many of them are traceable to the influence of the environment and the inheritance from the past. If the indi-vidual's view and character are the product of a long evolution, his actions which are the outcome of these cannot be free. The feeling of freedom may be an illusion of the self which lives in each moment of the present, ignoring the determining past. In answer to these difficulties, it may be said that the self represents a form of relatedness or organization, closer and more intimate than that which is found in animal, plant or atom. Self-determination means not determination by any fragment of the self's nature but by the whole of it. Unless the individual employs his whole nature, searches the different possibilities and selects one which commends itself to his whole self, the act is not really free.

Sheer necessity is not to be found in any aspect of nature; complete freedom is divine and possible only when the self becomes co-extensive with the whole. Human freedom is a matter of degree. We are most free when our whole self is active and not merely a fragment of it. We generally act according to our conventional or habitual self and sometimes we sink to the level of our subnormal self.

Freedom is not caprice, nor is Karma neces-sity. Human choice is not unmotivated or uncaused. If our acts were irrelevant to our past, then there would be no moral responsibility or scope for improvement. Undetermined begin-nings, upstart events are impossible either in the physical or the human world. Free acts cannot negate continuity. They arise within the order of nature. Freedom is not caprice since we carry our past with us. The character, at any given point, is the condensation of our previous history. What we have been enters into the "me" which is now active and choosing. The range of one's natural freedom of action is limited. No man has the uni-versal field of possibilities for himself. The varied possibilities of our nature do not all get a chance and the cosmic has its influence in permitting the development of certain possibilities and closing down others. Again, freedom is dogged by automatism. When we make up our mind to do a thing, our mind is different from what it was

before. When a possibility becomes an actuality, it assumes the character of necessity. The past can never be cancelled, though it may be utilized. Mere defiance of the given may mean disaster, though we can make a new life spring up from the past. Only the possible is the sphere of free-dom. We have a good deal of present constraint and previous necessity in human life. But necessity is not to be mistaken for destiny which we can neither defy nor delude. Though the self is not free from the bonds of determination, it can sub-jugate the past to a certain extent and turn it into a new course. Choice is the assertion of freedom over necessity by which it converts necessity to its own use and thus frees itself from it. "The human agent is free." He is not the plaything of fate or driftwood on the tide of uncontrolled events. He can actively mould the future instead of passively suffering the past. The past may become either an opportunity or an obstacle. Everything depends on what we make of it and not what it makes of us. Life is not bound to move in a specific direc-tion. Life is a growth and a growth is undeter-mined in a measure. Though the future is the sequel of the past, we cannot say what it will be. If there is no indetermination, then human con-sciousness is an unnecessary luxury.

Our demand for freedom must reckon with a universe that is marked by order and regularity. Life is like a game of bridge. The cards in the game are given to us. We do not select them. They are traced to past Karma but we are free to make any call as we think fit and lead any suit. Only we are limited by the rules of the game. We are more free when we start the game than later on when the game has developed and our choices become restricted. But till the very end there is always a choice. A good player will see possibilities which a bad one does not. The more skilled a player the more alternatives does he per-ceive. A good hand may be cut to pieces by unskillful play and the bad play need not be attrib-uted to the frowns of fortune. Even though we may not like the way in which the cards are shuffled, we like the game and we want to play. Sometimes wind and tide may prove too strong for us and even the most noble may come down. The great souls find profound peace in the consciousness that the stately order of the world, now lovely and luminous, now dark and terrible, in which man finds his duty and destiny, cannot be subdued to known aims. It seems to have a purpose of its own of which we are ignorant. Misfortune is not fate but providence.

The law of Karma does not support the doctrine of predestination. There are some who believe that only the predestination of certain souls to destruction is consistent with divine sovereignty. God has a perfect right to deal with his creatures even as a potter does with his clay. St. Paul speaks of "vessels of wrath fitted to destruction." Life eternal is a gracious gift of God. Such a view of divine sovereignty is unethical. God's love is manifested in and through law.

In our relations with human failures, belief in Karma inclines us to take a sympathetic attitude and develop reverence before the mystery of misfortune. The more understanding we are, the less do we pride ourselves on our superiority. Faith in Karma induces in us the mood of true justice or charity which is the essence of spirituality. We realize how infinitely helpless and frail human beings are. When we look at the warped lives of the poor, we see how much the law of Karma is true. If they are lazy and criminal, let us ask what chance they had of choosing to be different. They are more unfortunate than wicked. Again, failures are due not so much to "sin" as to errors which lead us to our doom. In Greek tragedy man is held individually less responsible and circumstances or the decisions of Moira [Fate] more so. The tale of Oedipus Rex tells us how he could not avoid his fate to kill his father and marry his mother, in spite of his best efforts. The parting of Hector and Andromache in Homer is another illustration. In Shakespeare again, we see the artist leading on his characters to their destined ends by what seems a very natural development of their foibles, criminal folly in Lear or personal ambition in Macbeth. The artist shows us these souls in pain. Hamlet's reason is puzzled, his will confounded.

He looks at life and at death and wonders which is worse. Goaded by personal ambition, Macbeth makes a mess of it all. Othello kills his wife and kills himself because a jealous villain shows him a handkerchief. When these noble souls crash battling with adverse forces we feel with them and for them; for it might happen to any of us. We are not free from the weaknesses that broke them, whatever we call them, stupidity, disorder, vacillation or, if you please, insane ambition and self-seeking. Today the evil stars of the Greek tragedians are replaced by the almighty laws of economics. Thousands of young men the world over are breaking their heads in vain against the iron walls of society like trapped birds in cages. We see in them the essence of all tragedy, something noble breaking down, something sublime falling with a crash. We can only bow our heads in the presence of those broken beneath the burden of their destiny. The capacity of the human soul for suffering and isolation is immense. Take the poor creatures whom the world passes by as the lowly and the lost. If only we had known what they passed through, we would have been glad of their company. It is utterly wrong to think that misfortune comes only to those who deserve it. The world is a whole and we are members one of another, and we must suffer one for another. In Christianity, it needed a divine soul to reveal how much grace there is in suffering. To bear pain, to endure suffering, is the quality of the strong in spirit. It adds to the spiritual resources of humanity.

⊚ CRITICAL QUESTIONS

1. Does the author's assertion that even though "the self is not free from the bonds of determination, it can subjugate the past to a certain extent and turn it into a new course" make sense? Why, or why not?

2. Do you think Radhakrishnan's analogy with a game of bridge is a good one? Give an argument in support of your answer.

3. What is the most important thing you learned from reading this selection? Explain why you think it is important.

11.6 WE ARE BOTH FREE AND DETERMINED

You might be thinking, "Hard determinism seems awfully hard. Human beings are not just pawns in the hands of heredity and environment. We are free. I am free. Indeed, right now, I can continue reading this book or I can stop, whichever is my pleasure. Yet Sartre's views seem unrealistic. I am not totally free. Heredity and environment clearly play some role. However, Radhakrishnan's ideas, though less radical than Sartre's with respect to the scope of human freedom, require me to believe in some kind of metaphysical notions about the self and reincarnation. I don't find that attractive. I don't, however, want to deny the law of causality. There must be some way to reconcile freedom and determinism."

If these are your thoughts, then you may like another answer that has been proposed to the problem of freedom and determinism, an answer called soft determinism. This position holds that every event has a cause, and this fact is compatible with human freedom. Hence, another name for soft determinism is compatibilism. According to the compatibilist, even if determinism is true, people ought to be held responsible for those actions they do voluntarily. Indeed, many compatibilists argue that responsibility makes no sense unless determinism is true because it makes no sense to hold anyone responsible for uncaused (undetermined) actions.

Notice that soft determinism is, like hard determinism, a kind of determinism. Both the soft and hard determinists agree that every event has a cause. However, they disagree about whether this is compatible with human freedom and about the implications for moral responsibility.

Of course the key question here is, are there any causes of my behavior over which I have control? And if so, which ones and how far does that control extend?

Nancy Holmstrom, Chair of the Department of Philosophy at Rutgers University, supports the compatibilist or soft determinism position but argues it is not sufficient to support this position by only arguing that an action is free if the agent's beliefs and desires are the cause of the action. This is not adequate as a defense of compatibilism because it does not consider the causes of the agent's beliefs and desires. The key issue for Holmstrom is whether or not we have control over the beliefs and desires that cause us to act the way we do.

◉ READING QUESTIONS

1. What does it mean to say that someone has control over his or her beliefs and desires, and why is this important for the free will debate?
2. What is a "second order volition" and what part does it play as a necessary condition of a free act?
3. Under what conditions are the causes of one's beliefs and desires coercive?
4. What are the conditions that need to exist before we can say that someone is a self-determining person?
5. Why does Holmstrom's view of compatibilism imply that most people today are not free?
6. What is one objection to Holmstrom's position, and how does she respond?

Firming Up Soft Determinism

NANCY HOLMSTROM

I

An important position on the question of freedom and determinism holds that determinism and predictability per se constitute no threat to the freedom and responsibility of an agent. What matters, according to this view, called soft determinism, is the basis on which the prediction is made or the nature of the conditions such that, given those conditions, the agent will do what he/she does. When the agent does what he does because of his beliefs and desires[1] to do it, then what the agent does is "up to him"; the causal chain goes through the person or the self, as it were. In such cases the agent can be said to be the cause of the action. Such actions are free. On the other hand, when the causes of an action, or, more generally, of what a person does, are not his/her beliefs and desires to do that action, then what happens is not "up to him" and the action is not free. However, it may not be compelled either. It is where the action is in contradiction to what the agent wants that the act can be said to be compelled. The agent is not responsible for the action because the action occurs in spite of him.

Among the objections that have been raised to this account of the distinction between free and unfree acts is that it provides an insufficient account of what it is for an agent to do an act freely. The problem is the source of the sources of one's allegedly free actions, that is, the sources of one's beliefs and desires. Many philosophers have felt that if an agent's beliefs and desires are themselves determined, then actions proceeding from them must be as unfree as actions that are not caused by the agent's beliefs and desires. For example, Richard Taylor bids us to suppose that

> while my behavior is entirely in accordance with my own volitions, and thus "free" in terms of the conception of freedom we are examining, my volitions themselves are caused. To make this graphic, we can suppose that an ingenious physiologist can induce in me any volition he pleases, simply by pushing various buttons on an instrument to which, let us suppose, I am attached by numerous wires. All the volitions I have in that situation are, accordingly, precisely the ones he gives me....
>
> This is the description of a man who is acting in accordance with his inner volitions, a man whose body is unimpeded and unconstrained in its motions, these motions being the effects of those inner states. It is hardly the description of a free and responsible agent. It is the perfect description of a puppet.[2]

The same point can be made by examples of beliefs and desires acquired by brainwashing, hypnosis, subliminal advertising, and so on. If a person acts because of beliefs and desires acquired in such ways, the action is clearly not free even though the action was done because of the agent's beliefs and desires. This shows that it is not the case that an act is free just because it is caused by the beliefs and desires of the agent to do the act. The standard soft determinist position is inadequate as it stands.

One way of dealing with the objection might be to distinguish freedom of action and freedom of will and to maintain that the act was free but the will was not. However, I think such examples show that these concepts cannot be so easily separated. Because the "will" is unfree in such cases, we would not call the act free. Taylor thinks his point applies much more generally than just to these sorts of examples and concludes that the standard conception of determinism cannot apply to a free act. He introduces, instead, a special notion of "agent causality." I prefer to explore a response to the above objection

From "Firming Up Soft Determinism," *The Personalist* (now the *Pacific Philosophical Quarterly*), vol. 58 (1977), pp. 39–51. Blackwell Publishing.

that remains within the standard compatibilist framework.

I think that the objection I raised to soft determinism shows that soft determinists have too limited a notion of what is required for an agent to be the source of his/her actions. All that they require is that the agent do what he or she pleases. They ignore the question of whether the agent has control over the sources of the actions, his/her desires and beliefs. Taylor inferred that if the desires causing an action are themselves caused then the action is not free. This does not follow. Just because some causes of desires and beliefs, such as brainwashing, make actions resulting from them unfree, it does not follow that any cause of desires and beliefs has the same implications for the freedom of actions resulting from them.

Since the notion of having control is the heart of the notion of freedom for me, let me stop to clarify the concept briefly. If I have control over x then x depends on what I do or do not do. I am an important part of the causal process producing x, such that if I did something different x would be different. Moreover, I must be conscious of x's dependence on me in order for x to be under my control. Whether some insect lives or not depends on whether or not I step on him as I walk down the street. But if I do not know he is there his life is not under my control. So for x to be under my control what I do or do not do must be an important part of the cause of x and I must know this. X therefore must depend on what I want or on my "will" in order for x to be under my control. Now since one can make more or less of a difference, be more or less important a part of the causal process, it therefore follows that one can have more or less control over something. The more control a person has the freer that person is. Clearly, then, a person is not simply free or unfree. Nor is every action simply free or unfree. Rather, there is a continuum between free and unfree, with many or most acts lying somewhere in between. When I say that an act is free what I mean is that the act falls on the free side of the continuum. Or, since there is no line in the middle of a continuum, it might be clearer to say that a free act falls in the direction of the free end of the continuum. Acts are more or less free according to how close they are to the free end of the continuum.

What I want to argue in this paper is that people can have differing amounts of control over what they desire and what they believe. People can be more or less important a part of the causal process leading to their having the desires and beliefs that they do. Our discussion thus far shows that only if they have control over their beliefs and desires do they really have control over their actions. The key question, then, is whether this idea of having control over one's beliefs and desires makes any sense and whether in fact we do have such control. Many people would probably say that while what we do is often up to us, what we believe and desire depends on factors completely beyond our control. Speaking generally, it depends on the way the world is; more specifically, it depends on our biological and psychological natures, the society in which we live, and our particular portion of it (that is, our class, race, ethnic group, and so on). Others would object that it makes no sense to separate the person or self from his/her desires and beliefs, and hence makes no sense to talk of the person having control over his/her desires and beliefs. My major purpose in this paper will be to give substance to the idea that people can have control over the sources of their actions—that is, have control over their desires and beliefs.

If an agent can be said to be the source of his/her beliefs and desires, then it makes sense to say that the agent is a self-determining being. This is a concept that many have taken to be at the heart of freedom, whether they be determinists, indeterminists, or hold to the idea of "agent causality." If we can give substance to this notion of a person having control over his desires and beliefs, we will have given substance to the notion of a self-determining being.

II

Before turning directly to the central task, I wish to raise another sort of counterexample to soft determinism. Some acts that are done because of the agent's desires and beliefs to do them are nevertheless unfree, but for reasons other than the source of those desires and beliefs. However, we will see that these counterexamples do not challenge the fundamental thrust of soft determinism because the examples are all such that we have reason to say that the actions in the examples are not truly self-determined.

A heroin addict steals some money and uses it to buy heroin, which he then takes. It might be said that all three acts (stealing, buying the drug, and taking it) are done because of the addict's desire to achieve a certain state and the belief that these are ways of achieving it. If we imagine that this addict does not want to be an addict, as is the case with most addicts, then these acts of his are crucially different from most acts done because of the agent's beliefs and desires. While the addict wants the heroin he also wants to not take the drug. Moreover, he wants a great number of things which he believes to be incompatible with taking the drug—for example, health, self-respect, an ordinary life, and so on. These contrary desires, values, and beliefs are greater in number and also are part of an integrated whole. The desire to take the drug is not part of such an integrated whole, but nevertheless it outweighs all these contrary desires and beliefs. A kleptomaniac's desire to steal would probably be similar. Most actions done because of the agent's desires are not in conflict with a greater number of his/her integrated desires and beliefs. I think it is this factor which leads compatibilists to reject such cases as not really counterexamples to their analysis of a free act as one resulting from the wants of the agent. An act resulting from such a conflict does not seem to proceed from the self as a free act must: It occurs in spite of the person. Moritz Schlick says, "We consider the man to be more or less unfree, and hold him less accountable, because we rightly view the influence of the drug as 'external,' even though it is found within the body; it prevents him from making decisions in the manner peculiar to his nature."[3] This integrated set of desires, beliefs and values might be said to constitute the person's nature or self as it is at that time. Acts proceeding from desires that are external to this and yet dominant would seem to be unfree. There are certain exceptions to this, however, which we will discover as we progress.

III

I wish at this point to introduce the notion of a second order volition as discussed by Harry Frankfurt in "Freedom of the Will and the Concept of a Person."[4] Someone has a volition of the second order when he wants to have a certain desire and, moreover, wants that desire to be his effective desire—that is, his *will*, in Frankfurt's terminology. The addict in our example may simply suffer from a conflict between the desire to take the drug and a number of contradictory or incompatible desires. However, he may, further, want that the latter desires be his effective desires. If so, then the addict's desire to take the drug is in conflict not only with a greater number of integrated desires and beliefs, but with a second order volition as well. Yet it still determines the addict's actions. By being in conflict with the will he wants to have, it is in conflict with the want with which he has thereby identified himself. Hence, when this desire determines action, the action is in sharp contrast to most acts done because of the agent's beliefs and desires. Instead of being an act that depends on the agent, that is "up to him," it happens against his will. This provides further grounds for saying that the act does not proceed from the self. Quite aside from the nature of the desire that is in conflict with the second order volition in our example (that is, the desire to take heroin), it would seem plausible to take as a sufficient condition for making an act unfree that it proceed from beliefs and desires that are in conflict with a second order volition. A necessary condition, then, of a free act is that it proceed from desires and beliefs that are consistent with second order volitions. This should be seen as a development of the compatibilist account of a free act as one caused by the self, specifically the agent's beliefs and desires.

IV

Consistency with an integrated set of beliefs and desires and with second order volitions is not sufficient for an act to be free. We saw at the outset that the source of the beliefs and desires causing an act is relevant to the freedom of that act.

The sorts of examples which first showed us that the soft determinist position was unsatisfactory as thus far presented were examples of acts done because of beliefs and desires that seemed in some way to have been forced upon the agent. Whether the person acquired beliefs and desires (volitions or the reasons for doing what he/she does) by being hooked up to a machine someone else controls, or by being brainwashed or exposed to subliminal advertising, the following is true. The beliefs and desires were acquired by measures taken by others in order to induce them, which measures were taken either explicitly against the person's will (brainwashing), and/or without his/her knowledge (subliminal advertising). (Taylor's case could be either.) Being ignorant of the measures taken to induce the beliefs and desires, the person is as much lacking in control over them as if they were taken explicitly against his/her will. In both cases the person, as an active determining being, is irrelevant to what happens. He/she has no control, and—more importantly—no possibility of control over the beliefs and desires he/she acquires. Actions done because of beliefs and desires acquired under such conditions are not free.

Now is it really necessary that a person's beliefs and desires be caused by other people in order for it to be the case that they were forced upon him/her? Although it was true of our original examples, I do not think it is a necessary condition. While it may sound odd to say they were the result of force or coercion where no persons were the cause, it can certainly be said that the desires were not acquired freely or even that they were acquired under coercive conditions. The issue about causation of beliefs and desires that is crucial to the freedom of acts resulting from them is whether the person enters into the causal process as an active determinant. If the person does not, then the beliefs and desires were not acquired freely, and acts resulting from them are not free because not self-determined. If, on the contrary, the beliefs and desires are opposed to the person's desires, first or second order, then acts resulting from them are unfree or compelled. All this can be true even though the causes of the beliefs and desires were not measures taken by others to induce them. Suppose that a person

lives under conditions of economic scarcity, which entails that not everyone will get what he/she needs and wants. A consequence of a person getting enough for himself and his family is that others will not have enough. A person in these conditions might, partly as a survival mechanism, come to desire that others not have enough—and might act on this desire. If this occurred, it seems to me that such an act would be an unfree one (although perhaps not at the very end of the continuum). If the person did not want to want that others not have enough, if in fact he/she wanted not to want this, then the desire would conflict with a second order volition. Acts resulting from such desires are unfree. However, in the absence of a conflicting or reinforcing second order volition, I would still wish to put the act on the unfree end of the continuum because the desires causing the act were produced under coercive conditions. The conditions were coercive because the person had no control over them, their existence was contrary to his/her desires, and his/her personality and character had little or no effect on their influence. Remove economic scarcity and the desire would be removed (although perhaps not immediately). Similar examples could be given of beliefs and desires caused by particular social systems and particular institutions within a social system.

V

Let us examine in some greater detail the conditions I have given under which desires could be said to have been acquired unfreely or coercively. It might be thought that my conditions apply too widely and would make too many desires turn out to have been unfreely acquired. For example, suppose a person has a strong desire to hear Bach because her parents regularly played Bach records in order to induce that desire. Her desire was acquired because of her parents' efforts to induce the desire. Their efforts consisted of intensively exposing her to the object they wished her to desire. If my conditions apply to such cases then her going to a concert as an adult because she wants to hear Bach played would be unfree—and this is an unattractive conclusion. However, my conditions do not lead to this conclusion, because the conditions I set are not met in the example. The child was not unaware of the causes of her later desire, which is what my condition requires; in fact it was by being aware of the music that was regularly played that she came to desire to hear it. Conceivably, but improbably, she was unaware that hearing the music was the cause of her later desire or that her parents regularly played it in order to produce that desire in her. However, these are different conditions from the one I gave. In general, where the measures taken to induce a desire simply amount to exposing a person to the object of the hoped-for desire, this does not meet my conditions, because the person cannot be unaware of the causes of the desire (although he/she may be unaware that they are the causes).

I am inclined to think that my conditions as they stand thus far are in need of revision in the other direction, that is, to make them apply more widely. Suppose that what was done to induce the desire was not mere exposure to the object, but rather conditioning. If they had conditioned her, the parents would have accompanied the playing of the music with pleasurable stimuli and they would have negatively reinforced any expressions of negative feeling toward the music. If this had been done, the desire would be the result of more than the interrelation of the person and the object of the desire, as is the case when the desire for something comes into being because of exposure to it. A desire that is the result of conditioning is the result of pleasures and pains that accompany the object, but are external to the person, the object, and the relation between them. When a person acquires desires and aversions for things because of pleasures and pains that are intrinsic to those things, such as the pleasures of eating good food, the pains of overeating, then those desires and aversions are freely acquired. Where the pleasures and pains are external, the person (that is, his/her personality, reasoning capacities, and so on) is bypassed in the process. This should make the process coercive. However, as my conditions stand they do not give this result. The person could be aware of the elements of the conditioning process (the music, the accompanying pleasures and pains), though unaware of the connections between them, the purposes behind them, and their effect. She was aware of the measures taken and therefore, if it were not explicitly against her will, the conditioning would not be coercive according to what I have said about coercion thus far. I take this to indicate that something more must be said.

In the hopes of working out how conditioning differs from mere exposure, let us go back to the example of the person who acquired a desire to hear the music of Bach because of repeated exposure to his music as a child. Whether the exposure was the deliberate work of others, as in our example, or not, acquisition of a desire through exposure differs from clearly coercive ways of acquiring desires. When people acquire a desire through being acquainted with the object or experience, they have the possibility of coming to have that desire or not. Whether they do or not will depend on facts about them: their aptitudes, beliefs, personality, other desires, and so on. Where this is the case they can be said to have control, or at least the possibility of control, over the desires they acquire. Where, on the other hand, the causes of their beliefs and desires would exist and would effectively operate regardless of the fact that their personality, character, other beliefs and desires are opposed to these causes, then they obviously have no chance of controlling what beliefs and desires they come to have.

We can distinguish, then, between cases where people can have control over their beliefs and desires and those where they cannot. Knowledge is necessary in order that a person have this possibility of control. In the account I gave of when a person could be said to have freely acquired his/her desires, I only required that the person have knowledge of the causes (and also that they not be against the person's will) in order that the causes not be coercive. Oftentimes, however, one needs to have more than simple knowledge of the causes. Conditioning is a case where the person being conditioned might know the causes, that is, might know the elements of the causal process, but might not know their interconnections or the purposes behind them. The person is acquainted with the causes but unaware that they are the causes or how and why they operate. If conditioning would operate regardless of whether a person knew the latter, then it is a causal process that the person cannot have any control over. Hence it is coercive.

Sometimes the efficacy of causal conditions depends on people's ignorance of them, that they are or may be causes, and how and why they operate. In such cases, people's ignorance of these facts would deprive them of whatever control knowledge might give them. People are less free to the extent that they operate on unconscious motives. Successful psychoanalysis can increase the patient's control and therefore freedom, by making conscious things that had hitherto been unconscious. Sometimes just knowing the purposes behind potential causes (for example, that it is designed to convince you, scare you, buy you off, or get you to buy something) can make a difference to whether those purposes are realized. Without the knowledge, one's attitudes towards these purposes cannot come into play and one cannot exercise any control over them. If the efficacy of the causes depends on one's ignorance of such facts about the causes, then the causes are coercive. It is where knowledge about the causes would have made a difference that ignorance makes the causes coercive. Causes of beliefs and desires are coercive where they operate contrary to the person's other beliefs, desires, character, and personality. This is so when the causes are explicitly against the person's will, or unknown to the person, or when they depend for their efficacy on the person's ignorance of certain facts about them. According to these conditions, conditioning would usually be coercive, which, I think, is as it should be.

Suppose one came to know that one was being conditioned and the knowledge made no difference to the efficacy of the causes. Is this a coercive way of acquiring desires? The answer depends on whether the conditioning process was against the person's will. If the causes operate against his/her will then they are coercive. On the other hand, suppose they are not operating against the person's will; in other words, suppose a person voluntarily chooses to be conditioned. A person might deliberately expose himself to conditions which will cause him to have (or not have) certain desires, for example, not to smoke. Once he puts himself into the situation, the causes operate independent of his other beliefs and desires, personality, and so on. His new effective desire not to smoke will be the result of conditioning, and we have said that conditioning is a form of coercion. However, I think that the circumstances of this kind of case make a significant difference. The person's self does enter into the causal process as an active determinant, whereas in most cases of conditioning this is not so. The person in our example who voluntarily has himself conditioned has a second order volition not to smoke, which is in conflict with his or her volition to smoke. If the second order volition were sufficiently strong to outweigh the first order volition by itself, then the new effective desire would be acquired in a completely free manner. However, it is not sufficiently strong to do this by itself. Causes that are independent of the person are necessary to change his desire. However, these other causes come into play only because of his second order volition. He had himself conditioned because he has a desire not to desire to smoke. So I think we can say that the cause of his new effective desire not to smoke is his second order volition. The new desire is not the result of coercion; it does spring from the self. However, it does not only spring from the self. It was not acquired in as free a manner as if the second order volition was sufficient by itself to cause it, but I would still put it towards the free end of the continuum.

What we have come up with is what we started with—and that is, to the extent that the causes of one's actions are themselves caused by things over which people have no control (even with knowledge of them), to that extent one's actions are unfree. What I have tried to do is to make sense of the idea of having control over one's desires. In order to say that one has control over one's desires it is necessary that what we identify as the self determines what one desires and what desires one acts on. To put together the criteria elaborated thus far: In order for actions caused by desires to be free, these desires must first of all not have been coercively acquired.

What this means has been explained. Knowledge was seen to be a key factor. Secondly, they must not be contrary to the person's second order volitions. This second condition implies that the person has second order volitions. We will not be able to say that these desires are the desires the person wants to have unless (a) he/she has second order volitions and unless (b) these volitions outweigh first order volitions in the case of a conflict. Thirdly, the desire must be in harmony with an integrated set of desires and beliefs—hence one's self—at that given time. This third requirement must be qualified. A desire causing a free action may be inconsistent with this integrated set if the set does not meet one of the necessary conditions and the desire fulfills both the conditions. If the set was coercively acquired and the conflicting desire was not, or if the conflicting desire is supported by a second order volition and the set is not, then an action caused by the conflicting desire would be free. Any person missing second order volitions is missing an important kind of control over his/her actions, and hence an important dimension of freedom. That is why an action that proceeds from a conflicting desire which is supported by a second order volition is freer than one that proceeded from the integrated set, where there are no effective second order volitions. This sort of situation could lead to a revision of the set—a restructuring of the self. However, lacking an integrated set which is responsible for his/her actions, the person is divided, and it is less possible for that person to be a self-determining being. Therefore, the person is most free when there is an integrated set which is in accordance with his/her second order volitions. Then we can say that this is a self-determining person.

VI

An objection that will almost certainly be raised to what I have said thus far is that I have failed to carry through the logic of my argument. If, in order to have control over one's actions (that is, for one's actions to be free), it is necessary to have control over the causes of one's actions (that is, one's desires), then in order to have control over them, it is also necessary to have control over *their*

causes, and in order to have control over them, it is necessary … In short, we are led to an infinite regress, or at least to a point where the person cannot possibly have any control—namely, a point before they are born. If it leads back to this point, then we can never have control over what we do. And so it seems we are led back to a choice of hard determinism, indeterminism, or a position like Taylor's.

I do not agree that the logic of my argument has to lead back to this point. In order to take this same analysis further back, one would have to make sense of having control over both (a) the integrated set of beliefs and desires and also over (b) one's second order volitions. Taking the former first, one way of having control over this integrated act would be to have effective second order volitions with respect to it. This is already part of my account. Aside from having effective second order volitions with respect to the integrated set of beliefs, desires, and so on, is there any other way in which one might be said to have or lack control over it? To give any other sense to how one might have control over this integrated set would require that some person or self be found to have control over it. But in the absence of a higher order volition, where and what is this entity that might but does not control this set? Unless some sense can be made of such an entity the idea remains incoherent, and my account thus far has not been shown to lead too far back.

To turn to (b), having control over one's second order volitions, we can make sense of this if we bring in the idea of third order volitions (wanting to want to want), and we could bring in volitions of still higher orders. I am not opposed to this but it is an empirical question just how far back we can go in any given case. Frankfurt deals with the point in the following way:

> There is no *theoretical* [my emphasis] limit to the length of the series of desires of higher and higher orders; nothing but common sense and, perhaps, a saving fatigue…. The tendency to generate such a series of acts of forming desires … leads to the destruction of a person…. It is possible, however, to terminate such a series of acts without cutting it off arbitrarily. When a person identified himself *decisively* with one of his first order desires, this

commitment "resounds" throughout the potentially endless array of higher orders.... The decisiveness of the commitment he has made means that he has decided that no further question about his second order volition, at any higher order, remains to be asked. It is relatively unimportant whether we explain this by saying that the commitment implicitly generates an endless series of confirming desires of higher orders, or by saying that the commitment is tantamount to a dissolution of the pointedness of all questions concerning higher orders of desire.[5]

A person does not have an indefinite number of orders of volition with respect to a given desire. Once we have reached the point where a person has identified him/herself with a particular volition, the idea of that person having control over his/her desires of that order through volitions of a higher order seems to make no sense, because that person does not go further back. The person, a discriminating being capable of choice among desires, has committed and identified him/herself with a particular volition. To go further back is to leave the person behind. To speak of identifying oneself with a volition requires the possibility of desires of more than one order, but it does not require an indefinite series.

Let us approach the question from a slightly different angle. A second order volition might be the result of a higher order volition, or of coercion, or of neither of these. If a second order volition results from a volition of a higher order, then the person can be said to have control over that volition. Suppose now that the person's second order volition was not the result of a higher order volition, but neither was it the result of coercion. This would be true where the person had no higher order volitions relevant to the second order volition, but where the causes would not have operated if there had been second order volitions in conflict. (If they would have operated anyway then they would be coercive.) In such cases, it seems to me that the volitions should be said to have been acquired freely. It certainly was not acquired unfreely. The person did not *lack* control, and would have had control if there had been higher order volitions. A person can be said to have acquired a second order

volition through coercion if the person has conflicting volitions of a still higher order which are ineffective against these causes. The person then lacks control over his/her second order volitions in an obvious way. Where the person has no volitions of a higher order, or where the person has decisively identified him/herself with the volition, Frankfurt and I have argued that something is wrong with saying that the person lacks control, because the person does not go further back. However, suppose that, if there were a conflicting higher order volition (although there isn't one), it would be ineffective. I am inclined to say that in this case as well, the person lacks control over his/her volitions and the causes are coercive. If this is correct, then a person lacks control over second order volitions if conflicting higher order volitions (whether the person has any or not) would be ineffective against them.

One might argue that because a person lacks control over his/her second order volitions it does not follow that he/she lacks control over his/her first order volitions or over his/her actions. I would want to distinguish between two sorts of cases. Recall that I distinguished two kinds of cases of second order volitions acquired through coercion: (a) ones in which there were conflicting volitions of a higher order, and (b) ones in which there were no volitions of a higher order, but if there had been they would have been ineffective. It seems to me that where the second order volitions result from coercion in the latter sort of case, actions proceeding from them are still free. The sense in which the second order volitions were coerced is a more extended hypothetical sense, and I therefore see little need to infer that the person's first order volitions and actions must also have been coerced. On the other hand, if the person's second order volitions are coerced as described in (a), the person lacked control and was coerced in more obvious and direct ways. Although it does not strictly follow, it seems more consistent with what I have been arguing to conclude that in such cases the person should be said to lack control over his/her first order volitions and his/her actions. I have argued that people have control over their actions when they have control over their causes (beliefs and desires), and that they have control over these when they are caused by second order volitions. If there are higher order volitions which are ineffective against the causes of the second order volitions, then the person has no control over these second order volitions. And it seems closer to the general line of argument I have been using, to conclude that in such cases they also have no control over their first order volitions and actions.

VII

As a prelude to concluding, I wish to consider the implications of my general and abstract analysis to the concrete question of just how free most people are today. We shall see that although my view implies that people can be free, though determined, it is also an implication of my view that most people are quite unfree today. The answer to this question of how free people are is not one that applies to all people just in virtue of their being human, but rather depends on who the people are and where and when they are living. It turns out, then, on my view, that human freedom is closely tied to social and political freedom and is not a distinct metaphysical question. (In considering this part of the philosophical question we are inevitably drawn into empirical issues, including political ones, so my own opinion on these matters will certainly intrude.)

Desires arise in us because of a whole complex set of conditions which affect one another. (Neither they nor their influence can actually be separated, so the following remarks are unavoidably artificial.) These determining conditions include physical and psychological conditions, which to some extent we share with others, but which also differ from person to person. People today are capable of some but not much control over these conditions. Greater knowledge, aided by money, gives a person greater possibilities of control, but there are still very definite limits which no one today is capable of transcending. Greater knowledge will give greater possibilities of human control, but it is probable that there will always be limits that one cannot transcend. What is possible is for a person to exercise some control over the form of the desires these conditions tend to produce, and also over whether and how these desires are acted upon.

How much control a person can exercise over the social and political conditions causing his/her desires depends on the particular social system in which the person lives, and also the place that the person occupies in the system. Some changes are possible in the latter in most societies but usually quite little. In any case, it is only within the framework allowed by that system and it is not possible within the framework of *any* present society for *most* people to change their positions within that framework. As for the framework itself, one cannot change the time in which one lives, and since what social systems are possible depends on the time and place, there is a certain inevitable limitation. However, there are many fewer inevitable limitations on the degree of control one can exercise over social causes than over physical causes—in the future, but also in the present. Given the limitations of time and place, there is great potential today for people to collectively control the social conditions under which they live, and hence the beliefs and desires these conditions tend to produce, even if there are some conditions they still would not be able to control. However, with some notable exceptions, the ability to control the social conditions in which one lives is only potential today, not actual. This is partially because people do not realize they have this ability. This lack of realization is strongly supported, of course, by the social system in which they live and by those who do control it. There is, again, the possibility of exercising some control over the form of the desires likely to be produced by these conditions, and also over whether and how these desires are acted upon. However, so long as one does not control the social causes of one's beliefs and desires, one does not have much chance of controlling the actual beliefs and desires one comes to have.

Leaving aside the nature of the influence, what is necessary in order to be able to exercise control over the influences acting upon one, is to be a certain kind of person, as well as to have knowledge and the cooperation of others. A person who is critical and discriminating and sees him/herself as actively shaping the world, history, and also him/herself, is capable of doing just that—not alone, but in cooperation with others. There are, of course, varying conditions where people may be more or less aware and/or more or less able not to be passive products. However, it seems that most people today are quite uncritical and undiscriminating and lack this self-conception. Many feel themselves to be more like passive products of history and their own particular environment—and their environment makes them feel that way. However, in the course of struggle against the oppressive aspects of their environment, they can come to realize their potential to bring the world under their conscious collective control. The realization of this is a first step towards changing the framework that keeps them without control. This capacity to change the world and consequently their own nature is unique to human beings. It gives them the potential of being free in the fullest sense that is possible in a deterministic world.

NOTES

1. I intend "beliefs" and "desires" to cover all mental sources of action whatever exactly these are.
2. Richard Taylor, *Metaphysics* (Englewood Cliffs, N.J.: Prentice Hall, 1963), p. 45.
3. Moritz Schlick, "When Is a Man Responsible?," in *Free Will and Determinism*, ed. Bernard Berofsky (New York: Harper & Row, 1966), p. 59.
4. Harry Frankfurt, "Freedom of the Will and the Concept of a Person," *The Journal of Philosophy* 68 (January 1971), pp. 5–20.
5. Frankfurt, "Freedom of the Will and the Concept of a Person," pp. 16–17.

◉ CRITICAL QUESTIONS

1. Do you think Holmstrom's assertion that greater knowledge "will give greater possibilities of human control" is true? Why or why not?
2. Do you think it is true that in struggling against oppressive forces people take the first step towards becoming a person who is "critical and discriminating" and that this is a move toward genuine freedom? Support your answer with an argument.

To access the *Voices of Wisdom*, 8th Edition, **Premium Website**, search for this book on CengageBrain.com.

CHAPTER TWELVE

What Am I?

I think, therefore I am is the statement of an intellectual who underrates
toothaches. *I feel, therefore I am* is a truth much more universally
valid, and it applies to everything that's alive.

MILAN KUNDERA

LEARNING OBJECTIVES

After studying this chapter students should be able to:
- explain the mind–body problem,
- distinguish interactionism, parallelism, and epiphenomenalism and state what all three have in common,
- distinguish identity theory, double-aspect theory, and neutral monism and state what all three have in common,
- describe behaviorism,
- define functionalism,
- identify Leibniz, Spinoza, Descartes, Cole, Turing, Hinrichs, Searle, and Bisson, and
- answer all the questions relating to the selections.

12.1 INTRODUCTION

To what does the word *I* refer? You might want to say that the word *I* refers to your body. This would mean that you are your body, and I am my body. That seems simple enough. Notice, however, the words *your* body or *my* body. Why do we say *my* body as if the body were something the *I* possessed? This way of talking seems to imply that we make a distinction between ourselves and our bodies. And, of course, we can lose parts of our bodies or even have parts of them replaced without losing or replacing ourselves.

Maybe "I" doesn't refer to the body but to something that goes on inside the body, like thoughts or sensations. So you are what you think, perceive, and feel. However, we run into the same problem, don't we? We speak of *my* thoughts, *my* perceptions, and *my* feelings. Also, these things are constantly changing, but is the "I" constantly changing? Are you a different person every time you have a different thought, feeling, or sensation?

If "I" does not refer to my body or my thoughts, perceptions, and feelings, maybe it refers to my mind. My mind is what *has* thoughts, perceptions, and feelings, so you might say it possesses them. And since my mind tells my body what to do, you might even say that my body is possessed by my mind. Or, at least, my mind inhabits my body.

As the above bit of thinking about the question "What am I?" indicates, the discussion sooner or later leads one to talk about the mind and the body. This seems natural enough since we normally think of ourselves as human beings, and we commonly think of humans as having minds and bodies. However, what precisely are the mind and the body, and how are they related to each other? These questions constitute what philosophers call the **mind–body problem**.

Generally speaking, the proposed solutions to the mind–body problem fall into two groups: dualistic and monistic. Dualistic theories hold that the mind and the body are two different substances. The mind is conscious, nonspatial, and private (only you have direct access to your own mind). The body is unconscious, spatial, and public (it can be viewed by others). How do these two substances, so defined, relate?

One theory, usually associated with René Descartes, is called **interactionism**. According to this theory, mind and body causally interact in the sense that mental events (e.g., thoughts) can cause physical events (e.g., walking) and physical events (e.g., taking a sleeping pill) can cause mental events (e.g., feeling sleepy). This seems plausible enough at first, but the problem of how two substances so radically different can causally affect each other has led to considerable controversy as well as to the development of other theories.

Some dualists who reject the idea of causal interactionism subscribe to **parallelism**. The German philosopher Gottfried Leibniz (1646–1716), for example, argued that a preestablished harmony exists between mental and physical events so that they run in parallel, like two clocks set to tick together. Mind and body appear to interact, but in fact they do not. A physical event occurs (e.g., a blow to the arm), and parallel to that event, but uncaused by it, a mental event (e.g., pain) occurs.

This seems somewhat fantastic, so other dualists have been led to yet a third theory called **epiphenomenalism**. According to this theory, mental events are by-products of physical events, as smoke is a by-product of fire. This means that physical events cause mental events, but mental events cannot cause physical events. Mental events are just things that happen when certain brain activities take place. The brain activity is what is primary; the mental activity is secondary.

Monistic solutions to the mind–body problem deny that the mind and the body are two different substances. For example, *materialism,* or *physicalism* as it is sometimes called, holds that so-called mental events are not different from physical events. There is no such thing as a mental substance above and beyond the physical. There are several varieties of materialism, but a popular version, called the **identity theory**, proposes that mental events are identical with brain processes in much the same way as lightning flashes are identical with electrical discharges.

Whereas some versions of materialism attempt to reduce mind to matter, *idealism* attempts to reduce matter to mind. If you read Berkeley, you may recall how such an argument progresses. Berkeley argued that because all we ever experience are sensations and because sensations are mental, matter is an unwarranted and unneeded inference. Only minds and mental events exist.

A third kind of monism is called the **double-aspect theory**. This view, maintained by the Dutch philosopher Baruch Spinoza (1632–1677), proposes that we rethink what we mean by mind and body (matter). Instead of thinking of these as things or *substances,* we should think of them as qualities, characteristics, or aspects.

There is one substance, Spinoza argued, that in itself is neither mental nor physical but has at least two different aspects or qualities called mind and body. A modern version of this theory was suggested by the famous British philosopher Bertrand Russell (see Section 1.4). Russell called his theory **neutral monism** and characterized it as the view that what exists is neither mental nor physical but neutral with respect to these distinctions.

Perhaps the mind–body problem arises only because we begin with faulty assumptions. If we focus on our normal experiences, we notice that we experience ourselves as embodied. Our bodies are not irrelevant to what we think and feel. We raise our arms without thinking about how to do it, and when someone kicks us, we yell. Our bodies seem to be more than mere shells or irrelevant dwelling places where our true selves just happen to be, sort of by accident.

Our brains are part of our bodies. They are an important part. I might accidentally cut off my finger, and although that unfortunate event would change me, it would not change me nearly as much as accidentally losing my brain. The relationship between brains and conscious minds is particularly close, and it is important to know how the brain works.

After the advent of the computer age, it did not take long for people to start suggesting that brains work like computers. Computers compute all sorts of information very rapidly. Perhaps the brain does the same thing. Maybe our minds are simply products of a very complex computing system we happen to call the brain. Then again, maybe not. Read further and see.

12.2 YOU ARE YOUR MIND

We return once again to Descartes, in particular to the last chapter of his *Meditations*. Let me remind you of his argument so far. Descartes was concerned with proving representational realism true. That is, he wanted to show for certain that physical objects really do exist outside our minds. He began by using his method of doubt to show that all our beliefs about an external world based on our sensations can be doubted. Hence, the most direct way to know the external world—namely, by sensation—is blocked by doubt. He then discovered that he could not doubt that he existed as a thinking thing as long as he was thinking because every time he doubted (thought) that he existed he proved that he existed (thought). So he found a certain foundation from which to begin, but he was trapped in his own mind.

Our selection in Section 8.3 ended with the second meditation and with Descartes knowing for certain that he existed as a thinking thing, but knowing nothing else. In the subsequent meditations, he sought a way out of his own mind by showing that God exists. If he could prove that God exists, he could be certain that at least one thing outside his own mind exists. He attempted this proof in *Meditation V* with his famous argument from perfection. Descartes argued that by God we mean a perfect being. A perfect being has all perfections. Existing is a perfection and, because a perfect being has all perfections, God must exist. Furthermore, God cannot be a deceiver because a perfect being must also have the perfection of goodness, and a perfectly good being would not deceive.

Along the way Descartes also tried to establish a rule for distinguishing true ideas from false. Ideas that are clear and distinct are true. He also thought he discovered the cause of error. We can use our will to choose to believe things that our understanding does not completely grasp. Hence, we can be confident that God is good and not the source of error. He also tried to show that material things are essentially different from mental things. Matter is extended in space and mind is not. So Descartes believed he had established with absolute certainty the existence of his own mind as a mental substance and the existence of a perfectly good God. How did he get from there to a world made up of physical objects external to our minds? In the *Meditation* that follows, Descartes made that move.

The standard interpretation of Descartes is that he not only establishes a mind–body dualism but also supports a theory of interactionism. According to this theory, the mind and body can causally interact even though one is a mental substance and the other is a physical substance. Recently, some philosophers have questioned whether Descartes did in fact support interactionism. Descartes corresponded about this very issue with Princess Elisabeth of Bohemia in May and June 1643. Elisabeth was puzzled about how interactive causation might happen because causation is a mechanical process requiring contact between bodies extended in space. But the mind is not extended in space and hence can have no contact with a physical body. So *how* do you raise your arm if your mind can have no contact with the muscles in your arm?

◉ READING QUESTIONS

1. What is the difference between having a mental image and having a pure understanding? Give an example of each.
2. According to Descartes, how does the mind or soul (what he here called "a thinking thing") differ from the body?
3. What did Descartes mean when he said that he could "conceive of my whole self" as something that lacks the power or ability to have mental images and to sense?
4. Restate in your own words the argument Descartes provided that led him to the conclusion that physical objects exist.
5. What did Descartes mean when he said that his mind was indivisible but his body was divisible?

Meditation VI

RENÉ DESCARTES

ON THE EXISTENCE OF MATERIAL OBJECTS AND THE REAL DISTINCTION OF MIND FROM BODY

It remains for me to examine whether material objects exist. Insofar as they are the subject of pure mathematics, I now know at least that they can exist, because I grasp them clearly and distinctly.

For God can undoubtedly make whatever I can grasp in this way, and I never judge that something is impossible for Him to make unless there would be a contradiction in my grasping the thing distinctly. Also, the fact that I find myself having mental images when I turn my attention to physical objects seems to imply that these objects really do exist. For, when I pay careful attention to what

From René Descartes's *Meditations on First Philosophy*, translated by Ronald Rubin (Claremont, CA: Areté Press, 1986), pp. 40–53. Reprinted by permission of Areté Press.

it is to have a mental image, it seems to me that it's just the application of my power of thought to a certain body which is immediately present to it and which must therefore exist.

To clarify this, I'll examine the difference between having a mental image and having a pure understanding. When I have a mental image of a triangle, for example, I don't just understand that it is a figure bounded by three lines; I also "look at" the lines as though they were present to my mind's eye. And this is what I call having a mental image. When I want to think of a chiliagon, I understand that it is a figure with a thousand sides as well as I understand that a triangle is a figure with three, but I can't imagine its sides or "look" at them as though they were present. Being accustomed to using images when I think about physical objects, I may confusedly picture some figure to myself, but this figure obviously is not a chiliagon—for it in no way differs from what I present to myself when thinking about a myriagon or any other many sided figure, and it doesn't help me to discern the properties that distinguish chiliagons from other polygons. If it's a pentagon that is in question, I can understand its shape, as I can that of the chiliagon, without the aid of mental images. But I can also get a mental image of the pentagon by directing my mind's eye to its five lines and to the area that they bound. And it's obvious to me that getting this mental image requires a special mental effort different from that needed for understanding—a special effort which clearly reveals the difference between having a mental image and having a pure understanding.

It also seems to me that my power of having mental images, being distinct from my power of understanding, is not essential to my self or, in other words, to my mind—for, if I were to lose this ability, I would surely remain the same thing that I now am. And it seems to follow that this ability depends on something distinct from me. If we suppose that there is a body so associated with my mind that the mind can "look into" it at will, it's easy to understand how my mind might get mental images of physical objects by means of my body. If there were such a body, the mode of thinking that we call imagination would only differ from pure understanding in one way: when the

mind understood something, it would turn a "inward" and view an idea that it found in itself, but, when it had mental images, it would turn to the body and look at something there which resembled an idea that it had understood by itself or had grasped by sense. As I've said, then, it's easy to see how I get mental images, if we suppose that my body exists. And, since I don't have in mind any other equally plausible explanation of my ability to have mental images, I conjecture that physical objects probably do exist. But this conjecture is only probable. Despite my careful and thorough investigation, the distinct idea of bodily nature that I get from mental images does not seem to have anything in it from which the conclusion that physical objects exist validly follows....

Now that I've begun to know myself and my creator better, I still believe that I oughtn't blindly to accept everything that I seem to get from the senses. Yet I no longer believe that I ought to call it all into doubt....

Accordingly, from the fact that I have gained knowledge of my existence without noticing anything about my nature or essence except that I am a thinking thing, [mind or soul] I can rightly conclude that my essence consists solely in the fact that I am a thinking thing. It's possible (or, as I will say later, it's certain) that I have a body which is very tightly bound to me. But, on the one hand, I have a clear and distinct idea of myself insofar as I am just a thinking and unextended thing, and, on the other hand, I have a distinct idea of my body insofar as it is just an extended and unthinking thing. It's certain, then, that I am really distinct from my body and can exist without it. In addition, I find in myself abilities for special modes of awareness, like the abilities to have mental images and to sense. I can clearly and distinctly conceive of my whole self as something that lacks these abilities, but I can't conceive of the abilities' existing without me, or without an understanding substance in which to reside. Since the conception of these abilities includes the conception of something that understands, I see that these abilities are distinct from me in the way that a thing's properties are distinct from the thing itself.

I recognize other abilities in me, like the ability to move around and to assume various postures.

These abilities can't be understood to exist apart from a substance in which they reside any more than the abilities to imagine and sense, and they therefore cannot exist without such a substance. But it's obvious that, if these abilities do exist, the substance in which they reside must be a body or extended substance rather than an understanding one—for the clear and distinct conceptions of these abilities contain extension but not understanding.

There is also in me, however, a passive ability to sense—to receive and recognize ideas of sensible things. But, I wouldn't be able to put this ability to use if there weren't, either in me or in something else, an active power to produce or make sensory ideas. Since this active power doesn't presuppose understanding, and since it often produces ideas in me without my cooperation and even against my will, it cannot exist in me. Therefore, this power must exist in a substance distinct from me. And, for reasons that I've noted, this substance must contain, either formally or eminently, all the reality that is contained subjectively in the ideas that the power produces. Either this substance is a physical object (a thing of bodily nature which contains formally the reality that the idea contains subjectively), or it is God or one of His creations which is higher than a physical object (something which contains this reality eminently). But, since God isn't a deceiver, it's completely obvious that He doesn't send these ideas to me directly or by means of a creation which contains their reality eminently rather than formally. For, since He has not given me any ability to recognize that these ideas are sent by Him or by creations other than physical objects, and since He has given me a strong inclination to believe that the ideas come from physical objects, I see no way to avoid the conclusion that He deceives me if the ideas are sent to me by anything other than physical objects. It follows that physical objects exist. These objects may not exist exactly as I comprehend them by sense; in many ways, sensory comprehension is obscure and confused. But these objects must at least have in them everything that I clearly and distinctly understand them to have—every general property within the scope of pure mathematics....

I'll note that mind differs importantly from body in that body is by its nature divisible while mind is indivisible. When I think about my mind—or, in other words, about myself insofar as I am just a thinking thing—I can't distinguish any parts in me; I understand myself to be a single, unified thing. Although my whole mind seems united to my whole body, I know that cutting off a foot, arm, or other limb would not take anything away from my mind. The abilities to will, sense, understand, and so on can't be called parts, since it's one and the same mind that wills, senses, and understands. On the other hand, whenever I think of a physical or extended thing, I can mentally divide it, and I therefore understand that the object is divisible. This single fact would be enough to teach me that my mind and my body are distinct, if I hadn't already learned that in another way.

Next, I notice that the mind isn't directly affected by all parts of the body, but only by the brain—or maybe just by the small part of the brain containing the so-called "common sense." Whenever this part of the brain is in a given state, it presents the same thing to the mind, regardless of what is happening in the rest of the body (as is shown by innumerable experiments that I need not review here)....

I know that sensory indications of what is good for my body are more often true than false; I can almost always examine a given thing with several senses; and I can also use my memory (which connects the present to the past) and my understanding (which has now examined all the causes of error). Hence, I need no longer fear that what the senses daily show me is unreal. I should reject the exaggerated doubts of the past few days as ridiculous. This is especially true of the chief ground for these doubts—namely, my inability to distinguish dreaming from being awake. For I now notice that dreaming and being awake are importantly different: the events in dreams are not linked by memory to the rest of my life like those that happen while I am awake. If, while I'm awake, someone were suddenly to appear and then immediately to disappear without my seeing where he came from or went to (as happens in dreams), I would justifiably judge that he was not a real man but a ghost—or, better, an apparition created in my brain. But, if I distinctly observe something's source, its place, and the time at which I learn about it, and if I grasp an unbroken connection between it and the rest of my life, I'm quite sure that it is something in my waking life rather than in a dream. And I ought not to have the slightest doubt about the reality of such things if I have examined them with all my senses, my memory, and my understanding without finding any conflicting evidence. For, from the fact that God is not a deceiver, it follows that I am not deceived in any case of this sort. Since the need to act does not always allow time for such a careful examination, however, we must admit the likelihood of men's erring about particular things and acknowledge the weakness of our nature.

◉ CRITICAL QUESTIONS

1. In the first *Meditation*, Descartes was skeptical about how confident we can be in distinguishing dreaming from waking. Then he became more confident about making the distinction. According to Descartes, how can dreaming be distinguished from waking? Do you agree? Why, or why not?

2. Has Descartes convinced you that you are made of two substances, a mental substance or mind—which is unextended in space, indivisible, and capable of pure understanding—and a body—which is extended in space, divisible, and capable of sensation? Present an argument to support your answer.

12.3 YOU ARE AN EMBODIED SELF

Descartes's notion that the mind causally interacts with the body has been criticized for a variety of reasons. One has to do with the mysterious nature of the supposed causality. How can an immaterial substance that is nonspatial cause a material substance (the spatial body) to do anything? Causality requires some sort of contact. But how can this contact take place?

Another problem has to do with a physical law called the *conservation of energy*. According to this well-established law in current physical theory, the amount of energy in the universe is constant. However, if minds can act on physical bodies, new energy is created every time the mind causes the body to act. So interactionism appears to stand in direct contradiction to known physical laws.

A more recent line of criticism derives from mounting evidence about the brain and how it operates. Many scientists and philosophers now believe that it is only a matter of time until we can explain human behavior in physical terms. The more we learn about the brain and how it works, the more it seems evident that so-called mental states totally depend on the way the brain functions. If we had never seen a computer and suddenly discovered one, we might suppose that it was operated by some little person inside. However, as we learn more about the computer and how it works, we realize that there is no little person, or self, inside. The computations it performs are due to a complex mechanical arrangement and a program that provides instructions. So too, the argument goes, is the human brain.

Another recent criticism of Descartes's notion of the self as mind does not focus on the issue of interactionism but attacks the very idea of the self that underlies the theory of interaction. Cartesian dualism is a refined and sophisticated version of Plato's soul–body dualism (see Section 10.3). Both types of dualism have been immensely influential in Western culture. In fact, most of us were raised to believe in some kind of dualism. The very way we talk about ourselves reflects a dualistic viewpoint. We talk and think about our bodies as if they were shells or containers we just happen to inhabit. In other words, being in a body is not a necessary or essential characteristic of who we are.

However, imagine a world in which we had no eyes or ears, no sense of touch or smell or taste. What would such a world be like? "We would be very isolated," you might plausibly respond. Quite so. And isn't Descartes's mind quite isolated as well?

In the next selection, Eve Browning Cole, professor of philosophy at the University of Minnesota, Duluth, summarizes a critique of Descartes that stems from feminist philosophy. She argues that Descartes's procedure and his notion of the self pays insufficient attention to the fact that the self is embodied and exists in a network of relations with others. This fault has led to sexism insofar as it has reinforced a masculine notion of the self as autonomous, detached, and dominant over matter.

READING QUESTIONS

1. What are some of the motivations, according to Cole, behind the philosophical discomfort with the physical body?
2. In what sense, according to Cole, is Descartes setting himself an artificial task?
3. Cole claims that if Descartes were working in collaboration with others, he could not easily entertain such radical doubts. Why?
4. What is the main point of the section entitled "The Uncertain Body"?
5. What is meant by "the relational self," and what difference would it have made if Descartes had begun his thought there?
6. In what sense is the concept of a radically isolated subject incoherent?

Body, Mind, and Gender

EVE BROWNING COLE

We have already had occasion to observe that much of Western philosophy has displayed a definite discomfort with the fact that human minds come in human bodies, that consciousness and the thought processes it underlies are embodied in more or less gross matter. It is not very difficult to understand some of the motivations behind this discomfort. For thoughts do not seem to be subject to the same limitations as ordinary physical objects; in imagination, I can accomplish things which seem to transcend the limits of space and time. Vivid memories defy the irrecoverability of the past, seeming to bring to life dead friends, bringing into the present past scenes, meals, and dreams. Dreams themselves are a powerful impetus toward regarding the mind as something more than or different from the physical "container" which it "inhabits" (though we shall soon see

reasons to question these terms). And personal identity, the "I" who is the location of my consciousness, stretches back in time to embrace the child I was, the adolescent I became, and the woman I am now, even though in the physical sense I can only claim to be exactly what I now am (the past being no longer present).

Thus there are certain prima facie reasons for at least questioning how consciousness, thought, dreams, and identity relate to the physical world. But we will see that quite often philosophers have gone much further than questioning the relationship, to the extent of privileging the mental over the physical, derogating the physical and the human body along with it to a secondary ontological status, counseling efforts to transcend the body in order to apprehend truth, and even regarding the fact that mental events can cause physical events as a miracle performed by God on a daily basis! While this last, far from being a majority view, seems to have been instead a desperate expedient recommended only by one philosopher (Malebranche), it is symptomatic of something having gone badly wrong at the philosophical starting point.

Let us look more closely at the way in which the relation between body and mind, and the status of the body in the grand scheme of things, become problematic for philosophy. As our companion in this inquiry we will choose René Descartes—whose philosophical outlook, especially as represented in the designedly popular work *Meditations on First Philosophy* (published in 1641), proved enormously influential and remains a standard component of introductory studies of Western philosophy today.

SOLITARY MEDITATIONS, RADICAL DOUBTS

Descartes's work came at an extremely crucial juncture for Western philosophy. He entered a philosophical milieu still largely dominated by the medieval scholastic tradition, itself based heavily on a theologized and incomplete digestion of the legacy of the ancient Greeks. Studying with the Jesuits at the college of La Flèche, he received a "classical" and rather intellectually conservative education. Descartes made a radical break with this tradition, however, and set institutional philosophy off in a wholly new direction. Seeking to provide a philosophical method which would be accessible to all who possess common sense, providing a set of "rules for the direction of the mind" which would be so simple that "even women" would be able to follow them, his contributions to philosophy were revolutionary and of inestimable worth and influence. His contribution to the topic of this chapter, however, is highly problematic; and the difficulties he bequeathed to subsequent modern Western thought are enormous.

The full title of Descartes's Meditations is *Meditations on First Philosophy: In Which the Existence of God and the Distinction Between Mind and Body Are Demonstrated.* This full title is instructive as to how Descartes himself viewed his purpose in the work, which is often read in modern terms as a refutation of skepticism or an essay in foundationalism. By his own description, it is a work of *metaphysics*.

Descartes begins by confessing that he has long been aware that false beliefs have formed a part of his world view, and that a general and total mental "housecleaning" would need to be undertaken, in order to discover which of his views should be retained and which discarded. The procedure for this belief-testing, which he now proposes to undertake (since he is at present free "from every care" and "happily agitated by no passions") is that of *doubting*. He will attempt to cast doubt on each of his present beliefs; only those that survive the doubt ordeal will be retained. Rather than holding up individual beliefs for scrutiny, however, he proposes to address their general bases:

> … [I]t will not be requisite that I should examine each [belief] in particular, which would be an endless undertaking; for owing to the fact that the destruction of the foundations of necessity brings with it the downfall of the rest of the edifice, I shall only in the first place attack those principles upon which all my former opinions rested.

This project raises several interesting issues. First, Descartes is firmly committed to a *hierarchical* view of the structure of his belief system. The metaphor of the edifice of opinion, an ordered structure in which there is a top-down organization of architectural form, is an epistemological image to which we return … when we discuss images of belief systems, and the power of the metaphors we choose to represent cognition.

But note also the extreme *solitude* of Descartes's project here. He is proposing to take apart and rebuild his entire belief structure in isolation from the rest of the world, and particularly from other human beings. The idea that an epistemological value test could reliably be applied in complete isolation from other knowers, that one's own relations of knowing the world could be tested through demolition and then rebuilt to stringent specifications entirely of one's own devising, is extraordinary. When we consider the contexts in which knowing takes place, in which knowledge is sought and constructed, few of these appear to be ones in which isolation is afforded or even desirable (we might think of archeological digs, science labs, classrooms, reading groups, research institutes, fact-finding missions to other countries, courtrooms, and other typical situations in which knowledge is found and formed in human minds; none is an individual-based project).

Thus Descartes is setting himself an *artificial* kind of task, in the dual sense that his knowledge-seeking environment is atypical and that the envisioned "new and improved" cognitive structure or edifice of opinion will be his *own* individual artifact.

But the solitariness of Descartes's project has also another implication/motivation. Only in radical isolation from the rest of the human social world can Descartes *fully* explore the reliability of his entire belief system. For if he were exploring in collaboration with others, if the meditations he undertakes were the work of a Cartesian task force, he would have to make concessions to the reliability of certain beliefs before the task force could begin its work. He would have to trust that the others were thinkers, perhaps even thinkers on a par with himself; that they were working with him rather than against him, that they could have and work toward a common goal, that their words could be understood, trusted, believed, taken more or less at face value. In other words, the Cartesian project could not motivate total doubt if it were not so solitary. The powerful skeptical doubts which Descartes is about to summon into existence will answer only to the call of an isolated individual human mental voice. They are creatures of solitude. Descartes's individualistic starting point has lasting and dramatic effects on his total project and its overall outcomes.

THE UNCERTAIN BODY

As the doubt program progresses, Descartes discards his trust in his senses as a source of reliable belief. Since (he reasons) the senses have deceived him in the past, it is advisable to suspend belief in sensory information for the duration of his meditations until he can uncover some justification for their occasional reliable operations. But the senses have been the source of his belief that he is an embodied creature, that he exists in or as a physical organism, in addition to being an originator of thoughts. Thus he must suspend his belief in the existence of the embodied Descartes and conceive of himself only as a locus of thoughts and other mental events, possibly not embodied at all, possibly embodied very differently from the way he has always pictured and experienced himself:

> I shall ... suppose, not that God who is supremely good and the fountain of truth, but some evil genius not less powerful than deceitful, has employed his whole energies in deceiving me; I shall consider that the heavens, the earth, colors, figures, sound, and all the other external things are nought but the illusions and dreams of which this genius has availed himself in order to lay traps for my credulity; I shall consider myself as having no hands, no eyes, no flesh, no blood, nor any senses, yet falsely believing myself to possess all these things; I shall remain obstinately attached to this idea....

Descartes will conceive of "himself as something independent of his body, and will discover in this incorporeal consciousness the one indubitable truth which will function for him as an Archimedean immovable point, from which his belief structure can be rebuilt. This point is the certain truth of his own existence.

Descartes has effectively divided himself, and his belief structure, into two components: the certain mind, the component in which he will repose confidence at least as to its existence, and the uncertain body, about whose reality he will remain in a state of doubt until complex argumentation proves a limited trustworthiness, a constricted and carefully policed reliability.

Armed with the certainty of his own existence (as an insular node of consciousness which may or may not be embodied), Descartes goes on to demonstrate the existence of God, the fact that God is neither a grand deceiver nor the kind of being who would tolerate such massive deception of his creatures, and finally infers that the senses' urgings toward belief are not in themselves so awfully unreliable after all.

But the body, on Descartes's showing, remains forever only a probability, never a certainty. Since certainty is the Cartesian Holy Grail, this means that the body is irredeemably a second-class citizen in the metaphysical scheme of things. First rank in Descartes's universe is held by "thinking things," nodes of consciousness that can through purely rational processes follow deductive argumentation to absolutely certain conclusions. The body cannot participate in this process with its own humble abilities, here conceived as sensation and perception; it either impedes the rational process or, tamed and disciplined, stands dumbly by and lets knowledge happen. Highest epistemological honors go to the elements of deductive reasoning processes: mathematical laws, logical principles, indubitable truths. These construct the knowable core of the world, and to them in human experience is superadded a "flesh" of more dubious nature: bodies, colors, touches, smells, and the entire organic contents of the universe.

This theme, the privileging of the mental over the physical, does not originate with Descartes by any means. It is familiar to readers of Plato, who describes the relationship of soul to body in vivid terms:

> ... [W]hen the soul uses the instrumentality of the body for any inquiry, whether through sight or hearing or any other sense—because using the body implies using the senses—it is drawn away by the body into the realm of the variable, and loses its way and becomes confused and dizzy, as though it were fuddled, through contact with things of a similar nature.... But when it investigates by itself, it passes into the realm of the pure and everlasting and immortal and changeless.... [*Phaedo* 79c–d]

Here the body is cast in the role of a bad companion, bad company for the soul to keep, company that drags it down to its own level and impedes its effective functioning. A nonphysical form of knowing, in which the soul or mind operates "by itself," is much to be preferred.

Two features of this way of discussing the relation of mind to body, common to Plato and Descartes, should be noted. First, it is striking how easily both drop into the mode of thought in which a human being becomes not one but two, and two *different*, kinds of entity. There quickly emerges a kind of logical and metaphysical distance between mind and body, an alienation that provokes disagreement about what to believe,

what to seek, how to behave. But secondly, this is not a disagreement among equals. The mind or soul is in Descartes's view the locus of certainty and value, in Plato's view the part of the human composite akin to the "pure" and "divine." Its relationship to the body is to be one of dominance; the body is to be subordinated and ruled.

An individual human being contains within the self, therefore, a fundamental power dialectic in which mind must triumph over body and must trumpet its victory in flourishes of "pure" rationality by means of which its soundness is demonstrated and ratified. Far from being an isolated peculiarity of a small handful of philosophers, moreover, this general dialectic is seen being set up and played out in many theaters of Western culture, from religion to popular morality, from Neoplatonism to existentialism....

FEMINIST CRITIQUES

We have already noted the extraordinary isolation of Descartes's metaphysical musings; he cuts off not only the instructions of his perceptive faculties, but also the entirety of his human social surroundings, to seek a certainty accessible only to the lone and insular conscious node "I." A feminist critique of Cartesian method might well begin with just this feature of his project.

The Cartesian ego, rather than being the ground for certainty and the Archimedean point which some philosophers have taken it to be, may in fact be the result of a mistaken abstraction. Feminist philosophers such as Caroline Whitbeck and Lorraine Code have convincingly argued that a preferable starting point for understanding the contents of human consciousness is *the relational self*, the self presented as involved in and importantly constituted by its connectedness to others. Each of us at this moment is connected as it were by invisible threads to an indefinite number of specific other human beings. In some cases, these connections are relatively remote; for example, we are all members of the same species and have biological similarities. Similarity is a relationship; therefore we are all related. Western culture has not tended to place much weight on this species relationship, however, and in some notorious institutions such as chattel slavery the reality of the relationship has been implicitly or explicitly denied. In other cases, the relationships in which we now stand are of deep significance in defining who we are, how we think, and how we act.

Starting with the concept of the relational self would greatly have changed the course of Descartes's meditations. If other persons are not just colorful wallpaper the design of which I contemplate from inside a mental fishbowl but actually part of who I am, then distancing myself from them in thought and supposing that I am the only consciousness in the universe becomes, if not impossible, extremely illogical. What would I hope to accomplish? If on the other hand I begin by granting them mentality and humanity, I will proceed by considering the specific ways in which their contributions to my mental life are made.

Paula Gunn Allen writes that, in Native American cultures, the question "Who is your mother?" is another and more profound way of asking who one is. In asking, one is inquiring about one of the most significant parts of a person's identity, for the influence of the mother and the mother's contribution to the child's self is considerable. In much the same way, we might begin a metaphysics of the self by asking "To whom am I related? In what ways? What contributions to my consciousness are presently being made, and by whom?" Such a beginning acknowledges the fundamental importance of sociality in human existence.

Here it might be objected that Descartes's ... methodological skepticism about the existence and reality of other minds remains a possible position even for a relational self. Haven't we merely sidestepped the skeptical possibility by granting the mentality and humanity of the others? Doesn't it really still seem possible that they are all phantasms, or robots, or results of direct C-fiber stimulation by a mad scientist on a distant planet?

Yes, skeptical possibilities remain and cannot be ruled out. But taking the standpoint of the relational self allows us to affirm that such possibilities *do not matter*. What matters is that relationships are granted metaphysical priority over isolated individuals, so that the embeddedness of the self in a social world becomes its primary reality. The exact nature of the individuals involved

becomes a matter of secondary importance. I grant at the outset that others make constitutive contributions to my experience, and I to theirs. This mutual interrelation becomes the ground for any further inquiry rather than functioning as a more or less uncertain inductive conclusion. Thus, to return to the problem of other minds, we can see that the philosopher's uncertainty about the mentality of the "foreign body" at the bus stop is a symptom of a flawed starting point rather than a genuine puzzle attending our reflective lives. The philosopher's mistake is to begin from isolation and attempt to reason himself back into society; we in fact begin in society and this is not an accidental but a deep truth about us.

We might go even further and argue that the concept of a radically isolated subject as the seat of consciousness is simply incoherent. We do not begin to think and speak in solitude, but in concert with our culture and with the specific representatives of the culture in whose care we find ourselves. We form ourselves in a collective process that is ongoing; our thoughts are never entirely our own, intersubjectivity is basic, while individual subjectivity is secondary and an abstraction.

Some feminist philosophers have analyzed the isolation of the ego and the "fishbowl" syndrome of some philosophy of mind in terms of differences between masculine and feminine gender socialization. Developmental psychologists have suggested that the structure and dynamics of relationships with other human beings differ profoundly for traditionally socialized men and women. Due largely to the fact that, in most cultures and historical epochs, women function as the primary caregiver for children of both sexes while men enter into the life of the family in a more intermittent way, it is to be expected that male children will form their earliest sense of themselves by *distinguishing* themselves from their female caregiver, realizing that they are members of the group from which the (distant, absent, or intermittently present) male family members derive. Female children will form their sense of themselves by *identifying* with the female caregiver, realizing that they share with her membership in the group of female family members. This early direction of the sense of self, either to distinguish oneself and differ from, or to identify oneself and resemble, leaves a lasting legacy in the child's heart and mind. The adult character which emerges from the socialization process is marked by the tendency toward either clear and stark ego boundaries (if male) or flexible and mobile ego boundaries (if female). A whole constellation of dispositions and traits goes alongside this basic distinction. The masculine ego, formed at a distance from its primary role exemplar, displays a lifelong tendency toward independence, distancing from others, and endless acts of "proving" the masculinity which it modeled, with some uncertainty, on the distant fellow *man*. The feminine ego, formed in close proximity to its primary role exemplar, has lifelong tendencies toward identifying with others, reciprocating feelings, being dependent on others and relating to them easily even confusing its own needs with those of others—since it early on perceived that part of being a woman was to place others first, as a primary caregiver must frequently do.

This developmental thesis about gender identity, though impossible to demonstrate empirically and almost certainty not cross-culturally or cross-racially, offers a tempting explanation for the philosophical model of the isolated self we have traced in Descartes and seen lurking behind the problem of other minds. The Cartesian ego is quintessentially *masculine* in its solitary doubting program, in its self-confidence about its quest, in its ambition ("proving" itself all on its own resources), and in its uneasiness....

By contrast, the relational self which some feminist philosophers have proposed as an alternative starting point for philosophy of mind, and for grounding our understanding of human experience generally, is more aligned with feminine identity development.

In addition to proposing that philosophers start from a conception of the human self as relational, as situated within a web of cultural and personal relationships which not only shape but do much to constitute its being and its thought, feminist philosophers have also criticized the Cartesian legacy for the relation between mind and body which it conveys.

We saw above that Descartes (and others) operate from a position that separates mind, self, consciousness, ego from the physical body these are said to "inhabit" or ... "animate." In Descartes, the distinction is so drastic that mind and body are said to share no attributes whatsoever; they are oppositionally defined and thus, metaphysically speaking, mutually exclusive. Consciousness is nonphysical, nonextended, and inhabits an order of being completely distinct from that in which the body lives. The body is a machine, operated by the mind in the case of the human being, mindless and purely mechanical in the case of other animals.

This drastic dualism is vulnerable to criticism from many different directions; feminist critics begin with the observation that in Western culture and throughout its history, we can observe a tendency to identify women with the natural, the physical, the bodily. Nature is personified as a female, a "mother"; women are portrayed as more closely linked to nature, less completely integrated into civilization and the cultural order, than men. Men are rational agents, makers of order and measure, controllers of history; women are emotional vessels, subjects of orders and measures, passive observers of history. No one describes this more clearly or more influentially for modern psychology than Sigmund Freud, who writes:

> The fact that women must be regarded as having little sense of justice is no doubt related to the predominance of envy in their mental life; for the demand for justice is a modification of envy and lays down the condition subject to which we can lay envy aside. We also regard women as weaker in their social interests and as having less capacity for sublimating their instincts than men.

Freud subsumes women into the domain of the natural, where instinct rules and justice is foreign.

Now, if man is to mind as woman is to body, as appears from much of the literature and iconography of Western culture throughout historical time, and if we adhere to a generally Cartesian view of the self as a purely mental entity, then the self of the woman becomes deeply problematic. Can women have Cartesian egos? Genuine selves? It would appear to be impossible if woman's essence is located in the domain of the bodily. Clearly some other and less dichotomously dualistic conception of the self must be sought. The associations between woman and body in Western culture have had a decidedly negative aspect, which feminist critics have stressed. The reduction of a woman's value to the culturally inscribed value of a certain feminine appearance and protest against that reduction have been strong themes of feminist criticism for several decades. Nevertheless, the appearance obsession which women are encouraged to develop in our culture, according to which a more-or-less single standard of feminine beauty applies to all women, no matter their age, race, build, or lifestyle, is as strong as ever and, some argue, gaining strength. In addition now to being slim, youthful, cosmetically adorned to the correct degree, fashionably dressed, and as light-skinned as possible (with of course a healthy tan to indicate white-skinned class-privilege), women must ideally have "hard bodies" with muscle-definition acquired by hours of grueling workouts and aerobic routines. That this formula cannot be met by the poor, those who don't have the time to devote to the pursuit of beauty, or those whose bodies resist the mold for whatever reason, does not mean that the standard does not hold its pristine severity over all women's heads equally. (Sadly, the appearance obsession does seem to be extending to men as well, but still seems to pertain to them in lesser degree.)

In a recent classroom discussion of trends in advertising, one young female student spoke out with sincere enthusiasm: "I can't wait till I get older! I'm going to eat whatever I want, wear whatever I want, and just not care!" An older female student turned to her and said, "Why wait? It isn't any easier to look different at age fifty than at age twenty." This exchange was instructive in many ways. There was anger in the second woman's voice; she heard herself as older being dismissed somehow from the class of viable potential beauties. There was a strange assumption behind the first woman's statements, to the effect that until some unspecified age, women are under an obligation to eat and to dress in ways other than those they would choose if not constrained. And there was in the second speaker's choice of the word *different* to describe an undisciplined woman the implicit admission that the *norm*, what it means to be non-different, is precisely the cultural ideal of the dieting and carefully dressed youthful appearance. But this is clearly false, as a simple glance at the immense variety of actual women's bodies in any real-life situation will immediately confirm. The so-called *norm* is in fact extremely rare. Yet an enormous amount of women's energy is devoted to its pursuit. Constant dieting, eating disorders such as anorexia and bulimia, compulsive exercising, and (not least of all) enormous cash investments in beauty and fashion, are all symptomatic of the power of the cultural ideal.

To connect with our previous discussion of the gendered distinction between mind and body, men generally do not in our culture tend to identify themselves and their worth as persons with the details of their physical bodies' appearances. While in recent years the standards of male attractiveness have undoubtedly become more exacting, men clearly feel more relaxed about not meeting these standards.

Let us summarize the contribution which the dualistic Platonic-Cartesian model of the self has made to our cultural conceptions of body and mind: (1) The body's relationship to the mind, in any given human being, is one of unruly bondage or servitude; mind properly dominates its body and directs its actions, while body properly obeys. (2) Mind's behavior and dispositions are, however, described in terms more appropriate to masculine gender identity (activity, ruling or hegemony, capacity for abstraction and objectivity, distanced contemplation, dispassionate analysis), while body's configurations tend toward feminine (passivity, subordination, unconscious physicality, sensuous and emotional implication, confusion). (3) Thus, while rationality becomes defined as a mostly masculine project, an adorned and disciplined physicality becomes the feminist project—leading to the contemporary obsession of middle-class women with weight and appearance generally. Women are given the cultural prescription to be docile bodies, adorned and available for participation in the rational schemes of the male-dominated social order. Thus the fact that in some basic respects the Cartesian ego is a masculine ego can be seen to have enormous reverberations throughout modern life. It is of no small significance to recognize that a certain outlook in the philosophy of mind provides a perfect recipe for male dominance and women's subordination.

Several important qualifications need to be made here, however. First, the neat gender dichotomy we have drawn in the ratio of proportion:

Male:Mind::Female:Body

does not appear to hold cross-racially. That is, nonwhite males in a white-dominated culture will be treated in much the same way as bodies are treated by minds in the Cartesian framework: They will be dominated, ruled, directed, used. Furthermore, white females will participate in this domination and rule, functioning as "minds" in a bureaucratic manner; and white women will benefit from skin privilege at the expense of the dominated nonwhite men and women. The non-white populations will be accorded *mental* attributes that correspond to the physical attributes of the body in the Cartesian scheme; they will be considered less than fully rational, emotional, "natural" or savage, sensuous, weak-willed, and so forth. So the factor of race does much to complicate a mind–body value map which takes *only* gender into account. This has led some feminist philosophers to hypothesize that *both* sexism and racism are more about power than they are about either sex or race.

A second qualification concerns the relationship between what, for want of a clearer word, we could call ideology and social reality. The rational man and the physical woman, intellectual masculinity and corporeal femininity, are creatures of ideology. This means that they are intensely value-laden concepts structuring culture and its expectations, rather than empirical generalizations drawn from observation of real women and real men. But ideology and reality touch one another at multiple points and reciprocally influence each other at these points of contact. It may be a strange-sounding philosophical thesis that rationality has been interpreted in terms defined as masculine, but it takes on a gruesomely real shape when a Berkeley philosophy professor announces to his classes that women can't do

logic, or when another philosophy professor writes to the secretary of the American Philosophical Association that white women and black people of both sexes display analytical capabilities inferior to those of white men. This is ideology shaping social reality with a vengeance.

Believing that the drastic dualism of the traditional picture of body's relation to mind, along with the inbuilt evaluatively hierarchical model of dominance and subordination which gives the model its working directives, are both deeply flawed, feminist philosophers look for alternatives.

A beginning point is to conceive of the human self as intrinsically embodied: An *embodied self can* displace the only questionably embodied Cartesian ego, the uncomfortably body-trapped Platonic soul, as a foundation for further inquiry into the nature of human experience. To conceive of the self as essentially or intrinsically embodied means to acknowledge the centrality of the physical in human psychology and cognition, for one thing. It means opening the door to the possibility of a bodily wisdom, to revaluing the physical human being, in ways that promise both better metaphysical schemes and more ethical models for human interaction. Breaking down the valuational hierarchy between mind and body, attempting to think of them as woven and melded together into what constitutes who we are and who we ought to be, eliminates the perhaps primary internal oppression model of mind over body. As a culture, however, we have learned to think of the body, and of those primarily identified with it, in terms of scorn (even when those latter people are ourselves). We have learned to privilege the "rational" over the emotional (conceived as proceeding from physical sources), the basely corporeal, the manual and tactile; to weigh technorationality over the mute testimony of nature and our own bodies. Those of us who are women have at times been encouraged to view our bodies with contempt when we perceive them as falling short of the beauty ideal or when we are addressed rudely in sexual terms by strangers. How can we begin to approach the relation of mind and body not as a *problem* but as a source of liberatory insight and joy?

French feminist philosophers, building on their national intellectual tradition, which placed the phenomenology of *lived experience at* center stage, have made exciting progress in constructing the basis for a liberatory philosophy of the body. They have argued that the dominant tradition in Western philosophy has made women's bodies problematic in two contradictory ways: In one way, woman and body are equated as essentially physical, and women's entire personalities become sexualized (think of the late Victorian habit of referring to women as a group with the phrase "the sex," as if men were "the nonsex"). In another direction, however, the sexualized woman is either ignored in philosophy, so complete is her subsumption under the rubric *Nature,* or she is philosophized about in male terms, and her (now highlighted in neon) sexuality is described in terms appropriate only to a certain specific cultural construction of *male* sexuality. She is thus obscured as a subject, discussed as an object.

This means that, for a genuinely liberatory philosophy of the body to be developed, women must reclaim in theory and in practice their own physicality, their own sexuality....

◉ CRITICAL QUESTIONS

1. What does it mean to say that "the Cartesian ego is quintessentially masculine" and to say that "the relational self ... is more aligned with feminine identity development"? Are these two claims plausible? Explain your answer.
2. According to Cole, how is the "appearance obsession" related to Descartes's views about the relationship between mind and body? Do you think Cole is right about this? Why, or why not?
3. What does Cole mean by the "embodied self"? Do you find her overall argument in support of this idea persuasive? Provide an argument in support of your answer.

12.4 YOU ARE A COMPUTING MACHINE

You probably don't like to think of yourself as a machine. After all, a machine is a thing, a mere "it," whereas you are a human being with a mind. I know I don't normally think of myself as a machine, and like you, I think of myself as something more than an impersonal thing. But what if we are "virtual" machines? That is, what if our conscious life is the result of a particular pattern of rules (software) being imposed on fixed structures (hardware)?

Alan Turing (1912–1954), a brilliant mathematician and computer scientist, proposed an operational test for deciding whether a computer can think. Turing argued that we can conclude that a computer can think if it can regularly beat a human opponent in the "imitation game." Two "contestants," according to this "game" show, are hidden from a human judge. One is a human and the other is a computer. They can communicate with the judge by typing messages on computer terminals. Both the human and the computer try to convince the judge, by their responses to questions posed by the judge, that they are human, conscious thinkers. If the judge cannot regularly spot the difference (pick out the computer responses from the human responses), the computer "wins" (is judged to have a mind!). If it quacks like a duck, it is a duck even if it doesn't look like one or walk like one or is made of the same stuff.

Turing's test reflects a view called **behaviorism**, which is a materialistic theory of the mind. According to this theory, so-called mental events are the same thing as behaviors or dispositions to behave. Thus, if I have a pain in my leg, I am disposed (have a tendency) to say "ouch" and rub the spot where it hurts. My behavior or my disposition to behave in such a fashion is the same as "experiencing pain in my leg."

If a computer behaves like a conscious mind in the Turing test, why not say it is conscious?

And why not work it the other way around? If a computing machine can behave in the same way a mind does, then perhaps a mind is a computing machine, or at least the brain that produces a mind is a computing machine. Perhaps it is just lingering prejudices about souls, or a kind of egocentric arrogance, that prevents us from recognizing that the brain is a very complex organic computing machine and our conscious life is a product of this complex computing system. Should comparing our human brain to a computer, such as the one recently featured on television, shown in one of the color plates, be unsettling to us?

Bruce Hinrichs, author of the next article, is a professor of psychology and humanities at Century College in Minnesota. He not only argues that the brain, which creates the mind, is a computing machine but also argues that this idea should not be nearly as upsetting to people as it often is.

◉ READING QUESTIONS

1. What are the two reasons why some people resist the brain–computer analogy, and how does Hinrichs counter those objections?
2. What are some important differences between a brain and a computer?
3. How does Hinrichs deal with the issue of how a brain creates a mind, and why does he think some people find his answer unsatisfactory?

Computing the Mind

BRUCE H. HINRICHS

For centuries, philosophers have puzzled over the mind–body problem—the captivating enigma that asks how subjective mental states are connected to our objective physical biology. In this century, neuroscientists have made spectacular achievements in describing the cellular and molecular actions of the nervous system, while cognitive psychologists have indirectly observed and measured mental and psychological functions, sometimes with ingenious experimental methodology and often borrowing brain-imaging techniques from neuroscience.

The most recent contributors to the mind–body topic are computer network experts who study how individual elements interact in a systematic way, producing computational processes which give rise to information processing and artificial intelligence. Pioneers such as Alan Turing, John von Neumann, Warren McCulloch and Walter Pitts, and, more recently, Patricia Churchland and Terrence Sejnowski have provided an analysis of systems at a higher level than the typical biomedical approaches of neuroscience and at a lower level than the macro states and behaviors favored by psychologists. By examining neural networks, these researchers hope to uncover just how individual cells combine to create emergent phenomena which are more than the sum of their parts.

Of course, in each cast the attention is on the human brain as the locus of mental and psychological functions. Computer guru Marvin Minsky

Bruce H. Hinrichs, "Computing the Mind: A Scientific Approach to the Philosophy of Mind and Brain," *The Humanist*, March–April (1998), Volume 58, 26–31. Copyright © 1998 American Humanist Association. Reprinted by permission of the author.

has called the brain a "meat machine" and a machine that "clanks softly." Viewing the brain as a soft computational machine allows an interesting commentary on the recent chess match lost by Garry Kasparov to the IBM computer sometimes called Deeper Blue (because it is an improved version of Deep Blue beaten by Kasparov the previous year). In this view, it was not man against machine as much as it was one type of machine—or process, if you prefer—against another. As was shown, one process happened to be better at chess than the other.

Critics complain that a digital computer lacks awareness or understanding, that it is just making unconscious computations. But a brain is a type of computer and it has awareness and understanding. A brain also just makes subconscious computations—by neurons creating electrical current and squirting transmitter chemicals. This, of course, is the essential mystery: how can these singularly objective cellular brain events transform into psychological states, moods, and behaviors? The consciousness we experience is apparently achieved via the interaction of billions of unconscious computational events, which in themselves have no awareness or understanding.

Certainly Deeper Blue was made and programmed by humans, but so was Kasparov! If we're giving credit to Deeper Blue's programmers, then let's give credit to the programmers of Kasparov: his parents, teachers, previous opponents, authors of books he read, and so forth. Also, some machines today are made by other machines, and someday computers will likely be made and programmed by other computers. So what? None of these truths diminishes human integrity, dignity, worth, goals, values, or self-actualization. There is no threat. Brains are better at some things, while silicon digital computers excel at others.

ANALOGIES

Years ago we were told that a human brain functions like a telephone switchboard. I still remember the scratchy 16mm movie that illustrated brain activity as a sequence of switchboard plugs being methodically pulled from and inserted into

an impressive array of holes. This analogy was readily embraced throughout society, in and out of schools, and it even sprouted in pedestrian places such as the silly 1972 Woody Allen movie *Everything You Always Wanted to Know About Sex But Were Afraid to Ask.* Allen depicts the brain as a command center for body actions (sex, in this case), which are initiated and regulated via telephone communication.

The days when a brain was likened to a telephone switchboard are thankfully long gone. In the modern zeitgeist, the idea seems humorously antiquated, belonging more properly to an era of bobby-soxers, air raid drills, and bomb shelters. But contemporary society need not go metaphor-less because—as is usually the case—when one analogy grows passe, another elbows its way into our collective hearts. The au courant brain metaphor, which is both ubiquitous and appropriate for the "information age," is that a brain is like a computer.

Our popular culture absorbs and reflects this analogy regularly—through such television characters as Commander Data of *Star Trek: The Next Generation,* who achieves consciousness with a "positronic" electronic matrix brain; through popular fiction like *The Terminal Man,* which features a man with epilepsy who has electrodes inserted into his brain; through newscasts which regularly report findings that certain traits are "hardwired" into the brain; and through movies such as *Brainstorm* (1983), *Total Recall* (1990), and *Until the End of the World* (1991), which envision machines that are able to interface with a living human brain and thereby access various mental functions, such as memories and dreams. Apparently, the brain–computer analogy is widespread and implicitly accepted throughout our culture. The brain has gone cyber.

IS A BRAIN LIKE A COMPUTER?

When first proposed in the 1960s, the brain–computer analogy was widely criticized, quite unfairly, on the basis that brains do very different tasks from computers. For example, it was noted that a brain is exquisitely excellent at visually recognizing a face or an object, while a computer is clunky and exceedingly slow at pattern recognition. On the other hand, a computer can do complex mathematical calculations at extremely high speed, while a brain is stumped by such tasks. While these indeed were and still are accurate observations, what makes this criticism a red herring is that it isn't the particular content of a computation that determines if something is like a computer; rather, it is the process used. In other words, it isn't what is done but how it's done that matters.

A more valid complaint of the brain–computer analogy is regarding the word *like*. The brain is not like a computer; it is a computer. Certainly a brain does not compute the same information that a PC does, but in the method—the manner in which it processes information—the brain is computing. For better or worse, your brain is a computer. Greetings, Data.

Not surprisingly, the idea that a brain is a computer receives a good deal of resistance and scoffing. One reason for this is that the term *computer* is often wrongly interpreted to exclusively denote serial digital computers. But the PC, like the slide rule, is just one example of a device that makes computations. A brain also is a computational device.

A second reason for resistance is that most nonexperts and even a few experts believe that a brain is more than a mere computer; that brain functioning in some way—perhaps at a subatomic or metaphysical level—results in the creation of emergent mental and emotional properties that would not be possible simply through computational processes. When this idea is presented with a rationale, it commonly is accompanied by quasi-scientific jargon. References to chaos theory and particle physics are currently in vogue, as if brains were the only substances on Earth that involve principles of quantum physics.

Arcane and illogical philosophical arguments are also often given. These imply that brains are somehow different than other matter in the universe and only brains can experience metaphysical transformations. Although these contentions certainly stimulate entertaining discussions, they are grossly speculative, controversial—even volatile when linked with religious beliefs—and extremely

unlikely to be resolved in the near future. So far, a materialist view is completely complementary to today's wide-ranging multidisciplinary empirical data.

What seems clear is that, whatever other qualities it may possess, a brain appears to be a kind of computer, a nature-made computer. Through a series of complex interactions, a brain takes incoming sensory signals, processes that information, and achieves a computational product, an output. Think of your senses as the keyboard or modem and your conscious mind as the monitor. The output of the brain includes regulation of body systems, emotions, behaviors, and thoughts, both conscious and unconscious. A brain does compute. Of course, exactly what it computes varies significantly from a PC or Macintosh.

This idea is typically a frightening one to people, although not to a majority of brain researchers and artificial intelligence experts who have calmly accepted it, at least at some fundamental level, despite disagreements over nuances. For our part, although we may have some trepidation, if we are willing to take an open-minded view, then it seems reasonable, even fun, to agree with the experts that a brain is a natural computer, the world's first computer, the best and brightest computer. There should be nothing threatening nor dehumanizing about this view. In fact, adopting this insight may help us to better understand and accept emotional, behavioral, and cognitive differences between people and the mental problems that beset us. However, even if we accept this framework, there are significant clarifications necessary, lest unwarranted conclusions be drawn.

WHAT KIND OF COMPUTER DO YOU HAVE?

A brain may be a computer, but it is a distinctly different sort of computer than the silicon chip models on our desks. The complex networking that is characteristic of both a PC and a brain is achieved in each case through the use of entirely different substances and different systems of organization. The cells (neurons) which permit communication within a brain are alive; a brain is a living computer. Brain cells require oxygen and involve complex biological processes driven by genetic codes. They are subject to malformations, irregularities, and damage via biological mechanisms (consider, for example, Alzheimer's disease). This simple realization leads us to the most enlightening fact that, since brain cells are alive and therefore are malleable and dynamic, it becomes difficult, perhaps impossible, to distinguish between hardware and software within the brain.

In contrast, a semiconductor computer uses cells that are essentially static, unchanged by the signals they carry; in a PC or Mac, the hardware is not significantly altered by the software program it runs. When the software is removed, the hardware is unchanged, back to normal, ready for more software. Brains don't work like that. A brain's hardware is pivotally changed by its software—a process that is at the heart of how a brain stores information (that is, remembers) and maintains continuity. As a brain takes in information through the senses, the cells which comprise the hardware are physically changed by the process.

Take language, for example. One brain may run an "English" program while another runs a "French" one. Each brain has been programmed through experience, and the software programs are now integral parts of the hardware of the brain. The hardware of each brain is importantly different from the other at the cellular level. They are different in a physical/chemical way that would be extremely difficult, if not impossible, to undo without doing damage to their structures; in a brain, the software is intricately intertwined with the hardware. The program (in this example, language) cannot be removed without altering the hardware. Even while asleep (and not dreaming), when one's conscious mind is "turned off," the nature of the software program is retained within the hardware so that, when one awakens, the same old memories, thoughts, and feelings are booted up and running.

MAKE UP YOUR MIND!

This insight may lead us to wonder what exactly it is about brains that allows them to create thoughts, memories, awareness, emotions—that

is, a mind. Where in the brain's biological processes are the key elements that give us consciousness? Are mental and emotional experiences a product of the brain's cellular interactions and therefore might be reproducible using inorganic networks that replicate brain networks? Or are conscious experiences dependent upon the biological characteristics of brain cells themselves? Does a mental experience—such as seeing, hearing, or feeling—depend on some particular quality of the individual cells of the brain, or is the computational interaction between the cells sufficient to produce awareness?

If it is the brain cells that are crucial for creating consciousness, then we may wonder which specific properties or characteristics of the cells are the necessary ones. Do other cells that have those properties then also have a mental life? Could mental experiences be replicated in a laboratory by reproducing those special cellular characteristics?

On the other hand, if mental experiences are produced not by particular aspects of the cells but instead by their interacting networks doing some sort of computing, then it should be possible to build a machine that could generate mental phenomena. If a silicon chip computer were built to exactly simulate brain connections, would it not feel? If not, why? What would be missing?

Of course, it is entirely possible—in fact, it is likely—that the creation of mental and emotional experiences depends on a unique combination of cellular characteristics and their interactions—that both biological cellular mechanisms and neural networks are necessary. In that event, it would take information about both neural nets and cell biology to understand and to artificially create a conscious mind.

When a brain creates a mind—when thoughts and emotions are formed by brain properties, states, conditions, and actions—then precisely what are the particular, distinctive elements involved? Are thinking, feeling, dreaming, and consciousness unique to humans or are these subjective experiences shared on some continuum with animals, insects, amoebae, perhaps even inorganic materials? In other words, are mental phenomena reproducible? Could a nonliving machine, if properly constructed, conceive a thought, feel, think, dream?

A SCIENTIFIC ANSWER

When we ask how it is that a brain creates a mind, it is somewhat similar to asking how any observed quality is created by its physical constituents. For example, how is it that rocks are hard, iron is magnetic, ice is cold, or, for illustrative purposes, water creates wetness? Just as wetness is a property or quality of water, the mind is a property or quality of the brain. Wetness is a state or condition that is created by the physical nature of water, and similarly we can conceptualize mental experiences as states or conditions created by the physical nature of the brain. Although this is not a perfect comparison—in fact, there are no perfect comparisons since a mind is the only thing we know to have subjectivity or awareness—still, we can use this comparison to help us achieve a better conceptual paradigm of the mind–brain connection.

When we attempt to explain a certain phenomenon, a scientific answer is one that describes the physical/chemical properties and interactions underlying the quality to be explained. For example, wetness is a quality that is scientifically explained by reference to certain properties and interactions of hydrogen and oxygen atoms. Following this paradigm, mental experiences can similarly be scientifically explained by detailing the specific brain substances and activities which generate them. Since the mind is one of the things a brain does, a scientific explanation of the mind would thus consist of a detailed description of the physical/chemical brain states and networks associated with each mental experience.

Though most people find this form of answer acceptable for explaining other things, it is typically found unsatisfactory for the question of how a brain creates a mind, since people want an answer of a different sort: one invoking the metaphysical or supernatural. Although the scientific approach may seem inadequate, it is how we explain other phenomena, and in those cases it is accepted. We don't ask how it is that water creates wetness; the how doesn't make sense, other than explaining wetness with reference to its underlying physical features. Perhaps this is the best approach to understanding the mind: to reduce mental experiences to their underlying physical features and not ask how it is that these features produce the mind.

It is disconcerting to hear critics reject a scientific approach to the mind because it doesn't include nonscientific ideas, such as the metaphysical, paranormal, or spiritual. But in any way that the mind can be examined empirically, a scientific approach is appropriate. This does not dehumanize us or diminish the value of the arts, emotions, self-discovery, and so on. Other valid approaches to understanding human experiences are, of course, welcomed. But science can provide one powerful piece of the puzzle.

It is likewise disconcerting to hear quasi-scientific explanations of the mind, which often are seductive enough to gain the favor of listeners. For example, Deepak Chopra often says that "a thought is a quantum event." Because of his use of scientific terminology, the hypothesis seems plausible. However, this is a confused idea. A thought is a personal, subjective experience produced by the brain, while quantum events are activities occurring at a subatomic level (for example, the interaction between an electron and a photon) which occur regularly in all physical matter in the universe, in and outside of our bodies. A thought is no more or less a quantum event than is wetness. The subjective experience of thinking is produced by actions of brain cells, which naturally include quantum events as do all physical acts.

We need to get over the idea that humans—and, in particular, the human mind—are somehow mysteriously or miraculously outside of nature. How a brain creates a mind is no more or less a mystery or a miracle than how rocks are hard, how magnets create fields, how electrons produce current, how light is both particle and wave, or how water is wet. Those who study the mind scientifically are interested in this area because it is one way of examining the human equation. It is a very practical approach that offers hope for people who have mental problems, such as Alzheimer's, Parkinson's, depression, or schizophrenia.

BASICS OF BRAIN AND MIND

The brain is a physical thing within the natural world, not a supernatural or metaphysical entity. Minds are not supernatural entities but personal experiences produced when brains are in a state of awareness of their own functioning, most probably a state created through the complex intercommunication between and among brain subcomputers for vision, hearing, language, attention, and other cognitive and perceptual functions. Minds are not substances; they are subjective experiences which the brain creates as a window into certain aspects of its own functioning. A brain, or a particular subdivision of the brain, is able to create an awareness of certain of its own states or functions—a kind of self-monitoring.

This concept of the mind may help us in speculating about why the mind exists. Why didn't a brain evolve without consciousness? What was the evolutionary impetus for the development of awareness? Viewing mental experiences as self-monitoring events helps us initiate some hypotheses about why consciousness would have evolutionary survival advantages over a non-conscious brain.

Although some experts have proposed that minds and brains are the same thing (in fact, some writers have recently begun to use the term brain–mind), minds, of course, are not brains any more than wetness is water. Minds are a quality or product of certain brain activity—one of the many things that a brain does, along with control of muscles, organs, and body housekeeping functions. While asleep, for example, a brain can be performing many functions, although consciousness (the mind) is temporarily turned off.

A brain has many tasks. One of the most interesting is the creation of thoughts, feelings, dreams, choices, personal identity, and awareness of the environment and the self—in other words, a conscious mind. The specific details of how the mind is created by the brain are yet to be unraveled and are likely to be complex and difficult to uncover and elucidate. Still, there is no reason to believe that these details are conceptually any more inaccessible to scientific investigation and scrutiny than any other complex phenomena. Nor is there any reason to feel threatened or dehumanized by such studies. In fact, people who scientifically study the mind are demonstrating a central focus of humanism: a high regard for understanding human nature and experience without supernatural biases. One thing on which it is easy to agree is that how the brain creates the mind is one of the most fascinating and exhilarating of all questions.

As you read these final words, consider for a moment the idea that an abundance of intricate electrical and chemical signals surging through your brain at this very moment is responsible right now for your awareness and attention; your seeing and understanding; your memories and emotions; your questions, concerns, and doubts; your creative impulses, curiosity, and emerging ideas; and any excitement you may now feel as the computer in your head invites you to explore its cyberspace. Happy computing!

⊚ CRITICAL QUESTION

1. Do you agree with Hinrichs that there is no good reason for people to feel "threatened or dehumanized" by scientific studies concerning how the brain produces a mind or consciousness? Provide an argument in support of your answer.

12.5 YOU ARE NOT A MACHINE

Have you ever wondered whether computers can think? Of course, they can think in the sense that they can process information. But I mean *really* think—that is, can they be conscious? If they can, perhaps our brains are like complex computers, vastly intricate machines that can process information in such a way that consciousness is the result.

As I pointed out in the introduction to this chapter, one set of answers to the mind–body problem is called *monism* because it denies that humans are made up of two radically different things, minds and bodies. One version of monism, usually called *materialism* or *physicalism*, claims that only bodies (matter) exist. The problem this answer must explain is why we have a conscious mental life (thoughts, feelings, sensations) that appears to be nonphysical in nature. Various kinds of physicalistic theories have been proposed in an attempt to solve this problem. I briefly mentioned the identity theory in the introduction. According to this theory, mental states are identical with brain states. When we think certain kinds of thoughts or dream certain sorts of dreams, certain sorts of physical events are happening in various parts of our brains, which can be observed and studied by science. One problem with this theory is that mental states seem to have characteristics different from those of physical states. For one thing, mental states are private, whereas physical states are publicly observable. For another, it appears unlikely that the same kind of brain state accompanies the same kind of thought or sensation. For example, I feel pain, you feel pain, and the other day Peanut, my fat blind cat, also felt pain when I accidentally stepped on his tail. Now my brain and your brain may be sufficiently alike so that our brain states may also be sufficiently alike. But the brain of my cat, and indeed the brains of many other animals, is quite different, and it seems unlikely that—even though we might have similar mental states (e.g., feeling pain)—we would have identical brain states. Also, for two things to be identical, they must have identical properties. A brain state, being physical, is located in space. But where in space is my feeling of being sorry that I stepped on my cat's tail? Is it 3 inches to the right of my left ear? Is it possible for a brain scientist to observe some kind of electrical event in my brain (a brain state) and read my thoughts? When I see Arthur the dog chasing Peanut the cat, can some scientist looking at my brain activity see the same thing? Hardly!

Materialists have their answers to these sorts of questions, but these kinds of problems with the identity theory have led some materialists to develop a different sort of theory, a theory called **functionalism**. There are different varieties of functionalism, but in general this theory holds that mental states are defined completely by their functions or causal relations. A mind is what a brain creates. Theoretically, something other than a brain could function as a mind—for example, a computer.

The slogan of functionalism is *not* the cry of the identity theorist that "the mind is nothing but the brain." Rather, drawing an analogy with computers, the slogan is "the mind is to the brain as a computer's software is to its hardware." The behavior of a computer is not explained, or at least not explained completely, by its physics and chemistry (hardware). It is explained by its program or "software" that manages the tasks the computer performs. The software of a computer is not identical with its hardware, and hence our minds are not identical with our brains. Nevertheless, the brain is a kind of computing machine, and the mind is the brain's program.

John Searle (b. 1932) is professor of philosophy at the University of California, Berkeley. In the following selection, taken from the 1984 Reith Lectures, Searle argues that machines cannot think (be conscious) and thus, by implication, that functionalistic theories of the mind fail. He offers what has become a classic example of a thought experiment in the field, the Chinese room argument, in order to show that no matter how complex and sophisticated digital computers may become, they will never be able to produce consciousness and hence the human brain must be significantly unlike a computer because the brain can cause consciousness.

Central to Searle's argument is a distinction between *syntax* (the grammatical rules that govern the arrangement of words in a sentence) and *semantics* (the meaning of a word or a sentence). Computers manipulate symbols according to syntax (a set of rules for their arrangement), but it does not follow that computers are aware of the meaning (semantics) of those symbols. If I knew only the syntax of Chinese, but not the semantics, could I be said to know Chinese?

⊛ READING QUESTIONS

1. According to Searle, what causes mental processes?
2. According to Searle, what is the "strong artificial intelligence (AI)" view?
3. What is one consequence of the strong AI view?
4. Why is Searle's refutation of the strong AI view independent of developments in computer technology?
5. What does Searle mean when he says, "the mind has more than a syntax, it has a semantics"?
6. What is the point of Searle's example of the Chinese room?
7. What four conclusions does Searle draw, and what are the premises on which they are based?

Can Computers Think?

JOHN SEARLE

... Though we do not know in detail how the brain functions, we do know enough to have an idea of the general relationships, between brain processes and mental processes. Mental processes are caused by the behavior of elements of the brain. At the same time, they are realized in the structure that is made up of those elements. I think this answer is consistent with the standard biological approaches to biological phenomena. Indeed, it is a kind of commonsense answer to the question, given what we know about how the world works. However, it is very much a minority point of view. The prevailing view in philosophy, psychology, and artificial intelligence is one which emphasizes the analogies between the functioning of the human brain and the functioning of digital computers. According to the most extreme version of this view, the brain is just a digital computer and the mind is just a computer program. One could summarize this view—I call it "strong artificial intelligence," or "strong AI"—by saying that the mind is to the brain, as the program is to the computer hardware.

This view has the consequence that there is nothing essentially biological about the human mind. The brain just happens to be one of an indefinitely large number of different kinds of hardware computers that could sustain the programs which

make up human intelligence. On this view, any physical system whatever that had the right program with the right inputs and outputs would have a mind in exactly the same sense that you and I have minds. So, for example, if you made a computer out of old beer cans powered by windmills; if it had the right program, it would have to have a mind. And the point is not that for all we know it might have thoughts and feelings, but rather that it must have thoughts and feelings, because that is all there is to having thoughts and feelings: implementing the right program.

Most people who hold this view think we have not yet designed programs which are minds. But there is pretty much general agreement among them that it's only a matter of time until computer scientists and workers in artificial intelligence design the appropriate hardware and programs which will be the equivalent of human brains and minds. These will be artificial brains and minds which are in every way the equivalent of human brains and minds.

Many people outside of the field of artificial intelligence are quite amazed to discover that anybody could believe such a view as this. So, before criticizing it, let me give you a few examples of the things that people in this field have actually said. Herbert Simon of Carnegie-Mellon University says that we already have machines that can literally

---

think. There is no question of waiting for some future machine, because existing digital computers already have thoughts in exactly the same sense that you and I do. Well, fancy that! Philosophers have been worried for centuries about whether or not a machine could think, and now we discover that they already have such machines at Carnegie-Mellon. Simon's colleague Alan Newell claims that we have now discovered (and notice that Newell says "discovered" and not "hypothesized" or "considered the possibility," but we have *discovered*) that intelligence is just a matter of physical symbol manipulation; it has no essential connection with any specific kind of biological or physical wetware or hardware. Rather, any system whatever that is capable of manipulating physical symbols in the right way is capable of intelligence in the same literal sense as human intelligence of human beings. Both Simon and Newell, to their credit, emphasize that there is nothing metaphorical about these claims; they mean them quite literally. Freeman Dyson is quoted as having said that computers have an advantage over the rest of us when it comes to evolution. Since consciousness is just a matter of formal processes, in computers these formal processes can go on in substances that are much better able to survive in a universe that is cooling off than beings like ourselves made of our wet and messy materials. Marvin Minsky of MIT says that the next generation of computers will be so intelligent that we will "be lucky if they are willing to keep us around the house as household pets." My all-time favorite in the literature of exaggerated claims on behalf of the digital computer is from John McCarthy, the inventor of the term "artificial intelligence." McCarthy says even "machines as simple as thermostats can be said to have beliefs." And indeed, according to him, almost any machine capable of problem-solving can be said to have beliefs. I admire McCarthy's courage. I once asked him: "What beliefs does your thermostat have?" And he said: "My thermostat has three beliefs—it's too hot in here, it's too cold in here, and it's just right in here." As a philosopher, I like all these claims for a simple reason. Unlike most philosophical theses, they are reasonably clear, and they admit of a simple and decisive refutation. It is this refutation that I am going to undertake in this chapter.

The nature of the refutation has nothing whatever to do with any particular stage of computer technology. It is important to emphasize this point because the temptation is always to think that the solution to our problems must wait on some as yet uncreated technological wonder. But in fact, the nature of the refutation is completely independent of any state of technology. It has to do with the very definition of a digital computer, with what a digital computer is.

It is essential to our conception of a digital computer that its operations can be specified purely formally; that is, we specify the steps in the operation of the computer in terms of abstract symbols—sequences of zeros and ones printed on a tape, for example. A typical computer "rule" will determine that when a machine is in a certain state and it has a certain symbol on its tape, then it will perform a certain operation such as erasing the symbol or printing another symbol and then enter another state such as moving the tape one square to the left. But the symbols have no meaning; they have no semantic content; they are not about anything. They have to be specified purely in terms of their formal or syntactical structure. The zeros and ones, for example, are just numerals; they don't even stand for numbers. Indeed, it is this feature of digital computers that makes them so powerful. One and the same type of hardware, if it is appropriately designed, can be used to run an indefinite range of different programs. And one and the same program can be run on an indefinite range of different types of hardwares.

But this feature of programs, that they are defined purely formally or syntactically, is fatal to the view that mental processes and program processes are identical. And the reason can be stated quite simply. There is more to having a mind than having formal or syntactical processes. Our internal mental states, by definition, have certain sorts of contents. If I am thinking about Kansas City or wishing that I had a cold beer to drink or wondering if there will be a fall in interest rates, in each case my mental state has a certain mental content in addition to whatever formal features it might have. That is, even if my thoughts occur to me in strings of symbols, there must be more to the thought than the abstract strings, because strings by themselves can't have any meaning. If my thoughts are to be *about* anything, then the strings must have a *meaning* which makes the thoughts about those things. In a word, the mind has more than a syntax, it has a semantics. The reason that no computer program can ever be a mind is simply that a computer program is only syntactical, and minds are more than syntactical. Minds are semantical, in the sense that they have more than a formal structure, they have a content.

To illustrate this point I have designed a certain thought-experiment. Imagine that a bunch of computer programmers have written a program that will enable a computer to simulate the understanding of Chinese. So, for example, if the computer is given a question in Chinese, it will match the question against its memory, or data base, and produce appropriate answers to the questions in Chinese. Suppose for the sake of argument that the computer's answers are as good as those of a native Chinese speaker. Now then, does the computer, on the basis of this, understand Chinese, does it literally understand Chinese, in the way that Chinese speakers understand Chinese? Well, imagine that you are locked in a room, and in this room are several baskets full of Chinese symbols. Imagine that you (like me) do not understand a word of Chinese, but that you are given a rule book in English for manipulating these Chinese symbols. The rules specify the manipulations of the symbols purely formally, in terms of their syntax, not their semantics. So the rule might say: "Take a squiggle-squiggle sign out of basket number one and put it next to a squoggle-squoggle sign from basket number two." Now suppose that some other Chinese symbols are passed into the room, and that you are given further rules for passing back Chinese symbols out of the room. Suppose that unknown to you the symbols passed into the room are called "questions" by the people outside the room, and the symbols you pass back out of the room are called "answers to the questions." Suppose, furthermore, that the programmers are so good at designing the programs and that you are so good at manipulating the symbols, that very soon your answers are indistinguishable from those of a native Chinese speaker. There you are locked in your room shuffling your Chinese symbols and passing out Chinese symbols in response to incoming Chinese symbols. On the basis of the situation as I have described it, there is no way you could learn any Chinese simply by manipulating these formal symbols.

Now the point of the story is simply this: by virtue of implementing a formal computer program from the point of view of an outside observer, you behave exactly as if you understood Chinese, but all the same you don't understand a word of Chinese. But if going through the appropriate computer program for understanding Chinese is not enough to give *you* an understanding of Chinese, then it is not enough to give *any other digital computer* an understanding of Chinese. And again, the reason for this can be stated quite simply. If you don't understand Chinese, then no other computer could understand Chinese because no digital computer, just by virtue of running a program, has anything that you don't have. All that the computer has, as you have, is a formal program for manipulating uninterpreted Chinese symbols. To repeat, a computer has a syntax, but no semantics. The whole point of the parable of the Chinese room is to remind us of a fact that we knew all along. Understanding a language, or indeed, having mental states at all, involves more than just having a bunch of formal symbols. It involves having an interpretation, or a meaning attached to those symbols. And a digital computer, as defined, cannot have more than just formal symbols because the operation of the computer, as I said earlier, is defined in terms of its ability to implement programs. And these programs are purely formally specifiable—that is, they have no semantic content.

We can see the force of this argument if we contrast what it is like to be asked and to answer questions in English, and to be asked and to answer questions in some language where we have no knowledge of any of the meanings of the words. Imagine that in the Chinese room you are also given questions in English about such things as your age or your life history, and that you answer these questions. What is the difference between the Chinese case and the English case? Well again, if like me you understand no Chinese and you do understand English, then the difference is obvious. You understand the questions in English because they are expressed in symbols whose meanings are known to you. Similarly, when you give the answers in English you are producing symbols which are meaningful to you. But in the case of the Chinese, you have none of that. In the case of the Chinese, you simply manipulate formal symbols according to a computer program, and you attach no meaning to any of the elements.

Various replies have been suggested to this argument by workers in artificial intelligence and in psychology, as well as philosophy. They all have something in common; they are all inadequate. And there is an obvious reason why they have to be inadequate, since the argument rests on a very simple logical truth, namely, syntax alone is not sufficient for semantics, and digital computers insofar as they are computers have, by definition, a syntax alone.

I want to make this clear by considering a couple of the arguments that are often presented against me.

Some people attempt to answer the Chinese room example by saying that the whole system understands Chinese. The idea here is that though I, the person in the room manipulating the symbols, do not understand Chinese, I am just the central processing unit of the computer system. They argue that it is the whole system, including the room, the baskets full of symbols and the ledgers containing the programs and perhaps other items as well, taken as a totality, that understands Chinese. But this is subject to exactly the same objection I made before. There is no way that the system can get from the syntax to the semantics. I, as the central processing unit, have no way of figuring out what any of these symbols means; but then neither does the whole system. Another common response is to imagine that we put the Chinese understanding program inside a robot. If the robot moved around and interacted causally with the world, wouldn't that be enough to guarantee that it understood Chinese? Once again the inexorability of the semantics–syntax distinction overcomes this maneuver. As long as we suppose that the robot has only a computer for a brain then, even though it might behave exactly as if it understood Chinese, it would still have no way of getting from the syntax to the semantics of Chinese. You can see this if you imagine that I am the computer. Inside a room in the robot's skull I shuffle symbols without knowing that some of them come in to me from television

cameras attached to the robot's head and others go out to move the robot's arms and legs. As long as all I have is a formal computer program, I have no way of attaching any meaning to any of the symbols. And the fact that the robot is engaged in causal interactions with the outside world won't help me to attach any meaning to the symbols unless I have some way of finding out about that fact. Suppose the robot picks up a hamburger and this triggers the symbol for hamburger to come into the room. As long as all I have is the symbol with no knowledge of its causes or how it got there, I have no way of knowing what it means. The causal interactions between the robot and the rest of the world are irrelevant unless those causal interactions are represented in some mind or other. But there is no way they can be if all that the so-called mind consists of is a set of purely formal, syntactical operations.

It is important to see exactly what is claimed and what is not claimed by my argument. Suppose we ask the question that I mentioned at the beginning: "Could a machine think?" Well, in one sense, of course, we are all machines. We can construe the stuff inside our heads as a meat machine. And of course, we can all think. So, in one sense of "machine," namely that sense in which a machine is just a physical system which is capable of performing certain kinds of operations, in that sense, we are all machines, and we can think. So, trivially, there are machines that can think. But that wasn't the question that bothered us. So let's try a different formulation of it. Could an artifact think? Could a man-made machine think? Well, once again, it depends on the kind of artifact. Suppose we designed a machine that was molecule-for-molecule indistinguishable from a human being. Well then, if you can duplicate the causes, you can presumably duplicate the effects. So once again, the answer to that question is, in principle at least, trivially yes. If you could build a machine that had the same structure as a human being, then presumably that machine would be able to think. Indeed, it would be a surrogate human being. Well, let's try again.

The question isn't: "Can a machine think?" or: "Can an artifact think?" The question is: "Can a digital computer think?" But once again we have to be very careful in how we interpret the question.

From a mathematical point of view, anything whatever can be described *as if* it were a digital computer. And that's because it can be described as instantiating or implementing a computer program. In an utterly trivial sense, the pen that is on the desk in front of me can be described as a digital computer. It just happens to have a very boring computer program. The program says: "Stay there." Now since in this sense, anything whatever is a digital computer, because anything whatever can be described as implementing a computer program, then once again, our question gets a trivial answer. Of course our brains are digital computers, since they implement any number of computer programs. And of course our brains can think. So once again, there is a trivial answer to the question. But that wasn't really the question we were trying to ask. The question we wanted to ask is this: "Can a digital computer, as defined, think?" That is to say: "Is instantiating or implementing the right computer program with the right inputs and outputs, sufficient for, or constitutive of, thinking?" And to this question, unlike its predecessors, the answer is clearly "no." And it is "no" for the reason that we have spelled out, namely, the computer program is defined purely syntactically. But thinking is more than just a matter of manipulating meaningless symbols, it involves meaningful semantic contents. These semantic contents are what we mean by "meaning."

It is important to emphasize again that we are not talking about a particular stage of computer technology. The argument has nothing to do with the forthcoming, amazing advances in computer science. It has nothing to do with the distinction between serial and parallel processes, or with the size of programs, or the speed of computer operations, or with computers that can interact causally with their environment, or even with the invention of robots. Technological progress is always grossly exaggerated, but even subtracting the exaggeration, the development of computers has been quite remarkable, and we can reasonably expect that even more remarkable progress will be made in the future. No doubt we will be much better able to simulate human behavior on computers than we can at present, and certainly much better than we have been able to in the past. The point I am making is that if we are talking about having mental states, having a mind, all of these simulations are simply irrelevant. It doesn't matter how good the technology is, or how rapid the calculations made by the computer are. If it really is a computer, its operations have to be defined syntactically, whereas consciousness, thoughts, feelings, emotions, and all the rest of it involve more than a syntax. Those features, by definition, the computer is unable to *duplicate* however powerful may be its ability to *simulate*. The key distinction here is between duplication and simulation. And no simulation by itself ever constitutes duplication.

What I have done so far is give a basis to the sense that those citations I began this talk with are really as preposterous as they seem. There is a puzzling question in this discussion though, and that is: "Why would anybody ever have thought that computers could think or have feelings and emotions and all the rest of it?" After all, we can do computer simulations of any process whatever that can be given a formal description. So, we can do a computer simulation of the flow of money in the British economy, or the pattern of power distribution in the Labour party. We can do computer simulation of rain storms in the home counties, or warehouse fires in East London. Now, in each of these cases, nobody supposes that the computer simulation is actually the real thing; no one supposes that a computer simulation of a storm will leave us all wet, or a computer simulation of a fire is likely to burn the house down. Why on earth would anyone in his right mind suppose a computer simulation of mental processes actually had mental processes? I don't really know the answer to that, since the idea seems to me, to put it frankly, quite crazy from the start. But I can make a couple of speculations.

First of all, where the mind is concerned, a lot of people are still tempted to some sort of behaviorism. They think if a system behaves as if it understood Chinese, then it really must understand Chinese. But we have already refuted this form of behaviorism with the Chinese room argument. Another assumption made by many people is that the mind is not a part of the biological world, it is not a part of the world of nature. The strong artificial intelligence view relies on that in its conception that the mind is purely formal; that somehow or other, it cannot be treated as a concrete product of biological processes like any other biological product. There is in these discussions, in short, a kind of residual dualism. AI partisans believe that the mind is more than a part of the natural biological world; they believe that the mind is purely formally specifiable. The paradox of this is that the AI literature is filled with fulminations against some view called "dualism," but in fact, the whole thesis of strong AI rests on a kind of dualism. It rests on a rejection of the idea that the mind is just a natural biological phenomenon in the world like any other.

I want to conclude this chapter by putting together the thesis of the last chapter and the thesis of this one. Both of these theses can be stated very simply. And indeed, I am going to state them with perhaps excessive crudeness. But if we put them together I think we get a quite powerful conception of the relations of minds, brains and computers. And the argument has a very simple logical structure, so you can see whether it is valid or invalid. The first premise is:

1. *Brains cause minds.*

Now, of course, that is really too crude. What we mean by that is that mental processes that we consider to constitute a mind are caused, entirely caused, by processes going on inside the brain. But let's be crude, let's just abbreviate that as three words—brains cause minds. And that is just a fact about how the world works. Now let's write proposition number two:

2. *Syntax is not sufficient for semantics.*

That proposition is a conceptual truth. It just articulates our distinction between the notion of what is purely formal and what has content. Now, to these two propositions—that brains cause minds and that syntax is not sufficient for semantics—let's add a third and a fourth:

3. *Computer programs are entirely defined by their formal, or syntactical, structure.*

That proposition, I take it, is true by definition; it is part of what we mean by the notion of a computer program.

4. *Minds have mental contents; specifically, they have semantic contents.*

And that, I take it, is just an obvious fact about how our minds work. My thoughts, and

beliefs, and desires are about something, or they refer to something, or they concern states of affairs in the world; and they do that because their content directs them at these states of affairs in the world. Now, from these four premises, we can draw our first conclusion; and it follows obviously from premises 2, 3 and 4:

Conclusion 1

No computer program by itself is sufficient to give a system a mind. Programs, in short, are not minds, and they are not by themselves sufficient for having minds.

Now, that is a very powerful conclusion, because it means that the project of trying to create minds solely by designing programs is doomed from the start. And it is important to re-emphasize that this has nothing to do with any particular state of technology or any particular state of the complexity of the program. This is a purely formal, or logical, result from a set of axioms which are agreed to by all (or nearly all) of the disputants concerned. That is, even most of the hardcore enthusiasts for artificial intelligence agree that in fact, as a matter of biology, brain processes cause mental states, and they agree that programs are defined purely formally. But if you put these conclusions together with certain other things that we know, then it follows immediately that the project of strong AI is incapable of fulfillment.

However, once we have got these axioms, let's see what else we can derive. Here is a second conclusion:

Conclusion 2

The way that brain functions cause minds cannot be solely in virtue of running a computer program.

And this second conclusion follows from conjoining the first premise together with our first conclusion. That is, from the fact that brains cause minds and that programs are not enough to do the job, it follows that the way that brains cause minds can't be solely by running a computer program. Now that also I think is an important result, because it has the consequence that the brain is not, or at least is not just, a digital computer. We saw earlier that anything can trivially be described as if it were a digital computer, and brains are no exception. But the importance of this conclusion is that the computational properties of the brain are simply not enough to explain its functioning to produce mental states. And indeed, that ought to seem a common-sense scientific conclusion to us anyway because all it does is remind us of the fact that brains are biological engines; their biology matters. It is not, as several people in artificial intelligence have claimed, just an irrelevant fact about the mind that it happens to be realized in human brains.

Now, from our first premise, we can also derive a third conclusion:

Conclusion 3

> Anything else that caused minds would have to have causal powers at least equivalent to those of the brain.

And this third conclusion is a trivial consequence of our first premise. It is a bit like saying that if my petrol engine drives my car at seventy-five miles an hour, then any diesel engine that was capable of doing that would have to have a power output at least equivalent to that of my petrol engine. Of course, some other system might cause mental processes using entirely different chemical or biochemical features from those the brain in fact uses. It might turn out that there are beings on other planets, or in other solar systems, that have mental states and use an entirely different biochemistry from ours. Suppose that Martians arrived on earth and we concluded that they had mental states. But suppose that when their heads were opened up, it was discovered that all they had inside was green slime. Well still, the green slime, if it functioned to produce consciousness and all the rest of their mental life, would have to have causal powers equal to those of the human brain. But now, from our first conclusion, that programs are not enough, and our third conclusion, that any other system would have to have causal powers equal to the brain, conclusion four follows immediately:

Conclusion 4

> For any artifact that we might build which had mental states equivalent to human mental states, the implementation of a computer program would not by itself be sufficient. Rather the artifact would have to have powers equivalent to the powers of the human brain.

The upshot of this discussion I believe is to remind us of something that we have known all along: namely, mental states are biological phenomena. Consciousness, intentionality, subjectivity, and mental causation are all a part of our biological life history, along with growth, reproduction, the secretion of bile, and digestion.

◉ CRITICAL QUESTIONS

1. Describe the two types of responses that Searle's argument received and his counter-response. Do you think his counter-response is convincing? Why, or why not?

2. Has Searle made his case to your satisfaction—that is, has he proved to you that a digital computer, in principle, cannot think or have a mind like a human mind? Provide an argument to support your answer.

12.6 YOU ARE MEAT

Many people don't like the idea that computers or computerized robots could ever be conscious in the way humans are conscious. They are made of metal, plastic, wires, and computer chips. Sure, George Lucas's robot characters in Star Wars (R2-D2 and C-3PO) made us laugh and feel sorry for them when they were damaged. We even feared for them when they were in danger. They seemed human, but we know they were only the products of Lucas's fertile imagination and the filmmaker's art.

Let's change the scene. Let's imagine that intelligent conscious and feeling robots like R2-D2 and C-3PO visit earth. Would they be amazed that we flesh-and-blood humans can think, feel, and communicate? Would thinking flesh and bone wow them? Perhaps they would deny, as many of us now do with regard to computerized robots, that these mobile meat containers were capable of conscious thought.

Terry Bisson (b. 1942), author of the next selection, is a member of the Authors Guild as well as the Science Fiction and Fantasy Writers of America. He is an award-winning author of many different kinds of stories, including both adult fiction and children's books. In the following science fiction fantasy, he imagines robots visiting a planet to study creatures that have been sending radio messages into outer space. What to their amazement, if not amusement, do they find? Read and see.

READING QUESTIONS

1. Why does the senior robot scientist refuse to believe that the creatures encountered and studied by Omigod are thinking meat?

2. Why is it important to make contact with intelligent beings in other parts of the universe?

They're Made Out of Meat

TERRY BISSON

"They're made out of meat."

"Meat?"

"Meat. They're made out of meat."

"Meat?"

"There's no doubt about it. We picked up several from different parts of the planet, took them aboard our recon vessels, and probed them all the way through. They're completely meat."

"That's impossible. What about the radio signals? The messages to the stars?"

"They use the radio waves to talk, but the signals don't come from them. The signals come from machines."

"So who made the machines? That's who we want to contact."

"They made the machines. That's what I'm trying to tell you. Meat made the machines."

"That's ridiculous. How can meat make a machine? You're asking me to believe in sentient meat."

"I'm not asking you, I'm telling you. These creatures are the only sentient race in that sector and they're made out of meat."

"Maybe they're like the orfolei. You know, a carbon-based intelligence that goes through a meat stage."

"Nope. They're born meat and they die meat. We studied them for several of their life spans, which didn't take long. Do you have any idea what's the life span of meat?"

"Spare me. Okay, maybe they're only part meat. You know, like the weddilei. A meat head with an electron plasma brain inside."

"Nope. We thought of that, since they do have meat heads, like the weddilei. But I told you, we probed them. They're meat all the way through."

"No brain?"

"Oh, there's a brain all right. It's just that the brain is made out of meat! That's what I've been trying to tell you."

"So ... what does the thinking?"

"You're not understanding, are you? You're refusing to deal with what I'm telling you. The brain does the thinking. The meat."

"Thinking meat! You're asking me to believe in thinking meat!"

"Yes, thinking meat! Conscious meat! Loving meat. Dreaming meat. The meat is the whole deal! Are you beginning to get the picture or do I have to start all over?"

Terry Bisson, "They're Made Out of Meat," *Omni* (April 1991), p. 54. Reprinted by permission.

"Omigod. You're serious then. They're made out of meat."

"Thank you. Finally. Yes. They are indeed made out of meat. And they've been trying to get in touch with us for almost a hundred of their years."

"Omigod. So what does this meat have in mind?"

"First it wants to talk to us. Then I imagine it wants to explore the Universe, contact other sentiences, swap ideas and information. The usual."

"We're supposed to talk to meat."

"That's the idea. That's the message they're sending out by radio. 'Hello. Anyone out there. Anybody home.' That sort of thing."

"They actually do talk, then. They use words, ideas, concepts?"

"Oh, yes. Except they do it with meat."

"I thought you just told me they used radio."

"They do, but what do you think is on the radio? Meat sounds. You know how when you slap or flap meat, it makes a noise? They talk by flapping their meat at each other. They can even sing by squirting air through their meat."

"Omigod. Singing meat. This is altogether too much. So what do you advise?"

"Officially or unofficially?"

"Both."

"Officially, we are required to contact, welcome and log in any and all sentient races or multi-beings in this quadrant of the Universe, without prejudice, fear or favor. Unofficially, I advise that we erase the records and forget the whole thing."

"I was hoping you would say that."

"It seems harsh, but there is a limit. Do we really want to make contact with meat?"

"I agree one hundred percent. What's there to say? 'Hello, meat. How's it going?' But will this work? How many planets are we dealing with here?"

"Just one. They can travel to other planets in special meat containers, but they can't live on them. And being meat, they can only travel through C space. Which limits them to the speed of light and makes the possibility of their ever making contact pretty slim. Infinitesimal, in fact."

"So we just pretend there's no one home in the Universe."

"That's it."

"Cruel. But you said it yourself, who wants to meet meat? And the ones who have been aboard our vessels, the ones you probed? You're sure they won't remember?"

"They'll be considered crackpots if they do. We went into their heads and smoothed out their meat so that we're just a dream to them."

"A dream to meat! How strangely appropriate, that we should be meat's dream."

"And we marked the entire sector unoccupied."

"Good. Agreed, officially and unofficially. Case closed. Any others? Anyone interesting on that side of the galaxy?"

"Yes, a rather shy but sweet hydrogen core cluster intelligence in a class nine star in G445 zone. Was in contact two galactic rotations ago, wants to be friendly again."

"They always come around."

"And why not? Imagine how unbearably, how unutterably cold the Universe would be if one were all alone...."

⊛ CRITICAL QUESTIONS

1. Would you react in a similar fashion to reports that entities on another planet encountered by human astronauts were intelligent, conscious, feeling machines? Explain your answer.
2. Why do the robot visitors decide to "erase the records" of their encounter with conscious meat beings? Do you think that "meat scientists" might react in a similar fashion upon discovering a planet with sentient entities that are machines "all the way through"?
3. How would you convince these robot scientists that you, as a "meat creature," can really think, rather than merely simulate or fake conscious thought?

To access the *Voices of Wisdom*, 8th Edition, **Premium Website**, search for this book on CengageBrain.com.

CHAPTER THIRTEEN

Who Am I?

My one regret in life is that I am not someone else.

WOODY ALLEN

LEARNING OBJECTIVES

After studying this chapter students should be able to:
- state the difference between a human being and a person,
- explain the problem of identity,
- state the relationship between the concepts of *anatta* and *amicca,*
- distinguish *jiva* from Atman,
- name the five aggregates,
- explain "turning the tables,"
- distinguish the ego theory of the self from the bundle theory,
- explain queer theory,
- identify Buddha, Nagasena, King Menander, Parfit, Dennett, Anzaldúa, and McCloskey, and
- answer all the questions relating to the selections.

13.1 INTRODUCTION

The question about what I am leads to questions about the nature of human beings, about what they are made of or what constitutes their being. It also leads to other questions, in particular questions about what a person is. It is here that the question of *what* begins to shade off into the question *of who.* Who are we? We are persons. Simple enough, right?

We must be careful to distinguish the concept of "person" from the concept of "human being." Human being refers to a biological species, one to which we happen to belong. Person, on the other hand, is not a biological concept. We can bring out the distinction by pointing to the example of the space alien E.T. It would appear that E.T. is a person, but certainly not a human being in the biological sense. This distinction is central to much of the debate about abortion because many claim that whereas a fetus belongs to the biological species human being, it is not a person, but only potentially a person.

To say that something is potentially a person indicates that personhood is something that may not always be present. Of course, we all know that persons can and do change. The fact that being a person is dynamic (a changing and developing process) leads to the issue of the identity of persons through time. Consider this puzzle: Are you the same person today as you were when you were five years old? If we mean by "same" a kind of strict identity such that if *A* is identical with *B,* then *A* and *B* have the same characteristics, the answer is obviously no. You have a different set of qualities today (such as size and age) than you did when you were five years old. If we mean by "same" similar but not absolutely identical characteristics, then the answer is yes.

But is similarity good enough? If I am only similar to my former self, then I have changed. And if I have changed, how much have I changed? For example, does it make sense to hold the person I am today responsible for the act of stealing cookies at age five? If my mother suddenly discovered that I, not my sister, stole the cookies and I lied about it, should she call me up and scold me many years later?

If we accept Descartes's views (see Chapter 12), then we might say that my identity consists in my soul substance, and because my soul has remained the same even though my body has changed, my mother should indeed scold me now no matter how different my body is now.

Many people believe in the soul. It is very popular. It not only takes care of the problem of identity through time but also gives the assurance of life beyond the death of the body. This belief does all that and makes us feel very special, important, and different from all those other living things with which we happen to share the planet. My identity is a soul. My person is a spiritual being. I am special.

But what if there were no souls? What if human identities (persons, if you will) were not everlasting, special, and unique souls but bundles of sensations, thoughts, memories, and experiences? What if the word "I" was merely a convenient way of talking about that bundle?

Puzzles about personal identity are closely related to other concerns about identity, such as how our sense of who we are is constructed in a social setting. Whether we are souls or not, we are social animals. We are born, we live, and we die in a social/cultural setting that is vitally important to who we are. If you were born in another country to a different family, you would be a very different person than you are now. Your religion might be different, along with many of your beliefs and values. Talk to people from other countries or other ethnic groups and see what I mean.

Social identity is closely tied to gender identity because how society treats us depends, in part, on our gender. Suppose you were born a different sex. Can you imagine yourself, if you are female, as a male? How might you be different? Can those of you who are male imagine yourselves as female? Would you like to be female? Would a sex-change operation make any real difference to who you are? Could you be a female in a male body? Could you be a male in a female body? Who are you? Think about it.

13.2 THERE IS NO SELF

Buddhism developed in India around 500 BCE and quickly came into conflict with some of the basic ideas of Hindu philosophy. Among the areas of conflict was the issue of the existence of the self. Hinduism and Buddhism gave very different answers to the question "Who am I?" Some Hindu philosophers answered, "You are the Atman" (for a discussion of the "Atman," see Section 10.4), and Buddhism responded with the assertion "There is no Atman." This is called *anatta* (also *Anatman*), or the no-self doctrine.

To understand this teaching, we must back up a moment to another Buddhist teaching called *anicca,* or impermanence. The doctrine of impermanence is a logical implication of the doctrine of dependent origination. If everything that exists is dependent on something else for its existence (as the thesis of dependent origination holds), there can be no independently existing things. This amounts to a denial of the existence of substances because substances are usually thought of as independently existing things. It also amounts to a denial of eternally permanent essences. And it is quite clear that some Indian philosophers regarded the Atman as an independently existing thing that is eternal and permanent.

If there are no substances and if everything is impermanent, it follows that what exists is in constant process. In contrast to Plato's essentialist metaphysics (see Section 10.3), Buddhism teaches a process view of reality. There are no Forms or essences, only ever-changing processes. Hence, according to Buddhist thought, we are wrong if we think of the *jiva* (individual soul or ego) as a permanent substance the way Plato did, or if we think of the Atman (universal Self) as a permanent substance the way some Hindu thinkers did. There is no soul, no ego, no Self, if we mean by any of those terms some independently existing substance or essence.

Note that Buddhists are not denying that you or I exist. They are only denying a particular philosophical view about our natures, the view that the word *I* refers to some unchanging substance called the self or soul. According to Buddhist philosophy, humans are made up of what they call the **five aggregates**. These consist of physical form, sensation, conceptualization, dispositions to act [Karmic constituents], and consciousness. There is no substance over and above these aggregates.

"What," I hear you say, "I am nothing but a collection of elements! How disappointing." It seems so to those of us raised with the idea that what is most important about us is our souls. If we have no souls, then we have no value, or so our culture has taught us. However, our cultural conditioning in this regard may blind us to the value of the Buddhist concept of *anatta*.

The no-self teaching had particular moral and religious value for Buddhism because once we are clear about the fact that there is no substantial self, we can be released from suffering and motivated to act with compassion. Suffering and selfishness arise from desiring things and clinging to them. However, if there is no self, then selfish desiring and clinging amount to one vast illusion, a dream from which those who know the truth about the self can awake. What appears at first glance to be a negative doctrine becomes positive once its moral and religious implications are understood.

The first selection in this section comes from the *Digha Nikaya* and is attributed to the Buddha himself. It deals with teachings about the permanence and existence of the soul found in Hindu philosophy. Buddhist monks found themselves in debate with Hindus on these issues, and this selection instructs them on how they can argue with their opponents and thereby show their opponents' views about the soul to be false. It is the classic expression of the sorts of arguments refined and elaborated in later Buddhism.

Note that this selection ends with a statement about the afterlife. Clearly one advantage of the doctrine that there is a soul is that one can explain life after death and reincarnation in terms of this soul persisting after the death of the body. However, if there is no soul, what, if anything, persists? Interestingly, the Buddhists affirmed a doctrine of continuity from one life to the next but denied there is a soul that is reborn or reincarnated. Rather what connects this life to the past or to the future is karma. You are the result of what you have done.

The second selection is the famous simile of the chariot found in the *Milinda-panha*. It would seem that if there is no soul, then all kinds of absurd things follow. King Menander (or Milinda), a Greek who ruled northwestern India in the second century BCE, was quick to point out these absurdities when the Buddhist monk Nagasena denied that his personal name referred to a permanent individual substance. Nagasena counterargued, using the king's own logic and the example of a chariot, to show that the king himself believed there is no chariot above and beyond its parts, yet he saw no problem in using the term *chariot* as a practical designation. So too with the word *I*. It is just a convenient way of talking, a mere sound, without any reference to something substantial.

As an interesting multicultural footnote on this ancient debate, I should call your attention to the fact that here Greek culture (represented by King Menander) encountered Indian Buddhist culture (represented by Nagasena) in public debate (there was an audience of Greeks and Indian monks who witnessed the exchange). Greek philosophers were fond of an argument called "turning the tables." One turns the table on one's debate opponents by using their own assumptions and arguments against them. So Socrates turned the table on a famous sophist named Protagoras by showing that his relativistic principle that stated "Man is the measure of all things" led to the conclusion that Protagoras's philosophical principle was false because Socrates (a man) thought (measures) it false. Supposedly the Greeks invented the technique of "turning the tables," but in this passage a Buddhist monk successfully used it on a Greek, much to the pleasure of the other monks and the grudging admiration of the assembled Greeks.

READING QUESTIONS

1. What is wrong with maintaining that the soul is sensation?
2. What is wrong with maintaining that the soul is not sensation?
3. What is wrong with maintaining that sensation is a faculty of the soul?
4. Because the notions of the soul and of surviving death are closely related, what must a Buddhist monk who rejects these theories of the soul believe about a perfected being who has died?
5. How did King Menander argue against Nagasena's assertion that the name Nagasena is only a practical designation and does not refer to any permanent individual?
6. How did Nagasena counter the King's argument?

False Doctrines about the Soul

THE BUDDHA

In regard to the soul, what are the views held concerning it?

It seems that either one holds the view that sensation is the soul or one holds the view that sensation is not the soul. One might also hold the view that the soul, while not identical to sensation, possesses the faculty or ability of sensation.

I have revised the translation of the *Digha-Nikaya* 256:21 by Henry Clarke Warren as found in *Buddhism in Translation* (Harvard University Press, 1896).

Where it is said, "Sensation is my soul," you should reply, "Brother, there are three sensations: the pleasant sensation, the unpleasant sensation, and the indifferent sensation. Which of these three sensations do you hold to be the soul? Whenever a person experiences a pleasant sensation, he does not at the same time experience an unpleasant sensation, nor does he experience an indifferent sensation; only the pleasant sensation does he then feel. This is also true of the others, for when one feels one sensation whether it be pleasant, unpleasant, or indifferent one does not feel the others."

Now all these sensations—pleasant, unpleasant, indifferent—are transitory, are due to causes, originate by dependence, and are subject to decay, disappearance, and cessation. While someone is experiencing a pleasant sensation, he thinks, "This is my soul." And after the cessation of this same pleasant sensation, he thinks, "My soul has passed away." The same is true of unpleasant and indifferent sensations. They are all subject to rise and disappearance. Accordingly, it is not possible to hold the view that sensation is my soul and that the soul is eternal.

If someone argues that sensation is not my soul, one should reply, "But, brother, where there is no sensation, is there any existence?" The answer is obviously no. Accordingly, it is not possible to hold the view that the soul has no sensation.

So, if sensation is the soul, then the soul is impermanent and not eternal and if sensation is not the soul, then the soul does not exist.

Suppose someone says that the soul has or possesses sensation as an ability but is not identical to it. In this case, a reply should be made as follows: "Suppose, brother, that utterly and completely, and without remainder, all sensation were to cease—if there were nowhere any sensation, pray, would there be anything, after the end of sensation, of which it could be said, "This am I?""

Accordingly, it is not possible to hold the views that the soul is sensation, the soul is not sensation, and that the soul possesses the faculty of sensation and still maintain that the soul is eternal.

From the time a monk no longer holds the view that sensation is the soul, no longer holds the view that the soul has no sensation, and no longer holds the view that the soul possesses the faculty of sensation, he ceases to attach himself to anything in the world, and being free from attachment, he is never agitated, and being never agitated, he attains to Nirvana [release from suffering]. He knows that rebirth is exhausted, that he has lived the holy life, that he has done what is required, and that he is no more for this world or any other. Now it is impossible that a monk whose mind is so freed should think that a perfect being exists after death, or does not exist after death, or both exists and does not exist after death, or neither exists nor does not exist after death.

And why do I say so?

I say so because a perfected being is released and in a state that goes beyond all expression, all communication, and all knowledge.

The Simile of the Chariot

Then King Milinda declared: "Listen to me, you five hundred ... lords and you eighty thousand monks! This Nāgasena says, 'There is no Person to be found here!' Is it possible to agree to that?"

And addressing the Venerable Nāgasena, he said: "If, Venerable Nāgasena, no Person [soul] is to be found, who then is it who gives you robes, food, lodgings, medicine—all the requisites

The translation of the "Simile of the Chariot" (from *The Milindapanho*) is by John S. Strong, *The Experience of Buddhism: Sources and Interpretations* (Belmont, CA: Wadsworth Publishing Company, 1995), pp. 92–94. Copyright © 1995 by Wadsworth, Inc.

for a mendicant? Who is it who enjoys the use of these things? Who keeps the precepts? Who practices meditation? Who experiences the path, the fruits, nirvāna? Who kills living beings? Who takes what is not given? Who engages in sinful pleasures? Who tells lies? Who drinks intoxicants? Who commits the five evil deeds that have karmic effects in this lifetime?

"From what you say it follows that there is no such thing as merit or demerit; there is neither doer nor causer of meritorious or demeritorious actions; there is no reward or punishment for good or evil deeds. If, Nāgasena, a man were to kill you, there would be no murder in that! Moreover, Nāgasena, you monks would have neither teacher nor preceptor: you are not even ordained! You say, 'Your majesty, my co-practitioners call me Nāgasena'; well, what is this 'Nāgasena'? Tell me, is the hair of the head 'Nāgasena'?"

"No, it is not, your majesty."

"Is the hair of the body 'Nāgasena'?"

"No, your majesty."

"What about nails, teeth, skin, flesh, sinews, bones, marrow, kidneys, heart, liver, pleura, spleen, lungs, colon, intestines, stomach, feces, bile, phlegm, pus, blood, sweat, fat, tears, lymph, saliva, snot, synovia, urine, brain—are any of these 'Nāgasena'?"

"No, your majesty."

"Well, then, sir, is your physical form (rūpa) 'Nāgasena'?"

"No, your majesty."

"Are feelings (vedanā) 'Nāgasena'?"

"No, your majesty."

"Are perceptions (saññā) 'Nāgasena'?"

"No, your majesty."

"Are karmic constituents (sankhārā) 'Nāgasena'?"

"No, your majesty."

"Is consciousness (viññāna) 'Nāgasena'?"

"No, your majesty."

"Perhaps the five skandhas all together—form, feelings, perceptions, karmic constituents and consciousness—are they 'Nāgasena'?"

"No, your majesty."

"Then is it something other than physical form, feelings, perceptions, karmic constituents, and consciousness that is 'Nāgasena'?"

"No, your majesty."

"Well, my friend, though I question you repeatedly, I do not find any 'Nāgasena.' 'Nāgasena' is but a sound! Who is this 'Nāgasena'? You are lying, my friend, you are telling falsehoods. There is no Nāgasena!"

Then the Venerable Nāgasena said to King Milinda: "Your majesty, you are a delicate, refined nobleman. If, in the middle of the day, you were to walk on the hot, burning, sandy ground and tread on rough, gritty, pebbly sand, your feet would hurt, your body would get tired, your mind would be distressed, and there would arise in you a consciousness of bodily suffering. Tell me, did you come on foot, or did you ride?"

"I did not come on foot, sir, I rode in a chariot."

"If that is the case, your majesty, tell me what is the chariot. Is the pole the chariot?"

"No, it is not, sir."

"Is the axle the chariot?"

"No, sir."

"Are the wheels the chariot?"

"No, sir."

"Is the frame the chariot?"

"No, sir."

"Is the banner staff the chariot?"

"No, sir."

"Is the yoke the chariot?"

"No, sir."

"Are the reins the chariot?"

"No, sir."

"Is the goad the chariot?"

"No, sir."

"Perhaps, your majesty, the pole, the axle, the wheels, the frame, the banner staff, the yoke, the reins, and the goad all together—are they the chariot?"

"No, sir, they are not."

"Then, your majesty, is it something other than the pole, the axle, the wheels, the frame, the banner staff, the yoke, the reins, and the goad that is the chariot?"

"No, sir, it is not."

"Well, your majesty, though I question you repeatedly, I do not find any chariot. 'Chariot' is but a sound! What is this chariot? You are lying, your majesty, you are telling falsehoods. There is no chariot! Your majesty, you are the supreme ruler over the whole of India, who are you afraid of that you should tell a lie? Listen to me, you five hundred … lords and you eighty thousand monks! This King Milinda says, 'I came in a chariot!' But when I ask him to tell me what the chariot is, he cannot produce a chariot. Is it possible to agree to such a thing?"

When he had thus spoken, the five hundred … lords applauded the Venerable Nāgasena, and said to King Milinda: "Now, your majesty, answer that if you can!"

And King Milinda said to the Venerable Nāgasena: "Good Nāgasena, I did not lie. The word *chariot* comes into existence, dependent on the pole, dependent on the axle, the wheels, the frame, the banner staff, the yoke, the reins, the goad; it is a designation, a description, an appellation, a name."

"Well said, your majesty! You truly understand the chariot! In the same way, your majesty, in my case, the word *Nāgasena* comes into existence, dependent on the hair of the head, dependent on the hair of the body, … dependent on the brain, dependent on physical form, on feelings, on perceptions, on karmic constituents, on consciousness. It is a designation, a description, an appellation, nothing but a name. But in the final analysis, the ultimate sense, there is no Person [soul] to be found herein…."

◉ CRITICAL QUESTIONS

1. Who do you think wins this debate, Nāgasena or King Menander? Why?

2. What unanswered questions do these readings leave you with? What do you think would be good answers to your questions?

13.3 DOWN WITH THE EGO

Suppose you found yourself in the following situation. You have agreed to participate in a psychological experiment. You are blindfolded and an object is placed in your left hand. When asked what the object is, you are unable to identify it. Your left hand is now placed in a box with a number of objects in it. You are still blindfolded so you cannot see them. You are asked to pick out the object that had been placed in your left hand, and you have no difficulty doing it. Now your right hand is put in the box, and you are asked to retrieve the object. You cannot. Now the blindfold is removed so that you can see which objects the right hand is picking up. Much to your astonishment, your left hand slaps your right hand whenever it picks up the wrong object. What would you make of this situation? What is going on here?

Those were the questions Roger Sperry and his colleagues asked in the 1960s when they began to get results like the ones above while they were conducting experiments with split-brain patients at the California Institute of Technology. Human brains are divided into two hemispheres. Each hemisphere controls and receives information from opposite sides of the body. The right hemisphere governs and gets information from the left side of the body, and the left hemisphere governs and gets information from the right side of the body. A large bundle of millions of nerves known as the *corpus callosum* connects these hemispheres and permits communication between the two sides of the brain. Neurosurgeons discovered that they could prevent seizures from moving from one hemisphere to another by cutting the *corpus callosum* without causing any obvious disruption in the cognitive life of the patients. However, controlled experiments like the one described above revealed differences between split-brain people and people whose *corpus callosum* was intact.

Researchers discovered that the information given to one hemisphere was unavailable to the other hemisphere in split-brain cases. In most people the left hemisphere controls speech, and people could not name an object placed in the left hand. The left hand could, however, select the object from among other objects because the right hemisphere remembered how it felt. The left hemisphere had no idea what the object was and so the right hand could not select the correct object. Once the blindfold was removed, the left hand (right hemisphere) could communicate to the right hand (left hemisphere) only by slapping it because the *corpus callosum* had been severed.

These experiments appear to indicate that there are two different streams of consciousness operating in a single brain. Are there two persons as well? Odd as it may sound, some people have argued that there are. Do we have two different minds associated with the two different hemispheres, but communicating with each other so quickly that we don't notice? If we have two different minds, are we two different persons? If so, who is the real me?

In the next selection Derek Parfit, a British philosopher who has taught at Oxford and in the United States, reflects on the implications of split-brain research for notions of what a person is. He argues that the split-brain experiments are inconsistent with an "ego theory" of self but are consistent with a "bundle theory." He discovers a remarkable similarity between his ideas of personal identity and ancient Buddhist notions of the "No-Self" (see Section 13.2).

⊚ READING QUESTIONS

1. According to Parfit, why do the split-brain cases support the view that there are two streams of consciousness?
2. What is the difference between the ego theory and the bundle theory of personal identity?
3. What point does Parfit make in his imaginary cases of teletransportation?
4. Explain what Parfit means when he says, "*Ordinary survival is about as bad as being destroyed and having a Replica.*"

Divided Minds and the Nature of Persons

DEREK PARFIT

It was the split-brain cases which drew me into philosophy. Our knowledge of these cases depends on the results of various psychological tests, as described by Donald MacKay. These tests made use of two facts. We control each of our arms, and see what is in each half of our visual fields, with only one of our hemispheres. When someone's hemispheres have been disconnected, psychologists can thus present this person two different written questions in the two halves of his visual field, and can receive two different answers written by this person's two hands. Here is a simplified imaginary version of the kind of evidence that such tests provide. One of these people looks fixedly at the centre of a wide screen, whose left half is red and right half is blue. On each half in a darker shade are the words, 'How many colours can you see?' With both hands the

From Derek Parfit, "Divided Minds and the Nature of Persons," *Mindwaves: Thoughts on Intelligence, Identity and Consciousness,* edited by Colin Blakemore and Susan Greenfield (Basil Blackwell, 1987), pp. 19–25. Footnotes deleted.

person writes, "Only one." The words are now changed to read, "Which is the only colour that you can see?" With one of his hands the person writes "Red," with the other he writes "Blue."

If this is how such a person responds, I would conclude that he is having two visual sensations—that he does, as he claims, see both red and blue. But in seeing each colour he is not aware of seeing the other. He has two streams of consciousness, in each of which he can see only one colour. In one stream he sees red, and at the same time, in his other stream, he sees blue. More generally, he could be having at the same time two series of thoughts and sensations, in having each of which he is unaware of having the other.

This conclusion has been questioned. It has been claimed by some that there are not two streams of consciousness, on the ground that the subdominant hemisphere is a part of the brain whose functioning involves no consciousness. If this were true, these cases would lose most of their interest. I believe that it is not true, chiefly because, if a person's dominant hemisphere is destroyed, this person is able to react in the way in which, in the split-brain cases, the subdominant hemisphere reacts, and we do not believe that such a person is just an automaton, without consciousness. The sub-dominant hemisphere is, of course, much less developed in certain ways, typically having the linguistic abilities of a three-year-old. But three-year-olds are conscious. This supports the view that, in split-brain cases, there *are* two streams of consciousness.

Another view is that, in these cases, there are two persons involved, sharing the same body. Like Professor MacKay, I believe that we should reject this view. My reason for believing this is, however, different. Professor MacKay denies that there are two persons involved because he believes that there is only one person involved. I believe that, in a sense, the number of persons involved is none.

THE EGO THEORY AND THE BUNDLE THEORY

To explain this sense I must, for a while, turn away from the split-brain cases. There are two theories about what persons are, and what is involved in a person's continued existence over time. On the *Ego Theory,* a person's continued existence cannot be explained except as the continued existence of a particular *Ego,* or *subject of experiences.* An Ego Theorist claims that, if we ask what unifies someone's consciousness at any time—what makes it true, for example, that I can now both see what I am typing and hear the wind outside my window—the answer is that these are both experiences which are being had by me, this person, at this time. Similarly, what explains the unity of a person's whole life is the fact that all of the experiences in this life are had by the same person, or subject of experiences. In its best-known form, the *Cartesian view,* each person is a persisting purely mental thing—a soul, or spiritual substance.

The rival view is the Bundle Theory. Like most styles in art—Gothic, baroque, rococo, etc.—this theory owes its name to its critics. But the name is good enough. According to the *Bundle Theory,* we can't explain either the unity of consciousness at any time, or the unity of a whole life, by referring to a person. Instead we must claim that there are long series of different mental states and events—thoughts, sensations, and the like—each series being what we call one life. Each series is unified by various kinds of causal relation, such as the relations that hold between experiences and later memories of them. Each series is thus like a bundle tied up with string.

In a sense, a Bundle Theorist denies the existence of persons. An outright denial is of course absurd. As Reid protested in the eighteenth century, "I am not thought, I am not action, I am not feeling; I am something which thinks and acts and feels." I am not a series of events, but a person. A Bundle Theorist admits this fact, but claims it to be only a fact about our grammar, or our language. There are persons or subjects in this language-dependent way. If, however, persons are believed to be more than this—to be separately existing things, distinct from our brains and bodies, and the various kinds of mental states and events—the Bundle Theorist denies that there are such things.

Bundle Theory

The first Bundle Theorist was Buddha, who taught "anatta," or the *No Self view.* Buddhists concede that selves or persons have "nominal existence," by which they mean that persons are merely combinations of other elements. Only what exists by itself, as a separate element, has instead what Buddhists call "actual existence." Here are some quotations from Buddhist texts:

> At the beginning of their conversation the king politely asks the monk his name, and receives the following reply: "Sir, I am known as 'Nagasena'; my fellows in the religious life address me as 'Nagasena.' Although my parents gave me the name ... it is just an appellation, a form of speech, a description, a conventional usage. 'Nagasena' is only a name, for no person is found here."

> A sentient being does exist, you think, O Mara? You are misled by a false conception. This bundle of elements is void of Self, In it there is no sentient being. Just as a set of wooden parts Receives the name of carriage, So do we give to elements The name of fancied being.

> [Buddha has spoken thus: "O Brethren, actions do exist, and also their consequences, but the person that acts does not. There is no one to cast away this set of elements, and no one to assume a new set of them. There exists no Individual, it is only a conventional name given to a set of elements."

Buddha's claims are strikingly similar to the claims advanced by several Western writers. Since these writers knew nothing of Buddha, the similarity of these claims suggests that they are not merely part of one cultural tradition, in one period. They may be, as I believe they are, true.

WHAT WE BELIEVE OURSELVES TO BE

Given the advances in psychology and neurophysiology, the Bundle Theory may now seem to be obviously true. It may seem uninteresting to deny that there are separately existing Egos, which are distinct from brains and bodies and the various kinds of mental states and events. But this is not the only issue. We may be convinced that the Ego Theory is false, or even senseless. Most of us, however, even if we are not aware of this, also have certain beliefs about what is involved in our continued existence over time. And these beliefs would

only be justified if something like the Ego Theory was true. Most of us therefore have false beliefs about what persons are, and about ourselves.

These beliefs are best revealed when we consider certain imaginary cases, often drawn from science fiction. One such case is *teletransportation.* Suppose that you enter a cubicle in which, when you press a button, a scanner records the states of all of the cells in your brain and body, destroying both while doing so. This information is then transmitted at the speed of light to some other planet, where a replicator produces a perfect organic copy of you. Since the brain of your Replica is exactly like yours, it will seem to remember living your life up to the moment when you pressed the button, its character will be just like yours, and it will be in every other way psychologically continuous with you. This psychological continuity will not have its normal cause, the continued existence of your brain, since the causal chain will run through the transmission by radio of your "blueprint."

Several writers claim that, if you chose to be teletransported, believing this to be the fastest way of travelling, you would be making a terrible mistake. This would not be a way of travelling, but a way of dying. It may not, they concede, be quite as bad as ordinary death. It might be some consolation to you that, after your death, you will have this Replica, which can finish the book that you are writing, act as parent to your children, and so on. But, they insist, this Replica won't be you. It will merely be someone else, who is exactly like you. This is why this prospect is nearly as bad as ordinary death.

Imagine next a whole range of cases, in each of which, in a single operation, a different proportion of the cells in your brain and body would be replaced with exact duplicates. At the near end of this range, only 1 or 2 per cent would be replaced; in the middle, 40 or 60 per cent; near the far end, 98 or 99 per cent. At the far end of this range is pure teletransportation, the case in which all of your cells would be "replaced."

When you imagine that some proportion of your cells will be replaced with exact duplicates, it is natural to have the following beliefs. First, if you ask, "Will I survive? Will the resulting person be me?," there must be an answer to this question. Either you will survive, or you are about to die. Second, the answer to this question must be either a simple "Yes" or a simple "No." The person who wakes up either will or will not be you. There cannot be a third answer, such as that the person waking up will be half you. You can imagine yourself later being half-conscious. But if the resulting person will be fully conscious, he cannot be half you. To state these beliefs together: to the question, "Will the resulting person be me?," there must always *be* an answer, which must be all-or-nothing.

There seem good grounds for believing that, in the case of teletransportation, your Replica would not be you. In a slight variant of this case, your Replica might be created while you were still alive, so that you could talk to one another. This seems to show that, if 100 per cent of your cells were replaced, the result would merely be a Replica of you. At the other end of my range of cases, where only 1 per cent would be replaced, the resulting person clearly *would* be you. It therefore seems that, in the cases in between, the resulting person must be either you, or merely a Replica. It seems that one of these must be true, and that it makes a great difference which is true.

HOW WE ARE NOT WHAT WE BELIEVE

If these beliefs were correct, there must be some critical percentage, somewhere in this range of cases, up to which the resulting person would be you, and beyond which he would merely be your Replica. Perhaps, for example, it would be you who would wake up if the proportion of cells replaced were 49 per cent, but if just a few more cells were also replaced, this would make all the difference, causing it to be someone else who would wake up.

That there must be some such critical percentage follows from our natural beliefs. But this conclusion is most implausible. How could a few cells make such a difference? Moreover, if there is such a critical percentage, no one could ever discover where it came. Since in all these cases the resulting person would believe that he was you, there could never be any evidence about where, in this range of cases, he would suddenly cease to be you.

On the Bundle Theory, we should reject these natural beliefs. Since you, the person, are not a separately existing entity, we can know exactly what would happen without answering the question of what will happen to you. Moreover, in the cases in the middle of my range, it is an empty question whether the resulting person would be you, or would merely be someone else who is exactly like you. These are not here two different possibilities, one of which must be true. These are merely two different descriptions of the very same course of events. If 50 per cent of your cells were replaced with exact duplicates, we could call the resulting person you, or we could call him merely your Replica. But since these are not here different possibilities, this is a mere choice of words.

As Buddha claimed, the Bundle Theory is hard to believe. It is hard to accept that it could be an empty question whether one is about to die, or will instead live for many years.

What we are being asked to accept may be made clearer with this analogy. Suppose that a certain club exists for some time, holding regular meetings. The meetings then cease. Some years later, several people form a club with the same name, and the same rules. We can ask, "Did these people revive the very same club? Or did they merely start up another club which is exactly similar?" Given certain further details, this would be another empty question. We could know just what happened without answering this question. Suppose that someone said: "But there must be an answer. The club meeting later must either be, or not be, the very same club." This would show that this person didn't understand the nature of clubs.

In the same way, if we have any worries about my imagined cases, we don't understand the nature of persons. In each of my cases, you would know that the resulting person would be both psychologically and physically exactly like you, and that he would have some particular proportion of the cells in your brain and body—90 per cent, or 10 per cent, or, in the case of teletransportation, 0 per cent. Knowing this, you know everything. How could it be a real question what would happen to you, unless you are a

566 CHAPTER 13 • Who Am I?

separately existing Ego, distinct from a brain and body, and the various kinds of mental state and event? If there are no such Egos, there is nothing else to ask a real question about.

Accepting the Bundle Theory is not only hard; it may also affect our emotions. As Buddha claimed, it may undermine our concern about our own futures. This effect can be suggested by re-describing this change of view. Suppose that you are about to be destroyed, but will later have a Replica on Mars. You would naturally believe that this prospect is about as bad as ordinary death, since your Replica won't be you. On the Bundle Theory, the fact that your Replica won't be you just consists in the fact that, though it will be fully psychologically continuous with you, this continuity won't have its normal cause. But when you object to teletransportation you are not objecting merely to the abnormality of this cause. You are objecting that this cause won't get you to Mars. You fear that the abnormal cause will fail to produce a further and all-important fact, which is different from the fact that your Replica will be psychologically continuous with you. You do not merely want there to be psychological continuity between you and some future person. You want to be this future person. On the Bundle Theory, there is no such special further fact. What you fear will not happen, in this imagined case, never happens. You want the person on Mars to be you in a specially intimate way in which no future person will ever be you. This means that, judged from the standpoint of your natural beliefs, even ordinary survival is about as bad as teletransportation. Ordinary survival is about as bad as being destroyed and having a Replica.

HOW THE SPLIT-BRAIN CASES SUPPORT THE BUNDLE THEORY

The truth of the Bundle Theory seems to me, in the widest sense, as much a scientific as a philosophical conclusion. I can imagine kinds of evidence which would have justified believing in the existence of separately existing Egos, and believing that the continued existence of these Egos is what explains the continuity of each

mental life. But there is in fact very little evidence in favour of this Ego Theory, and much for the alternative Bundle Theory.

Some of this evidence is provided by the split-brain cases. On the Ego Theory, to explain what unifies our experiences at any one time, we should simply claim that these are all experiences which are being had by the same person. Bundle Theorists reject this explanation. This disagreement is hard to resolve in ordinary cases. But consider the simplified split-brain case that I described. We show to my imagined patient a placard whose left half is blue and right half is red. In one of this person's two streams of consciousness, he is aware of seeing only blue, while at the same time, in his other stream, he is aware of seeing only red. Each of these two visual experiences is combined with other experiences, like that of being aware of moving one of his hands. What unifies the experiences, at any time, in each of this person's two streams of consciousness? What unifies his awareness of seeing only red with his awareness of moving one hand? The answer cannot be that these experiences are being had by the same person. This answer cannot explain the unity of each of this person's two streams of consciousness, since it ignores the disunity between these streams. This person is now having all of the experiences in both of his two streams. If this fact was what unified these experiences, this would make the two streams one.

These cases do not, I have claimed, involve two people sharing a single body. Since there is only one person involved, who has two streams of consciousness, the Ego Theorist's explanation would have to take the following form. He would have to distinguish between persons and subjects of experiences, and claim that, in split-brain cases, there are *two* of the latter. What unifies the experiences in one of the person's two streams would have to be the fact that these experiences are all being had by the same subject of experiences. What unifies the experiences in this person's other stream would have to be the fact that they are being had by another subject of experiences. When this explanation takes this form, it becomes much less plausible. While we could assume that "subject of experiences," or "Ego," simply meant "person," it was easy to believe that there are subjects of experiences. But if there can be subjects of experiences that are not persons, and if in the life of a split-brain patient there are at any time two different subjects of experiences—two different Egos—why should we believe that there really are such things? This does not amount to a refutation. But it seems to me a strong argument against the Ego Theory.

As a Bundle Theorist, I believe that these two Egos are idle cogs. There is another explanation of the unity of consciousness, both in ordinary cases and in split-brain cases. It is simply a fact that ordinary people are, at any time, aware of having several different experiences. This awareness of several different experiences can be helpfully compared with one's awareness, in short-term memory, of several different experiences. Just as there can be a single memory of just having had several experiences, such as hearing a bell strike three times, there can be a single state of awareness both of hearing the fourth striking of this bell, and of seeing, at the same time, ravens flying past the bell-tower.

Unlike the Ego Theorist's explanation, this explanation can easily be extended to cover split-brain cases. In such cases there is, at any time, not one state of awareness of several different experiences, but two such states. In the case I described, there is one state of awareness of both seeing only red and of moving one hand, and there is another state of awareness of both seeing only blue and moving the other hand. In claiming that there are two such states of awareness, we are not postulating the existence of unfamiliar entities, two separately existing Egos which are not the same as the single person whom the case involves. This explanation appeals to a pair of mental states which would have to be described anyway in a full description of this case.

I have suggested how the split-brain cases provide one argument for one view about the nature of persons. I should mention another such argument, provided by an imagined extension of these cases, first discussed at length by David Wiggins.

In this imagined case a person's brain is divided, and the two halves are transplanted into a pair of different bodies. The two resulting people live quite separate lives. This imagined case shows that personal identity is not what matters. If I was about to divide, I should conclude that neither of the resulting people will be me. I will have ceased to exist. But this way of ceasing to exist is about as good—or as bad—as ordinary survival.

Some of the features of Wiggins's imagined case are likely to remain technically impossible. But the case cannot be dismissed, since its most striking feature, the division of one stream of consciousness into separate streams, has already happened. This is a second way in which the actual split-brain cases have great theoretical importance. They challenge some of our deepest assumptions about ourselves.

CRITICAL QUESTION

1. Why does Parfit believe that the split-brain cases support the bundle theory? Do you find his argument convincing? Why, or why not?

13.4 WHERE AM I?

Location, location, location. This real estate slogan might well be the slogan of philosophers searching for the necessary and sufficient conditions that allow us to say that a person existing at one time (the five-year-old) is the same person existing at another time (the sixty-two-year-old).

It is natural to locate personal identity in the body. I am the same person just insofar as I am in the same body. This "body identity theory" works perfectly well most of the time. If we see someone who looks like our friend Sonia, we assume that she is Sonia. But things can go wrong. Sonia may have an identical twin or a remarkable look-a-like. There are at least three serious problems with the body identity theory. First, looks can be deceiving, as we just noted. Second, bodies change with time, so that the body of the sixty-two-year-old is very different from the body of the five-year-old. Third, our psychological life is left out of the picture. We are more than bodies. We are psychologies. So if someone looks like Sonia but has none of Sonia's memories or personality characteristics, we may doubt that she is Sonia.

We may be able to overcome these problems in a variety of ways. One way is to deny that incidents of deception amount to serious objections to the theory. The fact that I can be deceived does not invalidate my theory unless, of course, my theory claims that deception is not possible. Another way is to build into the "body identity theory" the notion of continuity. If my sixty-two-year-old body is physically continuous in important ways with my five-year-old body, then we can say I am the same person. Although I am not the same in any numerical sense, I am the same in the sense that I am the closest continuer of that other body. But what do we do about my psychological life? Is that located in my body in such a way that where my body is, there my psychological life is?

At this point we may wish to modify the body identity theory by including the brain. Because the brain appears to be the home of my conscious life, along with my memories and personality traits, we might say that it would be better to call the body identity theory a brain identity theory. Where my brain is, there is my home. There, in the brain, is where my psychological life takes place. Of course the physiology of the brain changes as much as the physiology of the body as we age, and surely we can just as easily (and probably more accurately) speak of different psychological lives associated with the same person. I have different bodies over time, but I also have different psychologies over time. Once again, now that we have a "body-brain-psychology" theory of identity, we have to build in some idea of continuity and thereby give up the idea of strict numerical identity. It seems that we should speak instead of similarities connected by continuous physical and psychological streams.

Just when we think we are out of the woods, science fiction steps in to complicate matters. Let's suppose that in the future, brain transplantations become as routine as heart transplantations are today. My body is dying from cancer. If a suitable recipient is found, my brain can be transplanted into that body. Assuming that my psychology will go with my brain, which is now located in a new body, where am I? "You are where your brain is," you might reply. Quite so. Now let's assume that bodies are in short supply, so my brain has to be kept alive in a vat, apart from any body, and constantly bathed with life-supporting fluids. So I am in the vat. Now suppose that our technology is such that we can keep organic brains alive that way for only so long. When time is running out, scientists decide to create a computer replica of my brain. They duplicate my psychology "line for line" as it were. Now where am I?

Don't panic. We are on a roll here. Suppose that now the computer replica brain and my biological brain both exist. Then, just as time is running out, a suitable recipient is found and my biological brain is transplanted into a new body. But there is still this computer replica brain out there in Sci-Fi-Land, bearing the exact same psychology as the newly transplanted biological brain. Where am I?

Daniel C. Dennett is currently the director of the Center for Cognitive Studies at Tufts University. In addition to being a philosopher, he is a sculptor, farmer, winemaker, and designer of museum computer exhibits. In the following selection, Dennett uses science fiction to explore conundrums about personal identity.

⊚ **READING QUESTIONS**

1. What are the alternative answers to the question "where am I" that Dennett faces after the surgery?
2. How does the idea of a "point of view" support the notion that Dennett is "wherever he thinks he is"?

3. What philosophical "revelation" occurs to Dennett when the radio links between his brain and body are broken?

Brainstorms

DANIEL DENNETT

Now that I've won my suit under the Freedom of Information Act, I am at liberty to reveal for the first time a curious episode in my life that may be of interest not only to those engaged in research in the philosophy of mind, artificial intelligence and neuroscience but also to the general public.

Several years ago I was approached by Pentagon officials who asked me to volunteer for a highly dangerous and secret mission. In collaboration with NASA and Howard Hughes, the Department of Defense was spending billions to develop a Supersonic Tunneling Underground Device, or STUD. It was supposed to tunnel through the earth's core at great speed and deliver a specially designed atomic warhead "right up the Red's missile silos," as one of the Pentagon brass put it.

The problem was that in an early test they had succeeded in lodging a warhead about a mile deep under Tulsa, Oklahoma, and they wanted me to retrieve it for them. "Why me?" I asked. Well, the mission involved some pioneering applications of current brain research, and they had heard of my interest in brains and of course my Faustian curiosity and great courage and so forth.... Well, how could I refuse? The difficulty that brought the Pentagon to my door was that the device I'd been asked to recover was fiercely radioactive, in a new way. According to monitoring instruments,

something about the nature of the device and its complex interactions with pockets of material deep in the earth had produced radiation that could cause severe abnormalities in certain tissues of the brain. No way had been found to shield the brain from these deadly rays, which were apparently harmless to other tissues and organs of the body. So it had been decided that the person sent to recover the device should *leave his brain behind*. It would be kept in a safe place where it could execute its normal control functions by elaborate radio links. Would I submit to a surgical procedure that would completely remove my brain, which would then be placed in a life-support system at the Manned Spacecraft Center in Houston? Each input and output pathway, as it was severed, would be restored by a pair of microminiaturized radio transceivers, one attached precisely to the brain, the other to the nerve stumps in the empty cranium. No information would be lost, all the connectivity would be preserved. At first I was a bit reluctant. Would it really work? The Houston brain surgeons encouraged me. "Think of it," they said, "as a mere *stretching* of the nerves. If your brain were just moved over an *inch* in your skull, that would not alter or impair your mind. We're simply going to make the nerves indefinitely elastic by splicing radio links into them."

Daniel C. Dennett, *Brainstorms: Philosophical Essays on Mind and Psychology*, pp. 310–323. Reprinted by permission of MIT Press. Footnotes deleted.

I was shown around the life-support lab in Houston and saw the sparkling new vat in which my brain would be placed, were I to agree. I met the large and brilliant support team of neurologists, hematologists, biophysicists, and electrical engineers, and after several days of discussions and demonstrations, I agreed to give it a try. I was subjected to an enormous array of blood tests, brain scans, experiments, interviews, and the like. They took down my autobiography at great length, recorded tedious lists of my beliefs, hopes, fears, and tastes. They even listed my favorite stereo recordings and gave me a crash session of psychoanalysis.

The day for surgery arrived at last and of course I was anesthetized and remember nothing of the operation itself. When I came out of anesthesia, I opened my eyes, looked around, and asked the inevitable, the traditional, the lamentably hackneyed post-operative question: "Where am I?" The nurse smiled down at me. "You're in Houston," she said, and I reflected that this still had a good chance of being the truth one way or another. She handed me a mirror. Sure enough, there were the tiny antennae poling up through their titanium ports cemented into my skull.

"I gather the operation was a success," I said, "I want to go see my brain." They led me (I was a bit dizzy and unsteady) down a long corridor and into the life-support lab. A cheer went up from the assembled support team, and I responded with what I hoped was a jaunty salute. Still feeling light-headed, I was helped over to the life-support vat. I peered through the glass. There, floating in what looked like ginger-ale, was undeniably a human brain, though it was almost covered with printed circuit chips, plastic tubules, electrodes, and other paraphernalia. "Is that mine?" I asked. "Hit the output transmitter switch there on the side of the vat and see for yourself," the project director replied. I moved the switch to OFF, and immediately slumped, groggy and nauseated, into the arms of the technicians, one of whom kindly restored the switch to its ON position. While I recovered my equilibrium and composure, I thought to myself: "Well, here I am, sitting on a folding chair, staring through a piece of plate glass at my own brain…. But wait," I said to myself, "shouldn't I have

thought, 'Here I am, suspended in a bubbling fluid, being stared at by my own eyes'?" I tried to think this latter thought. I tried to project it into the tank, offering it hopefully to my brain, but I failed to carry off the exercise with any conviction. I tried again. "Here am *I*, Daniel Dennett, suspended in a bubbling fluid, being stared at by my own eyes." No, it just didn't work. Most puzzling and confusing. Being a philosopher of firm physicalist conviction, I believed unswervingly that the tokening of my thoughts was occurring somewhere in my brain: yet, when I thought "Here I am," where the thought occurred to me was *here*, outside the vat, where I, Dennett, was standing staring at my brain.

I tried and tried to think myself into the vat, but to no avail. I tried to build up to the task by doing mental exercises. I thought to myself, "The sun is shining *over there*," five times in rapid succession, each time mentally ostending a different place: in order, the sun-lit corner of the lab, the visible front lawn of the hospital, Houston, Mars, and Jupiter. I found I had little difficulty in getting my "there's" to hop all over the celestial map with their proper references. I could loft a "there" in an instant through the farthest reaches of space, and then aim the next "there" with pinpoint accuracy at the upper left quadrant of a freckle on my arm. Why was I having such trouble with "here"? "Here in Houston" worked well enough, and so did "here in the lab," and even "here in this part of the lab," but "here in the vat" always seemed merely an unmeant mental mouthing. I tried closing my eyes while thinking it. This seemed to help, but still I couldn't manage to pull it off, except perhaps for a fleeting instant. I couldn't be sure. The discovery that I couldn't be sure was also unsettling. How did I know *where* I meant by "here" when I thought "here"? Could I *think* I meant one place when in fact I meant another? I didn't see how that could be admitted without untying the few bonds of intimacy between a person and his own mental life that had survived the onslaught of the brain scientists and philosophers, the physicalists and behaviorists. Perhaps I was incorrigible about where I *meant* when I said "here." But in my present circumstances it seemed that either

I was doomed by sheer force of mental habit to thinking systematically false indexical thoughts, or where a person is (and hence where his thoughts are tokened for purposes of semantic analysis) is not necessarily where his brain, the physical seat of his soul, resides. Nagged by confusion, I attempted to orient myself by falling back on a favorite philosopher's ploy. I began naming things.

"Yorick," I said aloud to my brain, "you are my brain. The rest of my body, seated in this chair, I dub 'Hamlet.'" So here we all are: Yorick's my brain, Hamlet's my body, and I am Dennett. *Now,* where am I? And when I think "where am I?" where's that thought tokened? Is it tokened in my brain, lounging about in the vat, or right here between my ears where it *seems* to be tokened? Or nowhere? Its *temporal* coordinates give me no trouble; must it not have spatial coordinates as well? I began making a list of the alternatives.

(1) *Where Hamlet goes, there goes Dennett.* This principle was easily refuted by appeal to the familiar brain transplant thought-experiments so enjoyed by philosophers. If Tom and Dick switch brains, Tom is the fellow with Dick's former body—just ask him; he'll claim to be Tom, and tell you the most intimate details of Tom's autobiography. It was clear enough, then, that my current body and I could part company, but not likely that I could be separated from my brain. The rule of thumb that emerged so plainly from the thought experiments was that in a brain-transplant operation, one wanted to be the *donor,* not the recipient. Better to call such an operation a body-transplant, in fact. So perhaps the truth was,

(2) *Where Yorick goes, there goes Dennett.* This was not at all appealing, however. How could I be in the vat and not about to go anywhere, when I was so obviously outside the vat looking in and beginning to make guilty plans to return to my room for a substantial lunch? This begged the question I realized, but it still seemed to be getting at something important. Casting about for some support for my intuition, I hit upon a legalistic sort of argument that might have appealed to Locke.

Suppose, I argued to myself, I were now to fly to California, rob a bank, and be apprehended. In which state would I be tried: In California, where the robbery took place, or in Texas, where the brains of the outfit were located? Would I be a California felon with an out-of-state brain, or a Texas felon remotely controlling an accomplice of sorts in California? It seemed possible that I might beat such a rap just on the undecidability of that jurisdictional question, though perhaps it would be deemed an inter-state, and hence Federal, offense. In any event, suppose I were convicted. Was it likely that California would be satisfied to throw Hamlet into the brig, knowing that Yorick was living the good life and luxuriously taking the waters in Texas? Would Texas incarcerate Yorick, leaving Hamlet free to take the next boat to Rio? This alternative appealed to me. Barring capital punishment or other cruel and unusual punishment, the state would be obliged to maintain the life-support system for Yorick though they might move him from Houston to Leavenworth, and aside from the unpleasantness of the opprobrium, I, for one, would not mind at all and would consider myself a free man under those circumstances. If the state has an interest in forcibly relocating persons in institutions, it would fail to relocate me in any institution by locating Yorick there. If this were true, it suggested a third alternative.

(3) *Dennett is wherever he thinks he is.* Generalized, the claim was as follows: At any given time a person has a point of view, and the location of the point of view (which is determined internally by the content of the point of view) is also the location of the person.

Such a proposition is not without its perplexities, but to me it seemed a step in the right direction. The only trouble was that it seemed to place one in a heads-I-win/tails-you-lose situation of unlikely infallibility as regards location. Hadn't I myself often been wrong about where I was, and at least as often uncertain? Couldn't one get lost? Of course, but getting lost *geographically* is not the only way one might get lost. If one were lost in the woods one could attempt to reassure oneself with the consolation that at least one knew where one was: one was right here in the familiar surroundings of one's own body. Perhaps in this case one would not have drawn one's attention to much to be thankful for. Still, there were worse plights imaginable, and I wasn't sure I wasn't in such a plight right now.

Point of view clearly had something to do with personal location, but it was itself an unclear notion. It was obvious that the content of one's point of view was not the same as or determined by the content of one's beliefs or thoughts. For example, what should we say about the point of view of the Cinerama viewer who shrieks and twists in his seat as the roller-coaster footage overcomes his psychic distancing? Has he forgotten that he is safely seated in the theater? Here I was inclined to say that the person is experiencing an illusory shift in point of view. In other cases, my inclination to call such shifts illusory was less strong. The workers in laboratories and plants who handle dangerous materials by operating feedback-controlled mechanical arms and hands undergo a shift in point of view that is crisper and more pronounced than anything Cinerama can provoke. They can feel the heft and slipperiness of the containers they manipulate with their metal fingers. They know perfectly well where they are and are not fooled into false beliefs by the experience, yet it is as if they were inside the isolation chamber they are peering into. With mental effort, they can manage to shift their point of view back and forth, rather like making a transparent Neckar cube or an Escher drawing change orientation before one's eyes. It does seem extravagant to suppose that in performing this bit of mental gymnastics, they are transporting *themselves* back and forth.

Still their example gave me hope. If I was in fact in the vat in spite of my intuitions, I might be able to train myself to adopt that point of view even as a matter of habit. I should dwell on images of myself comfortably floating in my vat, beaming volitions to that familiar body *out there*. I reflected that the ease or difficulty of this task was presumably independent of the truth about the location of one's brain. Had I been practicing before the operation, I might now be finding it second nature. You might now yourself try such a *trompe l'oeil*. Imagine you have written an inflammatory letter which has been published in the *Times*, the result of which is that the Government has chosen to impound your brain for a probationary period of three years in its Dangerous Brain Clinic in Bethesda, Maryland. Your body of course is allowed freedom to earn a salary and thus to continue its function of laying up income to be taxed. At this moment, however, your body is seated in an auditorium listening to a peculiar account by Daniel Dennett of his own similar experience. Try it. Think yourself to Bethesda, and then hark back longingly to your body, far away, and yet *seeming* so near. It is only with long-distance restraint (yours? the Government's?) that you can control your impulse to get those hands clapping in polite applause before navigating the old body to the rest room and a well-deserved glass of evening sherry in the lounge. The task of imagination is certainly difficult, but if you achieve your goal the results might be consoling.

Anyway, there I was in Houston, lost in thought as one might say, but not for long. My speculations were soon interrupted by the Houston doctors, who wished to test out my new prosthetic nervous system before sending me off on my hazardous mission. As I mentioned before, I was a bit dizzy at first, and not surprisingly, although I soon habituated myself to my new circumstances (which were, after all, well nigh indistinguishable from my old circumstances). My accommodation was not perfect, however, and to this day I continue to be plagued by minor coordination difficulties. The speed of light is fast, but finite, and as my brain and body move farther and farther apart, the delicate interaction of my feedback systems is thrown into disarray by the time lags. Just as one is rendered close to speechless by a delayed or echoic hearing of one's speaking voice so, for instance, I am virtually unable to track a moving object with my eyes whenever my brain and my body are more than a few miles apart. In most matters my impairment is scarcely detectable, though I can no longer hit a slow curve ball with the authority of yore. There are some compensations of course. Though liquor tastes as good as ever, and warms my gullet while corroding my liver, I can drink it in any quantity I please, without becoming the slightest bit inebriated, a curiosity some of my close friends may have noticed (though I occasionally have *feigned* inebriation, so as not to draw attention to my unusual circumstances). For similar reasons, I take aspirin orally for a sprained wrist, but if the pain persists I ask Houston to administer codeine to me *in vitro*. In times of illness the phone bill can be staggering.

But to return to my adventure. At length, both the doctors and I were satisfied that I was ready to undertake my subterranean mission. And so I left my brain in Houston and headed by helicopter for Tulsa. Well, in any case, that's the way it seemed to me. That's how I would put it, just off the top of my head as it were. On the trip I reflected further about my earlier anxieties and decided that my first post-operative speculations had been tinged with panic. The matter was not nearly as strange or metaphysical as I had been supposing. Where was I? In two places, clearly: both inside the vat and outside it. Just as one can stand with one foot in Connecticut and the other in Rhode Island, I was in two places at once. I had become one of those scattered individuals we used to hear so much about. The more I considered this answer, the more obviously true it appeared. But, strange to say, the more true it appeared, the less important the question to which it could be the true answer seemed. A sad, but not unprecedented, fate for a philosophical question to suffer. This answer did not completely satisfy me, of course. There lingered some question to which I should have liked an answer, which was neither "Where are all my various and sundry parts?" nor "What is my current point of view?" Or at least there seemed to be such a question. For it did seem undeniable that in some sense *I* and not merely *most of me* was descending into the earth under Tulsa in search of an atomic warhead.

When I found the warhead, I was certainly glad I had left my brain behind, for the pointer on the specially built Geiger counter I had brought with me was off the dial. I called Houston on my ordinary radio and told the operation control center of my position and my progress. In return, they gave me instructions for dismantling the vehicle, based upon my on-site observations. I had set to work with my cutting torch when all of a sudden a terrible thing happened. I went stone deaf. At first I thought it was only my radio earphones that had broken, but when I tapped on my helmet, I heard nothing. Apparently the auditory

transceivers had gone on the fritz. I could no longer hear Houston or my own voice, but I could speak, so I started telling them what had happened. In mid-sentence, I knew something else had gone wrong. My vocal apparatus had become paralyzed. Then my right hand went limp—another transceiver had gone. I was truly in deep trouble. But worse was to follow. After a few more minutes, I went blind. I cursed my luck, and then I cursed the scientists who had led me into this grave peril. There I was, deaf, dumb, and blind, in a radioactive hole more than a mile under Tulsa. Then the last of my cerebral radio links broke, and suddenly I was faced with a new and even more shocking problem: whereas an instant before I had been buried alive in Oklahoma, now I was disembodied in Houston. My recognition of my new status was not immediate. It took me several very anxious minutes before it dawned on me that my poor body lay several hundred miles away, with heart pulsing and lungs respirating, but otherwise as dead as the body of any heart transplant donor, its skull packed with useless, broken electronic gear. The shift in perspective I had earlier found well nigh impossible now seemed quite natural. Though I could think myself back into my body in the tunnel under Tulsa, it took some effort to sustain the illusion. For surely it was an illusion to suppose I was still in Oklahoma: I had lost all contact with that body.

It occurred to me then, with one of those rushes of revelation of which we should be suspicious, that I had stumbled upon an impressive demonstration of the immateriality of the soul based upon physicalist principles and premises. For as the last radio signal between Tulsa and Houston died away, had I not changed location from Tulsa to Houston at the speed of light? And had I not accomplished this without any increase in mass? What moved from A to B at such speed was surely myself, or at any rate my soul or mind—the massless center of my being and home of my consciousness. My *point* of view had lagged somewhat behind, but I had already noted the indirect bearing of point of view on personal location. I could not see how a physicalist philosopher could quarrel with this except by taking the dire and counterintuitive route of banishing all talk of persons.

Yet the notion of personhood was so well entrenched in everyone's world view, or so it seemed to me, that any denial would be as curiously unconvincing, as systematically disingenuous, as the Cartesian negation, "non sum."

The joy of philosophic discovery thus tided me over some very bad minutes or perhaps hours as the helplessness and hopelessness of my situation became more apparent to me. Waves of panic and even nausea swept over me, made all the more horrible by the absence of their normal body-dependent phenomenology. No adrenalin rush of tingles in the arms, no pounding heart, no premonitory salivation. I did feel a dread sinking feeling in my bowels at one point, and this tricked me momentarily into the false hope that I was undergoing a reversal of the process that landed me in this fix—a gradual undisembodiment. But the isolation and uniqueness of that twinge soon convinced me that it was simply the first of a plague of phantom body hallucinations that I, like any other amputee, would be all too likely to suffer.

My mood then was chaotic. On the one hand, I was fired up with elation of my philosophic discovery and was wracking my brain (one of the few familiar things I could still do), trying to figure out how to communicate my discovery to the journals; while on the other, I was bitter, lonely, and filled with dread and uncertainty. Fortunately, this did not last long, for my technical support team sedated me into a dreamless sleep from which I awoke, hearing with magnificent fidelity the familiar opening strains of my favorite Brahms piano trio. So that was why they had wanted a list of my favorite recordings! It did not take me long to realize that I was hearing the music without ears. The output from the stereo stylus was being fed through some fancy rectification circuitry directly into my auditory nerve. I was mainlining Brahms, an unforgettable experience for any stereo buff. At the end of the record it did not surprise me to hear the reassuring voice of the project director speaking into a microphone that was now my prosthetic ear. He confirmed my analysis of what had gone wrong and assured me that steps were being taken to re-embody me. He did not elaborate, and after a few more recordings, I found myself drifting off to sleep. My sleep lasted, I later learned, for the

better part of a year, and when I awoke, it was to find myself fully restored to my senses. When I looked into the mirror, though, I was a bit startled to see an unfamiliar face. Bearded and a bit heavier, bearing no doubt a family resemblance to my former face, and with the same look of spritely intelligence and resolute character, but definitely a new face. Further self-explorations of an intimate nature left me no doubt that this was a new body and the project director confirmed my conclusions. He did not volunteer any information on the past history of my new body and I decided (wisely, I think in retrospect) not to pry. As many philosophers unfamiliar with my ordeal have more recently speculated, the acquisition of a new body leaves one's *person* intact. And after a period of adjustment to a new voice, new muscular strengths and weaknesses, and so forth, one's *personality* is by and large also preserved. More dramatic changes in personality have been routinely observed in people who have undergone extensive plastic surgery, to say nothing of sex change operations, and I think no one contests the survival of the person in such cases. In any event I soon accommodated to my new body, to the point of being unable to recover any of its novelties to my consciousness or even memory. The view in the mirror soon became utterly familiar. That view, by the way, still revealed antennae, and so I was not surprised to learn that my brain had not been moved from its haven in the life-support lab.

I decided that good old Yorick deserved a visit. I and my new body, whom we might as well call Fortinbras, strode into the familiar lab to another round of applause from the technicians, who were of course congratulating themselves, not me. Once more I stood before the vat and contemplated poor Yorick, and on a whim I once again cavalierly flicked off the output transmitter switch. Imagine my surprise when nothing unusual happened. No fainting spell, no nausea, no noticeable change. A technician hurried to restore the switch to ON, but still I felt nothing. I demanded an explanation, which the project director hastened to provide. It seems that before they had even operated on the first occasion, they had constructed a computer duplicate of my brain, reproducing both the complete information processing structure and the computational speed of my brain in a giant computer program. After the operation, but before they had dared to send me off on my mission to Oklahoma, they had run this computer system and Yorick side by side. The incoming signals from Hamlet were sent simultaneously to Yorick's transceivers and to the computer's array of inputs. And the outputs from Yorick were not only beamed back to Hamlet, my body; they were recorded and checked against the simultaneous output of the computer program, which was called "Hubert" for reasons obscure to me. Over days and even weeks, the outputs were identical and synchronous, which of course did not *prove* that they had succeeded in copying the brain's functional structure, but the empirical support was greatly encouraging.

Hubert's input, and hence activity, had been kept parallel with Yorick's during my disembodied days. And now, to demonstrate this, they had actually thrown the master switch that put Hubert for the first time in on-line control of my body—not Hamlet, of course, but Fortinbras. (Hamlet, I learned, had never been recovered from its underground tomb and could be assumed by this time to have largely returned to the dust. At the head of my grave still lay the magnificent bulk of the abandoned device, with the word STUD emblazoned on its side in large letters—a circumstance which may provide archeologists of the next century with a curious insight into the burial rites of their ancestors.)

The laboratory technicians now showed me the master switch, which had two positions, labeled *B,* for Brain (they didn't know my brain's name was Yorick) and *H,* for Hubert. The switch did indeed point to *H,* and they explained to me that if I wished, I could switch it back to *B.* With my heart in my mouth (and my brain in its vat), I did this. Nothing happened. A click, that was all. To test their claim, and with the master switch now set at *B,* I hit Yorick's output transmitter switch on the vat and sure enough, I began to faint. Once the output switch was turned back on and I had recovered my wits, so to speak, I continued to play with the master switch, flipping it back and forth. I found that with the exception of the transitional click, I could detect no trace of a difference. I could switch in mid-utterance, and

the sentence I had begun speaking under the control of Yorick was finished without a pause or hitch of any kind under the control of Hubert. I had a spare brain, a prosthetic device which might some day stand me in very good stead, were some mishap to befall Yorick. Or alternatively, I could keep Yorick as a spare and use Hubert. It didn't seem to make any difference which I chose, for the wear and tear and fatigue on my body did not have any debilitating effect on either brain, whether or not it was actually causing the motions of my body, or merely spilling its output into thin air.

The one truly unsettling aspect of this new development was the prospect, which was not long in dawning on me, of someone detaching the spare—Hubert or Yorick, as the case might be—from Fortinbras and hitching it to yet another body—some Johnny-come-lately Rosencrantz or Guildenstern. Then (if not before) there would be *two* people, that much was clear. One would be me, and the other would be a sort of supertwin brother. If there were two bodies, one under the control of Hubert and the other being controlled by Yorick, then which would the world recognize as the true Dennett? And whatever the rest of the world decided, which one would be *me?* Would I be the Yorick-brained one, in virtue of Yorick's causal priority and former intimate relationship with the original Dennett body, Hamlet? That seemed a bit legalistic, a bit too redolent of the arbitrariness of consanguinity and legal possession, to be convincing at the metaphysical level. For, suppose that before the arrival of the second body on the scene, I had been keeping Yorick as the spare for years, and letting Hubert's output drive my body—that is, Fortinbras—all that time. The Hubert-Fortinbras couple would seem then by squatter's rights (to combat one legal intuition with another) to be the true Dennett and the lawful inheritor of everything that was Dennett's. This was an interesting question, certainly, but not nearly so pressing as another question that bothered me. My strongest intuition was that in such an eventuality I would survive so long as *either* brain-body couple remained intact, but I had mixed emotions about whether I should want both to survive.

I discussed my worries with the technicians and the project director. The prospect of two Dennetts was abhorrent to me, I explained, largely for social reasons. I didn't want to be my own rival for the affections of my wife, nor did I like the prospect of the two Dennetts sharing my modest professor's salary. Still more vertiginous and distasteful, though, was the idea of knowing *that much* about another person, while he had the very same goods on me. How could we ever face each other? My colleagues in the lab argued that I was ignoring the bright side of the matter. Weren't there many things I wanted to do but, being only one person, had been unable to do? Now one Dennett could stay at home and be the professor and family man, while the other could strike out on a life of travel and adventure—missing the family of course, but happy in the knowledge that the other Dennett was keeping the home fires burning. I could be faithful and adulterous at the same time. I could even cuckold myself—to say nothing of other more lurid possibilities my colleagues were all too ready to force upon my overtaxed imagination. But my ordeal in Oklahoma (or was it Houston?) had made me less adventurous, and I shrank from this opportunity that was being offered (though of course I was never quite sure it was being offered to *me* in the first place).

There was another prospect even more disagreeable—that the spare, Hubert or Yorick as the case might be, would be detached from any input from Fortinbras and just left detached. Then, as in the other case, there would be two Dennetts, or at least two claimants to my name and possessions, one embodied in Fortinbras, and the other sadly, miserably disembodied. Both selfishness and altruism bade me take steps to prevent this from happening. So I asked that measures be taken to ensure that no one could ever tamper with the transceiver connections or the master switch without my (our? no, *my*) knowledge and consent. Since I had no desire to spend my life guarding the equipment in Houston, it was mutually decided that all the electronic connections in the lab would be carefully locked: both those that controlled the life-support system for Yorick and those that controlled the power supply for Hubert would be guarded with failsafe devices, and I would take the only master switch, outfitted for radio remote control, with me wherever I went. I carry it strapped around my waist and—wait a moment—*here it is.* Every few months I reconnoiter the situation by switching channels. I do this only in the presence of friends of course, for if the other channel were, heaven forbid, either dead or otherwise occupied, there would have to be somebody who had my interests at heart to switch it back, to bring me back from the void. For while I could feel, see, hear and otherwise sense whatever befell my body, subsequent to such a switch, I'd be unable to control it. By the way, the two positions on the switch are intentionally unmarked, so I never have the faintest idea whether I am switching from Hubert to Yorick or *vice versa.* (Some of you may think that in this case I really don't know *who* I am, let alone where I am. But such reflections no longer make much of a dent on my essential Dennettness, on my own sense of who I am. If it is true that in one sense I don't know who I am then that's another one of your philosophical truths of underwhelming significance.)

In any case, every time I've flipped the switch so far, nothing has happened. *So let's give it a try....*

"THANK GOD! I THOUGHT YOU'D NEVER FLIP THAT SWITCH! You can't imagine how horrible it's been these last two weeks—but now you know, it's your turn in purgatory. How I've longed for this moment! You see, about two weeks ago—excuse me, ladies and gentlemen, but I've got to explain this to my ... um, brother, I guess you could say, but he's just told you the facts, so you'll understand—about two weeks ago our two brains drifted just a bit out of synch. I don't know whether my brain is now Hubert or Yorick, any more than you do, but in any case, the two brains drifted apart, and of course once the process started, it snowballed, for I was in a slightly different receptive state for the input we both received, a difference that was soon magnified. In no time at all the illusion that I was in control of my body—our body—was completely dissipated. There was nothing I could do—no way to call you. YOU DIDN'T EVEN KNOW I EXISTED! It's been like being carried around in a cage, or better, like being possessed—hearing my own voice say things I didn't mean to say, watching in frustration as my own hands performed deeds I hadn't intended. You'd scratch our itches, but not the way I would have, and you kept me awake, with your tossing and turning. I've been totally exhausted, on the verge of a nervous breakdown, carried around helplessly by your frantic round of activities, sustained only by the knowledge that some day you'd throw the switch.

"Now it's your turn, but at least you'll have the comfort of knowing I know you're in there. Like an expectant mother, I'm eating—or at any rate tasting, smelling, seeing—for *two* now, and

I'll try to make it easy for you. Don't worry. Just as soon as this colloquium is over, you and I will fly to Houston, and we'll see what can be done to get one of us another body. You can have a female body—your body could be any color you like. But let's think it over. I tell you what—to be fair, if we both want this body, I promise I'll let the project director flip a coin to settle which of us gets to keep it and which then gets to choose a new body. That should guarantee justice, shouldn't it? In any case, I'll take care of you, I promise. These people are my witnesses.

"Ladies and gentlemen, this talk we have just heard is not exactly the talk I would have given, but I assure you that everything he said was perfectly true. And now if you'll excuse me, I think I'd—we'd—better sit down."

◉ CRITICAL QUESTIONS

1. Would you, like Dennett, initially conclude that you are where your body is and not where your brain is? Why or why not?
2. Would you, like Dennett, be upset about the possibility of one of your brains becoming connected to another body? Why, or why not?
3. Where is your "self" located? Is it in your body or outside of your body? Is it in your brain and not in your body? Is it in your brain-body or some other place? Does it even make sense to ask where your "self is located? Support whatever answers you give with reasons.
4. Does the popular idea that our self is our soul solve any of Dennett's problems about where he is located? If so, how does it? If not, why not?

13.5 SOCIAL IDENTITY

How many languages do you speak? One? Two? Three or more? You probably speak more than you think.

"So why do you ask?" you may be thinking. I ask because when we focus on the question, "Who am I?" the issues relating to personal identity arise. This means that issues of ethnic and linguistic identity must soon be explored because our personal identities are shaped in a cultural and linguistic environment.

Recall that Eve Cole (see Section 12.3) takes Descartes to task for not only ignoring the embodied nature of the self but also for ignoring the relational self. She suggests that we might even begin a "metaphysics of the self" by asking, "To whom am I related?" Communication of some kind is essential to establishing relationships, and, for most of us, that means language is the vehicle by which we relate. You have all heard the slogan, "You are what you eat." Is it going too far to say, "You are your language"?

If you have grown up monolinguistic and securely centered within clear cultural borders, the slogan about you being your language may seem strange. However, if you have grown up in a borderland, between cultures, and multilinguistic, the slogan may not seem so strange. If we add to that experiences that have made you feel ashamed of your native tongue, then you can see more clearly how identity and language can be so closely related.

In the selection that follows, Gloria Anzaldúa (b. 1942) explores issues of identity and language based on her own personal experience as a Chicana. In the preface to the book from which this selection is taken, the author writes, "I am a border woman. I grew up between two cultures, the Mexican (with a heavy Indian influence) and the Anglo (as a member of a colonized people in our own territory). I have been straddling that tejas-Mexican border, and others, all my life."

As a poet and writer of fiction who has taught at various universities, Anzaldúa brings a particular insightful passion to her explorations of identity in a borderland. As you can imagine, borderlands are not always comfortable places. The discomfort and contradictions that often characterize life on the border not only shape one's identity, they make one more aware of the subtle ways our personal self is a social self.

◉ READING QUESTIONS

1. How, according to Anzaldúa, did Chicano Spanish arise?

2. What is linguistic terrorism, and what makes it so bad?

How to Tame a Wild Tongue

GLORIA ANZALDÚA

"We're going to have to control your tongue," the dentist says, pulling out all the metal from my mouth. Silver bits plop and tinkle into the basin. My mouth is a motherlode.

The dentist is cleaning out my roots. I get a whiff of the stench when I gasp. "I can't cap that tooth yet, you're still draining," he says.

"We're going to have to do something about your tongue," I hear the anger rising in his voice. My tongue keeps pushing out the wads of cotton, pushing back the drills, the long thin needles. "I've never seen anything as strong or as stubborn," he says. And I think, how do you tame a wild tongue, train it to be quiet, how do you bridle and saddle it? How do you make it lie down?

"Who is to say that robbing a people of
   its language is less violent than war?"
                              —Ray Gwyn Smith[1]

I remember being caught speaking Spanish at recess—that was good for three licks on the knuckles with a sharp ruler. I remember being sent to the corner of the classroom for "talking back" to the Anglo teacher when all I was trying to do was tell her how to pronounce my name. "If you want to be American, speak 'American.' If you don't like it, go back to Mexico where you belong."

"I want you to speak English. *Pa' hallar buen trabajo tienes que saber hablar el inglés bien. Qué vale toda tu educación si todavía hablas inglés con un* 'accent,'" my mother would say, mortified that I spoke English like a Mexican. At Pan American University, I, and all Chicano students were required to take two speech classes. Their purpose: to get rid of our accents.

Attacks on one's form of expression with the intent to censor are a violation of the First Amendment. *El Anglo con cara de inocente nos arrancó la lengua.* Wild tongues can't be tamed, they can only be cut out.

---

[1]Ray Gwyn Smith, *Moorland Is Cold Country*, unpublished book.

OVERCOMING THE TRADITION OF SILENCE

Ahogadas, escupimos el oscuro.
Peleando con nuestra propia sombra el
    silencio nos sepulta.

En boca cerrada no entran moscas. "Flies don't enter a closed mouth" is a saying I kept hearing when I was a child. *Ser habladorawas* to be a gossip and a liar, to talk too much. *Muchachitas bien criadas,* well-bred girls don't answer back. *Es una falta de respeto* to talk back to one's mother or father. I remember one of the sins I'd recite to the priest in the confession box the few times I went to confession: talking back to my mother, *hablar pa' 'tras, repelar. Hocicona, repelona, chismosa,* having a big mouth, questioning, carrying tales are all signs of being *mal criada.* In my culture they are all words that are derogatory if applied to women—I've never heard them applied to men.

The first time I heard two women, a Puerto Rican and a Cuban, say the word "*nosotras,*" I was shocked. I had not known the word existed. Chicanas use *nosotros* whether we're male or female. We are robbed of our female being by the masculine plural. Language is a male discourse.

> *And our tongues have become*
> *Dry   the wilderness has*
> *dried out our tongues   and*
> *we have forgotten speech.*
>
> —Irena Klepfisz[2]

Even our own people, other Spanish speakers *nos quieren poner candados en la boca.* They would hold us back with their bag of *reglas de academia.*

Oyé como ladra: el lenguaje de la frontera
Quien tiene boca se equivoca.

—Mexican saying

"*Pocho,* cultural traitor, you're speaking the oppressor's language by speaking English, you're ruining the Spanish language," I have been accused by various Latinos and Latinas. Chicano Spanish is considered by the purist and by most Latinos deficient, a mutilation of Spanish.

But Chicano Spanish is a border tongue which developed naturally. Change, *evolución, enriqueci-miento depalabras nuevaspor invención o adopción* have created variants of Chicano Spanish, un nuevo lenguaje. Un lenguaje que corresponde a un modo de vivir. Chicano Spanish is not incorrect, it is a living language.

For a people who are neither Spanish nor live in a country in which Spanish is the first language; for a people who live in a country in which English is the reigning tongue but who are not Anglo; for a people who cannot entirely identify with either standard (formal, Castillian) Spanish nor standard English, what recourse is left to them but to create their own language? A language which they can connect their identity to, one capable of communicating the realities and values true to themselves—a language with terms that are neither *español ni inglés,* but both. We speak a patois, a forked tongue, a variation of two languages.

Chicano Spanish sprang out of the Chicanos' need to identify ourselves as a distinct people. We needed a language with which we could communicate with ourselves, a secret language. For some of us, language is a homeland closer than the Southwest—for many Chicanos today live in the Midwest and the East. And because we are a complex, heterogeneous people, we speak many languages. Some of the languages we speak are:

1. Standard English
2. Working class and slang English
3. Standard Spanish
4. Standard Mexican Spanish
5. North Mexican Spanish dialect
6. Chicano Spanish (Texas, New Mexico, Arizona and California have regional variations)
7. Tex-Mex
8. *Pachuco* (called caló)

My "home" tongues are the languages I speak with my sister and brothers, with my friends. They are the last five listed, with 6 and 7 being closest to my heart. From school, the media and job situations, I've picked up standard and working class English. From Mamagrande Locha and from reading Spanish and Mexican literature, I've picked up

---

[2]Irena Klepfisz, "*Di Rayze Aheym*/ The Journey Home," in *The Tribe of Dina; A Jewish Women's Anthology,* Melanie Kaye/ Kantrowitz and Irena Klepfisz, eds. (Montpelier, VT: Sinister Wisdom Books, 1986), 49.

Standard Spanish and Standard Mexican Spanish. From *los recién llegados*, Mexican immigrants, and *braceros*, I learned the North Mexican dialect. With Mexicans I'll try to speak either Standard Mexican Spanish or the North Mexican dialect. From my parents and Chicanos living in the Valley, I picked up Chicano Texas Spanish, and I speak it with my mom, younger brother (who married a Mexican and who rarely mixes Spanish with English), aunts and older relatives.

With Chicanas from *Nuevo México* or *Arizona* I will speak Chicano Spanish a little, but often they don't understand what I'm saying. With most California Chicanas I speak entirely in English (unless I forget). When I first moved to San Francisco, I'd rattle off something in Spanish, unintentionally embarrassing them. Often it is only with another Chicana tejana that I can talk freely.

Words distorted by English are known as anglicisms or *pochismos*. The *pocho* is an anglicized Mexican or American of Mexican origin who speaks Spanish with an accent characteristic of North Americans and who distorts and reconstructs the language according to the influence of English.[3] Tex-Mex, or Spanglish, comes most naturally to me. I may switch back and forth from English to Spanish in the same sentence or in the same word. With my sister and my brother Nune and with Chicano *tejano* contemporaries I speak in Tex-Mex.

From kids and people my own age I picked up *Pachuco*. *Pachuco* (the language of the zoot suiters) is a language of rebellion, both against Standard Spanish and Standard English. It is a secret language. Adults of the culture and outsiders cannot understand it. It is made up of slang words from both English and Spanish. *Ruca* means girl or woman, *vato* means guy or dude, *chale* means no, *simón* means yes, *churro* is sure, talk is *peri*-quiar, *pigionear* means petting, *que gacho* means how nerdy, *ponte águila* means watch out, death is called *la pelona*. Through lack of practice and not having others who can speak it, I've lost most of the *Pachuco* tongue.

CHICANO SPANISH

Chicanos, after 250 years of Spanish/Anglo colonization have developed significant differences in the Spanish we speak. We collapse two adjacent vowels into a single syllable and sometimes shift the stress in certain words such as *maíz/maiz, cohete/cuete*. We leave out certain consonants when they appear between vowels: *lado/lao, mojado/mojao*. Chicanós from South Texas pronounce *f* as *j* as in *jue (fue)*. Chicanos use "archaisms," words that are no longer in the Spanish language, words that have been evolved out. We say *semos, truje, haiga, ansina*, and *naiden*. We retain the "archaic" *j*, as in *jalar*, that derives from an earlier *h* (the French *halar* or the Germanic *halon* which was lost to standard Spanish in the 16th century), but which is still found in several regional dialects such as the one spoken in South Texas. (Due to geography, Chicanos from the Valley of South Texas were cut off linguistically from other Spanish speakers. We tend to use words that the Spaniards brought over from Medieval Spain. The majority of the Spanish colonizers in Mexico and the Southwest came from Extremadura—Hernán Cortés was one of them—and Andalucía. Andalucians pronounce *ll* like a *y*, and their *d*'s tend to be absorbed by adjacent vowels: *tirado* becomes *tirao*. They brought el lenguaje popular, dialectos y regionalismos.[4])

Chicanos and other Spanish speakers also shift *ll* to *y* and *z* to *s*.[5] We leave out initial syllables, saying *tar* for *estar*, *toy* for *estoy*, *hora* for *ahora* (*cubanos* and *puertorriqueños* also leave out initial letters of some words). We also leave out the final syllable such as for *pa para*. The intervocalic *y*, the *ll* as in *tortilla, ella, botella*, gets replaced by *tortia* or *tortiya, ea, botea*. We add an additional syllable at the beginning of certain words: *atocar* for *tocar*, *agastar* for *gastar*. Sometimes we'll say *lavaste las vacijas*, other times *lavates* (substituting the *ates* verb endings for the *aste*).

---

[3]R. C. Ortega, *Dialectología Del Barrio*, trans. Hortencia S. Alwan (Los Angeles, CA: R. C. Ortega Publisher & Bookseller, 1977), 132.

[4]Eduardo Hernandéz-Chávez, Andrew D. Cohen, and Anthony F. Beltramo, *El Lenguaje de los Chicanos: Regional and Social Characteristics of Language Used by Mexican Americans* (Arlington, VA: Center for Applied Linguistics, 1975), 39.
[5]Hernandéz-Chávez, xvii.

We use anglicisms, words borrowed from English: *bola* from ball, *carpeta* from carpet, *máchina de lavar* (instead of lavadora) from washing machine. Tex-Mex argot, created by adding a Spanish sound at the beginning or end of an English word such as *cookiar* for cook, *watchar* for watch, *parkiar* for park, and *rapiar* for rape, is the result of the pressures on Spanish speakers to adapt to English.

We don't use the word *vosotros/as* or its accompanying verb form. We don't say *claro* (to mean yes), *imaginate*, or *me emociona*, unless we picked up Spanish from Latinas, out of a book, or in a classroom. Other Spanish-speaking groups are going through the same, or similar, development in their Spanish.

LINGUISTIC TERRORISM

> *Deslenguadas. Somos los del español deficiente.* We are your linguistic nightmare, your linguistic aberration, your linguistic *mestisaje,* the subject of your burla. Because we speak with tongues of fire we are culturally crucified. Racially, culturally and linguistically *somos huérfanos*—we speak an orphan tongue.

Chicanas who grew up speaking Chicano Spanish have internalized the belief that we speak poor Spanish. It is illegitimate, a bastard language. And because we internalize how our language has been used against us by the dominant culture, we use our language differences against each other.

Chicana feminists often skirt around each other with suspicion and hesitation. For the longest time I couldn't figure it out. Then it dawned on me. To be close to another Chicana is like looking into the mirror. We are afraid of what we'll see there. *Pena.* Shame. Low estimation of self. In childhood we are told that our language is wrong. Repeated attacks on our native tongue diminish our sense of self. The attacks continue throughout our lives.

Chicanas feel uncomfortable talking in Spanish to Latinas, afraid of their censure. Their language was not outlawed in their countries. They had a whole lifetime of being immersed in their native tongue; generations, centuries in which Spanish was a first language, taught in school, heard on radio and TV, and read in the newspaper.

If a person, Chicana or Latina, has a low estimation of my native tongue, she also has a low estimation of me. Often with *mexicanas y latinas* we'll speak English as a neutral language. Even among Chicanas we tend to speak English at parties or conferences. Yet, at the same time, we're afraid the other will think we're *agringadas* because we don't speak Chicano Spanish. We oppress each other trying to out-Chicano each other, vying to be the "real" Chicanas, to speak like Chicanos. There is no one Chicano language just as there is no one Chicano experience. A monolingual Chicana whose first language is English or Spanish is just as much a Chicana as one who speaks several variants of Spanish. A Chicana from Michigan or Chicago or Detroit is just as much a Chicana as one from the Southwest. Chicano Spanish is as diverse linguistically as it is regionally.

By the end of this century, Spanish speakers will comprise the biggest minority group in the U.S., a country where students in high schools and colleges are encouraged to take French classes because French is considered more "cultured." But for a language to remain alive it must be used.[6] By the end of this century English, and not Spanish, will be the mother tongue of most Chicanos and Latinos.

So, if you want to really hurt me, talk badly about my language. Ethnic identity is twin skin to linguistic identity—I am my language. Until I can take pride in my language, I cannot take pride in myself. Until I can accept as legitimate Chicano Texas Spanish, Tex-Mex and all the other languages I speak, I cannot accept the legitimacy of myself. Until I am free to write bilingually and to switch codes without having always to translate, while I still have to speak English or Spanish when I would rather speak Spanglish, and as long as I have to accommodate the English speakers rather than having them accommodate me, my tongue will be illegitimate.

---

[6]Irena Klepfisz, "Secular Jewish Identity: Yidishkayt in America," in *The Tribe of Dina*, Kaye/Kantrowitz and Klepfisz, eds., 43.

I will no longer be made to feel ashamed of existing. I will have my voice: Indian, Spanish, white. I will have my serpent's tongue—my woman's voice, my sexual voice, my poet's voice. I will overcome the tradition of silence.

> My fingers
> move sly against your palm
> Like women everywhere, we speak in
> code....
>
> —Melanie Kaye/Kantrowitz[7]

"VISTAS," CORRIDOS, Y COMIDA: MY NATIVE TONGUE

In the 1960s, I read my first Chicano novel. It was *City of Night* by John Rechy, a gay Texan, son of a Scottish father and a Mexican mother. For days I walked around in stunned amazement that a Chicano could write and could get published. When I read *I Am Joaquín*[8] I was surprised to see a bilingual book by a Chicano in print. When I saw poetry written in Tex-Mex for the first time, a feeling of pure joy flashed through me. I felt like we really existed as a people. In 1971, when I started teaching High School English to Chicano students, I tried to supplement the required texts with works by Chicanos, only to be reprimanded and forbidden to do so by the principal. He claimed that I was supposed to teach "American" and English literature. At the risk of being fired, I swore my students to secrecy and slipped in Chicano short stories, poems, a play. In graduate school, while working toward a Ph.D., I had to "argue" with one advisor after the other, semester after semester, before I was allowed to make Chicano literature an area of focus.

Even before I read books by Chicanos or Mexicans, it was the Mexican movies I saw at the drive-in—the Thursday night special of $1.00 a carload—that gave me a sense of belonging. "*Vámonos a las vistas*," my mother would call out and we'd all—grandmother, brothers, sister

and cousins—squeeze into the car. We'd wolf down cheese and bologna white bread sandwiches while watching Pedro Infante in melodramatic tearjerkers like *Nosotroslospobres*, the first "real" Mexican movie (that was not an imitation of European movies). I remember seeing *Cuando loshijosse van* and surmising that all Mexican movies played up the love a mother has for her children and what ungrateful sons and daughters suffer when they are not devoted to their mothers. I remember the singing-type "westerns" of Jorge Negrete and Miquel Aceves Mejía. When watching Mexican movies, I felt a sense of homecoming as well as alienation. People who were to amount to something didn't go to Mexican movies, or *bailes* or tune their radios to *bolero*, *rancherita*, and *corrido* music.

The whole time I was growing up, there was *norteño* music sometimes called North Mexican border music, or Tex-Mex music, or Chicano music, or *cantina* (bar) music. I grew up listening to *conjuntos*, three- or four-piece bands made up of folk musicians playing guitar, *bajo sexto*, drums and button accordion, which Chicanos had borrowed from the German immigrants who had come to Central Texas and Mexico to farm and build breweries. In the Rio Grande Valley, Steve Jordan and Little Joe Hernández were popular, and Flaco Jiménez was the accordian king. The rhythms of Tex-Mex music are those of the polka, also adapted from the Germans, who in turn had borrowed the polka from the Czechs and Bohemians.

I remember the hot, sultry evenings when *corridos*—songs of love and death on the Texas-Mexican borderlands—reverberated out of cheap amplifiers from the local *cantinas* and wafted in through my bedroom window.

Corridos first became widely used along the South Texas/Mexican border during the early conflict between Chicanos and Anglos. The *corridos* are usually about Mexican heroes who do valiant deeds against the Anglo oppressors. Pancho Villa's song, "*La cucaracha*" is the most famous one. *Corridos* of John F. Kennedy and his death are still very popular in the Valley. Older Chicanos remember Lydia Mendoza, one of the great border *corrido* singers who was called *la Gloria de*

[7]Melanie Kaye/Kantrowitz, "Sign," in *We Speak in Code: Poems and Other Writings* (Pittsburgh, PA: Motheroot Publications, Inc., 1980), 85.
[8]Rodolfo Gonzales, *I Am Joaquín/Yo Soy Joaquín* (New York: Bantam Books, 1972). It was first published in 1967.

Tejas. Her "*El tango negro*" sung during the Great Depression, made her a singer of the people. The everpresent *corridos* narrated one hundred years of border history, bringing news of events as well as entertaining. These folk musicians and folk songs are our chief cultural mythmakers, and they made our hard lives seem bearable.

I grew up feeling ambivalent about our music. Country-western and rock-and-roll had more status. In the 50s and 60s, for the slightly educated and *agringado* Chicanos, there existed a sense of shame at being caught listening to our music. Yet I couldn't stop my feet from thumping to the music, could not stop humming the words, nor hide from myself the exhilaration I felt when I heard it.

There are more subtle ways that we internalize identification, especially in the forms of images and emotions. For me food and certain smells are tied to my identity, to my homeland. Woodsmoke curling up to an immense blue sky; woodsmoke perfuming my grandmother's clothes, her skin. The stench of cow manure and the yellow patches on the ground; the crack of a .22 rifle and the reek of cordite. Homemade white cheese sizzling in a pan, melting inside a folded *tortilla*. My sister Hilda's hot, spicy *menudo, chile colorado* making it deep red, pieces of *panza* and hominy floating on top. My brother Carito barbequing *fajitas* in the backyard. Even now and 3,000 miles away, I can see my mother spicing the ground beef, pork and venison with *chile*. My mouth salivates at the thought of the hot steaming *tamales* I would be eating if I were home.

SI LE PREGUNTAS A MI MAMÁ, "¿QUÉ ERES?"

"Identity is the essential core of who
   we are as individuals, the conscious
   experience of the self inside."
                                   —Kaufman[9]

Nosotros los Chicanos straddle the borderlands. On one side of us, we are constantly exposed to the Spanish of the Mexicans, on the other side we hear the Anglos' incessant clamoring so that we forget our language. Among ourselves we don't say *nosotros los americanos, o nosotros los españoles, o nosotros los hispanos.* We say *nosotros los mexicanos* (by *mexicanos* we do not mean citizens of Mexico; we do not mean a national identity, but a racial one). We distinguish between *mexicanos del otro lado and mexicanos de este lado.* Deep in our hearts we believe that being Mexican has nothing to do with which country one lives in. Being Mexican is a state of soul—not one of mind, not one of citizenship. Neither eagle nor serpent, but both. And like the ocean, neither animal respects borders.

Dime con quien andas y te diré quien eres.
(Tell me who your friends are and I'll tell you who you are.)
                                   —Mexican saying

Si le preguntas a mi mamá, "¿Qué eres?" te dirá, "Soy mexicana." My brothers and sister say the same. I sometimes will answer "*soy mexicana*" and at others will say "*soy Chicana*" o "*soy tejana.*" But I identified as "*Raza*" before I ever identified as "*mexicana*" or "Chicana."

As a culture, we call ourselves Spanish when referring to ourselves as a linguistic group and when copping out. It is then that we forget our predominant Indian genes. We are 70–80% Indian.[10] We call ourselves Hispanic[11] or Spanish-American or Latin American or Latin when linking ourselves to other Spanish-speaking peoples of the Western hemisphere and when copping out. We call ourselves Mexican-American[12] to signify we are neither Mexican nor American, but more the noun "American" than the adjective "Mexican" (and when copping out).

Chicanos and other people of color suffer economically for not acculturating. This voluntary (yet forced) alienation makes for psychological conflict, a kind of dual identity—we don't identify with the Anglo-American cultural values and we

---

[9]Kaufman, 68.

[10]Chávez, 88–90.
[11]"Hispanic" is derived from Hispanis (*España,* a name given to the Iberian Peninsula in ancient times when it was a part of the Roman Empire) and is a term designated by the U.S. government to make it easier to handle us on paper.
[12]The Treaty of Guadalupe Hidalgo created the Mexican-American in 1848.

don't totally identify with the Mexican cultural values. We are a synergy of two cultures with various degrees of Mexicanness or Angloness. I have so internalized the borderland conflict that sometimes I feel like one cancels out the other and we are zero, nothing, no one. *A veces no soy nada ni nadie. Pero hasta cuando no lo soy, lo soy.*

When not copping out, when we know we are more than nothing, we call ourselves Mexican, referring to race and ancestry; *mestizo* when affirming both our Indian and Spanish (but we hardly ever own our Black ancestry); Chicano when referring to a politically aware people born and/or raised in the U.S.; *Raza* when referring to Chicanos; *tejanos* when we are Chicanos from Texas.

Chicanos did not know we were a people until 1965 when Caesar Chavez and the farmworkers united and *I Am Joaquín* was published and *la Raza Unida* party was formed in Texas. With that recognition, we became a distinct people. Something momentous happened to the Chicano soul—we became aware of our reality and acquired a name and a language (Chicano Spanish) that reflected that reality. Now that we had a name, some of the fragmented pieces began to fall together—who we were, what we were, how we had evolved. We began to get glimpses of what we might eventually become.

Yet the struggle of identities continues, the struggle of borders is our reality still. One day the inner struggle will cease and a true integration take place. In the meantime, *tenémos que hacer la lucha. ¿Quién está protegiendo los ranchos de mi gente? ¿Quién está tratando de cerrar la fisura entre la india y el blanco en nuestra sangre? El Chicano, si, el Chicano que anda como un ladrón en su propia casa.*

Los Chicanos, how patient we seem, how very patient. There is the quiet of the Indian about us.[13] We know how to survive. When other races have given up their tongue, we've kept ours. We know what it is to live under the hammer blow of the dominant *norteamericano* culture. But more than we count the blows, we count the days the weeks the years the centuries the eons until the white laws and commerce and customs will rot in the deserts they've created, lie bleached. *Humildes* yet proud, *quietos* yet wild, *nosotros los mexicanos-Chicanos* will walk by the crumbling ashes as we go about our business. Stubborn, persevering, impenetrable as stone, yet possessing a malleability that renders us unbreakable, we, the *mestizas* and *mestizos,* will remain.

---

[13]Anglos, in order to alleviate their guilt for dispossessing the Chicano, stressed the Spanish part of us and perpetrated the myth of the Spanish Southwest. We have accepted the fiction that we are Hispanic, that is Spanish, in order to accommodate ourselves to the dominant culture and its abhorrence of Indians. Chávez, 88–91.

◉ CRITICAL QUESTION

1. What did you learn about identity from reading this selection that you had not thought about before? Explain your answer.

13.6 GENDER IDENTITY

Gloria Anzaldúa (see previous section) grew up on a border. Deirdre (Donald) N. McCloskey crossed a border. The border was gender. Donald McCloskey became Deirdre McCloskey at the age of fifty-two. Donald had achieved fame as a professor of history and economics at the University of Iowa where Deirdre now teaches. In a book titled *Crossing: A Memoir*, Deirdre McCloskey tells her story, a story that raises basic questions about gender and identity.

Theories of gender and identity fall into two camps. Essentialist theories maintain that gender is determined by nature. According to this view, gender is fixed

and stable. It is something given, if not by evolutionary development, th
Nonessentialist theories maintain that gender is a social construction. It
unstable. It is not something given, but something constructed. One
breakthroughs of feminist theory was to separate the social from the biolo₅
such a way that what was formerly thought to be relatively unchangeable was recognized as changeable. Then liberation became possible.

While it is fairly common today to see gender (femininity and masculinity) as
social constructions and not biological (female and male) determinates, it is less common to see sexuality in the same way. We speak of sexual preference, as if our sexual
orientation is a matter of choice. We also speak about innate physiological factors
that supposedly determine whether someone is homosexual or heterosexual. Is sexuality as well as gender a social construction?

Gay/lesbian theory, building on the insights of feminist theory, focused not only
on the way sexuality is socially constructed but also on the way categories such as
normal and deviant are used in a normative way to assert and maintain social control.
To label something deviant, be it sexual or not, is to attach a negative value. Normal
is good; deviant is bad. Once behaviors are labeled bad, then the many practices of
social control, from denying legal rights to encouraging violence toward those
labeled deviant, appear justified. People often link the normal and the deviant labels
to essentialist theories. Thus certain sorts of sexuality become "natural" and other
kinds become "unnatural."

Queer theory, an area of academic study, emerged in the early 1990s. The word
queer, as used in queer theory, does not refer to homosexuality per se. The primary
meaning of queer is "peculiar," or "odd." Queer theory extends the concerns of
feminist theory and gay/lesbian theory to all sorts of sexual activities and identities
(homosexual, bisexual, heterosexual, transsexual, and so forth) in order to explore
the ways in which such identities are constructed and valorized by societies and ideologies. Sexuality can now be seen, thanks to the contributions of queer theory, as
an elaborate system of signs and codes that define what is "normal" and what is
"deviant" for a given society at a particular moment of history. In addition, this system of signs establishes identities. People come to think of themselves at a deep level
in terms of both gender and sexuality.

Is Deirdre the same person as Donald? Donald was male, married, a father who
existed in a complex web of social and professional relationships that reinforced his
gender and sexual identity. Donald had certain gestures, interests, ways of sitting
and walking, tastes, and more that Deirdre does not have. Yet Deirdre liberated
Donald. She allowed Donald to be what he always wanted to be: a woman. You
can see for yourself the result of Deirdre's physical transformation in one of the
book's color plates.

The following selection, from the Preface to *Crossing,* provides an occasion for us
to think not only about issues of gender and sexuality but also about issues of identity,
nature, and the ways society constructs such categories as normal and deviant.

◉ READING QUESTIONS

1. Explain what McCloskey means when she says, "My gender crossing was motivated by identity, not to be a balance sheet of utility"?

2. McCloskey writes, "Gender is not in every way natural." Why is this the case?

3. Why was McCloskey attracted to Christianity?

Crossing

DEIRDRE (DONALD) N. MCCLOSKEY

I want to tell you the story of a crossing from fifty-two-year-old man to fifty-five-year-old woman, Donald to Deirdre.

"A strange story," you say.

Yes, it's strange, statistically. All the instruments agree that what's usually called "transsexuality," permanently crossing the gender boundary, is rare. (The Latin in "transsexuality" makes it sound sexual, which is mistaken; or medical, which is misleading; or scientific, which is silly. I'll use plain English "crossing.") Only three in ten thousand want to cross the boundary of gender, a few of them in your own city neighborhood or small town. Gender crossing is no threat to male/female sex ratios or the role of women or the stability of the dollar. Most people are content with their birth gender.

But people do after all cross various boundaries. I've been a foreigner a little, in England and Holland and on shorter visits elsewhere. If you've been a foreigner you can understand somewhat, because gender crossing is a good deal like foreign travel. Most people would like to go to Venice on vacation. Most people, if they could magically do it, would like to try out the other gender for a day or a week or a month. The Venice visitors as a group can be thought of as all the "crossgendered," from stone butch dykes to postoperative male-to-female gender crossers, all the traversers, permanent or temporary, somber or ironic. A few people go to Venice regularly, and you can think of them as the crossdressers among these, wearing the clothing of the opposite gender once in a while. But only a tiny fraction of the crossgendered are permanent gender crossers, wanting to *become* Venetians. Most people are content to stay mainly at home. A tiny minority are not. They want to cross and stay.

On a trip to New York to see a friend after my own crossing I stood in the hall of photographs at Ellis Island and wept at the courage. Crossing cultures from male to female is big; it highlights some of the differences between men and women, and some of the similarities too. That's interesting. My crossing was costly and opposed, which is too bad. But my crossing has been dull, easy, comfortable compared with Suyuan's or Giuseppi's outer migrations.

Or compared with some people's inner migrations. Some people cross this or that inner boundary so radically that it would look bizarre, a slippage in the normal order of the universe, Stephen King material, if it were not so common. The most radical one is the crossing from child to adult, a crossing similar to mine that we all experience. I once saw a spoof scientific paper titled "Short Stature Syndrome: A Nationwide Problem." The strange little people, whose thoughts and actions were so different from normal, requiring the compulsory intervention of psychiatrists, and lots more money for the National Institute of Mental Health, were … children.

The word "education" means just "leading out." People are always leading themselves out of one life and into another, such as out of childhood and into each new version of adulthood. Not everyone likes to keep doing it, but the women I most admire have. My mother educated herself to earning her income and writing poetry after my father died. My roomer for a year in Iowa educated herself as a hospital chaplain after a third of a century teaching elementary school. My sister got a second degree in psychology, my former wife made herself into a distinguished professor. May Sarton, so glad to become by forced crossing an American rather than a Belgian woman, an English rather than a French poet and novelist and memoirist, kept crossing, crossing and looked forward at age seventy to "what is ahead—to clear my desk, sow the annuals, plant perennials, get back to the novel … like a game of solitaire that is coming out."

It's strange to have been a man and now to be a woman. But it's no stranger perhaps than having once been a West African and now being an American, or once a priest and now a businessman. Free people keep deciding to make strange crossings, from storekeeper to monk or from civilian to soldier or from man to woman. Crossing boundaries is a minority interest, but human.

My crossing—change, migration, growing up, self-discovery—took place from 1994 to 1997, beginning in my home in Iowa, then a year in Holland, then back in Iowa, with travels in between. As Donald and then as Deirdre I was and am a professor of economics and of history at the University of Iowa. From age eleven I had been a secret crossdresser, a few times a week. Otherwise I was normal, just a guy. My wife had known about the crossdressing since the first year of our marriage, when we were twenty-two. No big deal, we decided. Lots of men have this or that sexual peculiarity. Relax, we said. By 1994, age fifty-two, I had been married those three decades, had two grown children, and thought I might crossdress a little more. Visit Venice more too.

I visited womanhood and stayed. It was not for the pleasures, though I discovered many I had not imagined, and many pains too. But calculating pleasures and pains was not the point. The point was who I am. Here the analogy with migration breaks down. One moves permanently from Sicily to New York because one imagines the streets of New York are paved with gold, or at least better paved than the streets at home, not mainly because back in Catania since age eleven one had dreamed of being an American. Migration can be modeled as a matter of cost and benefit, and it has been by economic historians. But I did not change gender because I liked colorful clothing (Donald did not) or womanly grace (Donald viewed it as sentimentality). The "decision" was not utilitarian. In our culture the rhetoric of the very word "decision" suggests cost and benefit. My gender crossing was motivated by identity, not by a balance sheet of utility.

Of course you can ask what psychological reasons explain my desire to cross and reply with, say, a version of Freud. Some researchers think there is a biological explanation for gender crossing, because parts of the brains of formerly male gender crossers in postmortems are notably female. But a demand for an answer to why carries with it in our medicalized culture an agenda of treatment. If a gender crosser is "just" a guy who gets pleasure from it, that's one thing (laugh at him, jail him, murder him). If it's brain chemistry, that's another (commit him to a madhouse and try to "cure" him).

I say in response to your question Why? "Can't I just be?" You, dear reader, are. No one gets indignant if you have no answer to why you are an optimist or why you like peach ice cream. These days most people will grant you an exemption from the why question if you are gay: in 1960 they would not and were therefore eager to do things to you, many of them nasty. I want courtesy and the safety of a why-less treatment extended to gender crossers. I want the medical models of gender crossing (and of twenty other things) to fall. That's the politics. I am ashamed that from the 1960s and 1990s, in the political movements for black civil rights, women's liberation, gay rights, and opposition to the war in Vietnam, I had sound opinions but never really took a chance on them. Telling you my story is my last chance to be counted.

And incidentally, Why *do* you think you are the gender you were officially assigned to at birth? Prove it. How odd.

Ah. I think you need some treatment.

After a year of hesitation, and two years from well beginning, I found to my delight that I had crossed. Look by look, smile by smile, I was accepted. That doesn't make me a 100 per cent, essential woman—I'll never have XX chromosomes, never have had the life of a girl and woman up to age fifty-two. But the world does not demand 100 per cents and essences, thank God. An agnostic since adolescence, in my second year of crossing I came tentatively to religion and then could thank God in person, who made me inside in my comfort a woman.

I get weepy sometimes as I walk to the office, pick up my dry cleaning, shop at Prairie Lights bookstore, so pleased to Be. It's like someone who thought herself more French than American and one day was able to be French; or someone who always hoped to be a professional athlete and finally became one; or someone who felt herself a businesswoman and at last was seen as one. My game of solitaire came out.

I apologize for romanticizing sometimes the goodness of women and criticizing sometimes the badness of men. It's how I felt at the time. Forgive me, new to this place and starry-eyed. Perhaps my stories of Donald and then Dee and then Deirdre show enough bad women and good men to offset my romantic theories. In contrasting how men and women "are" I do not mean to recruit stereotypes or essentialisms that have been used to the disadvantage of other women. Women are not always more loving, or less interested in career. And certainly they are what in detail they "are" not on account of some eternal Platonic ideal or the imperatives of genetics. I am reporting how the difference in social practice seemed to me, admitting always that the difference might be, as the professors say, "socially constructed." Gender is not in every way "natural." "Feminine" gestures, for example, are not God's own creation. This of course I know. The social construction of gender is, after all, something a gender crosser comes to know with unusual vividness. She does it for a living.

I apologize, too, for any inaccuracies that remain despite my earnest attempts to get them out. I have tried to tell a true story. Yet none of the conversations and descriptions in the book are court transcripts. Each is something I believe I remember, ordered in the sequence I believe I remember, and intended to show how I heard and saw and thought at the time—my recollections, my ardent opinions, how I felt as I remember how I felt. I have been as careful as I can and have offered to show the manuscript to the main parties, some of whom could help.

The world does not tell stories. Men and women do, and I am merely a woman telling. It would be impossible to recount every single thing about your hour just passed, tiny things that illustrate character or position, much less to tell every single thing about three crowded years, or one side of a tangled life. Whether the result is God's own truth I don't know. Telling any story, from physics to fiction, is like placing stepping-stones through a garden, choosing what spots to miss in showing the path.

After the crossing I was eating lunch in Iowa City with a woman friend, another academic, and we spoke about how talk normalizes. She said, "This is the age of the candid memoir." So it seems. It's a good thing, we agreed, because talking to each other about who we are can make us mutually all human. Demonizing Others is the first stop on the railway to the gas chambers. Nowadays there are many books about the cross-gendered. Movies and television have stopped portraying them as dangerous lunatics in the mold of Anthony Perkins in *Psycho*. Since the 1960s, detested by those who value order above freedom, many kinds of people have spoken up: the raped women who kept their secrets, the unmarried mothers who kept theirs. In the 1950s a lot of people were keeping secrets, personal and state: the obedient wives, the hidden handicapped, the closeted homosexuals, the silenced socialists, the blacks under Jim Crow. After the liberation and the talk that followed they are no longer disgraceful Others or pathetic victims, or merely invisibles—"We don't have any homosexuals in Oklahoma"—but people whose stories are heard and talked about and might even be imagined as one's own. It's the difference between shame and life.

For this age of openness I praise the Lord, blessed be her holy name. I began to see that Christianity resembles the secular stoicism circa the 1930s in which I was raised, A. E. Housman to Hemingway, in that it promises no bed of roses. The world is mysterious from a human point of view, as both the stoic Housman and the Christian Gerard Manley Hopkins would say, and it contains bad news as well as good. I found Christianity in this way grown up, admitting sin. That *is* God's own truth.

And slowly as the story ended I began to hear the good news of forgiveness, the duty to offer it and the grace to receive.

◉ **CRITICAL QUESTION**

1. In your view, is gender identity natural or is it
   socially constructed? Support your answer with an
   argument.

To access the *Voices of Wisdom*, 8th Edition, **Premium Website**, search for this book
on CengageBrain.com.

CHAPTER FOURTEEN

Are Religious Claims True?

Philosophy begins in wonder and when philosophic thought has done its best, the wonder remains.

ALFRED NORTH WHITEHEAD

LEARNING OBJECTIVES

After studying this chapter students should be able to:
- define philosophy of religion,
- distinguish revealed from natural theology,
- explain the relationship between theism and ultimate reality,
- explain the ontological, cosmological, and teleological arguments,
- explain why the problem of evil poses a challenge to theism,
- define omnipotence and omniscience,
- describe Christian misogynist views,
- distinguish religious exclusivism, inclusivism, and pluralism,
- identify Anselm, Aquinas, Mackie, Hernandez, Augustine, Ruether, the Dalai Lama, and Prothero, and
- answer all the questions relating to the selections.

14.1 INTRODUCTION

Have you ever wondered whether God exists? Of course. Most people have. But have you wondered whether God's existence can be proved? Are there arguments that would convince any reasonable person? Is there evidence, I mean real, hard-core scientific evidence, that God exists? When I ask my students how many of them believe God exists, almost all of them raise their hands. But when I ask them how many think God's existence can be *proved*, most are skeptical. "It is," they say, "a matter of faith."

The existence of God is a metaphysical question central to a branch of philosophy called the **philosophy of religion**. As the name implies, this area of philosophy applies philosophical methods to the study of a wide variety of religious issues, including the existence of God. Philosophy of religion should be clearly distinguished from a type of theology called revealed theology. **Theology** literally means the "study of God." **Revealed theology** is a type of theology that claims that human knowledge of God comes through special revelations such as the Bible or the Qur'an. St. Thomas Aquinas (see Section 14.2) said that revealed theology provides "saving knowledge"—that is, knowledge that will result in our salvation.

– 590 –

Another kind of theology, called **natural theology**, has to do with the knowledge of God that is possible based on the use of "natural" reason—that is, reason unaided by special revelations. St. Thomas says that this sort of theology can provide us with some knowledge of God's nature and can demonstrate that God exists, but it cannot provide saving knowledge because, after all, even devils know that God exists.

Natural theology is sometimes called *rational theology* or *philosophical theology*. As this last name indicates, this kind of theology is more closely related to the philosophy of religion than is revealed theology. Both natural theology and the philosophy of religion rely solely on the use of human reason in their attempts to discover something about the divine. They do not assume the truth of some special revelation; they allow only what reason can prove.

Although both philosophy of religion and natural theology rely on reason rather than on revelation, they differ in the range of topics considered. Philosophy of religion studies a wide range of religious issues and different notions of what constitutes ultimate reality. **Theism** is just one sort of religious notion of ultimate reality. The *Tao* or Brahman-Atman, for example (see Chapter 10), both present conceptions of ultimate reality that appear quite different from theistic ideas. Needless to say, *nontheistic* philosophies have not been overly concerned with the issue of God's existence even though they have been concerned with the nature and existence of some kind of ultimate reality. However, *theistic* philosophies and the cultures—both Eastern and Western—influenced by theistic religions have regarded the topic of God's existence as an issue of immense significance.

One of the strongest arguments for the nonexistence of God is the apparent incompatibility between the existence of evil and the existence of an all-powerful and infinitely good God. Can such a God not prevent evil? Would he not want to?

Why he? Why use the masculine pronoun when referring to God? Is our concept of God hopelessly patriarchal? Is it a hangover from a past when men dominated societies and cultures, playing the role—often quite literally—of the divine? There are many different conceptions of God, including ideas about Goddesses. There are many different religions. Can they all be true? Are they all different but equally valid paths to salvation?

Although the existence of God is an important philosophical topic, we cannot lose sight of the fact that the philosophy of religion is also concerned with many other issues and questions. Our focus here is on a very narrow range of issues, mostly related to theism. However, there are many other philosophical problems we might consider. For example, how are religion and science related? Can there be genuine religious knowledge, or is religion primarily a matter of faith and hope? Is there life after death? How is religion related to ethics?

14.2 ARGUMENTS FOR GOD'S EXISTENCE

Do you think that the existence of God could be deduced from a definition of God? Your first inclination might be to deny that the existence of anything can be deduced from its definition. To define something is one thing, for it to exist is another matter. Once I have given you a definition of something you can always logically ask, "Are there any?"

For the most part, Anselm of Canterbury (1033–1109), a Christian monk and theologian, would agree with you that the existence of things cannot be deduced from their definitions. There was, however, one exception, or so Anselm thought. That exception was God. If we understand God as the greatest possible being that can be thought ("that than which nothing greater can be conceived" as Anselm puts it), then it follows that such a being must exist. Why does it follow? One purpose of the **ontological argument** for God's existence, as Anselm's argument has come to be called, is to show by purely a priori reasoning that God must exist outside the mind if a conception of God as that than which nothing greater can be thought exists in the mind.

Gaunilo, a contemporary of Anselm and also a Christian monk, thought there was something fishy with Anselm's argument. He was not quite sure what it was, but he applied what he took to be Anselm's reasoning to the idea of a perfect lost island in order to show by counterexample that something was indeed wrong with the ontological argument. The first selection below provides a small portion of their debate.

The a priori character of the ontological argument makes it not only difficult to follow but also makes some people a bit uncomfortable. This may be due to the fact that we are more comfortable with a posteriori arguments that begin with something empirical and argue for God's existence as an explanation. For example, how many of you have thought, "there must be a God because the universe just couldn't happen by itself? Something must have caused it. Things don't just pop into existence out of nothing." If you have had thoughts like this, you have been thinking along the lines of a cosmological argument. **Cosmological arguments** (there are several varieties) argue from the existence of the universe (world or cosmos) or some feature of it to the existence of God as its cause, its creator, or its explanation.

Cosmological arguments are very old and are found among ancient Greek and Indian philosophers. The Greek versions were most influential on Western thought. Aristotle (see Section 3.5) argued from the existence of motion to the existence of an Unmoved Mover as the explanation of motion. This Unmoved Mover he called "*ho theo*s" (the god), in part because it was unmoved (that is, nothing caused it to move) yet was responsible for the motion of other things. It is, if you will, a prime mover. Aristotle's argument was based on three principles that operate as assumptions in practically all cosmological arguments: (1) something cannot be the cause of itself, (2) something cannot come from nothing, and (3) there cannot be an infinite series of causes and effects.

Another type of a posteriori argument also stems from the Greeks. It is called the **teleological argument** (also called the argument from design) because it moves from noting that things that lack intelligence nevertheless behave for a purpose (*telos*). They appear to pursue goals and exhibit an order arranged or designed to achieve certain ends. Acorns grow up to be oak trees not fat blind cats. This sort of argument has proved particularly enduring and resurfaces in debates about evolution versus intelligent design.

Thomas Aquinas (ca. 1225–1274) was one of the most influential thinkers of the Christian tradition, and in the first part of his massive summation of theology, he presents not one but five arguments for the existence of God. The first three are versions of the cosmological argument, and the fifth one is a version of what has come to be known as the teleological argument.

As you think about these arguments ask yourself how important they are to religious faith. Do any of them prove the existence of the popular and widespread conception of God as a supernatural being who is concerned with the welfare of humanity?

1. Outline Anselm's argument for God's existence and describe his reasoning.
2. Explain Gaunilo's reasoning.
3. Summarize each of Aquinas's five ways as concisely as you can in premise and conclusion form.
4. In the second way, Aquinas claims that it is not possible for efficient causes (by which he means the agent or agency that brings about an effect) to "go on to infinity." Why is that not possible?
5. Why, according to Aquinas, do things that lack intelligence need to be directed by an intelligence?

The Ontological Argument

ANSELM OF CANTERBURY

Truly there is a God, although the fool hath said in his heart, There is no God.

And so, Lord, do thou, who dost give understanding to faith, give me, so far as thou knowest it to be profitable, to understand that thou art as we believe; and that thou art that which we believe. And, indeed, we believe that thou art a being than which nothing greater can be conceived. Or is there no such nature, since the fool hath said in his heart, there is no God? (Psalms xiii, 1). But, at any rate, this very fool, when he hears of this being of which I speak—a being than which nothing greater can be conceived—understands what he hears, and what he understands is in his understanding; although he does not understand it to exist.

For, it is one thing for an object to be in the understanding, and another to understand that the object exists. When a painter first conceives of what he will afterwards perform, he has it in his understanding, but he does not yet understand it to be, because he has not yet performed it. But after he has made the painting, he both has it in his understanding, and he understands that it exists, because he has made it.

Hence, even the fool is convinced that something exists in the understanding, at least, than which nothing greater can be conceived. For, when he hears of this, he understands it. And whatever is understood, exists in the understanding. And assuredly that, than which nothing greater can be conceived, cannot exist in the understanding alone. For, suppose it exists in the understanding alone: then it can be conceived to exist in reality; which is greater.

Therefore, if that, than which nothing greater can be conceived, exists in the understanding alone, the very being, than which nothing greater can be conceived, is one, than which a greater can be conceived. But obviously this is impossible. Hence, there is no doubt that there exists a being, than which nothing greater can be conceived, and it exists both in the understanding and in reality....

From *Anselm's Basic Writings*. Second edition. Translated by S. W. Deane (Peru, IL: Open Court Publishings, 1962), selections from the *Proslogion*. Copyright © 1962 by Open Court Publishing Company. Reprinted by permission.

GAUNILO'S CRITICISM

For example: it is said that somewhere in the ocean is an island, which, because of the difficulty, or rather the impossibility, of discovering what does not exist, is called the lost island. And they say that this island has an inestimable wealth of all manner of riches and delicacies in greater abundance than is told of the Islands of the Blest; and that having no owner or inhabitant, it is more excellent than all other countries, which are inhabited by mankind, in the abundance with which it is stored.

Now if someone should tell me that there is such an island, I should easily understand his words, in which there is no difficulty. But suppose that he went on to say, as if by a logical inference: "You can no longer doubt that this island which is more excellent than all lands exists somewhere, since you have no doubt that it is in your understanding. And since it is more excellent not to be in the understanding alone, but to exist both in the understanding and in reality, for this reason it must exist. For if it does not exist, any land which really exists will be more excellent than it; and so the island already understood by you to be more excellent will not be more excellent."

If a man should try to prove to me by such reasoning that this island truly exists, and that its existence should no longer be doubted, either I should believe that he was jesting, or I know not which I ought to regard as the greater fool: myself, supposing that I should allow this proof; or him, if he should suppose that he had established with any certainty the existence of this island. For he ought to show first that the hypothetical excellence of this island exists as a real and indubitable fact, and in no wise as any unreal object, or one whose existence is uncertain, in my understanding.

The Five Ways

ST. THOMAS AQUINAS

THIRD ARTICLE

Whether God Exists?

We proceed thus to the Third Article:—

Objection 1. It seems that God does not exist; because if one of two contraries be infinite, the other would be altogether destroyed. But the word "God" means that He is infinite goodness. If, therefore, God existed, there would be no evil discoverable; but there is evil in the world. Therefore God does not exist.

Obj. 2. Further, it is superfluous to suppose that, what can be accounted for by a few principles has been produced by many. But it seems that everything that appears in the world can be accounted for by other principles, supposing God did not exist. For all natural things can be reduced to one principle, which is nature; and all things that happen intentionally can be reduced to one principle, which is human reason, or will. Therefore there is no need to suppose God's existence.

On the contrary, It is said in the person of God: *I am Who am* (Exod. iii. 14).

I answer that, The existence of God can be proved in five ways.

The first and more manifest way is the argument from motion. It is certain and evident to our senses that some things are in motion. Whatever is in motion is moved by another, for nothing can be in motion except it have a potentiality for that towards which it is being moved; whereas a thing moves inasmuch as it is in act. By "motion" we mean nothing else than the reduction of something from a state of potentiality into a state of actuality. Nothing, however, can be reduced from a state of potentiality into a state of actuality, unless by

From *The Summa Theologica of St. Thomas Aquinas*, Part 1. Translated by the Fathers of the English Dominican Province. Copyright © 1911. New York: Benziger Brothers.

something already in a state of actuality. Thus that which is actually hot as fire, makes wood, which is potentially hot to be actually hot, and thereby moves and changes it. It is not possible that the same thing should be at once in a state of actuality and potentiality from the same point of view, but only from different points of view. What is actually hot cannot simultaneously be only potentially hot; still, it is simultaneously potentially cold. It is therefore impossible that from the same point of view and in the same way anything should be both moved and mover, or that it should move itself. Therefore whatever is in motion must be put in motion by another. If that by which it is put in motion be itself put in motion, then this also must needs be put in motion by another, and that by another again. This cannot go on to infinity, because then there would be no first mover, and, consequently, no other mover—seeing that subsequent movers only move inasmuch as they are put in motion by the first mover; as the staff only moves because it is put in motion by the hand. Therefore it is necessary to arrive at a First Mover, put in motion by no other; and this everyone understands to be God.

The second way is from the formality of efficient causation. In the world of sense we find there is an order of efficient causation. There is no case known (neither is it, indeed, possible) in which a thing is found to be the efficient cause of itself; for so it would be prior to itself, which is impossible. In efficient causes it is not possible to go on to infinity, because in all efficient causes following in order, the first is the cause of the intermediate cause, and the intermediate is the cause of the ultimate cause, whether the intermediate cause be several, or one only. To take away the cause is to take away the effect. Therefore, if there be no first cause among efficient causes, there will be no ultimate cause, nor any intermediate. If in efficient causes it is possible to go on to infinity, there will be no first efficient cause, neither will there be an ultimate effect, nor any intermediate efficient causes; all of which is plainly false. Therefore it is necessary to put forward a First Efficient Cause, to which everyone gives the name of God.

The third way is taken from possibility and necessity, and runs thus. We find in nature things that could either exist or not exist, since they are found to be generated, and then to corrupt; and, consequently, they can exist, and then not exist. It is impossible for these always to exist, for that which can one day cease to exist must at some time have not existed. Therefore, if everything could cease to exist, then at one time there could have been nothing in existence. If this were true, even now there would be nothing in existence, because that which does not exist only begins to exist by something already existing. Therefore, if at one time nothing was in existence, it would have been impossible for anything to have begun to exist; and thus even now nothing would be in existence—which is absurd. Therefore, not all beings are merely possible, but there must exist something the existence of which is necessary. Every necessary thing either has its necessity caused by another, or not. It is impossible to go on to infinity in necessary things which have their necessity caused by another, as has been already proved in regard to efficient causes. Therefore we cannot but postulate the existence of some being having of itself its own necessity, and not receiving it from another, but rather causing in others their necessity. This all men speak of as God.

The fourth way is taken from the gradation to be found in things. Among beings there are some more and some less good, true, noble, and the like. But "more" and "less" are predicated of different things, according as they resemble in their different ways something which is in the degree of "most," as a thing is said to be hotter according as it more nearly resembles that which is hottest; so that there is something which is truest, something best, something noblest, and, consequently, something which is uttermost being; for the truer things are, the more truly they exist. What is most complete in any genus is the cause of all in that genus; as fire, which is the most complete form of heat, is the cause whereby all things are made hot. Therefore there must also be something which is to all beings the cause of their being, goodness, and every other perfection; and this we call God.

The fifth way is taken from the governance of the world; for we see that things which lack intelligence, such as natural bodies, act for some purpose, which fact is evident from their acting always, or nearly always, in the same way, so as to obtain the best result. Hence it is plain that not fortuitously, but designedly, do they achieve their purpose. Whatever lacks intelligence cannot fulfil some purpose, unless it be directed by some being endowed with intelligence and knowledge; as the arrow is shot to its mark by the archer. Therefore some intelligent being exists by whom all natural things are ordained towards a definite purpose; and this being we call God.

Reply Obj. 1. As Augustine says: Since God is wholly good, He would not allow any evil to exist in His works, unless His omnipotence and goodness were such as to bring good even out of evil. This is part of the infinite goodness of God, that He should allow evil to exist, and out of it produce good.

Reply Obj 2. Since nature works out its determinate end under the direction of a higher agent, whatever is done by nature must needs be traced back to God, as to its first cause. So also whatever is done designedly must also be traced back to some higher cause other than human reason or will, for these can suffer change and are defective; whereas things capable of motion and of defect must be traced back to an immovable and self-necessary first principle.

◉ CRITICAL QUESTIONS

1. Who do you think is right, Anselm or Gaunilo? Why?
2. Which of the five ways do you find the most plausible and which do you find the least plausible? Why?
3. Assuming that there is a first cause of the universe as Aquinas argues, why must it be God? Would not a Big Bang as described by modern scientific cosmology do as well?

14.3 CAN EVIL AND GOD CO-EXIST?

If God is a perfectly good creator of this world in which we live, then how come evil and suffering exist?* We consider people good if they try to eliminate evil as much as they possibly can without thereby producing a greater evil or eliminating a greater good. Of course people are not God. For one thing, the power people have to prevent or eliminate evil is much less than God's power. There is the rub. God is all-powerful (**omnipotent**) as well as perfectly good. Surely such a God could and would eliminate evil. It is of little help to argue that maybe God does not know about all the evil that exists. God is **omniscient**. God knows everything.

What are we to conclude? Perhaps evil does not really exist. Perhaps God does not exist. Perhaps God is not perfectly good, or omnipotent, or all-knowing. Perhaps the existence of a perfectly good, all-powerful, and all-knowing creator God and the existence of evil are somehow logically compatible. But how can we show that?

J. L. Mackie (1917–1981) taught at Oxford University and is the author of the next selection. He made important contributions to many different areas of philosophy and formulated the deductive or logical form of the theological **problem of evil**. According to this argument, the existence of evil is logically incompatible with the existence of a perfectly good, all-knowing, and all-powerful creator God. That is a rather strong claim, and we need to pay careful attention to how Mackie develops his case. We may not be able to prove that God exists (see Section 14.2), but even if we fail it is still possible that God does exist. Mackie's argument takes us a step

---

*Some of this introductory material is from Gary E. Kessler, *Philosophy of Religion: Toward a Global Perspective* (Belmont, CA: Wadsworth Publishing Company, 1999), 224–225. Copyright © 1999 by Wadsworth Publishing Company. Reprinted by permission.

further because, if Mackie is right, those who embrace traditional theism are caught in a contradiction.

◉ READING QUESTIONS

1. According to Mackie, what additional propositions are needed in order to show that asserting the existence of an omnipotent, totally good God along with the existence of evil constitutes a contradiction?

2. According to Mackie, why is the claim that good cannot exist without evil a fallacious solution to the problem of evil?
3. What does Mackie think is wrong with the popular argument that evil is due to human free will?

Evil and Omnipotence

J. L. MACKIE

The traditional arguments for the existence of God have been fairly thoroughly criticised by philosophers. But the theologian can, if he wishes, accept this criticism. He can admit that no rational proof of God's existence is possible. And he can still retain all that is essential to his position, by holding that God's existence is known in some other, non-rational way.

I think, however, that a more telling criticism can be made by way of traditional problem of evil. Here it can be shown, not that religious beliefs lack rational support, but that they are positively irrational, that the several parts of the essential theological doctrine are inconsistent with one another, so that the theologian can maintain his position as a whole only by a much more extreme rejection of reason than in the former case. He must now be prepared to believe, not merely what cannot be proved, but what can be *disproved* from other beliefs that he also holds.

The problem of evil, in the sense in which I shall be using the phrase, is a problem only for someone who believes that there is a God who is both omnipotent and wholly good. And it is a logical problem, the problem of clarifying and reconciling a number of beliefs: it is not a scientific problem that might be solved by further observations, or a practical problem that might be solved by a decision or an action. These points are obvious; I mention them only because they are sometimes ignored by theologians, who sometimes parry a statement of the problem with such remarks as "Well, can you solve the problem yourself?" or "This is a mystery which may be revealed to us later" or "Evil is something to be faced and overcome, not to be merely discussed."

In its simplest form the problem is this: God is omnipotent; God is wholly good; and yet evil exists. There seems to be some contradiction between these three propositions, so that if any two of them were true the third would be false. But at the same time all three are essential parts of most theological positions: the theologian, it seems, at once *must* adhere and *cannot consistently adhere* to all three. (The problem does not arise only for theists, but I shall discuss it in the form in which it presents itself for ordinary theism.)

However, the contradiction does not arise immediately; to show it we need some additional premises, or perhaps some quasi-logical rules connecting the terms "good," "evil," and "omnipotent." These additional principles are that good is opposed to evil, in such a way that

From *Mind*, Vol. LXIV. No. 254 (1955):200–212. Reprinted by permission of Oxford University Press.

a good thing always eliminates evil as far as it can, and that there are no limits to what an omnipotent thing can do. From these it follows that a good omnipotent thing eliminates evil completely, and then the propositions that a good omnipotent thing exists, and that evil exists, are incompatible.

ADEQUATE SOLUTIONS

Now once the problem is fully stated it is clear that it can be solved, in the sense that the problem will not arise if one gives up at least one of the propositions that constitute it. If you are prepared to say that God is not wholly good, or not quite omnipotent, or that evil does not exist, or that good is not opposed to the kind of evil that exists, or that there are limits to what an omnipotent thing can do, then the problem of evil will not arise for you.

There are, then, quite a number of adequate solutions of the problem of evil, and some of these have been adopted, or almost adopted, by various thinkers. For example, a few have been prepared to deny God's omnipotence, and rather more have been prepared to keep the term "omnipotence" but severely to restrict its meaning, recording quite a number of things that an omnipotent being cannot do. Some have said that evil is an illusion, perhaps because they held that the whole world of temporal, changing things is an illusion, and that what we call evil belongs only to this world, or perhaps because they held that although temporal things *are* much as we see them, those that we call evil are not really evil. Some have said that what we call evil is merely the privation of good, that evil in a positive sense, evil that would really be opposed to good, does not exist. Many have agreed with Pope that disorder is harmony not understood, and that partial evil is universal good. Whether any of these views is *true* is, of course, another question. But each of them gives an adequate solution of the problem of evil in the sense that if you accept it this problem does not arise for you, though you may, of course, have other problems to face.

But often enough these adequate solutions are only *almost* adopted. The thinkers who restrict God's power, but keep the term "omnipotence,"

may reasonably be suspected of thinking, in other contexts, that his power is really unlimited. Those who say that evil is an illusion may also be thinking, inconsistently, that this illusion is itself an evil. Those who say that "evil" is merely privation of good may also be thinking, inconsistently, that privation of good is an evil. (The fallacy here is akin to some forms of the "naturalistic fallacy" in ethics, where some think, for example, that "good" is just what contributes to evolutionary progress, and that evolutionary progress is itself good.) If Pope meant what he said in the first line of his couplet, that "disorder" is only harmony not understood, the "partial evil" of the second line must, for consistency, mean "that which, taken in isolation, falsely appears to be evil," but it would more naturally mean "that which, in isolation, really is evil." The second line, in fact, hesitates between two views, that "partial evil" isn't really evil, since only the universal quality is real, and that "partial evil" is really an evil, but only a little one.

In addition, therefore, to adequate solutions, we must recognise unsatisfactory inconsistent solutions, in which there is only a half-hearted or temporary rejection of one of the propositions which together constitute the problem. In these, one of the constituent propositions is explicitly rejected, but it is covertly re-asserted or assumed elsewhere in the system.

FALLACIOUS SOLUTIONS

Besides these half-hearted solutions, which explicitly reject but implicitly assert one of the constituent propositions, there are definitely fallacious solutions which explicitly maintain all the constituent propositions, but implicitly reject at least one of them in the course of the argument that explains away the problem of evil.

There are, in fact, many so-called solutions which purport to remove the contradiction without abandoning any of its constituent propositions. These must be fallacious, as we can see from the very statement of the problem, but it is not so easy to see in each case precisely where the fallacy lies. I suggest that in all cases the fallacy has the general form suggested above: in order to solve the problem one (or perhaps more) of its constituent propositions is given up, but in such a way that it appears to have been retained, and can therefore be asserted without qualification in other contexts. Sometimes there is a further complication: the supposed solution moves to and fro between, say, two of the constituent propositions, at one point asserting the first of these but covertly abandoning the second, at another point asserting the second but covertly abandoning the first. These fallacious solutions often turn upon some equivocation with the words "good" and "evil," or upon some vagueness about the way in which good and evil are opposed to one another, or about how much is meant by "omnipotence." I propose to examine some of these so-called solutions, and to exhibit their fallacies in detail. Incidentally, I shall also be considering whether an adequate solution could be reached by a minor modification of one or more of the constituent propositions, which would, however, still satisfy all the essential requirements of ordinary theism.

1. "Good Cannot Exist without Evil" or "Evil Is Necessary as a Counterpart to Good"

It is sometimes suggested that evil is necessary as a counterpart to good, that if there were no evil there could be no good either, and that this solves the problem of evil. It is true that it points to an answer to the question "Why should there be evil?" But it does so only by qualifying some of the propositions that constitute the problem.

First, it sets a limit to what God can do, saying that God *cannot* create good without simultaneously creating evil, and this means either that God is not omnipotent or that there are *some* limits to what an omnipotent thing can do. It may be replied that these limits are always presupposed, that omnipotence has never meant the power to do what is logically impossible, and on the present view the existence of good without evil would be a logical impossibility This interpretation of omnipotence may, indeed, be accepted as a modification of our original account which does not reject anything that is essential to theism, and I shall in general assume it in the subsequent discussion. It is, perhaps, the most common

theistic view, but I think that some theists at least have maintained that God can do what is logically impossible. Many theists, at any rate, have held that logic itself is created or laid down by God, that logic is the way in which God arbitrarily chooses to think. (This is, of course, parallel to the ethical view that morally right actions are those which God arbitrarily chooses to command, and the two views encounter similar difficulties.) And *this* account of logic is clearly inconsistent with the view that God is bound by logical necessities—unless it is possible for an omnipotent being to bind himself, an issue which we shall consider later, when we come to the Paradox of Omnipotence. This solution of the problem of evil cannot, therefore, be consistently adopted along with the view that logic is itself created by God.

But, secondly, this solution denies that evil is opposed to good in our original sense. If good and evil are counterparts, a good thing will not "eliminate evil as far as it can." Indeed, this view suggests that good and evil are not strictly qualities of things at all. Perhaps the suggestion is that good and evil are related in much the same way as great and small. Certainly, when the term "great" is used relatively as a condensation of "greater than so-and-so," and "small" is used correspondingly, greatness and smallness are counterparts and cannot exist without each other. But in this sense greatness is not a quality, not an intrinsic feature of anything; and it would be absurd to think of a movement in favour of greatness and against smallness in this sense. Such a movement would be self-defeating, since relative greatness can be promoted only by a simultaneous promotion of relative smallness. I feel sure that no theists would be content to regard God's goodness as analogous to this—as if what he supports were not the *good* but the *better,* and as if he had the paradoxical aim that all things should be better than other things.

This point is obscured by the fact that "great" and "small" seem to have an absolute as well as a relative sense. I cannot discuss here whether there is absolute magnitude or not, but if there is, there could be an absolute sense for "great," it could mean of at least a certain size, and it would make sense to speak of all things getting bigger, of a universe that was expanding all over, and therefore it would make sense to speak of promoting greatness. But in *this* sense great and small are not logically necessary counterparts: either quality could exist without the other. There would be no logical impossibility in everything's being small or in everything's being great.

Neither in the absolute nor in the relative sense, then, of "great" and "small" do these terms provide an analogy of the sort that would be needed to support this solution of the problem of evil. In neither case are greatness and smallness *both* necessary counterparts *and* mutually opposed forces or possible objects for support and attack.

It may be replied that good and evil are necessary counterparts in the same way as any quality and its logical opposite: redness can occur, it is suggested, only if non-redness also occurs. But unless evil is merely the privation of good, they are not logical opposites, and some further argument would be needed to show that they are counterparts in the same way as genuine logical opposites. Let us assume that this could be given. There is still doubt of the correctness of the metaphysical principle that a quality must have a real opposite: I suggest that it is not really impossible that everything should be, say, red, that the truth is merely that if everything were red we should not notice redness, and so we should have no word "red"; we observe and give names to qualities only if they have real opposites. If so, the principle that a term must have an opposite would belong only to our language or to our thought, and would not be an ontological principle, and, correspondingly, the rule that good cannot exist without evil would not state a logical necessity of a sort that God would just have to put up with. God might have made everything good, though *we* should not have noticed it if he had.

But, finally, even if we concede that this is an ontological principle, it will provide a solution for the problem of evil only if one is prepared to say, "Evil exists, but only just enough evil to serve as the counterpart of good." I doubt whether any theist will accept this. After all, the *ontological* requirement that non-redness should occur would be satisfied even if all the universe, except for a minute speck, were red, and, if there were a corresponding requirement for evil as a counterpart to good, a minute dose of evil would presumably do. But theists are not usually willing to say, in all contexts, that all the evil that occurs is a minute and necessary dose....

4. *"Evil is due to Human Freewill"*

Perhaps the most important proposed solution of the problem of evil is that evil is not to be ascribed to God at all, but to the independent actions of human beings, supposed to have been endowed by God with freedom of the will. This solution may be combined with the preceding one: first order evil (e.g., pain) may be justified as a logically necessary component in second order good (e.g., sympathy) while second order evil (e.g., cruelty) is not *justified,* but is so ascribed to human beings that God cannot be held responsible for it. This combination evades my third criticism of the preceding solution.

The freewill solution also involves the preceding solution at a higher level. To explain why a wholly good God gave men free will although it would lead to some important evils, it must be argued that it is better on the whole that men should act freely, and sometimes err, than that they should be innocent automata, acting rightly in a wholly determined way. Freedom, that is to say, is now treated as a third order good, and as being more valuable than second order goods (such as sympathy and heroism) would be if they were deterministically produced, and it is being assumed that second order evils, such as cruelty, are logically necessary accompaniments of freedom, just as pain is a logically necessary pre-condition of sympathy.

I think that this solution is unsatisfactory primarily because of the incoherence of the notion of freedom of the will: but I cannot discuss this topic adequately here, although some of my criticisms will touch upon it.

First I should query the assumption that second order evils are logically necessary accompaniments of freedom. I should ask this: if God has made men such that in their free choices they sometimes prefer what is good and sometimes what is evil, why could He not have made men such that they always freely choose the good? If there is no logical impossibility in a man's freely choosing the good on one, or on several, occasions, there cannot be a logical impossibility in his freely choosing the good on every occasion. God was not, then, faced with a choice between making innocent automata and making beings who, in acting freely, would sometimes go wrong: there was open to him the obviously better possibility of making beings who would act freely but always go right. Clearly, his failure to avail himself of this possibility is inconsistent with his being both omnipotent and wholly good.

If it is replied that this objection is absurd, that the making of some wrong choices is logically necessary for freedom, it would seem that "freedom" must here mean complete randomness or indeterminacy including randomness with regard to the alternatives good and evil, in other words that men's choices and consequent actions can be "free" only if they are not determined by their characters. Only on this assumption can God escape the responsibility for men's actions; for if he made them as they are, but did not determine their wrong choices, this can only be because the wrong choices are not determined by men as they are. But then if freedom is randomness, how can it be a characteristic of *will*? And, still more, how can it be the most important good? What value or merit would there be in free choices if these were random actions which were not determined by the nature of the agent?

I conclude that to make this solution plausible two different senses of "freedom" must be confused, one sense which will justify the view that freedom is a third order good, more valuable than other goods would be without it, and another sense, sheer randomness, to prevent us from ascribing to God a decision to make men such that they sometimes go

wrong when he might have made them such that they would always freely go right.

This criticism is sufficient to dispose of this solution. But besides this there is a fundamental difficulty in the notion of an omnipotent God creating men with free will, for if men's wills are really free this must mean that even God cannot control them, that is, that God is no longer omnipotent. It may be objected that God's gift of freedom to men does not mean that he cannot control their wills, but that he always *refrains* from controlling their wills. But why, we may ask, should God refrain from controlling evil wills? Why should he not leave men free to will rightly, but intervene when he sees them beginning to will wrongly? If God could do this, but does not, and if he is wholly good, the only explanation could be that even a wrong free act of will is not really evil, that its freedom is a value which outweighs its wrongness, so that there would be a loss of value if God took away the wrongness and the freedom together. But this is utterly opposed to what theists say about sin in other contexts. The present solution of the problem of evil, then, can be maintained only in the form that God has made men so free that he *cannot* control their wills.

This leads us to what I call the Paradox of Omnipotence: can an omnipotent being make things which he cannot subsequently control? Or, what is practically equivalent to this, can an omnipotent being make rules which then bind himself? (These are practically equivalent because any such rules could be regarded as setting certain things beyond his control, and vice versa.) The second of these formulations is relevant to the suggestions that we have already met, that an omnipotent God creates the rules of logic or causal laws, and is then bound by them.

It is clear that this is a paradox: the questions cannot be answered satisfactorily either in the affirmative or in the negative. If we answer "Yes," it follows that if God actually makes things which he cannot control, or makes rules which bind himself, he is not omnipotent once he has made them: there are then things which he cannot do. But if we answer "No," we are immediately asserting that there are things which he cannot do, that is to say that he is already not omnipotent.

It cannot be replied that the question which sets this paradox is not a proper question. It would make perfectly good sense to say that a human mechanic has made a machine which he cannot control: if there is any difficulty about the question it lies in the notion of omnipotence itself.

This, incidentally, shows that although we have approached this paradox from the free will theory, it is equally a problem for a theological determinist. No one thinks that machines have free will, yet they may well be beyond the control of their makers. The determinist might reply that anyone who makes anything determines its ways of acting, and so determines its subsequent behaviour: even the human mechanic does this by his *choice* of materials and structure for his machine, though he does not know all about either of these: the mechanic thus determines, though he may not foresee, his machine's actions. And since God is omniscient, and since his creation of things is total, he both determines and foresees the ways in which his creatures will act. We may grant this, but it is beside the point. The question is not whether God *originally* determined the future actions of his creatures, but whether he can *subsequently* control their actions, or whether he was able in his original creation to put things beyond his subsequent control. Even on determinist principles the answers "Yes" and "No" are equally irreconcilable with God's omnipotence.

Before suggesting a solution of this paradox, I would point out that there is a parallel Paradox of Sovereignty. Can a legal sovereign make a law restricting its own future legislative power? For example, could the British parliament make a law forbidding any future parliament to socialise banking, and also forbidding the future repeal of this law itself? Or could the British parliament, which was legally sovereign in Australia in, say, 1899, pass a valid law, or series of laws, which made it no longer sovereign in 1933? Again, neither the affirmative

nor the negative answer is really satisfactory. If we were to answer "Yes," we should be admitting the validity of a law which, if it were actually made, would mean that parliament was no longer sovereign. If we were to answer "No," we should be admitting that there is a law, not logically absurd, which parliament cannot validly make, that is, that parliament is not now a legal sovereign. This paradox can be solved in the following way. We should distinguish between first order laws, that is laws governing the actions of individuals and bodies other than the legislature, and second order laws, that is laws about laws, laws governing the actions of the legislature itself. Correspondingly, we should distinguish two orders of sovereignty, first order sovereignty (sovereignty (1)) which is unlimited authority to make first order laws, and second order sovereignty (sovereignty (2)) which is unlimited authority to make second order laws. If we say that parliament is sovereign we might mean that any parliament at any time has sovereignty (1), or we might mean that parliament has both sovereignty (1) and sovereignty (2) at present, but we cannot without contradiction mean both that the present parliament has sovereignty (2) and that every parliament at every time has sovereignty (1), for if the present parliament has sovereignty (2) it may use it to take away the sovereignty (1) of later parliaments. What the paradox shows is that we cannot ascribe to any continuing institution legal sovereignty in an inclusive sense.

The analogy between omnipotence and sovereignty shows that the paradox of omnipotence can be solved in a similar way. We must distinguish between first order omnipotence (omnipotence (1)), that is unlimited power to act, and second order omnipotence (omnipotence (2)), that is unlimited power to determine what powers to act things shall have. Then we could consistently say that God all the time has omnipotence (1), but if so no beings at any time have powers to act independently of God. Or we could say that God at one time had omnipotence (2), and used it to assign independent powers to act to certain things, so that God thereafter did not have omnipotence (1). But what the paradox shows is that we cannot consistently ascribe to any continuing being omnipotence is an inclusive sense.

An alternative solution of this paradox would be simply to deny that God is a continuing being, that any times can be assigned to his actions at all. But on this assumption (which also has difficulties of its own) no meaning can be given to the assertion that God made men with wills so free that he could not control them. The paradox of omnipotence can be avoided by putting God outside time, but the freewill solution of the problem of evil cannot be saved in this way, and equally it remains impossible to hold that an omnipotent God *binds himself* by causal or logical laws.

CONCLUSION

Of the proposed solutions of the problem of evil which we have examined, none has stood up to criticism. There may be other solutions which require examination, but this study strongly suggests that there is no valid solution of the problem which does not modify at least one of the constituent propositions in a way which would seriously affect the essential core of the theistic position.

Quite apart from the problem of evil, the paradox of omnipotence has shown that God's omnipotence must in any case be restricted in one way or another, that unqualified omnipotence cannot be ascribed to any being that continues through time. And if God and his actions are not in time, can omnipotence, or power of any sort, be meaningfully ascribed to him?

⊚ CRITICAL QUESTIONS

1. Why did Mackie think that ascribing evil to human free will would not avoid the Paradox of Omnipotence? Do you agree? Explain your answer.

2. Do you find Mackie's argument convincing or not? Support your answer with an argument.

14.4 UNHEARD VOICES OF SUFFERING

Why do the righteous suffer? Why do bad, even horrible things, happen to innocent people? Why do the just often suffer injustice? Why is there so little justice in the world? Philosophers, theologians, poets, and others have endlessly debated these sorts of questions. They are also explored in religious scriptures such as the Book of Job (see the Hebrew or Jewish Bible [*Tanakh*] as well as the Christian Old Testament).

Job has become the paradigm of patient suffering in western literature. He is a man of virtue, blameless in all ways yet visited with great afflictions and heartache. Life is exceedingly unfair to this righteous man of Uz, the land where he lived. His friends counsel him to admit his sin but he refuses because he has done nothing wrong. It would be dishonest to admit that he deserves the calamity that has befallen his family. In a prologue to the Biblical poem that tells the story of Job, Satan, described as one of the "sons of God," wagers that Job will renounce God if he suffers enough.

Part of the story of Job (prose introduction and conclusion) circulated orally as a folktale in the second millennium, BCE in the Middle East. Modern scholars date the dramatic/poetic part of the text to the fifth or sixth century BCE. In the written version that appears as the Book of Job in the Bible, Job's wife tells him "to curse God and die" because Job's refusal to admit any guilt has brought great suffering to the family. However, Job dismisses her as one of the "foolish women" (Job 2:9–10) claiming that if they have received great blessings from God, why should they not receive evil? We hear from Job's wife no more in the story, but her voice is heard once more in the selection below.

Jack Hernandez, author of the following poem, is Director of the Norman Levan Center for the Humanities and Professor Emeritus of Philosophy and English at Bakersfield College, California. In his poem he imagines how Job's wife might have reacted to their suffering if given more of a voice.

⊚ READING QUESTIONS

1. What question does Job's wife put to Job?
2. When God puts things right and gives new children to Job and his wife, why is Job's wife still not satisfied?

3. Why has Job's wife spoken these words?

Job's Wife

JACK HERNANDEZ

Some say I told Job
To curse God and die,
But I have been maligned
In this, and ignored,
My anger not heard
My case not made
My voice erased.

Job was blameless,
Yes, but so was I,
The proverbial good wife
Working all the days of my life,
The bread of idleness
Never touching my lips,
Lips revered for wisdom.

I, too, trusted God,
Then my children died,
Seven sons, three daughters buried
Beneath a house, crushed.
What kind of God does this?
I put to Job who would not curse
The one who took his children.

And at the end, when overwhelmed
By a voice from the whirlwind
Job relented, content—
Too easily it seemed to me—
With replacements,
Only I mourned our first,
Growing ugly in my bitterness.

Even as three new daughters
Were praised for their beauty—
"Job's daughters," they were called—
I sat in blackness, remembering
Their sisters' loveliness lost
Like vineyards uprooted
Suddenly and without mercy.

For this I have become as stone
Have spoken these words,
Cast them forth
For my honor
For my solace
That my eyes might see
That my heart might beat again.

⊚ CRITICAL QUESTION

1. The Book of Job does not try to justify the ways of God to humans and neither does this poem about Job's wife. If that is not the purpose of this poem, what is its purpose? What does it tell us about suffering and evil?

Courtesy of Jack Hernandez at the Norman Levan Center for the Humanities, Bakersfield, CA.

14.5 RELIGION AND THE SUBORDINATION OF WOMEN

There is an old story about the reporter who was granted an interview with God. When the reporter returned, people eagerly asked, "Well, tell us. What is God like?"

"You will have to wait until I write my article," the reporter replied, "but I can tell you this much, she is black."

The punch line makes us smile because it is unexpected. But why is it unexpected? Why shouldn't God be female and black?

We have all been raised with certain images of God, and the dominant one in Western culture has been the image of a white male (usually old and bearded). Although the arguments for God's existence make no mention of God's sex, many who read the arguments undoubtedly imagine a male deity as the reference of these arguments. How many of you, as you read the arguments and read the word God, thought of a male deity? If you did, you can understand how these arguments reinforce, perhaps unconsciously and unintentionally, the idea that masculinity is creative, powerful, perfect, and intelligent. Other ideas beside patriarchal images of God have reinforced religious views of women as subordinate to men. Rosemary Ruether (b. 1936), author of the following selection and a pioneer in the area of feminist theology, examines how the body–soul dualism of Plato (see Sections 10.3, 12.2, and 12.3) influenced early Christian thinking about women. Ruether's focus is on Augustine of Hippo (354–430) one of the most influential theologians of the Christian church. However, Christianity is not the only religion that is misogynist. Views advocating the subordination of women to men can be found in almost all, if not all, religions including Judaism, Islam, Hinduism, and Buddhism—to name a few.

Misogynist ideas not only find their way into the teachings of religious leaders, but are also found in religious scriptures. Hence, they have the status of divine revelation for believers, which make them, in the eyes of some, beyond question. For example, the Hebrew Bible's (known as the Old Testament to Christians) account of creation subordinates Eve to Adam and assigns to her the main responsibility for inducing Adam to sin. This subordination of women to men is echoed in the Christian New Testament, as the following passage from I Timothy 2:11–15 indicates.

> Let a woman learn in silence with all submissiveness. I permit no woman to teach or to have authority over men; she is to keep silent. For Adam was formed first, then Eve and Adam was not deceived, but the woman was deceived and became a transgressor. Yet woman will be saved through bearing children, if she continues in faith and love and holiness, with modesty.

◉ READING QUESTIONS

1. What role did dualism play during the classical period in the subordination of women?
2. According to Ruether, what is the "ultimate core" of misogynism?
3. Briefly explain Augustine's views of women.

4. What are the "three basic images" of women in the Church Fathers, and how are they related to the dualistic viewpoint?
5. How does Ruether support her claim that the "female ascetic movement" expressed a kind of early women's liberation movement?

Is Christianity Misogynist?

ROSEMARY RUETHER

The oppression of women is undoubtedly the oldest form of oppression in human history. From the dawn of history the physical lightness of the woman's body (which has nothing to do with biological inferiority) and the fact that the woman is the childbearer have been used to subordinate the woman to the man in a chattel status and to deprive women of the leadership possibilities and the cultural development of the dominant group. The oppression of women can be seen as falling into two distinct cultural stages, corresponding to tribal societies and classical civilizations, while the liberation of women awaits the flowering of that modern civilization which has overcome the dichotomized reality principle of classical cultures. Religions have played a key role in both stages, since it was religion that formulated the world view and prescribed the rituals which inculcated that world view at each stage of consciousness.

The tribal period is one which must be studied much more carefully relative to the oppression of women. There was a time when the tribal period was seen as a time of female dominance, of "matriarchy," while the oppression of women came in only with private property and the division of labor in classical civilizations. Marxist theory preserved a version of this nineteenth century anthropology. The tribal period thus became a kind of "golden age" that served as a point of reference for the future liberation. It now appears clear that "matriarchy" was a method of reckoning descent through the mother, but this never entailed women as the power-holders in society. Agricultural societies clearly developed a different symbolism than hunting and nomadic societies. Women were innovators in the technology of agriculture at an early period and the connection of women and the earth as the sources of fecundity gave feminine symbols and feminine goddesses a primacy in agricultural religions.

In pastoral and hunting societies the disability of the woman, especially when pregnant, was more evident. In these societies strict segregation of women from the male hunting lodge, where the tribesmen prepared themselves for hunting and war, was developed. H. A. Hays, in his comprehensive volume on the history of the oppression of women, *The Dangerous Sex; The Myth of Feminine Evil* details the exorbitant disabilities heaped on women in these tribal societies. Normative sexuality was defined from the perspective of male sexuality. From this perspective the woman was seen as a deviant, an aberration. The vagina was seen as a wound, and the fact that a woman bled from the vagina a mark of castration. Terrible fears and taboos built up around this strange interpretation of woman's sexuality as a wound and a castration which might, through some evil influence, be visited upon the male penis. (It is interesting to see that Freud, whose views were taken to be "scientific," reproduces a psychological doctrine based essentially on this ancient misconception.) The aberrant or castrated sexuality of women was interpreted as "bad mana" from which men must rigidly protect themselves. Menstruation, childbirth, everything connected with the sexuality of women, and finally, even the very presence of women, came to be seen as "unclean"; a debilitating influence that might threaten the virility of the male. Women were isolated from each other and hedged in with elaborate purification rituals which often forced them to live by themselves in places of harsh segregation during large parts of their lives. Social relations were severely restricted, so that women, while preparing the food for the family, often were not

From Rosemary Ruether, *Liberation Theology: Human Hope Confronts Christian History and American Power* (New York: Paulist Press, 1972), pp. 95–114. Copyright © 1972 by The Missionary Society of St. Paul the Apostle in the State of New York.

allowed to sit at table with the men, but must hide in the back of the house lest their presence during the consumption of the strength-giving food cast an evil spell on male power.

By contrast, the male lodge became the place of male bonding and reinforcement in power. The relations of the males in the male lodge were at once both hierarchical and sadomasochistic, and these painful homosexual rituals were an intrinsic part of that male bonding that fit the tribesmen, as a caste, for hunting and war. Mysterious noises from the bullroarer and other instruments emitted from the male lodge, reinforcing the males in their sense of collective power, while frightening the women who were strictly excluded from knowing anything of what was taking place inside. Hays sees this male lodge and its rituals as the precursor of all those exclusively male fraternities, from armies to monasteries to press clubs, where men reinforce themselves in their power against women, and practice a strict pecking order among themselves.

The practices described by Hays as characteristic of hunting tribes would seem to have little connection with higher religions, yet, in fact, these practices were carried over into the great basins of civilization when hunting and nomadic peoples invaded and settled these regions. Israel was just such a tribe, and it canonized the ancient taboos and rituals of uncleanness against women in the Torah and the Talmud and thus passed down this set of attitudes and practices to the present day. This view of women as ritually unclean was transmitted to Christianity, in turn, and shapes to a remarkable extent the laws about women in classical Christian canon law. As Clara Maria Henning, one of the few Roman Catholic canon lawyers in the world, says in her article on the attitude toward women in Catholic canon law,[1] the basic concept of women in canon law is the ancient concept of uncleanness, extended into the Christian ascetic idea of woman as a sexual threat. Most of the laws having to do with

women revolve around elaborate exclusions from contact with priests and contact with the sacred ceremonies where priests preside.

These laws command women to cover their heads, forbid them to approach the altar during the celebration or to enter the sanctuary during Mass; exclude them from acting as servers at Mass, and even discourage them from singing and other participation. Not surprisingly, in the light of what we have said about the origins of these attitudes in ancient tribal taboos, the most vehement laws against women revolve around their sexual uncleanness during menstruation and childbearing. This view of women as unclean was crucial in the final demise of the institution of deaconesses in the early Church. It surrounded women with a ritual of purification after childbirth, and forbade her, at certain points in the Church's history, from taking communion or even entering the church during menstruation.

It might have been thought that the rise of the classical civilizations might have overcome these disabilities heaped upon women in hunting societies, since now mental quickness, rather than physical prowess, became the more important power. Woman's wit is clearly equal to that of the man. Therefore the transformation from physical to mental power should have given women the opportunity to overcome these ancient taboos. However, instead, the prejudice against women was translated into the intellectual sphere, and men reconfirmed their right to be the stronger by declaring that they alone possessed genuine mental power and all the spiritual virtues that went with it, while women were identified with the body and what was seen as the "lower psyche." Thus the actual capacity of women to intellectual equality and to parity within a civilization based on cultural rather than physical prowess was elaborately suppressed in classical civilizations by a cultural denial to women of these capacities and the institutionalization of this denial through the exclusion of women from opportunities for education and formation in higher culture. This exclusion of women from education lasted down into the late nineteenth century, when women fought a long battle to be admitted first to secondary and then to higher education, encountering

---

[1] See the article by Clara Maria Henning, "Canon Law and the Battle of the Sexes," in the *Images of Women in the Judaeo-Christian Tradition*, edited by Rosemary Ruether (Simon and Schuster, 1973).

male opposition at every step of the way. Not too surprisingly, the argument that was constantly used against the right of women to education was the insistence that woman lacked such capacity by nature, and that she was peculiarly tied up, psychosomatically, with childbearing, so that any diversion of her "blood" to her brain would divert it from the one place that it was necessary, namely her womb, and render her infertile! Clergymen were the warmest advocates of this particular piece of misinformation.[2]

Classical civilizations created a dualistic view of soul and body as an expression of their struggle to assert the ascendancy of the intellectual principle over the givenness of the human condition. But they also repressed the possibility for the liberation of women that arose out of that development, by equating soul-body dualism with male-female dualism, and thus reestablishing the subordination of women in new form. Christianity, in this respect, was the heir and bearer of the culture of classical civilization. And the study of the attitude toward women in the Church Fathers reveals dramatically both sides of this new development; the potential for the liberation of women through the affirmation of the superiority of the spiritual to the somatic principle, and the suppression of this possibility by equating the feminine with the bodily principle.

The dualistic anthropology, which Christianity absorbed from Platonism, created a distinct tension between its ascetic spirituality and the body-affirming doctrine of creation which was found in the Hebrew Scriptures. Eastern Christian theology tried to solve this conflict by defining the original creation as spiritual and monistic and ascribing the "gross" body and bi-sexuality to the fall.[3] Latin theology, in St. Augustine, for example, attempted to affirm the bi-sexual, bodily character of the original creation, but in a way that equated soul-body dualism with male-female dualism. Thus the spiritual image of God (made

in the image of the divine *Logos*—Christ) in man became essentially male, and femaleness was equated with the lower, corporeal nature.

For Augustine, the original Adam was unitary in person, but compound in nature, consisting of male spirit and female bodiliness. When Eve was taken from the side of Adam, she stood for the bodily "side" of man which was taken from him in order to serve him as a helpmate. But she is a helpmate solely for the task of procreation, in which she is alone indispensible. For any spiritual task, another male would be more suitable.[4] So the purpose of woman's existence was defined essentially in terms of childbearing. Other than this there is no reason for the existence of woman. Inexplicably, Augustine also affirms that Eve too has a rational spirit, being also a compound of body and spirit. But Augustine persists in speaking of woman, in relation to the male, as standing for the relation of body to spirit. Moreover, he consistently defines this relationship as woman's "nature."[5] He thus concludes that the male alone possesses the full image of God, whereas woman, when taken by herself, does not possess the full image of God, but only when taken together with the male who "is her head."[6] Woman is therefore defined as a *relative being,* who exists only in relationship to the male, who alone possesses full autonomous personhood. This view of woman is perhaps the ultimate core of misogynism.

This assimilation of male-female dualism into soul-body dualism conditions the definition of woman both in terms of the order of nature and in terms of the condition of the fall. In the order of nature woman is essentially subordinate to the man, just as the body is essentially subordinate to the mind in that right ordering of body to spirit that is defined as "original justice." (!) But because ascetic spirituality defined sin as the disordering of the flesh to the spirit, which made the mind the subject of passions, the equation of woman with body also made her peculiarly the

[2]See Rosemary Ruether, "Are Women's Colleges Obsolete," *Critic,* Oct.–Nov., (1968), pp. 58–64, for a summary of this struggle for women's education in America.
[3]Origen's, *de Principiis* and Gregory Nyssa's *de opiflcio hominis.*

[4]Augustine, *de grat. Ch. et pecc. orig.* 2,40; *de Genesi ad Lit.* 9,5.
[5]Augustine's *Confessiones* 13,32; *de opere Monach.* 40.
[6]Augustine, *de Trinitate* 7,7,10.

symbol of sin. This double definition of woman, as submissive body in the order of nature, and "carnality" in the disorder of sin, allows the Church Fathers to slip somewhat inconsistently from the second to the first, and attribute an inferiority in women that is sinful to woman's "nature." In some of the Church Fathers, such as Tertullian, the sinfulness of woman is equated with her primary responsibility for the original fall of man. Tertullian speaks of woman's role in the fall by such epithets as "the Devil's gateway," and sees her nature as permanently marked by her special guilt in causing the fall of man, leading up to the necessity for the death of Christ.[7]

St. Augustine is somewhat more temperate in his diatribes against Eve as the cause of the fall. Augustine's stress falls much more on the natural inferiority of women, as body, in the relation of body to mind in the right ordering of nature. For him, the fall could occur only when the mind consents to "go along," and not simply when the body "tempts." But this does not imply a milder view of sin, but rather a more contemptuous view of woman's ability to cause the fall "by herself."[8]

This assimilation of femaleness into bodiliness allows Augustine to explain woman's subjugation in the order of nature, but it makes for some contradiction when it comes to defending woman's redeemability; her capacity, like the male, to overcome the body and rise to the higher, spiritual nature (the Patristic definition of redemption). Augustine attempts to explain this contradiction by distinguishing what woman *is,* where she is equivalent to the male, and what she *symbolizes* in her bodily nature, where she stands for the subjugation of body to spirit in nature and that debasing carnality which draws the male mind down from its heavenly heights to "wallow in the flesh." As he puts it in his *Soliloquies:*

> I feel that nothing so casts down the manly mind from its heights as the fondling of woman and those bodily contacts which belong to the married state.[9]

But since Augustine identifies this that woman "symbolizes," with her "nature," this creates a strange schizophrenia in the relation of the male to the female in marriage. The man is exhorted to love his wife's spiritual nature, but to despise in her all her bodily functions as woman and wife:

> A good Christian is found, toward one and the same woman, to love the creature of God whom he desires to be transformed and renewed, but to hate in her the corruptible and mortal conjugal connection, sexual intercourse and all that pertains to her as a wife.[10]

It never occurs to Augustine that this definition of woman's nature in terms of what she "symbolizes" in the eye of the male perception, rather than in terms of what she is in herself, might be precisely a disorder in the eye of the male perceiver, and therefore in no sense a stance for the definition of woman's nature! But, for Augustine, as for the tradition of male dominance generally, this androcentric perspective, which reduced woman to "body" *vis à vis* the male eye, is never questioned, but is presumed. The essence of male ideology can be said to be contained precisely in this cultural relationship, where the woman is the one acted upon and defined by the male perception and "use," and her own self-definition and perspective are never heard or incorporated culturally. Women, as all oppressed people, live in a culture of silence, as objects, never subjects of the relationship.

The definition of woman as body lends itself to an identification of the female psyche and personality as peculiarly characterized by "carnal" traits. To woman's "mind" are attributed essentially the traits of pettiness, sensuality, materialism and maliciousness, while all the virtues of the mind, such as chastity, patience, wisdom, temperance, fortitude and justice, are equated with masculinity.[11] This comes about with a kind of spiritualizing of the primitive equation of all that is "strong" with the male; all that is weak with the female.

---

[7]Tertullian, *de cultu fem.* 1,1.
[8]Augustine, *de contin.* 1,23; *civitate Dei* 14,11; *de Genesi ad Lit.* 11,42.
[9]Augustine, *Soliloquies* 1,10.

[10]Augustine, *de sermone Dom. in Monte* 41.
[11]Eg. Leander of Seville, *de instit. Virg*; Ambrose, *de Cain et Abel* 1,4; Jerome, Ep. 130,17.

This definition of woman, both physically and psychically, in terms of the lower nature, creates a peculiar contradiction when it comes time to defend the ability of the "virgin" to overcome this lower nature and be redeemed.

It becomes characteristic of the Fathers, the ascetic writers especially, to speak of the virgin as having become "male," by transcending the female nature, physically and psychically. The very possibility of redemption through spiritualization is thus, for woman, "unnatural"; a transcendence of her "nature"; whereas the male ascetic is seen as being restored to his natural male spirituality through redemption. This view extended itself into a debate over the sexual character of the risen body. It was natural to conclude, therefore, that in the resurrection from the dead, there would be only males, females being transformed into males. (This is analogous to the racist view in Mormonism that only whites are redeemable, so the Negro can be saved only by being transformed into a white person.) Augustine and Jerome both assert that mankind will arise in both male and female bodies, but they too find the incompatibility so strong that they must modify this view by asserting that these bodies will be spiritual and lacking in all sensual libido, the female risen body in particular having been deprived of those organs having to do with intercourse and childbearing, so that the female body becomes "suited to glory rather than to shame."

What this angelic hysterectomy is supposed to mean is anyone's guess, but it illustrates graphically the dilemma of Patristic anthropology. They wish to affirm a doctrine of redemption that coheres with the original bodily, bi-sexual nature which God had declared "very good" in the beginning; but since they have declared this to be "very bad" and define redemption as the overcoming of the body, sexual relationship and female nature, they can only affirm this continuity by peculiarly mutilating redemption or creation or both in these particular characteristics.

The Fathers never entirely deny, although they often seem to forget, that woman too has a spiritual nature equivalent to that of the male. Indeed this affirmation is assumed in that view which allows the woman, as well as the man, to become a "virgin" and to rise to the "higher life" of monistic spirituality. But since woman is also made, in her bodily nature, peculiarly the symbol of body in relation to the (male) mind and associated with all the sensual and depraved characteristics of psychology through this corporeality, her salvation then is seen, not as an affirmation of her (feminine) nature, but a transcendence of her (feminine) nature to a higher (male) possibility. Such a view forces upon the female ascetic both a redoubled subjugation of her body and personality in ascetic practices, and also an abasement of her "image," so that she will no longer appear as an attractive female body before the male visual perception. This obsession with blotting out the female bodily image explains that peculiar concern in Patristic literature with matters of female dress, adornment and physical appearance which still agitates the relationship of the Vatican congregation for religious in its relation to its daughters! The woman must be stripped of all adornment that reveals or enhances her femininity. She must bear an unshapely dress and veil that conceal her face and limbs. Finally, she must literally destroy her physical appearance with dirt and fasting, so that she becomes unsightly. As Tertullian puts it, in his treatise, *de cultu feminarum:*

> It is time for you to know that not merely must the pageantry of fictitious and elaborate beauty be rejected by you, but even that natural grace must be obliterated by concealment and negligence, as equally dangerous to the glances of the beholder's eye.[12]

The definition of sin as sexual and bodily feeling, of course, creates that rigid view of the right purpose and use of sex characteristic of Augustine, that has traditionally denied the possibility of birth control. Since women are the childbearers, this means, in effect, the denial of the right of women to limit or control the effects of male sexual use of their bodies. When the denial of birth control is taken together with the view (also accepted by the Fathers), that woman stands in a chattel relation to the male in marriage, i.e., the husband has a proprietary

---

[12]Tertullian, *de cultu fem.* 2,2.

right over his wife's body, which forbids the wife to deny her husband sexual access to her at any time, the subordination of woman to biological necessity becomes complete.

Augustine believed that, in the original creation, there would have been bi-sexual, but non-sensual, reproduction.

In paradise woman would have been perfectly submissive to the male, just as the body would have been perfectly submissive to the mind. Just as every organ and muscle in the body would have been completely under the control and command of the mind; i.e., man would have been able to whistle tunes with his anus (!), so the female (body) would also have been perfectly submissive to the mind of the directing male. Man would have used the female body for reproduction, but in a completely dispassionate way, just as the farmer sows his seed in the furrow of a field. This act would have been entirely purposive; i.e., done solely for procreation, and would have been devoid of all sensual feelings.[13] Man's sexual organ would have been totally under the control of his rational mind, so that he would have moved it to its purpose just as he moves his hand or his foot now, without any rush of sensual feeling accompanying this act. Thus, in Augustine's view, rightly ordered sex is such as to be depersonalized, unfeeling and solely instrumental. It relates to the woman literally as a "baby making machine"; i.e., a body whose sole purpose for existence is to be used as the incubator of the male seed.

When, however, man sins, he loses the "original justice" of this ordering of body to mind. Sinful "carnality," signifying the revolt of the sensual principle against its "head," enters in. Then the male loses control over his sexual organ, which begins to respond with a "will of its own" to the female bodily presence. This Augustine sees as the exemplification of the principle of sin, whereby the "law of the members wars against the law of the mind."[14] For Augustine, then, the spontaneous tumescence of the male penis, in response to

sensual stimuli, and independent of conscious control, is the very essence of sin. He proceeded to construct his whole doctrine of the transmission of sin around this view.

Ideally, the married couple should give themselves to the sexual act solely for the purpose of procreation.

Otherwise they should be continent. However, since the fall, this dispassionate and wholly instrumental use of sex, such as would have existed in paradise is no longer possible. The sexual organs have been disordered by sin and so cause an unruly by-product of sensual pleasure, whether the couple will or not. Augustine sees this spontaneous libido as intrinsically sinful. It is forgiven to the married couple only if it is not intended, if it is despised by them, and their intention remains solely that of procreation. But the sinful character of the means, nevertheless, conditions the end product in the child, who is born thereby tainted with Original Sin.[15] This then is the means whereby the original sin of Adam, with its disordering of the relation of flesh to spirit, is transmitted from generation to generation through the sexual act.

If the couple actually intend to enjoy carnal pleasure, although also intending and not impeding procreation, Augustine sees this as sinful, but venially so, since it is allowable under that apostolic concession that it is better to "marry than to burn." It was this second purpose of the sexual act that was spoken of as the "remedy for concupiscence." But it is allowable only as a concession to weakness and is not a good in itself.[16] Finally, if the couple desires "only" carnal pleasure and impedes procreation (and this would include the rhythm method, for Augustine, which was practiced by the Manichaeans), the act is wholly sinful and equivalent to fornication.[17] Such a narrow view of sex follows from a depersonalized definition of the sexual relationship, which is seen either as instrumental or narcissistically carnal.

---

[13]Augustine, *civitate Dei* 14,26; *contra Julian* 3,13,27; *de grat. Ch. et pecc. orig.* 2,40.
[14]Romans 8,23; Augustine, *civitate Dei* 14,24; *de grat. Ch. et pecc. orig.* 2,41; *de nupt. et concup.* 1,6–7,27,33.
[15]Augustine, *de pecc. merit. et remiss.* 1,29; *de grat. Ch. et pecc. orig.* 1,27; 2,41–44; *de nupt. et concup.* 1,13,22; *adv. Julian,* 3,7; 5,14.
[16]Jerome, *Ep.* 48,14; Augustine, *de nupt, et concup,* 1,16; *de bono conj.* 6,11.
[17]Augustine, *de nupt et concup,* 1,17; *de bono conj.* 10,11; *de conj. adult.* 2,12.

The possibility of bodily relation as an interpersonal relationship or a vehicle of love, is essentially eliminated. Augustine does speak of a third purpose of marriage as a "symbol" of unity, mirroring the relationship of Christ to the Church, but he never develops this as an inter-personality that could be expressed through the sexual act itself.

Indeed this third purpose remains wholly undefined in his thought, and he speaks of the possibility of friendship between the married as arising only when the sexual act is no longer used, as in old people.[18]

This depersonalization of the sexual act and through it the depersonalization of woman must be seen as the reflection of that fundamental assimilation of male-female relation into soul-body relation. This implies a subject-object relationship between men and women. For the soul-body relationship corresponds to the subject-object relationship between the subject and that external reality which is reduced to the status of a "thing" to be "used." This subject-object relationship has, as its basic characteristic, the negating of the other as a "thou" or equivalent "subject," and therefore abolishes the possibility of a relation to the "other" as one of mutuality and intersubjectivity. The translation of male-female dualism in Christianity into soul-body dualism, therefore, blotted out in classical spirituality, the possibility of bodily relationship as a meeting of persons. It constricted it into the framework of a relation of a subject to an object to be "used." Woman, then, was defined literally as a "sex object," either to be rightly used, for procreation, or wrongly used, narcissistically, for carnal pleasure. In either case, woman as a person never appears in the relationship.

This view of sexuality determines the three basic images of women in the Church Fathers; woman as whore; woman as wife and woman as virgin. As whore, woman represents sinful carnality which is the essence of the fall. Here, woman is depicted as the bold strumpet, strutting forth in all her natural and artificial bodily allures. Here, woman incarnates the very character of the sensual principle in revolt against its "head," that subverts the right ordering between mind and sense.

As wife, woman is also defined as body, but now as submissive body, obedient to her "head," that stands for the proper relationship of the sensual to the intellectual principle. The ideal for the wife was one of total servility and meekness, even under harsh and unjust treatment. The wife is seen as having no personal rights autonomously, either over her mind or over her body. Mentally she is said to have "no head," but to submit to her husband who "is her head," while, on the bodily level the husband has complete proprietary rights to her body and the property of the household.[19] This rigid view of the mental and psychical subjugation of the wife is illustrated in a letter which Augustine wrote to the North African matron Ecducia.[20] This woman apparently had chosen a life of continence that had become contrary to her husband's wishes, although he had originally agreed to it. Augustine allows her to continue only because the husband had once agreed, but he severely rebukes her for her disposal of family property without her husband's permission. He enunciates the basic principles which guide his view, in the process. Women may never, independently, choose continence, or deny sexual use of their bodies to their husbands, because the woman has "no head of her own," but belongs to her husband, who "is her head," and it is a sin for the woman to refuse to her husband the "debt" of her body.

For Augustine, the ideal wife should receive no sensual pleasure from such sexual use, but submit her body solely as an instrument for procreation. Augustine even rationalizes Old Testament polygamy on these grounds, arguing that these ancient worthies gave themselves such excessive "marrying and giving in marriage," without experiencing any sensual pleasure, but solely in obedience to God's command to (hurry up and) increase and multiply, so they might all the sooner make up the whole of the race of Israel from which the messiah was to be

---

[18]Augustine, *de grat. Ch. et pecc. orig*, 2,39; *de nupt. et concup.* 1,19; *de bono conj.* 17; *de Genesi ad lit.* 9,7.

[19]Eg. John Chrysostom, *Epist. ad Ephes.; hom.* 13; *hom.* 22; and *hom.* 26,8.
[20]Augustine, *Ep.* 262, to Ecducia.

born. Polygamy was admissible for this purpose, although polyandry would have been unacceptable, since, as Augustine puts it, "nature allows multiplicity in subjugations, but demands singularity in dominations," just as many members may serve the one head in the body, and many slaves the one master, but not vice versa.[21]

Here we can see how fundamental it was for Augustine to equate male-female dualism with soul-body dualism in a way that defines that relationship essentially as one of domination and subjugation. The husband was, of course, exhorted to love his wife and not abuse her, but again this is said to be as he would "love his own body," and because it would demean his dignity as the "head" to do otherwise.[22] It is not because women have any autonomous dignity as persons, or rights over their own bodies relative to the male. Such a theory of married women in Christianity not only did not lift up the social position of women beyond what it had been in antiquity, but even fell below those modest legal rights to personal and economic autonomy which women had been winning under later Roman law. Thus the frequent claim that Christianity elevated the position of woman must be denied. It actually lowered the position of woman relative to the more enlightened legislation of later Roman society, and elevated woman only in her new role as "virgin."

For the Fathers, marriage has the lowest place of honor in the scheme of Christian life. Now that Christ has come, marriage is still allowable, but no longer necessary, since marrying and giving in marriage has been superceded by the new order of the Resurrection. The blessings upon procreation from the Old Testament, therefore, have been rescinded. Procreation is not forbidden, to be sure, but it has become redundant and distracting. It would be better if all men imitated the way of Christian perfection and refrained from procreation, so that the world could come to an end faster, and the new world of the Resurrection could dawn in its entirety, according to Augustine.[23] If a Christian is truly converted, he will become continent. The married life thus falls at the bottom of the hierarchy of virtue, falls below that 100-fold virtue of virginity, or the 60-fold virtue of widowhood.[24] The life of continence is the only life fully compatible with the Christian life of spiritual regeneration.

The highest ideal of life, then, for the woman is virginity. Here alone does woman rise to spirituality, personhood and equality with the male. But only at the expense of crushing out of her being all vestiges of her bodily and her female "natures" and rising to "unnatural manliness." But this regeneration is not seen as releasing the woman for a boldness and autonomy, since the condition for this release of her spiritual principle is that total abasement of her body and her female image which, *de facto,* lies under obedience to male authority. This assertion that female virginity in no way undid the hierarchical relation of male to female in the Church clearly ran into some real contradiction during the first period of the Christian ascetic movement. The Church Fathers, unwittingly, in their ascetic doctrines, released a movement of women's liberation which suggested a far fuller equality of male and female under the new order of the Resurrection. Again and again the early ascetic writers enunciated the principle that Eve was punished for her sin by the twofold marks of bearing children in sorrow and being under the authority of the husband. In choosing the life of virginity, the woman was declared to have thrown off both of these marks of Eve's punishment.[25] While it was fairly easy to see how the virgin no longer bore children in sorrow (since she bore no children at all), the implication of virginity as releasing women from male subjugation was clearly one that the Church Fathers were quite

---

[21]Augustine, *de bono conj.* 17–20; *de nupt. et concup.* 1,9–10.
[22]John Chrysostom, *Epis. ad Ephes.; hom.* 26,8; also Augustine, *de conj. adult.* 2,15.
[23]Compare Jerome, *adv. Jov,* 1,36; Augustine, *de nupt. et concup.* 1,14–15; *de bono conj.* 10,13; *de bono viduit,* 8–11; *de sancta virg.* 9,9,16.
[24]This common image contrasting marriage, widowhood and virginity according to the 30-, 60- and 100-fold harvest of Mark 4,20 is found repeatedly in the Fathers; eg. Cyprian, *de habitu virg.* 21; Athanasius, *Ep.* 48,2; Tertullian, *de exhort, cast.* 1; Jerome, *Epp.* 22,15; 48,3; 66,2; 120, 1,9; *Adv. Jov.* 1,3; Augustine, *de sancta virg.* 45; Ambrose, *de virg.* 1,60.
[25]Cyprian, *de habitu virg.* 22; Jerome, *Ep.* 130,8; *Comm. in Epist. ad Ephes.* 3,5; *adv. Helvid.* 22; Leander of Seville, *de instit. virg.*

unwilling to push to its logical conclusions. But there was a powerful movement of feminine asceticism in the fourth century and thereafter which clearly read this doctrine quite differently, and did indeed assume that the choice of the life of continence released them from male authority in general, and not merely in the literal sense that they had no husbands to whom to be subjugated. Thus many women flocked to the life of continence, either by refusing to marry or else by separating from their husbands to form communities of women, and were claiming thereby a freedom and equality with men. One peculiar expression of this was the "spiritual marriage" in which the virgin lived in a spiritual relationship with a male ascetic. In some cases this probably worked to the disadvantage of women, who were forced into a kind of housekeeper relationship.

But clearly, in the case of a strong-minded female ascetic, it could constitute something like a free love relationship, as is evident from some of Jerome's horrified descriptions of this possibility.[26] The idea that the woman who chose continence freed herself from the twofold curse of Eve of childbearing and male domination was leading many women in this period to abandon their children and household responsibilities, and depart to found communities of women. It was only with the greatest difficulty that the Church brought this female ascetic movement under control, but arguing simultaneously that, while virginity did raise the woman above her "female nature" to a virility and spiritual equality with the male, this in no way detracted from male authority, because the condition for this spiritualization was her self-abasement, humility and obedience to God (*de facto* exercised by male authority in the Church). The insistence that the male alone could represent Christ in the priesthood (since he alone possesses that spiritual image of God that mirrors the divine Word), and the continuation of the Jewish ideas of woman's uncleanliness, operated to exclude women from any positions of authority in the Church and thus to insure that, however high a woman might rise in the female ascetic ranks,

there would always be a male authority above her. Needless to say this tension between the female ascetic movement and male authority is exploding all over again in contemporary Catholicism, having been successfully repressed for fourteen hundred years!

Thus the potential of the female ascetic movement to express the liberation of women within the framework of classical religion was largely repressed in Christianity through the very dualism in which the liberation of the spiritual principle from the body was perceived.

At each point the women found femininity equated with bodiliness to re-subordinate her, even as an ascetic, to the right of the stronger, now interpreted spiritually as the right of the male to monopolize intellectual power and identify it with masculinity.

Nevertheless the ascetic movement in late antiquity did raise up a new cultural ideal of the "spiritual woman," who, through the conquest of the body, could rise to spiritual personhood equal to that of the male and could even achieve the life of intellectual contemplation that led to the ultimate *summum bonum* of communion with God. Women now, for the first time, were conceded the possibility of the highest spiritual achievement, from which they were generally excluded among Greek philosophers (although late antiquity did see one great woman philosopher, Hypatia). Judaism, by contrast, systematically excluded women from living the life of the scholar. In Christianity women, normally, and in great numbers, were admitted to the highest ideals of ascetic spirituality. Fourth and fifth century Christianity, moreover, saw a great flowering of cultural imagery related to spiritual femininity. Much of the literature of the period was constructed around the figure of the woman as seer, muse or revealer of spiritual truths, from the figure of "Dame Church," who speaks to the worried Christian in the *Shepherd of Hermas* in the second century, to "Dame Philosophia" who is Boethius' muse in prison four centuries later. As the Virgin Psyche, the feminine principle in the soul was represented as the human partner in the nuptial mystery of the communion of the soul with Christ in mystical ecstasy. As the Bridal Church, woman represents mankind in its eschatological union with God. All

---

[26]Jerome, *Ep.* 117.

these images of spiritual womanhood were gathered together to make up that Mariology which flowered, together with the ascetic movement, in the fourth and fifth centuries. The culmination of this elevation of spiritual femininity was the doctrine of Mary's Assumption, a characteristic doctrine of this period of the Church's history. The doctrine of the Assumption grew up first in Egypt in the early fourth century, in the cradle of Christian asceticism, and spread from there essentially along with the spread of the ascetical movement. In the doctrine of the Assumption, the "Spiritual Woman" was raised to the very heavens, to take her place beside the Jewish Ancient of Days and his Son Messiah who once had ruled from the Cherubim Throne in exclusive patriarchal splendor. An early precedent for this, however, was set within Judaism itself which used the femininity of the word "spirit" in Hebrew to speak of God's Spirit as the "Eldest daughter of Yahweh," "who sits at his right hand." Christianity inherited this tradition in the form of Sophia piety that also merged with Mariology in the Eastern Church.

But in ascetical Christianity this elevation of spiritual womanhood was done at the price of despising all real, living women, sex and fecundity, and the sublimation of the feminine into an ethereal love object for the sublimated sexual libido of the male ascetic. It should not surprise us, therefore, that Mariology has done little for the liberation of women, concretely and historically, when we realize to what extent it was created by and has always been the spirituality of male ascetics, serving as a substitute fantasized love object for a repressed male sexual libido, thereby guarding this from turning back to any real, physical expression of love with the dangerous daughters of Eve! Yet perhaps the task of Christians today is not merely to vilify the inhumanity of this tradition both to the affections of men and the natural somatic persons and full development of women. Rather we must realize how this ideology fits in with a strange but real struggle of mankind for transcendence of their given situation and the achievements of spiritual personhood, which seems to lie behind this aberrant fear of the body and its feelings. Without discarding these achievements, we today must find out how to pour them back into a full-bodied sense of creation and incarnation, as male and female, who can begin to stand as personalized, autonomous selves and therefore as full persons for each other, not merely against the body, but in and through the body.[27]

---

[27]A fuller exposition of the material of this chapter is found in my chapter on "Misogynism and Virginal Feminism in the Fathers of the Church," in the book edited by this author, *Images of Women in the Judaeo-Christian Tradition* (Simon and Schuster, 1973).

◉ CRITICAL QUESTIONS

1. Do you think the androcentric view of women that Ruether describes persists to this day? Present evidence to support your answer.

2. Do you think that Christianity is misogynist? Provide an argument in support of your answer.

14.6 ARE ALL RELIGIONS TRUE?

Suppose there were only one religion in the world. Let's call it the religion of Bliss. Suppose further that most people were Blissians. They participated in its rituals and conducted their lives, for the most part, according to its teachings. There were some dissenters, some anti-Blissians, but very few.

One consequence of this imaginary situation would probably be that the teachings of Bliss would seem true. There would be no real alternatives, no other religions teaching different doctrines or disputing the truth of Bliss. No one would have to worry about what attitude to take toward rival religions. It would not be necessary. Blissians would have a monopoly on religious truth.

We do not live in such a world. Instead we live in a world with diverse religious traditions that have been and are in conflict. We cannot avoid contact with people of other faiths and the very existence of such religious pluralism calls into question the truth of each. In the diverse religious world in which we live, we must develop some view about how our religion, if we profess one, relates to the others.

One possibility is to claim that only members of our religion will be saved because only our religion teaches the true path to salvation. Truth belongs to us exclusively. Another possibility is to claim that, although other religions teach some truth and although others can be saved, *our* religion teaches the *full* truth. It is the fulfillment of what the others have only dimly glimpsed. This sort of *inclusivism* seems more charitable than the *exclusive attitude,* but it is not as charitable as a third possibility, which is often called *pluralism.* According to pluralism, all religions are valid paths to salvation.

If we adopt a pluralistic attitude, we need some sort of explanation of why the teachings of all these valid religions appear so different and often seem to conflict. One possibility is to argue that the differences are real but relate to trivial matters. On important issues there is basic agreement. Another possibility is to argue that the differences are not real but apparent. On the surface the different religions seem to contradict each other, but when properly understood, they do not. Or one might admit that these are real differences, even on important matters, but claim that these differences do not affect the salvific value of each of the great traditions.

In addition to the attitudes of exclusivism, inclusivism, and pluralism, one might argue that today religions interpenetrate one another. Religions no longer exist isolated from one another, but in mutual relationship. What others believe and do helps us to better understand our own religions.

We live, as it were, in a religious supermarket with competing brand names and products. Suppose we are shopping. How do we decide what to buy? Do we judge all the other religions by the standards of our own religion? Do we judge the other religions by their own standards? Do we develop some neutral set of rational criteria that allow us to judge impartially and fairly the truth claims of each?

Perhaps this whole business of judging the truth of other religions is misguided. Perhaps it simply cannot be done or, even if it could, it misses the point. Perhaps we should concentrate on cooperation among the various religions on important moral and social issues, like helping the poor and stopping violence and war.

Maybe the question, "Are all religions true?" is misleading. It is certainly ambiguous. Does it mean that the teachings of the various religions are true? Does it mean that the rituals and rites practiced by the various religions are effective? Does it mean that the social organizations of the various religions are conducive to building community? If we restrict its meaning only to the teachings, does the question mean that before a religion is true all (every single one) of its teachings (however trivial) must be true? Further, the question seems to presuppose that there is some sort of religious truth that humans are capable of discovering. Perhaps there is no such thing as objective, absolute truth. What we call "truth" is nothing more than human constructions and conventions that reflect cultural values and biases. Perhaps truth is localized and relative to particular historical periods. After all, many different religions and societies have managed to flourish and survive on this planet while responding to the problems of human existence in very different ways. Perhaps what works for each is the only truth there is.*

His Holiness the Fourteenth Dalai Lama (born in 1935 as Tenzin Gyatso) is both the spiritual leader of Tibetan Buddhism and the political leader of the Tibetan people. He was forced into exile by the invasion and annexation of Tibet by the Chinese in 1959. Since then he has traveled the world supporting his people, teaching the precepts of Buddhism, and seeking independence for his homeland. He likes to say that he is no more than "a simple Buddhist monk." This "simple monk" won the Nobel Peace Prize in 1989.

In his book, *Freedom in Exile: The Autobiography of the Dalai Lama* (Harper-Collins, 1990), he defines religion as follows:

> What is religion? As far as I am concerned, any deed done with good motivation is a religious act. On the other hand, a gathering of people in a temple or church who do not have good motivation are not performing a religious act when they pray together....**

---

*This introductory material comes from Gary E. Kessler, *Philosophy of Religion: Toward a Global Perspective* (Belmont, CA: Wadsworth Publishing Company, 1999), pp. 529–530. Copyright © 1999 by Wadsworth Publishing Company. Reprinted by permission.
**For more on Tibetan Buddhism, see Gary E. Kessler, *Ways of Being Religious* (Mountain View, CA: Mayfield Publishing Company, 2000).

⊚ READING QUESTIONS

1. What are the two primary sources of conflict related to religion?
2. Why does the Dalai Lama consider religion relevant to the modern world?
3. What is the most significant obstruction to interreligious harmony?
4. Why is dialogue among religions so important? What else is needed in order to overcome religious conflict?
5. How does the Dalai Lama propose to deal with the problems that arise from the fact that different religions all claim to be the one "true" religion?

The Role of Religion in Modern Society

THE DALAI LAMA

It is a sad fact of human history that religion has been a major source of conflict. Even today, individuals are killed, communities destroyed, and societies destabilized as a result of religious bigotry and hatred. It is no wonder that many question the place of religion in human society. Yet when we think carefully, we find that conflict in the name of religion arises from two principal sources. There is that which arises simply as a result of religious diversity—the doctrinal, cultural, and practical differences between one religion and another. Then there is the conflict that arises in the context of political, economic, and other factors, mainly at the institutional level. Interreligious harmony is the key to overcoming conflict of the first sort. In the case of the second, some other solution must be found. Secularization and in particular the separation of the religious hierarchy from the institutions of the state may go some way to reducing such institutional problems. Our concern in this chapter is with interreligious harmony, however.

This is an important aspect of what I have called universal responsibility. But before examining the matter in detail, it is perhaps worth considering the question of whether religion is really relevant in the modern world. Many people argue that it is not. Now I have observed that religious belief is not a pre-condition either of ethical conduct or of happiness itself. I have also suggested that whether a person practices religion or not, the spiritual qualities of love and compassion, patience, tolerance, forgiveness, humility, and so on are indispensable. At the same time, I should make it clear that I believe that these are most easily and effectively developed within the context of religious practice. I also believe that when an individual sincerely practices religion, that individual will benefit enormously.

People who have developed a firm faith, grounded in understanding and rooted in daily practice, are in general much better at coping with adversity than those who have not. I am convinced, therefore, that religion has enormous potential to benefit humanity. Properly employed, it is an extremely effective instrument for establishing human happiness. In particular, it can play a leading role in encouraging people to develop a sense of responsibility toward others and of the need to be ethically disciplined.

On these grounds, therefore, I believe that religion is still relevant today. But consider this too: some years ago, the body of a Stone Age man was recovered from the ice of the European Alps. Despite being more than five thousand years old, it was perfectly preserved. Even its clothes were largely intact. I remember thinking at the time that were it possible to bring this individual back to life for a day, we would find that we have much in common with him. No doubt we would find that he too was concerned for his family and

loved ones, for his health and so on. Differences of culture and expression notwithstanding, we would still be able to identify with one another on the level of feeling. And there could be no reason to suppose any less concern with finding happiness and avoiding suffering on his part than on ours. If religion, with its emphasis on overcoming suffering through the practice of ethical discipline and cultivation of love and compassion, can be conceived of as relevant in the past, it is hard to see why it should not be equally so today. Granted that in the past the value of religion may have been more obvious in that human suffering was more explicit due to the lack of modern facilities. But because we humans still suffer, albeit today this is experienced more internally as mental and emotional affliction, and because religion in addition to its salvific truth claims is concerned to help us overcome suffering, surely it must still be relevant.

How then might we bring about the harmony that is necessary to overcome interreligious conflict? As in the case of individuals engaged in the discipline of restraining their response to negative thoughts and emotions and cultivating spiritual qualities, the key lies in developing understanding. We must first identify the factors that obstruct it. Then we must find ways to overcome them.

Perhaps the most significant obstruction to interreligious harmony is lack of appreciation of the value of others' faith traditions. Until comparatively recently, communication between different cultures, even different communities, was slow or nonexistent. For this reason, sympathy for other faith traditions was not necessarily very important—except of course where members of different religious lived side by side. But this attitude is no longer viable. In today's increasingly complex and interdependent world, we are compelled to acknowledge the existence of other cultures, different ethnic groups, and, of course, other religious faiths. Whether we like it or not, most of us now experience this diversity on a daily basis.

I believe that the best way to overcome ignorance and bring about understanding is through dialogue with members of other faith traditions. This I see occurring in a number of different ways. Discussions among scholars in which the convergence and perhaps more importantly the divergence between different faith traditions are explored and appreciated are very valuable. On another level, it is helpful when there are encounters between ordinary but practicing followers of different religions in which each shares their experiences. This is perhaps the most effective way of appreciating others' teachings. In my own case, for example, my meetings with the late Thomas Merton, a Catholic monk of the Cistercian order, were deeply inspiring. They helped me develop a profound admiration for the teachings of Christianity. I also feel that occasional meetings between religious leaders joining together to pray for a common cause are extremely useful. The gathering at Assisi in Italy in 1986, when representatives of the world's major religions gathered to pray for peace, was, I believe, tremendously beneficial to many religious believers insofar as it symbolized the solidarity and a commitment to peace of all those taking part.

Finally, I feel that the practice of members of different faith traditions going on joint pilgrimages together can be very helpful. It was in this spirit that in 1993 I went to Lourdes, and then to Jerusalem, a site holy to three of the world's great religions. I have also paid visits to various Hindu, Islamic, Jain, and Sikh shrines both in India and abroad. More recently following a seminar devoted to discussing and practicing meditation in the Christian and Buddhist traditions, I joined an historic pilgrimage of practitioners of both traditions in a program of prayers, meditation, and dialogue under the Bodhi tree at Bodh Gaya in India. This is one of Buddhism's most important shrines.

When exchanges like these occur, followers of one tradition will find that, just as in the case of their own, the teachings of others' faiths are a source both of spiritual inspiration and of ethical guidance to their followers. It will also become clear that irrespective of doctrinal and other differences, all the major world religions are concerned with helping individuals to become good human beings. All emphasize love and compassion, patience, tolerance, forgiveness, humility, and so on, and all are capable of helping individuals to develop these. Moreover, the example given by the founders of each major religion clearly demonstrates a concern for helping others find happiness

through developing these qualities. So far as their own lives were concerned, each conducted themselves with great simplicity. Ethical discipline and love for all others was the hallmark of their lives. They did not live luxuriously like emperors and kings. Instead, they voluntarily accepted suffering—without consideration of the hardships involved—in order to benefit humanity as a whole. In their teachings, all placed special emphasis on developing love and compassion and renouncing selfish desires. And each of them called on us to transform our hearts and minds. Indeed, whether we have faith or not, all are worthy of our profound admiration.

At the same time as engaging in dialogue with followers of other religions, we must, of course, implement in our daily life the teachings of our own religion. Once we have experienced the benefit of love and compassion, and of ethical discipline, we will easily recognize the value of others' teachings. But for this, it is essential to realize that religious practice entails a lot more than merely saying, "I believe" or, as in Buddhism, "I take refuge." There is also more to it than just visiting temples, or shrines, or churches. And taking religious teachings is of little benefit if they do not enter the heart but remain at the level of intellect alone. Simply relying on faith without understanding and without implementation is of limited value. I often tell Tibetans that carrying a *mala* (something like a rosary) does not make a person a genuine religious practitioner. The efforts we make sincerely to transform ourselves spiritually are what make us genuine religious practitioners.

We come to see the overriding importance of genuine practice when we recognize that, along with ignorance, individuals' unhealthy relationships with their beliefs is the other major factor in religious disharmony. Far from applying the teachings of their religion in our personal lives, we have a tendency to use them to reinforce our self-centered attitudes. We relate to our religion as something we own or as a label that separates us from others. Surely this is misguided? Instead of using the nectar of religion to purify the poisonous elements of our hearts and minds, there is a danger when we think like this of using these negative elements to poison the nectar of religion.

Yet we must acknowledge that this reflects another problem, one which is implicit in all religions. I refer to the claims each has of being the one "true" religion. How are we to resolve this difficulty? It is true that from the point of view of the individual practitioner, it is essential to have a single-pointed commitment to one's own faith. It is also true that this depends on the deep conviction that one's own path is the sole mediator of truth. But at the same time, we have to find some means of reconciling this belief with the reality of a multiplicity of similar claims. In practical terms, this involves individual practitioners finding a way at least to accept the validity of the teachings of other religions while maintaining a wholehearted commitment to their own. As far as the validity of the metaphysical truth claims of a given religion is concerned, that is of course the internal business of that particular tradition.

In my own case, I am convinced that Buddhism provides me with the most effective framework within which to situate my efforts to develop spiritually through cultivating love and compassion. At the same time, I must acknowledge that while Buddhism represents the best path for me—that is, it suits my character, my temperament, my inclinations, and my cultural background—the same will be true of Christianity for Christians. For them, Christianity is the best way. On the basis of my conviction, I cannot, therefore, say that Buddhism is best for everyone.

I sometimes think of religion in terms of medicine for the human spirit. Independent of its usage and suitability to a particular individual in a particular condition, we really cannot judge a medicine's efficacy. We are not justified in saying this medicine is very good because of such and such ingredients. If you take the patient and the medicine's effect on that person out of the equation, it hardly makes sense. What is relevant is to say that in the case of this particular patient with its particular illness, this medicine is the most effective. Similarly with different religious traditions, we can say that this one is most effective for this particular individual. But it is unhelpful to try to argue on the basis of philosophy or metaphysics that one religion is better than another. The important thing is surely its effectiveness in individual cases.

My way to resolve the seeming contradiction between each religion's claim to "one truth and one religion" and the reality of the multiplicity of faiths is thus to understand that in the case of a single individual, there can indeed be only one truth, one religion. However, from the perspective of human society at large, we must accept the concept of "many truths, many religions." To continue with our medical analogy, in the case of one particular patient, the suitable medicine is in fact the one medicine. But clearly that does not mean that there may not be other medicines suitable to other patients.

To my way of thinking, the diversity that exists among the various religious traditions is enormously enriching. There is thus no need to try to find ways of saying that ultimately all religions are the same. They are similar in that they all emphasize the indispensability of love and compassion in the context of ethical discipline. But to say this is not to say that they are all essentially one. The contradictory understanding of creation and beginninglessness articulated by Buddhism, Christianity, and Hinduism, for example, means that in the end we have to part company when it comes to metaphysical claims, in spite of the many practical similarities that undoubtedly exist. These contradictions may not be very important in the beginning stages of religious practice. But as we advance along the path of one tradition or another, we are compelled at some point to acknowledge fundamental differences. For example, the concept of rebirth in Buddhism and various other ancient Indian traditions may turn out to be incompatible with the Christian idea of salvation. This need not be a cause for dismay, however. Even within Buddhism itself, in the realm of metaphysics there are diametrically opposing views. At the very least, such diversity means that we have different frameworks within which to locate ethical discipline and the development of spiritual values. That is why I do not advocate a super or a new world religion. It would mean that we would lose the unique characteristics of the different faith traditions.

Some people, it is true, hold that the Buddhist concept of *shunyata,* or emptiness, is ultimately the same as certain approaches to understanding the concept of God. Nevertheless, there remain difficulties with this. The first is that while of course we can interpret these concepts, to what extent can we be faithful to the original teachings if we do so? There are compelling similarities between the Mahayana Buddhist concept of *Dhar-makaya, Sambogakaya,* and *Nirmanakaya* and the Christian trinity of God as Father, Son, and Holy Spirit. But to say, on the basis of this, that Buddhism and Christianity are ultimately the same is to go a bit far, I think! As an old Tibetan saying goes, we must beware of trying to put a yak's head on a sheep's body—or vice versa.

What is required instead is that we develop a genuine sense of religious pluralism in spite of the different claims of different faith traditions. This is especially true if we are serious in our respect for human rights as a universal principle. In this regard, I find the concept of a world parliament of religions very appealing. To begin with, the word "parliament" conveys a sense of democracy, while the plural "religions" underlines the importance of the principle of a multiplicity of faith traditions. The truly pluralist perspective on religion which the idea of such a parliament suggests could, I believe, be of great help. It would avoid the extremes of religious bigotry on the one hand, and the urge toward unnecessary syncretism on the other.

Connected with this issue of interreligious harmony, I should perhaps say something about religious conversion. This is a question which must be taken extremely seriously. It is essential to realize that the mere fact of conversion alone will not make an individual a better person, that is to say, a more disciplined, a more compassionate, and a warm-hearted person. Much more helpful, therefore, is for the individual to concentrate on transforming themselves spiritually through the practice of restraint, virtue, and compassion. To the extent that the insights or practices of other religions are useful or relevant to our own faith, it is valuable to learn from others. In some cases, it may even be helpful to adopt certain of them. Yet when this is done wisely, we can remain firmly committed to our own faith. This way is best because it carries with it no danger of confusion, especially with respect to the different ways of life that tend to go with different faith traditions.

Given the diversity to be found among individual human beings, it is of course bound to be the case that out of many millions of practitioners of a particular religion, a handful will find that another religion's approach to ethics and spiritual development is more satisfactory. For some, the concept of rebirth and karma will seem highly effective in inspiring the aspiration to develop love and compassion within the context of responsibility. For others, the concept of a transcendent, loving creator will come to seem more so. In such circumstances, it is crucial for those individuals to question themselves again and again. They must ask, "Am I attracted to this other religion for the right reasons? Is it merely the cultural and ritual aspects that are appealing? Or is it the essential teachings? Do I suppose that if I convert to this new religion it will be less demanding than my present one?" I say this because it has often struck me that when people do convert to a religion outside their own heritage, quite often they adopt certain superficial aspects of the culture to which their new faith belongs. But their practice may not go very much deeper than that.

In the case of a person who decides after a process of long and mature reflection to adopt a different religion, it is very important that they remember the positive contribution to humanity of each religious tradition. The danger is that the individual may, in seeking to justify their decision to others, criticize their previous faith. It is essential to avoid this. Just because that tradition is no long effective in the case of one individual does not mean it is no longer of benefit to humanity. On the contrary, we can be certain that it has been an inspiration to millions of people in the past, that it inspires millions today, and that it will inspire millions in the path of love and compassion in the future.

The important point to keep in mind is that ultimately the whole purpose of religion is to facilitate love and compassion, patience, tolerance, humility, forgiveness, and so on. If we neglect these, changing our religion will be of no help. In the same way, even if we are fervent believers in our own faith, it will avail us nothing if we neglect to implement these qualities in our daily lives. Such a believer is no better off than a patient with some fatal illness who merely reads a medical treatise but fails to undertake the treatment prescribed.

Moreover, if we who are practitioners of religion are not compassionate and disciplined, how can we expect it of others? If we can establish genuine harmony derived from mutual respect and understanding, religion has enormous potential to speak with authority on such vital moral questions as peace and disarmament, social and political justice, the natural environment, and many other matters affecting all humanity. But until we put our own spiritual teachings into practice, we will never be taken seriously. And this means, among other things, setting a good example through developing good relations with other faith traditions.

⊚ CRITICAL QUESTIONS

1. Do you agree that "it is unhelpful to try to argue on the basis of philosophy or metaphysics that one religion is better than another"? Why, or why not?
2. Do you think that it is important to develop a "genuine sense of religious pluralism"? Present reasons in support of your answer.
3. What, from the Dalai Lama's point of view, is the "whole purpose of religion"? Do you agree? Why, or why not?

14.7 ARE ALL RELIGIONS THE SAME?

You may have had conversations with friends or relatives about whether all religions are essentially alike. If you have, the discussion sooner or later probably got around to the issue of in what ways they may or may not be essentially the same. Someone might have said, "Oh, all of them believe in God." And someone else might have asserted that they basically teach the same moral code. Perhaps someone else claimed they are the same in some respects and not in others. Maybe some used the popular image of a mountain with one summit but different religious paths leading to that summit. Whatever positions people staked out about religious sameness and difference, all most likely agreed that religious tolerance was a good thing and deplored religious intolerance.

We tend to think that if we acknowledge the sameness or near sameness of all religions, then we are promoting religious tolerance, which is something the world sorely needs in an age when religious conflict can too quickly turn into religious violence. Of course we know that there is little sense in being asked to tolerate a religion very much like your own. That is easy. Tolerance becomes a virtue only when it requires you to grant the same rights and privileges as you wish granted to your own religion to other religions that are very different from your own.

One difficulty that many face when they get into conversations with others about religion is ignorance. Many Americans know very little about religions other than Christianity and Judaism. They also know very little about the differences within their own religious traditions. It is easy to be either tolerant or intolerant with respect to religions you know next to nothing about beyond their name.

Stephan Prothero, Professor of Religion at Boston University and author of the best selling book, *Religious Literacy*, is the author of the next selection taken from the introduction to his latest book, *God is Not One*. He argues that claims about the sameness of all religions mask the many differences that exist. He also argues that it is dangerous to deny religious differences. Why? Read and see.

1. What is "Godthink," and why does Prothero call it a "rabbit hole"?
2. Why is it important to understand religious people as they are, not as well-intentioned perennial philosophers imagine them?
3. How does Prothero answer the question, "Is religion toxic or tonic"?
4. What is the "four-step approach" to understanding the world's religions?

God Is Not One

STEPHEN PROTHERO

At least since the first petals of the counterculture bloomed across Europe and the United States in the 1960s, it has been fashionable to affirm that all religions are beautiful and all are true. This claim, which reaches back to *All Religions Are One* (1795) by the English poet, printmaker, and prophet William Blake, is as odd as it is intriguing.[1] No one argues that different economic systems or political regimes are one and the same. Capitalism and socialism are so obviously at odds that their differences hardly bear mentioning. The same goes for democracy and monarchy. Yet scholars continue to claim that religious rivals such as Hinduism and Islam, Judaism and Christianity are, by some miracle of the imagination, essentially the same, and this view resounds in the echo chamber of popular culture, not least in Dan Brown's multi-million-dollar *Da Vinci Code* franchise.

The most popular metaphor for this view portrays the great religions as different paths up the same mountain. "It is possible to climb life's mountain from any side, but when the top is reached the trails converge," writes philosopher of religion Huston Smith. "At base, in the foothills of theology, ritual, and organizational structure, the religions are distinct. Differences in culture, history, geography, and collective temperament all make for diverse starting points.... But beyond these differences, the same goal beckons."[2] This is a comforting notion in a world in which

religious violence often seems more present and potent than God. But is it true? If so, what might be waiting for us at the summit?

According to Mohandas Gandhi, "Belief in one God is the cornerstone of all religions," so it is toward this one God that all religious people are climbing. When it comes to divinity, however, one is not the religions' only number. Many Buddhists believe in no god, and many Hindus believe in thousands. Moreover, the characters of these gods differ wildly. Is God a warrior like Hinduism's Kali or a mild-mannered wanderer like Christianity's Jesus? Is God personal, or impersonal? Male, or female (or both)? Or beyond description altogether?

Like Gandhi, the Dalai Lama affirms that "the essential message of all religions is very much the same."[3] In his view, however, what the world's religions share is not so much God as the Good—the sweet harmony of peace, love, and understanding that religion writer Karen Armstrong also finds at the heart of every religion. To be sure, the world's religious traditions *do* share many ethical precepts. No religion tells you it is okay to have sex with your mother or to murder your brother. The Golden Rule can be found not only in the Christian Bible and the Jewish Talmud but also in Confucian and Hindu books. No religion, however, sees ethics alone as its reason for being. Jews understand *halakha* ("law" or

From *God is Not One: The Eight Rival Religions that Run the World—and Why Their Differences Matter*, (New York: Harper One, 2010), pp. 1–15; 22–23; 343–345. Copyright © 2010 Stephen Prothero.

"way") to include ritual too, and the Ten Commandments begin with how to worship God.

To be fair, those who claim that the world's religions are one and the same do not deny the undeniable fact that they differ in some particulars. Obviously, Christians do not go on pilgrimage to Mecca, and Muslims do not practice baptism. Religious paths do diverge, Huston Smith admits, in the "foothills" of dogma, rites, and institutions.[4] To claim that all religions are the same, therefore, is not to deny the differences among a Buddhist who believes in no god, a Jew who believes in one God, and a Hindu who believes in many gods. It is simply to claim that the mathematics of divinity is a matter of the foothills. Debates over whether God has a body (yes, say Mormons; no, say Muslims) or whether human beings have souls (yes, say Hindus; no, say Buddhists) do not matter, because, as Hindu teacher Swami Sivananda writes, "The fundamentals or essentials of all religions are the same. There is difference only in the non-essentials."[5]

This is a lovely sentiment but it is dangerous, disrespectful, and untrue. For more than a generation we have followed scholars and sages down the rabbit hole into a fantasy world in which all gods are one. This wishful thinking is motivated in part by an understandable rejection of the exclusivist missionary view that only you and your kind will make it to heaven or Paradise. For most of world history, human beings have seen religious rivals as inferior to themselves—practitioners of empty rituals, perpetrators of bogus miracles, purveyors of fanciful myths. The Age of Enlightenment in the eighteenth century popularized the ideal of religious tolerance, and we are doubtless better for it. But the idea of religious unity is wishful thinking nonetheless, and it has not made the world a safer place. In fact, this naive theological groupthink—call it Godthink—has made the world more dangerous by blinding us to the clashes of religions that threaten us worldwide. It is time we climbed out of the rabbit hole and back to reality.

The world's religious rivals do converge when it comes to ethics, but they diverge sharply on doctrine, ritual, mythology, experience, and law. These differences may not matter to mystics or philosophers of religion, but they matter to ordinary religious people. Muslims do not think that the pilgrimage to Mecca they call the hajj is inessential. In fact, they include it among the Five Pillars of Islam. Catholics do not think that baptism is inessential. In fact, they include it among their seven sacraments. But religious differences do not just matter to religious practitioners. They have real effects in the real world. People refuse to marry this Muslim or that Hindu because of them. And in some cases religious differences move adherents to fight and to kill.

One purpose of the "all religions are one" mantra is to stop this fighting and this killing. And it is comforting to pretend that the great religions make up one big, happy family. But this sentiment, however well-intentioned, is neither accurate nor ethically responsible. God is not one. Faith in the unity of religions is just that— faith (perhaps even a kind of fundamentalism). And the leap that gets us there is an act of the hyperactive imagination.

ALLERGIC TO ARGUMENT

One reason we are willing to follow our fantasies down the rabbit hole of religious unity is that we have become uncomfortable with argument. Especially when it comes to religion, we desperately want everyone to get along. In my Boston University courses, I work hard to foster respectful arguments. My students are good with "respectful," but they are allergic to "argument." They see arguing as ill-mannered, and even among friends they avoid it at almost any cost. Though they will debate the merits of the latest Coen brothers movie or U2 CD, they agree not to disagree about almost everything else. Especially when it comes to religion, young Americans at least are far more likely to say "I feel" than "I think" or (God forbid) "I believe."

The Jewish tradition distinguishes between arguing for the sake of victory (which it does not value) and "arguing for the sake of God" (which it does).[6] Today the West is awash in arguments on radio, television, and the Internet, but these arguments are almost always advanced not in service of the truth but for the purpose of ratings or self-aggrandizement or both. So we won't argue for anyone's sake and, when others do, we don't see anything godly in it. The ideal of religious tolerance has morphed into the straitjacket of religious agreement.

Yet we know in our bones that the world's religions are different from one another. As my colleague Adam Seligman has argued, the notion of religious tolerance assumes differences, since there is no need to tolerate a religion that is essentially the same as your own.[7] We pretend these differences are trivial because it makes us feel safer, or more moral. But pretending that the world's religions are the same does not make our world safer. Like all forms of ignorance, it makes our world more dangerous. What we need on this furiously religious planet is a realistic view of where religious rivals clash and where they can cooperate. Approaching this volatile topic from this new angle may be scary. But the world is what it is. And both tolerance and respect are empty virtues until we actually know something about whomever it is we are supposed to be tolerating or respecting.

PRETEND PLURALISM

Huston Smith's *The World's Religions* has sold over two million copies since it first appeared in 1958 as *The Religions of Man*. One source of its success is Smith's earnest and heartfelt proclamation of the essential unity of the world's religions. Focusing on the timeless ideals of what he calls "our wisdom traditions," Smith emphasizes spiritual experience, keeping the historical facts, institutional realities, and ritual observances to a minimum. His exemplars are extraordinary rather than ordinary practitioners—mystics such as Islam's al-Ghazali, Christianity's St. John of the Cross, and Daoism's Zhuangzi. By his own admission, Smith writes about "religions at their best," showcasing their "cleaner side" rather than airing their dirty laundry, emphasizing their "inspired" philosophies and theologies over wars and rumors thereof. He writes sympathetically and in the American idioms of optimism and hope. When it comes to religion, Smith writes, things are "better than they seem."[8]

When Smith wrote these words over a half century ago, they struck just the right chord. In the wake of World War II and the Holocaust, partisans of what was coming to be known as the Judeo-Christian tradition were coming to see Protestantism, Catholicism, and Judaism as three equal expressions of one common faith. Meanwhile, fans of Aldous Huxley's *The Perennial Philosophy* (1945) and Joseph Campbell's *The Hero with a Thousand Faces* (1949) were denouncing the longstanding human tendency to divide the world's religions into two categories: the false ones and your own. The world's religions, they argued, are different paths up the same mountain. Or, as Swami Sivananda put it, "The Koran or the Zend-Avesta or the Bible is as much a sacred book as the Bhagavad-Gita.... Ahuramazda, Isvara, Allah, Jehovah are different names for one God."[9] Today this approach is the new orthodoxy, enshrined in bestselling books by Karen Armstrong and in Bill Moyers' television interviews with Joseph Campbell, Huston Smith, and other leading advocates of the "perennial philosophy."

This perennialism may seem to be quite pluralistic, but only at first glance. Catholic theologian Karl Rahner has been rightly criticized for his theory that many Buddhists, Hindus, and Jews are actually "anonymous Christians" who will make it to heaven in the world to come. Conservative Catholics see this theory as a violation of their longstanding conviction that "outside the church there is no salvation." But liberals also condemn Rahner's theology, in their case as condescending. "It would be impossible to find anywhere in the world," writes Catholic theologian Hans Küng, "a sincere Jew, Muslim or atheist who would not regard the assertion that he is an 'anonymous Christian' as presumptuous."[10]

The perennial philosophers, however, are no less presumptuous. They, too, conscript outsiders into their tradition quite against their will. When Huxley's guru Swami Prabhavananda says that all religions lead to God, the God he is imagining is Hindu. And when my Hindu students quote their god Krishna in their scripture the Bhagavad Gita (4:11)—"In whatsoever way any come to Me, in that same way I grant them favor"—the truth they are imagining is a Hindu truth. Just a few blocks away from my office stands the Ramakrishna Vedanta Society. Its chapel looks conspicuously like a mainline Protestant church, yet at the front of this worship space sit images of various Hindu deities, and around the room hang symbols of the world's religions—a star and crescent for Islam, a dharma wheel for Buddhism, a cross for Christianity, a Star of David for Judaism. When my friend Swami Tyagananda, who runs this Society, says that all religions are one, he is speaking as a person of faith and hope. When Huston Smith says that all religions are one, he is speaking in the same idiom.

I understand what these men are doing. They are not describing the world but reimagining it. They are hoping that their hope will call up in us feelings of brotherhood and sisterhood. In the face of religious bigotry and bloodshed, past and present, we cannot help but be drawn to such vision, and such hope. Yet, we must see both for what they are, not mistaking either for clear-eyed analysis. And we must admit that there are situations where a lack of understanding about the differences between, say, Sunni and Shia Islam produces more rather than less violence. Unfortunately, we live in a world where religion seems as likely to detonate a bomb as to defuse one. So while we need idealism, we need realism even more. We need to understand religious people as they are—not just at their best but also their worst. We need to look at not only their awe-inspiring architecture and gentle mystics but also their bigots and suicide bombers.

RELIGION MATTERS

Whether the world's religions are more alike than different is one of the crucial questions of our time. Until recently, most sociologists were sure that religion was fading away, that as countries industrialized and modernized, they would become more secular. And religion is receding today in many Western European countries. But more than nine out of every ten Americans believe in God, and, with the notable exception of Western Europe, the rest of the world is furiously religious. Across Latin America and Africa and Asia, religion matters to Christians who praise Jesus after the birth of a child, to Muslims who turn to Allah for comfort as they are facing cancer, and to Hindus who appeal to the goddess

Lakshmi to bring them health, wealth, and wisdom. And it still matters in Western Europe, too, where Catholic attitudes toward women and the body, for example, continue to inform everyday life in Spain and Italy, and where the call to prayer goes up five times a day in mosques from Amsterdam to Paris to Berlin.

But religion is not merely a private affair. It matters socially, economically, politically, and militarily. Religion may or may not move mountains, but it is one of the prime movers in politics worldwide. It moves elections in the United States, where roughly half of all Americans say they would not vote for an atheist, and in India, which has in the *Hindutva* (Hinduness) movement its own version of America's Religious Right. Religion moves economies too. Pilgrims to Mecca and Jerusalem pump billions of dollars per year into the economies of Saudi Arabia and Israel. Sales of the Bible in the United States alone run roughly $500 million annually, and Islamic banking approaches $1 trillion.[11]

All too often world history is told as if religion did not matter. The Spanish conquered New Spain for gold, and the British came to New England to catch fish. The French Revolution had nothing to do with Catholicism, and the U.S. civil rights movement was a purely humanitarian endeavor. But even if religion makes no sense to you, you need to make sense of religion to make sense of the world.

In the twenty-first century alone, religion has toppled the Bamiyan statues of the Buddha in Afghanistan and the Twin Towers in New York City. It has stirred up civil war in Sri Lanka and Darfur. And it has resisted coalition troops in Iraq. In many countries, religion has a powerful say in determining what people will eat and under what circumstances they can be married or divorced. Religious rivalries are either simmering or boiling over in Myanmar, Uganda, Sudan, and Kurdistan. The contest over Jerusalem and the Middle East is at least as religious as it is economic or political. Hinduism and Buddhism were key motivators in the decades-long civil war that recently ravaged Sri Lanka. And religion remains a major motivator in Kashmir, where two nuclear powers, the Hindu-majority state of India and the Muslim-majority state of Pakistan, remain locked in an ancient territorial dispute with palpable religious overtones. Our understanding of these battlefields is not advanced one inch by the dogma that "all religions are one."

TOXIC AND TONIC

The beginning of the twenty-first century saw dozens of bestselling books in both Europe and the United States by so-called New Atheists. Writers such as Richard Dawkins, Sam Harris, Daniel Dennett, Christopher Hitchens, and Michel Onfray preach their own version of Godthink, aping the perennial philosophers by loading all religions into one boat. This crew, however, sees only the shared sins of the great religions—the same idiocy, the same oppression. Look at the Crusades, 9/11, and all the religiously inspired violence in between, they say. Look at the ugly legacies of sexist (and sexually repressed) scriptures. Religion is hazardous to your health and poisonous to society.

Of course, religion does not exist in the abstract. You cannot practice religion in general any more than you can speak language in general. So generalizing about the overall effects of religion is a hazard of its own. Nonetheless, the main thesis of the New Atheists is surely true: religion *is* one of the greatest forces for evil in world history. Yet religion is also one of the greatest forces for good. Religions have put God's stamp of approval on all sorts of demonic schemes, but religions also possess the power to say no to evil and banality. Yes, religion gave us the Inquisition. Closer to our own time, it gave us the assassinations of Egypt's president Anwar Sadat by Islamic extremists, of Israel's prime minister Yitzhak Rabin by a Jewish gunman, and of India's prime minister Indira Gandhi by Sikh bodyguards. But religion also gave us abolitionism and the civil rights movement. Many, perhaps most, of the world's greatest paintings, novels, sculptures, buildings, and musical compositions are also religiously inspired. Without religion, there would be no Alhambra or Angkor Wat, no reggae or Gregorian chant, no *Last Supper* by Leonardo da Vinci or *Four Quartets* by T. S. Eliot, no Shusaku Endo's *Silence* or Elie Wiesel's *Night*.

Political scientists assume that human beings are motivated primarily by power, while economists assume that they are motivated primarily by greed. It is impossible, however, to understand the actions of individuals, communities, societies, or nations in purely political or economic terms. You don't have to believe in the power of prayer to see the power of religious beliefs and behaviors to stir people to action. Religion was behind both the creation of the Islamic Republic of Pakistan in 1947 and the founding of the state of Israel in 1948, both the Iranian Revolution of 1979 and the Reagan Revolution of the 1980s.

When I was a professor at Georgia State University in Atlanta, I required my students to read Nazi theology. I wanted them to understand how some Christians bent the words of the Bible into weapons aimed at Jews and how these weapons found their mark at Auschwitz and Dachau. My Christian students responded to these disturbing readings with one disturbing voice: the Nazis were not real Christians, they informed me, since real Christians would never kill Jews in crematories. I found this response terrifying, and I still do, since failing to grasp how Nazism was fueled by ancient Christian hatred of Jews as "Christ killers" allows Christians to absolve themselves of any responsibility for reckoning with how their religion contributed to these horrors.

After 9/11 many Muslims absolved themselves too. The terrorists whose faith turned jets into weapons of mass destruction—who left Qurans in their suitcases and shouted *"Allahu Akbar"* ("God is great") as they bore down on their targets—were not real Muslims, they said. Real Muslims would never kill women and children and civilians. So they, too, absolved themselves of any responsibility for reckoning with the dark side of their tradition.

Is religion toxic or tonic? Is it one of the world's greatest forces for evil, or one of the world's greatest forces for good? Yes and yes, which is to say that religion is a force far too powerful to ignore. Gandhi was assassinated by a Hindu extremist convinced that he had given too much quarter to Muslims when he agreed to the partition of India and the creation of Pakistan. But Gandhi's strategy of *satyagraha,* or nonviolent resistance, was inspired by religion too, deeply influenced by the Jain principle of *ahimsa* (noninjury) and by the pacifism of Jesus's Sermon on the

Mount. Yes, religion gave the United States the racist hatred of the Ku Klux Klan, but it also put an end to discriminatory Jim Crow legislation.

Today it is impossible to understand American politics without knowing something about the Bible used to swear in U.S. presidents and evoked almost daily on the floor of the U.S. Congress. It is impossible to understand politics in India and the economy of China without knowing something about Hinduism and Confucianism. At the dawn of the twentieth century, in *The Souls of Black Folk* (1903), W. E. B. DuBois prophesied that "the problem of the Twentieth Century is the problem of the color-line." The events of 9/11 and beyond suggest that the problem of the twenty-first century is the problem of the religion line.[12]

KOYAANISQATSI

What the world's religions share is not so much a finish line as a starting point. And where they begin is with this simple observation: something is wrong with the world. In the Hopi language, the word *Koyaanisqatsi* tells us that life is out of balance. Shakespeare's *Hamlet* tells us that there is something rotten not only in the state of Denmark but also in the state of human existence. Hindus say we are living in the *kali yuga,* the most degenerate age in cosmic history. Buddhists say that human existence is pockmarked by suffering. Jewish, Christian, and Islamic stories tell us that this life is not Eden; Zion, heaven, and Paradise lie out ahead.

Religious folk worldwide agree that something has gone awry. They part company, however, when it comes to stating just what has gone wrong, and they diverge sharply when they move from diagnosing the human problem to prescribing how to solve it. Christians see sin as the problem, and salvation from sin as the religious goal. Buddhists see suffering (which, in their tradition, is *not* ennobling) as the problem, and liberation from suffering as the religious goal. If practitioners of the world's religions are all mountain climbers, then they are on very different mountains, climbing very different peaks, and using very different tools and techniques in their ascents.

Because religious traditions do not stay static as they move into new centuries, countries, and circumstances, the differences inside each of the world's religions are vast. Religious Studies scholars are quick to point out that there are many Buddhisms, not just one. And so it goes with all the world's religions. Christians align themselves with Roman Catholicism, Orthodoxy, and Protestantism, and fast-growing Mormonism may well be emerging as Christianity's fourth way. Jews call themselves Orthodox, Conservative, Reform, Reconstructionist, and secular. Hindus worship a dizzying variety of gods in a dizzying variety of ways. And as every American and European soldier who fought in Iraq and Afghanistan can attest, Shia and Sunni Islam are in many respects quite distinct.

While I do not believe we are now witnessing a "clash of civilizations" between Christianity and Islam, it is a fantasy to imagine that the world's two largest religions are in any meaningful sense the same, or that interfaith dialogue between Christians and Muslims will magically bridge the gap. You would think that champions of multiculturalism would warm to this fact, glorying in the diversity inside and across religious traditions. But even among multiculturalists, the tendency is to pretend that the differences between, say, Christianity and Islam are more apparent than real, and that the differences *inside* religious traditions just don't warrant the fuss practitioners continue to make over them. Meanwhile, the worldwide Anglican Communion splinters over homosexuality, and in the United States hot-button issues such as abortion and stem-cell research drive Protestants into two opposing camps.

For more than a century, scholars have searched for the essence of religion. They thought they found this holy grail in God, but then they discovered Buddhists and Jains who deny God's existence. Today it is widely accepted that there is no one essence that all religions share. What they share are family resemblances—tendencies toward this belief or that behavior. In the family of religions, kin tend to perform rituals. They tend to tell stories about how life and death began and to write down these stories in scriptures. They tend to cultivate techniques of ecstasy and devotion. They tend to organize themselves into institutions and to gather in sacred places at sacred times. They tend to instruct human beings how to act toward one another. They tend to profess this belief or that about the gods and the supernatural. They tend to invest objects and places with sacred import. Philosopher of religion Ninian Smart has referred to these tendencies as the seven "dimensions" of religion: the ritual, narrative, experiential, institutional, ethical, doctrinal, and material dimensions.[13]

These family resemblances are just tendencies, however. Just as there are tall people in short families (none of the men in Michael Jordan's family was over six feet tall), there are religions that deny the existence of God and religions that get along just fine without creeds. Something is a religion when it shares enough of this DNA to belong to the family of religions. What makes the members of this family different (and themselves) is how they mix and match these dimensions. Experience is central in Daoism and Buddhism. Hinduism and Judaism emphasize the narrative dimension. The ethical dimension is crucial in Confucianism. The Islamic and Yoruba traditions are to a great extent about ritual. And doctrine is particularly important to Christians.

The world's religious rivals are clearly related, but they are more like second cousins than identical twins. They do not teach the same doctrines. They do not perform the same rituals. And they do not share the same goals.

DIFFERENT PROBLEMS, DIFFERENT GOALS

After I wrote *Religious Literacy: What Every American Needs to Know—and Doesn't* (2007), I received many letters and emails from readers confessing their ignorance of the world's religions and asking for a single book they could read to become religiously literate. This book [*God is Not One*] is written for them. It attends to the idiosyncrasies of each of the great religions: for example, Yoruba practitioners' preoccupation with power, Daoists' emphasis on naturalness, and Muslims' attention to the world to come.

At the heart of this project is a simple, four-part approach to the religions, which I have been using for years in the classroom and at lectures around the world. Each religion articulates:

- a *problem*;
- a *solution* to this problem, which also serves as the religious goal;

- a *technique* (or techniques) for moving from this problem to this solution; and
- an *exemplar* (or exemplars) who chart this path from problem to solution.

For example, in Christianity …

- the problem is sin;
- the solution (or goal) is salvation;
- the technique for achieving salvation is some combination of faith and good works; and
- the exemplars who chart this path are the saints in Roman Catholicism and Orthodoxy and ordinary people of faith in Protestantism.

And in Buddhism …

- the problem is suffering;
- the solution (or goal) is nirvana;
- the technique for achieving nirvana is the Noble Eightfold Path, which includes such classic Buddhist practices as meditation and chanting; and
- the exemplars who chart this path are *arhats* (for Theravada Buddhists), *bodhisattvas* (for Mahayana Buddhists), or *lamas* (for Vajrayana Buddhists).

This four-step approach is admittedly simplistic. You cannot sum up thousands of years of Christian faith or Buddhist practice in four sentences. So this model is just a starting point and must be nuanced along the way. For example, Roman Catholics and Protestants are divided about how to achieve salvation, just as Mahayana and Theravada Buddhists are divided about how to achieve nirvana (or whether nirvana is an "achievement" at all). One of the virtues of this simple scheme, however, is that it helps to make plain the *differences* across and inside the religious traditions. Are Buddhists trying to achieve salvation? Of course not, since they don't even believe in sin. Are Christians trying to achieve nirvana? No, since for them suffering isn't something that must be overcome. In fact, it might even be a good thing.…

BIG QUESTIONS

Every year I tell my BU undergraduates that there are two worthy pursuits for college students. One is pre-professional—preparing for a career that will put food on the table and a roof overhead. The other is more personal—finding big questions worth asking, which is to say questions that cannot be answered in a semester, or even a lifetime (or more). How do things come into being? How do they cease to be? How does change happen? How does anything stay the same? What is the self? Who (or what) is God? What happens when we die? As predictably as fall follows summer, incoming college students bring into classrooms big questions of this sort. Just as predictably, many professors try to steer them toward smaller things—questions that can be covered in an hour-long lecture, and asked and answered on a final exam. But the students have it right. At least in this case, bigger is better.

Before I came to describe myself as religiously confused, I thought I had the answers to the big questions. I now know I didn't even have the questions right. If, as Muhammad once said, "Asking good questions is half of learning," I was at best a half wit.[14] Today I try to follow the advice of the German poet Rainer Maria Rilke to "love the questions themselves," not least this one from the American mystic Walt Whitman:

> ... what saw you to tell us?
> What stays with you latest and deepest? of curious panics
> Of hard-fought engagements or sieges tremendous what deepest remains?[15]

NOTES

1. The sole surviving copy of this book can be found at the Huntington Library and Art Gallery in San Marino, California. See it online at: http://www.blakearchive.org/exist/blake/archive/work.xq?workid=aro&java=yes. Blake wrote, "As all men are alike (tho infinitely various), so all religions ... have one source," which he referred to as "the Poetic Genius."
2. Huston Smith, *The World's Religions: Our Great Wisdom Traditions* (New York: Harper San Francisco, 1991), 73.
3. Dalai Lama, *An Open Heart: Practicing Compassion in Everyday Life* (Boston: Little, Brown, 2001), 8–9.
4. Smith, *World's Religions*, 73. "Those who circle the mountain, trying to bring others around to their paths, are not climbing," Smith adds.
5. Swami Sivananda, "The Unity That Underlies All Religions," http://www.dlshq.org/religions/unirel.htm.
6. See Reuven Firestone, "Argue, for God's Sake—or, a Jewish Argument for Argument," *Journal of Ecumenical Studies* 39, no. 1–2 (2002): 47–57.
7. Adam B. Seligman, "Tolerance, Tradition and Modernity," *Cardozo Law Review* 24, no. 4 (2003): 1645–56. In addition to writing sociological works

on this topic, Seligman runs The Tolerance Project and the International Summer School on Religion and Public Life (http://www.issrpl.org).
8. Smith, *World's Religions*, 5, 388–89.
9. Sivananda, "Unity That Underlies All Religions."
10. Hans Küng, *On Being a Christian*, trans. Edward Quinn (Garden City, NY: Doubleday, 1976), 98.
11. Tracy McNicoll, "Courting Islamic Cash in France," *Newsweek*, September 21, 2009, 12.
12. W. E. B. DuBois, *The Souls of Black Folk Etches and Sketches* (Chicago: A. C. McClurg, 1903), 23. I first heard this argument from Eboo Patel of the Interfaith Youth Core.
13. Ninian Smart, *Dimensions of the Sacred: An Anatomy of the World's Beliefs* (Berkeley: Univ. of California Press, 1996).
14. James Fadiman and Robert Frager, eds., *Essential Sufism* (New York: HarperCollins), 82.
15. Rainer Maria Rilke, *Rilke on Love and Other Difficulties*, trans. John J. L Mood (New York: Norton, 1975), 25; Walt Whitman, "The Wound-Dresser," in his *Leaves of Grass* (Philadelphia: David McKay, 1891–92), 242.

◉ CRITICAL QUESTION

1. Do you agree with Prothero that not recognizing the many differences among the various religions is dangerous? Why or why not?

To access the *Voices of Wisdom*, 8th Edition, **Premium Website**, search for this book on CengageBrain.com.

Glossary

absolute skepticism. *See* skepticism.

Advaita Vedanta. A school of Hindu philosophy that teaches that reality is nondual (*advaita*).

aesthetics. A subdivision of the field of axiology (value theory) that has to do with philosophical reflection on a range of concepts such as beauty, harmony, and structure that are relevant to art and experiences of nature.

Allah. The Muslim name for God. Allah is viewed as a unitary sovereign, creator God of infinite mercy and goodness whose will is absolute.

altruism. The view holding that one ought to do what is in the best interest of others.

ambiguity. The word *ambiguity* refers to instances when linguistic meaning is unclear. For example, the word "bank" is ambiguous because without specified context it is unclear whether it refers to a place to keep money, the side of a river, or a type of shot in pool.

analytic statement. A statement that is necessarily true by virtue of the meaning of the words. According to Hume, such statements are about the relations of ideas, and it is not logically possible for their negation to be true. They are the opposite of synthetic statements.

anarchism. The political theory that governments, by their very nature, are immoral and should not be formed. It is based on the idea that only the individual has ultimate moral authority.

anatta (Anatman). A Buddhist term meaning "no-self," refers to the Buddhist doctrine that there is no Atman. It is the denial of the notion that a substance exists that constitutes the human self or soul.

anicca. A Buddhist term meaning "impermanence." According to this teaching, there are no eternal substances, essences, or ideal Forms (as in Plato's theory of Forms).

anomalies. New events that are inconsistent with prevailing laws and theories.

a posteriori. Latin meaning "following from" or "after," characterizes reasoning based on sense experience and identifies human experience as the place from which ideas come. Knowledge that comes from experience is called a posteriori.

a priori. Latin meaning "prior to" or "before," refers to reasoning based on reason (in contrast to sense experience) and identifies ideas as innate (acquired *prior* to sense experience) or as valid independent of experience. Mathematical knowledge is frequently characterized as a priori because its truth does not depend on sense experience.

Atman. Usually translated "Self." According to some schools of Hindu philosophy, it is pure consciousness or consciousness itself and constitutes the essence of all reality. It is to be distinguished from the ego, or individual self.

axiology. A branch of philosophy concerned with developing a theory of value. Ethics (moral value) and aesthetics (artistic value) are two main subdivisions.

behaviorism. The view that mental states are either equivalent to the behaviors of an organism or the dispositions to behave.

Brahman. A Sanskrit term that can refer to the creator God or, as in Shankara, to the source and essence of all reality. Sometimes translated as "Godhead," indicating the essence of the divine.

categorical imperative. A command or law that is unconditional. Such a law instructs us to do something regardless of the consequences. According to Kant, this is the principle of all morality. Kant characterized it as the highest moral law and formulated it in several ways, one of which states that humans should be treated as ends, not means.

cognitive relativism. The view that truth and standards of knowledge are relative rather than absolute. (*See* ethical relativism.)

coherence theory of truth. The theory that some proposition is true if and only if it is logically implied by some other true statement.

commonsense skepticism. *See* skepticism.

communism. A political and economic theory that rejects private ownership and maintains that the ideal society is classless.

compatibilism. *See* soft determinism.

compensatory justice. The sort of justice that demands the correct distribution of benefits to those who have suffered unfair hardship. Affirmative action programs are often justified on these grounds.

constructivists. Critics of foundationalism (see below) who maintain that rationality is a social construction.

correspondence theory of truth. The theory that some proposition is true if and only if it corresponds to the facts.

cosmological argument. An a posteriori argument from the existence of the universe (cosmos) to God as the cause, creator, or explanation of the universe's existence.

covering law model. A concept of explanation in the philosophy of science which holds that science explains events by reference to some natural law that includes (covers) the events.

critical theory. This type of theory developed out of the Marxist tradition and differs from "traditional theory" in explicitly seeking to develop ideas that liberate humans from social conditions that limit choices and opportunities. It is at once explanatory, practical, and normative.

Dao (Tao). A concept central to Chinese philosophy, usually translated as "The Way." It has a variety of meanings but often refers to the way of nature or the way reality functions.

de (te). A Chinese word meaning "excellence" or "power," often translated as "virtue."

deductive-nomological model. Another name for the covering law model (see above).

democracy. The political theory stating that the people are sovereign and have the right to rule.

deontological ethical theory. A theory (such as Kant's) that stresses the importance of the motive of doing one's duty as a determining factor in assessing the moral value of actions. It is the motive for, not the consequences of, actions that morally count.

descriptive. A concept that is usually contrasted with normative (what ought to be) and is used to refer to a type of reflection that seeks to describe the way things are in *fact*.

determinism. Also called simple determinism, the belief that every event has a cause—that is, for every event, there is a set of conditions such that, if the conditions are repeated, the event is repeated.

dharma. A Sanskrit term meaning "duty," "teachings," or "doctrines." In Hindu philosophy, it often refers to the moral law and order believed to be inherent in nature.

direct realism. *See* realism.

distributive justice. The fair distribution of benefits such as wealth, privileges, rights, and honors among the members of a society.

divine command theory. A position holding that what makes an action morally right is the fact that God commands or wills it.

double-aspect theory. The view that the mind and body are two different aspects of one substance, which is itself neither mental nor physical. *See* neutral monism.

dualism. A metaphysical theory that two fundamentally different things, usually characterized as mind and matter (body), are real.

egalitarianism. The view that all persons, just because they are persons, should share equally in all benefits and burdens.

Eightfold Path. The way of attaining enlightenment as taught by Buddhism; this path consists of right views, right thought, right speech, right action, right livelihood, right effort, right mindfulness, and right concentration.

empiricism. An epistemological theory holding that (1) knowledge derives from sense experience and (2) knowledge claims are verified by reference to sense experience.

epiphenomenalism. Refers to a theory that mental events are by-products of physical events.

epistemology. A branch of philosophy concerned with developing a theory of knowledge and truth.

ethical absolutism. A view that maintains that moral principles are universal and some of them ought never be violated or compromised.

ethical emotivism. The view that moral value derives from how people feel.

ethical nihilism. The view that moral value has no basis.

ethical relativism. A view that claims that there are no universal moral principles and the moral value of human actions depends upon social conventions and historical context.

ethical skepticism. The position that the existence of moral truth and the possibility of ethical knowledge is doubtful.

ethics. A subdivision of axiology concerned with the study of moral value.

eudaimonia. Usually translated as "happiness" or "living well" and can be thought of as self-realization. Aristotle uses the concept to refer to the final good or purpose of human action, namely, to realize or actualize essential human nature.

evidentialism. The view that we should have good evidence in support of a position before we accept it as true.

existentialism. A philosophical movement that takes as its starting point reflection on the concrete existence of humans and what it means to be a human being living in the sort of world in which we actually live.

fatalism. The view that some or all events are predetermined by an impersonal force or power.

five aggregates. These are physical form, sensation, conceptualization, dispositions to act, and consciousness. According to Buddhism, they constitute the processes that make up the individual.

five pillars of Islam. These are the five central practices of Islam: (1) witnessing that there is no God but Allah and that Muhammad is his Apostle; (2) *salat*, or mandatory prayers; (3) *zakat*, or mandatory alms; (4) fasting during the holy month of Ramadan; and (5) *hajj*, or pilgrimage to Mecca.

formal principle of justice. People ought to be treated fairly with respect to relevantly similar (or relevantly different) traits.

Forms. *See* theory of Forms.

foundationalism. The claim that rationality and knowledge rest on a firm foundation of self-evident truths or truths characterized as so reliable that no further justification is required.

Four Noble Truths. The name for the heart of the Buddha's teaching: (1) life is suffering; (2) the cause of suffering is craving; (3) suffering can be overcome; and (4) the Eightfold Path, or the Middle Way, of right understanding, thought, speech, action, livelihood, effort, mindfulness, and concentration is the way to attain release from suffering.

functionalism. A theory about the mind, holding that mental states are completely defined as functions of physical processes.

hard determinism. The theory that every event has a cause and that this fact is incompatible with the existence of free will. Hence, human beings should not be held morally responsible for their actions because it is impossible for them to do other than what they do.

hedonism. A moral theory holding that the highest or greatest good is pleasure.

hypothetico-deductive method. Sometimes called the "scientific method" because it involves deducing predictions that can be experimentally tested in order to check some hypothesis.

ideology. In a positive sense ideology refers to any system of beliefs and values that justify cultural, religious, and political practices. In a negative sense it refers to a system of beliefs and values that justify practices and institutions by concealing their social and historical origins.

incommensurable. A term that means not only incompatibility but also a degree of difference so fundamental that no value judgments are possible about incompatible views because they are based on a completely different set of assumptions.

idealism. A metaphysical theory that only ideas (minds and mental events) are real or that they are more real, valuable, and enduring than material things. In an ethical context, *idealistic* is sometimes used to refer to a person who lives by ideals or to a view based on principle.

identity theory. The view that mental events are identical with brain events.

indirect realism. *See* realism.

innate ideas. Refers to ideas we are born with, a concept used by rationalists to characterize the state of the human mind prior to sense experience.

interactionism. The theory that the mind and body, though they are two distinct and different substances, nevertheless can causally affect one another.

karma. From a Sanskrit word meaning "action"; it often refers to the consequences of actions and the natural moral law that governs actions called the law of karma ("You reap what you sow").

laissez-faire capitalism. An economic theory based on the idea of a totally free market.

law of noncontradiction. A cannot be A *and* not-A in the same respect and at the same time.

Li. A Confucian concept meaning order, ceremony, custom, and propriety.

libertarianism. The theory that human choice is not caused (determined) by antecedent events. Human beings are free agents with the power to decide contrary to the influence of character and inclination.

Hence, when deciding freely, humans can and should be held morally responsible. This term is also used in a political context to name a movement that supports the idea that the role of government ought to be severely restricted and individual freedom ought to be maximized.

logical positivism. A type of positivism (*see* positivism) that claims only those statements that are in principle capable of falsification are meaningful.

materialism. Also called physicalism, the metaphysical view holding that matter alone is real. Negatively, it is the denial of the existence of immaterial, mental, and spiritual reality. In an ethical context, it also refers to a value system that prizes material goods and possessions above other things.

material principle of justice. This refers to some specific trait on which decisions of distribution, retribution, and compensation are made—for example, all those who work 2 years get a 10 percent bonus.

mechanism. The view that the universe operates like a machine according to the law of cause and effect. It is the opposite of a teleological view.

metaphysics. A major branch of philosophy concerned with developing a theory of what is genuinely real.

methodical skepticism. *See* skepticism.

Middle Way. This term is used in general to characterize Buddhist teaching and practice as a middle way between extremes. It also has a variety of specialized meanings, such as specific reference to the Fourth Noble Truth or the Eightfold Path.

mind–body problem. The problem of defining what mind and body are and stating clearly how they are related.

monism. A metaphysical theory holding that reality is one.

Muslim. Literally it means "one who submits to Allah's will" and refers to the members of the Islamic religion.

Naiyayika. An Indian school of philosophy concerned with a whole range of philosophical issues, but most often associated with advancing a theory of knowledge called *pramana* (*see* pramana).

natural theology. *See* theology.

neutral monism. The view that what exists is neither mental nor physical, but neutral with respect to these properties. (*See* double-aspect theory.)

normal science. A term referring to the practice of accumulating knowledge by careful applications of scientific methods working within a given model or paradigm.

normative. This concept, often contrasted with descriptive, refers to a type of reflection that seeks to discover the way things *ought* to be. It has to do with norms (rules for correct behavior).

Nyaya. A school of Hindu philosophy that emphasizes logic and holds that there are four sources of knowledge: correct perception, correct inference, correct comparison, and correct testimony.

omnipotent. A traditional metaphysical attribute of God that means all-powerful.

omniscient. A traditional metaphysical attribute of God that means all-knowing.

objective idealism. The view that reality is a manifestation of an absolute mind.

ontological argument. An argument for God's existence that attempts to deduce the existence of God from a concept of God as that than which nothing greater can be conceived.

ontology. A major subdivision of metaphysics that focuses on the study of being as such.

paradigm. A scientific achievement so deep and impressive that it defines the daily practice for a particular community of scientists.

parallelism. The theory that mental and physical events parallel one another in a coordinated manner but do not causally interact.

philosophy. From the Greek word for "love of wisdom," it has been defined in a variety of ways, one of which is the notion that philosophy is the rational attempt to formulate, understand, and answer fundamental questions.

philosophy of art. A study of the nature of art and related topics such as artistic taste and value.

philosophy of religion. The use of philosophical methods to study a variety of religious issues such as the relation of faith to reason, God's existence, life after death, and the nature of religious experience.

philosophy of science. The use of philosophical methods to critically analyze the assumptions and key concepts of science.

pluralism. The metaphysical theory holding that there are many different realities and that they are not reducible to a single reality or to only two basic realities. Also used in a different context to refer to a society characterized by a variety of different cultural groups.

political philosophy. Philosophical reflection on the nature and justification of government.

positivism. A view holding that modern science and its methods are the sole trustworthy guide to the truth.

postmodernism. This term is used in a variety of contexts but when referring to art it frequently designates a type of art that self-consciously tries to go beyond the modernist movement by revealing the subtle ways in which conventional notions of beauty reflect gender, class, religious, political, and historically specific ideologies that claim universal and absolute value for what is culturally relative. More broadly it emphasizes that "truth" is a contested concept and offers a critique of ideological claims to objectivity.

pragmatic theory of truth. A theory that holds some statement is true if and only if that statement "works" in the broad sense of being useful.

pragmatism. A philosophical movement, which developed in the United States, stressing that, in determining both the meaning and truth of our beliefs, we must pay attention to their implications for our behavior.

pramana. The means of knowledge developed in Indian philosophy: correct perception, correct inference, correct comparison (analogy), and reliable testimony.

predestination. The belief that some or all events (including the salvation of some people) are predetermined by a personal divine power.

primary qualities. *See* secondary qualities.

problem of evil. In the broad sense, the problem of explaining and making sense of evil. In the theological sense, the difficulty of reconciling the existence of evil with the existence of a perfectly good, all-powerful, creator God.

problem of freedom and determinism. If all events are caused, how can human actions be free?

problem of induction. The problem of providing a rational justification for inductive reasoning. Hume claimed we could not provide such a justification, and so our trust in inductive reasoning was rooted in custom or habit, not reason.

problem of the one and many. Is reality fundamentally one thing or many things?

process ontology. The view that change is a basic feature of reality and that all aspects of reality are interrelated.

rationalism. An epistemological theory holding that all genuine knowledge derives from reason and is justified a priori (independent of sense experience). It is the opposite of empiricism.

realism. The view that objects exist apart from a mind that knows them. *Representational* or *indirect realism* holds that sensations put us indirectly in touch with the real objects that they represent; *direct realism* holds that we are directly in touch with physical objects via our senses.

reincarnation. The view that souls or karmic effects can become attached to successive physical bodies and hence be reborn over and over again.

ren (jen). A Confucian concept commonly translated as "benevolence" or "humanity," it refers to the highest human virtue or excellence.

representational realism. *See* realism.

retributive justice. A corrective distribution of burdens to persons who undeservedly enjoy benefits or to those who are guilty of failing to fulfill their responsibilities. Legal penalties for breaking the law are examples of the application of this principle.

revealed theology. *See* theology.

revolutionary science. This concept is contrasted with normal science and refers to a paradigm shift or revolution in a fundamental framework for conducting scientific research.

sabi. A Japanese aesthetic value that associates beauty with what is natural.

samsara. A Buddhist and Hindu concept referring to the life of suffering and the constant round of birth, death, and rebirth in which we are trapped.

scientism. The strong belief that science can solve all or almost all of the problems that plague human existence.

secondary qualities. The objects of the five senses (sounds, colors, odors, flavors, and textures) are called secondary because they exist in the mind. *Primary qualities* (extension, figure, motion, rest, solidity, and number) are traits of physical objects that exist apart from the mind.

Shi'i. A branch of Islam that believes Allah gave the right to rule to the religious leaders (*imams*).

skepticism. In its absolute form, an epistemological theory contending that knowledge is not possible. *Commonsense skepticism* and *methodical skepticism* are not so absolute. The former doubts some but not all knowledge claims, and the latter uses doubt as a tool in the search for truth.

social contract theory. A theory of political sovereignty claiming that the authority of government derives from a voluntary agreement among all the people of a society to form a political community and to obey the laws laid down by the government they collectively select.

socialism. An economic system based on collective ownership of the means of production, rational economic planning, and the equal distribution of goods and services.

social philosophy. The study of issues relating to social policy and justice.

Socratic method. The method of critical analysis Socrates developed in an effort to uncover the essential qualities of various concepts.

soft determinism. Also called compatibilism because, according to this theory, determinism (the fact that every event has a cause) is compatible with the existence of human freedom. Human beings can and should be held morally responsible for whatever they voluntarily do.

standpoint epistemology. The claim that our social and historical situations substantially impact our understanding of knowledge.

subjective idealism. The view that physical objects do not exist apart from their perception.

sublation. Literally meaning "to carry or wipe away," often used in logic for the activity of contradicting, negating, or correcting. The concept is used by Shankara in conjunction with the distinction between appearance and reality. Appearance is sublatable, but reality is not.

substance ontology. A view holding that permanence is the basic feature of reality and that one or more substances exist independently in the sense that they would exist even if other things did not.

Sufism. A mystical movement in Islam that teaches the possibility of a direct and immediate experience of Allah.

Sunni. A branch of Islam that believes Allah gave the right to rule to the whole community.

synthetic statement. A statement whose truth value depends on the way the world is. According to Hume, they are about matters of fact, and it is possible for their negation to be true. They are the opposite of analytic statements.

tabula rasa. Meaning "blank tablet or slate," a term some empiricists use to characterize the state of the human mind prior to sense experience. It stands in contrast with the concept of innate ideas.

teleological argument. An a posteriori argument for God's existence, begins with the premise that the world exhibits purposeful order and concludes that this order is the result of the actions of a divine intelligence.

teleological ethical theory. A theory maintaining that good consequences constitute the moral rightness of an action.

teleology. The word comes from the Greek *telos* (goal, purpose, or end) and logos (word, reason, or study), hence, literally, "the study of ends or goals." It often refers to the position that the universe has a goal, purpose, or final cause and that everything that happens contributes toward achieving that goal or outcome. In ethics, it refers to those theories stressing that the consequences or outcomes of actions are what determines their moral value.

theism. The view that God is the infinite, unitary, all-powerful, perfectly good, self-existent cause of all things and is a personal being who created the universe out of nothing and directs it according to teleological laws.

theocracy. The political theory holding that God is and ought to be the ruler of human societies and the government must rule according to God's laws and through God's representatives.

theodicy. In the broad sense, any proposed solution to the problem of evil. In the narrow sense, any solution to the problem of evil that reconciles the existence of evil with the existence of God.

theology. The study of divine reality or God, sometimes divided into *natural theology*, which deals with possible knowledge about God based on the use of reason alone, and *revealed theology*, which claims knowledge about God based on special revelations.

theory of Forms. A Platonic theory claiming that Forms or concepts constitute essences that exist in their own right, as entities independent of the world of appearances in which they may be manifest.

totalitarianism. A political theory claiming that the state's entitlement to rule extends to all aspects of life and that the authority of the state is beyond question.

underdetermination thesis. This thesis claims that some scientific theory is always underdetermined to a greater or lesser degree by the evidence because different explanations can be supported by the same data.

utilitarianism. A moral theory holding that the value of an action resides in its utility or use for the production of pleasure or happiness.

vagueness. Linguistic meaning is vague when the range of applicability is unclear. For example, the word "bald" is vague because it is unclear precisely how much hair must be missing before the word applies.

wabi. A Japanese aesthetic value usually characterized by simplicity of style.

Wuwei. A Chinese word meaning "no action," refers to acting unselfishly, naturally, and spontaneously.

xiao (hsiao). The Confucian virtue of filial love, loyalty, obedience, and piety.

yi. The Confucian term for what is fitting or appropriate.

yin and yang. A Chinese concept referring to the basic opposites that make up reality and are complementary. Yin is the passive force, and yang the active force.

APPENDIX TWO

Pronunciation Guides

CHINESE

Two methods are in wide use today for romanticizing (translating into a Latin-based alphabetical system) Chinese words. One is called Wade-Giles and the other Pinyin. I have used Pinyin instead of Wade-Giles because it is the official romanticization system endorsed by the Chinese government. However, my selections use the older Wade-Giles spelling, which requires a pronunciation guide because some of the sounds indicated by the letters do not, to an English speaker, correspond to the sounds in Chinese.

a as in father	ch pronounced as j
e as in end	k pronounced as g
i as in the initial e in eve	p pronounced as b
o as in go	t pronounced as d
u as in rude	ts or tz pronounced as tz or dz
ü as in menu	hs pronounced as sh
ai as in ice	j pronounced as r
ao as in out	ch', k', p', ts', tz' pronounced as in English
ou as in obey	

SANSKRIT

Vowels

1. *e, ai, o,* and *au* are long and are pronounced as in *gray, aisle, open,* and *cow.*
2. *ā, ī, ū,* with lines over them (macrons) are long and are pronounced as in *father, machine,* and *rude.*
3. The same vowels without macrons are short as in *but, tin,* and *full.*
4. *r* is sounded as in *rill* and is lightly trilled.

Consonants

5. *c* as in *church*, *j* as in *jungle*, *ṣ* as in *s'hip*, *s* as in *sun*, and *jn* as in *gyana*.
6. Aspirated consonants should be pronounced distinctly: thus *bh* as in *caB-House*, *dh* as in *maD-House*, *gh* as in *doG-House*, *jh* as in *fudGE-House*, *kh* as in *rocK-House*, *ph* as in *toP-Hat*, and *th* as in *goaT-Herd*.

Accent

7. Words of two syllables are accented on the first syllable: *GIta*.
8. Words of more than two syllables are accented on the penult (second syllable from end) when the penult is long or has a short vowel followed by two or more consonants: *veDANta*.
9. Words of more than two syllables are accented on the antepenult (third syllable from the end) in cases where the penult is short and not followed by two consonants: *UpaniSHAD*.

ARABIC

Letters are pronounced in the usual English manner unless indicated otherwise in the following list.

a	fl*a*t	o	n*o*t
ah	f*a*ther	oo	f*oo*d
ay	p*ay*	ōō	f*oo*t
ee	s*ee*	ow	h*ow*
e	l*e*t	u	b*u*t
i	h*i*gh	a	*a*bout
i	p*i*ty	izm	tribal*ism*
ō	n*o*	j	*j*et

Some Examples

caliphs (*kay* lifs)   salat (sa *laht*)
dhikr (*dhi* kar)   Qur'an (kor *an*)
faqih (fa *kee*)   Shi'i (*Shee* ee)